THE WEST IN THE WORLD

RENAISSANCE TO PRESENT

THIRD EDITION

DENNIS SHERMAN

John Jay College
City University of New York

JOYCE SALISBURY

University of Wisconsin–Green Bay

Boston   Burr Ridge, IL   Dubuque, IA   Madison, WI   New York   San Francisco   St. Louis
Bangkok   Bogotá   Caracas   Kuala Lumpur   Lisbon   London   Madrid   Mexico City
Milan   Montreal   New Delhi   Santiago   Seoul   Singapore   Sydney   Taipei   Toronto

Published by McGraw-Hill, an imprint of The McGraw-Hill Companies, Inc., 1221 Avenue of the Americas, New York, NY 10020. Copyright © 2008, 2006, 2004, 2001. All rights reserved. No part of this publication may be reproduced or distributed in any form or by any means, or stored in a database or retrieval system, without the prior written consent of The McGraw-Hill Companies, Inc., including, but not limited to, in any network or other electronic storage or transmission, or broadcast for distance learning.

This book is printed on acid-free paper.

1 2 3 4 5 6 7 8 9 0 WCK/WCK 0 9 8 7

ISBN: 978-0-07-331671-0
MHID: 0-07-331671-7

Editor in Chief: *Michael Ryan*
Publisher: *Lisa Moore*
Sponsoring Editor: *Jon-David Hague*
Marketing Manager: *Pamela Cooper*
Marketing Specialist: *Clare Cashen*
Media Project Manager: *Magdalena Corona*
Director of Development: *Lisa Pinto*
Developmental Editors: *Susan Gouijnstook, Karen Helfrich*
Production Editor: *Chanda Feldman*
Manuscript Editor: *Patricia Ohlenroth*
Art Director: *Jeanne Schreiber*
Design Manager: *Cassandra Chu*
Text and Cover Designer: *Linda Beaupre*
Art Editor: *Emma Ghiselli*
Illustrator: *Parrot Graphics*
Photo Research Coordinator: *Alexandra Ambrose*
Photo research: *Christine Pullo*
Production Supervisor: *Richard DeVitto*
Composition: *10.5/12 by ProGraphics, Inc.*
Printing: *45# Publishers MattePlus, Quebecor-World*

Cover: Portrait of Paquius Proculus and his wife. Roman Fresco from Pompeii, c. 55-79 C.E., © Scala/Art Resource, NY; Trading at the harbour of Curmos, Ilumination, Paris, studio of the Boucicaut master, c.1412, © akg-images; The Geography Lesson by Pietro Longhi, c. 1750-52, © akg-images; St. Martin in the Fields by William Logsdail, 1888, © Tate Gallery, London / Art Resource

Credits: The credits section for this book begins on page C-1 and is considered an extension of the copyright page.

Library of Congress Cataloging-in-Publication Data

Sherman, Dennis.
    The West in the world : a history of western civilization / Dennis Sherman, Joyce Salisbury. — 3rd ed.
        p. cm.
    Includes bibliographical references and index.
    ISBN-13: 978-0-07-331671-0 (v.3 : alk. paper)
    ISBN-10: 0-07-331671-7 (v.3 : alk. paper)
    1. Civilization, Western—History—Textbooks. I. Salisbury, Joyce E. II. Title.
CB245.S465 2009
909'.09821—dc22

                                      2007043955

The Internet addresses listed in the text were accurate at the time of publication. The inclusion of a Web site does not indicate an endorsement by the authors or McGraw-Hill, and McGraw-Hill does not guarantee the accuracy of the information presented at these sites.

www.mhhe.com

DENNIS SHERMAN

DENNIS SHERMAN is Professor of History at John Jay College, the City University of New York. He received his B.A. (1962) and J.D. (1965) degrees from the University of California at Berkeley, and his Ph.D. (1970) from the University of Michigan. He was visiting Professor at the University of Paris (1978–1979, 1985). He received the Ford Foundation Prize Fellowship (1968–1969, 1969–1970), a fellowship from the Council for Research on Economic History (1971–1972), and fellowships from the National Endowment for the Humanities (1973–1976). His publications include *A Short History of Western Civilization*, Eighth Edition (coauthor), *Western Civilization: Sources, Images, and Interpretations*, Seventh Edition, *World History: Sources, Images, and Interpretations*, Third Edition, a series of introductions in the Garland Library of War and Peace, several articles and reviews on nineteenth-century French economic and social history in American and European journals, and several short stories in literary reviews.

JOYCE SALISBURY

JOYCE SALISBURY recently retired from the University of Wisconsin–Green Bay, where she taught history to undergraduates for almost twenty years. She continues to teach at various local colleges and universities. She received a Ph.D. in medieval history from Rutgers University in New Jersey. She is a respected historian who has published many articles and has written or edited ten books, including the critically acclaimed *Perpetua's Passion: Death and Memory of a Young Roman Woman*, *The Beast Within: Animals in the Middle Ages*, *Encyclopedia of Women in the Ancient World*, and *The Blood of Martyrs*. Salisbury is also an award-winning teacher, who was named *"Professor of the Year for Wisconsin in 1991"* by CASE (Council for Advancement and Support of Education), a prestigious national organization.

What's the best way to write an interesting, accessible, and accurate account of the West's complex history? This question confronts everyone who approaches this huge and important task. On the one hand, we believed strongly that different authors' perspectives would give readers a sense of the richness of the past. On the other hand, we wanted a seamless narrative that read like a good story. We decided that a careful, two-author collaboration would best enable us to achieve both goals. We brought our different backgrounds, research interests, and teaching experiences to the table. We talked over our ideas and read and struggled with one another's words. Throughout, we never lost sight of our goal: to bring the compelling history of the West in the world to students of the twenty-first century.

DENNIS SHERMAN: I was in the twelfth grade in west Los Angeles when I first realized I had a flair for history. Our teacher wisely gave us much latitude in selecting topics for two lengthy papers. I chose ancient Egypt (I liked the National Geographic visuals) as my first topic, and Tasmania as the second. (I was the only one who seemed to know that Tasmania was an island below Australia). Assembling the material and writing the papers just came easily to me, as did any questions our history teacher posed in class (though I was an otherwise fading-into-the-background student). I more or less blundered into different majors in college and then slid through law school (which taught me how to be succinct) before returning to history. At the beginning of my first semester of graduate school, I met my advisor who asked me what courses I wanted to take. I ticked off four selections: History of South Asia; Nineteenth Century Europe; Twentieth Century America; European Intellectual History. "You're a generalist," he said. Indeed I was. He wisely counseled me to narrow my focus. However, throughout my studies and professional career I have found the big picture—the forest rather than the trees—the most interesting aspect of history.

A few years later I moved to the front of the classroom and, never forgetting what it was like to be a student, found my heart in teaching. Teaching and writing about the sweep of Western civilization within the broadest possible context has remained my greatest interest over the years. That is why I have written this book with Joyce.

JOYCE SALISBURY: I grew up in Latin America (10 years in Brazil and 5 in Mexico). Through those years, I attended American schools filled with expatriates. There I studied a curriculum of Western culture, which in those days was equated with European history. But even as a young girl, I knew I wasn't getting the whole story. After all, we celebrated Mardi Gras (a Christian holiday) to an African drumbeat, and the national museum of Mexico was bursting with Napoleonic artifacts. I knew that the history and culture of the West was intimately tied to that of the rest of the world.

In the more than twenty years that I've been teaching Western civilization, I've brought this global perspective to the classroom, and now Dennis and I have brought it to this book. It is very satisfying to me to work with my students as we trace the unfolding history of the West and to see that all my students—with their own rich and varied cultural backgrounds—recognize their stories within the larger narrative. In Spring 2007, I had the opportunity to implement intensively my commitment to the integration of Western and global history: I signed on to the University of Virginia's Semester at Sea, and had the wonderful experience of teaching Western Civilization (as well as other courses) to students as we cruised around the world. This was indeed the opportunity to teach the West in the world!

BRIEF CONTENTS

CONTENTS

CHAPTER 18

CHAPTER 19

CHAPTER 20

LIST OF PRIMARY SOURCE DOCUMENTS

THINKING ABOUT DOCUMENTS

LIST OF MAPS

THINKING ABOUT GEOGRAPHY

LIST OF FEATURES

PREFACE

The study of Western civilization prepares students to understand who they are, where they come from, and how they might shape the future. Our deep commitment to this enterprise inspired us to write the first edition of *The West in the World*. We trace the major events of our history through an accessible narrative—the story of the development of the West is an interesting one, and we want to present it as such. We have been particularly conscious of including critical thinking tools and pedagogical features to engage students actively in the content. The text is designed to help students acquire the body of knowledge and abilities that will mark them as well-educated people of the twenty-first century.

GOALS OF *THE WEST IN THE WORLD*

Western civilization influences—and is influenced by—peoples all over the world today; it remains a fascinating (and at times controversial) subject. While many have studied the strong contributions of the West to the world, too often the reverse influences have not been stressed. In fact, one of the hallmarks of Western civilization has been its power to be transformed through contact with people outside its center. This quality has contributed to the West's capacity to keep changing as it embraces new ideas, new people, and new challenges. We chose the title of this book—*The West in the World*—to emphasize this characteristic, and we have written the story of the West in a way that reveals its complex interactions with the surrounding world. When we first prepared to write this book, we set out to accomplish six goals, which we continue to strive toward in this new edition:

1. Demonstrate the complex relationship between Western and world history.

To address this first goal, we dealt with the thorny issue of the relationship between Western and world history. Historians have coined the term "Western civilization" to identify societies that seemed to share certain historical traditions and cultural traits. Today, historians, journalists, and cultural commentators usually use "the West" to refer, roughly, to Europe and some other areas of the world such as the Americas, Australia, and New Zealand that came to be dominated by Europeans and their culture over the past few centuries

In this book, we present the concept of Western civilization as an ever-changing pattern of culture that first emerged in the ancient Middle East and that then moved west through the Mediterranean lands, north to Europe, and, in the sixteenth century, across the Atlantic.

In this new edition, we have added "The Global Context" essays through which we have widened our focus to consider specifically how people have thought about the West, what developments marked non-Western civilizations, and what lines of communication linked Western and other civilization.

We have also added more Global Connections essays that appear throughout chapters, and in which we narrow our focus to a particular set of connections between the West and the world. Throughout the narrative we have tried to emphasize the importance of the interactions—economic, social, and cultural as well as political—that have created our modern civilization that in the twenty-first century is in many ways a world civilization.

2. Weave a strong social-history "thread" into the political/cultural framework.

To meet our second goal, we integrated social history, including women's history, throughout this text, acknowledging that people of all ages and walks of life have affected the course of history. Social historians have sometimes written about "the masses" while losing touch with the individual men and women whose lives have shaped the past. We frequently "stop the music" for a moment to let the words and experiences of individuals illustrate broad developments, and in addition we have presented biographical portraits of people who experienced some of the developments discussed in each chapter.

3. Convey the drama and interest inherent in the story of the past.

To meet our third goal, we sought to capture both the art and science of history. We strove for an engaging narrative of Western civilization (the "art") that would also analyze the events, individuals, ideas, and developments (the "science"). We designed the book to draw students in as they follow the unfolding of Western culture from its earliest roots to the present.

4. Integrate unique pedagogical features that enhance the narrative and support student learning.

To fulfill our fourth goal, we have designed a number of unique pedagogical features that complement and support the narrative. For example, we treat art works and maps in an unusual way. Each illustration is discussed in the text itself rather than presented as a separate, optional feature or mere ornamentation. This approach not only brings the past alive for today's highly visual audience, it also helps teach students how to interpret art works and other illustrations.

For example, we analyze a painting of a nineteenth-century middle-class family to show gender roles, attitudes toward children, the place of servants, and relationships to the outside world. Similarly, we use a beautiful Rubens painting of the miracles of Saint Ignatius Loyola to comment on the theology and sensibilities of sixteenth-century Catholicism. All this is discussed within the narrative of the text. Visuals serve as sources of history and encourage students to arrive at richer insights than they would have gained solely through reading the text. In this edition we have also included "Thinking About Art," a feature designed to extend chapter discussion of a particular image and to prompt analysis and critical thinking (see the description of this new feature in the "New Features" section on p. xxv).

Maps are also treated as more than a visual aid. Each map comes with an analytical guide that encourages readers to consider connections between geography, politics, and other developments. A picture by itself is not worth a thousand words, but in this text the illustrations and maps serve as a central feature for learning.

5. Meet the growing interest in science and technology.
An enthusiasm for science and technology has been a hallmark of Western civilization. Like many developments in the story of the West, this enthusiasm has ebbed and flowed over time. To meet the growing interest among today's students and scholars, we emphasize these topics throughout the narrative. For example, a discussion of medieval technology reveals the significant inventions that brought mechanical power to a central point in society, and students will also see how other cultures—like early Muslim societies—performed surgery, dispensed drugs, and established hospitals. Even in the modern period, we discuss the experience of going to a doctor in addition to reporting on new developments in medicine, such as antiseptics, anesthetics, and antibiotics. Consistent with our use of art as history, illustrations such as Caroline Naudet's "Journey of a Dying Man to the Other World" are used to reveal both typical medical practices and common attitudes toward physicians.

6. Create an accessible text of manageable length.
To achieve our final goal of making this book an attractive size, we selected a length that is unusual for a Western civilization textbook. Long texts, while of great value, can be intimidating to students in their level of detail and can make the assigning of supplementary readings difficult, if not impossible—we've all had this experience. Brief texts, while leaving plenty of time for additional readings, are typically lacking in necessary coverage and detail, thus making it a remarkable challenge for the authors to achieve the kind of braided, nuanced narrative that history deserves. Medium in length, *The West in the World* is long enough to present a strong, rich narrative while allowing instructors the flexibility to use other sources and books as supplements. In this new edition, we've redesigned the text to make it more accessible for students.

With each chapter and each round of revision, we reminded ourselves of these six goals and asked our reviewers to hold us accountable for achieving them.

NEW TO THE THIRD EDITION

CHAPTER BY CHAPTER CHANGES

We have made substantial changes both in content and in pedagogical features in this third edition of *The West in the World*. We have revised the content throughout in response to students', professors', and reviewers' comments, keeping us current on the latest scholarship and on what actually goes on in today's classrooms. Following are some of the key changes we've made to specific chapters:

CHAPTER 1
- Expanded coverage of ancient Persians, including discussion of Cambyses and Darius, new document on Persians.
- Increased coverage of ancient history and science
- Expanded coverage of the Hittites
- Substantial revision of Egypt discussion

CHAPTER 2
- Revised presentation of periods of ancient Greece history
- Several new illustrations to clarify the periodization
- Increase on science and drama with new document
- New "Global Connections" that emphasizes coverage of science
- Expanded section on Greek women and their roles

CHAPTER 3
- Expanded discussion on Alexander's reception in Persia
- Two new documents

CHAPTER 4
- Increased coverage on the Roman military, including new section on the wars with Macedon and Greece
- Revisions throughout to emphasize Romans' political identity and the changes it experienced
- New document on the Roman constitution
- Revised end-of-chapter questions to make them more analytical

CHAPTER 5
- Extensive new section on the second century crisis and the military monarchy
- New map that shows trade goods during the empire
- Timeline enhanced to show dynasties
- New discussion and illustrations on changing burial practices

CHAPTER 6
- Much expanded discussion on the nuances of *jihad* and how the idea changed over time (both here and in Chapter 8)
- New document to expand understanding of relationships between Islam and conquered peoples

CHAPTER 8

- A continued discussion (begun in Chapter 6) on the changing Muslim attitudes toward *jihad* in response to the Crusaders
- Expanded coverage of townspeople's views of the world
- New discussion of "Peace of God" and "Truce of God" to examine medieval violence

CHAPTER 9

- Revised section on Ockham
- Expanded discussion of the Hundred Years' war with a new section on the Battle of Agincourt and Dauphin's treatment of Joan of Arc
- Expanded discussion of Wars of the Roses
- New section on Russian identity—east or west?
- Expanded discussion on Black Death including a new document on the experience of the plague
- New document on a Franciscan missionary's interaction with the Mongols

CHAPTER 10

- New section on the arrival of Greek scholars and texts into Italy after the fall of Constantinople in 1453
- New discussion of the founding of the Platonic Academy in Florence
- Heavily revised section on family
- New Document on Northern Renaissance
- New explanation of "Christian humanism" mentioning Erasmus and Ximenez

CHAPTER 11

- Expanded discussion on Charles V's attempts to reconcile Lutherans and Catholics before 1555
- Expanded discussion of witchcraft
- Expanded treatment of Spain, including reign of Ferdinand and Isabella, establishment of the Inquisition
- Expanded discussion of the reign of Edward VI of England
- New section and image on Protestant iconoclasm
- New discussion on the role of women in Protestantism, with a new document
- New document on Loyola's views on education

CHAPTER 12

- New section on the East India Companies—English and Dutch
- Revised discussion on the influence of the Dutch traders
- Expanded description of *encomienda* system

CHAPTER 13

- Expanded description of the Dutch Republican form of government
- New discussion and illustration of Dutch shipbuilding

CHAPTER 15

- Expanded treatment of the Great Colonial Rivalry

CHAPTER 20

- New Global Connections essay on the consequences of the opium trade in China
- Expanded treatment of imperialism
- New document on theories about race and imperialism

CHAPTER 23

- Reorganized chapter to focus on the interwar period
- Added new Biography essay on Virginia Woolf
- New document on Stalin's collectivization process

CHAPTER 24

- This is a new chapter devoted to an expanded treatment of World War II
- New documents on the Nazi death camps, women workers during the war, and Japanese Kamikaze attacks on U.S. ships

CHAPTER 26

- Expanded and updated with new material on recent developments such as global warming

NEW FEATURES

We believe that telling a good story is only part of the task facing those who teach the history of the West. Instructors also have to engage students in the enterprise of learning, and the more actively engaged they are, the more they learn. Therefore, we have designed and included a number of new pedagogical features to help students participate actively in the learning process. These can be used by students alone or become part of classroom activity.

- Increased coverage of World War II. We have added a **new chapter on World War II.** Interest in this topic has been growing, and the chapter emphasizes both the drama of the period and how the war became a historical turning point.
- **New Global Context Essays.** When we wrote our first edition in 2000, we knew that the unfolding story of the West required a new global awareness. This approach has been so popular that we have strengthened it in each subsequent edition. In this edition, we have added several essays that consider "The Global Context." The new **The Global Context** essays appear after Chapters 1, 5, 15, and 24, and they cover the ancient, medieval, early modern, and modern eras. These essays explore what historians have considered the "West" at different times and how the West related to the rest of the world. They also provide a general sense of what was going on elsewhere in the world, with an accompanying map, so that students may keep a global perspective as they study the history of the West.

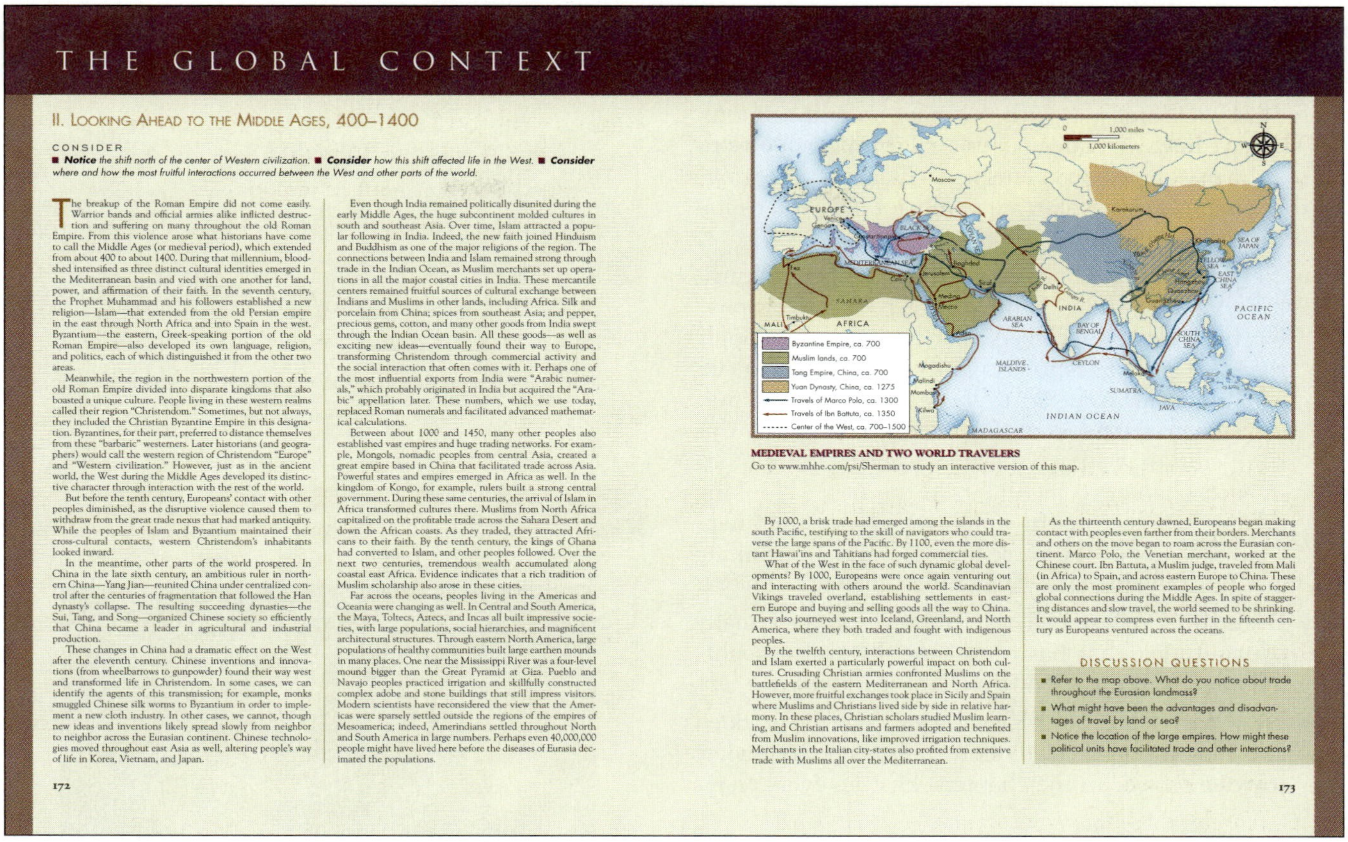

THE GLOBAL CONTEXT

II. Looking Ahead to the Middle Ages, 400–1400

CONSIDER

■ ***Notice*** *the shift north of the center of Western civilization.* ■ ***Consider*** *how this shift affected life in the West.* ■ ***Consider*** *where and how the most fruitful interactions occurred between the West and other parts of the world.*

The breakup of the Roman Empire did not come easily. Warrior bands and official armies alike inflicted destruction and suffering on many throughout the old Roman Empire. From this violence arose what historians have come to call the Middle Ages (or medieval period), which extended from about 400 to about 1400. During that millennium, bloodshed intensified as three distinct cultural identities emerged in the Mediterranean basin and vied with one another for land, power, and affirmation of their faith. In the seventh century, the Prophet Muhammad and his followers established a new religion—Islam—that extended from the old Persian empire in the east through North Africa and into Spain in the west. Byzantium—the eastern, Greek-speaking portion of the old Roman Empire—also developed its own language, religion, and politics, each of which distinguished it from the other two areas.

Meanwhile, the region in the northwestern portion of the old Roman Empire divided into disparate kingdoms that also boasted a unique culture. People living in these western realms called their region "Christendom." Sometimes, but not always, they included the Christian Byzantine Empire in this designation. Byzantines, for their part, preferred to distance themselves from these "barbaric" westerners. Later historians (and geographers) would call the western region of Christendom "Europe" and "Western civilization." However, just as in the ancient world, the West during the Middle Ages developed its distinctive character through interaction with the rest of the world.

But before the tenth century, Europeans' contact with other peoples diminished, as the disruptive violence caused them to withdraw from the great trade nexus that had marked antiquity. While the peoples of Islam and Byzantium maintained their cross-cultural contacts, western Christendom's inhabitants looked inward.

In the meantime, other parts of the world prospered. In China in the late sixth century, an ambitious ruler in northern China—Yang Jian—reunited China under centralized control after the centuries of fragmentation that followed the Han dynasty's collapse. The resulting succeeding dynasties—the Sui, Tang, and Song—organized Chinese society so efficiently that China became a leader in agricultural and industrial production.

These changes in China had a dramatic effect on the West after the eleventh century. Chinese inventions and innovations (from wheelbarrows to gunpowder) found their way west and transformed life in Christendom. In some cases, we can identify the agents of this transmission; for example, monks smuggled Chinese silk worms to Byzantium in order to implement a new cloth industry. In other cases, we cannot, though new ideas and inventions likely spread slowly from neighbor to neighbor across the Eurasian continent. Chinese technologies moved throughout east Asia as well, altering people's way of life in Korea, Vietnam, and Japan.

Even though India remained politically disunited during the early Middle Ages, the huge subcontinent molded cultures in south and southeast Asia. Over time, Islam attracted a popular following in India. Indeed, the new faith joined Hinduism and Buddhism as one of the major religions of the region. The connections between India and Islam remained strong through trade in the Indian Ocean, as Muslim merchants set up operations in all the major coastal cities in India. These mercantile centers remained fruitful sources of cultural exchange between Indians and Muslims in other lands, including Africa. Silk and porcelain from China; spices from southeast Asia; and pepper, precious gems, cotton, and many other goods from India swept through the Indian Ocean basin. All these goods—as well as exciting new ideas—eventually found their way to Europe, transforming Christendom through commercial activity and the social interaction that often comes with it. Perhaps one of the most influential exports from India were "Arabic numerals," which probably originated in India but acquired the "Arabic" appellation later. These numbers, which we use today, replaced Roman numerals and facilitated advanced mathematical calculations.

Between about 1000 and 1450, many other peoples also established vast empires and huge trading networks. For example, Mongols, nomadic peoples from central Asia, created a great empire based in China that facilitated trade across Asia. Powerful states and empires emerged in Africa as well. In the kingdom of Kongo, for example, rulers built a strong central government. During these same centuries, the arrival of Islam in Africa transformed cultures there. Muslims from North Africa capitalized on the profitable trade across the Sahara Desert and down the African coasts. As they traded, they attracted Africans to their faith. By the tenth century, the kings of Ghana had converted to Islam, and other peoples followed. Over the next two centuries, tremendous wealth accumulated along coastal east Africa. Evidence indicates that a rich tradition of Muslim scholarship also arose in these cities.

Far across the oceans, peoples living in the Americas and Oceania were changing as well. In Central and South America, the Maya, Toltecs, Aztecs, and Incas all built impressive societies, with large populations, social hierarchies, and magnificent architectural structures. Through eastern North America, large populations of healthy communities built large earthen mounds in many places. One near the Mississippi River was a four-level mound bigger than the Great Pyramid at Giza. Pueblo and Navajo peoples practiced irrigation and skillfully constructed complex adobe and stone buildings that still impress visitors. Modern scientists have reconsidered the view that the Americas were sparsely settled outside the regions of the empires of Mesoamerica; indeed, Amerindians settled throughout North and South America in large numbers. Perhaps even 40,000,000 people might have lived here before the diseases of Eurasia decimated the populations.

172

Byzantine Empire, ca. 700
Muslim lands, ca. 700
Tang Empire, China, ca. 700
Yuan Dynasty, China, ca. 1275
Travels of Marco Polo, ca. 1300
Travels of Ibn Battuta, ca. 1350
Center of the West, ca. 700–1500
EUROPE
AFRICA
INDIA
INDIAN OCEAN
PACIFIC OCEAN

MEDIEVAL EMPIRES AND TWO WORLD TRAVELERS

Go to www.mhhe.com/psi/Sherman to study an interactive version of this map.

By 1000, a brisk trade had emerged among the islands in the south Pacific, testifying to the skill of navigators who could traverse the large spans of the Pacific. By 1100, even the more distant Hawai'ins and Tahitians had forged commercial ties.

What of the West in the face of such dynamic global developments? By 1000, Europeans were once again venturing out and interacting with others around the world. Scandinavian Vikings traveled overland, establishing settlements in eastern Europe and buying and selling goods all the way to China. They also journeyed west into Iceland, Greenland, and North America, where they both traded and fought with indigenous peoples.

By the twelfth century, interactions between Christendom and Islam exerted a particularly powerful impact on both cultures. Crusading Christian armies confronted Muslims on the battlefields of the eastern Mediterranean and North Africa. However, more fruitful exchanges took place in Sicily and Spain where Muslims and Christians lived side by side in relative harmony. In these places, Christian scholars studied Muslim learning, and Christian artisans and farmers adopted and benefited from Muslim innovations, like improved irrigation techniques. Merchants in the Italian city-states also profited from extensive trade with Muslims all over the Mediterranean.

As the thirteenth century dawned, Europeans began making contact with peoples even farther from their borders. Merchants and others on the move began to roam across the Eurasian continent. Marco Polo, the Venetian merchant, worked at the Chinese court. Ibn Battuta, a Muslim judge, traveled from Mali (in Africa) to Spain, and across eastern Europe to China. These are only the most prominent examples of people who forged global connections during the Middle Ages. In spite of staggering distances and slow travel, the world seemed to be shrinking. It would appear to compress even further in the fifteenth century as Europeans ventured across the oceans.

DISCUSSION QUESTIONS

- Refer to the map above. What do you notice about trade throughout the Eurasian landmass?
- What might have been the advantages and disadvantages of travel by land or sea?
- Notice the location of the large empires. How might these political units have facilitated trade and other interactions?

173

- **New Global Connections essays:** "Global Connections" essays, which focus on important connections between the West and the non-Western world, appear in half of the book's chapters. They illustrate varying degrees of interaction between the West and the world, and in each essay, we have reinforced the notion that the West has always developed within a world context. We have also used Global Connections to consider history from the perspective of non-Westerners. For this edition, we have written two new **Global Connections** essays: "Transforming Science in Asia Minor" (Chapter 2), and "Opium and the West in China" (Chapter 20).
- **New Thinking About Documents** boxes. In this third edition we have integrated the primary source documents at appropriate locations within the chapters, and have provided accompanying pedagogical tools—**Thinking About Documents**—to help engage students in these important historical tools. We have also changed many of the primary documents

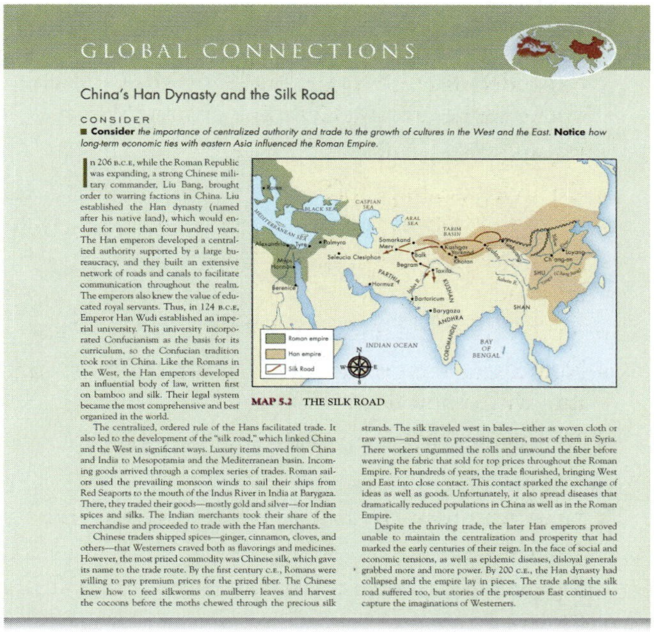

GLOBAL CONNECTIONS

China's Han Dynasty and the Silk Road

CONSIDER

■ **Consider** *the importance of centralized authority and trade to the growth of cultures in the West and the East.* **Notice** *how long-term economic ties with eastern Asia influenced the Roman Empire.*

In 206 B.C.E, while the Roman Republic was expanding, a strong Chinese military commander, Liu Bang, brought order to warring factions in China. Liu established the Han dynasty (named after his native land), which would endure for more than four hundred years. The Han emperors developed a centralized authority supported by a large bureaucracy, and they built an extensive network of roads and canals to facilitate communication throughout the realm. The emperors also knew the value of educated royal servants. Thus, in 124 B.C.E, Emperor Han Wudi established an imperial university. This university incorporated Confucianism as the basis for its curriculum, so the Confucian tradition took root in China. Like the Romans in the West, the Han emperors developed an influential body of law, written first on bamboo and silk. Their legal system became the most comprehensive and best organized in the world.

Roman empire
Han empire
Silk Road
INDIAN OCEAN
BAY OF BENGAL

MAP 5.2 THE SILK ROAD

The centralized, ordered rule of the Hans facilitated trade. It also led to the development of the "silk road," which linked China and the West in significant ways. Luxury items moved from China and India to Mesopotamia and the Mediterranean basin. Incoming goods arrived through a complex series of trades. Roman sailors used the prevailing monsoon winds to sail their ships from Red Seaports to the mouth of the Indus River in India at Barygaza. There, they traded their goods—mostly gold and silver—for Indian spices and silks. The Indian merchants took their share of the merchandise and proceeded to trade with the Han merchants.

Chinese traders shipped spices—ginger, cinnamon, cloves, and others—that Westerners craved both as flavorings and medicines. However, the most prized commodity was Chinese silk, which gave its name to the trade route. By the first century C.E., Romans were willing to pay premium prices for the prized fiber. The Chinese knew how to feed silkworms on mulberry leaves and harvest the cocoons before the moths chewed through the precious silk strands. The silk traveled west in bales—either as woven cloth or raw yarn—and went to processing centers, most of them in Syria. There workers ungummed the rolls and unwound the fiber before weaving the fabric that sold for top prices throughout the Roman Empire. For hundreds of years, the trade flourished, bringing West and East into close contact. This contact sparked the exchange of ideas as well as goods. Unfortunately, it also spread diseases that dramatically reduced populations in China as well as in the Roman Empire.

Despite the thriving trade, the later Han emperors proved unable to maintain the centralization and prosperity that had marked the early centuries of their reign. In the face of social and economic tensions, as well as epidemic diseases, disloyal generals grabbed more and more power. By 200 C.E., the Han dynasty had collapsed and the empire lay in pieces. The trade along the silk road suffered too, but stories of the prosperous East continued to capture the imaginations of Westerners.

in response to reviewers' comments. Our pedagogical philosophy is that students should be encouraged to engage with the primary source documents as tools for historical study, as with the maps and illustrations. Thus, we have extended our critical thinking questions to primary source documents in each chapter. We hope these might serve as starting points for class discussion or writing assignments.

■ **New Thinking About Art** boxes. The active learning encouraged by "Thinking About Geography" has been so well received, that we decided to apply the same principles to art. Throughout the text, we carefully analyze the art to show how the pieces may serve as primary sources for historical study. In this third edition, we have selected a special piece of art in each chapter to highlight, in the new "Thinking About Art" feature, in which we extend the chapter discussion of the piece and add critical thinking questions to encourage students to analyze the work.

■ **Beautifully redesigned,** the third edition is a visually dynamic text that has been carefully and thoughtfully developed to support student learning.

■ **New Key Dates** and **Key Terms.** We have added two new pedagogical tools to help students review topics discussed in the chapters. First, in every chap-

THINKING ABOUT ART

Karl Friedrich Schinkel, *Medieval Town on a River,* 1815

■ FIGURE 18.3
In this 1815 painting, Karl Friedrich Schinkel depicts an imaginary medieval town. A stunning Gothic cathedral dominates the people below, as well as the scene itself. ■ **What** impression of medieval life do you think the artist intended to convey to viewers? ■ **In what ways** does this painting represent Romanticism? ■ **Why** might Schinkel have chosen to make the cathedral so prominent? ■ **Consider** how the scene in this painting might contrast with a realistic urban scene of the nineteenth century.

ter, we have included one or more Key Dates chronology. Second, at the end of each chapter, we have added a list of Key Terms that are highlighted in the chapter and linked to our expanded glossary.

■ **Expanded coverage of key topics.** In response to comments from students and teachers, we have expanded our coverage of several topics, including science and technology, the ancient world, and imperialism. See the chapter by chapter list of changes for more detailed information on expanded coverage.

KEY DATES

ANCIENT EGYPT CIVILIZATION

ca. 2700–2181 B.C.E.	Old Kingdom
2181–2140 B.C.E.	First Intermediate Period
ca. 2060–1785 B.C.E.	Middle Kingdom
ca. 1785–1575 B.C.E.	Second Intermediate Period
1570–1085 B.C.E.	New Kingdom
ca. 1504–1482 B.C.E.	Pharaoh Hatshepsut
ca. 1377–1360 B.C.E.	Pharaoh Akhenaten
1290–1223 B.C.E.	Pharaoh Ramses II

KEY TERMS

Tennis Court Oath, p. 507	*sans-culottes,* p. 512	Thermidorian reaction, p. 520
Bastille, p. 508	Jacobins, p. 513	Directory, p. 521
Declaration of Rights of Man and Citizen, p. 509	Committee of Public Safety, p. 517	Napoleonic Code, p. 523
Civil Constitution of the Clergy, p. 511	*levée en masse,* p. 518	Continental System, p. 525

ENDURING FEATURES

In addition to our new features, we have retained, and in some cases expanded, several elements and pedagogical features that have been part of the previous editions of the book.

■ **Strong Narrative.** Students and instructors often complain that history texts are dry. We agree. The strong narrative approach of this book reflects our belief that the various dimensions of an historical era—political, intellectual, social, and cultural—are best presented as part of an integrated whole rather than separate chapters or occasional references in a discussion. The story of the West is a compelling one, and we have worked hard to tell it in a lively way that includes analysis (the "why" of history) as well as events and ideas (the "what"). For example, in Chapter 7, the discussion of Charlemagne's wars and his relation with the papacy are framed in a larger theoretical discussion of the benefits of linking politics with religion. Similarly, in Chapter 11, a chronology of warfare is informed by an analysis of technological and social change.

■ **Biographies.** Each chapter features a biographical essay of a man or woman who embodies major themes from the chapter. The individuals selected are not necessarily the most celebrated nor the most typical, but instead are powerful illustrative examples. Each biography serves as a reminder of the major themes—another kind of review—and provides a concrete way to discuss some of the more abstract concepts covered. As well, each biography includes questions that guide students to think critically about the individual's life and connect it with the chapter's themes. We designed the biographies to bring the past to life, and to encourage students to think about how large developments affect individuals. For example, the biography of Isabelle D'Este, found in Chapter 10, illustrates the Renaissance by her patronage of the arts, her political struggles, and her strong family ties. Similarly, the biography of Jean-Jacques Rousseau in Chapter 14 analyzes his life and examines how it reflects the broad themes of the Enlightenment.

BIOGRAPHY

Isabella d'Este (1474–1539)

CONSIDER

■ **Consider** how Isabella's life sheds light on the importance of patronage during the Renaissance, the position of women, and the significance of family ties.

Isabella d'Este was born the daughter of a duke in 1474 in the small Duchy of Ferrara, just south of Venice. She grew up in a court that both appreciated Renaissance education and art and succumbed to the violence that marked fifteenth-century Italy.

When Isabella was only 2, her father's nephew attacked the palace in an effort to seize power from the duke. Before Isabella was 8 years old, Venetian armies had invaded Ferrara to try to dominate the small duchy. Yet Isabella's father was a skillful diplomat and withstood these and many other challenges. In the process, his daughter began learning about Renaissance diplomacy.

The young girl was educated in the best humanist tradition. Her tutors taught her to read the great classics of the Roman world in the original Latin. She learned quickly and spoke Latin fluently at an early age. She also was an accomplished musician and excelled at singing and playing the lute.

When she was 6 years old, Isabella's parents began searching for a suitable future husband for her. They approached the family of the nearby Duke of Mantua to discuss a betrothal between Isabella and their eldest son, Francesco. When representatives of

■ FIGURE 10.2
Isabella d'Este.

Francesco's family interviewed the young child, they wrote back to the prospective in-laws that they were astonished at her precocious intelligence. They sent Francesco's parents a portrait of the lovely black-eyed, blond child, but assured that "her marvelous knowledge and intelligence are far more worthy of admiration [than her beauty]." A betrothal was arranged that would unite the two houses trying to maintain independence from their powerful neighbors, Milan and Venice.

Duchess of Mantua, Diplomat, and Patron of the Arts

Isabella and Francesco were married in 1490, when she was 15. An elaborate ceremony joined the two families, and in her old age, Isabella proudly wrote of her memories of the gifts, decorations, and lavish banquet that marked this turning point of her life.

Under the skillful rule of Francesco and Isabella, Mantua rose to the foremost rank of the smaller Italian city-states. Isabella involved herself in the art of diplomacy throughout the couple's reign. She wrote more than two thousand letters—many of them to popes, kings, and other Italian rulers. In one letter to her husband, Isabella assured him that he could concentrate completely on military matters, for "I intend to govern the State . . . in such a manner that you will suffer no wrong, and all that is possible will be done for the good of your subjects." This talented woman was as good as her word, for when Francesco was captured in 1509 and imprisoned, Isabella ruled in his stead and valiantly saved the city from invasion.

Like other Italians influenced by Renaissance pseudoscience, Isabella avidly believed in astrology. She embarked on no important venture without consulting her astrologers. But she also took an interest in the real-world findings of the time. She received correspondence about Columbus's discovery of America and the "intelligent and gentle" natives she found there.

Yet the educated duchess is most remembered as a patron of the arts. She wrote explicit instructions for the works she commissioned: One painting prompted her to pen as many as forty letters. Recognizing excellence, she wanted to commission a work from Leonardo da Vinci, but the artist never found the time to oblige her. (See Document 10.1.)

With a love of literature nurtured since her youth, Isabella accumulated a library that became one of the best in Italy. She took advantage of the new printing industry to acquire the first editions of the great classics as well as the contemporary works of Petrarch and Dante. Her requests for these editions show her appreciation of beauty even in her search for literature: She asked for books printed on parchment (instead of paper) and bound in leather.

When Isabella was 64 years old, Francesco died. The aging duchess turned to her many children and grandchildren for comfort and companionship. She took particular delight in one grandchild who could recite Virgil at the age of only 5. Isabella died in 1539, a year after losing her husband. In the last months of her life, a great scholar of the age called her "the wisest and most fortunate of women"—an apt epitaph for someone who so personified the Renaissance spirit.

■ **Chapter Previews and Summaries.** Each chapter opens with a short preview and telling anecdote that, together, set the stage for understanding the material. We have included "Study" and "Notice" prompts to help students think critically about the main themes of the chapter. Chapters then end with a summary of key themes. Rather than dry outlines, these features instead preserve the engaging narrative style while satisfying the pedagogical dictum: "Tell them what they'll learn; teach them, then tell them what they have learned." The chapter previews and reviews help students stay focused on the main themes in the narrative.

A WORLD DIVIDED

WESTERN KINGDOMS, BYZANTIUM, AND THE
ISLAMIC WORLD, CA. 376–1000

| STUDY | Germanic life, values, and the establishment of their kingdoms in western Europe ■ The Byzantine Empire, its characteristics and relationship with its neighbors ■ Islamic religion, life, and expansion. |
| NOTICE | That as the Roman Empire breaks up, the Islamic world confronts the West. |

"The harsh nature of war! The malevolent fate of all things! How proud kingdoms fall, suddenly in ruins! Blissful housetops that held up for long ages now lie torched, consumed beneath a huge devastation." These lines, written by Radegund, a nun living in sixth-century Gaul, poignantly express the turbulent world in which she lived. The Roman Empire was no longer a political unit that people could rely on for peace within its borders. The once mighty empire had fragmented into three culturally distinct parts separated by religion, language, and loyalties.

In the west, Germanic invaders established new kingdoms and converted to Christianity. Popes in Rome slowly became a force to be acknowledged in the west. In the east, the political form of the Roman Empire continued at least nominally for another thousand years. However, centered in the great city founded by Constantine, and separated from Rome, Byzantium began developing its own distinct character. The language of government changed to Greek, and people began to mingle more with the Slavic tribes to the north than with the Latins in the west. Finally, the desert of Arabia produced a prophet, Muhammad, who profoundly influenced the religious beliefs of millions. Followers of the new religion of Islam swept out of the desert and conquered the eastern and southern shores of the Mediterranean, as well as most of Spain. These three civilizations—the heirs of Rome—existed in uneasy, sometimes violent, proximity. Their differences and conflicts would remake the map of the Mediterranean basin and shatter the Roman unity that had graced the land for so long.

175

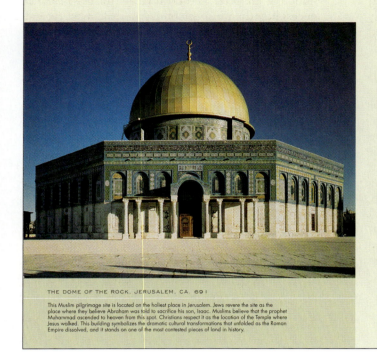

THE DOME OF THE ROCK, JERUSALEM, CA. 691

This Muslim pilgrimage site is located on the holiest place in Jerusalem. Jews revere the site as the place where they believe Abraham was told to sacrifice his son, Isaac. Muslims believe that the prophet Muhammad ascended to heaven from this spot. Christians respect it as the location of the Temple where Jesus walked. This building symbolizes the dramatic cultural transformations that unfolded as the Roman Empire dissolved, and it stands on one of the most contested pieces of land in history.

SUMMARY

After the sixth century, the Mediterranean world of the old Roman Empire underwent a dramatic transformation. The Roman Empire in the west dissolved in the face of the rising Germanic kingdoms. The empire persisted in the east, but in a drastically changed form known as the Byzantine Empire. In the south, armies of the new religion of Islam conquered vast territories to create a new society and culture. Islam arose in part as a reaction to the Byzantine Empire and Christianity. Although they worshiped the same God as Christians and Jews, Muslims worshiped in a different way. Consequently, they developed a new way of life that led to a vigorous synthesis of the cultures of the many lands they conquered.

The emergence of this third culture in the lands of the old Roman Empire brought warfare, suffering, and religious tensions, but also a rejuvenated intellectual life. The West and Byzantium did not adopt Islamic religion, but they learned much from Muslim philosophers, scientists, and poets. From this time forward, the interactions among these three great cultures—western European, Byzantine, and Muslim—would profoundly shape the history of the West.

- **Clear Headings and Marginal Notes.** Each chapter has clear thematic titles and precise headings that guide students through the narrative. Throughout, brief marginal notes help students focus on the key concepts, terms, and events and provide a tool for reviewing the chapter.

poster shown in Figure 16.7, printed just after France became a republic, is a typical example. The poster announces principles at the core of the Republic: "Unity, indivisibility of the Republic. Liberty, equality, fraternity, or death." A triangle of authorities—"God, People, Law"—shines its blessings on these principles. Also blessed are the liberty trees that symbolize the Revolution, the one at the left topped by a "liberty cap"; the one at the right, by a helmet from France's citizen army.

In the name of reason and revolutionary principles, the government revamped the calendar, making the months equal in length and naming them after the seasons. Weeks were made ten days long, with one day of rest. (This change eliminated Sunday, a day of traditional Christian importance.) September 22, 1792—the date of the declaration of the Republic—became the first day of Year I. The new metric system of weights and measures based on units of 10 was introduced and eventually would spread beyond France's borders to countries throughout the world.

■ FIGURE 16.7
A republican poster.

THE REVOLUTION SPREADS OUTSIDE OF FRANCE

Sister republics
Since 1792, France had fended off various coalitions of European powers. After initial defeats, France's citizen armies had gone on the offensive. During the struggles that ensued, France incorporated lands on its northern and eastern borders, claiming that these additions conformed to France's "natural boundaries" of the Rhine and the Alps. By 1799, more victories on the battlefield enabled France to set up "sister" republics in Holland, Switzerland, and Italy. To these areas, the French brought their own Enlightenment-inspired revolutionary principles and legislation. However, the gains carried a tremendous price tag. Hundreds of thousands died in the fighting, and the constant warfare disrupted trade and created shortages of essential goods.

Outside opinion
The Revolution also powerfully influenced opinion outside France. Initially many groups in nearby countries supported the Revolution and its principles. However, part of that support rested on seeing France, a powerful rival, weakened. As people began to understand the seriousness of the attacks on monarchy and aristocracy and the threat to their own political independence, support waned. Still, many intellectuals and liberal political groups continued to uphold the ideals of the Revolution, at least until 1793 when the Revolution took a more radical turn.

The Revolution helped promote other developments farther away. In Poland, patriots tried to use inspiration from France to assert independence from Russia. Despite some initial successes, however,

their efforts failed. In Ireland, the revolutionary doctrines of liberty, equality, and natural rights touched many, encouraging them to rise against their British lords and make Ireland a republic. Irish patriots even anticipated a French invasion to help their own rebellion, although the invasion never took place.

Uprisings

In the Caribbean, slaves in France's lucrative colony of St. Domingue (Haiti) took heart from revolutionary principles and revolted. As Figure 16.8, a French print, reveals, the 1791 slave uprising struck fear in the hearts of white settlers. Slaves, outnumbering white settlers, attack a plantation. Women and men fall under the knives, swords, and cannon of the slaves, while plantation buildings go up in flames. Reports from French settlers, such as the wealthy Madame de Rouvray, described how the slaves "slaughtered and torched much of the countryside hereabouts," and warned, "how can we stay in a country where slaves have raised their hands against their masters?"

After much maneuvering and the abolishing of slavery by the National Convention in February 1794, the rebel leader Toussaint L'Ouverture and his black generals gained control of St. Domingue. The determined group would go on to successfully oppose English, Spanish, and French armies, turning the island into the independent republic of Haiti in 1804.

RESISTANCE TO THE REPUBLIC RISES

Despite the Reign of Terror and efforts to establish a Republic of Virtue, violent resistance to the Republic persisted and, in some cases, grew. Its leadership consisted primarily of local aristocrats and notables, officials who had fallen out of favor with the Jacobins, Girondin sympathizers, and members of the

- **Reminder Dates.** Many instructors and reviewers have told us that students lack a sense of chronology. We believe that this problem stems in part from the way history texts are written—as the narrative progresses in a linear way, students lose track of simultaneous developments, and indeed of the dates themselves. We have added several features to strengthen readers' sense of chronology. For example, we include dates in the chapter titles and many of the chapter subheadings. We have also sprinkled important dates throughout the narrative and whenever key individuals are named. We have also added new **Key Dates** tables within the chapter discussions.

- **"The Big Picture" Time Lines.** As a significant feature to address the understanding of chronology, we have included a time line at the beginning of each chapter. These timelines, called "The Big Picture," show blocks that indicate the large events, periods, or dynasties that will be covered within the chapter.

- **Thinking About Geography.** Because a sense of geography is essential to the study of history, we have included a wealth of full-color maps, and we treat them uniquely. As instructors know very well, too often students just glance at maps without understanding them or engaging them critically. The "Thinking About Geography" feature provides analytical exercises that invite students to delve into the meaning of each map. We hope this approach will not only help students remember particular maps, but will also get them into the habit of actively seeking to understand how geographic features shape human events.

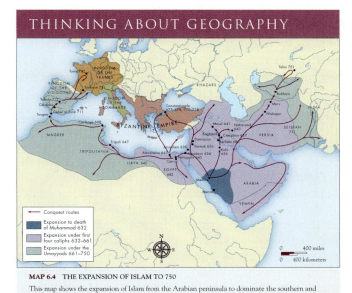

MAP 6.4   THE EXPANSION OF ISLAM TO 750

This map shows the expansion of Islam from the Arabian peninsula to dominate the southern and eastern Mediterranean. It also gives the dates of the expansion. ■ Which sections of the Byzantine Empire were lost to the Muslims? ■ Notice the scale on the map. Consider the difficulties in governing such a large area. ■ Locate Mecca, Damascus, and Baghdad—each in turn would become the capital of the Muslim world. Which regions might be most influenced by the change in capitals? Where might the Islamic rulers be most likely to focus their efforts while based in each city?

■ **Glossary and Pronunciation Guide.** One of the challenges for history students is learning the vocabulary that shapes our discipline. We retain many of the features that make this process easier. All these terms—and others—are highlighted in bold type, collected in new end-of-chapter Key Terms lists, and briefly defined in the Glossary at the end of the book (that is conveniently marked by a color border to make it easy to locate). All the words, except the most simple, come with a pronunciation guide. This feature allows students to readily review terms, while giving them the confidence in pronunciation to help make the terms part of their vocabulary.

■ **Review, Analyze, and Anticipate.** At the end of each chapter are questions that not only ask students to think about the material discussed within the chapter, but also encourage them to place the material within the context of what has come before and what is coming next. The summary paragraphs included within these sections offer continuous reviews and previews of material, once again helping students to retain the larger picture while learning new details.

■ **Beyond the Classroom.** Like all teaching faculty, we hope that education goes beyond the textbook. At the end of each chapter, we have included annotated bibliographies of some of the most useful works in the field. These books are arranged to match the main headings of the chapters so students can more easily follow their interests. Our extensive online support materials are also part of our "beyond the classroom" concept, as students can have access to many research tools through our online "Primary Source Investigator" (PSI), sample quizzes, map exercises, and many other multimedia tools.

A NOTE ABOUT THE DATING SYSTEM

The various civilizations across the world do not all use the same dating system. For example, Muslims use the date 622 (when the Prophet fled from Mecca to Medina) as year 1 in their history. The Hebrew calendar counts the Western year 3760 B.C.E. as year 1—which some consider to be when the world was created.

Before about the seventh century, people in the West (and in many other parts of the world) used dating systems based on rulers. That is, they might say "in the third year of the reign of Emperor Vespasian." Beginning in about the seventh century, many people in the West began to use a dating system that counts backward and forward from the birth of Christ, which Westerners consider year 1. Events that took place "Before Christ," designated as B.C., were counted backward from year 1. Thus, something that happened 300 years before Christ's birth was dated 300 B.C. Events that took place after the birth of

---

GLOSSARY

Note to users: Terms that are foreign or difficult to pronounce are transcribed in parentheses directly after the term itself. The transcriptions are based on the rules of English spelling; that is to say, they are similar to the transcriptions employed in the *Webster* dictionaries. Each word's most heavily stressed syllable is marked by an acute accent:

A

Absolute monarch (máh-nark) A seventeenth- or eighteenth-century European monarch claiming complete political authority.

Absolutism (áb-suh-loo-tism) (Royal) A government in which all power is vested in the ruler.

Abstract expressionism (ex-présh-un-ism) A twentieth-century painting style infusing nonrepresentational art with strong personal feelings.

Acropolis (uh-króp-uh-liss) The hill at the center of Athens on which the magnificent temples—including the Parthenon—that made the architecture of ancient Athens famous are built.

Act of Union Formal unification of England and Scotland in 1707.

Afrikaners Afrikaans speaking South Africans of Dutch and other European ancestry.

Age of Reason The eighteenth-century Enlightenment; sometimes includes seventeenth-century science and philosophy.

Agora In ancient Greece, the marketplace or place of public assembly.

Agricultural revolution Neolithic discovery of agriculture; agricultural transformations that began in eighteenth-century western Europe.

Ahura Mazda In Zoroastrianism, the beneficial god of light.

Ahriman In Zoroastrianism, the evil god of darkness.

Akkadian (uh-káy-dee-un) A Semitic language of a region of ancient Mesopotamia.

Albigensians (al-buh-jén-see-unz) A medieval French heretical sect that believed in two gods—an evil and a good principle—that was destroyed in a crusade in the thirteenth century; also called Cathars.

Alchemy The medieval study and practice of chemistry, primarily concerned with changing metals into gold and finding a universal remedy for diseases. It was much practiced from the thirteenth to the seventeenth century.

Allies (ál-eyes) The two alliances against Germany and its partners in World War I and World War II.

Al-Qaeda A global terrorist network headed by Osama bin Laden.

Anarchists (ánn-ar-kissts) Those advocating or promoting anarchy, or an absence of government. In the late-nineteenth- and early-twentieth-century, anarchism arose as an ideology and movement against all governmental authority and private property.

Ancien Régime (áwn-syáwn ráy-zhéem) The traditional political and social order in Europe before the French Revolution.

Antigonids (ann-tíg-un-idz) Hellenistic dynasty that ruled in Macedonia from about 300 B.C.E. to about 150 B.C.E.

Anti-Semitism (ann-tye-sém-i-tism) Prejudice against Jews.

Apartheid "Separation" in the Afrikaans language. A policy to rigidly segregate people by color in South Africa, 1948–1989.

Appeasement Attempting to satisfy potential aggressors in order to avoid war.

Aramaic (air-uh-máy-ik) A northwest Semitic language that spread throughout the region. It was the language that Jesus spoke.

Archon (áhr-kahn) A chief magistrate in ancient Athens.

Areopagus (air-ee-áh-pa-gus) A prestigious governing council of ancient Athens.

Arete (ah-ray-táy) Greek term for the valued virtues of manliness, courage, and excellence.

Arianism (áir-ee-un-ism) A fourth-century Christian heresy that taught that Jesus was not of the same substance as God the father, and thus had been created.

Assignats (ah-seen-yáh) Paper money issued in the National Assembly during the French Revolution.

Astrolabe (áss-tro-leyb) Medieval instrument used to determine the altitudes of celestial bodies.

Augury (áh-gur-ee) The art or practice of foretelling events though signs or omens.

Autocrat (áuto-crat) An authoritarian ruler.

Autocracy (au-tóc-ra-cee) Government under the rule of an authoritarian ruler.

Axis World War II alliance whose main members were Germany, Italy, and Japan.

B

Baby boom The increase in births following World War II.

Babylonian Captivity Period during the fourteenth century in which seven popes chose to reside in Avignon instead of Rome. Critics called this period the "Babylonian Captivity" of the papacy.

Bailiffs Medieval French salaried officials hired by the king to collect taxes and represent his interests.

Balance of power Distribution of power among states, or the policy of creating alliances to control powerful states.

Balkans States in the Balkan Peninsula, including Albania, Bulgaria, Greece, Romania, and Yugoslavia.

Baroque (ba-róak) An artistic style of the sixteenth and seventeenth centuries stressing rich ornamentation and dynamic movement; in music, a style marked by strict forms and elaborate ornamentation.

Bastard feudalism (feúd-a-lism) Late medieval corruption of the feudal system replacing feudal loyalty with cash payments.

After the sixth century, the Mediterranean world of the old Roman Empire underwent a dramatic transformation. The Roman Empire in the west dissolved in the face of the rising Germanic kingdoms. The empire persisted in the east, but in a drastically changed form known as the Byzantine Empire. In the south, armies of the new religion of Islam conquered vast territories to create a new society and culture. Islam arose in part as a reaction to the Byzantine Empire and Christianity. Although they worshiped the same God as Christians and Jews, Muslims worshiped in a different way. Consequently, they developed a new way of life that led to a vigorous synthesis of the cultures of the many lands they conquered.

The emergence of this third culture in the lands of the old Roman Empire brought warfare, suffering, and religious tensions, but also a rejuvenated intellectual life. The West and Byzantium did not adopt Islamic religion, but they learned much from Muslim philosophers, scientists, and poets. From this time forward, the interactions among these three great cultures—western European, Byzantine, and Muslim—would profoundly shape the history of the West.

REVIEW, ANALYZE, AND ANTICIPATE

REVIEW THE PREVIOUS CHAPTER

Chapter 5—"Territorial and Christian Empires"—followed the difficulties of the late Roman Empire and studied Diocletian's reforms in which he tried to reorganize and preserve the empire, and Constantine's movement of the capital to the east.

1. *What elements of Diocletian's reforms did the Byzantine emperors continue? Why did many of these reforms endure more in the east than in the west?*

2. *Review the reasons Constantine moved his capital. In what ways did his decision prove to be sound in the face of the events of the fifth and sixth centuries?*

ANALYZE THIS CHAPTER

Chapter 6—"A World Divided"—shows how three distinct cultures emerged in the old territory of the Roman Empire.

1. *Review the various characteristics of the societies of the Byzantine Empire, the Muslim lands, and the western kingdoms. What are the strengths and weaknesses of each?*

2. *Compare and contrast the beliefs of Christianity, Judaism, and Islam.*

3. *What accounted for the rapid expansion of Islam?*

4. *As the Slavs converted to Christianity, they established cultural patterns that would affect Europe for millennia. Review the Slavic settlements and their conversion to Christianity.*

5. *Review the main elements of Muslim culture, including the forces of unity and disunity that helped shape the lands of Islam.*

ANTICIPATE THE NEXT CHAPTER

Chapter 7—"The Struggle to Bring Order"—will trace the development of the Western kingdoms, and in Chapter 8—"Order Restored"—we will see the three powers—Byzantium, Islam, and the West—confront each other again on the battlefield.

1. *Which of the western kingdoms do you expect to emerge first as the most powerful? Why?*

2. *Over what territory and what issues do you expect the three great powers to clash? Why?*

BEYOND THE CLASSROOM

THE MAKING OF THE WESTERN KINGDOMS, CA. 376–750

Brown, Peter. *The Rise of Western Christendom: Triumph and Diversity, A.D. 200–1000.* Boston: Blackwell, 1997. A highly readable narrative with a breadth of coverage presented by a master historian. Includes the Persian empire and the differing development of the eastern and western church.

Glob, P.V. *The Bog People; Iron Age Man Preserved.* Translated by R. Bruce-Mitford. Ithaca, NY: Cornell University Press, 1969. A fascinating archaeological study of Iron Age people and their culture, based on the excavations of corpses from the bogs.

Grant, Michael. *The Fall of the Roman Empire.* New York: Macmillan, 1990. A highly illustrated text illuminating why the fall of the western Roman Empire has been regarded as one of the most significant transformations in history.

Noble, T.F.X. *The Republic of St. Peter: The Birth of the Papal State, 680–825.* Philadelphia: University of Pennsylvania Press, 1984. A clear study of the growth of the papacy in these early, little-studied centuries.

Christ were also dated from the hypothetical year 1 and were labeled A.D., which stands for the Latin *anno Domini*, meaning "in the year of the lord."

In the twentieth century, many historians, scholars and others who recognized that the West was not solely Christian, wanted a dating designation that could apply more easily to non-Christians and that could be used more universally in a global context. They kept the same numerical system—counting backward and forward using the hypothetical date of Jesus's birth—but changed the designations. Now the common usage is "B.C.E.," which means "Before the Common Era," and "C.E.," the "Common Era"—and we have adopted this system in the third edition of *The West in the World*. The events described in the first four chapters all took place in B.C.E. In Chapter 5, we've marked all dates with C.E., but because everything after that time is C.E., we then drop the designation.

SUPPLEMENTS

PRIMARY SOURCE INVESTIGATOR ONLINE

McGraw-Hill's Primary Source Investigator (PSI), now available online at www.mhhe.com/psi, is designed to support and enrich the text discussion in *The West in the World, 3/e*. PSI gives instructors and students access to more than 650 primary and secondary sources including documents, images, maps, and videos. Students can use these resources to formulate and defend their arguments as well as further their understanding of the topics discussed in each chapter. All assets are also indexed alphabetically as well as by type, subject, place, and time period, allowing students and instructors to locate resources quickly and easily.

STUDENT RESOURCES IN PSI

Primary Source Documents: This database, which has been updated for *The West in the World*, 3e, includes items from a wide range of contemporary accounts. Each document is accompanied by a detailed description and a series of critical thinking questions that draw students into the content and engages them in thoughtful analysis.

Images: This extensive collection includes photographs of artifacts and buildings as well as contemporary paintings, engravings, and drawings. Each image is also accompanied by a description and critical thinking questions.

Interactive Maps: Each map's legend is interactive, allowing students to see historical change over time and to compare various factors in the order of their choice.

Sites: Organized by chapter, this feature lists reliable Internet sites that provide further information on particular topics. These can be particularly useful to students who are searching for dependable research sources.

Books: This list includes both standard texts as well as the most recent scholarship on topics within each chapter, another valuable resource for student researchers.

Movies: This list includes both educational and commercial films.

Events: More than simply a timeline, this feature includes annotated entries of important events in chronological order.

NEW! Online Reader: New for The West in the World, *3e*, the Online Reader gives students an opportunity to try their hand at historical analysis. Based upon sources found in PSI, the reader's modules ask students to evaluate sources and formulate their own interpretation of an historical event, providing valuable skills for their own research.

NEW! Writing Guide: New for The West in the World, *3e*, the online Writing Guide offers both general assistance for writing college papers, as well as specific tips for history papers. Topics include research, paragraph and argument creation, a comparison of style guides, information on plagiarism and source citation, and much more.

INSTRUCTOR RESOURCES IN PSI

Faculty Guide: The Faculty Guide provides easy reference to all learning assets, both in the text and on PSI, available to teachers and students. Each chapter is accompanied by a rich list of resources, including **PowerPoint slides, image bank, outline maps, book maps,** and **test bank questions,** all keyed to the chapter. Resources are organized within chapters by A-Heads to streamline lecture and assignment preparation. Icons allow users to quickly differ-

ADDITIONAL RESOURCES FOR INSTRUCTORS

- The **Online Learning Center for Instructors** at www.mhhe.com/sherman3 contains several instructor tools including a link to the faculty guide on Primary Source Investigator (www.mhhe.com/psi), and PowerPoint presentations for each chapter. The instructor side of the OLC is password protected to prevent tampering. Please contact your local McGraw-Hill representative for details.

- A **Computerized Test Bank,** McGraw-Hill's **EZ Test** allows you to quickly create a customized test using the publishers supplied test banks or your own questions. You decide the number, type and order of test questions with a few simple clicks. **EZ Test** runs on your computer without a connection to the Internet.

- **Videos** on topics in world history are available through the Films for Humanities and Sciences collection. Contact your local McGraw-Hill sales representative for further information.

- **Classroom Performance System (CPS).** The Classroom Performance System brings ultimate interactivity to *The West in the World*. CPS is a wireless response system that gives you immediate feedback from every student in the class. With CPS you can ask subjective and objective questions during your lecture, prompting every student to respond with their individual, wireless response pad, and providing you with instant results. A complete CPS Tutorial is available at www.einstruction.com.

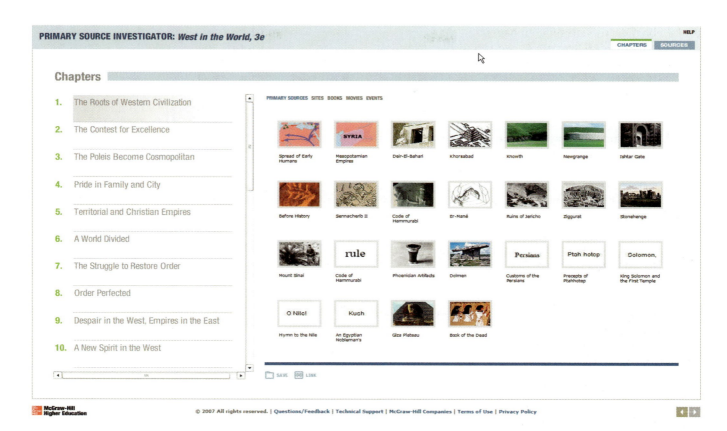

entiate between text and PSI sources. Each asset is listed by title and includes a brief annotation.

In addition to assets, the Faculty Guide also includes a chapter overview, a list of themes, lecture strategies, discussion suggestions, suggestions for further reading, and chapter-specific film recommendations. These, too, are organized by chapter and A-Head to make classroom implementation simple.

ADDITIONAL RESOURCES FOR STUDENTS

- The **Online Learning Center for Students** at www. mhhe.com/sherman3 provides students with a wide range of tools that will help them test their knowledge of the book. It includes chapter overviews, interactive maps, multiple choice and essay quizzes, matching and identification games, as well as primary source indexes for further research.

- Two **After the Fact Interactive** units are available for use with *The West in the World:* After the Fact Interactive: Tracing the Silk Roads" for volume 1 (ISBN: 0072818433), and "After the Fact Interactive: Envisioning the Atlantic World" for volume 2 (ISBN 0072818441). These rich, visually appealing modules on CD-ROM allow students to be apprentice historians, examining a variety of multimedia primary source material and constructing arguments based on their research.

- **Videos** Created and narrated by Joyce Salisbury, this three-video collection illuminates the author's lectures on the Middle Ages with the sculpture and fine art of the times. Available to adopters through your local McGraw-Hill representative, this unique series contains a video on each of the following topics: medieval women, medieval Judaism, and medieval life. A wide range of videos on classic and contemporary topics in history is available through the Films for the Humanities and Sciences collection. Instructors can illustrate classroom discussion and enhance lectures by selecting from a series of videos that are correlated to complement *The West in the World.* Contact your local McGraw-Hill sales representative for further information.

ACKNOWLEDGMENTS

We have nurtured this book through many drafts, and every page has benefited from the advice of numerous reviewers, some of whom we have gone back to several times. For their thoughtful comments and generous contribution of time and expertise, we would like to thank the following reviewers:

For the Third Edition

April Brooks, *South Dakota State University*; Daniel Patrick Brown, *Moorpark College*; Kathleen Carter, *High Point University*; Laura Cruz, *Western Carolina University*; Philip Daileader, *College of William and Mary*; Cassie Farrelly, *Fordham University*; Beth Fickling, *Coastal Carolina Community College*; Ginger Guardiola, *Colorado State University*; Jennifer Hedda, *Simpson College*; Barry Jackisch, *Gannon University*; Molly Johnson, *University of Alabama–Huntsville*; William Kinsella, *Northern Virginia Community College*; Todd Larson, *Xavier University*; Elizabeth Lehfeldt, *Cleveland State University*; William Lipkin, *Union County College*; Nancy Locklin, *Maryville College*; Karl Loewenstein, *University of Wisconsin–Oshkosh*; Michael Loughlin, *Ohio Northern University*; Jack Pesda, *Camden County College*; Penne Prigge, *Rockingham Community College*; Dana Sample, *University of Virginia's College at Wise*

For the Second Edition

Joseph Appiah, *Virginia Community College*; Douglas C. Baxter, *Ohio University*; Jonathan Bone, *William Patterson University*; Suzanne Bowles, *William Patterson University*; April Brooks, *South Dakota State University*; Katherine Clark, *University of Kansas*; Sandi Cooper, *City University of New York*; Florin Curta, *University of Florida*; Norman C. Delany, *Del Mar College*; David D. Flaten, *Plymouth State College*; Marsha L. Frey, *Kansas State University*; Bruce Garver, *University of Nebraska at Omaha*; Carla Hay, *Marquette University*; Holly Hurlburt, *Southern Illinois University*; Andrew Keitt, *University of Alabama at Birmingham*; Dave Kelly, *Colorado State University*; Jason Knirck, *Humboldt State University*; Mark W. McLeod, *University of Delaware*; Carol Menning, *University of Toledo*; Jeffrey Lee Meriwether, *Roger Williams University*; Zachary Morgan, *William Patterson University*; Michael Myers, *University of Illinois*; Max Okenfuss, *Washington University*; Jack Pesda, *Camden County College*; Dolores Davison Peterson, *Foothill College*; Paul Rempe, *Carroll College*; Harry Rosenberg, *Colorado State University*; Shawn Ross, *William Patterson University*; Glenn Sanders, *Oklahoma Baptist University*; Marc Schwarz, *University of New Hampshire*; David Stefanic, *Saint Mary's College*; Aliza Wong, *Texas Technical University*; Michael A. Zaccaria, *Cumberland County College*

For the First Edition

Edward Anson, *University of Arkansas*; William S. Arnett, *West Virginia University*; Richard Berthold, *University of New Mexico*; Robert Blackey, *California State University–San Bernardino*; Hugh Boyer, *Michigan Technical University*; Carol Bresnahan-Menning, *University of Toledo*; April Brooks, *South Dakota State University*; Nathan Brooks, *New Mexico State University*; Blaine T. Browne, *Broward Community College*; Donald Butts, *Gordon College*; Frederick Corney, *University of Florida*; Jeffrey Cox, *University of Iowa*; Florin Curta, *University of Florida*; Norman Delaney, *Del Mar College*; Robert Dise, *University of Northern Iowa*; Chris Drake, *Houston Community College–Northwest*; Lawrence G. Duggan, *University of Delaware*; Laird Easton, *California State University–Chico*; Gregory Elder, *Riverside Community College*; Nancy Erickson, *Erskine College*; Chiarella Esposito, *University of Mississippi*; Gary Ferngren, *Oregon State University*; Nancy Fitch, *California State University–Fullerton*; Elizabeth Lane Furdell, *University of North Florida*; Frank Garosi, *California State University–Sacramento*; Don Gawronski, *Mesa Community College*; Paul Goodwin, *University of Connecticut*; Anita Guerrini, *University of California–Santa Barbara*; Louis Haas, *Duquesne University*; Alice Henderson, *University of South Carolina–Spartanburg*; Jennifer Hevelone-Harper, *Gordon College*; Steven Hill, *Wake Technical Community College*; Laura J. Hilton, *Ohio State University*; Karen Holland, *Providence College*; David Hudson, *California State University–Fresno*; Gary Johnson, *University of Southern Maine*; Jonathan G. Katz, *Oregon State University*; Andrew Keitt, *University of Alabama–Birmingham*; Charles Killinger, *Valencia Community College*; Lisa Lane, *Mira Costa College*; John Livingston, *University of Denver*; David Longfellow, *Baylor University*; Donna Maier, *University of Northern Iowa*; James I. Martin Sr., *Campbell University*; Carol Miller, *Tallahassee Community College*; Eileen Moore, *University of Alabama–Birmingham*; Frederick I. Murphy, *Western Kentucky University*; Max J. Okenfuss, *Washington University*; Michael Osborne, *University of California–Santa Barbara*; Jack Pesda, *Camden County College*; Russell Quinlan, *Northern Arizona University*; Patricia Ranft, *Central Michigan University*; Roger Reese, *Texas A&M University*; Harry Rosenberg, *Colorado State University*; Constance M. Rousseau, *Providence College*; Jay Rubenstein, *University of New Mexico*; Claire Sanders, *Texas Christian College*; Alan Schaffer, *Clemson University*; Daryl Schuster, *University of Central Florida*; Marc Schwarz, *University of New Hampshire*; David Shearer, *University of Delaware*; Arlene Sindelar, *University of Central Arkansas*; James Sisson, *Central Texas College*; Ronald D. Smith, *Arizona State University*; Saulius Suziedelis, *Millersville University of Pennsylvania*; Hunt Tooley, *Austin College*; Kevin Uhalde, *Northern Illinois*

University; David Ulbrich, *Kansas State University*; Bruce Venarde, *University of Pittsburgh*; Charlotte Wells, *University of Northern Iowa*; Michael Wilson, *University of Texas–Dallas*; Robert Wise, *University of Northern Iowa*; Bill Wrightson, *American River College*

In addition to our reviewers and focus group participants, we would also like to thank Jon-David Hague, sponsoring editor; Karen Helfrich, developmental editor; Susan Gouijnstook, Chanda Feldman, and the rest of the third edition team, whose efforts have made this a better book. We also thank Lauren Johnson, developmental editor for the previous edition. Last, but certainly not least, we would like to thank the many professors who choose to use this text in their classrooms. It is they who will fulfill our hope for this text—that it will bring the past to life for many undergraduates and will perhaps awaken in them a love for history and an awareness that understanding the past is the key to our future.

TO YOU, THE STUDENT: HOW TO USE THIS BOOK

WELCOME TO THE STUDY OF WESTERN CIVILIZATION! The word "West" does not refer to one geographic location, but rather a series of cultures that first emerged in the ancient Middle East, spread to the Mediterranean world and Europe, and eventually crossed the seas to the Americas and elsewhere. Today, there is scarcely any culture in the world not touched by the West. Yet from the beginning, the West has also been powerfully influenced by its interactions with cultures outside its moving center. *The West in the World* emphasizes this global, interactive quality rather than analyzing the West's story in isolation. To get the most out of this book, we suggest you use the process described below as you read each chapter. (Try these same techniques with textbooks in your other courses, too—you'll likely find them just as valuable there.)

1. Preview the chapter. Find out what the chapter is about before you start reading it. Look at the chapter "study" and "notice" points at the beginning, and read the preview that appears next to the opening illustration. These two features set the stage for what you are about to read. You might also want to go to the end of the chapter, where there are two tools to help you focus on what is important: 1.) See the list of "Key Terms," so you will watch for them as you read; 2.) glance at the "Analyze This Chapter" questions, because they will give you an idea of the most important points in the chapter. Finally, a chapter outline from our online study guide is also available at www.mhhe.com/sherman3.

2. Read the chapter as you would a good story. Try to get engaged in the narrative. That is, don't read the chapter too slowly. However, *do* notice each sub-heading in the chapter—these signal what's coming next. Also, resist the urge to highlight *everything!* The margin notes we have provided tell you what topics are covered in the paragraphs you are reading, so just highlight the portion that explains the main points of the margin note. For example, in Chapter 4, under the heading "Wars of the Mediterranean," the margin note says "First Punic War." Within that paragraph, we suggest that you just highlight who fought and what was the outcome. Then when you review the chapter to study for your tests, you will be able to keep track of the flow of history.

3. Examine and think about the illustrations. We've also included descriptions and analyses of the illustrations. When you come to an illustration, pause and look carefully at it. This process will help you get used to interpreting visual sources. One illustration in each chapter is set apart with a series of critical thinking questions. This feature—"Thinking About Art"—allows you to practice interpreting visual sources and to experience how historians use art as a window into the past. The illustrations in each chapter will also trigger your memory of the chapter's content when you study the chapter later.

Here are a few general questions to guide you as you read and analyze illustrations:

- Read the discussion of the image within the text and read the caption label. Identify who is the artist (if known). What is the date of the illustration? Where was it created? What is the subject?
- What information might the artist have been attempting to convey to the viewer about this subject? What seems to be the artist's attitude about the subject?
- With the aid of the chapter discussion, try to look at the illustration as if it were a document: What would it be saying to you?
- What might the illustration reveal about a society, about how people behaved, how they thought, what they believed, and what they valued?
- How might this illustration add to the written narrative or support some conclusions in the text?

4. Examine and think about the maps. Geography plays a huge role in history, so it's vital that you know how to read and interpret maps. We've provided "Thinking About Geography" questions with each map to help you understand how it fits in with the chapter as a whole. Try to answer the questions (even if you're not sure how)—they'll help you review the material in the chapter. Also, sharpen your map skills by practicing the interactive map exercises for each chapter in the online study guide.

Here are a few general questions to guide you as you read and analyze maps:

- Broadly, what does the map show?
- Look more closely at the map's contours and examine its labels and its key. What specific information is emphasized within the map?
- What relationships or interactions are conveyed by the map elements?
- How does the map and the information if contains relate to events described in the chapter's narrative?
- How might geography help explain, for example, an era's political and military developments?

5. Use the primary source documents in each chapter. Within each chapter's narrative are relevant primary sources. Each source, "Thinking About Documents," begins with a brief introduction and questions to help you analyze the document and connect it to chapter topics. Working with primary documents is the heart of the historian's craft, and these document boxes let you experience the creative part of historical research.

In addition to the questions accompanying each document, try to answer the following general questions, which can help you analyze each document and its relevance to chapter topics and themes:

- Read the title and introduction. Who is the author of the document?
- When was this account written and for what purpose?
- Who is the intended audience?
- Is the account reliable? Is it an eyewitness account? Does the author have obvious bias about the subject?
- What does this document reveal about the subject or issues it discusses?
- How does this document relate to events and concepts discussed in the chapter?
- How might this document add to the chapter narrative or support some conclusions in the text?
- What does this document—line by line—reveal about a society, about how people behaved, how they thought, and what they believed?

Consider each document as a window on to another aspect of the political, cultural, and social environment of the times. If you are particularly interested in one document, you may want to conduct further research.

6. Examine and think about the "Biography," and "Global Connections" features. These boxes provide more information about the time period covered in the chapter. Information in the chapter connects directly to these features, so watch carefully for these relationships. These two features can serve as an additional review of the chapter while helping you understand one topic more deeply. By answering the "consider" questions at the head of each box, you build your critical-thinking skills while you review.

7. Review the timelines and "Key Dates" charts. Some people may lose track of chronology—that is, the sequence in which major developments and events occurred—while they're reading narrative histories. The chapter's timeline and Key Dates charts will help you keep track of chronology. The timeline at the beginning of the chapter gives you the large developments that will help you preview and review the material. The "Key Dates" charts help summarize important events covered in the chapter. As you examine these, make sure everything in them is familiar. If you see something you don't understand in a timeline or "Key Dates" chart, go back into the chapter to fill in the gaps. These timelines and chronologies make excellent review tools.

8. Review "Key Terms." These terms should be familiar to you if you looked at them as you previewed the chapter. Now review them again to be sure you know the definitions and the historical significance of each term. Check any unfamiliar terms in the Glossary at the end of the book. When you study for tests, review the Key Terms again to remind you of important concepts discussed in the chapter.

9. Review the chapter. Answer the "Review, Analyze, and Anticipate" questions at the end of the chapter, even if you just compose your responses in your mind. Better yet, talk over your responses with other students in your class. The "Review the Previous Chapters" questions will help you connect the material you just read with preceding chapters; the "Analyze This Chapter" questions focus on the material in the current chapter; and the "Anticipate the Next Chapter" questions point you to future chapters. Don't worry if you don't know what's coming next. Making educated guesses helps you build your thinking skills. Even more important, you'll soon realize that history is a seamless web that is only artificially divided into chapters.

10. Conduct further research. Do you have to write a paper, or are you simply curious and want to learn more? Are you looking for more primary or secondary sources on a specific topic? The readings listed at the end of each chapter will get you started with a list of texts at your school library. The online Primary Source Investigator (www.mhhe.com/psi) contains hundreds of additional primary source documents, along with help on how to use them, images, interactive maps, relevant links, and practice quizzes. You have everything you need to succeed in your studies.

11. Consider the larger Global Context. In each chapter you study the unfolding history of Western Civilization, and throughout you have seen how the West developed in constant interaction with other parts of the world. To help you understand the relationship more clearly, we have included four essays called "The Global Context." These essays can be found after Chapters 1, 5, 15, and 24. Before you read the essays, think about the prompt questions included at the beginning of each essay; keep these questions in mind as you read. Look carefully at the map and work through the questions for discussion at the end of the essay. You can also go online to www.mhhe.com/psi/Sherman to study an interactive version of the map. The sense of Global Context you will gain from these essays will make the narrative of the West in the following chapters much more vivid. The goal is to really understand the relationship between the West and the World.

The steps described above should help you better understand the story of *The West in the World*. We hope you enjoy the unfolding history of the West as much as we have enjoyed bringing it to you.

PEDRO BERRUGUETE, *FEDERICO DA MONTEFELTRO AND HIS SON GUIDOBALDO*, CA. 1476

This portrait shows the founder of the dynasty of Urbino—a soldier of fortune who was made duke by the Pope in 1474. The artist used oil paint and a new sense of realism to depict the duke with everything that mattered to him: the armor of a soldier, the book of a scholar, the support of the papacy shown by the tiara in the upper left corner, and the presence of his son, an heir to perpetuate his dynasty. Strong, well-rounded individuals such as this brought a dramatic new spirit to the West.

CHAPTER 10

A New Spirit in the West

THE RENAISSANCE, CA. 1300–1640

STUDY	Characteristics of the Renaissance ■ Politics of the Italian city-states ■ Urban life ■ Artistic and scientific developments ■ Renaissance ideas in France and England.
NOTICE	How ideas of individualism and Greco-Roman values permeated all facets of this movement.

"This age is dominated by great men [who] labored much to aggrandize themselves and to acquire glory. And yet, would it not have been better if they had undertaken fewer enterprises and been more afraid of offending God and of persecuting their subjects and neighbors?" With these words, a contemporary biographer of Louis the Spider, king of France during the Renaissance, pinpointed both the strengths and weaknesses of this new age: Talented individuals accomplished much, yet often to the neglect of those in their care.

The Renaissance (which means "rebirth") was mainly a cultural movement that emphasized the study of Greek and Roman classics and praised individual achievement. It first emerged in Italy in the fourteenth century and then spread throughout Europe as the disasters of the fourteenth century broke down the old medieval structures. Renaissance ideas fostered especially striking accomplishments in literature, architecture, and the visual arts. Politics, as well, came under the influence of the age: Princes and monarchs governed their states in new ways, developing innovative military strategies and novel ways of conducting diplomacy. At the same time, public policies in these centuries often worsened the lot of the poor and the powerless. Nevertheless, this era was an exciting, vibrant time that ushered Europe from the medieval world toward the modern one.

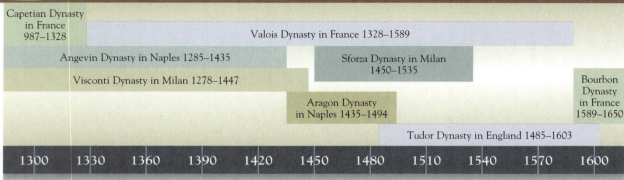

TIMELINE: THE BIG PICTURE

Capetian Dynasty in France 987–1328

Valois Dynasty in France 1328–1589

Angevin Dynasty in Naples 1285–1435

Sforza Dynasty in Milan 1450–1535

Visconti Dynasty in Milan 1278–1447

Bourbon Dynasty in France 1589–1650

Aragon Dynasty in Naples 1435–1494

Tudor Dynasty in England 1485–1603

1300 1330 1360 1390 1420 1450 1480 1510 1540 1570 1600

A New Spirit Emerges: Individualism, Realism, and Activism

In the late thirteenth century, Cimabue, an important painter from the Italian city-state of Florence, was walking in the countryside and saw a young shepherd boy drawing sheep on a rock. The painter recognized the boy's talent and took him on as an apprentice. The young shepherd, Giotto (ca. 1267–1337), flourished under his master's tutelage, and stories arose about the youth's talent for realistic painting—and his independent spirit. He was said to have once painted a fly on the nose of a face that Cimabue was painting, and the fly was so lifelike that the master tried to brush it off several times before he grasped his student's joke. Giotto grew up to vastly surpass his master and create paintings of such realism and emotional honesty that they helped change the direction of painting. As the new century dawned, there would be others like Giotto who creatively broke new ground.

The Renaissance: A Controversial Idea

For centuries historians have struggled with the very idea of whether this age beginning in the fourteenth century in Italy constituted a turning point—the **Renaissance.** People living in fourteenth-century Italy themselves identified this era as characterized by a return to the sources of knowledge and standards of beauty that had created the great civilizations of classical Greece and Rome. ("Classical literature," as they defined it, covered a period from about 800 B.C.E. to about 400 C.E.) Francesco Petrarch (1304–1374), an Italian writer who studied the classics and wrote poetry, was an early proponent of Renaissance ideas. Petrarch lamented because he felt that he could find no one in his own times who could serve as a model of virtuous behavior—he mirrored the example of many in the fourteenth century who despaired of their times (see Chapter 9). However, through his studies, he came to revere figures from antiquity who seemed to understand proper values and follow them regardless of worldly distractions. Petrarch even wrote letters to ancient figures, and in one such letter to the Roman historian Livy, he wrote: "I only wish, that I had been born in your time or you in ours. . . . I have to thank you . . . because you have so often helped me forget the evils of today." Later Renaissance thinkers would follow Petrarch's example and see in ancient Greece and Rome the models to shape a new world.

Yet, they overstated their case—medieval scholars had never lost touch with the Latin texts, and no one gazing at the Gothic cathedrals and the magnificent illuminated manuscripts of the Middle Ages can doubt that medieval people had an exquisite sense of beauty. Indeed, most of the qualities that we identify with the Renaissance had existed in some form throughout the Middle Ages. For this reason, some modern scholars have suggested that the Renaissance should not be considered a separate historical era. Others argue that a different spirit clearly emerged during the period that we have come to call the Renaissance.

Medieval antecedents

In its simplest sense, the Renaissance was an age of accelerated change that began in Italy and that spread new ideas more rapidly than ever. Many people, especially urban dwellers, questioned medieval values of hierarchy, community, and reliance on authority, and replaced them with a focus on ambitious individualism and realism (both of which had to some extent existed in the Middle Ages, but received new emphasis). Some no longer used the classic texts to reinforce the status quo as had become common in the medieval universities; instead, they studied to transform themselves. Petrarch eagerly noted that the texts "sow into our hearts love of the best and eager desire for it." As they strove for excellence, the men and women of the Renaissance ushered in a new age.

Thus, many historians identify the Renaissance as a unique state of mind or set of ideas about everything from art to politics. Having first sprouted in Italy in the fourteenth century, these ideas slowly spread north as the prevailing medieval culture was rocked by the disasters of the fourteenth century. Just as historians disagree about the nature of the Renaissance, they also differ on exactly why these new ideas took root in Italy. What was it about the Italian situation in the early fourteenth century that made that land ripe for fresh ideas about individualism and realism and that fostered the rise of enterprising people?

WHY ITALY?

Because the people of the Renaissance themselves believed the heart of their rebirth was a recovery of the spirit of classical Greece and Rome, the ancient ruins provided a continuing stimulus for such reflections. As Petrarch mapped the ruins, he said the pastime was wonderfully pleasant "not so much because of what I actually saw, as from the recollection of our ancestors, who left such illustrious memorials of Roman virtue . . ." For Petrarch and others, these ruins were an ever-present reminder of an age that they believed was dramatically different from their own—an age they sought to recapture.

The new appreciation of classical authors caused a resurgence of interest in the Greek classics that had been neglected in the West for so long. In 1396, the Florentines invited a Greek scholar from Byzantium to lecture at the University of Florence, but this first step received a huge impetus in the mid-fifteenth century when Constantinople fell to the Turks. (See Chapter 9.) Many eastern scholars fled to Italy, bringing their language skills and Greek manuscripts with them. Over the next decades, new translations of some of the greatest Greek works became fully integrated into Western culture. The study of Greek texts would make a dramatic impact on religious studies, as we will see in Chapter 11.

A fresh reading of the classics certainly stimulated in some literate Italians a desire to recover a spirit of classical greatness, but were readings alone enough to change a culture's sensibilities so dramatically? Some historians argue instead that the tumultuous politics of the Italian city-states particularly favored the

growth of new ideas. Incessant warfare among the states opened the door for skilled, innovative leaders to come forward. These leaders in turn surrounded themselves with talented courtiers who willingly broke from tradition to forward their own careers as they pleased their princes. A new spirit found fertile ground in these ambitious, upwardly mobile men.

Others point to the Black Death that entered Italy in 1348 as the catalyst that transformed the old order (see Chapter 9). The plague's drastic reduction of the *Plague disruptions* population engendered huge economic changes. Prices plummeted, and trade in luxuries such as silk, jewelry, spices, and glass quickened. Italy was ideally placed to profit from this commerce, for throughout the Middle Ages, the Italian city-states had dominated trade in the eastern Mediterranean. During the fourteenth century, individuals, families, and institutions accumulated a good deal of capital, and men and women used some of this money to support the arts. Some have vividly suggested that the Renaissance became one long shopping spree that supported the talented artists whose vision helped define this controversial era—the bridge that began to move Western history from the Middle Ages to modernity.

A MULTIFACETED MOVEMENT

At its core, the Renaissance emphasized and celebrated humans and their achievements. It thus revived an advocacy of individualism that the West had not seen since the time of ancients. As the Italian writer Giovanni Pico della Mirandola (1463–1494) optimistically wrote in his *Oration on the Dignity of Man*, "Man is rightly . . . considered a great miracle and a truly marvelous creature," and in addition to this, Pico said that people could determine their own destiny. This optimistic faith *Individualism* in the human potential was an exciting new idea. Renaissance thinkers asserted a powerful belief in the human ability to choose right and wrong and to act on these choices.

During the Renaissance, Europeans favored a biblical verse from Genesis that described humans as being created in God's "image and likeness." Figure 10.1 shows one portion of the Italian artist Michelangelo's (1475–1564) revered painting on the ceiling of the Sistine Chapel. In this image, the realistic and beautifully proportioned figure of Adam mirrors the physical beauty of the Creator. Michelangelo also portrayed Adam as more than a piece of inert clay waiting for the divine spark to bring him life. Instead, Adam reaches up to God, meeting him halfway in the act of Creation. For Michelangelo and many other artists of the time, man was indeed created in God's

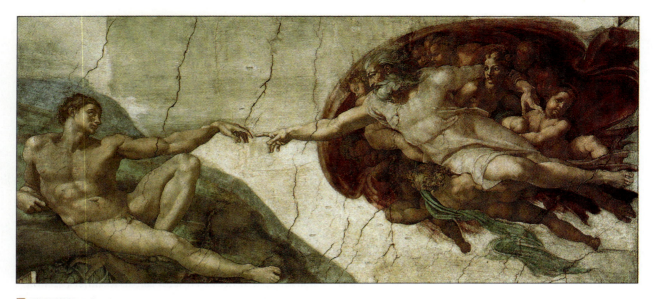

■ FIGURE 10.1

Michelangelo, *Creation of Adam*, from the Sistine Chapel, 1508–1512.

image—not merely spiritually and morally, but also as a creator himself, shaping his own destiny. Here Michelangelo echoes Pico in expressing this idea that was the essence of Renaissance thought.

Renaissance men and women also prided themselves on their accurate view of the world. This form

Realism

of realism appears vividly in the art of the period. Throughout the rest of this chapter, the various examples of artwork from these centuries show a realistic portrayal of the world.

Another prevailing theme in the Renaissance came with the emergence of activism. Petrarch himself succinctly expressed the energetic spirit of the age, writing, "It is better to will the good than to know the truth." In other words, being wise was not enough; one had to exert one's will actively in the

Activism

world to make a difference. Leon Battista Alberti (1404–1472) expressed the same sentiment: "Men can do all things if they will." As we see, Michelangelo's Adam in Figure 10.1 participates in his own creation by reaching up to receive the spark of life, and people were encouraged to imitate this active involvement.

A final characteristic of this new spirit was that it was secular—that is, it did not take place in the

A secular spirit

churches, monasteries, or universities that were dominated by religious thought. That is not to say Renaissance thinkers were antireligious, for they were not— Petrarch explained quite clearly: "Christ is my God; Cicero is the prince of the language I use." While most believed deeply in God and many worked in the church, their vocation was to apply the new spirit to this world, not the next.

Renaissance thinkers felt that the spirit of the classical worlds of Greece and Rome had been reborn before their very eyes. In part, they were right. This vital new age witnessed a renewed belief in human beings' capacity to perfect themselves, to assess the world realistically, and to act vigorously to make an impact on their society. The key to this transformation was education.

HUMANISM: THE PATH TO SELF-IMPROVEMENT

The urban dwellers of the Italian cities knew that education was the key to success. Men entering business had to be trained at least in reading, writing, and mathematics. In Florence at the beginning of the fourteenth century, the number of students enrolled in private schools testifies to the value practical Florentines placed on education: Out of a total population of about 100,000, some 10,000 youths attended private schools to obtain a basic education. Of those, about 1,000 went to special schools to learn advanced business mathematics. However, another 500 pursued a more general liberal education. From these latter emerged an educational movement that defined and perpetuated the Renaissance spirit and changed the course of Western thought.

Petrarch departed from the traditional medieval course of study and from his father's desire that he prepare for a career in law. Instead, he pur-

Humanist curriculum

sued a general study of classical literature. The cities of Italy spawned many young men like Petrarch, who wanted an education separated from the church-dominated universities that had monopolized learning for centuries. Such students sought to understand the causes of human actions through the writings of the ancients, and in turn improve themselves. The humanities—literature, history, and philosophy—thus formed the core of the ideal Renaissance education, which aimed to shape students so that they could excel in anything. Proponents of this teaching method were called **humanists.**

Humanists stressed grammar (particularly Latin and Greek so students could read the classics), poetry, history, and ethics. Following the ancient Roman model, humanists capped off their education with rhetoric, the art of persuasive speaking, which prepared men to serve in a public capacity. Although this course of study may not appear revolutionary, it proved to be.

The early humanists' passion for classical texts led them to search out manuscripts that might yield even greater wisdom from the ancients. As they read and compared manuscripts, they discovered that mistakes had crept into texts that had been painstakingly copied over and over in the medieval monasteries. So the early humanists carefully pored over the many copies of texts to compile accurate versions. These techniques established standards for historical and literary criticism that continue today. Our debt to these literary scholars is incalculable as we enjoy accurate editions of works written thousands of years ago.

The Renaissance emphasis on study and self-improvement inspired some writers to comment on educational theory. Christine of Pizan (1365–ca. 1430) *Self-improvement books* was a professional writer who worked in the French court. She supported herself and her children through her works of poetry and prose. Reflecting the interests of the times, she also wrote several pedagogical treatises: one instructing women on their roles in society (*The Book of Three Virtues*), a manual of good government for the French Dauphin (*The Book of Deeds of King Charles V*), and even a military handbook (*The Book of Feats of Arms and of Chivalry*).

In the same vein, many others authored self-improvement books. The best known of these is *The Book of the Courtier*, by the Italian author Baldassare Castiglione (1478–1529). In this popular work, the author summarizes the expected behavior of men of the court. For Castiglione, native endowments were only the beginning—a courtier had to cultivate military skills, a classical education, and an appreciation of art through music, drawing, and painting. Castiglione turned the Renaissance ideal of an active, well-developed individual into a social ideal of the aristocracy.

Other humanists proposed more formal educational settings. One educator (Guarino da Verona) established a model secondary school at Mantua, in Italy, called the "Happy House," which taught humanities, religion, mathematics, and physical education. The school even included lessons on diet and dress; no facet of the whole human was neglected in the effort at improvement.

Urban families who prized education for their sons also expected their daughters to be educated, but not to the same degree. The eminent Italian humanist Leonardo Bruni *Women humanists* (1374–1444) wrote an oft-quoted letter praising a humanist—but not a full—education for women. For example, he argued that rhetoric in particular was inappropriate for women: "For why exhaust a woman with the concerns of . . . [rhetoric] when she will never be seen in the forum?" His comments reveal the crux of the matter: Women could be educated, but they were not to use their education in a public way, and since rhetoric was central to the humanists, educated Renaissance women were caught in a paradox.

As one example, Isotta Nogarola (1418–1466) earned much recognition from her family and some family friends for her learning. However, as soon as she tried to engage in a public dialogue (through letters), male humanists reprimanded her and deemed her "immoral" for her public display. She retired into the seclusion of her study, just as other women took refuge in convents to pursue their research.

Rulers, of course, were exempt from such prohibitions of public use of education, and royal women made good use of the latest Renaissance notions of study. Queens such as Elizabeth I of England (r. 1558–1603) and Isabella of Castille (r. 1474–1504) employed their education to rule effectively, support the arts, and encourage the new educational methods. The Biography of Isabella d'Este (on page 308) describes the life of one Italian woman who possessed so much political authority that she became a renowned patron of the arts and of education.

Humanists applied their skills in many areas of life. Some—called **civic humanists**—involved themselves in politics, treating the public arena as their artistic canvas. Others applied their skills at literary criticism to the Bible and other Christian texts. The most influential of these **Christian humanists** came from outside Italy. As we will see in Chapter 11, men such as the Spanish Cardinal Ximénez de Cisneros (1436–1517) and the Dutchman Desiderius Erasmus (ca. 1469–1536) transformed the study of the Bible and paved the way for dramatic changes in religious sensibilities.

Humanist scholarship was crucial in shaping the new spirit of the Renaissance, but it was not sufficient in itself. Scholars and artists and talented young men

BIOGRAPHY

Isabella d'Este (1474–1539)

CONSIDER

■ **Consider** how Isabella's life sheds light on the importance of patronage during the Renaissance, the position of women, and the significance of family ties.

Isabella d'Este was born the daughter of a duke in 1474 in the small Duchy of Ferrara, just south of Venice. She grew up in a court that both appreciated Renaissance education and art and succumbed to the violence that marked fifteenth-century Italy.

When Isabella was only 2, her father's nephew attacked the palace in an effort to seize power from the duke. Before Isabella was 8 years old, Venetian armies had invaded Ferrara to try to dominate the small duchy. Yet Isabella's father was a skillful diplomat and withstood these and many other challenges. In the process, his daughter began learning about Renaissance diplomacy.

The young girl was educated in the best humanist tradition. Her tutors taught her to read the great classics of the Roman world in the original Latin. She learned quickly and spoke Latin fluently at an early age. She also was an accomplished musician and excelled at singing and playing the lute.

When she was 6 years old, Isabella's parents began searching for a suitable future husband for her. They approached the family of the nearby Duke of Mantua to discuss a betrothal between Isabella and their eldest son, Francesco. When representatives of

■ FIGURE 10.2
Isabella d'Este.

would have made little impact without the generosity of patrons such as Isabella, who supported the new talent and assiduously purchased their productions. The spirit of the Renaissance thrived on the money that flowed abundantly (albeit unevenly, as we will see) in the Italian cities.

THE GENEROSITY OF PATRONS: SUPPORTING NEW IDEAS

The talented writers and artists of the Renaissance depended on generous patrons to support them. During the early Renaissance, cities themselves served as artistic patrons, stimulating the creation of art by offering prizes and subsidies for their talented citizens. Guilds, too, served as artistic patrons, commissioning great public monuments to enhance the spaces of their cities. The public art that graced the streets and squares enhanced the reputation of the city itself and in turn forwarded the new ideas of the gifted artists.

In time, warfare and internal strife caused cities to have less money to use in support of art, and patronage was taken over by wealthy individuals. In addition to Isabella d'Este, many other rulers, such as the Medici in Florence and the Sforza in Milan, used their wealth to stimulate the creation of spectacular works of art. In return, patrons gained social and political status by surrounding themselves with objects of beauty or intellect.

Cosimo de Medici (1389–1464) offers a perfect model for the impact of patrons in the Renaissance. Cosimo supported intellectuals and artists, and personally financed the acquisition of manuscripts. His fascination with the Greek philosopher Plato led him to make perhaps his greatest contribution to the intellectual life of the West: He founded the Platonic Academy, hiring the famous Neoplatonic scholar Marsilio Ficino (1433–1499) to guide the studies. Ficino translated the works of Plato, and wrote works that demonstrated that Pla-

Francesco's family interviewed the young child, they wrote back to the prospective in-laws that they were astonished at her precocious intelligence. They sent Francesco's parents a portrait of the lovely black-eyed, blond child, but assured that "her marvelous knowledge and intelligence are far more worthy of admiration [than her beauty]." A betrothal was arranged that would unite the two houses trying to maintain independence from their powerful neighbors, Milan and Venice.

Duchess of Mantua, Diplomat, and Patron of the Arts

Isabella and Francesco were married in 1490, when she was 15. An elaborate ceremony joined the two families, and in her old age, Isabella proudly wrote of her memories of the gifts, decorations, and lavish banquet that marked this turning point of her life.

Under the skillful rule of Francesco and Isabella, Mantua rose to the foremost rank of the smaller Italian city-states. Isabella involved herself in the art of diplomacy throughout the couple's reign. She wrote more than two thousand letters—many of them to popes, kings, and other Italian rulers. In one letter to her husband, Isabella assured him that he could concentrate completely on military matters, for "I intend to govern the State . . . in such a manner that you will suffer no wrong, and all that is possible will be done for the good of your subjects." This talented woman was as good as her word, for when Francesco was captured in 1509 and imprisoned, Isabella ruled in his stead and valiantly saved the city from invasion.

Like other Italians influenced by Renaissance pseudoscience, Isabella avidly believed in astrology. She embarked on no important venture without consulting her astrologers. But she also took an interest in the real-world findings of the time. She received correspondence about Columbus's discovery of America and the "intelligent and gentle" natives he found there.

Yet the educated duchess is most remembered as a patron of the arts. She wrote explicit instructions for the works she commissioned: One painting prompted her to pen as many as forty letters. Recognizing excellence, she wanted to commission a work from Leonardo da Vinci, but the artist never found the time to oblige her. (See Document 10.1.)

With a love of literature nurtured since her youth, Isabella accumulated a library that became one of the best in Italy. She took advantage of the new printing industry to acquire the first editions of the great classics as well as the contemporary works of Petrarch and Dante. Her requests for these editions show her appreciation of beauty even in her search for literature: She asked for books printed on parchment (instead of paper) and bound in leather.

When Isabella was 64 years old, Francesco died. The aging duchess turned to her many children and grandchildren for comfort and companionship. She took particular delight in one grandchild who could recite Virgil at the age of only 5. Isabella died in 1539, a year after losing her husband. In the last months of her life, a great scholar of the age called her "the wisest and most fortunate of women"—an apt epitaph for someone who so personified the Renaissance spirit.

tonism and Christianity shared a belief that humans were permeated with divine love and that the goal of humanity was to rise upward toward the Divinity. These studies shaped the glorification of human accomplishments that were to be the hallmark of the Renaissance, and they were made possible by the powerful patronage of Cosimo and other leaders.

Not only rulers, but rising bourgeoisie could enhance their social status by owning works of art, and this activity served to spur the production of art. Document 10.1 describes Isabella d'Este trying to contract a painting.

The church also supported the arts. Religious fraternities commissioned many paintings, and popes financially backed numerous artists. Like cities and individuals, churches gained status through their patronage, but churches also recognized a religious purpose of art. Many people attributed miraculous power to visual portrayals of religious themes

Religious patronage

and churchmen supported this belief. For example, the Florentines customarily brought an image of the Virgin Mary (called the *Madonna of Impruneta*) down from the hills to Florence in times of crisis, and in 1483, a procession of the Madonna was credited with stopping a destructive, month-long rainfall.

Such ceremonies also served the civic purpose of bringing the faithful together in a public way. The painting in Figure 10.3 shows a religious procession in Venice, in which the sacred Eucharist was paraded through the square encased in a magnificently ornate carrier. The painting reinforces the way these religious festivities united the residents and indeed celebrated the beautiful public spaces of the city itself.

Thus, dynamic city life and a new emphasis on education stimulated new ideas, and generous patronage helped them grow. However, the new spirit spread rapidly by the late Renaissance owing to a revolutionary advance in technology.

■ DOCUMENT 10.1

Isabella d'Este Implores Leonardo da Vinci to Paint for Her

In 1504, Isabella d'Este of Mantua (see Biography in this chapter) wrote letters to Leonardo da Vinci soliciting a painting. Although she never received her painting, these letters show the tensions that often arose between purchasers' desires and artists' aesthetic inclinations, and shed light on the all-important process of patronage. ■ **What** *specific painting does Isabella want?* ■ **What** *are your thoughts about how specific her request is?* ■ **Notice** *how Leonardo's uncle gets involved (see Letter 2).* ■ **What** *does the uncle's participation suggest about the relationship between family connections and patronage?*

Letter 1. "To Master Leonardo Vinci, the painter. M. Leonardo,—Hearing that you are settled at Florence, we have begun to hope that our cherished desire to obtain a work by your hand may be at length realised. When you were in this city, and drew our portrait in carbon, you promised us that you would some day paint it in colours. But because this would be almost impossible, since you are unable to come here, we beg you to keep your promise by converting our portrait into another figure, which would be still more acceptable to us; that is to say, a youthful Christ of about twelve years, which would be the age He had attained when He disputed with the doctors in the temple, executed with all that sweetness and charm of atmosphere which is the peculiar excellence of your art. If you will consent to gratify this our great desire, remember that apart from the payment, which you shall fix yourself, we shall remain so deeply obliged to you that our sole desire will be to do what you wish, and from this time forth we are ready to do your service and pleasure, hoping to receive an answer in the affirmative." Mantua, May 14, 1504.

Letter 2. On the 27th of May, Angelo del Tovaglia replied:—
"I received the letter of Your Highness, together with the one for Leonardo da Vinci, to whom I presented it, and at the same time tried to persuade and induce him, with powerful reasons, to oblige Your Excellency by painting the little figure of Christ, according to your request. He has promised me without fail to paint it in such times and hours as he can snatch from the work on which he is engaged for this Signory. I will not fail to entreat Leonardo, and also Perugino, as to the other subject. Both make liberal promises, and seem to have the greatest wish to serve Your Highness. Nevertheless, I think it will be a race between them which is the slower! I hardly know which of the two is likely to win, but expect Leonardo will be the conqueror. All the same, I will do my utmost."

Source: Julia Cartwright, *Isabella d'Este: Marchioness of Mantua, 1474–1539*, vol. 1 (New York: E. P. Dutton, 1903), pp. 324–327.

■ FIGURE 10.3

Gentile Bellini, *Procession of Eucharist.*

THE INVENTION OF THE PRINTING PRESS: SPREADING NEW IDEAS

Throughout the Middle Ages, precious texts had to be laboriously copied by hand, making books relatively scarce and expensive. As we saw in Chapter 1, one of the significant advantages to the growth of civilization is the ability for more people to read and have access to the written word. In Asia (China and Korea) inventors had developed a way to reproduce texts and pictures more quickly—wood-block printing. With this technique, images and some text were carved into wooden blocks and then could be mass produced by printing. This technique had spread to the West by the late fourteenth century. By the early fifteenth century, Asian printers replaced wooden type with bronze type, which was much more durable and offered a more consistent print. This method, too, rapidly spread to the West.

In the 1440s, these early printing techniques reached their culmination with the development of moveable type and the adaptation of an oil press to print pages more rapidly. A German silversmith named Johannes Gutenberg (ca. 1400–1470) is credited with bringing all these innovations together to produce the first printed Bible in 1455. Suddenly, literature became more available and thereby ultimately affecting all of Western civilization. Figure 10.4 depicts a printing shop in the late fifteenth century. At the right of the image, a worker sets the type in a tray so as to match the lettering in the manuscript in front of him. The printer at the left presses a plate of type on the paper, producing copies that are admired (and perhaps proofread) by the worker in the foreground. The worker standing at the left mixes the ink that will be applied to the letters to produce the image on the paper.

The development and proliferation of the printing press was a testimony to the growing confidence that there was a market for books. In addition to a demand for their product, print shops also needed something to print on. Paper technology gave them the necessary cheap medium to replace the expensive parchment used during the Middle Ages. The technique of papermaking came to Europe from China through the Muslim world. By the fourteenth century, Italian paper mills were using old rags to make inexpensive, yet high-quality, paper. Although some wealthy patrons, such as Isabella d'Este, often preferred the more traditional parchment, the future lay with the new paper.

Printing presses spread rapidly through Europe—by the 1480s many Italian cities had established their own presses, and by 1500 there were about a thousand presses all over the continent. Previously, valuable books, painstakingly copied by hand, belonged to the patron who paid for the copy. Now the literary world looked to a broader reading public for support, consequently igniting a rapid spread of ideas that carried the new spirit throughout Europe. Subsequent notions—from the excitement of international discoveries to intellectual challenges to religious ideology—also spread rapidly. The pace of change in Western civilization quickened as the European presses circulated ideas with unprecedented speed.

All the elements were in place for the transformation of thought that we have come to know as the Renaissance. The study of classical texts had helped change people's views of themselves and their approach to the world. Money flowed in support of talented and enterprising individuals, and technology helped spread the ideas rapidly. Finally, men actively implemented these ideas in many fields, from art to business to politics.

■ FIGURE 10.4
A printing shop.

THE POLITICS OF INDIVIDUAL EFFORT

The medieval power struggle between emperors and popes left an enormous power vacuum in northern Italy. This vacuum allowed small city-states, or cities that controlled the surrounding countryside, to become used to independence. As the fourteenth century opened, most of the northern cities were free communes (see Chapter 8) with republican forms of government, but as the fourteenth century progressed, changes occurred.

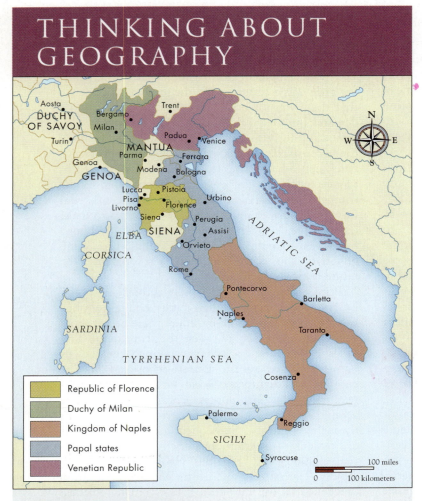

MAP 10.1   ITALY IN 1454

This map shows the political divisions of Italy in the fifteenth century. ■ **Notice** the location of the major city-states of the north. **Which** were likely to be most immediately threatened by the expansion of the Papal states? ■ **Locate** Venice. **Consider** why it was so well placed to dominate trade in the eastern Mediterranean. **Which** states were threatened by Venice's expansion into the peninsula? ■ **Locate** the Kingdom of Naples. **What** contributed to Naples' relative isolation from the politics of the northern states?

THE ITALIAN CITY-STATES

These city-states engaged in almost constant warfare over their borders and commercial interests, and within the cities, classes and political factions fought for control of the government. In such unstable times, most of the republican governments were under pressure, and strong men with dictatorial power took over. As we saw in Chapter 9, mercenary armies had become a significant feature of warfare, and they also became a force in Italian politics as city-states hired army captains (called *condottieri*) with their armies to come fight their wars. These mercenaries frequently ravaged the countryside, bringing more misery than protection to the population. Through the fourteenth and fifteenth centuries, city-states would see repeated internal and external strife as they wrestled with their neighbors and with internal governing. These turbulent times brought misery to many but opportunity to others. Sometimes strong, talented individuals rose to positions of authority without constitutional or hereditary legitimacy. The Duke of Urbino portrayed in the chapter-opening illustration is one such successful mercenary captain. These rulers introduced a new kind of politics and perhaps inadvertently stimulated the new spirit of the Renaissance.

Map 10.1 shows Italy in 1454. Notice that the northern areas consisted of a patchwork quilt of city-states. Among these, Venice, Milan, and Florence were the largest and most powerful. Popes controlled the large, central strip of the peninsula, and the Kingdom of Naples dominated the south. It was the competition among the northern states that fueled the politics of individual effort that so influenced Renaissance ideas such as individualism and activism.

The Italian city-states fell into two general categories: republics and principalities. Republics featured the institutions of the medieval city communes, in which an urban elite governed. For the most part, Venice and Florence preserved the republican form of government during most of the Renaissance. Principalities, on the other hand, were ruled by one dynasty. Milan and Naples were the most notable examples of this form of government.

FLORENCE: BIRTHPLACE OF THE RENAISSANCE

Florence at the beginning of the fourteenth century was a vibrant republic where Renaissance ideas seem to have been first fostered. Florence prided itself on its republican form of government in which eligible men held office by random selection. But the city was an uneasy republic indeed, fragmented by local rivalries that always threatened to break out into violence within the urban spaces themselves. Only guild members could participate in the government, and an oligarchy of the leading families was frequently able to control the government. Florence was badly hit by the plague—in 1348 alone, almost 40 percent of its population was killed, and its

THINKING ABOUT DOCUMENTS

■ DOCUMENT 10.2

Friar Savonarola Ignites a "Bonfire of the Vanities"

Luca Landucci ran a small apothecary shop in Florence and kept a diary chronicling these turbulent times. This excerpt from 1497 describes the notorious incident in which the reforming friar Savonarola (whom Landucci calls Fra Girolamo) ordered his followers— young boys—to collect Florentine artworks and burn them in the square. ■ **What** *kinds of objects did the friar's followers collect?* ■ **Who** *supported the friar?* ■ **Was** *Landucci sympathetic to Savonarola?* ■ **Why** *was Florence a particularly appropriate place for this act?*

27th February (the Carnival). There was made on the *Piazza de' Signori* a pile of vain things, nude statues and playing-boards, heretic books, Morganti [poems], mirrors, and many other vain things, of great value, estimated at thousands of florins. Although some lukewarm people gave trouble, throwing dead cats and other dirt upon it, the boys nevertheless set it on fire and burnt everything, for there was plenty of small brushwood. And it is to be observed that the pile was not made by children; there was a rectangular woodwork measuring more than *12 braccia* [about 23 feet] each way, which had taken the carpenters several days to make, with many workmen, so that it was necessary for many armed men to keep guard the night before, as certain lukewarm persons, specially certain young men called *Compagnacci* wanted to destroy it. The *Frate* was held in such veneration by those who had faith in

him, that this morning, although it was Carnival, Fra Girolamo said mass in *San Marco*, and gave the Sacrament with his hands to all his friars, and afterwards to several thousand men and women; and then he came on to a pulpit outside the door of the church with the Host, and showing it to the people, blessed them, with many prayers: *Fac salvum populum tuum Domine*, etc. There was a great crowd, who had come in the expectation of seeing signs; the lukewarm laughed and mocked, saying: "He is excommunicated, and he gives the Communion to others." And certainly it seemed a mistake to me, although I had faith in him; but I never wished to endanger myself by going to hear him, since he was excommunicated.

SOURCE: Luca Landucci, *A Florentine Diary from 1450 to 1516*, trans. Alice de Rosen Jervice (London: Dent, 1927), pp. 130–131.

---

economy, too, was badly damaged as cloth production declined. Warfare with Milan in the early fifteenth century bankrupted many of the city's leading commercial families and created a massive public debt. In their troubles, the Florentines turned to the wealthiest banking family in Europe—the Medici. The republic got more than it bargained for.

In 1434, Cosimo de' Medici took control of the Florentine oligarchy and exiled his rivals. In the tradition of Caesar Augustus, whom he admired, Cosimo concentrated power in his household while ostensibly keeping a republican form of government. Under this shrewd family, Florence and the arts flourished. Cosimo's grandson, Lorenzo the Magnificent (r. 1469–1492), epitomized the ideal Renaissance ruler. A great statesman, he was also a patron of the arts, a poet, and an athlete.

The Medici

Yet even Lorenzo could not bring peace to the contentious Florentine people. During his life he faced intrigue and assassination attempts and had to use all his diplomatic skills to preserve Florence from foreign foes. Late in his tenure, voices began to be raised against the Renaissance ideals that he so actively supported. Shortly after Lorenzo's death, the rule of the Medici could not withstand the growing pressures from outside and within the city.

In 1494, French armies invaded the countryside around Florence, and the city-state was again buffeted with financial and material woes. The French armies found an ally within the city in the person of a fiery preacher who had objected to the rule of the Medici and to the passionate acquisition of money and art that had dominated the early Renaissance.

Savonarola

Girolamo Savonarola (1452–1498) was a courageous, yet uncompromising, man who had resented the rule of the Medici and accused the clergy of corruption from the papacy on down. He argued vigorously against the lust for money that motivated citizens in the high-tempo Florentine economy. Perhaps most of all, he despised humanism, which he believed poisoned everything from art to religion by placing humans in the spotlight. The passionate preacher clearly recognized the changing times, but he advocated a different response to these changes.

Helped by the disruptions caused by the French invasions, Savonarola was able to arrange for the Medici to be expelled from the city and for a republic to be reintroduced. But Savonarola also wanted to return people's sensibilities to what he perceived to be a more pious age. He preached against nude paintings and sculptures, and in 1497 presided over a public "burning of the vanities"—a huge bonfire into which people tossed ornaments, pictures, cards, and other "frivolous" items. This event is described by an eyewitness in Document 10.2.

Eventually, the monk's zeal sparked opposition. The pope chafed at Savonarola's attacks and finally excommunicated him and forbade him to preach. Savonarola himself came to an ironic, fiery end: He was condemned, hung, and his body was burned in the public square of Florence—exactly where the "vanities" had been burned.

Like the other great figures of the age, Savonarola was a product of the Renaissance—he felt the same civic pride and shared the same love of education. But, instead of responding to these forces with a sense of humanism and realism, he looked for a spiritual reaction, a religious renewal that he believed should shape the future. In time, northern Europeans picked up Savonarola's call for religious renewal, but not yet. In Florence the Medici were restored by the sixteenth century, and the republic was formally dissolved in 1530.

At first glance, it may seem incongruous that the stormy political history of Florence spawned the creative ideas that we have come to identify with the Renaissance. However, the very environment that made people feel they had to be actively involved in their city and fight for their own interests stimulated the driving individualism that characterized this age. Politicians vied to prove themselves superior to their rivals, often by supporting artists whose products contributed to their own status. In the republican turmoil, the Renaissance was born.

VENICE: THE SERENE REPUBLIC?

Venice preserved its republic with much less turmoil than Florence, although there, too, an oligarchy ruled. Venice's constitution called for only its aristocratic merchant families—numbering about 2,000—to serve in its Great Council. From among this number, they chose one man to serve as the council leader, or *doge,* for life, but most men were in their 70s before being elected to this office. This rule by the elders made political life in Venice remarkably stable—indeed, the city called itself the "Most Serene Republic." This title underplayed the ever-present factional strife that plagued the Italian cities, but Venetians were able to suppress the strife, and many believed their self-proclaimed myth of serenity.

This peace also stemmed from the prosperity generated by overseas trade, which Venice dominated owing to its advantageous location on the Adriatic Sea. Map 10.2 shows how Venice's location perfectly situated it to take advantage of the *Overseas trade* lucrative trade in the eastern Mediterranean. From Venice's earliest history, it enjoyed a privileged position in the trade with Byzantium, and as we saw in Chapter 8, during the Fourth Crusade in 1204, the Venetians led in the conquest of Constantinople itself. The painting of St. Mark's

Square in Figure 10.3 shows not only the wealth of Venice, but the domed church in the background reveals the continuing influence of Byzantium on the aesthetics of the city that was formed by interactions with the east. The end of the crusader kingdoms did not end the Venetian dominance of trade, and at the beginning of the Renaissance, wealth continued to pour into the Serene Republic. To consolidate its hold on the eastern Mediterranean, Venice built an empire of coastal cities and islands—as shown on Map 10.2.

Venice was built on a collection of islands in a lagoon, and the Grand Canal that continues to mark its main thoroughfare is a perfect representation of the city's maritime orientation. Of the city-state's total population of about 150,000 people, more than 30,000 were sailors. Venice's navy boasted forty-five galleys—large warships with sails and oars—and three hundred hefty sailing ships.

In the beginning of the fifteenth century, Venice began to engage in a policy of expanding into the Italian mainland—the city-state wanted to secure its food supply as well as its overland trade routes. Map 10.2 shows the cities that became Venetian dependencies. Although this expansionist policy made sense to the Venetians, it understandably upset the neighboring states of Milan and Florence.

The Venetians perhaps should have looked more carefully at their maritime holdings, for Turkish expansion in the eastern Mediterranean (with the capture of Rhodes) seriously challenged Venetian supremacy in the seas. (See Chapter 11 for the subsequent confrontation.)

Through the Renaissance, however, this calm republic helped forward the progress of the new spirit. Its leaders wanted to grace their city with the magnificent new art, so their patronage brought talent to the fore, and their ships helped disseminate the new ideas along with the Italian trade goods.

MILAN AND NAPLES: TWO PRINCIPALITIES

Milan's violent history mirrored that of Florence, but this city-state more quickly moved from a republican form of government to an hereditary principality. During the thirteenth century, rival political factions in the city had constantly vied for power. In desperation, the commune invited a soldier from a family named Visconti to come in and keep the peace; he stayed on to rule as prince and established a dynasty that reigned in Milan from 1278 to 1447. The Visconti family recognized the volatility of Italian politics and focused on the military strength that had brought them to power in the first place. After fending off attempts to establish a republic, the Visconti established a principality that coveted the lands of the rest of northern Italy. Only the diplomatic and

THINKING ABOUT GEOGRAPHY

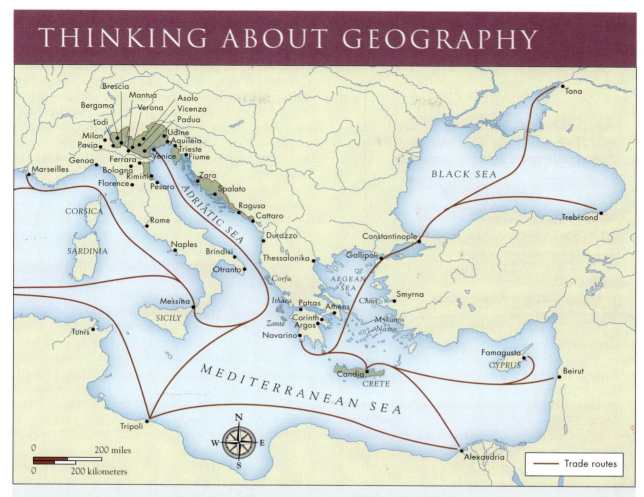

MAP 10.2 THE VENETIAN EMPIRE IN THE FIFTEENTH CENTURY

This map shows the Venetian empire, with the red lines indicting the main trade routes of Venice's prosperous commercial ventures. ■ **Notice** Venice's dominance of the Adriatic Sea. **Locate** Crete. **Consider** how control of these two areas would facilitate Venice's ascendancy of the trade in the eastern Mediterranean. ■ **Locate** the Muslim cities of Tripoli, Tunis, Alexandria, and Beirut. **Consider** how trade with these centers might facilitate cross-cultural interactions.

military talents of Florence, Venice, and its other neighbors kept this aggressive principality in check. Finally, in 1447, the Visconti dynasty ended when the prince died without an heir—the door was open for a new power struggle in Milan.

In 1450, another strong dynasty took power. The Sforza family kept the city-state's proud military tradition, yet also served as patrons of the arts to enhance their own political reputations. The Sforza continued to rule until the early sixteenth century, though always under the pressure of growing republican aspirations.

The Kingdom of Naples in the south was the only region of Italy that preserved a feudal form of government ruled by an hereditary monarchy. In the early fourteenth century, Naples was ruled by Angevin kings who were descendants of the king of France. Under these kings, the ideas of the Renaissance came to the feudal and rural south. Giotto (the shepherd-painter whose story opened this chapter) and Boccaccio (see Chapter 9) spent time in Naples under the patronage of King Robert (r. 1309–1343), and even Petrarch called Robert "the only king of our times who has been a friend of learning and of virtue." However, after Robert's rule, Naples became a battleground with claimants from the Angevins and the Spanish Aragonese competing for the throne.

Naples

KEY DATES

Dates are for period of rule

RENAISSANCE RULERS

1364–1380	Charles V the Wise, France
1434–1464	Cosimo de'Medici in Florence
1461–1483	Louis XI the Spider, France
1469–1492	Lorenzo the Magnificent de'Medici, Florence
1490–1539	Isabella d'Este, Mantua
1492–1503	Pope Alexander VI
1503–1513	Pope Julius II
1509–1547	Henry VIII of England
1515–1547	Francis I of France
1558–1603	Elizabeth I of England

In 1435, the king of Aragon, Alfonso the Magnanimous (r. 1435–1458), was able to reunite the crowns of Naples and Sicily. He worked to centralize his administration but was unable fully to subdue his barons, and Naples remained a feudal kingdom. Alfonso was a passionate devotee of Italian culture and served as a patron of the Renaissance. However, the dynastic claims on this throne by other kings in Europe would disrupt Italian politics in years to come.

THE PAPAL STATES

As Map 10.1 shows, the papacy was not just a spiritual presence. When the popes returned to Rome after their sojourn in Avignon (see Chapter 9), they found their traditional lands reduced and many under the control of their neighbors. They faced the question of whether they were to be more secular or more spiritual leaders. One supporter of papal rule said that "virtue without power would be ridiculous." Therefore, like the Italian princes, the Renaissance popes strove to resume control of central Italy and succeeded.

As rulers of central Italy, the popes had a particular advantage in that their rule was a **theocracy** that derived its legitimacy from God (and election by the college of cardinals), so that issues of republicanism and tyranny did not apply. However, their religious role also brought complications. For example, as worldly rulers in the Italian tradition, they were expected to improve the fortunes of their fam-

ilies, so they frequently (and accurately) fell prey to the charge of nepotism as they created positions for their relatives. The popes also looked backward to their medieval struggles with the Holy Roman Emperors to control Italy (see Chapter 8), so many felt they had a right—indeed an obligation—to expand papal lands on the peninsula. All these factors helped propel the popes into the frequently violent sphere of Italian politics. But they also leaped into the exciting, brilliant world of Renaissance creativity.

Just as other Italian princes discovered that art could enhance their prestige, the popes, too, became avid patrons of the arts. In doing so, they transformed Rome into one of Europe's major cultural centers. Figure 10.5 shows Pope Sixtus IV (r. 1471–1484) seated in as much grandeur and surrounded by as much wealth as any king. His courtiers talk among themselves while the pope receives the humanist Platina (kneeling in the center). This painting commemorated the founding of the Vatican library, to be run by Platina. Even today, the library remains a major learning center. The cardinal standing in the center of the painting later became Pope Julius II. The courtiers on the left are Sixtus's nephews, who later participated in a plot to murder one of the Medicis. This painting depicts the Renaissance love of learning—as well as its penchant for nepotism and intrigue.

Papal patronage

To increase (or even maintain) their secular power, the popes waded into the quagmire of Italian politics, and by the end of the Renaissance, a pope was elected from an influential family—the Borgia. Like many other Renaissance princes, the Borgia Pope Alexander VI (r. 1492–1503) tried to reclaim his lands from his acquisitive neighbors. Alexander also proved worldly in his personal life; gossips gleefully circulated accounts of his sexual escapades. He still upheld the tradition of Renaissance family life, however, favoring his illegitimate children by placing them in advantageous positions. The pope's warrior son, Cesare Borgia (ca. 1475–1507), seemed a candidate for uniting Italy under Alexander's authority. For his daughter Lucrezia, Alexander arranged three marriages designed to advance the family's dynastic aims. Isabella d'Este (featured in this chapter's Biography on page 308) arranged one of these marriages to protect the Este family's interests. All these manipulations came to nothing, however: Alexander died suddenly, and the family's ambitions failed. The reputation of the papacy as a spiritual authority also declined.

The Borgia family

One of the most memorable of the Renaissance popes, Julius II (r. 1503–1513) embodied the ambitious values of the times, but without the scandals that had plagued Alexander. Julius was as perfect a Renaissance ruler as Florence's Lorenzo de' Medici. A patron of the arts, he made Rome a cultural hub on a par with the greatness of Florence. He was also an experienced warrior, personally leading his armies into battle as he carried on Alexander's expansionist policies. Julius II summoned Michelangelo to Rome and commissioned him to decorate the ceiling of the Sistine Chapel (see Figure 10.1). Michelangelo also worked on the new St. Peter's Church in Rome that was being built at the time. Although Julius and Michelangelo had a stormy relationship, the patron helped his artist produce some of the most beautiful work of the Renaissance. But such creations cost money, and, as we will see in Chapter 11, many people, especially in northern Europe, began to criticize these popes for what some called worldly extravagance.

Julius II

■ FIGURE 10.5

Melozzo da Forlí, *Sixtus IV Receives Platina, Keeper of the Vatican Library.*

THE ART OF DIPLOMACY

The wars, shifting alliances, and courtly intrigue of Italian politics sparked a new interest (and expertise) in the art of diplomacy. Not since the early Byzantine state had courtiers devoted such attention to the details of successful diplomacy. States exchanged ambassadors to facilitate official communication and sent spies to maintain advantages.

The most noted writer on political skill and diplomacy was Niccolò Machiavelli (1469–1527), whose book *The Prince* still influences many modern-day political thinkers. Machiavelli recognized the danger confronting Florence in the fifteenth century as French armies threatened the independence of the city-states, and he wrote to offer advice about how to survive—indeed prevail—in these turbulent times. His was an eminently practical guide that looked at politics with a cold-blooded realism that had not been seen before. For Machiavelli, the most important element for a successful ruler (the prince) was his strength of will. He insisted that while princes might appear to have such traditional virtues as charity and generosity, they could not rely on these traits to hold power. They

Machiavelli

must actually be ruthless, expedient, strong, and clever if they were to maintain their rule. As he said, "It is better for a ruler to be feared than loved."

Machiavelli's blunt description of political power articulated a striking departure from medieval political ideals. During the Middle Ages, the perfect ruler was Louis IX of France (r. 1226–1270) (described in Chapter 8), who proved so virtuous that he was made a saint. With the Renaissance, men like Cosimo de' Medici and Cesare Borgia—self-made rulers who methodically cultivated their talents and grasped power boldly—took power. Machiavelli's book captured the new statecraft and showed realistic politics often meant a brutal disregard for ethics. Indeed, many Europeans living during the Renaissance showed a social indifference and personal immorality that we might find dismaying today.

Individualism as Self-Interest: Life During the Renaissance

In spite of efforts to hone their diplomatic skills to a fine art, many Italians still resorted to brute force to get what they wanted. In all the city-states, some individuals came to power by stimulating social strife among competing factions or even using violence to vanquish their rivals. Taking part in politics could also get one in deep trouble. Petrarch's father, for example, like many other men of his time, made the mistake of supporting a losing political struggle in Florence, and the victors punished him by amputating his hand. Individuals struggling to better themselves politically and economically often did so at the expense of their neighbors.

Aside from the occasional opportunity to improve one's social position, Renaissance cities still had a clearly defined social hierarchy. The Florentines referred to these divisions as the "little people" and the "fat people." The "little people" consisted of merchants, artisans, and workers, and made up about 60 percent of the population. Slaves and servants assumed even lower status, beneath the "little people." The "fat people" included well-to-do merchants and professionals, and made up about 30 percent of the population. The wealthiest elite—bankers and merchants owning more than one-quarter of the city's wealth—made up only 1 percent of the population.

Whenever there is a great disparity between rich and poor in a situation of some social mobility, crime tends to run high. This was true throughout Renaissance Europe. One Florentine merchant, Luca Landucci, who kept a detailed diary of the events of his age, regularly wrote of crime and punishment as he heard his neighbors gossip about the shocking misdeeds of the day. In one diary entry, he repeats news of a young woman who killed a child for the pearl necklace the girl was wearing. In another, he tells of the townspeople watching as a man was beheaded for "coining false money." Luca's dreary lists of crimes seem endless.

Rising crime

Many people blamed wanderers for the alarming rise in crime. According to such observers, soldiers discharged from mercenary armies, the poor fleeing poverty in cities and countryside, and other displaced persons made the highways more dangerous than ever. Italy and other states tried to control crime, but their methods were usually ineffective as well as misplaced. As in other times of rapid social change, rulers increased the regulation of social behavior. For example, in England in 1547 a new law stipulated that vagabonds be branded and enslaved for two years. The law tells us a great deal about Renaissance society's intense fear of crime and strangers.

Growing Intolerance

Renaissance governments enacted harsh legislation on people they found threatening, from prostitutes to paupers. This same impulse contributed to an increasing intolerance of other religions and cultures, as evidenced by an intensifying prejudice against Jews. In Italy, Christians passed laws against sexual relations between Christians and Jews, and authorities in Rome reputedly burned 50 Jewish prostitutes to death for having intercourse with Christian men. Laws also restricted Jews to certain parts of cities and required them to wear identifiable clothing. In some instances the clothing included colors that had been set aside for prostitutes. This cruel association left Jewish women open to ridicule, criticism, and sometimes abuse from non-Jewish neighbors.

Persecution of Jews existed during the Middle Ages—thirteenth-century kings of England and France had expelled Jews from their lands, and communities of Jews had experienced periodic violence. (As we saw in Chapter 9, Jews were subjected to particular violence in the wake of the bubonic plague.) However, increasing prejudice in the fifteenth century led to large-scale expulsions of Jewish communities from many cities and countries. Vienna began expelling Jews in 1421, and many other German cities followed. Figure 10.6 is taken from a fifteenth-century Hebrew manuscript, and it shows Jews driven from a German town. The group was allowed to take their animals and a wagon for the women, children, and elderly as they headed down the hills seeking a new home. Most German Jews moved eastward into Poland and Russia, and the center of Judaism shifted from western Europe to the East.

Ferdinand and Isabella forced all of Spain's Jews to leave in 1492, causing one of the largest movements of peoples in the era. Portugal did the same in 1497. Many Iberian Jews fled to the Muslim lands in North Africa, and some people today still trace their ancestry back to this exodus. As a result of this intolerance, western Europe lost the talents of the many Jews who had inhabited these lands for centuries.

Economic Boom Times

The new ideas of the Renaissance (both good and bad) developed against the backdrop of the fourteenth-century crises but were fostered in the fifteenth century by a vigorous economic life. Individualism was stimulated by the economic potential, and excess money made the all-important patronage possible. Growing commerce and industries brought money into Italy, stimulating the local economy and allowing wealthy people to indulge their desire for beauty and comfort.

Venice shone as the greatest merchant city in the world, importing tons of cotton, silk, and spices every year and exporting woolen cloth and mounds of silver coins to pay for their imports. As the sixteenth century opened, 1.5 million pounds of spices came through Venice alone every year. Venetians did not simply rest on their commercial wealth; some enterprising citizens developed and manufactured new products—most prominently, forks and windowpane glass—that would in time sweep through the world.

By contrast, Milan and Florence were craft-industrial cities. Florence, with its 270 workshops, led the way in wool cloth making. Renaissance Italy also profited from

Wool and silk

another new industry: silk. As early as the twelfth century, travelers had smuggled silkworms into Italy from China so that Italians could begin to produce the precious fabric locally. But the industry really blossomed after the thirteenth century, when the Chinese silk loom appeared in Italy. Italians powered the looms with waterwheels and produced large amounts of silk cloth. In the fourteenth century, one city had a silk mill employing 480 spindles rapidly spinning the precious silk. By the fifteenth century, Florence boasted eighty-three workshops devoted to silk production. The wealth let Florence take part in the thriving economy generated by the cloth trade network that connected countries like Italy and the Netherlands all the way to the New World. In the wake of this prosperous trade, even a shopkeeper in Florence wrote excitedly about his first taste of sugar brought in from overseas.

But the most profitable industry was banking. Throughout the Middle Ages, the development of banking and commerce had been impeded by

Banking

the Christian belief in the immorality of usury, or charging interest, but enterprising merchants found ways around the prohibition. Some people offered gifts in gratitude for a loan of money, thus effectively paying back more than they borrowed. However, the easiest way to collect interest was by changing money and making a profit on the exchange rate. By the thirteenth century, Christians all over Europe began to engage in the lucrative trade of money lending, but it was the Italian bankers of the Renaissance who really first perfected the art of using money to make money. In the process, many raked in fortunes—for example, the rich families in Florence purchased

■ FIGURE 10.6

Jews driven from a German city, Hebrew manuscript, ca. 1427.

state-guaranteed government bonds that paid over 15 percent interest. It is not surprising that the "fat people" got even "fatter" as the Renaissance rolled on.

SLAVERY REVIVED

The booming economy of the Renaissance led to new institutional oppression—the revival of slavery in Europe. Why was slavery reintroduced precisely when even serfs were being freed from their bondage? Some historians suggest that the labor shortage of the late fourteenth century caused by the bubonic plague drove people to look for fresh hands. However, this explanation is not satisfactory, because the new slaves were by and large not used in agriculture or industry. Instead, it seems that newly wealthy people trying to make their lives more comfortable looked to new sources for scarce domestic help.

Slavery had some complex facets. Renaissance families, for example, often considered slaves part of the household. One Florentine woman in 1469 wrote a letter to her husband asking him to acquire a slave girl to care for their young child or a "black boy" to become the child's playmate. Occasionally slaves bore children fathered by their owners, who sometimes raised them as legitimate heirs. Figure 10.7 is a portrait of a slave named Katharina drawn by Albrecht Dürer (1471–1528), a popular engraver commissioned to render portraits of many famous people. Katharina was in the service of a Portuguese commercial agent living in Antwerp who became friends with Dürer in 1520. This portrait shows the high regard in which this owner held Katharina. She is well dressed, and the fact that she sat for a portrait shows that she was a valued member of the household.

The Venetians, positioned near the eastern Mediterranean, capitalized on this trade first, dealing mostly in Muslim and Greek Orthodox slaves obtained through warfare or simply taken captive. Between 1414 and 1423, Venetian traders sold about 10,000 slaves in their markets. Most of these slaves were young girls sold into service as domestic servants. The fall of Constantinople to the Turks in 1453 (see Chapter 9) led to a decline in slaves from eastern lands, and Europeans began to look for new sources of captives. In the early fifteenth century, the Portuguese conquered the Canary Islands off the western coast of Africa, and what had been a trickle of

Sources of slaves

African slaves into Europe swelled. In the following decades, Portuguese traders eager to compete with the wealthy Venetians brought some 140,000 sub-Saharan African slaves into Europe.

Many people questioned the reestablishment of slavery in Europe. The church disapproved of it, and numerous slaveowners considered it too expensive in the long run. Slavery gradually disappeared in Europe by the end of the Renaissance. However, the precedent had been reestablished, and traders would later find a flourishing slave market in the New World (see Chapters 12 and 15).

FINDING COMFORT IN FAMILY

In the rugged world that emphasized individual achievement, the family assumed central importance as the one constant, dependable structure in Renaissance society. Men and women believed they could count on their kin when all else failed and highlighted these connections in art, literature, and the decisions they made in their daily lives. The emphasis on family loyalty was not limited to the upper classes. Artisan workshops, for example, were family affairs in which fathers trained sons and sons-in-law to carry on the family business.

Family ties also defined ethics in a world in which morality seemed relative. In a book about family written by Leon Battista Alberti (1404–1472), a Florentine architect, the author argued that whatever increased a man's power to help his family was good. Riches, however gained, fell into this category. Still, as Isabella d'Este proved, nothing beat a good marriage alliance for improving a family's standing.

Marriage alliances

Plans for such beneficial alliances began as early as the birth of a girl, when wealthy Florentine fathers would open an account with the public dowry fund, which paid as much as 21 percent interest. Family alliances depended on both parties bringing resources to the match. Wealthy families with sons wanted to be certain that their resources would not be diminished by marriage. Thus, parents of girls had to ensure that their daughters could bring enough money to an alliance to ensure a match with well-placed families. The dowry fund was implemented to guarantee that a girl had a sizeable dowry when she reached marriageable age. Some Renaissance families could not afford dowries for all their daughters and encouraged some to enter convents (which required smaller dowries). Indeed, the number of convents in Florence increased from only five in 1350 to forty-seven in 1550.

Of course, all these efforts to secure important family alliances had an equal impact on men and women. In the literature and art of the period, too, both men and women appear, but here women played

■ FIGURE 10.7

Albrecht Dürer, *Portrait of Katharina*, 1520.

a strikingly different role than they did in real life. Frequently following the medieval traditions of courtly love, women were given a prominent place as idealized beings who inspired men. Dante Alighieri (1265–1321) (discussed in Chapter 9), whose *Divine Comedy* stands at the cusp between the Middle Ages and the Renaissance, featured a young woman, Beatrice, as his guide into heaven. Petrarch devoted many sonnets to Laura, a young woman who served as his inspiration. Painters, too, portrayed numerous women, many of them nudes who represented idealized beauty and longing for perfection. Artists may have played with the notion of idealized women, but Renaissance men depended on real women to preside over the haven that was their family and their security for the future.

CHILDREN'S LIVES

Though idealized visions of women signaled the importance of the continuity that families provided, and Renaissance families wanted and loved their children, child-rearing practices undermined the hopes of many a proud parent. Privileged families of the Renaissance believed that it was unhealthy (and perhaps even unsavory) for women to breast-feed their infants. Therefore, they customarily sent their newborns to live with peasant women, who were paid to serve as wet nurses until the children were weaned. Some nurses took meticulous care of these infants; others were less attentive. Peasant mothers suffered from poor diets themselves and had insufficient milk to nurse a fosterling along with her own infants. Foster babies faced other dangers in the villages as well: Criminal records tell horrifying stories of death in the countryside, such as that of a peasant man who murdered four children under the age of 8. Florentine city-dwellers hearing such tales sometimes worried about their children's safety in the countryside, but the force of custom sent infants away to depend on the kindness of strangers.

Wealthy urban parents reclaimed their children when they were weaned, at about 2 years old. These young strangers then had to fit into large households teeming with older children, stepchildren, and a host of other relatives. With busy parents and stepparents, children often formed their principal attachment with an older sibling or aunt or uncle. The artist Andrea Mantegna was commissioned to paint a cycle of frescoes for the Gonzaga family, who ruled the Duchy of Mantua, and Figure 10.8 shows one portion of this magnificent work. Against the stunning background of the city, the painter shows a man with presumably three of his sons. The youngest in the foreground holds tightly to the eldest's hand, perhaps reflecting the situation in many crowded settings as older children cared for younger.

Childhood hardships

■ FIGURE 10.8

Andrea Mantegna, *The Cardinal Francesco Gonzaga Returning from Rome.*

Child-rearing experts warned parents against pampering their offspring, and in general the parents obeyed. Ironically, in this culture of wealth and luxury, people raised their children with a degree of strictness that may seem extreme to us today. One writer (the Dominican Giovanni Dominici), for example, urged mothers to prepare children for hardship by making them sleep in the cold on a hard chest instead of a bed. To toughen them, parents fed children bitter-tasting objects such as peachstones and sometimes gave them "harmless" nausea-inducing herbs so as to accustom them to illness. A humanist (Filarete) writing about an ideal school recommended that children be fed only tough meat so they would learn to eat slowly. This same writer recommended that children eat standing up until they were 20 years old. Many parents let their children sleep only six to eight hours a night to keep them from getting lazy.

Within these strict guidelines, boys and girls were treated quite differently. One humanist (Paola da Certaldo) advised feeding and clothing boys well. For girls, he recommended: "Dress the girl well but as for eating, it doesn't matter as long as it keeps her alive; don't let her get fat."

At about 7 years old, middle-class boys were sent to school to learn reading and mathematics and to ready themselves for the complex world of Renaissance economics. As the boys prepared for careers, fathers arranged marriages for their young daughters. Girls were married relatively young—between 17 and 20 years old (although sometimes younger)—to bridegrooms in their 30s who had established their careers. (See Isabella d'Este's biography.) Many brides, still children themselves when they began having babies, did not survive the experience of giving birth. One Florentine man recorded in his memoirs that, between 1390 and 1431, he had four wives who gave him a total of 24 children. The first three wives died in childbirth.

The harshness of childhood took its toll on many boys and girls; mortality among children reached astonishing rates. In fifteenth-century Florence, 45 percent of children died before the age of 20, most of them girls. The 1427 census in Florence showed a surprising gender ratio: 100 women to every 110 men. This statistic reversed the situation that had prevailed through the High Middle Ages, when women outnumbered men.

An Age of Talent and Beauty: Renaissance Culture and Science

Renaissance life had its unsavory side—as rich men struggled to get richer, powerful men worked for more power, and small children sometimes suffered. But at the same time, Renaissance society produced some astonishingly talented people whose works have transformed not only our ideas about beauty but also the very appearance of the world we live in today. During the Renaissance—as in classical Athens—people expected art to be a public thing, to be available to and appreciated by people as they strolled through the cities. Public art nurtured civic pride.

Artists and Artisans

During the Renaissance, many upper-class boys pursued humanistic literary studies to prepare for the day they would play a public role in city life, but their families generally discouraged them from following careers in the visual arts. Filippo Brunelleschi (1377–1446), for example, greatly displeased his father when he declared his interest in sculpting and architecture; his family had fully expected Filippo to become a physician or a notary. Michelangelo's father dismissed his son's interest in art as "shameful." Peasant boys, too, had little chance at a career in the arts, for without family connections, there was little chance of entry into the art world. If a country boy was a talented artist, he would probably not have the good fortune to be discovered like the shepherd Giotto whose story opened this chapter.

The majority of Renaissance artists came from artisan families. As boys worked as apprentices in artisan workshops, masters recognized and supported genius. Botticelli, the great Florentine painter, was apprenticed at age 13, as was Michelangelo. These examples were typical—a boy entering adulthood had to learn to take his place in the world, and that place often began in the artisan workshops. As a young man developed his skill, people began to recognize that he was no longer a simple craftsman, an artisan, making goods, but instead an artist, a creator of beauty.

Women ordinarily were excluded from taking this path. Yet, in spite of this lack of official acceptance, a number of female artists won renown during the Renaissance. Two, in particular, were highly respected by their contemporaries. Sofonisba Anguissola (ca. 1532–1625) achieved fame as an artist through her skill and the support of her wealthy, aristocratic father. More typical was the case of Lavinia Fontana (1552–1614), the daughter of an artist who trained in her father's workshop. Despite these successes, the public role of artists precluded many women from active careers in art. For example, Anguissola delayed marriage until she was in her late 40s so she could paint—a privilege that most Renaissance fathers did not grant.

Late in the Renaissance, artists overall gained new respect—wealthy patrons stopped viewing them as simply manual laborers and began to recognize them as artists. Michelangelo even earned the title "Il Divino," the Divine One. Europeans during the Renaissance valued genius, and these artistic geniuses obliged by creating magnificent works.

Architecture: Echoing the Human Form

The most expensive investment a patron of the arts could make was in architecture, and artists competed for these lucrative contracts. In the process, they designed innovative churches and other buildings that contributed to the prestige of their cities. Where did architects learn these new ideas? Part of the answer comes from the training of architects. Artisans did not consider architecture a separate craft, so there was no direct apprenticeship for this profession that rigidly inculcated old design ideas. Indeed, the greatest architects had all trained for other fields: Brunelleschi, for example, was a goldsmith, and Alberti a university-trained

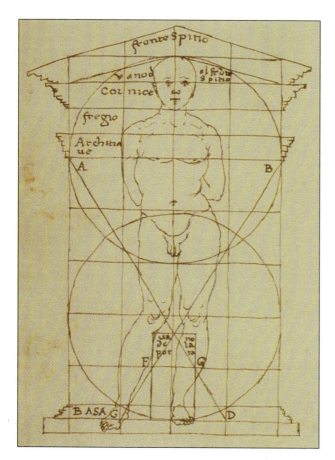
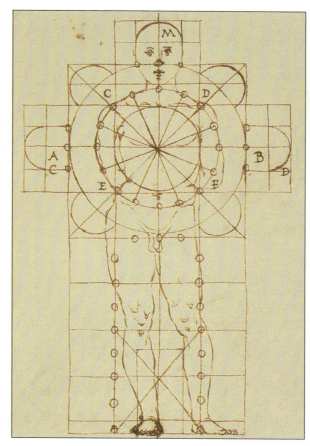

■ FIGURE 10.9

Francesco di Giorgio Martini, human-proportion architecture.

humanist. The Renaissance passion for the glory of classical Greece and Rome led would-be architects to look carefully at the old ruins that had stood for so long; their love of the individual caused them to put humans at the center of their enterprise. The resulting architecture, while looking back to classical models, was strikingly and beautifully new.

Instead of soaring Gothic cathedrals dominated by vertical heights, architects followed classical models of balance and simplicity and combined circular forms with linear supports to break up the monotony of vertical lines. Instead of creating structures that made humans seem small and insignificant before God, they built to glorify the human form and proportions. The fifteenth-century architectural drawings pictured in Figure 10.9 show the ideal of buildings designed along human proportions. The drawing on the left shows a front view of a building with a man standing to indicate the proper proportions, while the one on the right shows a floor plan with the man lying down in the building.

The most influential architectural treatise, *On Building* by Alberti, dominated the field for centuries and expressed an architectural aesthetic that echoed that

Human architecture

of the ancient Greeks. Alberti argued that buildings should mirror the human body in their supports and openings, and this sentiment is shown in Figure 10.9. Repeating the same principle, Michelangelo claimed that anyone who had not mastered anatomy and painting of the human form could not understand architecture. "The different parts of a building," he explained, "derive from human members." Thus, much of the architecture of the Renaissance was created in the image and likeness of the human form.

It is easy to miss the subtleties of human proportion within architecture as we look at the graceful buildings, but there is no overlooking one of the architects' debts to Rome—domes instead of Gothic spires now began to rise with more frequency over the skylines of Renaissance cities. Figure 10.10 shows the cathedral of Florence, with its dome designed by Brunelleschi. The architect had admired the Pantheon dome in Rome (see Chapter 4), and he wanted to erect a massive dome to span the huge base of the new cathedral in Florence. However, Brunelleschi realized that the Roman dome was not suitable to the large space, so the architect creatively took the Gothic technique of using architectural ribs to create a magnificent new structure for

Domes

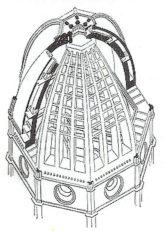

■ FIGURE 10.10
Brunelleschi's dome of the Florence Cathedral, 1420–1436.

■ FIGURE 10.11
Michelangelo, *David*, 1504.

the city. Brunelleschi designed the dome of the Florence cathedral with an inner and outer shell, both attached to the eight ribs of the octagonal structure. The drawing in Figure 10.10 shows the structural design. Between the two shells the architect placed sixteen ribs to strengthen the dome. The two shells thus supported each other and shared the weight of the whole. Many Florentines predicted that the dome would collapse, yet Brunelleschi's handiwork continues to dominate the skyline of Florence.

The Renaissance study of architecture also extended beyond individual buildings to town planning in general. In the fifteenth century, planners began to dream of laying out towns in the simple and logical grid pattern that characterizes our modern cities. Indeed, older European cities still feature a medieval center with curved and random streets surrounded by tidy, post-Renaissance grids. In Latin America, by contrast, towns founded by fifteenth-century Europeans were created in a grid pattern centered on the town square. On the peripheries of such towns, however, streets wove randomly in the tradition of the villages that predated the Renaissance town centers. All these new ideas about buildings and street planning reshaped the cities of the West.

Town planning

SCULPTURE COMES INTO ITS OWN

Just as Brunelleschi's admiration of the ancients led him to re-create domed architecture, sculptors also drew from classical models. Italians, who had admired free-standing images from the ancient world, began to demand similar beauty for their cities. City communes and individuals commissioned life-sized figures to stand free in the public spaces of cities.

Figure 10.11 shows Michelangelo's widely admired statue of David, the biblical figure who killed the giant Goliath. The statue stands more than 18 feet high and took the master three years to carve from a block of

Michelangelo's David

supposedly flawed marble. The work exhibits all the innovations of Renaissance sculpture: It is a huge, free-standing nude that depicts the classical ideal of repose, in which the subject rests his weight on one leg in a pose called **contra posto.** The figure exemplifies the confidence and the glorification of the human body that marked Renaissance pride.

Michelangelo's statue shows another hallmark of Renaissance spirit—an exuberant praise of realism; the sculptor knew anatomy and realistically portrayed the human body. Renaissance sculptors had to look at life carefully in order to reproduce it with such accuracy, and the audience, too, was led to an appreciation of realism through admiring the great sculptures that graced the public areas.

The statue also carried a political message, a common characteristic of the civic humanism of the day. In 1494, when the French invasion of Florence caused a temporary fall of the Medici rule, the newly restored Republic of Florence had commissioned Michelangelo to create a work with a patriotic theme—something that would celebrate the overthrow of the family that had dominated the city for so long. The sculptor chose David the "giant killer" to symbolize the republic's ousting of the goliath Medici. Michelangelo portrayed David before his fight with Goliath—the youth is confident and defiant, just as Florence saw itself confronting the rest of the world. In this masterpiece, art joined with politics in the best Renaissance tradition.

PAINTING FROM A NEW PERSPECTIVE

The shepherd Giotto di Bondone (ca. 1267–1337), whose artistic talents were recognized by a Florentine master, was to revolutionize painting for Florence and the West. The young apprentice who fooled his master with a painting of a fly turned his talents to magnificent religious paintings, and he created realistic figures that showed a full range of human expression. For example, his images of the Virgin Mary were not portrayed as remote queens of heaven, but instead painted as realistic young girls struggling to be caring mothers.

Figure 10.12 shows Giotto's fresco of the *Lamentation over Christ*, in which the faithful mourn the death of Christ. The painting looks back to medieval tradition with gold leaf on the halos and the theme of the painting. However, the painter points to the future with his three-dimensional figures and a new realistic portrayal of emotion. Giotto's talent was recognized during his lifetime, and his paintings were in great demand. Toward the end of his life, his city of Florence issued a proclamation that in part cap-

■ FIGURE 10.12

Giotto, *Lamentation over Christ*, ca. 1305.

tures the painter's influence: "Many will profit from his knowledge and learning and the city's beauty will be enhanced." Painters following Giotto built on his techniques and further revolutionized this visual art.

Like architects and sculptors, Renaissance painters developed striking new techniques, including oil painting on canvas and the perfection of portraiture. However, perhaps their best-known innovation was **linear perspective,** which allowed painters to enhance the realism of paintings by creating the illusion of three-dimensional space on a two-dimensional surface. The Florentines—and Brunelleschi in particular—proudly claimed to have invented this technique of painting. Whether they did or not is probably irrelevant; regardless of who invented linear perspective, the Florentines perfected it.

Linear perspective

Before beginning to paint, Brunelleschi organized the painting around a central point and then drew a grid to place objects precisely in relation to each other. His real innovation, however, came when he calculated the mathematic ratios by which objects seem to get smaller as they recede from view. In this way, he knew exactly how big to paint each object in his grid to achieve a realistic illusion of receding space. In commenting on Brunelleschi's creations, Alberti asserted that a painting should be pleasing to the eye, but also should appeal to the mind with optical and mathematical accuracy. And here is the essence of these complex works: They used all the intellectual skill of the artists to create images profoundly appealing to the senses.

Perspective also grew from and appealed to the Renaissance emphasis on the individual, for it assumed

Raphael, *The School of Athens*, 1510–1511

■ FIGURE 10.13

Raphael was commissioned by Pope Julius II to create a fresco for his library. In this magnificent fresco, the artist portrayed famous ancient philosophers, such as Euclid, Pythagoras, and Socrates. In the center are Plato and Aristotle. Plato (looking remarkably like Leonardo da Vinci) is on the left with his hand pointing in the air reminding viewers of the realm of ideas. He is speaking to Aristotle whose hand presses downward to earth, reminding viewers of his more earthly approach to knowledge. Raphael has included a self-portrait on the right (in a black hat) and a brooding Michelangelo sitting in the center foreground. ■ **Identify** the following characteristics of the Renaissance: individualism, appreciation of the classics, and perspective. ■ **Why** would the Pope find this a suitable subject matter for the papal library? ■ **Why** do you think Raphael included portraits of his artist contemporaries in the company of the philosophers?

that a painting would be viewed from one single spot in front of the work. As one art critic wrote, "Every painting that used perspective proposed to the spectator that he was the unique center of the world." In other words, the painter designed the painting with the eye of the beholder in mind. For the next four hundred years, Renaissance ideas of perspective and space set the standard for Western painting.

The painter Raphael (1483–1520) was widely regarded as one of Italy's best painters of the High Renaissance (the late fifteenth and early sixteenth centuries). During his lifetime, he **Raphael** was much acclaimed as an artist who could portray transcendent themes with all the realism of fifteenth-century Italian life, and modern critics agree. His reputation gained him the coveted commission to paint a fresco for Pope Julius II's library, and Figure 10.13 shows the fresco he painted—the *School of Athens*. Raphael created this fresco just as Michelangelo was painting the Sistine Chapel ceiling (see Figure 10.1).

SCIENCE OR PSEUDOSCIENCE?

The Renaissance passion for direct observation and realistic assessment that led to such magnificent achievements in the visual and literary arts catalyzed a process that ultimately led to the scientific accomplishments of the seventeenth century. During the fourteenth and fifteenth centuries, however, much scientific inquiry was shaped by a desire to control as well as understand the world. This combination led to the pursuit of what we consider pseudoscientific studies.

As the biography of Isabella d'Este indicated, astrology was extremely popular during these centuries. Even some popes hired **Astrology and alchemy** their own astrologers. The bright appearance of Halley's comet in 1456 provoked a flurry of both dire and inspiring prophecies. For example, one humanist physician explained the outbreak of syphilis in Europe in terms of a conjunction of the planets Saturn, Jupiter, and Mars in the sign of Cancer. **Alchemy was the early practice of chemistry, but the alchemists' interests were dramatically different from those of modern scientists.** Their main goal was to find a "philosopher stone" that would turn base metals into gold. This science was perhaps even more popular than astrology.

Such pseudoscience aside, the Renaissance did succeed in combining visual arts with scientific observation. The study of linear **Mathematics and anatomy** perspective, for example, depended on an understanding of mathematics, and scholars spread the use of Arabic numerals to replace the Roman numerals that had previously dominated the West. The use of these numbers facilitated higher orders of calculations, like algebra, which was also learned from the Muslims. Realistic sculpture and painting required a study of anatomy, and this science also progressed. Amidst these advancements, the Renaissance saw the birth of a man who came to represent the entire range and combination of talents that so defined this age.

LEONARDO DA VINCI: THE "RENAISSANCE MAN"

Leonardo da Vinci (1452–1519) personifies the idea of the "Renaissance man"—the person who can supposedly do anything well. As a young man, he had

■ FIGURE 10.14

Leonardo da Vinci, *Mona Lisa*, ca. 1504.

contributed to the architecture of Florence by helping to make the golden ball that topped Brunelleschi's dome (see Figure 10.10), but he excelled in much more than architecture and sculpture.

This multitalented Italian served in the courts of a number of patrons, from the Medici to the Sforza of Milan—even Isabella d'Este **Painting** had tried to woo him. At these courts, Leonardo painted magnificent portraits and beautiful religious works. Figure 10.14 shows Leonardo's celebrated *Mona Lisa*, probably the most famous portrait from the Renaissance. Her famous hint of a smile and calm pose were strikingly original at the time and inspired many later portraits.

Although Leonardo's skill as a painter would have satisfied most men longing for greatness, he saw this medium only as a beginning, a means to a larger end. "Painting should increase the artist's knowledge of the physical world," he explained.

Leonardo left a collection of notebooks that showed his intense interest in the world. His drawings of plants revealed **Scientific notebooks** a skill and meticulousness that any botanist would envy, and his sketches of water in motion would have impressed the most accomplished of engineers. Leonardo's imagination seemed boundless—his sketches included tanks and other war machines, a submarine, textile machines, paddle boats, a "horseless carriage," and many other inventions that lay in the future.

Leonardo also took an interest in the inner workings of the human body. Although some medieval physicians conducted dissections, the practice was not common. During the Renaissance, however, physicians and scholars began to approach the study of the human body empirically by regularly dissecting cadavers. At the time, both artists and physicians saw dissection as a way to improve their portrayal of the human form. Like many other artists, Leonardo dissected cadavers to understand anatomy and thereby make his paintings as realistic as possible (as well as to satisfy his insatiable curiosity). Figure 10.15 shows Leonardo's sketches and descriptions of human shoulders and arms, including their intricate network of veins and capillaries. The drawing of the head of an old man whose body Leonardo had dissected suggests the artist's awareness of humanity even in his mechanical analysis of the body.

Figure 10.16, a depiction of a child in the womb, reveals the wide range of Leonardo's interests as well

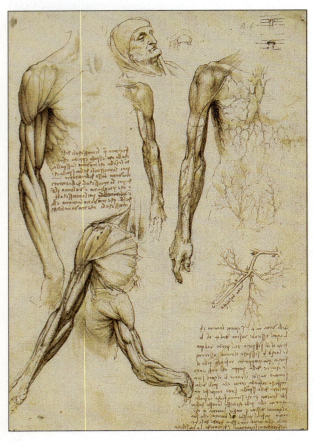

■ FIGURE 10.15

Leonardo da Vinci, study of a shoulder and arm.

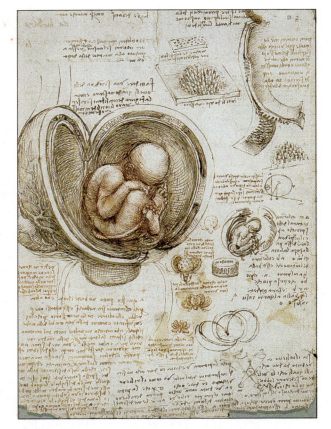

■ FIGURE 10.16

Leonardo da Vinci, child in womb.

as his scientific curiosity. It is the oldest surviving illustration in the West of the actual position of an unborn child. To make this drawing, Leonardo secured a dispensation to dissect a deceased pregnant woman. In addition to capturing the correct positioning, the drawing also explains the function of the placenta.

King Francis I of France (r. 1515–1547) once said of Leonardo, "No other man had been born who knew so much." Unfortunately for the future of science and engineering, Leonardo's voluminous notebooks were lost for centuries after his death. In retrospect, perhaps Leonardo's greatest achievement was that he showed how multitalented human beings could be. He proved the humanists' belief that an educated man could accomplish anything in all fields. Leonardo died at the court of Francis I, who had proudly served as his patron.

Renaissance of the "New Monarchies" of the North: 1453–1640

As we saw in Chapter 9, the medieval political structures of Europe began to fall apart under the pressures of the many disasters of the fourteenth century. The monarchies of the fifteenth century could no longer rely on feudal contracts and armies of mounted knights and began to search for new ways to rule their countries. To bypass their sometimes unreliable nobility, monarchs concentrated their royal authority by appointing bureaucrats who owed their status only to the will of the king or queen. As they looked for new sources of income to pay growing mercenary armies, kings and queens kept imposing new taxes and, in general, were receptive to new ideas to help them consolidate their power. Many hired Italians trained in the humanist tradition to work in their courts, and slowly and fitfully from the late thirteenth through the sixteenth centuries, the ideas of the Renaissance spread to northern European countries. As Renaissance notions traveled north and bore fruit in the courts of powerful rulers, the ideas were further transformed. This migration of ideas also accelerated the changes triggered by the disasters of the fourteenth century.

France: Under the Italian Influence

France offers a case study in how slowly and sporadically Renaissance ideas moved and how much this new spirit depended on the patronage of monarchs. The French king Charles V (r. 1364–1380), known as "the Wise," encouraged Renaissance learning among

his subjects, gathering a circle of intellectuals around him. However, this early flowering of learning withered when his mentally unstable son, Charles VI (r. 1380–1422), took power. Integration of Renaissance ideals in this northern court would have to wait until the end of the Hundred Years' War in 1453 (discussed in Chapter 9).

France eventually triumphed in the Hundred Years' War, but a new threat from the neighboring state of Burgundy immediately arose. As we saw in Chapter 9, Burgundy had allied with England to weaken France, and England's defeat did not weaken Burgundy's land hunger. As Map 10.3 shows, the rulers of Burgundy were trying to forge a state between France and the Holy Roman Empire, and their hundred-year expansion represented a real threat to France. Instead of leading armies in the old chivalric manner, however, the French king, Louis XI (r. 1461–1483) skillfully brought a new kind of diplomacy to bear in confronting this next challenge. His contemporaries called him "Louis the Spider" because he spun a complex web of intrigue and diplomatic machinations worthy of Machiavelli—bribing his allies and murdering his enemies. Louis subsidized Swiss mercenaries who eventually defeated the Burgundian ruler. France then seized the Duchy of Burgundy and added the sizeable new territory to its lands. (As Map 10.3 shows, the Low Countries remained in the hands of Mary, the Duke of Burgundy's daughter, and this later formed part of the inheritance of her grandson, Charles V, whose fortunes we will follow in Chapter 11). Louis left France strong and prosperous and well placed to play a powerful political role in the coming centuries. Document 10.3 offers a contemporary's view of this complex king.

Louis the Spider

As Map 10.3 shows, the French kings succeeded in slowly taking the lands from the nobles who had retained their holdings since the Middle Ages. With its increasing strength, France next began expanding across the Alps into Italy to assert dynastic claims in Naples, because, as we saw previously, the French royal family was related to the rulers in Naples. However, the French came back with much more than wealth. Nobles leading mercenary armies in the Italian campaigns of 1494 came in search of land and left feeling dazzled by the cultural accomplishments of the Italian Renaissance. In a letter to his courtiers back home, the French king Charles VIII (r. 1483–1498) gushed about discovering the "best artists" in Italy. He returned home with some 20 Italian workmen whom he instructed to build "in the Italian style." The aesthetic ideals of Italy thus moved north with the retreating French armies, and the early Renaissance spirit in France was reawakened.

Italian influence increased further with the substantial growth of the French court, which opened positions to Italian humanists and diplomats. France's

Map labels

ENGLAND

NORTH SEA

HOLY ROMAN EMPIRE

London

Bruges
Antwerp
Calais
Brussels
FLANDERS
Etaples

Scheldt R.
Meuse R.
Rhine R.
Moselle R.

PICARDY
Amiens

Rouen

Reims
Marne R.
Verdun
Metz
ALSACE

Paris
CHAMPAGNE
Toul
LORRAINE

Brest

NORMANDY

ORLEANS
Orléans
Blois

BRITTANY

MAINE
Tours
Amboise
Bourges

DUCHY OF BURGUNDY

Dijon
FRANCHE-COMTE

Loire R.
Nantes

ANJOU

POITOU

AUVERGNE

Lyons

SAVOY

ANGOULEME

Bordeaux
Dordogne R.

GUIENNE

Grenoble
DAUPHINE

Avignon

Toulouse

LANGUEDOC

PROVENCE

Marseilles

Perpignan
CERDAGNE
ROUSSILLON

MEDITERRANEAN SEA

N
W E
S

0   100 miles
0   100 kilometers

Legend

— Holy Roman Empire boundary

--- Ile de France boundary

Royal domain in 1461

Areas added to 1483

Areas added to 1498

Areas added to 1515

Areas added to 1547

Areas added to 1559

Burgundian areas in 1477: those in the Holy Roman Empire to be inherited by the Habsburgs; those to the West by France.

Semi-independent areas

MAP 10.3   FRANCE IN THE FIFTEENTH AND SIXTEENTH CENTURIES

This map shows the growth of the royal domain of the French kings from 1461 through 1559.
■ **Locate** the Duchy of Burgundy that extends from Flanders down to Savoy. **Consider** why this state posed such a threat to the French kings. ■ **Locate** Avignon, where the popes had lived for so long. **Consider** why many in Europe accused those popes of being pro-French.

■ DOCUMENT 10.3

A Courtier Describes a Suspicious King—Louis the Spider

point of view

Philippe de Commynes (ca. 1447–1511) served Louis XI and wrote an account of the king's reign shortly after Louis' death in 1483. Commynes had been raised at the court of Burgundy until he found it politically expedient to change sides and work for France. Thus, he was well placed to view the king with the eye of an outsider as well as a courtier. ■ **What** *qualities did Commynes value in the king and* **which** *did he criticize?* ■ **Would** *Machiavelli have considered Louis a good prince? Why or why not?* ■ **What** *qualities do you think made him a successful monarch?*

The King had ordered several cruel prisons to be made; some were cages of iron, and some of wood, but all were covered with iron plates both within and without, with terrible locks, about eight feet wide and seven high. . . . I lay in one of them eight months together in the minority of our present King. . . . However, I have seen many eminent and deserving persons in these prisons, with these nets about their legs, who afterwards came forth with great joy and honor, and received great rewards from the King. . . .

It may be urged that other princes have been more given to suspicion than he, but it was not in our time; and, perhaps, their wisdom was not so eminent, nor were their subjects so good. They might too, probably, have been tyrants, and bloody-minded; but *fair?* our king never did any person a mischief who had not offended him first, though I do not say all who offended him deserved death. I have not recorded these things merely to represent our master as a suspicious and mistrustful prince; but . . . that those princes who may be his successors, may learn by his example to be more tender and indulgent to their subjects, and less severe in their punishments than our master had been: although I will not censure him, or say I ever saw a better prince; for though he oppressed his subjects himself, he would never see them injured by anybody else. . . .

I knew him, and was entertained in his service in the flower of his age, and at the height of his prosperity, yet I never saw him free from labor and care. Of all diversions be loved hunting and hawking in their seasons; but his chief delight was in dogs. As for ladies, he never meddled with any in my time; for about the time

very effected

of my coming to his court he lost a son, at whose death he was extremely afflicted, and he made a vow to God in my presence never to have intercourse with any other woman but the queen; and though this was no more than what he was bound to do by the canons of the church, yet it was much that his self-command should be so great, that he should be able to persevere in his resolution so firmly, considering that the queen (though an excellent princess in other respects) was not a person in whom a man could take any great delight. . . .

He was involved [in warfare that]. . . lasted till his death, and many brave men lost their lives in it, and his treasury was exhausted by it; so that he had but a little time during the whole year to spend in pleasure, and even then the fatigues he underwent were excessive. When his body was at rest his mind was at work, for he had affairs in several places at once, and would concern himself as much in those of his neighbors as in his own, putting officers of his own over all the great families, and endeavoring to divide their authority as much as possible. When he was at war he labored for a peace or a truce, and when he had obtained it, he was impatient for war again. He troubled himself with many trifles in his government, which he had better have let alone: but it was his temper, and he could not help it; besides, he had a prodigious memory, and he forgot nothing, but knew everybody, as well in other countries as in his own.

workaholic + divide

Source: A. R. Scoble, trans. and annotator, *The Memories of Philip de Commines* (London: G. Bell & Sons, 1884), II, 75–81.

---

kings employed more officials than any other state in Europe—one estimate places the number of bureaucrats at more than 4,000 during the reign of Francis I (r. 1515–1547). (Leonardo da Vinci was among those brought to France by this powerful and sophisticated patron.) Under Francis's rule, humanist literature flourished, and the new learning influenced university curricula from languages to mathematics to law. The king even ordered Castiglione's *The Book of the Courtier* to be translated into French and read to him nightly.

Italians in France

The French Renaissance did not merely copy the Italian movement. Indeed, many works by French artists and writers during this period show a unique blend of humorous skepticism and creative power. The imag-

inative humanist François Rabelais embodies this unmistakable French version of Renaissance ideals. His books *Pantagruel* and *Gargantua*—bawdy tales about giants with enormous appetites—are masterpieces of satire. Both stories continue to captivate modern readers. France had left its own mark on the Renaissance spirit.

ENGLISH HUMANISM

When Henry VII (r. 1485–1509) became king in England after the Wars of the Roses (see Chapter 9), he succeeded in taming the rowdy and independent nobility and established a strong, centralized monarchy. Under the dynasty that he initiated, England again prospered. The English monarchs now turned their attention to the new spirit emanating from the south as they began to surround themselves with courtiers and art that served as the hallmarks of the courts of new monarchs. Delayed because of internal strife, the English Renaissance (1500–1640) gained momentum just as the Italian movement waned.

During the reign of Henry VII, English scholars intrigued by Renaissance thought traveled to Italy and studied under noted humanists. They frequented the newly established Vatican library and consulted with Platina, the papal librarian shown in Figure 10.5, and then returned home brimming with new ideas. By 1500, these scholars had so transformed the curriculum at Oxford that England could offer as fine a classical education as Italy.

Henry VIII (r. 1509–1547) proved an even more vigorous patron of Renaissance learning than his father. As we will see in Chapter 11, Henry met the French king Francis I and tried to outdo that Renaissance prince in splendor and patronage. The English king cultivated interest in astronomy, literature, and music—all the fields advocated by the humanists. Still, the talented monarch was outdone by his Lord Chancellor, Sir Thomas More (1478–1535).

More published a biography of the humanist Pico della Mirandola that revealed the author's debt to the Italian movement. The English scholar mastered classical learning and the humanist curriculum and applied his skills in public life in the best tradition of civic humanism. More's masterpiece, however, was *Utopia*, a work that commented on contemporary evils while offering a vision of a society free of poverty, crime, and corruption. More's work, with its visions of exploration and decidedly political orientation, points to distinct characteristics of the English Renaissance. More's studies gave him strong views on religion, which, as we will see in Chapter 11, led to a fatal conflict with his king.

Thomas More

Many Englishwomen also wrote during this Renaissance. The first wife of Henry VIII, Catherine of Aragon (1485–1536) had grown up with a love of the new learning encouraged by her mother, Isabella of Castille. When Catherine came to England, she stimulated interest among courtiers and scholars in the proper education of women. Consequently, Englishwomen wrote more publicly than their Italian counterparts. In fact, Italian travelers to England wrote disparagingly of the "brazen and violently assertive" Englishwomen. This tradition of education strongly influenced Queen Elizabeth I (r. 1558–1603), under whose rule England prospered and the Renaissance flowered.

Renaissance queens

RENAISSANCE LONDON: A BOOMING CITY

Sixteenth-century London—a vibrant city—scintillated during the English Renaissance, expanding physically and intellectually. Between 1560 and 1603, the population almost doubled, from 120,000 to more than 200,000, and travelers flocked there to see its wonders. Figure 10.17 shows a 1616 painting of London by Claes von Visscher. In this cityscape, the great sailing ships that made London a bustling commercial hub waft by, along with small vessels that supplied the city's growing population. Rows of houses stand in front of St. Paul's cathedral, which dominates the skyline.

In the foreground of the painting is the south bank of the Thames, which had been a center of prostitution from the time of the Roman settlement of London. The south bank remained the unseemly quarter of the city, inhabited by criminals and prostitutes, and notorious for its violent forms of entertainment such as bear baiting and dog fights. The

The south bank

■ FIGURE 10.17
Claes von Visscher, *Map of London*, detail, 1616.

south bank also housed private prisons, including the infamous "clink" that housed some of the fiercest criminals. Yet, the south bank was also home to the theaters where crowds gathered to watch the plays of the great Renaissance dramatists. The two tall, round structures in the foreground are examples of these theaters. The one on the right is inaccurately labeled "The Globe." Known as Shakespeare's theater, the building had burned down in 1613, before Visscher painted his London scene. During the late-sixteenth century, however, the Globe served as a backdrop for the work of the greatest writer England has ever produced, and crowds today gather to see plays performed in a newly rebuilt Globe Theater on the south bank of the Thames.

"The Globe"

ENGLAND'S PRIDE: WILLIAM SHAKESPEARE

The new social mobility of the Renaissance permitted William Shakespeare (1564–1616) to rise to prominence. William's father, a modest glove maker, married a woman above his station, the daughter of a wealthy landowner. Shakespeare probably attended the local school in Stratford-upon-Avon and received a humanist education. At the age of 18, the young scholar married Anne Hathaway, about eight years his elder, who was pregnant with their first child. In 1592,

William S.

William journeyed to London, where he worked as an actor and wrote comedies, histories, and tragedies. This master of the English language articulated all the Renaissance ideals: Shakespeare's love of the classics showed in his use of Roman histories in his plays (*Julius Caesar*) and in his study of Roman playwrights that offered him models of theater. Furthermore, Hamlet's words, "What a piece of work is man," expressed Renaissance optimism in human accomplishment; *Romeo and Juliet* re-created the story of "star-crossed lovers" (a reference to the Renaissance love of astrology) in the streets of Italy. *The Tempest* featured Renaissance magicians, and Shakespeare's histories described the fortunes of princes as surely as Machiavelli's analysis of history and politics had. In Shakespeare's hands, the ideals of the Renaissance were given a new enduring form—popular theater that reached the masses. However, some modern literary critics believe the great playwright accomplished much more than perfecting Renaissance ideas. Some claim that by expressing complex human emotions in magnificent language, Shakespeare created an understanding of humanity for the West. In this, perhaps, we can see the ideals of the Renaissance come full circle—the early humanists in Italy transformed themselves by the texts they read, and Shakespeare used the written word to shape our understanding of who we are. Western civilization was dramatically transformed.

SUMMARY

In the crucible of the fourteenth century—in which plague, famine, warfare, and religious instability swirled—new ideas percolated in the turbulent Italian city-states. Scholars and statesmen alike resuscitated a pride in human dignity, a confidence in human activism, and a fascination with classical ideals, and they expressed these ideas primarily in the secular arena. Writers, painters, and politicians looked with new realism at the world around them and strove to exert an impact on it. Although all these ideas had a precedent in the Middle Ages, nevertheless, their prevalence and novel applications created a new spirit that historians call the Renaissance.

This age of the Renaissance ushered in a period that had both great and shameful aspects. In booming economies, Italian city-states were able to support architects and artists who created masterpieces that have set Western standards of beauty for centuries. At the same time, many of these enterprising individualists turned a blind eye to social problems—increased crime, new slavery, and growing anti-Semitism.

The new ideas of the Renaissance flowed northward with humanist courtiers and talented artists and artisans. In the process, they helped transform the old feudal monarchies. At the same time, scholars in each country put their own stamp on the Renaissance spirit. For example, France gloried in court architecture and brilliant satire, and England most notably brought these ideas to the popular theater.

As we will see in Chapter 11, Spain and Germany, too, would mold the praise of individualism and literary criticism to their own interests. Like Savonarola in Florence, German humanists applied Renaissance ideas to spiritual matters. Their efforts would eventually bring about an upheaval in religion as great as the Renaissance revolution in art and ideas.

KEY TERMS

Renaissance, p. 304

humanist, p. 307

civic humanists, p. 307

Christian humanists, p. 307

condottieri, p. 312

doge, p. 314

theocracy, p. 316

contra posto, p. 325

linear perspective, p. 325

alchemy, p. 327

REVIEW, ANALYZE, AND ANTICIPATE

REVIEW THE PREVIOUS CHAPTER
Chapter 9—"The West Struggles and Eastern Empires Flourish"—told of the disasters of the fourteenth century that contributed to the breakdown of medieval structures. It also told of the rise of empires in the East that would soon cast a long shadow on politics in the West.

1. *Review the political order of northern Europe in the Middle Ages and contrast it with the political life of fourteenth-century Italy. How did the turbulent politics of Italy contribute to the growth of Renaissance thought?*

2. *Contrast medieval art, architecture, and literature with that of the Renaissance artists and humanists.*

ANALYZE THIS CHAPTER
Chapter 10—"A New Spirit in the West"—considers the characteristics we have come to associate with the term "Renaissance." It looks at the politics and social life of the Italian city-states that fostered these ideas and the magnificent accomplishments in the arts and science that accompanied them. It also follows the fortunes of the "new monarchies" of the north as Renaissance ideas spread.

1. *Review the characteristics of the Renaissance and consider what contributed to the development.*

2. *One theme this chapter traces is the relationship between ideas—like individualism and realism—and actual events and accomplishments. Analyze some aspects of life and accomplishments of Renaissance Italy in light of these values and consider how they were related.*

3. *How did Renaissance ideas spread northward, and how were they transformed in France and England?*

ANTICIPATE THE NEXT CHAPTER
Chapter 11—"Alone Before God"—will explore political developments as northern monarchs jockey for increased power. It will also explore major changes in religious beliefs.

1. *How do you think Renaissance ideas like individualism and scholarly criticism of texts might influence traditional religious convictions?*

2. *What states do you think will emerge as the strongest in the sixteenth century, and what areas do you think they might threaten the most?*

BEYOND THE CLASSROOM

A NEW SPIRIT EMERGES: INDIVIDUALISM, REALISM, AND ACTIVISM

Eisenstein, Elizabeth. *The Printing Revolution in Early Modern Europe*. New York: Cambridge University Press, 1983. Studies the shift from script to print and looks at the relationship between changes in communication and other developments.

Goldthwaite, Richard A. *Wealth and the Demand for Art in Italy, 1300–1600*. Baltimore: Johns Hopkins University Press, 1993. An original and important look at art in relationship to the society and economy that produced it.

King, Margaret L., and Albert Rabil. *Her Immaculate Hand: Selected Works by and About the Women Humanists of Quattrocento Italy*. Asheville, NC: Pegasus Press, 1998. Presents writings of women humanists to illuminate an often-neglected side of the Renaissance.

Marek, G. *The Bed and the Throne: Isabelle d'Este*. New York: Harper & Row, 1976. A dazzling story of culture, art, and politics through the life of this talented ruler.

Naubert, Charles G. *Humanism and the Culture of Renaissance Europe*, 2nd ed. Cambridge: Cambridge University Press, 2006. A clear yet comprehensive description of the movement from its inception in Italy to its spread northward—definitely the place to begin.

Plumb, J.H. *The Italian Renaissance*. New York: Mariner Books, 2001. A narrative that skillfully engages readers with no background in the subject and, at the same time, offers new insights to scholars.

THE POLITICS OF INDIVIDUAL EFFORT

Burckhardt, Jacob. *The Civilization of the Renaissance*. New York: Modern Library, 2002. A reissued edition of the nineteenth-century classic that began serious historical analysis of the Renaissance.

Femia, Joseph V. *Machiavelli Revisited*. Cardiff: University of Wales Press, 2002. Looks at the impact of Machiavelli's pivotal work *The Prince* while guiding the reader through the maze of contradictory interpretations.

Jones, P.J. *The Italian City-State: From Commune to Signoria*. Oxford: Clarendon Press, 1997. An impressive, scholarly study of the political history of the Italian city-states.

Rosenberg, Charles M. *Art and Politics in Late Medieval and Early Renaissance Italy, 1250–1500*. South Bend, IN: University of Notre Dame Press, 1991. Considers the interaction of art and politics from various points of view.

INDIVIDUALISM AS SELF-INTEREST: LIFE DURING THE RENAISSANCE

Brucker, Gene. *Florence: The Golden Age, 1138–1737*. Berkeley: University of California Press, 1998. A beautifully illustrated history by a prominent historian who brings the past vividly to life, including great families, common folk, wars, and artistic achievements.

Haas, Louis. *The Renaissance Man and His Children*. New York: St. Martin's Press, 1991. Sheds light on how Florentine parents (primarily fathers) viewed, reared, and cared for their children.

Herlihy, David, and C. Klapisch-Zuher. *Tuscans and Their Families*. New Haven, CT: Yale University Press, 1985. A well-written, fascinating study of families—the classic in the field.

King, Margaret L. *Women of the Renaissance*. Chicago: University of Chicago Press, 1991. A short, accessible summary of women in the family, the church, and participating in high culture.

McIntosh, Marjorie. *Controlling Misbehavior in England, 1370–1600*. Cambridge: Cambridge University Press, 2002. An in-depth study of the growing efforts of states to regulate behavior they deemed threatened public order.

Trexler, Richard. *Public Life in Renaissance Florence*. Ithaca, NY: Cornell University Press, 1991. Describes the way Florentines from Dante to Michelangelo interacted with one another, with foreigners, and with their God.

AN AGE OF TALENT AND BEAUTY: RENAISSANCE CULTURE AND SCIENCE

Baxandall, Michael. *Painting and Experience in Fifteenth Century Italy: A Primer in the Social History of Pictorial Style*. Oxford: Oxford University Press, 1988. A brilliant work that shows the intersection between life in Florence and painters' expression of those experiences. A study of both painting and social history.

James, Frank A. *Renaissance and Revolution: Humanists, Scholars, Craftsmen and Natural Philosophers in Early Modern Europe*. New York: Cambridge University Press, 1994. A clear and engaging survey of the history of science and technology between 1400 and 1750.

Kaufmann, Thomas D. *The Mastery of Nature: Aspects of Art, Science and Humanism in the Renaissance*. Princeton, NJ: Princeton University Press, 1993. A rich collection of essays that contribute to the study of art history and the history of science.

Paletti, John T., and Gary M. Radke. *Art in Renaissance Italy*. New York: Harry N. Abrams, 1997. A good survey.

RENAISSANCE OF THE "NEW MONARCHIES" OF THE NORTH: 1453–1640

Bloom, Harold. *Shakespeare: The Invention of the Human*. New York: Riverhead Books, 1998. A controversial but influential study of all Shakespeare's plays that argues that Shakespeare shaped the way we define ourselves.

Kendall, P.M. *Louis XI, the Universal Spider*. New York: W.W. Norton, 1971. A remarkable presentation of the French king Louis XI as one of the formidable personalities of Europe and one of the shapers of the modern world.

Martin, John J. *The Renaissance: Italy and Abroad*. New York: Routledge, 2002. A collection of essays that illustrates the current status of Renaissance studies, revealing its diversity and complexities.

www.mhhe.com/sherman3

- Unfamiliar words? See our Glossary at the back of the book for pronunciation and definitions.

- Need help studying? See our web page for map exercises, practice quizzes, and additional study resources.

- Need help writing a paper? Access hundreds of primary documents, maps, images, and a guide to writing history papers on our Primary Source Investigator site at **www.mhhe.com/psi.**

HANS HOLBEIN THE YOUNGER, *ERASMUS OF ROTTERDAM*, CA. 1523

As Humanist ideas of scholarship and individualism spread north, they influenced a revolution in Christian thought, first led by the man portrayed here. Erasmus is shown resting his hands on a Greek book inscribed "The Labors of Herakles," a tribute to his Herculean task of revising biblical translations based on the study of ancient languages. He is placed in a room with hints of Renaissance design, reminding viewers of his debt to the Italian scholars. This quiet portrait reveals a pious man, seeking God alone. It does not reveal how this new approach to religion ripped at the social fabric as warfare and bloodshed tore through Europe.

"ALONE BEFORE GOD"

RELIGIOUS REFORM AND WARFARE, 1500–1648

STUDY	Dynastic warfare ▪ Protestant religious reform ▪ Catholic Reformation ▪ Religious wars ▪ Changes in society.
NOTICE	How new religious ideas significantly and sometimes violently changed European politics and society.

"They used thumbscrews, which they cleverly made out of their pistols, to torture the peasants, as if they wanted to burn witches. . . . They put one of the captured peasants in the bake-oven and lighted a fire in it." This horrifying description of war in Germany (by a soldier, Jakob von Grimmelshausen) characterizes a period in European history when many innocents suffered horrible deaths. Rulers launched their armies at each other in an attempt to win new territory and enhance their power, and these armies fighting with new weapons unleashed untold misery.

At the same time, new ideas about how to worship God began to spread throughout Europe—religious reformers introduced an intellectual revolution that would not only alter how people viewed their relationship with God, but would also redefine their ideas about society, politics, and the very nature of human beings. However, as monarchs confronted the religious diversity boiling within their countries, they increased the violence: Civil wars over religion erupted and brought this period to a bloody close.

Out of this turmoil came a reform in religion that split the Christian body into many Christian churches. In the course of this reform, many men and women who were spared the bloodshed of warfare were killed for their beliefs. This religious reform also generated more subtle changes in society—ideas of love, marriage, education, and charity were transformed as some people rethought their relationship to God. The West was irrevocably changed.

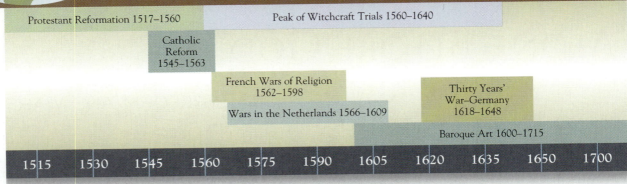

Protestant Reformation 1517–1560

Peak of Witchcraft Trials 1560–1640

Catholic Reform 1545–1563

French Wars of Religion 1562–1598

Wars in the Netherlands 1566–1609

Thirty Years' War–Germany 1618–1648

Baroque Art 1600–1715

1515 1530 1545 1560 1575 1590 1605 1620 1635 1650 1700

THE CLASH OF DYNASTIES, 1515–1555

IN 1520, TWO OF THE most powerful kings in Europe met in France to hold a tournament and discuss matters of state. Francis I (r. 1515–1547) of France had invited Henry VIII (r. 1509–1547) of England to his court to seek an alliance against his powerful enemy, the Holy Roman Emperor Charles V (r. 1519–1556). Francis hoped to impress Henry with his extravagant wealth, but the ostentatious display generated only more rivalry. Each king approached the meeting with as much state as he could muster. The kings, their followers, and even their horses wore clothing made of silver and gold thread. Silk and gold decorated the walls of the French palace and even the tents on the palace grounds that offered shade from the noonday sun. The meeting was dubbed the "Field of the Cloth of Gold." All this opulence underscored the character of the sixteenth century—there was money to spend and kings thought excess bought power. However, Francis had offended Henry by outspending him, and he did not get the alliance he sought. Instead, much to Francis's dismay, Henry met with Charles V, who approached the king in a frugal and reserved manner—and received his alliance. The struggle for land and power between Francis I and the Holy Roman Emperor would not take place on a golden tournament field; instead, these kings opened a violent century by warfare, while Henry waited to see who would be left standing. The Italian city-states—too small to compete on fields of golden cloth—became the battleground in this bitter contest.

The kings of France and England ruled strong, unified states, but at the beginning of the sixteenth century, nation-states were not necessarily the ideal political form. Indeed, kings sought to extend their reach even further and acquire multinational empires like that held by the Holy Roman Emperor, Charles V. Ignoring considerations of common culture or the difficulties of holding large empires, each king believed simply that bigger was better.

LAND-HUNGRY MONARCHS

Charles V was the grandson of Ferdinand and Isabella of Spain (see page 354). Thanks to the prudent dynastic marriages of his ancestors, he had inherited a sprawling, multinational empire. Map 11.1 shows the Habsburg lands of Charles V, which included the Netherlands, Spain, and lands in Austria, and highlights all the battles to indicate how warfare dominated Charles's reign. The map also shows the extensive empire of the Ottoman Turks that threatened Charles in the East.

As we saw in Chapter 9, events in the eastern Mediterranean had complicated western European rivalry, for the empire of the Ottoman Turks had gained strength. After the Turks conquered Constantinople in 1453, they consolidated their rule and developed a sophisticated administration and a well-trained military. Under Suleiman I the Magnificent (r. 1520–1566), the Turks began to advance again, this time toward the very heart of Europe. Map 11.2 *Turkish expansion* shows the sixteenth-century advance of the Ottoman Empire and indicates why western Europeans felt threatened by the growing power of the Muslims.

In 1521, the Turks marched up the Danube valley and seized Belgrade and Hungary, creating a panic throughout central Europe. By 1529, they were outside the walls of Vienna, the core of the Austrian Habsburg lands. At the same time, Turkish ships proved so effective in the eastern Mediterranean that all the western rulers wondered how long they could

THINKING ABOUT GEOGRAPHY

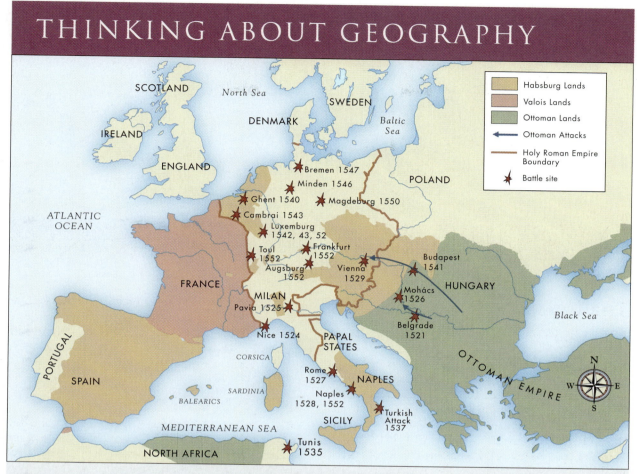

MAP 11.1   EUROPE IN 1526—HABSBURG-VALOIS WARS

This map shows the political division of Europe in 1526, highlighting the Habsburg lands inherited by Charles V and the Ottoman Empire on his borders. ■ **Notice** Charles V's extensive holdings. **Why** would the French king have felt threatened by his powerful neighbor? ■ **Locate** the Ottoman Empire and notice its proximity to Charles's territory. ■ **Notice** all the battles Charles fought. **Consider** the impact of all this warfare both on the people and on the ability of the emperor to rule.

hold onto their share of the lucrative sea trade in that area. For Charles V in particular, however, the Ottoman Empire had become a major, distracting presence in the east as he struggled to extend his empire in the west. All these monarchs had to grapple with new complexities in their seemingly endless struggles with each other, for the scale of warfare was increasing, and the old rules no longer applied.

THE CHANGING RULES OF WARFARE

As we saw in Chapter 9, the mounted knights of the Middle Ages were being replaced by infantry, and by the sixteenth century, that trend was complete. The primary reason for this change was military technology.

By 1500, Europeans had improved on the unreliable early guns of the Hundred Years' War. Now, guns with 50-inch-long barrels gave marksmen a good deal of power and accuracy, and soon the Spanish developed the musket, a 6-foot-long gun that could shoot lead bullets up to 200 yards. Armed with these weapons, soldiers could do a great deal more damage. As one observer noted: "Often and frequently . . . a virile brave hero is killed by some forsaken knave with a gun." Indeed, warfare was now dramatically changed, and kings had to pay the price in men and materials for new armies.

The new weapons dictated different military strategies. Now, captains arrayed their troops in a series of long, narrow lines. The infantrymen carried

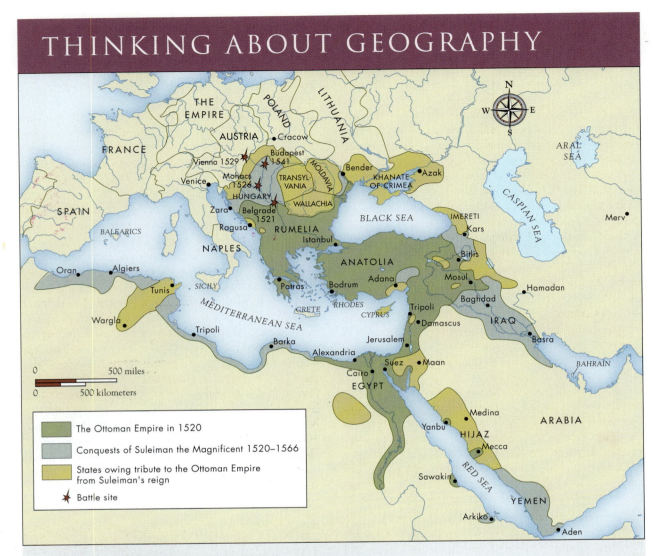

MAP 11.2   THE OTTOMAN EMPIRE, 1520–1566

This map shows the remarkable growth of the Ottoman Empire under Suleiman the Magnificent.
■ **Notice** the spread of the Muslims into the Balkan area. **Consider** the long-term effects of this expansion and the resulting blending of peoples in this region. ■ **Locate** Vienna. **Consider** its strategic location as a gateway into Europe from the east. **Consider** the impact on western Europe if Vienna should fall.

muskets, and were backed by tight formations of pike-wielding foot soldiers. In this new kind of warfare, sheer numbers often determined a king's success, so monarchs strove to bolster the size of their armies. At the beginning of the century, most armies had fewer than 50,000 men; Charles V's forces boasted a whopping 148,000 (although they were widely dispersed through Charles's extensive lands).

Growing armies

To enlarge their armies, rulers had to resort to creative new ways to fill their ranks. In part, kings relied on mercenaries, hiring soldiers of fortune who offered their services to the highest bidder, but these were never sufficient. Traditionally, kings claimed the right to draft an army from among the able-bodied men of the land. Originally, these draftees were required only to fight on their home soil, but in 1544 Henry VIII sent his conscripts overseas. No one objected, and a useful precedent was set that helped kings boost their foreign armies. Sometimes men did not wait to be drafted into the growing armies, but instead volunteered. These soldiers joined up for various reasons—some wanted to escape poverty or the hardships of village life; others sought adventure. Martin Guerre, described in the Biography, was one such villager; he volunteered for the wars probably to escape the responsibilities of family life.

Not surprisingly, armies made up of poorly paid mercenaries, conscripts, and volunteers brought new problems to the art of making war. Officers repeatedly complained of soldiers' lack of discipline, and they imposed drilling and strict penalties for disobedience. Military leaders developed other strategies as well to manage their expanding forces. The Spanish evolved a complex military administration, which included the first battlefield hospitals. The Dutch introduced standardized caliber weapons to help solve the problem of supplying larger numbers of infantrymen. Feeding and outfitting armies was still no easy matter, however. Wives, children, prostitutes, and servants trailed behind the lines to take advantage of the regular pay that the armies offered their men. These followers also needed to eat, of course, and at times they plundered the countryside through which the army moved.

Modernized warfare carried a high price. Heavy artillery was especially costly for both offensive and defensive forces. Not only did armies have to spend valuable currency to equip their armies with cannons, but rulers had to rebuild cities into massive fortresses with forts and gun emplacements to guard against opposing artillery. The new warfare also required larger navies, and ships, too, were expensive. Between 1542 and 1550, England spent more than twice its royal revenue on military campaigns. Other European powers also bankrupted themselves on these incessant wars. For example, between 1520 and 1532, Charles V borrowed an astounding 5.4 million gold coins from rich merchants to pay his troops—still, he could not compensate them completely. At his death, Francis I owed bankers one full year's income of all the crown lands.

WINNERS AND LOSERS

Kings were seldom able to deliver a decisive victory in this seemingly endless warfare, and small victories were soon avenged. Therefore, very few combatants "won" these military contests or profited at all. However, some individuals were able to gain a huge profit. Bankers who lent money to kings recklessly supplying ever larger armies struck it rich. Guns and ammunition manufacturers, especially in the Netherlands, also profited hugely.

Overall, however, losers vastly outnumbered winners in these wars. As armies ballooned, so did casualties. With the increasing use of bullets and gunpowder, the nature of combat injuries also changed. **Casualties of war** In the Middle Ages, battlefield surgeons had been skilled at treating sword injuries; in the sixteenth century, surgeons more often had to amputate limbs crushed by artillery shells (as happened to Martin Guerre; see the Biography). As one soldier wrote of the new guns: "Would to God that this unhappy weapon had never been invented." In Figure 11.1, a painting by the Dutch artist, Pieter Brueghel (ca. 1525–1569), the wounded men's artificial limbs are depicted as particularly short. In this way, Brueghel emphasized the loss and disability that came with amputation. To survive, many legless or armless veterans resorted to begging in the towns and villages of Europe.

The wars of this period also contributed to inflation and ruined harvests, both of which tormented even noncombatants. Horrified contemporary witnesses repeatedly described the legions of poor, starving civilians who wandered the landscape in search of food and died along the way. One French writer told of "some thousands of poor people, . . . subdued like skeletons, the majority leaning on crutches and dragging themselves along as best they could to ask for a piece of bread." People weakened by hunger and traveling through the countryside also fell prey to all manner of diseases. In the sixteenth century, outbreaks of plague, typhoid fever, typhus, smallpox, and influenza took a terrible toll.

■ FIGURE 11.1

Pieter Brueghel the Elder, *The Cripples*, 1568.

Martin Guerre (1524–1594)

CONSIDER

■ **Notice** what this case reveals about the tumultuous sixteenth century, when people resorted to magic to solve problems, foreign wars disrupted families, and changing religious ideas split communities.

In 1527, a peasant family moved from their village in the Basque country, on the border between France and Spain, to a village in southern France. The Guerre family prospered in their new home and by the time their young son, Martin, was fourteen, his parents had contracted a promising marriage for him with the daughter of a relatively well-to-do peasant family nearby.

Martin and his new bride, Bertrande, spent their wedding night in the Guerre household, where neighbor women gave them a heavily seasoned drink designed to stimulate their ardor and fertility. The potion failed. Martin remained impotent for eight years, while the village discussed whether he was "under a spell" and teased him mercilessly for not fulfilling his duty. Finally, an old woman told the young couple how to lift the spell through special prayers and cakes. The marriage was consummated, and Bertrande became pregnant immediately and bore a son. Martin, however, was not a happy young man. After quarreling with his father one day in 1548, the 24-year-old fled the village and was not heard from for years.

Martin traveled to Spain, where he served in the Spanish army in Flanders and France. During the fighting, he was shot in the leg; the limb then had to be amputated. Still, he sent no word to his village. In his absence, his parents died. Bertrande remained under the care of Martin's uncle Pierre as she raised their son and awaited the return of her husband.

Then, in 1556, a man strolled into the village and claimed to be Martin Guerre. He was actually an imposter, Arnaud du Tilh, who had left his own French village after a dissolute youth and joined the Spanish army fighting in Flanders. He had met Martin and learned about his life and marriage. Now, when Arnaud was ready to settle down into a new life, Martin's village seemed to offer that opportunity.

The village welcomed Arnaud as the lost Martin, and Bertrande took him in as her husband. If she had doubts about the newly passionate "Martin," she apparently set them aside. The couple harmoniously lived together for three years, during which Bertrande gave birth to two daughters.

Soon dissension arose in the village as Protestant ideas began to spread through the region. Bertrande's parents became Protestant, and Arnaud may have been drawn to Protestant ideas as well. As in so many villages throughout Europe, a split in religion caused tensions in previously unified villages, and these religious ideas may have exacerbated the suspicions that were growing in Bertrande's family. Arnaud and Martin's uncle increasingly began to quarrel over land and ideas, which caused Pierre to question Arnaud's very identity. Finally, Pierre had Arnaud arrested, and charged him with impersonating his nephew. At Arnaud's trial, hundreds of villagers testified for both sides. Some were certain that Arnaud was the real Martin; others felt equally convinced that he was not. Most of them simply could not decide. The case went to appellate court, where the legal tide seemed about to turn in Arnaud's favor. However, one day during the appeal proceedings, the real Martin Guerre, outfitted with crutches and a peg leg, suddenly limped into the courtroom to reclaim his identity and his family.

Peasant, Soldier, and Reluctant Family Man

The imposter was condemned to death, and Bertrande was judged an innocent victim of Arnaud's duplicity and returned to her husband. Over the coming years, Martin and Bertrande had two more sons. The historical records reveal nothing about Bertrande's response to Martin's return. In 1594, Martin died.

This extraordinary case was recorded by a contemporary witness, Jean de Coras, who was fascinated by the motivations of the various parties. Coras's account was widely circulated throughout France, although the author did not live long enough to enjoy the fame. The Protestant Coras was killed in the French wars of religion—a few months after the Saint Bartholomew's Day Massacre in 1572. Villagers related the tale of the impersonation of Martin Guerre for centuries.

THE HABSBURG-VALOIS WARS, 1521–1544

All these costs of making war still did not deter kings from their drive for land and power, and the city-states of Italy—where both Francis I and Charles V had dynastic claims—became the battlefield. Thus began the Habsburg-Valois Wars, named after the ruling houses of Austria and France. These wars were fought sporadically for about twenty-five years.

The wars devastated the Italian city-states, demonstrating that only large states could successfully field large enough armies for the new warfare. Charles also learned a hazard in using mercenary troops, for in 1527 the emperor was unable to pay them, and his enraged armies stormed Rome in search of booty to cover their pay.

Weary imperialists

Neither Charles nor Francis could win a decisive victory, so the two men finally negotiated a peace in

1544, and by its terms, Francis agreed to renounce his claim on Italy. Charles, too, wearied by all his problems, and in ill health, troubled by gout, decided to give up his imperial ambitions. He abdicated his various thrones between 1555 and 1556 and split his extensive holdings. He bestowed his Austrian and German lands to his brother Ferdinand I (r. 1558–1564) and the Low Countries, Spain, and Naples to his son Philip II (r. 1556–1598). Weary and disheartened, the ailing Charles V retired to a palace in Spain, where he died two years later. From this point on, these two branches of the Habsburg family went their separate ways.

During the wars, the kings had been willing to ally with unlikely partners. Sometimes Francis sought help from the Turks against Charles, and at times both Catholic kings courted critics of the church—"Lutherans"—to help against the other's Catholic forces. However, the treaty that ended the war attempted to present the Catholic kings as a united front against religious diversity that had flourished in their lands. Charles and Francis agreed to focus their energies on defeating "Muslims and Lutherans" who were threatening the Christian world. The Muslims had been a traditional enemy, but who were these Lutherans who appeared in the sixteenth century and who by 1544 seemed such a threat to the Christian kings?

A TIDE OF RELIGIOUS REFORM

The powerful medieval Christian church had called itself "Catholic," which meant "universal." In the hands of reformers, however, "Catholic" began to mean the traditional church, which even in the Middle Ages had come under criticism. Medieval critics had questioned some of the beliefs and practices of the church—its power, its wealth, and its insistence on obedience to the pope as necessary for spiritual salvation. The last point was central, because from the beginning, Christians had focused on salvation—everything from the best way to worship God to getting into heaven after death. As the sixteenth century opened, criticism began to intensify and many people wondered if their salvation was in good hands.

THE BEST PATH TO SALVATION?

The church had promised Christians that the path to salvation lay in the hierarchy of the church and its sacramental system that offered grace to the faithful through the seven **sacraments.** To further confirm this, the Fourth Lateran Council in 1215 (described in Chapter 8) had declared that there was no salvation outside the church. Churchmen also promised that the faithful would be supported by the community of Christians, including the Virgin Mary, all the saints,

and the congregations on earth. No Catholic believer, the church claimed, would have to face God alone in the afterlife.

A new popular piety and personal mysticism, along with the spread of Renaissance ideas of individualism, began to raise questions about this path to salvation. Catholicism had emphasized the need for an ordained priest—a "father confessor"—to hear one's confession and offer absolution. This new sensibility of popular piety allowed individuals seeking God to seek Him directly through prayer, breaking the chain of mediators that had marked the Catholic church. Many men and women who called themselves the Brethren of the Common Life tried to create a devout personal relationship between themselves and Christ, to supplement the complex Catholic theology. This style of popular religion was called the **devotio moderna** ("modern devotion"), and it influenced many subsequent believers.

One pious follower of the *devotio moderna*, Thomas à Kempis (1380–1471), is reputed to be the author of the best articulation of their ideas in *The Imitation of Christ* (1425). In this profoundly influential text, Thomas argued that personal piety and ethics were as important as religious dogma. In Thomas's view, individuals could work toward salvation by focusing on their own spiritual growth, and many agreed passionately with Thomas's assertion: "Blessed is the soul which hears the Lord speak within it and receives consolation from his mouth." Many longed for this kind of personal contact with God that, as Thomas pointed out, would make society as a whole more spiritual. As devoted Christians began to experiment with new forms of a Christian life, intellectuals began to contemplate some of the more complicated aspects of Christian thought.

DESIDERIUS ERASMUS: "PRINCE OF HUMANISTS"

As humanism spread to northern Europe, scholars applied the techniques of humanist education to Christian thought. The greatest Christian humanist was Desiderius Erasmus (1466–1536), who became known as the "Prince of the Humanists." Erasmus (shown in the chapter opening painting on page 336) knew firsthand that some elements of the church needed reform, because he was born in Holland as the illegitimate son of a supposedly celibate priest. He studied at a school that was the center of the Brethren of the Common Life and grew up imbued in the new devotion that called for people to approach God directly in their hearts. Erasmus became a priest and went to study in a traditional university in Paris, which he hated. He dropped out of school, complaining that the university offered "theology as stale as their eggs."

The young priest then went to England, where his intellect was awakened by the humanists in Henry VIII's

THINKING ABOUT DOCUMENTS

Germans Rage Against Papal Exploitation

These two documents, written in 1480 and 1503, reveal that some in Germany raged against what they saw as exploitation of Germans by a distant pope. These documents show that Luther's critique launched in 1517 would find fertile soil. ■ *What were the main criticisms of the church expressed in these documents?* ■ *Notice the angry rhetoric of these texts.* *How will that contribute to the coming of the Reformation?*

1. Critique of Church Wealth, CA 1480. Author anonymous.

It is as clear as day that by means of smooth and crafty words the clergy have deprived us of our rightful possessions. For they blinded the eyes of our forefathers, and persuaded them to buy the kingdom of heaven with their lands and possessions. If you priests give the poor and the chosen children of God their paternal inheritance, which before God you owe them, God will perhaps grant you such grace that you will know yourselves. But so long as you spend your money on your dear harlots and profligates, instead of upon the children of God, you may be sure that God will reward you according to your merits. For you have angered and overburdened all the people of the empire. The time is coming when your possessions will be seized and divided as if they were the possessions of an enemy. As you have oppressed the people, they will rise up against you so that you will not know where to find a place to stay.

2. Against Abuses in Indulgences, Myconius, 1512

Anno 1512. Tetzel gained by his preaching in Germany an immense sum of money which he sent to Rome. A very large sum was collected at the new mining works at St. Annaberg, where I heard him for two years. It is incredible what this ignorant and impudent monk used to say. . . . He declared that if they contributed readily and bought grace and indulgence, all the hills of St. Annaberg would become pure massive silver. Also, that, as soon as the coin clinked in the chest, the soul for whom the money was paid would go straight to heaven. . . . The indulgence was so highly prized that when the agent came to a city the bull was carried on a satin or gold cloth, and all the priests and monks, the town council, schoolmaster, scholars, men, women, girls and children went out in procession to meet it with banners, candles, and songs. All the bells were rung and organs played. He was conducted into the church, a red cross was erected in the center of the church, and the pope's banner displayed. . . .

Source: Oliver J. Thatcher and Edgar H. McNeal, *A Source Book for Mediaeval History* (New York: Charles Scribner's Sons, 1905), pp. 336–340

London. Erasmus became great friends with Thomas More and began a course of study based on a humanist curriculum. His interests remained religious, however, and he turned the humanist emphasis on original texts to biblical studies. He learned Greek so he could immerse himself in the mental world of the New Testament, and like the Italian humanists, he insisted that language study had to be the starting point for any education: "Our first care must be to learn the three languages, Latin, Greek, and Hebrew, for it is plain that the mystery of all Scripture is revealed in them." In this statement, we can see the literary work of the humanists applied to the highest Christian purpose.

Erasmus's greatest contribution to the intellectual life of the West was his critical edition of the New Testament. To approach this, Erasmus rejected the officially accepted version of the Bible—Jerome's (ca. 340–420) Latin translation, called the Vulgate—and returned to the Greek and Hebrew texts to create a new rendition. Erasmus even corrected portions of the Vulgate, and his edition became the basis for later translations of the Bible.

The humanist also criticized corruption in the church in many writings. For example, he wrote a satire, *Julius Excluded from Heaven* (1517), in which he showed the famous Renaissance warrior-pope Julius II

Religious satires

(see Chapter 10) unable to enter heaven, even though popes had always claimed to hold its keys. His most famous satire, however, was *The Praise of Folly* (1511), in which he used his sharp wit to promote a greater spirituality in religion. In this book, his character, Folly, catalogs vices, and in the process makes fun of the author himself, his friends, and the follies of everyday life. His attacks also probed deeply into many of the religious practices of the day, and as readers laughed at his attacks on people who "worshiped" the Virgin Mary over her son and popes who did not live like Jesus, their ideas on worship itself began to change.

Perhaps even more than his disappointment at church corruption, it was his humanist love of education that led him to propose a radically different approach to Christian life. Erasmus argued that Christians should read the Bible directly, rather than relying on priests to interpret it for them: "I would that even the lowliest women read the Gospels and the Pauline Epistles. And I would that they were translated into all languages." A scholar to the core, Erasmus did not advocate separation from the church, but a contemporary of his recognized the long-term impact of the humanist's thought, saying that "Erasmus laid the egg Luther hatched." Revolution in religious thinking had been planted, and the letters in Document 11.1 reveal the anger that served as fertile ground.

LUTHER'S REVOLUTION

Martin Luther (1483–1546), the intelligent son of an upwardly mobile family in Germany, was an improbable revolutionary. His father, a successful mine owner, expected him to further the family fortune by becoming a lawyer, but young Luther's life took a dramatically different turn. During a fierce thunderstorm, Luther was struck to the ground by a bolt of lightning. Frightened, Luther cried out to Saint Anne (the Virgin Mary's mother): "Help me and I will become a monk." He survived the storm and fulfilled his vow (much to his father's initial disapproval). Luther threw himself into his new calling—becoming a monk, priest, and doctor of theology—but he remained plagued with a deep sense of sin and a deep fear of damnation. He even believed he actually saw the devil during the torments of his conscience.

For all Luther's study, prayer, and attempts to live a Christian life, he still did not believe he could ever be worthy of salvation. Even the church's promise of grace in the sacraments and "good works" of the church brought him no comfort. Finally, he found peace in the Bible, especially its statement that the "just shall live by his faith" (Rom. 1:17). Luther interpreted this statement as meaning that people were saved only through God's mercy, not through their own efforts to live as good Christians. Faith alone—not ritual—would save their souls. For Luther, Christ's sacrifice had been complete and for all time, so humans did not have to do anything else for their own salvation. This central point of Luther's belief is called "justification by faith."

Inflamed by his newfound belief, Luther challenged church doctrine over the issue of indulgences. Through the Middle Ages, the Catholic Church had developed a complex understanding of how people are forgiven for their sins, including confession, penance, and absolution. As part of this process, churchmen claimed that people had to perform certain "works"—like prayers, fastings, pilgrimages, or similar activities—to receive forgiveness for their sins. If people died before completing full repentance for their transgressions, they could expect to suffer for them in purgatory before they could enter heaven, and late medieval people had come to believe it would be virtually impossible for anyone to do full penance for their sins before death.

In the Middle Ages, the pope had begun to alleviate some people's fears by offering an "indulgence," a remission of the need to do penance for sins. The pope claimed to control a "treasury of merit"—an infinite supply of good works that had been done by the saints and the Virgin Mary from which he could draw to remit sins. These remissions came in the form of "indulgences," documents that popes gave people in return for certain pious acts. Dating from the fourteenth century, a pious act might be a contribution of money to the church.

In 1517, Pope Leo X had issued a special indulgence to finance the construction of a new St. Peter's Church in Rome that would replace an old, smaller one. Johann Tetzel, a well-known Dominican friar, appeared to sell these indulgences to rich and poor alike in Germany and sent the money to Leo. Tetzel was reputed to have used the crude words: "As soon as the coin in the coffer rings, the soul from purgatory springs." Luther, horrified by this apparent trafficking in God's grace, wrote a series of statements decrying the selling of these indulgences and protesting the flow of money from Germany to Rome. Figure 11.2 shows an engraving that apparently depicts the sale of indulgences.

Attack on indulgences

Jörg Breu, *The Sale of Indulgences,* ca. 1530

■ FIGURE 11.2

The artist of this engraving intended to show churchmen (called pardoners) on the right watching the pardoner on the left issue indulgences to the faithful lining up in the center. ■ **Notice** the clothing of both the pardoners and the faithful. **What** signs of wealth do you see in their clothing—furs, fabrics, etc.? **What** other signs of wealth do you see in the pardoners? ■ **How** would viewers recognize that indulgences were being "sold" here? ■ **Do** you think the artist was criticizing the practice? **Why** or why not?

Tradition says that Luther tacked his list of arguments—the Ninety-Five Theses—to the door of the church in Wittenberg, but he may well have simply sent it to his bishop. It seems that Luther merely wanted to engage a scholarly debate on the subject, but too many people were profoundly interested in this topic. The inflammatory theses were soon translated into German and circulated even more widely than if they had been publicly posted on the church doors— they spread rapidly throughout Germany and beyond by way of the printing press. Their clearly drawn arguments and the passion that lay beneath them appealed to many intellectuals who criticized the church and to Germans who had begun to resent German money going to Italy. With Luther's strong words, "It is foolish to think that papal indulgences . . . can absolve a man," the battle lines were drawn.

Ninety-Five Theses

Luther's commitment to individual conscience over institutional obedience catalyzed major changes in his life that in turn shaped the emergence of the reformed church. It is somewhat ironic that within a generation, reformers would be enforcing institutional obedience with as much enthusiasm as the Catholics ever had. However, Luther himself pursued the logical consequences of his ideas. In Luther's new understanding, the monastic life made no religious sense; in the presence of God's grace, there was no need for heroic renunciations. Therefore, he left the monastery and married Katherina von Bora, a former nun, and wrote influential works on Christian marriage. He also composed moving hymns that transformed religious services. Furthermore, because he came to his understanding of religion through reading the Bible, he believed that it should be accessible to everyone, so he translated it into German. Indeed, this translation became his most influential legacy. Not only did it make the Bible available to an even wider group of readers, it also, through its popularity, helped shape the form of the developing German language.

PROTESTANT RELIGIOUS IDEAS

Luther articulated a core of beliefs that subsequent religious groups would share, even as they departed from "Lutheranism." Christian churches (except the Roman Catholic and Eastern Orthodox) that share these beliefs today are called **Protestant.** The word derives from the "protest" of some German princes at the Diet (assembly) of Speier in 1529. Over the objection of the Lutheran princes, that body decided to protect the Catholic Church's right to offer services in Lutheran lands while denying the same privilege to Lutherans. The name "Protestant" remained long after the issue had been resolved.

For Luther and subsequent Protestant reformers, at the heart of religious belief lay a faith in God's mercy that transcended the need for any "good works." The Protestants thus conceived of a "priesthood of all believers," in which women and men were responsible for their own salvation. There was no need for an ordained priesthood to convey grace to believers by performing the sacraments. Church leaders (whom Protestants called ministers, pastors, or preachers) could teach, preach, and guide Christian followers, but they could not help them achieve salvation. Each person stood alone before God throughout his or her life, and on judgment day prayers to saints and to the Virgin Mary were no more helpful than prayers offered by any other Christian. When people's spiritual quests combined with the Renaissance sense of individualism, it changed even the path to God.

Priesthood of all believers

With their emphasis on the individual's relationship to God, Protestants rejected many of the elements that had characterized the medieval church. No longer were the faithful to venerate saints or the Virgin Mary, so many claimed the relics of saints and martyrs that filled the churches of Europe were worthless. Protestant faithful would not become pilgrims traveling to the great cathedrals and saints' shrines in search of blessings or miracles. Indeed, the statues of the saints and other icons seemed to many Protestants to promote idolatry, and there was periodic Protestant **iconoclasm,** or destroying of the sacred images in the churches. (See Figure 11.4.)

Just as Protestants downplayed the importance of the priesthood and the intercession of saints, they restricted the significance and number of the sacraments. In the Middle Ages, Catholics had identified seven sacraments important for salvation (including marriage and the last rites at death). Most (but not all) Protestant reformers accepted only two sacraments—baptism and the Eucharist (the celebration of Christ's Last Supper before his Crucifixion). Furthermore, they rejected **transubstantiation,** which said that the bread and wine offered up at mass were turned into the actual body and blood of Christ—a transformation that only an ordained priest could perform. Although Protestants may have rejected transubstantiation, they held various views on how Christ was present in the Eucharist, but because the bread and wine were not transformed, any believer could celebrate the Last Supper. As other Protestant groups branched off from Luther's initial thinking, they would emphasize some points of this theology over others. However, all of them shared the same basic principles: salvation by faith, not works; the Bible as the sole authority; and a "priesthood" made up of all believers.

Sacraments

These ideas spread rapidly in large part because they offered a simple and elegant answer to the question that had plagued so many: "How do I know I am saved?" Printing presses produced pamphlets and flyers offering these notions to the literate of towns and manors, and popular preachers told peasants in villages about Luther's challenge. Luther's seeds of revolution disseminated widely and found fertile soil.

The Reformed Church Takes Root in Germany

Luther's attack on tradition and hierarchy could not go unnoticed. In July 1519, at the Leipzig Debate, the Catholic theologian Johann Eck forced Luther to look at the logical consequences of his stand on indulgences and actually to deny the authority of popes and councils. After this turning point, Luther was more and more ready to make a full break with Rome. Finally, in 1521, Luther was called to appear before Charles V at the Diet of Worms to defend his views. Though confronted with over a thousand years of tradition, Luther nevertheless adhered to his understanding of scripture, and he reputedly made the famous reply: "To go against conscience is neither right nor safe. Here I stand, I cannot do otherwise." During the Middle Ages, many men and women who had similarly stood by their beliefs had been executed for their stance. The political situation in Germany in the sixteenth century saved Luther from this fate—and turned his personal stance into a religious revolution.

Under pressure from Charles V to recant, Luther sought and received the protection of his prince, the powerful Frederick the Wise of Saxony. Figure 11.3 shows Frederick surrounded by Protestant reformers under his protection. Frederick, at the center of the image, has an imposing presence, with his gold chains and richly embroidered clothing. The reformers gather behind him, Martin Luther at the prince's right arm. This painting suggests the degree to which the Reformation drew strength from the support of powerful local leaders.

In addition to reasons of conscience, German princes had other motives for supporting Luther's ideas. The reformer's call to stop sending German money to Rome suited princes who felt the sharp sting of inflation. Princes could also benefit from confiscating wealthy Catholic properties (like churches and monasteries) in the name of religion. Luther's call for a break with Rome also appealed to a growing sense of German nationalism as distinct from the international Christendom represented by the Catholic Church. Some princes may have hoped that any weakening of the pope's authority would also diminish the power of the Holy Roman Emperor Charles V, whose authority derived in part from papal support. A weakened emperor meant more opportunities for the princes to bolster their own power.

Many poor, too, rallied to Luther's banner of religious reform, and this support took a particularly

■ FIGURE 11.3

Lucas Cranach the Younger, *Martin Luther and the Wittenberg Reformers*, sixteenth century.

violent form in Germany. Spurred on by fiery preachers, peasants who suffered from hunger, inflation, and skyrocketing manorial dues made Luther's attack on religious abuses part of their revolutionary program. In 1524, German peasants circulated the "Twelve Articles," in which they demanded such things as a reduction of manorial dues and services and preservation of their rights to use meadows and woods. These wants dealt directly with the peasants' concerns, but they couched their demands in references to Scripture—a direct consequence of Luther's call for people to conduct their lives in accordance with their biblical readings. The "Twelve Articles" claimed to "give a Christian reason for the disobedience or even the revolt of the entire peasantry," and further promised "[if any of] the articles here set forth should not be in agreement with the word of God . . . we will willingly

Peasants' war

recede from [it]." This widely circulated pamphlet linked Protestant theology directly with revolution, and Germany erupted.

In 1524, a violent peasant war broke out. As the peasants took up arms and stormed manor houses, they called for support from Luther's religious reformers. However, Luther was no John Ball (the religious leader who had led the peasant revolt in England in 1381). He advocated religious reform, not social revolution, for he believed the Bible called for people to obey secular rulers. Appalled by the violence in the countryside, Luther wrote a treatise called "Against the Robbing and Murdering Hordes of Peasants," in which he reprimanded peasants for defying legitimate government. He also urged those in power to "smite, slay and stab" rebellious peasants, but the nobility needed no urging from Luther to protect their privileges. The rebellion was brutally suppressed—more than 100,000 peasants were killed. The princes appreciated Luther's support of their repression and judged the movement perfectly consistent with their political needs. The Protestant Reformation thus found a warm welcome in the courts of many German princes.

By the time Charles V could turn his attention from the wars in Italy in the west and the Turkish threat in the east back to his German lands, the reformed church had taken firm root. At this point, Charles was in no position to uproot Lutheranism, which was supported by many of the great princes of the land. Furthermore, Charles's armies contained many Lutherans—as early as 1527, men among the rioting troops in Rome purportedly were calling for a silk rope to hang the pope. The emperor could not govern any longer without some accommodation.

Charles first tried to demand that his subjects come together under one religion. In 1530, he commanded all Lutherans to return to Catholicism or be arrested, but it was too late. Too many princes were willing to form a military alliance rather than obey. Then, Charles tried compromise. In the 1540s, he encouraged talks between Lutherans and Catholics about the possibility of reconciliation, but these failed as well. By the 1550s, Lutheranism had captured about half the population of the empire.

In 1555, Charles's successor, Ferdinand, met with the German princes to negotiate a compromise to settle the religious turmoil. The resulting Peace of Augsburg established the Lutheran Church as a legitimate alternative to Catholicism in Germany. By this treaty, each prince defined his principality as either Catholic or Lutheran. This compromise is known by the Latin phrase, *"cuius regio, eius religio,"* which means, "who rules determines the religion." Residents of any principality who did not agree with their prince's religious decision were free to move to a more congenial location. The Catholic emperor Ferdinand, the pope,

Peace of Augsburg

and many churchmen did not like this concession to Lutheranism, which split the unity of the Christian church. However, they had no choice but to accept the compromise forced by the strong German princes.

The Augsburg treaty opened the door for the Reformation to fragment Christian Europe into a complex mix of different Christian sects. In addition, other monarchs and princes besides those in Germany saw the advantage in separating from Rome. Scandinavian kings, for instance, followed the example of German princes in supporting Lutheranism. These conversions left many problems unsolved—what about groups other than Lutherans? What about dissenting voices within either Catholic or Protestant principalities? What was the relationship between the state and religion? While these questions smoldered, the fire of religious reform continued to spread through Europe.

BRINGING REFORM TO THE STATES IN SWITZERLAND

While Luther's call for reform was the first to gain a large audience, his was not a solitary voice. Shortly after Luther's challenge, reformers in Switzerland successfully challenged old religious ideas. Switzerland consisted of a loose confederation of states (called *cantons*) in which many residents were ready for change, and the very independence of the cantons facilitated acceptance of new religious ideas. In addition, many of the young men from the Swiss cantons served as mercenaries in the seemingly insatiable armies of Europe, and service generated a growing disdain for the established order. Just as in Germany, dissatisfaction and growing national spirit combined with a desire for religious reform.

The first leader of the Reformation in Switzerland was Ulrich Zwingli (1484–1531), who lived in the northern canton of Zurich. Zwingli had been strongly influenced by Erasmus's writings, and when he served as a chaplain with Swiss mercenaries, his longing for religious reform became joined with a desire to remove the Swiss confederation from the horrible wars.

Zwingli

In 1519 (a mere two years after Luther's challenge with his Ninety-Five Theses), Zwingli became the priest of the main church in Zurich, and from there he began his own attack on traditional church practices. He believed Christians should practice only those things found in Scripture, so his church in Zurich rejected such things as the veneration of saints, pilgrimages, purgatory, clerical celibacy, and most of the sacraments. In 1523, the city government in Zurich approved Zwingli's reforms, and Zurich became a Protestant city.

Zwingli and Luther shared many ideas, but would Protestants join together and form one church to oppose Catholicism? One German prince—Philip of Hesse—saw the advantages of consolidation and brought Luther and Zwingli together in 1529 at a meeting in Marburg to try to bring about an alliance. Although the two reformers agreed on virtually all points of doctrine, the meeting fell apart over their respective understanding of the nature of Christ's presence in the celebration of the Eucharist. Zwingli insisted the remembrance was symbolic, whereas Luther insisted that Christ's body was present as well as his spirit. As neither man could compromise with his conscience, there would be no united Protestant church or state. The new reformed churches would go their separate ways.

Just as in Germany, Protestantism came to the Swiss cantons with violence. In 1529, civil wars broke out between Protestant and Catholic cantons, and Zwingli himself died on the battlefield in 1531. The cantons reached a resolution similar to that of the later Peace of Augsburg in Germany—each canton would determine its own religion. However, the fires of reform stirred in more consciences and continued to spread, bringing both more hope and more violence.

ANABAPTISTS: THE RADICAL REFORMERS

The reforms of Luther and Zwingli appealed to many people, but were implemented by princes or urban governments. However, many people saw power and religion as incompatible. New groups took a more radical turn in their efforts to reform the church and to keep it untainted by politics, and these reformers seemed threatening even to Protestants like Lutherans and Swiss reformers. Most members of these sects were referred to by their opponents as "Anabaptists," meaning "rebaptizers," (although many of them preferred to be called simply "Baptists") because they believed baptism should be reserved for adults, who could make a conscious choice to receive the grace of the sacrament. The radical sects drew heavily from peasants and artisans, especially those suffering from poverty and the relentless warfare of the period.

Confrontation between Anabaptists and the rest of society stemmed mainly from the Anabaptists' views on the relationship between church and state. Many radical reformers advocated a complete separation of these two institutions. They even argued that the "saved" (or the "elect") should not participate in government (including serving in the armies that were vigorously recruiting in the villages). One especially pacifist form of Anabaptism emerged in the Netherlands, developed by Menno Simons (1496–1561). Simons led his followers, the Mennonites, into Germany and Poland; eventually members of this sect emigrated to the United States, where they settled as early as the seventeenth century.

Church vs. state

While most Anabaptist groups were pacifists, others became revolutionaries fighting for what they believed was a religious cause—the ushering in of a biblically promised age of peace and prosperity during which the "meek shall inherit the earth." Some saw the horrors of war and famine in the sixteenth century as the expected biblical disasters and chose to take up arms to help fight against those who had previously oppressed the poor. In Germany in 1534, a fiery preacher named Melchior established a sect (called the Melchiorites) that gained political control of their city of Munster. They burned all books but the Bible, abolished private property, and introduced polygamy as they settled down to await the expected second coming of Christ. Lutherans and Catholics alike believed this was a threat to society, so they captured the city and massacred the Melchiorites. Thereafter, the radicals were persecuted by Catholics and other Protestants alike.

Radical reformers

CALVINISM AND THE GROWING MIDDLE CLASS

As we have seen, the Swiss cantons with their prosperous middle class had voiced religious longings and aspirations under the guidance of Zwingli. In the mid-sixteenth century, another voice also appealed to many of these well-to-do people in cities throughout Europe. Many people found intellectual and spiritual satisfaction in the teachings of the brilliant French scholar John Calvin (1509–1564). While preparing for a career in law, Calvin had studied many humanist writings, and in about 1533, Calvin read some of Martin Luther's works. He experienced a profound calling to Protestant theology, as he said: "God by a sudden conversion subdued and brought my mind to a teachable frame." The new reformer soon experienced pressure from royal authorities who in the reign of Francis I began a periodic suppression of reformers. Calvin had to flee France to avoid persecution and found a safe haven in the Swiss city of Geneva, where he published the first edition of his master work, *The Institutes of the Christian Religion* (1536).

What was the nature of Calvin's vision that appealed particularly to the hardworking and often prosperous middle classes? Calvin accepted the basic elements of Protestant belief that Luther had articulated, but he added his own emphasis. Whereas Luther had focused on salvation as the goal of human struggle, Calvin urged people to recognize the majesty, power, and justice of God. Perhaps Calvin's greatest contribution to Reformation thought was to redirect theological speculation from individual salvation to a larger question of humans' place in the universe.

When he turned to the question of salvation, Calvin again emphasized the power of God, shown in **predestination,** the belief that God preordained who

■ FIGURE 11.4

Destruction of images by Calvinists in the Netherlands, 1566.

how believers could establish underground groups to adopt Calvinism even where civil authorities were hostile. These techniques worked. The Netherlands were particularly receptive to Calvinist thought. In addition, many French cities soon amassed substantial Calvinist minorities, called **Huguenots.** German cities, too, began attracting Calvinist minorities—a problem because the Peace of Augsburg recognized only Lutheranism and Catholicism as acceptable religions. The Scot John Knox (1514–1572) was dazzled by Calvin in Geneva and returned to Scotland, where he established Calvinism as the predominant form of Protestantism. Like Knox, others from the British Isles were drawn to the exciting ideas of the reformers.

Protestant reliance on individual conscience made believers uncomfortable with much of the religious art that had dominated Christian worship in the West. In addition, many Protestants believed that religious art smacked of idol worship, drained precious resources better used on the poor, or simply distracted worshipers from focusing on the word of God. These concerns caused believers in many regions to attack religious art. Most of the Reformation leaders disapproved of such violence, but nevertheless, much religious art was destroyed in Protestant countries. This iconoclasm is reminiscent of the eighth-century conflict that had destroyed so much art in the eastern Orthodox lands. (See Chapter 6.) The engraving in Figure 11.4 shows people destroying religious art in the Netherlands. Statues are tumbled, precious windows broken while soldiers are unable (or unwilling) to stop the violence.

would be saved or damned, even before a person was born. Calvin explained that if God were *only* just, everyone would be damned, for all people were sinful. However, God tempered his justice with mercy, reaching down into the flames of damnation and plucking some souls out to share salvation. Calvin called these souls that were predestined to be saved the "elect"; the rest would experience eternal damnation. Many believers who, like Luther, felt that humans could do nothing to earn their salvation, found comfort in the concept of predestination. Although predestination was at the core of Calvin's beliefs, he never stressed it as much as his followers in subsequent generations did.

Predestination

Many people seeking new paths to God were drawn to Geneva to join the exciting religious movement there. One such spiritual seeker was an ex-nun, Marie Dentière, who with her new husband was in the forefront of the reform movement in Geneva. Document 11.2, a letter from Marie to Queen Marguerite of Navarre, reveals a tension that arose as part of the Reformers' theology: If all were responsible for their own salvation, did that mean women could preach and be leaders in the movement? Calvin, like Luther before him, rejected the idea that women should be leaders, but Marie expressed the ideas of many women—before and after her—that they, too, should be educated and preach the word of God.

As Calvinism took hold, Geneva became a vibrant center for Calvinist missionary work. Between 1555 and 1562, Calvin dispersed 100 preachers to the far-flung corners of Europe. Calvin had impressive organizational abilities, and he laid out directions for organizing congregations that explained

Spread of Calvinism

HENRY VIII AND THE ENGLISH CHURCH

In England in the 1520s, men with Protestant sympathies gathered to discuss some of Luther's writings that had been smuggled in. Perhaps even more exciting to the reformers was William Tyndale's English translation of the New Testament, which began to circulate in England in 1526. Protestant sympathies were growing on the island, but they would bear fruit from the actions of an unlikely ally—the king himself.

Henry VIII (r. 1509–1547), the proud king who appeared in state at the "Field of the Cloth of Gold," was not initially a reformer. In fact, he had written an attack against Martin Luther in 1521 called the *Defense of the Seven Sacraments*, and Pope Leo X awarded him the title "Defender of the Faith" for his support. (Ironically, Protestant English monarchs still retain this title.) Although many English people

THINKING ABOUT DOCUMENTS

■ DOCUMENT 11.2

Marie Dentière Defends Reformation Women's Rights

In 1539, Marie Dentière (ca. 1495–1561) wrote a letter to Queen Marguerite of Navarre in which she defends the right of women to be active participants in the reformed churches. Selections from that letter appear below. Marie had been an abbess who left her monastery in the 1520s to come to Geneva and help bring about the Calvinist reform there. Within a few years, even the reformers in Geneva suppressed Dentière's work because it was written by a woman. ■ **What** *does Marie say was the purpose of her writing?* **Notice** *she gives several reasons.* ■ **What** *arguments does she marshal in favor of women's studying and preaching?* ■ **Notice** *the emphasis on literacy as she describes the Hebrew grammar book her daughter wrote.* ■ **Are** *her arguments consistent with the theology of the reformers?* ■ **Why** *do you think her writings were suppressed?*

My very honored lady, since the true lovers of truth desire to know and understand how they ought to live in these very dangerous times, so too we woman ought to know how to flee and to avoid all errors, heresies, and false doctrines, such as those of false Christians, Turks, infidels or others suspect in doctrine, as your writings have already very well demonstrated. . . .

I have not only wished, my lady, to write this letter for you but also to give courage to other women held in captivity, so that they will not fear exile from their countries, relatives, and friends, like I was, for the word of God. And principally I write for the poor little women, who desire to know and understand the truth; those who do not know which path, which way they ought to take, so that in the future they are not so tormented and afflicted within themselves, but rather they will rejoice, be consoled, and be moved to follow the truth, which is the Gospel of Jesus Christ. And also [I write] to give courage to my little daughter, your god-daughter, to give the printers a small Hebrew grammar that she has written in French for the use and benefit of other little girls. . . . Because as you well know, the female sex is more shameful than the other, and not without reason. For until now, the scriptures have been hidden from them and no one dared say a word [about it], and it seemed that women should neither read nor hear anything of holy letters, which is the principal reason, my lady, that moved me to write to you, hoping in God that in the future women will no longer be so scorned as in the past. Because from day to day God changes the heart of his people for the better, which, I pray, will soon be so throughout the land. . . .

Not only would some slanderers and adversaries of the truth want to accuse us of too great audacity and boldness, but also some of the faithful say that women are too bold to write to one another about holy scripture. To them one can allowably respond that all those who have written and who have been named in holy scripture are not judged to be too bold, since several [women] are named and praised in holy scripture as much for their good morals, actions, behavior, and examples as for their faith and doctrine. . . .

Although there has been some imperfection in all women, nevertheless men have not been exempt from it. Why is it so necessary to criticize women, seeing that a woman never sold or betrayed Jesus, but a man named Judas. Who are the ones, I ask you, who have invented and fabricated so many ceremonies, heresies, and false doctrines on earth, if not men? And the poor women have been seduced by them. Never was a woman found to be a false prophet, although they have been fooled by them. By this I do not wish to excuse the great malice of some women, which can surpass all measure, but there is no reason to make a general rule of it without any exception as some do daily. . . .

Therefore, if God has given grace to some good women, revealing something good and holy to them through his holy scriptures, will they dare not write, tell, or declare it to one another for the sake of the slanderers of the truth? Ah, it would be too impudent to wish to hinder them, and it would be too foolish to hide the talent that God has given us. He gives us grace to persevere until the end. Amen.

Source: Marie Dentière, "A Very Useful Letter written and composed by a Christian woman from Tournai, sent to the Queen of Navarre, sister of the King of France, Against the Turks, Jews, Infidels, False Christians, Anabaptists, and Lutherans (Geneva, 1539)," trans. and ed. Elisabeth Wengler.

---

wanted religious reform and some felt a strong antipathy toward the pope, it did not seem as if their king would lead them in a break with Rome. But Henry's desperate need for a male heir changed all this.

Remembering the devastating Wars of the Roses (Chapter 9) that had brought his Tudor dynasty to power, Henry believed he needed a male heir to secure the succession. His wife of eighteen years, Catherine of Aragon, had failed to produce one. Henry began to believe that God disapproved of this marriage, for he had married the widow of his brother

Seeking a male heir

(a practice normally forbidden) and had received special permission from the pope to do so. Henry also had fallen in love with a beautiful and bright young woman, Anne Boleyn. Anne did not want to become another of the king's mistresses, so she held off his amorous advances, insisting on a promise of marriage; first, Henry needed an annulment from the pope to end his first marriage.

Ordinarily, such royal annulments were easy to obtain because the popes had traditionally acquiesced to royal wishes. However, just as Charles V's absence from Germany in the Italian Habsburg-Valois Wars allowed Lutheranism to take hold, it also facilitated religious reform in England. Henry wanted his divorce in 1527, just as Charles V's troops were sacking Rome and virtually holding Pope Clement VII prisoner. The pope needed the goodwill of Charles to restore order and Henry's queen, Catherine, was Charles V's aunt. The pope dragged his feet in granting Henry his annulment.

In 1533, Anne Boleyn, persuaded that the king would marry her, became pregnant. Now Henry was running out of time for his annulment, for he wanted Anne's child to be born legitimate. Henry's two principal advisors—Thomas Cranmer, archbishop of Canterbury, and Thomas Cromwell—devised a way for Henry to get his annulment. Parliament passed an act making the archbishop of Canterbury the highest ecclesiastical official in England (cutting off the pope's authority). Then Thomas Cranmer ruled that Henry's marriage to Catherine was "null and void," so Henry was free to marry Anne. He did so, and three months later, much to the king's dismay, she gave birth to a girl, the future Queen Elizabeth. (Henry finally had a male heir by his third wife, after Anne was beheaded for adultery, but the king would eventually marry six women in his quest for heirs and personal happiness).

Henry's annulment

Henry had gotten his annulment, but the force of religious reform he had unleashed continued its momentum. Parliament passed a number of measures designed to control the Catholic clergy and finally passed an "Act of Supremacy" (1534) that declared the king the "supreme head of the Church of England." This break with the papacy established the Church of England as a separate church (that later was also called Protestant), but not everyone in England welcomed this major reform. The most notable dissenter was the humanist Thomas More (1478–1535) (see Chapter 10), whose conscience would not allow him to obey a secular ruler in matters of faith, and he refused to swear an oath acknowledging the king's ecclesiastical supremacy. More was beheaded for his dissent, and this man of high integrity died blessing the king who had been his great friend, saying: "I die the king's good servant, but God's first."

Church of England

Henry's position toward the reformers vacillated throughout his life. He did not support all the Protestant religious ideas—for example, he reaffirmed transubstantiation, which all the Protestants rejected. In fact, he considered himself a Catholic, although not a "Roman" Catholic. However, the powerful king readily implemented Reformation ideas that enriched his coffers and weakened the power of the Catholic Church. He shared the reformers' rejection of the monastic life and dissolved all the monasteries in England, confiscating their extensive lands and wealth. The king's treasury bulged from the confiscations, and many English religious reformers were satisfied with his new policies. However, the Church of England (also called the Anglican Church) really became Protestant under the reign of Henry's son.

Henry's third wife, Jane Seymour, finally bore him a son, Edward, in 1537. However, the boy was sickly when he took the throne upon Henry's death in 1547. Edward VI (r. 1547–1553) was a bright youth who was fond of Protestant theology, but he was young. Because of Edward's age, England was in fact ruled by a council of regents who wanted to solidify Protestantism in England.

Edward VI

The painting in Figure 11.5 shows the young king at the center of the portrait, with his dying father on the left. The composition reveals the difficulties faced by the rule of a minor during these tumultuous times. The dying king, extending his right arm, transmits his blessing to rule, but the portrait includes many others with the father and son. On the right is the full Privy Council, which was to manage England during the boy king's minority. Seated next to Edward is his uncle, Edward Seymour, who served as the first Lord Protector of England. Seymour's successor, John Dudley, the duke of Northumberland, is seated next to him. During Edward VI's brief six-year reign, both dukes would try to usurp power.

Beneath the young king in the painting, the pope and monks are crushed by the Scriptures, while outside the window, iconoclastic Protestants destroy churches and images. Indeed, during the regency of the young king, Catholicism came under attack in England.

Archbishop Thomas Cranmer issued a Protestant manual of worship, *The Book of Common Prayer*, and Parliament issued an "Act of Uniformity" in 1549, making the prayer book's use mandatory for religious service throughout the kingdom. It seemed as if the Church of England was securely established, but the English would suffer more upheavals before religious peace reigned.

The 16-year-old Edward died without an heir, and the kingdom next went to his elder sister, Mary (r. 1553–1558), daughter of Catherine of Aragon, Henry's first wife. A staunch Catholic, Mary promptly set about undoing the Protestant reforms and returning England to the protective bosom of Rome. Although many prominent Protestants had fled to the continent upon Mary's accession, the queen attempted to force remaining Protestants to renounce their beliefs. "Bloody Mary" ordered some 280 Protestants burned for "religious treason," including Archbishop Cranmer, who had originally granted Henry VIII his divorce. The English public was even more upset by her marriage to Charles V's son Philip II, the Catholic king of Spain. However, the marriage did not produce an heir who could continue her Catholic policies.

"Bloody Mary"

■ FIGURE 11.5

Anonymous, Edward VI and the pope.

Upon Mary's death, the throne went to her half-sister, Anne Boleyn's daughter, Elizabeth I (r. 1558–1603), whose rule would earn her the affectionate nickname "Good Queen Bess."

Elizabeth I

Elizabeth (shown in Figure 11.6) proved a brilliant politician who skillfully positioned herself at the center of a contentious court. As the portrait in Figure 11.6 shows, she portrayed herself as a haughty, yet gracious queen who cared deeply for her subjects. She also remained unmarried (the ermine on her left arm in the painting is the symbol of virginity) and used that condition for her own diplomatic advantage by holding out the possibility of marrying into other European royal houses. Though arrogant and vain, Elizabeth was also a shrewd and frugal ruler who well deserved her people's grateful affection.

In matters of religion, Elizabeth did not worry about the fine points of theology. The young queen was appalled at the violence and destruction caused by the religious controversies, and she felt deeply responsible for maintaining peace in her realm while allowing people to follow their consciences. However, she was insistent on loyalty above all else, and she persecuted Catholics, who she felt had divided loyalties. She wanted to unify England around a Protestant core but also allow her loyal subjects latitude in religious practice and belief. For example, the prayer book that she instituted let people of differing convictions pray together in a national church. This moderate approach was effective: For awhile, England basked in a time of peace that fostered an intellectual flowering (see Chapter 10) and an era of international expansion (see Chapter 12).

By the end of the seventeenth century, the old medieval notion of a Europe united under the protection of a uniform Christianity had evaporated. Map 11.3 shows the religious diversity that characterized Christian Europe at the end of the sixteenth century. Lutheran and Anglican churches were accepted by princes and rulers. Calvinists formed a solid minority in many

Europe divided

areas. Many rulers struggled to grapple with even this degree of diversity. Yet Protestantism, by its very nature, had the potential to yield even more divisions. Once the door had opened for individuals to define their own way to God, there was no limit to the paths that people might create. However, the Catholic Church could not ignore these theological controversies and cries for reform, and in the sixteenth century, Catholicism searched its own conscience.

■ FIGURE 11.6

William Segan (attrib.), *Portrait of Elizabeth I*, 1585.

THE CATHOLIC REFORMATION

Even before Luther circulated his devastating criticism, many leaders in the Catholic Church were working to reform abuses and bring to Catholic worship new insights about textual criticism of Christian humanism. Girolamo Savonarola (1452–1498) in Florence, for example, had urged reform of the Renaissance papacy (see Chapter 10). His was not an isolated voice, though, for even popes in the early sixteenth century called councils and promulgated decrees aimed at reform. However, the popes faced a tough challenge in implementing reforms at that time, because the Habsburg-Valois Wars occupied the attention of the Catholic kings Charles V and Francis I, who, in normal times, would have backed the papacy. These wars also carried a high financial price for the popes—during the sack of Rome in 1527, for example, imperial troops made off with mounds of gold coins from the papal treasury. To recover their losses, the popes stepped up the sort of fund-raising that had so incited Luther. Practical reform had to wait for peace.

THE STIRRING OF REFORM IN SPAIN

In the fifteenth century, Spain emerged from its medieval decentralization and became a strong, unified kingdom. In 1469, Isabella (r. 1474–1504) and Ferdinand (r. 1479–1516) married, joining the kingdoms of Castille and Aragon (see Map 8.5). They immediately set about reducing the power of the nobility and establishing a centralized power. As part of their consolidation of royal authority, the two monarchs obtained permission from the pope to establish their own Inquisition directed against converted Jews and former Muslims who were suspected of secretly practicing their old faith. This newly-established court brought great suffering to many of Spain's loyal citizens.

Ferdinand and Isabella became known as the "Catholic monarchs," emphasizing their faith and the degree to which they believed they carried the banner of an invigorated Catholicism. As part of their goal of a centralized and religiously homogenous Spain, they resumed the Reconquest of the peninsula that had dominated the history of medieval Spain. The monarchs besieged Granada, the last Muslim stronghold in the south of Spain, and conquered it in 1492.

The religious zeal that grew out of the crusade against Granada continued after the fall of the city. In the same year, all Jews were expelled from Spain. Some 150,000 were given four months to leave. As we will see in Chapter 12, the same crusading zeal would extend across the Atlantic. By 1492, Spain was well placed to take the lead in fostering Catholicism against the forces of Protestantism.

As part of their dynastic aims, Ferdinand and Isabella had arranged marriages for their children to the leading families of Europe. Their daughter Joanna became the wife of the Habsburg archduke, and her son Charles V became heir to both Spain and the Habsburg lands. With such pious grandparents, it is not surprising that Charles V was so vigorous in his support of Catholicism.

The most influential religious figure in Spain during this time was Cardinal Ximénez de Cisneros (1436–1517). He was confessor to the queen, Bishop of Toledo, Grand Inquisitor, and regent of Spain after Ferdinand's death. It was Ximénez who brought humanist ideas into Spain.

Ximénez was particularly impressed with Erasmus's emphasis on scholarly study of Scripture and the works of the church fathers, and he wanted to strengthen this kind of education in Spain. In 1498, Ximénez received permission from the Borgia pope Alexander VI to found a new university at Alcalá de Henares that would feature humanist approaches to theological and ecclesiastical studies. The high quality of the scholarship at the school drew notice with the publication of the *Complutensian Polyglot Bible* (1520), an edition of the Bible written in three columns that compared the

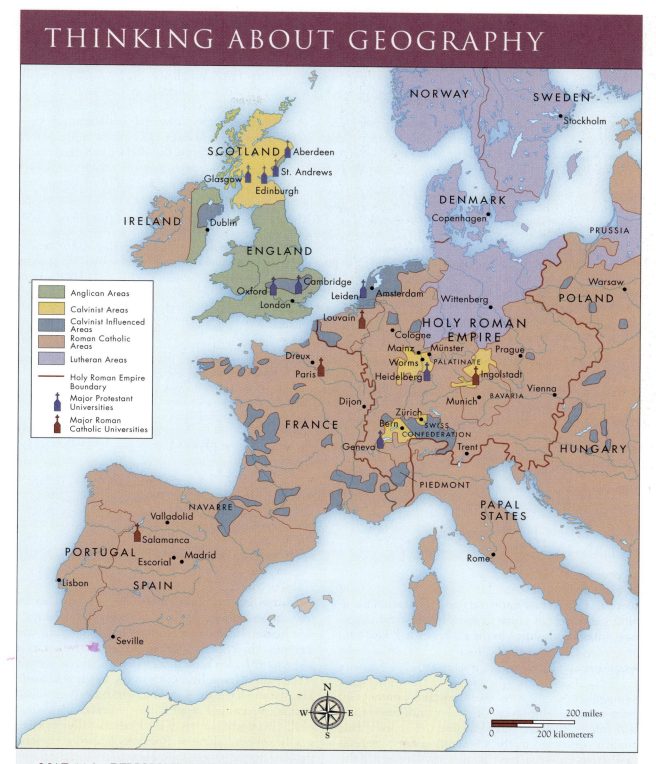

Legend:
- Anglican Areas
- Calvinist Areas
- Calvinist Influenced Areas
- Roman Catholic Areas
- Lutheran Areas
- Holy Roman Empire Boundary
- Major Protestant Universities
- Major Roman Catholic Universities

MAP 11.3   RELIGIONS IN EUROPE, CA. 1600

This map shows the distribution of the major centers of Catholics and Protestants in Europe at the end of the sixteenth century. ■ **Notice** the contrast between those countries that had established Protestant churches and those in which the Protestants (especially the Calvinists) constituted a significant minority. **Where** might the Protestant minorities be most likely to confront religious turmoil?

■ DOCUMENT 11.3

Ignatius Loyola Argues for Education as a Solution

In August 1554, Ignatius Loyola wrote a letter in which he reveals his desire to stop the growth of Protestantism. In this letter, he advocates education as the best way to stop Catholics from embracing the Protestant theology. ■ **What** *does Loyola argue are the main reasons for the spread of Protestant beliefs?* ■ **What** *solutions does he propose?* ■ **How** *effective do you think his suggestions will be?* ■ **Do** *you think there will be other social effects of such an emphasis on education?* **What** *might these effects be?*

Seeing the progress which the heretics have made in a short time, spreading the poison of their evil teaching throughout so many countries and peoples . . . it would seem that our society . . . should be solicitous to prepare the proper steps, such as are quickly applied and can be widely adopted, thus exerting itself to the utmost of its powers to preserve what is still sound and to restore what has fallen sick of the plague of heresy, especially in the northern nations.

The heretics have made their false theology popular and presented it in a way that is within the capacity of the common people. They preach it to the people and teach it in the schools, and scatter booklets which can be bought and understood by many, and make their influence felt by means of their writings when they cannot do so by their preaching. Their success is largely due to the negligence of those who should have shown some interest; and the bad example and the ignorance of Catholics, especially the clergy, have made such ravages in the vineyard of the Lord. Hence it would seem that our Society should make use of the following means to put a stop and apply a remedy to the evils which have come upon the Church through these heretics.

In the first place, the sound theology which is taught in the universities and seeks it foundation in philosophy, and therefore requires a long time to acquire is adapted only to good and alert minds. . . . It would be good to make a summary of theology to deal with topics that are important but not controversial, and with great brevity. . . . In this way theologians could be produced in a short time who could take care of the preaching and teaching in many places. . . .

The principal conclusion of this theology, in the form of a short catechism [instructional manual] could be taught to children, as the Christian doctrine is now taught, and likewise to the common people who are not too infected or too capable of subtleties. This could also be done with the younger students in the lower classes, where they could learn it by heart. . . .

Another excellent means for helping the Church in this trial would be to multiply the colleges and schools of the society in many lands, especially where a good attendance could be expected. . . .

The heretics write a large number of booklets and pamphlets, by means of which they aim at taking away all authority from the Catholics, and especially from the society, and set up their false dogmas. It would seem expedient, therefore, that our here also write answers in pamphlet form, short and well written, so that they can be produced without delay and bought by many. In this way the harm that is being done by the pamphlets of the heretics can be remedied and sound teaching spread. These works should be modest, but lively. . . .

Source: Ignatius Loyola, *Monumenta Ignatiana*, vol. 12 (Madrid, 1904), pp. 259–262, in Robert E. Van Voorst, *Readings in Christianity*. (New York: Wadsworth Publishing, 1996), 211–213.

Hebrew, Greek, and Latin versions. This scholarship represented a high point in humanistic learning and new critical techniques in the study of the Bible.

THE SOCIETY OF JESUS

Throughout its history, the Catholic Church had been reformed by monastic and mendicant orders that infused new life and ideas into the church. This pattern continued in the sixteenth century. Several new orders emerged, but the most influential was the Society of Jesus, whose members were called Jesuits. The Society of Jesus was founded by Ignatius of Loyola (1491–1556), a soldier in the service of the Span-

Jesuits established

ish monarch. In battle a cannon-ball shattered Loyola's legs, and he had a long and painful recovery—his legs had to be set and rebroken twice (without anesthesia) because they were healing crookedly. During his recuperation, Loyola read stories of Christian saints and

decided to dedicate himself as a soldier of Christ. Loyola trained himself for a spiritual life with the same rigor that marked his military practice. In his quest, he was influenced by Thomas à Kempis's *The Imitation of Christ* and wrote his own book that offered a Catholic version of the personal search for God. In the widely read work, *The Spiritual Exercises,* Loyola taught how spiritual discipline could satisfy people's desire to reach up to God while obeying the orders of the Catholic Church. Here was the perfect combination of Catholic orthodoxy with the longings expressed by Protestant reformers.

In 1540, the pope established the Society of Jesus as a religious order, and the Jesuits, who vowed perfect obedience to the papacy, became the vanguard of reformed Catholicism. These men devoted themselves to education, sharing Cardinal Ximénez's belief that a Christian humanist education would combat the threat of Protestantism. Their schools became among the best in Europe, drawing even some Protestants who were willing to risk their children's conversion to Catholicism in exchange for the fine education. Document 11.3 contains a letter from Loyola that explains his recognition of the importance of education.

Jesuits also served as missionaries to bring Catholicism to the New World (see Chapter 12). However, in time the new shock troops of the papacy became controversial in their own right—the vigor with which they pursued their aims and the vehemence of their support of the papacy alienated some Catholics and Protestants alike. But there is no question that in the sixteenth century and beyond, the Jesuits would be a powerful force in the reformed Catholicism.

Figure 11.7, a painting by the Flemish artist Peter Paul Rubens (1577–1640), captures the spirit of reformed Catholicism. *The Miracles of St. Ignatius* was commissioned in 1620 to be placed in the Jesuits' first church in Antwerp in 1622 on the occasion of the canonization of Ignatius of Loyola. The painting shows the saint performing miracles: easing the pain of childbirth (on the right), reviving a suicide victim long enough for the dying man to take the last rites (in the foreground), and casting out demons (on the left). The image praises traditional Catholic doctrine, showing the efficacy of saints by representing them as intermediaries between people and God. In the same way Loyola is positioned in the vertical center of the painting. Rubens also affirms the importance of the sacrament of "last rites" (attacked by the Protestants) by depicting it as the occasion of a miracle. Finally, this work points out that, in less than a century, Loyola's accomplishments had earned him the status of sainthood and his Society of Jesus had become the army of the new Catholicism.

Rubens's painting is an example of a new style of painting (and the arts in general) called **baroque,** which also served to forward the ideas and spirit of reformed Catholicism. Baroque art was characterized by passion, drama, and awe, and was designed to involve the audience. Catholic patrons, in particular, spurred this art that spoke as eloquently of Catholic doctrine and passion as a Jesuit sermon. However, before either the new art style or the energetic order of Jesuits could be effective, the church had to agree on its doctrine in response to the Protestant critique.

Baroque art

■ FIGURE 11.7

Peter Paul Rubens, *The Miracles of St. Ignatius*, 1620.

THE COUNCIL OF TRENT, 1545–1563

With the conclusion of the Habsburg-Valois Wars, the Catholic monarchs could focus on the divisive religious questions of the day. After the treaty of 1544 that ended the wars, church leaders from all over Europe gathered in northern Italy at Trent, and the council met intermittently from 1545 to 1563. Charles wanted the council to concentrate on reforming abuses, and they confronted this thorny issue honestly, establishing stern measures to clean up clerical corruption, ignorance, and apathy. They even banned the selling of indulgences and the office of indulgence-seller (like the pardoners shown in Figure 11.2). But the real work of the council took place when they confronted the theological debate that had driven the Protestants from the church. As these leaders clarified their beliefs, it became obvious that there would be no compromise with Protestant Christianity.

The Council of Trent determined that Catholics did *not* stand alone before God. Rather, they claimed, the community of the faithful, both living and dead, could help a Catholic to salvation. Thus prayers to the saints and to the Virgin Mary *did* matter. The

Reforming corruption

Affirming doctrine

PROTESTANT AND CATHOLIC REFORMERS

ca. 1320–1384	John Wycliffe
1415	Jan Hus executed
1511	Erasmus, *Praise of Folly*
1517	Martin Luther, *Ninety-Five Theses*
1519	Zwingli's reform in Switzerland
*1520	Ximénez, *Complutensian Polyglot Bible*, Spain
1521	Luther at Diet of Worms
1534	Henry VIII's Act of Supremacy in England
1536	Calvin, *Institutes of Christian Religion*
*1540	Loyola found "Society of Jesus"
*1545–1563	Council of Trent
*1515–1582	Teresa of Avila

for the count's soul. The painting depicts heaven as filled with saints and the souls of other saved individuals, who also pray for the count and help him enter their community. By all these means, the picture visually reaffirms the theology established at the Council of Trent.

While debating and refining their beliefs, the churchmen attending the council looked to two authorities—Scripture and tradition. Armed with these pillars of Christian thought, they **Scripture and tradition** prepared to answer Luther and the other Protestants, who recognized only their own consciences and the complete authority of the Holy Book. Catholics, the Trent council argued, could draw strength from the body of practices that the faithful had accumulated over the course of a millennium. With its doctrine thus established, the Catholic Church showed a new strength and confidence. Dissenters had gone to other sects, leaving a vigorous corps of dedicated believers to challenge the Protestants head-on.

CATHOLICS ON THE OFFENSE

Throughout this period, as we have seen with baroque art, many Catholics expressed their faith with more passion and mystical emotion than they had shown in centuries. Teresa of Avila, Spain (1515–1582), a sixteenth-century mystic who quickly became a saint, exemplified this newfound energy. The daughter of a converted Jew, Teresa entered a convent and experienced a series of visions. Not only a mystic, Teresa was an active reformer, establishing new convents for women as part of her dedication to a reinvigorated Catholicism. Her mystical writing, *Way of Perfection*, ensured her influence, for it inspired the pope to declare her a "Doctor of the Church" (which means that her writings were worthy of study). Soon she became the patron saint of Spain, replacing Saint James (Santiago), who had held that honor throughout the Middle Ages. The example of Teresa and other mystics offered the church a strong weapon to show skeptics the deep and passionate faith that came with Catholic worship. However, they also used stronger measures than the writings of gentle mystics.

Reinvigorated, and considering themselves at war with Protestants, the Catholics moved to repress opposition to their views. The Spanish Inquisition took a forceful role **Spanish Inquisition** in this battle over religious diversity. (This court was separate from the Papal inquisition that, as we saw in Chapter 8, had been introduced into Europe in the thirteenth century.) Inquisitors now added Lutherans and Calvinists to converted Jews and Muslims in their definition of suspect populations and launched a new round of public trials and executions. In 1542, the Inquisition was reestablished

church also affirmed the existence of purgatory and the power of prayer and even indulgences to free souls from their punishment.

These churchmen further departed from the Protestants by declaring that Christians needed both faith and good works to go to heaven. For Catholics, the sacraments by their very nature conveyed grace, so the council reaffirmed the existence of all seven rites. In further rejection of Protestant criticism, Catholics supported the idea of transubstantiation, by which priests presided over the transformation of the wine and host into the blood and body of Christ.

Like Rubens, the Spanish painter El Greco ("the Greek") (1547–1614) was a baroque painter who reaffirmed Catholic theology. El Greco's painting *Burial of the Count of Orgaz* (Figure 11.8) **El Greco** is less about the burial of one man than about the theological stance of the Council of Trent. The dead count does not face his maker alone. Instead, he is buried with the full ceremony of the church presided over by the bishop. El Greco also shows saints Augustine and Stephen miraculously appearing and helping with the burial. The count's way to heaven is paved by the prayers of the living who surround the scene and the Virgin Mary, who sits between the dead man and Jesus as an intermediary in Rome, as the popes also felt compelled to take extreme measures to protect Catholics themselves from incorrect ideas. In addition, the papacy began to publish an "Index of Prohibited Books" in 1557, which it updated and reissued regularly. (The index was finally abolished in 1966.)

While such measures aimed to control people's beliefs, the church looked to the Spanish king to champion the Catholic cause in the political and military arena. **Philip II** (r. 1556–1588), Charles V's heir to the kingdoms of Spain and the Netherlands, had an unparalleled zeal for both the Catholic religion and empire. Philip moved his capital from Toledo, the cramped medieval city, to the newly built city of Madrid, chosen because it was the geographic center of the Iberian Peninsula.

Philip faced two dire threats to the Catholic faith: the Turks in the eastern Mediterranean and the Protestants in the north. In 1571, he assembled a league that included a number of Italian city-states and set out to challenge the Turks' supremacy in the Mediterranean. The Venetians, with their large fleet and who were highly motivated by their trading interests in the eastern Mediterranean, were particularly eager to join Philip's navy. Outfitted with 208 galleys—sleek warships rowed by slaves and armed with cannons—Philip's navy confronted the Turks' 230 warships at the Battle of Lepanto, off the coast of Greece. Figure 11.9 depicts what the scene may have looked like. In this graphic image, cannons

Philip II

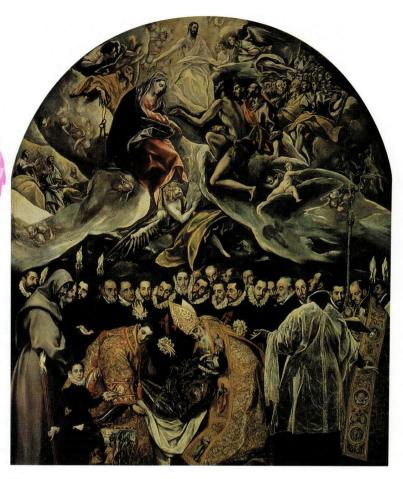

■ FIGURE 11.8

El Greco, *Burial of the Count of Orgaz*, ca. 1586.

■ FIGURE 11.9

The Battle of Lepanto.

blaze and battering rams thrust forward as the galleys draw together.

When the smoke cleared after this spectacular battle, Philip's coalition had scored a decisive victory. The Turks lost two hundred warships, the Europeans only ten. Tens of thousands of men on both sides died in the fighting, and contemporary witnesses described the sea as running red with blood. Nevertheless, the success at Lepanto raised Catholics' spirits throughout the West. The navy had proved that Turkish power in the Mediterranean was not invincible after all. Indeed, some Western Catholics began toying with the idea of invading the Ottoman Empire itself. But the Catholic monarchs had other adversaries in mind. Again, the kings of Europe went to war. This time, though, they marched against the Protestants in a series of battles that would drag on for a century and tear apart the soul of Europe.

Europe Erupts Again: A Century of Religious Warfare, 1559–1648

The Reformation had done far more than just establish alternative Christian sects—it raised the possibility that individuals might follow their own consciences in matters of religion. In a society in which the church served as the central institution in people's lives, this radical new idea struck at the very foundation of European politics and social realities. From the time the Roman emperor Constantine supported the Catholic Church (see Chapter 5), people always assumed that there was an identity of belief between rulers and subjects. Political loyalty was considered a religious phenomenon; the Protestant Reformation questioned this assumed fact.

In fact, the wars of religion that scourged Europe from 1559 to 1648 involved much more than the proper way to worship God. They also centered on the question of what constituted a state—specifically, whether one state could encompass various religious expressions. Like the peasant wars in Germany in 1524, these new hostilities involved religion, but they had significant economic, political, and social dimensions as well.

French Wars of Religion, 1562–1598

By the 1550s, Calvinism had gained a good deal of strength in France among the peasants and in the towns of the south and southwest (including villages like that of Martin Guerre in the Biogra-

phy). Although the French Calvinists (Huguenots) remained a minority—only about 7 percent of the population—they were well organized. Local congregations governed by ministers sent representatives to district assemblies that in turn coordinated their efforts with a national assembly and even mustered troops from local churches. This impressive minority even began to recruit members from the nobility— possibly 40 percent of French nobles had become Huguenots. Great noble families took the lead in forwarding their religious (and in turn political) interests—the Guises led the Catholics, and the Bourbons championed the Huguenots. By the mid-sixteenth century, French Protestantism was a force to be reckoned with and the French kings took notice.

Francis I (r. 1515–1547) and his heir, Henry II (r. 1547–1559), were both powerful kings who based their authority in part on a strong Catholic stance. However, this royal power was broken by a freak accident. King Henry was celebrating the wedding of his daughter by fighting in a joust (the war game still much beloved by the nobility), but during the last joust of the day, his opponent's lance shattered, gouging Henry's eye. Henry died of complications of this wound, leaving his widow, the Italian Catherine de' Medici, to rule as regent for her young sons from 1559 to 1589.

Catherine tried to preserve royal control, but her efforts were impeded by the struggle for power between the Guises and the Bourbons, both of whom had family ties to the monarchy and hoped to inherit the throne. Politics here intertwined with religion and the time was ripe for civil war. Fighting broke out in 1562, when the Duke of Guise massacred a Huguenot congregation, and it continued for about thirty-six years (with brief respites). The Huguenot forces, though outnumbered, were too well organized to be defeated. The most infamous point of these wars was the Saint Bartholomew's Day Massacre, which took place on August 23, 1572, just when peace seemed imminent.

A religious compromise seemed to be on the horizon with a marriage between Catherine's daughter and the Bourbon leader of the Huguenots, Henry of Navarre. However, the mutual suspicions and desire for revenge had not subsided—the Guise family persuaded the young king Charles IX (r. 1560–1574) that the Huguenot gathering for the wedding was a plot against the crown. The king then ordered his guard to kill all the Protestant leadership. On the morning of St. Bartholomew's Day, the soldiers unleashed a massacre against Protestants.

> **Catholics vs. Huguenots**

> **Saint Bartholomew's Day Massacre**

■ FIGURE 11.10

Françoise Dubois, *St. Bartholomew's Day Massacre*.

Although the young bridegroom escaped assassination, many others did not. Thousands were murdered, and the painting shown in Figure 11.10 depicts a contemporary witness's memory of the slaughter. The massacre raged for six days, and as the image shows, it was particularly brutal. Women and infants were not spared, and the painting shows that even corpses were mutilated as religious fervor introduced a bloodbath. This violence did not end the wars, however. Civil war continued in France until King Henry III (r. 1574–1589) was assassinated, leaving no heir.

The next in line for the throne was Henry of Navarre—the Protestant bridegroom who survived the massacre. Recognizing that the overwhelmingly Catholic population would not accept a reformist king, he converted to Catholicism, reputedly saying, "Paris is worth a mass." Sympathetic to both religions, the new king Henry IV (r. 1589–1610) issued the Edict of Nantes (1598), which ended the religious wars and introduced religious toleration in France. However, a subsequent king (Louis XIV, discussed in Chapter 13) who believed that a nation was defined by loyalty to one religion would overturn Henry's policy. But for the time being at least, France gained a small respite from the violence of intolerance. The rest of Europe was not so lucky.

Peace in France

A "COUNCIL OF BLOOD" IN THE NETHERLANDS, 1566–1609

In addition to Spain, the Catholic king Philip II ruled over the Netherlands, which consisted of seventeen provinces. (Today these provinces are Netherlands, Belgium, and Luxembourg.) Trouble began when Philip began to exert more control over the provinces—he restructured the Catholic Church to weaken the local aristocracy, he insisted on billeting troops locally, and he levied new taxes, all of which offended the Dutch.

In response, riots broke out in 1566 and Dutch Protestants, though still a tiny minority, rebelled against their Spanish, Catholic overlords. In a spasm of violence, they destroyed Catholic Church property, smashing images of saints and desecrating the host. Philip was enraged. Vowing to silence the rebels, he sent the largest land army ever assembled into the Netherlands to crush the Protestants and bring the province back under his Catholic rule. In 1572, organized revolt broke out and war officially began.

Revolt breaks out

Philip's crackdown ignited a savage forty-year contest in which the Spanish general, the "iron duke of Alba" presided over a slaughter of thousands of Protestants in what he called a "Council of Troubles," but what the Protestants called the "Council of Blood." Calvinist preachers retaliated by giving their congregations complete license to kill the invaders. To protect themselves, the towns of the Netherlands even opened their dikes to flood their country rather than give in to Philip's armies. The Dutch found an able leader in William of Orange, a nobleman known for his wise counsel, who took charge in 1580. William was assassinated four years later, and the murderer was publicly tortured to death as blood continued to flow in the Netherlands.

The defiance of the Dutch cost Philip more than the loss of soldiers and huge amounts of gold to finance the wars. It also diverted his attention northward, away from his victory over the Turks at Lepanto in 1571. Preoccupied by events in the Netherlands, he failed to ride the wave of widespread Christian antipathy toward the Turks and launch a decisive campaign against the enemy in the eastern Mediterranean.

Philip also tried to "save" England from the Protestantism that Henry VIII had introduced. Philip had married Henry's Catholic daughter Mary (r. 1553–1558), and when she died without an heir, the Spanish king proposed matrimony to her sister, Elizabeth **Armada against England** I. But the Protestant Elizabeth refused his attentions and even dared support the Netherlands against him. Philip struck back by hurling the full force of his navy against England, sending a huge fleet across the English Channel in 1588. What happened next stood in stark contrast to Philip's triumph at Lepanto. Instead of scoring an easy victory, the Spanish Armada was wiped out by the well-armed English ships and the sudden onslaught of violent storms in the North Sea (what the English would later call a "Protestant wind").

Philip never succeeded in subduing the Protestants in the Netherlands; the conflict dragged on until the deaths of both Philip and Elizabeth. In 1609, the two sides finally drew up an agreement that gave the northern provinces virtual independence. The final recognition of an independent **Netherlands split** Netherlands would have to wait until the Peace of Westphalia in 1648. After the final settlement, Protestants in the southern provinces moved north to escape continuing Spanish rule in the south, so the two provinces became divided along religious lines. The northern provinces became the Protestant Dutch Republic, and the southern (and French-speaking) Spanish Netherlands (which later became Belgium) remained Catholic. But this solution still could not quell the religious tensions tearing at Europe. Instead, the wars shifted east, where they culminated in the bloodiest engagement of them all.

THE THIRTY YEARS' WAR, 1618–1648

The Peace of Augsburg had only temporarily answered the question of religious diversity in the Holy Roman Empire. For fifty years after Augsburg, pressure mounted as more and more people followed their consciences and as diverse spiritual beliefs proliferated in the principalities. These tensions reached the boiling point in 1618, when a Catholic prince took over Bohemia (in the modern Czech Republic) and set out to vanquish the substantial Protestant minority in his state. Protestant Bohemian nobles responded by throwing the prince's representatives out the castle window in Prague. The hapless officials landed unhurt in a pile of manure, but the Catholic explanation was that their fall had been broken by angels. The two sides seemed to have irreconcilable points of view.

But the Holy Roman Empire's political structure contained a unique feature that made religious tensions much harder to resolve than by merely pushing bureaucrats out of **War breaks out** windows. The essential problem was that Protestant and Catholic electors (princes who elected the Holy Roman Emperor) were roughly equal in number. If Bohemia went to a Protestant prince, the balance of power would shift away from the ruling Catholic Habsburgs. Fearing this possibility, the Holy Roman Emperor Ferdinand II (r. 1619–1637) went to war to reclaim Bohemia for Catholicism. His action provoked a civil war that began over the key issue of the authority of the emperor over the princes in Germany, but that quickly turned international as Protestants and Catholics across the Holy Roman Empire faced each other in battle.

The first twelve years of the war were marked by the success of Emperor Ferdinand's forces, and it seemed as if the Catholic Habsburgs would be able to roll back the Protestant gains in the German lands. The powerful Catholic Maximilian of Bavaria put an army at Ferdinand's disposal that won a stunning victory over the Bohemians at the Battle of White Mountain in 1620 (shown on Map 11.4). The Bohemian rebels were killed or exiled, and it seemed as if the war was over. However, the Protestants continued their struggle, but with few gains.

In 1624, the emperor received considerable help when a soldier of fortune came to offer his services to the Catholic cause. Albrecht von Wallenstein, a minor Bohemian nobleman, recognized that the emperor needed **Wallenstein** a new army if he was to succeed, and Wallenstein offered to raise the force if he could billet it and raise its supplies wherever it happened to be stationed. Ferdinand agreed, and by 1627 Wallenstein's army had begun to conquer the northern region of the empire— the center of Protestant strength. Ferdinand grew so

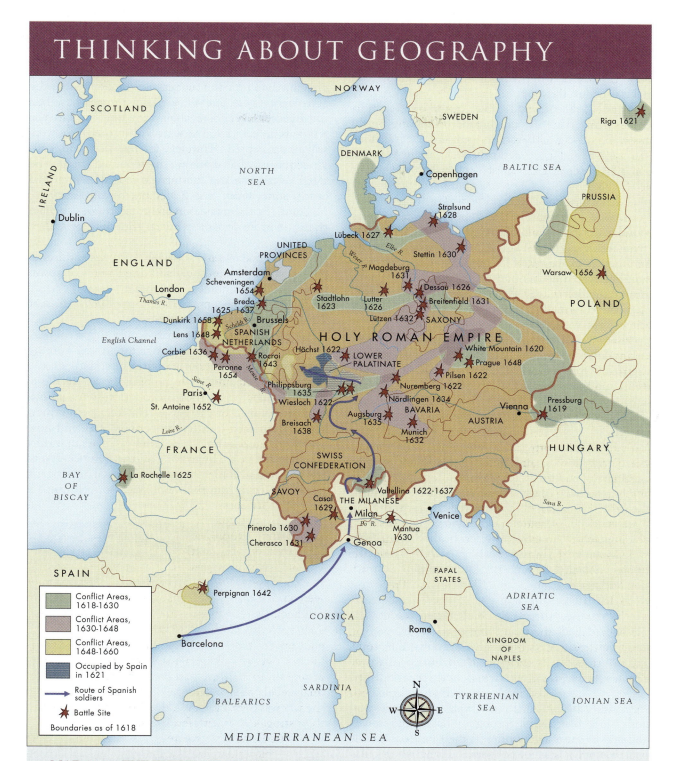

MAP 11.4   THE THIRTY YEARS' WAR, 1618–1648

This map shows the major participants and the main battles of the long war that took place on German territory. ■ **Notice** the location of Swedish lands. **Consider** why the king of Sweden became involved in this war. ■ **Compare** this map with Map 11.3. **Consider** which regions were Protestant and which were Catholic. **Which** regions departed from their religious interests to fight primarily for political reasons?

confident that he issued the Edict of Restitution in 1629, ordering all territories lost to Protestants since 1552 to be restored to Catholics. Wallenstein—brilliant general and opportunist—became one of the richest men in the empire.

By 1630, the tide and nature of the war began to change. With help from abroad, Protestants made gains, but the war began to shift from a religious struggle to a purely political quest—to weaken the power of the Habsburgs; for example, the Catholic French king was willing to join Protestants in support of this cause. Protestant forces found a worthy champion in the Swedish king Gustavus Adolphus (r. 1611–1632), who was appalled by Ferdinand's treatment of Protestants, and at the same time, he feared a Habsburg threat to Swedish lands around the Baltic Sea (see Map 11.4). A decisive battle was fought at Lutzen in 1632, where Gustavus's armies beat Wallenstein's forces. Unfortunately, Gustavus was killed in that battle, so the Swedish forces did not follow up on the victory. (The German princes eventually forced Ferdinand to turn against Wallenstein, and the emperor had his general assassinated a few months later.)

From religion to politics

Gustavus's successes opened the final phase of the war (from 1632–1648), during which the emperor lost all his previous gains. The Protestant princes raised new armies, and by 1635, Ferdinand had to agree to suspend the Edict of Restitution and to grant amnesty to most of the Protestant princes. In return, the Protestants joined the imperial troops in driving the Swedes out of German lands. However, the Catholic French declared open war on Ferdinand in 1635, and for the next thirteen years, French and Swedish troops rampaged through the lands, causing destruction and devastation.

By the 1640s, the war had reached a stalemate. The kings and princes who had started the hostilities had all died, and their successors (as well as civilians) were exhausted. Both sides laid down their arms and took stock of their losses. This war had raged with a violence that astonished even contemporary witnesses used to sixteenth-century battle methods, for armies on both sides had swept through villages and towns and laid to waste everything in their paths. The war had exacted a staggering price: Germany's population had plummeted (although historians do not agree on the figures, some suggest a population loss as high as 30 percent). The economy, too, was damaged. Spain had gone bankrupt and would never recover its standing as a leader on the European stage. France and Sweden emerged somewhat victoriously, gaining some land at the expense of the exhausted German states.

Devastation

PEACE AT WESTPHALIA

The series of agreements that ended the Thirty Years' War are collectively known as the Peace of Westphalia, named for the region of Germany where the agreements were drafted. German princes now had the freedom to choose their own religion, but the religious desires of individuals within the states were still not accepted. However, for the first time, Calvinism was included among the tolerated faiths. The religious landmark of Europe was roughly established along north-south lines. The northwest—England, Holland, Scandinavia, and the northern German states—was Protestant, whereas the south remained Catholic.

The war had marked political overtones at the end, and the treaty accordingly addressed issues of power beyond religious choice. The peace set the political geography of Europe for the next century and established a precedent for diplomacy that would shape the way nations resolved political problems in the coming centuries. Map 11.5 outlines the aftermath of the Peace of Westphalia. The representatives at Westphalia conducted all these negotiations with an eye toward "balance of power," a relatively new principle that emerged in fifteenth-century Italy and now applied to European politics. They believed that they could ensure peace by making all the European powers roughly as strong as their neighbors. This strategy would dominate European diplomacy for centuries.

Political results

KEY DATES

POLITICS OF THE AGE OF REFORMATION

1521–1544	Habsburg-Valois Wars
1524–1525	German peasants revolt
1529	Turks besiege Vienna
1555	Religious Peace of Augsburg, Germany
1562–1598	French wars of religion
1566–1609	Wars in the Netherlands
1571	Battle of Lepanto
1572	St. Bartholomew's Day Massacre, France
1588	Spanish Armada attacks England
1618–1648	Thirty Years' War
1648	Peace of Westphalia

THINKING ABOUT GEOGRAPHY

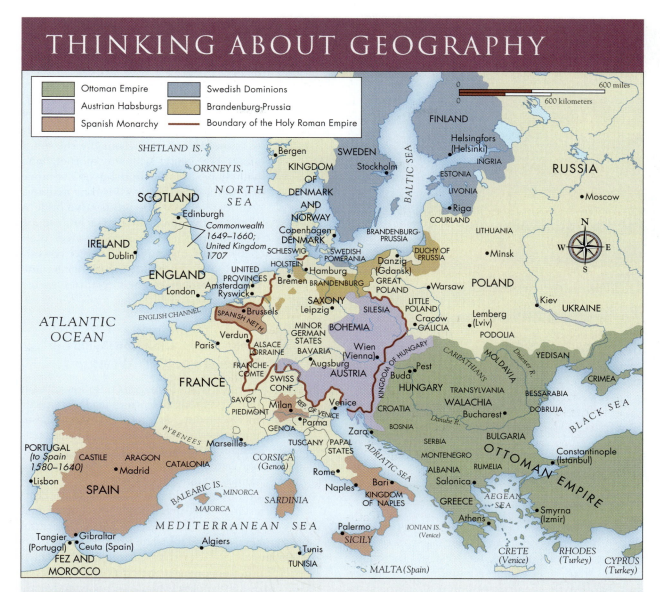

Legend:
- Ottoman Empire
- Austrian Habsburgs
- Spanish Monarchy
- Swedish Dominions
- Brandenburg-Prussia
- Boundary of the Holy Roman Empire

MAP 11.5   EUROPE IN 1648

This map shows the political configuration of Europe after the Peace of Westphalia that ended the Thirty Years' War. ■ **Notice** which countries appear large and cohesive after the settlement of Westphalia, and see the description in the text of the countries that gained the most. ■ **Notice also** the countries that control territories distant from their main nations. **Which** of these more remote areas might become centers of conflict in the future?

LIFE AFTER THE REFORMATION

The early modern wars of religion were finally over. Christians with different beliefs would now have to learn to coexist. As the storms of religious rage subsided, Europeans began noticing the dramatic changes in other aspects of everyday life and thought that the Protestant Reformation had provoked.

NEW DEFINITIONS OF COURTSHIP AND MARRIAGE

When the Protestants excluded marriage as a sacrament, the institution changed in ways they could not have foreseen. After Martin Luther left the monastery and married Katherina, the couple formed a loving partnership and raised five children (along with

■ FIGURE 11.11

Gerard Ter Borch, *The Suitor's Visit*, 1658.

marriage, and daughters had some say in vetoing disagreeable matches. Courtship customs grew more complex, as men and women evaluated whether they would have a "harmonious" union. In Figure 11.11, a painting titled *The Suitor's Visit*, a young man calls on a woman in one of many visits intended for the couple to get to know each other. Presumably, the suitor greets the young woman's mother, who will chaperone the courtship and approve the joining of the families that marriage still represented. The prospective bride is in the background playing her lute; young women in these years cultivated their skills at making music and clever conversation so as to beguile potential mates and convince them of their qualities as life partners.

FORGING A LINK BETWEEN EDUCATION AND WORK

The Christian humanists from Erasmus on urged everyone to learn to read. As we saw in Document 11.3, reformed Catholicism under the Jesuits also stressed education as central to a Christian life, and parochial schools and armies of nuns gave young children the rudiments of education. Protestants, too, urged study. As Luther and others emphasized Bible study as part of essential Christian behavior and translated the Book into vernacular languages, the next logical step was to broaden literacy. Luther encouraged the cities and villages in Saxony to establish publicly funded schools, and many Protestants followed his call. A Bohemian reformer, Jan Amos Comenius (1592–1670) wrote: "All alike, boys and girls, both noble and ignoble, rich and poor, in all cities and towns, villages and hamlets, should be sent to school." This egalitarian notion would take centuries to implement, but it established a new educational goal in the West.

Valuing literacy

The painter Jan Steen's depiction of an early-seventeenth-century classroom (shown in Figure 11.12) embodies the Protestant ideals of education. This is a village school where both boys and girls study. The strict schoolmaster slaps a boy's hand in reprimand for the poorly done assignment on the floor, while the boy cries. The girl on the boy's right smiles rather too gleefully at his distress. This scene must have played out repeatedly in the many small village schools that began to spring up as more children began to receive formal education.

Although education was intended primarily to help people study the Bible and learn to serve as their own

caring for orphans). Luther explored this relationship in his writings and saw in marriage part of God's plan for humanity. Calvin, too, rejected the church fathers' "too superstitious admiration of celibacy" and extolled the benefits of conjugal partnerships. Although divorce was not easy in any of the Protestant groups, it was possible. With all these changes, the ideal of marriage shifted. Couples began to expect "mutual love between man and wife," instead of simply duty that bound extended families together. The Catholic Church also was influenced by the new marital values, and in the late sixteenth century, church manuals began to use the word "love" to refer to conjugal relations.

People still did not marry just for love, however; instead, families continued to arrange suitable matches between young people. Arranged marriages were an essential and logical part of a view that valued family prosperity and continuity more than an individual's happiness. Individuals were seen as mere moments in the larger life of the family. Nevertheless, something new was going on in family relations. Although parents still negotiated a suitable match, prospective couples were allowed to consider their compatibility before

Courtship

spiritual guides, it also had profound implications for the way people viewed work. In response to critics who complained about educating "rustics," the Bohemian educational reformer Comenius answered that universal education would help everyone avoid "that idleness which is so dangerous to flesh and blood." His words hinted at a new philosophy that stressed the value of work.

Valuing work

In the Middle Ages, "those who work" were relegated to the bottom of the social scale. The upper crust consisted of only those who could live off the income of their land and did not need to work to survive. The bourgeoisie—the middle class—that was becoming more and more prosperous since the Renaissance began to change that view and brought a new valuing of work into the consciousness of Western society. The Protestant reformers that appealed to many of the residents of these growing urban areas lent religious support to new ideas about work. In Luther's writings, even women were defined by the work they did. He described the ideal wife as follows: "She likes working. . . . She girds her loins and stretches her arms, works with energy in the house."

Calvin, too, believed that men and women were "called" to work and that work itself was a virtuous activity. Centuries later, the German sociologist Max Weber, in *The Protestant Ethic and the Spirit of Capitalism* (1904), would argue that Calvinists' emphasis on work legitimized and therefore boosted the growth of capitalism in the West. Many Calvinists believed that hard work, efficiency, and frugality all indicated a person predestined to salvation. Not surprisingly, then, Protestants embraced what has come to be called the "work ethic" with fervor. Historians dispute the details of Weber's thesis, but his argument still offers us an insight into the way religious ideas shaped modern-day views of work in the West. In the Catholic Middle Ages, people had seen work as the curse of Adam laid on the damned; in the Protestant early modern period, work became God's gift to a saved humanity.

ANXIETY AND SPIRITUAL INSECURITY

The striking revolution in thought that the Protestant reformers introduced also prompted some spiritual anxiety and insecurity among Christians. In part, this unease stemmed from the hardship spawned by the relentless warfare of the period. The "community of the faithful" that Catholicism once represented had fragmented, and for Protestants encouraged to "stand alone before God," the new religious individualism often felt frightening.

The new mind-set began to raise questions about charitable institutions and their relationship with religious bodies. Where once the universal church looked after the poor and widows and orphans, now separate congregations had to care for

Charitable institutions

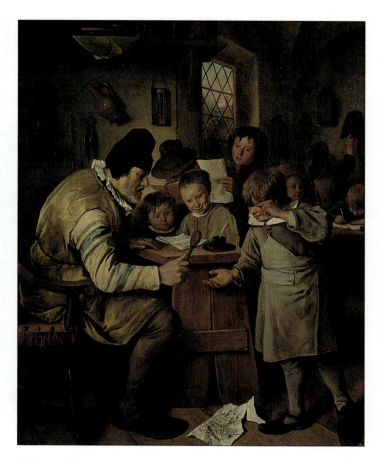

■ FIGURE 11.12

Jan Steen, *The Village School*, ca. 1655.

their own. The question of who was responsible for whom sometimes became quite murky, and a sense of individual responsibility for one's own plight slowly replaced a collective sense of charity. For example, civic authorities began to consider ways to help the needy, building workhouses for the poor and passing laws prohibiting begging. Such laws could never completely succeed, given the scale of need that we saw in the painting of the "Cripples" in Figure 11.1. Yet, more and more societies tried designing institutional solutions to the problems of poverty.

Figure 11.13 depicts a girls' dining hall in a Protestant orphanage in Amsterdam. The painting emphasizes the institutional quality of charity in the early seventeenth century. The orphans are dressed alike, for example, and the girls in the foreground serve watery soup for dinner while the matrons watch.

As communities redivided themselves along religious loyalties, many people's sense of personal anxiety increased. The Catholic Church had also provided community support and at least the hope of miraculous cures for the sick and troubled. Men and women could themselves pray to saints or the Virgin Mary for help, and priests could say prayers

Decline of "magic"

for members of their congregation in need. The Catholic Church even turned a blind eye to "white" magic (like that described in the village of Martin Guerre in the Biography), but Protestants rejected saints and any forms of "magic." As village rituals split apart, it became harder to define "community." As changing times and beliefs generated anxieties, some people began looking for scapegoats.

Jan Victors, *The Girls' Dining Hall in the Reformed Parish Orphanage*, ca. 1651.

■ FIGURE 11.14

Salvator Rosa, *Witches at Their Incantations* (detail), late seventeenth century.

SEARCHING FOR SCAPEGOATS: THE HUNT FOR WITCHES

Catholics and Protestants alike shared a long-standing, deeply-held belief in charms and potions that could affect people. These might be as benign as healing magical cures and love potions, or as harmful as spells to bring bad weather, illness, or crop failure. Traditionally, Catholic priests offered prayers and counter charms to combat the power of people—often, but not always, called witches—who had the knowledge to cast spells. Protestant preachers argued regularly against "superstitious magical practices," but some remained attached to charms and spells, and in England witchcraft accusations usually remained tied to spell-casting.

In the sixteenth century, especially on the Continent, some began to link a fear of witches to "diabolism," or the idea that magical powers came because of a pact with the devil. **Fear of the devil** Martin Luther himself claimed to have confronted the devil several times and constantly remained alert to the presence of this evil being. Church authorities began to stress that witches were in league with the devil and performed mysterious ceremonies in his service. To stamp out the devil's assistants, many accused supposed witches, putting them on trial and executing them.

People in the sixteenth century were fascinated by the possibility of witchcraft. The best-known work on the subject was the *Malleus Maleficarum* (the "Hammer of Witches"), which had been written in the late fifteenth century (before the start of the Reformation) for inquisitors to try witches. However, by 1669 it had been reissued in 40 editions and had become extraordinarily popular, appealing to Protestants and Catholics alike. In France alone, 345 books about witchcraft were published between 1550 and 1650.

There is no real evidence that any of the convicted "witches" engaged in pacts with the devil. Instead, many people were forced to "confess" under torture. Others may have thought they were confessing to using simple charms only to discover that they were convicted of diabolism.

Figure 11.14, a painting from the seventeenth century, reveals the characteristics of witches as imagined by many Europeans of this period. Those accused of witchcraft were predominantly female (90 percent of those executed for witchcraft were women), many of whom were old. In this picture, the witches prepare magic potions drawn from body parts taken from the corpse hanging on the left and the heart impaled on the sword in the center. At the right, a witch carries an infant who will be killed and whose body will be used for magical purposes. In the center is a broomstick. People believed that witches rode these and used them to apply hallucinogenic potions to their vaginas.

Catholics and Protestants alike persecuted witches, and the trials in Europe peaked between 1560 and 1640. Although precise numbers elude us, more than 100,000 people were executed for witchcraft, and 200,000 may have endured trials. These trials are probably the most disturbing indicator of the rampant anxiety stirred by the intellectual and social changes of the sixteenth century.

Persecutions

By the eighteenth century, the witchcraft panic ebbed and the trials gradually ceased, as men and women adjusted to the religious diversity that had split their countries and their communities. However, the ideals of the Protestant Reformation—individualism, a desire for marital harmony, an emphasis on hard work, and a staunch reliance on conscience—left a permanent mark on European society.

SUMMARY

Through the sixteenth century, the monarchs of the unified states of Europe—England, France, Spain, and the Holy Roman Empire—struggled to snatch power, wealth, and land from each other. The wars that resulted accomplished little except to bankrupt some of the kings, leave the European countryside in ruins, and inflict misery on the people. Meanwhile, religious revolutionaries stepped up their criticism of the thousand-year history of Christian tradition. These Protestants effected a reformation that spurred century-long religious warfare and that split Christendom as people followed their own paths to God. The religious quest had political ramifications as well—kings involved themselves in the Catholics' and Protestants' conflict in part to try to exert religious hegemony over their own lands and to gain land from their neighbors.

When the century of religious wars in Europe ended, it left a legacy of economic devastation, social and political change, and an intellectual revolution that transformed Western culture. More boys and girls in village schools began to read and write, men and women hoped to find love in marriage, and people began to take more pride in work over leisure. Nevertheless, the Protestant revolution failed to stop the competition for Christian souls. In the centuries to come, Europeans would take the battle between Protestants and Catholics across the seas, as they discovered lands that were new to them.

KEY TERMS

sacraments, p. 343

devotio moderna, p. 343

justification by faith, p. 345

indulgence, p. 345

purgatory, p. 345

Protestant, p. 346

iconoclasm, p. 346

transubstantiation, p. 346

predestination, p. 349

Huguenots, p. 350

Jesuits, p. 356

baroque, p. 357

REVIEW, ANALYZE, AND ANTICIPATE

REVIEW THE PREVIOUS CHAPTER

Chapter 10—"A New Spirit in the West"—described the characteristics that we have come to identify with the Renaissance. In addition, Chapter 10 also discussed the complex political structure of Italy that engaged popes as well as princes in power politics.

1. *Which Renaissance characteristics also describe the ideas of the Protestant reformers? Consider how the Renaissance influenced the Protestant Reformation.*

2. *Review the policies of Renaissance popes as they strove to become political powers in Italy. How did those policies contribute to the Reformation?*

ANALYZE THIS CHAPTER

Chapter 11—"Alone Before God"—follows the expansion of warfare until it engulfed all of Europe in the sixteenth century. It also looks at the new religious ideas that split the Catholic Church and brought about a change in life in the West.

1. *Review the various religious beliefs of the different Protestant sects and consider the relationship of these ideas to the different social and economic groups who were attracted to them.*

2. *How did the differing appeal help lead to the century of religious warfare? What were the results of this warfare?*

3. *Review the reform movements of the Catholic Church. How did the church respond to the critique of the Protestants?*

4. *How did the Reformation help contribute to changing social and cultural patterns that marked seventeenth-century Europe?*

ANTICIPATE THE NEXT CHAPTER

Chapter 12—"Faith, Fortune, and Fame"—looks at the European expansion into much of the rest of the world that took place at the same time Europe was wracked with the religious wars discussed in Chapter 11.

1. *Based on the strengths and weaknesses of the various states discussed in Chapter 11, which countries do you think might take the lead in the explorations and which might be left behind? Why?*

2. *Which Christian churches do you think might be most vigorous in missionary activities? Review Chapter 11's discussion of the characteristics of each sect's relative theology as you decide.*

BEYOND THE CLASSROOM

THE CLASH OF DYNASTIES

Bonney, Richard. *The European Dynastic States, 1494–1660.* Oxford: Oxford University Press, 1991. A rich survey that includes eastern as well as western Europe and provides an excellent overview (although it does exclude England).

Braudel, Fernand. *The Mediterranean and the Mediterranean World in the Age of Philip II.* New York: Harper & Row, 1972. An extraordinary analysis of the Mediterranean world that, in its consideration of geography, ecology, social history, economic history, and politics, offers a broad background for the period.

Davis, Natalie Zemon. *The Return of Martin Guerre.* Cambridge, MA: Harvard University Press, 1983. The classic study of Martin Guerre (the subject of the Chapter 11 Biography).

Parker, Geoffrey. *European Soldiers, 1550–1650.* New York: Cambridge University Press, 1997. A short, beautifully illustrated look into the lives of European soldiers.

Parker, Geoffrey. *The Grand Strategy of Philip II.* New Haven: Yale University Press, 1998. Reconsiders the reign of Philip II and shows that the king was more of a strategic thinker than many have thought, and explores his failings in that light.

A TIDE OF RELIGIOUS REFORM

Bainton, Roland H. *Here I Stand: A Life of Martin Luther.* New York: Meridian, 1995. First published in 1950, remains the best and most sensitive study of the man and his impact.

Baylor, Michael G. *The Radical Reformation.* New York: Cambridge University Press, 1991. Collects letters and other documents to illustrate the rich diversity and the fragile unity that existed in the political thinking of some of the major radical reformers in Germany.

Edwards, Mark, Jr. *Printing, Propaganda and Martin Luther.* Berkeley, CA: University of California Press, 1994. A study of the literature that tried to redefine the church and its beliefs.

Haigh, Christopher. *English Reformations: Religion, Politics, and Society Under the Tudors.* Oxford: Clarendon Press, 1993. A scholarly work that draws on a wealth of primary materials from catechisms to churchwardens' accounts to offer a full picture of the English Reformation.

McGrath, Alister E. *Reformation Thought: An Introduction,* 3rd ed. Oxford: Blackwell, 2001. The best starting point for anyone wanting to understand the ideas of the Reformers set within their historical context.

Scribner, R.W. *The German Reformation,* 2nd ed. New York: Palgrave Macmillan, 2003. A brief and accessible analysis of the appeal of the Reformation to common people.

THE CATHOLIC REFORMATION

Ahlgren, Gillian. *Teresa of Avila and the Politics of Sanctity.* Ithaca, NY: Cornell University Press, 1996. Considers Teresa's struggle in the context of a world that did not always look kindly on an outspoken woman.

Birley, Robert. *The Refashioning of Catholicism, 1450–1700: A Reassessment of the Counter Reformation.* Washington: Catholic University Press, 1999. Offers a comprehensive, balanced, historical view of the Catholic Reformation by a prominent historian of Catholicism. Its strength is placing these ideas into the context of the times.

O'Malley, John. *Trent and All That: Renaming Catholicism in the Early Modern Era.* Cambridge: Harvard University Press, 2002. The best overview of early modern Catholicism that explains the intellectual and historical developments in an engaging way.

EUROPE ERUPTS AGAIN: A CENTURY OF RELIGIOUS WARFARE, 1559–1648

Holt, Mack P. *The French Wars of Religion, 1562–1629,* 2nd ed. Cambridge: Cambridge University Press, 2005. A brief, clear description of the events of these wars as well as an analysis of the issues that formed the backdrop of the warfare, clarifying a complex time.

Knecht, R.J. *The French Wars of Religion: 1554–1598.* New York: Longman, 1989. A good survey.

MacCaffrey, Wallace. *Elizabeth I: War and Politics, 1588–1603.* Princeton, NJ: Princeton University Press, 1992. Recounts the conduct of the war with Spain and describes the diplomacy of alliances of the period.

Parker, Geoffrey. *The Thirty Years' War*. New York: Routledge, 1997. A readable general history by one of the foremost military historians.

LIFE AFTER THE REFORMATION

Harrington, Joel. *Reordering Marriage and Society in Reformation Germany*. Cambridge, England: Cambridge University Press, 1994. A provocative and sound interpretation.

Thomas, Keith. *Religion and the Decline of Magic*. 1971. An important book that investigates many sources to study the changing character of religious beliefs and the replacement of "superstition" with science.

Weber, Max. *The Protestant Ethic and the Spirit of Capitalism*. Los Angeles: Roxbury Publishing, 1998. Originally published in 1904, this study of how the Reformation helped create the modern world has generated much controversy, but has also shaped much of the historical thinking about the Reformation.

www.mhhe.com/sherman3

- Unfamiliar words? See our Glossary at the back of the book for pronunciation and definitions.

- Need help studying? See our web page for map exercises, practice quizzes, and additional study resources.

- Need help writing a paper? Access hundreds of primary documents, maps, images, and a guide to writing history papers on our Primary Source Investigator site at **www.mhhe.com/psi.**

DON FRAN. DE AROBE. 5 6. A

PORTRAIT OF DON FRANCISCO DE AROBÉ, DETAIL FROM *THE MULATTO GENTLEMEN OF ESMERALDAS*, BY ANDRÉS SÁNCHEZ GALLQUE, 1599

Globalization changed the world beginning in the fifteenth century as Europeans and Africans encountered native peoples in the New World. This portrait is part of a larger portrait of three men in Ecuador in the service of the Spanish king, Philip III. The subject here, Francisco, was of mixed African descent, a Christian, and the governor of a settlement in Ecuador. He represents the new blending of peoples and cultures, and this portrait, the oldest surviving signed and dated painting from colonial South America, reveals the kind of changes that came about as people moved across the seas.

FAITH, FORTUNE, AND FAME

STUDY	The world imagined ■ Discovery of new lands and sea routes ■ Confrontation of cultures ■ The growth of a world market and commercial revolution.
NOTICE	How the mingling of various cultures transformed all of them to some degree.

"To serve God and the King, to give light to those who are in darkness, and to grow rich, as all men desire to do." With these words, the Portuguese explorer Bartholomeu Dias (1450–1500) explained purposes that drove men to sail their ships across uncharted oceans during the sixteenth and seventeenth centuries. At the same time that Italian Renaissance ideas spread and the Reformation created new martyrs, daring Europeans ventured where they had never gone before. Kings and queens sponsored these explorers in the hopes that the new territories and riches they promised would give monarchs an advantage over their dynastic rivals.

The adventurers traveled by ship east to China, Japan, and other places in the Pacific, and west to strange new islands and continents. As they journeyed, they met peoples living in great empires in the East and in the mountains and jungles of South and Central America. They traded with many others from tribes and kingdoms in sub-Saharan Africa, the Caribbean, and North America. The interactions among the many cultures prompted the emergence of new markets and the discovery of unusual products that whetted Europeans' appetites for yet more novelties. Some men like Don Francisco shown in the chapter-opening portrait were able to prosper in the new global environment, but not all were so successful. Sadly, the commingling also led to the transmission of deadly new diseases and other hardships. Europeans were irrevocably altered by these cultural contacts, and so were the cultures they encountered.

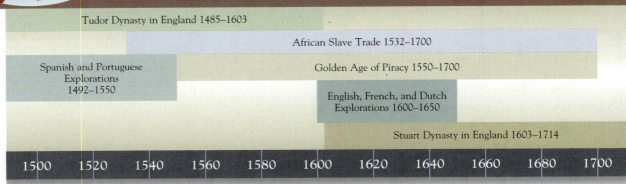

Tudor Dynasty in England 1485–1603

African Slave Trade 1532–1700

Spanish and Portuguese
Explorations
1492–1550

Golden Age of Piracy 1550–1700

English, French, and Dutch
Explorations 1600–1650

Stuart Dynasty in England 1603–1714

| 1500 | 1520 | 1540 | 1560 | 1580 | 1600 | 1620 | 1640 | 1660 | 1680 | 1700 |

THE WORLD IMAGINED

IN 1498, FOUR PORTUGUESE SHIPS led by Vasco da Gama sailed south from Europe and rounded the southern tip of Africa to reach India in the east. Gaspar Correa accompanied this journey, keeping a careful chronicle that told of the exciting, frightening voyage. In order to sail south with prevailing northwesterly winds, the navigators could not hug the shore, but instead had to direct the ships southwest, tacking into the wind and going far away from the sight of land into the unknown sea. For two months, Vasco da Gama tacked out to sea to make sure when they turned to shore, the ships would "double the cape," skirting the African continent. Correa wrote of the hardships of this venture into the Atlantic: "The fury of the sea [made] the ships seem every moment to be going to pieces. The crews grew sick with fear and hardship, . . . and all clamored for putting back to Portugal. . . . At times they met with such cold rains that the men could not prepare their food. All cried out to God for mercy upon their souls." Vasco da Gama finally ordered the ships about and they sailed southeast again. They circled the southern tip of Africa and with much celebration they headed northeast toward India.

The ships were to face much more hardship. They pulled into great rivers in Africa looking for food and for people to tell them where they were. They ate unknown fruits—one so toxic it made their gums swell and their teeth loosen. The captain ordered his ill men to rinse their mouths with urine to ease their gums, and the cure worked. Somehow, through all the adversity the crews carried on, and finally docked in India at a city where citizens flocked to the shore, amazed at the Western ships. Correa succinctly and accurately described the confrontation between East and West: "All were much amazed at seeing what they had never before seen." Vasco da Gama's crew was not unique in the fifteenth century; brave sailors sailed east and west from Europe, and the world was transformed as Europeans and indigenous peoples almost everywhere were "amazed" at their new confrontation.

THE LURE OF THE "EAST"

Western Europeans had long coveted goods from the "East," which they generally considered China and India. When they used the name "China," they also meant Japan and the other lands of eastern Asia. When they referred to "India," they included southeast Asia and the many islands dotting the Pacific, and although Vasco da Gama reached the mainland of India,

Eastern trade

he would have been content to land on any of the Pacific islands. More than just a geographic entity, though, the East, in many Europeans' minds, was the source of valuable luxury goods.

Since the Middle Ages, Europe had lusted after the silks, fine carpets, pottery, and precious jewels produced in the East. Europeans were so impressed by these exotic goods that they praised the Chinese as the "finest craftsmen in the world." Yet it was the spices from the Orient that riveted westerners' attention. European diets were bland, and those who depended only on local seasonings—garlic, saffron, and the ever-present salt—found the food tiresome. Recipes of the time and records showing commercial demand reveal that people clamored for cloves, cinnamon, coriander, and pepper in particular—all available only in the East. Throughout the Middle Ages, these products came overland through the Byzantine Empire into western Europe.

But after 1400, intensifying warfare in eastern Europe and Asia made overland travel difficult. (See Chapter 9 for the increased threat posed by the Turks.) Europeans began looking for new trade routes through the eastern Mediterranean to satisfy their appetite for spice. They revived centuries-old memories of journeys to the East by reading accounts like that of the Venetian explorer Marco Polo (1254–1324), who wrote detailed descriptions of his visits to China (see Chapter 9). These works were incorrect in much of their geography, however; for example, Marco Polo believed that Japan was 1,500 miles east of China. Furthermore, most of these older accounts contained exaggerated descriptions of botanical and biological features of eastern lands. Nevertheless, no tale of the exotic "East" seemed too far-fetched to fifteenth-century European imaginations.

■ FIGURE 12.1

"Monstrous races" pictured in manuscript of Marco Polo's travels, fifteenth century.

IMAGINED PEOPLES

Since the time of the Roman scholar Pliny the Elder (23–79), people had heard of unusual races of people who inhabited parts of the world outside the Mediterranean. Pliny's works had been read, copied, and embellished over the centuries, and by the fifteenth century, explorers expected to find beings as bizarre as dog-headed humans, headless people, one-legged "sciopods," and—south of the equator—"antipods," whose feet reportedly faced backward.

Figure 12.1 shows an illustration from a fifteenth-century manuscript about the travels of Marco Polo. Although Marco Polo never claimed to have seen such creatures, later Europeans imagined that he did. On the left of the illustration is a blemmyae, a headless man whose face is located on his chest. In the center is a sciopod, a one-legged creature believed to use his large foot as a parasol against the sun. These two beings are greeted by a cyclops approaching from the right.

A more plausible person the explorers expected to meet was "Prester John," supposedly a rich and powerful Christian king reigning in the heart of Africa. By the Renaissance, Europeans hoped to enlist this king as an ally against the Muslims. However, the search for both Prester John and the fascinating creatures in Marco Polo's tales was stymied by an inaccurate geographic sense of the world that, like the descriptions of the "monstrous races," the explorers had inherited from the ancients.

PTOLEMY'S MAP

During the fifteenth century, western Europeans acquired the *Geography* of Ptolemy (ca. 100–ca. 178).

This guide had been translated from Greek, reproduced by the new printing presses, and widely distributed. Now Renaissance explorers had a picture of the world that they could use to venture into the Atlantic, or the "green sea of darkness," as the Arabic commentators called it.

Ptolemy's worldview

Ptolemy portrayed the world as a globe, divided into the familiar 360 degrees of longitude. Figure 12.2, from a 1482 edition of the *Geography*, shows Ptolemy's map of the world. This ancient geographer believed that the world consisted of three continents—Asia, Africa, and Europe—and two oceans—the Indian Ocean and the Western Ocean. The map is surrounded by figures representing the many winds so crucial to a sailing society. In addition to mistaking the number of continents, Ptolemy made two major errors. He underestimated the extent of the oceans, suggesting that land covered three-fourths of the earth's surface, and he miscalculated the earth as being one-sixth smaller than its true size. With only Ptolemy's map to guide them, later explorers understandably expected the journey east to be shorter than it really was. During this age of discovery, however, the theories of Ptolemy dissolved in the face of experience.

THE WORLD DISCOVERED

The explorers expected to capitalize on Europe's desire for Eastern goods and bring back wealth for themselves and their sovereigns. Sixteenth-century rulers were desperate for money to field their expensive armies,

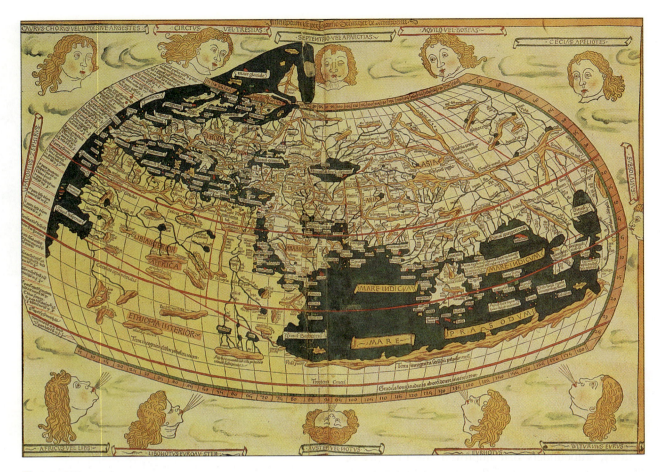

■ FIGURE 12.2

Ptolemy's image of the world.

and the conquest of Constantinople by the Turks in 1453 increased the price of the valuable spices as they imposed steep taxes on the goods. This costly trade siphoned precious metals away from an already coin-poor western Europe, and monarchs were willing to reward anyone who hunted for new wealth. Brave, enterprising men eager for fame and fortune took up the challenge.

FAME, FORTUNE, AND FAITH: THE DRIVE TO EXPLORE

Though the lure of wealth motivated explorers and the sovereigns who funded them, some adventurers had other incentives for embarking on these risky travels. As Bartholomeu Dias implied in the quotation that introduced this chapter, religion also served as a major impulse for Europeans to seek new worlds. Christians during the fifteenth and sixteenth centuries felt besieged by the Islamic empire of the Ottoman Turks that loomed on Europe's eastern border (see Chapter 11). Some voyages aimed to find allies against the Turks. For example, the Portuguese Prince Henry the Navigator (1394–1460) sponsored voyages down the coast of Africa to search for "Prester John." The Reformation within Europe also stimulated explorations and migrations, as Catholics sought converts to Catholicism overseas and Protestants looked for new lands where they could practice their faith. Faith joined with fame and fortune to drive Europeans across the seas.

NEW TECHNOLOGIES AND TRAVEL

Europeans had a passion for adventure, but they also needed strong navigational tools and skills if they were to survive these hazardous journeys. Fortunately for them, sailors in the Middle Ages had perfected instruments to help them sail out of sight of land. One device, the **quadrant,** aligned with the fixed North Star at night to let navigators determine their latitude. However, this was not useful in the Southern Hemisphere, where the North Star was not visible. Sailors going south had to confront uncharted heavens as well as unmapped lands. During the day, sailors in both Northern and Southern hemispheres could check their calculations

Navigation instruments

Finally, mapmakers had gained experience in charting the seas and lands and could graphically document their travels with some accuracy. Earlier skilled seafarers like the Vikings who first discovered North America lacked the cartography skills to allow them to reproduce their long sea voyages with as much certainty as the sixteenth-century explorers. Navigators felt confident in their charts, and the newly discovered map of Ptolemy, though inaccurate, at least gave them a basic sense of direction.

Sailors lacked only the ships to carry them safely on long ventures. The galleys that had ruled the Mediterranean in the fourteenth century had large, square sails, but their locomotion came primarily from the many slaves who rowed the big ships. These ships were unsuitable for long distances and had little extra space left in their holds to store the provisions necessary for a lengthy sea voyage.

All this changed in the late fifteenth century, when the Portuguese built ships that marked the highest development of a long evolution of Mediterranean sailing ships. In the Middle Ages, shipbuilders had developed a new kind of sail rigging that

Improved ships allowed ships to maneuver near shore in uncertain winds. By the sixteenth century, shipbuilders had improved the mobility of the sails and the rigging of the ropes so that the sails could be moved readily. Figure 12.3 shows a sixteenth-century watercolor of Portuguese caravels—the small (70 to 80 feet long) ships that conquered the great seas. The large square sails allowed the ships to move in the direction of the wind, or downwind. The real secret to long-distance sailing, however, was the lateen, a triangular, mobile sail at the rear (furled in Figure 12.3). This device not only let the ship sail faster, it also allowed it to sail at an angle to the wind and thus progress upwind—a crucial advantage for traveling into the prevailing westerly winds of the Atlantic. This ship, with its absence of oar banks, stands in striking contrast to the Mediterranean galleys shown in Figure 11.9. The ships had to be heavy to withstand the storms of the Atlantic, and this weight gave the West an unforeseen advantage: They could support heavy cannons, giving them a military advantage over the lighter ships of the east that sailed the calmer Indian ocean. On these innovative vessels, the Portuguese set out on voyages of discovery that changed the world.

THE PORTUGUESE RACE FOR THE EAST, 1450–1600

As the chronicler of Vasco da Gama's voyage described in the account at the beginning of this chapter, the Portuguese explorers had an immediate goal in mind:

FIGURE 12.3

Sixteenth-century watercolor of Portuguese ships.

to venture south around Africa to the Indian Ocean and trade directly with natives in India for spices and other luxury items. This route would eliminate the troublesome role of the Ottoman Turks as key players in the eastern Mediterranean trade network. Beginning in 1418, Prince Henry the Navigator (1394–1460) of Portugal sponsored annual expeditions down the west coast of Africa. Bartholomeu Dias continued Henry's work with great success, rounding the southern tip of Africa in 1488. King John II of Portugal (r. 1481–1495), expecting this route to yield the riches of the East, named the tip the "Cape of Good Hope." But Dias never reached India. His frightened crew had experienced the storms and hardships that Correa described, but Dias did not maintain the iron control that Vasco da Gama would, and his crew mutinied as he sailed north along the eastern coast of Africa. He was forced to return home. In 1498, his countryman Vasco da Gama (ca. 1460–1524) set out with four ships to complete Dias's ill-fated voyage to India. He succeeded and returned to Portugal with ships laden with spices worth sixty times the cost of the journey.

Portuguese explorers scored spectacular successes in opening up the trade to the east. As one pleasant surprise, they discovered that "India" was not simply one location—it included the Moluccas, "spice islands,"

THINKING ABOUT GEOGRAPHY

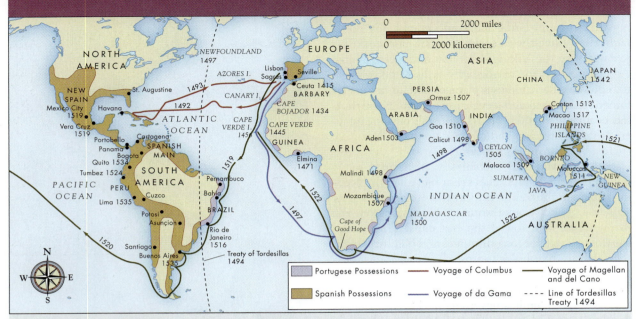

MAP 12.1   **EXPLORATION AND CONQUEST: FIFTEENTH AND SIXTEENTH CENTURIES**

This map shows the routes and dates of the explorations of the fifteenth and sixteenth centuries, as well as the possessions claimed by the Spanish and Portuguese. ■ **Notice** the differences in the patterns of settlement in the Americas, Africa, and Asia. **What** do you think accounted for those differences? ■ **Notice** the location of the Treaty of Tordesillas line that divided up the world between Portugal and Spain. **Notice** how the wealthiest and most populated regions went to Portugal. **How** did this treaty influence the differing settlement patterns of the Spanish and the Portuguese?

from which wafted the delightful aroma of cloves as the Portuguese ships approached. As Map 12.1 shows, the Portuguese established a string of *Trading outposts* trading outposts throughout the East. In these small settlements, Europeans lived peacefully near native settlements in a mutually profitable relationship. Portugal's successful entry into the Indian Ocean trade struck a dramatic blow to the economy of the Muslims, who had previously held a monopoly on that trade. At the same time, their neighbors, the Spanish, took a quite different approach. Spain's explorers sailed westward in hopes of reaching the fabulous Orient, believing Ptolemy's claim that the land of plenty lay just over the horizon.

SPAIN'S WESTWARD DISCOVERIES, 1492–1522

Christopher Columbus (1446–1506) perhaps best exemplifies Spain's travel ambitions. The son of an Italian (Genoese) weaver, Columbus traveled to Portugal in 1476 to learn about Portuguese shipbuilding

and sailing. During his visit, he became captivated by the accounts of Marco Polo and the *Geography* of Ptolemy. Inflamed by images of glory and wealth, he asked the Portuguese king to sponsor him on a trip west to Asia. The king rejected him; like many others, he dismissed Columbus as a vague dreamer. Columbus then presented his idea to the Spanish monarchs Ferdinand and Isabella. The queen, impressed with Columbus's proposal, made him an admiral in 1492 and financed his expedition.

Columbus embarked on his journey with three ships, the *Niña*, the *Pinta*, and the *Santa María*. In October, the small fleet landed on an island in the Caribbean *Columbus's discoveries* Sea. According to the admiral's account, as he stepped ashore, Columbus "claimed all the lands for their Highnesses, by proclamation and with the royal standard displayed." According to Columbus, the many islanders who watched him did not object to his claims, so he accepted this as their tacit agreement—ignoring the language barrier that separated them. Subsequent explorers followed his lead, claiming ownership of already inhabited lands.

Figure 12.4 is a contemporary woodcut that was intended to capture this incident, and it shows all the essential elements: The King of Spain, on the left, gives Columbus the authority for his voyage. The three ships are featured in the center, and Columbus is shown landing on an island to claim it for the king. The island is depicted as a place as fanciful as any in the literature of imaginative travel, with exotic trees and beautiful, naked natives. The reality of the landing proved much less idyllic.

Columbus made four voyages between 1492 and 1502, during which he established settlements on several more Caribbean islands and visited the northern coast of South America and Central America. On his third voyage, he brought women from Spain to ensure the permanence of the settlements. The explorer was not a good administrator, and when Spain sent a judge to look into a revolt in the new lands, Columbus was brought back to Spain in chains. Though he was later released and made a final fourth voyage to the New World, Columbus never received the riches and acclaim he sought. Throughout these years, the Italian adventurer apparently felt sure that he had found Asian islands. He even referred to the natives as "Indians" because he was certain he was in the general region of "India." Columbus never realized that he had discovered a world unknown by virtually all Europeans. Instead, he clung to the image of the world he had imagined. His continued misconceptions encouraged other voyagers, who would soon prove him wrong.

As the Spanish and Portuguese both raced to claim lands on their way east, they inevitably came into conflict. The Catholic sovereigns of Spain and Portugal appealed to the pope to divide the world into two spheres of influence. In the 1494 Treaty of Tordesillas (shown on Map 12.1), the Spanish received exclusive rights to the lands west of a line drawn 370 leagues (about 1,200 miles) west of the Cape Verde Islands off the west coast of Africa, and the Portuguese received rights to the lands east of the line. This agreement (which was virtually ignored by the other European monarchs) was one of many attempts to apportion the world without regard for the opinions of indigenous residents.

Treaty of Tordesillas

Soon, subsequent travelers convinced Europeans that Columbus was wrong and that a great new landmass had been found. The most influential of these explorers was Amerigo Vespucci (1451–1512), an educated "Renaissance man" who worked for the Medici family of Florence (discussed in Chapter 10). In 1499, Vespucci set off on a voyage of discovery that took him westward from Spain and across the vast ocean to South America. During his voyage, he took careful navigational measurements and wrote colorful letters

■ FIGURE 12.4
Woodcut of Columbus landing.

to his Medici patron, which were widely circulated. In the introduction to these works, Amerigo's publisher even suggested that Vespucci's name be given to the *Mundus Novus* (the "New World") he had popularized with his maps and vivid tales of a continent across the ocean. The suggestion caught on, and the name "America" became attached to the western landmass that newly captured the European imagination. See Document 12.1 for an example of one of Vespucci's vivid descriptions.

After Vespucci's voyages, people set out purposefully to visit the new continent. For example, the Spanish adventurer Vasco Núñez de Balboa (1475–1517) trekked across the Isthmus of Panama, eventually reaching the Pacific Ocean on the other side. Besides adding to the evidence that a new continent existed, Balboa's discovery intensified the race to the riches of the East. New men with even bigger dreams of wealth joined the rush.

Circumnavigating the globe

Ferdinand Magellan (ca. 1480–1521) was one of these men. A Portuguese explorer in the service of Spain, Magellan began the first expedition that succeeded in encircling the world. He sailed west from Spain in 1519 with three ships and discovered (and named) the Straits of Magellan at the southern tip of South America. The straits gave him access to the Pacific Ocean (which he also named). He and his crew braved the huge expanses of ocean and withstood mutinies. In 1521, Magellan was killed while interfering in a local war in the Philippines. His navigator, Sevastian Elcano (ca. 1476–1526), finished the journey to Asia and through the Indian Ocean back to Spain. Elcano's

■ DOCUMENT 12.1

Amerigo Vespucci Describes the New World

In 1499, the naval astronomer Amerigo Vespucci wrote a letter to Lorenzo d'Medici of Florence (see Chapter 10) describing his travels. The letter serves as a valuable early source for European impressions of the new lands. ■ ***How** does Vespucci demonstrate that observation of the New World is more important than speculations about it?* ***How** might such observations foster a scientific attitude?* ■ ***What** plants does he find most interesting?* ***How** might this narrative persuade people that there would be profits to be made in the New World?* ■ ***Consider** how Vespucci describes the native peoples, and **how** these descriptions might shape future interactions.* ■ ***Consider** how his account is very engaging.* ***How** might this narrative make him so influential that "America" was named after him?*

It appears to me, most excellent Lorenzo, that by this voyage most of those philosophers are controverted who say that the torrid zone cannot be inhabited on account of the great heat. I have found the case to be quite the contrary. I have found that the air is fresher and more temperate in that region than beyond it, and that the inhabitants are also more numerous here than they are in the other zones, for reasons which will be given below. Thus it is certain that practice is of more value than theory.

Thus far I have related the navigation I accomplished in the south and west. It now remains for me to inform you of the appearance of the country we discovered, the nature of the inhabitants, and their customs, the animals we saw, and of many other things worthy of remembrance which fell under my observation. After we turned our course to the north, the first land we found to be inhabited was an island at ten degrees distant from the equinoctial line. When we arrived at it we saw on the sea-shore a great many people, who stood looking at us with astonishment. We anchored within about a mile of the land, fitted out the boats, and twenty-two men, well armed, made for land. The people, when they saw us landing, and perceived that we were different from themselves—because they have no beard and wear no clothing of any description, being also of a different color, they being brown and we white—began to be afraid of us, and all ran into the woods. With great exertion, by means of signs, we reassured them and negotiated with them. We found that they were of a race called cannibals, the greater part or all of whom live on human flesh.

Your excellency may rest assured of this fact. They do not eat one another, but, navigating with certain barks which they call 'canoes,' they bring their prey from the neighboring islands or countries inhabited by those who are enemies or of a different tribe from their own. They never eat any women, unless they consider them outcasts. These things we verified in many places where we found similar people. We often saw the bones and heads of those who had been eaten, and they who had made the repast admitted the fact, and said that their enemies always stood in much greater fear on that account.

Still they are a people of gentle disposition and beautiful stature. They go entirely naked, and the arms which they carry are bows and arrows and shields. They are a people of great activity and much courage. They are very excellent marksmen. . . .

Nearly half the trees of this island are dye-wood, as good as that of the East. We went from this island to another in the vicinity, at ten leagues' distance, and found a very large village, the houses of which were built over the sea, like Venice, with much ingenuity. While we were struck with admiration at this circumstance, we determined to go and see them; and as we went to their houses, they attempted to prevent our entering. They found out at last the manner in which the sword cuts, and thought it best to let us enter. We found their houses filled with the finest cotton, and the beams of their dwellings were made of dye-wood. We took a quantity of their cotton and some dye-wood and returned to the ships.

Your excellency must know that in all parts where we landed we found a great quantity of cotton, and the country filled with cotton-trees, so that all the vessels in the world might be loaded in these parts with cotton and dye-wood.

Source: Amerigo Vespucci, "Letter to Lorenzo de'Medici," in *The Great Events by Famous Historians*, vol. VIII, ed. Rossiter Johnson (The National Alumni, 1905), pp. 351–356.

---

voyage took three years and he returned home with only one ship. But that ship was packed with enough spices not only to pay for the cost of the expedition, but also to make the crew very rich.

Magellan's and Elcano's successful circumnavigation of the globe revealed not that the world was round (they knew that), but its true size. It also demonstrated the impracticality of sailing to the Orient by way of the Pacific. The Spanish would have to search for new sources of wealth—this time in the New World.

THE NORTHERN EUROPEANS JOIN THE RACE, 1600–1650

England, France, and the Netherlands came late to the race for the riches of the New World. Understandably, they were unwilling to accept the terms of the Treaty of Tordesillas. Instead, they began their own explorations. They started by looking for a "northwest passage" to the East that would parallel the southern route around South America. In about 1497, the

Genoese captain John Cabot (1450–1498) and his son Sebastian (1476–1557), who both had settled in England, received a letter from the English king Henry VII (r. 1485–1509) authorizing them to take possession for England any new lands unclaimed by any Christian nation. So empowered, father and son sailed across the North Atlantic to Newfoundland and Maine. They found codfish so plentiful that their ships could not pass through the thick schools of fish. However, the voyage was immediately disappointing because they neither reached Asia nor returned laden with spices.

The French also hunted for a northwest passage to the East. In 1534, Jacques Cartier led three voyages that explored the St. Lawrence River in what is today Canada. He and his crew got as far as Montreal, but the great waterway led only inland, not out to the Pacific Northwest. An early settlement effort in the region of Quebec in 1541 failed, owing to the harsh winter and indigenes' hostility. In about 1600, Samuel de Champlain (ca. 1567–1635) made another try at establishing a settlement in North America. He founded Quebec, signing treaties with the natives to secure the settlement. Canadian settlements remained small in both size and number through the seventeenth century, but their existence ensured the continuous presence of European traders and missionaries in this northern land.

Settlements in Canada

When the much sought after northwest passage proved elusive, northern Europeans shifted their journeys of discovery farther south and began to confront the Iberians directly. The Dutch established trading posts in the Spice Islands, and Dutch warships proved their superiority and expelled the Portuguese from the islands that we now know as Indonesia. The Dutch also redesigned their ships to haul more cargo than the small Portuguese caravels that had first mastered the oceans. They then dominated the lucrative spice trade, founding colonies in strategic locations to protect their growing trade empire. As one example, they colonized the tip of South Africa to facilitate their eastern trade and planted colonies in North America (most famously on Manhattan Island) and in the Caribbean.

Dutch colonies

The English, for their part, began to install settlements along the North American Atlantic seaboard in the seventeenth century: By 1700, about 250,000 colonists lived along the coast. Many of these people moved there to escape the religious persecution that swept Europe in the seventeenth century. For this reason, they traveled west with their entire families, with the intent to stay. Their presence irrevocably altered the face of North America. Map 12.2 shows the status of the European colonization in about 1700, and it illustrates how the northern European countries had joined the Spanish and Portuguese in their race around the world.

English colonies

the Dutch taking over · *persecution*

CONFRONTATION OF CULTURES

When the Europeans arrived in the New World, it was already abundantly populated by peoples who had lived there in resilient societies for millennia. From as early as 35,000 B.C.E., small groups of people walked from Asia northward across a land bridge from Siberia to Alaska. Slowly, over tens of thousands of years, families, clans, and tribes moved southward and settled throughout North, Central, and South America. At first all these tribes pursued a highly effective hunting-and-gathering existence, with devastating consequences for their future development. As the hunters came through North America, they confronted great herds of large mammals—horses, elephants, camels, and giant ground sloths. Within a few centuries of human arrival, all those large mammals were extinct, probably because of effective hunting. However, this meant that there were no more large animals in North America for domestication—this would represent a fatal disadvantage when the Amerindians confronted Europeans millennia later.

hunters

THE ORIGINAL AMERICANS

In about 5500 B.C.E., tribes in central Mexico first developed agriculture, which, as we saw in Chapter 1, allowed large settled populations to become established. These civilizations would become tempting, wealthy targets for European explorers. Agriculture spread north and south from there, but very slowly. The differing latitudes and varied growing seasons of the large American continents caused agriculture to diffuse more slowly in the Americas than it had in Europe and Asia, where crops spread primarily within similar latitudes. In the Americas, for example, it took about 3,500 years for maize (what we usually call corn) and beans to spread 700 miles from Mexico to the southern farmlands of the modern United States.

Agriculture

latitude affecting growth

Some North American tribes—in Canada and the great central plains of the modern United States—maintained their hunting and gathering culture; others—mostly in the southwest and east—developed agricultural societies that permitted fairly large concentrations of population. With the early use of agriculture in Central America and the western mountains of South America, populations grew large and elaborate empires—the Maya, Aztec, Inca, and others—developed. These civilizations thrived mainly through the cultivation of maize. This highly nutritious, versatile crop originally grew wild in the New World, but had been cultivated for so long that it no longer grew without human help. Maize offered high yields with very little effort. Cultivators worked only about fifty

maize

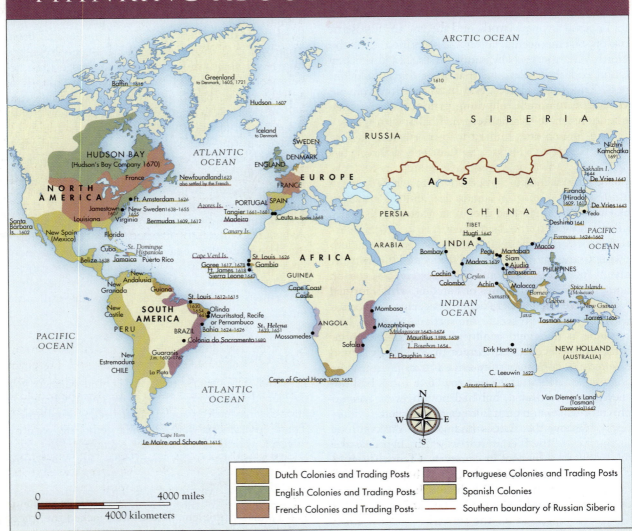

MAP 12.2 EUROPEAN EXPANSION, CA. 1700

This map shows the world around 1700, when Europeans had farther expanded throughout the globe. ■ **Notice** where the people from the various countries settled. **Compare** the different settlement patterns of the Americas and Africa and Asia. **What** accounts for this difference?
■ **Compare** this map with Map 12.1. **Consider** what caused the major differences.

days a year to produce an abundant crop that could be eaten even before it was ripe.

In these maize-growing societies, men cut and burned brush to clear the land to plant the grain, and women ground the hard kernels into flour to make tortillas, or flat bread. Girolamo Benzoni, a traveler in Central and South America in 1541, drew women in the process of making the essential corn-bread (Figure 12.5). The woman on the right boils the husked corn with lime, and then the woman on

the left grinds it to make flour for the woman at the center cooking the dough on the griddle.

The Incas, a people living in the Andes Mountains of South America, also cultivated a crop indigenous to that region—potatoes. An excellent alternative to maize, which did not grow in the high country, this hardy vegetable grew easily in the adverse conditions and high altitudes of mountain ranges and provided a hearty food supply. Once planted, potatoes required little work to harvest and prepare. Incas living in the mountains dried potatoes for long-term storage.

The small amount of time required to cultivate and harvest maize and potatoes left many days free for other work, and the great Central and South American empires developed a religious and aristocratic culture that demanded human labor for immense building projects. The Maya, Aztecs, and Incas built magnificent cities and roads and imposing pyramids. These constructions seem even more remarkable when we realize that they were built with Stone Age technology and without use of the wheel and (in most places) without the help of powerful, domesticated animals. Among these civilizations, only the Incas had domesticated the llama and alpaca as beasts of burden; throughout the rest of North and South America, people raised only dogs and fowl.

Map 12.3 shows the locations of the large South American empires as they existed when the Europeans arrived in the fifteenth century. The illustration shows the narrow Isthmus of Panama, which formed an effective geographic barrier between the two major empires, and which also served to disadvantage the merindians in developing increasingly complex societies. For example, the Aztecs in Mexico invented a wheel, but because they lacked draft animals, the wheel remained a children's toy. The Incas had domesticated the llama, but had no wheel to convert this animal into an effective beast of burden.

In Mexico, the Aztecs had located their capital at the great city of Tenochtitlán, built on a lake and accessible only by boat or causeway. (Tenochtitlán is the site of present-day Mexico City.) The Aztecs called themselves Meshica, where we get the word "Mexico." The Aztecs had conquered all the surrounding local tribes and claimed tribute from the vanquished, including humans sacrificed to the demanding Aztec gods who people believed claimed human blood to delay an inevitable destruction of Aztec society. Much of the visual information we have on the South American tribes comes from manuscripts written in the sixteenth century after the Spanish conquests. Authors included drawings within these books—many created by the Amerindians themselves. From these drawings, we can gain information about life before and after the Spanish invasions. Figure 12.6 is one such drawing, which shows the ritual human sacrifice. In the sacrificial ceremony, victims were forced to the top of a pyramid and stretched over a stone. A priest then used a sharp, stone knife to cut out the victim's heart and offer it—still beating—to the god. The voracious demand for such tribute from the subject peoples catalyzed resentment among them—a force that the new conquerors from Europe would find useful in overpowering the Aztecs.

Empire building

Aztec Empire

domesti capod

■ FIGURE 12.5
Women preparing corn for tortillas, ca. 1541.

EARLY CONTACTS

Christopher Columbus set the tone for the relationship between the original Americans and Europeans when he claimed land in the New World for the Spanish monarchs and when he treated the people as sources of revenue for the Spanish crown. With few exceptions, subsequent European explorers viewed the native peoples in the same way. Sometimes they traded with them; other times they used them as labor. Still other times, they killed or enslaved the men and women they found living in the new lands.

Explorers of the New World believed they encountered a major problem: These lands lacked the spices and luxury goods of the East that had brought so much immediate wealth to merchants. These new explorers had to find other forms of riches to bring home. Sometimes they enslaved natives, but this was not particularly lucrative. Instead, they searched for silver and gold to take back to Europe. According to one contemporary observer, when an Amerindian asked a Spaniard what Europeans ate, the Spaniard responded, "Gold and silver." (We do not know whether this exchange actually took place, but the anecdote testifies to the insatiable European appetite for precious metals.)

European contacts with the North American tribes took place about twenty-five to one hundred years later than the early South and Central American contacts, and some of the early European chroniclers of these engagements offer interesting details about the local customs. For example, a shipwreck stranded a Spaniard, Cabeza de Vaca (ca. 1409–ca. 1560) with his three companions (including an African slave) in

THINKING ABOUT GEOGRAPHY

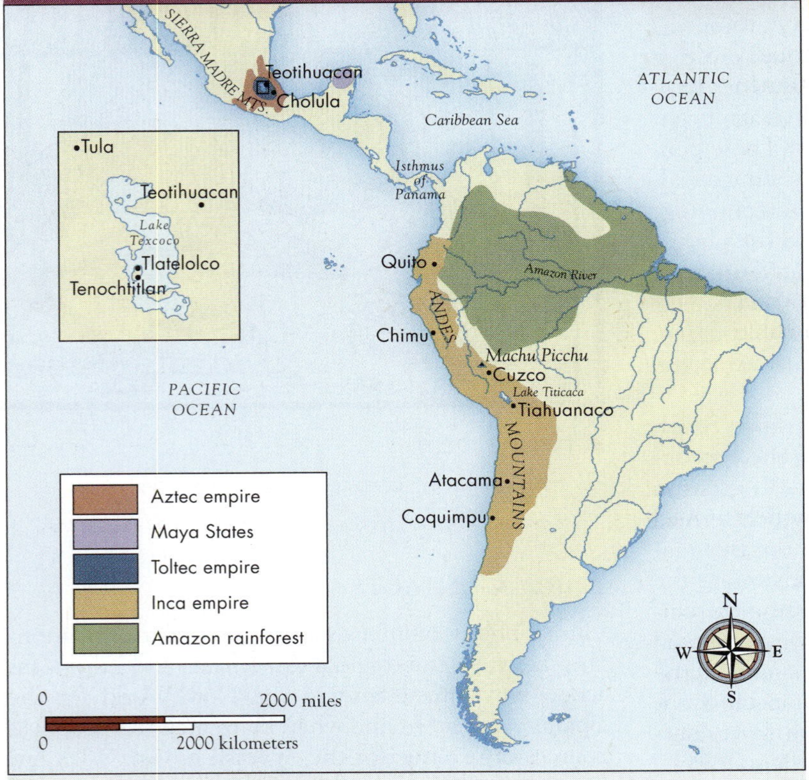

MAP 12.3   INDIGENOUS EMPIRES IN THE AMERICAS, CA. 1500

This map shows the locations of the Inca and Aztec Empires in North and South America. ■ **Notice** how distant the Inca Empire is from the Aztec and Maya in Mesoamerica. **How** might these distances and geographic barriers have contributed to the striking differences among these populations?

---

me two or three days." His account of hunger, hospitality, and warfare among the Amerindians shaped many Europeans' views of the original Americans.

An English chronicler observed more prosperous, but equally generous, tribes in what would become the colony of North Carolina. In 1584, Arthur Barlow accompanied an expedition that established excellent relations with the tribes—trading goods and hospitality with these "very handsome and goodly people, in their behavior as mannerly and civil as any of Europe."

We are also fortunate to have a visual record of this tribe of agriculturists, for an artist, John White, accompanied three voyages to this colony of Roanoke. White's detailed watercolors were copied by an engraver in the Netherlands and published in 1590; they remain an excellent source of information about life in some North American tribes before the impact of Europeans. The village White portrays in Figure 12.7 is prosperous and orderly and shows the abundant food available. In the upper left of the etching, Amerindians hunt deer. In the hut at the upper right, a watchman makes "continual cries and noise" to frighten animals and birds from the fields, which grow maize and pumpkins on the right and tobacco in the circular field on the left. Villagers celebrate the abundance by dancing (lower right) and feasting (center).

Amerindians

However, within a few years, relations between Europeans and Amerindians had soured, and the attractive village White painted was destroyed. As a subsequent chronicler of the new colony wrote, "Their amicable relations with the natives were now to receive a rude shock, from which they never recovered." An Amerindian stole a silver cup, and although he returned it, the colonists wanted to teach a lesson about property. "For this enormous offence the English burned the town and barbarously destroyed the growing corn." Strife like this was repeated many times, and the two cultures that newly confronted each other beginning in the sixteenth century would engage in increasing conflict.

Deteriorating relations

---

southwest North America. For eight years, they wandered among the southern nomadic tribes until they encountered a Spanish colony in 1536. Cabeza de Vaca wrote of his experiences shortly after his return to Spain, and his narrative stimulated interest in the New World.

North American contacts

Cabeza de Vaca told most profoundly about the scarcity of food among these tribes of the Southwest, who lived on cactus fruit and game. The Spaniards were welcomed, and they worked side by side with the tribes they visited. The author wrote how he was pleased to be given an animal hide to scrape and tan for leather, for he "scraped it very deep in order to eat the parings, which would last

food

problems

CONQUEST OF THE GREAT EMPIRES, 1520–1550

While in the Caribbean, the Spanish explorer Hernando Cortés (1485–1547) heard of a fabulously rich society to the west. Their curiosity aroused, he and 600 men sailed across the Gulf of Mexico in search of gold and glory. These Spanish soldiers of fortune were known as **conquistadors.** When Cortés landed on the Yucatan peninsula in southeast Mexico, the people he met there told him of a wealthy civilization in the interior (the Aztecs). As Cortés moved inland, he acquired a gift that proved more valuable to his quest than anything else—the slave woman Malinche.

Cortés's explorations

According to later Spanish sources, Malinche was a princess whose father had died when she was young. The girl's mother gave her to local slave traders when the mother remarried, and the traders included the young woman in their gifts to Cortés. Malinche spoke four Amerindian languages, including the Nahuatl of the Aztecs, and she easily learned Spanish. She converted to Christianity and took the baptismal name of Marina. Malinche was constantly at Cortés's side, interpreting and advising him on matters of policy and customs as he made his way west. The various peoples they encountered on their journey recognized her importance, calling Cortés "Malinche's Captain."

Eventually Cortés's group marched 250 miles into the interior of Mexico and reached the Aztec capital of Tenochtitlán. There, Cortés and Malinche met with Montezuma II (1502–1520), the Aztec emperor. Figure 12.8 depicts this meeting. This drawing was taken from a valuable cloth that was painted in the mid-sixteenth century by a Mexican tribe that helped Cortés conquer the Aztecs. (Unfortunately, the original cloth has disappeared, but a copy was made in Mexico in the eighteenth century.)

Confronting the Aztecs

By skilled use of images, the painter emphasized the role of Malinche in the conquest. In the illustration, Cortés and Malinche use the same gesture, showing that they speak with one voice. Montezuma sits in state, his nobles standing behind him. The Aztecs have gathered gifts for Cortés, drawn at the bottom of the page. The illustration foreshadows the coming European conquest: In the center of the picture the Aztec royal headdress moves toward Cortés; in the upper-right corner, the hand of God reaches down to bless the proceedings.

Cortés knew that to transport the riches of the Aztecs back to Spain, he first had to vanquish this

■ FIGURE 12.6

Aztec human sacrifice, ca. 1570, in the *Codex Magliabecchiano*.

■ FIGURE 12.7

Amerindian village in North America. Theodore DeBry, *Grands et Petits Voyages*, 1590.

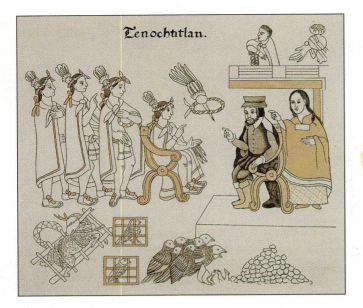

FIGURE 12.8

Cortés and Malinche meet Montezuma. *Lecuzo de Tlaxcala,* sixteenth century, copied in eighteenth century.

mighty civilization. With the help of Malinche, he garnered the support of nearly 100,000 people from neighboring tribes who were eager to throw off the Aztec yoke. Even with the advantage of gunpowder, armor, horses, and fierce dogs, it took him nearly a year to subdue the empire, and contemporary witnesses captured the violence of the struggle. Bernal Díaz del Castillo described the capture of the last stronghold: "I have read of the destruction of Jerusalem, but I know not if that slaughter was more fearful than this—the earth, the lagoons, and the buttresses were full of corpses and the stench was more than any man could bear." In 1522, Cortés proclaimed the Aztec Empire "New Spain," and he prepared to rule. Although he had fathered a son with Malinche, he gave her as a bride to one of his soldiers and presented her with expensive estates to thank her for her help.

The Inca Empire fell to another conquistador, Francisco Pizarro (ca. 1475–1541). In 1532, Pizarro landed on the west coast of South America and began to march to Cuzco, the Incan capital. (See Global Connections box.) The Inca rulers had just endured a five-year civil war over a disputed succession, and the newly victorious ruler, Atahualpa, apparently underestimated the Spanish. Atahualpa came unguarded to meet with Pizarro, and he was promptly captured. He offered a roomful of gold as his ransom, which the Spanish accepted. After collecting the ransom, they killed their hostage. The Incas fought fiercely for a few years after the fall of their leader, but they were

Aztecs conquered

Incas conquered

unable to overcome the Spanish technical advantages. A new order arose in South America.

How did these small numbers of Europeans manage to conquer the impressive Amerindian empires? They gained a clear advantage from their steel weapons, horses, and high organization (including writing, which allowed them to communicate effectively). However, in the long run, their greatest weapon was biological—germs they brought from Europe. When previously isolated populations mingle, it is common for epidemics to break out, but the confrontation between Europeans and Amerindians was particularly devastating because the New World had no history of interaction with domesticated animals. The most devastating acute diseases that Eurasians faced came initially from their animals: measles, tuberculosis, flu, whooping cough, and perhaps most deadly, smallpox. With thousands of years of exposure to these diseases, Europeans had developed immunities. Amerindians had not. In what turned out to be a biological tragedy that clinched the European conquest, disease and death followed the colonists everywhere they ventured. As one Huron woman said of the Jesuit missionaries, "They set themselves up in a village where everyone is feeling fine; no sooner are they there but everyone dies except for three or four people. They move to another place, and the same thing happens."

Germs

LIFE AND DEATH UNDER EUROPEAN RULE, 1550–1700

The goal of the newly established European colonial empires was to enrich the home countries. To meet this aim, the colonists exploited natural resources and Amerindian peoples to their fullest. The Spanish crown divided up the lands, placing "viceroys" in charge of each section. These royal representatives were responsible for delivering to the crown the profits taken from the new lands. The crown claimed one-fifth of all gold and silver mined in the New World, and the treasure ships departed the coasts of the Americas heavily laden.

To get the human labor he needed to search and mine for precious metals, Christopher Columbus proposed enslaving the native peoples. Queen Isabella rejected the plan, for she considered the New World peoples her subjects. Instead, the Spanish developed a new structure, called the encomienda system, to provide the conquerors with labor. Under this system, the crown would grant an encomienda, which gave conquistadors and their successors the right to the labor of a certain number of Amerindians. Theoretically, in exchange for labor, the Spanish owed the natives protection and an introduction to the Christian faith.

Enforced labor

The Inca Empire Falls

CONSIDER

■ **Consider** *how technological differences between the Incas and the Spanish contributed to the brutality of the Spanish rule.*
Notice *how internal problems and Spanish military technology led to the Incas' defeat.*

Ten years after Hernando Cortés had sailed from Spain and conquered the Aztec Empire in Mexico in 1521, another conquistador, Francisco Pizarro, set off to seek his own fortune in the New World. He landed on the west coast of South America—which included the 2,500-mile border of the mountainous Inca Empire. (See Map 12.3.) The Inca ruler used a hierarchic bureaucracy to govern a population of about 11.5 million peasants.

Before Pizarro even landed in South America, the great Inca Empire had endured deep troubles. Powerful earthquakes accompanied by giant waves had pounded the coast. Lightning had struck the palace of Huayna Capac. Messengers had also told Huayna that strange beings with beards had landed on the coast. In the midst of these disasters, the ruler remembered a prophecy claiming that during the reign of the twelfth ruler, strange men would invade and destroy the empire. Huayna was the eleventh. On his deathbed, he purportedly advised his subjects to submit to the newcomers, who would surely arrive soon in fulfillment of the prophecy.

But the empire's ruling house had suffered other problems as well. Civil war between two half brothers over the succession erupted after the death of Huayna Capac. Atahualpa, Huayna's illegitimate son, challenged Huascar, the legitimate heir. In 1533, Atahualpa captured Huascar, but resistance to Atahualpa's rule continued in the region of Cuzco. (See Map 12.3.) At this volatile moment, Pizarro arrived. Some of Huascar's supporters claimed that their god, Viracochas, had sent the armed men to place Huascar on the throne. This account of Inca beliefs on the eve of Pizarro's conquest was recorded in the early sixteenth century by the conquerors themselves. Historians have used it in part to explain how Pizarro—with a force of only 62 mounted men and 106 foot soldiers—could overwhelm between 100,000 and 400,000 armed Incas. Yet, it was neither their fatalism nor Pizarro's temporary alliance with Huascar that gave the Spanish the advantage; it was their technological superiority.

In the sixteenth century, warfare had honed both the weapons and the tactical skills of the Spanish. Their horses made a huge difference, adding power and reach to the mounted soldier. Pizarro wrote that the horsemen "did all the fighting, because the . . . Indians hold the footsoldiers in slight account." Furthermore, the Spanish fighters' steel swords, spears, and pikes so outmatched the Incas' most effective weapon, the sling, that the armored invaders could engage many Indians without much fear of injury themselves. Yet, even with these advantages, the Spanish took seven years to fully conquer the extensive empire. Despite the Incas' lack of advanced weaponry, they quickly assessed the Spanish tactics and bravely exploited what weaknesses they could find.

Due to the cultural and technological chasm between the Spanish and the Incas, the conquest took on unprecedented brutality. One conquistador wrote, "I can bear witness that this is the most dreadful and cruel war in the world. For between Christians and Muslims there is some well-feeling. . . But in this Indian war there is no such feeling on either side. They give each other the cruelest deaths they can imagine." After finally crushing the Incas, the Spanish had little inclination to treat their captives with any humanity. The early Spanish rule—with its forced labor programs—proved as brutal as the conquest itself.

The encomiendas lasted only through the sixteenth century, but this system was replaced by other forms of labor servitude, like the *repartimiento*, which required adult males to devote a certain number of days of labor annually to Spanish economic enterprises, such as plantations (called haciendas) or mines. Sometimes these contracts stipulated a lifetime of labor (though the subject peoples remained personally free); other times, the Amerindians had to work for the Spanish for a fixed number of years. Life under these contracts proved extremely harsh—hard labor and shortage of food—and many laborers died while working for their new overseers.

For the Spanish, the arrangement yielded untold wealth, exemplified by the silver mine in Bolivia—the Potosí—shown in the painting in Figure 12.9. In the background of this picture, workers and pack-trains climb steep peaks that lead to the veins of ore. The workers' homes are shown in the middle of the painting. In the foreground, other local Amerindians process the ore. First they watch a hydraulic wheel crush the raw ore; then they pound the ore with large hammers until it is reduced to powder. The waterwheel is fed by long canals that convey melting snow and rainwater from the mountain. The last step in the process was to mix the ore with mercury and convert it into a paste. This technique, brought from Europe in 1557, increased silver production tenfold. From 1580 to 1620, the great age of Spanish imperialism was financed by the silver extracted primarily from the Potosí mine.

■ FIGURE 12.9

The Potosí silver mine in Bolivia, ca. 1584.

Figure 12.9 also hints at the amount of work necessary to run sixteenth-century mines and the reason that the mine owners saw the enforced labor of the locals as essential. The Spanish crown gave the mine owners of the Potosí the conscripted labor of 13,300 Amerindians. These workers had to report to the mine on Monday morning and toil underground until Saturday evening. The mine owners did not provide meals; throughout the work week, the men's wives had to bring them food. Many workers perished under the inhumane conditions.

Not everyone accepted this colonial brutality as a natural consequence of the need for silver. The most severe critic among these was the Dominican friar Bartolomé de Las Casas (1474–1566). In his book *The Tears of the Indians,* Las Casas wrote: "There is nothing more detestable or more cruel, than the tyranny which the Spaniards use toward the Indian." Historians have disagreed about the exact number of lives lost in the Spanish domination of Central and South America, but all the estimates are shocking. Diseases, overwork, and warfare took a terrible toll on indigenous people everywhere in the New World. When Columbus landed in 1492, for example, the population of the Caribbean Islands was about 6,000,000 people, and fifty years later, it numbered only a few thousand. The native population of Peru fell from about 1,250,000 in 1570 to just 500,000 in 1620. Mexico fared worse: About 24 million native individuals died between 1519 and 1605. Many fell victim to diseases, overwork, and the abuse

Amerindian mortality

that Las Casas had described. Some Europeans abhorred this destruction, but many saw it as merely a source of worry about where to get enough labor to work their mines and the plantations.

In another tragic turn of events, Las Casas proposed a solution that he thought might free the native workers from their burden of labor. He suggested that the king of Spain offer Spanish men and women a license to settle in the New World. In addition to land, each license would give permission for the holder to import a dozen African slaves to the Americas. In his old age, Las Casas recognized the problems with this policy. To his regret, the plan brought a shameful new injustice to the New World: the African slave trade.

THE AFRICAN SLAVE TRADE

By the beginning of the seventeenth century, the new rulers in the Americas were facing alarming labor shortages. The original Americans had died in huge numbers just as colonists stepped up the need for labor in their profitable enterprises. As we saw earlier, mining required countless workers. The sprawling plantations built to exploit demand for new crops also desperately depended on large numbers of ill-paid workers.

Sugar is the overriding example. Although sugarcane grew in Egypt and North Africa, it remained scarce and expensive. Europeans discovered that the cane flourished in the New World and began to cultivate it avidly in hopes of satisfying the intense European craving for its sweet flavor. Sugar also fueled a new vice—the alcoholic beverages (like rum) that it helped make. Throughout the Caribbean and in Brazil, colonists established grand sugar plantations and began using African slaves to work them. On the plantations, like the one in Barbados shown in Figure 12.10, workers tended the sugarcane and harvested it with large, sharp knives—a practice that often led to serious injuries. Then the cane had to be crushed to extract its juice. In this illustration, the cane is crushed in the background with grindstones. In the center, the crushed cane is cooked in vats to produce molasses, and then the product is distilled into rum (in the lower left). The whole process was guided by overseers like the one in the foreground holding his stick to beat any recalcitrant slaves.

Sugar plantations

Sugar and other plantations (for example, cotton in North America) were designed to produce enough of their specified crop to satisfy a world market. Plantation owners took a consuming interest in the success of

■ FIGURE 12.10

Sugar plantation engraving, 1667.

these endeavors. Indeed, the German naturalist Maria Merian (see the Biography on page 399) wrote that she was ridiculed in the colony of Surinam, in South America, because she was interested in things other than sugar. This monoculture, or focus on a single crop, forced the plantations to trade with the rest of the world for all their remaining necessities, including labor.

As we saw in Chapter 10, slavery on a small scale began to be reintroduced into Europe during the Renaissance, and the sixteenth-century warfare escalating between Christians and Muslims stimulated even more enslavements in North Africa. For example, in 1627 Muslim pirates from the Mediterranean raided distant Iceland and enslaved nearly 400 descendants of the Vikings. Current studies suggest that between 1580 and 1680, some 850,000 Christian captives were enslaved in Muslim North Africa. Some of these captives who escaped or were ransomed engaged in their own slaving raids against Muslims as a form of revenge.

This growth of slavery between Christians and Muslims likely suggested to Europeans a solution for the labor shortages in the New World. *African slaves* In 1532, the first slave shipments departed from Africa to transport slaves directly across the Atlantic to the plantations of the West Indies and Brazil. Before 1650, only about 7,000 slaves annually crossed the Atlantic, but the figure doubled to about 14,000 between 1650 and 1675. Before the 1680s, the Atlantic slave trade almost

exclusively provided slaves for these sugar plantations. During the seventeenth century, blacks brought to North America came from the Caribbean, not directly from Africa—many had European surnames and knew a European language. A significant fraction of these early "servants for life" in North America became free, and some appear in the early records of the colonies (even in the South) as freeholders and voters. By the eighteenth century, the rise in plantations in North America caused slaves to be imported directly from Africa in large numbers (see Chapter 15).

The slave trade generated huge profits, not only for the Europeans, but also for African chiefs who supplied slaves to the traders. Because of long, but periodic, contact with Europe for millennia, Africans had substantial resistance to European disease, so they survived in larger numbers than the Amerindians had. Slavery had always been part of African warfare, and as early as the seventh century, Muslims profited from slaves brought across the Sahara Desert. However, in the sixteenth century the huge profits created a new scale of trade—chiefs traded slaves to the Europeans in exchange for guns to gain advantage over their traditional rivals. Some tribes (such as the Congo in central Africa) were initially opposed to the trade, but became heavily involved to stay competitive with their neighbors. *Impact in Africa*

The political consequences of the trade in Africa varied. In the kingdom of the Congo, the Portuguese quest for slaves weakened the monarchy and led to local warfare and a decentralization of power. In the military kingdom of Dahomey on the west coast of Africa, kings made the slave trade a royal monopoly and profited enormously. When the trade ended, however, the resulting economic depression in Dahomey led to severe political disturbance. Although this discussion shows it is possible to treat the slave trade as one more manifestation of the growing world economy, one cannot ignore the fact that the trade of human beings rendered incalculable costs in human misery.

By 1700, traders delivered about 30,000 slaves each year, and that number continued to escalate into the late eighteenth century. Packed tightly into the holds of ships and subjected to lack of food, water, and sanitary facilities, as many as 25 percent of these human beings died in transit. Anyone who survived the trip then faced new horrors: starvation and overwork and sometimes harsh physical discipline by their owners.

Some slaves ran away. In Brazil, in particular, many escapees fled into the forest and founded their own communities. The largest of the settlements was Palmares, which the Portuguese attacked in 1692 and destroyed three years later. Although it is impossible to get exact figures, it seems the community consisted of perhaps 10,000 fugitives who had formed a kingdom and designated a king and a council of elders. Other slaves devised more subtle forms of rebellion, including slow labor. In one interesting instance, an African woman in Surinam told the naturalist Maria Merian (see the Biography on page 395) that the slaves practiced birth control to avoid bringing children into slavery. Although we know that Africans practiced some birth control in Africa, we cannot know for sure that it took a new purpose under slavery, but it may have.

Slave rebellions

GATHERING SOULS IN THE NEW LANDS

Early explorers were partially motivated to travel by their desire to spread the Christian faith, and this desire only increased as Europeans found so many "heathens" around the world. Cultures all over the world became exposed to the Christian message. Many missionaries worked to alleviate the misery caused by the conquests, but others traveled from Europe with the zeal of crusaders and with the dogged insensitivity of the *conquistadors*. Some of them baptized natives in large groups, with no concern for their spiritual inclinations. Columbus and other early explorers, ignorant of native culture, wrote that the indigenous peoples had no religious sensibilities and thus should be easily converted. As a result, subsequent mission-

aries believed they were offering the benefits of religion to people who had none.

This attitude led to even further ill treatment of native peoples. In 1543, for example, the archbishop of "New Spain" (Mexico) tried 131 people for heresy, including 13 Aztecs, who he (rightly) believed practiced old forms of piety. In 1555, the Council of Mexico resolved not to ordain anyone of Indian, African, or mixed background—the priesthood was to be reserved for those of European descent. The suspicion extended even to churchmen sympathetic to native peoples. The Spanish crown had banned the writings of Bartolomé de Las Casas that decried Iberian treatment of Amerindians, and the Spanish Inquisition included them on its list of forbidden books.

A significant turning point in the conversion of the indigenous peoples of Mexico came in 1531, when a native convert named Juan Diego claimed to have seen the Virgin Mary. As Diego explained it, Mary had commanded him to build a church in her honor, and when he needed proof of this command, the Virgin ordered him to gather roses within his cloak and take them to the bishop. Although it was not the season for the flower, Diego claimed to have found them and when he unfolded his cloak in the presence of the bishop, all claimed to see a miraculously formed image of the Virgin Mary left on the cloak. The Virgin of Guadalupe (named for the region near Mexico City where she reportedly appeared) became the patroness of Mexico, and Juan Diego's cloak with the Virgin's image remains in her shrine, where pilgrims gather to see it. Figure 12.11 shows an eighteenth-century reproduction of the image on the cloak painted on wood. For many Mexicans, she lent credence to their belief that Christianity did not belong only to Europeans. Her shrine remains a major pilgrimage site today, and reproductions of the image have been widely circulated. Juan Diego, too, remained a venerated figure, and in 2002, he was declared a saint.

Virgin of Guadalupe

Some missionaries to the Americas proved acutely sensitive to the needs of the new converts and accommodated Christian practice to local religious ways. Las Casas was one such missionary; another was Marie de l'Incarnation (1599–ca. 1669), a French nun who founded a convent in Quebec to teach native Canadian girls. Marie not only cared for the young women who came to her convent, she also learned the Algonquin language and translated some religious writings into that language to make them accessible to the Algonquin-speaking peoples.

Missionaries

Missionaries generally paid more attention to the spiritual salvation of New World natives than to that of the African slaves brought to the Americas. A striking exception to this rule was the Portuguese missionary Pedro Claver (1580–1654), who has now been declared a Catholic saint. Claver settled in Colombia in 1610 and was horrified by the plight of the slaves who worked the plantations. From then on, whenever he signed his name, he added the vow "forever a servant to Africans." He lived up to that vow, converting many Africans to Christianity while caring for their physical needs. He even built and worked in a leper colony, caring for sick, neglected Africans.

Elsewhere across the world, European missionary work took on decidedly different forms than it did in the Americas. In Asia, the missionaries succeeded in their aims only after they acknowledged the validity and strengths of the local cultures. For example, some Jesuit priests in Japan adopted the status of Zen Buddhist priests and strictly observed Japanese etiquette. The Japanese were quite receptive to the missionaries, and by 1580, Jesuits claimed over 100,000 conversions in Japan. The goodwill ended in about 1600, when trade disputes unleashed a Japanese persecution of Christians that was so brutal it virtually stamped out Christianity on the island. The Jesuit Roberto de Nobili in 1605 carried this policy of religious accommodation to its logical extreme in India by dressing in the robes of an Indian holy man, studying Sanskrit, and refusing all contact with fellow Europeans.

The Chinese proved more suspicious of the westerners, at first denying them entry to their country. Nevertheless, a Jesuit—Matteo Ricci (1552–1610)—approached them with Western gifts (such as a mechanical clock) and gained admission to the court of the Ming emperor, Wan-li (r. 1573–1620). While practicing his faith at the Chinese court, Ricci adopted much that was Chinese. He dressed as a Confucian scholar, for example, and preached the Christian message in terms consistent with Chinese ethics. By 1605, 17 missionaries were working in China. Not all the missionaries working in China were as tolerant as Ricci, and many condemned Confucianism as paganism.

As Christianity spread around the world, Christian practice changed as it accommodated the needs of new converts. Mexican Christians, for example, venerated the dark-skinned image *Christianity transformed* of the Virgin of Guadalupe with a vigor unappreciated in Europe. Brazilian and Haitian converts worshiped in the Christian tradition, all the while acknowledging spiritual customs brought from Africa. Chinese Christians continued their practice of venerating ancestors, much to the chagrin of some European priests. In all these cases, the Catholic Church was itself transformed even as it transformed those around it. In time, Protestant worship, too, would be affected—the use of African rhythms in gospel music in modern North American churches offers one vivid example.

■ FIGURE 12.11

Pedro Antonio Fresquis, Image of the Virgin of Guadalupe, ca. 1790.

THE WORLD MARKET AND COMMERCIAL REVOLUTION

Europeans had long traded over extensive distances; after all, it was the spices and silks of the Far East that had first lured them across the Atlantic. During the twelfth and thirteenth centuries, Europeans had enjoyed a growing commerce (see Chapter 8), creating northern and southern trade routes that brought goods through the Middle East from the farthest reaches of Asia. These centuries introduced a commercial revolution that greatly expanded the opportunities for many in the growing towns of the Middle Ages. However, the disasters of the fourteenth century (see Chapter 9) put the brakes on this growth, and this commercial contraction lasted almost until

■ FIGURE 12.12

Jan Vermeer, *Young Woman with a Water Pitcher*, ca. 1664.

probably from the Orient. Both objects are set on a tablecloth of tapestry from India. The woman's clothing is made of oriental silk—an unusual luxury for everyday dress. Even the woman's movement to open a window suggests wealth, for expensive, leaded glass windows originally had been used only in churches. Vermeer completes this picture of prosperity with a leather map of the world hanging on the wall—a fitting symbol of the new global commerce.

What exactly stepped up the global demand for luxury goods? In part, the demand was fueled by population growth in the sixteenth and seventeenth centuries. During the sixteenth century, the number of Europeans expanded from about 80 million to 105 million as Europe recovered from the devastation of the Black Death. These increases continued. As the population steadily rose, goods became scarce. Demand intensified and drove prices up. In the sixteenth century, cereal prices escalated about fivefold, and the price of manufactured goods tripled. Contemporary witnesses repeatedly expressed shock at the inflation. As one sixteenth-century Spaniard lamented, "Today a pound of mutton costs as much as a whole sheep used to." People complained, but no one had concrete solutions to the problem.

Inflation

At mid-century, some Europeans began blaming the influx of precious metals from the New World for their inflation woes. Their frustration was understandable. The Potosí mine alone yielded millions of Spanish coins a year, which poured unchecked into the European economy, moving rapidly from one country to the next. As just one example of the interconnected economy, the massive Spanish ships that transported silver across the Atlantic depended on French canvas for their sails. Silver coins from the New World paid for those sails. As one French author wrote, "They may have the ships, but we have their wings." Economists can trace Spanish silver from Europe to as far as China, where European merchants snapped up the silks and spices that initially inspired the explorations. Yet the flood of coins into Europe was only part of the picture. In truth, the "price revolution" stemmed from a combination of the new money, a surge in population growth, and unprecedented appetites for new goods.

the middle of the sixteenth century. Now, the navigation of the seas and the exploration of new lands reopened and reshaped this pattern of production and commerce. By the end of the sixteenth century, Europeans were trading in a world market, on a scale larger than they had ever experienced.

HIGH PRICES AND PROFITS: TRADING ON THE WORLD STAGE

In Figure 12.12, the Dutch artist Jan Vermeer (1632–1676) captures some of the themes of this new commercial age. Vermeer painted many everyday scenes praising the tranquillity and order of the prosperous Netherlands. However, these serene images also testify to the bustling world market that made middle-class townspeople so wealthy. Indeed, the lifestyle hinted at in this painting would have been unimaginable in the Middle Ages. Vermeer depicts a young woman gently grasping a water pitcher. The pitcher is made of silver, possibly from the Potosí mine in Bolivia (see Figure 12.9). The jewel box to the right of the pitcher lies open, revealing pearls

THE RISE OF COMMERCIAL CAPITALISM

Inflation always hurts those with fixed incomes, but high prices also provide incentives for enterprising people to make a profit. The energetic sixteenth-century pursuit of trade stimulated new forms of pro-

■ DOCUMENT 12.2

✱ Thomas Mun Praises Trade

Thomas Mun (1571–1641) was a director in the East India Company, and in 1630 he wrote a "Discourse on England's Treasure by Foreign Trade," which was published in 1664. In this excerpt, Mun shows that he shared the mercantilist view that trade could enrich the kingdom. ■ **What** *benefits does Mun say will accompany a vigorous foreign trade?* ■ **What** *does he consider a favorable balance of trade?* **How** *are these views consistent with mercantilist thought, and* **how** *do they differ from your understanding of modern economic life?*

Although a Kingdom may be enriched by gifts received, or by purchase taken from some other Nations, yet these are things uncertain and of small consideration when they happen. The ordinary means therefore to increase our wealth and treasure is by Foreign Trade, wherein we must ever observe this rule: to sell more to strangers yearly than we consume of theirs in value. For suppose that when this Kingdom is plentifully served with the Cloth, Lead, Tin, Iron, Fish and other native commodities, we do yearly export the overplus to foreign countries to the value of twenty-two hundred thousand pounds; by which means we are enabled beyond the Seas to buy and bring in foreign wares for our use and Consumptions, to the value of twenty hundred thousand pounds: By this order duly kept in our trading, we may rest assured that the kingdom shall be enriched yearly two hundred thousand pounds, which must be brought to us in so much Treasure; because that part of our stock which is not returned to us in wares must necessarily be brought home in treasure. . . .

Let Princes oppress, Lawyers extort, Usurers bite, Prodigals wast, and lastly let Merchants carry out what money they shall have occasion to use in traffique. Yet all these actions can work no other effects in the course of trade than is declared in this discourse. For so much Treasure only will be brought in or carried out of a Commonwealth, as the foreign Trade doth over or under balance in value. And this must come to pass by a Necessity beyond all resistance. So that all other courses (which tend not to this end) howsoever they may seem to force money into a Kingdom for a time, yet are they (in the end) not only fruitless but also hurtful; they are like to violent flouds which bear down their banks, and suddenly remain dry again for want of waters.

Behold then the true form and worth of foreign trade, which is *The great Revenue of the King. The honour of the Kingdom. The Noble profession of the Merchant. The School of our Arts. The supply of our wants. The employment of our poor. The improvement of our Lands. The Nursery of our Mariners. The walls of the Kingdoms. The means of our Treasure. The Sinnews of our wars. The terror of our Enemies.* For all which great and weighty reasons, do so many well-governed States highly countenance the profession, and carefully cherish the action, not only with Policy to increase it, but also with power to protect it from all foreign injuries; because they know it is a Principal in Reason of State to maintain and defend that which doth support them and their estates.

Source: Thomas Mun, from *England's Treasure By Forraign Trade*, 1664, in *Modern History Sourcebook*, www.fordham.edu/halsall/mod/1664 mun-engtrade.html.

---

duction and economic concepts that together have been called the "commercial revolution," but might more accurately be termed a "commercial acceleration," during which trading practices developed in the Middle Ages spread and flourished. During this vital era, a set of business practices (and perceptions) arose that we know as capitalism. The word *capitalism* was actually not used until the nineteenth century. By the mid-seventeenth century, however, some individuals were called **capitalists,** a word indicating how they handled money. Capitalists were people who chose to invest their funds in business activities in order to make more money (capital). For these **entrepreneurs,** the most lucrative business opportunity was the growing world trade. Document 12.2 presents a seventeenth century testimonial on the benefits of this long-distance trade.

Dutch entrepreneurs led the way in implementing capitalist ideas as they engaged in worldwide trade. For example, merchants in Amsterdam built huge warehouses to store goods so that they could control supplies and keep prices high. Through new strategies like this and through individual initiative (rather **Capitalist ideas** than through government policy), the Netherlands became the leading commercial center in Europe in the sixteenth century. Indeed, it was this very success that generated the wealth depicted in the households painted by Vermeer.

Capitalist initiative gave rise to fluctuations in demand for goods. We can follow an early example of this economic cycle in the tulip industry. Tulips originally were imported into the Netherlands from Turkey, in the sixteenth century. A Dutch botanist discovered how to grow the many varied colors of this versatile flower. By 1634, buyers not only in the Netherlands but also all over Europe were so enthralled by the exotic and beautiful plants that one rare tulip bulb sold for 1,000 pounds of cheese, four oxen, eight pigs, twelve sheep, a bed, and a suit of clothes.

Investors rushed to take advantage of the lucrative tulip market and the supply of the bulbs ballooned. Three years later, however, the increased supply drove down the price, ruining many who had gambled on the rare flower. Novice capitalists learned the hard way about the cruel whims of the market economy.

People with moderate means also yearned to participate in promising financial ventures. To accommodate them, businesses built **Joint-stock companies** upon medieval concepts of trading partnerships and developed an innovative entity called the **joint-stock company.** This new economic structure allowed ordinary investors to buy shares in commercial ventures that were run by boards of directors. With successes in such investments, modest capitalists might generate enough money to set out on their own and gamble on higher-risk opportunities. These joint-stock companies made it easier to raise enough capital for trading ventures around the world. Amsterdam was the site of the first stock exchange, and enterprising people in the colony of New York began trading shares at a tree at the end of Wall Street.

In the seventeenth century, English and Dutch merchants formed exceptionally efficient joint-stock companies that helped them dominate trade in Asia: the English East India Company, founded in 1600, and the Dutch United East India Company, known by its initials VOC (*Vereenigde Oost-Indische Compagnie*), founded in 1602. Although both companies enjoyed government support, they were privately owned by merchant investors. Their charters granted them remarkable powers—they could buy, sell, and even wage war in the companies' interests. These companies immediately generated huge profits and both contributed to the early formation of a global network of trade.

MERCANTILISM: CONTROLLING THE BALANCE OF TRADE

With so much money at stake, western European governments attempted centralized regulation of their economies—**mercantilism**—to profit from the expanded global trade. Mer- **Economic nationalism** cantilism was based on the assumption that the amount of worldwide wealth was fixed, so countries competed to get a larger piece of the pie. This was essentially economic nationalism, in which governments controlled their economies to increase their acquisition of hard currency. The simple principle "buy low, sell high" led these governments to discourage imports, particularly expensive ones, and encourage exports. In 1586, one Spanish bureaucrat asked King Philip II to forbid the import of candles, glass trinkets, jewelry, cutlery, and other such items, because these sorts of "useless" luxuries drained away precious Spanish gold. Such policies aimed to create a favorable balance of trade and fill bank vaults with gold.

Mercantilist governments passed laws to ensure a favorable trade balance. They imposed tariffs on imports and discouraged manufacturing in their colonies to force them to buy exports from the home country. **Economic regulations** Thus, hard currency would flow from the colonies to enrich royal treasuries in Europe. In fact, mercantilist policy encouraged the founding of new colonies to create new markets to purchase European exports. When other things failed, governments debased their coins to try to maintain a favorable balance.

Some governments even tried to keep wages low so that citizens would have little discretionary income with which to buy expensive imports. All these efforts were meant to enrich the states, not the fortunes of wealthy citizens. Mercantilist policies placed the state before the individual. They achieved their goal, vastly enriching the powerful monarchies of western Europe. Sadly, they also financed the destructive wars that swept over Europe through the mid-seventeenth century (discussed in Chapter 11). Mercantilist economic policy would continue to shape government policy into the eighteenth century (as we will see in Chapter 15).

THE GROWTH OF BANKING

Neither private capitalism nor mercantilism could have succeeded without innovations in banking practices. Medieval ideas that forbade charging interest and that kept royal treasuries locked in chests in royal bedrooms had become obsolete. In this new age, people needed easier access to a lot of money, and they refined banking techniques that had been developed in the late Middle Ages in the Italian cities of the Renaissance. Medieval bankers had developed bills of exchange and complex account books to facilitate commerce, but in the late fifteenth century, bankers added checks, bank drafts, and sophisticated double-entry bookkeeping to their skills, all of which made commercial ventures easier than ever.

Through the sixteenth century, private bankers handled most financial transactions. The Fuggers of Germany were the most successful at this profession, taking over a role that the Medicis in Florence had dominated in the fifteenth century. The Fugger family became so wealthy **State banks** that they even lent money to Emperor Charles V. With the emergence of mercantilist ideas about economics serving the state, this kind of practice waned. Instead, government banks developed that controlled profits going to individuals. The Bank of Amsterdam was founded in 1609, followed by the Bank of Sweden in 1657, and the Bank of England in 1694. However, new banking policies could not ensure that even mercantilist governments would grow rich.

THE DANGER OF OVERSPENDING: SPAIN LEARNS A LESSON

At first, Europeans believed that the wealth flowing into Europe from the New World was the primary payoff from their explorations. Entire countries became rich, and imperial powers grew in previously unheard-of ways. Spain immediately capitalized on the new wealth, its treasure ships offering unlimited prosperity and power to the monarchs. Yet, the vast influx of silver was deceiving, and the Spanish king spent it wastefully on the incessant wars that dominated the sixteenth and early seventeenth centuries.

Consequently, the Spanish crown had to declare bankruptcy several times in the course of the sixteenth and seventeenth centuries. Spain's financial troubles hurt merchants in Germany and Italy, but the real burden fell on the Spanish taxpayers, who were soon saddled with debt. Instead of relieving their debt burdens, the politics of empire only added to them. Spanish domination of the New World passed to the governments of other countries (notably Holland and England) that proved more efficient in fiscal matters.

Ultimately, much of the gold and silver that motivated the expansionist countries did not even end up in Europe. A large percentage of this currency eventually flowed to the East for the purchase of luxury items. As Spain discovered, these precious metals were not enough to keep profligate governments in power.

REDEFINING WORK ROLES

The commercial revolution both enlarged the scale of business and redefined the way people viewed their work. While most people still worked the land, in the cities, which served as the nerve centers of the new economies, people experienced the most remarkable shifts in how they made their living. As the middle class rose to economic power on the dual waves of trade and hard work, the lives of urban women in particular diverged dramatically from earlier times. In the early Middle Ages, women had labored in the stores and workshops of Europe's cities. They dominated trades that they had controlled in the home—textile making and brewing, for example. Women had such a presence in these fields that feminine forms of certain words (ending in "ster") derived from these jobs—for instance, "webster" (from "weaver") and "brewster" (from "brewer")—arose and even became common surnames. Women also owned taverns in such numbers that an instruction manual written for merchants in 1515 assumed that the innkeeper would

Women's work

be a woman and gave instructions on "how to ask the *hostess* how much one has spent."

Still, women's access to the workforce came primarily through their families. Daughters, like most sons, mastered trades in the family workshops, just as Maria Merian (in the Biography on page 399) learned printing from her stepfather. Wives worked with their husbands, and widows frequently ran businesses and took their husbands' place in the guilds. During the late Middle Ages, men slowly began to replace women in some of the most lucrative jobs, like cloth making, and just as in banking and commercial enterprises, this late-medieval trend accelerated in the early modern period.

Into the sixteenth century, as work generated more capital and power, it began losing its association with the family and became more linked to the public political arena. Many people (women and men alike) believed that public work and control of money were more appropriately managed by men than women. Late in the sixteenth century, cities accordingly began to issue ordinances restricting women's entry into guilds, which had taken on markedly political overtones. For example, a ruling in France in 1583 limited silk-making apprentices (who had previously been predominantly female) to only two males per master. In another example, a 1508 ordinance in the Netherlands referred to a "brotherhood and sisterhood" of a guild, but the reissued ordinance in 1552 mentioned only a "brotherhood of trimmers." By 1563, when the ordinances were again revised, even widows' rights had been omitted.

Leaving the workforce

Similar examples emerged at local levels throughout Europe. As the commercial revolution spread and urban merchants grew powerful, the old divisions of those who worked and those who did not began to blur. Instead, the growing middle class began to divide the world between those who worked outside the home in the public, political arena, and those who worked inside the home. Urban women, relegated increasingly to the domestic sphere, lost much of their visibility in the public arena.

PIRACY: BANDITRY ON A WORLD SCALE, 1550–1700

The expansion of trade into the Atlantic and Pacific brought with it another nettlesome problem: a rise in piracy. Piracy was as old as Mediterranean shipping, when seagoing robbers had preyed mercilessly on the ponderous merchant roundships that moved goods through the inland sea. As the pace of the world economy quickened, pirates moved to take advantage. From about 1550 to about 1700, a "pirate belt" developed that stretched from the West Indies to East Asia. The new entrepreneurial raiding coincided with the weakening of the great Turkish, Spanish, and Chinese empires that we saw in Chapter 11, because these navies could no longer effectively patrol their territorial waters.

Piracy as a way of life actually had a somewhat benign origin—monarchs had often issued licenses for people to steal from other countries in unofficial warfare. Before the seventeenth century, the word *pirate* rarely appeared. Instead, seagoing raiders were called **privateers** or *corsairs,* terms meaning that they had the authorization of formal commissions from their rulers. Even as late as the eighteenth century, the United States Constitution gave Congress the right to issue letters of "marque and reprisal," essentially to hire pirate ships. Privateers earned their profits from captured booty, and in the freewheeling raids that took place on the open seas, it was impossible to distinguish them from pirates acting on their own. The ships that were robbed probably did not draw any distinction between the two.

Early privateers

The difficulties of discerning pirate from privateer may be seen in the famous early English privateers,

particularly Francis Drake (ca. 1540–1596). By 1571, Drake had become a major force in the Caribbean, and this champion of the British was considered a ruthless pirate by the Spanish. Drake had numerous bases on land and gained the admiration and support of unconquered Amerindians and Spanish-hating escaped slaves. With the backing and affection of Queen Elizabeth I (r. 1558–1603), Drake and his fellow privateers relentlessly harassed the Spanish ships they found sailing in the Caribbean.

The fortunes of Drake's compatriot, Walter Raleigh (ca. 1554–1618), showed how fragile royal support of these independent captains could be. Elizabeth backed Raleigh in his flamboyant enterprises, even knighting her champion. However, her successor, James I (r. 1603–1625) found the privateer less useful. As James began to have political difficulties with English Protestants, he sought an alliance with Spain (as we will see in Chapter 13). As a token of good will to Spain, James imprisoned Raleigh in the Tower of London and executed him in 1618.

Pirates included many Africans who had been captured as slaves, because after seizing wealthy slave-trading ships, pirates frequently gave the slaves the choice to continue on their way or join the pirate band. The eighteenth-century trial records of a pirate on the ship *Whydah* indicates that about 30 to 50 of the men on his ship were African and one was an Amerindian. The freedom of the pirate life drew many who had few choices elsewhere.

Pirate life

With all its hazards—from fickle royal supporters to war on the high seas—the pirate life could bring amazing riches even for those without a royal patron. Pirate cities sprang up based solely on the illicit trade. For example, Algiers in North Africa became a prosperous Muslim pirate city, and Malta in the Mediterranean was its Christian counterpart. Other pirate cities dotted the Caribbean from the coast of the Yucatán to the islands of the West Indies. These cities served as havens for the violent, reckless sea raiders and their families. They also were places where talented outsiders could rise to positions of considerable power. For example, a poor North African shepherd boy rose through the pirate ranks to become "king" of Algiers in 1569. During the eighteenth century, several women even took command of pirate ships.

By the mid-eighteenth century, however, governments began expanding their navies and set out to suppress the buccaneers. The British admiralty discouraged privateering because it lured sailors away from serving in the navy. The age of informal warfare came to a close and accounts of the bandits' careers retreated to literary works that romanticized their lives. For example, literary pirates made their victims walk the plank; real pirates would not have wasted

KEY DATES

EXPLORING THE WORLD

1492	Columbus sails to North America
1494	Treaty of Tordesillas
1497	John Cabot lands in North America
1498	Vasco da Gama rounds Africa
1499	Amerigo Vespucci maps New World
1514	Portuguese reach China
1519–1521	Magellan's crew circumnavigates globe
1522	Cortés conquers Aztec Empire
1531	Virgin of Guadalupe appears
1532	African slave trade begins
1532	Pizarro conquers Incan empire
1534	Jacques Cartier explores Canada
1577–1580	Francis Drake circumnavigates the world
1607	Jamestown colony founded
1620	English establish colony at Plymouth, Massachusetts

time on such rituals. If they wanted to kill their captives, they unceremoniously threw them overboard.

THE WORLD TRANSFORMED

The booming world market that stimulated the movement of goods and the enterprise of pirates also served to spread other aspects of European culture around the world. During the sixteenth century, more than 200,000 Spanish people, 10 percent of them women, migrated to Latin America. In the next century, comparable numbers of English, French, and Dutch settled in North America. These immigrants became a new ruling class that transfused much of European culture into the New World. They built cities featuring the grid pattern that marked Renaissance urban planning and placed their churches in the city centers.

EUROPEAN CULTURE SPREADS

The new immigrants brought their languages and religions, but also unique livestock, tools, plants, and other goods that transformed the lives of native peoples. When European horses escaped (or were stolen), for example, some indigenous peoples took them into their midst. The Plains Indians in the southwest of North America soon made horses central to their way of life. In time, guns, liquor, and many other goods also found their way into the many native cultures.

Plants from Europe, some of them intentionally cultivated, made their mark on the New World as
Plants well. For example, Europeans brought wheat to make the bread that had long served as their dietary staple. Along with their domesticated plants, they also transported their traditional farming methods. Figure 12.13 shows Amerindians cultivating wheat on a Spanish plantation. The laborers use the same kinds of tools, including the overburdened donkey in the lower-left corner, that their European peasant counterparts had employed.

Europeans unwittingly altered the ecology of the New World in many other ways. As we have seen, they brought diseases that ravaged native populations. Less destructive but equally ubiquitous, plants transported to the New World spread with vigor. A sixteenth-century Inca observer (Garcilaso de la Vega) described how quickly the ecology of Peru had been transformed by invasive plants: "Some of them are becoming mischievous, such as the mustard, mint, and camomile, which have spread. . . [and] the first endives and spinach multiplied in such a way that a horse could not force its way through them." Inadvertent transportation of weed seeds also displaced native species. Dandelions are a particularly apt example of a European weed that spread acciden-

■ FIGURE 12.13
Amerindians planting wheat in America.

tally as people, plants, and animals moved across the sea.

Europeans traveling and trading in Africa and Asia took New World plants to other regions of the world, transforming local consumption habits and economies. Africa, for example, received sweet potatoes and maize in the sixteenth century. In the Congo, the Portuguese introduced maize, although at first the tribes dismissed the vegetable as more suitable for pigs than human beings. In time, these plants became so central to the local culture that people no longer remembered that they were once strange imports. Because the societies of east Asia kept most Europeans at arm's length, they were less influenced by European culture than were the peoples of North and South America, and it would take several more centuries for European trade to exert its full impact in that region.

Finally, the populations themselves mixed as immigrants settled among native societies. Because European men greatly outnumbered women from their home continent, many of them married native and slave women or **Population mixing** kept them as concubines. Generations of children born of mixed background, called *mestizos*, preserved aspects of both their parents' cultures. These generations ultimately made the Americas vastly different from Europe in spite of common languages, religions, and political structures.

Festival Scene Painted on a Screen, Mexico, ca. 1650

■ FIGURE 12.14

Artists often have a particular talent for portraying life at a particular time, and this painting reveals the blending of cultures that took place in the villages of Mexico in the seventeenth century. ■ **What** features mark Spanish influence and which are Amerindian? ■ **Notice** the Spanish clothing worn by the Amerindians and mestizos spinning on the pole in the center in a traditional native celebration. ■ **Notice** the Spanish guitar being played by the native in the foreground. ■ **What** other festival features can you identify? ■ **Notice** the hazy Spanish castles in the background. **What** might the artist have intended by placing these features of his homeland in this picture? ■ **What** conclusions might you draw about the blending of cultures in Mexico from this painting?

Figure 12.14 reveals much about the cultural blending that marked the Americas.

EUROPEAN CULTURE TRANSFORMED

Europeans were as much transformed by contact with the New World as the original Americans were by their European conquerors. In one of the less savory examples of this exchange, the earliest explorers to the New World probably brought back a virulent form of syphilis. New archaeological excavations have revealed that some form of syphilis existed in Europe from classical times, but this new strain of the sexually transmitted disease ravaged Europe until the twentieth century, when the advent of penicillin offered a cure. The disease never took the kind of toll on Europeans that plagues such as smallpox and measles imposed on native populations. Nevertheless, its presence caused much misery and made some people more cautious about sexual activity.

New foods changed Europeans' diets and even the landscape. It is difficult to imagine Ireland without the hardy, nutritious potatoes that flourish today in that rocky land, but until the conquest of the Incas, the population of Ireland had to strug- *New foods* gle to sustain itself. The tomato—a New World fruit that people first rejected as poisonous—was eventually embraced as an aphrodisiac and became an often-used ingredient in European cuisine. Maize spread more slowly, for Europeans, like the Africans, did not initially view it as a food fit for humans. However, as early as 1500, it began thriving in Spain, from where it soon spread to Italy (near Venice) and eventually to the rest of Europe. Maize had immediate use as animal feed and peasant fare and allowed farming families to sell their more expensive wheat.

In addition to new staples, certain food stimulants from the Americas proved enormously popular in Europe. Chocolate, for example, came to Spain from Aztec Mexico in about 1520 in the form of loaves and tablets that were *New stimulants* boiled into a drink. A luxury at first, chocolate became a common beverage by the eighteenth century. Tea, too, had been a rare treat in the Middle Ages, when some traders brought small amounts from China. Over time, more and more Europeans developed an unquenchable thirst for tea, making the East India Company rich in the process.

Coffee appeared in Europe for the first time in the early seventeenth century and replaced tea and chocolate as the most popular stimulant drink. Coffee seems to have first come from Africa and then spread to the Muslim lands—it was in Mecca by 1511, and Istanbul in 1517. By 1615, coffee reached Venice, and merchants spread the product rapidly through Europe

Maria Sibylla Merian (1647–1717)

CONSIDER

■ **Notice** *how Merian's life exemplifies this exciting age that combined deep religious faith, world exploration, scientific curiosity, and astonishing opportunities for enterprising women and men.*

Maria Sibylla was born in Frankfurt, Germany, the daughter of a well-known engraver and publisher and his second wife, Johanna. Maria's father also had a keen interest in the explorations of the age. He published editions of *Grands et Petites Voyages*, which contained accounts of journeys to the New World (including the illustration shown in Figure 12.7). Although he died in 1650 when Maria was only three years old, she grew up to excel in the same fields that had so captivated her father. Maria's mother married a painter and art dealer, and the young girl cultivated her artistic interests and skills in her stepfather's workshop.

In her later years, Maria remembered acquiring an additional passion: "I have been concerned with the study of insects. This led me to collect all the caterpillars I could find in order to study their metamorphoses . . . and to work at my painter's art so that I could sketch them from life and represent them in lifelike colors."

Maria married Johann Andreas Graff, an artist and publisher, in 1665, and the couple had two daughters. Ten years later, she published her first book of copperplate engravings. This work consisted solely of illustrations of flowers and some insects. It contained no text but was used to provide patterns for artists and embroiderers, who preferred to work from an illustration rather than from life. This work established Merian's reputation as an artist and naturalist, and she was included in a contemporary book on German art.

Naturalist, Artist, and Traveler

A few years later, she published *Wonderful Transformation and Singular Flower-Food of Caterpillars*. This work contained her detailed observations and commentaries on the habits of caterpillars and was hailed as "amazing."

Yet Merian's scientific work was soon interrupted by dramatic changes in her personal life. In 1685, she was consumed with a fervor for religious renewal. With her elderly mother and two daughters, she joined a radical Protestant sect, the Labadists, in the Netherlands. The group established a community of the "elect," who held their property in common and lived in isolation from what they saw as a sinful world. When Merian's husband pleaded with her to return to him and bring home their daughters, she refused. He acquired a divorce and remarried.

After some years, the closed Labadist community must have felt too confining to the talented, curious Merian. She and her daughters left the group and settled in Amsterdam, the thriving port city that bustled with exotic goods and hummed with exciting tales of travel. Recognized for her previous work, Merian was welcomed into the circle of naturalists in Amsterdam.

Despite the attractions of her new life, Merian continued to find fascination in insects. In 1699, she and her daughter Dorothea sailed from Amsterdam to Surinam, the Dutch colony on the

■ FIGURE 12.15

Maria Sibylla Merian. Frontispiece to Merian *Der Rupsen*, 1717.

northern shore of South America. The Labadists had established a community there, but it had failed due to the hardships of the tropics. Merian might well have heard about Surinam during her earlier stay with the Labadists and decided to go there to study tropical insects, butterflies, and plants.

The devoted naturalist lived in Surinam for two years. With the help of Amerindians and African slaves, she collected thousands of specimens and made hundreds of drawings of plant and insect species unknown in Europe. In 1701, she returned to Amsterdam and several years later published *Metamorphosis of the Insects of Surinam* in both Dutch and Latin. Her drawings were praised as "the most beautiful work ever painted in America" (see Figure 12.16). Merian lived the rest of her days in Amsterdam, consulted by other naturalists and continuing to seek out interesting new caterpillar specimens. Her book remained widely read by naturalists well into the next century.

from there. Physicians praised the drink as medicinal for many ailments, from heart disease to "short breath, colds which attack the lungs, and worms." By the eighteenth century, coffee was so central to European society that even the social life of the West began to be centered at coffee shops.

But it was tobacco that made the biggest impression on European culture. Columbus saw Amerindians smoking it and brought the plant back home as an object of curiosity. Europeans cultivated tobacco at first for medicinal purposes—one sixteenth-century Parisian claimed that it cured all ills—and the plant then spread rapidly all over the world. By the mid-seventeenth century, it had reached as far as China, where virtually the entire population took up the smoking habit. The difficulties of planting tobacco also stimulated settlement expansion. Because the crop rapidly depletes the soil, in an age without chemical fertilizers colonists seeking to profit from the lucrative crop constantly had to annex and cultivate new lands.

Tobacco

The New World's reshaping of European culture unfolded slowly. New products became available gradually, whetting appetites for yet more novelties. The commercial revolution stimulated the movement of goods all over the world, creating more and more demand that fueled further explorations and commerce. Ironically, the demand for spices, and particularly pepper, that had originally served as the main force behind the voyages of exploration waned by the eighteenth century. Europeans had found other, more intriguing products to satisfy their restless desire for culinary novelties.

A NEW WORLDVIEW

When Europeans first set off across the seas, they had a false, though highly imaginative, view of what they would find. The world proved larger and far more diverse than they had ever imagined, and travelers began to study and write about the new reality. Amerigo Vespucci, the Italian mapmaker and chronicler we met earlier, wrote with awe in 1499 about New World flora: "The trees were so beautiful and so fragrant that we thought we were in a terrestrial paradise. Not one of those trees or its fruit was like those in our part of the globe." Such early descriptions were followed by more systematic studies in the seventeenth century. For example, in 1648 a Dutch prince sponsored an expedition that published the *Natural History of Brazil*, followed by many other books by naturalists cataloging the wonders of the Americas.

Scientific observations

■ FIGURE 12.16

Spiders and Ants on a Guava Tree. Maria Sibylla Merian, *Metamorphosis*, plate 18, ca. 1705.

Figure 12.16 shows an illustration from *Metamorphosis of the Insects of Surinam* by Maria Sibylla Merian (1647–1717) (see Biography). In this painstakingly rendered illustration, one can see both the detail that marked these kinds of studies and the artist's fascination with the exotic. Merian drew a guava tree (one of the fruits that Vespucci had found so strange) populated with spiders and ants. In the drawing, most of the spiders are eating ants. One of them, however, is shown attacking a nest of hummingbird eggs. Here Merian was illustrating a story told to her by the Surinam locals. (In fact, spider attacks on birds' nests are extremely rare.) This illustration, with its blend of careful attention to detail and elements of fantasy, typifies the European fascination with the newly discovered world.

The new maps created as explorers traveled the global coastlines and great rivers were almost as precise as the naturalists' drawings. These representations offered a much more realistic picture of the world than Ptolemy's map that guided Columbus. The map in Figure 12.17 shows the globe flattened out. This projection method, which let sailors plot

Mercator maps

■ FIGURE 12.17

Mercator projection of the world in 1608.

straight-line courses, was developed by the Flemish cartographer Gerhard Mercator (1512–1594), who first published in 1569. Many modern European maps are still based on this technique.

The **mercator projection** was a huge step forward in mapmaking, but it still allowed for some measure of geographic illusion. By flattening out the map and placing Europe in the center, mapmakers could not help distorting their graphic representation of the world. Greenland, for example, appears much larger than it is, India becomes smaller, and Asia is divided, thus seeming to have less mass than it really does. Not surprisingly, the Mercator map encouraged the illusion that Europeans occupied the center of the world. This idea shaped Europeans' future mapmaking techniques and their attitudes and actions toward the rest of the globe.

SUMMARY

By the early sixteenth century, Western culture was no longer contained within Europe. Lured by faith, fame, and fortune, Europeans sailed all over the world. They also settled in the new-found lands, conquering and colonizing the Americas and establishing trading posts in the East. Merchants and entrepreneurs followed the explorers and established a world market that stimulated the growth of commercial capitalism, new banking techniques, and widespread popular interest in economic opportunity. Some governments began to set economic policy and tried to control the flow of money to and from their countries.

In this great movement of peoples and confrontation of cultures, Europeans generated enormous wealth—and equally unprecedented misery. Native populations were virtually eliminated by warfare, disease, and abuse, and hundreds of thousands of Africans were enslaved and taken by force from their homelands. The resultant blending of peoples, ideas, and goods profoundly affected the entire world and whetted European appetites for yet more exploration and conquest.

KEY TERMS

quadrant, p. 376

astrolabe, p. 377

conquistadors, p. 385

encomienda, p. 386

hacienda, p. 387

capitalist, p. 393

entrepreneur, p. 393

joint-stock company, p. 394

mercantilism, p. 394

privateer, p. 396

mercator projection, p. 401

REVIEW, ANALYZE, AND ANTICIPATE

REVIEW THE PREVIOUS CHAPTER

Chapter 10—"A New Spirit in the West"—analyzed the revolution in thought that we have come to call the Renaissance, and in Chapter 11—"Alone Before God"—we saw how the new ideas were put into practice in religion. Chapter 11 also told the story of the struggles of European states as they competed with each other to claim superiority.

1. *Review the characteristics of Renaissance thought and consider how they contributed to the sixteenth-century interest in discovering previously unknown areas of the world.*

2. *Review the Chapter 11 discussion of sixteenth-century European warfare and religious reforms. How did these wars and reforms affect the global exploration that was occurring at the same time?*

ANALYZE THIS CHAPTER

Chapter 12—"Faith, Fortune, and Fame"—describes and analyzes the European explorations and conquests that spread Western culture around the world and, in turn, transformed Europe.

1. *Review the areas of Spanish and Portuguese exploration and consider where these early efforts forced England, France, and the Netherlands to focus their attention. Which areas turned out to be most profitable in the long run? Why?*

2. *Consider the complex relationship between technology, commercial exchange, and the lure of exploration and conquest and review how this relationship was expressed in this chapter.*

3. *What advantages did the Spanish have in their conquests in the New World? How did the Spanish perceptions of the natives shape their treatment of them?*

ANTICIPATE THE NEXT CHAPTER

Chapter 13—"The Struggle for Survival and Sovereignty"—returns to the events occurring on the European subcontinent and explores political and religious tensions as nobles struggled for power with kings claiming ever more privileges.

1. *As kings in the seventeenth century strive to exert control over their nobles, who might they ally with given the new wealth generated in the years of commercial revolution and discovery?*

2. *What social group do you think might develop an economic theory to challenge mercantilism? Why?*

BEYOND THE CLASSROOM

THE WORLD IMAGINED

Friedman, John Block. *The Monstrous Races in Medieval Art and Thought.* Cambridge, MA: Harvard University Press, 1981. The best study on this subject—scholarly, fascinating, and well illustrated.

Russell, Jeffrey B. *Inventing the Flat Earth: Columbus and Modern Historians.* Westport, CT: Greenwood, 1991. Studies the origin of the myth that only Columbus believed the earth was round.

THE WORLD DISCOVERED

Greenhill, Basil. *The Evolution of the Sailing Ship, 1250–1589.* Annapolis, MD: Naval Institute Press, 1996. A clear explanation of the technology of sailing ships that does not get bogged down in unduly technical language.

McNeill, William. *History of the Human Community,* 5th ed. Englewood Cliffs, NJ: Prentice Hall, 1996. A look at world history showing the complex interactions that have always marked our global society.

Subrahmanyam, Sanjay. *The Portuguese Empire in Asia, 1500–1700: A Political and Economic History.* New York: Longman, 1993. A comprehensive look at the economic and diplomatic history of the whole Portuguese Asian empire.

CONFRONTATION OF CULTURES

Berlin, Ira. *Many Thousands Gone.* Cambridge, MA: Harvard University Press, 1998. A sensitive study of the changing nature of the history of African-American slavery in mainland North America.

Diamond, Jared. *Guns, Germs, and Steel.* New York: W.W. Norton, 1997. A Pulitzer Prize–winning analysis of the interactions of cultures around the world that is utterly riveting.

Fagan, Brian M. *Clash of Cultures.* New York: W.H. Freeman, 1984. Concentrates on the first period of European exploration and settlement beginning in 1488.

Karlen, Arno. *Men and Microbes: Diseases and Plagues in History and Modern Times.* New York: Touchstone, 1996. A detailed look at the history of diseases, demonstrating how infections are always part of the changing natural and social human environment. Particularly strong on modern times.

Pagden, Anthony. *European Encounters with the New World: From Renaissance to Romanticism.* New Haven, CT: Yale University Press, 1993. A fascinating study of the ways in which European ideas were changed by encounters with the peoples of the New World.

Palmer, Colin. *The First Passage: Blacks in the Americas (1501–1617).* New York: Oxford University Publishing Press, 1995. A comprehensive study that includes differences among African cultures and the changes that went on in Africa as a result of the African diaspora.

Standard, David E. *American Holocaust: Columbus and the Conquest of the New World.* New York: Oxford University Press, 1993. Describes in horrible detail the mass destruction of the New World societies in the wake of European contact.

Thornton, John. *Africa and Africans in the Making of the Atlantic World, 1400–1680.* Cambridge: Cambridge University Press, 1992. Offers the controversial perspective that Africans were voluntary and active participants in the Atlantic world.

GLOBAL CONNECTIONS

Andrien, Kenneth J., and Rolena Adorno. *Transatlantic Encounters: Europeans and Andeans in the Sixteenth Century.* Berkeley: University of California Press, 1991. A particularly good analysis of the warfare of the period as well as economic conditions after the conquest.

Rostoworowski de Diez Canseco, Maria. *History of the Inca Realm*. Cambridge: Cambridge University Press, 1999. A thorough and readable account drawing from the latest scholarship.

Wachtgel, Nathan. *The Vision of the Vanquished: The Spanish Conquest of Peru Through Indian Eyes, 1530–1570*. New York: Barnes and Noble, 1971. A comprehensive, readable account sensitively drawn from the few sources giving the Indian point of view.

THE WORLD MARKET AND COMMERCIAL REVOLUTION

Braudel, Fernand. *Civilization and Capitalism, 15th to 18th Centuries*, 3 vols. Translated by S. Reynolds. New York: Harper & Row, 1981. A celebrated author's detailed economic history that analyzes patterns in European and world economy—particularly rich in details.

Magnusson, Lars. *Mercantilism: The Shaping of an Economic Language*. New York: Routledge, 1994. A book that directly deals with how nations could increase their wealth specifically through international trade.

Smith, Alan K. *Creating a World Economy: Merchant Capital, Colonialism and World Trade, 1400–1825*. Boulder, CO: Westview Press, 1991. Deals with the first world economy, an entity that was shaped by the emergence of merchant capital in early modern Europe.

THE WORLD TRANSFORMED

Crosby, A.W. *Ecological Imperialism: The Biological Expansion of Europe, 900–1900*. Cambridge: Cambridge University Press, 1986. Discusses the expansion of Europeans and the animals, weeds, and pathogens that accompanied them.

Davis, Natalie Zemon. *Women on the Margins: Three Seventeenth-Century Lives*. Cambridge, MA: Harvard University Press, 1997. Explores seventeenth-century culture through the lives of three women—a Catholic missionary, a Jewish storyteller, and the Protestant Merian (described in the chapter's Biography box).

Fuentes, Carlos. *The Buried Mirror: Reflections on Spain and the New World*. Boston: Houghton Mifflin, 1992. A fascinating essay by one of Mexico's greatest writers on the blending of cultures of Spain and the New World.

www.mhhe.com/sherman3

- Unfamiliar words? See our Glossary at the back of the book for pronunciation and definitions.

- Need help studying? See our web page for map exercises, practice quizzes, and additional study resources.

- Need help writing a paper? Access hundreds of primary documents, maps, images, and a guide to writing history papers on our Primary Source Investigator site at **www.mhhe.com/psi.**

CHARLES LEBRUN, *CHANCELLOR SEGUIER*

Chancellor Pierre Seguier (1588–1672) was an ambitious courtier to the French king Louis XIV, and a
member of France's new nobility that earned position by service to the crown, the noblesse de robe. In this
painting, Seguier's office is symbolized by the formal robes he wears, rather than by arms. Several well-
dressed pages surround him, one holding an umbrella over his head as if he were a minor monarch. His
face conveys a sense of pleased assurance with the position he has gained. Charles Lebrun (1619–1690),
like several other leading artists of the day, served as painter to Louis XIV and for eighteen years created
decorations for the king's Versailles palace.

THE STRUGGLE FOR SURVIVAL AND SOVEREIGNTY

EUROPE'S SOCIAL AND POLITICAL ORDER, 1600–1715

STUDY	Stresses in traditional society ▪ Absolutism in France ▪ The state in eastern Europe ▪ Constitutionalism in England and the Netherlands.
NOTICE	The intertwined struggles both in society and politics.

"This poor country is a horrible sight," wrote the abbess of a French town in January 1649. "[I]t is stripped of everything. The soldiers take possession of the farms . . . there are no more horses . . . the peasants are reduced to sleeping in the woods . . . and if they only had enough bread to half satisfy their hunger, they would indeed count themselves happy." France had just emerged a victor from the Thirty Years' War (discussed in Chapter 11) only to find itself embroiled in a series of internal revolts. These revolts, like many others erupting throughout Europe, signaled new strains on European society from the bottom to the top of the traditional order.

For the vast majority—peasants who worked the fields—pressures came from powers outside their control. The landowning aristocracy required service and obedience; governmental officials demanded ever more taxes and military service; and the impersonal forces that most people attributed to luck, fate, or God brought bad weather, failed harvests, and plagues. Sometimes peasants fled their aristocratic masters or turned violently against isolated governmental officials. However, against the fates and well-armed soldiers, they were powerless.

For those at the top of society, the pressures came from central governments and monarchs. Kings, struggling with the increasingly heavy burdens of war and governance, chipped away at aristocratic independence year after year. They argued that "the royal power is absolute. . . . The prince [king] need render account of his acts to no one." Elites insisted that "our privileges and liberties are our right and due inheritance, no less than our very lands and goods." This contention between monarch and aristocrat sometimes broke out in violence, at other times led to compromises, and often severely strained the elite order.

These two struggles—the first faced by the vast majority on the bottom, the second by the dominant elites on top—colored the West's social and political life during the seventeenth and early eighteenth centuries. This chapter follows these intertwined conflicts in four areas—France, eastern Europe, England, and the Netherlands—where the story took different turns.

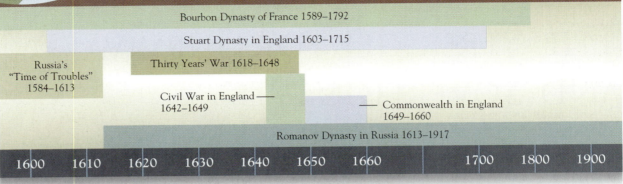

Bourbon Dynasty of France 1589–1792

Stuart Dynasty in England 1603–1715

Russia's "Time of Troubles" 1584–1613

Thirty Years' War 1618–1648

Civil War in England 1642–1649

Commonwealth in England 1649–1660

Romanov Dynasty in Russia 1613–1917

1600 1610 1620 1630 1640 1650 1660 1700 1800 1900

STRESSES IN TRADITIONAL SOCIETY

"IT IS NECESSARY THAT SOME command and others obey," explained a French judge and legal scholar in 1610. "Sovereign lords address their commands to the great; the great to the middling, the middling to the small, and the small to the people." This description captures the traditional social order that reigned in the West during the seventeenth century. Indeed, people took this order for granted. The structure was based on a hierarchy of ranks, and each rank, from nobility to peasantry, had its set status and occupations. Within each rank were subranks. For example, a hierarchy of titles and offices determined position among the nobility. Artisans divided themselves into masters, journeymen, and apprentices. Within the peasantry, landholders stood above laborers, and all looked down on serfs. Each rank distinguished itself through conventions, dress, duties, and etiquette. Finally, within all these ranks, position went hand in hand with family, itself ranked with men at the top, followed by women, and then children at the bottom.

Together the ranks made up the "body politic," with kings and nobles serving as the head and arms, and artisans and peasants as hands and feet. All worked together to perpetuate life as an organic whole. Everywhere, the church and religious sentiments sanctified this organic social hierarchy. Indeed, the social structure paralleled what Westerners saw as the larger, hierarchical order of the universe—the **Great Chain of Being.** In the Great Chain, everything—from God to the angels, humans, animals, and plants—existed in an ordered, permanent arrangement. During the seventeenth century, new forces tested the smooth running of this traditional society.

MOUNTING DEMANDS ON RURAL LIFE

Facing new demands from many quarters, rural life declined. At the beginning of the century, life for most Europeans typically centered on small, self-sufficient villages that contained a few to a hundred families. A church or manor served as the center of communal activities. Strangers attracted intense scrutiny, and most authorities were local people whom everyone knew. When bad harvests, plagues, or war struck, the villagers received little help from the outside.

The majority of people lived in crowded one-room houses made of timber, thatch, and mud, with one or two narrow windows. At one end of the house stood a stone hearth used for light, cooking, and heat. Wood and peat, which fired the stove, were often in short supply, and the villagers struggled to stay warm during the winters. Grain, in the form of black bread and porridge, made up most meals, though in some areas meat, vegetables, fruits, and dairy products supplemented diets. A few treasured pots, pans, and utensils served all.

In Figure 13.1, Louis le Nain (1593–1648), a French artist known for his realistic paintings of peasant life, shows a farmyard scene in rural France. The faces of these people express a grimness; clearly they have known hard times and would endure difficulties again and again. Many seventeenth-century Europeans were poorer even than those in this painting. According to one observer in 1696, "They suffer from exposure: winter and summer, three-fourths of them are dressed in nothing but half-rotting tattered linen, and wear throughout the year wooden shoes and no other covering for the foot."

As in past centuries, the family functioned as both a social and an economic unit. Women and men married for practical as well as sentimental reasons. The land, wealth, skills, and position one held counted for much in a potential marriage partner. Husband, wife, and children lived together, and most marriages, whether happy or not, lasted until death. At various times, relatives, domestics, and laborers might live for a while in the household. Finally, although everyone worked together in the fields, men generally did the heaviest work, while women gardened, raised poultry, and supervised dairy producing.

The family

Fathers, older children, and other relatives might also participate with mothers in raising and socializing young children. Nevertheless, children were not considered at the center of family life, and girls were less valued than boys. Indeed, parents often sent children away to other households to work as apprentices, domestics, or laborers if they could earn more there. Infant mortality ran high; of the five or more children to whom a woman was likely to give birth, only two or three lived beyond 5 years. Parents valued and cared for their children, but in a time of grinding poverty, it is not surprising that parents also viewed children as either assets or liabilities in the struggle for survival; great emotional entanglements with them were risky.

The stresses on these common people are strikingly revealed by the population decreases that occurred during the first half of the seventeenth century. The devastation from the seemingly endless wars took many lives, especially in German lands. The old enemies—poverty, disease, and famine—also roared through these decades. Unusually severe winters—advancing glaciers marked the 1600s as part of the "little ice age"—froze rivers and fields, and wet summers destroyed crops. Suffering, malnutrition, illness, and, too often, death followed. "The staple dish here consists of mice, which the inhabitants hunt, so desperate are they from hunger," reported provincial officials in northern France in 1651. "They devour roots which the animals cannot eat . . . not a day passes but at least 200 people die of famine in the two provinces."

Population changes

Bad times also meant postponed marriages, fewer births, and an increase in the number of deaths among infants and children. Europeans already married late compared to the rest of the world. On average, men waited until their late twenties to wed; women until their mid-twenties. Sometimes so many people died,

Louis le Nain, *The Cart*, 1641

■ FIGURE 13.1

This painting by Louis le Nain provides a glimpse of everyday life in rural France during the mid-seventeenth century. Here women and children of varying ages stand on a cart or tend a few animals. One woman sits with her baby on the ground; another has slung a large pot over her back, perhaps in preparation for gathering water. In the background stands a modest house. ■ **What** does this painting reveal about how these people spend their time? ■ **What** roles do women and children play in this rural economy? ■ **Why** do you think there are no men shown in this painting? ■ Considering his portrayal of the figures and details in this painting, **what** impression of rural life do you think the artist wanted to convey to viewers?

wandered away in search of food, or fled to the cities that whole villages were abandoned. Conditions improved a bit during the second half of the century, though only enough for the European population to maintain itself and perhaps grow slightly. Life expectancy, which varied by social class and region, was probably less than 30 years (in part, because of high infant mortality).

New demands from central governments cut into traditional patterns of rural life. With every new outbreak of war, governmental officials intruded more and more into villages in search of army conscripts. People resisted, and for good reason. Military service took men out of the fields, increasing the burden on

■ FIGURE 13.2

The rich noble, the poor peasant.

the women, children, and elderly who had to shoulder the men's share of the labor. Soldiers embroiled in nearby battles plundered what they could from the villages they passed.

Officials also came with new tax assessments, even though peasants already owed much to those above them. Traditional taxes to the government, tithes to the church, and rents to large landowners used up more than half of the already scant wealth peasants produced. Figure 13.2, a mid-seventeenth-century print, caustically depicts some of the peasants' grievances. On the left, the well-dressed noble sits authoritatively on his padded chair to receive the peasant ("thin as the noble's terrier"), who is bringing money in his right hand, fruits and vegetables in his left hand, and a sack of wheat at his feet. Above the noble is a spider and a fly caught in its web. As the caption on the lower left states, "The noble is the spider and the peasant the fly." The noble says, "You must pay or serve." The peasant can only reply, "To all masters, all honors."

Peasants avoided collectors and hid what assets they could. In countless incidents, peasants and city-dwellers across Europe rose against increasing taxes and attacked the hated collectors. In the 1630s, for example, French peasants rose against tax increases and forced temporary concessions from local officials, only to have those victories reversed by the state. Farther south, in 1647, women demanding more bread led riots that swept through the city of Palermo in Spanish-occupied

Tax revolts

Italy. Rebels in the city chanted, "down with taxes!" As in France, government forces eventually reversed early victories and crushed the revolt.

Other intrusions further eroded the traditional isolation that characterized rural life. Officials and merchants ventured more and more often to the countryside to buy grain for cities, creating food shortages in rural villages. Moreover, as members of the local nobility departed for capital cities and the king's court, new officials appeared and began administering affairs and rendering judgments in courts. For good or ill, villagers found themselves increasingly drawn into the web of national affairs.

PRESSURES ON THE UPPER ORDERS

Monarchs faced pressures of their own, especially the demands of war. In the competition for territory and status, kings won by fielding ever larger armies and mustering the resources needed to support them. During the seventeenth century, armies doubled and redoubled in size, as did the central governments that supported them (see Chapter 11). The costs of making war and supporting government increased accordingly. Governments devoted half or more of their income to the military, and monarchs desperate for money levied more and more taxes just to stay even. The ability to collect taxes could make or break a ruler. More than anything else, a king's unrelenting demands for more taxes sparked widespread resistance to his rule.

Competing centers of power added to the kings' problems. Independent town officials, church leaders, and provincial officials tried to hold on to their authority over local matters. Religious dissidents, for their part, guarded what independence they could. Finally, those who resented the royal tax collectors resisted the crown's reach. But the greatest threat to monarchical power came from aristocrats, who tried to retain as much of their social and economic dominance as possible. These nobles often challenged royal policies and decried royal "tyranny" as a violation of divine law. They guarded their traditional rights and local authority, and many of them refused to give up their tax exemptions. Should the crown falter, they stood ready to take back any powers they might have lost.

Competing centers of power

Monarchs argued with, fought, and schemed against these forms of opposition. They justified their power as a divine right, because they represented God on earth, and surrounded themselves with compliant advisors and admirers. As Document 13.1 reveals, their favored supporters, such as France's court preacher and royal tutor, Bishop Jacques Bossuet (1627–1704), backed them. Bossuet declared, "The whole state is included in him [the monarch], the will of all the people is enclosed within his own."

■ DOCUMENT 13.1

Bishop Bossuet Justifies Monarchical Absolutism

In their efforts to acquire as much power as possible, European monarchs and their supporters sought justifications for monarchical rights. One of the most explicit and influential justifications was written and preached by Jacques Bénigne Bossuet (1627–1704), a French bishop and tutor to the son of Louis XIV. In the following excerpt from his Politics Drawn from the Very Words of Holy Scripture, *Bossuet argues for the divine right of kings.* ■ **What,** *according to Bossuet, are the nature and properties of royal authority?* ■ **How** *does Bossuet justify the various qualities of royal authority?* ■ **How** *absolute is the power of kings?*

Article I

There are four characters or qualities essential to royal authority: First, royal authority is sacred; second, it is paternal; third, it is absolute; fourth, it is ruled by reason. . . .

Article II

Royal authority is sacred.

Proposition 1

God established kings as his ministers and rules peoples by them.

We have already seen that all power comes from God. "The prince," St. Paul adds, "is the minister of God to thee for good. But if thou do that which is evil, be afraid; for he beareth not the sword in vain; for he is the minister of God, a revenger to execute wrath upon him that doeth evil."

Thus princes act as ministers of God, and as his lieutenants on earth. It is by them that he exercises his rule. . . .

Proposition 2

The person of kings is sacred.

It thus appears that the person of kings is sacred and that to make an attempt on their lives is a sacrilege. . . .

The title of Christ is given to kings; and they are everywhere called christs, or the anointed of the lord. . . .

Proposition 3

The prince must provide for the needs of the people.

It is a royal right to provide for the needs of the people. He who undertakes it at the expense of the prince undertakes royalty: this is why it has been established. The obligation to care for the people is the foundation of all the rights that sovereigns have over their subjects. . . .

Article I

The royal authority is absolute.

. . . The prince is by his office the father of his people; he is placed by his grandeur above all petty interests; even more: all his grandeur and his natural interests are that the people shall be conserved, for once the people fail him he is no longer prince. There is thus nothing better than to give all the power of the state to him who has the greatest interest in the conservation and greatness of the state itself. . . .

Proposition 4

Kings are not by this above the laws. . . .

Kings therefore are subject like any others to the equity of the laws both because they must be just and because they owe to the people the example of protecting justice; but they are not subject to the penalties of the laws; or, as theology puts it, they are subject to the laws, not in terms of its coactive power but in terms of its directive power.

Source: J.B. Bossuet, *Politics Drawn from the Very Words of Holy Scripture* (1709), in *Western Societies, A Documentary History*, vol. II, Brian Tierney and Joan Scott (New York: McGraw-Hill, 1984), pp. 11–13.

Yet the kings used more than words and "yes-men" in this power struggle. Bypassing representative institutions, they sent their royal law courts into the provinces as a way to extend their authority. Sometimes they appointed new local leaders to gain allies. Other times, they attracted aristocrats from the provinces to the royal court, thereby creating a power vacuum that they then filled with their own men. When great nobles resisted being turned into obedient officials, rulers often turned to the lesser nobility or members of the wealthy middle class—men such as Chancellor Seguier, whom we met in the opening of this chapter on p. 400. Such royal servants received titles or land and were elevated to high office as compensation for their loyalty.

Women also became entwined in these struggles between monarchs and aristocrats. With the royal courts growing in size, many women became important friends and unofficial advisors to kings and influential aristocrats. They used their intelligence, wit, services, and advice to gain privileged positions in royal courts. There they won titles, offices, lands, money, and advantageous marriages for themselves and their families. Mothers encouraged their daughters not to let good marriage opportunities pass by. "It is true that [the proposed groom] is some fifteen years older than you," wrote one aristocratic mother in 1622. "[B]ut . . . you are going to marry a man . . . who has spent his life honorably at court and at the wars and has been granted considerable payments by the king." Royal mistresses also achieved important positions in the king's household. Françoise d'Aubigné (Marquise de Maintenon), mistress (and, secretly, wife) of France's king Louis XIV, influenced court appointments and founded a royal school for the daughters of impoverished nobles in 1686. Some mistresses even persuaded kings to acknowledge their children as "royal bastards" and grant them titles and privileges. This system of elevated royal authority has been called **royal absolutism** because the kings of the day commanded more loyalty, control, and resources than their predecessors had, and because they justified their right to rule as an absolute. However, no monarch gained true absolute power. Most people understood that even the strongest ruler, divinely ordained, was vaguely subject to tradition and law. As one seventeenth-century French jurist explained, the king's power "seems to place him above the law, . . . [but] his rank obliges him to subordinate his personal interests to the general good of the state." Further, with so many local centers of power, with scores of nobles who persisted in their independent ways, and with too much information to control, no king in this era could hope to dominate everything. Some monarchs even found themselves on losing ends of internal battles for power.

Royal absolutism

Royal Absolutism in France

In western Europe, the efforts of French kings to maximize their power exemplified the development of royal absolutism. Building upon the work of predecessors who had enhanced the power of the monarchy, Louis XIV (r. 1643–1715) took personal control of the French monarchy in 1661. By then, France had supplanted Spain as the most powerful nation in Europe. Under Louis' long rule, royal absolutism reached its peak and inspired other monarchs to emulate his style.

Henry IV Secures the Monarchy

French absolutism had its immediate roots in the reign of Henry IV (r. 1589–1610). When Henry IV ascended the French throne in 1589, his country had endured several decades of wars between Protestants and Catholics, combined with conflicts between different political factions. Law and order had broken down, and powerful nobles had reasserted their authority. The finances of the central government lay in disarray, and French prestige abroad had sunk to a low level.

The talented, witty Henry, in his prime at 36, set out to change all this. He defused the religious turmoil by issuing the Edict of Nantes (see Chapter 11), which granted to Huguenots (French Protestants) religious toleration and control of some two hundred fortified cities and towns as a guarantee against future oppression. He appealed to the traditional nobility by developing an image as a cultured warrior-king who could be trusted to enforce the law. He catered to rich lawyers, merchants, and landowners by selling new governmental offices, which often came with ennoblement as well as prestige. This growing elite became known as the nobility of the robe because their robes of office, rather than the arms borne by the traditional nobility of the sword, represented their power (see p. 404). Many of these nobles gladly paid annual fees for the right to pass their offices on to heirs. For the peasantry, Henry suggested that prosperity should bring "a chicken in the pot of every peasant for Sunday dinner." Not surprisingly, Henry's authority and popularity soared.

With the help of his able, methodical administrator, the duke of Sully (1560–1641), Henry also launched a comprehensive program of economic reconstruction. Agriculture and commerce benefited from the increased security of life and property brought by better law enforcement; from improved transportation facilitated by the repair of roads, bridges, and harbors; and from the freeing of trade, thanks to lower internal tariff barriers. The monarchy even subsidized and protected new industries that produced luxuries such as glass, porcelain, lace, silk, tapestries, fine leather, and textiles. Sully's efficient collection of taxes and administration of expenditures produced a rare budget surplus.

Henry also dreamed of making France secure from ambitious foreign states and of ensuring his country a supreme position in all of Europe. However, the powerful Spanish and Austrian Habsburgs on France's borders stood in his way. In 1610, he prepared to join his armies for a campaign against his rivals. Yet before he could set out, he was assassinated by a fanatic, and his plans died with him.

Richelieu Elevates Royal Authority

For several years after Henry's death, his Italian wife, Marie de Médicis (1573–1642), ruled as regent for their son, the young Louis XIII (r. 1610–1643). Marie kept opponents at arm's length, but made little headway in strengthening the position of the monarchy. Then in 1624, one of her favorite advisors, Cardinal Richelieu (1585–1642), became chief minister and began exercising power from behind the throne. Having come from a minor noble family and possessing a keen intellect, the arrogant and calculating Richelieu handled the young king deftly and controlled others through a skillful blend of patronage and punishment. His twofold policy was to make royal power supreme in France and to maneuver France into a position of dominance in Europe. To Louis XIII, Richelieu promised "to ruin the Huguenot party, to abase the pride of the nobles, to bring back all your subjects to their duty, and to elevate your name among foreign nations to the point where it belongs."

KEY DATES

THE POLITICS OF ABSOLUTISM

1533–1584	Reign of Ivan IV the Terrible in Russia
1589–1610	Reign of Henry IV in France
1640–1688	Reign of Frederick William in Prussia
1643–1715	Reign of Louis XIV in France
1648–1653	The Fronde in France
1683	Siege of Vienna by Ottoman forces
1685	Revocation of the Edict of Nantes in France
1688–1713	Reign of Frederick I in Prussia
1689–1725	Reign of Peter the Great in Russia
1713–1714	Peace of Utrecht
1721	Treaty of Nystad

With the royal army at his disposal, Richelieu boldly destroyed the castles of nobles who opposed the king; he disbanded their private armies and executed a number of the most recalcitrant among them. When Huguenot nobles in the southwest rebelled, Richelieu sent in the army and stripped the Huguenots of the special military and political privileges that Henry IV had granted them. Only their religious liberties remained intact. To dilute local centers of political power, the dynamic minister divided France into some thirty administrative districts, placing each under the control of a powerful *intendant,* who was an agent of the crown. He chose these intendants from the ranks of the middle class and recently ennobled people and shifted them around frequently, lest they become too sympathetic with their localities. Finally, Richelieu plunged France into the Thirty Years' War in Germany (see Chapter 11). His purpose was to weaken the Habsburgs, chief rivals of the French monarchs for European supremacy.

By the time of his death in 1642, Richelieu had firmly secured royal power in France and elevated France's position in Europe. Nevertheless, the imperious cardinal, having more than doubled taxes to promote his policies, had gained few friends. Far more French subjects rejoiced in his death than mourned his passing.

MAZARIN OVERCOMES THE OPPOSITION

Richelieu was succeeded by his protégé, Cardinal Jules Mazarin (1602–1661). Louis XIII's death in 1643, a few months after that of his great minister, left the throne to Louis XIV, a child of 5. Mazarin, who began his career as a gambler and diplomat, played the same role in the early reign of Louis XIV and his regent, Anne of Austria (1601–1666), that Richelieu had played during the reign of Louis XIII.

Early on, Mazarin, Anne, and the child-king faced a series of wide-ranging, uncoordinated revolts that forced them to flee Paris. Known collectively as the **Fronde** (the name of a child's slingshot game, which implied that the participants were childish), these revolts stemmed primarily from French subjects' objections to high taxes and increasing royal power. Between 1648 and 1653, ambitious nobles, footloose soldiers returning from war, urban artisans, and even some peasants fought the monarchy and its supporters in what amounted to a civil war at times. Bad harvests added to the chaos and suffering: "People massacre each other daily with every sort of cruelty," wrote an observer in 1652. "The soldiers steal from one another when they have denuded everyone else . . . all the armies are equally undisciplined and vie with one another in lawlessness." Nobles conspired and shifted alliances for their own gains, resulting in growing disillusionment with their cause. Gaining support from city-dwellers and peasants longing for peace, and shrewdly buying off one noble after another, Mazarin quashed the revolts by 1653. The crown gradually reasserted itself as the basis for order in France.

The Fronde

The Fronde was paralleled by other revolts during the 1640s in Spain, the Italian states, and much more seriously, in England. In each case, the catalysts included new taxes, the demand for more men and supplies for the military, and monarchies' efforts to acquire more power. In the Spanish provinces of Catalonia and Portugal, as well as in the Italian states of Naples and Sicily, rebels murdered tax officials, peasants took up arms, and local nobles joined the fray. Localities demanded and sometimes got concessions, but many of these victories proved short lived when the crown reasserted its authority. As we will see, matters grew much worse in England. Taken together, these mid-century rebellions served as a warning to monarchs not to push unpopular policies too far—and to the aristocracy not to underestimate the power of the crown.

THE SUN KING RISES

Upon Mazarin's death in 1661, the 23-year-old Louis XIV finally stepped forward to rule in his own right. "Up to this moment I have been pleased to entrust the government of my affairs to the late Cardinal," he announced. "It is now time that I govern them myself." With his regal bearing and stolid build, young Louis fit the part well. His lack of intellectual brilliance was offset by a sharp memory, a sense of responsibility, and a capacity for tedious work. "One reigns

■ DOCUMENT 13.2

Louis XIV Describes Monarchical Rights and Duties

For many, France's Louis XIV embodied the nearly all-powerful king—at least in his glorious appearance and style, if not always in his deeds. Louis XIV probably wielded more power than any other seventeenth-century European monarch. In the following excerpts from his writings, he describes his view of kingship to his son. ■ **In what ways,** *according to Louis, should a king take steps to maintain his authority?* ■ **How** *does Louis XIV justify the obedience owed to kings?*

"Homage is due to kings, and they do whatever they like. It certainly must be agreed that, however bad a prince may be, it is always a heinous crime for his subjects to rebel against him. He who gave men kings willed that they should be respected as His lieutenants, and reserved to Himself the right to question their conduct. It is His will that everyone who is born a subject should obey without qualification. This law, as clear as it is universal, was not made only for the sake of princes: it is also for the good of the people themselves. It is therefore the duty of kings to sustain by their own example the religion upon which they rely; and they must realize that, if their subjects see them plunged in vice or violence, they can hardly render to their person the respect due to their office, or recognize in them the living image of Him who is all-holy as well as almighty.

"It is a fine thing, a noble and enjoyable thing, to be a king. But it is not without its pains, its fatigues, and its troubles. One must work hard to reign. In working for the state, a king is working for himself. The good of the one is the glory of the other. When the state is prosperous, famous, and powerful, the king who is the cause of it is glorious; and he ought in consequence to have a larger share than others do of all that is most agreeable in life."

Source: J.M. Thompson, *Lectures on Foreign History, 1494–1789* (Oxford: Blackwell, 1956), pp. 172–174.

only by dint of hard work," he warned his own son. Haunted by childhood memories of fleeing in terror across the tiled rooftops of Paris during the Fronde revolts, he remained determined to prevent further challenges from rebellious aristocrats. By his mother, Mazarin, and a succession of tutors, Louis had been convinced that he was God's appointed deputy for France. Supporting him was the most famous exponent of royal absolutism, Bishop Bossuet, who argued that the monarchy "is sacred, it is paternal, it is absolute, and it is subject to reason . . . the royal throne is not that of a man but the throne of God Himself." As Document 13.2 indicates, Louis XIV learned these lessons well. In words commonly attributed to Louis, *"L'état, c'est moi"* ("I am the state").

However, Louis could not possibly perform all the functions of government personally. The great bulk of the details was handled by a series of councils and bureaus and administered locally by the intendants. Distrusting the traditional nobility, Louis instead usually appointed members of modest noble backgrounds to the important offices of his government. Well supervised by the industrious king, the administrative machinery hummed along.

To raise his stature, Louis XIV initiated massive public-works projects that glorified him, his government, and his reign. His greatest architectural project was a new palace. Hating the tumult of Paris, with its streets teeming with commoners, he selected Versailles, 11 miles southwest

Versailles

of the city, as the new seat of government. There, as many as 35,000 workmen toiled for more than forty years to turn marshes and sand into Europe's most splendid palace and grounds.

Figure 13.3 shows Versailles in 1668. Over the next forty-three years, successive teams of workers added rear gardens and more than doubled the size of the buildings. This painting, which shows the roads, paths, and gardens of Versailles geometrically laid out, gives a sense of the scale of the project. In the foreground to the right, the royal coach, with its train of followers, arrives at the front gates. The exterior of Versailles was designed in long, horizontal, classic lines. The interior boasted a lavish baroque style with richly colored marbles, mosaics, inlaid woods, gilt, silver, silk, velvet, and brocade. Ceiling-to-floor windows and mirrors and crystal chandeliers holding thousands of candles illuminated the salons and halls. In terms of sheer capacity, the palace could house 5,000 people and serve thousands more visitors each day. It faced hundreds of acres of groves, walks, canals, pools, terraces, fountains, statues, flower beds, and clipped shrubs—all laid out in formal geometric patterns symbolizing the triumph of engineering over nature. So dazzling was this hallmark of royal absolutism that other European monarchs soon attempted to copy it.

Louis used Versailles, images of himself, and symbols to enhance his authority among the nobility and everyone else. "The peoples over whom we reign, being unable to apprehend the basic reality of things,

■ FIGURE 13.3

Pierre Patel the Elder, *Versailles*, 1668.

usually derive their opinions from what they can see with their eyes," he explained. Figure 13.4, a painting by an anonymous seventeenth-century artist, shows Louis—in the center astride a white horse—as he rides into the gardens at Versailles. His favored courtiers throng around him, hoping to be seen by him and others more than to see him. Servants mingle in the crowd as well. Above is the king's chosen symbol, the sun, with its light radiating out. As Louis put it, "The symbol that I have adopted and that you see all around you represents the duties of a Prince . . . endlessly promoting life, joy and growth." It is "the most dazzling and most beautiful image of the monarch."

The "Sun King" finally moved to Versailles in 1682. Once established there, he lured the men and women of the nobility away from their local centers of power where they might make trouble and turned them into domesticated court "butterflies." He subjected them to a complex system of etiquette and favoritism that made every aspect of Louis' daily life the center of their concern. Court became a theater where those already in favor, as well as aspiring favorites, had to scheme for gifts, patronage, and position. Winners might secure lucrative rewards, and losers might spend themselves broke trying to stay in the race.

Despite the grandeur of Versailles, this glittering monument to royal absolutism had its critics. In her novel *The Princess of Clèves* (1678), the Countess de Lafayette complained that at Versailles "everybody was busily trying to better their position by pleasing, by helping, or by hindering somebody else." The court **Versailles' critics** reportedly seethed with gossip, scandal, and intrigue. Critics such as Pierre Jurieu, a French Calvinist pastor who fled to Holland, lamented that the king "is the idol to which are sacrificed princes, great men and small, families, provinces, cities, finances and generally everything." Resentful nobles once proudly drawing high status from their lands and lineage came to depend on the approval of and service to the king as the primary route to power. Many hard-toiling, heavily taxed French commoners also grumbled about living in the reflected glory of a pretentious monarch.

To enhance the glory of his court, Louis XIV subsidized and attracted to Versailles leading French artists and literary figures. The elegance, the sense of order, and the formalism of royalty all found expression in much of the **"Classical" literature** literature of this **classical style** in French culture. Pierre Corneille (1606–1684), for

■ FIGURE 13.4
Louis XIV on horseback at Versailles.

who like many nobles felt slighted and grew to resent the king, chronicled life at Versailles in his forty-volume *Memoirs*.

While the literature of the seventeenth century amused monarchs, the visual arts of the period positively glorified them. Kings and aristocrats still favored **Visual arts** the baroque style of painting and architecture (see Chapter 11). As they saw it, the baroque's swirling forms and massive, ornamental elegance perfectly reflected their wealth and power. Yet during the second half of the seventeenth century, classicism, with its emphasis on control and restraint, began to gain favor. The appealing paintings of French artists Claude Lorraine (1600–1682) and Nicolas Poussin (1594–1665) helped classicism win official approval in France. Both men spent much time in Italy, studying the Renaissance masters and the Italian landscape. Figure 13.5 embodies their style. In this painting, Lorraine has framed the foreground figures with trees under a radiant sky. The Italian landscape is geometrically balanced, the figures are in classic dress, and the scene exudes calm and discipline. Here is an idyllic vision, a scene designed to elevate the minds of viewers. Compared to the baroque, the classical style shows a logic that echoed the sense of order pervading the Versailles court of the Sun King.

Versailles, the arts, and all other aspects of government cost money. Louis assigned the talented Jean-Baptiste Colbert (1619–1683) to manage his finances. An engine of efficiency, Colbert toiled endlessly, supervising the details of the **Colbert** French economy while also promoting culture by founding the Royal Academy of Sciences in 1666 and subsidizing the arts. In keeping with his bourgeois origins, he chose service to the king as his means of advancement. His family shared in his success, becoming ministers, gaining high offices in the church, marrying well, and securing top positions in the military.

Promoting mercantilistic economic policies (see Chapter 12), Colbert protected industries with high tariffs while subsidizing exports and new industries. To encourage France's growing empire and the commerce it generated, he built a large navy. Finally, Colbert worked to ensure a worldwide reputation for the uniformly high quality of French products. He subjected manufacturing to the most minute regulation and supervision: So many threads of such and such quality and color must go into every inch of this textile and that lace. Although Colbert's restrictive mercantilistic controls in the long run stifled initiative and economic change, French products earned wide acclaim for their quality. By his death in 1683,

example, wrote elegant plays modeled on the ancient Greek tragedies. Human beings' conflicts with their own nature and with the workings of fate and the universe furnished the plots. Even more exquisite were the perfectly rhymed and metered couplets of Jean Racine's (1639–1699) dramas. Finally, in his profound comedies, Jean-Baptiste Molière (1622–1673) satirized pompous scholars, social climbers, false priests, and quack physicians. Louis and his court had little to fear from this literature. On the contrary, they appreciated its formal order and laughed along with other audiences at its satire, which was aimed at humankind in general rather than at specific ruling regimes.

At court and elsewhere, many members of the elite also read historical romances. Perhaps the most popular of these was *Grand Cyrus* by Madeleine de Scudéry (1608–1701), a writer who rose from an impoverished background. The fact that this book was published under the name of the author's brother, Georges, hints at the difficulties women faced in expressing their cultural talents. Other forms of literature included letters and memoirs. The courtier Madame de Sévigné (1626–1696), for example, wrote almost two thousand letters to her daughter that reported what the king said and did as well as news of marriages, deaths, gossip, fads, and conspiracies that marked life at the court of Louis XIV. The duke of Saint-Simon (1675–1755),

Colbert had balanced the budget and promoted relative prosperity despite Louis XIV's lavish expenditures.

During the following decades, however, Louis embarked on policies that undermined much of what Colbert had accomplished. The

Revocation of the Edict of Nantes king's demands for religious conformity and his military ambitions ranked among the most destructive of these policies. Huguenots (French Protestants) paid the highest price for his religious intolerance. In 1685, Louis revoked the Edict of Nantes, which in 1598 had granted tolerance to the Protestant minority. Then he outlawed Protestantism and ordered Protestant churches demolished. The duke of Saint-Simon lamented that the "ultimate results [of the reversal] were the depopulation of a fourth part of the kingdom and the ruin of our commerce . . . the country was given over to the authorized ravages of dragoons [armed troops], which caused the death of, literally, thousands of innocent people of all ages and both sexes." Although Huguenots were forbidden to emigrate, perhaps as many as 200,000 did, taking their wealth and skills with them to Protestant-friendly areas in Europe and America, "enriching them and causing their cities to flourish at the expense of France," according to Saint-Simon. Up to a million Huguenots who remained in France went underground.

Nor was Louis content to rule in peace as the leader of Europe's most powerful nation. During the last four

Wars of aggression decades of his 72-year reign, he fought four wars of aggression. The same old reasons prompted him to lead France into battle: more territory, more glory, and more wealth. He set his sights on the Spanish and Austrian Habsburg lands on France's eastern borders and on the Dutch, France's most powerful commercial rivals on the Continent. He put his war minister, the marquis of Louvois (1639–1691), in charge of organizing France's huge military establishment on the model of a complex business, replete with supply depots and hospitals. While Louvois introduced strict discipline, uniforms, and promotions based on merit, Sébastien de Vauban (1633–1707) designed sturdy fortifications and brilliant siege operations. It was a common saying that whereas a city defended by Vauban was safe, one besieged by Vauban was doomed. Louis initiated his foreign adventures in the War of Devolution (1667–1668), waged against Spain for French claims in the Spanish Netherlands and Franche-Comté (Burgundy). When victory seemed within reach, the United Provinces, England, and Sweden joined Spain to prevent France from upsetting the balance of power. The Treaty of Aix-la-Chapelle

■ FIGURE 13.5

Claude Lorraine, *The Marriage of Isaac and Rebekah (The Mill)*, 1640.

(1668) brought Louis only minor gains (see Map 13.1). In 1672, Louis turned against the Dutch, whom he blamed for organizing the alliance against him and who were France's chief trade competitors. The Dutch stopped the invading French only by opening the dikes and flooding the land. Dutch diplomacy brought Spain, Sweden, Brandenburg, and the Holy Roman Empire into an alliance against the French. Louis fought them to a standstill and gained some valuable territories in the Peace of Nijmegen (1679). In the following years, Louis made enemies of the Austrians by refusing to help in their war against the Turks, and he alienated Europe's Protestants by turning against the Huguenots. Fearful that he intended to upset the balance of power and dominate the Continent, much of Europe formed the Grand Alliance against him. The eight-year War of the League of Augsburg (1689–1697) gained France little territory at the cost of much bloodshed and misery. Louis' final struggle, the War of the Spanish Succession, was fought over French claims to the Spanish throne and the partition of Spanish holdings in the Netherlands and Italy. The war lasted eleven years (1702–1713), and the Grand Alliance defeated French and Spanish forces in a series of battles. Beaten, impoverished, and facing revolts fueled by despair and opposition to taxation, Louis XIV was forced to accept the Peace of Utrecht (1713), which ended Louis' ambitions to create a partnership of Bourbon monarchs in France and Spain—with France the senior partner. Map 13.1 depicts France in 1661, when Louis XIV took control of the monarchy, and the territories he eventually acquired. In the end, he possessed little more than what he had started with some fifty years earlier, and he had even fewer holdings in North America.

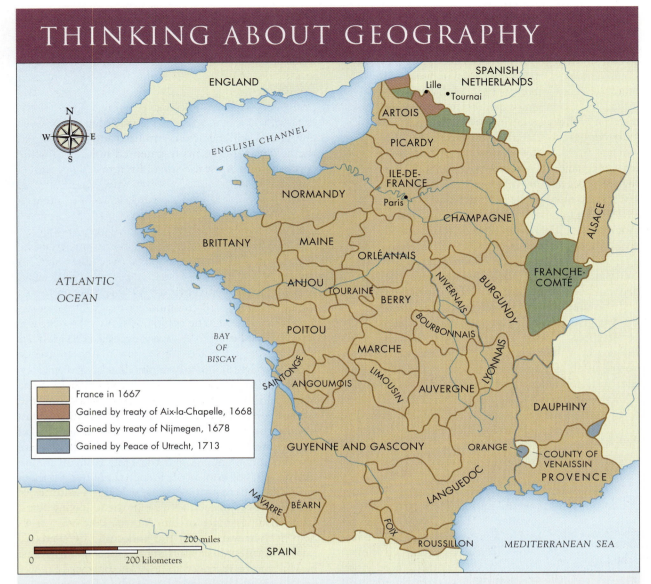

MAP 13.1   FRANCE UNDER LOUIS XIV, 1661–1715

This map shows France's provinces and the territorial gains it made during the reign of Louis XIV.
■ **Notice** that most of Louis' gains came from Spanish lands and German states on France's eastern border. **What** might this imply about vulnerable areas of Europe and changing power relationships?
■ **Consider** how little France's gains were despite almost endless, costly wars. **What** were the likely consequences for France's finances and the popularity of its monarch?

Louis XIV died only two years after the Peace of Utrecht. He had long outlived his popularity. One widely circulated letter from an aristocratic critic, Archbishop Fénélon, complained that "for thirty years, your principal ministers have . . . overthrown all the ancient maxims of the state in order to increase your authority beyond all bounds. . . . For the sake of getting and keeping vain conquests abroad, you have destroyed half the real strength of your own state."

As the coffin carrying Louis XIV's body was drawn through the streets of Paris, some of his abused subjects cursed his name.

The Sun King had built the French state into the envy of Europe, and his glittering court at Versailles outshone all others. His success relied on knowing how to use the old system, modified by preceding state-builders such as Richelieu, to his advantage. He tamed rather than fought the nobility, who at the same time remained the crown's most important ally and potent competitor. Clearly, strong central governments enjoyed advantages, and none were stronger than France's under Louis XIV. For many monarchs, France under Louis XIV became the model of absolutism. However his expenditures and wars created unprecedented misery for most commoners saddled with relentlessly rising taxes, more military service, and famines. Recognizing that the continued power of the state required some support of the people, Louis' successors would try to avoid his mistakes and ameliorate the worst threats to the lives of French people.

Assessing Louis XIV

THE STRUGGLE FOR SOVEREIGNTY IN EASTERN EUROPE

In eastern Europe, people struggled just as fiercely to survive and to define sovereignty as they did in the west. However, the two regions differed sharply, and those differences affected the outcomes of battles over these issues. States east of the Elbe River (see Map 13.2) were less commercially developed than those in western Europe. Instead of farms worked by legally free and mobile peasants, estate agriculture (large landed estates owned by lords and worked by their serfs) dominated those economies. By the sixteenth century, the nobles who owned these estates had reversed the medieval trends toward greater freedom for the peasantry and the growth of towns. Most people who worked the fields sank into serfdom, bound to the land and owing ever-increasing services to their lords. The middle classes in the towns also declined, failing to gain in numbers and wealth like their counterparts in western Europe. Finally, most central governments at the beginning of the seventeenth century proved weaker than those in western European states, as powerful nobles retained much independence. Despite all this, several monarchs decided to change things in their own favor.

CENTRALIZING THE STATE IN BRANDENBURG-PRUSSIA

In Brandenburg-Prussia, the "Great Elector" Frederick William (r. 1640–1688) inherited a scattered patchwork of poorly managed lands weakened by years of war and population decline. He faced a number of other problems as well. His army was tiny—too weak to keep foreign forces out of his lands or to discipline internal opponents. His nobles, or *Junkers*, had an independent streak and had found ways to avoid most taxes. Finally, his cities remained uncooperative, asserting their long-established political and economic independence.

Frederick William set out to correct the situation. He believed that the key was to strengthen his standing army. Only then could he gain control of his lands and make Brandenburg-Prussia a desired ally in international affairs. During the 1640s, he more than tripled the size of his army. This new strength and effective diplomacy won him several new territories at the end of the Thirty Years' War (see Map 13.2). With energy and skill, he next centralized and administered the governments of his fragmented holdings—while continuing to boost the size of his army. He prevailed over the Estates—the representative assemblies of the realm—and acquired the crucial authority to collect taxes. He then used his newly powerful army to enforce tax payments and organize state resources. In a pivotal compromise with landed aristocrats, he allowed them complete control over their serfs in return for support and service in his bureaucracy and army. Through mercantilistic policies, he protected industries, improved communications, and promoted agriculture. Though he could not afford a lavish court like that of Louis XIV, Frederick William's policies ratcheted up his power. "Hold fast to the eminence of your superior position . . . [and] rely on your own strength," he advised his son. At the Great Elector's death in 1688, Brandenburg-Prussia was well on the road to becoming a major player in European politics. He also left a legacy of military values and reliance on armed might that would influence much of Prussia's subsequent history.

In 1701, his son, Frederick I (r. 1688–1713), increased the dynasty's status by acquiring the title of King of Prussia in return for helping the Holy Roman Emperor in a war against France. He used state revenues to turn his Berlin court into a great social and cultural center. By his death in 1713, Brandenburg-Prussia had become a respected force in eastern Europe.

AUSTRIA CONFRONTS THE OTTOMANS AND EXPANDS ITS CONTROL

Austria's Leopold I (r. 1657–1705), facing extreme local, language, and ethnic differences within his diverse lands, could not hope to acquire the same power as that enjoyed by Louis XIV in France or even Frederick William in Prussia. Localities retained considerable autonomy, especially in matters of taxation. The practical Leopold focused on securing his own Habsburg lands, rather than cementing the minimal control he had over the Holy Roman Empire, and allied himself closely with the Catholic Church. He gained the allegiance of the nobles by making them his chief advisors and granting them rights to exploit lands and the peasants on them. Some peasants revolted, but as elsewhere in Europe, they did not pose a serious challenge to authorities.

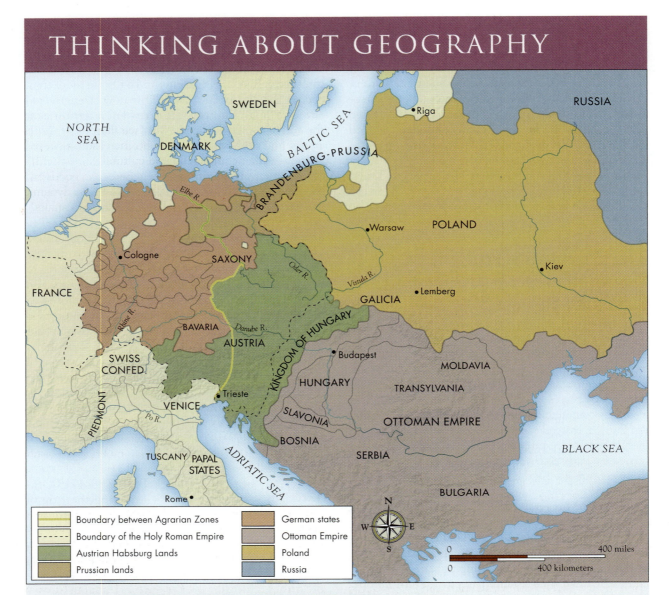

MAP 13.2   CENTRAL AND EASTERN EUROPE, 1648

This map shows the border between the western and eastern agrarian zones, running from the mouth of the Elbe River south to Trieste on the Adriatic Sea. ■ **Notice** which states are to the east of this line. **What** might this imply about social differences between eastern and western European states? **What** problems might these differences pose for eastern European states such as Australian and Brandenburg-Prussia, which controlled provinces to the west of this line?

With the help of Poland's king, Jan Sobieski (r. 1674–1696), Leopold also fought the Ottoman Turks, who controlled most of Hungary as part of their large and still-powerful empire. The Ottoman rulers had their own problems maintaining authority in the face of competition from bandit armies, mutinous army officers, and squabbling elites. However, in times of crisis, the sultans usually managed to bring these forces under control. In 1683, Ottoman forces pushed into Austrian lands and laid siege to the capital, Vienna. Leopold and Sobieski's forces saved the city and then brought most of Hungary under Austrian control (see Map 13.3 on page 416). During the following decades, Ottoman power and imperial leadership would deteriorate as weakened rulers struggled against political corruption, provincial revolts, and military insubordination.

After his victory in Vienna, the Austrian king tried to install his own nobility in Hungarian lands and ally himself with powerful Hungarian nobles at the expense of the peasantry. He succeeded only partially, and the still-independent Hungarian nobles remained a thorn in the side of the Austrian monarchy. Facing west, Leopold helped build a coalition that stood against Louis XIV. By the Austrian king's death in 1705, the Habsburg state had become one of the most powerful in Europe.

RUSSIA AND ITS TSARS GAIN PROMINENCE

Even farther east, the Russian monarchy slowly rose to prominence. Already in the sixteenth century, Ivan IV ("the Terrible") (r. 1533–1584) had added both to the authority of the Russian *tsars* (*caesars*, or emperors) and to the span of territories over which they ruled. He destroyed the remaining power of the Mongols in southeastern Russia and annexed most of their territory. Next, he began Russia's conquest of Siberia. Within his expanding state, Ivan ruled as a ruthless autocrat, creating his own service gentry to bypass powerful nobles and using torture and terror to silence all he saw as his opponents.

A difficult period known as the "Time of Troubles" (1584–1613) followed Ivan IV's death. Ivan's feeble-minded son Fyodor ruled ineffectively

The Romanovs

and left no successor upon his death in 1598. Great nobles vied for power among themselves and against weak tsars. To end the political chaos, a group of leading nobles in 1613 chose the 17-year-old Michael Romanov (r. 1613–1645) to rule as tsar. He began a dynasty that ruled Russia for over three hundred years.

Despite the political stability Michael and his immediate successors brought, discontent among those below the tsar and the nobility mounted during the century as the authorities increasingly restricted the freedom of the masses. The notorious Law Code of 1649, for example, merged peasants and slaves into a class of serfs and gave the landowning nobility the power to treat them as property. In a spate of uprisings between the late 1640s and early 1670s, the lower classes rebelled against landowners and officials by killing them and looting or burning their estates. The discontent reached a climax in the late 1660s and early 1670s with the revolts of Cossacks ("free warriors") in south Russia led by Stenka Razin. A shrewd, seasoned warrior, Razin claimed to "fight only the boyars and the wealthy lords. As for the poor and the plain folk, I shall treat them as brothers." His rebel army marched north, and many towns opened their gates to welcome Razin's forces, now swelling with the addition of discontented peasants and the urban poor. Russian soldiers finally caught, tortured, and executed Razin, and the uprisings tapered off.

By the final decades of the seventeenth century, the Romanov tsars had shored up the government's central administration and extended their authority throughout the country. Lured by visions of wealth from access to Siberian furs, Russians had driven eastward into

Russian expansion

Asia, establishing fortified settlements, bringing indigenous peoples under their control (in the process decimating them with raids and diseases such as smallpox), and planting their flag on the shores of the Pacific. Moreover, through increased trade and travel, Russia's commercial and cultural contacts with the West expanded, bringing new European goods and ideas into the country. The stage was set for a dynamic tsar to propel Russia more fully into European affairs.

This new, energetic emperor came in the person of Peter I ("the Great") (r. 1689–1725). Standing nearly seven feet tall, Peter seemed born to rule. At the age of 17, he seized the reins of government from his elder sister.

Peter the Great

He soon concluded that the best way to bolster his own political and military power was to copy Western practices. To this end, he traveled to western Europe and learned as much as he could about Western politics, customs, and technology.

Back home, he took decisive steps to solidify his authority. In 1698, he crushed a revolt of his bodyguards and silenced critics with a ruthlessness that cowed all potential troublemakers. "Every day was deemed fit and lawful for torturing," wrote an observer. He also made five years of education away from home and state service requirements for the nobility and allowed movement within the ranks only through merit. Peter applied the bureaucratic system of western European monarchs to both central and local government to secure his rule. He also brought Western technicians to Russia in large numbers and protected new industries with mercantilistic policies. Western social customs were introduced to the upper and middle classes of Russian society, such as bringing Russian women out of seclusion to appear in Western dresses at official dinners and social gatherings. In addition, Peter banned the long beards and flowing Oriental robes that Russian men traditionally wore. When the patriarch of the Russian Orthodox Church opposed the tsar's authority and some of his westernizing policies, Peter took control of the church and confiscated much of its wealth. Henceforth, the Orthodox Church served as a powerful instrument of the Russian government.

All these reforms left the peasantry in even worse straits than before. Peasants made up 97 percent of Russia's population during Peter's reign, and they became tied down in a system of serfdom bordering on slavery. The taxes they were forced to

Russia's military establishments

pay ballooned by a whopping 500 percent, and their feudal obligations and military service increased. Nowhere was peasant life harsher than in Russia, and Peter's efforts to westernize the nobility only widened

Legend:
- Brandenburg-Prussia
- Prussian acquisitions in 1688
- Russian territory in 1693
- Seized by Peter the Great from Sweden, 1694–1725
- Austrian Habsburg territory in 1657
- Austrian Habsburg territory in 1718
- Ottoman Empire in 1699
- Boundary of the Holy Roman Empire

0 400 miles
0 400 kilometers

MAP 13.3   CENTRAL AND EASTERN EUROPE, 1640–1725

This map shows the changing political landscape in central and eastern Europe during the seventeenth and early eighteenth centuries. ■ **Notice** how Russia's expansion to the west increased its contact with European commerce and affairs. **How** might this alter the balance of power in Europe? ■ **Notice** the gains made by the Austrian Habsburgs against the Ottomans. **What** might the declining fortunes of the Ottoman Empire have implied for the future of this part of the Western world? ■ **Locate** Poland-Lithuania. **What** problems face this country, hemmed in by three growing powers?

the gap between the educated elites and the enserfed peasantry.

To keep Russia in step with the West and support his ambitions for territorial expansion, Peter devoted particular attention to his military establishment. He built a navy and patterned his expanded and modernized conscript army on the model of Prussia. Recruits were drafted for life and even branded with a cross on their left hand to deter desertion. Officials arbitrarily assigned serfs to work in mines and manufacturing establishments to supply the military with equipment and arms.

Peter meant to use his new military might. Figure 13.6 depicts the clean-shaven tsar Peter the Great in heroic military pose. Clad in armor and carrying a sword, Peter asserts his authority over all potential rivals, who offer him their swords. Beneath the feet of his horse lays a defeated dragon. Above, an angel crowns Peter with divine authority. The tsar waged numerous military campaigns over his long reign, and he designed many of his great reforms to strengthen and modernize his armed forces. In the background of the painting, his troops surge to victory in a mighty battle.

Lacking warm-water access to the west, Peter tried to seize lands bordering the Black Sea that the Ottoman Turks held. Though they had weakened during the seventeenth century, the Ottoman

Conflict with Sweden Turks remained a formidable obstacle, and Peter's armies could not dislodge them. Frustrated, Peter turned northwest toward Sweden, which controlled lands bordering the Baltic Sea. Under King Gustavus Adolphus (r. 1611–1632), this Nordic country had become the dominant military power in northeastern Europe in the early seventeenth century (see Chapter 11). At the opening of the eighteenth century, Sweden held large areas east and south of the Baltic in addition to the homeland, and it ranked second only to Russia in size. Much of its success and the power of its monarchs came from the almost constant wars it fought during the seventeenth century. However, it lacked the population and resources to hold its far-flung territories for very long. Though Peter initially lost battle after battle to his brilliant Swedish adversary, Charles XII (r. 1697–1718), his persistence finally paid off. In the Battle of Poltava (1709), the Russians destroyed the Swedish army and managed to wound Charles.

Through the Treaty of Nystad in 1721, Russia received the Swedish Baltic provinces and some Polish territories (see Map 13.3). On the shores of the Baltic Sea, Peter triumphantly built a modern capital, St. Petersburg, that faced west. Reigning from this

■ FIGURE 13.6

Louis Karavack, *Peter the Great.*

new court, he emulated the cultured, royal ways of the West to enhance his personal authority. At his death in 1725, Russia had taken its place as a major player on the European stage.

THE VICTORY OF THE NOBILITY IN POLAND

Not all the eastern European states drifted toward monarchical absolutism. In Poland, the competition between the monarchy and the nobility took a different turn—with severe consequences for the nation. In the sixteenth and seventeenth centuries, Poland seemed poised to become a major power. Taking advantage of Russia's "Time of Troubles" (1584–1613), the Poles had captured Moscow for a few years until the Russians finally drove them out in 1613. In reality, however, the Polish nation, which included Lithuania in a dual kingdom, was far from strong. Sprawling over a large area between Russia and the German states, it had no natural, protective

The Rise and Fall of the Mughal Empire In India

CONSIDER
■ **Consider** *the similarities between European and Mughal monarchs, particularly Louis XIV of France and Aurangzeb of India.*
Notice *the policies that weakened their respective states.*

While monarchs in Europe struggled to consolidate their authority during the seventeenth century, powerful rulers rose in the Asian states. These emperors would become strong enough to rival the Western powers and control relations with European traders. The Asian leaders had a proud history. During the sixteenth century, the Mughals [Moguls], a fierce Islamic Turkish tribe, had swept into the Indian subcontinent and established a flourishing realm ruled by able emperors such as Babur (1483–1530) and Akbar (1542–1605).

In 1605, the 38-year-old Jahangir succeeded the great Mughal leader Akbar and assumed the title of "the world-subduing emperor." In his memoir, he described the lavish ceremonies accompanying his crowning. During the festivities, the high officials of the empire, "covered from head to foot in gold and jewels, and shoulder to shoulder, stood round in brilliant array, also waiting for the commands of their sovereign."

By that time, the Portuguese had already established a flourishing trading base on the west Indian coast. As the seventeenth century unfolded, the Mughals also allowed the English, French, and Dutch to establish trading bases in India, but without power to be of any concern. The Mughals themselves paid little attention to foreign trade, but welcomed the revenues from the commerce into their treasuries.

Though Jahangir wielded power arbitrarily, he also felt compelled to follow certain traditions and laws. In his view, to bring "prompt punishment to the man who violates the laws of his country is an alternative with which no person entrusted with the reins of power is authorized to dispense." Jahangir also struggled to bring unruly sections of his empire more firmly under his control, at one time ordering a bloody campaign against rebellious Afghans. The Mughal emperor recorded how prisoners from one battle were paraded before

him "yoked together, with the heads of the seventeen thousand slain in the battle suspended from their necks." Reflecting on the burdens of office, Jahangir lamented, "There is no pain or anxiety equal to that which attends the possession of sovereign power, for to the possessor there is not in this world a moment's rest." Nevertheless, the emperor gave his wife, Nur Jahan, a major role in running the government. He also managed to find time to support and enjoy sports, literature, and art as well as to smoke opium regularly. He completed his *Memoirs* before his death in 1627.

An eventual successor, Aurangzeb, became Mughal emperor in 1658 and held power for almost fifty years. One of his chroniclers, Bakhta'war Khan, claimed it was "a great object with this Emperor that all Muslims should follow the principles of the religion." The biographer also boasted that his emperor "has learned the Qur'an by heart." But Aurangzeb's reign marked both the apex of Mughal power and the beginning of its end. By the time of his death in 1707, reckless spending, endless military campaigns, and persecution of Hindus and Sikhs had weakened the regime. Widespread rebellions broke out, which Aurangzeb's weaker successors failed to overcome. In the 1720s, one observer, Khafi Khan, reported that many townships "have been so far ruined and devastated that they have become forests infested by tigers and lions, and the villages are so utterly ruined and desolate that there is no sign of habitation on the routes."

As the Mughal empire disintegrated, rivals quickly took power. Europeans traders also gained influence—especially the British and French, who were competing for the Indian trade in textiles, spices, and sugar. By the mid-eighteenth century, the land controlled by Aurangzeb's successors had dwindled to Delhi. Meanwhile, the British and French forged strategic political alliances with Indian states and jockeyed for a dominant position on the subcontinent.

boundaries either to the east or to the west. Ethnic and religious divisions undermined the Polish rulers' hopes for unity, and the economy stumbled. In the late Middle Ages, a sizeable overland commerce between the Black and Baltic Seas had flowed across Poland. However, with the shifting of commercial routes and centers to the west in the sixteenth century, Poland's commerce withered. Worse, the Polish nobility, protective of its own power and fearful of an alliance between merchants and the king, deliberately penalized merchants by passing legislation to restrict trade. The great mass of the Polish people remained serfs, bound to the estates of the powerful nobility.

In the face of such forces, only a strong central government could have ensured stability for Poland.

Yet this was precisely where Poland proved weakest. For many years, Poland's nobles had been gaining the upper hand, and they closely guarded their power to elect the king. When King Sigismund II died in 1572, ending the long-ruling Jagellon dynasty, the nobles saw to it that no strong king ascended the throne. They monopolized the legislative body (the "Diet") and, to safeguard their rights, required a unanimous vote to pass any measure. This system guaranteed political anarchy in which, in the words of a mid-seventeenth-century observer, "there is no order in the state," and "everybody who is stronger thinks to have the right to oppress the weaker."

Over the course of the seventeenth century, revolts by Ukrainian Cossack warriors and wars with Russia,

Sweden, and Brandenburg-Prussia resulted in the loss of Polish territories. Rivalries among the Polish nobles worsened the chaos. Moreover, Tatar slave raiders carried off many people. Incursions and internal wars destroyed towns, and the once-thriving Jewish populations were pushed from their homes and often slaughtered. Tens of thousands of Jews were murdered in the pogroms (organized persecutions) that swept through Poland between 1648 and 1658. Protestants also suffered at the hands of the Catholic majority. Not surprisingly, Poland's population declined sharply in these years. By the beginning of the eighteenth century, it lay vulnerable to surrounding powers that boasted stronger central governments.

THE TRIUMPH OF CONSTITUTIONALISM

As the tendency toward absolutism intensified in central Europe, another major struggle began to unfold in a small island nation far to the west. Kings desiring absolute power in England faced a situation significantly different from that in France. In France, the nobility had little history of common action between classes and lost their solitary struggle against absolutism. In England, however, there had been a tradition of joint parliamentary action by nobles and commoners who owned land, and this helped contribute to a different outcome in the struggle for sovereignty. Instead of government residing in the person of an absolute monarch, it rested in written law—constitutions, not kings, would come to rule.

THE NOBILITY LOSES RESPECT

For over one thousand years, the English had taken for granted the idea of separate social classes. Peasants and members of the middle classes showed the high nobility an unmistakable deference, turning out to greet them when they emerged, gazing downward and holding their hats respectfully in their hands. Even upwardly mobile landowners with some wealth (the "gentry") knew that they ranked well below the "peers" (the old nobility). In England, there were only about four hundred noble families and they jealously guarded their exclusive position. Commentators wrote that "nobility is a precious gift" and accepted this privilege as the natural order of things: "Men naturally favor nobility."

By the beginning of the seventeenth century, several disturbing incidents pointed to ominous cracks in the wall of privilege. One member of the gentry actually jostled and swore at an earl as the two passed in a narrow passageway, and some tenant farmers neglected to turn out, hats in hand, to welcome passing noblemen. Later, a Protestant sect, the Quakers, enacted a religious policy that forbade members to take off their hats to men in authority. Something had changed and nobles no longer seemed so essential nor so noble.

What explained this apparent loss of respect for the English upper crust? We can find a partial answer in the shifting role of money. In the early modern world, the old wealth of the nobility had declined relative to the "new money" of merchants and other enterprising individuals. Furthermore, the medieval base of noble power, the military, had also declined. No longer were nobles in charge of defending the realm; mercenary armies made up of commoners now took care of these matters. England had a relatively large sector of independent craftsmen compared to other countries, and noblemen depended more on "free labor"—that is, on wage laborers who could enter into contracts for their labor. These differences led commoners increasingly to feel they could control their own lives rather than defer to their "betters." In addition, education had become the key to upward mobility. More and more, knowledge and service, rather than birth, seemed the measure of a man.

New wealth

The members of the nobility did not relinquish their traditional place easily. Indeed, critics complained that noblemen were becoming more arrogant than ever in exerting their privileges. Sometimes, nobles even exceeded the bounds of propriety. In 1635 the earl of Arundel lost his temper when the mayor of a city did not turn out to greet him in the traditional way. The earl sought out the mayor, grabbed his staff of office, and proceeded to beat him with it, shouting, "I will teach you to . . . attend Peers of the Realm!"

As early as the sixteenth century, laws throughout Europe had begun to supplement tradition in keeping the social classes separate, and England was no different. Governments issued **sumptuary laws** to regulate what kinds of clothing were appropriate for members of each social class. For example, an individual could not wear velvet unless he had an independent income of over 100 pounds a year, and laborers could not wear cloth costing more than 2 shillings a yard. These laws were supposed to preserve social distinction, but the newly rich recognized that the path to gaining social respect lay in part in *looking* noble. Thus, men and women insisted on purchasing luxurious clothing to rival that of the highest classes. In 1714, a Sicilian traveler observed: "Nothing makes noble persons despise the gilded costume so much as to see it on the bodies of the lowest men in the world." Now, it seemed, there was no visual marker of a person's noble status.

Sumptuary laws

The nobles had more success in guarding their property rights than their fashion privileges. In 1671,

■ FIGURE 13.7

Anthony Van Dyck, *James Stuart, Duke of Richmond and Lennox,* ca. 1630.

Parliament passed game laws giving the nobility the exclusive prerogative to hunt on their own lands. The new mandates even allowed them to set lethal trapguns to kill poachers. Not surprisingly, these laws only exacerbated the common people's anger, as the poor continued to poach simply to survive in times of hunger. Still, many members of the nobility tried to hang on to their privilege while others pressed to undo them.

The portrait of James Stuart, a member of the royal family, shown in Figure 13.7, captures the arrogance and complacency of the typical English nobleman of 1630, who was oblivious to the gathering social storm that would soon disrupt his idyllic world. James stands proudly dressed in the opulent clothing of the nobility that the sumptuary laws carefully tried to preserve. His stockings are made of the finest silk, and the lace at his throat is expensive and handcrafted. Adorning

his jacket sleeve is a sun image embroidered in silver thread—an early forerunner of Louis XIV's trademark symbol. The painting portrays James with his huge hunting dog, again proclaiming his privileged position through his hunting rights. The dog gazes up adoringly at his master with the kind of deference that James had come to expect. Sadly for members of the nobility, they would receive fewer and fewer admiring glances from their fellow humans.

PROTESTANTISM REVITALIZED

A good deal of social criticism also came from Protestants, many of whom believed that the implementation of Reformation ideas in England had not gone far enough. Because many Protestants were involved in the increasingly lucrative commerce, their wealth helped make their concerns more visible. For many, the compromise of Elizabeth I (discussed in Chapter 11) that allowed worshipers of many beliefs to share one Church of England was unacceptable. These critics believed that the Church of England (the Anglican Church) should be "purified"—that is, trimmed of any practice that lacked biblical precedent or smacked of Catholicism. They especially objected to priestly garments and the elaborate rituals of the Anglican Church. Some wanted to eliminate bishops altogether, preferring rule by church elders instead. (This was the practice common in Scotland, where Protestant churches came to be called "Presbyterian"—"ruled by elders").

In their zeal, many Protestants became increasingly anti-Catholic, and their political actions were shaped by this prejudice. Other Protestants even wanted to purify daily life, objecting to theater, cockfights, and other seemingly frivolous activities. Although individuals disagreed among themselves on exactly how they wanted the Church of England purified, they all concurred that change was essential. Many members of this loose group of critics, called **Puritans,** became influential members of Parliament.

Puritans in England reconsidered the political relationship between monarchs and their subjects, wondering about competing loyalties between law and conscience, for example. These questions formed the backdrop of a struggle for sovereignty that dominated the seventeenth century. As early as 1561, the Scottish reformer John Knox warned Queen Mary of Scotland that monarchs were responsible to their subjects: "If their princes exceed their bounds, Madam, no doubt they may be resisted, even by power." This was tantamount to a call to revolution. As Puritans gathered to discuss the purification of the church, they could not help but consider the possibility of political action.

James I Invokes the Divine Right of Kings

Because Queen Elizabeth I had died childless, the throne went to her cousin, the king of Scotland, who became King James I of England (r. 1603–1625). As soon as James heard of Elizabeth's death, he rushed to England brimming with great plans. He made promises to many who greeted him on his way south to London, rapidly knighted thousands of gentry, and even ordered an accused thief hanged without a trial—assuming incorrectly that as king he had the right to do so. Many of his subjects turned out to see their affable new monarch, but, unfortunately for him, he would not prove as popular, nor as politically shrewd as "Good Queen Bess."

The honeymoon of the new monarch and his people faded rather quickly, for unlike his predecessor, he was unable to mollify **Religious problems** the varying religious beliefs of his people. He was a Calvinist, yet he favored Anglicanism, and his most enduring heritage was the translation of the Bible he commissioned, the King James Bible, which remains widely admired as both religion and beautiful literature. However, the king managed to offend his subjects who hoped for his support for religious change. At the beginning of his reign, Calvinists approached the king, hoping to eliminate the Anglican episcopal system and bring it in line with the Presbyterian Scottish practice with which the king was familiar. They were sadly disappointed, for James threatened to "harry them out of the land" if they did not conform to Anglicanism.

James also offended his Catholic subjects, banning Jesuits and seminary priests. In 1605, a conspiracy of Catholics planned to blow up Parliament while it was in session. The plot failed and the conspirators were executed. Yet, the "gunpowder plot," as it came to be known, increased the anti-Catholic feelings in the country, which were exacerbated when James planned a political marriage between his son and a Catholic Spanish princess. Although the marriage negotiations fell through, the attempt alienated Calvinists and Anglicans alike.

Thus by 1610, there was much animosity between the king and many of his subjects. James thought the English ungrateful and they found him arbitrary and arrogant. Unlike Elizabeth before him, James was disinclined to compromise his theoretical **Divine right** notions of divine right monarchy. Even before he ascended the throne, James had written two treatises in which he asserted the divine right of kings, and in 1610 he presented this position to a skeptical Parliament. As he put it, "Kings have power of . . . life and death; [they are] judges over all their subjects and in all causes, and yet account-

able to none but God." This position was consistent with his hasty execution of the accused thief, but it offended many Puritans in the House of Commons, as well as many Lords who viewed the king as subject to the law of the land.

During James's rule, the English colonies in North America grew. In part, the attention to the New World stemmed from James's financial difficulties: The first permanent English colony, named **Colonies** Jamestown after the monarch, was founded in Virginia in 1607. James hoped to generate new income from the Virginia colonies, which in 1619 had imported slaves from Africa to grow tobacco, an increasingly popular crop. Colonial settlement was also forwarded by James's high-handed attitude toward religious dissidents. When the king threatened to harry nonconformists out of the land, some took him literally and emigrated to North America to establish colonies. They avoided Jamestown, which was sympathetic to the Church of England, and instead landed farther north, founding their first colony in Plymouth, Massachusetts, in 1620. The New World was not to be the solution to either James's religious or fiscal problems. He died leaving a shortage of money and an oversupply of ill will among both Parliament and Protestants.

Charles I Alienates Parliament

James's son, Charles I (r. 1625–1649), inherited both his father's rule and his policies. This sober monarch, continuing to invoke the divine right of kings, considered himself answerable only to God, not Parliament. His relationship with his subjects deteriorated rapidly. He approached Parliament in the same way his father had—calling it when he needed money and disbanding it when the members demanded concessions.

Showing a remarkable insensitivity to his Protestant subjects, Charles married a sister of the Catholic king Louis XIII of France. Soon after his wedding, Charles granted concessions to English Catholics, even allowing the queen and her entourage to practice **Concessions to Catholics** Catholic rituals in the court itself. English Protestants were horrified at what they saw as outrageous behavior by the family of the titular head of the Church of England. Charles responded to critics by persecuting Puritans, whom he viewed as disloyal. More Puritans fled to North America, settling so many colonies in the northeast that the region came to be called New England. Meanwhile, the situation in old England grew more desperate.

As we saw in Chapter 11, warfare had become extremely expensive, and Charles's costly and fruitless wars with Spain and France had so strained his

MAP 13.4 THE ENGLISH CIVIL WAR, 1642–1649

This map shows England during the civil war years, the locations of the parliament and royalist supporters, and the major battles. ■ **Notice** the scale of the map and **consider** how this might have affected the progress of the war. ■ **Notice** the regions that initially supported the king and **consider** why the royalist drew from rural rather than the urban centers.

However, the temporary compromise between the king and Parliament came to an end when troubles in Ireland caused both to agree to send troops. However, their alliance ended there. The question of who would command the army remained. Parliament did not trust the king to suppress his religious sympathies to fight the Catholic Irish, and the king did not trust Parliament to share control of any army it raised. In the end, Parliament appointed officers to raise an army, and Charles withdrew from London to raise an army of his own. The Irish no longer seemed the immediate enemy for either side.

"GOD MADE MEN AND THE DEVIL MADE KINGS": CIVIL WAR, 1642–1649

As Map 13.4 shows, the alignments in the English civil war show some divisions in English life. The rural areas were more likely to support the king, and the Puritan strongholds in the cities followed the forces of Parliament. In response to Charles's call for support, noblemen, cavalry officers, and Irish Catholics rallied to his banner. His royalist supporters were called Cavaliers, or horsemen, as a reference to medieval knights who fought for their kings. Back in London, Parliament recruited an army 13,000 strong, drawn from the commoners, merchants, a few noblemen, Scots, and Puritans. All these generalizations, however, are drawn in broad strokes, and frequently the choice to support one side or another derived from private decisions based sometimes on religion and sometimes on long-standing personal grudges against neighbors.

The strength of the parliamentary forces, called **Roundheads** for their short haircuts, stemmed mainly from their skilled infantry, the support of major sections of the navy, and their religious conviction. Parliament's forces also benefited from the leadership of Oliver Cromwell, a Puritan who not only forwarded the cause of revolutionary change in Parliament, but who took charge of the army and forged it into a formidable force called the New Model Army. The royalists had more experience in battles and more skilled generals. The lines were drawn—the royalist forces led by the king fought a civil war against the forces led by Cromwell.

finances that he even tried to pawn the crown jewels. The king called Parliament several times in the 1620s, only to disband them repeatedly. Things came to a head in 1640, when the Scots, who also objected to the king's high-handed religious policies, invaded the north of England. To raise the army and funds he needed to fight the Scots, Charles called Parliament again. This time, Parliament forced him to agree that he could not disband them without their consent. The first crack in Charles's armor of divine right had appeared. The "Long Parliament," as it came to be called, continued to meet from 1640 to 1653. Over time, it acquired a measure of power and established protections for the religious freedom of Anglicans and Puritans alike.

Parliament gains power

By 1646, Parliament forces had won a series of victories, and Charles surrendered to the Scots, who later turned him over to Parliament in exchange for their back military pay. While the king was moved from prison to prison as royalists conspired to free him, leaders of Parliament confronted new challenges: a series of social upheavals as more and more people were drawn into the turbulent events of the 1640s.

Charles captured

Women from all social groups participated in unprecedented numbers in the English civil war. In their husbands' absence, a number of noble women defended their fortified castles against parliamentary forces, inspiring many accounts of "great heroics" considered surprising in the "weaker sex." Working women disguised as men also passed themselves off as Roundhead soldiers. In 1643, Charles issued a proclamation intending to prevent women from joining the army: "Let no woman presume to counterfeit her sex by wearing man's apparel under pain of the severest punishment which law shall inflict." However, the king was in no position to enforce this edict, and women continued to serve as soldiers. It is impossible to know exactly how many women fought for their cause, but the fact that Charles tried to legislate their exclusion suggests that at least he and his advisors thought the numbers significant.

Women in war

Women were well suited as spies, because people expected them to be noncombatants. One such woman, Jane Whorwood, dedicated herself fiercely to the king's cause. The tall redhead repeatedly tried to free Charles during his imprisonment after 1646. She smuggled money to him and once brought in acid to weaken the metal bars so that he could break free. One of Charles's aides described Whorwood as "the most loyal person to King Charles I in his miseries."

Other previously uninvolved members of society also jumped into the fray. After 1646, radicals, both men and women, raised new demands for social justice. Their complaints stemmed mostly from the severe economic problems that had hamstrung England in the 1640s. A series of bad harvests caused food shortages and rising prices, and disabled soldiers returning home discovered they could no longer earn a living. Crime increased as people stole to feed their families, and the social order deteriorated. One contemporary observed: "Necessity dissolves all laws and government, and hunger will break through stone walls." From these difficult circumstances, groups of radical Protestants arose. Known as **Levellers,** they insisted that social justice become part of Parliament's agenda. A pamphlet sympathetic to their cause claimed that "God made men and the Devil made kings."

Levellers

Levellers were as varied a group as the Puritans, encompassing people with a broad array of agendas. In general, however, they harked back to a tradition of English religious radicals like John Ball (see Chapter 9), and espoused as their goal to "level" social differences. To that end, they advocated some reforms of Parliament. For example, they believed Parliament should be chosen by the vote of all male heads of households, which would represent a dramatic broadening of the vote. Furthermore, they wanted members of Parliament to be paid, so that even those with no independent income could serve. Although these ideas may seem natural to us, they posed a major threat to those who believed that only property brought privilege.

THE KING LAID LOW

In the midst of these controversies, the civil war broke out again in 1648 as Charles encouraged his supporters to rise up to free him. Cromwell's forces promptly crushed the uprisings, and some army leaders concluded that they would never come to peaceful terms with the king. With Cromwell's support, they demanded that Charles be tried for treason. The majority of Parliament members refused to take this extreme step, but in December 1648 invading soldiers purged Parliament of the cautious. The remaining members, scornfully called the Rump Parliament by opponents and historians, brought the king to trial.

The Rump Parliament tried Charles as a king, rather than deposing him first and then trying him as a private citizen. In other words, they wanted to find the *king* guilty, not just the man. This bold act represented a direct clash between two theories of government—one claiming that the king stood above Parliament, the other declaring that he must answer to it. This unprecedented, highly public trial became the first in history to receive full press coverage. Newspapers had initially emerged in England in 1641, on the eve of the civil war; by 1649, six licensed newspapers recorded the testimony in the trial and provided differing opinions on the proceedings.

Charles was accused of claiming to rule by divine right: He who had been "trusted with a limited power to govern . . . had conceived a wicked design to . . . uphold in himself an unlimited and tyrannical power to rule according to his will. . . ." Though he genuinely believed in divine right, Charles refused to answer this or any other charge. Instead he claimed that Parliament had no right to bring charges against him at all. He gained much popular support over the few days of the trial as he consistently reiterated his position, rising above a stutter that had plagued him all his life in order to express his views firmly

■ FIGURE 13.8

Weesop, *Execution of Charles I*, 1649.

and with dignity. He challenged Parliament to justify "by what power I am called hither." Both sides clearly understood the magnitude of the trial's central question: Who had sovereignty? Charles claimed that God had sovereignty and had delegated it to the king; the Puritans in Parliament claimed that they had sovereignty. There was no room for compromise, and neither side gave way. Charles was found guilty and sentenced to die.

On January 30, 1649, the condemned king was led to a scaffold erected in front of Whitehall Palace. His public execution inspired a rash of etchings and paintings. Figure 13.8 depicts the crowds who gathered to watch, including women, whose interest in the execution seemed remarkable to contemporary commentators. Many in the crowd were sympathetic to their king. Jane Whorwood, for example, who had worked tirelessly to free Charles, ran forward to greet the king as he walked to the scaffold. Figure 13.8 shows some of these sympathizers; note the old man in the foreground, leaning on his cane and crying, and the woman fainting in the center.

Charles executed

Charles bravely addressed the few people near him on the scaffold and repeated his views on sovereignty: "I must tell you that the liberty and freedom [of the people] consists in having a government. . . . It is not for having a share in government. Sir, that is nothing pertaining to them. A subject and a sovereign are clear different things." Charles then laid his head on the block, and the executioner severed it cleanly with

one blow. The man on the side of the platform in Figure 13.8 holds the king's head up to show the crowd. The monarchy had ended, and a new form of government arose to take its place: a republic in which sovereignty rested with representatives of those who owned property. England called its new republic the Commonwealth.

A PURITAN REPUBLIC IS BORN: THE COMMONWEALTH, 1649–1660

As the Rump Parliament began to rule the republic, chaos erupted throughout the realm. The new commonwealth faced warfare outside its borders and dissension within. Fortunately, Parliament had an able champion in Oliver Cromwell (1599–1658). While Parliament ruled, Cromwell with his army controlled the policies.

Rebellions broke out in Catholic Ireland and Protestant Scotland, and Cromwell led his army to those lands, putting down the revolts so brutally that the Irish still remember his invasion with anger. However, Cromwell was effective and brought Scotland and Ireland tightly under English rule. Yet Parliament had more to worry about than just these expensive wars.

Within England, Levellers continued to agitate for social reform, and many of their leaders were imprisoned. Then, in 1649, a gathering of women entered the House of Commons bringing a petition asking for

"those rights and freedoms of the nation that
you promised us." One member of Parliament taunted
the women, saying their
public stance was "strange," to which a petitioner responded, "It was strange that you cut
off the king's head." These were odd times
indeed, and many wondered whether Parliament's victory in the civil war had created
more disorder than it had resolved.

Domestic distress

The 1649 cartoon in Figure 13.9 expresses
the fears of royalists and moderates alike during this difficult era and serves to illustrate the
tumultuous times of the Commonwealth. In
this complex image, axe-wielding men (representing the Roundheads) chop down "the
Royal Oak of Britain," England's longtime
symbol of authority and tradition. The oak
teeters, threatening to fall and take with it the
Bible, the Magna Carta, and the traditional
rule of law. Soldiers assist the woodsmen in
destroying the tree and the order it represents.
The pigs in the center symbolize the common people, being "fattened for the slaughter." Oliver
Cromwell stands at the left, supervising the destruction. Below his feet is hell, although he is oblivious
to how close he is to damnation. While this cartoon
clearly vilifies Cromwell and all he embodied, it also
reveals the disorder that had torn at England since the
civil war began. Could the parliamentary forces under
Oliver Cromwell resolve these fears and tensions?

Parliament seemed incapable of uniting the various constituents that demanded action after Charles's
death. In 1653, when the House of Commons considered a proposal to dismantle Cromwell's large army,
the general lost patience. He disbanded Parliament altogether, named
himself "Lord Protector" of the Commonwealth of England, Scotland, and Ireland, and
established a military dictatorship—the republic
remained only as an ideal. Cromwell faced the same
problems that had confronted Parliament and the
king—foreign wars and religious struggles. A pious
Puritan, Cromwell set out to make England the model
of a Protestant land, banning horse races, cockfights,
and even theater. He ultimately proved as intolerant of Anglicans as they had been of Puritans, and
he alienated most of the population with his intrusive policies. The brief experiment with a rule purely
by Parliament had failed, and a military dictatorship
could not be popular in a land with such a tradition of
participatory government.

Lord Protector

WHO HAS THE POWER TO RULE?

Charles's trial and execution, and the disorder that followed, did not resolve the issue of who had the ultimate

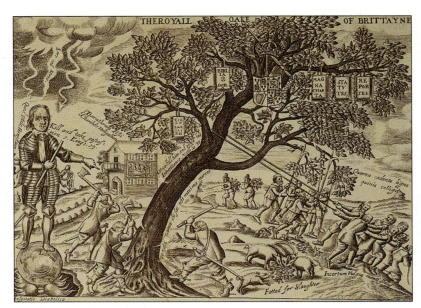

■ FIGURE 13.9

The Royal Oak of Britain, 1649.

power in England. In 1651, the English philosopher
Thomas Hobbes (1588–1679) wrote a political treatise, *The Leviathan*, that offered an
answer to this question in the form of
a new theory of government. Perhaps
shaken by the chaos of the civil war, Hobbes harbored a pessimistic view of human nature. He claimed
that everyone was driven by a quest for power and
that given the chance, people would try to exercise
their power at the expense of their neighbors—even
if it meant taking their property and their lives. In
this "state of nature" where there was no controlling
authority, Hobbes described human life as "solitary,
poor, nasty, brutish and short." However, he held out
a ray of hope. Humans, he explained, recognized their
inability to live peacefully, so they created a "social
contract" by which they erected a ruler above them.
By this contract, subjects willingly surrendered their
sovereignty to a ruler who, in turn, agreed to rule over
them absolutely.

Thomas Hobbes

With this explanation, Hobbes reconciled the
Protestant views of sovereignty—in which the people
held the right to rule—with absolute monarchy,
where the ruler (the king or "Lord Protector") possessed sole sovereignty. In the famous frontispiece of
The Leviathan, shown in Figure 13.10, Hobbes visually portrayed the benefits of his system. The ruler is
shown at the top wielding the sword and scepter of
absolute power. Even more significant, he comprises
all the people of the land—he is the "body politic."
The king derives his power from his subjects, without
whom he would not exist. However, with this delegated power, he presides over an orderly and peaceful countryside and village. Church, state, the army,

■ FIGURE 13.10

Frontispiece of *The Leviathan* by Thomas Hobbes, 1651.

and Parliament are all neatly ordered along the sides of the page. This tidy, comforting vision stands in stark contrast to the chaos shown in Figure 13.9 and reveals Hobbes's hope that absolute monarchy would guarantee peace in the land.

Hobbes omitted a key point in his thesis: Absolute rule is only as effective as the ruler. Although Cromwell preserved order (albeit while offending many), he failed to develop an institution that could maintain the Puritan republic. When he died in 1658, he named his son Richard his successor. However, the young man could not lead with the same energy and fervor that his father had shown. Under pressure from members of Parliament, Richard resigned, and the right to govern again returned to the people's representatives.

THE MONARCHY RESTORED, 1660–1688

Sobered by the chaos that had followed Charles's execution, Parliament decided to reinstate the monarchy. It invited Charles II (r. 1660–1685), son of the executed king, to resume the throne. Ships sailed from England to Holland to escort the king home from his place of exile. Among those in attendance when the king returned was Samuel Pepys (see Biography on page 432), an English diarist who became noted for the detailed accounts he kept of events from 1660 to 1669. According to Pepys, the people of England greeted their new king with much fanfare and excitement. Charles II came home to a restored monarchy that had all the luxury that his father had enjoyed— and all the problems that had plagued this troubled institution.

Samuel Pepys devoted several pages of his diary to Charles's coronation in 1661. "So glorious was the show with gold and silver," he wrote, "that we were not able to look at it, our eyes at last being so much overcome with it." Like most of his countrymen, Pepys drank ale with wild abandon during the celebration—the years of Puritan temperance seemed to melt away in a haze of drunkenness.

Yet, not everyone got caught up in the celebration. Former Cromwell supporters saw the Restoration in a very different light. John Bunyan (1628– 1688), for example, who had fought with Cromwell, was imprisoned in 1660 for preaching against the Restoration. His original sentence of three months was extended to twelve years because he refused to stop preaching. After his release in 1672, he continued to preach and wrote his masterpiece, *Pilgrim's Progress,* in 1678. Probably the most widely read book by an English author, *Pilgrim's Progress* tells of a hero named Christian and his search for salvation through an allegorical world. This tale of hope and confidence in the human power to prevail through times of tribulation was balanced by Bunyan's lesser-known work, *The Life and Death of Mr. Badman* (1680). In this allegory, Bunyan criticized the loose life of Restoration England by describing the journey of a man who goes straight to hell. Bunyan's works strongly suggested that the Restoration had definitely not solved the political struggles of England.

John Bunyan

Charles II grappled with the same fiscal problems that had plagued James I and Charles I, but he had to face a Parliament that had proven its strength during the civil wars. The king was bound by law to call Parliament at least every three years, and the members of Parliament had severely curtailed royal power over taxation. Like his predecessors, Charles needed money, and to buttress his revenues without the restrictions Parliament imposed, the new king tried to exert more control over the colonies in North America. He increased the customs duties permitted by the Navigation Acts (imposed in 1651) and fought a war with the Dutch in 1665. This conflict ended in a treaty that gave the English New York in exchange for Dutch control of Surinam in South America.

Fiscal problems

Charles's international dealings were hampered by disasters at home. In 1665, England experienced a plague of frightening intensity—70,000 people died in London alone.

Plague and fire

The following year, a devastating fire broke out in London, engulfing the city and destroying 13,000 dwellings and eighty-seven churches, including the venerable St. Paul's Cathedral. After the fire had died out, Charles ordered the city rebuilt and hired the skilled architect Sir Christopher Wren to redesign the main buildings. Wren's masterpiece, the new St. Paul's Cathedral, still marks the London skyline.

In addition to these disasters, the issue of religion again came to the fore. Charles had Catholic sympathies, and to circumvent Parliament, he had several times turned to the Catholic king Louis XIV of France for help and money. The Protestant Parliament, wary of Charles's granting concessions to Catholics, passed the "Test Act" in 1673. The law required an oath of Protestant loyalties to prevent Catholics from holding public offices, but legislation could not affect the king's conscience, nor alleviate Parliament's fears of Catholicism. In 1685, Charles died after converting to Roman Catholicism on his deathbed.

Charles's successor, his brother James II (r. 1685–1688), was not able to avoid direct confrontation with the Protestant Parliament. A Catholic, James demanded in vain that Parliament repeal the Test Act, and he proceeded to place Catholics in high office in violation of Parliament's law. Many English feared that James would adopt Louis XIV's policies against Protestants and even try to institute absolute rule. They may well have been right, but the members of Parliament were not going to wait and see. In 1688, when James's Catholic wife produced a Catholic heir to the throne of England, leading members of Parliament took action.

THE GLORIOUS REVOLUTION

To preempt James, Parliamentary leaders turned to the king's eldest daughter, Mary, a Protestant and the wife of William of Orange of the Netherlands. William staunchly opposed the policies of the Catholic Louis XIV, so both his politics and his religion suited the English Protestants. William gathered a fleet and an army of 14,000 men and landed in England in November 1688. He marched slowly and peacefully toward London, while most of the English population rallied to his side. Recalling Charles I's fate, James decided to flee to France "for the security of my person." Louis XIV received his Catholic counterpart with kindness.

William and Mary

The Irish Catholics did not welcome the new Protestant king. Indeed, they thought of James II as a Catholic hero, and Irish leaders conspired with James to help him retake his throne while the French king helped fund this enterprise. Early in his reign William led an army into Ireland and ruthlessly suppressed what he saw as Catholic treason. Abandoning both Ireland and his claim to the throne, James lived out his life in lavish exile in France, leaving the Irish to bear the brunt of William's wrath. The new king reduced Ireland to colonial status and offered new opportunity for English landlords to take possession of Irish Catholic lands. Irish anger toward the English festered and would grow, but William's victory was cheered in England.

William and Parliament turned to the immediate task of establishing the legitimacy of his kingship. Parliament decided that James's flight from England constituted an abdication of the throne. The sovereignty that, according to Hobbes,

England's Bill of Rights

the people had surrendered to their king had been returned to Parliament, who now had the right to install a new monarch. Parliament determined to clarify its relationship with the king, and in 1689 it passed a Bill of Rights firmly stating that kings were subject to the laws of the land, thus creating a constitutional monarchy—the triumph of **constitutionalism.** Within the Bill of Rights, William agreed to "deliver

KEY DATES

ENGLISH CIVIL WAR

1625	Charles I becomes king
1629	Charles dissolves Parliament
1642	Outbreak of civil war
1649	Charles I executed
1649–1660	Commonwealth in England
1651	Hobbes, *The Leviathan*
1660	Restoration of monarchy with Charles II
1685	James II becomes king
1688	Glorious Revolution
1689	William and Mary become monarchs
1690	Locke, *Second Treatise of Government*

BIOGRAPHY

Samuel Pepys (1633–1703)

CONSIDER

■ **Notice** *that Pepys' diary shows how the political events of the day—the Glorious Revolution and the growing importance of Parliament—affected his life.* ■ **Consider** *the effects of educational opportunities on the lives of seventeenth-century people.*

Samuel Pepys was born in London on February 23, 1633, the fifth of eleven children. Only he and two of his siblings survived childhood. Samuel's father was a relatively modest tailor and his mother was the sister of a butcher. Nevertheless, the family had relatives who included landed gentry, lawyers, and a physician. The Pepyses were Puritans, and although Samuel uncharitably recalled his mother as "quarrelsome and feeble-minded" and his father as "always needing some kind of aid," the family did provide him with the educational opportunities he needed to succeed.

As a young boy, Pepys was sent to live with an uncle and attend the same grammar school where the young Oliver Cromwell had been educated. Samuel must have seemed a promising student, for when he was about 13 he returned to London to attend St. Paul's School, a stronghold of Puritanism and classical learning. He won scholarships to attend Cambridge University and received his bachelor's degree in 1654. After graduating, he found a job as secretary to a distant relative who had taken an important position in Cromwell's new Commonwealth.

A year later, Pepys married Elizabeth, the 15-year-old daughter of a French Protestant refugee. She brought no dowry to the marriage, though Samuel was probably drawn to her beauty—throughout his diary, he repeatedly made notes about attractive

women. His domestic life proved stormy, but he wrote often about being pleased with his marriage during the more harmonious times in his household. Pepys complained that Elizabeth was untidy and that she mismanaged the household. For his part, Samuel was no model husband; he always kept his wife short of money and was relentlessly unfaithful to her. He recorded the details of his infidelities and of Elizabeth's pained reactions to them. Elizabeth died young and childless in 1669, and Samuel never remarried.

Enterprising Clerk, Member of Parliament, and Diarist

Through the late seventeenth century, Pepys was an active participant and a careful chronicler of the major events of the era. While still at Cambridge, he witnessed the execution of Charles I and supported the Commonwealth as a clerk. However, he must have harbored royalist sympathies, for his political career blossomed in 1660 with the Restoration. Pepys accompanied the fleet that escorted the new monarch back to England, and his contacts on that journey ensured him a position suited to his many talents.

Pepys began his diary in 1660 and for nine years detailed the events of his times, both great and small. In this extraordinary text, we have

this kingdom from popery [Catholicism] and arbitrary power" and to preserve freedom of speech, election, and the rule of law. The bill secured the position of Protestantism in England by ruling that "no person embracing Catholicism or married to a Catholic is eligible to succeed to the throne." Through this bloodless **Glorious Revolution,** Parliament had finally demonstrated that the power to rule rested with the people through their representatives, rather than absolutely with the king. After this, Parliament began to meet annually, which was a practical way to secure its authority.

ROYALISM RECONSIDERED: JOHN LOCKE

Many English men and women were proud of their bloodless "revolution" that so peacefully changed their monarch, but others were uncertain about the

legality of this step. The English philosopher John Locke (1623–1704) wrote an influential political tract—*The Second Treatise of Government* (1690)—to justify "to the world [and] the people of England" the Revolution of 1688, and proclaim the legitimacy of William. Locke did much more—he articulated a new relationship between king and subjects that provided a theoretical framework for constitutional forms of government. Like Hobbes, Locke believed that power originally rested with the people and that citizens themselves established a monarchy to keep order. However, whereas Hobbes had said that the people turned over their sovereignty completely to the monarch, Locke claimed that they retained it but created a contract of mutual obligations with their ruler. Locke argued that if the king broke the contract, the people had the right to depose him and install a new monarch, just as Parliament had done during the Glorious Revolution.

FIGURE 13.11

J. Hayls, *Samuel Pepys*, 1666.

an eyewitness account of the devastating plague that scourged London in 1665, followed by the great fire the year after. Pepys juxtaposed historical events with the most intimate details of his daily life, from the food he ate to the arguments he had with his wife. He stopped keeping his diary in 1669 because his eyesight was failing him.

Pepys took an active role in political life by working in the naval office. In 1685 he was even elected to the House of Commons. He continued to receive the benefits of royal patronage under the reigns of Charles II and James II, but the Glorious Revolution of 1688 caused his fortunes to change. He lost the parliamentary election in 1689, and in the following year he was arrested on suspicion that he supported the deposed James II. Pepys had always been more interested in observing political events rather than engaging passionately in them, and when he was released from prison he removed himself from political life. He spent the rest of his years reading, playing music, and exchanging letters with friends, including such eminent scholars as Isaac Newton. His last years were devoted to building a substantial library that he bequeathed at his death to his alma mater, where it still remains intact and unaltered. He died peacefully in 1703.

Pepys wrote his diary in a shorthand that was used by clerks in the seventeenth century; Newton used the same shorthand for taking his notes. The four-volume, handwritten, leatherbound diary written in a forgotten code lay ignored on the library shelves until the nineteenth century. Then, an undergraduate of the college took on the gigantic task of transcribing the diary (omitting the erotic passages) and it became an instant success. Modern editions of the complete diary continue to engage readers with its direct picture of seventeenth-century England. It has ensured that Samuel Pepys will not be forgotten.

Locke's political theories were not intended to support full democracies—in his time, the "people" meant only those who owned property. He did not intend for individuals, such as the landless Levellers, to threaten property owners. Nor did he view women as sharing in the popular sovereignty of the privileged social order. Locke's highly influential rhetoric, in which he claimed natural rights of "life, liberty, and property," actually applied to relatively few people in 1690. However, in time, his theory would broaden to form the basis for democracy as well as constitutional monarchy.

Parliament soon had the opportunity to exert its king-making authority once again. William and Mary died without an heir, so the crown went to James II's Protestant daughter, Anne. Queen Anne (r. 1701–1714) also died without an heir, whereby the Protestant Stuart dynasty evaporated. Parliament then passed the

Hanover dynasty

crown to George I (r. 1714–1727), a great-grandson of James I, who ruled the German principality of Hanover, introducing the Hanoverian dynasty to England. This peaceful transition demonstrated once and for all that the struggle for sovereignty in England was over—Parliament ruled.

THE NETHERLANDS MAINTAIN A REPUBLIC

The English nobles asserted their rights over the king by exercising their authority through a parliament that ruled over a highly centralized government. This struggle created a strong constitutional monarchy that preserved popular sovereignty while creating a state that would prove highly stable. Another way for people to preserve their sovereignty was to resist a strong central government in order to strengthen

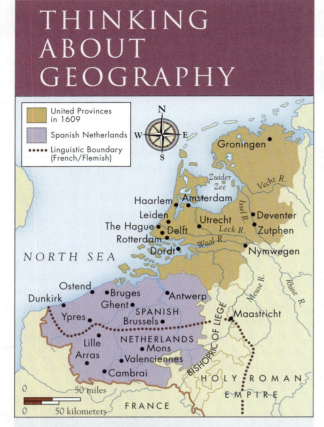

THINKING ABOUT GEOGRAPHY

Map legend:
- United Provinces in 1609
- Spanish Netherlands
- Linguistic Boundary (French/Flemish)

Map labels: Groningen, Zuider Zee, Vecht R., Haarlem, Amsterdam, Leiden, Utrecht, Deventer, The Hague, Delft, Leck R., Zutphen, Rotterdam, Waal R., Nymwegen, Dordt, NORTH SEA, Meuse R., Rhine R., Ostend, Bruges, Antwerp, Dunkirk, Ghent, SPANISH, BISHOPRIC OF LIEGE, Maastricht, Ypres, Brussels, Lille, NETHERLANDS, Mons, Arras, Valenciennes, Cambrai, HOLY ROMAN EMPIRE, FRANCE

Scale: 0 — 50 miles / 0 — 50 kilometers

MAP 13.5   THE UNITED PROVINCES AND THE SPANISH NETHERLANDS, 1609

This map shows the location of the Netherlands in Europe and its division into two separate states. ■ **Notice** the scale of this map. **Consider** how small the United Provinces were. **What** about their location contributed to their wealth and importance in the seventeenth century? ■ **Notice** the proximity of the Catholic Spanish Netherlands to France. **Consider** how this region might have served as a buffer for the Protestant United Provinces.

local institutions. In the seventeenth century, the Netherlands developed this political structure that also gave power to the people instead of to absolute rulers. They instituted another form of constitutionalism that structured the government around consent of the propertied.

When the Low Countries split in 1609, the southern Catholic regions remained subject to the absolutist monarch, Philip III of Spain. Map 13.5 shows the division of the Low Countries in 1609. The Spanish Netherlands of the south (now Belgium) formed

a buffer between the United Provinces of the north and the divine right monarchy of France. In the United Provinces, which became largely Calvinist after the wars with Catholic Spain, a Protestant state developed that successfully resisted any attempts at royal absolutism.

The United Provinces

The United Provinces—also known as the Dutch Republic—was the only major European power to maintain a republican form of government throughout the seventeenth century. Each province was governed locally by an assembly (called the State) made up of delegates from cities and rural areas. In reality, the States were dominated by an oligarchy of wealthy merchants. The union of the provinces was only a loose confederation, with each province sending deputies to the States General, a national assembly that implemented provincial assembly decisions.

Executive power at the local level was vested in governors (Stadholders) of each province. At the national level, executive power was given to the Council of State, made up of deputies drawn from the provinces.

This remarkable decentralization worked effectively for local issues, but had some drawbacks for implementing foreign policy. During the 1650s, Holland—the largest province—began to take an informal lead in directing the state's foreign policy in the first two wars against England. After 1672, William III, a prince of the hereditary house of Orange, became the captain-general of the republic's military forces against France. The House of Orange had a permanent vote in the States General and served as a unifying point. However, William of Orange exercised more power once he became king of England in 1689 than he ever had in the Netherlands. Document 13.3 provides a description of the governmental structure of the Dutch Republic. The 1648 Treaty of Westphalia that ended the Thirty Years' War (see Chapter 11) formally recognized the Republic of the United Provinces.

What were the special circumstances that led the Netherlands to develop and maintain this strong sense of local sovereignty when other areas of Europe were moving to centralized governments?

Dutch prosperity

In large part, such political independence was facilitated by prosperity. The seventeenth century has been called the "golden age" of the United Provinces, for this small region was a tremendous European and colonial power. Amsterdam became the commercial and financial center of Europe as ships brought huge quantities of herring from the North Sea, as well as sugar, tobacco, glass, and many other items from around the world, through the bustling port.

In addition to commerce, the Dutch prospered through skilled shipbuilding that was the wonder of

■ DOCUMENT 13.3

An Ambassador Describes the Dutch Government

Sir William Temple (1628–1699) was an English diplomat who served as ambassador to the Netherlands in 1668 and again in 1674. He negotiated the marriage of William of Orange to Princess Mary of England. This political insider was an acute observer of the government of the United Provinces of the Netherlands as shown in this account. ■ **Notice** *which powers remained in the hands of the Prince and which in the assembly of the States General.* ■ **How** *does this division of rights compare with the governmental forms described in Document 13.1?* ■ **What** *might be the strengths and weaknesses of this form of government?*

In the first constitution of this government, after the revolt from Spain, all the power and rights of Prince William of Orange, as Governor of the Provinces, seem to have been carefully reserved. But those which remained inherent in the Sovereign, were devolved upon the assembly of the States-General, so as in them remained the power of making peace and war, and all foreign alliances, and of raising and coining of monies: in the Prince, the command of all land and sea forces, as Captain-general and Admiral, and thereby the disposition of all military commands, the power of pardoning the penalty of crimes, the chusing of magistrates upon the nomination of the towns; for they presented three to the Prince, who elected one out of that number. Originally the States-General were convoked by the council of State, where the Prince had the greatest influence: nor, since that change, have the States used to resolve any important matter without his advice. Besides all this, as the States-General represented the sovereignty, so did the Prince of Orange the dignity, of this State, by public guards, and the attendance of all military officers; by the application of all foreign ministers, and all pretenders at home; by the splendor of his court and magnificence of his expence; supported not only by the pensions and rights of his several charges and commands, but by a mighty patrimonial revenue in lands and sovereign principalities and lordships, as well in France, Germany, and Burgundy, as in thy several parts of the Seventeen Provinces; so as Prince Henry was used to answer some that would have flattered him into the designs of a more arbitrary power, that he had as much as any wise Prince would desire in that State; since he wanted none indeed, besides that of punishing men, and raising money; whereas he had rather the envy of the first should lie upon the forms of the government, and he knew the other could never be supported, without the consent of the people, to that degree which was necessary for the defense of so small a State against so mighty Princes as their neighbors.

Source: *The Works of Sir William Temple*, vol. I (London, 1814), pp. 118–119 in *Modern History Sourcebook*, www.fordham.edu/halsall/mod/17dutch.html.

Europe. Not only did they design remarkable ships that could sail with fewer crew members than more traditional ships, they also built them quickly and cheaply. They obtained timber, pitch, and rigging from the nearby Baltic regions, and they used the most modern technology for the assembly: mechanical saws, hoists for masts, and the manufacture of interchangeable parts. Contemporary witnesses were amazed to report that given two months' notice, Dutch shipbuilders could turn out a warship every week for the rest of the year. Figure 13.12 shows an engraving of a Dutch shipyard that was the envy of the rest of Europe. It is no wonder that silver from the New World found its way into the coffers of Dutch builders.

The Dutch also grew rich from their activities as major slave traders in the New World. The population of Amsterdam grew from about 30,000 people in 1570 to 200,000 by 1660, and the growth was testimony to the wealth and opportunities people saw there. Its financial importance was secured in 1609 by the foundation of the Exchange Bank of Amsterdam, the greatest public bank in northern Europe. Europe-

ans were astonished by the prosperity and enterprise of the Dutch.

The Dutch had other elements that contributed to their resistance of absolutism. The Dutch aristocracy was not as wealthy as that of England or France, for example. Their wealth lay more in commerce than in land, so the aristocracy had more in common with the merchants of their land than they did with the landed gentry in England or with the nobility at the court of Versailles. Furthermore, in the United Provinces, the Protestant faith cultivated an ideology of moderation—rather than the aristocratic excess that marked the nobility of other states. That is not to say that the seventeenth-century United Provinces espoused notions of egalitarian democracy—the nobility were as interested in trying to increase their power as those of other countries. They were just not able to exert much centralized control over the prosperous, Protestant residents that were the wonder of Europe.

Overall, the Dutch exhibited an unusual degree of religious toleration for their time. They even

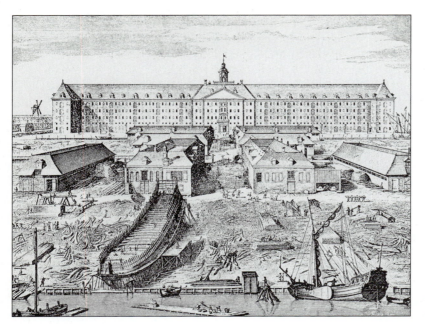

■ FIGURE 13.12

Anonymous, *Engraving of a Dutch Shipyard*.

■ FIGURE 13.13

Rembrandt van Rijn, *Syndics of the Cloth Guild*, ca. 1661.

the open-minded assemblies stimulated the spread of ideas through the press. The United Provinces became a leading center for book publishing and transmitted ideas, even revolutionary ones, all over Europe. In 1649, for example, an anonymous pamphlet published in the Netherlands attacked Cromwell's government for not supporting the ideas of the Levellers. The pamphlet called for an "equality of goods and lands" and condemned the government that "hangs a poor man if he do steal, when they have wrongfully taken from him all his maintenance."

The refugees streaming into the Netherlands included some destitute travelers and in some ways burdened the small country. The Dutch, however, generously assisted the needy, who never sank to the same depths of hardship that faced the poor in many other European cities. In his brief stay in the Netherlands, Samuel Pepys recorded in his diary the provisions the Dutch made for the poor. He observed a guesthouse, "where it was very pleasant to see what neat preparation there is for the poor." He further noted that there were special entertainment taxes to raise money for the needy.

The wealthy middle classes treated themselves well also. For example, they commissioned paintings that depicted their unique way of life. The Dutch artist Jan Vermeer (see Chapter 12) was one of several whose talents flourished in the free Dutch environment. Even more celebrated was the Dutch artist Rembrandt van Rijn (1606–1669), whose brilliant use of light and forceful expressiveness made him among the greatest of western European painters.

In the painting *Syndics of the Cloth Guild* (Figure 13.13) Rembrandt portrays the serious, successful merchants who had been chosen to manage the wealthy guild. The artist captures the proud intensity with which they work over a book on the table. In the uniformity in their clothing, they stand in striking contrast to the man in Figure 13.7 on page 424, who boasts luxurious designs and fabrics that set him apart from people precisely like these successful syndics. Rembrandt offered this painting to the cloth guild in thanks for their charity—the painter, who had fallen on hard times, needed coal to heat his house for the winter, and the cloth guild had provided it.

allowed Catholics and Jews to practice their religions, a policy that encouraged religious refugees to flock to the Netherlands from all over Europe. These refugees greatly enriched the cultural and economic life of the republic. Not only did the United Provinces attract intellectuals, such as René Descartes from France and John Locke from England, but

Religious toleration

The preeminence of the Dutch in the seventeenth century began to wane by the beginning of the next century. The economies of England and France had gathered strength both in Europe and abroad and encroached on the commercial empire forged by the Dutch. Yet the two geographically small countries of England and the Netherlands had contributed much to the political development of the West. Both established the sovereignty of the people through constitutionalism—England through Parliament, and the Netherlands through local autonomy. For all their tremendous impact for the future, at the opening of the eighteenth century both nations seemed hardly whispers in a Europe dominated by strong monarchs proclaiming a divine right to rule.

SUMMARY

For upper-crust members of Western societies, the seventeenth century was a period of both comfort and struggle. The comfort came from these elites' continued dominance. From the beginning to the end of the century, they held most of the riches, status, and power. Those below them sometimes revolted, but the real threats came from competing colleagues and the monarch above. The efforts by monarchs to increase their power, to become "absolute" in both theory and practice, sparked intense struggles within states. In some places, such as France, Prussia, and Russia, strong monarchs offering order and stability won. In other places, such as Poland, England, and the Netherlands, powerful nobles—sometimes allied with commoners—overcame kings.

For the vast majority who toiled the fields, the period offered struggle without much comfort. In western Europe, demands from expanding central governments for taxes and conscripts only aggravated the hardships wrought by unusually bad harvests and disease. In eastern Europe, landowning nobles added to these problems by burdening peasants under an increasingly heavy yoke of serfdom.

Thus the structure of this hierarchical society may have loosened enough for some people in western Europe to improve their lot. However, that structure only tightened in eastern Europe. For all of Europe, war, revolt, and even revolution shook societies without breaking the traditional hierarchies. Nevertheless, some traditions started to crumble. Important changes in science and thought were already afoot that would soon transform the intellectual foundations of Western society.

KEY TERMS

Great Chain of Being, p. 406

royal absolutism, p. 410

Fronde, p. 411

classical style, p. 413

Estates, p. 417

sumptuary laws, p. 423

Puritans, p. 424

Roundheads, p. 426

Levellers, p. 427

constitutionalism, p. 431

Glorious Revolution, p. 432

REVIEW, ANALYZE, AND ANTICIPATE

REVIEW THE PREVIOUS CHAPTER

Chapter 11—"Alone Before God"—examines the Reformation, which shattered the unity of Western Christendom, and the entwined religious and dynastic wars that followed. Chapter 12—"Faith, Fortune, and Fame"—told how several European powers expanded overseas during this same period and grew rich from the commerce developed in their colonies.

1. Analyze how the religious divisions and wars of the sixteenth and seventeenth centuries laid the groundwork for both the growth of absolutism in France and central Europe as well as the struggle against it in England and the Netherlands.

2. In what ways might the competition for overseas empires and the commerce that resulted have affected the power of central governments and their responsibilities? How might the Netherlands' political structure have contributed to its commercial expansion?

ANALYZE THIS CHAPTER

Chapter 13—"The Struggle for Survival and Sovereignty"—describes how kings and nobles battled for power, the resolutions of those struggles, and their impact on the millions of people outside the elites.

1. Analyze the ways monarchs tried to increase their power.

2. What groups opposed the increase in monarchical power, and what political theories were developed to support their positions?

3. In what ways might the term "absolutism" also apply to the Mughal emperors?

4. How do you explain why in some areas monarchs won the battle for sovereignty, whereas in others they lost?

5. *Describe the struggles peasants throughout Europe faced during the seventeenth century. How did their conditions differ in western and eastern Europe?*

ANTICIPATE THE NEXT CHAPTER
Chapter 14—"A New World of Reason and Reform"—examines the changing intellectual foundations of the West.

1. *What kinds of intellectual changes do you think might undermine the traditional social and political order during the seventeenth and eighteenth centuries? Why?*

2. *What groups and institutions are most likely to be threatened by or resist intellectual changes? Why?*

BEYOND THE CLASSROOM

STRESSES IN TRADITIONAL SOCIETY
Braudel, Fernand. *Civilization and Capitalism: The Structures of Everyday Life.* New York: Harper & Row, 1981. An excellent survey by an important historian that details the transformations in economic and social history.

Bush, Michael. *Noble Privilege.* New York: Holmes & Meier, 1983. Analyzes the role of the nobility in the seventeenth century.

Chartier, Roger, ed. *A History of Private Life, Vol. III: Passions of the Renaissance.* Cambridge, MA: Harvard University Press, 1989. Part of a fine series that describes the creation of the sphere of private life.

Gottlieb, Beatrice. *The Family in the Western World from the Black Death to the Industrial Age.* Oxford: Oxford University Press, 1994. A thorough survey of the transformations in family life.

ROYAL ABSOLUTISM IN FRANCE
Bercé, Yves-Marie. *The Birth of Absolutism.* London: Macmillan, 1996. A solid examination of French absolutism from the reign of Louis XIV to 1789.

Muchembled, Robert. *Popular Culture and Elite Culture in France, 1400–1750.* Baton Rouge, LA: Louisiana State University Press, 1985. Examines popular culture and the means by which higher authorities attempted to destroy it.

Treasure, Geoffrey. *Louis XIV.* London: Longman, 2001. A well-written study of the king and his times.

THE STRUGGLE FOR SOVEREIGNTY IN EASTERN EUROPE
Goffman, Daniel. *The Ottoman Empire and Early Modern Europe.* Cambridge: Cambridge University Press, 2002. An informative recent survey of the topic.

Hughes, Lindsey. *Russia in the Age of Peter the Great.* New Haven, CT: Yale University Press, 1998. The most recent study of this important figure.

Kirby, David G. *Northern Europe in the Early Modern Period: The Baltic World, 1492–1772.* London: Longman, 1990. A good survey of the region during this period.

Wilson, Peter H. *Absolutism in Central Europe.* London: Routledge, 2000. A good comparative study of absolutism in Prussia and Austria.

GLOBAL CONNECTIONS
Richards, John F. *The Mughal Empire.* Cambridge: Cambridge University Press, 1993. A solid, useful survey of Mughal history.

THE TRIUMPH OF CONSTITUTIONALISM
Coward, Barry. *The Stuart Age: A History of England, 1603–1714.* White Plains, NY: Longman, 1995. A readable and balanced narrative of the whole course of the history of England.

van Deursen, A.Th. *Plain Lives in a Golden Age: Popular Culture, Religion, and Society in Seventeenth-Century Holland.* Translated by M. Ultree. New York: Cambridge University Press, 1991. A fascinating analysis of how laborers, peasants, and sailors made their living.

Durston, Christopher, ed. *Culture of English Puritanism, 1560–1700.* New York: Saint Martin's Press, 1996. A look into the lives and times of the English Puritans.

Fraser, Antonia. *The Weaker Vessel.* New York: Knopf, 1984. A detailed, illustrated, and comprehensive study of women in seventeenth-century England.

Gaunt, Peter. *Oliver Cromwell.* Cambridge, MA: Blackwell, 1995. A good study on the life and career of the Lord Protector.

Hill, Christopher. *A Nation of Change and Novelty: Radical Politics, Religion, and Literature in Seventeenth-Century England.* London: Routledge, 1990. A history of the revolution by an eminent historian.

Miller, John. *Restoration and the England of Charles II,* 2nd ed. White Plains, NY: Longman, 1997. Clarifies the complex issues of the major political and religious themes surrounding the Restoration.

Sharpe, Kevin. *Culture and Politics in Early Stuart England.* Stanford, CA: Stanford University Press, 1994. A revisionist look at the culture and politics in England at this time.

www.mhhe.com/sherman3

- Unfamiliar words? See our Glossary at the back of the book for pronunciation and definitions.

- Need help studying? See our web page for map exercises, practice quizzes, and additional study resources.

- Need help writing a paper? Access hundreds of primary documents, maps, images, and a guide to writing history papers on our Primary Source Investigator site at **www.mhhe.com/psi.**

FRONTISPIECE TO MARCO VINCENZO CORONELLI'S ATLAS, 1691

In this frontispiece from an atlas, a globe and ship occupy center stage and represent the West's exploration of the world. Just above, the banner of a trumpeting angel reads, "Yet farther"—words that contrast sharply with the traditional medieval expression "No farther." Drawings of the numerous instruments that characterized the new age of exploration and science occupy the periphery of the image.

A New World of Reason and Reform

THE SCIENTIFIC REVOLUTION AND THE ENLIGHTENMENT, 1600–1800

STUDY	The traditional worldview ▪ The modern scientific worldview ▪ Spreading science ▪ The Enlightenment.
NOTICE	The connections between the Scientific Revolution and the Enlightenment.

In 1655, French scientist Blaise Pascal (1623–1662) retired from his studies and began recording his thoughts in writing. "Man is but a reed, the most feeble thing in nature; but he is a thinking reed," he wrote. "All our dignity consists, then, in thought . . . by thought I comprehend the world." Pascal's words hint at the changes emerging in scholars' thinking about ideas, the world, and the place of humans in it.

We can detect more clues about these changes in the artwork on page 436. The 1691 world atlas itself, published by the accomplished Venetian mapmaker and mathematician Marco Coronelli (1650–1718), echoes the overseas expansion of Europe, already two centuries old. It also reveals the underlying culture of the Renaissance, which stressed learning and exploration through reading and art. Coronelli chose this illustration to open his new atlas. With the images of a ship, the earth, scientific instruments, and the provocative phrasing "Yet farther," he declared the end of limits to the search for knowledge. The entire illustration suggests a people proudly using science to fuel their growing power—over other peoples as well as nature itself.

Buoyed by the accumulation of scientific discoveries, this optimism about the power of thought and the search for knowledge grew and spread throughout the West during the eighteenth century. Widening circles of intellectuals and the reading public learned about the new ways of thinking being applied to all fields, from politics and religion to economics and criminology. Despite resistance from church and state, this dawning of what became known as the Age of Reason would gather strength, filter down through the ranks of society, and form the intellectual foundation for life in the modern West. Certainly the West was not unique in reasoning about the world. In the centuries preceding Europe's Renaissance, the Chinese had made many scholarly and scientific advances. The Arabs had not only prized learning and science, but also had provided Europeans with tools such as translations of Greek science and Arabic numerals that were essential for Europe's scientists. On the other hand, by the sixteenth century most European scientists had university educations, whereas non-Western civilizations lacked institutions comparable to the medieval universities in places such as Bologna, Paris, and Oxford. Moreover, during the seventeenth and eighteenth centuries, the Islamic, Chinese, Japanese, and other civilizations of the world declined to question their traditional ways. Only Westerners challenged the standard assumptions of their civilization. The power and attitudes that the West gained from this intellectual exploration helped redefine Western civilization and distinguish it from the non-Western world.

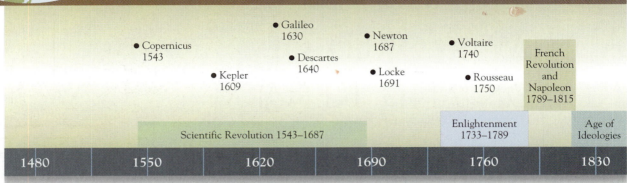

- Copernicus 1543
- Kepler 1609
- Galileo 1630
- Descartes 1640
- Newton 1687
- Locke 1691
- Voltaire 1740
- Rousseau 1750

French Revolution and Napoleon 1789–1815

Scientific Revolution 1543–1687

Enlightenment 1733–1789

Age of Ideologies

1480   1550   1620   1690   1760   1830

QUESTIONING TRUTH AND AUTHORITY

ON JUNE 22, 1633, THE well-known Italian scientist Galileo Galilei (1564–1642) knelt in a Roman convent before the cardinals who served as judges of the Inquisition. The cardinals informed Galileo that he was "vehemently suspected of heresy." They also showed him the customary instruments of torture, though they did not use them. Next, they ordered him to deny "the false opinion that the sun is the center of the universe and immovable, and that the earth is not the center of the same"—views that Galileo had supported in a book he published the previous year. Threatened with being tried and burned as a heretic, Galileo had to denounce his views as heresy. The court and papacy sentenced Galileo to house arrest in Florence for the rest of his life and forbade him to publish on the topic again. Nevertheless, Galileo would not change his mind. The sequence of events leading to Galileo's trial and conviction is a story of its own, but the conflict lay at the core of a major development of the age: the Scientific Revolution.

THE OLD VIEW

Until the sixteenth century, most European scholars shared the standard medieval understanding of the physical nature of the earth and the universe. This understanding was based on a long legacy stretching back to the views of the fourth-century B.C.E. Greek philosopher Aristotle. His ideas had been modified in the second century C.E. by Ptolemy of Alexandria and then passed on through Byzantine and Arab scholars to medieval European thinkers. After the thirteenth century, Europeans translated Aristotle's works into

Latin and merged his thinking with Christian ideas about the universe.

According to this Christian medieval understanding, illustrated in the woodcut in Figure 14.1, the earth rested at the center of an unchanging universe. Around it in ascending order rose the perfect spheres of air, fire, the sun, the planets, and the stars (the "firmament"), with God (the "prime mover") just beyond. The signs of the zodiac are recorded on one band in the illustration, revealing the importance of astrology. Westerners accounted for the succession of day and night by explaining that this finite universe rotated in precise circles around the earth once every twenty-four hours. The heavenly abode of angels consisted of pure matter, and the earthly home of humans was made of changeable, corrupt matter. This universe was clear, finite, and satisfyingly focused on the earthly center of God's concern.

The earth-centered universe

Common sense supported this worldview. A glance at the sky confirmed that the sun and stars indeed circled around the earth each day. Under foot, the earth felt motionless. To careful observers, the motion of planets, whose position often changed, was more perplexing. To explain this mystery, Ptolemy and others had modified their theories, concluding that planets moved in small, individual orbits as they traveled predictably around the earth. People had lived by the wisdom of the ancients and authoritative interpretations of the Bible for centuries. Accordingly, investigation of the physical universe generally consisted of making deductions from these long-accepted guides.

UNDERMINING THE OLD VIEW

During the fifteenth and sixteenth centuries, new problems began undermining this traditional view.

Authorities of all kinds—including Aristotle—came into question during the Renaissance. Some of this questioning stemmed from the Renaissance search for classical writings, which led scholars to discover and read the works of Greek authorities who contradicted Aristotle. **Neoplatonism,** based on the ideas of Plato, stressed the belief that one should search beyond appearances for true knowledge; truth about both nature and God could be found in abstract reasoning and be best expressed by mathematics. Neoplatonic **Hermetic doctrine** provided especially powerful alternatives to Aristotelian thought.

According to Hermetic doctrine, based on writings mistakenly attributed to Hermes Trismegistus (supposedly an ancient Egyptian priest), all matter contained the divine spirit, which humans ought to seek to understand. Among many scholars, this doctrine stimulated intense interest in botany, chemistry, metallurgy, and other studies that promised to help people unlock the secrets of nature. The Hermetic approach also held that mathematical harmonies helped explain the divine spirit and represented a crucial pathway to understanding God's physical world. This approach encouraged scholars to use mathematics and to measure, map, and quantify nature. Moreover, Hermetic doctrine also held that the sun was the most important agency for transmission of the divine spirit, and thus rightly occupied the center of the universe. Finally, these beliefs fostered the idea of the natural magician who could unleash the powers of nature through alchemy (the study of how to purify and transform metals, such as turning common minerals into gold), astrology (the study of how stars affect people), and magic. Scholars often saw no distinction between seeking to understand the harmony, oneness, and spiritual aspects of the natural world and what we would call scientific observation and experimentation. Although Hermetic doctrine often proved not useful, all these ideas encouraged investigators to question traditionally accepted knowledge.

Hermetic doctrine

Figure 14.2, an illustration from a book on alchemy by the German Heinrich Khunrath shows these close connections between spiritual beliefs and the "science" or "Hermetic art" of alchemy. At the left, the author prays in a small chapel. Lettering on the drapery of the chapel states, "When we attend strictly to our work, God himself will help us." At the center, musical instruments and a pair of scales rest on a table, representing the links among music, harmony, and number so characteristic in alchemy. The inscription on the table reads, "Sacred music disperses sadness in evil spirits." On the floor lie containers and other apparatus used to mix materials, and at the upper right are flasks and other storage containers.

■ FIGURE 14.1

The medieval view of the universe, 1559.

In addition to new ideas and beliefs, geographic exploration during the Renaissance also upset traditional assumptions. The discovery of the New World, for example, disproved Ptolemaic geography. Furthermore, overseas voyages stimulated demand for new instruments and precise measurements for navigation. This demand, in turn, encouraged research, especially in astronomy and mathematics.

Exploration

Finally, the recently invented printing press enabled even out-of-favor scholars to publish their findings, which spread new ideas and discoveries even further. Renaissance rulers supported all these efforts in hopes of gaining prestige as well as practical tools for war, construction, and mining. Church authorities did the same at times, especially backing research in astronomy in the hopes of improving the calendar to date Easter more accurately.

The printing press

Like the Renaissance, the Reformation also unleashed forces that provoked the questioning of long-held views. Most researchers had religious motives for their work, though those motives were not necessarily grounded in tradition. In particular, they yearned for insights into the perfection of God's universe.

■ FIGURE 14.2

Heinrich Khunrath, *The Laboratory and the Chapel*, 1609.

give church some power [handwritten margin note]

As we read in Chapter 11, the Reformation shattered confidence in religious authorities. By upsetting hallowed certainties, sixteenth- and seventeenth-century scholars hoped to establish new, even sounder certainties and thereby regain a sense of mastery over nature.

DEVELOPING A MODERN SCIENTIFIC VIEW

Even with these rumblings of change, no sudden breakthrough cleared away the centuries-old understanding of nature. Most scientific work still proceeded slowly, as did scholarly and public acceptance of its findings. Investigators had to demonstrate the effectiveness of their new methods again and again to convince even their colleagues. Indeed, few scholars suggested a wholesale rejection of traditional authorities; most simply chipped away at old notions. By the end of the seventeenth century, however, an entirely new scientific view of reality, initiated by just a handful of scholars, had replaced the traditional view. To understand this startling shift, we need to trace developments in astronomy, physics, and scientific methodology.

ASTRONOMY AND PHYSICS: FROM COPERNICUS TO NEWTON

During the sixteenth and seventeenth centuries, astronomy and physics attracted the most systematic attention from scholars. Researchers in these fields became particularly dissatisfied with the inability of Aristotelian theory to explain, simply and efficiently, careful observations and mathematical calculations of the stars. The Ptolemaic system for predicting planetary movements seemed overly complex and cumbersome to these scholars. Their findings would dramatically alter Westerners' perceptions of nature and of the earth's place in the universe. As the English poet John Donne complained in 1611, "New philosophy calls all in doubt."

Nicolaus Copernicus (1473–1543), a Polish clergyman with an interest in astronomy, astrology, mathematics, and church law, took the first steps in this intellectual adventure. Like so many other northern European scholars, he crossed the Alps to study in an Italian university. There he became influenced by the rediscovery of Greek scholarship, Neoplatonism, and the Hermetic doctrine. Copernicus sought a simpler mathematical formulation to explain how the universe operated. His search convinced him

Nicolaus Copernicus

earth not center, moving [handwritten margin note]

that the earth was *not* at the center of the universe. Instead, he believed that the sun "sits upon a royal throne" in that location, "ruling his children, the planets which circle around him." Moreover, Copernicus concluded that the earth was not stationary: "What appears to be a motion of the sun is in truth a motion of the earth." According to Copernicus, the earth moved in perfect, "divine" circles around the sun, as did other bodies in the universe. Day passed into night because the earth turned on its axis. Figure 14.3 shows this view of the universe. At the center is the sun, circled by the earth ("this globe of mortality") and other planets, all bounded by an infinity of stars ("fixed" and "immovable") and the heavens ("the palace of happiness . . . the habitat for the elect"). This change from an earth-centered (geocentric) to a sun-centered (heliocentric) universe would become known as the **Copernican revolution.** Copernicus worked on his **heliocentric model** of the universe for almost twenty-five years. However, fearing ridicule and disapproval from the clergy, he waited until 1543—what became the year of his death—to publish it. Few people outside a limited circle of scholars knew of his views, and even fewer accepted them. Nevertheless, Catholic and Protestant authorities who were wedded to the earth-centered system soon recognized the threat to the Christian conception of the universe that these ideas represented. They denounced the Copernican system as illogical, unbiblical, and unsettling to the Christian faith. [handwritten: Christians] One Protestant associate of Martin Luther complained that "certain men . . . have concluded that the earth moves. . . . It is want of honesty and decency to assert such notions publicly. . . . It is part of a good mind to accept the truth as revealed by God and to acquiesce in it."

Still, Copernicus's thinking had some supporters. An Italian monk, Giordano Bruno (1548–1600), tested Catholic authorities by openly teaching and extending Copernican thought, arguing that "the universe is entirely infinite because it has neither edge, limit, nor surfaces." Bruno also professed a series of unusual religious notions. Outraged, the Catholic Inquisition burned Bruno at the stake. [handwritten: what did he believe?] Nevertheless, Copernicus's views began to influence other scholars who were investigating the physical nature of the universe.

The Danish aristocrat Tycho Brahe (1546–1601) did not share Copernicus's belief in a heliocentric universe, nor did he grasp the sophisticated mathematics of the day. Still, he became the next most important astronomer of the sixteenth century. He persuaded the king of Denmark to build for him the most advanced astronomy laboratory in Europe. There he recorded thousands of unusually accurate, detailed observations about the planets and stars over a period of twenty years—all without a telescope. His discoveries of a new star in 1572 and a comet in 1577 undermined the Aristotelian belief in a sky of fixed, unalterable stars moving in crystalline spheres. Although Brahe mistakenly concluded

Tycho Brahe

[handwritten vertical margin: don't mess with the church]
[handwritten vertical margin: Tycho Brahe]

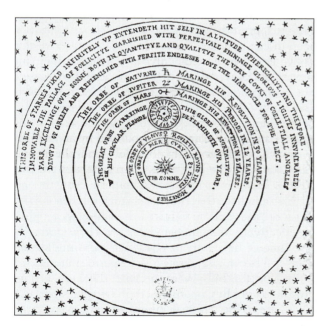

■ FIGURE 14.3
Tycho Brahe, the Copernican view of the universe, 1576.

that some planets revolved around the sun, which itself moved around the earth, other astronomers with better understandings of mathematics would use his observations to draw very different conclusions.

Tycho Brahe's assistant, Johannes Kepler (1571–1630), built on Brahe's observations to support the Copernican heliocentric theory. A German Lutheran from an aristocratic family, Kepler—like other Hermetic scholars—believed in an underlying mathematical harmony of mystical significance to the physical universe. He sought one harmony that would fit with Brahe's observations. Between 1609 and 1619, he announced his most important findings: the three laws of planetary motion. After determining the first law—which stated that the planets moved in ellipses around the sun—he excitedly wrote, "It was as if I had awaken from a sleep." The second law declared that the planets' velocity varied according to their distance from the sun. The third law concluded that the physical relationship between the moving planets could be expressed mathematically. Kepler thus showed "that the celestial machine . . . is the likeness of [a] clock," further undermining the Aristotelian view and extending the Copernican revolution.

Johannes Kepler

[handwritten vertical margin: Kepler 3 laws]

Document 14.1 reveals that in 1597, Kepler responded to a letter from Galileo Galilei, the Italian astronomer, physicist, and mathematician discussed at the beginning of this chapter. Although Galileo expressed a reluctance to publicize his beliefs in Copernican ideas, Kepler encouraged him to take the risk. "Be of good cheer, Galileo, and appear in public. If I am not mistaken there are only a few among the distinguished mathematicians of Europe who would dissociate themselves from us. So great is the power of truth."

Galileo Galilei

Galileo already believed that the world could be described in purely mathematical terms. "Philosophy," he wrote, "is written in this grand book, the universe, which stands continually open to our gaze. . . . It is written in the language of mathematics, and its characters are triangles, circles, and other geometric figures without which it is humanly impossible to understand a single word of it. . . ." Galileo also felt that harmonies could be discovered through experimentation and mathematics. By conducting controlled experiments such as rolling balls down inclines, he demonstrated how motion could be described mathematically. He rejected the old view that objects in their natural state were at rest and that all motion needed a purpose. Instead, he formulated the principle of inertia, showing that bodies, once set into motion, will tend to stay in motion. He thus overturned Aristotelian ideas and established rules for experimental physics.

Galileo, hearing about the recent invention of the telescope, then studied the skies through a telescope that he built in 1609 out of a long tube and magnifying

■ DOCUMENT 14.1

Kepler and Galileo Exchange Letters About Science

Many leading European scholars of the Scientific Revolution feared publishing their views, which were often unpopular with religious authorities. Such scholars sometimes turned to each other for support, as the following late-sixteenth-century letters between Kepler and Galileo suggest. Here the two men discuss their beliefs in Copernican theory. ■ **Why** *is Galileo reluctant to publish his views on the Copernican position?* ■ **How** *does Kepler respond to Galileo's concerns?*

Galileo to Kepler: "Like you, I accepted the Copernican position several years ago. I have written up many reasons on the subject, but have not dared until now to bring them into the open. I would dare publish my thoughts if there were many like you; but, since there are not. I shall forbear."

Kepler's Reply: "I could only have wished that you, who have so profound an insight, would choose another way. You advise us to retreat before the general ignorance and not to expose ourselves to the violent attacks of the mob of scholars. But after a tremendous task has been begun in our time, first by Copernicus and then by many very learned mathematicians, and when the assertion that the Earth moves can no longer be considered something new, would it not be much better to pull the wagon to its goal by our joint efforts, now that we have got it under way, and gradually, with powerful voices, to shout down the common herd? Be of good cheer, Galileo, and come out publicly! If I judge correctly, there are only a few of the distinguished mathematicians of Europe who would part company with us, so great is the power of truth. If Italy seems a less favorable place for your publication, perhaps Germany will allow us this freedom."

Source: Giorgio de Santillana, *The Crime of Galileo* (Chicago: University of Chicago Press, 1955), pp. 11, 14–15.

lenses. He saw that the moon's surface, instead of being a perfect heavenly body, was rugged (like the earth's), with craters and mountains indicated by lines and shading. The telescope also revealed that Jupiter had moons and that the sun had spots. These observations confirmed the view that other heavenly bodies besides the earth were imperfect and further convinced him of the validity of Copernicus's hypothesis. For years, Galileo had feared the disapproval of the Catholic Church. Now, however, he was ready to publicly argue that "in discussions of physical problems we ought to begin not from the authority of scriptural passages, but from sense-experiences and necessary demonstrations." Galileo published his findings in 1610.

Six years later, the church attacked his proposition that "the earth is not the center of the world nor immovable, but moves as a whole, and also with a daily motion." This statement, the church said, was "foolish and absurd philosophically, and formally heretical." To back up its claim, the church cited the authority of both the Bible and itself. For the next several years, Galileo kept his thoughts to himself. In 1632, believing that the church might be more open, he decided again to present his views. To avoid challenging the church, he submitted his book to the official church censors and agreed to some changes they demanded. Finally he published his *Dialogue on the Two Chief Systems of the World*—in Italian rather than the less-accessible Latin. This text advocated Copernicanism, portrayed opponents of the Copernican system (such as the Jesuits) as simpletons, and brought Galileo directly into public conflict with conservative forces in the Catholic Church. Because Galileo could show that his book had already been approved by church officials, prosecutors had to use questionable evidence against him. Figure 14.4, painted by an anonymous artist, shows Galileo, wearing a black suit and hat, sitting alone facing church officials. Behind him a man records the trial, while surrounding them are observers—some members of the clergy, others lay people. In the lower left, two men discuss or argue the issues being decided within; above them some members of the audience look out toward the viewers and the greater world. As we saw at the beginning of the chapter, the Roman Inquisition ultimately forced Galileo to renounce his views.

News of Galileo's sensational trial spread throughout Europe, as did fear of publishing other radical views. Soon, however, his book was translated and published elsewhere in Europe, and his views began to win acceptance by other scientists. Even though Galileo admitted that the new science was beyond the grasp of "the shallow minds of the common people," he effectively communicated its ideas to his peers. By the time of his death in 1642, Europe's intellectual elite had begun to embrace the Copernican outlook.

In England, Isaac Newton (1642–1727) picked up the trail blazed by Copernicus, Brahe, Kepler, and Galileo. Late in life, Newton described his career modestly: "I do not know what I may appear to the world; but to myself I seem to have been only like a boy playing on the seashore, and diverting myself in now and then finding

Isaac Newton

a smoother pebble or a prettier shell than ordinary, while the great ocean of truth lay all undiscovered before me." Newton may have held himself in humble regard, but his accomplishments were astonishing.

In 1661, Newton entered Cambridge University, where he studied the ideas of Copernicus and Galileo as well as the advantages of scientific investigation. He distinguished himself enough in mathematics to be chosen to stay on as a professor after his graduation. Like most other figures of the Scientific Revolution, Newton was also profoundly religious and, as indicated by Document 14.2, hoped to harmonize his Christian beliefs with the principles of science. He also believed in alchemy and elements of Hermeticism.

Starting in his early 20s, Newton made some of the most important discoveries in the history of science. He developed calculus and investigated the nature of light; he also formulated and mathematically described three laws of motion: inertia, acceleration, and action/reaction. Yet he is best known for discovering the law of universal attraction, or gravitation. After working on the concept for years, he finally published it in 1687 in his great work *Principia (The Mathematical Principles of Natural Knowledge)*. In the book, he stated the law with simplicity and precision: "Every particle of matter in the universe attracts every other particle with a force varying inversely as the square of the distance between them and directly proportional to the product of their masses." In his view, this law applied equally to all objects, from the most massive planet to a small apple falling from a tree.

Newton's Principia

Newton had managed to synthesize the new findings in astronomy and physics into a systematic explanation of physical laws that applied to the earth as well as the heavens. This Newtonian universe was infinite and had no center. Uniform and mathematically describable, it was held together by explainable forces and was atomic in nature. Essentially, everything in the universe consisted of only one thing: matter in motion.

THE REVOLUTION SPREADS: MEDICINE, ANATOMY, AND CHEMISTRY

Although astronomy and physics led the way in dramatic scientific findings, researchers in other fields made important discoveries as well. Many of these advances also had roots in the sixteenth century.

■ FIGURE 14.4
Trial of Galileo.

For example, several scholars developed new ideas in the related fields of medicine, anatomy, and chemistry.

In medicine, a flamboyant Swiss alchemist-physician known as Paracelsus (1493–1541) strongly influenced the healing arts. A believer in Hermetic doctrine, Paracelsus openly opposed medical orthodoxy and taught that healers should not look for truth in libraries ("the more learned, the more perverted," he warned) but in the Book of Nature. "I have not been ashamed to learn from tramps, butchers, and barbers," he boasted. As a teacher and wandering practitioner, he treated patients, experimented with chemicals, recorded his observations, and developed new theories. Paracelsus concluded that all matter was composed of salt, sulfur, and mercury—not the traditional earth, water, fire, and air. Rejecting the standard view that an imbalance in the humors of the body caused disease, he instead looked to specific chemical imbalances to explain what caused each illness. He also encouraged research and experimentation to find natural remedies for bodily disorders, such as administering mercury or arsenic at astrologically correct moments. Though rejected by most established physicians, Paracelsus's ideas became particularly popular among common practitioners and would later influence the study of chemistry.

Paracelsus

Other researchers founded the modern science of anatomy. In the sixteenth century, Andreas Vesalius (1514–1564), a Fleming living in Italy, wrote the first comprehensive textbook on the structure of the human body based on careful observation. Figure 14.5 shows the 28-year-old Vesalius displaying one of his studies on human anatomy from his 1543 treatise, *On the Fabric of the Human Body*. This figure is one of more

■ DOCUMENT 14.2

Isaac Newton: God in a Scientific Universe

Like Galileo and Descartes, Newton was well aware that his ideas had profound implications for theology. His views, he realized, might even be considered contrary to religious doctrine. Yet Newton was a deeply spiritual man and took pains to distinguish the appropriate realms of science and religion. In the following selection from Opticks *(1704), his analysis of light, Newton emphasizes that his ideas and systems still allow room for God in the universe.* ■ **What** *is Newton's view of the role played by God in the universe?* ■ **Might** *scientists today have any objections to these ideas? If so,* **what** *might they be?*

All these things being consider'd, it seems probable to me, that God in the Beginning form'd Matter in solid, massy, hard, impenetrable moveable Particles, of such Sizes and Figures, and with such other Properties, and in such Proportion to Space, as most conduced to the End for which he form'd them; and that these primitive Particles being Solids, are incomparably harder than any porous Bodies compounded of them; even so very hard, as never to wear or break in pieces; no ordinary Power being able to divide what God himself made one in the first Creation. . . .

It seems to me farther, that these Particles have not only a *Vis inertiae*, accompanied with such passive Laws of Motion as naturally result from that Force, but also that they are moved by certain active Principles, such as is that of Gravity, and that which cause Fermentation, and the Cohesion of Bodies. These Principles I consider, not as occult Qualities, supposed to result from the specifick Forms of Things, but as general Laws of Nature, by which the Things themselves are form'd; their Truth appearing to us by Phaenomena, though their Causes be not yet discover'd. . . .

Now by the help of these Principles, all material Things seem to have been composed of the hard and solid Particles abovemention'd, variously associated in the first Creation by the Counsel of an intelligent Agent. For it became him who created them to set them in order. And if he did no, it's unphilosophical to seek for any other Origin of the World, or to pretend that it might arise out of a Chaos by the mere Laws of Nature; though being once form'd, it may continue by those Laws for many Ages.

Source: Sir Isaac Newton, *Opticks*, 4th ed. (London: 1730), pp. 400–402.

than two hundred woodcut illustrations showing the composition of the body, stage by stage. Vesalius himself dissected cadavers, as suggested by the scalpel resting on the table. A notable aspect of this illustration is that Vesalius boldly looks the viewer in the eye, perhaps to challenge directly the old, authoritative assumptions about human anatomy. Nevertheless, his dissections of human bodies brought him into conflict with traditional physicians and scholars. Disgusted, he finally gave up his scientific studies and became the personal physician to Emperor Charles V.

Andreas Vesalius

Despite relentless criticism, other scholars continued anatomical research. A line from a poem written for the opening of the Amsterdam Anatomical Theatre in the early seventeenth century reflects the sense that this research needed special justification: "Evil doers who while living have done damage are of benefit after their death." In other words, the body parts of criminals "afford a lesson to you, the Living." The most important of these researchers was William Harvey (1578–1657), an Englishman who, like Vesalius, studied at the University of Padua in Italy. Harvey dissected hundreds of animals, including dogs, pigs, lobsters, shrimp, and snakes. He discovered that the human heart worked like a pump, with valves that

William Harvey

allowed blood to circulate through the body: "The movement of the blood occurs constantly in a circular manner and is the result of the beating of the heart." Yet, despite this mechanistic view, he also considered the heart the physical and spiritual center of life—in his words, "the sovereign of everything."

By the seventeenth century, anatomists and others benefited from several newly invented scientific instruments, such as the microscope. Anton van Leeuwenhoek (1632–1723), a Dutchman, became the chief pioneer in the use of this instrument. In observations during the 1670s, he described seeing "little animals or animalcules" in water from a lake. "It was wonderful to see: and I judge that some of these little creatures were above a thousand times smaller than the smallest ones I have ever yet seen, upon the rind of cheese, in wheaten flour, mould and the like." Leeuwenhoek discovered what would later be identified as bacteria in his own saliva: "little eels or worms, lying all huddled up together and wriggling . . . This was for me, among all the marvels that I have discovered in nature, the most marvellous of all."

Anton van Leeuwenhoek

Around this same time, Robert Boyle (1627–1691), an Irish nobleman particularly interested in medical chemistry, helped lay the foundations for modern

FIGURE 14.5

Andreas Vesalius, 1543.

chemistry. Drawing inspiration from Paracelsus, Boyle attacked many assumptions inherited from the ancients and began a systematic search for the basic elements of matter. Relying on the experimental method and using new instruments, he argued that all matter was composed of indestructible atoms that behaved in predictable ways. Boyle also discovered a law—which still bears his name—that governs the pressure of gases. His exacting procedures set a standard for the scientific practice of chemistry.

Robert Boyle

THE METHODOLOGY OF SCIENCE EMERGES

The scientists who challenged traditional views in their fields also used new methods of discovery—of uncovering how things worked and of determining "truth." Indeed, this innovative methodology lay at the heart of the Scientific Revolution. Earlier techniques for ascertaining the truth—by referring to long-trusted authorities and making deductions from their propositions—became unacceptable to the new scientists. They instead emphasized systematic skepticism, experimentation, and reasoning based solely on observed facts and mathematical laws. The two most important philosophers of this methodology were Francis Bacon and René Descartes.

Francis Bacon (1561–1626), an English politician who was once lord chancellor of England under James I, took a passionate interest in the new science. He rejected reliance on ancient authorities and advocated the collection of data without preconceived notions. From such data, he explained, scientific conclusions could be reached through inductive reasoning—drawing general conclusions from particular concrete observations. "Deriv[ing] axioms from . . . particulars, rising by gradual and unbroken ascent, so that it arrives at the most general axioms of all. This is the true way," he proclaimed. In addition, Bacon argued that scientific knowledge would be useful knowledge: "I am laboring to lay the foundation not of any sect or doctrine, but of human utility and power." He believed that science would benefit commerce and industry and improve the human condition by giving people unprecedented power over their environment.

Francis Bacon

Figure 14.6, the title page from Bacon's 1620 book *New Instrument,* graphically depicts these views. The illustration shows a ship of discovery sailing out from the western end of the Mediterranean Sea into the unknown. Below is the quotation, "Many shall venture forth and science shall be increased." Here is an optimistic assertion that knowledge is limitless and that science constitutes a voyage of discovery—a view that would be echoed again and again, as we saw in the picture at the beginning of this chapter. As Figure 14.6 suggests, Bacon thus became a noted propagandist for the new science as well as a proponent of the empirical method.

Despite his brilliance, Bacon did not have a thorough understanding of mathematics and the role it could play in the new science. His contemporary, René Descartes (1596–1650), would be the one to excel in this arena. Born in France, René Descartes received training in scholastic philosophy and mathematics at one of France's best Jesuit schools and took a degree in law. He entered military service and served during the Thirty Years' War. During his travels, he met a Dutch mathematician and became interested in the new science. An ecstatic experience in 1619 convinced him to commit to a life of the mind. He spent his most productive years as a mathematician, physicist, and metaphysical philosopher in Holland. In 1637, he published his philosophy and scientific methodology in the *Discourse on Method*—in French, not Latin. The book presented an eloquent defense of skepticism and of abstract **deductive reasoning**—deriving conclusions that logically flowed from a premise. "Inquiries should be directed, not to what others have thought, nor to what we ourselves conjecture, but to what we can clearly and perspicuously

René Descartes

FIGURE 14.6

Title page of Francis Bacon's *New Instrument*, 1620.

behold and with certainty deduce; for knowledge is not won in any other way."

Descartes questioned all forms of authority, no matter how venerable—be it Aristotle or even the Bible. He tried to remove systematically all assumptions about knowledge and advocated doubting the senses, which he claimed could be deceptive. Taken to its logical conclusion, his argument left him with one God-given experiential fact—that he was thinking. "I think, therefore I am" became his starting point. From there he followed a rigorous process of deductive reasoning to draw a variety of conclusions, including the existence of God and the physical world. He argued that there were two kinds of reality: mind, or subjective thinking and experiencing; and body, or objective physical matter. According to this philosophy, known as **Cartesian dualism,** the objective physical universe could be understood in terms of extension (matter occupying space) and motion (matter in motion). "Give me extension and motion," vowed Descartes, "and I will create the uni-

verse." He considered the body nothing more than "an earthen machine." In his opinion, only the mind was exempt from mechanical laws.

Descartes emphasized the power of the detached, reasoning individual mind to discover truths about nature. Unlike Bacon, he put his faith in mathematical reasoning, not in empirical investigation. By challenging all established authority, by accepting as truth only what could be known by reason, and by assuming a purely mechanical physical universe, Descartes established a philosophy and methodology that became the core of the new science.

SUPPORTING AND SPREADING SCIENCE

Only a small group of people actually participated in the **Scientific Revolution.** Of these, a handful of women managed to overcome barriers to take part as patrons for scientists or as scientists themselves. Men ignored or discounted their work, and scientific societies usually excluded them. The few women engaged in science such as the naturalist Maria Sibilla Merian (see Biography, page 399) and the German astronomer Maria Winkelmann (1647–1717) had to rely on their own resources or work in collaboration with their husbands.

Few scientific scholars—whether male or female—got far without calling on a network of peers and soliciting the support of wealthy patrons. To spread their ideas, these scientists needed to publish their works,

KEY DATES	
THE SCIENTIFIC REVOLUTION	
1543	Copernicus's heliocentric model published
1543	Vesalius, *Fabric of the Human Body*
1609–1619	Kepler, three laws of planetary motion
1620	Bacon, *New Instrument*
1633	Trial of Galileo
1637	Descartes, *Discourse on Method*
1662	English Royal Society founded
1687	Newton, *Principia*
1690	Locke, *Essay Concerning Human Understanding*
1697	Bayle, *Historical and Critical Dictionary*

interact with like-minded colleagues, and gain the backing of prestigious elites. Fortunately for them, these elites were eager to comply.

COURTS AND SALONS

Governments and wealthy aristocrats served as benefactors and employers of scientists. Kepler, for example, received help from the imperial court, serving in Bohemia as Rudolf II's official mathematician. Galileo became court mathematician to Cosimo de' Medici in Tuscany. Vesalius served as physician to Holy Roman Emperor Charles V, and Harvey as royal physician in England.

Queen Christina of Sweden, like several other monarchs, invited scholars and artists to her court. Figure 14.7 shows her in 1649 with the French philosopher and mathematician René Descartes (on the right pointing to papers). Books, papers, and instruments attest to the importance of the new science at this meeting. In this Protestant country, the religious figure on the far right seems to indicate that there is little conflict between science and religion. The artist portrays Christina, a deeply religious person (who would later become a Catholic), as an interested and gracious benefactor helping to bring to light scientific findings.

Rulers had their own motives—namely practicality and prestige—for assisting scholars and scientists. Royals especially hoped that scholarship and scientific inquiry would yield discoveries that would enhance the strength and prosperity of the state. For example, they sought experts in building projects, armaments, mapmaking, navigation, and mining. They also tried to burnish their own reputations as powerful, educated people by patronizing scholarship, science, and the arts. In this way, support of science became a supposed hallmark of good government. Enticed by this assistance, learned people gathered at royal courts, which gradually filled rooms with new tools, machines, exotic plants and animals, and books.

Beyond the court, people formed private salons and local academies where those interested in science could meet. In the 1540s, the first academy for scientific study was established in Naples. Women ran several important salons where scientists discussed their findings along with literature, art, and politics. Some scientists even found benefactors at these meetings.

THE RISE OF ROYAL SOCIETIES

During the second half of the seventeenth century, central governments stepped up their support of scientific experimentation, publications, and acade-

■ FIGURE 14.7

Queen Christina and Descartes, 1649.

mies. In 1662, for example, Charles II chartered the Royal Society in England; four years later, Louis XIV's finance minister, Jean Baptiste Colbert, founded the Académie des Sciences in France. These organizations, and others patterned after them, furnished laboratories, granted subsidies, brought scientists together to exchange ideas, published their findings, and honored scientific achievements. This governmental support of science added to the growing prestige of science and the scientific community.

RELIGION AND THE NEW SCIENCE

Religious organizations played a mixed role in the spread of the new science. Traditionally, the Catholic Church supported scholarship and learning in general, including natural science. Moreover, religious orders staffed most universities, and many key figures of the Scientific Revolution held university positions. Numerous leading scholars also felt a profound sense of spirituality. Copernicus, for example, who dedicated his work to the pope, was a cleric, as were many other natural scientists. Although we may be tempted to assume that the skepticism inherent in the scientific method would lead to atheism, the great scientists attacked neither faith nor established religion. Nor were they dispassionate investigators holding themselves apart from the spiritual nature of their age. They often believed in magic, ghosts, and witchcraft, and typically considered alchemy, astrology, and numerology (predicting events from numbers) valuable components of natural science. Galileo, though he later decried his trial as the triumph of "ignorance, impiety, fraud and deceit," remained a believing Catholic. Even Robert Boyle, who like others came to think of the universe as a machine, attributed its origin to God: "God, indeed, gave motion to matter . . . and established those rules of motion, and that order amongst things . . . which we call the laws of nature." Newton agreed: "This most beautiful system of the sun, planets, and comets, could only proceed from the counsel and dominion of an intelligent and powerful Being. . . . He endures forever, and is everywhere present. . . ."

Nevertheless, the new science did challenge certain tenets of faith and the traditional Christian conception of God's place in the ordering of the world. Neither Protestant nor Catholic leaders welcomed Copernican ideas and the implications of the new science. The Catholic Church, itself ordered in a hierarchy that paralleled the old view of the universe, stayed particularly committed to established authorities. Moreover the church's condemnation of Galileo in 1633 discouraged scientific investigations throughout much of Catholic Europe. Descartes was not alone in deciding not to publish ideas incorporating Copernican assumptions. As he explained in 1634, "It is not my temperament to set sail against the wind . . . I want to be able to live in peace . . . out of sight." Although the French government would actively promote science, after the mid-seventeenth century most scientific work and publishing took place in Protestant areas—particularly in England and the Netherlands.

The New Worldview

By the end of the seventeenth century, the accumulation of convincing scientific findings and the support for those findings among the educated elites had broken the Aristotelian-medieval worldview and replaced it with the Copernican-Newtonian paradigm. According to the new view, the earth, along with the planets, moved around the sun in an infinite universe of other similar bodies. The natural order consisted of matter in motion, acting according to mathematically expressible laws. Scientific

The Copernican-Newtonian paradigm

truths came from observing, measuring, experimenting, and making reasoned conclusions through the use of sophisticated mathematics. Religious truths still had their place, and the orderliness of nature reflected God's design (see Document 14.2 on page 444). However, science now claimed precedence in explaining the material world.

In the sixteenth and early-seventeenth centuries, great thinkers such as Copernicus and Galileo had been ridiculed and persecuted for their ideas. By the late-seventeenth and early-eighteenth centuries, Isaac Newton's fate revealed the acceptance of the new paradigm among educated elites. Famous and popular, Newton became a member of Parliament, served for many years as director of the Royal Mint, and was knighted by Queen Anne.

Laying the Foundations for the Enlightenment

In the course of the eighteenth century, the ideas of the Scientific Revolution spread widely and were applied in stunning new ways. With this broadening, the eighteenth century witnessed the birth of a major cultural movement known as the **Enlightenment.** At the heart of this movement lay the firm conviction—especially among intellectuals—that human reason should determine understanding of the world and the rules of social life. "[H]ave the courage to use your own intelligence," and leave your "self-caused immaturity," exhorted the German philosopher Immanuel Kant (1724–1804). "All that is required for this enlightenment is freedom, and particularly . . . the freedom for man to make public use of his reason in all matters."

The Enlightenment hit its full stride in the middle decades of the eighteenth century, when it particularly influenced literate elites of Europe and North America. Yet, its roots stretched back to the end of the seventeenth century. At that time, the thinking that would characterize the Enlightenment emerged in the writings of people who popularized science, applied a skeptical attitude toward religious standards of truth, and criticized accepted traditions and authorities.

Science Popularized

Unevenly educated and facing challenging findings, members of scientific societies often struggled to understand one another's work. For the nonscientific public, the problem of communicating new, complex ideas was even worse. Late in the seventeenth century, several talented writers, nonscientists themselves but believing that science had established a new standard of truth, began explaining in clear language the meaning of science to the literate public. For example, the French writer Bernard de Fontenelle (1657–1757) enjoyed a long, brilliant career as a popularizer of science. In *Conversations on the Plurality of Worlds* (1686), he presented the Copernican view of the universe in a series of conversations between an aristocratic woman and her lover under starry skies. The English essayist and publisher, Joseph Addison (1672–1719), in the March 12, 1711, issue of his newspaper, *The Spectator,* said that he hoped to bring "philosophy out of closets and libraries, schools and colleges, to dwell in clubs and assemblies, at tea-tables and in coffee-houses." He aimed his daily paper not only at men, but at women "of a more elevated life and conversation, that move in an exalted sphere of knowledge and virtue, that join all the beauties of the mind to the ornaments of dress, and inspire a kind of awe and respect, as well as love, in their male beholders." Other writers also targeted women. In 1737, for example, *Newtonianism for Women* was published in Naples and was soon translated into English. Writings such as these helped make science fashionable in elite circles.

By the mid-eighteenth century, this popularization of science merged with another foundation of Enlightenment thinking: the belief that every educated man and woman should

Teaching science

be familiar with the nature and methods of science. Figure 14.8, an illustration from a British book on the arts and sciences, depicts this connection between science and education. Here a teacher instructs three young men in the principles of astronomy by demonstrating the planetary movements on a new machine—the orrery. The stuffed animals hanging from the ceiling underscore the importance of natural history. Atop the bookcase and on the floor are seminal instruments of science—an air pump, a microscope, a telescope, and a globe. A human skeleton hangs in the closet.

Soon scientific ideas were being taught to children of the middle and upper classes. For example, the year 1761 saw the publication of *The Newtonian System of Philosophy, Adapted to the Capacities of Young Gentlemen and Ladies,* a book engagingly advertised as the "Philosophy of Tops and Balls." In it, a fictional boy named Tom Telescope gave lectures on science topics to children while also teaching the virtues of good manners and citizenship. The book proved immensely popular, going through many editions in Britain and in other countries.

Many of these books emphasized Newton—and for understandable reasons. Enlightenment think-

■ FIGURE 14.8

Science, education, and enlightenment, 1759.

ers saw this brilliant Englishman as the great synthesizer of the Scientific Revolution, an astute observer who rightly described the universe as ordered,

Glorifying Newton: Reason and nature

mechanical, material, and set into motion by God. From Newton, they concluded that reason and nature were compatible: Nature functioned logically and discernibly; therefore, what was natural was also reasonable. Many writers of the day agreed with the spirit of a poem written for Newton by the English author Alexander Pope upon the scientist's death in 1727:

Nature and Nature's Laws lay hid in Night.
God said, "Let Newton be," and all was Light.

In simple terms, Newton had become a European cultural hero, as Figure 14.9 suggests. At the left-center of this allegorical painting, a great urn "wherein is

■ FIGURE 14.9

Giovanni Battista Pittori, *Allegorical Monument to Isaac Newton,* 1727–1730.

applied scientific thinking to human psychology. This English philosopher did not hold the mind exempt from the mechanical laws of the material universe. In his *Essay Concerning Human Understanding* (1690), Locke pictured the human brain at birth as a blank sheet of paper that sensory perception and reason filled as a person aged. "Our observation, employed either about external sensible objects or about the internal operations of our minds perceived and reflected on by ourselves, is that which supplies our understanding with all the materials of thinking." Locke's empirical psychology rejected the notion that human beings were born with innate ideas or that revelation was a reliable source of truth. What we become, he argued, depends solely on our experiences—on the information received through the senses. Schools and social institutions should therefore play a major role in molding the individual from childhood to adulthood. These ideas, like those of Newton and the Scientific Revolution, also set the stage for the skeptical questioning of received wisdom.

> The psychology of John Locke

SKEPTICISM AND RELIGION

Locke's ideas, along with those of Newton and the Scientific Revolution, set the stage for the questioning of established wisdom that came to define the Enlightenment. Among several writers, skepticism—or doubts about religious dogmas—mounted. Pierre Bayle (1647–1706), a French Huguenot forced to flee to the Dutch Republic because of Louis XIV's religious persecutions, became the leading proponent of skepticism in the late seventeenth century. In his *News from the Republic of Letters* (1684), Bayle bitterly attacked the intolerance of the French monarchy and the Catholic Church. In most of Europe, where religious principles shared by ruler and ruled underlay all political systems, nonconformity was a major challenge. Therefore, the book earned him condemnation in Paris and Rome. Eventually, however, Bayle would have the last word. In 1697 he published the *Historical and Critical Dictionary,* which contained a list of religious views and beliefs that Bayle maintained did not stand up to criticism. Bayle cited human reason and common sense as his standard of criticism: "Any particular dogma, whatever it may be, whether it is advanced on the authority of the Scriptures, or whatever else may be its origins, is to be regarded as false if it clashes with the clear and definite conclusions

> Pierre Bayle

supposed to be deposited the Remains of the deceased Hero" is displayed. Above the urn shines a beam of light, broken into the colors of the spectrum by a prism—a bow to Newton's famous prism experiments. At the right are pages filled with mathematical calculations; below them, a globe and measuring instruments. Various figures in classical dress admire these objects and perhaps discuss Newton's ideas. The entire painting glorifies not only Newton, but all of science.

Enlightenment thinkers also admired the ideas of Newton's compatriot John Locke (1632–1704), who of the natural understanding." Bayle also argued that "morals and religion, far from being inseparable, are completely independent of each other." For Bayle, a person's moral behavior had little to do with any particular religious doctrine or creed. With these stands, Bayle pushed much harder than Galileo in challenging the Catholic Church and other religious beliefs. He became recognized as an international authority on religious toleration and skeptical criticism of the Bible.

New information and arguments added weight to Bayle's criticism of biblical authority. For example, geological discoveries suggested that life on Earth had actually begun earlier than biblical accounts claimed. Investigators also began casting doubt on reports of miracles and prophecies. David Hume (1711–1776), a first-rate Scottish philosopher and historian, carried the skeptical argument even further. In *An Essay Concerning Human Understanding* (1748), he insisted that nothing—not even the existence of God or our own existence—could be known for sure. Reality consisted only of human perceptions. To Hume, established religions were based on nothing but "hope and fear." Reason demanded that people live with skeptical uncertainty rather than dogmatic faith.

David Hume

BROADENING CRITICISM OF AUTHORITY AND TRADITION

Travel writing had a long history, and by the eighteenth century many Enlightenment thinkers had read explanations of China's lucid Confucian traditions as well as accounts of customs and beliefs in Islamic, Buddhist, and Hindu lands. Several writers— among them Baron de Montesquieu (1689–1755), a wealthy judge in a provincial French court, and the French author Voltaire (1694–1778)—used comparisons of place and time to criticize authority and tradition during the early decades of the eighteenth century. Journeying abroad and writing about their experiences gave such people a new perspective on their home societies. Montesquieu and Voltaire, for their part, chastised European customs in general and French institutions in particular for being contrary to reason and good ethics.

Travel writings of Montesquieu and Voltaire

Both presented the traveler as an objective observer. In his best-selling book *Persian Letters* (1721), Montesquieu bitingly satirized the customs, morals, and practices of Europeans from the point of view of two Persian travelers. Through this comparative perspective, Montesquieu painted the French as lacking in both good morals and effective government. Voltaire, in his widely read *Letters Concerning the*

English Nation (1733), similarly criticized French politics and Catholic intolerance. In the island nation, "one thinks freely and nobly without being held back by any servile fear." Like many people, Voltaire idealized England because it allowed greater individual freedom, religious differences, and political reform than most other countries, especially France. England was also enviably prosperous and was the home of Newton and Locke, so admired in France. Many French intellectuals wanted for their own country what the English already seemed to have.

Other writers took a new historical perspective to criticize tradition and trumpet rapid change. For them, the tools of science and reason enabled people to surpass their historical predecessors, even the admired Greeks and Romans of antiquity. History became a story of relentless human progress, and people living in the eighteenth century stood on the brink of unprecedented historical achievements. Some people, such as the American scientist and philosopher Benjamin Franklin (1706–1790), embraced the idea of progress with an almost religious fervor: "The rapid Progress of *true* Science now occasions my regretting sometimes that I was born so soon. It is impossible to imagine the Height to which may be carried . . . the Power of Man over Matter, . . . all diseases may by sure means be prevented, . . . and our lives lengthened at pleasure."

History and progress

THE ENLIGHTENMENT IN FULL STRIDE

Building on the foundations of science, skepticism, and criticism, Western intellectuals systematically investigated the ethical, political, social, and economic implications of science after the 1730s. For them, nature—with its laws, order, simplicity, and rationality—served as a guide for human thought and society. "The source of man's unhappiness is his ignorance of Nature," claimed France's influential Baron d'Holbach (1723–1789). The Marquis de Condorcet argued, "The Time will therefore come when the sun will shine only on free men who know no other master but their reason (see Document 14.3). These optimistic intellectuals pushed for reform and change, using critical and empirical reasoning to back up their arguments. Specifically, they urged people to shrug off the shackles of tradition and custom and to participate in the accelerating progress of civilization. The spark of reason would soon dispel ignorance and enlighten all human understanding. Indeed, it was this image that lent the Enlightenment its name.

■ DOCUMENT 14.3

Condorcet Lauds the Power of Reason

No one lauded the power of reason and the Enlightenment, or had more hope for the future—thanks to the Enlightenment—than the French mathematician and philosophe, *the Marquis de Condorcet (1743–1794). The following is an excerpt from his* Sketch of the Progress of the Human Mind, *a book tracing human "progress" over time, which he completed in 1794.* ■ **What** *"hopes" does Condorcet have for the future of humanity? According to Condorcet,* **what** *will open the door to such great progress?*

Our hopes for the future condition of the human race can be subsumed under three important heads: the abolition of inequality between nations, the progress of equality within each nation, and the true perfection of mankind. Will all nations one day attain that state of civilization which the most enlightened, the freest and the least burdened by prejudices, such as the French and the Anglo-Americans, have attained already? Will the vast gulf that separates these peoples from the slavery of nations under the rule of monarchs, from the barbarism of African tribes, from the ignorance of savages, little by little disappear? . . .

In answering these three questions we shall find in the experience of the past, in the observation of the progress that the sciences and civilization have already made, in the analysis of the progress of the human mind and of the development of its faculties, the strongest reasons for believing that nature has set no limit to the realization of our hopes.

If we glance at the state of the world today we see first of all that in Europe the principles of the French constitution are already those of all enlightened men. We see them too widely propagated, too seriously professed, for priests and despots to prevent their gradual penetration even into the hovels of their slaves; there they will soon awaken in these slaves the remnants of their common sense and inspire them with that smoldering indignation which not even constant humiliation and fear can smother in the soul of the oppressed. . . .

The time will therefore come when the sun will shine only on free men who know no other master but their reason; when tyrants and slaves, priests and their stupid or hypocritical instruments will exist only in works of history and on the stage; and when we shall think of them only to pity their victims and their dupes; to maintain ourselves in a state of vigilance by thinking on their excesses; and to learn how to recognize and so to destroy, by force of reason, the first seeds of tyranny and superstition, should they ever dare to reappear amongst us.

Source: Jean Antoine Nicholas Caritat, Marquis de Condorcet, *Sketch for a Historical Picture on the Progress of the Human Mind,* trans. June Barraclough [London: Weidenfeld and Nicolson (Orion Books), 1955], pp. 236–237, 244.

THE PHILOSOPHES

Although Enlightenment ideas bubbled up throughout Europe and North America, France was the true heart of the movement. There Enlightenment thinkers came to be called *philosophes*, the French term for "philosophers." In a sense, the questions these thinkers grappled with were philosophical: How do we discover truth? How should we live our lives? Yet the *philosophes* were not traditional philosophers. Coming from both noble and middle-class origins, they were intellectuals—though often not formally trained by or associated with a university. They tended to extend, apply, or propagandize others' ideas rather than initiate new concepts themselves. They also wrote more plays, satires, histories, novels, encyclopedia entries, and short pamphlets than formal philosophical treatises. Finally, they considered themselves part of a common intellectual culture, an international "republic of letters" held together by literature, correspondence, and private gatherings. In the eyes of leading *philosophes* such as Jean Le Rond d'Alembert (1717–1783), this republic of letters should "establish the laws of philosophy and taste for the rest of the nation."

The witty, versatile François Arouet, who took the pen name Voltaire (1694–1778), best represented the *philosophes*. The son of a Parisian lawyer, Voltaire received a fine classical education from the Jesuits and soon denounced their religious doctrine. He became the idol of French intellectuals while only in his 20s, and the enemy of many others. He soon ran afoul of state authorities, who imprisoned him in the Bastille for writing verses that criticized the crown. Released, he became embroiled in a dangerous conflict with a prominent nobleman and again landed in the Bastille. By promising to leave the country, he gained his freedom. In England, he encountered the ideas of Newton and Locke and came to admire English parliamentary government and the nation's religious tolerance. As we saw, he popularized Newton's and Locke's ideas and extolled the virtues of English society in his writings.

Slipping back into France, Voltaire hid for a time under the protection of Émilie du Châtelet (1706–1749), a wealthy woman who became his lover and

Voltaire

match. Châtelet had already shown brilliance as a child. By the age of 12, she could speak four languages and had already translated Greek and Latin texts. Her mother worried that she would not find a mate because she "flaunts her mind, and frightens away the suitors her other excesses have not driven off." In 1733, she insisted on joining a group of male intellectuals who met regularly at a Parisian coffeehouse, donning men's clothes after the management refused to admit her because of her gender. Voltaire lived openly with Châtelet and her husband. In the great hall of their country chateau, she hung rods, pipes, and balls from the ceiling for her experiments in physics. She made her reputation by publishing a three-volume work on the German mathematician and philosopher Leibnitz and translating Newton's *Principles of Mathematics*. A *philosophe*, accomplished scientist, and leading proponent of Newtonian thought in her own right, Châtelet helped Voltaire gain a better understanding of the sciences and their significance. When she died in childbirth in 1749, the despondent Voltaire accepted an invitation from King Frederick II of Prussia to join his court. However, they soon argued, and Voltaire returned to France.

Émilie du Châtelet

Having made both a fortune in financial speculations and a rich network of friends and acquaintances, Voltaire was not without resources. He wrote poetry, drama, history, essays, letters, and scientific treatises—ninety volumes in all. The novel *Candide* (1759) became his best-known work. In this dark satire, Voltaire created the epitome of the "ivory-tower" intellectual, ridiculed the pretensions of the nobility and clergy, and skewered the naiveté of optimists who believed that "this is the best of all possible worlds and all things turn out for the best." He aimed his cynical wit especially at the Catholic church and Christian institutions. His *Philosophical Dictionary* became the most famous, wide-ranging attack on supernatural religion and churches. Voltaire mounted several campaigns for religious toleration, coming to the defense of individuals attacked by prejudice. In his *Treatise on Tolerance* (1763), he attacked the mentality that led to the torture and murder of a Protestant merchant, Jean Calas, on the false charges of murdering his son for threatening to convert to Catholicism. "Christians ought to tolerate one another. I will go even further and say that we ought to look upon all men as our brothers. What! call a Turk, a Jew, a Siamese, my brother? Yes, of course, for are we not all children of the same father, and the creatures of the same God?" Celebrated as a national hero and lionized internationally, Voltaire's popularity reveals the widespread acceptance of Enlightenment thought throughout the West by the late eighteenth century.

THE ENCYCLOPEDIA

No work better summarizes the philosophy of the Enlightenment than the *Encyclopedia*, a collaborative effort by many *philosophes* under the editorship of Denis Diderot (1713–1774) and Jean le Rond d'Alembert. In the preface, the editors stated their aim: "to overturn the barriers that reason never erected" and "contribute to the certitude and progress of human knowledge." The *Encyclopedia* embodied the notion that reason alone could be used to discover, understand, or clarify almost anything. This massive work explored the complete spectrum of knowledge, offering articles on subjects ranging from music to machinery interpreted through the "lens" of the *philosophes'* criticism and empiricism. The authors wrote with supreme self-importance: "I can assure you," said d'Alembert in a 1752 letter, "that while writing this work I had posterity before my eyes at every line."

The first volume of the *Encyclopedia* was published in 1751. Figure 14.10 shows one of its many illustrations. In this image of a chemical laboratory, two chemists and their assistants work. Each piece of equipment is numbered in the illustration and labeled in the text. At the bottom of the picture is a "table of affinities," a system used to organize and symbolize each chemical substance. The illustration conveys a sense of both the practicality of chemistry and its ordered progress. Although the study of chemistry and the hundreds of other topics covered in the *Encyclopedia* at first glance may appear innocent enough, they were saturated with the philosophy of the Enlightenment. Church authorities and their

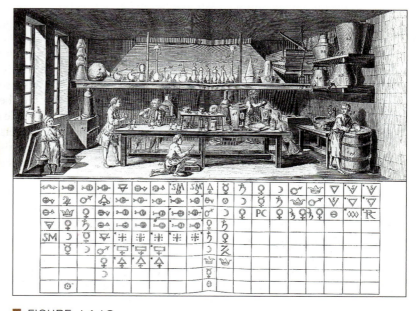

■ FIGURE 14.10

Chemistry, the *Encyclopedia*, 1751.

governmental allies therefore saw the *Encyclopedia* as a direct threat to the status quo. They censored it, halted its publication, and harassed its editors. Thanks in great part to the persistence of Diderot, who fought the authorities and managed a difficult group of contributing authors, the project was finally completed in 1772.

BATTLING THE CHURCH

Diderot's struggle to publish the *Encyclopedia* was part of a wider conflict between the *philosophes* and the church. Both sides spent much time and effort attacking each other. In countries such as France and Italy, where clerics were strongly entrenched in government, officials censored the writings of the *philosophes* and threatened to imprison or exile them. Governmental censorship was usually more nominal than real. However Diderot and others trying to publish "offensive" books constantly worried about these threats: "How many times did we awake uncertain if . . . we would be torn from our families, our friends, our fellow citizens. . . ." French authors often sent their works to Holland or Switzerland for publication, and private companies then made a business of smuggling the books back into France across Swiss or Dutch borders.

Sometimes the *philosophes'* "crime" was promoting toleration of religious minorities, whether Christian or otherwise. Montesquieu and Voltaire, in France, were among several who attacked discrimination against Jews, for example. These views were particularly controversial because religious tolerance—formal and informal—was not the rule. Most governments maintained a state religion, rooted in law and viewed as the custodian of received views, that discriminated against nonmembers. For example, Denmark barred Catholic priests from entering the country, and the Catholic Inquisition remained active in Spain.

Some *philosophes*, such as Baron d'Holbach and David Hume, verged on atheism in their attacks on organized religion. "The Christian religion not only was at first attended by miracles, but even now cannot be believed by any reasonable person without one," Hume claimed. However, few Enlightenment thinkers pushed matters that far. Most believed in some form of deism—that an impersonal, infinite Divine Being created the universe but did not interfere with the world of human affairs. The prominent author and political philosopher Thomas Paine (1737–1809) stated, "I believe in one God, and no more; and I hope for happiness beyond this life. . . . I do not believe in the creed professed by the Jewish church, by the Roman church, by the Greek church, by the Turkish church, by the Protestant church, nor by any church that I know of. My own mind is my own church." These ideas, like other ideas of the

Deism

Enlightenment, gained momentum over the course of the eighteenth century. In the long run, the church probably lost more supporters among the upper and middle classes than it gained by so ardently attacking the *philosophes* and their ideas.

REFORMING SOCIETY

The *philosophes* thought long and hard about reforming society. They wrote and argued about the relationship between the individual and society, and reevaluated the functioning of traditional social institutions. Applying their critical reasoning to fields from government to education, they generated influential ideas for reform.

> **Political thought: Montesquieu and Rousseau**

The most important political thinkers of the Enlightenment—Montesquieu and the Swiss-born writer Jean-Jacques Rousseau (1712–1778)—built on John Locke's work. Locke had pleaded eloquently for the "natural rights"—life, liberty, and property—of human beings. In his *Second Treatise on Civil Government* (1690), Locke had argued that to safeguard these rights, individuals agree to surrender a certain amount of their sovereignty to government. However, the powers of the government, whether it be monarchical or popular, were strictly limited. No government was allowed to violate the individual's right to life, liberty, and property. If it did, the people who set it up could and should overthrow it—something the English had done in their Glorious Revolution, according to Locke.

An admirer of Locke and the English system of government, Baron de Montesquieu analyzed political systems from a relativistic perspective. In his widely acclaimed political masterpiece, *The Spirit of the Laws* (1748), Montesquieu argued that political institutions should conform to the climate, customs, beliefs, and economy of a particular country. For instance, limited monarchy is most appropriate for countries of moderate size, like France; and republics for small states, like Venice or ancient Athens. Each form of government had its virtues and vices.

Not only did Montesquieu approve of Locke's doctrine of limited sovereignty, but he specified how it could best be secured—by a separation of powers and a system of checks and balances. The alternative, he warned, was tyranny and an end to liberty: "There would be an end to everything, were the same man or the same body, whether of the nobles or of the people, to exercise those three powers, that of enacting laws, that of executing the public resolutions, and of trying the causes of individuals." This theory, equally applicable to monarchies and to democracies, became Montesquieu's greatest practical contribution to political thought. In North America, framers of the U.S. Constitution incorporated his ideas into their structuring of the United States government, creating separate executive, judicial, and legislative branches of government.

Rousseau offered a more radical political theory than Montesquieu's (See Biography). In his *Discourse on the Origin of Inequality* (1755), Rousseau argued that people in the "primitive" state of "noble savagery" were free, equal, and relatively happy. Only when some of them began marking off plots of ground, claiming them as their own and thereby founding civil society, did the troubles begin. Private property created inequality and the need for laws and governments to protect people from crime and wars. In *The Social Contract* (1762), Rousseau began by challenging his contemporaries: "Man is born free; and everywhere he is in chains." He then offered a solution to this conflict between individual freedom and social restrictions. In an ideal state, he argued, people entered into a compact with one another, agreeing to surrender their individual liberty, which was driven by self-interest, to the whole society. In return, the individual gained freedom by virtue of being part of the society's "general will," which was driven by the common good. "This means nothing less than that [the individual] will be forced to be free," explained Rousseau. Although Rousseau never made it clear just how the general will operated in practice, he believed that the people themselves—rather than a monarch or a parliamentary body—should make laws. His controversial ideas would powerfully influence the development of democratic theory over the next two centuries. For some, *The Social Contract* would support participatory democracy, whereas for others, Rousseau's emphasis on conforming to the general will would justify authoritarian political systems.

Although critical and combative, neither Rousseau, Montesquieu, nor the other *philosophes* were political or social revolutionaries. They did not champion the lower classes, whom they dismissed as ignorant, prone to violence, and, in Voltaire's words, "inaccessible to the progress of reason and over whom fanaticism maintains its atrocious hold." Diderot, of humble parents, admitted that he wrote "only for those with whom I should enjoy conversing . . . the philosophers; so far as I am concerned, there is no one else in the world." Most *philosophes* hoped for painless change from above rather than a revolutionary transfer of power to the still-unenlightened "masses." Many shared Voltaire's belief that enlightened absolutism—rule by a well-educated, enlightened monarch—offered the best chance for the enactment of Enlightenment reforms such as religious toleration, rule subject to impartial laws, and freedom of speech (see Chapter 15).

If the functioning of the universe and politics could be described by understandable, rational laws, why should the same not hold true for economic activity? Several Enlightenment thinkers turned their thoughts to this question and attacked mercantilism, the system of regulated national economics that still operated throughout much of Europe. A group of French think-

ers known as Physiocrats, led by François Quesnay, personal physician to Louis XV, began to teach that economics had its own

Economic ideas: The Physiocrats and Adam Smith

set of natural laws. The Physiocrats believed that the most basic of these laws was that of supply and demand, and that these laws operated best under only minimal governmental regulation of private economic activity. This doctrine, which became known as *laissez-faire* (noninterference), favored free trade and enterprise. In France, the Physiocrats saw land and agriculture as the main source of national wealth. Other economists would build on their ideas and apply them to different settings.

In 1776, Adam Smith (1723–1790), a Scottish professor of philosophy who associated with the Physiocrats while traveling in France, published *Wealth of Nations*. The book became the bible of laissez-faire economics. By nature, Smith argued, individuals who were allowed to pursue rationally their own economic self-interest would benefit society as well as themselves. Focusing on Britain's economy, Smith emphasized commerce, manufacturing, and labor rather than agriculture as the primary sources of national wealth. Anticipating the industrial age that would first emerge in Britain, he concluded that "the greatest improvement in the productive powers of labor . . . have been the effects of the division of labor." For Smith as well as the Physiocrats, laissez-faire economics held the key to national wealth—whether a nation was built on agriculture or industry.

What Smith and the Physiocrats did for economics, the Italian Cesare Beccaria (1738–1794) did for criminology and penology. Beccaria wrote *On Crimes and Punishments* (1764), an international best-seller, to protest "the cruelty of punishments and the irreg-

KEY DATES

THE ENLIGHTENMENT

1733	Voltaire, *Letters Concerning the English Nation*
1748	Montesquieu, *The Spirit of the Laws*
1751	The *Encyclopedia*
1759	Voltaire, *Candide*
1762	Rousseau, *Social Contract*
1764	Beccaria, *On Crimes and Punishments*
1776	Smith, *Wealth of Nations*
1792	Wollstonecraft, *Vindication of the Rights of Women*

BIOGRAPHY

Jean-Jacques Rousseau (1712–1778)

CONSIDER

■ **Consider** *how Rousseau's work and life reflect the ideas and efforts of other Enlightenment thinkers.*

Jean-Jacques Rousseau described himself as a "singular soul, strange, and to say it all, a man of paradoxes." A celebrity both admired and hated in his own time, he wrote more deeply on a wide range of subjects than any of his contemporaries.

"My birth was my first misfortune," Rousseau once stated wryly. His mother died shortly after he was born in 1712 in the Republic of Geneva. His father, a watchmaker, raised him to the age of 10, and then abandoned him to a series of homes where he served unhappily as an apprentice. One day in 1728, returning late from walking in the countryside, he found the gates of Geneva closed. Anticipating punishment from his master for his tardiness, he turned around and set off on the first of a series of wanderings that would mark the rest of his life.

He lived for much of the next ten years as the guest and lover of a baroness, Madame de Warens. In his own words, Rousseau became her "piece of work, student, friend. . . ." Rousseau addressed Madame de Warens as "Momma," and she referred to him as "my little one." This was the first of Rousseau's numerous relationships, many of them with older women. Yet he also lived as a recluse for long stretches of time during which he educated himself.

In 1742 the shy Rousseau arrived in Paris. He would often live there, though he harbored "a secret disgust for life in the capital," with its "dirty stinking little streets, ugly black houses, . . . poverty, [and] beggars." He first gained attention in Paris by writing about music and by joining the cultural circles. He also earned a modest income by serving as secretary to aristocratic patrons and by copying music. In 1745, Thérèse Levasseur, a young laundress, became his lifelong companion and ultimately his wife. The couple would have four children and abandon them all to a foundling hospital for adoption.

Singular Soul, Controversial Thinker

In 1749, Rousseau entered an essay contest that abruptly changed his life. He won the competition by arguing that progress in the arts and sciences corrupted rather than improved human conduct. Suddenly he was controversial and famous. "No longer [was I] that timid man, more ashamed than modest. . . . All Paris repeated [my] sharp and biting sarcasms. . . ." Buoyed by his new-found fame, he contributed several articles on music and political economy to the *Encyclopedia*, edited by his close friend Denis Diderot. He came to know and eventually quarrel with most of the leading figures of the Enlightenment.

Rousseau went on to publish several critical and widely circulated books, including *Discourse on the Origin of Inequality* (1755), *Julie* or *The New Heloise* (1761), *Émile* (1762), and *The Social Contract* (1762). These writings inspired not only learned responses, but ardent mail from ordinary readers. One reader of *The New Heloise*, a novel focusing on the conflict between so-

ularities of criminal procedures, . . . to demolish the accumulated errors of centuries." He argued that criminal laws and

Criminology, penology, and slavery

punishments, like all other aspects of life, should incorporate reason and natural law. Good laws, he explained, promoted "the greatest happiness divided among the greatest number." Criminal law should strive to deter crime and rehabilitate criminals rather than merely punish wrongdoers. In Beccaria's view, torture and capital punishment made no sense; indeed, only new penal institutions that mirrored natural law could transform convicted criminals.

Other Enlightenment thinkers used similar arguments to denounce slavery. Abbé Guillaume Raynal (1713–1796), an outspoken and widely read critic of slavery, argued that this institution and many other practices of European and American colonists were irrational and inhumane. In the name of natural rights, he called for a slave rebellion. An article in the authoritative *Encyclopedia* asserted similar views, declaring that all enslaved individuals "have the right to be declared free. . . ." These arguments, like the ideas of Beccaria and, in politics, of Montesquieu and Rousseau, would resound again and again through eighteenth-century Western society.

Becoming "enlightened" required education. Diderot claimed that the *Encyclopedia* was written so "that our children, by becoming more educated, may at the same time become more virtuous and happier. . . ." Many Enlightenment thinkers based their ideas on the psychological ideas of John Locke, which emphasized the power of education to mold the child into the adult. These thinkers often

Education

attacked organized religion in particular for controlling education.

Rousseau became the outstanding critic of traditional education. In *Émile*, he argued that teachers should appeal to children's natural interests and goodness rather than impose discipline and punishment. "Hold childhood in reverence," he counseled. "Give nature time to work." He also pushed for less "artificial demands and personal feelings, wrote, "Ever since I read your blessed book I have burned with love of virtue. . . . Feeling has taken over once again." Yet the books also inspired scorn. Peasants once stoned Rousseau's house, for example, after a pastor attacked him from the pulpit. Authorities issued more serious threats. In 1762 Parisian officials ordered *The Social Contract* burned and Rousseau arrested. He fled to Geneva, only to discover that officials there were also seeking his arrest. Again he escaped, moving from place to place and finding shelter with friends whom he quickly lost after bitter arguments. Figure 14.11 shows him in the distinctive fur hat and collar he often wore during this period, when he was a guest of the English philosopher David Hume.

In the last fifteen years of his life, Rousseau felt persecuted and depressed. "I appear," he wrote, "as the enemy of the Nation." He published stunning, often exaggerated self-revelations in his *Confessions*, disclosing his affairs, lies, and quarrels.

A difficult man and a tortured soul, Rousseau was also a superb writer whose *New Heloise* became the most widely read novel of his age. He counts among the most important educational theorists in history and became an accomplished composer and musical theorist. Author of one of the most striking autobiographical works ever written, he also proved an extremely influential philosopher and political theorist. "I am different," he wrote, "alone on earth. . . . Whether nature did well or ill to break the mould in which she formed me, this is something one can only judge after reading me." Sixteen years after Rousseau's death in 1778, France's revolutionary government moved his body to a place of honor near Voltaire's burial site in Paris.

■ FIGURE 14.11

Allan Ramsay, *Jean-Jacques Rousseau*, 1766.

cial" schools, maintaining that nature and experience were better guides to independent thinking and practical knowledge—at least for males. "I hate books," he pointed out. "They only teach us to talk about things we know nothing about." By emphasizing practical education, learning by doing, and motivating rather than requiring the child to learn, Rousseau's *Émile* became one of the most influential works on modern education. His ideas on the education of females, however, were not so modern. Like most men of his time ("enlightened" or not), he believed that girls should be educated to fulfill their traditional domestic roles as wives and mothers.

In theory at least, the Enlightenment emphasis on individualism opened the door to the idea of equality between men and women. Several intellectuals explored this controversial issue.

The "woman question" Early in the period, some challenging books on the "woman question" were published by female authors. In one of the best-known of these, *A Serious Proposal to the Ladies* (1694), the English writer Mary Astell (1666–1731)

argued that women should be educated according to the ideas of the new science—reason and debate— rather than tradition. Later, she explained that men seem to know more than women because "boys have much time and pains, care and cost bestowed on their education, girls have little or none. The former are early initiated in the sciences" and "have all imaginable encouragement" while "the latter are restrained, frowned upon, and beaten." In other writings, she questioned the inequality of men's and women's roles: "If all Men are born Free, how is it that all Women are born Slaves?" Later in the eighteenth century, the British author Mary Wollstonecraft (1759–1797) published *Vindication of the Rights of Women* (1792), in which she analyzed the condition of women and argued forcefully for equal rights for all human beings. Like Astell, Wollstonecraft stressed the need to educate women: "If she be not prepared by education to become the companion of man, she will stop the progress of knowledge and virtue; for truth must be common to all, or it will be inefficacious with respect to its influence on general practice."

Few male writers went that far. Although some men supported better education for women, most held the traditional view that women were weaker than men and best suited for domestic rather than public affairs. According to Immanuel Kant, who spoke so optimistically and eloquently about education and enlightenment, "laborious learning or painful pondering, even if a woman should greatly succeed in it, destroy the merits that are proper to her sex." The editors of the *Encyclopedia* also ignored contributions from women, instead praising those who remained at home. Some of Rousseau's writings were particularly influential among women, primarily because they glorified child rearing, maternalism, and emotional life. Rousseau never suggested that women were independent beings equal to men. For him, "Woman is made to please and to be subjugated to man."

THE CULTURE AND SPREAD OF THE ENLIGHTENMENT

The Enlightenment glittered especially in Paris, and salon meetings became the chief social setting for this intellectual culture. These meetings were hosted by wealthy Parisian patrons, usually women of the aristocracy or upper-middle class. In an environment lush with art, music, and wealth, the *philosophes,* powerful

Salon meetings

nobles, diplomats, statesmen, artists, and well-educated conversationalists gathered regularly to read, listen to, and debate the ideas of the Enlightenment. They also discussed—and sometimes influenced—economic policies, wars, and the king's choice of ministers. The German critic Friedrich Grimm (1723–1807), who published a private newsletter on Parisian life, described the salons of Julie de Lespinasse, who lived openly with the *philosophe* d'Alembert: "Her circle met daily from five o'clock until nine in the evening. There we were sure to find choice men of all orders in the State, the Church, the Court—military men, foreigners, and the most distinguished men of letters. Politics, religion, philosophy, anecdotes, news, nothing was excluded from the conversation." These salon meetings became self-conscious forums for arbitrating and molding public opinion through the open use of reason.

As leaders, patrons, and intellectual contributors to these gatherings, women played a particularly important role in the Enlightenment. Independent, witty, powerful women governed the potentially unruly meetings and discussions by enforcing rules of polite conversation. One of the most famous of these patrons was Madame Marie-Thérèse Geoffrin (1699–1777), a rich middle-class widow who served as a model and mentor for other women leaders of salons. Figure 14.12, a painting by Anicet Charles Lemonnier, shows a salon meeting at her home in 1755.

■ FIGURE 14.12

Anicet Charles Lemonnier, *An Evening at Madame Geoffrin's in 1755,* 1812.

Léonard Defrance, *At the Shield of Minerva*, 1781

■ FIGURE 14.13

In this painting, French artist Léonard Defrance depicts a street scene in front of a bookstore in France. ■ **What** might the packages of books bound for or being delivered from Spain, Portugal, Rome, and Naples suggest about the spread of Enlightenment ideas throughout Europe? ■ **In what ways** does this painting imply that people of all classes were being touched by books and perhaps Enlightenment ideas? ■ **Why** do you think the artist included a member of the clergy so prominently in this painting?

Madame Geoffrin, wearing a blue dress and looking at the viewer, sits at the left next to Bernard de Fontenelle, 98-year-old popularizer of science. Above is a bust of Voltaire, the Enlightenment hero living in exile at the time. Women with the right intellectual and social qualifications attended this and other salons, but the star invitees were usually men.

Smaller meetings in other French and foreign cities, from Berlin to Philadelphia, paralleled the Parisian salon meetings. Moreover, all these meetings went hand in hand with an extensive international correspondence carried out by participants. For some, letter writing, like good conversation in the salons, was an art. People also read and discussed Enlightenment ideas in local academies, Freemason lodges, societies, libraries, and coffeehouses. In addition, most municipalities had clubs where the social and intellectual elites could mingle.

Even bookstores, where people could purchase books or pay small fees to read recent works, became hotbeds of Enlightenment ideas. Figure 14.13 shows an eighteenth-century bookstore. In the doorway stand two women, reading books. Just outside are packages of books being delivered from or

Bookstores

to Spain, Portugal, Rome, and Naples. In the street, apparently drawn to the bookstore, are people of all classes, from a peasant with his scythe at the left to a cleric in his white robes at the center. The name of the bookstore, "The Shield of Minerva," refers to the Roman goddess of wisdom. In a growing number of bookstores such as this, all sorts of works became increasingly available, from religious tracts and chivalric tales to new novels and Enlightenment literature.

These gatherings and interchanges spread the ideas of the Enlightenment throughout society and enhanced the social respectability of intellectuals. They also helped create a common intellectual culture that crossed class lines and political borders and that contributed to an informed body of public opinion. People who participated in these interchanges came to sense that they could freely express ideas as well as debate political and social issues. By the last quarter of the eighteenth century, Enlightenment ideas could be heard even in the camps of the *philosophes'* traditional opponents—the clergy, governmental officials, and monarchs. As we will see, these ideas pushed some monarchs to enact "enlightened" reforms and encouraged many other people to demand revolutionary change.

SUMMARY

The great intellectual revolution of the seventeenth and eighteenth centuries was fueled by advances in science. Brimming with new scientific ideas and discoveries, Western civilization relinquished its medieval assumptions and embarked on an innovative journey unique among the cultures of the world. This change in direction became one of the main forces behind the power and dynamism that came to characterize the West. Through science, Westerners hoped to gain greater control over the material world and nature.

Enlightenment thinkers carried these daring aspirations further, self-consciously leading a mission of reform and freedom from the shackles of tradition. By striking the match of reason, they believed, people could at last dispel the darkness of the past and liberate themselves as never before. Thus enlightened, humanity as a whole could move from childhood to adulthood. As the *philosophe* Baron d'Holbach proclaimed, "The *enlightened man*, is man in his maturity, in his perfection; who is capable of pursuing his own happiness; because he has learned to examine, to think for himself, and not to take that for truth upon the authority of others."

Many participants in Enlightenment circles have since been criticized as self-concerned dilettantes reluctant to take on the risks of real reform. Most historians, however, see the *philosophes* as thoughtful, sincere, and sometimes brilliant thinkers. The *philosophes* clearly left a mark on Western culture. Their ideas, like those of the seventeenth-century scientists, threatened the traditional order, especially the church. As their primary legacy, they widened the gap between religiously influenced doctrines and accepted scholarly thought. Equally significant, they set the intellectual stage for a series of revolutions that would soon sweep America and Europe. Above all, their way of thinking—stressing reason, individualism, and progress—would form the intellectual foundation of modern Western society and further distinguish this civilization from its non-Western counterparts.

KEY TERMS

Neoplatonism, p. 443

Hermetic doctrine, p. 443

Copernican revolution, p. 444

heliocentric model, p. 444

empirical method, p. 449

deductive reasoning, p. 449

Cartesian dualism, p. 450

Scientific Revolution, p. 450

Enlightenment, p. 452

philosophes, p. 456

REVIEW, ANALYZE, AND ANTICIPATE

REVIEW THE PREVIOUS CHAPTERS
Chapter 12—"Faith, Fortune, and Fame"—told how several European powers expanded overseas during the fifteenth, sixteenth, and seventeenth centuries and grew rich from the commerce. Chapter 13—"The Struggle for Survival and Sovereignty"—focused on how kings and nobles battled for power, the resolutions of those struggles, and their impact on the millions of people outside the elite.

1. *Analyze how the expansion of Europe might have stimulated scientific research.*

2. *In what ways did the effort of monarchs to increase their power and create stability relate to the promotion of science and the desire for greater intellectual certainty?*

ANALYZE THIS CHAPTER

Chapter 14—"A New World of Reason and Reform"—examines the changing intellectual foundations of the West.

1. *List and analyze the differences between the new scientific views of the world and traditional medieval views. How did standards for ascertaining the "truth" differ between these two perspectives?*

2. *Analyze the beliefs and motives of three central figures in the Scientific Revolution. What barriers did they have to overcome to present their views?*

3. *Do you think the Enlightenment merely popularized the Scientific Revolution, or did it accomplish something more?*

4. *In what ways did the Enlightenment threaten traditional views and authorities?*

ANTICIPATE THE NEXT CHAPTER

In Chapter 15—"Competing for Power and Wealth"—the struggles of Western powers over land, position, and commerce, as well as the economic and social changes affecting life in several Western societies during the eighteenth century, will be examined.

1. *What kinds of reforms—actual changes in governments and institutions—would most likely flow from Enlightenment ideas?*

2. *What social groups might try to adopt the ideas of the Enlightenment as a basis for demanding political and social reforms? Why might some monarchs consider enacting Enlightenment ideas?*

BEYOND THE CLASSROOM

QUESTIONING TRUTH AND AUTHORITY

Kuhn, Thomas S. *The Structure of Scientific Revolutions*, 2nd ed. Chicago: University of Chicago Press, 1970. A landmark analysis of the nature, causes, and consequences of transformations in scientific concepts.

Mandrou, Robert. *From Humanism to Science*. Atlantic Highlands, NJ: Humanities Press, 1979. A description of how the role of intellectuals changed between 1480 and 1700.

Teresi, Dick. *Lost Discoveries: The Ancient Roots of Modern Science—From the Babylonians to the Maya*. New York: Simon & Schuster, 2003. A recent book that focuses on discoveries from non-Western societies that predated Europe's Scientific Revolution.

DEVELOPING A MODERN SCIENTIFIC VIEW

Cohen, H.F. *The Scientific Revolution*. Chicago: University of Chicago Press, 1994. An analysis of when and where modern science began.

Dear, Peter. *Revolutionizing the Sciences: European Knowledge and Its Ambitions, 1500–1700*. Princeton: Princeton University Press, 2001. A survey of the main ideas of science and its new institutions.

Feingold, Mordechai. *The Newtonian Moment: Isaac Newton and the Making of Modern Culture*. New York: Oxford University Press, 2004. A well illustrated book that focuses on Newton and how his ideas affected eighteenth-century culture.

Hall, Rupert A. *The Revolution in Science, 1500–1750*. London: Longman, 1983. A useful introduction to the developments in science during this period.

Schiebinger, Londa. *The Mind Has No Sex? Women in the Origins of Modern Science*. Cambridge, MA: Harvard University Press, 1990. An examination of the participation of women in science and stresses how science reflected male biases.

Shapin, Steven, *The Scientific Revolution*. Chicago: University of Chicago Press, 1996. A concise, new interpretation questioning whether there was a "scientific revolution."

Westfall, Richard. *The Construction of Modern Science: Mechanisms and Mechanics*. New York: Cambridge University Press, 1977. A good survey of scientific developments during the seventeenth century that emphasizes the importance of mathematics and mechanics.

SUPPORTING AND SPREADING SCIENCE

Jacob, Margaret C. *The Cultural Meaning of the Scientific Revolution*. New York: Alfred A. Knopf, 1988. Examines the evolution of science within its political, social, and cultural context.

Moran, Bruce T., ed. *Patronage and Institutions: Science, Technology and Medicine at the European Court, 1500–1750*. Rochester, NY: Boydell Press, 1991. Examines the role of royal courts in supporting and shaping science during this period.

LAYING THE FOUNDATIONS FOR THE ENLIGHTENMENT

Imhof, Ulrich. *The Enlightenment*. Oxford: Blackwell, 1994. A recent examination and evaluation of the Enlightenment.

Outram, Dorinda. *The Enlightenment*. Cambridge: Cambridge University Press, 2005. Presents the various interpretations of the Enlightenment.

Sklar, Judith. *Montesquieu*. Oxford: Oxford University Press, 1987. A concise, well-written study of Montesquieu and his ideas.

THE ENLIGHTENMENT IN FULL STRIDE

Besterman, Theodore. *Voltaire*, 3rd ed. Chicago: University of Chicago Press, 1976. A useful biography of this major Enlightenment figure.

Darton, Robert. *The Business of Enlightenment: A Publishing History of the Encyclopedia, 1775–1800*. Cambridge, Mass.: Belknap Press, 1979. A well-written social history and analysis of the publication of the *Encyclopedia*.

Gay, Peter. *The Enlightenment: An Interpretation*, 2 volumes. New York: Alfred A. Knopf, 1966–1969. A classic study, exhaustive, but with a strong point of view.

Goodman, Dena. *The Republic of Letters: A Cultural History of the French Enlightenment*. Ithaca, NY: Cornell University Press, 1994. A study of the cultural and intellectual life of eighteenth-century France that concentrates on the role played by the salons.

Lougee, Carolyn. *Le Paradis des Femmes. Women, Salons, and Social Stratification in Seventeenth-Century France*. Princeton, NJ: Princeton University Press, 1976. Analyzes the foundations and importance of the French salons, emphasizing the role played by women in them.

Melton, J.V.H. *The Rise of the Public in Enlightenment Europe*. Cambridge: Cambridge University Press, 2001. Connects publishing and the reading public during the Enlightenment.

www.mhhe.com/sherman3

• Unfamiliar words? See our Glossary at the back of the book for pronunciation and definitions.

• Need help studying? See our web page for map exercises, practice quizzes, and additional study resources.

• Need help writing a paper? Access hundreds of primary documents, maps, images, and a guide to writing history papers on our Primary Source Investigator site at **www.mhhe.com/psi.**

PHILIP VAN DIJK, *BRISTOL DOCKS AND QUAY*, CA. 1780

This painting shows the British port of Bristol, one of many European port cities that benefited from the lucrative overseas trade that grew during the eighteenth century. On the left, ships arrive and dock on the well-protected canal, where they are loaded and unloaded. On the quay are workers, merchants, and families—some of the many who directly benefited from the activity. Around them are well-kept shops, homes, and buildings that reflect the prosperity of this commercial center and the wealth drawn from Britain's colonial empire.

CHAPTER 15

COMPETING FOR POWER AND WEALTH

THE OLD REGIME, 1715–1789

STUDY	Statebuilding and warfare ▪ Enlightened absolutism ▪ Country and city life ▪ Culture of the elite ▪ Culture for the lower classes ▪ The American Revolution.
NOTICE	The connections between politics, war, and society during the eighteenth century.

"A reasonable man is always happy if he has what is necessary for him according to his condition [social rank], that is to say, if he has the protection of the laws, and can live as his father lived before him," wrote a French observer in 1747. The political lesson behind these words was clear. "Essential . . . to the good of a nation is being governed in one constant and uniform manner." Most people living in the eighteenth century would have nodded their heads in agreement. Indeed, they actively upheld the social order—ranked, governed, and sanctioned as it was by tradition and Christian teachings.

Despite this affirmation of stability, change was afoot in these years. During the seventeenth century, kings and queens had struggled with nobles in their own countries for control and with other monarchs to increase their nations' sway. In their continuing competition for power and wealth, eighteenth-century kings and queens tried to strengthen their states while gaining status—often through war—in the international arena. Below them, ambitious aristocrats flexed their muscles, sometimes challenging their monarchs, sometimes forging alliances with them, and often reveling in the new wealth and culture that now lay within their reach. They, along with the growing number of commoners, began to see much promise in the new ways to produce food and organize manufacturing, all fueled by accelerating commerce—especially with overseas colonies, as reflected in the painting facing this page. Moreover, many elites—including some monarchs themselves—also recognized the strength of Enlightenment ideas and began to think of ways to institute "enlightened" reforms. At the base of Western society, the mass of peasants and workers toiled, as they always had. However, their numbers were increasing, and their ways of life were slowly adjusting to the pressures of change. This society and its politics would later be known as the Old Regime, but many living at the time detected the quickening pulse of a new era.

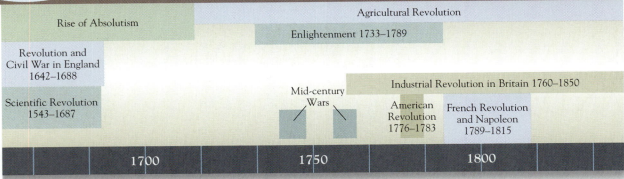

Rise of Absolutism

Agricultural Revolution

Enlightenment 1733–1789

Revolution and
Civil War in England
1642–1688

Mid-century
Wars

Industrial Revolution in Britain 1760–1850

Scientific Revolution
1543–1687

American
Revolution
1776–1783

French Revolution
and Napoleon
1789–1815

1700   1750   1800

STATEBUILDING AND WAR

IN AUGUST 1715, THE OLD and sad Louis XIV fell ill. His legs swelled and turned black as gangrene set in. Remarkably, he had outlived both his son and grandson. On his deathbed, Louis warned his 5-year-old great-grandson, who would succeed him as Louis XV (r. 1715–1774), not to "imitate my love of building nor my liking of war." Neither Louis XV nor many other rulers of the time managed to follow this advice for long. War and building might cost lives and drain royal treasuries, but they made a spectacular show of power in a competitive world. The rulers of Europe clung to their statebuilding ways, straining to secure their central governments and ensure their own position at the top.

During the seventeenth century, this competitiveness had plunged Europe into a series of bloody conflicts—the very battles Louis XIV regretted on his deathbed (see Chapter 13). In western Europe, the violence stopped with the Peace of Utrecht in 1713–1714. Seven years later, the Treaty of Nystad (1721) ended the conflicts in eastern Europe (see Map 15.1). For a while, the two treaties held. Monarchs throughout Europe tried to adhere to the principle of a **balance of power** to prevent any one state or alliance from dominating the others. Nevertheless, anyone hoping for an extended period free of war would be sorely disappointed. Up-and-coming states such as Prussia and Britain bristled with ambition and vied with their established competitors for power, prestige, and wealth. Their struggles spread beyond the borders of Europe to overseas colonies on continents from North America to Asia, in this sense turning European wars into global conflicts. As we will see, this competition subjected millions of people to a fresh round of hardship and irrevocably altered the fate and fortunes of nations throughout the West.

RISING AMBITIONS IN EASTERN EUROPE

Within Europe, the fiercest competition took place in eastern Europe. There, Russia and Brandenburg-Prussia were on the rise. Under Peter the Great, Russia had already defeated Sweden, grabbing much of the northeastern Baltic coast in the process. Russia next hoped to take advantage of the sprawling but weak Polish state farther west (see Chapter 13) and to benefit from the decline of the Ottoman Empire, which controlled the Black Sea to Russia's south. Brandenburg-Prussia also saw opportunities in Poland, which divided and bordered its lands. This militaristic state also coveted some of the holdings of the bloated Austro-Hungarian Empire to the south, which in turn intended to hold its own in the power struggle. Someone would have to pay the price for all these ambitions.

Peter the Great had done much to turn Russia toward the west and make it a great power. By the time of his death in 1725, he had modernized Russia's government and military, established Russia as the dominant power in northeastern Europe, and pressured the Russian nobility into the state bureaucracy and army officer corps. In the process, he made many enemies, from the peasants who paid dearly for Peter's accomplishments to all those who had a stake in the very social, cultural, and religious traditions that Peter attacked. His successors would have to face these enemies and shoulder the task of sustaining Russia's expansion to the south and west.

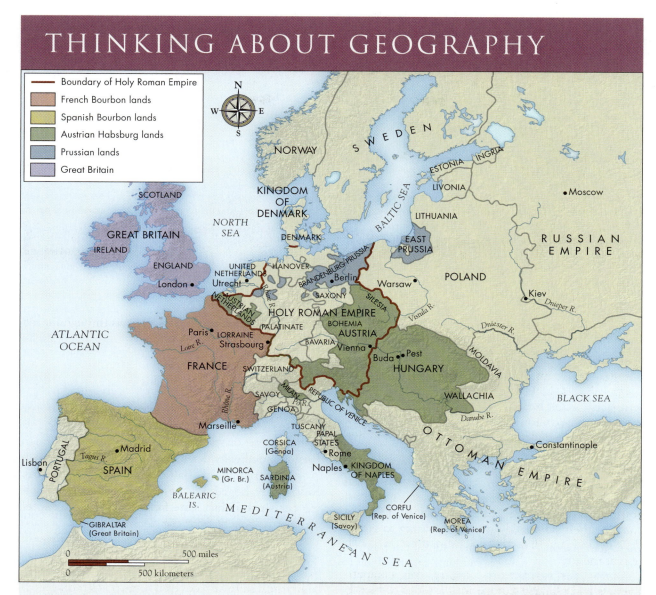

MAP 15.1 EUROPE, 1721

This map shows Europe after the Treaties of Utrecht (1714) and Nystad (1721). ■ **Notice** that although France and Spain are ruled by Bourbon monarchs, the two nations remain separate. **How** might their union have altered the balance of power in Europe? ■ **Locate** the large states in eastern Europe. **Which** of these states, despite their size, are declining powers? ■ **Notice** the lands controlled by Austria. **Why** might this power's holdings be vulnerable?

Six mediocre rulers followed Peter—including an infant, a boy of twelve, and a mentally unstable tsar. Despite this shaky leadership, Russia held its ground. From 1725 to 1762, its population increased, and the landowning elite grew wealthier than ever. The nobility took back some of the authority it had lost to Peter, diminishing the service it owed to the state; in 1762, nobles freed themselves of all such obligations. Nevertheless, they still staffed the bureaucracy and

military officer corps. Moreover, nobles cracked down even more on their serfs, reducing their status to that of mere property. The 1767 Decree on Serfs made the situation crystal clear: "Serfs and peasants . . . owe their landlords proper submission and absolute obedience in all matters."

New leadership in expanding Russia

The decades of weak leadership ended when a dynamic new leader ascended the Russian throne.

■ DOCUMENT 15.1

Landlords and Serfs in Russia

During the eighteenth century, Russian serfs probably fared worse than peasants elsewhere in Europe. Toward the end of the century, Alexander Radischev published a description of Russian serfs and their treatment by noble landowners. For this daring act, the author was imprisoned by Catherine II. ■ ***In what ways*** *does the landowner described in this excerpt treat his serfs?* ■ ***How*** *does the author criticize this treatment of serfs?*

A certain man left the capital, acquired a small village of one or two hundred souls [i.e., serfs], and determined to make his living by agriculture. . . . To this end he thought it the surest method to make his peasants resemble tools that have neither will nor impulse; and to a certain extent he actually made them like the soldiers of the present time who are commanded in a mass, who move to battle in a mass, and who count for nothing when acting singly. To attain this end he took away from his peasants the small allotment of plough land and the hay meadows which noblemen usually give them for their bare maintenance, as a recompense for all the forced labor which they demand from them. In a word, this nobleman forced all his peasants and their wives and children to work every day of the year for him. Lest they should starve, he doled out to them a definite quantity of bread. . . . If there was any real meat, it was only in Easter Week.

These serfs also receive clothing befitting their condition. . . . Naturally these serfs had no cows, horses, ewes, or rams. Their master did not withhold from these serfs the permission, but rather the means to have them. Whoever was a little better off and ate sparingly, kept a few chickens, which the master sometimes took for himself, paying for them as he pleased.

In a short time he added to his two hundred souls another two hundred as victims of his greed, and proceeding with them just as with the first, he increased his holdings year after year, thus multiplying the number of those groaning in his fields. Now he counts them by the thousands and is praised as a famous agriculturalist.

"Barbarian! What good does it do the country that every year a few thousand more bushels of grain are grown, if those who produce it are valued on a par with the ox whose job it is to break the heavy furrow? Or do we think our citizens happy because our granaries are full and their stomachs empty?"

Source: Alexander Radischev, *A Journey from St. Petersburg to Moscow* (1790).

Catherine the Great (r. 1762–1796) grew up an obscure princess from one of the

Catherine the Great

little German states. For political reasons, her family married her to young Peter III (r. 1762), the tyrannical and intellectually limited grandson of Peter the Great and heir to the Russian crown. He soon rejected her in all ways, and after he became tsar, he quickly lost most of his supporters as well. Catherine had no intention of languishing in obscurity. "I did not care about Peter," she later wrote, "but I did care about the crown." Less than a year after he took the throne, Catherine conspired with a group of aristocratic army officers, who assassinated him and declared Catherine tsarina of Russia.

The new empress used her striking intelligence, charm, and political talent to assert her own power and expand Russian territory and might. Well educated, she thought of herself as attuned to Enlightenment ideas. She often corresponded with French *philosophes* such as Denis Diderot, who spent some time at St. Petersburg as her guest. In 1766, she congratulated Voltaire for triumphing "against the enemies of mankind: superstition, fanaticism, ignorance, quibbling, evil judges, and the power that rests in their hands." Voltaire returned the favor with constant praise for

Catherine. She relaxed the traditionally tight constraints on the press in Russia and she confiscated church lands—policies that seemed in line with Enlightenment thinking. Her educational reforms, by which she established new local schools, teachers' colleges, and schools for girls, also suggested a forward-thinking monarch. Most stunningly, Catherine convened a legislative commission, half of whose members were commoners (some even peasants), to reform Russia's legal code. She wrote the *Instruction* (1767) to that commission herself, relying on the works of key Enlightenment figures such as Montesquieu and Beccaria. Her *Instruction* called for equality before the law, the abolition of torture, and other liberal reforms.

These programs promised more than they delivered. The commission members squabbled among themselves, and in the end, the effort yielded only minor reforms before it was finally abandoned. Catherine's early talk of easing the burdens on the peasantry also came to little; in return for the support of noble landowners, she allowed them to subjugate the peasants even further. As Document 15.1 suggests, some observers criticized the treatment of Russia's serfs. For example, Alexander Radischev argued, "What good does it do the country that every year a few thousand more bushels of grain are grown, if those who produce it are valued on a par with the ox whose job it is to break the heavy furrow?" Catherine imprisoned him.

In 1768, Catherine provoked a war against the Ottoman Empire. The event seems to have signaled her turn away from enlightened reform and toward power politics. A massive insurrection by Russian serfs in 1773 under the leadership of a Don Cossack, Yemelyan Pugachev (1726–1775), further soured her on reform. Pugachev claimed to be Catherine's murdered husband, a "redeemer tsar," and promised his followers land and freedom. Thousands of serfs in southwestern Russia turned against their masters—slaughtering hundreds of landlords and officials—and demanded an end to their plight. Catherine's army managed to put down the rebellion, but only with great difficulty. When some disgruntled followers betrayed Pugachev, the army captured him and tortured him to death.

Catherine proved more successful in her ambitious foreign policy. She defeated the Turks in 1774, extending Russia to the Black Sea and the Balkan Peninsula. Map 15.2 shows Russia's expansion to the south and west during the eighteenth century. For the Ottoman Empire, this defeat marked another step in an unstoppable decline.

Catherine then turned on Poland. At the beginning of the eighteenth century, Poland was the third-largest country in Europe.

The partition of Poland Yet, as we saw in Chapter 13, it lacked natural boundaries and a strong central government. Weak and without allies, it became a power vacuum that proved all too tempting to its ambitious neighbors. In 1772, Russia, Prussia, and Austria—having plotted Poland's demise among themselves—annexed slices of Polish territory. This aggression at long last stirred the Polish government to action. The Diet passed sweeping reforms, improved the lot of commoners, and gave the central government power to act effectively. These changes came too late. Poland still could not match the combined armies of its enemies, and in 1795, the three aggressors divided the remainder of the hapless nation among themselves. Map 15.2 shows the eventual dismemberment of Poland, which left Russia, Prussia, and Austria the dominant powers in eastern Europe. When Catherine died in 1796 after thirty-five years of rule, Russia had grown to an ominous size and had taken its place as a major power in world affairs.

In east-central Europe, the small but rising Brandenburg-Prussia set its sights on the Austrian Empire, a large power struggling to maintain control over its far-flung lands. From 1713 to 1740, the vigorous Frederick William I ruled Prussia. The king was obsessed with unquestioned absolutism,

Forging a military state in Prussia

centralized bureaucratic administration, and, above all, the military. His martial uniforms and preoccupation with Prussian soldiery earned him the label the "Sergeant King."

Frederick William's mental image of the perfect military dominated his policies and Prussian society. While he employed his army for road and canal building as well as traditional military service, some 70 percent of the state's budget went to the armed forces, whose size he more than doubled during his reign. Rather than relying on mercenaries, the king required all men to register for military service in local units commanded by German noble officers. The localities, in turn, had to recruit and support these regiments, and soldiers were billeted among the civilian population.

No other state in Europe could boast such a high proportion of men, from peasant to noble, in the military. Nor could any other state point to such a regimented society. In Prussia, the higher ranks of the military and state bureaucracy were reserved for the nobility; the middle classes were clearly prevented from rising to noble status; and the peasantry was a subordinate, overburdened people, often still serfs living in almost slavelike relationships to their land-owning masters.

Despite the martial tenor of life in Prussia, the king left a surprisingly progressive legacy. Frederick William I avoided wars, promoted a strong economy, welcomed Protestant and Jewish refugees, and filled the treasury. In 1740, he passed all that he had built, intact, on to his talented son Frederick II (r. 1740–1786), later known as Frederick the Great. The new king soon used this army—the fourth largest in Europe—and the money his father had accumulated to make a bold bid for Austrian lands.

In the same year that Frederick II ascended the throne in Prussia, Maria Theresa (r. 1740–1780) became empress of the Austrian Habsburg dominions. Austria was not a tightly controlled, militaristic state like Prussia. Rather, it had already

Austria tries to hold on

lost most of the indirect control it once held over the central German states as head of the Holy Roman Empire. Austria's own lands contained a complex array of language groups and consisted of some semi-autonomous territories. Austria could barely control Hungary, and its nobility fully dominated its serfs, who paid most taxes directly to their lords rather than to the crown. As a result, Maria Theresa could afford only a relatively small army.

The empress's father had feared that these weaknesses might prove Austria's undoing when he died. Moreover, there was only weak precedent for a female ruler of Habsburg lands. Therefore, he spent the final twenty years of his life securing agreement among all the European powers (embodied in a document called the Pragmatic Sanction) that his daughter would

THINKING ABOUT GEOGRAPHY

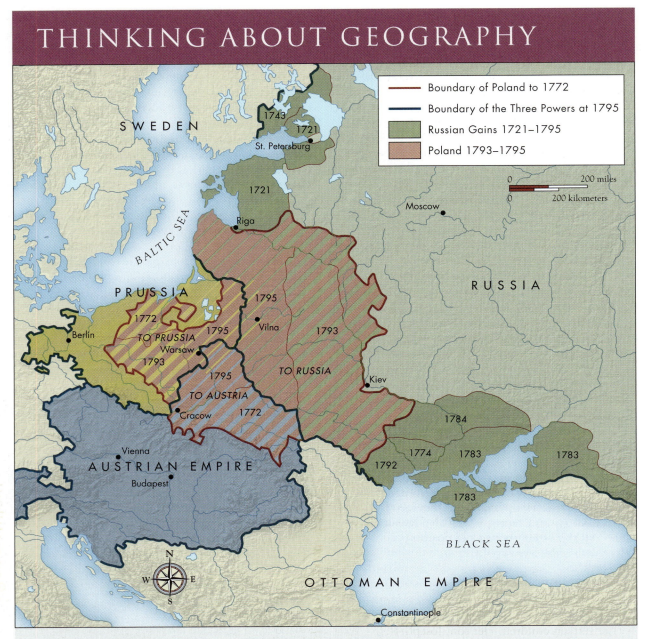

MAP 15.2   THE EXPANSION OF RUSSIA AND THE PARTITION OF POLAND, 1721–1795

This map shows eastern Europe during the eighteenth century. ■ **Notice** the division of Poland.
In what ways did the partition of Poland benefit Russia, Prussia, and Austria? **How** might Poland's
decline change the balance of power? ■ **Notice** the expansion of Russia and Prussia. **Where** might
these rising powers look for further expansion?

succeed him without question. In spite of his diligence, when he died in 1740, competitors arose to challenge her authority. As for the principle of balance of power among states implying a desire for peace, Frederick II of Prussia dismissed the idea bluntly: "The fundamental rule of governments is the principle of extending their territories."

As soon as Maria Theresa took the crown, Frederick challenged her authority, a common occurrence when a succession was questionable in any way. Acting on his maxim that "the safety and greater good for the state demands that treaties should be broken under certain circumstances,"

The mid-century land wars

the Prussian king marched his troops into Silesia (see Map 15.3), the richest of the Habsburg provinces. He also shrewdly forged alliances with other German states against Austria. His aggressive scheming plunged most of the major European states into a series of wars for the mastery of central Europe.

The War of the Austrian Succession dragged on for eight years (1740–1748). Maria Theresa rallied Hungarian arms to her defense and repelled Prussia's allies—Bavarians, Saxons, French, and Spanish. The conflict eventually turned into a military stalemate, which led to a 1748 peace treaty that ended the hostilities. Maria Theresa had managed to preserve the Habsburg state as a major power, but she had been unable to dislodge Frederick from Silesia.

Neither she nor her advisors intended to tolerate this robbery of their fair province by the upstart Prussians—even if it meant starting negotiations for an alliance with their traditional rival, France. Frederick grew fearful of being isolated by his enemies and left vulnerable to invasions. In 1756, when he signed an alliance with Great Britain—Prussia's opponent only a few years earlier—Maria Theresa solidified a new alliance with France.

The Diplomatic Revolution Document 15.2 reveals how difficult the change of allies was for Maria Theresa. This astounding shift of alliances—the so-called Diplomatic Revolution—suddenly transformed former enemies into friends. Meanwhile, Maria Theresa shored up Austria's internal resources by honing her government's control over taxation, diminishing burdens on the peasantry, and reorganizing the bureaucracy. All this strengthened her position as a ruler who could command strong forces and who enjoyed backing from a powerful ally. Figure 15.1, a painting by Habsburg court artist Martin Meytens, shows the empress with her husband (seated on the left) and thirteen of her sixteen children. Her son, Joseph, heir to the throne, stands in a favored place at the center of the star floor. As this painting suggests, even though she led Austria through wars, Maria Theresa often chose to present herself as a good mother to both her family and her nation.

Not one to wait for his enemies to strike first, Frederick reopened hostilities by overrunning Saxony in 1756, initiating the Seven Years' War (1756–1763). However, Frederick soon found himself at bay as France and Austria—now joined by Russia and Sweden, both of which hoped to gain lands at Prussia's expense—closed in on him from all directions. His only backing came from Britain, which saw an opportunity to weaken its longtime opponent, France. After holding off his enemies for six years, the exhausted Prussian king finally seemed near defeat. "I believe all is lost," he confessed in private. Then in 1762 his luck revived. The Russian tsarina Elizabeth, one of his most reviled enemies, died. Her successor, the weak Peter III, happened to admire Frederick and suddenly pulled Russia out of the war. The remaining allies soon lost stomach for the fight. The peace in 1763 left matters much as they had been before the war began, but as we will see (pages 316–319), the fighting in Europe spread to India, the Caribbean, and North America.

Having narrowly escaped destruction, Frederick spent the remaining twenty-three years of his life reconstructing his war-ravaged territories. He encouraged agriculture, subsidized and protected industry, and invited immigrants into his well-governed territories. At no time, though, did he neglect his army or lose his sense of practicality. Indeed, in 1772 he joined Austria and Russia in the first partition of Poland. Map 15.3 shows Prussia's expansion under Frederick, first at the expense of the Austrian Empire when he took Silesia, and then at the expense of Poland as

■ FIGURE 15.1

Martin Meytens, *Maria Theresa and Her Family*, 1750.

■ DOCUMENT 15.2

Austria's Empress Explains the Diplomatic Revolution

During the eighteenth century; alliances among European states often shifted. They changed most dramatically in the 1756 "Diplomatic Revolution" preceding the Seven Years' War (1756–1763). In the following excerpt, Empress Maria Theresa of Austria explains why she turned toward her traditional adversary, France, to form a coalition against the newly allied Prussia and Great Britain. ■ **Why** *does Maria Theresa forge an alliance with France?* **What** *problems does she anticipate in allying Austria with France?*

"I have not abandoned the old system, but Great Britain has abandoned me and the system, by concluding the Prussian treaty, the first intelligence of which struck me like a fit of apoplexy. I and the king of Prussia are incompatible; and no consideration on earth will ever induce me to enter into any engagement to which he is a party. Why should you be surprised if, following your example in concluding a treaty with Prussia, I should now enter into an engagement with France?

"I am far from being French in my disposition, and do not deny that the court of Versailles has been my bitterest enemy, but I have little to fear from France, and I have no other recourse than to form such arrangements as will secure what remains to me. My principal aim is to secure my hereditary possessions. I have truly but two enemies whom I really dread, the king of Prussia and the Turks; and while I and Russia continue on the same good terms as now exist between us; we shall, I trust, be able to convince Europe, that we are in a condition to defend ourselves against those adversaries, however formidable."

Source: Maria Theresa, William Coxe, *History of the House of Austria*, vol. 3 (London: Bohn, 1847), pp. 363–364.

---

he used the territory to unify the main portions of his country. The map also shows Prussia's chief competitor, Austria, with its more far-flung territories. By the time of his death in 1786, Frederick had raised Prussia to the status of a great power and shared the leadership of central Europe with Austria.

WARFARE IN THE EIGHTEENTH CENTURY

The nature of wars fought by these eighteenth-century nations had evolved and changed from earlier times. Now armies consisted primarily of professional forces whose size and elaborate organization mirrored the centralized, bureaucratic governments they served. Officers were paid as full-time servants of the state in both peace and war. However, the troops they commanded were not all so "professional." Conscripts, volunteers, mercenaries, and even criminals made up their rank and file. In this sense, armies served as a depository for men without means and for those seen as threats to the social order. Officers tried to tame these motley groups by stressing harsh discipline and incessant drilling.

Weapons and tactics were also changing. Reliable muskets; bayonets that no longer hindered fire; mobile cannons; and skilled coordination of troops, artillery, and cavalry all made warfare potentially more destructive than ever. Still, generals typically avoided all-out battles, preferring to expend their resources judiciously. "I do not favor pitched battles, especially at the beginning of a war," said Marshall Saxe, a leading French officer and writer on war tactics, in 1732. "I am convinced that a skillful general could make war all his life without being forced into one." Even Frederick the Great—not one to shy away from warfare—expressed this preference in his *Instructions for His Generals* (1747): "The greatest secret of war and the masterpiece of a skillful general is to starve his enemy." Instead of embarking on grand, decisive battles, then, eighteenth-century generals focused on building fortifications, initiating and maintaining sieges, securing supply lines, gaining superior positions, and piling up small advantages. Moreover, most military campaigns lasted only four or five months a year. Meanwhile, life outside the military—commerce, farming, culture, travel, and politics—went on as usual.

Yet, as Frederick the Great recognized, "war is [ultimately] decided only by battles and is not finished except by them." Outright fighting, when it finally occurred, took a heavy toll in human lives. Typically, soldiers arranged themselves in dense rows at least three men deep and fired their muskets, row by row, on command. Each side hurled artillery fire into the opposing troops and sent the cavalry charging in. Casualties mounted, but at the end of the day generals usually pulled their forces back from the battle with enough survivors to fight again.

Maritime battles cost fewer lives than land wars but could be crucial in the overall outcome of war. The largest ships of war in the eighteenth century carried up to one hundred cannons. Figure 15.2, a cutaway view of a French warship, shows cannons poking out of the top three decks. Sailors are depicted at drill

[Marginal handwritten notes: "more organized & government", "improvement? or not?", "war tactics"]

THINKING ABOUT GEOGRAPHY

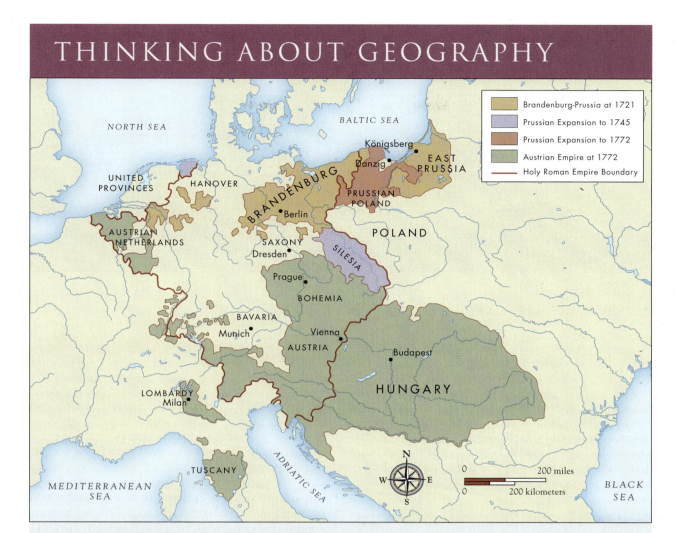

MAP 15.3   PRUSSIA AND THE AUSTRIAN EMPIRE, 1721–1772

This map shows two growing eighteenth-century powers, Prussia and Austria. ■ **Compare** the holdings of these two states. **Which** do you think might be considered the stronger? **What** problems face both in creating a strong, unified state? ■ **Notice** France to the west and Russia to the east—both large and unified states. **Where** are Austria and Prussia most likely to compete with each other or expand?

and at rest. At the upper right are officers' quarters, and the bottom decks house supplies, including livestock. Often firing at each other at point-blank range, many warships were destroyed or suffered grievous damage in these brutal clashes, and thousands of sailors perished.

A single battle, whether on land or sea, rarely led to a definitive outcome. More likely, the relentless draining away of money and men prompted diplomats to come to the bargaining table and end the war. This hemorrhaging of money and men was not missed by critics of the military, especially Enlightenment thinkers, who denigrated the old warrior culture as irrational and wasteful. Their criticisms, however, could neither prevent nor end wars in a society in

Enlightenment [handwritten margin note]

which most people still regarded war as a normal— perhaps necessary—part of life.

WESTERN EUROPE AND THE GREAT COLONIAL RIVALRY

Like eastern Europe, western Europe experienced its own brand of statebuilding and rivalry for power. In this region as well as overseas, France and Britain uneasily shared dominance. Their seventeenth-century rivals, Spain and Holland, were declining. On the continent, Spain—lacking the finances, manpower, and royal leadership that made it such a power in the late sixteenth and early seventeenth centuries—could no longer threaten France. Holland—damaged by three

weaker Spain [handwritten margin note]

■ FIGURE 15.2

An eighteenth-century French warship, from *Iconographic Encyclopaedia*, 1851.

Anglo-Dutch wars and economic warfare with Britain during the seventeenth century—had gradually lost much of its trade and international position. Overseas, however, Spain as well as Portugal had managed to hold onto most of their lands. In the Americas, they remained great colonial powers, controlling most of the territory stretching from Mexico to the South American continent. There, they dominated the Amerindians, disrupting their cultures and turning them into laborers on large plantations and in mines, which still produced massive loads of gold and silver for shipment to Europe. Holland also had retained its Pacific colonies, which supported a valuable coffee and spice trade. However, the Dutch had lost some of their empire in Asia and much of their sea power to the British. With Spain and Holland thus occupied, France and Britain became the primary colonial rivals (see Map 15.4).

Louis XIV had made France a model of absolutism. However, the French monarchy never again achieved the clout it had enjoyed under his guidance. To be sure, France remained a first-rank power with a large army, a centralized bureaucracy, and a growing economy. Yet, even during the last decades of his reign, Louis XIV's stature diminished. Thoughtful people criticized him for dragging France into what they saw as meaningless foreign conflicts. Louis' expensive wars and unreformed taxation policies also depleted the treasury. As Voltaire reported in 1751, "In the minds of the majority of his subjects, he lost during the last three years of his life all the prestige of the great and memorable things he had accomplished. . . . "

After Louis' death in 1715, French nobles in governmental councils and France's *parlements*—the thirteen judicial courts that had to sign royal decrees before those documents could become law—angled for a restoration of the powers they had lost to the king. The *parlements* claimed to speak for the nation, though in fact they voiced only the interests of the elites. The nobles bargained with the crown, sometimes to the point of open defiance. They faced a stubborn opponent. The young Louis XV, who had ascended the throne at the age of 5, would rule for almost sixty years. Like Louis XIV, he asserted that "sovereign power resides in my person only . . . my courts [*parlements*] derive their existence and their authority from me alone . . . to me alone belongs legislative power without subordination and undivided."

Despite his longevity and support from some able ministers, Louis XV governed far less effectively than his predecessor had. Ignoring administrative matters, he allowed his royal bureaucracy to weaken. As resistance from the *parlements* ate away at the king's authority, France's fiscal pressures from old debts and continued military expenditures grew. The rising tensions centered on the issue of taxes. Specifically, the crown wanted to tap France's wealth by raising taxes, but the nobility sidestepped this move by using the *parlements* to protect their tax exemptions. Moreover, private tax farmers still controlled the collection of taxes, keeping one-third for themselves. Clearly, the monarchy was missing out on large sources of revenue. In 1716, the crown had tried to change this system. The effort led to the creation of a private bank, promoted by a brilliant Scottish financier, John Law, with the power to produce its own notes as legal tender and to monopolize overseas commerce. Within just a few years, however, overspeculation in his Mississippi Company had brought the bank to ruin the "Mississippi Bubble,"

The French monarchy in decline

trade

new rivals

problems in France

private bank

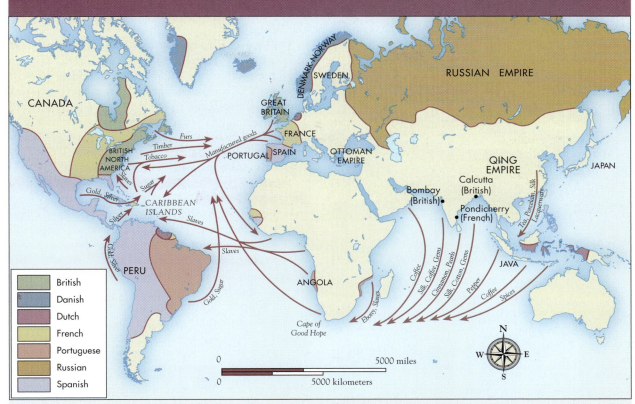

MAP 15.4 OVERSEAS COLONIES AND TRADE, 1740

This map shows Europe's colonies and overseas trade patterns during the mid-eighteenth century.
- **Locate** British and French holdings. **Where** are conflicts most likely to break out between these two powers? ■ **Identify** the triangular trade structure across the Atlantic. **Why** was slavery so central to this structure? ■ **Notice** what goods dominated trade. **Which** goods were Europeans most interested in selling and buying? **Why?**

leaving France saddled again with its inefficient old system.

Nothing drained money from the treasury more than wars. By avoiding major wars until 1740, the crown achieved relative financial stability. Thereafter the story changed, as France was drawn into a series of costly conflicts with continental and colonial rivals. Struggling to fund these endeavors and lacking the appropriate financial institutions and taxable resources, France staggered under a relentlessly expanding debt.

In the 1770s, the king and his chancellor finally dissolved the *parlements* and tried to enact an ambitious program of reform. The move came too late. The inept Louis XV had never projected the image of a dynamic, reforming, enlightened monarch. On the contrary, he had a reputation for living lavishly within his opulent court. Underground pamphlets accused him of allowing his mistress and his sexual taste for girls to distract him from attending properly to courtly matters and the demanding business of managing the state. By the end of his reign, he had earned the dislike and even hatred of his subjects. Louis XV's death in 1774 was met with conspicuous silence, and his tardy reform program evaporated.

Hoping to gain popularity, Louis' successor, Louis XVI (r. 1774–1792), quickly restored the *parlements* and their powers. Again, these aristocratic bodies thwarted new plans for financial reform—even those offered by talented ministers. In France, unlike in most other European powers, the crown and the nobility failed to find a satisfactory way of working together. Again and again, reform efforts faltered, annoying those hoping for change. As frustrations intensified, the crown became increasingly isolated from traditional sources of support within the country.

France needed all the strength it could muster to compete for colonies and stature with Great Britain, where a much different situation had evolved. In 1714, a year before Louis XIV's death, Queen Anne had died. The crown passed to George I (r. 1714–1727), the first of the German Hanoverian line. The British monarchy had already sustained damage from the civil war and revolution of the seventeenth century (see Chapter 13). Though the king remained the chief executive of the state, ordained by God and tradition, Parliament now had the upper hand. Divided into the House of Lords (for nobles only) and House of Commons (elected representatives of commoners), Parliament controlled critical functions such as taxation, lawmaking, and the process for bringing grievances to the monarchy. Clearly, king and Parliament had to find a way to work together rather than in opposition.

Making the British system work

The answer came in the form of a new institution: the cabinet system. Under this structure, the king chose members of Parliament, usually from the House of Commons, to serve as his ministers. If he hoped to enact policies, he had to select ministers who could command plenty of votes. These men tended to be the leaders of the major groups, or parties, in the House of Commons. By the eighteenth century, two groups dominated the House. Whigs, favoring commercial interests and a strong Parliament, remained staunchly opposed to any return of the Catholic Stu-

arts to the crown. Whigs also championed popular rights more than the conservative Tories did. Tories usually favored large landowners and a strong monarchy and had stood less firmly against the Stuarts than the Whigs had.

Differences between the two groups came to a head in 1714. That year, the Tories considered supporting James, a Catholic Stuart raised in France, against George I. An unsuccessful rebellion in favor of James discredited the Tories in the eyes of the monarchy. In 1746, the English army put down another rebellion in Scotland that had attempted to support a Catholic Stuart. This latest fiasco further alienated the Tory leadership from the British crown.

For these reasons, George I and his son George II (r. 1727–1760) selected their ministers from the Whigs rather than the Tories. The two kings' lack of talent and public support made them all the more dependent on Whig leadership for governance. That leadership came in the person of Robert Walpole (1676–1745). Already recognized as a superb speaker and leading Whig in the House of Commons, Walpole became First Lord of the Treasury and the most important minister in George I's Privy Council in 1721. Much of Walpole's prominence derived from his successful handling of a financial crisis after an overseas trading company collapsed in 1720 (the South Sea Bubble). After that coup, he brought in other Whigs who could control votes in Parliament. He flattered and "managed" the monarch to remain in favor. Through patronage—control over money, contracts, offices, and honors—and the manipulation of elections, he ensured the dominance of the Whigs and his own leadership for twenty years.

Many complained about this pattern of political corruption, which both Whigs and Tories used. One critic—the British artist William Hogarth (1697–1764)—produced many prints lambasting British political and social life. In Figure 15.3, one of a series of works on British elections, Hogarth shows a corrupt political campaign in progress. At the center, a voter emerges drunk from a riotous tavern. He has been bribed and is being instructed how to vote, which at the time was done publicly. At the left, the Tory candidate is purchasing cheap jewelry for a woman on the balcony. He makes his purchase from a Jewish merchant, despite his own anti-Jewish record in Parliament.

Walpole's successors continued his strategy of patronage to ensure parliamentary support, and the Whigs held office for another twenty years. By the middle of the eighteenth century, a pattern had emerged. A group of ministers—themselves led by a prime minister, chosen from Parliament, who could command enough votes in the House of Commons to pass legislation—served the monarch and remained responsible to Parliament. Unlike in France, where most political debate took place outside the government, in Britain, debate occurred within Parliament between the party in power and the "loyal opposition." People thus perceived the nation as being governed by the rule of law rather than the whim of a monarch. This system often moved slowly, but it worked.

Although Britain's government may have been more representative than France's, it was far from democratic. Only some 200,000—most of them the wealthiest males—could vote. Rich landowners and powerful local elites staffed the government. Not surprisingly, Parliament listened most carefully to representatives of the 400 families whose massive estates included one-fourth of Britain's arable land. British officials did not seek to exempt themselves from taxation, as did most of their counterparts in France, but instead ruled along with the crown by controlling Parliament.

Prosperity formed the foundation of Britain's strong position in these years. The middle class in particular agreed with the popular British author and observer Daniel Defoe that "the greatness of the British nation is not owing to war and conquests . . . it is all owing to trade, to the increase of our commerce at home, and the extending it abroad." Goods poured into Britain from India and North America. The nation transformed itself into an agricultural exporter and a flourishing manufacturing center. By the middle of the eighteenth century, Great Britain had become Europe's leading economic power. It pursued its interest in European affairs through diplomacy, alliances, and the subsidizing of its allies' arms. Its naval dominance alone made it a formidable opponent. After 1740, Britain used both its economic strength and its military might in the great midcentury wars with France that stretched across three continents. To understand this story, we must shift our attention to the West's overseas colonies and the nature of trade among them.

Colonies, trade, and war More than anything else, France and Britain fought over colonies. For both countries, foreign trade quadrupled in the eighteenth century, and a large part of that increase derived from transactions with colonies. The two nations also made their greatest profits from trade across the Atlantic. However, their overseas presence differed crucially. The French had only 56,000 colonists living in North America in 1740—a fraction of the British colonial population. Yet French colonists carried out an extensive, highly profitable fur trade. Further, because

■ FIGURE 15.3

William Hogarth, *Canvassing for Votes—The Election*, 1754.

of their small numbers and trade arrangements, they experienced limited conflict with Amerindians.

British colonists, clustered along the eastern seaboard, had a different experience. First, they grew rapidly—from 250,000 in 1700 to 1.7 million in 1760. As they occupied and exploited more and more land, they pushed the Amerindians out. Their expansion, combined with resistance from local tribes, led to savage battles. The fighting, in turn, convinced the colonists that removing or even exterminating the Amerindians was justified. As they became more firmly established, the British colonists bought manufactured goods from Britain in return for tobacco, rice, cotton, and indigo dye, much of which Britain re-exported to the European continent.

These North American colonists participated in the even more lucrative triangle of trade that connected Europe, Africa, and the Americas and that centered on the Caribbean (see Map 15.4). The British and French, along with the Dutch and Spanish, held islands there that supported sugar, rum, coffee, and dyestuffs trade **The triangle of trade** produced by slave labor. In particular, the demand for sugar and coffee seemed endless. European craving for these items grew so much that, for many, they became necessities rather than occasional luxuries.

At the heart of this thriving colonial commerce was the slave trade (see Chapter 12). Slavery was long common throughout Africa and in other societies. For centuries, Islamic merchants had purchased slaves through well-established African networks and transported them by caravan across the Sahara Desert to the Mediterranean basin or by ship from east African ports across the Indian Ocean to Asia.

The slave trade

By the eighteenth century, the dramatic demand for slaves in the Americas shifted Africa's slave trade westward to the Atlantic coast. Ships from Europe carried manufactured goods (most notably, guns) and gin to western Africa and traded them for slaves—two-thirds of them males, because they best provided heavy labor. Usually captured by African middlemen, slaves languished in pens in towns or forts on the African coast. European trading ships then carried them across the Atlantic in a perilous two-month sea voyage known as the **Middle Passage.**

Figure 15.4, an 1846 watercolor, suggests what conditions were like below decks on a slave ship. Typically, slaves were packed like cargo into the holds of ships "where the light of day does not penetrate." As many as 700 slaves—naked, branded, and shackled—might be crammed into one ship. A French writer describing these voyages told of a "continuous state of alarm on the part of the white men, who fear a revolt, and . . . a cruel state of uncertainty on the part of the Negroes, who do not know the fate awaiting them." In Document 15.3, Olaudah Equiano, a captured African, describes how this middle-passage experience soon made him "so sick and low" that he "wished for the last friend, death."

Traders took most of their slaves to the West Indies and Brazil; less than 10 percent went to North American destinations. After unloading their human cargo, the ships filled up with sugar, rum, and other goods—sometimes stopping farther north in the American colonies to take on additional products such as cotton, tobacco, timber, and furs. From there, the ships returned to Europe. Merchants then re-exported many of these products to other European nations.

Disease, abuse, and suicide took the lives of many slaves. In addition, African women often suffered the horror of rape by their captors. Those who survived the Middle Passage were then sold for profit and put to work on a plantation or in the mines or households of colonists. Figure 15.5 depicts slaves harvesting sugarcane on a West Indies plantation. Men, women, and children share the difficult work. In the foreground, a manager on horseback gives orders to a slave, who looks up deferentially to his master. On the right, sugarcane is being loaded into a cart, to be carried to the mill in the distant background. Slaves suffered from poor diets, inadequate housing, broken families, and stiff corporal punishment. The uprooting, the trauma of transportation, and the harsh conditions in the colonies stripped much away from these people. Still, slaves often resisted their masters by working slowly, sabotaging equipment, running away, and revolting. Despite their lack of freedom, slaves built hybrid cultural traditions from African, American, and European sources.

Within the slave societies of Brazil, the West Indies, and North America, the notion of race was becoming tied to slavery, adding to earlier notions of racial prejudice. The unprecedented dependence on slavery and the associated development of racism would stain these societies in ways that would persist to this day.

The consequences of the slave trade also rippled through sub-Saharan Africa. Traditional trade routes north to the Mediterranean and east to the Indian Ocean disintegrated as more lucrative commerce shifted west to the Atlantic coast of Africa. To supply more human cargo to the Europeans, West African kingdoms raided inland tribes. Bloody internal wars erupted—more deadly than ever thanks to the guns supplied by Europeans to the Africans.

Because many slaves perished in the Americas, and the plantations that depended on them kept expanding, the demand for fresh supplies of slaves increased relentlessly. This rising need perpetuated the triangular commerce among Europe, Africa, and the Americas. European traders took 50,000 to 100,000 slaves across the Atlantic each year during most of the eighteenth century. By the time slave trafficking abated in the mid-nineteenth century, more than 11 million Africans had been ripped from their homes, transported across the Atlantic, and sold into slavery. Another 4 million died resisting seizure or while in transport.

■ FIGURE 15.4

A transatlantic slave ship.

■ DOCUMENT 15.3

Olaudah Equiano Describes the Middle Passage

The slave trade between Africa and the Americas involved the horrors of capture and the "Middle Passage," a harrowing two-month voyage across the Atlantic. In the account below, Olaudah Equiano (1745–1797)—a west African who was captured by slave raiders when he was 10 years old—describes the ocean journey. He survived the voyage and twenty-one years of slavery before purchasing his freedom. ■ ***How*** *were captured Africans treated on the slave ship?* ■ ***In what ways*** *did they try to resist?*

The first object which saluted my eyes when I arrived on the coast was the sea, and a slave ship which was then riding at anchor and waiting for its cargo. These filled me with astonishment, which was soon converted into terror when I was carried on board. I was immediately handled and tossed up to see if I were sound by some of the crew, and I was now persuaded that I had gotten into a world of bad spirits and that they were going to kill me. . . .

I was not long suffered to indulge my grief; I was soon put down under the decks, and there I received such a salutation in my nostrils as I had never experienced in my life; so that with the loathsomeness of the stench and crying together, I became so sick and low that I was not able to eat, nor had I the least desire to taste anything. I now wished for the last friend, death, to relieve me; but soon, to my grief, two of the white men offered me eatables, and on my refusing to eat, one of them held me fast by the hands and laid me across I think the windlass and tied my feet while the other flogged me severely. I had never experienced anything of this kind before, and although not being used to the water I naturally feared that element the first time I saw it, yet nevertheless if I could have gotten over the nettings I would have jumped over the side, but I could not; and besides, the crew used to watch very closely over those of us who were not chained down to the decks, lest we should leap into the water, and I have seen some of these poor African prisoners most severely cut for attempting to do so, and hourly whipped for not eating. This indeed was often the case with myself. . . .

One day when we had a smooth sea and moderate wind, two of my wearied countrymen who were chained together (I was near them at the time), preferring death to such a life of misery, somehow made through the nettings and jumped into the sea; immediately another quite dejected fellow, who on account of his illness was suffered to be out of irons, also followed their example; and I believe many more would very soon have done the same if they had not been prevented by the ship's crew, who were instantly alarmed. Those of us that were the most active were in a moment put down under the deck, and there was such a noise and confusion amongst the people of the ship as I never heard before, to stop her and get the boat to go after the slaves. However, two of the wretches were drowned, but they got the other and afterwards flogged him unmercifully for thus attempting to prefer death to slavery. In this manner we continued to undergo more hardships than I can now relate, hardships which are inseparable from this accursed trade.

Source: Olaudah Equiano, *The Interesting Narrative of the Life of Olaudah Equiano, or Gustavus Vassa, the African, Written by Himself,* 2 vols. (London, 1789).

Planters and merchants on both sides of the Atlantic profited from this trade, and European cities serving as slave-trade ports flourished, particularly in England. The coastal town of Liverpool, for example, grew from a small town to a major city in the eighteenth century. In 1750, its slave merchants and fleet of almost two hundred ships carried almost half of Europe's slave trade. Thousands of men from Liverpool worked on both merchant and naval ships, and more than a dozen banks and several insurance companies served slave-trade merchants. The wealth spread outward from Liverpool, helping to finance Britain's burgeoning industry as well as its rising position on the world stage. "Our West-Indies and African Trades are the most nationally beneficial of any we carry on. . . . The Trade to Africa is the branch which renders our American Colonies and Plantations so advantageous

■ FIGURE 15.5

A West Indies sugar plantation, 1823.

to Great Britain," argued one British defender of the slave system in 1746. "The daily bread of the most considerable part of our British Manufacturers are owing primarily to the labor of Negroes." Although the statement may be an exaggeration, slavery generated much commerce and wealth in this eighteenth-century Atlantic economy, whether by direct or indirect means.

As Europeans' commercial activities, profits, and presence increased in the Americas, so did competition and friction, especially between the French and the British. In North America, British colonists along the eastern seaboard pushed inland, beyond the Appalachian Mountains into the Ohio Valley. The French strengthened their holdings by building forts along the Great Lakes and the large rivers of the St. Lawrence and Mississippi valleys. When the War of the Austrian Succession broke out in Europe in 1740, Britain and France soon locked horns on the Continent as well as overseas. Most of the fighting took place in the Americas, however. Wins and losses on each side balanced out, and by the time the conflict ended in 1748, each side had settled for what it had held in the beginning.

Fighting on three continents

The peace would not last long. In 1755, war—sometimes known as the French and Indian War—erupted again, this time initiated by a British offensive against a French stronghold near Pittsburgh in North America. At the same time, the two powers were also competing in India, each trying to take advantage of the declining power of the Mughals (India's Muslim rulers—see Global Connections). After 1715, the subcontinent had split apart into bickering, independent kingdoms. India became a fertile ground for the British and French, working through their chartered trading companies and backed by their superior weapons of war, to make deals, gain influence, and line up allies among India's opposing princes and political factions. In 1759, British colonialist and soldier Robert Clive (1725–1774), representing Britain's East India Company, explained how a combination of force and bribery could gain the company and England "absolute possession of these rich kingdoms" in India that would provide "an income yearly of upwards of two million sterling." Moreover, he added, Britain would gain advantages over "the several European nations engaged in the commerce here," especially "against the French." This competition between the British and French for trade and imperial power developed into an undeclared war that, after 1756, coalesced with the hostilities breaking out across Europe (the Seven Years' War), the Caribbean, and North America.

In this widespread war, which involved Asians and Amerindians as well as Europeans, France invested most of its energy and resources in the European arena, whereas Britain focused on the battle overseas. Initially, the French, assisted by the Amerindian allies they had gained, held their own in North America. Then the British, with their superior navy and more extensive population, began capturing French strongholds one by one. The fall of Quebec in 1759 opened all of Canada to British forces. British naval power overwhelmed the French and their Spanish allies in the Caribbean as well. In India, the British also prevailed, crushing the French and subduing several resisting Indian states. During the succeeding decades, as Map 15.5 reveals, the British increasingly took direct control over areas around their bases of power.

Figure 15.6 also attests to this British success. This late eighteenth-century painting shows William Kirkpatric, a British officer, with his attendants—a group of Indian princes and merchants. Kirkpatric's prominence reflects his authority over those around him and his sword reveals the source of his power. The British had to conquer native forces as well as the French to increase their holdings in the Indian subcontinent. The papers on the table represent the taxes collected by British authorities and suggest the imposition of British law over local states. In the background stands a magnificent estate, suggesting

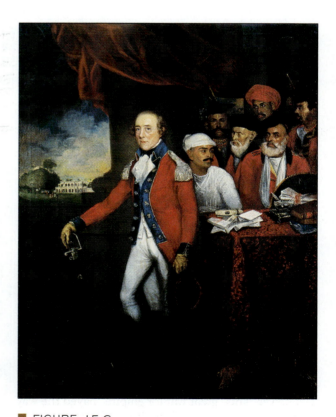

■ FIGURE 15.6

Thomas Hickey, *Colonel Kirkpatric with his Assistants.*

Western Africa, Brazil, and the Atlantic Slave Trade

CONSIDER
■ **Consider** *the consequences of the slave trade for the societies of western Africa and Brazil.* **Notice** *how Brazilian masters dealt with their slaves.*

Drawn by commercial opportunities, European vessels flocked to the west coast of Africa during the seventeenth and eighteenth centuries. The new trade, especially the lucrative and rapidly expanding commerce in slaves, turned west Africans' attention toward the Atlantic Ocean as well. European textiles, metal goods, and firearms poured into west Africa off the European ships. From Brazil and other lands in the Americas came new crops, such as manioc and maize, to supplement the yams, millet, and bananas that served as staples for sub-Saharan Africans. Prosperous port cities emerged, and west African states such as Dahomey and Asante gained power.

Other African societies weakened, and once-powerful kingdoms fell in the turmoil and wars provoked by slaving. In 1730, an officer of the Dutch West India Company involved in the slave trade concluded, "The great quantity of guns and powder which the Europeans have from time to time brought" to west Africa have caused "terrible wars among the kings, princes . . . of those lands, who made their prisoners of war slaves." Moreover, the profits from slaving made many Africans "forget all labor." Consequently, there was now "very little trade among the coast Negroes except in slaves." Other methods of obtaining slaves only worsened the turmoil and dislocations that were tearing African societies apart. According to Alexander Falconbridge, a British surgeon who served on slaving ships during the 1780s, "There is great reason to believe that most of the negroes shipped off from the coast of Africa are *kidnapped*." As a result, "continual enmity is thus fostered among the negroes of Africa, and all social intercourse between them destroyed."

The slave trade shaped the Portuguese colony, Brazil, as well. During the eighteenth century, Europeans shipped millions of slaves across the Atlantic; more than a third of them went to Brazil. Although most slaves worked on large plantations producing crops such as sugar and tobacco for export, many also served as domestics and manual laborers. The English navigator Captain William Dampier, stopping in Brazil, reported that everyone kept slaves in their houses except "people of the lowest degree of all." Tradesmen, he continued, "buy Negroes, and train them up to their several Employments," and "Many of the Portugueze, who are Batchelors, keep these black Women for Misses."

Another British traveler to Brazil, Henry Koster, reported that all slaves in Brazil "follow the religion of their master." Many were "baptized in lots before they left their own shores," whereas others were converted upon arrival in Brazil. "The system of baptizing the newly imported negroes," he reported, rendered the slaves "more tractable." Over time, these slaves learned to speak Portuguese, while "their own dialects are allowed to lie dormant until they are, by many of them, quite forgotten." Many slaves died from diseases such as yellow fever or from brutal working conditions and poor nutrition. However, Koster claimed that slaves adapted to "the habits of their masters." At the same time, their masters "imbibe[d] some of the customs of their slaves; and thus the superior and his dependent are brought nearer to each other."

The trans-Atlantic slaving connection between west Africa and Brazil continued into the nineteenth century. In 1888, Brazil—by then an independent nation—became the last state in the Americas to abolish slavery.

---

how colonial holdings and commerce created great wealth in the officer's homeland.

Maps 15.6 and 15.7 show the changing fortunes of France and Britain in North America between 1755 and 1763. The Treaty of Paris, which ended the fighting in 1763, gave Britain control of Canada and of France's holdings east of the Mississippi. Britain also received France's West Indian possessions, except for Guadeloupe and Martinique, and most of France's holdings in India. British control over most of India dates from this period. France and several other nations still retained important overseas colonies, but Britain now reigned as the top colonial and commercial power. This "great war for empire" paved the way for the British to establish their worldwide empire in the nineteenth century.

THE TWILIGHT OF MONARCHIES? THE QUESTION OF ENLIGHTENED ABSOLUTISM

In both Britain and France, the eighteenth-century monarchies were in decline, but for different reasons. In Britain, the monarchs ruled in partnership with Parliament. However, the kings were undistinguished, and Parliament continued to gain the upper hand. In France, the successors to Louis XIV lacked the interest, talent, and support to make the monarchy dynamic or popular. The twin threats to the crown in these nations—the growing complexity of effective governance, and demands from elites to share power—arose elsewhere as well.

THINKING ABOUT GEOGRAPHY

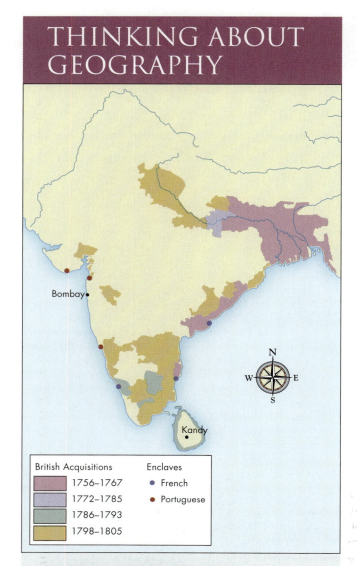

MAP 15.5   INDIA, 1756–1805

This map shows British acquisitions in India between 1756 and 1805. ■ **Notice** where the British concentrated their holdings in the subcontinent. **What** connections might these holdings have to trade and transportation? ■ **Notice** where the French and Portuguese maintained some presence. **Why** might that limited presence have been important to the French and Portuguese?

However, in several other nations, monarchs managed to maintain their authority—often by justifying their rule in innovative ways and instituting new policies. In the second half of the eighteenth century, some of these monarchs styled themselves as "enlightened," or attuned to Enlightenment beliefs and willing to initiate reforms for the good of the state and its people. Some historians have distinguished these rulers from their predecessors, calling them "enlightened absolutists" or simply "enlightened." Yet, how valid is this characterization? Several historians claim that these monarchs primarily followed the long tradition of trying to buttress the central government's power and efficiency. Other historians argue that they genuinely initiated reforms in line with Enlightenment thinking.

The most sensational of the self-described enlightened monarchs was Frederick the Great (Frederick II) of Prussia. Even as a boy, Frederick loved music, poetry, and philosophy. After ascending to the throne, he still found time to perform in concerts as an accomplished flutist in his Palace of San Souci. There he also hobnobbed with towering cultural figures such as Voltaire, savored books in his library, and carried on a lively correspondence with leading French intellectuals. He knew and spoke the phrases of the Enlightenment. Like several other monarchs, he also wanted to display his awareness of culture and intellectual life to help justify his position as monarch. He described "the good monarch" as one who behaved "as if he were each moment liable to render an account of his administration to his fellow citizens." He claimed to act only in the common interest of the people, declaring himself to be "the first servant of the state" rather than a divinely appointed ruler.

Frederick the Great

At the end of the Seven Years' War (1756–1763), the second of his two wars of aggression, Frederick made some attempts at "enlightened" reforms. For example, he initiated codification of the laws, abolished torture, and ended most capital punishment. Believing that "all religions, if one examines them, are founded on superstitious systems, more or less absurd," he proclaimed religious toleration. Nevertheless, he considered Jews "useless to the state" and taxed them heavily. He advocated public education, but spent very little on it compared with what he spent on his army. In his economic policy, Frederick did share the Physiocrats' appreciation of the importance of agriculture and tried to introduce new methods of cultivation (see page 459). Yet he did nothing to free the serfs or lessen their burdens. Neither his wars nor his involvement in the partition of Poland revealed any hint of "enlightened" principles different from the monarchs who preceded him.

No one tried more sincerely to be "enlightened" than Joseph II of Austria (r. 1780–1790). "Since I have ascended the throne," he said in 1781, "I have made *philosophy* the legislator of my empire." Viewing his rule as a moral and holy calling, Joseph issued thousands of decrees. Unfortunately, he lacked the practical sense of Frederick the Great. He did change laws that had previously

Joseph II

MAPS 15.6 AND 15.7   NORTH AMERICA, 1755 AND 1763

These maps show North America before and after the Seven Years' War. ■ **Notice** France's large holdings in 1755. **What** advantages helped the British defeat France in this part of the world? **What** new problems faced Britain as a result of this victory? ■ **Notice** what other competitors to the British remained in North America after 1763. **Assess** their relative strength.

limited freedom of the press and religion (including Judaism). He also restricted the death penalty, promoted education, and enacted and tried to enforce equality before the law.

Nevertheless, Joseph still ruled as an autocrat, antagonizing most of the powerful groups in his lands. Even peasants, unable to understand exactly what all the decrees meant, failed to support him. His well-meaning but ill-conceived efforts—to centralize the administration of the widely dispersed Habsburg territories, to replace the numerous languages of his subjects with German, to subordinate the strongly entrenched Roman Catholic Church, and to free the serfs in a society still based on feudalism—all backfired. Opposition and even open revolt swelled in his lands. In 1787, Joseph lamented, "[I] hope that when I am no more, posterity will examine, and judge more equitably . . . all that I have done for my people." His

vision would not come to pass. Within a few years of his death in 1790, most of his reforms were abolished and the Habsburg lands reacquired their old, conservative ways.

Other monarchs, such as those of Sweden, Sardinia, Spain, and Portugal, attempted or enacted reforms that could be seen as enlightened. In Russia, Catherine the Great certainly prided herself on being "enlightened" (see page 470). She once described the true aim of monarchy as "not to deprive People of their natural Liberty; but to correct their Actions, in order to attain the supreme good." Ultimately, however, Catherine failed to put most of her reforms into practice. Instead, she resorted to the tried-and-true tactic of appeasing elites at a price paid by the peasantry.

Certainly these monarchs found it easier to manifest their "enlightenment" in style rather than substance. Moreover, they rarely lost sight of traditional goals: to increase their own military and economic power. Few attempted to

enact fundamental social, political, or economic reforms dictated by Enlightenment thought. Even those who tried, such as Joseph II in Austria, generally failed to overcome opposition to those reforms from tradition-minded people.

Nevertheless, thoughtful observers of the eighteenth century—looking for tendencies and possibilities for reform rather than revolutionary change—believed that several rulers displayed the enlightened spirit of the times. Despite great obstacles to reform within the traditional order, some of these rulers made progress toward fulfilling the *philosophes*' agenda of promoting more religious tolerance, humane social institutions, and rational administration. In the eyes of contemporaries, they earned the label "enlightened."

Finally, from another perspective, **enlightened absolutism** also may have reflected a growing sense that, in the long run, monarchs could no longer *claim* to embody the state. The need for governmental efficiency had grown too much to be entrusted to a poorly qualified individual who happened to be a king or queen. If the institution of monarchy were to survive, kings and queens had to justify their position in these new, ostensibly "enlightened" ways.

CHANGES IN COUNTRY AND CITY LIFE

Eighteenth-century European monarchs and officials faced not only the risky politics and wars of their times, but also the changes unfolding in their very societies. Especially in western Europe, new economic and social forces began to upset old traditions (see Chapter 13). For some, these changes created a sense that life was improving and would continue to do so. For others, the changes only deepened their misery. The greatest shifts emerged in the countryside, where the vast majority of the population (some 80 percent) lived and depended on agriculture for their livelihood and very survival.

Historically, toiling in the fields within Europe's traditional subsistence economies produced little more than enough food to survive. During the late seventeenth and eighteenth centuries, new methods of agricultural production that had originated in Holland spread to England and then to other areas of western Europe. These innovative methods allowed fewer people to work the fields and still produce far more food than they needed. The new techniques and the changes flowing from them became so important that they are known as the agricultural revolution.

THE AGRICULTURAL REVOLUTION

Most early-eighteenth-century farmers used methods that differed only marginally from those employed in previous centuries. They grew the same crops year after year, left one-third to one-half of the land fallow (unplanted) to allow the soil to replenish itself with nutrients for the next planting, and saved only enough fodder to feed small numbers of domestic animals during the winters. Individual families worked small strips of land, and large, uncultivated fields, brushlands, and forests (the "commons") were reserved for general use by the community. Traditional community practices usually determined decisions about crops, animals, and land use. Overall, only a small minority of people made their living outside of agriculture, and an even smaller percentage had the good fortune to afford luxuries.

This traditional, agricultural economy had the potential to support a limited measure of population growth. In the eighteenth century, population increases stepped up the demand for food, and hence for hands to clear fields, drain swamps, terrace hillsides, carry water, and till the soil. Most of these efforts were simply an intensification of old methods for increasing agricultural yields, and the growing population consumed most of the extra food they produced. Something had to change if large numbers of Europeans hoped to increase their standard of living and provide enough food for people living in the cities as well as the countryside.

At the heart of the **agricultural revolution** lay two developments: first, the introduction of new crops and the use of new farming techniques that

dramatically boosted agricultural yields; and second, the transformation of rural lands farmed for subsistence into large, controlled properties that produced crops for commerce. The primary agricultural advances came first in Holland and Britain, where farmers began experimenting with new crops such as clover, turnips, and legumes, as well as the potato from America. These crops replenished the soil rather than depleted it, and therefore could be grown on lands that farmers periodically had to leave fallow. Farmers now used the new crops to feed livestock during the hard winters. More cattle meant more protein-rich dairy products; more horses and oxen eased the workload for humans and provided transportation; and more sheep produced more wool. All this livestock, improving with new crossbreeding practices, yielded more meat, leather, and soap as well as manure with which to fertilize fields. Other new foods, such as nutrient-rich potatoes, also made the land more productive than ever before. Some landowners became renowned for their farming innovations. In England, for example, Charles

■ FIGURE 15.7

The fields of Gloucestershire, England.

"Turnip" Townshend (1674–1738) experimented with crop rotation and growing turnips. His compatriot, Jethro Tull (1674–1741), advocated the use of a seed drill and manure, which made planting more efficient and productive.

Not all farmers adopted the new agricultural methods. For many, traditional ways were comfortably familiar. Even those who realized how much profit they might make by selling their surpluses in the cities and other distant markets needed money to fund the new farming methods. They also required control over larger tracts of land to introduce the new crops, apply the innovative methods, and specialize in certain products—whether sheep for wool, grain for flour, or cattle for meat and dairy.

By all means, fair and foul, these market-oriented landowners dispossessed individuals of their small plots and communities of their commons to enclose land with fences, hedges, and walls as their own. *Enclosures* Figure 15.7, a mid-eighteenth century English painting, shows a large, rich estate in Gloucestershire, England. The fields are consolidated and enclosed. In the center, organized groups of men and women workers toil on the harvest while wagons haul away the produce, destined for commerce rather than local consumption. Other fields are carefully planned and managed for the marketplace. Gone are the small farms, subsistence crops, and open fields that used to dominate the English countryside. After 1750, Britain's Parliament furthered this trend by authorizing a wave of these enclosures. Over the decades, wealthy landowners created large, controlled tracts that yielded products for the market. They reserved only a small part of their land for their own needs or bought their food elsewhere. Through this process, thousands of small, independent landowners, sharecroppers, and tenant farmers lost their land—and the status and security that had come with it. Rural communities disintegrated, eroding the support and human interactions that had so characterized life in the country.

MANUFACTURING SPREADS IN THE COUNTRYSIDE: COTTAGE INDUSTRY

The spreading agricultural revolution became one force pushing, forcing, or freeing people to work more in nonagricultural jobs. When families lost their self-sufficient farms, they had to find new sources of income to supplement the meager day-labor wages their landowning employers paid them. Manufacturing seemed to offer a solution. Growing commerce, particularly overseas trade, had heightened demand for manufactured goods—and thus workers to produce them. Traditionally, well-paid urban artisans had done this sort of work. Now, with demand high and rural workers available by the thousands, merchants turned to the countryside to increase production and take advantage of the cheap labor. Moreover, by shifting more production itself to the countryside, merchants avoided urban guild regulations that historically had controlled wages and the quantity and quality of goods.

All these changes stimulated the growth of cottage industry, also known as the "putting-out system." This system, which had already existed in the sixteenth and seventeenth centuries but to a much smaller degree, worked in a specific way. An entrepreneur provided raw materials (usually for production of textiles such as wool or linen) and sometimes equipment (such as a handloom or a spinning wheel) to peasants. The entrepreneur might be anyone—from a city merchant to a rural landowner—who managed to amass enough money to make an initial investment in raw materials and perhaps equipment. Peasants, who sought employment during times of the year when there was less need for agricultural labor, worked in their homes (hence the term "cottage industry") to turn these raw materials into finished products. Mainly, they spun wool into yarn and wove the yarn into cloth. Sometimes enterprising peasants contracted out raw material to other spinners to keep weavers busy, since weavers depended on spinners to provide a steady supply of yarn. Women and children often worked while men were off performing day-labor for large landowners. The entrepreneur periodically returned, paid for the peasants' labor by the piece, and distributed the finished products to distant markets.

As Figure 15.8 shows, whole families participated in cottage-industry work. Women and children usually washed, combed, and spun the raw material into thread, while men often wove the yarn on looms. In this print, members of a rural household in Ireland beat and comb flax into linen, which will later be spun and woven. The light streaming in from the open window, the smiling laborers, and the little girl playing with a dog all distract our attention from the realities of the work: the dark, cramped quarters of single-room cottages and the tedious nature of this labor.

Cottage industry spread rapidly during the eighteenth century, particularly in Great Britain and parts of France and Germany. In addition to textiles, all sorts of goods—from buttons and housewares to knives, nails, and clocks—were produced through this system. The quality of these products varied, and relations between merchants and laborers often broke down over accusations of theft and disputes over wages. Still, more and more people came to depend on the system. For many of these workers, cottage-industry labor changed from a part-time to a full-time occupation.

The primary appeal of the work was its availability. Cottage industry allowed many people to remain in rural areas in a time of shrinking demand for farm workers. It also helped large families keep up, and enabled young people to get an earlier start on marriage. On the other hand, the pay rarely rose above starvation wages, and the labor was drudgery.

Wherever it spread, cottage industry extended the money economy and the web of the commercial marketplace. Along with the agricultural revolution, the growth of cottage industry helped set the stage for an even greater economic transformation that would eventually sweep from Britain throughout the West and into the non-Western world: the industrial revolution.

MORE PEOPLE, LONGER LIVES

As these new economic and social forces began to alter traditional ways of life, Europe's population jumped from approximately 110 million in 1700 to 190 million in 1800. Figure 15.9 reveals the population growth throughout most of Europe during the eighteenth century. Relatively large populations help explain the strength of three major powers—England (along with Ireland), France, and Russia (note that much of Russia's increased population came from territorial expansion). Earlier marriages, more and better food, and fewer plagues raised the birthrate and lowered the death rate. Agricultural and commercial prosperity, along with improvements in the transportation of food, reduced the number and severity of famines in many areas. In particular, the widespread cultivation of the potato during the second half of the eighteenth century made this cheap, nutritious food available to millions. A spate of good weather helped to improve harvests. In some areas, new urban sanitation practices—cleaning wells, draining swampy areas, and burying refuse—probably improved health as well.

Surprisingly, medical practices rarely contributed to better health. Certainly the medical field saw some advances. Inoculation against smallpox, for example, spread to Europe from the Middle East during the eighteenth century, although it was not used widely until the last decades of the century. Surgeons also

Population growth

Eighteenth-century medicine

■ FIGURE 15.8
Cottage industry.

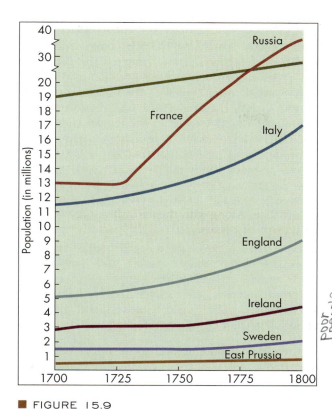

FIGURE 15.9

Population growth in Europe, 1700–1800.

made some improvements in the treatment of battle-field injuries. For instance, they learned to treat soldiers for shock before operating, and to clean wounds around the trauma.

Despite these signs of progress, eighteenth-century medicine was still dangerous. Figure 15.10 provides a glimpse into a German hospital. In just one room, a bewildering array of medical procedures takes place. At the center, a surgeon saws off the leg of a patient. At the right lies a woman with a grotesquely swollen leg; just behind her, a woman prepares to give birth. At the far left, a priest administers last rites to a dying patient. In the background, women distribute food, men haul a body away, and sufferers lie crowded together in beds. French hospitals were no better. The French encyclopedist Denis Diderot described the Hôtel-Dieu in Paris, considered one of France's finest hospitals at the time: "Imagine a long series of communicating wards filled with sufferers of every kind of disease who are sometimes packed three, four, five or even six into a bed, the living alongside the dead and dying, the air polluted by this mass of unhealthy bodies, passing the pestilence of their afflictions from one to the other, and the spectacle of

suffering and agony on every hand. That is the Hôtel-Dieu."

DEEPENING MISERY FOR THE POOR

The eighteenth-century population explosion exacted an ironic price. Stiffening competition for food drove prices up, while competition for jobs kept wages down. As a result, more and more people fell into poverty. A governmental commission in Austria reported to Empress Maria Theresa that "the peasants live in a condition of real slavery. . . . In their ruinous huts, the parents sleep on straw, the children naked on the wide shelves of earthenware stoves . . . all the charges of the Kingdom are born by the peasants, who are the sole taxpayers." Despite a widespread sense that people were better off than ever and that things would improve, in truth more people meant more misery.

In a desperate attempt to survive, poor people fled to the cities, hoping to find work in trade and manufacturing or as day-laborers and domestics. Only some of them managed to find jobs; the rest were left to fend for themselves. A large percentage of urban dwellers missed out on the new wealth and opportunities of the cities. They eked out a living at little more than a subsistence level, and their lot worsened as more and more of them crowded in from the countryside.

Indeed, the surplus of workers; inflation; and disasters such as war, disease, and failed harvests hit the poor in cities and countryside alike. In France, economist Jacques Turgot (1727–1781) described the disastrous harvest of 1769: "The people could exist only by exhausting their resources, by selling at a miserable price their articles of furniture and even their clothes. Many of the inhabitants have been obliged to disperse themselves through other provinces to

FIGURE 15.10

A German hospital, 1746.

seek work or to beg, leaving their wives and children to the charity of the parishes. . . ." One Spanish official described how "wives and children are without work, and all, piled together in cities or large towns, live at the expense of charity. . . ." Even for those who found steady employment, wages simply did not keep pace with escalating prices.

In bad times, food riots and tax revolts broke out in cities and rural areas across Europe. A rise in the price of grain often sparked attacks on merchants, granaries, and convoys of grain slated for armies. People turned on officials as well, blaming them for not keeping grain prices affordable or for allowing food to be shipped out to higher bidders elsewhere. Crime increased and more people slept along the sides of rural roads and city streets. Crowds of mothers pushed into foundling hospitals, desperate to leave children they could not care for. Some foundling hospitals established lotteries to determine which children they could afford to take in.

This deepening of poverty put a huge strain on traditional systems for aiding the poor, such as through the church or private charity. Some people were reduced to begging and to teaching their children this dubious art. Some authorities sympathized; others turned a blind eye. As one French official put it, "Beggary is the apprenticeship of crime; it begins by creating a love of idleness . . . in this state the beggar does not long resist the temptation to steal." A few countries devised legislation, such as the English Poor Laws, that required the impoverished to work on public projects or in workhouses. Officials used these sorts of laws more to control and discipline the poor than to help them. Often the same institution served as a workshop for the unfortunate, a hospital, and a prison. True, the poor had always suffered. Now, however, the population boom pushed their numbers to overwhelming new heights.

PROSPERITY AND THE BOURGEOISIE

Like the agricultural revolution, urban growth made life worse for some and better for others. Those who gained most during this era were the middle and aristocratic classes, particularly those who seized opportunities in commerce and industry and in the expanding governmental bureaucracies. The urban middle class—in French, the *bourgeoisie*—expanded and found itself in a particularly odd situation. Wealthier than most, the bourgeoisie lived off their investments in trade, manufacturing, or land rather than working with their hands like their fellow commoners. They also found ways to avoid the restrictions of the guild system of production. While those laboring "below" them envied and resented their success, the bourgeoisie tried to distance themselves from "less respectable" commoners.

Middle-class people also had difficult relationships with those above them—the aristocracy. Successful members of the bourgeoisie resented the privileges enjoyed by the aristocracy, but—even more strongly—they wanted those privileges for themselves. They longed to join the aristocracy, and they were willing to spend money to do it. Money got them titles and offices, large estates, and judicious marriages—the trappings of success that they hoped would earn them acceptance into the ranks of the aristocracy. The aristocrats, for their part, viewed this method of "social climbing"—and the people who attempted it—with disdain. As they saw it, true nobility derived from birth, not wealth.

Nevertheless, the bourgeoisie persisted and thrived. These merchants, manufacturers, and professionals made money, expanded their businesses, invested in government bonds, and took chances on shaky financial schemes. They valued hard work and the accumulation of money. Moreover, they had the means to purchase a vast variety of luxuries, from coffee and chocolate to wallpaper, cotton clothing, and watch chains—goods produced outside the home, often even outside the country. For them, the market—rather than the household—supplied staples as well as conveniences and luxuries.

Over time, the richest among the bourgeoisie might manage to gain entrance into the aristocracy. Yet even if they could not get into the courts, estates, and homes of the aristocracy, the bourgeoisie developed a public culture of their own. They educated their children at universities, and attended public theaters, music halls, and galleries. They filled tearooms, coffeehouses, literary societies, and clubs, and devoured newspapers, journals, and books written especially for them. Over time, they acquired their own sense of identity, as well as an impatience when further opportunities to rise in society were denied them.

THE CULTURE OF THE ELITE: COMBINING THE OLD AND THE NEW

The culture of the bourgeoisie and the aristocracy reflected the continuance of old trends along with the new developments that characterized the eighteenth century. For example, the courts of Europe still sponsored painters, composers, and musicians. In their private halls, aristocrats savored these artists' paintings, concerts, and operas. The prevailing spirit remained classical, inspired by the Greek and Roman appreciation for formal symmetry, proportion, and reason. On the other hand, artistic styles were changing. Several artists and authors put a new emphasis on emotion and nature in their works, an artistic trend sometimes referred to as the **cult of sensibility.** Audiences for these new cultural forms expanded, and the stream of literature being published for the growing numbers of literate westerners swelled.

THE ADVENT OF THE MODERN NOVEL

Much of the reading public consisted of members of the middle class, and, not surprisingly, the modern novel reflected middle-class tastes. A compelling story, complex and varied characters, and realistic social situations formed the core of this new literary form. Novels also conveyed current ideas, manners, news, and information in witty and dramatic ways. In several popular novels, the English writer Daniel Defoe (1660–1731) wrote about individuals who planned ahead and used their entrepreneurial skills to meet challenges. The adventures of a character in a Defoe novel might take place at home in England or on exotic islands, as in *Robinson Crusoe* (1719). Similarly, Defoe's book *Moll Flanders* (1722) tells of a woman of lower-class origins who manages to navigate through all sorts of difficult situations, from prisons to a position in high society, in England and America.

Samuel Richardson (1689–1761) and Henry Fielding (1707–1754), also British, used the novel to analyze human personality, emotions, and psychology. In *Pamela, or Virtue Rewarded* (1740), Richardson recounts the story of a servant girl who tries to retain her "virtue" in the face of her wealthy employer's sexual advances. The book's characters and circumstances powerfully reflected contemporary realities, and the novel inspired a wave of similar works. Henry Fielding, for one, expanded on Richardson's effort, weaving a rich tapestry of English society in his novel *Tom Jones* (1749).

Many novels appealed particularly to women readers. British writer Fanny Burney (1752–1840) gained fame with the publication of her novel *Evelina or A Young Lady's Entrance into the World* (1778). The book portrays a provincial girl who makes a life for herself in London. Although the story ends with a marriage, it also reveals the social restrictions and dangers facing eighteenth-century women who tried to live an independent life. Burney would go on to publish several other popular novels.

During the second half of the century, novels and works of poetry by authors such as Jean-Jacques Rousseau in France and Johann Wolfgang von Goethe (1749–1832) in the German states emphasized emotion, relationships, and social problems. These authors presented the emotions as natural virtues, rejecting the artificiality of formal manners. Their style, which would become known as romanticism, grew in popularity during the last quarter of the century.

PRIDE AND SENTIMENT IN ART AND ARCHITECTURE

Unlike literature, the fine arts still typically reflected the tastes of the dominant aristocracy. Artists vied with one another for commissions to paint the portraits of royals and aristocrats, depicting their proud subjects adorned with plumes, buckles, silks, brocades, and laces. The scenes might include children and dogs and, in the background, lavish estate grounds. The distinctive clothing, haughty poses, and elaborate settings marked subjects as members of the landowning elite.

Many paintings showed intimate scenes of aristocratic private life—meetings, picnics, flirtations, and conversations among the upper classes. In Antoine Watteau's (1684–1721) popular paintings, for example, the context might be classical mythology, but the figures were eighteenth-century aristocrats. In *A Pilgrimage to Cythera* (a mythical island of love), shown in Figure 15.11, aristocrats wander leisurely through an idyllic garden of nature. Cupids at the left and Venus at the right bless the scene. The line between life, mythology, and the social roles played by the subjects blurs in this lush scene. The painting also has an underlying seriousness, as the lovers, reluctantly preparing to depart to the everyday world, enjoy a moment of life that will pass too quickly.

■ FIGURE 15.11

Antoine Watteau, *A Pilgrimage to Cythera*, 1717.

Jean-Baptiste Greuze, *The Father's Curse*

■ FIGURE 15.12

In this eighteenth-century painting, French artist Jean-Baptiste Greuze depicts a dramatic family conflict between a father, issuing a curse, and his son, who is departing for the army. ■ **What** does this depiction reveal about the roles of men, women, and children in this family? ■ **Why** might viewers of this scene be touched and fascinated? ■ **Why** might the father have been so disturbed by his son's departure? ■ **What** alternatives other than the army might have been available to this son? **Consider** how the structure and lighting of the painting reflects the drama of its content.

artists

Whereas the aristocracy tended to populate Watteau's works, other artists painted well-received, sentimental scenes of ordinary people experiencing dramatic moments. Figure 15.12, a painting by the French artist Jean-Baptiste Greuze (1725–1805), shows one of these works. Here, the father at the left curses his departing son, who is determined to find his own way through life by joining the army. The young man's mother and other members of the family try in vain to reconcile the two men and to prevent the breakup of the family on such a painful note. In an accompanying painting, the grief-stricken son returns to find his father on his death bed. William Hogarth's works (see Figures 15.3 and 15.14) also explored everyday experiences in the lives of ordinary

people, but usually from a satirical or moralistic perspective.

Eighteenth-century architecture could not portray sentiments in the same detail as paintings, but buildings in the baroque style still expressed well the gaudy splendor of the eighteenth-century monarchs and their courts. At the same time, architects began deemphasizing size and instead relied on multiple curves and lacy, shell-like ornamentation to convey a sense of pleasing luxury. This style is usually referred to as **rococo**. Some new government buildings and urban residences followed a more neoclassical style, which stressed clarity of line and form modeled on Greek and Roman ideals.

Gardens complemented the buildings they accompanied, extending them and reflecting the mix of old and new tastes. As we saw in Louis XIV's Versailles palace (see Chapter 13), the French garden in particular emphasized rational, geometric forms marked off by hedges. Here, nature was shown completely tamed by human power and reason. By contrast, the eighteenth-century English garden looked freer and more natural. In fact, these gardens were not natural at all. Landscape architects designed them to imitate a vision of nature or to turn the grounds of an estate into an idealized version of nature. This managing of nature in English gardens was a compromise between old and new ideas about human beings' place in the natural world.

REACHING NEW HEIGHTS IN MUSIC

Of all the eighteenth-century arts, music left the most profound legacy. Much of it reflected the tastes of its royal, aristocratic, and ecclesiastical patrons. Composers and musicians, therefore, usually stuck to established forms, and music was typically heard as a pleasing background to conversations, balls, and other social occasions in the bastions of the aristocracy. Increasingly, however, music was played in public concert halls to a larger audience. Opera houses opened everywhere, and composers could now hope to make money from paying audiences as well as from court and aristocratic patronage. Several cities became well-known musical centers, but Vienna topped them all. This Austrian city became the musical heart of Europe, drawing hundreds of musicians who competed for favor there.

The first half of the eighteenth century saw the high point of baroque music, a style that had originated in the seventeenth century and that was still favored in royal courts and aristocratic homes. The greatest practitioners of the baroque style were Johann Sebastian Bach (1685–1750) and George Frideric Handel (1685–1759). Bach was a member of a German family long distinguished by its musical talent. Noted in his own lifetime chiefly as an organist rather than a composer, he created a vast array of great music for organ, harpsichord, clavichord (forerunner of the piano), orchestra, and chorus. Sadly, much of Bach's work has been lost. Much of his music was religiously inspired, but he also wrote a large amount of secular music. Handel was born in central Germany in the same year and same region as Bach. He studied Italian opera in Germany and Italy and wrote forty-six operas himself. He also became court musician in Hanover. Later, he made his home in England, as did the elector, who became King George I of England. Handel wrote an enormous quantity of music—both instrumental and vocal—all of it marked by dignity, formal elegance, and harmony.

Baroque music

During the last decades of the century, the restrained baroque style gave way to the more melodic "classical" style, with its striking depth, structure, and emotion. Franz Joseph Haydn (1732–1809) and Wolfgang Amadeus Mozart (1756–1791) led the way. Their most stunning work was the symphony; by the end of their careers, they had created symphonies of rich harmonic complexity and emotional depth within the restrained classical form. During his long career in Vienna, Haydn wrote more than a hundred symphonies in addition to scores of compositions for other forms, particularly chamber music. Toward the end of his career, he became so popular that he left noble patrons and signed a lucrative contract with his music publisher.

The classical style

Haydn became a friend and a source of inspiration for the young Mozart (see Biography). Figure 15.13 shows the 7-year-old Wolfgang playing the piano. Accompanying him are his father on the violin and his sister, who is singing. Here the performers are exquisitely dressed for their aristocratic audience. Ultimately, Mozart composed more than six hundred works and excelled in all forms, but he became most appreciated for his symphonies, piano concertos, and operas. His music was stunningly clear, melodic, elegant, and graceful. In his hands, the classical style reached its peak.

THE GRAND TOUR

The music, art, and literature of the elites was part of a broader, cosmopolitan culture that spilled across national boundaries. This culture manifested itself in elaborate styles of dress, polished manners, and highly structured conversation. French was its international language. The growing popularity of travel and travel literature added to the sense of a common European cultural identity, at least among elites. Indeed, the wealthy often considered the grand tour a necessary part of education. Travelers on the tour stopped in main cities to indulge in coffeehouses, storefront window displays, public gardens, theaters, opera houses, and galleries. They might also visit art dealers or public auctions to purchase quality paintings. Family connections offered them accommodations and introduced them to local society, Enlightenment salons, or potential candidates for marriage. The tour usually continued to historical ruins, which featured revered models of Greek and Roman antiquity that further strengthened the viewers' sense of a common cultural identity.

CULTURE FOR THE LOWER CLASSES

The lower classes were not without cultural outlets that fit their lives and provided a sense of common identity. For peasants, artisans, and the urban poor, culture typically came in the form of shared recreation, songs, tales, and the passing down of wisdom at gatherings and celebrations. Many of these activities also coincided with religious gatherings and celebrations.

FESTIVALS AND POPULAR LITERATURE

Villagers worked together and celebrated together—at fairs, harvests, plowings, weddings, and religious holidays. Numerous festivals and public ceremonies had seasonal themes that were of particular importance and interest to people so dependent on agriculture. Other celebratory events related to the Christian calendar and centered on holidays, such as Christmas and Easter. Traditional weddings involved a community procession and festivities as well as a religious ceremony, and they featured music, dancing, feasts, games, and play. In the cities, artisans participated in their own organizations that combined recreational activities with mutual aid and religious celebrations.

Certain forms of literature also became popular among ordinary people. Literacy was growing, thanks to the printing press, the demands of business, and an increase in the number of primary schools. By the end of the eighteenth century, some 40 to 60 percent of the population in England and France could read (more men than women). With the rise in literacy, popular literature also expanded. Stirring religious tracts, almanacs, and tales of chivalric

BIOGRAPHY

Wolfgang Amadeus Mozart (1756–1791)

CONSIDER

■ **Consider** *how Mozart's career reflected eighteenth-century society—still dominated by the aristocracy but with a growing middle class interested in the culture of the day.*

Musicians quickly recognized the young Wolfgang Amadeus Mozart as a unique genius. His father, Leopold, a well-known Austrian composer and violinist, called him the "miracle which God let be born in Salzburg." Born in 1756, Wolfgang wrote his first compositions when he was just 5 years old. He embarked on the first of many tours throughout Europe as a 6-year-old child prodigy, playing the clavier with his elder sister, Nannerl, also a child prodigy, and his father (see Figure 15.12). They played at several royal courts for monarchs such as Louis XV of France, Maria Theresa of Austria, and George III of Britain. They also performed at the homes of leading nobles as well as in public theaters. Wolfgang's father, always eager to promote his young son, wrote that "our great and mighty Wolfgang seems to know everything at the age of seven that a man acquires at the age of forty."

By the time he had reached 14, Mozart had composed several concertos, sonatas, and an opera. Announcements for his performances stressed his virtuosity. For example, for a concert in Italy, the 14-year-old would play "A Symphony of his own composition; a harpsichord concerto which will be handed to him, and which he will play on first sight; a sonata handed him in like manner, which he will provide with variations, and afterwards repeat in another key. . . ." The boy could play the organ and violin almost as well. After hearing Mozart in 1771, one well-known composer said, "This boy will cause us all to be forgotten." The prestigious Haydn, who strongly influenced Wolfgang's music, would later tell Wolfgang's father that "your son is the greatest composer known to me. . . ."

Child Prodigy, Musical Genius

In 1781, Mozart settled in Vienna as a teacher and composer. Short, slim, with engaging blue eyes and a full head of fine hair, the young man enjoyed an active social life, including billiards and dancing. Yet music preoccupied him. He wrote, "You know that I am, so to speak, swallowed up in music, that I am busy with it all day—speculating, studying, considering." Keenly aware of his own talents, he at times arrogantly criticized other musicians' limitations. He felt certain that he could outshine any rival.

In 1782, despite the doubts of his father and sister, Mozart married Constanze Weber, a singer. Mozart wrote that "as soon as we were married, my wife and I both began to weep" for joy. Their marriage seems to have been happy. They would have six children, of whom only two survived. Neither parent managed the family finances well. Even though Mozart became brilliantly successful as a composer, a virtuoso pianist, and a teacher; received numerous commissions and fees; and attained appointment as royal chamber composer to Emperor Joseph II of Austria, he continually borrowed money to support his growing family.

■ **FIGURE 15.13**

The Mozarts.

Wolfgang could never quite satisfy his demanding and increasingly distant father. Hearing that Leopold had fallen seriously ill in 1787, Mozart wrote a letter of consolation that included his own views on death: "As death . . . is the true goal of our existence, I have formed during the last few years such close relations with this best and truest friend of mankind that his image is no longer terrifying to me but rather very soothing and consoling." Leopold died a month later. In July 1791, a stranger appeared at Wolfgang's door with a commission to write a requiem in secrecy. Mozart was still working on the project in December when he died in relative poverty. He was just 35. Although he probably had succumbed to an infection and fever, unsubstantiated rumors circulated for years that a competitor had poisoned him.

valor—typically, small, cheap booklets—circulated widely. More often, however, the "literature" of ordinary people was passed on orally. At night, people might gather to share folktales and songs that told of traditional wisdom, the hardships of everyday life, the hopes of common people, the dangers of life in the forests or of strangers who could be monsters or princes, and the ways to get along in life.

In the past, elites had fully participated in this popular culture, but during the eighteenth century they increasingly abandoned it to the lower classes. The "respectable" classes now often considered the leisure activities of ordinary people too disorderly and crude. Nevertheless, the middle and upper classes read some of the same popular literature enjoyed by the lower classes. Moreover, everyone—aristocrats and peasants alike—might be found at village festivals, fairs, and sporting events or enjoying jugglers, acrobats, magic lantern shows, and touring troops of actors. Men of all classes watched and wagered on cockfights and dogfights. Other sports, such as soccer and cricket, gained popularity and drew large, animated crowds.

GIN AND BEER

All the social classes also engaged in drinking—whether wine or brandy in the privacy of a wealthy home, or gin and beer in popular taverns. Especially in England, the ravages of drinking gin seemed to grow to alarming proportions. Figure 15.14, another moralistic work by William Hogarth, graphically depicts the evils of gin drinking in England. At the center a pox-ridden, impoverished, and drunken woman lets her baby fall over a wooden rail. Near her, a man slowly starves to death. In the background, workers haul bodies away, a man hangs himself in an upstairs tenement, children drink glasses of gin, and buildings collapse for want of repair. The scene is one of physical, social, and moral decay from excessive alcohol consumption. Though this image is an exaggeration, the actual problems caused by drinking were so extensive that in 1751 the British government passed a heavy tax on cheap gin to curtail its consumption.

RELIGIOUS REVIVALS

Popular culture also merged with deeply felt spiritual beliefs and religious activities. Despite the many secular trends of the period, Christianity still stood at the center of Western culture and life. Churches rather than the state ran the schools and hospitals. The poor, aged, and crippled relied on churches for social services. Church bells announced the time of day everywhere, and religious holidays marked the year.

Within this Western religious culture, popular piety persisted. Indeed, especially among Protestants, a sense grew among ordinary churchgoers that official churches were becoming bureaucratized, complacent, and unresponsive to peoples' spiritual needs. In response, religious revivals spread from community to community and across national borders. In the German and Scandinavian states, pietism—which minimized dogma and formal ritual in favor of inner piety, holy living, and the private emotional experience of worshiping—gained strength. Revival movements in Britain and its North American colonies attracted thousands to huge gatherings.

Pietism

The greatest of these revival movements was Methodism, founded in England by John Wesley (1703–1791). While studying for the Anglican ministry at Oxford, Wesley and a band of fellow students became disillusioned with the spiritual emptiness that had fallen upon the Anglican Church as well as its subservience to the government and the aristocracy. The group's lives became such examples of piety and moderate regularity that their fellow students branded them "Methodists" in derision. Methodism stressed

■ FIGURE 15.14

William Hogarth, *Gin Lane*, 1750.

humble faith, abstinence, and hard work. Barred from preaching in the Anglican churches, Wesley rode horseback from one end of England to the other until well into his 80s, preaching the "glad tidings" of salvation in thousands of sermons in streets, fields, and anywhere else he could find even a small audience. He claimed "to lower religion to the level of the lowest people's capacities."

Among Catholics, similar movements—such as Jansenism in France and Italy and Quietism in Spain—spread among elites and others. East European Jews had their own revivalist movement with the founding of the Hasidic sect in the 1740s. Hasidim (meaning "most pious") spread throughout Poland, rejecting formalism, stressing simplicity, and engaging in loud, joyful singing prayers. These religious movements revealed the power with which spiritual matters still influenced people in the West. Nevertheless, like the broader cultural forms of the time, religious revivals left the overall social order intact.

FORESHADOWING UPHEAVAL: THE AMERICAN REVOLUTION

For most of the eighteenth century, neither wars, colonial rivalries, nor changes in country and city life upset the fundamental social and political stability of Western societies. In the last quarter of the eighteenth century, however, new forces erupted that would ultimately transform the West. The first of these disturbances occurred in Britain's thirteen North American colonies. This upheaval shifted the tide of events in North America and foreshadowed a far deeper and broader revolution that would strike at the heart of Europe itself.

INSULTS, INTERESTS, AND PRINCIPLES: THE SEEDS OF REVOLT

By the mid-eighteenth century, over two million people lived in the colonies. The seaboard cities in particular flourished, benefiting from a thriving commerce with Europe, Africa, and the West Indies. The colonists thought of themselves as British. Furthermore, the thirteen colonies in theory were part of Great Britain, governed in the same way and therefore subject to British trade regulations. In practice, however, the colonists often acted as they pleased, even if that meant quietly ignoring those regulations. They developed their own patterns of local government, manipulated British governors, and worked around British mercantilist policies.

Tensions between the island nation and these prospering colonies arose just after the Seven Years' War ended in 1763. Feeling that they had helped defend the American colonists against the hostile French and Indians, the British expected the colonists to help pay off the huge debt incurred in the fighting. To tighten their control over the colonial empire for which Britain had just fought so long and hard, British officials enacted new commercial regulations and taxes. Perhaps the most irritating of these was the Stamp Act of 1765, which taxed printed documents such as newspapers, pamphlets, and wills.

New commercial regulations and taxes

The colonists reacted to the new policies with complaints, boycotts, protest meetings, outrage, and sometimes riots. Because colonists were not represented in Britain's Parliament, headlines in newspapers and pamphlets screamed, "No taxation without representation!" In their Stamp Act Congress of 1765, colonists announced that they were "entitled to all the inherent rights and liberties of his [the king's] natural born subjects within the kingdom of Great Britain." Local circumstances and the distance from Britain meant that "the only representatives of these colonies are persons chosen therein by themselves, and that no taxes ever have been, or can be constitutionally imposed on them, but by their respective legislatures." The British compromised, repealing most of the taxes, but many colonists were still not satisfied.

Both sides translated their disagreements into ideological terms. American newspapers, propagandists, and political groups, echoing Enlightenment ideas, argued that violation of their fundamental rights justified a fight for independence. Most people in Britain stood against rebellion and for parliamentary sovereignty as a matter of principle. They argued that they were making only reasonable and minimal demands on the colonies.

In the end, each side felt backed into a corner. The notion of full independence gained appeal among the colonists. American political leaders who were critical of British policies organized the First Continental Congress in 1774, hoping to persuade Parliament to abandon its efforts to directly control colonial affairs. In response, King George III increased British armed forces in America, convinced that "blows must decide whether they are to be subject to the Country or Independent."

A WAR FOR INDEPENDENCE

The first "blows" were exchanged in 1775 between British troops and American militiamen in New England. The Second Continental Congress appointed George Washington (1732–1799) its military commander, setting the course for armed rebellion and independence. On July 4, 1776, that Congress issued the Declaration of Independence, written primarily by Thomas Jefferson (1743–1826) and based on the ideas of John Locke and other Enlightenment thinkers. Citing "self-evident" truths; "inalienable" natural rights such as "Life, Liberty, and the pursuit of Happiness"; and "a long train of abuses" to reduce the people under "absolute Despotism," the Declaration passionately justified rebellion.

Odds favored the stronger British forces, and at first they had the upper hand. Indeed, many British leaders viewed the rebel troops with disdain, one official calling the rebels a "rude rabble without a plan." Nevertheless, despite much internal division, an American victory at Saratoga in 1777 persuaded the French to help the Americans with money, ships, and troops against France's longtime enemy. The Dutch and Spanish eventually declared war on Britain, increasing the stakes for the British. Now British possessions in the West Indies, the Mediterranean, and perhaps even India hung in the balance. In 1781 the victory of the French fleet off Virginia forced a large British army to surrender at Yorktown. This indignity convinced the British that the effort to keep the American colonies was not worth the costs. After two years of negotiations, the combatants drew up the Treaty of Paris in 1783. Britain agreed to recognize American independence and ceded to the United States the lands between the Mississippi River to the west, Canada to the north, and Spanish Florida to the south.

CREATING THE NEW NATION

By 1787, a new American constitution established a central government balanced by a separation of powers and strong states' rights. A Bill of Rights was soon enacted, protecting individual liberties and separating church and state. These principles, though lofty, did not apply to everyone. Although the Declaration of Independence had proclaimed that "all men are created equal" as a "self-evident" truth, one-fifth of the people remained slaves, and only property owners and men could vote. Nevertheless, the new nation had instituted—to an unprecedented degree—popular control, personal freedom, and formal toleration.

Some historians deem the American rebellion a war for independence, and others call it a revolution. At the time, people throughout the West—not just in America and Great Britain—viewed the events as dramatic and significant. A growing body of European readers avidly followed the action in newspaper accounts. Many of these readers saw the American Revolution as a victory for Enlightenment ideas. The French in particular celebrated the Revolution as a triumph in their own competition with their British rivals. They did not realize at the time that the debts incurred by France and the ideas promoted by the American Revolution would soon come back to haunt the French monarchy.

War for independence or revolution?

SUMMARY

On the surface, life between 1715 and 1789 seemed to change only incrementally for most Westerners. The vast majority still lived in the countryside and worked the fields. Moreover, society and politics in the so-called Old Regime remained dominated by the aristocracy and, in most places, the monarchy. As in the seventeenth century, cultural forms still reflected elite tastes and the traditional values of commoners below them.

Below the surface, however, the West changed in crucial ways during this period. The political balance of power shifted as Russia and Prussia rose in the east while Britain gained prominence in the west. Success in the international arena often reflected how well central governments conducted their internal affairs. Some monarchs managed to dominate or work with the nobility, enact reforms, and even take on the trappings of "enlightened" rulers, whereas others—such as the French kings—failed in these ways. More important, mushrooming commerce, the agricultural revolution, and the spreading of cottage industry altered the ways by which millions of people earned a living, and these changes generated enormous new wealth. Finally, across the Atlantic in Britain's North American colonies, the American Revolution posed a challenge to the status quo that the French would soon take up in a much more fundamental way. These developments, combined with the spread of Enlightenment ideas, mark the eighteenth century as a period in which westerners—knowingly or not—laid foundations for the great transformations to come.

KEY TERMS

REVIEW, ANALYZE, AND ANTICIPATE

REVIEW THE PREVIOUS CHAPTERS

Chapter 13—"The Struggle for Survival and Sovereignty"—told the story of kings and nobles battling for power, the results of those struggles, and their impact on millions of people throughout the West. Chapter 14—"A New World of Reason and Reform"—shifted focus to the changing intellectual foundations of the West.

1. *In what ways was the eighteenth century a continuation of the struggle between monarchs and elites that had marked the seventeenth century?*

2. *Analyze how Enlightenment ideas—themselves stemming from the Scientific Revolution—affected Western society and especially politics during the eighteenth century.*

ANALYZE THIS CHAPTER

Chapter 15—"Competing for Power and Wealth"—examines the battles of Western powers over land, position, and commerce, as well as the economic and social changes affecting eighteenth-century life in the West.

1. *Which nations do you think were the biggest winners and which the biggest losers in this period? How do you explain their varying fortunes?*

2. *How did eighteenth-century rulers try to shore up and justify their own powers and those of their central governments?*

3. *Analyze the impact of slavery on Africa, the Americas, and Europe.*

4. *Analyze the benefits and costs of the growing commerce, the agricultural revolution, and cottage industry.*

5. *Why might this period be considered one of both growing prosperity and deepening social misery?*

6. *Delineate the differences between elite and popular culture during this period. How do you explain those differences?*

ANTICIPATE THE NEXT CHAPTER

Chapter 16—"Overturning the Political and Social Order"—will examine the great upheaval in France that shook and transformed the West.

1. *Why might the French monarchy have been particularly vulnerable to a revolution?*

2. *In what ways might the American Revolution—as a revolution and in its principles—have foreshadowed the political upheaval that would break out in France?*

BEYOND THE CLASSROOM

STATEBUILDING AND WAR

Anderson, M.S. *Europe in the Eighteenth Century, 1713–1783*, 3rd ed. London: Longman, 1987. A thorough survey of the period.

Davis, Ralph. *The Rise of the Atlantic Economies*. Ithaca, NY: Cornell University Press, 1973. A survey of the early modern economic history of the countries on the western fringe of Europe and their colonies in North and South America.

de Madariaga, Isabel. *Catherine the Great: A Short History*. New Haven, CT: Yale University Press, 1990. A solid, useful study.

Jasanoff, Maya. *Edge of Empire: Lives, Culture, and Conquest in the East, 1750–1850*. New York: Knopf, 2005. A well-written reinterpretation of British imperialism and its consequences.

MacDonagh, G. *Frederick the Great*. New York: St. Martin's Press, 2001. A fine, comprehensive biography.

Manning, Patrick. *Slavery and African Life: Occidental, Oriental and African Slave Trades*. Cambridge: Cambridge University Press, 1990. A wide-ranging study that demonstrates how the external slave trade affected African societies.

Weigley, R.F. *The Age of Battles: The Quest for Decisive Warfare from Breitenfeld to Waterloo*. Bloomington: Indiana University Press. 1991. A study of the period between 1631 and 1815 when economic, social, and technological circumstances enabled governments to concentrate large forces in the field.

GLOBAL CONNECTIONS

Conniff, Michael, and Davis, Thomas. *Africans in the Americas: A History of the Black Diaspora*. New York: St. Martin's Press, 1998. Excellent coverage of the slave trade and the African diaspora.

THE TWILIGHT OF MONARCHIES? THE QUESTION OF ENLIGHTENED ABSOLUTISM

Gagliardo, John G. *Enlightened Despotism*. Arlington Heights, IL: AHM Publishing, 1967. A respected examination of the topic in its European context.

Scott, H.M., ed. *Enlightened Despotism*. Ann Arbor, MI: University of Michigan Press, 1990. A book of essays by leading historians analyzing Europe's rulers and nobility.

CHANGES IN COUNTRY AND CITY LIFE

Blum, Jerome. *The End of the Old Order in Rural Europe*. Princeton, NJ: Princeton University Press, 1978. A comprehensive study of life in rural Europe from the early eighteenth to the mid-nineteenth centuries; especially good on the abolition of serfdom.

Chambers, J.D., and G.E. Mingay. *The Agricultural Revolution*. London: Batsord, 1966. Covers various aspects of the agricultural revolution, such as enclosures and technological improvements, and relates agriculture to the socioeconomic life of the period.

Clarkson, Leslie A. *Proto-Industrialization: The First Phase of Industrialization?* London: Macmillan, 1985. Stresses the importance of cottage industry for the beginning of industrialization.

THE CULTURE OF THE ELITE: COMBINING THE OLD AND THE NEW

Black, Jeremy. *Eighteenth-Century Europe*. London: Macmillan, 1990. A thorough survey of the period.

Watt, Ian. *The Rise of the Novel*. Berkeley, CA: University of California Press, 1957. A study of the intellectual and social conditions that produced the novel in eighteenth-century England.

CULTURE FOR THE LOWER CLASSES

Burke, Peter. *Popular Culture in Early Modern Europe*. New York: Harper & Row, 1978. A survey of popular culture from the Renaissance to the French Revolution.

Muchembled, Robert. *Popular Culture and Elite Culture in France, 1400–1750*. Baton Rouge, LA: Louisiana State University Press, 1985. An examination of popular culture and the means higher authorities used to destroy it.

FORESHADOWING UPHEAVAL: THE AMERICAN REVOLUTION

Weintraub, Stanley. *Iron Tears: America's Battle for Freedom, Britain's Quagmire: 1775–1783*. New York: Free Press, 2005. A fresh look at the war from various perspectives.

Wood, Gordon. *The American Revolution: A History*. New York: Random House, 2002. A fine survey and important interpretation.

www.mhhe.com/sherman3

- Unfamiliar words? See our Glossary at the back of the book for pronunciation and definitions.
- Need help studying? See our web page for map exercises, practice quizzes, and additional study resources.
- Need help writing a paper? Access hundreds of primary documents, maps, images, and a guide to writing history papers on our Primary Source Investigator site at **www.mhhe.com/psi.**

MOVING INTO THE MODERN WORLD

CONSIDER

■ **Consider** the ways in which the meaning of the West had changed by the eighteenth century. ■ **Notice** how the civilizations of the West compared to other civilizations in the world.

The world had changed dramatically since Europe began its "expansion" in the fifteenth century. By the mid-eighteenth century, the West had been sending out explorers, making new commercial contacts, establishing links, and racking up conquests in the non-Western world for almost three centuries. Had Europe's expansion changed the meaning of the West?

During the eighteenth century, the actual "boundaries" of the West did begin to shift. Russia brought under its direct control lands to the east in Siberia. By the second half of the century, Russians easily outnumbered those regions' indigenous inhabitants. It also pushed its borders south, particularly in the Caspian Sea region. Russia's growing empire blurred any line between the West and the non-Western world on the Eurasian landmass. Across the Atlantic, Europeans had colonized parts of the Americas so thoroughly that large sections of the Western hemisphere were much more than mere outposts. Though thousands of miles away from Europe, they were becoming part of the West itself.

If not in control of other major regions of the world, people from the West were certainly in increasing contact with other cultures and civilizations across the globe. From the broadest perspective, Westerners shared important similarities with several of these civilizations. For example, all had economies based on agriculture and handicrafts; the factories, railroads, and steamships that would mark the industrial era in the West were yet to come. Moreover, several Asian civilizations had enough wealth and military might to put them in the same league as the European nations.

China, for instance, remained the dominant power in east Asia. By 1750, Qing emperors (1644–1911) had extended their control far into central Asia and the south. In those regions, they made Vietnam, Burma, and Nepal their vassal states. The long rule of the talented emperor Qianolong (Chi'en Lung) (1736–1795) marked the height of the Qing (Chi'ing) dynasty. Wealthy, sophisticated, well-organized, and powerful, Qing China controlled the degree of contact it had with the West and supported its own trading networks throughout east and southeast Asian lands. China and other east Asian societies benefited from the West's growing thirst for their unique products as well as from crops that originated in the Americas. Farther east, Tokugawa shoguns had unified the Japanese islands and secured their rule. Like the Chinese, they managed to keep Western people at arm's length while promoting their own conservative values, such as adherence to a carefully ranked society and Confucian principles.

By the dawn of the eighteenth century, three powerful Islamic empires governed by Turkish dynasties had come to dominate southern and southwestern Asia. The Mughals ruled most of the Indian subcontinent and commanded a formidable, cosmopolitan society. The Safavid dynasty reigned in Persia, prospering as a trade link between the East and West. The powerful Ottomans had expanded from their base in Anatolia into eastern Europe, southwestern Asia, and north Africa. As recently as 1683, they had mustered enough force to lay siege to Vienna, the capital of the Habsburg's Austrian empire. But the days of all three Islamic empires were already numbered. By 1750, the Safavid empire had disappeared entirely, much of Mughal India was disintegrating and falling under British rule, and the Ottomans were losing control over various provinces.

Meanwhile, in the Western hemisphere, the Spanish and Portuguese ruled most of Latin America. A varied mix of Europeans, Africans, and Amerindians populated those lands. In the Caribbean, Western administrators governed societies populated predominantly by African slaves. Farther north, firmly established British and French colonies were spreading west at the expense of indigenous peoples. The twin disasters of disease and violence had already reduced these natives to a fraction of their numbers from 250 years earlier.

In Africa, states and societies based on kinship groups continued to develop as they had for centuries. Societies in West Africa and on the east African coast maintained long-established trade with Muslims from the north and east. By the eighteenth century, Islam had spread through these African societies. But the growing slave trade to the west generated wealth in Atlantic port cities and power in West Africa's coastal kingdoms, while creating great turmoil and human loss throughout much of sub-Saharan Africa.

Most of Oceania remained scarcely touched by the West during this time. Only toward the end of the eighteenth century did Europeans begin settling in Australia and initiating substantial contact with that land's aboriginal peoples. During that same period, a number of Western explorers, merchants, missionaries, and settlers arrived on islands throughout the Pacific.

In the mid-eighteenth century, European ships carried goods and people overseas in astounding numbers and with great regularity. Some sailed to Western ports; others, to lands beyond Europeans' control. Demand in the West for goods such as sugar, tea, coffee, and tobacco, along with demand in China for silver, fueled this long-distance commerce. As the same time, a burgeoning hunger for slave labor forced millions of enslaved Africans across the Atlantic into the Americas.

In some areas, Western nations were chipping away at holdings of competitors such as the Ottomans in southeastern Europe and western Asia and the Mughals in southern Asia. In other areas, such as North America beyond the Atlantic colonies and Oceania, Western societies were starting to overwhelm indigenous peoples. But in vast regions of the world, eighteenth-century Europeans gained access only on coastlines. East Asian societies easily kept them at bay, remaining in

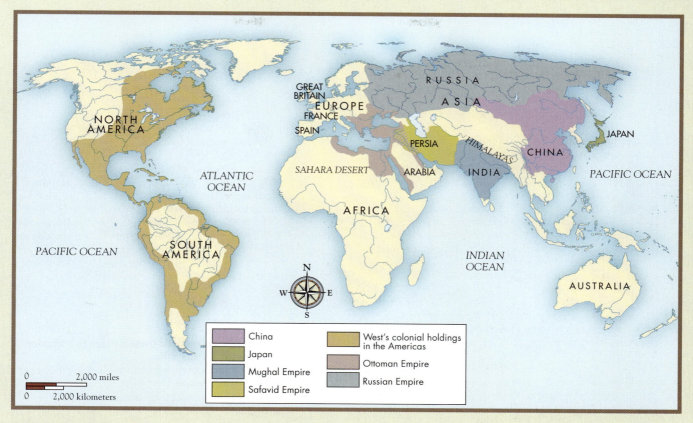

THE WORLD, CA. 1700

Go to www.mhhe.com/psi/Sherman to study an interactive version of this map.

control of their own affairs. Western newcomers had only recently made inroads into lands of the once powerful Mughal and Safavid empires. The Ottomans, though declining economically and politically, nevertheless managed to retain control over most of their lands. And in Africa, much of the continent remained too difficult for the West to penetrate.

Western explorers still sailed and marched off in search of new opportunities. However, they were limited to the most remote regions—Oceania, the frozen stretches of the far north and south, jungle-choked lands in South America and sub-Saharan Africa. In many ways, the mid-eighteenth-century world was growing more tightly interconnected. At the same time, that world was becoming a stage for widespread competition and conflict between states and civilizations.

DISCUSSION QUESTIONS

- **In what ways** might one look at the "Atlantic world" (areas with easy access to the Atlantic Ocean) as an interactive whole?

- **What** geographic considerations might help account for the West's lack of control over various areas of the world outside the Atlantic world?

JEAN-PIERRE HOUEL, *THE STORMING OF THE BASTILLE*, CA. 1789

On July 14, 1789, a crowd of Parisians stormed the Bastille, a castle-prison that stood as a symbol of all that was oppressive under the Old Regime. For most people, this event marked the beginning of the French Revolution.

OVERTURNING THE POLITICAL AND SOCIAL ORDER

THE FRENCH REVOLUTION AND NAPOLEON, 1789–1815

STUDY	Causes of the French Revolution ▪ Creating a new order in France ▪ The radical Republic ▪ The rise and fall of Napoleon Bonaparte.
NOTICE	How the French Revolution and Napoleon transformed politics and society.

France was beginning to stir. On October 17, 1787, Arthur Young, a British farmer and diarist traveling through France, described "a great ferment amongst all ranks of men, who are eager for some change, without knowing what to look to, or to hope for." People whom Young talked with in Paris concluded that "they are on the eve of some great revolution in the government."

Two years later, the French Revolution brought the French monarchy to its knees. During the following ten years, revolutionaries eliminated the monarchy, overturned the social system of France's Old Regime, and transformed France's institutions. Moreover, the Revolution, with its compelling banner of "Liberty, Equality, Fraternity," proved so potent that its impact spread far beyond the borders of France. It soon spawned wars that engulfed most of Europe for more than two decades. Riding the twin forces of revolutionary turmoil and war, one individual—Napoleon Bonaparte—would rise to a legendary pinnacle of power. He would rule over a new French empire and a nearly conquered continent. In the process, Napoleon spread the ideals of the French Revolution well beyond France. This tide of change, turmoil, and war mounted by the French Revolution and Napoleon would eventually subside, but for France—and for much of Western civilization—the course of history had shifted permanently.

TIMELINE: THE BIG PICTURE

American Revolution 1776–1783

The French Revolution and Napoleon 1789–1815

Enlightenment

Early Phases 1789–1793

Restoration 1815–1830

The Terror 1793–1794

The Directory 1795–1799

The Thermidorian Reaction 1794–1795

Napoleon in Power 1799–1815

Age of Ideologies

Industrial Revolution in Britain

1787	1794	1801	1808	1815

"A GREAT FERMENT": TROUBLE BREWING IN FRANCE

ARTHUR YOUNG RECOGNIZED DISCONTENT PERCOLATING among the French population, but there was good reason for people everywhere to assume that any crises would pass without a fundamental change in the monarchy or social order. The French monarchy had remained intact for centuries. Both Louis XVI and his predecessor, Louis XV, ruled over the leading nation on the Continent—a country more populous, wealthy, and educated than ever. Although neither king could claim much popularity, Louis XVI could at least bask in the glory of supporting the American revolutionaries in their victory over the British, France's chief competitor.

Then what caused the "great ferment" in France described by our British traveler? Below the surface bubbled growing complaints within France's social orders. Members of the aristocracy and middle classes, many influenced by the ideas of the Enlightenment, wanted more rights and power from the monarchy. Peasants suffered hardships that could, as in the past, create disorder and uprisings. However, the immediate, visible problem came from a conflict over France's finances.

THE FINANCIAL CRISIS WEAKENS THE MONARCHY

When Louis XVI ascended the throne in 1774, he inherited a large—and constantly growing—national debt. Much of that debt had been incurred financing wars and maintaining the military (see Chapter 15). Yet this debt should not have broken a nation as rich as France. Great Britain and the Netherlands had

higher per-capita debts than France, but these countries also boasted taxation systems and banks to support their debts. France lacked an adequate banking system, and most of the national debt was short term and privately held. Moreover, France's taxation system offered little help. The French nobility, clergy, and much of the bourgeoisie controlled the bulk of France's wealth and had long been exempt from most taxes. Nearly all direct taxes fell on the struggling peasantry. There was no consistent set of rules or method for collecting taxes throughout the country, and private tax collectors diverted much revenue from the treasury into their own pockets. Unless something was done, royal bankruptcy loomed ahead.

The taxation system

To stave off financial ruin, Louis XVI appointed the Physiocrat Jacques Turgot (1727–1781), a friend of Voltaire, as his minister of finance in 1774. Turgot proposed to abolish guilds, eliminate restriction on the commerce in grain, institute a small new tax on landowners, and cut down on expenses at court. However, people who benefited from the old system soon engineered his dismissal, and his modest reform measures were rescinded. A succession of ministers tried all kinds of temporary solutions, but to no avail. Costs incurred to support the Americans in their war of independence against England made matters worse. Now interest payments on the debt ate up half of all government expenditures. Bankers began refusing to lend the government money.

Reform efforts

Desperate, Louis called an Assembly of Notables in 1787 and pleaded with these selected nobles, clergy, and officials to consent to new taxes and financial reforms. Still they refused, as did the judges (all members of the nobility) in the *parlement*, or law court, of Paris when Louis turned to them. Instead, leading nobles and officials demanded a meeting of an old representative institution, the Estates General. They fully expected to control these proceedings and thereby assert their own interests. With bankruptcy imminent and nowhere else to turn for help, the king gave in. No one knew it at the time, but Louis' decision set the stage for turning France's financial crisis into a political and social movement of epic proportions.

The Underlying Causes of the Revolution

Louis' financial woes were just the most visible part of France's problems. When these tensions combined with the conflicts tugging at the fabric of French society, a dangerous blend resulted. One of the most troubling conflicts stemmed from the relationship between the monarchy and the nobility. For centuries, the French nobility, less than 2 percent of the population, had been the foundation on which the monarchy established its rule. However, the nobility was also the monarchy's chief rival for power, and it had grown increasingly assertive during the eighteenth century (see Chapter 15). Through institutions such as the *parlements* that they controlled, nobles resisted ministerial efforts to tax them. More and more, nobles claimed to be protecting their rights as well as France itself from "ministerial despotism." So when the monarchy turned to this group for financial help, the nobles refused for two reasons. First, they wanted to protect their own financial interests. Second, they used the crisis to assert their independence. Indeed, they argued that they represented the nation. They established a price for their cooperation: a greater share of power. Understandably, France's kings refused to pay that price. Thus, when the Assembly of Notables turned a deaf ear to Louis' pleas in 1787 and instead demanded a meeting of the Estates General, the king faced a financial crisis that was linked to a virtual revolt of his own nobility.

Revolt of the nobility

Louis might have thought he could find allies within the middle class in his standoff with the nobility. After all, French and other European kings had occasionally turned to wealthy members of this class for support in the past. Nevertheless, as events would prove in the tumultuous months of 1789, the middle class had changed—it now nursed its own set of grievances. This growing social sector—having almost tripled during the century to some 9 percent of the population—had benefited greatly from France's general prosperity and population boom after 1715. Many talented, wealthy, and ambitious members of the middle class managed to gain the high offices,

Middle-class demands

titles, and privileges enjoyed by the nobility. Others rubbed shoulders and shared ideas with the nobility in salons and did their best to copy the nobles' style of life. Moreover, most had found ways to avoid paying heavy taxes.

However, numerous members of the bourgeoisie—particularly younger administrators, lawyers, journalists, and intellectuals—had encountered frustrating barriers to the offices and prestige enjoyed by the nobility. They also had grown impatient with the monarchy's failure to enact reforms that would benefit them specifically. By 1789, many applauded broad attacks on the privileged orders and the status quo. An example of such an attack was Abbé Emmanuel-Joseph Sieyès' widely circulated pamphlet *What Is the Third Estate?* According to Sieyès, "If the privileged order should be abolished, the nation would be nothing less, but something more." The sorts of reforms that these middle-class critics had in mind were no more palatable to the monarchy than those of the nobility.

People from both the middle class and the nobility had begun expressing ideas and using highly charged political terms that profoundly threatened the monarchy. In the decades before 1789, salon meetings and new publications had spread key ideas of the Enlightenment to an increasingly literate public, particularly the aristocratic and middle-class elite in Paris and other French cities (see Chapter 14). These ideas emphasized the validity of reason and natural rights and questioned long-established institutions. They also undermined notions of the divine rights of kings and traditional ways of life—all while intensifying expectations of rapid reforms. In addition, terms such as "nation," "citizen," and "general will" had increasingly cropped up in the political discourse and reflected a growing sense that politics should include more than the concerns of the monarch and a tiny elite. So, when nobles asserted their own interests against the king, they often used language and ideas that attacked monarchical absolutists as unjustified tyrants and that accused the king's minister of "despotism." Middle-class men and women shared these sentiments and later extended them to demands for legal equality.

Enlightenment ideas and language

Thus, given all the resentments brewing among the nobility and the middle class, Louis and his often unpopular ministers risked much after they exposed themselves to discussions of reform within the Estates General. Three other developments—all beyond the powers of the king, nobility, and middle class—added an underlying sense of disappointment, desperation, and disorder among the French people in these decades.

First, a gap opened between rosy expectations and frightening realities. Before 1770, France had enjoyed a long period of prosperity. This growing wealth engendered a sense of rising expectations—that economically, things would keep getting better and better.

Disappointed expectations After 1770, a series of economic depressions struck, turning these high expectations into bitter disappointment and frustration. Worse, in 1788 the countryside suffered unusually bad harvests. In May and July of that year, hailstorms wiped out crops throughout France. Drought and then the most severe winter in decades followed. The price of bread soared, and with it came hunger, desperation, and even starvation. Droves of peasants crowded into the cities in search of jobs and help, but the agricultural depression had already spread there and had thrown thousands of artisans and laborers out of work. In the spring of 1789, peasants and urban poor looking for food turned to violence in France's cities and villages. Women led groups demanding grain and lower prices for flour. Desperate people attacked bakeries and stores of grain wherever they could find them. Arthur Young wrote, "the want of bread is terrible: accounts arrive every moment from the provinces of riots and disturbances, and calling in the military, to preserve the peace of the markets." The populace angrily blamed governmental figures and "parasitical agents" of the Old Regime for their plight.

By 1789, many pamphlets and cartoons portraying the connection between suffering and France's privileged orders circulated throughout France. Figure 16.1 is an apt example of these publications. This illustration shows the thin "common man," who represents the vast majority of the people, carrying three heavy figures from the privileged classes on his back. In front, wielding a whip and claiming feudal rights, is the king, representing oppressive royal power. Just above him is a clergyman in robes, brandishing papers representing the threat of an inquisition and clerical privileges. In back rides a judge with a list of the jealously guarded rights of the noble-controlled *parlements*. The illustration depicts the common man as a naked beast kept under control by reins, chains, and a blindfold. He crawls pitifully across barren fields, bleeding from the hands, knees, and loins, while his tormentors spur him on.

The second unsettling development came with the increasing demands for political participation and governmental reform throughout the West in the Demands for political participation years before 1789. These movements, arising in various countries, were led by ambitious elites. In Poland, agitation for independence from Russian influence surfaced between 1772 and 1792. Across the Atlantic, what started as a tax revolt in Britain's North American colonies turned into the American Revolution and war for independence that directly involved French aristocrats and common soldiers alike, and led to government without a king (see Chapter 15). In the Dutch Republic, demands for reform in the 1780s erupted into open revolt in 1787. In the Austrian Netherlands (Belgium and Luxembourg), elites rose against the reforms initiated by Emperor Joseph II in 1787. Well-informed French elites, keeping abreast of these disturbances, began to surmise that they, too, might successfully challenge the political status quo.

The economic hardship and political uprisings across Europe were damaging enough. A third problem—the French people's disrespect for their own king—made matters Unpopular kings worse. For much of the eighteenth century, France had been ruled by the unremarkable, unpopular, and long-lived King Louis XV. Unlike some of his European counterparts, neither he nor his successor, Louis XVI, managed to forge an effective alliance with the nobility or consistently assert their authority over it. Nor did they succeed in enacting reforms or even give the impression of being "enlightened" monarchs. Louis XVI had little particular taste or talent for rule, and his unpopular Austrian wife, Queen Marie Antoinette, increasingly drew fire for her supposed extravagance and indifference to those below her. According to a widely circulated story, she dismissed reports that the poor could not buy bread with the phrase, "Let them eat cake!"

■ FIGURE 16.1

France's privileged orders.

Though the story was untrue, it reflected the growing anger against the king and queen.

Desperate to stave off the immediate threat of bankruptcy, the relatively weak Louis XVI looked for support. Instead of able allies, he found a jealous nobility, a disgruntled middle class, a bitter and frustrated peasantry, and an urban poor made desperate by hunger.

THE "TENNIS COURT OATH"

In this ominous atmosphere, Louis XVI summoned the Estates General in 1788. This representative body, which had not met since 1614, was divided into France's three traditional orders, or estates: the first estate, the clergy, owned over 10 percent of France's best land; the second estate, the nobility, owned more than 20 percent of the land; and the third estate, the so-called commoners, included the bourgeoisie, the peasantry, and the urban populace. During the early months of 1789, elections of representatives to the Estates General were held. All men who had reached the age of 25 and who paid taxes could vote. In thousands of meetings to draw up lists of grievances to present to the king, people found their political voices and connected their dissatisfactions with inflating expectations of reform. Hundreds of pamphlets appeared and public debate spread widely. Each of the three estates elected its own representatives. Because the third estate made up more than nine-tenths of the total population, Louis XVI agreed to grant it as many seats as the other two estates combined. However, by tradition, the three estates sat separately, and each group had one vote.

The Estates General

In April 1789, delegates began streaming into Versailles armed only with *cahiers*, or the lists of grievances from all classes of people, that had been called for by the king. Of the 600 representatives of the third estate, not one came from the peasantry. Except for a handful of liberal clergy and nobles elected to the third estate, these delegates—mostly ambitious lawyers, petty officials, administrators, and other professionals—were all members of the bourgeoisie. They fully expected to solve the financial crisis quickly and then move on to addressing the long lists of complaints that they had been accumulating for years. Most bourgeois representatives, like many liberal nobles, wanted to create a constitutional government with a national assembly that would meet regularly to pass taxes and laws.

After religious services and a solemn procession in Paris, the delegates met in Versailles on May 5. Immediately they debated the voting system. The two privileged estates demanded that, according to custom, the three estates meet separately and vote by order—that is, each estate cast one vote. This procedure would place power squarely in the hands of the nobility, which controlled most of the first estate as well as its own order. The third estate demanded that all the orders meet jointly and that delegates vote by head. This method would favor the third estate, for not only did this order boast as many members as the other two combined, but a number of liberal clergy and nobles in the first and second estates sympathized with the reforms called for by the third estate. All sides realized that the outcome of this voting issue would be decisive.

The delegates haggled for six weeks. Louis waffled from one side to the other. Finally, the third estate, backed by some clergy from the first estate, took action and declared itself the National Assembly of France on June 17 and invited the other two estates to join it in enacting legislation. Three days later, when the third estate deputies arrived at their meeting hall, they found it locked. Adjourning to a nearby building that served as an indoor tennis court, they took the **Tennis Court Oath,** vowing not to disband until France had a constitution.

The National Assembly

Figure 16.2 dramatizes and glorifies this act of defiance. The painting is based on a pen and ink drawing by Jacques-Louis David (1748–1825), a talented contemporary painter and active supporter of the Revolution. In the center of the picture, the presiding officer, Jean-Sylvain Bailly (1736–1793) (soon to become mayor of Paris), raises his arm in a pledge and reads the oath aloud. Below him, from left to right, a white-robed Carthusian monk represents the second estate, a black-robed Catholic curate the first estate, and the brown-clad Protestant minister the third estate. These same three figures also stand for France's main religious groups: the secular clergy, the regular clergy, and Protestantism. All three figures join, symbolizing the transformation of the meeting into the newly formed National Assembly. Around these figures, representatives also take the oath. From above, light streams through billowing curtains as if blessing the heroic activities below, and members of the populace approvingly watch the scene.

On June 23, the king met with the three estates in a royal session. He offered many reforms but also commanded the estates to meet separately and vote by order. Then the king, his ministers, and members of the first two estates regally filed out. The third-estate representatives, however, defiantly remained seated. When the royal master of ceremonies returned to remind them of the king's orders, Count Mirabeau (1749–1791), a liberal nobleman elected by the third estate, jumped to his feet. "Go and tell those who sent you," he shouted, "that we are here by the will of the people and will not leave this place except at the point of the bayonet!" When the startled courtier dutifully repeated these words to his master, Louis XVI, with characteristic weakness, replied, "They mean to stay. Well, damn it,

■ FIGURE 16.2

School of Jacques-Louis David, *The Tennis Court Oath*.

let them stay." A few days later, the king reversed himself and ordered the three estates to meet jointly and vote by head. The third estate had won the first round.

STORMING THE BASTILLE

The monarchy might have been able to reassert control had not the new National Assembly received unexpected support from two sources: the Parisian populace and the French peasantry. Both groups had been suffering from the unusually poor economic conditions initiated by bad harvests. Revolutionary events raised expectations in hard times, making these people in the city and countryside particularly volatile. The first important disturbances broke out in Paris, whose population of 600,000 made it one of the largest cities in Europe. In early July, rumors that the king was calling the professional troops of the frontier garrison to Versailles raced through the streets of Paris. Alarmed, residents concluded that the king meant to use force against them. Then Louis dismissed his popular finance minister, Jacques Necker (1732–1804). This move seemed to confirm the fears of the third estate, who saw Necker as an ally.

At this critical juncture, the common people of Paris acted on their own. On July 14, riotous crowds of men and women searching for arms marched on the Bastille, a gloomy old fortress-prison in a working-class quarter. Few people were actually in the weakly guarded Bastille, but it symbolized the old order. Many died in the confused battle. With the help of mutinous troops, however, the crowd eventually took the Bastille, hacked its governor to death, and paraded around Paris with his head on a pike. "This glorious day must amaze our enemies, and finally usher in for us the triumph of justice and liberty," proclaimed a Paris newspaper.

The scene on page 502, one of many paintings and drawings made to celebrate this event, reveals the importance of this famous battle. The Bastille is portrayed as a massive castle that, against all odds, has come under attack by commoners and troops who have rallied to the side of the people. Only a few cannons seem necessary, for the people supposedly have heroic revolutionary spirit and numbers enough to surge forward and somehow storm across the bridge toward the Bastille entrance. The picture poignantly captures the symbolism of the act—the Bastille, representing the old feudal regime of the past, falls because of corruption within and the heroic power of an outraged people fighting under the revolutionary banner of Liberty, Equality, and Fraternity. In fact, this show of force by the artisans, shop owners, and laborers of Paris stayed the king's hand and sparked uprisings in other cities across France. Under pressure, royal authority began to crumble.

THINKING ABOUT DOCUMENTS

■ DOCUMENT 16.1

New Laws End the Feudal System in France

During the summer of 1789, revolutionary activities swept France. On July 14, a mob stormed the Bastille, symbolizing a violent tearing down of the ancien régime. In the countryside, the peasantry rose against the nobility. Cracking under these pressures, nobles in the National Assembly moved on August 4 and 5 to abolish their own feudal rights and privileges. The following excerpts describe some of the laws passed to end the feudal system. ■ **What** *conclusions about the grievances underlying the French Revolution might this document support?* ■ **What** *does this document reveal about the rapidly declining position of the aristocracy?* ■ **In what ways** *did these laws transform the ancien régime?* ■ **How** *did these laws change the relationship between commoners and nobility, as well as between citizens and the king?*

ARTICLE I. The National Assembly hereby completely abolishes the feudal system. It decrees that, among the existing rights and dues, . . . all those originating in or representing real or personal serfdom or personal servitude, shall be abolished without indemnification.

IV. All manorial courts are hereby suppressed without indemnification. . . .

V. Tithes of every description, as well as the dues which have been substituted for them . . . are abolished, on condition, however, that some other method be devised to provide for the expenses of divine worship, the support of the officiating clergy, for the assistance of the poor, for repairs and rebuilding of churches and parsonages, and for the maintenance of all institutions, seminaries, schools, academies, asylums, and organizations to which the present funds are devoted.

VII. The sale of judicial and municipal offices shall be suppressed forthwith. Justice shall be dispensed *gratis*.

IX. Pecuniary privileges, personal or real, in the payment of taxes are abolished forever. Taxes shall be collected from all the citizens, and from all property, in the same manner and in the same form. . . .

X. . . .All the peculiar privileges, pecuniary or otherwise, of the provinces, principalities, districts, cantons, cities and communes, are once for all abolished and are absorbed into the law common to all Frenchmen.

XI. All citizens, without distinction of birth, are eligible to any office or dignity, whether ecclesiastical, civil or military; and no profession shall imply any derogation.

Source: James Harvey Robinson, ed., *Translations and Reprints from the Original Sources of European History*, vol. I, no. 5 (Philadelphia: University of Pennsylvania Press, 1898), pp. 2–5.

Uprisings in the countryside echoed events in Paris. That July and August, peasants throughout France revolted against their lords. Burning tax rolls, the peasantry attacked manors, reoccupied enclosed lands, and rejected the traditional rights of noble landowners—dues on land, flour mills, wine presses, and law courts, and the tithes (taxes) landlords charged their tenants. These revolts intensified with the spreading of unfounded rumors that bands of brigands, perhaps assembled by nobles, were on the loose in the countryside. Panicked by this "Great Fear," many nobles—including one of the king's brothers—fled France and became known as the *émigrés* (exiles).

Peasant revolts

The "Great Fear"

THE END OF THE OLD ORDER

Now the nobility as well as the monarchy was in retreat. The National Assembly—dominated by the middle-class deputies from the third estate but now including many deputies from the clergy and nobility—tried to pacify the aroused peasantry. On August 4, during a night session of the National Assembly, one nobleman after another stood up and renounced his traditional rights and privileges in an effort to make the best of a bad situation. A leader of the Assembly hailed the "end of feudalism." As Document 16.1 shows, the National Assembly quickly decreed the end of serfdom, traditional dues owed to landlords, special taxation rights, and privileged access to official posts. The peasantry seemed pacified for the time being.

Success spurred the National Assembly to take further steps. The most important of these actions occurred on August 26, when the Assembly proclaimed the **Declaration of Rights of Man and Citizen.** Enlightenment ideas and phrases similar to those in the American Declaration of Independence filled this document. "Men are born and remain free and equal in rights," it stated. The natural rights included "liberty, property, security, and resistance to oppression." Sovereignty—supreme authority—rested with the nation as a whole, not the monarchy. Enacted laws should express the "general will"—a term and idea made popular by Jean-Jacques Rousseau (see Chapter 14). The

Declaration of Rights of Man and Citizen

document proclaimed freedom of opinion "even in religion," freedom of the press, and freedom from arbitrary arrest. In 1791, this spirit would lead to the liberation of France's Jews from old legal disabilities.

Some of these rights, such as freedom of the press, applied to women as well as men, but only men gained the full measure of new social and political rights. In the months and years that followed, many women objected to this limitation. Organizing groups and writing petitions and pamphlets, these women demanded to be included. In 1791, Olympe de Gouges (1748–1793), a writer and strong supporter of the Revolution, wrote one of the best-known and more challenging pamphlets, the *Declaration of the Rights of Women*. She argued that women should have the same political and social rights as men: "The only limits on the exercise of the natural rights of woman are perpetual male tyranny; these limits are to be reformed by the laws of nature and reason." Some members of the government, such as the Marquis de Condorcet (1743–1794) voiced similar demands. However, their arguments fell on deaf ears.

Despite this rising tide of defiance, Louis refused to sign the August decrees. Instead, he once more assembled troops around Versailles and Paris. In answer to this new threat of force, on October 5 and 6, a huge crowd of Parisian women, already infuriated by high bread prices and food shortages, marched eleven miles through the rain to

■ FIGURE 16.3
Parisian women march to Versailles.

March to Versailles Versailles. The contemporary print shown in Figure 16.3 depicts the marchers, armed with pikes, axes, swords, and cannon. With the exception of the well-dressed, reluctant figure at the left, their faces express a striking determination and authority. (Notice the woman riding in the cart with the cannon and the woman at the front to the far right).

At Versailles, the marchers surrounded the palace. With the help of members of the recently formed National Guard—units of armed civilians under Lafayette—they forced the king and his family to accompany them back to Paris, bringing him closer to the people and away from the protected isolation of Versailles and the king's aristocratic advisors. As the carriage bearing the royal family rolled toward the capital, where the royal family would be virtually imprisoned in the Tuileries Palace, the surrounding crowd of women and men shouted jubilantly, "We have the baker [the king], the baker's wife, and the little cook boy! Now we shall have bread!" Although this image of women taking political action into their

own hands made them heroines of the Revolution in some eyes, others would nervously look back on the women's behavior as something inappropriate and even frightening. Most men were not ready to accept such a change in women's traditional roles.

A few days later, the National Assembly moved its sessions to Paris. The third estate, building on the anger and hunger of the peasantry and the urban poor, had triumphed. The old order had disintegrated.

THE CONSTITUTIONAL MONARCHY: ESTABLISHING A NEW ORDER

Flushed with success, the National Assembly now turned to the task of transforming French institutions. Guiding principles were represented by the revolutionary banner "Liberty, Equality, and Fraternity." At that time, the idea of liberty meant freedom from arbitrary authority and freedom of speech, press, conscience, assembly, and profession. Equality meant equal treatment under the law and equality of economic opportunity—at least for men. Fraternity meant comradeship as citizens of the nation. During the next two years, the Assembly passed a series of sweeping reforms that altered almost all aspects of life in France.

Liberty, Equality, Fraternity

The central government, now based on national sovereignty, was transformed into what amounted to a constitutional monarchy. The National Assembly served as its legislature, and the king (still an important symbol of authority for many) remained its chief executive officer. Because

Constitutional monarchy

MAPS 16.1 AND 16.2   REORGANIZING FRANCE IN 1789

These maps show France's historic provinces, each with its own political identity (Map 16.1, left), and the nation's revolutionary departments after 1789 (Map 16.2, right). ■ **Notice** the different sizes of the old provinces and the almost equal size of the new departments. ■ **Notice** that the historic names of the provinces have been eliminated, and most of the new departments are named for geographical features (mountains, such as the Alps; rivers, such as the Seine). **Consider** why France's Assembly reorganized the nation in this way.

only tax-paying males could vote and win election to office, the bourgeoisie firmly held the reins of power. For the time being, the governance of France was decentralized. To undermine old loyalties and the power of the provincial nobility, the National Assembly created eighty-three newly named departments, each almost equal in size and administered by locally elected assemblies and officials (Maps 16.1 and 16.2). Similarly, the National Assembly took France's judicial system out of the hands of the nobility and clergy. It created new civil and criminal courts, with elected judges. France's complex, unequal system of taxation was also swept away, replaced by uniform taxes on land and the profits of trade and industry.

The new government linked reform of the Catholic Church with the financial problems it faced. Repudiating France's debt was out of the question because part of it was owed to members of the bourgeoisie. To pay for its expenditures, the National Assembly issued what amounted to paper money called *assignats*. To back up the *assignats*, pay off the debt, and at the same time bring the church under governmen-

tal control, government officials confiscated and sold church property.

This seizure of property constituted a major step toward the nationalization of the church. Next the Assembly dissolved all convents and monasteries and prohibited the taking of religious vows. People would elect the clergy, including non-Roman Catholics, and the state would pay their salaries. These measures were incorporated in the Civil Constitution of the Clergy, to which all members of the clergy were required to take an oath of allegiance in order to perform their functions and draw their salaries. This last step proved too much for many religious officials, for it threatened the very independence of the clergy. Pope Pius VI called the oath of allegiance "the poisoned fountainhead and source of all errors." Approximately half the clergy of France, including nearly all the bishops, refused to take the oath. This defection of the "nonjuring clergy" created a long-lasting division among France's Catholic population. Many, especially rural

Civil Constitution of the Clergy

women, fought against this disturbance of their religious life, vowing to defend their faith "with the last drop" of blood. The Revolution would lose the support of many French citizens who felt loyal to the old church and their local priests.

THE KING DISCREDITED

Louis XVI must have bitterly resented these changes, for they diluted his power and put Paris under the control of his former subjects. Nonetheless, he managed to make things even worse for himself. On June 20, 1791, the royal family, in disguise, escaped from Paris and headed by coach to France's northeastern frontier, where Louis hoped to find supporters and perhaps reverse the tide of events. Unfortunately for him and his family, a postmaster recognized them just before they could reach safety. Officials arrested the royal family in Varennes and returned them to Paris. To save face, the government concocted a thin story about the royal family being kidnapped, but in many eyes the king and queen had now become traitors.

Flight of the royal family

In October 1791, the National Assembly gave way to the Legislative Assembly, with all new representatives elected under the new rules. In only two years, and with relatively little bloodshed, France had been made over. A written constitution ruled supreme over the diminished monarchy. The church lost its independence from the state. The nobility forfeited its special rights and privileges. Men gained individual rights and liberties and legal equality. Though excluded by the reformers, women would nevertheless continue to voice demands for political and social rights and play important roles as the Revolution evolved. France now boasted a more democratic electoral system than England or the United States. Events had already gone well beyond anything our British traveler, Arthur Young, might have imagined two years earlier.

REACTIONS OUTSIDE FRANCE

Outside France, writers and reformers in Europe and the United States hailed the French Revolution or the principles underlying it. In elegant salons, elites spiritedly discussed these dramatic events, and in newspapers and pamphlets, writers dissected and debated their meaning. Supporters established societies in Britain and in states along France's eastern borders. Some activists, such as the American writer Tom Paine, traveled to Paris to participate directly. In Britain, Charles Fox, a leader of the Whigs, called the Revolution "much the greatest event that ever happened, and much the best." Others argued against the French Revolution. The most famous attack was launched by Edmund Burke in his *Reflections on the*

Revolution in France (1790). This British statesman argued that France moved too quickly in the name of abstract notions of natural rights and justice. As a result, revolutionaries replaced a despotic monarchy with anarchy. In his view, societies should evolve slowly, drawing reforms from the long historical experience of a national culture. Good government came from good habits. Reforms worked well when based on a nation's best traditions.

Most governments opposed the Revolution when they realized the threat it posed to their own security. If a revolution could rise in France, end aristocratic privileges, and undermine the monarchy, the same might happen elsewhere. Officials welcomed and listened to the aristocratic émigrés who fled France. They suppressed pro-revolutionary groups within their borders. Within a few years, most states joined coalitions to fight against the revolutionary armies.

TO THE RADICAL REPUBLIC AND BACK

The new government, launched with such optimism in October 1791, lasted less than a year. Up to that point, the bourgeoisie and the peasants had been the primary beneficiaries of the Revolution. The bourgeoisie had gained political control over the country and social mobility. The peasantry had won freedom from feudal obligations. To the many peasant landowners who owned their land before the Revolution were now added others who had seized the lands of émigré nobles or had purchased confiscated church lands (though many of these lands went to middle-class buyers).

However, other groups remained quite dissatisfied. The royal family and much of the aristocracy and high clergy yearned for the restoration of their traditional positions. On the other hand, many Parisians urged a more radical approach to the Revolution. These shopkeepers, artisans, bakers, innkeepers, and workers had won little beyond theoretical rights and legal equality. Those who owned no property still could not vote, yet they had supplied much of the physical force and anger that had saved the third estate and made the reforms possible. Increasingly, these men and women formed organizations, held meetings, and intently discussed the numerous pamphlets, petitions, and newspapers printed daily in Paris. Some of these clubs became egalitarian meeting places for women and men; others, such as the Society of Revolutionary Republican Women, insisted that women should participate more fully in the Revolution. Many of the most politically active came to be known as the *sans-culottes* because

Sans-culottes

they wore long pants instead of the fashionable knee breeches of the elites. A pamphlet described a *sans-culotte* as "a man who has no mansions, no lackeys to wait on him, and who lives quite simply. . . . He is useful, because he knows how to plough a field, handle a forge, a saw, or a file, how to cover a roof or how to make shoes and to shed his blood to the last drop to save the Republic." Typically the *sans-culottes* carried pikes and addressed people as "Citizen" or "Citizeness." Eventually they and their supporters gained control over the municipal government of Paris—the Commune.

Leadership for this urban populace fell into the hands of radical members of the bourgeoisie, who

The Jacobin Club

allied themselves with the *sans-culottes* and favored overthrow of the monarchy and extension of the Revolution. Well organized and ably led, these radicals came together in numerous clubs that formed to debate and plan political matters. The Jacobin Club, which had hundreds of affiliated clubs outside of Paris, became the most important of these political organizations. Its membership included more than 200 deputies, and over time, militant radicals gained strength within the organization.

WAR AND THE BREAKDOWN OF ORDER

Events—particularly the rumors of war that had begun circulating throughout France—soon played into the hands of the Parisian radicals. The monarchs of Austria and Prussia, fearing the spread of revolutionary ideas to their own lands and urged on by French émigrés, began to make threatening moves and to issue meddlesome warnings to the French revolutionaries. In France, many groups welcomed the prospect of war, though for different reasons. The royal family and its supporters believed a French victory would enhance the prestige and power of the throne; even a French defeat could help by restoring the Old Regime and royal power. Radicals, who wanted to turn France into a republic, believed that war would expose the inefficiency and disloyalty of the king and topple the monarchy.

The war that broke out in April 1792 became the first of a series of conflicts that would span twenty-three years and ultimately embroil most of the Western world. At first, inflation, food shortages, and breakdowns of order hampered France's war effort. The French armies suffered from lack of experienced leadership; nearly all the high-ranking officers were members of the nobility and had either fled or been deposed. The Austrian and Prussian armies badly defeated the French and advanced toward Paris. Panic broke out in the city. "Everywhere you hear the cry that the king is betraying us, the generals are betraying us, that nobody is to be trusted . . . that Paris will be taken," exclaimed an observer. When the Prussian

commander, the duke of Brunswick, announced that he would deliver the royal family "from their captivity," French radicals rightly accused Louis XVI and Marie Antoinette of being in treasonable communication with the enemy. On August 10, local leaders in Paris organized a huge Parisian crowd of men and women who attacked the king's palace. The royal family fled for their lives to the Legislative Assembly. The invading crowd wrecked the interior of the palace and slaughtered hundreds of the king's guards. The Legislative Assembly suspended and imprisoned the hapless Louis XVI. Under pressure from the people of Paris, it called elections—this time with almost all men enjoying the right to vote—for a National Convention to draw up a new, more radical constitution.

Meanwhile, one of the Jacobin leaders, Georges-Jacques Danton (1759–1794), used his great skills as an orator and organizer to gather recruits for the army and rush them to the front. As the

Panic and massacres

recruits prepared to leave Paris to meet the invading Prussians, rumors—spurred by the propaganda of radical journalists like Jean-Paul Marat (1743–1793)—spread that reactionary clergy and nobles planned to murder their wives and children. Frightened and enraged people began murdering members

KEY DATES	
THE FRENCH REVOLUTION (1789–1799)	
1787	Assembly of Notables
May 5, 1789	Meeting of the Estates General
June 20, 1789	Tennis Court Oath
July 14, 1789	Fall of the Bastille
August 4, 1789	Renunciation of noble privileges
August 26, 1789	Declaration of Rights of Man and Citizen
October 5–6, 1789	March to Versailles
June 20, 1791	Flight to Varennes
October 1791	Legislative Assembly
April 1792	War breaks out
September 1792	France declared a republic
January 1793	Louis XVI executed
1793–1794	The Terror
1795–1799	The Directory

■ DOCUMENT 16.2

The Jacobins' Revolutionary Politics

*In the years following 1789, the Jacobin Club of Paris became the most influential political club in the city and, with many affiliated clubs outside of Paris, the most important in France. The Jacobins pushed politics in an increasingly more radical direction. The following document, which they circulated on September 12, 1792, reveals some of the club's evolving goals and tactics. ■ **What** is the club's vision of the monarchy and its supporters? ■ **What** does the club stand for? ■ **What** tensions within France does this document expose?*

Since the 10th of August conspirators have expiated their offences; the public spirit has risen again; the sovereign, recovered possession of its rights, triumphs at length over the scoundrels leagued against its liberty and its welfare. Nevertheless, the people of Paris have felt the necessity of preserving an imposing attitude and of exercising a strict surveillance over the Minions and agents of the traitor, Louis the Last. Be apprehensive, brothers and friends, lest new intrigues shall follow the baffled intrigues. The head, the cause and the pretext of the machinations still lives! Despotism moves in the darkness; let us be ready to engage in a combat to the death with it, under whatever form it presents itself. . . .

Let us impress our minds then with the spirit of the orders of the electoral body of Paris; they alone can save us from all sorts of despotism and the dangers of convulsions too long a time prolonged, etc.

These orders are in substance:

The purgatorial examination of the National Convention, in order to reject from its midst the suspected members who may have escaped the sagacity of the primary assemblies;

The revocability of the deputies to the National Convention who have attacked or who attack by any motions the rights of the sovereign;

The sanction, or the popular revision of all the constitutional decrees of the National Convention;

The entire abolition of royalty and the penalty of death against those who may propose to reestablish it;

The form of a republican government.

These, friends and brothers, are the important matters which the electors, the Commune, and the Primary Assemblies of Paris, invite us to discuss earnestly in order to fortify and encompass the National Convention with your opinion upon these matters.

Source: F. M. Anderson, ed., *The Constitution and Other Select Documents Illustrative of the History of France 1789–1901*, (Minneapolis: H. W. Wilson Co., 1904), pp. 127–128.

---

of the nonjuring clergy (who would not swear allegiance to the new order) and nobles being held in the prisons of Paris. During the first three weeks of September 1792, more than a thousand fell victim to these massacres.

In the elections for the National Convention, held amid this hysteria, republicans—favoring elimination of the monarchy altogether and the creation of a French republic—won a sweeping victory. Document 16.2 reveals how the Jacobin club of Paris, branding the king "Louis the Last," pushed for a republic and legislators who favored Jacobin views. Most of the conservative elements fearfully stayed away from the polls. This Convention ruled France for the next three years, taking the Revolution down a new, more radical road.

National Convention

RADICAL REPUBLICANS STRUGGLE FOR POWER

The struggle for political dominance among the different Jacobin factions intensified after the election. The Girondins, so called because many of their leaders came from the vicinity of Bordeaux in the department of the Gironde, had once been the most powerful and radical faction of the Legislative Assembly. Because they had sat on the speaker's left, they had come to be known as "the Left." In the new National Convention, the Girondins found themselves on the Right as the more conservative faction. Now the Left consisted mostly of members of the Jacobin political club from Paris. These Jacobins came to be called "the Mountain" because they occupied the highest seats in the convention hall.

Girondins and Jacobins

On September 22, 1792, the National Convention declared France a republic. The government then disposed of the king, who had squandered most of his support since his flight to Varennes in 1791. The Convention tried Louis and found him guilty of treasonable communication with the enemy. An extended debate ensued over whether to execute the king, with most of the Girondins opposed and the Mountain in favor. On January 21, 1793, the Convention voted by a narrow margin to execute Louis.

The Republic

Figure 16.4 depicts the scene of Louis's execution. On the platform,

Execution of the king

Louis addressed the crowd for the last time: "I die innocent." An eyewitness described how the executioners "dragged him under the axe of the guillotine, which with one stroke severed his head from his body." The revolutionary government adopted the newly invented guillotine as its instrument of choice because it considered the device more efficient and therefore humane than other methods of execution, such as hanging and the axe. Here an executioner holds up the head of the king for the troops and crowd to view. An observer reported that a few seconds later, "cries of 'Vive la Républic' [long live the Republic] were heard . . . and in less than ten minutes this cry, a thousand times repeated, became the universal shout of the multitude, and every hat was in the air." The troops, with their backs to the crowd, are there to witness what is presented as a patriotic event. Although other executions would not have the same significance or draw the same crowds, this scene would be repeated thousands of times over the next two years. Beheadings not only served as affirmations of revolutionary justice, they also provided entertainment—people often rented chairs and purchased food, drinks, and souvenirs, including miniature guillotines. Those who could not attend might purchase widely sold prints such as the one pictured.

Ten months later the queen, Marie Antoinette, followed Louis XVI to the guillotine. These executions sent a shudder of horror through the royal courts of Europe, as did the new French army recruits' surprising success against the Austrian and Prussian coalition. The hastily assembled revolutionary armies,

Internal and external enemies

swelling with numbers and enthusiasm, had checked the advancing Austrian and Prussian armies at Valmy in September 1792. France now went on the offensive. Alarmed, Britain, the Dutch Netherlands, Spain, Portugal, Sardinia, and Naples joined Austria and Prussia in a great coalition against France.

This new external threat was compounded by internal threats to the revolutionary government. The peasants of the Vendée region in western France, stirred up by the nonjuring clergy and others, rebelled against the republican government. "We want our king, our priests and the Old Regime," cried the rebels. Figure 16.5 shows a young aristocratic general leading the rebels in the midst of one of the close-quarter

■ FIGURE 16.4

Execution of Louis XVI.

■ FIGURE 16.5

Pierre-Narcisse Guérin, *Henri de la Rochjacquelein,* 1817.

BIOGRAPHY

Manon Roland (1754–1793)

CONSIDER
■ **Consider** what Manon Roland's life reveals about the attitudes underlying the Revolution and the rapidly changing events that disrupted people's lives.

Manon Roland, describing herself as a "friend of humanity" and "lover of liberty," welcomed the French Revolution "with rapture." Born in 1754 into the family of a Parisian engraver, she learned to read by the age of 4. By her early 20s, she was fluent in two foreign languages, had mastered the Greek and Roman classics, and embraced the ideas of Rousseau. She also rejected her Catholic faith and formed a lasting hatred for the pretensions of the aristocracy—and of the royal family in particular. She married a lawyer twenty years her senior who gained a position as inspector of manufacturers in Lyons. At the outbreak of the Revolution in 1789, she was at the center of a group of idealistic intellectuals and admirers who met regularly in Lyons. She argued for a republic rather than a constitutional monarchy and demanded that the royal family be put on trial.

The turmoil of revolutionary events created opportunities for the couple. In 1791, the city government of Lyons sent Manon's husband to Paris as a negotiator. Manon accompanied him, thrilled to be at the political center of France. They attended meetings of the Jacobin Club, and Manon quickly gathered around her a social circle of men, including Robespierre, whom she would later describe as "ardent, jealous, avid for popularity." The Rolands also associated with Girondins.

Manon's husband often attended gatherings of this circle, and Manon let him do all the public speaking for both of them.

Upholding the traditional, formal role of a proper wife, mother, and homemaker, she mostly listened. "I knew the role that suited my sex, and I never abandoned it," she noted. Similarly, she did not argue for the rights of women or even invite other women to these gatherings, but she often resented men's attitudes toward women: It takes "a great deal of patience or vanity to hear with cool head, from men's own mouths, the value they attach to their superiority over us." Yet she was more politically and intellectually ambitious than her husband. Often, she was the force behind her husband's words and the author of writings that came out under his name. Figure 16.5 shows this strong woman looking directly at the viewer, pen in hand.

In 1792, with the rise to power of the Girondins, Manon's husband was offered the high post of minister of the interior. She talked him into accepting it and, from behind the scenes, shared his new position of power and prominence. It was she who did most of the necessary writing—the instructions, circulars, and public announcements—and who accepted visitors eager to get an audience with the busy minister.

Events, however, moved too rapidly for Manon Roland as her life and the Revolution took more radical turns. She fell in love with Buzot, a young Girondin in her circle. She told her husband of her feelings, and although the two honored the form of their marriage out of a sense of propriety and discipline, they were

battles that often occurred in the Vendée revolt. Standing in tall boots and yellow pants, a white sash around his waist, and his wounded right arm in a sling, Rochjacquelein fires a gun at the enemy, so close in front of him that we see to the right the opposing bayonet just inches away. Behind Rochjacquelein stand his equally determined but more modestly dressed peasant guerilla followers, one with a rifle, another with only a pitchfork to stress the popularity of this rebellion. Above flies the white flag of the rebel Royalist cause that is echoed by the sacred heart pinned to the hero's chest. Rochjacquelein would survive this battle only to be killed in 1794. However, the uprising he helped lead spread until some sixty of the eighty-three departments suffered revolts. Lyons, France's second largest city, rose against the government in May. Toulon, the chief French naval base on the Mediterranean, invited in the British fleet to help in the fight against France's radical government. All-too-real enemies outside and within France's borders surged forward to fight against the Revolution.

THE TERROR

Faced with a seemingly inevitable demise of their cause and threatened by radical demands from the *sans-culottes*, the leaders of the Mountain decided to take drastic action. For support they turned to the Paris Commune, as the city government was called, which radicals and the *sans-culottes* controlled. The *sans-culottes* wanted to carry the Revolution even further, toward more direct democracy and governmental controls over the price of bread. Although the Mountain's leaders did not fully agree with the *sans-culottes*, they were willing to work with them to gain supremacy.

The National Convention, now dominated by the Mountain and surrounded by a threatening Parisian crowd of women and men urged on by *sans-culotte* leaders, voted the ***Committee of Public Safety*** expulsion and arrest of their chief competitors, the Girondin leaders, on June 2, 1793. To pacify the

FIGURE 16.6
Manon Roland.

miserable together. Manon made new political enemies, particularly Danton and the more radical Jacobins. The radical press called her a whore and her salon a hotbed of intrigue. Then the Girondins began to lose power, and Manon's husband's career stumbled as well. He resigned from office two days after the execution of the king in early 1793. The Revolution had gone too far even for Manon Roland, who wrote that she was "ashamed of it. It has been dishonored by scoundrels." Over the next few months both Rolands drew criticism from the press and their political enemies. Threatening groups of *sans-culottes* lurked in front of their apartment.

Too late, the Rolands tried to flee Paris. On May 31, 1793, Manon's husband, like many other Girondins, was arrested. He soon escaped, but then Manon suffered the same fate. After languishing in jail for months and writing her memoirs (modeled on Rousseau's *Memoirs*), she was tried on November 8, 1793, and found guilty of crimes against the Republic. That same day, she was escorted to the very guillotine where her longtime enemies Louis XVI and Marie Antoinette had perished. On the platform, she raised her eyes to David's statue representing liberty and lamented, "O Liberty, what crimes are committed in thy name." Upon hearing of her death, her husband committed suicide. Just weeks later, her love, Buzot, facing arrest himself, also committed suicide.

Revolutionary events that had drawn Manon to Paris and initially fulfilled her hopes quickly spun out of control. At the forefront of change in 1789, she found herself left behind and labeled an enemy of the Revolution just four years later. For Manon Roland and so many like her who rose with the Revolution, the wry statement of a moderate observer held true: "The Revolution . . . devours its children."

sans-culottes, the National Convention also agreed to enact the Law of the Maximum to control the price of bread, flour, and other essentials. Finally, the Convention drafted a democratic constitution based on universal male suffrage that promised rights to education and even subsistence (a job or poor relief). However, the Convention soon suspended the constitution and formed the 12-member **Committee of Public Safety** to guide the country. The committee had two main tasks: to secure the Republic against its enemies—both internal and external—and to carry out a radical republican program. With the vast authority granted by the Convention, it enjoyed dictatorial powers. The committee came under the ideological leadership of the gifted and feared Maximilien Robespierre (1758–1794). A lawyer from the provinces when elected to the Estates General in 1789, he quickly rose to head the Jacobin Club in Paris. This stern, determined idealist was influenced by Rousseau and was bent upon the creation of a virtuous republic. In pursuit of this dream, Robespierre and his fellow committee members struggled both to appease and control the unpredictable, threatening *sans-culottes*.

To protect the Republic from its internal enemies and to satisfy demands from the *sans-culottes* for immediate action, the Committee of Public Safety instituted a Reign of Terror. "We must annihilate the enemies of the Republic at home and abroad, or else we shall perish," Robespierre warned. He justified the Terror by arguing that in this time of revolution, "the first maxim of our politics ought to be to lead the people by means of reason and the enemies of the people by terror." Accordingly, agents of the committee searched out and summarily tried anyone suspected of being counterrevolutionaries. Even those who had once supported the Revolution—such as the Girondins, whose views had fallen out of favor—were arrested and executed. Jean-Sylvain Bailly, shown leading the 1789 Tennis Court Oath in Figure 16.2; Manon Roland (see Biography); and Olympe de Gouges, the woman who argued so strongly for revolutionary

> **Reign of Terror**

principles in the beginning, fell to the guillotine. Though many people became victims of arbitrary justice, officials used the Terror most often where real threats arose—regions in revolt and vulnerable areas near France's borders. During this violent phase of the Revolution, probably between 200,000 and 400,000 victims of the Terror went to prison. Some 25,000 to 50,000 died in jail or at the hands of executioners.

To secure the Republic against external enemies, the government ordered a **levée en masse,** or general call-up of all men, women, and children to serve the nation. As able-bodied young men were rapidly trained and rushed to the front, the army swelled to 850,000 men—a number that far exceeded the forces of France's opponents. Everyone else was supposed to contribute to the war effort by collecting or manufacturing supplies for the troops and by bolstering spirit. Women stitched clothing and served as nurses, children made bandages, and old men delivered stirring, patriotic speeches. This united activity for defense of the country produced an intense national patriotism. One soldier wrote home from the front to explain his feelings: "When *la patrie* calls us to her defense, we ought to fly there. . . . Our life, our wealth, and our talents do not belong to us. It is to the nation, *la patrie*, that all that belongs." With the officer corps now open to talent and the massive mobilization of men, materials, and spirit, the citizen armies turned back coalition forces by the end of 1793. By the summer of the following year, they carried the war beyond France's borders.

Levée en masse

THE REPUBLIC OF VIRTUE

While fighting this war, Robespierre and the Committee of Public Safety carried out their radical republican program. They attempted to reform institutions and infuse all aspects of French life with revolutionary politics. They intended to create a Republic of Virtue based on Rousseauian ideas of reason and natural law.

First, they targeted those institutions that, in their view, represented the worst of the Old Regime. Many officials saw the Catholic Church in this negative light and sold church buildings, turned them into warehouses, or rededicated them as "temples of reason." Angry radicals disfigured religious statues, even sending some wooden figures of saints to the guillotine and melting down church treasures. The most enthusiastic radicals searched out nonjuring clergy for prosecution and pressured even the clergy that had sworn to uphold the Revolution to leave their vocations. Some radical leaders hoped that the new festivals established to celebrate the Revolution would provide a sufficient substitute for Christian rituals. Other revolutionaries tried to create new beliefs, such as the Cult of Rea-

Attacking the Catholic Church

son, to replace Christianity. Robespierre tried in vain to institute his own deistic Cult of the Supreme Being.

The National Convention also enacted legislation that took the rules governing family life and education away from the church and placed them in state hands. Marriage became a civil rather than a religiously ordained act. New rules for divorce allowed thousands of couples to end marriages they would have been bound to under church rules. Births were registered at city halls rather than local churches. Women could sue for equal inheritance for the first time. Education became a responsibility of the state. New legislation mandated free primary schooling for all girls and boys and state-run secondary schooling, though in fact the government had neither the funds nor enough trained teachers to support such a system.

Family life and education

Women—especially those living in the cities—welcomed the new marriage, divorce, inheritance, and education laws, for they increased women's rights. However, the Jacobins had no desire to free women from their traditional role in the private sphere. Rather, they rejected women's participation in politics and outlawed female associations such as the Society of Revolutionary Republican Women. Jacobins declared that women's primary duties lay in nurturing children. They concluded that women had no proper role as active citizens and that women's political groups only disrupted the republican order. As one member of the government explained, "It is horrible, it is contrary to all laws of nature for a woman to want to make herself a man."

The new government went far beyond simply rooting out opponents of the Revolution and attacking institutions tied to the Old Regime. It also tried to create support for the Republic by infusing the objects and activities of everyday life with revolutionary symbols. The figure of Liberty replaced royal symbols on everything from coins and statues to plates and posters. Patriotic groups planted liberty trees throughout France. Women adopted the flowing robes and hairstyles of ancient Greece that reflected rejection of the traditional social order. People sported revolutionary ribbons on their hats. Songs such as the "Marseillaise," rallying the "children of the nation . . . against . . . the bloody standard of tyranny!" rang out among crowds and troops. Plays and paintings that supported the Revolution were encouraged. Officials promoted festivals that featured revolutionary symbols, mass loyalty oaths, and patriotic celebrations. Titles of all kinds were discarded and replaced with the terms "citizen" and "citizeness."

Revolutionary symbols

Pamphlets and posters spread throughout France, proclaiming what the Republic stood for. The 1792 poster shown in Figure 16.7, printed just after France became a republic, is a typical example. The poster announces principles at the core of the Republic: "Unity, indivisibility of the Republic. Liberty, equality, fraternity, or death." A triangle of authorities—"God, People, Law"—shines its blessings on these principles. Also blessed are the liberty trees that symbolize the Revolution, the one at the left topped by a "liberty cap"; the one at the right, by a helmet from France's citizen army.

In the name of reason and revolutionary principles, the government revamped the calendar, making the months equal in length and naming them after the seasons. Weeks were made ten days long, with one day of rest. (This change eliminated Sunday, a day of traditional Christian importance.) September 22, 1792—the date of the declaration of the Republic—became the first day of Year I. The new metric system of weights and measures based on units of 10 was introduced and eventually would spread beyond France's borders to countries throughout the world.

THE REVOLUTION SPREADS OUTSIDE OF FRANCE

Since 1792, France had fended off various coalitions of European powers. After initial defeats, France's citizen armies had gone on the offensive. During the struggles that ensued, France incorporated lands on its northern and eastern borders, claiming that these additions conformed to France's "natural boundaries" of the Rhine and the Alps. By 1799, more victories on the battlefield enabled France to set up "sister" republics in Holland, Switzerland, and Italy. To these areas, the French brought their own Enlightenment-inspired revolutionary principles and legislation. However, the gains carried a tremendous price tag. Hundreds of thousands died in the fighting, and the constant warfare disrupted trade and created shortages of essential goods.

Sister republics

The Revolution also powerfully influenced opinion outside France. Initially many groups in nearby countries supported the Revolution and its principles. However, part of that support rested on seeing France, a powerful rival, weakened. As people began to understand the seriousness of the attacks on monarchy and aristocracy and the threat to their own political independence, support waned. Still, many intellectuals and liberal political groups continued to uphold the ideals of the Revolution, at least until 1793 when the Revolution took a more radical turn.

Outside opinion

The Revolution helped promote other developments farther away. In Poland, patriots tried to use inspiration from France to assert independence from Russia. Despite some initial successes, however,

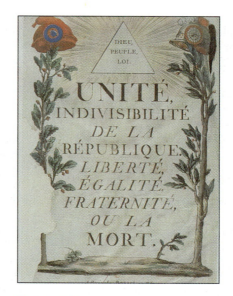

■ FIGURE 16.7

A republican poster.

their efforts failed. In Ireland, the revolutionary doctrines of liberty, equality, and natural rights touched many, encouraging them to rise against their British lords and make Ireland a republic. Irish patriots even anticipated a French invasion to help their own rebellion, although the invasion never took place.

Uprisings

In the Caribbean, slaves in France's lucrative colony of St. Domingue (Haiti) took heart from revolutionary principles and revolted. As Figure 16.8, a French print, reveals, the 1791 slave uprising struck fear in the hearts of white settlers. Slaves, outnumbering white settlers, attack a plantation. Women and men fall under the knives, swords, and cannon of the slaves, while plantation buildings go up in flames. Reports from French settlers, such as the wealthy Madame de Rouvray, described how the slaves "slaughtered and torched much of the countryside hereabouts," and warned, "how can we stay in a country where slaves have raised their hands against their masters?"

After much maneuvering and the abolishing of slavery by the National Convention in February 1794, the rebel leader Toussaint L'Ouverture and his black generals gained control of St. Domingue. The determined group would go on to successfully oppose English, Spanish, and French armies, turning the island into the independent republic of Haiti in 1804.

RESISTANCE TO THE REPUBLIC RISES

Despite the Reign of Terror and efforts to establish a Republic of Virtue, violent resistance to the Republic persisted and, in some cases, grew. Its leadership consisted primarily of local aristocrats and notables, officials who had fallen out of favor with the Jacobins, Girondin sympathizers, and members of the

■ FIGURE 16.8

Slave rebellion in St. Domingue (Haiti), 1791.

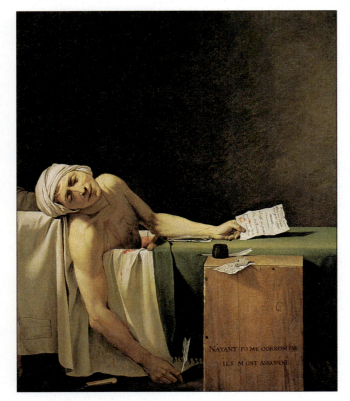

■ FIGURE 16.9

Jacques-Louis David, *The Death of Marat*, 1793.

nonjuring clergy who had gone underground. They gathered additional support from remaining royalists, conservative peasants who had already gained most of what they wanted, opponents of military conscription, and the many citizens who remained loyal to Catholicism and their nonjuring priests. Of the many armed revolts that broke out across France, the most important occurred in the Vendée, a region in western France (see pages 515–516). In what amounted to a regional civil war that raged for most of 1793 and dragged on for years thereafter, both sides committed atrocities and thousands lost their lives before republican soldiers gained the upper hand.

Figure 16.9 reveals another form of resistance and the symbols of conflict during the radical phase of the Revolution. The painting, by the politically active artist Jacques-Louis David, depicts the death of Jean-Paul Marat, a journalist and leading radical deputy, in July 1793. Marat, ironically already suffering from a terminal skin condition, was working in his bathtub when Charlotte Corday, a supporter of the Girondins, assassinated him. Corday felt that it was her duty to kill Marat because of his persistent demands for more executions. This painting shows the mortally wounded Marat with pen and paper still in his hands and Corday's knife on the floor. David and others eulogized Marat as a martyr for the Revolution. On the side of his writing stand are the words, "Not having been able to corrupt me, they assassinated me." Corday, widely denounced but convinced that she had "avenged many innocent victims," was soon guillotined.

Meanwhile, discontent with Robespierre and his policies increased. With the defeat of the invading coalition armies and the suppression of internal rebellion, most people no longer saw any need for the Terror— *Thermidorian reaction* yet the Terror only intensified. When the influential Danton counseled moderation, Robespierre sent him and his most prominent followers to the guillotine. No one, not even the members of the National Convention, felt safe. Finally, on July 27, 1794 (9 Thermidor on the Revolutionary calendar, and thus referred to as the **Thermidorian reaction**), the Convention overthrew Robespierre. In an ironic ending, the Jacobin leader died by the guillotine: the same device to which he had sent so many others to their deaths.

REACTION: THE "WHITE" TERROR AND THE DIRECTORY

With the leader of the Terror now dead, the propertied bourgeoisie quickly gained control of the government. Eliminating the "Red" Terror of the Committee of Public Safety, they replaced it with the "White" Terror of reaction. They executed the former terrorists and imprisoned many supporters of Robespierre, including the painter, Jacques-Louis David. Armed bands of bourgeois hirelings roved around beating and killing Jacobins. Restrictive measures of Robespierre's regime were repealed, and many individuals, weary of the Republic's code of discipline and restraint, reveled in an outburst of licentious living. Middle- and upper-class women wore more revealing clothing; mistresses appeared more publicly, even in the political arena. On the other hand, women of the poor in the small towns and countryside often turned back to the Catholic Church. They hoped that a return to God would end the turmoil of the revolutionary years.

A new constitution in 1795 reflected conservative reaction. The right to vote for members of the legislative bodies was limited to the wealthier property owners. Executive functions were placed in the hands of five directors—the **Directory.** Men of reasonable competence staffed the Directory (1795–1799), but they failed to restore tranquility. War dragged on, governmental finances unraveled further, and brigands terrorized the countryside and the cities. The five directors tried to balance threats from the royalists on the Right and the Jacobins on the Left. They turned against the *sans-culottes* by removing price controls and had to be saved by governmental forces when the *sans-culottes* stormed the Convention in May 1795. Five months later, the government barely put down a royalist uprising, thanks to a quick-acting artillery officer named Napoleon Bonaparte. The directors finally resorted to purges to control the legislature and increasingly relied on the army for support. All in all, the situation was ripe for the arrival of a strongman who could bring both order at home and peace abroad.

NAPOLEON BONAPARTE

Within France, the Revolution provided unprecedented opportunities for ambitious soldiers of talent. Most prerevolutionary army officers had come from the nobility, and had fled the country or lost their commands as the Revolution gathered momentum. This leadership drain, as well as the need to expand the army, created a huge demand for skilled officers. Napoleon Bonaparte, a talented artillery officer, stepped in to take full advantage of these opportunities.

NAPOLEON'S RISE TO POWER

Born into a poor but well-known family on Corsica in 1769, just a few months after the Mediterranean island was transferred from the Republic of Genoa to France, Napoleon was hardworking, assertive, independent, and even arrogant as a youth. These qualities would stay with him for the rest of his life. The young Napoleon attended French military school (where he proved particularly strong in mathematics) and received his commission as second lieutenant when he was just 16. When the Revolution broke out in 1789, Napoleon was already familiar with Enlightenment ideas and resented the aristocratic pretensions of those around him. He quickly sided with the revolutionaries. In 1793, he attracted attention during the recapture of Toulon. Two years later, when he happened to be in Paris, the National Convention called on him to quell a threatening Parisian crowd. Using artillery—his legendary "whiff of grape-shot"—Napoleon quickly dispersed the crowd and became the hero of the Convention. He fell in love with and married the politically well-connected Josephine de Beauharnais (1763–1814), a 32-year-old widow eager to provide security for her children.

Napoleon then used his growing prominence to secure command of the French army still fighting in northern Italy. Calling his forces "soldiers of liberty" and announcing to the people of Italy that "the French army comes to break your chains," he skillfully galvanized the lethargic French forces into defeating the Austrians and Sardinians. Along with loads of Italian art, Napoleon sent home glowing reports of his exploits. In 1797, he personally negotiated a favorable Treaty of Campo Formio with Austria, which recognized French expansion and the creation of the Cisalpine Republic in northern Italy (Map 16.3). Over the next two years, French armies moved south, helping to set up more French-controlled republics throughout the Italian peninsula. Napoleon's successes in Italy established his reputation as a brilliant military leader and able statesman.

Italian campaign

Turning toward the British, Napoleon and the Directory concluded that an expedition to Egypt would deal a telling blow to British commerce with its colonies in Asia. Egypt could also serve as the foundation for a new French colony. Moreover, a conquest there might enhance Napoleon's image as a daring, heroic conqueror. Yet, despite some spectacular battlefield successes, the expedition failed; Admiral Nelson (1758–1805), who became one of Britain's most admired naval commanders, destroyed the French fleet at the Battle of the Nile on August 1, 1798. The French land campaign in Egypt and Syria persisted for a while, but it was doomed by a lack of supplies and reinforcements. Napoleon avoided personal disaster by slipping back to France with a few chosen followers, cleverly controlling the

Expedition to Egypt

Map legend:
- French Republic at 1792
- Annexed to France 1792-1795
- Sister Republics

Labels on map: NORTH SEA, ENGLAND, BATAVIAN REPUBLIC 1798, Amsterdam, PRUSSIA, AUSTRIAN NETHERLANDS (BELGIUM) AND RHINELAND PROVINCES 1795, Paris, BAVARIA, ATLANTIC OCEAN, FRANCE, AUSTRIAN EMPIRE, Geneva, HELVETIC REPUBLIC 1798, Bordeaux, SAVOY 1792, Turin, Milan, VENICE, Campoformio, Lyons, PIEDMONT, Venice, CISALPINE REPUBLIC 1797, Genoa, OTTOMAN EMPIRE, Marseilles, NICE 1792, TUSCANY, ROMAN REPUBLIC 1798, ADRIATIC SEA, SPAIN, CORSICA, NAPOLEON'S INVASION OF EGYPT 1798, Rome, PARTHENOPIAN REPUBLIC 1799, SARDINIA, Naples, 200 miles, 200 kilometers, MEDITERRANEAN SEA, SICILY

MAP 16.3   FRANCE AND ITS SISTER REPUBLICS

This map shows the expansion of France and the creation of its sister republics between 1792 and 1798. ■ **Notice** the dates of annexation and creation of sister republics. **Consider** who was most threatened by these developments. ■ **Notice** the arrow indicating Napoleon's invasion of Egypt in 1798. **Why** might Napoleon have moved against British interests in Egypt rather than Great Britain itself?

reports from Egypt and emphasizing the expedition's scientific explorations and exotic discoveries (he sent 165 scholars to Egypt in hopes that they might help him control the country) as well as its few victories.

Meanwhile, matters took a bad turn for France's government, the Directory. The expedition to Egypt prompted Great Britain, Austria, and Russia to join in a new coalition. These allies inflicted defeats on French armies and threatened to invade France itself. Eyeing this foreign threat, as well as bankruptcy, insubordinate army commanders, and disruptions in the countryside, rival factions within France vied for power. One conservative faction, led by a member of the Directory, Abbé Sieyès, concluded that a coup d'état would gain them needed control over the government. This situation provided Napoleon with another opportunity to advance his career. Sieyès and others conspired with him to overthrow the Directory on November 9, 1799 (18 Brumaire). The conspirators expected that the 30-year-old military hero would make a popular figurehead representing authority, and they would actually govern the country. As events would prove, they were very mistaken.

Coup d'état

NAPOLEON CONSOLIDATES CONTROL

Napoleon quickly outmaneuvered his partners. He had a new "short and obscure" constitution drawn up and accepted by members of the old legislature. In a national plebiscite where people could vote to accept or reject the new constitution, the French overwhelmingly approved it (though the government falsified the results to give it a more lopsided victory). As one observer explained, people "believed quite sincerely that Bonaparte . . . would save us from the perils of anarchy." Napoleon named himself "first consul" and assumed the powers necessary to rule—all with the ready support of the Senate. The remaining two consuls, as well as voters and the handpicked legislative bodies they thought they were electing, had only minimal powers. Next, Napoleon placed each of France's eighty-three departments under the control of a powerful agent of the central government—the *prefect*. Thus at both the local and the national levels, Napoleon ended meaningful democracy in France.

First consul

With the touch of a skilled authoritarian politician, Napoleon proceeded to gather support. He welcomed former Old Regime officials as well as moderate Jacobins into his service. By approving the end of serfdom and feudal privileges as well as all transfers of property that had occurred during the Revolution, he won favor with the peasantry. He gained the backing of the middle class by affirming the property rights and formal equality before the law that adult males had secured during the Revolution. He welcomed back to France

all but the most reactionary émigrés, most of whom had come from France's old aristocracy. The educated elite admired Napoleon for patronizing science and inviting leading scientists to join him in his government. To deter opposition, he created a secret police force, suppressed independent political organizations, and censored newspapers and artistic works. Finally, for those who displayed the highest loyalty and the most spectacular achievements (particularly in the military), he created the prestigious Legion of Honor.

Keenly aware of the political and social importance of religion—once calling religion "excellent stuff for keeping the common people quiet"— Napoleon made peace with the pope and ended the ten-year struggle between the French revolutionary governments and the Roman Catholic church. Their Concordat (formal agreement) of 1801 declared the Catholic religion the religion of the majority of the French people, but ensured freedom for Protestants. Later, Napoleon granted new rights to Jews, as well. Under his rule, the clergy was paid by the state and required to take an oath of allegiance to the state. Confiscated Catholic Church property was not returned.

The Concordat

REFORMING FRANCE

Napoleon followed up this pattern of blending compromise and authoritarian control with a remaking of France's legal, financial, and educational systems. The Civil Code of 1804 (the Napoleonic Code), for example, generally affirmed the Enlightenment-inspired legal reforms that the early French revolutionaries had sought. Progressives throughout Europe and even overseas would embrace this law code. For men, the code guaranteed legal equality, careers open to talent, and paternal authority over women, children, and property. In particular, it catered to middle-class employers by forbidding strikes and trade unions. At the same time, the code rejected many of the rights and liberties gained in 1789 as well as the more radical measures enacted after 1792. For women, the code represented a clear defeat. Rather than granting them legal or political equality, it gave power over property and the family to men and left married women legally and economically dependent on their husbands. The code also severely restricted the right to divorce, particularly for women. These measures reflected Napoleon's belief that women belonged in the home and that their concerns should center on domestic life.

Napoleonic Code

To stabilize France financially, Napoleon established the Bank of France to handle governmental funds and issue money. To promote economic health, he involved the state in a huge

Finance and education

FIGURE 16.10

Jacques-Louis David, *Napoleon's Coronation*.

However, two problems lurked beneath this promising exterior. First, Napoleon had an insatiable craving for public recognition and legitimacy. He satisfied this need at least partially with a bold move in 1804. That year, with the approval of the Senate and the French people in a lopsided plebiscite, Napoleon formally established France as an empire—and then crowned himself emperor.

As Jacques-Louis David's painting in Figure 16.10 reveals, Napoleon controlled all aspects of the coronation. Although he invited Pope Pius VII (seated behind him) to preside over the ceremony, it is Napoleon—ever the self-made man—who takes matters into his own hands. As splendidly dressed spectators look on, Napoleon raises a crown, preparing to place it on the kneeling Josephine's head to make her his empress. He has already boldly crowned himself emperor with a laurel wreath that alludes back to Roman emperors and Charlemagne, crowned emperor by the pope in the year 800. Aware of the importance of details, Napoleon had shrewdly instructed his ardent supporter David to paint the reluctant pope raising his hand in blessing.

The new emperor then elevated members of his family to princely status and granted new titles and honors to his wealthy supporters who had proved themselves, usually as officers on the battlefield.

program of public works, supported certain industries, and established price controls. To restructure educational institutions, he created a long-lasting system of secondary schools tied to the University of France and infused it with patriotic trappings. Napoleon also actively supported scientific research and rewarded surgeons, chemists, mathematicians, and other scientists with governmental posts and honors.

CREATING THE EMPIRE

Napoleon's rise to power hinged on his ability to remove external military threats as well as internal disruptions. This he managed by crossing the Alps in 1800 with a French army to crush the Austrian forces in Northern Italy and knock Austria out of the coalition of powers opposing France. Next, he made peace with Russia and persuaded Great Britain to sign the Peace of Amiens in 1802.

In the first five years of his rule, Napoleon scored spectacular successes. Law and order reigned at home, and he secured peace abroad. Public morale was high. Napoleon's vision of a centralized, paternalistic state that would make France the model of a modern nation through reason, authority, and science seemed almost real.

KEY DATES

THE AGE OF NAPOLEON

1796–1797	The Italian campaign
1798	The Egyptian campaign
1799	Napoleon's coup d'état
1801	Concordat with the Roman Catholic Church
1802	Peace of Amiens
1804	Napoleonic Code
	Napoleon crowned emperor
1805	Battle of Austerlitz
1807	Treaty with Russia
	Napoleon's Continental System imposed
1812	Invasion of Russia
1814	Napoleon exiled to Elba
1815	Battle of Waterloo

Later, he divorced Empress Josephine, whose relationship with Napoleon became more formal than intimate, and who failed to produce a male heir. He married Princess Marie-Louise of Austria, giving him a stronger image as legitimate royalty.

In addition to his hunger for formal recognition, Napoleon had a second problem. He had risen to prominence and power through his military conquests. "I am an upstart soldier," he admitted. "My domination will not survive the day when I cease to be strong, and therefore feared." *Need for conquests* These martial ties would push Napoleon to seek still greater conquests on the battlefield. "Conquest has made me what I am; only conquest can maintain me." Yet even when battle after battle brought him victory, war also came at great cost and risk.

WAR AND CONQUEST

The interests of Great Britain and Napoleon clashed too often for their peace to last long. By the end of 1803, the two countries were again *Battle of Trafalgar* at war, and by 1805, the ambitious Napoleon had to battle a new coalition of European powers. That year, he marched to the English Channel with a huge army and seemed poised to invade England. Before him stretched 24 miles of water and British sea power. To overcome those barriers, Napoleon amassed a combined French and Spanish fleet and plotted his next move. Alert for any opportunity, he suddenly turned his army eastward, surrounded an exposed Austrian army, and on October 20, forced it to surrender. The next day, however, England's Admiral Nelson sighted the combined French and Spanish fleets off Cape Trafalgar on the southwest point of Spain and annihilated them. Although Nelson perished early in the battle, his navy's victory saved Great Britain from the menace of an invasion and limited Napoleon's conquests to the European continent.

On land, Napoleon fared much better—in fact, he seemed invincible. His success stemmed in part from his independent units that could move quickly and then join in a mass attack. Equally important, he possessed an unusually talented officer corps and enjoyed the loyalty of a large number of nationalistic citizen-soldiers. The strategy of sending a mass of spirited soldiers in a column of attack aimed at dividing opposing forces served Napoleon well. Fighting alongside his troops, he cleverly used these military strengths to crush the combined forces of Austria and Russia at Austerlitz in December 1805. Prussia made the mistake of declaring war on France after it was too late to join the Austrians and Russians. As the French troops moved east through villages and cities, people reported *Military strengths*

how "the dreadful cry was heard in the streets, 'the French are coming!'" Napoleon virtually obliterated the Prussian forces. When the Russian troops began massing again, Napoleon moved eastward and decisively defeated them in the great Battle of Friedland (1807). Although the resulting Treaties of Tilsit (July 1807) were technically between equals, they actually left Russia only a junior partner to France. France commanded the greater resources, and Napoleon expected to have his way on the European continent.

Despite all these triumphs, Napoleon still could not find a way to get his troops across the Channel to attack England directly. He finally hit on an alternative plan—the Continental *The Continental System* System—that he hoped would destroy his rival's commercial economy by preventing the importation of British goods into continental Europe. To implement the plan, he ordered a continent-wide blockade against British ships, confiscated all British goods, and set French privateers upon British merchant ships. Britain responded with new regulations that amounted to its own blockade on shipping to continental ports. Now the naval war between France and Britain affected even neutral states, including the United States.

By 1810, Napoleon had redrawn the map of Europe (Map 16.4) and the political balance of power. He had dismembered Prussia and abolished the Holy Roman Empire. Now most *The new European order* German states were unified into the Confederation of the Rhine. Holland and the Italian peninsula had come under French control. Spain was a dependent state, and Austria, Russia, and a diminished Prussia had become reluctant allies of France. Only Great Britain and still-defiant parts of Spain and Portugal remained active opponents.

In those areas annexed to France, Napoleon ruled directly and imposed all of France's laws and institutions. In dependent states, he installed French-controlled governments to rule with the help of local elites. He usually made members of his family monarchs in these areas—his brother Louis, king of Holland, his brother Jérôme, king of Westphalia, and his brother Joseph, king of Spain. As Document 16.3 suggests, some of France's "enlightened" institutions and policies were introduced. These usually included constitutional government, equality before the law, careers open to talent, the Napoleonic Civil Code, civil rights to Jews and other religious minorities, and the creation of similar public works improvements—schools, roads, bridges—that Napoleon supported in France. Wherever Napoleon conquered, except Russia, he abolished serfdom. At the same time, the reforms included tax increases and conscription quotas to help finance and provide soldiers for Napoleon's armies.

THINKING ABOUT GEOGRAPHY

Legend:
- French Empire
- Satellite Kingdoms
- Allies of Napoleon
- Hostile to Napoleon
- Confederation of the Rhine Boundary
- Major battles

MAP 16.4 EUROPE, 1810

This map shows Europe at the height of Napoleon's empire. ■ **Notice** the extent of area Napoleon controlled—directly and indirectly. **Where** would you expect Napoleon's rule to exert the greatest impact? **What** geographical problems did Napoleon face trying to control his empire? ■ **Locate** those areas that remained hostile to Napoleon. **How** might geography help explain why those areas retained their independence?

THE IMPACT OVERSEAS

Naturally, Napoleon's policies exerted their greatest impact in Europe, but other areas—particularly in the Western Hemisphere and the British Empire—also felt the effects of his rule and expansion. In the Caribbean, Napoleon failed to put down the black population's struggle for independence and freedom in Saint Domingue (Haiti) (see page 519). He also

cut his losses in North America and sold Louisiana to the United States.

The Napoleonic Wars had dramatic consequences in the colonies of Spain and Portugal in the Americas. Discontent with colonial rule had been mounting during the eighteenth century. In particular, the colonists resented the economic and political restrictions imposed by the "mother" country. As the native-born "Creoles" began to outnum-

■ DOCUMENT 16.3

Napoleon Issues an Imperial Decree at Madrid

When Napoleon scored military successes outside of France, he demanded more from the conquered peoples than subservience to French rule. Typically, he applied some of the same reforms and institutions of the French Revolution to the conquered lands. This policy is shown in the following decree, issued from Napoleon's imperial camp at Madrid on December 4, 1808. ■ **What** *benefits might Napoleon have been hoping for by issuing this decree?* ■ ***In what ways*** *are these measures consistent with the spirit of the French Revolution?*

To date from the publication of the present decree, feudal rights are abolished in Spain.

All personal obligations, all exclusive fishing rights and other rights of similar nature on the coast or on rivers and streams, all feudal monopolies (*banalités*) of ovens, mills, and inns are suppressed. It shall be free to every one who shall conform to the laws to develop his industry without restraint.

The tribunal of the Inquisition is abolished, as inconsistent with the civil sovereignty and authority.

The property of the Inquisition shall be sequestered and fall to the Spanish state, to serve as security for the bonded debt.

Considering that the members of the various monastic orders have increased to an undue degree and that, although a certain number of them are useful in assisting the ministers of the altar in the administration of the sacraments, the existence of too great a number interferes with the prosperity of the state, we have decreed and do decree as follows:

The number of convents now in existence in Spain shall be reduced to a third of their present number. This reduction shall be accomplished by uniting the members of several convents of the same order into one.

All regular ecclesiastics who desire to renounce the monastic life and live as secular ecclesiastics are at liberty to leave their monasteries. . . .

In view of the fact that the institution which stands most in the way of the internal prosperity of Spain is that of the customs lines separating the provinces, we have decreed and do decree what follows:

To date from January 1 next, the barriers existing between the provinces shall be suppressed. The custom houses shall be removed to the frontiers and there established.

Source: James Harvey Robinson, ed., *Readings in European History,* vol. II (Boston: Ginn, 1904), p. 512.

---

ber the Spanish- and Portuguese-born settlers, the ties of loyalty to home countries weakened. The successful revolt of the English colonies to the north and the birth of the United States also impressed colonial liberals and intellectuals. Spanish colonists' attachment to Spain faltered further when Napoleon overthrew the Spanish king and placed his own brother, Joseph Bonaparte, on the throne. By 1810, many colonists were in open revolt.

Revolt in Latin America

Over the next ten years, Spain struggled to regain its colonies. In 1814, Argentina drove off a Spanish army and won its independence. Elsewhere, Simón Bolívar (1783–1830), known as "The Liberator," led the fight for independence against Spanish forces. Figure 16.11 shows him in heroic pose, probably to symbolize his military campaigns in Venezuela, Colombia, Ecuador, and Peru. The painting is modeled on a well-known work by David that portrays Napoleon leading his troops across the Alps. Bolívar points upward while a wind blows at his back—a traditional posture of victory.

As Map 16.5 shows, by 1822 almost all of Spain's colonies, as well as Portugal's huge colony of Brazil, had gained their independence. Nevertheless,

■ FIGURE 16.11

Simón Bolívar.

THINKING ABOUT GEOGRAPHY

areas of influence. Sea power enabled it to capture and take over French and Dutch colonies in Africa, Asia, and America. In addition, England began trading more briskly with South America. However, one of England's strategies—its counterblockade of Napoleonic Europe—had a major, unintended drawback. By enforcing the blockade, England ended up embroiled in the War of 1812 with the United States. That war, in turn, spread farther north when the United States attempted to invade Britain's loyal colonies in Canada.

In the decades that followed, states from Asia to the Americas that reformed their own governments and laws would look to the Napoleonic Code and adopt parts of it. In this way, some of the ideals of the Enlightenment and the French Revolution would be translated through the Napoleonic Code to many areas around the globe.

Adopting the Napoleonic Code

MAP 16.5   **LATIN AMERICA AFTER INDEPENDENCE**

This map shows that within a twelve-year period Spain and Portugal lost most of their possessions in the Americas. ■ **Notice** that in several areas there are differences between the date of independence from the colonial power and the date of separation from other states. **What** might these differences mean? ■ **Locate** those territories still held by European nations. **What** might differentiate these territories from those that gained their independence?

DECLINE AND FALL

Napoleon had an even more ambitious vision—to rule Europe as the head of a single imperial administration. Before he could make his vision real, new problems plagued him. Even at the height of his power, Napoleon and his empire suffered from dangerous weaknesses. Between 1808 and 1812, three crucial vulnerabilities—flawed policies, resistance to his rule, and overextension of his military reach—would intensify and erode Napoleon's power.

The Continental System that Napoleon devised to cripple England economically was not working well enough. With control of the sea, Great Britain applied an effective counterblockade against the Napoleon-dominated Continent. Port cities and industries relying on external commerce suffered. Smuggling further weakened the system. In some areas, such as Holland and Russia, the restrictions of the system became a constant source of irritation and resentment against the French. In the long run, the Continental System stiffened opposition to Napoleon on the Continent and failed to weaken England. Again and again, that island nation would finance Napoleon's enemies.

Flawed policies

Bolívar's and other's hopes for unity within Spain's old colonies soon faded as various South American regions began dividing into separate states. Most of these new states would adopt the Napoleonic Code as their basis of civil law, and oppressive white minorities would rule them for many years.

Napoleon's dominance over the European continent inspired England to step up its overseas expansion and tighten control over its own colonies and

Francisco de Goya, *The Executions of the Third of May, 1808*

■ FIGURE 16.12

This 1814 painting by the great Spanish artist Francisco de Goya shows French soldiers executing Spanish citizens in retaliation for riots against French troops who had occupied Madrid. ■ **What** information might Goya have been trying to convey to Spanish viewers? ■ **What** does this suggest about the French occupation of Spain? ■ **What** associations might viewers have to the central figure in white? ■ **Why** might Goya have decided to paint the sky over the monastery ink-black?

People across Europe had other reasons besides the Continental System to resist Napoleon's rule. In the wake of France's conquering armies, a new national spirit developed among many subject peoples. In Spain, for example, Napoleon had no sooner placed his brother Joseph on the Spanish throne when his unwilling subjects rose up against him. The painting in Figure 16.12 by the influential Spanish artist Francisco de Goya depicts the popular resistance in Spain to the Napoleonic occupation and the reprisals that resulted.

Growing resistance

Here, in a night scene on May 3, 1808, a firing squad of anonymous French soldiers brutally executes citizens in retaliation for riots against French troops in Madrid. The magnitude of the French atrocity is emphasized by the central figure, who resembles a crucified Christ about to be shot. Monks and commoners, selected at random for execution, surround the man at the center, and the bodies of those already executed lie scattered on the bloody earth around him. Goya, who painted this scene six years after the actual event, intended the work as a statement against the evils of war.

The Madrid rebellion and reprisals by Napoleon's soldiers inspired other Spanish uprisings and organized resistance against French troops in the years to come. Larger French armies, even when led by Napoleon himself, managed only limited success against the hit-and-run guerrilla tactics used by the Spanish. England took advantage of the situation by sending supplies and troops to Spain under the duke of Wellington (1769–1852), the British commander who would plague Napoleon's forces to the end. Spain became a running abscess that drained Napoleon's military strength.

In Prussia, similar national sentiments encouraged the government—partly in secret—to modernize its army and civil institutions in preparation for liberation from France. In Austria, the government again declared war on Napoleon in a premature effort to free itself from subservience to the French emperor. In Holland, opposition to Napoleon's policies ran so strong that in 1810 he had to annex the country to France to bring it under control. All this resistance drained French forces and raised the specter of open revolt at the least opportunity.

Napoleon himself created that opportunity by overextending his imperial reach. Successes on the battlefield added to his growing dreams of *Overextension* creating an empire ruled from Paris that would encompass all of Europe. Russia, already chafing against the commercial restrictions of the Continental System and harboring its own ambitions for expansion in eastern Europe, stood as the main barrier to Napoleon's dreams. In 1812, these conflicting ambitions soured the alliance between Russia and France. *Invasion of Russia* Against the advice of his closest associates, Napoleon decided to invade Russia. Amassing an immense army of more than 600,000, he plunged into the vastness of Russia. Half of his troops, however, were unenthusiastic conscripts from dependent states. The Russian army retreated into the interior of their huge country, following a scorched-earth policy and luring Napoleon ever farther from his base of supplies. "We believed that once in Russia, we need do nothing but forage—which, however, proved to be an illusion. . . . All the villages were already stripped before we could enter," wrote Jakob Walter, a German conscript in Napoleon's army. One of Napoleon's aides explained the deepening problem: "We were in the heart of inhabited Russia and yet we were like a vessel without a compass in the midst of a vast ocean,

knowing nothing of what was happening around us." At Borodino, the Russians turned and made a stand. In one of the bloodiest battles of the nineteenth century—taking a toll of more than 80,000 casualties—the two armies fought until the Russians withdrew.

The French army may have won the battle, but it failed to destroy Russia's forces. In September, Napoleon's Grand Army, weakened by battlefield losses and even more so by hunger, fatigue, and disease, finally entered Moscow. Tsar Alexander I, however, refused to capitulate. The future looked even worse for the French when a fire destroyed much of Moscow, leaving the invaders without enough shelter or supplies to ride out the notorious Russian winter. "Here in the white country we'll all have to die of hunger," wrote Hohann Wärncke, a German soldier in Napoleon's army. Napoleon began his retreat, but too late. The winter caught his forces overburdened with loot. Tens of thousands of them froze, starved, or succumbed to disease. Russian Cossacks, riding out of the blizzards, cut down or captured thousands more. Many of Napoleon's men surrendered to Russian forces. Of the original 600,000 who marched into Russia, fewer than 100,000 struggled home.

Napoleon himself was able to dash back to France. Behind him, one nation after another, aided by British money, joined the Russians in a war of liberation. Back home, Napoleon raised new conscripts for his army and again *Defeat at Leipzig* rushed them eastward. At Leipzig in central Germany, in October 1813, allied armies at last decisively defeated Napoleon. The next year, the allies entered Paris and exiled Napoleon to the island of Elba, off the coast of Italy.

Napoleon still had some fight left in him. While the allies squabbled over the peace settlement and discontent weakened France's new government under Louis XVIII, Napoleon escaped back to France. "Soldiers! In exile I heard your voice," he announced. "Now I have landed [in France]." He quickly raised yet another army from the remains of his old, still loyal supporters. However he was finally defeated in June 1815 by British and Prussian forces *Waterloo* at Waterloo in Belgium. This time his captors imprisoned him on the bleak island of St. Helena in the South Atlantic. "Posterity will do me justice," he wrote while in exile. "The truth will be known; and the good I have done will be compared with the faults I have committed." Six years later, Napoleon died, probably of stomach cancer.

SUMMARY

In 1815, a king from the old house of Bourbon again ruled France. Many aristocrats and royalists hoped to turn back the clock to the days before 1789, when they enjoyed unchallenged power and prestige. However, too much had changed. The Revolution had destroyed a French monarchy based on the divine right of kings. French aristocrats might still boast impressive titles, but the revolutionaries and Napoleon had secured legal equality for French men, if not women. Members of the middle class, though no longer enjoying the control they had exercised during the revolutionary years, would not relinquish the opportunities for position and prestige that they had gained. The peasantry, which had played such an important role during the early months of the Revolution, would never again be burdened by the traditional dues and services they once owed to lords. Finally, the Catholic Church had forever lost the lands and position it had once possessed before the Revolution.

Napoleon's connection to the Revolution was contradictory. He subverted key elements of the Revolution by removing the substance from representative institutions and eliminating freedom of speech and press. On the other hand, he preserved other elements of the Revolution by affirming the end of feudalism, protecting the rights of property, and ensuring equality before the law for men; through his conquests, he spread the ideas and institutions of the Revolution beyond France's borders. When he maximized the political and military power of the state by rationalizing the government, he acted like an eighteenth-century enlightened despot.

Finally, the French Revolution and Napoleon created two potent, long-lasting images. First, people had learned that a popular revolution could topple the government and social order of even the most powerful country. This image would inspire revolutionaries and unnerve those representing the status quo for decades to come. Second, Westerners also saw in Napoleon a nationalistic, charismatic leader who could suddenly seize power and exert his will with ease. This compelling image would inspire other individuals who envisioned themselves as potential Napoleons. Perhaps even more important, it would seduce people who yearned for easy, decisive solutions to complex problems.

After 1815, the old forces of order tried desperately to reassert their control. Although they scored some temporary successes, the ideas and institutions of the Revolution, spread by the armies of the French Republic and Napoleon, had taken root permanently in France and beyond its borders. The French Revolution had become a watershed event, and those who ignored it did so at peril.

KEY TERMS

Tennis Court Oath, p. 507

Bastille, p. 508

Declaration of Rights of Man and Citizen, p. 509

Civil Constitution of the Clergy, p. 511

sans-culottes, p. 512

Jacobins, p. 513

Committee of Public Safety, p. 517

levée en masse, p. 518

Thermidorian reaction, p. 520

Directory, p. 521

Napoleonic Code, p. 523

Continental System, p. 525

REVIEW, ANALYZE, AND ANTICIPATE

REVIEW THE PREVIOUS CHAPTERS
Chapter 14—"A New World of Reason and Reform"—revealed how Enlightenment ideas challenged traditional values and institutions in the West. Chapter 15—"Competing for Power and Wealth"—followed the battles of Western powers over land, position, and commerce as well as the economic and social changes affecting eighteenth-century life in the West.

1. *In what ways were Enlightenment ideas reflected in the values and reforms of the French Revolution?*

2. *Do you think the French Revolution conformed to or contradicted the main political trends of the eighteenth century?*

3. *In what ways did Napoleon embody the eighteenth-century trend toward "enlightened absolutism?"*

ANALYZE THIS CHAPTER
Chapter 16—"Overturning the Political and Social Order"—examines the great upheaval in France that shocked and transformed the West.

1. *Analyze the roles of France's aristocracy, bourgeoisie, peasantry, and urban workers in causing the French Revolution.*

2. *What might Louis XVI have done to keep his throne?*

3. *Why do you think the Revolution turned more radical, resulting in the establishment of a republic and leading to the Reign of Terror?*

4. *How do you explain Napoleon's rise? Was his rise a logical consequence of revolutionary events?*

5. *Analyze Napoleon's accomplishments. Do you think they were worth the costs?*

ANTICIPATE THE NEXT CHAPTER
In Chapter 17—"Factories, Cities, and Families in the Industrial Age"—the industrial revolution and its accompanying social changes will be examined.

1. *With the industrial revolution beginning in Britain at about the same period as the French Revolution on the continent, in what ways should this period be considered a watershed ushering in the modern era?*

BEYOND THE CLASSROOM

"A GREAT FERMENT": TROUBLE BREWING IN FRANCE

Chartier, Roger. *The Cultural Origins of the French Revolution*. Translated by Lydia G. Cochrane. Durham, NC: Duke University Press, 1991. Examines the developments that contributed to the cultural destabilization of the Old Regime.

Doyle, William. *The Oxford History of the French Revolution*. Oxford: Oxford University Press, 2003. A thorough, highly respected survey.

Furet, François. *Interpreting the French Revolution*. Cambridge: Cambridge University Press, 1981. An important book that refutes the traditional theory of the French Revolution as a bourgeois revolution.

Landes, Joan. *Women and the Public Sphere in the Age of the French Revolution*. Ithaca, NY: Cornell University Press, 1988. Explores the historical evolution of the male-oriented public sphere and the consignment of women to the private realm of domesticity.

Lefebvre, Georges. *The Coming of the French Revolution*. Translated by R.R. Palmer. Princeton, NJ: Princeton University Press, 1947. A landmark analysis of the social structure of prerevolutionary France and the opening phase of the Revolution.

Schama, Simon. *Citizens: A Chronicle of the French Revolution*. New York: Random House, 1990. A popular, well-written narrative of events.

THE CONSTITUTIONAL MONARCHY: ESTABLISHING A NEW ORDER

Andress, David. *The French Revolution and the People*. New York: Continuum, 2004. A book that focuses on the impact of the Revolution on ordinary people.

Hunt, Lynn. Politics, *Culture and Class in the French Revolution*. Berkeley, CA: University of California Press, 1984. Focuses on the political culture of language, dress, and festivals created by the revolutionaries.

Jones, P. *The Peasantry in the French Revolution*. New York: Cambridge University Press, 1988. Examines the role of the peasantry in the revolutionary events from 1789–1799.

TO THE RADICAL REPUBLIC AND BACK

Higonnet, Patrice. *Goodness Beyond Virtue: Jacobins During the French Revolution*. Cambridge: Harvard University Press, 1998. A study of the Jacobins, their ideas, and the Terror.

Hufton, Olwen. *Women and the Limits of Citizenship in the French Revolution*. Toronto: University of Toronto Press, 1992. Analyzes attitudes toward women during the French Revolution that led to female exclusion from the rights of citizenship.

Kennedy, Emmet. *A Cultural History of the French Revolution*. New Haven, CT: Yale University Press, 1989. Examines the role of the arts, clubs, and intellectual institutions during the Revolution.

Lyons, Martyn. *France Under the Directory*. New York: Cambridge University Press, 1975. A brief yet wide-ranging survey of the Directory period.

Palmer, Robert R. *Twelve Who Ruled: The Committee of Public Safety During the Terror*. Princeton, NJ: Princeton University Press, 1970. A well-written account of the Terror and its leaders.

NAPOLEON BONAPARTE

Broers, Michael. *Europe under Napoleon, 1799–1815*. London: Edward Arnold, 2002. Examines how Napoleon's rule affected people in conquered nations.

Connelly, Owen. *Blundering to Glory: Napoleon's Military Campaigns*. Wilmington, DE: Scholarly Resources, 1987. An assessment of Napoleon's military strategy and achievements.

Lyons, Martyn. *Napoleon Bonaparte and the Legacy of the French Revolution*. New York: St. Martin's Press, 1994. A solid reevaluation of Napoleon and his legacy.

Schom, Alan. *Napoleon Bonaparte: A Life*. New York: HarperCollins, 1998. An up-to-date, critical biography of Napoleon.

www.mhhe.com/sherman3

- Unfamiliar words? See our Glossary at the back of the book for pronunciation and definitions.

- Need help studying? See our web page for map exercises, practice quizzes, and additional study resources.

- Need help writing a paper? Access hundreds of primary documents, maps, images, and a guide to writing history papers on our Primary Source Investigator site at **www.mhhe.com/psi.**

J.M.W. TURNER, *DUDLEY, WORCESTERSHIRE*, 1832

In his 1832 watercolor of Dudley, Worcestershire, a city of about 23,000 in 1831 in the heart of Britain's industrial Black Country, British painter J.M.W. Turner shows the transformation of old towns and traditional landscapes wrought by the industrial revolution. In the foreground on one of the canals that crisscrossed this region, barges laden with cargo—typically coal for fuel, iron ore for smelting, and lime for flux, all plentiful in the region and used in the production of iron—dock for unloading and wait to receive goods from factories along the banks. The vessel at the right carries hoops of sheet iron destined for one of Dudley's finishing shops. The numerous mills' chimneys and coal-fired hearths produce dense clouds of polluting smoke that dim the city and encrust it with soot. On the right, a white and orange glow bursts from iron furnaces. In the background, the church steeples and battlements of a ruined castle rise into the moonlighted sky, indicating how the old town has had to adapt to the new realities of modern industry where work never seems to stop. Charles Dickens (1812–1870), who visited the region during the 1830s, would describe it as "cheerless," a "mournful place" filled with "tall chimneys, crowding on each other and presenting that endless repetition of the same dull, ugly form," chimneys that "pour out their plague of smoke, obscured the light, and made foul the melancholy air."

CHAPTER 17

FACTORIES, CITIES, AND FAMILIES IN THE INDUSTRIAL AGE

THE INDUSTRIAL REVOLUTION, 1780–1850

STUDY	■ Causes of the industrial revolution ■ New markets, machines, and power ■ The spread of industrialization ■ The benefits and burdens of industrialization ■ Life in the growing cities ■ Public health and medicine ■ Family ideals and realities.
NOTICE	The social consequences of industrialization.

In 1828, a German visitor described Britain as a land where the "new creations springing into life every year bordered on the fabulous." These creations were the machines and factories of the **industrial revolution** that were replacing agriculture and handicrafts as the basis of the traditional economy. They turned industrial cities like Manchester into what the French writer Alexis de Tocqueville called "the greatest stream of human industry" that "flows out to fertilize the whole world."

However, this wave of industrial developments, which made Britain wealthy and envied, brought disturbing consequences in its wake: great swings of economic prosperity and depression and a new working class harnessed to the rhythm of machines. A British journal in 1826 spoke of a growing "accumulation of misery endured by thousands" in industrial areas. A few years later, the French consul in Edinburgh argued, "Who would want the prosperity of Liverpool and Manchester in France . . . beside these base miseries offered by manufacturing establishments?"

These "miseries" haunted not only the new factories and mines. Workers hoping for jobs crowded into unprepared cities. There, life for them as well as for middle-class employers, professionals, and shopkeepers was rapidly changing. In bad times, unemployment and business failures made urban life particularly harsh. In prosperous times, filth and disease still marked these cities. Here even the family, which for so long labored together as a cooperating unit of economic life, was shifting under the weight of new ideas and pressures. Western societies were entering the industrial age.

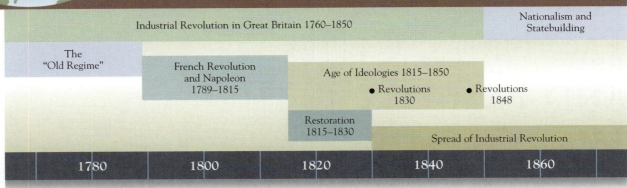

Industrial Revolution in Great Britain 1760–1850

Nationalism and Statebuilding

The "Old Regime"

French Revolution and Napoleon 1789–1815

Age of Ideologies 1815–1850

● Revolutions 1830

● Revolutions 1848

Restoration 1815–1830

Spread of Industrial Revolution

1780   1800   1820   1840   1860

THE INDUSTRIAL REVOLUTION BEGINS

IN THIS NEW ERA, BRITAIN led the way. There a middle-class couple such as Richard and Elizabeth Cadbury (see the Biography on pp. 560–561) might expect to work hard and see the cloth and dry goods store they opened in 1794 support them and their several children. Thirty-five years later their sons, Benjamin and John, had become wealthy retailers and manufacturers.

Others did not consider the industrial age such a boon. One railroad worker told of a day when two thousand of his coworkers lost their jobs: "They were all starving, the heap of them, or next door to it." This worker had recently injured his leg at work and was laid up for one month, living "all that time on charity; on what the chaps would come and give me. When I could get about again, the work was all stopped, and I couldn't get none to do. . . . I went to a lodginghouse in the Borough, and I sold all my things—shovel and grafting-tool and all, to have a meal of food. When all my things was gone, I didn't know where to go. . . . Now I'm dead beat, though I'm only twenty-eight next August."

Stories about successful merchants like the Cadburys and less fortunate laborers like this railroad worker give us a glimpse at the two faces of Britain's industrial revolution. Year by year, the work and home lives of these people and others changed only gradually. However, between the 1780s and 1850s—little more than a single lifetime—astonishing developments transformed economic and social life in Britain.

The scene pictured in Figure 17.1 captures some of what that transformation meant to people. In the foreground of this 1851 painting is a romanticized vision of nature and the countryside, featuring trees, bushes, rock formations, hills, and a road winding around a lake. On the left, a couple, perhaps enjoying a picnic, relax with their dog—all apparently at one with nature. In the distance looms Manchester, which between 1780 and 1851 grew from a small country town to a large, industrialized city. Manchester's numerous factory chimneys belch clouds of smoke into the air. The sense of contrast is striking: In the city, people grind out the new wealth of this civilization, all while enduring crowds and filth away from the imagined delights of nature and the rural life they once knew.

In the mid-eighteenth century, most British people had lived in the countryside. Women and men who laboriously spun fibers into thread and yarn and then wove it into cloth with the aid of only simple tools and handlooms barely noticed the few new machines that could quickly spin American cotton into thread and weave it into cloth by the thousands of yards. At the edges of forests where wood was available for smelting iron, most iron masters still forged metal using slow methods inherited from their ancestors. To transport their goods to markets, these people, like their predecessors from centuries back, relied on coaches drawn by horses over rutted dirt roads, and on wooden ships pushed by currents and winds across the seas. Steam engines, already present for several decades, were inefficient and rare outside of coal mines.

By 1850, things had changed dramatically. Over half of Britain's population, which had more than doubled during the period, now lived in cities. Cotton factories churned out hundreds of millions of yards of cloth that were sold throughout the world every year and were driving those who still made cloth the old way out of business. New mines, machines, and production techniques made vast quantities of iron

■ FIGURE 17.1

William Wyld, *View of Manchester*, 1851.

cheap to produce, easy to work, and available every-where. Railroads carried people and merchandise to their destinations quickly, inexpensively, and reliably. Recent generations of efficient coal-burning steam engines powered these factories, foundries, and rail-roads. Waves of inventions and innovations built on earlier breakthroughs cheapened production while improving quality. Entrepreneurs and business organizations applied these machines and production methods to other industries in Britain and elsewhere in the West. Although marked by periodic crises and downturns, a self-sustaining process of economic growth and technological change had been achieved and would continue through the decades after 1850.

What created this phenomenon—which French observers in the 1820s termed an "industrial revolution"—and why did it happen first in the West and particularly in Britain?

A BOOMING COMMERCIAL ECONOMY IN THE WEST

Why the industrial revolution emerged first in the West rather than in other civilizations such as China or India is difficult to say. Before 1500, Europeans enjoyed no fundamental advantages in how they produced goods over their Asian counterparts; in some areas, such as iron and steel production, they even lagged behind. Many qualities, such as intellectual traditions and politics, differentiated Eastern civilizations from the West and may help explain the early appearance of the industrial revolution in the West. However, the rise of commerce during the sixteenth, seventeenth, and eighteenth centuries distinguished the West economically. Civilizations elsewhere usually participated in this growing commerce only reluctantly. China, for example, may have produced luxury goods dearly desired by Westerners, but, except for gold and silver, the Chinese wanted little in trade from the West (see Global Connections on page 538). Moreover, the occupation of merchant had a low social status in China, further discouraging any potential bloom of commerce in that part of the world. In the West, however, the growth of commerce encouraged people to produce more agricultural and manufactured goods and sell them for a profit in the marketplace. Merchants and entrepreneurs became devoted to "buying low" and "selling high," thereby amassing more and more wealth. The growth of commerce helped create the potential markets, producers, entrepreneurs, and capitalists that would fuel the industrial revolution in the West.

The Western and non-Western worlds

Cross-Cultural Misunderstandings: China and Great Britain

CONSIDER
■ **Consider** the contrasting views about China held by the British and Chinese. **Notice** the British response to China's isolation.

As industrialization spread in England during the last decades of the eighteenth century, British merchants sought new markets across the globe for their manufactured goods. China constituted a huge potential market for trade. In 1776, the British economist Adam Smith concluded that China's home market was "perhaps in extent not much inferior to the market of all the different countries of Europe put together." Indeed, during the eighteenth century, China under the Qing (Ch'ing) dynasty enjoyed considerable peace, prosperity, and population growth. But the emperors had always limited European merchants' access to China. Moreover, the Qing, determined to minimize foreign influences on their society, imposed strict restrictions on Western commerce within China.

Eager to widen the opening to China, the East India Company persuaded the British government to send an experienced diplomat, Lord George Macartney, to China in 1792. There, Macartney presented a formal request from King George III for a lessening of trade restrictions. But Emperor Qianlong (Ch'ien Lung) (r. 1736–1796), a capable and humane ruler, rejected the request. In a letter to King George III, he stressed that China "possesses all things in prolific abundance and lacks no product within its own borders." Therefore, China had "no need to import manufactures of outside barbarians [Europeans] in exchange for our own produce." Clearly, in the emperor's mind, it was the British who "yearned after the blessings of our civilization" and not the reverse. Indeed, Qianlong expressed sympathy for the British, condemned as they were to "the lonely remoteness of your island, cut off from the world by intervening wastes of sea." He went on to lament the persistent desire of Christian missionaries for greater access to China. The Chinese had no need for these missionaries, he argued.

"Ever since the beginning of history, sage Emperors and wise rulers have bestowed on China a moral system [Confucianism] and inculcated a code, which from time immemorial has been religiously observed by the myriads of my subjects." The emperor ended his letter by denying all British requests for greater access to China. He also threatened to treat any future violations of his rules harshly: "Do not say that you were not warned in due time!"

Lord Macartney, in turn, criticized the Chinese. "Morality is a mere pretense in their practice, though a common topic of their discourse." As for science, the Chinese, he claimed, considered it a mere "intruder." However, Macartney admitted that China was "an old first-rate man of war, which a succession of vigilant officers has continued to keep afloat." And in the government as well as the family, he observed, authority was "usually exercised with kindness and indulgence."

In 1816, the British tried again, sending Lord Amherst on a similar mission to China. This effort, too, met with failure. However, British observers had even more positive things to say about China than Lord Macartney had. One official under Lord Amherst noted that the "lower orders of Chinese seem to me more neat and clean than any Europeans of the same class." Many other Western observers who traveled in China during the first half of the nineteenth century agreed with Robert Fortune's conclusion: "In no country in the world is there less real misery and want than in China."

By this time, however, China's population growth was outstripping its economic growth. The government struggled to cope with its people's needs, but poverty worsened. Local banditry rose and rebellions broke out with alarming frequency. The weakening Qing empire was losing its ability to meet the growing challenges from the British and the West.

BRITAIN'S UNIQUE SET OF ADVANTAGES

Commerce also helps explain why Britain industrialized first. During the sixteenth and seventeenth centuries, commercial activity in England intensified along with English sea power *Commercial vigor* and overseas holdings. In the eighteenth century, Britain became Europe's leading commercial and colonial power (see Chapter 15). Britain's economy efficiently turned out goods for export, and the island nation enjoyed considerable access to expanding markets—both internal, from its rapidly growing and relatively wealthy population, and external, from its colonies and established commercial connections.

Commercial vigor, however, is not enough to answer the question of why Britain led the industrial revolution. Other areas of Europe enjoyed advantages that would be important for industrialization. For example, during the first half of the eighteenth century, Holland's agriculture and financial institutions were second to none. France was the wealthiest nation in the West. Britain, however, boasted a unique combination of advantages that, when added to its commercial leadership, laid a solid foundation for the birth of the industrial revolution.

Water transportation—far cheaper and quicker than overland shipping—played a crucial role in moving the coal, iron, cloth, and machines pumped out by Britain's new factories and mines. Already crisscrossed with countless navigable rivers (see Map 17.1), Britain enhanced its natural internal transportation system even more by building an extensive network of canals after 1760.

Transportation

Certain raw materials—especially coal, iron, and cotton—also had an essential part in the island's industrialization. Britain's American colonies harvested large quantities of cotton. The British countryside not only contained plentiful deposits of coal, but they were often conveniently located near iron deposits where foundry workers used the two materials in the newer processes of smelting to make iron products.

Raw materials

An expanding population and a particularly large and mobile force of both skilled and unskilled workers gave Britain another advantage. Already less tied to villages than others in many parts of the continent, this class of rural laborers grew as waves of enclosures in the eighteenth century made many small farmers landless (see Chapter 15). These men and women could fill the rising demand for cheap industrial labor in the cities.

Labor

Britain had the capital to invest in industry for several reasons. First, its growing agricultural and commercial prosperity made it one of the wealthiest countries—per capita—in Europe. Second, it gained an unusual ability to amass and mobilize that wealth into capital for potential investment, thanks to the development of a national banking system. Third, unlike most of its continental competitors, Britain was long free of internal tariff barriers, had a uniform and stable monetary system, and—since the Glorious Revolution of 1688 (see Chapter 13)—had a government that sympathized with business interests. All this encouraged wealthy individuals and families to risk money on commerce and industry. Therefore, inventors, innovators, and those who saw an opportunity could more easily find the means to start an industrial enterprise in Britain than elsewhere in Europe.

Capital

Finally, and according to some analysts, most importantly, entrepreneurship—at the heart of industrialization—was more socially acceptable in England than elsewhere. Members of England's aristocratic families—especially younger sons left without inherited lands—often sought careers in commerce and manufacturing. Social barriers between them and the business-minded middle class were lower than elsewhere. More than in most European nations, British merchants and **entrepreneurs** occupied a strong, respected place in society. On the other hand, in France, for

Entrepreneurship

THINKING ABOUT GEOGRAPHY

Coal-producing Areas

Major Areas of Metal Goods Production, ca 1750

Canals Built between 1760 and 1800

Navigable rivers

MAP 17.1 EIGHTEENTH-CENTURY ENGLAND

This map shows England's system of navigable waterways and areas of coal and iron production in the eighteenth century. ■ **Consider** the advantages of England's natural resources for industrialization. **How** did the English add to those advantages during the second half of the eighteenth century?

example, most elites looked on commerce and industry as a means—often regrettable—to gain money to purchase office, estates, and aristocratic status; as soon as possible, French aristocrats usually left commerce or distanced themselves from their businesses.

In short, Britain had the most potential both to nurture and to take advantage of Europe's first industrial stirrings. Yet, what was it that finally transformed this potential into reality? Oddly, the crucial development came with advances in agriculture.

A REVOLUTION IN AGRICULTURE

The agricultural revolution, with its new crops, methods of rotating crops, breeding of animals, and enclosures of open fields, spread in Britain during the late seventeenth and eighteenth centuries (see Chapter 15). Production increased, as did profits for the large landowners who shipped their crops to markets near and far. Declining food prices enabled more British families to purchase manufactured goods such as shoes, knives, and cloth. As the agricultural revolution picked up speed, fewer and fewer people produced more and more food. The new, large-scale farmers grew crops and livestock to feed the growing number of people working in factories, digging in the mines, and building their lives in the cities. Moreover, these well-to-do, enterprising landowners could use their profits to invest in the many business and commercial opportunities becoming available.

By 1850, the majority of Britain's population no longer raised food or lived in the countryside. Most lived and worked in cities and factory towns. Whether people were better off in these urban centers is a question we will turn to later. For now, the stage was set for Britain's industrial revolution.

NEW MARKETS, MACHINES, AND POWER

As wealth increased and people moved away from subsistence farming toward the burgeoning urban centers, the demand for manufactured goods reached unheard-of levels. Inventors and entrepreneurs rushed to fill this demand, dreaming up new machines and designing novel manufacturing methods. The machines, gaining complexity almost every year, seemed like mechanical wonders. The methods of production transformed the workplace. Coal and steam provided all the power necessary to make these machines and production methods work. Manufactured goods poured forth, available to all with the money to purchase them.

THE RISING DEMAND FOR GOODS

The old methods of production—slow, unreliable, and costly—could not satisfy the rising clamor for manufactured goods (see pages 487–488). In fact, the population growth in Britain and Europe alone created an ever-expanding pool of potential customers for low-cost clothing, nails, pottery, knives, and so forth. Eager overseas buyers, particularly in the colonies, offered raw materials in return for Britain's manufactured goods. At home, Britain's own successful farmers and merchants added to the demand.

Between the middle decades of the eighteenth century and 1850, inventors and entrepreneurs introduced new machines and *Inventors and entrepreneurs* methods that began to satisfy these hungry markets. Most inventors were practical men who embodied the widespread British interest in devices, gadgets, and machines of all kinds and had more talent as curious tinkerers than as scientific thinkers. Industrial entrepreneurs were also practical. Sometimes inventors themselves, they more often used the new devices and processes invented by others. Entrepreneurs purchased machines, employed workers, ran factories and mines, and found the necessary capital and markets.

Some entrepreneurs were landowning aristocrats; others rose from rags to riches. Many were Protestant dissenters, such as Calvinists and Quakers, who had been discriminated against by the dominant Anglican Church. Denied careers in government, they jumped at the opportunities presented by commerce and industry. Most, however, came from the middle classes. They took advantage of journals that promoted new techniques and ideas, divided and re-divided the processes of production, and trained a work force unaccustomed to working with machines in factory conditions. Buying raw materials from both local and distant suppliers, they promoted their products to the public. Through their resourcefulness and sometimes outright greed, they pursued profits. Navigating a risky competitive environment, they often reinvested their profits in their shops and factories, buying new machines and boosting production. The story of how they took advantage of new markets in the early decades of the industrial revolution is a narrative of new developments in cotton, iron, and steam.

COTTON LEADS THE WAY

Changes in cotton production came first and with dramatic results. Before 1750, most thread and yarn was spun by women and woven into cloth by men who worked in rural cottages or small urban shops. Using only simple spinning wheels and handlooms, these laborers produced thread, yarn, and cloth of uneven quality. How much they produced was limited by many things—the supply of fiber, farmwork that took them away from their spinning and weaving, the wages paid by the entrepreneurs who organized much of this work, and, above all, the tools and methods they used.

In 1733, John Kay (1704–1764) invented a device called the flying shuttle, which doubled the speed at which cloth could be woven on a loom. The shuttle in turn, intensified the demand for thread.

Weaving and spinning

In the 1760s, James Hargreaves (d. 1778) invented the spinning jenny, which revolutionized thread production. By 1812, one spinner could produce as much cotton thread as 200 spinners had in 1760. Other inventions, such as Richard Arkwright's (1732–1792) water frame and Edmund Cartwright's (1743–1823) power loom, allowed weavers to turn cotton into cloth in tremendous quantities. Two American developments added to the acceleration in textile production: Eli Whitney's (1765–1825) cotton gin (1793), which efficiently removed seeds from raw cotton; and the expanding slave plantation system in the South. Indeed, British manufacturers' growing demand for cotton became an important force perpetuating slavery in the cotton-growing areas of the United States.

By 1850, British cotton manufacturers had boosted cloth production from less than 40 million yards per year during the 1780s to more than 2,000 million yards per year. Cotton had become hugely popular and, alone, accounted for some 40 percent of British exports.

IRON: NEW PROCESSES TRANSFORM PRODUCTION

Machines for the new cotton industry were just one source of a growing demand for iron. Armies needed guns and cannons; civilians needed nails and pans. Until the eighteenth century, British iron makers were limited by the island nation's dwindling forests, for they knew how to smelt iron ore only with charcoal, which came from wood. Even during the days of plentiful charcoal, ironworkers had only their own and their animals' muscle power with which to work the iron into usable forms. Most of this iron production came out of small family firms or homes of artisans.

In 1708, Abraham Darby discovered an efficient way to smelt iron with coal in a blast furnace. This

■ FIGURE 17.2

Philip James de Loutherbourg, *The Coalbrookdale Ironworks at Night*, 1801.

innovation would make the iron industry a key driver of the industrial revolution. By the end of the century, other new processes enabled iron makers to double production again and again. As suggested by Figure 17.2, foundry workers began using steam engines to operate smelting furnaces, drive forge hammers to shape the iron, and roll the iron into sheets. The Coalbrookdale ironworks became one of England's most important industrial centers, renowned for its production of pig iron and casting of cylinders for steam engines. In the center of Loutherbourg's painting, blistering flames and sulfurous clouds of smoke billow out from the coke hearth. To the right stand an engine house and a casting building. In the foreground, two dray horses haul a loaded cart along a road leading out from the ironworks. People standing along the road and to the left are dwarfed by the larger scene as well as the derelict industrial artifacts lying along the road. The painting suggests that the town—located in the rolling, wooded hills of central England—is being transformed into an industrial inferno. Ironworks such as these, with their tall, smoke-belching furnaces, were joining cotton factories as symbols of the industrial revolution.

Smelting with coal

THE STEAM ENGINE AND THE FACTORY SYSTEM

Both the cotton and the iron industries created ever higher demand for power. At the beginning of the eighteenth century, people had to rely on muscle,

■ FIGURE 17.3

François Bonhomme, *Workshop with Mechanical Sieves*, 1859.

wind, and water to supply the energy to do their work. Early mills used water power, which meant that their owners had to build them near waterfalls. A drought in the summer or a cold snap in the winter could threaten to dry up or freeze this essential power source.

The steam engine, first used in the early eighteenth century to pump water out of deepening coal mines, provided a solution and would become the industrial revolution's most important technological advance. Portable and easily controlled, the earliest models were nevertheless not yet efficient enough for widespread application. Over the course of the eighteenth century, inventors such as Thomas Newcomen (1663–1729) and James Watt (1736–1819) improved the power and efficiency of these engines. Watt, a skilled craftsman backed by the daring entrepreneur Matthew Boulton (1728–1809), worked for years on the engine, making several design changes and eventually converting the reciprocal motion of the piston into a rotary motion. Now steam engines could be used not only to pump coal mines but also to drive the other new machines of the day, such as powering bellows for iron forges, mills for grains, and looms for textiles. The steam engine came to symbolize the new industrial age.

Reliable power from steam engines also made it possible for entrepreneurs to locate factories away from water power sites and build even larger cotton, iron, and other factories. In huge buildings, entrepreneurs hoped to guard their industrial secrets and mold a new labor force. Hundreds of workers, who produced goods in a repetitive series of steps and specialized tasks, tended rows of machines. The **factory system** had emerged. "The principle of the factory system . . . is to substitute mechanical science for hand skill, and the partition of a process into its essential constituents, for the division or graduation of labor," explained Andrew Ure, a professor of applied science, in 1835 (see Document 17.1). As we will see, factories generated unprecedented wealth for their owners and investors, but brought new hardships for the people who toiled in them.

Figure 17.3 reveals the nature of the factory system. This realistic 1859 painting of a factory interior in France shows the mixture of raw materials (zinc ore), machines, and division of labor that epitomized factories in the industrial age. In the upper left and center, workers bring ore from the mines and dump it into machines for initial washing and processing. After the ore is split and sorted, workers shovel it

■ DOCUMENT 17.1

Andrew Ure Defends Industrial Capitalism

From the beginning, industrialization had its critics and defenders. Andrew Ure, a British doctor, was one of the most effective public advocates of industrial capitalism. In the following excerpt from his 1835 book The Philosophy of Manufacturers, *Ure focuses on the factory system and its consequences for workers.* ■ **What** *is the essence of the factory system?* ■ **How**, *according to Ure, does this system affect workers?*

In my recent tour, continued during several months, through the manufacturing districts, I have seen tens of thousands of old, young, and middle-aged of both sexes, many of them too feeble to get their daily bread by any of the former modes of industry, earning abundant food, raiment, and domestic accommodation, without perspiring at a single pore, screened meanwhile from the summer's sun and the winter's frost, in apartments more airy and salubrious than those of the metropolis, in which our legislative and fashionable aristocracies assemble. In those spacious halls the benignant power of steam summons around him his myriads of willing menials, and assigns to each the regulated task, substituting for painful muscular effort on their part, the energies of his own gigantic arm, and demanding in return only attention and dexterity to correct such little aberrations as casually occur in his workmanship. The gentle docility of this moving force qualifies it for impelling the tiny bobbins of the lace-machine with a precision and speed inimitable by the most dexterous hands, directed by the sharpest eyes. Hence, under its auspices, and in obedience to Arkwright's polity, magnificent edifices, surpassing far in number, value, usefulness, and ingenuity of construction, the boasted monuments of Asiatic, Egyptian, and Roman despotism, have, within the short period of fifty years, risen up in this kingdom, to show to what extent, capital, industry, and science may augment the resources of a state, while they meliorate the condition of its citizens. Such is the factory system, replete with prodigies in mechanics and political economy.

The principle of the factory system then is, to substitute mechanical science for hand skill, and the partition of a process into its essential constituents, for the division or graduation of labour among artisans. On the handicraft plan, labour more or less skilled, was usually the most expensive element of production— *Materiam superaba opus*; but on the automatic plan, skilled labour gets progressively superseded, and will, eventually, be replaced by mere overlookers of machines.

By the infirmity of human nature it happens that the more skilful the workman, the more self willed and intractable he is apt to become, and, of course, the less fit a component of a mechanical system, in which, by occasional irregularities, he may do great damage to the whole The grand object therefore of the modern manufacturer is through the union of capital and science, to reduce the task of his workpeople to the exercise of vigilance and dexterity,— faculties, when concentred to one process, speedily brought to perfection in the young. In the infancy of mechanical engineering, a machine-factory displayed the division of labour in manifold gradations—the file, the drill, the lathe, having each its different workmen in the order of skill: but the dexterous hands of the filer and driller are now superseded by the planing, the key-groove cutting, and the drilling machines; and those of the iron and brass turners by the self-acting slide-lathe.

Source: Andrew Ure, *The Philosophy of Manufacturers* (Charles Knight, 1835).

into large ovens to be melted down. Men, women, and children work together in this hot, noisy building; the men have the more authoritative and skilled jobs (a foreman sits in the rear to the left), while the women and children are assigned to sorting and splitting chunks of ore.

COAL: FUELING THE REVOLUTION

As the industrial revolution hit its stride, the demand for coal also intensified. Steam engines devoured coal as fuel. Iron makers required more and more coal to run their furnaces. Britain's doubling population needed coal to heat their homes.

People poured huge amounts of money and labor into digging mines, extracting the coal, and developing the roads, canals, and rails necessary to trans-

port the mineral to waiting customers. Coal not only fueled the industrial revolution; mining and manufacturing became so entwined that it was hard for people to think of one without the other.

RAILROADS: CARRYING INDUSTRIALIZATION ACROSS THE LAND

The advent of the railroad age brought everything together. In the eighteenth century, horses had pulled carts along rails radiating out from mines, hauled barges along the growing network of canals, and pulled carriages along roads. Only wind in the sails of ships could move heavy cargoes and passengers across the seas.

During the 1820s, as steam engines began to power ships, the British inventor George Stephenson

William Powell Frith, *The Railway Station*, 1862

■ FIGURE 17.4

William Powell Frith's 1862 painting, *The Railway Station*, was viewed by thousands and helped make him one of England's most popular painters. It depicts the crowd in London's Paddington Station just before the departure of the Great Continental Express. ■ **In what ways** does this painting celebrate the connection between railroads and modern urban life? ■ **Why** might viewers have found this scene so interesting? ■ **In what ways** does the building enshrine the railroad and people in this scene?

(1781–1848) developed the practical modern railroad. In 1830 his new train, "the Rocket," initiated the Liverpool-to-Manchester railway line. The Rocket's speed (16 miles per hour) and reliability excited the imaginations of everyone. People eagerly invested in railway companies, rode the new lines out of curiosity, and traveled by rail to vacation spots.

The railway carried heavy freight with unprecedented ease and speed. By 1850, trains were chugging over 2,000 miles of track in Britain, reaching astonishing speeds of up to 50 miles an hour. Steaming across bridges and through tunnels to the railway stations dotting the land, the new locomotives embodied the power and the promise that seemed to characterize the industrial age. Optimistic observers such as the British politician Edward Stanley argued that "of all the promoters of civilization, the Railway System of communication will be amongst the foremost in its effects, for it cannot fail to produce many and mighty changes in manufactures, in commerce, in trade, and in science."

Figure 17.4 by the popular British artist William Powell Frith captures the drama and excitement of the railroad age. The Great Continental Express is about to depart from Paddington Station in London. At the center is a middle-class family. The mother kisses her son, who is holding a cricket bat and is being sent away to school with his brother. Farther right, a bearded foreigner whose dress suggests wealth haggles over the fare with a cab driver. A wedding party bids adieu to a bride and groom. Behind them, a boy sells newspapers to departing passengers, and a soldier in a red uniform kisses his plump baby goodbye. On the far right, two well-known London detectives arrest a criminal as he steps into the train. Behind them, workers load luggage onto carriage roofs. On the far left, working-class people hurry toward the third-class cars, and porters push luggage toward the train. Above the bustling platform and trains, the wrought-iron-ribbed ceiling and numerous hanging lamps mark the train station as one of London's appealing industrial wonders.

■ FIGURE 17.5

The Crystal Palace Exhibition.

The railroad seemed to pull together all the trends that emerged during the industrial revolution. It ignited demand for an array of related products—coal-thirsty steam engines to power the trains, iron to build the rails and cars, cloth and leather to make furnishings, and bricks and glass to erect the new stations. Like the cotton factories, iron foundries, and coal mines, the railroad industry created new jobs while destroying old ones. In addition, it left its own permanent mark on the land and neighborhoods it affected. As Charles Dickens (1812–1870) described in *Dombey and Son* (1846), a new rail line meant that "houses were knocked down; streets broken through and stopped; deep pits and trenches dug in the ground; enormous heaps of earth and clay thrown up . . . everywhere carcasses of ragged tenements, and fragments of unfinished walls and arches, and piles of scaffolding, and wilderness of bricks, . . . mounds of ashes blocked up rights of way." All this "wholly changed the law and custom of the neighborhood," before the railroad "trailed smoothly away, upon its mighty course of civilization and improvement."

Finally, like the other new industries, the railroads could be a risky investment opportunity. Some own-

Effects of the railroad

ers and investors grew fabulously wealthy; others suffered devastating financial losses. Just as the cotton and iron industries continued to face competition from older methods such as the putting-out system (cottage industry), handicrafts, small family firms, and agriculture, the railroads had to fight to steal business from the roads and canal systems that were expanding across Britain at the same time. Those who had thrown their lot in with the railroads need not have worried too long about the wisdom of their investment, however. Like the cotton and iron factories, the railways were the wave of the future, and they rolled inexorably across the British landscape.

BRITAIN'S TRIUMPH: THE CRYSTAL PALACE EXHIBITION

In 1851, that shining future was put on display for all the world to admire. That year, London hosted the first international industrial fair at the glass-and-iron Crystal Palace. At this dazzling exhibit, millions of visitors came to gaze reverently at the British miracle.

Figure 17.5 shows the interior of the Crystal Palace—its arching glass roof like a cathedral, its steel

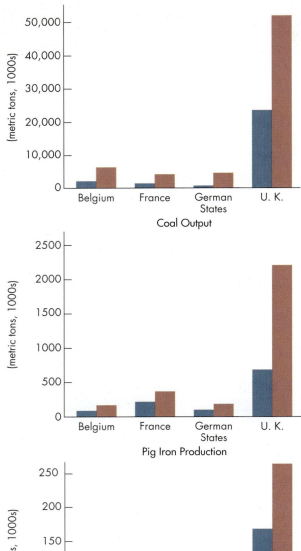

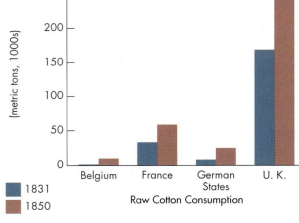

■ 1831
■ 1850

■ FIGURE 17.6

Industrial production in Europe, 1831–1850.

THE INDUSTRIAL REVOLUTION

1760s	Hargreave's spinning jenny
1793	Whitney's cotton gin
1800	500 steam engines in use
1830	Liverpool-to-Manchester railway line
1834	*Zollverein* founded
1842	Chadwick report on sanitation
1851	Crystal Palace Exhibition

to have fashioned, in so short a time, so novel and so vast a structure . . . the gates of which may . . . be thrown open to the world at large, for many years to come." To Wyatt and many others in 1851, the Crystal Palace was at once an architectural masterpiece and a jewel of mass production that could not help but appeal to popular taste. In addition to admiring the building itself, visitors could view displays from various nations.

The awe-inspiring palace confirmed economic realities. Britain produced more than half the world's cotton cloth and iron, and, despite periodic downturns, the nation enjoyed sustained economic growth. Britain had become the world's first industrialized nation.

INDUSTRIALIZATION SPREADS TO THE CONTINENT

It was not until after 1830 that industrialization spread with much force outside Britain (see Figure 17.6). Before then, people from France, the German states, and elsewhere were interested in Britain's economic wonders. Some traveled to Britain to copy machines, and others enticed British technicians and capital to their own countries. A few modern industrial shops and machines sprang up on the continent, but overall, agriculture and tradition still dominated economic life there.

After 1830, industrialization spread to certain regions, especially Belgium, northeastern France, the northern German states, and northwestern Italy (see Figure 17.6). These areas had plenty of urban laborers, deposits of iron and coal, and developed

Governmental aid

framing a testament to modern engineering. Matthew Wyatt, one of the directors of the exhibition, proudly described the construction of the palace as an industrial triumph: "But for the perfect system of discipline, which frequent practice in directing the labour of masses of workmen has now made general throughout England, it would have been impossible

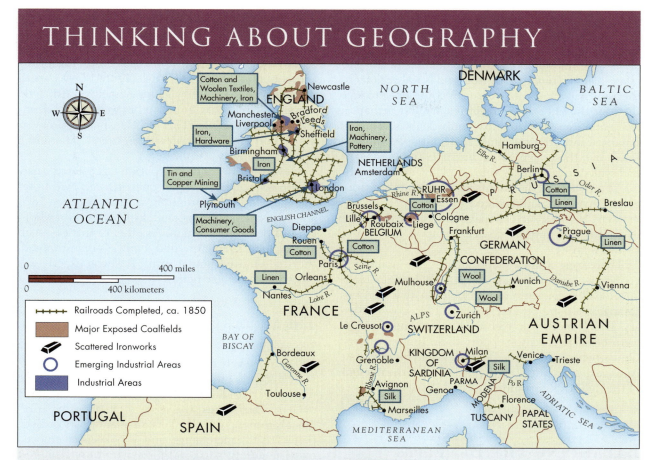

MAP 17.2   THE INDUSTRIAL REVOLUTION IN EUROPE, 1850

This map reveals the spread of industrialization in Europe by 1850. ■ **Locate** industrial areas. **What** connections are there between these areas, resources—such as coalfields—and access to transportation by water or rail? **Compare** the extent of British industrialization to that in continental nations. ■ **Notice** the location of railways. **What** does this suggest about the kinds of areas that early railways were intended to serve?

transportation facilities. Envious of British wealth, pressured by British competition, and recognizing the military potential of cheap iron and rail transportation, continental governments took a more active role in supporting industrialization than British rulers had. They enacted tariffs to protect their manufacturers from British goods and they subsidized new industries. Railroads, partially financed by governments and foreign capital, led rather than followed the advent of other industries, widening markets and creating demand for coal and iron. These countries could not yet hope to catch up to Britain. At mid-century, a German official complained that Germany would never "be able to reach the level of production of coal and iron currently attained in England." But soon Germany and other nations would manage to industrialize more selectively and

quickly, thanks to the groundwork that Britain had laid.

As Map 17.2 indicates, by 1850 large industrial centers had arisen in Belgium, France, and those areas of northern Germany bounded by the 1834 *Zollverein* (a customs union that eliminated tariffs between independent German states). Other regions, particularly around Milan in northern Italy and in the northeastern United States, had also begun to industrialize.

Most of southern, central, and eastern Europe, however, remained virtually untouched by industrial development. Lacking well-placed resources, efficient transportation, mobile work forces, commercialized agriculture, and capital for investment, these regions retained their traditional and rural character. The vast majority of people

Remaining traditional economies

in these areas remained in the countryside tied to subsistence farms or, especially in the east, large agricultural estates. Small villages rather than booming cities were the rule. Wealthy urban elites might purchase manufactured goods from industrial regions to the west, but their own countries could not produce them in the same way. Governments and perhaps a few ambitious and wealthy individuals sometimes imported the latest machines and built a few railroad lines, but these signs of industrialization primarily had symbolic or military value. Relying on old methods of production, merchants in these lands had trouble selling their manufactured goods in international markets. Nations, such as Spain and Russia, that once exported cloth saw their sales dry up in the face of British textiles.

There were a few exceptions in these traditional economies. For example, Austria's Bohemian lands developed a spinning industry, and a few factories sprang up around St. Petersburg and Moscow in Russia. Even so, British technicians and industrialists were often needed to support these limited efforts. On the whole, all these countries would have to wait before experiencing both the benefits and the burdens of the industrial revolution.

BALANCING THE BENEFITS AND BURDENS OF INDUSTRIALIZATION

How did industrialization affect everyday life for Europeans? To answer this complex question, we might first explore the impact of the new machines, factories, and railroads on people's work conditions, home lives, and social relationships. It is also important to ask who received the lion's share of the new wealth.

Foreign observers marveled at Britain's wealth; indeed, to this day many of us associate machines, factories, and railroads with prosperity. *New wealth* Statistics seem to confirm this impression: Britain's national product increased more than threefold between 1780 and 1850. The population in Europe also surged during the same period and absorbed some of the new wealth. Probably thanks to better food supplies (especially cultivation of the potato), earlier marriages, and declining mortality rates, Europe's population *Population growth* balloned from fewer than 175 million in 1780 to 266 million in 1850. During this same period, Britain's population more than doubled.

These startling numbers suggest a sense of economic well-being on the part of Europeans, but they also frightened some contemporaries. In his influential *Essay on the Principle of Population* (1798), British economist Thomas Malthus (1766–1834) warned that population growth would inevitably outstrip food supplies. A few years later, another well-known economist, David Ricardo (1772–1823), argued that overpopulation would restrict wages to no more than subsistence levels.

Nevertheless, industrialization generated new wealth so rapidly that personal income rose faster than population growth in these years. Between 1800 and 1850, per-capita income skyrocketed by a whopping 75 percent in Britain. As other countries—such as Belgium, Germany, and France—industrialized, they too enjoyed similar gains. But who exactly was receiving these new riches?

THE MIDDLE CLASS

The middle classes (bourgeoisie), still a minority of the population even in Britain, prospered. The newest, most dynamic group within the middle classes were the industrial entrepreneurs—the factory and mine owners. They gained the most, some amassing enormous fortunes. Many bankers, smaller factory owners, professionals, merchants, and shopkeepers enjoyed more modest gains, as did those who earned interest and profits from investing their savings in industrial and commercial ventures. All investments, however, did not pay off. Some loans were not repaid. People took financial risks, and some lost their bets. Firms failed all the time, and periodic economic downturns spawned a string of losses and bankruptcies.

Still, over the long haul, the middle class as a whole benefited the most from industrialization. As their wealth and numbers grew, so did their prestige, political power, and cultural influence. The Scottish philosopher and scholar James Mill (1773–1836) claimed that the "heads that invent . . . the hands that execute, the enterprise that projects, and the capital by which these projects are carried into operation" all come from the middle class. Marked by their modest, sober clothing, the middle class gradually displaced the once glittering aristocracy who were still tied by tradition to the land. This process unfolded slowly, and some aristocrats and landowners managed to adjust quite well to the change.

THE WORKING CLASSES

The picture is far less clear for the working classes— those who labored in the factories, tended the machines, and toiled in the mines. For people who shifted from the agricultural life or jobs as artisans to work as factory laborers, industrialization may have hurt more than it helped, especially in its earlier decades. These people worked six days a week, twelve to sixteen hours a day, earning only subsistence-level wages. William Harter, a British silk manufacturer, justified the long hours to a parliamentary commission: Reducing the hours of labor "would instantly much reduce the value of my mill and machines . . . every machine is valuable in proportion to the quantity of work which it will turn off in a given time." In textile factories, whole families typically labored together. Women's earnings were between one-third and two-thirds of men's, and children's wages were a mere fraction of that. As a result, factory owners employed women and children whenever possible to save money, and they even contracted with orphanages to provide cheap child laborers.

Figure 17.7, an 1853 woodcut, shows the interior of a cotton factory. Here the supervisor of an English

Factory labor cotton factory whips a boy as a woman in tattered clothing looks on. Whipping was one way in which supervisors disciplined child workers to the rhythms of the machinery. In the scene's background, women and men tend the spinning machines while three other men talk, apparently unconcerned by the violence. Middle-class reformers such as Frances Trollope (1780–1863) used pictures like these to decry the harsh treatment of children in the cotton mills. One governmental investigation of child labor described how children "were rendered pale, weak and unhealthy" from "labouring for hours like little slaves." Employers, anxious to keep their machines running and wages low, replied that "it was absolutely necessary that the children should be employed within the mills from six o'clock in the morning till seven in the evening, summer and winter." Document 17.2 reveals some of the typical factory rules that employers insisted were necessary to keep their machines running smoothly and profitably.

After the 1820s, factory workers' wages started to climb. By the 1840s or 1850s, they were earning more than their agricultural counterparts. This change did not make them rich, however, for most of them had to spend some two-thirds of their income on food alone. In 1842, Flora Tristan reported that most workers in English factories "lack clothing, bed, furniture, fuel, wholesome food—even potatoes!" and that their bodies were "thin and frail, their limbs feeble, their complexions pale, their eyes dead."

Money was only one variable in the quality-of-life equation. Industrial workers faced job insecurity, physical dangers, and painful changes unique to their way of life. The worst insecurity centered on employment itself. Even in good times, some firms failed. During

■ FIGURE 17.7

Factory labor, 1853.

economic downturns and crises, such as the "Great Hunger" of the 1840s, wages plummeted below subsistence levels, and many workers *Insecurity* lost their jobs. For these industrial laborers there was no unemployment insurance to turn to, and no foraging, cottage industry, or gardening that people living in the countryside could resort to in hard times.

The work itself carried a high risk of severe physical injury. Factory owners made no provisions for safety. In cotton factories, children regularly climbed under and on top of the equip- *Risks of injury* ment to free jammed machines, collect cotton, and tie broken threads; many young workers suffered terrible injuries to their hands and even lost fingers. Long hours and exposure to chemicals, dust, smoke, and industrial residue all led to ill health. Indeed, industrial populations had a far shorter life expectancy and higher incidence of disease and deformity than rural populations. In the 1840s, the military turned down 90 percent of volunteers from some urban areas for health reasons—double the rate of rejection for rural volunteers.

THINKING ABOUT DOCUMENTS

■ DOCUMENT 17.2

Factory Owners Establish Discipline for Workers

Employers and overseers in the new factories needed workers who would labor in rhythm with the machines and according to the demands of industrial capitalism. To these ends, they instituted rules and disciplinary measures. The following document discusses such measures, which went into effect at a Berlin factory in 1844. ■ **What** *problems do employers face, as suggested by these rules?* **How** *might a labor union argue against some of these rules?*

In every large works, and in the co-ordination of any large number of workmen, good order and harmony must be looked upon as the fundamentals of success and therefore the following rules shall be strictly observed.

1. The normal working day begins at all seasons at 6 A.M. precisely and ends, after the usual break of half an hour for breakfast, an hour for dinner and half an hour for tea at 7 P.M., and it shall be strictly observed. . . .

Workers arriving 2 minutes late shall lose half an hour's wages; whoever is more than 2 minutes late may not start work until after the next break; or at least shall lose his wages until then.

4. Repeated irregular arrival at work shall lead to dismissal. This shall also apply to those who are found idling by an

official or overseer, and refused to obey their order to resume work.

6. No worker may leave his place of work otherwise than for reasons connected with his work.

7. All conversation with fellow-workers is prohibited; if any worker requires information about his work, he must turn to the overseer or to the particular fellow-worker designated for the purpose. . . .

Source: Sidney Pollard and Colin Holmes, *Documents of European Economic History*, vol. 1 (St. Martin's Press, 1968).

Besides job insecurity, injury, and ill health, the new industrial age brought other lifestyle changes that are harder to evaluate. Industrial workers experienced a new rhythm of labor that no longer bore any resemblance to the natural rhythms of daylight and seasonal changes. Now, workers toiled unrelentingly to keep pace with the machines and schedules of the factory owner. Employers and their stewards maintained workplace discipline with fines, curses, and whippings. Children who could not keep up were beaten at times (see Figure 17.7); some were even chained to their machines. There were no slack days, like the traditional Monday of preindustrial times. Wages took the form of cash, which workers had to save and apportion carefully over the week for food and housing despite the temptations of alcohol and other leisure activities. At the end of the long workday, laborers trudged home to poor housing clustered around noisy mills or mine entrances or to cheap, overcrowded rooms and cellars of industrial cities.

Lifestyle changes

The question remains: Did the overall quality of life improve for the working classes in the early decades of the industrial revolution? One way to judge is to ask what would have happened to these people without industrialization. Communal villages and agricultural labor had their advantages. In a widely popular poem, "The Deserted Village," (1770) Oliver Goldsmith lamented the loss of rural life:

Ill fares the land, to hastening ills a prey
Where wealth accumulated . . .
But a bold peasantry, their country's pride
When once destroyed, can never be supplied.

People growing up on farms and in small villages at least had traditions they could rely on. But this traditional life also had its own harsh side. Poverty was no stranger to the countryside, nor was child labor, cold, uncertainty, and squalor in windowless hovels. One contemporary, Frederick Eden, argued that the difficulties experienced by small farmers and villagers were only "temporary" and a small price to pay for "the greater good which may be expected from the improvement." However we evaluate all this, life in the city did give the working class something no one could have foreseen: a new sense of class consciousness, an awareness of their own unique burdens and hardships that emboldened them into action and alarmed the onlooking middle classes.

DEVELOPING WORKING-CLASS CONSCIOUSNESS

Because industrial workers lived in the same areas, labored in the same oppressive buildings, grappled with similar problems, socialized and commiserated together, and joined the same trade or civic organizations, they began to see them-

Workers' organizations

selves as a separate class. This sense of solidarity came partly from a tradition among artisans and craftsmen of membership in guilds. Although guilds were made illegal after 1791 and were opposed by middle-class people committed to gaining control over the workplace, other workers' organizations such as fraternal societies, trade organizations, and mutual aid societies persisted. These groups laid the foundation for the emergence of trade unions, made legal (though severely restricted) in England in 1824 and elsewhere after 1850.

Figure 17.8, a nineteenth-century trade union membership certificate, reveals the pride and values in union labor during this industrial age. Like most unions of the period, the Associated Shipwright's Society—a British shipbuilders' union—was made up of skilled workers. Toward the top of this membership certificate is a blue shield; above it are two hands clasped in brotherhood, below it are the words, "WE ARE AS ONE." In the center is a construction site where ships are being built. Just above are pictures of ships, particularly the steamships that carried people and commerce throughout the world. On the bottom of the certificate are pictures of some of the typical benefits of union membership, including accident insurance, retirement income, and death payments. By mid-century, labor leaders had

formed the beginnings of national unions, such as the Grand National Consolidated Trades Union in Britain in 1834, the National Trades Union in the United States in 1834, and the General Workers' Brotherhood in Germany in 1848.

Sometimes workers turned to violence against what they saw as threats from industrialization by destroying the new machines. After 1811, English hand weavers, losing their work to the new power looms, went on rampages, smashing the machines to pieces or campaigning to get rid of them. Glove makers, too, destroyed the new stocking frames that threatened their jobs. These forms of protest came to be known as **Luddism** in honor of a legendary (and perhaps fictitious) leader, Ned Ludd. The British Parliament quickly named industrial sabotage a capital offense and heavily suppressed the violence. Nevertheless, sporadic episodes of violence continued to erupt for several years, not only in Britain but elsewhere as the industrial revolution spread. In the 1830s, silk workers in Lyons, France, rose up against attempts to lower their pay. In 1836, Spanish workers burned a textile factory in Barcelona. During the 1840s, several governments had to call out troops against strikers.

Luddism

Most of these efforts brought few concrete results in the period before 1850. In addition to the power wielded by wealthier classes and governments, many internally divisive forces chipped away at the fledgling working-class solidarity. Labor leaders, for example, who usually came from the more skilled trades—the cabinetmakers, printers, tailors, masons, and blacksmiths—tended to look down on unskilled industrial workers. Most women were not invited to join worker organizations, though they forged some of their own trade associations. Other loyalties based on religion, region, trade, or even neighborhood undermined worker unity. Sometimes the only connection holding laborers together was a sense of shared problems, the belief that workers had a right to a "just wage," and the impression that their employers were exploiters rather than economic partners.

Despite the forces dividing them, workers' sense of themselves as a separate, unique class strengthened over time. Increasingly, members of the middle class began to see them as dangerous and even savage. As we will see in following chapters, with the sharpening of working-class consciousness, the power of the traditional artisan groups and the peasantry would decline—quickly in the decades after 1850, especially in highly industrialized places such as Britain, Belgium, and parts of Germany. The process would unfold more gradually in moderately industrialized places, such as France, and slowly in most of southern and eastern Europe.

For good or ill, industrialization was transforming everyday life across Europe. The economic and human balance shifted from the countryside to the

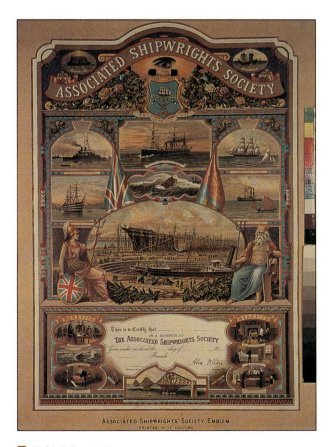

■ FIGURE 17.8
Trade union membership certificate.

■ DOCUMENT 17.3

A Middle-Class Reformer Describes Workers' Housing

During the first half of the nineteenth century, most urban workers gained little more than just enough to get by. Their dwellings reflected their precarious existence. The following is a description of housing in Nantes, France, during the 1830s. ■ **What** *most bothers the author about workers' housing?* ■ **In what ways** *are housing conditions connected to public health problems?*

"If you want to know how he [the poorer worker] lives, go—for example—to the Rue des Fumiers which is almost entirely inhabited by this class of worker. Pass through one of the drain-like openings, below street-level, that lead to these filthy dwellings, but remember to stoop as you enter. One must have gone down into these alleys where the atmosphere is as damp and cold as a cellar; one must have known what it is like to feel one's foot slip on the polluted ground and to fear a stumble into the filth: to realise the painful impression that one receives on entering the homes of these unfortunate workers. Below street-level on each side of the passage there is a large gloomy cold room. Foul water oozes out of the walls. Air reaches the room through a sort of semi-circular window which is two feet high at its greatest elevation. Go in—if the fetid smell that assails you does not make you recoil. Take care, for the floor is uneven, unpaved and untiled—or if there are tiles, they are covered with so much dirt that they cannot be seen. And then you will see two or three rickety beds fitted to one side because the cords that bind them to the worm-eaten legs have themselves decayed. Look at the contents of the bed—a mattress; a tattered blanket of rags (seldom washed since there is only one); sheets sometimes; and a pillow sometimes. No wardrobes are needed in these homes. Often a weaver's loom and a spinning wheel complete the furniture. There is no fire in the winter. No sunlight penetrates [by day], while at night a tallow candle is lit. Here men work for fourteen hours [a day]."

Source: Sidney Pollard and Colin Holmes, *Documents of European Economic History*, vol. 1 (New York: St. Martin's Press, 1968), pp. 494–495.

city. Now the dramatic social transformations took place in the growing urban centers where, as one young worker described London in the 1820s, "a wilderness of human beings" lived.

LIFE IN THE GROWING CITIES

The unprecedented growth of cities from 1780 to 1850 stemmed from a combination of forces. Population was increasing in both urban and rural areas. Enclosures of land by market-oriented landowners that dispossessed individuals of their small farms and communities of their commons further uprooted rural families. These pressures pushed people from the land. At the same time, the cities, with their promise of jobs and the lure of beer halls and theaters, attracted people in droves. Industrial towns sprang up where none had existed before. Towns ballooned into cities, and already large cities grew even more imposing. Some of the most spectacular urban growth happened in industrial cities, such as Manchester, which expanded from 25,000 in 1772 to 367,000 in 1850; and Birmingham, Leeds, and St. Etienne in France, which more than tripled in size. Other already substantial cities, such as London and Paris, became increasingly crowded and sprouted new suburbs.

Urban growth

Most cities flourished through industrial activity, such as mining and manufacturing. Other areas scarcely touched by industrialization, such as Naples, St. Petersburg, and Vienna, also grew dramatically through the expansion of governmental bureaucracies and traditional commerce.

THE PROMISE AND PITFALLS OF WORK IN THE CITIES

Industry, however, had the strongest pull. It inevitably attracted new commerce and gave rise to a broad range of consumer and service needs. Women flocked to the textile factories, but even more women living in the cities worked as domestics. Many young women came for what jobs they could find, perhaps hoping to send home part of their pay and still save enough to start a new life. The building trades drew growing numbers of men, who sometimes left their wives and children in the countryside to survive on a patch of land and dwindling cottage industry employment. Many men periodically returned to the countryside, particularly in winter when construction slowed, or during planting and harvest times.

LIVING WITH URBAN GROWTH

Industrialization and urbanization also altered the landscape that people traveled through to reach the cities. Forests shrank as people cut down more and more trees for construction of cities, mines, factories, and railroads. The same mines and railroads cut scars into the land, and the cities and factories ate up rural landscapes. Rivers once fit for fish or drinking became polluted with industrial and human wastes.

Approaching the cities, travelers saw smoke in the air from the dirty coal fires used to heat buildings and from the engines of industry. In the city, and particularly in the poor working-class areas, *Environmental changes* the air smelled foul, for there were no modern sewers, sorely inadequate toilet facilities, and not enough clean water. Garbage and animal waste collected in the streets until heavy rains washed them away. In Manchester, only two-thirds of the houses had toilets, and many of those flushed into inadequate cesspools. Human and animal waste mixed in rivers that people used for drinking water. Charles Dickens' description of the fictionalized Coketown in his novel *Hard Times* (1854) would have struck a familiar chord for nineteenth-century travelers to Britain's industrial cities: "It was a town of machinery and tall chimneys, out of which interminable serpents of smoke trailed themselves for ever and ever. . . . It had a black canal in it, and a river that ran purple with ill-smelling dye, and vast piles of buildings full of windows where there was a rattling and a trembling all day long, and where the piston of the steam-engine worked monotonously up and down."

Overwhelmed by these surroundings, newcomers to the cities tended to settle in areas where they knew someone else. Whole neighborhoods grew up populated by people who had come from the same rural region. This tendency led to a sense of segregation and separate identities within the cities, as people familiar with one another clustered together.

Few neighborhoods were planned. Indeed, the expansion of most cities became increasingly uncontrolled. The rampant growth created far more problems for the working class than for anyone else. The middle classes, for example, most likely lived in lower-floor apartments in the more desirable sections of town and had *Different neighborhoods* the benefit of some running water. They also could afford to employ servants. It was in the working-class sections and poverty-stricken areas that the social ills and squalor of the age reached their worst levels. As the manufacturer and socialist Frederich Engels (1820–1895) described, "The houses are packed from cellar to attic and they are as dirty inside as outside." In the Irish quarter of London, as many as 38 people crowded into small buildings down narrow alleys where the walls were crumbling, and "piles of refuse and ashes lie all over the place and the slops thrown out into the street collect in pools which emit a foul stench." In the bad quarters lived "the poorest of the poor. Here the worst-paid workers rub shoulders with thieves, rogues and prostitutes."

Document 17.3 describes conditions where poor workers lived. Figure 17.9, a mid-nineteenth-century woodcut by the French artist Gustave Doré (1832–1883), also portrays the squalor and crowding of a London slum. In the center, a young child carries a baby, perhaps because her mother is working. Around her in the alley, dejected men, women, and children stand listlessly. Dark tenements tower over them, and laundry sags from clotheslines. Though criticized for overdramatizing the plight of the poor, Doré effectively conveys the anguish of unemployment, poverty, and crowding marring this rich city. As this and other works by novelists such as Charles Dickens, Elizabeth Gaskell, Frances Trollope, and Honoré de Balzac showed, the burgeoning cities were fostering a whole set of social concerns.

WORRYING ABOUT URBAN SOCIETY: RISING CRIME

One of those social concerns centered on patterns of criminal behavior. People in the upper classes complained about crime and the social disorder it implied. Had cities become hotbeds of crime, as some middle-class observers claimed, or were these critics simply overly worried about their own safety and well-being?

Crime certainly plagued people in the West long before the industrial revolution. In rural areas, along highways, and in the preindustrial cities of Europe, crimes ranging from pickpocketing to murder occurred all too frequently. Professional thieves reportedly ran rampant in Germany, England, and France in past centuries.

In the early stages of industrialization, theft and robbery in particular did rise in the cities. Crowds provided prime opportunities for pickpockets. In urban taverns and dance halls, men sometimes fell into violent brawling, sometimes over women. In these establishments, alcohol flowed freely and almost certainly played a role in outbreaks of fighting. The widening gaps between rich and poor and the desperation of living in hard times also made tempers short. Finally, the anonymity of life in the city and the tempting array of luxury items to steal made crime harder to resist.

Whether justified by the realities of more crime or not, the specter of urban crime and fear of disorder prompted new efforts to improve law enforcement. In 1829, under the leadership of Robert Peel, *Crime and law enforcement* Parliament passed a law establishing the first modern police force in London. Peel's new police, called "Bobbies" in his honor, emphasized regular patrols by uniformed officers as a way to deter crime and present a visual image of security. Both the middle and the working classes accepted the Bobbies, in part because the police were not allowed to be engaged for political purposes such as domestic espionage, and in part because people saw

■ FIGURE 17.9

Gustave Doré, *A London Slum*.

them as the first line of defense against all disorder. By the early 1830s, there were some 3,000 uniformed officers in the force.

The frightening consequences of rapid urbanization were becoming all too apparent. Year by year, the cities grew more densely packed and seemingly more dangerous. In bad times, they teemed with desperate people hoping to find jobs; in good times, they drew even more people eager to take advantage of the available work and other opportunities. Contemporaries associated the cities with overcrowding, filth, crime, moral degeneracy, and an unruly working class. "They [the working class] live precisely like brutes . . . they eat, drink, breed, work and die," complained a middle-class British observer in 1850. "The richer and more intelligent classes are obliged to guard them with police." Perhaps most disturbing, however, was the disease and death that haunted urban centers.

PUBLIC HEALTH AND MEDICINE IN THE INDUSTRIAL AGE

People had good reason to fear for their health and safety in the growing cities, especially in the poorer sections of town. On average, city-dwellers fell ill more often and died at a far earlier age than their rural counterparts. Within the cities, the poor lived half as long as the rich.

Industrialization itself was dangerous. The new machines maimed factory workers, and cave-ins, floods, and explosions killed miners. Various diseases stemmed directly from mining and manufacturing. Coal miners became ill and died from black-lung disease. Cotton workers developed brown-lung disease. In textile factories, women suffered particularly high mortality rates. Metalworkers, especially grinders, developed lung diseases from inhaling shavings. Poisonings from mercury, lead, and phosphorus used in industrial processes also increased.

THE DANGER OF DISEASE

The greatest danger came from infectious diseases. They were the great causes of sickness and death before the nineteenth century, and the rapid growth of crowded cities that lacked sanitation facilities made matters worse. People living in working-class quarters and urban slums were most vulnerable. Tuberculosis and diphtheria thrived in the most heavily populated areas and killed millions during the nineteenth century.

Worse, plagues periodically swept through cities. Cholera epidemics struck Europe several times, causing great panic as people in city after city awaited the arrival of the illness (see Map 17.3). Suggested remedies included taking several measures to restore warmth to the body, giving laudanum (opium dissolved in alcohol), and seeking medical aid. In 1831 alone, cholera killed some 100,000 in France and 50,000 in England.

People disagreed about the causes of diseases. Some observers blamed illnesses on physical weakness and immorality of individuals. In these critics' view, disease was rooted in inferior genetic background, overindulgence, degenerate lifestyle, poor hygiene, and irresponsibility. Only self-help could solve the problem, they argued.

Causes of disease

Other commentators and some doctors theorized that disease spread through contagion—that people caught diseases from one another. This theory had more to do with magic, belief in the devil, or a desire to keep the ill out of sight than any notion of modern germ theory. It seemed to explain sexually transmitted diseases like syphilis, but could not answer the question of why some people contracted various diseases while others did not. In these commentators' minds, quarantine offered the best solution to fighting contagious diseases.

Most doctors eventually concluded that disease stemmed less from personal contact than from environmental forces. They believed in "miasma," the centuries-old notion that people caught diseases by breathing fumes given off by human waste, rotting vegetables, decaying flesh, marshes, or stagnant ponds. They also blamed poor diets for weakening resistance to these sources of disease. In a widely respected 1840 study, the French physician Louis Villermé attributed the prevalence of disease in the working-class slums of Lille to the cellars and crowded rooms where "the air is never renewed," where "everywhere are piles of garbage, of ashes, of debris from vegetables picked up from the streets, of rotten straw," where "one is exhausted in these hovels by a stale, nauseating, . . . odor of filth, odor of garbage." This helped him and others explain why people living in barracks, workhouses, and the worst parts of cities more often fell ill and died.

SEEKING MEDICAL CARE

None of these theories about disease aided individuals seeking medical care. Doctors may have been well-meaning, but in 1850, anyone visiting a doctor was more likely to be hurt than helped. Most people consulted physicians reluctantly and had little trust in the power of treatments or medicine. To our twentieth-century sensibilities, medicine in the early 1800s can indeed seem quite alarming. To alleviate a fever, for example, doctors often turned to traditional cures such as initiating bloodletting by opening a vein or applying leeches to the skin, or they recommended laxatives to purge the "bad humors" and fluids from the body. Physicians routinely pre-

Doctors

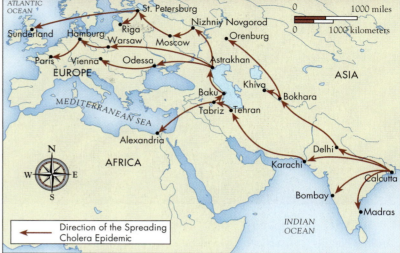

THINKING ABOUT GEOGRAPHY

MAP 17.3   THE SPREAD OF A CHOLERA EPIDEMIC

This map shows the spread of a cholera epidemic, which originally broke out in eastern India in 1817 and struck France and England so hard in the 1830s. ■ **Notice** how, over time, the epidemic spread north and west. **Consider** what this reveals about the growing connections between the Western and non-Western worlds.

scribed pills that at best did nothing and more likely contained toxic substances such as mercury. Frequently, the addictive drug laudanum was suggested for the treatment of pain, sleeping problems, difficulties with children, and a variety of other complaints. Such treatments more often led to fluid depletion, poisoning, and addiction than any improvement of the patient's condition.

More benignly, doctors might recommend fresh-air cures or "taking the waters" at health spas. Many of the wealthy traveled to coastal resorts and centers in Caldas da Rainha in Portugal, Bath in England, and Baden-Baden in Germany for these health cures. They may have gained some temporary relief from conditions such as arthritis, but they more likely enjoyed the lively social events and casinos that also attracted them to these spas.

Figure 17.10, an 1820 print by the French artist Caroline Naudet (1775–1839), reveals popular attitudes toward physicians. Titled *Journey of a Dying Man to the Other World*, the print depicts a wealthy doctor in black robes leading a procession that includes a dying man, a clergyman pointing up, a surgeon with a

■ FIGURE 17.10

Caroline Naudet, *Journey of a Dying Man to the Other World*, 1820.

fluttering bat over his head, a sinister-looking apothecary carrying an enema device, and an undertaker. The solemn physician carries a banner that describes the traditional treatment for diseases: "To give a clyster [enema], after that to bleed, finally to purge."

Many sufferers looked for treatments opposed by ordinary doctors to cure their ailments. Homeopathy, which emphasized the use of herbal drugs and natural remedies, gained in popularity during the period. Other options—from vegetable laxatives, claimed to be effective for all ills, to faith healers—saw wide use. These alternatives at least gave sufferers a sense of controlling their own health.

Alternative medicine

As for surgery, people turned to this option only as a last resort. Surgical methods became safer in the first half of the nineteenth century, but anesthesia and antiseptics still lay in the future. Those who managed to survive the pain of an operation faced a likelihood of dying from an infection afterward.

Surgery

PROMISING DEVELOPMENTS FOR PUBLIC HEALTH

Despite all the dangers, the period had a few bright spots for the future of public health. Improvements in diet probably held the most promise. Many nutritious foods had become more available than ever, especially potatoes, which were an affordable, rich source of vitamin C and minerals; dairy products, which helped newborns survive infancy and childhood; and meat, which contained high-grade proteins. Inexpensive cotton underwear, thanks to the new cot-

ton mills, kept people warmer and cleaner than before. The smallpox vaccine, developed during the eighteenth century and made into a safe form in 1796 by Edward Jenner in England, would virtually erase a disease that had once afflicted almost 80 percent of Europeans and killed millions. The discovery of anesthetics—nitrous oxide and, after 1846, ether and chloroform—began to make surgical trauma bearable.

Other developments showed some potential as well. Following the lead of a small group of influential French physicians, European doctors applied scientific methods to medicine and made great strides in pathology and physiology. Hospitals proliferated and increasingly became places to observe the sick and gather information. New laboratories allowed doctors to conduct more experiments. Professional organizations and educational institutions for doctors and nurses formed, and governments, particularly in France, began taking some responsibility for medical education and licensing.

New developments in medicine

Many doctors no longer relied solely on a patient's description of the problem. Physical examinations became common—feeling the pulse, sounding the chest, taking the blood pressure, looking down the throat. Some doctors used the new stethoscope, which became a crucial tool for diagnosing bronchitis, pneumonia, and pulmonary tuberculosis (commonly called consumption). Among the upper classes, the family physician was even gaining some favor as a respected social contact and confidant.

In England, Edwin Chadwick (1800–1890) initiated a campaign to improve public health. In his 1842 report for a parliamentary commission, *The Sanitary Condition of the Laboring Population of Britain*, he emphasized that the accumulation of human and animal waste near people's dwellings was a crucial cause of disease. He proposed a system of underground tunnels that would allow constantly running water to carry waste out of the city.

Nevertheless, the gains from these promising new developments would not come until the second half of the nineteenth century. In Britain, one of every three people still died of contagious diseases in the decades surrounding 1850. Health, therefore, remained a great public and private concern. It was not the only concern that crossed the lines between public and private life, however. The day-to-day events in everybody's lives, whether in illness or health, unfolded within a crucial setting: the family. In this period of industrialization and urbanization, the family as an institution and the roles within it began to shift in the face of enormous economic and social pressures.

FAMILY IDEALS AND REALITIES

The ways that people come together into families and the roles they play in their families usually evolve slowly, if at all. During this period, however, the middle class redefined accepted notions of the family, and working-class families struggled under the new pressures beleaguering them. In subtle but important ways, family ideals and realities were changing.

MIDDLE-CLASS IDEALS: AFFECTION, CHILDREN, AND PRIVACY

With their numbers, wealth, and status in urban societies rising, the middle class not only developed its own ideas about what the proper family should be; it propagated those ideas as the norm for everyone else. The result was an evolution of, rather than a break from, old notions about the family. Compared with families of earlier times, the ideal middle-class family emphasized emotional bonds, attention to children, and privacy.

People were supposed to marry because of affection, love, and emotional compatibility. Social rank and wealth remained important, but these values exerted less influence than they had in the past. Love could bridge social and economic gaps. Indeed, one of the great themes in the flood of new novels that appeared during the nineteenth century centered on this very conflict: the tension between *Marriage* love and money in marriage. In stories that ended happily, love won out—though most characters in these plots never were relegated to a life of poverty as a consequence of their choice.

The new middle-class family was smaller and more child-centered than before. Europeans were choosing to limit the size of their families, *Family size* and by mid-century this preference led to declining rates of population growth. Women gave birth to fewer children—two or three rather than the five or six of an earlier era—and more infants than ever survived the first, riskiest years of life. Unlike workers and peasants, middle-class parents did not have to view their children as economic assets—as hands to work the fields, help with the crafts, or labor in the factories. Wealthier urban parents could afford to raise perhaps just two or three children as fulfilling products of a good home. More than ever, children came to be seen as innocent, impressionable, vulnerable persons who should be separated from the corrupting influences of adult society. Mothers and fathers *Children* began investing more time, effort, and other resources in child rearing. Boys, especially, needed training and education designed to ensure their success as adults in the changing urban world. To arm them with these essentials, parents extended the time period of childhood and economic dependence. All this required planning and intensified emotional ties between parents and children. Parents increasingly centered their attention and family activities on children.

More than ever, mothers and fathers idealized their home as a private "haven in a heartless world," separate from and above the world of paid work. The home represented the reward for competing on the job—a protected, glorified *The home* place for a satisfying personal life. There husband and wife could enjoy the delights of material possessions and, hopefully, the rewarding intimacy of family life. As indicated by the growing number of popular books by authors such as Jane Austen (1775–1817), Mary Ann Evans (1819–1880) (writing under the pen name George Eliot), and Charlotte Brontë (1816–1855), home was a setting of many appealing, moralizing dramas where the virtues of prudence, love, sacrifice, self-reliance, and persistence could usually overcome all obstacles.

SEPARATE SPHERES: CHANGING ROLES FOR MIDDLE-CLASS WOMEN AND MEN

With the rise of industrialization and urban life, the roles of middle-class husbands and wives grew more and more separate. In the seventeenth and eighteenth centuries, most middle-class families had worked together as one economic unit—sharing the responsibilities of running a shop or business and living near their place of work in back rooms, upstairs, or next door. During the nineteenth century, the tasks assigned to men and women, and the private world of home and the public place of paid work, became increasingly distinct. As the locus of work shifted from the home to the factory, store, or office, women lost their traditional employments that contributed to the family economy. Paid employees working outside the home now occupied the role previously played by women who had run thriving family businesses. The new

■ FIGURE 17.11

Carolus Duran, *The Merrymakers.*

economic growth also allowed middle-class families to afford the homes, servants, and leisure previously reserved for the elite. Eventually, the ability of middle-class women to devote more time to their homes and families without having to do paid work, and to hire servants to lighten domestic burdens, became symbols of social success. The home became women's sphere, and within the home, child rearing began requiring far more maternal attention than ever. As the task of raising children and socializing them with the values and training needed for success expanded, so did the responsibilities of motherhood. Becoming "rational mothers," fully able to meet the new demands of child rearing, turned into a revered duty.

The man was supposed to be the respected economic provider who operated primarily in his sphere: the competitive world of work outside the home. He was expected to behave in an authoritative, competent, and controlled manner. These qualities reflected the legal and economic realities of the time. Under British common law and the Napoleonic Code on the Continent, for example, a man had legal authority over his wife and children. He also had control over his wife's personal property as well as over any money earned by her. Furthermore, only men could vote. Most positions in the middle-class world of work were reserved for men. Those jobs usually required specialized skills in planning and information managing—abilities that came primarily from formal schooling. Young men were more likely than women to receive a formal education in areas of study such as accounting or law. Through apprenticeships and clerkships in commerce, industry, or finance, men also found many opportunities to equip themselves for success in the growing industrial-urban economy.

The man's sphere

Women faced a very different set of cultural expectations. A host of marriage manuals, medical tracts, advice books, and religious dictates reminded women that their place was within the domestic sphere. A woman should provide emotional support for her husband and cultivate a virtuous home environment to counteract the amoral, competitive marketplace. She should care for the children, make sure the house was clean and the meals served, supervise domestic servants (a requirement for any middle-class home), and manage other domestic tasks from sewing to administering household accounts.

The woman's domestic sphere

In the mid-nineteenth-century painting shown in Figure 17.11, Carolus Duran depicts two middle-class women at home. The center of the women's attention, and the painting, is a playful child sitting on her mother's lap and reaching for a pet bird or figurine. Across the table from the two well-dressed women, a maid or house servant leans toward the child with a folded paper figurine, perhaps in mock play with the bird. On the lower right are more pet-like figurines. Indeed, middle-class families often considered pets as much a part of domestic life as the food and drink on the table.

In some ways, a middle-class woman's domestic sphere extended outside the home. She might manage the family's social life, for example, or lead in religious matters. If she had the time and means, she might also participate in philanthropic activities, social movements such as temperance or the abolition of slavery, and certain cultural events—but only as long as these activities added to her image as virtuous, dutiful, maternal, supportive, and sensitive. These activities put women in a position of power as representatives of the family in religious, social, and cultural matters and often gave them the last word on such matters within the family.

Involvement in politics was out of the question for most women. A few middle-class women joined movements to gain political and legal rights, but their efforts did not lead to real reforms during this period. Nor did paid work fit the domestic image. Although a woman might serve without wages as a clerk or secretary in her husband's store or office, paid work outside the home was considered inappropriate and generally not available to married women. Even for unmarried women, only occupations directly connected to the domestic role, such as governess, elementary schoolteacher, lady's companion, or seller of women's clothing were deemed acceptable. There were exceptions, especially in cultural fields such as painting and writing, but most people raised a skeptical, disapproving eyebrow at women who had such careers.

At home, a wife was expected to be the counterpart to her controlled, strong husband. "In every thing . . . that women attempt, they should show their consciousness of dependence" on men, explained Elizabeth Poole Sandford in her widely read book, *Woman in her Social and Domestic Character* (1842). Law hindered most married women from acquiring economic independence and generally placed them, as well as children, under the formal power and protection of men. Women were to be emotional and even frail, and therefore capable of only domestic tasks. The training of young women reinforced these qualities. Instead of a secondary schooling or professional education, women's formal training focused on religion, music, and perhaps languages. Any other skills a young woman might need, she picked up at home.

Educators and scientists generally agreed that women were ill suited for occupations outside the home and that they lacked the emotional control, mental acuity, and assertiveness of men. Doctors usually held the same views, and even believed that menstruation incapacitated women and that women had no interest in sex. Clothing, too, emphasized this vision of women's proper role. Middle-class husbands wore prudent and practical clothing for the world of work—trousers and jackets in modest black or gray. Their wives endured tight corsets and full decorative skirts more suited for display than action.

In short, the middle-class ideal was a small, private family bonded by love and authority. In such a family, the wife and husband willingly fulfilled the expected roles of their separate spheres. Families measured their success in achieving this ideal by the luxury items they bought, collected, and self-consciously displayed; by the accomplishments of their children; by how well their lives matched the uplifting dramas that the novels and paintings of the day depicted; and by their participation in appropriate social, religious, and philanthropic activities.

Middle-class success is well illustrated by the economic and social rise of wealthy commercial and industrial families such as the Cadburys (see Biography on page 560). The 1824 drawing by E. Wall Cousins in Figure 17.12 shows the still-modest Cadbury shops on Bull Street in Birmingham. To the right is Richard's original dry-goods (linens) store; to the left, his son John's tea and coffee shop. The plate-glass windows and the dress of people on the street indicate the store's intention to appeal to middle-class and wealthy clients. Above are the family's apartments, which include plants and pets. When the business expanded, the Cadburys moved away from this store to a suburban house, with separate nursery and schoolrooms for the children. The idea of separate rooms for children, and for eating, cooking, reading, and socializing was new and reflected the growing wealth of the middle class and how the idea of

Middle-class success

differentiation—separate areas for different tasks and the division of labor—already spreading in the industrial world affected the domestic sphere as well.

WORKING-CLASS REALITIES

The middle class assumed that its vision of the proper family served as the standard for all. However, this vision did not fit the urban and industrial realities facing the far more numerous working classes.

Industrialization pulled many working-class women away from their homes and into factory jobs. Employers preferred to hire women because they worked for lower salaries and seemed more pliable than men. In the early decades, young children often accompanied their mothers, providing even cheaper labor and falling victim to the harsh, disciplined factory environment. During the 1830s and 1840s, public outcry against child labor (led by middle-class reformers, not the working class) prompted women to leave their younger children at home in care of an older child or neglectful "babyfarmers," women who took in far too many children. Many mothers resorted to drugging their children with laudanum to keep them out of harm's way while the adults were at work.

Women workers

Middle-class critics demanded reforms that would limit women's ability to work away from home, although working-class women objected that they had no better alternatives. As one group of women factory workers from Manchester pointed out, "Hand loom has been almost totally superseded by power loom weaving, and no inconsiderable number of females, who must depend on their own exertions, . . . have been forced . . . into the manufactories, from their total inability to earn a livelihood at home." During recessions, women's plight worsened. Employers laid off the more highly paid men first, leaving women with the overwhelming burden of managing both a paid job and all the domestic tasks at home.

Working-class and peasant families were being pulled apart in other ways as well. Adolescent boys left home to seek work in the mines or cities. Daughters, too, sought jobs as factory laborers or as domestics in middle- or upper-class homes. In the cities, women were all the more vulnerable during economic downturns when low-paying jobs disappeared.

PROSTITUTION

Hard times left unmarried and married women alike in particularly desperate straits. To survive, some women turned to prostitution, which grew along with Europe's mushrooming cities. In 1850, there were probably some 30,000 prostitutes in Paris and

The Cadburys

CONSIDER

■ **Consider** why the Cadburys benefited so greatly from the industrial revolution and how members of the family exhibited typical nineteenth-century middle-class values.

By the late eighteenth century, the Cadburys were a well-established Quaker family of shopkeepers in western England. Young Richard Tapper Cadbury used his father's connections to find positions as an apprentice and journeyman to drapers (selling retail cloth and dry goods) in Gloucester and London. In 1794, his father helped him again, giving him money to start his own cloth and dry goods store on a main street in Birmingham, one of Britain's leading industrial cities.

In 1800, Richard, his wife, Elizabeth, and their growing family moved into an apartment above their shop on Bull Street. Middle-class families such as the Cadburys typically lived in the same building as their business until they could afford to buy a separate home.

Elizabeth Cadbury, like most middle-class women of moderate means, worked in the family enterprise but had received no professional training. She picked up skills on the job, helping rather than leading, and taking over for her husband when he was away. As a married woman, Elizabeth had no independent legal identity and could not have owned a business on her own. Formally, their family business belonged to Richard, but like many businesses during the period, it also functioned as an informal partnership between the couple. In addition to working in the business, Elizabeth was also responsible for running the household, which included eight children and young apprentices.

Draper retailers such as the Cadbury family played a major role in the revolution of Britain's textile industries. Like producers, retailers benefited from the new sources of supply and expanding demand for cloth. The Cadbury shop expanded and brought in enough income for Richard and Elizabeth to rent a house and land for a garden on the outskirts of Birmingham in 1812. The younger children, their nurse, and their pets moved there. Elizabeth and her older daughters traveled back and forth, managing the two households.

A Rising Middle-Class Family

Richard and Elizabeth's sons eventually apprenticed in retail businesses in different cities—Benjamin as a draper, John as a tea and coffee dealer. The daughters had no such training. Instead they learned what they could from their mother as they helped in the shop, house, and garden.

John (1801–1889) opened a tea and coffee store next door to his parents' shop (see Figure 17.12). He and his first wife, who died in 1828, lived over the shop. When John accumulated enough money, he also opened a plant to manufacture the cocoa and chocolate for which the family name would become so famous. In 1834, John and his second wife, Candia, moved their home away from the city, with its filth and crowds, to a new, planned middle-class suburb just outside of Birmingham. Candia generally stayed at home, busy with her domestic tasks and gardening, while John rode to

50,000 in London. Unemployment and the dangers of solitude were probably the main forces driving women to prostitution. Many prostitutes had come from outside the cities and had no family to help them. Others were out-of-work domestics, seamstresses in need of income during a slow season, daughters of unemployed workers, or women abandoned after being impregnated by masters or lovers. Low wages also led to prostitution; a woman earned as much money in one night prostituting herself as she could acquire after an entire week of work at the factory.

Many of these women worked as prostitutes for relatively short periods, and only part time. While the work helped them financially, it also exposed them to venereal disease, which ran rampant during this period. Finally, in some people's minds, prostitution linked working-class women to images of urban crime and immorality. To middle-class moralists, prostitutes embodied unrestrained sexuality and therefore were the ultimate outcasts. However, despite its dangers, prostitution would persist as a sign of the difficulties that many working families faced in Europe's growing cities.

STRESS AND SURVIVAL IN THE WORKING CLASSES

The new tensions swirling through working-class family life had severe consequences for some. Peasant, artisan, and working-class families had worked together as economic units for longer than the middle class had, and industrialization and urbanization corroded this unity. The stresses proved so great that some families broke apart, leaving a growing number of women to work and manage households on their own.

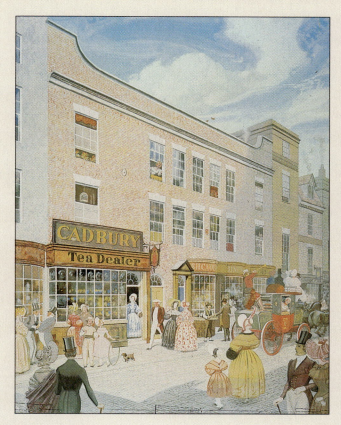

■ FIGURE 17.12

E. Wall Cousins, *The Cadbury Shops*, 1824.

town every day to take care of business and political affairs. Candia could not look after the family business as her mother-in-law Elizabeth had, for the demands of child rearing had grown and the training necessary for John's more complex business had increased. John and Candia's spheres were much more distinct than the elder Cadburys' had been.

In 1861, John's sons, Richard and George, took over their father's failing business. They visited a chocolate factory in Holland that was using a new process to transform cocoa beans into cocoa and chocolate. In 1866, they successfully introduced that process into their own factory. This new technique helped them to break the near monopoly that French chocolate products had previously enjoyed in the British market. In the decades that followed, the brothers built Cadbury into a prosperous cocoa and chocolate manufacturing firm. Richard painted the designs for fancy Cadbury chocolate boxes that idealized children and their innocence, using his own children as models.

In 1879, the brothers moved their firm from industrialized Birmingham to a rural site they called Bournville. There they introduced improved conditions for their workers and a private social security program, reforms well ahead of their time. George, holding firmly to the Quaker views of his parents and grandparents, had long taught in a Birmingham "adult school" for workingmen. Concluding that poor housing lay at the root of many social evils, he began building high-quality working-class housing that featured gardens. By 1900, that community included 313 houses and served as a model for British "garden cities" and "garden suburbs."

In 1901, George and members of his family acquired the *London Daily News* and other newspapers, which they used to express their Liberal Party views. By this time, Cadbury, which had grown unevenly from the seeds planted by Richard and Elizabeth in 1794, had become a vast, worldwide company.

However, the picture was not all bleak. As a rule, the family survived, providing a haven for workers and a home for children. Like peasants' and artisans' families, many working-class families clung to the old putting-out system or the newer piecework system, in which entrepreneurs distributed jobs, such as tailoring or decorating, to workers at their homes. Unions, better wages, and new social policies would ease the burdens on workers in the decades after 1850. In the end, most families adjusted and found ways to meet the many challenges of the industrial age.

SUMMARY

Industrialization meant unprecedented, sustained economic growth, and it soon became a measure of whether people considered a society "modern" or "traditional." Carrying in its wake fundamental changes in literally all aspects of life, industrialization altered the ways people worked, what they could buy, how they lived their lives, and where they stood on the social ladder. Its railroads, dams, bridges, factories, and mines transformed the land, the rivers, and the air. Nations that industrialized left others behind in the competition for wealth. That wealth was all too easily translated into power, leaving traditional agrarian societies in the West vulnerable to their industrialized neighbors.

The new riches pumped out by the machines of industry also propelled the West into an even stronger position to dominate over unindustrialized, non-Western societies throughout the world. Decade after decade, a widening gap of wealth and power opened up between the industrializing regions of the West and nonindustrializing regions of Asia, Africa, and Latin America.

At the same time, the cities grew. There, old ties to traditional communities and beliefs loosened; long-established religions even lost some of their influence. Despite a host of social problems, the cities had a vibrancy and an image of opportunity that continued to attract people. While some people lost when they migrated to the cities, others gained, whether by hard work, luck, or the advantages of birth. Perhaps life in the countryside, with its slower pace and simpler pleasures, simply could not compete with what the city promised.

Through these decades, most families found ways to adapt to new circumstances. Middle-class families responded to their improving positions by developing a compelling new set of ideals about how men and women should behave. Working-class families did their best to hold themselves together in the face of divisive forces; looking to the future, workers began seeing themselves as a new class of people who just might have the power to determine their own fate.

This growing awareness by both classes added to the fundamental changes being wrought by industrialism. Conflict—whether in an intellectual realm, at the work site, in the courts, or on the barricades—would often be the result. These conflicts, along with those stemming from the French Revolution, would profoundly shape social and political life in the West in the decades to come.

KEY TERMS

industrial revolution, p. 535   factory system, p. 542   Luddism, p. 551

entrepreneurs, p. 539

REVIEW, ANALYZE, AND ANTICIPATE

REVIEW THE PREVIOUS CHAPTER

Chapter 16—"Overturning the Political and Social Order"—examined the revolution that transformed France and whose consequences were felt throughout the West. The chapter also focused on the role Napoleon played during that period and the battles he waged throughout Europe until his final defeat in 1815.

1. Who do you think were the main beneficiaries of the French Revolution and the industrial revolution? Were they the same groups?

2. In what ways might the French Revolution and the industrial revolution be related?

ANALYZE THIS CHAPTER

Chapter 17—"Factories, Cities, and Families in the Industrial Age"—analyzes the industrial revolution and urbanization.

1. How do you explain why Britain industrialized before other European nations and non-Western societies such as China?

2. Compare the consequences of industrialization for the middle class and the working class.

3. In what ways did moving from the countryside to the city change people's lives during this period?

4. Analyze how the family and ideas about women's and men's roles altered within the middle class. In what ways were circumstances different for working-class families?

ANTICIPATE THE NEXT CHAPTER

In Chapter 18—"Coping with Change"—we will examine the political developments, theories of change, and revolutionary movements of the period between 1815 and 1850.

1. What sorts of problems do you think the industrial revolution will pose for governments? What policies might they adopt to solve those problems?

2. Consider which ideas about the industrial revolution might be favored by people sympathetic to the workers. What about people sympathetic to middle-class employers?

BEYOND THE CLASSROOM

THE INDUSTRIAL REVOLUTION BEGINS

Brown, Richard. Society and Economy in Modern Britain, 1700–1850. New York: Routledge, 1991. Argues that Britain's industrial development was gradual and quite regionally varied.

Landes, David. The Wealth and Poverty of Nations. New York: W.W. Norton, 1999. Connects cultures to economic development in a broad international context.

O'Brien, Patrick K., and Roland Quinault, eds. The Industrial Revolution and British Society. Cambridge: Cambridge University Press, 1993. Essays by noted scholars that stress the origins and consequences of the industrial revolution in Britain.

GLOBAL CONNECTIONS

Pomeranz, Kenneth. The Great Divergence: China, Europe, and the Making of the Modern World Economy. Princeton: Princeton University Press, 2000. A bold comparison of economic development in Europe and Asia.

NEW MARKETS, MACHINES, AND POWER

Deane, Phyllis. The First Industrial Revolution, 2nd ed. Cambridge: Cambridge University Press, 1979. A respected account of British industrialization and its consequences.

Landes, David S. The Unbound Prometheus: Technological Change and Industrial Development in Western Europe from 1750 to the Present. London:

Cambridge University Press, 1969. A classic treatment of technological development in a broad social and economic context.

Mokyr, Joel. *The Lever of Riches: Technological Creativity and Economic Progress*. New York: Oxford University Press, 1992. An attempt to explain why technological creativity occurred in some places and not in others.

INDUSTRIALIZATION SPREADS TO THE CONTINENT

Pollard, Sidney. *Peaceful Conquest: The Industrialization of Europe, 1760–1970*. Oxford: Oxford University Press, 1981. Charts the process of industrialization as it spread from Britain to the European continent.

Stearns, Peter. *The Industrial Revolution in World History*. New York: Westview Press, 1998. A wide-ranging interpretation.

BALANCING THE BENEFITS AND BURDENS OF INDUSTRIALIZATION

Chinn, Carl. *Poverty Amidst Prosperity: The Urban Poor in England, 1834–1914*. Manchester: Manchester University Press, 1995. Focuses on the poverty created by the industrial revolution.

Nardinelli, Clark. *Child Labor and the Industrial Revolution*. Bloomington, IN: Indiana University Press, 1990. A sympathetic portrait of the topic.

Thompson, E.P. *The Making of the English Working Class*. New York: Random House, 1966. A remarkable book of sympathy and insight that has been hugely controversial and influential.

LIFE IN THE GROWING CITIES

Lawton, Richard, and Robert Lee, eds. *Urban Population Development in Western Europe from the Late Eighteenth to the Early Twentieth Century*. Liverpool: Liverpool University Press, 1989. Examines urban growth throughout western Europe.

Traugott, Mark, ed. *The French Worker: Autobiographies from the Early Industrial Era*. Berkeley, CA: University of California Press, 1993. Presents a working-class perspective on the effects of industrialization.

PUBLIC HEALTH AND MEDICINE IN THE INDUSTRIAL AGE

Porter, Roy. *A Medical History of Humanity*. New York: W.W. Norton, 1998. A wide-ranging and interesting survey that covers the period well.

FAMILY IDEALS AND REALITIES

Honeyman, Katrina. *Women, Gender and Industrialization in England, 1700–1850*. New York: St. Martin's Press, 2000. Analyzes connections between work and gender roles.

Maynes, Mary Jo. *Taking the Hard Road*. Chapel Hill, NC: University of North Carolina Press, 1995. Examines German and French workers' lives during the industrial revolution.

Tilly, Louise, and Joan Scott. *Women, Work and Family*. New York: Holt, Rinehart and Winston, 1978. A classic study of the family as an economic unit, especially during the first half of the nineteenth century.

www.mhhe.com/sherman3

- Unfamiliar words? See our Glossary at the back of the book for pronunciation and definitions.

- Need help studying? See our web page for map exercises, practice quizzes, and additional study resources.

- Need help writing a paper? Access hundreds of primary documents, maps, images, and a guide to writing history papers on our Primary Source Investigator site at **www.mhhe.com/psi.**

ANTON ZIEGLER, *THE BARRICADE IN MICHAELER SQUARE ON THE NIGHT OF MAY 26TH*

This painting by the Austrian artist Anton Ziegler depicts the "glory days" of the 1848 revolutions. In the image, men and women of various classes in Vienna guard a revolutionary barricade made of paving stones, timbers, and carts. Behind the barricade, a community of people stands ready to help one another politely in the common effort (notice the man aiding a woman across a wooden footbridge). The atmosphere has an almost festive quality, and nothing in the picture hints at the violence and loss of life that came with this turbulent year.

CHAPTER 18

COPING WITH CHANGE

IDEOLOGY, POLITICS, AND REVOLUTION, 1815–1850

STUDY	The Congress of Vienna ■ Ideologies ■ The Restoration ■ Revolution and reform ■ 1848.
NOTICE	The sets of beliefs about the world that shaped politics and social action.

Prince Clemens von Metternich (1773–1859), Austria's conservative and powerful minister of foreign affairs, discussed ideas in candlelit salons as easily as he wielded power in somber cabinet meetings. Like other cosmopolitan aristocrats born into traditional eighteenth-century societies, he spoke French as well as the German of his birthplace. In 1820, five years after the fall of Napoleon, he wrote to his ally, Tsar Alexander I (r. 1801–1825) of Russia. "Kings have to calculate the chances of their very existence in the immediate future," he complained. "Passions are let loose and league together to overthrow everything which society respects as the basis of its existence; religion, public morality, laws, customs, rights, and duties, all are attacked, confounded, overthrown, or called to question."

Metternich, Alexander I, and people everywhere were struggling to adjust to the political and social forces unleashed by the French Revolution and Napoleon's domination of Europe. The industrial revolution, wherever it set its roots, spawned another set of problems along with the wealth it created. Together, these waves of change were undermining traditional political, social, and economic orders.

Some, such as Metternich, fought to maintain the old order; others, displaying the "passions" Metternich complained about, fought for all-encompassing reforms. People on all sides turned to ideologies—sets of ideas, attitudes, and beliefs about how the world is and should be—to try to cope with the new realities of Western life in the nineteenth century. One of those realities was the possibility of revolution again raising its unpredictable head. The outcomes of these struggles of ideologies and politics would profoundly shape much of nineteenth-century history.

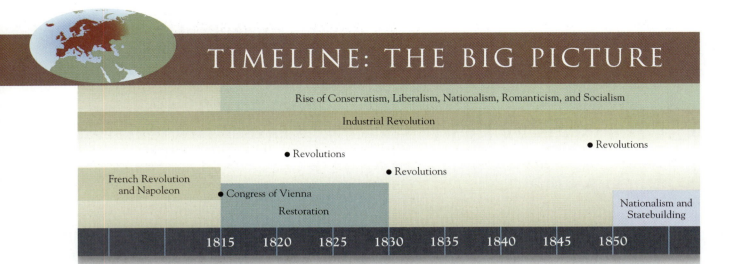

TIMELINE: THE BIG PICTURE

Rise of Conservatism, Liberalism, Nationalism, Romanticism, and Socialism

Industrial Revolution

● Revolutions

● Revolutions

French Revolution and Napoleon

● Congress of Vienna

Restoration

● Revolutions

Nationalism and Statebuilding

1815   1820   1825   1830   1835   1840   1845   1850

THE CONGRESS OF VIENNA: A GATHERING OF VICTORS

IN THE AUTUMN OF 1814, the leaders of the powers who had finally vanquished Napoleon gathered to redraw territorial boundaries and fashion a lasting peace. The conference also attracted representatives of every state in Europe, hundreds of dispossessed princes, agents of every interest, and adventurers. Nearly everyone who thought he or she was somebody of importance in "high circles" attended. The representatives reveled in the glittering gatherings and entertainments. In addition to the public conferences, many private meetings took place—though just how private remains uncertain, for Austrian spies regularly opened letters and searched wastebaskets. Elsewhere, in newspapers from St. Petersburg, Rome, and Paris to London and even Boston, people closely followed the daily events in the beautiful Austrian capital. Something immensely important and exciting seemed to be unfolding there.

The four major victors over Napoleon—Great Britain, Prussia, Russia, and Austria—set peace terms with France around the time of Napoleon's overthrow in April, and these four dominated the congress. The able Lord Castlereagh (1769–1822) represented Great Britain and the experienced Baron Hardenberg (1750–1822) represented Prussia. Russia's tsar, the unsteady Alexander I, headed his own delegation. The elegant, arrogant Metternich led the Austrian delegation and became the most influential figure of the congress.

The victors

Jean-Baptiste Isabey's formal portrait of the principal figures at the Congress of Vienna (Figure 18.1) gives a sense of the seriousness of this event and the ideals that the victors represented. From left to right,

Austria's polished Metternich stands before a chair, Great Britain's Castlereagh sits with crossed legs, and the elderly Talleyrand (1754–1838) of France rests with his right arm on the table. In a fine but businesslike eighteenth-century salon, these powerful men are gathered around a table to participate in the reading and signing of crucial documents. Their clothing marks them as members of the aristocracy: Almost all the men sport gold trim and knee breeches with high stockings; some wear military coats and carry swords reflecting victory in the field over Napoleon. Most display medals symbolizing their achievements and position. Yet these clothes also hint at change: Most of the figures in the painting lack the more elegant clothing and wigs of the eighteenth century. Above the men, as if approving of what they are doing, hangs a symbol of the restoration of the old regime: a portrait of a king draped in regal robes.

As guiding principles in the negotiations, the conferees decided on "legitimacy" and "stability." By *legitimacy* they meant that territories should once more be placed under the control of the old ruling houses of the traditional order. By *stability* they meant establishing and maintaining a balance of power within Europe, with particular focus on restraining France. The main powers agreed that the settlement should apply to all of Europe.

Legitimacy and stability

Yet the conferees proved lenient in their settlement toward France. Thanks to the victors' desire to turn France into an ally rather than a resentful enemy and to Talleyrand's diplomatic skills, France, the original force behind all the turmoil, escaped the proceedings with only light penalties. Having already restored the French throne to the Bourbons, the powers merely reduced France roughly to

■ FIGURE 18.1

Jean-Baptiste Isabey, *The Congress of Vienna.*

its 1789 boundaries. Because of Napoleon's 100-day return (see p. 530), they also required France to pay an indemnity of 700 million francs, return stolen art treasures, and submit to occupation by allied forces until the indemnity was paid.

To confine France within its frontiers and discourage future French aggression, the powers established strong buffer states along France's borders. As Map 18.1 shows, Prussia received *Territorial arrangements* a sizable block of territory along the Rhine; the Austrian Netherlands (Belgium) and the Dutch Netherlands were unified; Piedmont-Sardinia in northern Italy was enlarged; and the old monarchy was restored in Spain.

Trading among themselves, the four main powers took new territories. Great Britain gained several strategic islands and colonies, all of which boosted its sea power and overseas dominance. Prussia added some areas in central Europe. Russia acquired control over a reduced, nominally independent Poland, thereby edging farther into the heart of central Europe. Russia also took Finland from Sweden, which

in turn got Norway at the expense of Napoleon's ally, Denmark. Austria gained Lombardy and Venetia in northern Italy as well as the permanent presidency over the weak German Confederation—the thirty-nine German states that remained after Napoleon's destruction of the Holy Roman Empire.

Although they displayed little concern for the wishes of the peoples being placed under the control of one power or the other, the conferees did produce a settlement that contributed to a century of freedom from Europewide war. Moreover, thanks to the persistent efforts of the British, the powers agreed in principle to abolish the slave trade. They also achieved—at least temporarily—their conservative goals of promoting legitimacy and stability that meant so much to them.

THE CONCERT OF EUROPE: SECURING THE VIENNA SETTLEMENT

Metternich and his colleagues, pleased with their handiwork, set up the political machinery for perpetuating

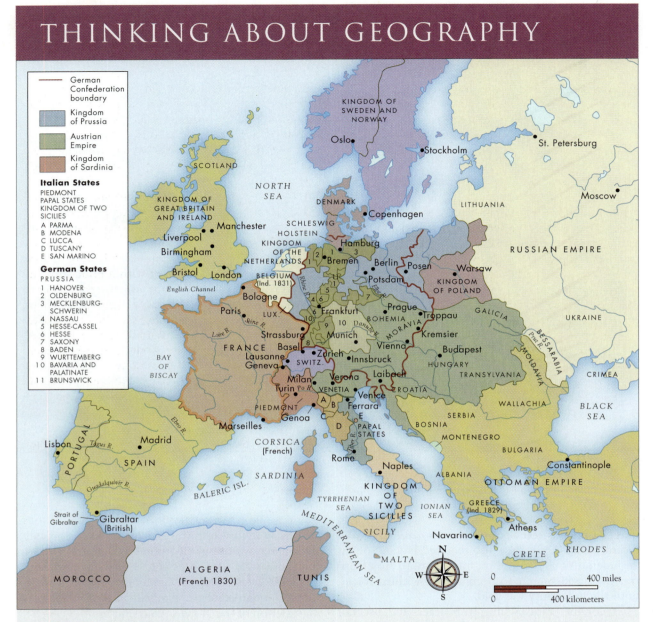

Legend:
- German Confederation boundary
- Kingdom of Prussia
- Austrian Empire
- Kingdom of Sardinia

Italian States
PIEDMONT
PAPAL STATES
KINGDOM OF TWO SICILIES
A PARMA
B MODENA
C LUCCA
D TUSCANY
E SAN MARINO

German States
PRUSSIA
1 HANOVER
2 OLDENBURG
3 MECKLENBURG-SCHWERIN
4 NASSAU
5 HESSE-CASSEL
6 HESSE
7 SAXONY
8 BADEN
9 WURTTEMBERG
10 BAVARIA AND PALATINATE
11 BRUNSWICK

MAP 18.1 EUROPE, 1815

This map shows Europe after the Congress of Vienna in 1815. ■ **Compare** this map with that of Napoleon's empire in Chapter 16 (Map 16.4). **What** are the main changes? ■ **Locate** the enlarged states—the Netherlands, Prussia, and Piedmont-Sardinia. **Why** did the Congress of Vienna strengthen these states? ■ **Consider** the effect of the settlement on the major European powers. **Did** the settlement severely punish France?

The Holy Alliance

the Vienna settlement. Conveniently at hand was the Holy Alliance, conceived by Alexander I to establish and safeguard the principles of Christianity. Russia, Austria, and Prussia—the three bastions of conservatism—formed the nucleus of this alliance.

Though Metternich and professional diplomats put little faith in it, the Holy Alliance did symbolize a commitment to preserving the Vienna settlement. Perhaps more important, it suggested a possible willingness to intervene in other countries in support of its conservative principles.

The Quadruple Alliance, also known as the Concert of Europe, proved a much more earthly agency for perpetuating the Vienna settlement. Austria, Russia, Prussia, and Great Britain created this military alliance in November 1815 to guarantee the Vienna settlement. The powers agreed to hold periodic meetings to discuss common problems. In 1818, France completed its payment of indemnities and joined the Alliance.

The Concert of Europe

Soon this conservative partnership showed its strength. In 1821 it authorized an Austrian army to put down an insurrection in Naples against King Ferdinand I. The Neapolitan liberal rebels, no match for the Austrian troops, were soon defeated and their leaders executed, imprisoned, or exiled. In 1822 the Alliance, despite Britain's withdrawal, authorized France to intervene against a liberal revolt in Spain. A French army streamed across the Pyrenees and easily crushed the rebellion. That same year, the conservative powers supported Alexander's proposal to send a Russian fleet to help put down the revolt of Spain's Latin American colonies (see Chapter 16).

The great strength of the Alliance, however, remained bound within the European continent. Across the Atlantic Ocean, President Monroe of the United States announced what would come to be called the Monroe Doctrine: The United States would regard any interference on the part of European powers in the affairs of the Western Hemisphere as an "unfriendly act." British support of the doctrine—stemming from Britain's own economic interests in Latin America—killed any further thought of Holy Alliance intervention in the Western Hemisphere, for Great Britain enjoyed unchallenged dominance of the seas.

IDEOLOGIES: HOW THE WORLD SHOULD BE

The principles underlying the settlement at Vienna and the international cooperation to enforce it reflected the deep conservatism of Metternich and many others during these years. Their conservatism was more than just a whim or political mood. Under the impact of the French Revolution and the industrial revolution, the centuries-old aristocratic order and agriculturally based society had started to crumble. Intellectuals in particular tried to grasp these changes by exploring ideologies, or sets of beliefs about the world and how it should be. These ideologies exerted immense power. People wrote, marched, fought, and died for them. Indeed, they fueled many of the struggles that would erupt in the years to come and ultimately would shape our very definition of the modern world.

CONSERVATISM: RESTORING THE TRADITIONAL ORDER

The changes initiated during the French Revolution and supported by Enlightenment ideas threatened and even terrified conservatives. They wanted desperately to preserve the traditional way of life. Conservatism provided the ideas to refute Enlightenment and revolutionary principles and all those who stood behind them. At the heart of conservatism lay a belief in order and hierarchy. The social and political order, conservatives believed, should be based on a hierarchy of authoritative institutions whose legitimacy rested on God and tradition. As conservatives saw it, the revolutionary notion of equality was wrong. The elite was equipped to rule; the rest were not. The most formidable enemy was the bourgeoisie, "this intermediary class" ready to "abandon itself with a blind fury and animosity . . . to all the means which seem proper to assuage its thirst for power," according to Metternich. Conservatives also warned that the idea of individualism promoted by the Enlightenment and favored by the rising middle class would fragment society and lead to anarchy. In the mind of a conservative, all change was suspect. If change did come, it should take the form of slow evolution of social and political institutions.

In 1790, the influential Anglo-Irish writer and statesman Edmund Burke (1729–1797), horrified with the outbreak of the French Revolution, outlined some of the principles of conservatism (see p. 512). He argued that the revolutionaries' radical reforms based on abstract reason and notions of equality unraveled hard-won victories against savagery: "[I]t is with infinite caution that any man ought to venture upon pulling down an edifice which has answered . . . for ages the common purposes of society." The monarchy and nobility should be preserved because they, like the church, were established links to an organic past and the best hopes for preserving the order necessary for societies to thrive.

Burke

The French writers Joseph de Maistre (1753–1821) and Louis de Bonald (1754–1840) represented a later generation of conservative thinkers who proved more rigid and ultraroyalist than Burke. As Document 18.1 suggests, they attacked everything about the French Revolution and Enlightenment as contrary to religion, order, and civilization. De Maistre called the French Revolution an "insurrection against God." Both writers argued that authority rightly rests in the monarchy and the church, both of which derive that authority from God. "When monarchy and Christianity are both attacked, society returns to savagery," declared de Bonald. These conservatives felt that deep down, humans were more wicked than good, more irrational than rational.

de Maistre and de Bonald

■ DOCUMENT 18.1

A Conservative Theorist Attacks Political Reform

Many conservatives resented the reforms sparked by the French Revolution. The extremely conservative theorist Joseph de Maistre was no exception. In the following excerpt from his Essay on the Generative Principle of Political Constitutions, *published in Russia in 1810 and then Paris in 1814, de Maistre attacks written constitutions and the reform of political institutions.* ■ **On what basis** *does de Maistre object to written constitutions?* ■ **Would** *any political reforms have merit according to de Maistre?*

"Every thing brings us back to the general rule—*man cannot create a constitution; and no legitimate constitution can be written.* The collection of fundamental laws, which must essentially constitute a civil or religious society, never has been written, and never will be, *a priori.* It is only when society finds itself already constituted, without being able to say how, that it is possible to make known, or explain, in writing, certain special articles; but in almost every case these declarations or explanations are the effect of very great evils, and always cost the people more than they are worth.

". . . Not only does it not belong to man to create institutions, but it does not appear that his power, *unassisted*, extends even to change for the better institutions already established. . . . *Nothing* [says the philosopher, Origen] . . . *can be changed for the better among men, without God.* All men have a consciousness of this truth, without being in a state to explain it to themselves. Hence that instinc-

tive aversion, in every good mind, to innovations. The word *reform*, in itself, and previous to all examinations, will be always suspected by wisdom, and the experience of every age justifies this sort of instinct.

". . . To apply these maxims to a particular case . . . the great question of parliamentary reform, which has agitated minds in England so powerfully, and for so long a time, I still find myself constrained to believe, that this idea is pernicious, and that if the English yield themselves too readily to it, they will have occasion to repent."

Source: Scholars' Facsimiles & Reprints (New York: Delmar, 1977), reprinting of the edition of Joseph de Maistre, *Essay on the Generative Principle of Political Constitutions* (Boston: Little and Brown, 1847).

Only the time-tested traditions and institutions could hold the bad impulses of humans in check. All means, including fear and violence, should be used to roll back the changes from the French revolutionary and Napoleonic periods and return to societies dominated by monarchs, aristocrats, and clergy.

Not surprisingly, people from these same three groups found conservatism most appealing. Conservatism also attracted many who believed in a Christian view of society, particularly members of the established churches rather than religious minorities. Some even saw the revolutionary and Napoleonic periods as divine retribution for the presumption and evil that had long marred human beings. In the international field, conservatism was epitomized by Metternich's policies, the Holy Alliance, and the Concert of Europe. In domestic policies, this conservatism was characterized by the restoration of power to the traditional monarchs and aristocrats, the renewed influence of Christianity, and the suppression of liberal and nationalistic movements.

Appeal of conservatism

However, conservatives faced formidable opponents, even during the early years after the fall of Napoleon. The French Revolution had turned the ideas of liberalism into a powerful, persistent force. The

clash between conservatism and liberalism had just begun and would endure into the twentieth century.

LIBERALISM: INDIVIDUAL FREEDOM AND POLITICAL REFORM

In contrast to conservatism, liberalism drew on the promises of the French Revolution and the Enlightenment. Conservatives sought to maintain traditional society; liberals fought to change it. Liberals wanted a society that promoted individual freedom, or liberty. However, many laws, customs, and conditions of the traditional order stood in their way. Liberals therefore opposed the dominance of politics and society by monarchs, aristocrats, and clergy, and governments' arbitrary interference with individual liberty. To the extent that these elements of the traditional order remained in place, liberals demanded reform and fought resisting conservatives.

From the Enlightenment and the theories of John Locke, liberals adopted ideas about natural laws, natural rights, toleration, and the application of reason to human affairs (see Chapter 14). From political thinkers such as Montesquieu, they took the idea that governmental powers should be separated

Sources of liberalism

and restricted by checks and balances. From the French and American Revolutions, they drew on the principles of freedom, equality before the law, popular sovereignty, and sanctity of property.

Liberalism reflected the aspirations of the middle class, which was gaining wealth but lacked political and social power in the traditional order. Not surprisingly, then, liberals advocated government limited by written constitutions, the elimination of political and social privileges, and extension of voting rights to men of some property and education (most liberals stopped short of suggesting universal male suffrage or extension of the vote to women.) In addition, liberals desired representative institutions where none existed and an extension of the right to participate in representative institutions that remained the preserve of the aristocratic and wealthy elite. They demanded that governments guarantee the sanctity of property and individual rights, such as freedom of the press, speech, assembly, and religion.

Certain economic policies also had great importance to liberals and reflected the stake that the middle class had in commerce and industry. The **Smith** Scottish economist Adam Smith (1723–1790) formulated the ideas that guided economic liberalism (see page 459). In *The Wealth of Nations* (1776), Smith argued that economics, like the physical world, had its own natural laws. The most basic economic law was of supply and demand, he explained. When left to operate alone, economic laws, like an "invisible hand," would keep the economy in balance and, in the long run, create the most wealth. According to Smith, self-interest—even greed—was the engine that motivated people to work hard and produce wealth: "It is not from the benevolence of the butcher, the brewer, or the baker that we expect our dinner, but from their regard to their own interest." Governments should therefore follow a policy of laissez-faire (hands-off), limiting their involvement in the economy to little more than maintaining law and order so that an unfettered marketplace could flourish.

Other liberal economic thinkers extended Smith's ideas. The British economist Thomas Malthus (1766–1834) cast gloom on hopes for **Malthus and Ricardo** progress among workers. He argued that population would always increase more than food supplies, resulting in poverty and death by "the whole train of common disease, and epidemics, wars, plague and famine." Malthus concluded that workers themselves are "the cause of their own poverty," because they lacked the moral discipline to avoid sexual activity. The politically influential Englishman David Ricardo (1772–1823) refined Malthus's arguments into the "iron law of wages," explaining that wages would always sink to subsistence levels or below because higher salaries just caused workers to multiply, thereby glutting the labor market and lowering wages. He emphasized that the economy was controlled by objective laws. The lessons for these "classical" liberals (to distinguish them from modern American liberals, who usually favor government programs to regulate certain economic and social affairs) were clear: no intervention in economic matters by government, no tariffs or unions that artificially raise prices or wages, and no restrictions on individual enterprise.

Over time, liberalism evolved and developed several variations. The English philosopher Jeremy Bentham (1748–1832) and his followers advocated a kind of liberalism that became particularly influential in Britain. Known as utilitarianism, it **Bentham** held that all activities and policies should be judged by the standard of usefulness. "Nature has placed mankind under the governance of two sovereign masters, *pain* and *pleasure*," explained Bentham. What was useful, the utilitarians decreed, was what created more pleasure than pain; the best laws and policies were therefore those that promoted "the greatest good for the greatest number" of people. Bentham's utilitarians fought for more governmental intervention in economic and social affairs than other liberals. For example, they supported reforms to protect women and children workers in factories and to improve urban sanitation. Democracy was implicit in utilitarianism, for the best way for the greatest number to maximize their own happiness was for each person to vote. Nevertheless, most liberals during this period actually opposed democracy. They feared the supposedly unruly "masses" and hoped to keep government in the hands of the propertied and well educated. They **Mill** would not start to embrace democratic reforms until the middle of the nineteenth century. At that time, some of them, such as John Stuart Mill (1806–1873) (see Biography on page 572), would also begin arguing for major social programs to protect workers and even the right to vote for women.

As we saw earlier, liberalism appealed especially to the rising middle classes, who were prospering from commerce and industry and wanted political power along with their growing wealth and confidence. Liberals had faith that history was on their side, that liberalism, like progress, was inevitable and that the forces they opposed were of the past. That optimism gave them strength to fight against the conservative forces of tradition and rally to protect their gains.

NATIONALISM: A COMMON IDENTITY AND NATIONAL LIBERATION

Like the liberals, nationalists harbored a spirit of optimism. They, too, were aroused by the French Revolution, for it promoted the idea that sovereignty

BIOGRAPHY

John Stuart Mill (1806–1873) and Harriet Taylor (1807–1858)

CONSIDER

■ **Consider** why Mill is labeled a leading proponent of liberalism. ■ **Compare** the Mill family and the Cadbury family discussed in Chapter 17.

John Stuart Mill and Harriet Taylor were one of the most famous and extraordinary couples of the nineteenth century. Born in 1806, John described his own childhood as "remarkable." His father, the well-known liberal philosopher James Mill (1773–1836), raised John according to the cut-and-dried principles of Jeremy Bentham's utilitarianism. John learned Greek at the age of 3, Latin when he was 7, logic at 12, and economics at 13. On their daily walks, James encouraged little John to summarize assigned readings for him. He wanted to turn John's mind into a logical machine for radical thought and utilitarian reform.

In 1822, John and several other young men founded the liberal Utilitarian Society. John, like other liberals, had great faith in the power of knowledge and reason to right human errors: "Knowledge has triumphed. It has worked the downfall of much that is mischievous." For the young Mill, utilitarianism was virtually "a religion." In 1823, John took his first job with the East India Company, the vehicle of British rule in India. He would remain with that company for thirty-five years, reading dispatches from the company's agents in India and drafting replies.

In 1826 he suffered a "crisis." Recoiling from his sterile, intellectualized upbringing, John came to doubt the value of his education and ambition, concluding that neither of these qualities led to happiness. He turned to romanticism—a movement that featured the lush music and especially the writings of Wordsworth,

Goethe, and other cultural icons of the day. In time, he came to believe that "poetry is higher than logic, and . . . the union of the two is philosophy."

During these same years, 19-year-old Harriet Hardy had married John Taylor, a wealthy partner in a wholesale drug firm. Taylor adored his intellectual wife, who was bolder and more brilliant than he. However, after giving birth to two children, Harriet began to lose interest in John. She increasingly found sex with him an unpleasant imposition and criticized marriage as a sexual contract that was unfair to women.

Extraordinary Victorians

In 1830 Harriet Taylor and John Stuart Mill met. They became "intimate and confidential friends." Mill was a constant visitor to the Taylor household and a frequent companion to Harriet in London. Although their relationship created a scandal in London society, John Taylor, unwilling to see his wife unhappy, acquiesced in it.

In 1843, Mill published A *System of Logic*, the first of several major works that marked him as one of the leading thinkers of the nineteenth century. In 1851, Harriet published anonymously *The Enfranchisement of Women*, which argued for universal suffrage and more equal companionship between men and women. Mill would go on to publish *On Liberty* (1859), his most famous political work, in which he argued for freedom of thought

rested not in a monarch or a church, but in the people, and that they, banded together, constituted the nation. Nationalism promised to unify nations, liberate subject peoples from foreign rule, create a sense of fraternity among members of a national community, and lead that community to a common destiny. At its core was a feeling of cultural identity among distinct groups of people who shared a common language and traditions and who belonged in a nation-state of their own.

France became an early source of nationalist sentiments. There a sense of membership in the state became especially important when the Revolution transformed the kingdom into a nation. Popular sovereignty, wider political participation, and abolition of old provincial boundary lines gave the French a feeling of solidarity among themselves and with the national government. Universal

The French Revolution

conscription into the revolutionary armies added to feelings of fraternity in a righteous cause and helped make those armies strong. Powerful new symbols, such as the tricolor flag, stood for national unity and willingness to sacrifice for the sake of the nation.

Nationalism also moved people who did not yet share a state. In the German-speaking areas, for example, scholars and intellectuals developed a cultural basis for nationalism. Writers such as Johann Gottfried von Herder (1744–1803) fostered a sense of common national identity arising from German folk culture and oral traditions. Georg Wilhelm Friedrich Hegel (1770–1831) provided philosophical

Cultural nationalism

and historical bases for German nationalism and the importance of the national state. Romantics such as Ernst Moritz Arndt (1769–1860) urged Prussians, Austrians, Bavarians, and others with common roots to "be Germans, be one, will to be one by love and

and warned against the tyranny of the majority. In 1869, he published *The Subjection of Women*, which made him one of the leading feminists of the century. It is fundamentally wrong, he said, for society to "ordain that to be born a girl instead of a boy, any more than to be born black instead of white, or a commoner instead of a nobleman, shall decide the person's position through all life."

Mill was happy to describe most of his works as jointly produced by himself and Harriet. But Mill may have been too generous in his praise of her role. Just how much she contributed has long been a matter of heated debate. In 1849, two discreet years after John Taylor's death, Mill and Harriet Taylor married. They were proud that their relationship was based on rationality, intellectual companionship, affection, and intimacy, but not sex. They imagined their marriage as a utopian union of equals. It lasted until 1858, when Harriet died.

In the years before his death in 1873, Mill was elected to the House of Commons, where he argued for liberal reforms such as the abolition of capital punishment, feminist reforms such as the extension of suffrage to women, and socialist reforms such as poor relief. Figure 18.2 shows a caricature drawing of Mill that was published in the widely read journal *Punch* in 1867. Readers could easily recognize the famous liberal intellectual (depicted with an unusually large head). The illustration shows him leading women, who are demanding the right to vote, by pushing aside resisting men with his arm and his logical arguments. He concluded that "the social problem of the future" would center on "how to unite the greatest individual liberty of action with a common ownership in the raw material of the globe."

Thus Harriet and John embodied many nineteenth-century trends. Liberalism, romanticism, and socialism all played a role

■ FIGURE 18.2
John Stuart Mill.

in their lives. In addition, what brought them together was the middle-class ideal—affection, companionship, the shared life at home. In other ways, however, they did not reflect the times at all. Their views on marriage and relations between men and women, for example, the long triangular relationship with John Taylor, and the intensity of their intellectual collaboration all alarmed many of their contemporaries. Only in the decades to come would these unusual views gain more favor.

loyalty, and no devil will vanquish you." Groups and secret societies such as Young Germany—usually composed of students, intellectuals, and members of the middle class—promoted a sense of national identity and unity.

In Italy, Poland, and elsewhere, nationalists formed similar organizations and intellectuals created interest in national languages and folk culture. Scholars resurrected and developed languages from previous eras and elevated myths to national histories. Schoolteachers taught these languages and histories to their students and thereby spread a sense of ethnic unity. Nationalists used this growing interest in language and history to proclaim their nation's special mission— for example, of the Czechs to become leaders of the Slavs, or the Italians to lead Europe again as it had during Roman times.

Nationalism promised a new sense of community as the old order with its traditional allegiances declined.

It offered a sense of strength and unity that appealed to many peoples: to those threatened with foreign domination, such as the Spaniards and Italians under the French during the Napoleonic era; to those dissatisfied with the dominance of one ethnic group, such as Czechs, Magyars, or Serbs under the Germans within the Habsburg Empire; and to those feeling suppressed by what they considered foreign domination, such as the Greeks under the Ottomans, the Poles under the Russians, and the Italians under the Austrians.

Sense of community

From such sources, it was a short step to calls for national liberation and political unification. Nationalism soon acquired attributes of a religion and became a powerful political force. For example, the Italian nationalist Giuseppe Mazzini (1805–1872), who

National liberation and unification

founded the revolutionary Young Italy movement in 1831, called Italy "the purpose, the soul, the consolation of our thoughts, the country chosen of God and oppressed by men." Some nationalist leaders such as Mazzini began demanding loyalty and solidarity from members of their organizations.

Before 1848, most nationalists supported liberal causes, for liberals also struggled for national rights. Both liberals and nationalists typically believed that sovereignty should rest with the people, united by common loyalties and language. They also had faith that change would bring political, social, and economic progress. Campaigns by liberals to promote agricultural improvement and industrial development often merged into German, Italian, and Hungarian calls for national unity.

Later, nationalists would ally themselves with conservatives, for both believed in the value of historical traditions and in an organic society over the rights of the individual. Nationalism would also become more entwined with notions of national superiority and special national missions that so often appealed to conservatives. All nationalists, however, insisted that each nation of people, unified into a self-governing state, should be the primary focus of political loyalty and that the political boundaries of the state should be the same as ethnic boundaries of the people. The widespread political and emotional appeal of nationalism made it an increasingly powerful ideology over the course of the century.

ROMANTICISM: FREEDOM, INSTINCT, AND SPONTANEITY

The origins of nationalism in literature and history also made it attractive to believers in romanticism. This ideology became the dominant spirit in literature and art during the first half of the nineteenth century. Its significance stretched beyond culture, however. Romanticism reflected a new recognition that human beings were complex, emotional, and only sometimes rational creatures. In a civilization that was growing ever more scientific, materialistic, industrial, and urban, romanticism became a counterweight for the human experience. It stood against eighteenth-century classicism and the Enlightenment and the ideals of reason and order that so characterized those eras. Instead, romanticism emphasized individual freedom and spontaneity.

Origins of romanticism can be traced back to Jean-Jacques Rousseau, the acclaimed writer and philosopher we met in Chapter 14. Though *Rousseau* a central figure of the Enlightenment, Rousseau had stressed feeling, instinct, emotions, and love of nature. He described walking away from the city into the fields and woods, stretching himself out on the ground, digging his fingers and toes into the dirt, kissing the earth, and weeping for joy. In several of his most widely read writings, he seemed to idealize love, childhood, and "the noble savage."

Other strands of romanticism came from the German "Storm and Stress" (Sturm und Drang) literature of the late eighteenth century. German writers gave much weight to inner feelings fully experienced and expressed by *"Storm and Stress" literature* sensitive individuals. Johann Wolfgang von Goethe provided a model of the emotional individual searching for love and self-understanding in his novel *The Sorrows of the Young Werther* (1774). Like Rousseau, Goethe had many interests. He delved into philosophy, science, and public affairs as well as literature. His masterpiece, the philosophical drama *Faust*, featured a medieval scholar who, dissatisfied with the fruits of knowledge, sells his soul to the devil in return for earthly pleasure and wisdom. In Goethe's medieval interests, his emotional spontaneity, and his love of nature and of individual personality, this renowned writer exemplified the heart of romanticism.

All these qualities explored by Rousseau and Goethe came to characterize the work of succeeding romantic writers and artists. Many romantics expressed a new interest in the Middle Ages. They *Reviving the Middle Ages* revived the popularity of medieval tales, Gothic architecture, the Knights of the Round Table, and heroic figures, thereby turning the medieval era from the "Dark Ages" into the "Age of Faith."

This fascination with the Middle Ages reflected romanticism's passionate concern with the drama of history. Written by scholars such as Thomas Babington Macaulay (1800–1859) in Great Britain, history was literary and exciting, featuring *History* heroic individuals, great accomplishments, and national struggles. These same themes were explored by the Prussian philosopher Hegel. In Hegel's view, history was a great spiritual drama of heroic individuals that would lead to a new sense of national identity and freedom.

Romanticism also stressed the emotion of Christianity and the mystical presence of God in nature. According to romantic theologians, the important part of religion was the feeling of dependence on an infinite God rather than religious dogma or institutions. In his widely *Christianity* read book, *The Genius of Christianity*, the French writer François Auguste-René de Chateaubriand (1768–1848) described in lush words how "every thing in a Gothic church reminds you of the labyrinths of a forest; every thing excites a feeling of religious awe, of mystery, and of the Divinity." In part, religious revivals during the late eighteenth and early nineteenth centuries, with their stress on piety and emotional outpourings, reflected these spiritual qualities of romanticism.

The connections among the love of nature, the spiritual presence of God, and the power of emotions were most striking in the romantic literature, art, and music of the period. In the literary realm, the English poets William Wordsworth (1770–1850) and Samuel Taylor Coleridge (1772–1834) became closely associated with the beautiful lake country of northwest England—Wordsworth by birth and Coleridge by adoption. Together the two men traveled to Germany, where they fell under the influence of German romanticists. They collaborated on *Lyrical Ballads* (1798), which included Wordsworth's "Lines Composed a Few Miles Above Tintern Abbey" and Coleridge's "Rime of the Ancient Mariner." Both writers glorified nature and sensed a brooding, mystical presence of the divine. Wordsworth saw in nature a higher wisdom than what scholars might offer:

Literature

> One impulse from a vernal wood
> May teach you more of man,
> Of moral evil and of good
> Than all the sages can.

Wordsworth's and Coleridge's ardent appreciation of nature, their introspective concern for the individual, and their preoccupation with the spiritual rather than the material made them leaders among Britain's many romantic poets.

In France, Germaine de Staël (1766–1817) led the romantic movement in literature. Although she admired the passionate Rousseau, she attacked most Enlightenment thinkers for not being free enough. She turned to writing in order to grapple with her own emotional experiences with several lovers and to argue for living the passionate life. Often writing about female heroes and genius in works such as *Corinne*, de Staël also looked to history for a vision of another, better world. She and other romantics created an image of the ideal romantic heroine who followed her emotions rather than tradition or reason—a model that some tried to follow in life. Also in France, George Sand (Amandine Dupin Dudevant) (1804–1876) became an extraordinarily creative writer and an unconventional, even threatening woman. Abandoning her tyrannical husband for an independent life in Paris, Sand became an intellectual leader whose private life included several love affairs with well-known people. At her own convenience, she dressed as a man or a woman. Like several other women writers, she also took a male pseudonym to add legitimacy to her writings. Several of her novels explored romantic love and featured strong, intensely emotional heroines.

Leading romantic painters also stressed emotional images. Figure 18.3, an oil painting by the German artist Karl Friedrich Schinkel, shows an idealized image of a medieval town at twilight. In the center stands a magnificent Gothic cathedral, its spires stretching toward the heavens above. The parting clouds and setting sun seem to bless this church and town. Below, humble workers bring abundant supplies from the river. They are dwarfed by the cathedral, the central stairs leading up to the cathedral, the high-arching bridge that echoes the arches of the cathedral, their finely built town on the right, and nature above. The painting contains the key elements of romanticism: glorification of nature, religious mysticism, adoration of an idealized medieval era, and expression of emotion.

Art

The romantic love of magnificent landscapes can be found in Figure 18.4. This 1817 painting emphasizes the theme of the poet both immersed in nature and conjuring up a majestic natural setting like a god. Here the robed poet with his harp stands on a cliff, his arm stretched out to the swirling heavens above. Below him, waters rage and a knight on a white horse (lower left) gallops off into the distance. In the background stands a medieval castle built into the mountains.

In music, a number of romantic composers followed in the footsteps of Ludwig van Beethoven (1770–1827). The music of this famed German composer overflowed the bounds of classic forms, becoming freer, more individualistic, and emotional than anything that had come before. Beethoven composed his *Pastoral Symphony* as a musical link to nature. "How happy I am," he wrote in 1810, "to be able to stroll in the woods, among the trees, bushes, wild flowers and rocks. No one can love the country as much as I do." The lyrics to one of his choral works explain his feelings about music:

Music

> When the magic of sound holds sway
> and works bring inspiration,
> glorious things must appear,
> darkness and turmoil become light.

One critic explained that romantic music should "paint to the eyes of the soul the splendors of nature, the delights of contemplation, the character of nations, the tumult of their passions, and the languor of their sufferings. . . ."

The painting by the Austrian artist Josef Danhauser shown in Figure 18.5 brings together leading figures of romantic art and literature. At the center, the Hungarian virtuoso and composer Franz Liszt plays the piano for his friends. Standing, from left to right, are the French writer Victor Hugo, the Italian violinist Niccolò Paganini, and the composer Antonio Rossini. Sitting are the French writers Alexandre Dumas, George Sand (characteristically in men's clothing), and Daniel Stern (Marie d'Agoult, who had a long-term liaison with Liszt). Above the

Karl Friedrich Schinkel, *Medieval Town on a River*, 1815

■ FIGURE 18.3

In this 1815 painting, Karl Friedrich Schinkel depicts an imaginary medieval town. A stunning Gothic cathedral dominates the people below, as well as the scene itself. ■ **What** impression of medieval life do you think the artist intended to convey to viewers? ■ **In what ways** does this painting represent Romanticism? ■ **Why** might Schinkel have chosen to make the cathedral so prominent? ■ **Consider** how the scene in this painting might contrast with a realistic urban scene of the nineteenth century.

group shows a portrait of Lord Byron and a bust of Beethoven, the deceased "saints" of romantic poetry and music.

Through much of romanticism, strands from all the ideologies combined and recombined in a variety of ways. Nationalism, for example, played a promi- nent role in some roman- tics' lives. In the 1820s, England's romantic poet Lord Byron (1788–1824) fought for Greek national inde- pendence against the Turks (see Figure 18.7). Some

Connections to nationalism

of Frederic Chopin's (1810–1849) dramatic music self-consciously evoked nationalistic sentiments for his native Poland, which was still under Russian rule. The Italian Giuseppe Verdi (1813–1901) and the German Richard Wagner (1813–1883), who devel- oped the opera into a fully integrated art form of music, theater, ballet, and special effects, were among many other composers whose works brought together romantic and openly nationalistic themes.

Liberals, too, found comfort in various aspects of romanticism, which helps explain the movement's wide appeal. By breaking sharply with past forms, romanticism attracted lib-

Connections to liberalism

eral and revolutionary spirits. Indeed, many romantic writers and artists sided with liberal causes. Germaine de Staël, for example, in her own life as well as in her novels, histories, and political tracts, fostered romanticism and liberalism in France. Few liberal romantics, however, were more popular than the French writer Victor Hugo (1802–1885), who idealized the masses of underprivileged humanity and preached redemption and purification through suffering.

At the same time, certain dimensions of romanticism appealed to conservatives as well—especially the return to the past, the emphasis on Christianity, and the stand against

Connections to conservatism

the rationalism of the Enlightenment. Sir Walter Scott (1771–1832), who in novel and verse glorified the Middle Ages and his native Scotland, was a conservative. So was the French writer François Auguste-René de Chateaubriand, who advocated a return to mystic Catholicism and dreamed of noble Indians in tropical America.

Romanticism found expression in many cultural forms—in the new English gardens that imitated nature rather than confining it to geometric forms, in the image of the artist as a nonconforming genius, in the glorification of walks down wooded lanes, in the popularity of the Grimm fairy tales that evoked images of medieval life, and in the sentimentalization of love in life and literature. In its qualities, its popularity, and its persistence, romanticism proved to be more than a casual change of taste or a mood. It reflected the revolutionary social, political, and intellectual developments of the era.

EARLY SOCIALISM: ENDING COMPETITION AND INEQUITIES

Romantics questioned the existing system from cultural and emotional perspectives. **Socialists** questioned it from social and economic perspectives. As socialists saw it, the common people—the workers—were missing out on the astounding power and wealth generated by the industrial revolution. Socialists called for a reordering of society so as to end the competition and class divisions that caused inequalities and suffering. Such calls made the socialists enemies of both the conservative and liberal camps.

During the early decades of the nineteenth century, a few intellectuals—some of whom came to be called Utopian Socialists—contended that society should be based on cooperation rather than com-

■ FIGURE 18.4

John Martin, *The Bard*, 1817.

■ FIGURE 18.5

Josef Danhauser, *Liszt at the Piano*, 1840.

petitive individualism and that property should be owned communally. One of the first of these early socialists was the French nobleman Henri de Saint-Simon (1760–1825). During the French Revolution,

Saint-Simon abandoned his noble title. Turning to

Utopian Socialists land speculation, he made and lost a fortune. He and his followers believed that society should be reorganized on the basis of a "religion of humanity," that all people should work, and that the inheritance of private property should be abolished. In Saint-Simon's ideal world, women would be elevated from their inferior social positions. Superior artists,

Saint-Simon scientists, engineers, and business people would be rewarded according to the formula: "from each according to his capacity, to each according to his deserts." Saint-Simon's influential followers became convinced that the best scientists and managers could use their expertise to plan and run prosperous societies for the benefit of everyone.

Charles Fourier (1772–1837) was also an early Utopian Socialist who, like Saint-Simon, gathered

Fourier a following. A Frenchman who had been a traveling salesman, he advocated doing away with economic competition, which he saw as the very source of evil. In his utopian society, agriculture and industry would be carried on by voluntary cooperatives whose members would pool their resources and live in communal apartment houses (*phalansteries*). Housework and child care would be a shared responsibility of the community. Women, like men, would have the right to work and to control their own money. Fourier also considered traditional marriage too restrictive sexually. Work and pleasure would merge as people did as they pleased while still carrying out the tasks their society required to survive. People would be paid according to the labor, capital, and talent that each contributed.

In fact, the communities that Fourier's followers established in the United States and Europe rarely lasted for long. Fourier's ideas, however, inspired many people looking for a more joyful, communal alternative to the competitive industrial societies spreading in the West.

Robert Owen (1771–1858) had different ideas. Born in Wales, Owen quickly made an industrial for-

Owen tune in Manchester and bought large cotton mills in New Lanark, Scotland. Early in the nineteenth century, he set out to make New Lanark a model community. He raised wages, shortened work hours, improved working conditions, abolished child labor, provided educational and recreational facilities for employees, and established sickness and old-age insurance. Productivity in his mills soared, and profits rose. Owen spent years drawing up plans for model socialist communities, which he envisioned as being located in rural settings and as mostly self-sufficient. The plans called for community members to raise children together and for women to share in governing. Like Fourier, Owen advocated loosen-

ing the bounds of marriage to create greater sexual freedom for women and men. Several such communities were established in America, most notably New Harmony, Indiana. However, all soon succumbed to internal disagreements and economic difficulties. The efforts cost Owen most of his fortune. He retained his fame, especially within the labor movement and among those establishing modest workers' cooperatives. However, he died in 1858 without having created a lasting alternative to the harsh industrial capitalism he deplored.

In the 1830s, several Frenchwomen began linking socialist demands with calls for the emancipation of women. The most famous of these women was Flora Tristan (1801–1844), a Frenchwoman *Tristan* influenced by Fourier's ideas. French law discriminated against women in many ways, including automatically awarding custody of children to fathers after a marital separation. When Tristan's abusive husband was awarded their children, she fought back. Eventually she turned this dispute into a campaign to end discrimination against women within marriage, in the law, and on the job. She traveled throughout Europe and Latin America, speaking passionately for unions and the creation of centers for the care and education of workers. In her *Worker's Union* (1843), she argued that equality between women and men could free the whole working class and transform civilization.

These and other early socialists recognized both the significance of the industrial revolution and its possibilities. They attacked the unbridled pursuit of profits in an unregulated, industrial economy. Only a well-organized society, they explained, could eliminate the misery of industrial capitalism and promote happiness. Most also attacked middle-class restrictions on women, emphasized the importance of sensual pleasure, and questioned traditional Christianity. The wave of socialist thought that these leaders unleashed became profoundly influential by the middle decades of the nineteenth century. As it evolved, it took on a more revolutionary quality, and it bore the distinctive stamp of one of the most authoritative thinkers of the nineteenth century: Karl Marx.

"SCIENTIFIC SOCIALISM": KARL MARX AND *THE COMMUNIST MANIFESTO*

"A specter is haunting Europe—the specter of Communism," announced Karl Marx (1818–1883) in 1848. "Let the ruling classes tremble at a Communist revolution." Born into a German middle-class family, his father was a Jewish lawyer who had converted to Christianity. A brilliant student, Marx attained his doctorate in philosophy and history, but he was denied an academic position because of his radical views. After embarking on a career in journalism, he was exiled from Germany for his attacks on censorship and his economic views; later France exiled him because of his revolutionary socialist ideas. He spent the last thirty-four years of his life in London researching, writing, and trying to build organizations to put his ideas into action. Marx collaborated with his friend Friedrich Engels (1820–1895), son of a wealthy German manufacturer, in writing the seminal work, *The Communist Manifesto* (1848). This treatise, along with the later *Das Kapital*, contained the fundamentals of what Marx called "scientific socialism."

Marx argued that economic interest, more than anything else, drove human behavior. He also thought that the dominant characteristic of each historical epoch was its prevailing system of economic production—how people made a living. In his view, politics, religion, and culture were all shaped mainly by economic and social realities.

Economic interest

Marx also described how human societies in each historical era became divided into the "haves" and the "have-nots." The haves owned the means of economic production—in nineteenth-century Britain, for example, the industrial capitalists who owned the machines and factories. They also controlled the state and the ideas that dominated their societies. The have-nots were the exploited laborers—for example, Britain's industrial working class. Each side consisted of classes of people with opposing interests. As Marx wrote, "[T]he history of all hitherto existing society is the history of class struggle." At a certain point, economic and social change would bring these class struggles to a revolutionary crisis. The French Revolution, he explained, was an example of one of those conflicts coming to a violent head, as the bourgeoisie (the middle-class capitalists) overcame the aristocracy (the feudal landlords.)

Class struggle

Marx focused much of his analysis on his own industrial society of the nineteenth century. In this society, he explained, the bourgeoisie (capitalists) exploited workers by paying them only subsistence wages rather than compensating them for the true value created by their work. "These labourers, who must sell themselves piecemeal, are a commodity, like every other article of commerce," Marx lamented. At the same time, Marx saw capitalists as locked in a competitive struggle with one another. This contest forced them continually to introduce new, costly machines and build larger factories: "Constant revolutionizing of production, uninterrupted disturbance of all social conditions, ever-lasting uncertainty and agitation distinguish the bourgeois epoch from all earlier ones." Soon, Marx warned, greater and greater quantities of

Industrial capitalism

goods would be produced by a system running out of control. Eventually, the relentless competition and the periodic economic crises that plague industrial societies would thin the ranks of the bourgeoisie. At the same time, the working class would grow stronger as its numbers and consciousness increased. Inevitably, the workers—with "nothing to lose but their chains" and with "a world to win"—would revolt, seize the factories, destroy the capitalist system, abolish private property, and establish a classless socialist society.

Marx only hinted at the general nature of this new socialist society. His writings suggest that the elimination of capitalism would end the division of society into classes of haves (capitalists) and have-nots (workers). The state itself would eventually wither away, for its only purpose was to protect the interests of the haves against the have-nots. Freed from exploitation and the pressures of capitalist competition, all people would lead more varied, cooperative, creative lives—in this sense, free and truly human.

Socialist society

Marx's socialism gained immense appeal. Because he based much of his analysis on evidence and logic, it attracted intellectuals and students. Because his socialism reflected the social and emotional turmoil being produced by the industrial revolution, especially the suffering of the working poor, it spoke convincingly to workers and their leaders. During the second half of the nineteenth century, Marx's socialism would become a major force in the West.

Appeal of socialism

RESTORATION AND REPRESSION

Socialism as well as the other ideologies reflected the political and social realities of their era, particularly the efforts of people to understand and cope with changes that either threatened them or offered promise. In the three decades following 1815, however, socialism played only a limited part in the great struggles for policies and power. During these years, it was the forces representing conservatism, liberalism, and nationalism that instead took center stage.

The struggles for influence and power among believers of these ideologies took place in pamphlets and newspapers, in courts and parliaments, in universities and police barracks, and in streets and fields throughout Europe. In the first years after the defeat of Napoleon, conservatism held sway in international and diplomatic affairs. The Vienna agreements and the cooperative arrangements to repress the threat of revolution in Europe epitomized this ideology. Conservatism also prevailed in domestic politics across most of Europe.

THE RETURN OF THE BOURBONS IN FRANCE

When the victorious armies of the coalition powers entered France and deposed Napoleon in the spring of 1814, they brought "in their baggage" the members of the Bourbon royal family who had fled the Revolution. In their wake trooped the émigré nobility. The brother of the guillotined Louis XVI was placed on the throne as Louis XVIII (r. 1814–1824). (The son of Louis XVI, who had died in prison without having ruled, was considered Louis XVII.)

Louis XVIII

The "restored" king ruled with an odd mixture of conservatism and moderation. He issued a charter that retained Napoleon's administrative and legal system as well as civil and religious liberties. He also placed lawmaking in the hands of a two-chamber legislature. However, only a small, wealthy elite could vote, and the king kept most of the power.

Nevertheless, Louis XVIII used his authority with moderation, thinking that a mild leadership style would help ensure his hold on the crown and tranquillity in France. Most of the returned émigrés, however, had little appreciation for his relaxed rule—they were more conservative and angry than he was and wanted action. Led by the king's younger brother, Comte d'Artois, these ultraroyalists controlled the legislature. Through the rest of Louis XVIII's reign, they agitated for a return of their privileges and indemnification for their lost lands.

After Louis XVIII's death in 1824, d'Artois was crowned King Charles X (r. 1824–1830); he followed more conservative policies that favored the old aristocracy and the Catholic Church. He offered money to indemnify those who had lost land in the Revolution and gave the church greater control over education. Those policies provoked growing opposition to his rule. When elections increased the size of the opposition, he dissolved the Chamber of Deputies. In the face of still-increasing opposition, he abolished freedom of the press and drastically restricted the right to vote.

Charles X

REACTION AND REPRESSION IN THE GERMAN STATES

The Germanies in 1815 consisted of thirty-seven little states and two large ones—Prussia and Austria. All belonged to the German Confederation, which lacked an army, a treasury, and even a flag. Austria and Prussia politically dominated the German lands. Both states were firmly conservative, if not reactionary.

In multilingual Austria, the Habsburg emperor and Metternich, the conservative diplomat we met at the beginning of the chapter, held sway. The Austrian leaders had good reason to fear liberalism and national-ism like the plague, for the empire included many ethnic groups—including Hungarians, Czechs, Serbs, and Italians—with their own languages and customs. In the wake of the French Revolution, they began to stir with national consciousness. Metternich used all means—police, spies, censorship, and travel restrictions—to ensure the status quo. The only possible threats to conservative control came from within some of the small states in the weak German Confederation, and Austria enjoyed permanent presidency over that organization.

Metternich

When students and professors formed organizations and staged festivals that supported liberal and nationalistic principles, conservative officials became alarmed. "We want a constitution for the people that fits in with the spirit of the times and with people's own level of enlightenment," explained one student. "[A]bove all, we want Germany to be considered *one* land and the people *one* people."

The murder of a conservative dramatist by a member of a student organization, Karl Sand, gave Metternich his opportunity to strike. After Sand's trial and public execution, Metternich called the princes of the leading German states to Carlsbad and had them draw up a set of harsh decrees outlawing the organizations. He also issued an ominous warning: "The duty of especial watchfulness in this matter should be impressed upon the special agents of the government." The Carlsbad Decrees established strict censorship and supervision of classrooms and libraries. Spies and police terrorized liberal students and professors. Although Sand became a political martyr in the eyes of many young nationalists, the crackdown worked: The small liberal and nationalistic movements evaporated.

Carlsbad Decrees

In Prussia, the conservative, militaristic Hohenzollern kings reigned. Behind them stood the equally conservative landed aristocracy, the *Junkers*. The Junkers served as officers in the Prussian army and filled the key posts in the civil service and administration. They had no sympathy for any reforms that seemed even faintly liberal or nationalistic, and they reversed many of the changes of the Napoleonic era. However, to better connect its separated territories, Prussia began making commercial treaties with its smaller German neighbors, providing for the free flow of trade among them. By 1834, nearly all the states of the German Confederation except Austria had joined the Prussian-sponsored **Zollverein** (customs union), which would prove of great importance in the march toward national unity.

Prussia

RESTORATION IN ITALY

Austria dominated Italy even more completely than Germany. Metternich described Italy as only a "geographical expression." Austria annexed the northern states of Lombardy and Venetia outright. Most other states were ruled by Austrian princes or under Austria's protection and guidance. Piedmont-Sardinia in the northwest was free from Austrian control, but its ruling House of Savoy was no less conservative than Metternich.

In 1815, the deposed aristocracy and clericals trooped back to the Italian states intent on regaining their old positions. They and their Austrian masters soon sent nearly all the Italian intelligentsia to prison or exile. When revolts in Naples, Sicily, and Piedmont flared up in 1820, the forces of order quickly used overwhelming force to put them down.

The Papal States in central Italy were no exception in this period of restoration. Pope Pius VII revived the Inquisition, reconstituted the *Index* of prohibited books, annulled Napoleonic laws of religious toleration, and even did away with French innovations such as street lighting. His successor, Pius VIII, followed equally conservative ideas. In 1829, he condemned almost everything even faintly liberal, including secular education and civil marriage.

CONSERVATISM IN RUSSIA

Russia remained a vast agricultural nation with a feudal social structure and a tiny urban bourgeoisie. The Orthodox Christian Church, dominated by an upper clergy drawn from the aristocracy, served as an arm of the government. After fighting against the French, suffering a ravaging invasion in 1812, and playing a major role in Napoleon's defeat, Russia commanded considerable respect and power in Europe. Russia's tsar was the unstable Alexander I—at first a man open to reform, such as granting the Poles a constitution and proclaiming religious toleration, and later more of a reactionary mystic who resumed religious repression. He fell under the influence of Metternich in international affairs and his own aristocratic magnates at home. At his death in 1825, Russia remained a champion of autocracy and conservatism.

His successor, Nicholas I (r. 1825–1855), was an austere autocrat whose military career wedded him to the concepts of discipline and authority. When he assumed the throne in December 1825, a group of his young liberal military officers—hoping to write a constitution and free the serfs—revolted. Nicholas immediately crushed these "Decembrists" and bitterly turned against any hints of liberalism. He followed a policy of demanding submission of every-

one to the autocracy and to the Orthodox Church. Although the Decembrists would later gain a reputation as liberal political martyrs, Russia's government now stood as a bastion of conservatism and would remain so for many decades.

HOLDING THE LINE IN GREAT BRITAIN

Although Great Britain had for years been a home of representative government, conservatives dominated its government in 1815. Property qualifications so severely restricted the suffrage that only about 5 percent of adult males could vote. The distribution of seats in Parliament was so distorted that a relatively small number of families dominated the House of Commons. Furthermore, the emerging industrial cities of the north were scarcely represented at all. The conservative landed aristocracy and the Tory Party, which had seen the country through the Napoleonic Wars, had a firm grip on power.

Things became even more restricted when an economic depression left thousands of returning veterans jobless. Luddite riots (see page 551) and the specter of revolutionary activity prompted the government to take strong measures against the restless workers. The climax came in 1819 when troops charged on a crowd that had assembled in St. Peter's Fields, outside Manchester, to listen to reform speeches. A number were killed and hundreds injured in this "Peterloo Massacre."

Peterloo Massacre

Figure 18.6, a print by George Cruikshank, shows the troops of the conservative British government breaking up this rally for liberal and radical political reform. On the platform, women and men wave banners demanding universal suffrage, religious freedom,

■ FIGURE 18.6

George Cruikshank, *The Peterloo Massacre*, 1819.

and liberty; a banner is topped with liberty caps, a radical symbol from the French Revolution. This depiction of the violence that erupted at St. Peter's Fields near Manchester seeks to evoke sympathy for the reformers. It portrays merciless troops on horseback striking down and trampling nonresisting women, men, and children. An army officer on horseback repeats orders from a higher authority, "Cut them down." A participant confirmed this depiction: "Women, white-vested maids, and tender youths, were indiscriminately sabred or trampled. . . . In ten minutes from the commencement of the havoc the field was an open and almost deserted space." Parliament would not back down. It soon passed the Six Acts of 1819, which further restricted public meetings and facilitated prosecution of radicals.

The government treated the Irish no less harshly. The Irish had long been ruled and exploited as a conquered people. In the 1801 Act of Union, Britain formally absorbed Ireland into the United **Ireland** Kingdom. In this predominantly Catholic land, the Protestant minority controlled most of the land and political power. The Catholic peasantry suffered from such acute poverty that the threat of famine was not uncommon. Irish nationalists organized to agitate for the right to send elected Catholic representatives to Parliament. In 1829, fearing a civil war in Ireland, the conservative British government reluctantly passed the Catholic Emancipation Act, which allowed Roman Catholics to become members of Parliament.

A WAVE OF REVOLUTION AND REFORM

Despite conservative efforts to maintain order and halt change during the years after 1815, liberal and nationalistic causes simmered just under the surface. The demands for greater political participation and recognition of national identity strengthened and spread. Moreover, Europeans could no longer ignore the changes stemming from early industrialization and urbanization. In some cases, revolts and revolutions broke out. In other cases, people clamored for and gained major reforms.

THE GREEK WAR FOR INDEPENDENCE

A hint of the problems to come occurred during the 1820s, when Greeks mounted a national liberation movement against their Ottoman Turk overlords. The Ottoman Empire still sprawled over vast territories, from the north African coast and southwest Asia to southeastern Europe, but it had been weakened by internal dissension and external threats. By 1815, revolts had enabled Serbia to gain virtual independence, and in Egypt, Mehemet Ali ruled with only nominal subordination to the Ottomans. The Greek revolt began in 1821, which resulted in the death of many defenseless Turks. After the Turks met Greek insurrections with force and atrocities, romantic and liberal idealists formed an international movement to support Greek independence. Britain's well-known romantic poet Lord Byron was one of several who traveled to Greece to contribute to the cause. He brought money and enlisted in a regiment, but lost his life to malaria at Missolonghi.

Figure 18.7, by the romantic French artist Eugène Delacroix (1798–1863), captures Greece's struggle for independence. The year is 1826, during the months when the Turks laid siege to the Greek stronghold of Missolonghi and the garrison of 4,000 finally succumbed to 35,000 attackers and the Ottoman fleet. The remaining defenders blew up the city and themselves rather than surrender to the Turks. Greece is represented as a beautiful, defenseless peasant woman and a classical symbol of liberty. Under a dark, foreboding sky, she kneels on what are both the ruins of Missolonghi's city walls and the stone remains of Greek culture in a desperate, mute appeal for aid. But it is already too late for the martyred freedom fighter (perhaps evoking the memory of the fallen Byron), whose arm is thrust forward toward the viewer. Behind the woman, a Turkish soldier strikes a victorious pose. The painting, like the Greek cause in Europe, blends the themes of romanticism, liberalism, and nationalism that so characterized the era.

In the end, intervention by Great Britain, France, and Russia finally secured Greek independence. Although Europeans thought of Greece sympathetically as Christian and as the birthplace of European civilization, these countries' motives had more to do with their own greedy hopes of gains at the expense of the Turks than genuinely supporting the Greek revolutionaries. They achieved their objective, but this dramatic chapter in Greek history still revealed the strength of nationalistic movements and the power of liberal and romantic ideals to fuel these movements.

LIBERAL TRIUMPHS IN WESTERN EUROPE

In 1830, a new series of revolutions tested and sometimes overwhelmed established governments. In France, a struggle arose for liberal reforms against the reactionary King Charles X. Since ascending the throne in 1824, Charles had tried to reverse the moderate policies of his predecessor, Louis XVIII, and return France to the days before the French Revolution. He aligned himself

The July Revolution in France

with the most extreme ultraroyalists and the Catholic Church, angering the wealthy bourgeoisie and even the peasantry with his reactionary policies. Support for his regime weakened and he lost control over the Chamber of Deputies, the most representative of France's two-chamber legislature. His efforts to dissolve the Chamber, censor the press, and narrow the electoral laws only stiffened liberal opposition. In July 1830, things came to a head. Liberals in Paris joined with workers outraged by rising food prices. Workers took to the streets of Paris and set up barriers against the king's unenthusiastic troops. Uprisings—fueled by hunger, suspicions of hoarding, and resentment against taxes—spread throughout France. After three days of haphazard fighting, the insurgents gained the upper hand. Charles X, the last Bourbon king of France, fled to Great Britain.

Figure 18.8, a painting by Horace Vernet, reveals how the victors in France's revolution of 1830 interpreted the dramatic events of that year. In the center of the painting, the new constitutional monarch, Louis-Philippe, rides victoriously to the Hôtel de Ville (city hall), the seat of power in Paris. Before him a man carries the French revolutionary tricolor flag, replacing the old Bourbon flag of Charles X. Louis-Philippe's horse picks his way through the paving stones, which the people of Paris had used to construct barricades and hurl at the royal troops. In the foreground, rich and poor walk arm-in-arm with regular and irregular soldiers in victory; a wealthy man stops to drop alms into a basket for the poor or fallen. Women and men of all classes hail the new king and the revolutionary cause.

While many in France had hoped for a republic to replace the Bourbon monarchy, more conservative liberals took control and created a constitutional "bourgeois monarchy" under Charles X's cousin, Louis-Philippe (r. 1830–1848). Recognizing that a new, more liberal era had dawned in France, Louis-Philippe assumed the role of "citizen king," casting aside the clothes and ornaments of royalty and dressing in the style of his Parisian upper-middle-class supporters. He reduced property qualifications for voting, thereby doubling the electorate (though still only the property-owning elite could vote).

The year 1830 also brought revolutionary trouble in the Belgian provinces of the kingdom of the Netherlands. The union forced on Belgium (predominantly Catholic) and the Netherlands (mainly Calvinist) at Vienna had never been a happy one. Although numerically a minority, the Dutch staffed most of the country's political institutions. As one Belgian nationalist put it in 1830, "By what right do two million Dutchmen command four million Belgians?" Desires for national liberation combined with tensions over high food prices to fuel a revolt in Au-

Revolution in Belgium

■ FIGURE 18.7

Eugène Delacroix, *Greece on the Ruins of Missolonghi*, 1827.

gust 1830. When the half-hearted efforts of the Dutch government failed to suppress the revolt, Austria and Russia threatened to intervene. Britain and France resisted the intervention and secured Belgian independence. Belgium soon adopted a liberal constitution.

By that time, liberal reformers had also scored successes in Switzerland, making that country the first to grant universal male suffrage. In 1834, a new constitution introduced at least the form of liberal institutions to Spain as well.

Switzerland and Spain

TESTING AUTHORITY IN EASTERN AND SOUTHERN EUROPE

As Map 18.2 shows, revolutionaries also tested regimes in eastern and southern Europe. In November 1830, a Polish nationalistic movement led by students and army cadets tried to end Russian rule. They managed to establish a provisional government in Warsaw, but

■ FIGURE 18.8

Horace Vernet, *The Duc d'Orléans Proceeds to the Hôtel-de-Ville, July 31, 1830*, 1833.

conflict within different social groups and among reformers weakened that government. Russian troops soon defeated the revolutionaries. Nicholas sent thousands of Poles to Siberia in chains and began a harsh program of Russification to crush any hint of Polish independence.

Poland

In Italy, nationalists began gathering in secret societies called *Carbonari*. (The word means "charcoal burners," suggesting an image of common people meeting around charcoal fires.) The Carbonari had long plotted for political freedom and national unification. In 1831, liberal and nationalist revolutions broke out in central Italy, but Austrian forces promptly suppressed them. The movement again went underground, but was kept alive under the leadership of the romantic nationalist Giuseppe Mazzini (1805–1872).

Italy

LIBERAL DEMANDS IN GREAT BRITAIN

In Britain, conservatives had to contend not only with demands for liberal reforms but also with pressures rising from early industrialization and urbanization. Despite the Peterloo Massacre and the restrictive Six Acts, Britain had already shown signs of political flexibility in response to public opinion in the 1820s. By 1822, it had deserted the conservative Concert of Europe. The government repealed laws preventing laborers from organizing unions and removed civil restrictions against nonconforming Protestants and Catholics. Yet these measures, however encouraging to liberals, did not get at the fundamental issue that had raised reform demands for decades: broadening popular participation in the government.

Now the industrial middle class, gaining in wealth and number, added weight to radicals' demands to extend the right to vote and relocate political strength from the countryside to the underrepresented industrial cities. However, the conservative Tories, who controlled Parliament, remained unwilling or unable to effect electoral reform. In 1830, elections brought the more liberal Whigs to power. These Whigs believed that moderate reform rather than reactionary intransigence was the best way to preserve elite institutions from revolutionary change. Worried that the July Revolution in France might spread to Britain, and facing increasing public demonstrations for reform as well as violent acts of protest, the Whigs decided to bend rather than break. They introduced the Reform Bill of 1832, which answered some of the demands. Speaking in favor of the bill, the English historian and politician Thomas Babington Macaulay warned that "now, while the crash of the proudest throne of the Continent [France] is still resounding in our ears . . . now, while the heart of England is still sound," the Reform Bill must be passed. After considerable effort, the Whigs finally enacted the new law.

Reform Bill of 1832

The Reform Bill did not grant the universal manhood suffrage called for by radicals, but it lowered property qualifications so that most upper-middle-class men (still a small minority) could vote. More important, the bill redistributed electoral districts, taking power away from the "rotten boroughs" (no-longer-important towns and rural areas) and giving it to the underrepresented cities where commercial and industrial elites dominated. The political struggle to pass the bill enabled the House of Commons to gain power over the House of Lords, which had opposed the law. The long era of dominance by the conservative landed aristocracy was ending. More liberal property owners, including the commercial and industrial bourgeoisie, rose to power. From that point on, Britain's leading political groups realigned themselves into the modern Conservative and Liberal parties.

Britain's government soon turned to other reforms. Britain had for several decades led in the antislavery movement, abolishing its own slave trade in

1807 and pushing the Congress of Vienna to declare against the trade in 1815. Europeans, however, often violated principled declarations against slavery and shipped hundreds of thousands more African slaves to the Americas—especially to the Caribbean and Brazil. In 1833, Parliament bowed to humanitarian radicals and Protestant reformers and abolished slavery in Britain's colonies. Fifteen years later, France would follow suit by abolishing slavery in its colonies, and in 1888, Brazil joined the list, ending slavery in the Americas.

Antislavery

Britain's Parliament and reformers also tried to cope with growing pressures exerted by the industrial revolution. Several new laws aimed to ease some of the disturbing harshness of industrial employment. Between 1833 and 1847, Parliament forbade the employment of women and children in underground mines, prohibited the employment of children under 9 in textile mills, and limited children 9 or older and women to ten hours a day in those factories. Other legislation also reflected the British economy's shift from agriculture to industry. In the name of free trade and lower bread prices, liberals mounted a major attack on the Corn Laws, which imposed tariffs on grain imports. An anti-Corn Law movement spread throughout the country, accusing the aristocratic landowners who benefited from the Corn Laws of being enemies of the middle and working classes. Victory for the movement came in 1846 with the repeal of the Corn Laws. The repeal reduced the price of bread, but it also opened up the possibility that employers—knowing that workers could afford the cheaper bread—would slash wages.

Economic and social reforms

Corn Laws

These liberal principles and reforms, however, only added to the suffering of millions facing the horrible potato famine in Ireland. This mostly rural and impoverished population relied on the potato for food. In 1845, a new, unknown fungus attacked potato plants, ruining the crop. Famine spread as the crops failed year after year. Despite some charitable assistance, Britain's liberal government concluded that the state should not meddle in the economy. More than a million died in Ireland and another million fled overseas while Britain's liberals—often sympathetic and believing that the free market would alleviate the distress—held fast to their principles and did little.

Irish famine

Nor were liberal reforms enough for the hard-pressed urban workers. They were bitterly aware that they had been bypassed by the Reform Bill of 1832:

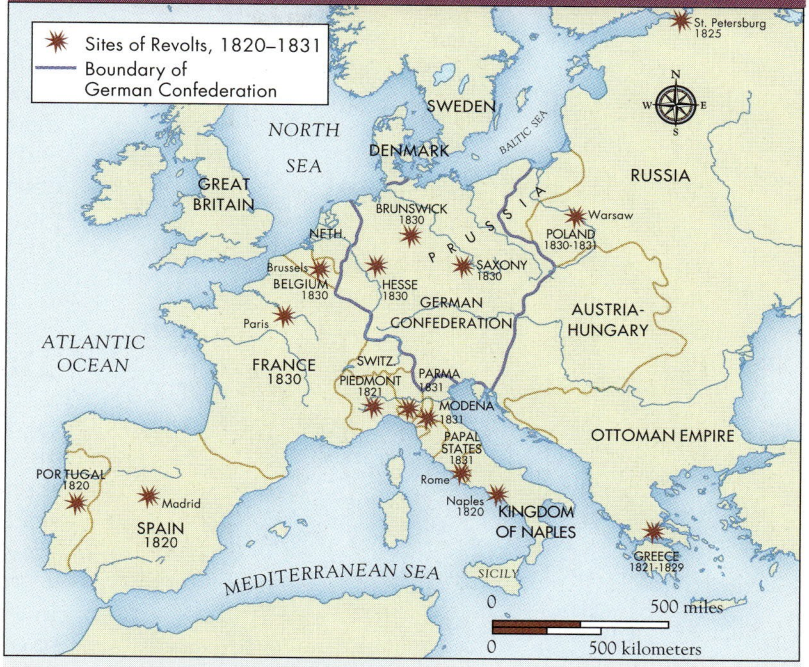

MAP 18.2   EUROPEAN REVOLTS, 1820–1831

This map shows the locations of revolts in Europe between 1820 and 1831. ■ **Notice** the geographic extent of these revolts. **What** problems might this have posed for the efforts of the Concert of Europe to maintain the status quo through international cooperation? ■ **Consider** which of these revolts had the most lasting consequences.

"The Reform Act has effected a transfer of power from one domineering faction to another, and left the people as helpless as before," explained one of their leaders. They also complained that Britain's unprecedented national prosperity had not benefitted workers: "With all these elements of national prosperity, and with every disposition and capacity to take advantage of them, we find ourselves overwhelmed with public and private suffering." In 1838, working-class leaders took action and drew up The People's Charter. The document called for several democratic reforms, including universal male suffrage, election by secret ballot, and the removal of property qualifications for office. "We perform the duties of freemen; we must have the privileges of freemen," announced the charter.

Chartism

The so-called **Chartists** presented their demands twice to Parliament, which summarily rejected them.

KEY DATES

COPING WITH CHANGE

1814–1815	Congress of Vienna
1815	The Quadruple Alliance (Concert of Europe)
1819	Carlsbad Decrees
	Peterloo Massacre
1820	Revolts in Naples, Sicily, and Piedmont
1822	Revolt in Spain
1825	Decembrists revolt in Russia
1829	Greek independence
1830–1831	Revolutions in France, Belgium, Poland, and Italy
1832	British Reform Bill
1833	Britain abolishes slavery in its colonies
1834	*Zollverein* founded
1838	Chartist movement begins
1846	Repeal of Corn Laws in Britain
1846–1848	Irish famine
1848	*The Communist Manifesto*
	The revolutions of 1848

Nevertheless, the movement persisted within the working class for years. Women aided the cause by raising money and passing petitions for signatures. They also, unsuccessfully, demanded that the charter include provisions for female suffrage. Finally, in April 1848, the Chartists planned a huge demonstration in London to back up their petition. The frightened government and middle classes prepared to use force to control the gathering, as they had several times against strikes and workers' protests. However, when the reforms were refused once more, only a few mild protests arose, and the Chartist movement sputtered out. Nevertheless, Britain's political parties were becoming aware of the growing influence of the working classes and began considering ways to win their favor.

In Britain, then, reforms designed to meet demands for broader representation and manage the social consequences of industrialization and urbanization were under way by the 1840s. Under pressure, Britain's government bent enough to satisfy much of the middle class. The discontented working classes were not yet powerful enough to force their views on the resisting government. Liberalism, the strongest ideology challenging Britain's traditional order, remained a force for reform rather than revolution.

On the continent, however, nations followed a different path. Throughout western Europe, liberal and nationalistic movements gained stunning successes in these same years. In eastern and southern Europe, these two ideologies also rose and served notice, but, with the exception of Greece, the conservative forces of order beat them down. In 1848, however, the complicated interplay among all these movements finally reached a volatile turning point.

THE DAM BURSTS: 1848

On New Year's Day, 1848, one could look back to 1830 and conclude that the forces that had opened the gates to a wave of revolutions and reforms had since been held under control. In February 1848, everything would change.

Trouble had already been brewing across Europe. In 1846 and 1847, poor harvests had driven up food prices and even brought famine. These disasters, along with financial crises, undermined markets for manufactured goods, created business failures, and left thousands of workers jobless. Governments tried to maintain order, but the growing resentments of liberals, nationalists, and now socialists, who blamed governments for failing to enact overdue reforms, made things even more difficult.

Antigovernment groups had also begun taking on a disturbing complexity and variety. Some protesters wanted only to widen political participation and institute accepted liberal reforms; others demanded full democracy. Several ethnic groups desired national autonomy; workers wanted jobs and rights. Together, the potential opposition to established governments not only loomed large but also cut across class and ideological lines. Intense, shared opposition to the status quo masked any differences these groups might have had. As the pressure of their frustration mounted, the economic crisis threatened to unlock the floodgates.

THE "GLORY DAYS"

The dam broke first in France. Louis-Philippe's constitutional monarchy had allied moderate conservatives and moderate liberals into a regime of wealthy property owners. Presenting itself as *France* the bearer of national patriotism and political caution, the government managed to quiet both conservative and radical opponents during the 1830s. However, beneath the surface of this apparently stable regime, discontent grew. The king and his chief minister during the 1840s—the moderately liberal historian François Guizot—opposed any further extension of the suffrage. Workers, who had not shared in the relative prosperity of the period, clamored for the right to vote and the right to organize unions, but got neither. The poor harvests and financial crises in 1846 and 1847 heightened frustration with the regime. In Paris, more than 40 percent of the workforce were without a job. One Parisian radical complained, "While half of the population of Paris dies of starvation, the other half eats for two."

The parliamentary opposition and bourgeois reformers began holding banquets to rally support for widening the right to vote. When a banquet to be held in Paris on February 22 in honor of George Washington's birthday (the United States served as a symbol of democracy in this period) promised to attract thousands of sympathetic workers, the government tried to prohibit the event. Opposition erupted in the Parisian streets. King Louis-Philippe tried to quiet people by dismissing his unpopular prime minister, Francois Guizot (1787–1874). Long in office, Guizot's response to those not rich enough to have the right to vote was, "Get rich, then you can vote." The king's effort at appeasement failed. A shot fired during a brawl between a crowd and troops guarding government houses unnerved the troops, who fired a murderous volley into the mob and set off a full-scale insurrection. Barricades against governmental troops flew up all over Paris, and when the king's citizen militia, the National Guard, began taking the rebels' side, Louis-Philippe followed Guizot into exile.

Figure 18.9 depicts the triumph of the revolutionaries and the already simmering political battles to come. In the center, the well-dressed liberal and romantic poet Alphonse de Lamartine (1790–1869) stands with his arm raised in front of the Paris city hall. He persuades the crowd to keep the tricolor flag to represent the new republic rather than the more radical red flag, carried by a woman in plain dress riding a white horse on the left. On the right, troops and ordinary citizens march under the flag in unity. On the left, citizens bring objects of wealth gathered to support the new republic. At the bottom are the paving stones used in the battle and a fallen victim of the struggle.

Lamartine and a group of bourgeois liberals proclaimed the Second Republic and hastily set up a provisional government. The new ruling body was republican in sentiment, but tellingly, it had only one prominent radical member: the socialist writer Louis Blanc (1811–1882). The provisional government immediately called for the election by universal male suffrage of an assembly to draw up a new constitution. Yet that government turned down demands for political and economic rights by the new woman's newspaper, *The Voice of Women*, and by women's political clubs. Under the pressure of the Paris populace, the provisional government did admit workers to the National Guard, and therefore access to arms.

Document 18.2 reveals that the government, in response to popular demand for the "right to work," also set up national workshops. The workshops—an idea once proposed by Louis Blanc—

National workshops

■ FIGURE 18.9

Henri-Félix Emmanuel Philippoteaux, Revolutionary triumph in Paris, 1848.

THINKING ABOUT DOCUMENTS

■ DOCUMENT 18.2

France's Provisional Government Issues Decrees

Shortly after the 1848 revolution that ended the July Monarchy in France, the victors established a new provisional government. They issued the following decrees relating to workers on February 25, 1848—the day after creating the provisional government. ■ **What** *do these decrees suggest about possible causes of the revolution?* ■ **What** *might be the advantages and disadvantages of issuing these decrees?*

The provisional government of the French republic decrees that the Tuileries shall serve hereafter as a home for the veterans of labor.

The provisional government of the French republic pledges itself to guarantee the means of subsistence of the workingman by labor.

It pledges itself to guarantee labor to all citizens.

It recognizes that workingmen ought to enter into associations among themselves in order to enjoy the advantage of their labor. . . .

The provisional government of the French republic decrees that all articles pledged at the pawn shops since the first of February, consisting of linen, garments, or clothes, etc., upon which the loan does not exceed ten francs, shall be given back to those who pledged them.

The provisional government of the republic decrees the immediate establishment of national workshops. The minister of public works is charged with the execution of the present decree.

Source: James Harvey Robinson, ed., *Readings in European History*, vol. II (Boston: Ginn, 1904), pp. 560–561.

---

however, were a parody of Blanc's socialist vision. Blanc lamented that they were deliberately planned so as to ensure failure. In this ill-designed undertaking, laborers were assigned to hastily arranged projects. When more laborers enrolled than could be used, the surplus workers were paid almost as much as the employed ones to remain idle. To make matters worse, tens of thousands of job-hungry laborers rushed to Paris to join the workshops. The resulting demoralization of labor and the cost to the taxpayers frightened peasant and bourgeois property owners alike. Elections held in April 1848 swept conservative republicans and monarchists back into office.

As Map 18.3 reveals, the February explosion in Paris set central Europe aflame with revolt. One core

Austria

of the revolutions settled in Vienna, the seat of the Habsburg government. After news of the Paris events arrived in Vienna, Austrian students, middle-class reformers, and workers charged into the streets, clamoring for an end to Metternich's system. There, as elsewhere in the streets of Europe's cities, women joined men in the effort, building the barricades, taking care of the wounded, supplying the fighters with meals, and sometimes taking part in battles against armed forces. The painting on page 587 captures the flavor of this revolutionary activity. As the uprising gained momentum, Metternich fled for his life. The Habsburg emperor, Ferdinand I, hastily abolished the country's most repressive laws, ended serfdom, and promised constitutional reform.

In Hungary, the Magyars, under the leadership of the eloquent Louis Kossuth (1802–1894), rose and demanded national autonomy from Austria. The Czechs followed suit in Bohemia and called for a Pan-Slavic congress to meet at Prague. In Austria's Italian provinces of Lombardy and Venetia, the rebellious populace drove the

Hungary

Austrian forces into defensive fortresses and declared their independence. By June 1848, it appeared that the Habsburg Empire was splintering along ethnic lines and that its German core would commit to liberal reforms.

When the Hohenzollern ruler of Prussia, Frederick William IV (r. 1840–1861), heard of events in Austria, he granted some reforms and promised a liberal constitution. Nevertheless, as Document 18.3 suggests, the news from Paris and Vienna

Prussia

sent middle-class liberals and artisans demonstrating in the streets of Berlin, the capital of Prussia. Frederick William sent in the troops, but their brutality stiffened support for the revolutionary cause. A few days later, he withdrew his troops and promised more reforms and support for German national unity. Hohenzollern Prussia, like Habsburg Austria, appeared on the road to liberal government.

In several other German states, rulers quickly gave in to revolutionary demands. Then a self-appointed group of liberal leaders made a bold move: They called for a popularly elected assembly representing all German states to meet at Frankfurt to construct a liberal German nation. "[A]t last the great opportunity had arrived for giving to the German people the liberty which was their birthright and to the German fatherland its unity and greatness," explained a participant. Three crucial questions confronted the Frankfurt Assembly: (1) whether German-speaking portions of the multilingual Habsburg Empire and other states should be included in the projected German nation, (2) what should be done with non-German ethnic groups living within German states, and (3) who should head the new nation. After almost a year of debate, the assembly decided on a smaller Germany and offered the crown to the king of Prussia.

Frankfurt Assembly

Meanwhile, in Italy several states established new constitutions. The movement for national unification kept alive by the idealist Giuseppi Mazzini found additional strength. He backed up his ideas with action: "Insurrection—by means of guerrilla bands—is the true method of warfare for all nations desirous of emancipating themselves from a foreign yoke," he explained. Just one year after the first revolt broke out in France, popular demonstrations brought down the papal government and forced Pius IX to flee Rome. Mazzini soon gained a foothold as head of the newly formed Republic of Rome.

Italy

THE RETURN TO ORDER

For the revolutionaries of 1848, a new, victorious age seemed to have dawned. Within a few months, the old governments almost everywhere had been swept from power or seriously weakened. The upheavals were so widespread that at one point Tsar Nicholas I of Russia exclaimed to Britain's Queen Victoria, "What remains standing in Europe? Great Britain and Russia." Unfortunately for the revolutionaries, however, the forces of order showed resiliency and even new strength when events took more radical turns.

In France, divisions rose among those once unified against the monarchy. The more conservative peasantry and landowners in the countryside stepped back from the radical reforms demanded by Parisian artisans, shopowners, and intellectuals. The gap also widened between the middle class, which felt that reforms had gone far enough or even too far, and workers, who agitated for more social programs. These divisions reached a boiling point when the Constitutional Assembly, which had been elected in the late spring of 1848, abolished the national workshops. Officials told the workers to join the army or go look for work in the provinces. The desperate men and women of the Paris working class resorted to arms and barricades. For four days, war raged in the streets of Paris between the working class, armed with National

June Days in France

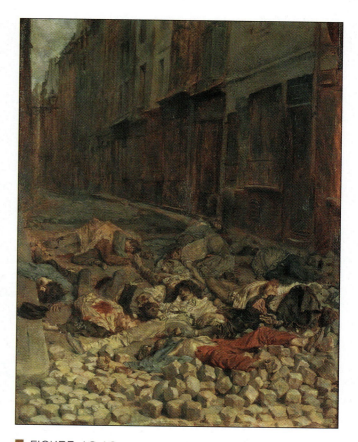

■ FIGURE 18.10

Jean-Louis-Ernest Meissonier, *Memory of Civil War (The Barricade)*, 1849.

Guard rifles, and the regular army. The French liberal writer and politician Alexis de Tocqueville (1805–1859), an observer of the events, described the June Days as "the revolt of one whole section of the population against another. Women took part in it as well as men . . . and when at last the time had come to surrender, the women were the last to yield."

Figure 18.10 depicts the fate of the revolutionary workers of Paris during the "June Days" of 1848. Here the paving stones used so successfully for the barricades in February 1848 are scattered in the rout of the revolutionaries. The revolutionaries and the radical demands they represented—symbolized by the red, white, and blue of a fallen fighter's clothing—lie crushed by army troops, who this time have willingly fired on the people. The artist, Meissonier (1815–1891), witnessed these defenders "slain, shot down, thrown from the windows, covering the ground with their corpses, the earth not yet having drunk up all the blood." Meissonier intended his painting to serve as "a sober warning to the rebels of the future." When the last barricade had fallen during the bloody June Days, some 1,500, mostly workingmen, had perished. Several hundred were sent overseas to French colonial

THINKING ABOUT GEOGRAPHY

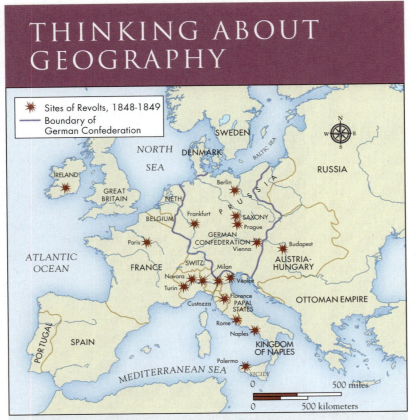

Sites of Revolts, 1848-1849
Boundary of German Confederation

MAP 18.3   EUROPEAN REVOLTS, 1848–1849

This map shows the location of the 1848–1849 revolutions.
■ **Consider** the possible reasons for the eruption of so many revolutions over this wide geographic area. ■ **Compare** this map with Map 18.2. What do the two maps reveal about the breadth of revolutionary activity between 1820 and 1849 and the challenges faced by the conservative forces of order?

gary, they had the help of the reactionary Nicholas I of Russia, whose army overwhelmed the Magyar rebels. In Italy, Austrian might (and in Rome, French arms) eventually prevailed.

In Prussia, Frederick William IV fell under the influence of his militaristic and reactionary Junker advisors. Heartened by the news from Vienna that the Habsburgs had regained their position, he spurned the German crown offered him by the Frankfurt Assembly, contemptuously calling it "a crown from the gutter." His rejection of the crown blasted the Frankfurt Assembly's hopes for a united, liberal Germany. He accused liberals in the Frankfurt Assembly of "fighting the battle of godlessness, perjury, and robbery, and kindling a war against monarchy," and his Prussian troops drove the point home by ousting the few remaining liberals determined to keep the assembly alive.

Prussia

Figure 18.11 (on page 592) reveals much of what happened in Prussia and elsewhere. The painting by Adolph Menzel shows a funeral that the city of Berlin staged for the fallen on Sunday, March 22, 1848. More than 300 people had lost their lives in the fighting that raged during the early days of the revolution. Caskets are piled in a monumental pyramid. To the left of the church, the black, red, and gold flags of a (hopefully) united Germany flutter outside the optimistic townspeople's houses. To the left, university students, who played a vital role in the revolution, stand at attention. To the right, people energized by the revolution watch the procession, discuss recent events, and read announcements. Groups of the newly armed militia and mourners who supported the revolutionary cause move across the square. Victory once seemed to be in the revolutionaries' grasp. As the only sketched-in figures on the far left suggest, when the revolutionaries suffered reversals a few months later, Menzel lost the heart to finish the painting. His canvas stands as a testament to this "unfinished" revolution.

prisons. Louis Blanc fled to Great Britain. The events widened the cleavage between radical urban Paris and conservative rural France—a cleavage that would long complicate France's public life. As a final insult to the revolutionaries, the December presidential elections swept Louis-Napoleon Bonaparte (1808–1873), nephew of Napoleon Bonaparte, to victory. Promising something for everyone and projecting an image of order and authority, Louis-Napoleon held office for three years and then destroyed the republic in 1851 by taking power for himself in a coup d'état.

In Austria, the revolutionaries' inexperience and the rivalries among various ethnic groups gave the Habsburgs the upper hand. Playing off one group against another and using their still-formidable military force, the Austrian rulers beat down the liberal and national revolts one after the other. In Hun-

Austria and Hungary

WHAT HAPPENED?

By 1850, the conservative forces of order had regained control. What happened? How could so many victories

■ DOCUMENT 18.3

German Liberals and Nationalists Rally for Reform

The February 1848 revolution ending Louis-Philippe's regime and establishing a republic in France inspired many others throughout Europe who thirsted for reform. In Germany, liberals and nationalists rallied in hopes of uniting the German states and initiating liberal reforms. In the following selection, Carl Schurz (1829–1906) describes his participation in those events and the feelings he shared with others. ■ **Why** *did the fall of Louis-Philippe in France have such a strong effect on Schurz?* ■ **What** *reforms did Schurz long for?*

One morning, toward the end of February, 1848, I sat quietly in my attic-chamber, working hard at my tragedy of "Ulrich von Hutten," [a sixteenth-century German knight] when suddenly a friend rushed breathlessly into the room, exclaiming, "What, you sitting here! Do you not know what has happened?"

"No; what?"

"The French have driven away Louis Philippe and proclaimed the republic."

I threw down my pen—and that was the end of "Ulrich von Hutten." I never touched the manuscript again. We tore down the stairs, into the street, to the market-square, the accustomed meeting-place for all the student societies after their midday dinner. Although it was still forenoon, the market was already crowded with young men talking excitedly. There was no shouting, no noise, only agitated conversation. What did we want there? This probably no one knew. But since the French had driven away Louis Philippe and proclaimed the republic, something of course must happen here, too. . . . We were dominated by a vague feeling as if a great outbreak of elemental forces had begun, as if an earthquake was impending of which we had felt the first shock, and we instinctively crowded together. . . .

The next morning there were the usual lectures to be attended. But how profitless! At last we closed with a sigh the notebook and went away, impelled by a feeling that now we had something more important to do—to devote ourselves to the affairs of the fatherland. And this we did by seeking as quickly as possible again the company of our friends, in order to discuss what had happened and what was to come. In these conversations, excited as they were, certain ideas and catchwords worked themselves to the surface, which expressed more or less the feelings of the people. Now had arrived in Germany the day for the establishment of "German Unity," and the founding of a great, powerful national German Empire. In the first line the convocation of a national parliament. Then the demands for civil rights and liberties, free speech, free press, the right of free assembly, equality before the law, a freely elected representation of the people with legislative power, responsibility of ministers, self-government of the communes, the right of the people to carry arms, the formation of a civic guard with elective officers, and so on—in short, that which was called a "constitutional form of government on a broad democratic basis." Republican ideas were at first only sparingly expressed. But the word democracy was soon on all tongues, and many, too, thought it a matter of course that if the princes should try to withhold from the people the rights and liberties demanded, force would take the place of mere petition. Of course, the regeneration of the fatherland must, if possible, be accomplished by peaceable means. . . . Like many of my friends, I was dominated by the feeling that at last the great opportunity had arrived for giving to the German people the liberty which was their birthright and to the German fatherland its unity and greatness, and that it was now the first duty of every German to do and to sacrifice everything for this sacred object.

Source: Carl Schurz, *The Reminiscences of Carl Schurz* (New York: The McClure Co., 1907), vol. 1, pp. 112–113.

---

by liberals, nationalists, workers, and students be turned into defeats so quickly?

There are several explanations. First, the alliances among middle-class liberals, radicals, socialists, artisans, and workers was one of convenience (their shared opposition to the status quo) *Internal divisions* rather than genuine fellowship. After revolutionary forces gained power, the interests of the various groups proved too divergent for the alliances to endure. These divisions emerged most clearly in France, where the frightened middle class and conservative peasantry broke with the Parisian working classes. Lamartine, a poet and leading politician at the time, explained how the revolutionaries were divided into two groups: the republicans "were inspired by the hatred of royalty," while the socialists "were inspired . . . by the progress of humanity. The republic and equality was the aim of the one; social renovation and fraternity the aim of the other. They had nothing in common but impatience . . . and hope. . . ."

Second, liberal and nationalistic forces worked best together when out of power; in power, they often stood at cross-purposes. This lack of harmony between liberals and nationalists was particularly pronounced in central Europe, where the nationalist aspirations of

Holding power: Liberalism vs. nationalism

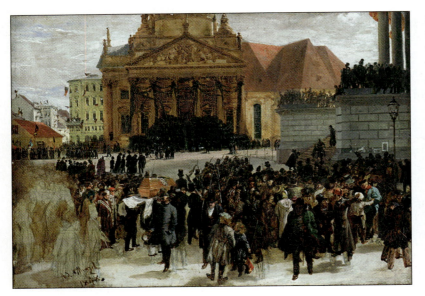

■ FIGURE 18.11

Adolph Menzel, *The March Casualties Lying in State*, 1848.

German, Polish, Magyar, Croatian, Serbian, and other groups conflicted with efforts to form new governments with liberal institutions. For example, liberals in the Frankfurt Assembly who sought to unify Germany turned against other nationalities who rose up against German rule in Austria and Prussia.

Third, the strength of conservatism should not be underestimated. With industrialization just begin-ning to emerge in central Europe, the middle and working classes—both discontented with the conservative status quo—were still weak. Revolutionary leaders were inexperienced as well. In Germany, for example, the journalist Carl Schurz explained the failure of the Frankfurt parliament: "That parliament was laboring under an overabundance of learning and virtue and under a want of . . . political experience."   **Conservatism**

Finally, once the shock of initial defeat at the hands of revolutionaries had faded, the seasoned leaders of the forces of order marshaled their resources, drew on their own armies and those of allies, and overcame the divided revolutionary forces.   **Force**
After they reestablished control, conservative leaders tore up most of the reforms and imprisoned, executed, or exiled revolutionaries. In December 1848, Pope Pius IX summarized the views of angry conservatives: "We . . . declare null and of no effect, and altogether illegal, every act" of reform during 1848. In fact, a few liberal reforms, such as the abolition of serfdom in Austria and Hungary and the limited constitutions in Piedmont and Prussia, would survive, but the great changes and power that for a few months seemed within the grasp of revolutionaries were gone.

SUMMARY

In 1815, the conservative forces of order tried to secure their own survival by repressing all those heartened by the principles and reforms of the French Revolution and the Enlightenment. Change became the enemy of conservatives, but the industrial revolution and the growing strength of ideologies such as liberalism, nationalism, and socialism strengthened demands for change.

In the early 1820s, a cycle of revolution and reform timidly emerged. In 1830, revolutionary forces posed a broader challenge, gaining some important victories in western Europe. The cycle returned in full force in 1848, as revolutions broke out through Europe and scored victory after victory. Those victories proved short-lived. By 1850, conservatives were back in power. This quick reversal of fortunes has led many historians to call the revolutions of 1848 "the turning point at which modern history failed to turn."

Yet the revolutions of 1848 left several important legacies. In a few cases, some liberal reforms were retained; in other cases, reforms in modified forms would be passed in succeeding years. Moreover, the overall failure of 1848 did not necessarily ensure a permanent victory for conservatism. As industrialization and urbanization spread year by year, traditional life and the old order it represented kept crumbling. Perhaps most significant, participants and observers had witnessed the power of ideologies, as well as economic and social realities, to galvanize people into political action.

However, the reestablished governments had learned important lessons from 1848, too, and would try to secure their positions with new vigor. They repaired the dam that broke in February 1848. For the time being, at least, everything seemed under control.

KEY TERMS

REVIEW, ANALYZE, AND ANTICIPATE

REVIEW THE PREVIOUS CHAPTER

Chapter 17—"Factories, Cities, and Families in the Industrial Age"—analyzed the industrial revolution and urbanization. Chapter 16—"Overturning the Political and Social Order"—examined the revolution whose consequences were felt throughout the West.

1. *In what ways might the developments described in Chapter 18 be considered a reaction to the French Revolution and industrial revolution discussed in the previous two chapters?*

2. *What forces stemming from the French Revolution and industrial revolution did conservatives try to repress or contain? To what extent do you think conservatives succeeded?*

ANALYZE THIS CHAPTER

Chapter 18—"Coping with Change"—analyzes the struggles between competing ideologies and political forces during the period between Napoleon's fall and the revolutions of 1848.

1. *Analyze the ideas of conservatism and policies of the forces of order in the years between 1815 and 1830.*

2. *In what ways did the ideas and actions of liberals, nationalists, and socialists challenge conservatives between 1815 and 1850?*

3. *In what ways did romanticism become a new cultural movement and an important ideology?*

4. *Analyze the commonalities in the several revolutions and movements for reform that developed between 1820 and 1848.*

ANTICIPATE THE NEXT CHAPTER

In Chapter 19—"Nationalism and Statebuilding"—the movements for national strength and unity will be examined.

1. *What "lessons" do you think governments and different social groups will have learned from the decades just preceding 1850 and, in particular, the revolutions of 1848?*

2. *Why might the ideologies of liberalism, nationalism, and socialism—which apparently suffered a stunning defeat between 1848 and 1850—persist and even grow in strength in the following decades?*

BEYOND THE CLASSROOM

THE CONGRESS OF VIENNA: A GATHERING OF VICTORS

Bridge, F. R. *The Great Powers and the European States System, 1815–1914.* London: Longman, 1980. A thorough diplomatic history of the period.

Chapman, Tim. *Congress of Vienna: Origins, Processes, and Results.* London: Taylor & Francis, 1998. A well-written study that covers the topic well.

IDEOLOGIES: HOW THE WORLD SHOULD BE

Arblaster, Anthony. *The Rise and Decline of Western Liberalism.* Oxford: B. Blackwell, 1984. An analysis of the evolution and key components of liberalism.

Beecher, Jonathan. *Charles Fourier: The Visionary and His World.* Berkeley, CA: University of California Press, 1986. Traces the development of Fourier's ideas through his early years to his emergence as a political prophet and founder of one of the most significant early socialist movements.

Porter, Roy, and Mikulas Teich, eds. *Romanticism in National Context.* Cambridge: Cambridge University Press, 1988. A series of essays on romanticism by noted historians.

Smith, Denis Mack. *Mazzini.* New Haven, CT: Yale University Press, 1999. A recent biography of this important figure by a well-known historian.

RESTORATION AND REPRESSION

Jardin, André, and André-Jean Tudesq. *Restoration and Reaction, 1815–1848.* Cambridge: Cambridge University Press, 1988. A solid survey of France during this period.

Sheehan, James J. *German History, 1770–1866.* New York: Oxford University Press, 1989. A comprehensive, exhaustive examination of the changes in German social, political, and economic history.

Sked, Alan. *The Decline and Fall of the Habsburg Empire, 1815–1918.* London: Longman, 1989. Studies the growing problems facing the Habsburg Empire during the nineteenth century.

A WAVE OF REVOLUTION AND REFORM

Church, Clive. *Europe in 1830: Revolution and Political Change.* London: Allen & Unwin, 1983. Examines the revolutions that swept across Europe in a comparative context.

Fortescue, William. *Revolution and Counter-Revolution in France, 1815–1852.* London: Blackwell, 2002. A useful survey of the topic and France during this period.

THE DAM BURSTS: 1848

Price, Roger. *The Revolutions of 1848.* Atlantic Highlands, NJ: Humanities Press International, 1989. A useful, wide-ranging survey.

Sperber, Jonathan. *The European Revolutions, 1848–1851.* Cambridge: Cambridge University Press, 1994. A brief yet thorough account that covers the tumultuous events throughout Europe.

www.mhhe.com/sherman3

- Unfamiliar words? See our Glossary at the back of the book for pronunciation and definitions.

- Need help studying? See our web page for map exercises, practice quizzes, and additional study resources.

- Need help writing a paper? Access hundreds of primary documents, maps, images, and a guide to writing history papers on our Primary Source Investigator site at **www.mhhe.com/psi.**

ADOLPH MENZEL, *THE DEPARTURE OF WILLIAM I FOR THE ARMY ON JULY 31, 1870*, 1871

This 1871 painting by German artist Adolph Menzel suggests that the inhabitants of Prussia's capital, Berlin, greeted a statebuilding war against France with an outburst of Prussian patriotism and broader German nationalism. Menzel depicts King William I's departure on July 31, 1870, from Berlin to his military headquarters in Mainz to help lead the war against France. On the left, in a white satin-lined coach, the king and his wife pass under cast-iron and glass street lamps along the fashionable tree-lined avenue *Unter den Linden*. The monarch salutes the crowd, while the tearful queen covers her face with a handkerchief. The crowds are celebrating not only the king, but also their own success and anticipated victory. Flags billow in the breeze—both the Prussian and the black, white, and red German flags, signaling a moment of growing national unification. In the distance stands Berlin's new redbrick city hall, evidence of Prussia's growing political and economic power that supports the bold military effort.

CHAPTER 19

NATIONALISM AND STATEBUILDING

UNIFYING NATIONS, 1850–1870

STUDY	Italian unification ▪ German unification ▪ National unity in North America ▪ Nationalism in France and Russia.
NOTICE	The conflict of forces for and against national unification.

On May 31, 1860, just three weeks after landing in Sicily, the Italian nationalist leader Giuseppe Garibaldi toured Palermo, Sicily's main city. He entered the city at the head of a band of one thousand volunteer soldiers to begin the liberation of southern Italy from the old, Austrian supported Bourbon king. He called for "Italians" to "put an end, once and for all, to the miseries of so many centuries," and "prove to the world that it is no lie that Roman generations inhabited this land." An eyewitness described how "the popular idol, Garibaldi, in his red flannel shirt, with a loose colored handkerchief round his neck . . . was walking on foot among those cheering, laughing, crying, mad thousands." As he moved through the streets, "the people threw themselves forward to kiss his hands, or, at least, to touch the hem of his garment, as if it contained the panacea for all their past and perhaps coming suffering."

In the decades between 1850 and 1870, millions of others in the Italian states—and in regions ranging from the Americas in the west to the Ottoman Empire in the east—would rally, fight, and die in the name of national unity. In Europe, maps had to be redrawn as new nation-states emerged. In the United States, a wrenching battle was entered in the name of preserving the Union. Political leaders would use nationalistic appeals to build stronger states as well as to tear apart multinational empires. Nationalism was evolving from the ideals of earlier decades to the realities of power politics.

TIMELINE: THE BIG PICTURE

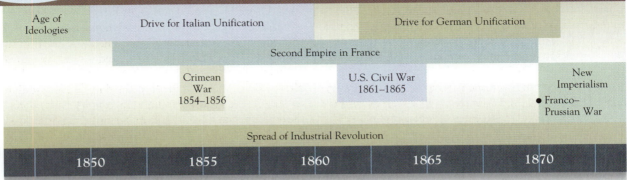

Age of Ideologies	Drive for Italian Unification		Drive for German Unification	
	Second Empire in France			
	Crimean War 1854–1856	U.S. Civil War 1861–1865		New Imperialism
				● Franco–Prussian War
Spread of Industrial Revolution				
1850	1855	1860	1865	1870

BUILDING UNIFIED NATION-STATES

"EVERY GERMAN HEART HOPED FOR IT," wrote the baroness Spitzemberg in Berlin in 1871. "United into one Reich, the greatest, the most powerful, the most feared in Europe; great by reason of its physical power, greater still by reason of its education and the intelligence which permeates it!" So the baroness expressed her longing for national unification, a passion felt by many others in the West.

In the two decades after 1850, no political force was stronger than nationalism. It pushed people toward national unity in Italy and Germany and *Nationalism* threatened to tear the Habsburg and Ottoman Empires apart. In the United States, the principle of national unity helped spark a brutal civil war. In France and elsewhere, rulers enacted major reforms designed to bolster national unity and their authority as leaders of a nation of citizens. All these efforts were intended to build strong, unified nation-states led by central governments that could enjoy the support of their citizens.

Unlike in 1848, however, the nationalist political figures were neither revolutionaries nor idealists. As one advocate of Italian unification observed, "To defeat cannons and soldiers, cannons *Political realism* and soldiers are needed." From positions of established power, this new generation of leaders molded nationalism to fit harsh political realities. They focused their eyes on practical policies, not ideals. They gambled, compromised, manipulated, and fought to achieve their goals. Few struggled more persistently and cleverly than Count Camillo di Cavour (1810–1861).

THE DRIVE FOR ITALIAN UNIFICATION

Cavour was born into a well-to-do, noble family living in Piedmont-Sardinia, a small, but relatively powerful independent state in northern Italy that also included the island of Sardinia. As a young man, he gambled, played the stock market, experimented with agricultural techniques, and succeeded in business— a pattern of taking calculated risks he would *Cavour* later try to follow in politics. By the 1840s, he had become committed to Italian unification. Shortly before the revolution of 1848, he founded the newspaper *Il Risorgimento (The Resurgence)*, which passionately argued for a unified Italy. In 1850, Piedmont-Sardinia's king Victor Emmanuel II (r. 1849–1878) made Cavour his minister of commerce and agriculture and, two years later, prime minister.

Cavour's goals were clear. First, he wanted to modernize Piedmont economically and thereby win strength and respect for his homeland. Second, he sought to make Piedmont *Cavour's leadership* the central engine of the drive for national unification. Third, he advocated forming a new Italian state as a constitutional monarchy under Piedmont's king rather than a democratic republic or a confederation under the pope. To achieve all these ends, Cavour lowered tariffs, built railroads, and balanced Piedmont's budget. He supported the nationalistic Italian National Society and its Feminine Committee, which worked toward national unification with Piedmont at the helm. Finally, he employed diplomacy and Piedmont's relatively small army to gain international support for the struggle against the primary obstacle to unification—Austria.

When the Crimean War broke out between Russia and the Ottoman Empire in 1854, Cavour saw an opportunity. He brought Piedmont in on the side of Great Britain and France, countries that had joined the Ottoman Turks against Russia. Cavour hoped to gain the friendship and support of France and Britain and thereby elevate Piedmont-Sardinia's status among the European powers. "I believe that the principal condition for the improvement of Italy's fate," he explained to the Parliament of Piedmont in 1855, "is to lift up her reputation once more . . . to prove that Italy's sons can fight valiantly on battlefields where glory is to be won." Victory in the east, he claimed, "will help the future state of Italy more than all that has been done by those people who hoped to regenerate her by rhetorical speeches and writings."

His risky plan may have paid off. At the Paris Peace Conference in 1856, which ended the war, he pleaded Piedmont's case against Austria so skillfully that he captured the attention of the international community. Two years later, Cavour and France's emperor Napoleon III met at a French resort to discuss ways to move against Austria, a competitor of France on the Continent and the chief barrier to Cavour's hopes for Italian unity. The two decided to provoke Austria into a war against Piedmont and thereby bring France into the fray. "Together we began to . . . search of those grounds for war which were so difficult to find," explained Cavour in a note to his king. Then "we discovered what we had been trying so hard to find," a way to manipulate Austria into a war that "would not alarm the other continental powers." After Austria declared war, France would help Piedmont drive the Austrians out of Lombardy and Venezia, and these two states would then be annexed to Piedmont-Sardinia. In return, Piedmont would cede the two small, French-speaking provinces of Savoy and Nice to France and allow a kingdom of Central Italy to be created for Napoleon III's cousin.

In 1859, after Cavour mobilized the Piedmontese army and refused an Austrian demand to reverse the act, the unsuspecting Austrians declared war on Piedmont. French armies, using new railroad lines, poured across the Alps to fight alongside the Piedmontese. In the bloody battles of Magenta and Solferino, the French and Piedmontese ousted the Austrians from Lombardy. But to the dismay of Cavour, Napoleon III suddenly made a separate peace at Villafranca with Austria that gave Piedmont Lombardy and left Venetia in Austrian hands. Cavour's side now had momentum, however. Nationalists in other Italian states, inspired by Piedmont's success, rose to the cause of national unity. By early 1860, most of northern and central Italy had joined Piedmont voluntarily.

War with Austria

At this pivotal point in the action, the raw-boned nationalist Giuseppe Garibaldi (1807–1882) made a daring exploit. Garibaldi had long struggled to create a unified and republican Italy— organizing people, conducting campaigns of guerilla warfare, and leading insurrections. Often in exile, he had become a well-known figure in Europe and the Americas. In May 1860, accompanied by a thousand civilian warriors dressed in red shirts, he sailed for Sicily in southern Italy, where many peasants had already launched a revolt. "It is the duty of every Italian to succor them [the Sicilians in revolt] with words, money, arms, and above all, in person," he announced (see Document 19.1). Garibaldi's goal was nothing less than the conquest of the Kingdom of Naples, the largest and most populous of the Italian states, and then Rome itself. Cavour officially condemned the seemingly foolhardy expedition but secretly assisted it.

Garibaldi

As Figure 19.1 suggests, Garibaldi's exploits read like an adventure novel. He heroically lands at the island of Sicily to fight for Italian unification. In the background, his band of volunteer soldiers (the "Red Shirts") pours from three ships and marches in rough formation. Carrying a sword and a flag representing Italian unity, Garibaldi is welcomed by admiring children, women, men, and a priest. In rapid succession, he conquered Sicily, crossed the Strait of Messina, and triumphantly entered Naples (see Map 19.1 on page 600). The opposing troops had little heart for their own cause. Many, along with civilian women and men by the thousands, joined Garibaldi after his first victories. Made ever bolder by his conquests, the confident Garibaldi advanced north toward Rome.

Not wanting to lose control of the rapidly changing situation and fearing that an attack on Rome by Garibaldi might lead France and Austria to come to the aid of the pope, Cavour sent troops southward in September 1860, gained control over the Papal States, and then skirted the area around Rome. King Victor Emmanuel, marching at the head of his army, met Garibaldi's forces south of Rome. Garibaldi yielded to Victor Emmanuel and his Piedmontese troops. Two years later, Garibaldi, hoping to annex Rome as the capital of Italy, fomented an unsuccessful uprising. The gallant patriot soon retired to his farm on the rocky island of Caprera.

The Kingdom of Italy was formally declared in March 1861, with Victor Emmanuel II as monarch and the Piedmontese Constitution of 1848 as the national charter. The king, along with a parliamentary government elected by limited suffrage, would rule. The red, white, and green Piedmontese flag now flew over all of Italy, from the Alps to Sicily, except in Venetia and Rome (see Map 19.1). These two provinces (with the exception of the Vatican palace) joined the Italian state in 1866 and 1870, respectively.

Kingdom of Italy

Garibaldi Landing in Sicily

■ FIGURE 19.1

This painting illustrates for the public Giuseppe Garibaldi and his band of soldiers landing in Sicily in May 1860. This landing and the campaign that followed played an important role in the unification of Italy. ■ **How** has the artist depicted Garibaldi, who stands in the center of the picture, and the "Red Shirts" soldiers behind him? ■ **In what ways** might this depiction glorify Garibaldi's exploits and the unification movement? ■ **Consider** how the people surrounding Garibaldi are presented to viewers.

Sadly, Cavour did not live to enjoy the fruits of his labors. Less than three months after the birth of his beloved Italian nation, he died. Paunchy, with ill-fitting glasses, he had never cut an impressive figure. Nor had he made a particularly powerful orator. "I cannot make a speech," he once said, "but I can make Italy."

GERMANY "BY BLOOD AND IRON"

Like Italy, Germany as we understand it did not exist in 1850, except in the hearts of nationalists. Most of the many German states belonged to the loose Germanic Confederation, but this organization, under the dominance of Austria, did not function as a unified nation. Would someone like Piedmont's Count Cavour rise to overcome the obstacles to German unification? By 1860, no one of this caliber had yet stepped forward.

Prussian leadership

The best hope for German unity rested with Prussia, which had achieved a position of strength thanks to its economic expansion and leadership over the Zollverein, a German customs union that fostered industrialization in Prussia and the Rhineland (see p. 580). By 1853, every German state except

THINKING ABOUT DOCUMENTS

■ DOCUMENT 19.1

Garibaldi Appeals to Italians for Support

The campaign that resulted in the unification of Italy required not just idealism, but also a realistic outlook and daring action. With his political manipulations, Cavour provided the realism. With his invasion of Sicily in 1860, Guiseppe Garibaldi provided the daring action. To support the invasion, Garibaldi issued his Proclamation for the Liberation of Sicily. ■ ***How*** *does Garibaldi appeal to Italians outside of Sicily for support?* ■ ***In what ways*** *does this proclamation echo the appeal of nationalism?*

Italians!—The Sicilians are fighting against the enemies of Italy, and for Italy. It is the duty of every Italian to succour them with words, money, and arms, and, above all, in person.

The misfortunes of Italy arise from the indifference of one province to the fate of the others.

The redemption of Italy began from the moment that men of the same land ran to help their distressed brothers.

Left to themselves, the brave Sicilians will have to fight, not only the mercenaries of the Bourbon, but also those of Austria and the Priest of Rome.

Let the inhabitants of the free provinces lift their voices in behalf of their struggling brethren, and impel their brave youth to the conflict.

Let the Marches, Umbria, Sabina, Rome, the Neapolitan, rise to divide the forces of our enemies.

Where the cities suffice not for the insurrection, let them send bands of their bravest into the country.

The brave man finds an arm everywhere. Listen not to the voice of cowards, but arm, and let us fight for our brethren, who will fight for us tomorrow.

A band of those who fought with me the country's battles marches with me to the fight. Good and generous, they will fight for their country to the last drop of their blood, nor ask for other reward than a clear conscience.

"Italy and Victor Emmanuel!" they cried, on passing the Ticino. "Italy and Victor Emmanuel!" shall re-echo in the blazing caves of Mongibello.

At this cry, thundering from the great rock of Italy to the Tarpeian, the rotton Throne of tyranny shall crumble, and, as one man, the brave descendants of Vespro shall rise.

To Arms! Let me put an end, once and for all, to the miseries of so many centures. Prove to the world that it is no lie that Roman generations inhabited this land.

Source: Public Documents, *The Annual Register*, 1860 (London, 1861), pp. 281–282.

Austria had joined the Zollverein. However, Prussia was torn by the political struggle between liberals in the legislature and the conservative aristocracy. The two sides fought over plans to strengthen Prussia's military. When Prussia's new king, William I, and his military advisors proposed to double the size of the army, the liberals, who distrusted Prussian militarism and hoped to gain a stronger role for the legislature in the Prussian government, defeated the measure. Faced with a deadlock between these uncompromising forces and convinced that his royal authority was being threatened, William I called on Otto von Bismarck (1815–1898).

"I was born and raised as an aristocrat," Bismarck once explained. He would remain loyal to Prussia's

Bismarck landowning aristocracy for the rest of his life. As a young man, Bismarck showed little promise of future greatness. While attending university, he spent more time gambling than studying. A religious conversion in 1846 and marriage seemed to give him more of a sense of purpose. He entered politics in 1847 and came to believe that only an alliance of conservatism and nationalism

could preserve the aristocracy and strengthen Prussia. His enemies were the liberals, who had failed in 1848, and Austria, Prussia's chief competitor and supposed senior partner within the German states.

Bismarck assumed the office of prime minister of Prussia in 1862. With the backing of the king, the aristocracy, and the army, he promptly defied the liberals in the legislature, violated the constitution, and ordered taxes collected for military reform. "Necessity alone is authoritative," he argued. He would pursue a policy of realism—**Realpolitik**—to achieve his goals. "Not by speeches and majority resolutions," Bismarck rumbled, "are the great questions of the time decided—that was the mistake of 1848 and 1849— but by blood and iron." As the prime minister argued, Germans looked to Prussia for leadership not because of its liberalism, but because of its power.

Like Cavour in Italy, Bismarck sought out political opportunities, created them when they failed to materialize, **Wars for unification** and did not hesitate to take calculated risks, including war. In 1864, Denmark provided his first opportunity when it tried to incorporate

THINKING ABOUT GEOGRAPHY

MAP 19.1 THE UNIFICATION OF ITALY

This map shows the unification of Italy in the years after 1859.
■ **Locate** Lombardy and Nice. **Consider** how much Piedmont gave
up and gained in its bargain for French support. ■ **Find** the route of
Garibaldi's campaign. **Why** might this have been so important—and
threatening—to Piedmont's plans to unify Italy? ■ **Consider** the importance of those territories still outside of the Italian state in 1860.

tlement—Schleswig and Holstein
were to be ruled jointly by Prussia
and Austria—Bismarck shrewdly
planted the seeds for a future conflict with Austria.

Bismarck soon used this unworkable arrangement to stir up
trouble with
Austria. He   ***Austro-Prussian War***
obtained the
support of Italy by promising Austria's province of Venezia as a prize.
He gained Russia's sympathy by
supporting its intervention against
rebellious subjects in Poland. He
neutralized Napoleon III by personal persuasion and deception. Finally, as Document 19.2 suggests,
he manipulated domestic politics
to achieve his ends. In 1866, Bismarck took a risk by using threats
and maneuvers to provoke Austria
into declaring war on Prussia. Austria was twice the size and population of Prussia and had long
dominated central Europe. Nevertheless, Prussia's modern and mobile armies managed to overwhelm
the surprised Austrian forces in just
seven weeks. Austria suffered four
times as many casualties as Prussia, in great part because of the fast-
firing needle-guns used by Prussian troops and the army's use of
railroads to move forces quickly to
battlefields. Bismarck boldly expelled Austria from the German
Confederation and even annexed
several German states that had
sided with Austria. Nevertheless,
hoping for Austrian support in the
future, Bismarck refused the desires
of Prussia's king and army leaders
to annex Austrian territories.

Prussia now controlled the
newly created North German
Confederation. Despite some democratic forms, such as a legislative
body (the Reichstag) elected by
universal male suffrage, the gov-
ernment was fundamentally an **autocracy**. The legislature had no control over the
chancellor—appointed by and   ***Franco-Prussian War***
responsible only to the king
or his cabinet—and little control over the budget or
armed forces. However, some of the southern German
states, with larger Catholic populations than Prussia,

Schleswig and Holstein, two small provinces lying
between Prussia and Denmark. The provinces' legal
status had been disputed for decades. Posing as a
defender of German nationalism, Prussia promptly
declared war on Denmark, pulling Austria—anxious
to retain leadership of the German Confederation—
in as Prussia's reluctant ally. In the complicated set-

■ DOCUMENT 19.2

Bismarck Masters Politics in Prussia

Like Cavour in Italy, Otto von Bismarck became a master of both politics and war in his effort to unify Germany under Prussia. Just before Prussia's war with Austria in 1866, Bismarck, despite his conservatism, instituted a constitution that included universal male suffrage. In the following excerpt from his Memoirs, *Bismarck describes his support for universal suffrage.* ■ **What** *exactly does Bismarck mean by "universal suffrage"?* ■ **Why** *might he support this apparently democratic institution?*

Looking to the necessity, in a fight against an overwhelming foreign Power, of being able, in extreme need, to use even revolutionary means, I had had no hesitation whatever in throwing into the frying-pan, by means of the circular dispatch of June 10, 1866, the most powerful ingredient known at that time to liberty-mongers, namely, universal suffrage, so as to frighten off foreign monarchies from trying to stick a finger into our national omelette. . . .

The acceptance of universal suffrage was a weapon in the war against Austria and other foreign countries, in the war for German Unity, as well as a threat to use the last weapons in a struggle against coalitions. In a war of this sort, when it becomes a matter of life and death, one does not look at the weapons that one seizes, nor the value of what one destroys in using them: one is guided at the moment by no other thought than the issue of the war, and the preservation of ones external independence; the settling of affairs and reparation of the damage has to take place after the peace. Moreover, I still hold that the principle of universal suffrage is a just one, not only in theory but also in practice, provided always that voting be not secret, for secrecy is a quality that is indeed incompatible with the best characteristics of German blood. . . .

The counterpoise to this lies in the influence of the educated classes, which would be greatly strengthened if voting were public, as for the Prussian Diet. It may be that the greater discretion of the more intelligent classes rests on the material basis of the preservation of their possessions. . . . Every great state-commonwealth that loses the prudent and restraining influence of the propertied class, whether that influence rests on material or moral grounds, will always end by being rushed along at a speed which must shatter the coach of state, as happened in the development of the French Revolution.

Source: Otto von Bismarck, *The Memoirs,* trans., A.J. Butler (Howard Fertig, 1890).

---

still lay outside Bismarck's grasp (see Map 19.2). He wisely recognized that these remaining, reluctant states might join the fold if German nationalism could be rallied against a common, foreign threat. France, Bismarck decided, might just fit the bill.

Bismarck's opportunity to confront France came in 1870 when the Spanish crown was offered to a Hohenzollern prince—a relative of Prussia's William I. When Bismarck persuaded the reluctant prince to accept the Spanish offer, the French immediately took alarm at the prospect of being surrounded by Hohenzollerns. The French exerted heavy pressure on Prussia, and both the prince and King William yielded. However, the unsatisfied French ministers demanded more. After a meeting at Ems between the French ambassador and the Prussian king, the chancellor saw an opportunity to provoke the French into war. Cleverly editing the Ems telegraph dispatch so as to make it appear that the French ambassador and the Prussian king had insulted each other, he published it to the world. The French government was offended and walked into Bismarck's trap. Buoyed by public demands for action, France declared war.

The chancellor had taken his greatest risk, for France seemed to possess enough military might and economic resources to humble Prussia. As France's confident prime minister stated, "We go to war with a light heart." Again, however, the able Prussian troops quickly scored resounding successes. One French army was surrounded at the fortress city of Metz. The Prussians encircled another French army at Sedan, forcing it to surrender. Napoleon III himself was one of the captives. When this news reached Paris, the liberals overthrew the government of the Second Empire and declared the Third French Republic. Paris held out for a few more months, surrounded by the Germans, but finally surrendered in January 1871.

On January 18, 1871, Bismarck called the heads of all the German states to Versailles in France. Gathering in the Hall of Mirrors, the dignitaries proclaimed Prussia's king William I, emperor of the new German Empire; he would rule until 1888. Figure 19.2 celebrates that moment. In this well-known painting by Anton von Werner, who witnessed the event, Prussian officers hail William, who stands at the left. But the center of the painting belongs to Bismarck, dressed in white, the architect of this historical moment. He alone holds the document proclaiming the new empire that he, more than anyone else, had built. The dramatic scene is set in France's historic symbol of monarchical power, the Versailles palace. By choosing this location, Bismarck drove home

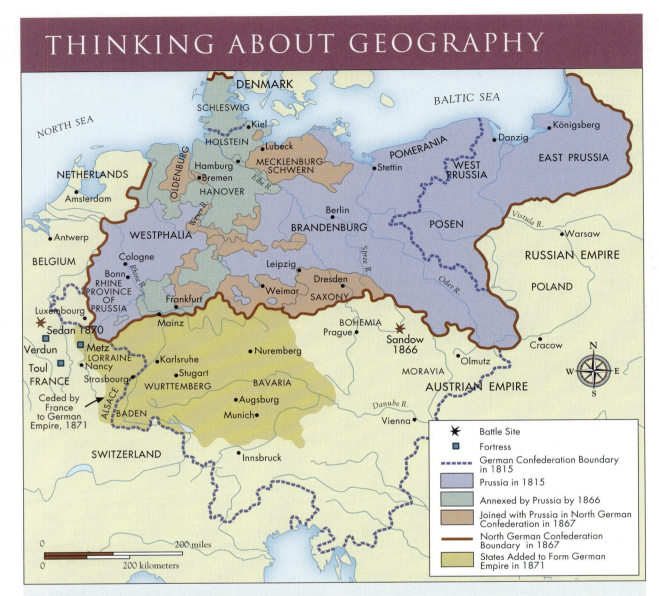

MAP 19.2   **THE UNIFICATION OF GERMANY**

This map shows the steps taken to achieve German unification in 1871. ■ **Notice** the positions of Prussia and Austria before 1866. **What** does this reveal about the rivalry between these two countries for control over the German states? ■ **Notice** the changes in 1866, 1867, and 1871. **What** does this show about the importance of Prussia's triumph over Austria in 1866 and over France in 1871? **Who** might be most threatened by a powerful Germany after 1871?

the point that Prussia had achieved German unity by defeating France in war. He also wanted to make it crystal clear that Germany, now in possession of France's rich provinces of Alsace and Lorraine and owed a war indemnity of 5 billion francs in gold from the French, had replaced the humiliated France as Europe's leading continental power.

The constitution that Bismarck had drafted for the North German Confederation became the constitu-tion for the new German Empire. Its twenty-five states retained control over many domestic matters, but Prus-sia dominated the union. Known as the Second Reich (Germans honored the old Holy Roman Empire as the First Reich), the powerful nation included a large and rapidly growing population, a vibrant industrial econ-omy, and a feared military. Bismarck, of course, remained chancellor and lived to rule over his creation for the next nineteen years. In Germany, as in Italy, a clever,

■ FIGURE 19.2

Anton von Werner, *Proclamation of the German Empire*.

realistic political leader had employed diplomacy and war to transform the unruly forces of nationalism into German unification.

THE FIGHT FOR NATIONAL UNITY IN NORTH AMERICA

The struggle for unification flared up in other parts of the West besides Italy and Germany. Between 1800 and 1861, the United States' political institutions had evolved along democratic and *The United States* nationalistic lines. Almost all white men had gained the right to vote. A modern, broad-based political party system had formed and wrestled political power from the elite circles of the old colonial well-to-do. The nation had expanded westward to the Pacific Ocean, conquering the Amerindians and displacing them to reservations. When Mexico stood in the way of expansion, it also lost its lands to the United States armed forces. Commercial interests led the United States across the Pacific to Japan (see Global Connectionson page 605). Finally, American culture began to free itself from strictly European influence. Citizens proudly thought of themselves and their institutions as having a distinct flavor within Western civilization.

However, as the nineteenth century progressed, the nation labored under growing regional differ-ences. The North was an expanding, urban, industrial society based on free labor. Figure 19.3, a *North-South divisions* lithograph of the Stillman, Allen & Co. Novelty Iron Works of New York City, illustrates one of the many manufacturing facilities growing up in the North's cities in the middle decades of the nineteenth century. The South remained agricultural, dependent on plantation crops such as cotton, and based on slave labor. Figure 19.4, a painting by Charles Giroux, portrays this rural society with its large population of slaves. The North enjoyed a growing population and generally favored federal over state power. The South, worried that its influence over national policies was slipping away, emphasized states' rights over federal power. In the decades before 1861, these two regions, with their increasingly different societies and interests, clashed politically on several occasions.

It was the issue of slavery, though, that gave these clashes a dangerous emotional intensity and tied together the other problems dividing the North and the South. By the early 1800s, the northern states had eliminated slavery. However, the institution persisted in the South, where agriculture, and especially cotton plantations, reigned supreme. There, *Slavery* slaveholders viewed slaves as the very basis of their wealth, power, and status. Meanwhile, in the free-labor North, antislavery sentiment grew. "[T]his government cannot endure permanently half slave and half free," declared Abraham Lincoln (1809–1865) in 1858, just two years before the nation elected him president.

In 1861, all these regional differences, fueled by the question of whether to abolish slavery, ignited a bloody war between the North, led by Lincoln, and the South under Jefferson Davis (1808–1889). The conflict raged for four years until the North finally defeated the Southern armies. Ultimately the war took more than 600,000 lives, making it the bloodiest conflict in the Western *The Civil War* world since the end of the Napoleonic Wars. Lincoln had achieved his primary goal: to reestablish national unity and affirm the power of the national government. In the aftermath, slavery was abolished in the United States.

Farther north, a different struggle for national independence and unity had been unfolding in Canada. William Lyon Mackenzie (1795– *Canada* 1861), a nationalist politician, called for Canadians to "put down the villains [the British] who oppress and enslave our country" and gain "freedom from British tribute." Britain responded to a rebellion in 1837 by granting Canada some control over its own domestic affairs. Nevertheless, the Canadian territories were not yet joined into a single nation, and Canadians feared the growing power of the United States. Demands for union and complete nationhood increased. Finally, in 1867, the British North American Act united Canada into a single nation with its own constitution.

DIVIDED AUTHORITY IN THE AUSTRIAN AND OTTOMAN EMPIRES

Nationalism pulled Austria's multiethnic empire apart rather than bringing it together (see Map 19.3). Czechs, Serbs, Romanians, Magyars (Hungarians), and **Austria** other ethnic groups wanted to form their own, independent nations rather than rally behind Austria, which was predominantly German.

Austria's emperor, Francis Joseph (r. 1848–1916), was no reformer or politician in the mold of Bismarck, Cavour, or Lincoln. Under pressure from liberals and nationalists, he agreed in 1860 to a mod-

■ FIGURE 19.3

A northern factory.

■ FIGURE 19.4

Charles Giroux, *Cotton Plantation*.

erate decentralization of the empire and the creation of a parliament. After Austria's defeat by Prussia in 1866, the dominant German minority in Austria compromised with the assertive Magyars rather than fight **Austria-Hungary, 1867** them over issues of nationality. Their agreement, the Compromise of 1867, set up the **Dual Monarchy** of Austria-Hungary. Each country had its own separate parliament, but the two were united under a common ruler, the head of the House of Habsburg. This arrangement was essentially an alliance between the Germans of Austria and the Magyars of Hungary against other competing ethnic groups. The empire therefore divided authority in an effort to control even more threatening movements for national independence. This arrangement did not please other national groups, especially the Czechs, who would persistently demand equality with the Hungarians.

Like the Austrians, the Ottoman rulers also had to struggle with the divisive forces of nationalism. In 1850, the Ottoman Empire was still extensive. From its **The Ottoman Empire** base in Turkey, it maintained control over much of southeastern Europe as well as over provinces stretching from North Africa to the Persian Gulf. However the empire, often referred to as "the sick man of Europe," was in decline. Powerful, ambitious neighbors—especially the Russians, who attacked the Turks in 1853 and again in 1877—maneuvered to take advantage of the Ottomans' weaknesses. But **Balkan nationalism** the greatest threats to the empire's integrity came from its restless Balkan provinces in southeastern Europe. In this area nationalism rose, producing the same sort of movements for independence that had weakened the Austrian Empire.

By 1830, the Ottoman Empire had already lost Serbia and Greece to independence movements (see Map 19.4). Nationalism had fueled an unsuccessful revolt by the Romanians in 1848 as well. In 1856, the Romanians gained international support as part of the settlement of the Crimean War. Over the next twenty years, they pressed the Ottomans for their freedom, finally winning full independence in 1878.

Nationalist movements also cropped up among the Bulgars. Encouraged by Serbia and Russia, the Bulgars revolted in 1876. Each side in the conflict committed atrocities, but those committed by the Turks especially shocked Europeans. That year, Bosnia and Herzegovina also rose against the Turks. Serbia and Russia then joined forces against the Ottoman Empire. By 1878, international agreements, most notably the Treaty of Berlin, had secured the independence of Bulgaria and placed Bosnia and Herzegovina under Austro-Hungarian rule. Movements for national independence, with the aid of powers eager to take advantage of the empire's declin-

Japan Opens to the West

CONSIDER

■ **Consider** *the options available to the Japanese when faced with growing Western pressures.* **Notice** *how quickly the Japanese "Westernized" as a measure of self-defense.*

In 1853, after two centuries of self-imposed isolation from the West, the Japanese witnessed an intimidating sight: an American squadron of well-armed, steam-powered ships under Admiral Perry sailing uninvited into Edo (Tokyo) Bay. Perry's instructions from the American government stressed the United States' desire to "establish commercial intercourse with a country whose large population and reputed wealth hold out great temptations to mercantile enterprise." Should friendly negotiations fail, the instructions continued, Perry should "change his tone" and threaten force. Perry took the charge to heart: "The World has assigned this duty to us."

During the 1830s and 1840s, the Japanese had watched with growing alarm as the Chinese failed to limit Western access into their empire. Now Japan faced a vital question: Should it resist the technologically superior West by arms? Or should it open itself to Westerners but adapt to them in ways that would make Japan a power in its own right?

Some Japanese, such as the scholar and official Sahuma Shozan, thought that the newly arrived Americans "were exceedingly arrogant, and the resulting insult to our national dignity was not small." But, Sahuma continued, the best response was to accept trade with the West and learn Western ways. "In order to master the barbarians," Sahuma recommended learning Western languages and science. His motto would become famous throughout Japan: "Eastern ethics and Western science."

Other Japanese, such as the conservative Tokugawa Nariaki, a high official in the Tokugawa Shogunate government, recommended an aggressive armed response to Perry: Despite prohibitions against them, "the Americans who arrived recently and fired heavy guns in salute were arrogant and discourteous, their actions an outrage." Tokugawa warned that it is the practice of foreigners "first to seek a foothold by means of trade and then go on to propagate Christianity and make other unreasonable demands."

But Japan's efforts to resist Perry's encroachment proved futile. Soon the well-armed Western ships intimidated the Tokugawa government into signing unequal treaties with the United States. Japan also signed agreements with Britain, Russia, France, and the Netherlands that opened the country to trade and foreign presence.

Fifteen years after Perry's arrival, the 250-year-old Tokugawa Shogunate collapsed in a revolution led by powerful aristocrats who ushered into power the boy emperor, Meiji ("Enlightened Rule"). Weakened by decades of population growth, declining agricultural productivity, popular revolts, and failed efforts at reform, the Shogunate gave way. According to Count Ito, a leader of the Meiji Restoration, members of the new government "set themselves to the task of introducing Western civilization into Japan." These leaders quickly dismantled the country's traditional military and social order. Using French, German, British, and American ways, they created a new conscript army, introduced universal education, established a written constitution, and began industrializing the economy. In 1889, Ito declared success: "If we . . . compare the present state of affairs with that which existed some twenty years ago, we shall not exaggerate if we say that the country has undergone a complete metamorphosis."

Within a few decades, Japan had transformed itself on its own terms. Formerly a feudal society with a preindustrial economy, it was now a modern industrialized nation. By the end of the nineteenth century, the new Japan—an amalgam of Western influences and Japanese culture—had become a rising imperial power. It would soon constitute one of the West's most formidable competitors.

---

ing strength, had ended Turkish control throughout most of the Balkans. However, these developments also left a jumble of dissatisfied groups and nationalities—a few who had their own states, some who longed for political independence, and others who did not like being annexed by Austria-Hungary.

Using Nationalism in France and Russia

The power of nationalism to motivate people to join revolutionary organizations, form new political allegiances, follow powerful politicians, and go to war in the name of national unity made itself clear in Italy and Germany. Under different conditions, nationalism weakened and dismembered long-established multinational states such as the Austrian and Ottoman Empires.

Nationalism also pushed governments in well-established states to reach out to citizens for support. These governments tried to justify and sustain their authority by performing public services, and they bolstered their power by promoting the idea of national greatness. They paid more attention to everyday life so as to maintain social peace and cultivate loyalty to the nation—and especially to its leaders. These efforts to channel nationalism into statebuild-

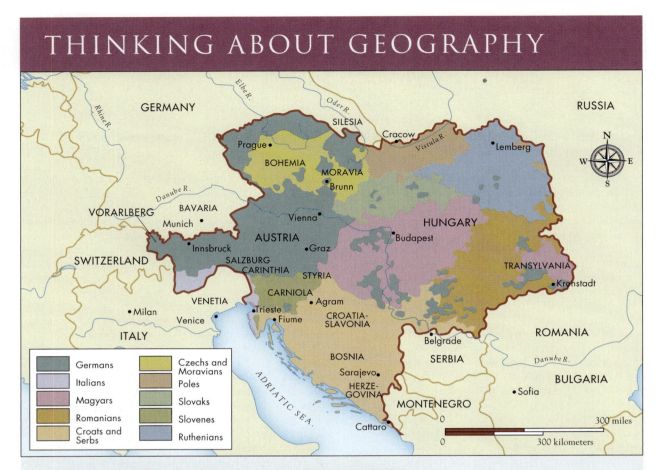

MAP 19.3   LANGUAGE GROUPS OF AUSTRIA-HUNGARY

This map shows the concentrations of language groups in Austria-Hungary at the end of the nineteenth century. ▪ **What** does this map reveal about the difficulties facing the Austro-Hungarian Empire in an age of growing nationalism? **In what areas** is the empire most vulnerable? ▪ **Notice** the surrounding states. **What** language groups might find support from outside the empire's borders?

ing are especially well illustrated by the paths that France and Russia took after 1850.

NAPOLEON III AND THE SECOND EMPIRE

In France, Louis-Napoleon Bonaparte, nephew of Napoleon Bonaparte, promised reform while creating a regime based on authoritarian nationalism. Louis-Napoleon was originally elected president of France's Second Republic in 1848 (see page 590). He benefited from his illustrious name, his appeal to property owners longing for order, and his well-publicized promises to link democracy from below with reforming leadership from above. When the National Assembly refused to change the constitution so that he could run for a second term, he organized a coup d'état and seized power on December 2, 1851. Resistance was limited, although hun-

Napoleon III

dreds were killed and thousands were arrested and deported. He quickly granted universal male suffrage, and during the following year, he held two plebiscites in which more than 90 percent of the voters supported him, establishing the Second Empire and making him hereditary emperor—Napoleon III. "I believe," he confidently wrote, "that there are certain men who are born to serve as the means for the march of the human race. . . . I consider myself to be one of these."

Building upon his uncle's legend, Napoleon III tried to convince citizens that he would lead the nation to new heights in domestic as well as foreign affairs. Napoleon III kept the elected legislature firmly under his thumb by minimizing its authority over his ministers and manipulating the electoral machinery. When it served his purposes, he encouraged industrialization and economic growth by promoting railroad construction, public works, and financial institutions—policies that appealed to the middle and working classes. His prefect of Paris, Georges Haussmann (1809–1891), rebuilt Paris into an envied model of a modern, wealthy, powerful capital (see Chapter 20). To project a progressive image, Napoleon also directed the building of hospitals, nurseries, and homes for the aged. To gain support from workers, he kept bread prices low, instituted a system of voluntary social insurance, encouraged cooperatives, and partially legalized labor unions.

The French emperor's foreign adventures gained him prestige at first, but lost him everything in the end. He brought France into the Crimean War and played the glorious host to the peace conference that ended that conflict. In addition, he tried to increase French influence in the Italian peninsula by joining Piedmont in a war against Austria, but he underestimated the strength of Italian nationalism; that nation unified without becoming beholden to France. In 1862, his armies marched into Mexico City and set up a Habsburg prince, Maximilian, as puppet emperor for France. A few years later, problems at home and a threatening army from the United States forced Napoleon to withdraw his troops, leaving the doomed Maximilian to the mercy of Mexican forces. French artist Edouard Manet (1832–1883) depicts the scene on June 19, 1867 (Figure 19.5). In an arena with spectators looking over the brick wall, as if this were a ritual killing at the end of a bullfight, a Mexican firing squad aims and fires at point-blank range, executing Maximilian and two of his generals. However Maximilian did not die immediately; the soldier on the far right is casually reloading his rifle as if anticipating that the emperor would have to be given a final degrading *coup de grâce*. The soldiers are in uniforms similar to those of the French army to emphasize France's role in this affair. The Mexican fiasco added to the growing unpopularity of Napoleon III with the French people.

Meanwhile, declining prosperity further weakened Napoleon's position within France. Trying to allay the mounting discontent of liberals and workers, he made one concession after another. By 1870, the

Fall of Napoleon III

liberal parliament had begun gaining the upper hand. That year, the ailing and discouraged Napoleon III blundered into a war with Prussia. Defeated and captured, he and his government fell.

ALEXANDER II AND RUSSIA

Napoleon III had stood for order, reform from above, and national grandeur. Until he faltered, the French gave up their liberal sentiments for those ends. In Russia, Tsar Alexander II made similar appeals in an effort to overcome that country's troubles.

By 1850, Russia had earned a reputation as the most conservative of European powers. Its government

KEY DATES	
NATIONALISM AND STATEBUILDING	
1851	Louis Napoleon becomes emperor of France
1854–1856	Crimean War
1860	Italian unification
1861	Russia frees the serfs
1861–1865	U.S. Civil War
1866	Austro-Prussian War
1867	Canadian independence and unification
	Creation of Austro-Hungarian Dual Monarchy
1868	Meiji Restoration in Japan
1870	Franco-Prussian War
1871	German unification

■ FIGURE 19.5

Edouard Manet, *The Execution of Emperor Maximilian*, 1868.

THINKING ABOUT GEOGRAPHY

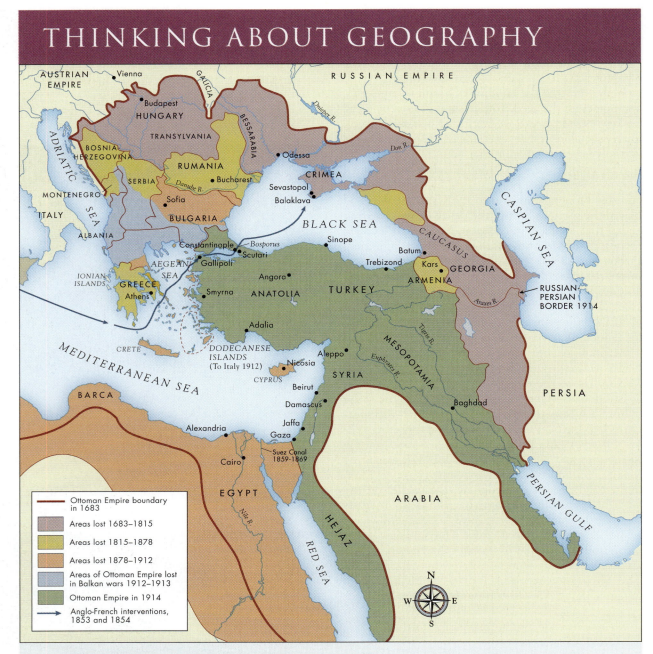

MAP 19.4 THE DECLINE OF THE OTTOMAN EMPIRE, 1683–1914

This map shows the loss of territory from the Ottoman Empire between 1683 and 1914. ■ **Who** were the Ottomans' main European rivals in this region? ■ **Notice** in particular those areas lost during the nineteenth and early twentieth centuries. **Consider** why the growth of nationalism became such a threat to the empire.

remained autocratic under the tsar, its feudalistic society still bound serfs to the land

Russia's autocracy and their lords, and its large army enjoyed an aura of near invincibility. After the Crimean War, it became clear that things would have to change.

In 1853, war broke out between Russia and the Ottoman Turks. Although the causes for this outbreak of hostilities were complex, Russia hoped to snatch territory from the weakening Ottoman Empire. In addition, Russia sought to gain shipping access to the world

Crimean War

from the Black Sea through the Turkish Straits and gain influence in the Near East. Early the next year, after the Russian navy sank the Ottoman fleet in a single devastating battle, France, Britain, and Piedmont-Sardinia, driven by their own ambitions rather than principles, joined the Ottoman Turks and poured their military forces into the Black Sea. They laid siege to Russia's naval base, Sebastopol, on the Crimean Peninsula.

The war dragged on until 1856, and both sides fought with gross incompetence. The flavor of this war, and in particular one suicidal charge by the British light cavalry, would be immortalized in a poem by Alfred, Lord Tennyson:

'Forward, the Light Brigade!'
Was there a man dismay'd?
Not tho' the soldier knew
Some one had blunder'd:
Their's not to make reply,
Their's not to reason why,
Their's but to do and die:
Into the valley of Death
Rode the six hundred

Thanks to new telegraph lines and expanded press coverage, the public in the West could follow the conflict closely. People learned almost immediately, in graphic detail, about the horrific loss of life both on the Crimean battlefield and in the pitifully inadequate medical facilities (see Biography). More than 250,000 soldiers died, most of them from disease caused by poor sanitation, starvation, and lack of medical assistance. In the end, no one could claim much of a victory, but Russia, whose massive military no longer looked so formidable, was humbled.

Even before the Crimean disaster, peasant revolts and workers' protests had plagued Russia. In all of Europe, only Russia still allowed serfdom, which left millions tied to the land. Russia's serfs deeply resented the labor and dues they owed for the right to farm lands, and protests and insurrections broke out with alarming frequency. Between 1825 and 1855, more than five hundred serf rebellions occurred in Russia. Food shortages struck all too often, yet most aristocrats took little responsibility for the suffering of their serfs. Many within the privileged class feared rebellion.

The peasants' low standard of living is revealed in Figure 19.6, a photograph of peasants in a Russian village during the second half of the nineteenth century. The man on the left wears tattered clothes. He and all the others stand barefoot in the mud street and beside the simple houses. This image contrasts sharply with Figure 19.7, an 1861 photograph that shows a noble landowner standing on the front steps of his mansion and reading a decree to some of his

■ FIGURE 19.6
Peasants in a Russian village.

■ FIGURE 19.7
A noble's estate in Russia, 1861.

BIOGRAPHY

FLORENCE NIGHTINGALE (1820–1910)

CONSIDER

■ **Consider** *how Nightingale's experience reveals the different ways war can alter people's lives.* ■ **How** *does her life illustrate the problems caused by the social limitations on women during this period (see chapter 17)?*

In October 1854, a British journalist in Constantinople reported the successes enjoyed by the British army in the Crimean War. He also described in dramatic detail the horrendous condition of the army's medical facilities where the wounded and sick languished and died.

One of the many readers outraged by the report was Florence Nightingale. Just three years earlier, in a private note, she had written, "What am I that their [other women's] life is not good enough for me? . . . why, oh my God, cannot I be satisfied with the life that satisfied so many people?" The war, which was causing so much suffering on and off the battlefield, suddenly created an opportunity for Nightingale to take control of her own life, gain fame as "the Lady with the Lamp," and be hailed as a national heroine.

Born in 1820 into an upper class family, she received an unusual classical education—including several languages, philosophy, history, and science—from her father. Her mother tried to train her to conform to the domestic responsibilities of her class—the domestic rituals, long meals, and formal sociability Florence resisted. She complained that "daughters are now their mothers' slaves . . . they are considered their parents' property, they are to have no other pursuit, nor power, nor independent life, unless they marry." She rejected suitors, explaining, "I have a moral and active nature which requires satisfaction, and that would not find it in his [a husband's] life."

Instead, she pleaded with her family to allow her to train as a nurse. They responded with rage, for at the time nursing was considered a menial occupation reserved for the lowest classes. Her society offered few opportunities for "respectable" women to gain independence, and Florence described the suffering caused by these restrictions: "I see the numbers of my kind who have gone mad for want of something to do."

"Angel of the Crimea" and Medical Reformer

Her frustration and torment with family life became entwined with her anguished spiritual life. She first reported hearing God speak to her when she was 16. The depth of her despair is revealed by her petitions to God: "Forgive me, God & let me die—this day let me die." But she also looked to God for purpose: "God has something for me to do for him—or he would have let me die some time ago."

Her chance for a purposeful life came in 1854 when reports of the lack of proper medical care for sick and wounded British soldiers in the Crimean War appeared in the newspaper. Despite her family's opposition, Nightingale had managed to gain some training as a nurse in Germany, France, and Ireland. Now she was serving as superintendent of the Hospital for Invalid Gentlewomen in London. Using her family's wealth and political connections, she obtained from the British government a commission to lead a team of 38 nurses to Turkey.

---

assembled serfs. Well-dressed members of his family watch from the stairs and the second-floor balcony, while household servants stand by attentively.

Not surprisingly, serfs conscripted into Russia's armies showed a distinct lack of enthusiasm. Their sullenness finally helped make Russia's leaders see that their country was being left behind by the other powers. The country simply lacked the social support, armaments, and railroads (it took Russia months instead of weeks to move troops and supplies to the Crimean front) to win a modern war. Moreover, because serfs were bound to the land, Russia lacked a large mobile labor force to support industrialization and thereby keep up with nations to the west.

The new tsar, Alexander II (r. 1855–1881), was a complex, well-educated individual who recognized Russia's problems from the moment he took office. He was determined to introduce reforms to strengthen and modernize Russia and prop up his own rule. Like Napoleon III's policies, Alexander's **"Great Reforms"** came from above but proved much more far-reaching and dramatic. In 1861, Alexander freed Russia's 22 million serfs and, a few years later, 25 million state-owned peasants. "It is better to abolish serfdom from above than to wait until the serfs begin to liberate themselves from below," he told a group of his nobles. This bold move, occurring at almost the same time that millions of slaves were emancipated in the United States, put an end to a notorious form of human bondage and transferred land to the freed peasantry. In Figure 19.7, the noble landowner is reading the decree that abolished serfdom. Document 19.3 (on page 612) reveals one serf's reactions to this decree. However, emancipation did not make the peasants fully independent and self-sufficient. In general, they received the poorest land, owed payments for their land and

Alexander II's "Great Reforms"

On November 4, 1854, they arrived at the barrack hospital at Scutari—a suburb outside Constantinople near the Black Sea (see Map 19.4). In a November 14 letter, she described conditions at Scutari: "We have no room for corpses in the wards. . . . Not a sponge, nor a rag of linen, not anything have I left. . . . These poor fellows have not had a clean shirt nor been washed for two months before they came here. . . . I hope in a few days we shall establish a little cleanliness." She advocated fresh air, sunshine, hygiene, and diet. Figure 19.8, a lithograph of a ward at Scutari, shows Nightingale holding up her lamp and organizing care for the patients. Images such as this gave her the label "Lady with the Lamp."

Within six months and despite opposition, incompetence, and corruption within the British army, she transformed the medical facility, and the death rate fell from 40 percent to 2 percent. Her fame quickly spread. The *London Times* declared, "There is not one of England's proudest and purest daughters who at the moment stands on as high a pinnacle as Florence Nightingale."

The end of the war in 1856 did not end her efforts. Her best-selling *Notes on Nursing* (1859) became a primary text for nurses, and the nursing school she established in London (1860) became a model for similar institutions in Europe, Australia, and North America. Suffering from what she called "nervous fever," she spent much of the rest of her life in her own sickbed battling the sense of despair that had risen during her youth. Nevertheless, she used her prestige, political connections, and writings to campaign for reform of mili-

FLORENCE NIGHTINGALE IN THE MILITARY HOSPITAL AT SCUTARI.

■ FIGURE 19.8

J.A. Benwell, Florence Nightingale in the military hospital, 1856.

tary health-care, public sanitation, and social policy. In 1907, three years before her death, she was honored as the first woman to be awarded the British National Order of Merit. The "Angel of the Crimea" had revolutionized nursing and transformed military and public health care in the West.

freedom, and were tied by collective ownership to their village commune, the *mir,* whose elected officials assigned parcels of land and determined what could be planted.

Other reforms made the judicial system more independent, created local political assemblies (*zemstva*) with elected officials, encouraged primary and secondary education by opening thousands of new schools, and reduced military service. However, expectations for further reform rose too fast for Alexander and came to haunt him. His efforts to relax control over Poland and grant amnesty to thousands of Poland's political prisoners seemed only to provoke a major Polish revolution in 1863, leading Alexander to repress the divisive nationalistic uprisings there and elsewhere within Russia's empire. To counter budding nationalism among minorities, he tried to force them to adopt the Russian language and

culture. The universities he reopened became centers of intellectual discontent. Nor did his emancipation of the serfs end peasant rebellions.

Alexander intended to transform Russia into a modern authoritarian state that could command the allegiance of its citizens and wield power through a reformed, supported military. At best, he succeeded only partially. Certainly some of his reforms created important, long-lasting changes, but he did not turn his nation into a modern, national monarchy. Alexander himself, though called the "tsar liberator," was never popular. After an assassination attempt in 1866, he became more close-minded and increasingly turned Russia into a police state. Unrest still simmered among Russia's different nationalities. In addition, dissatisfaction among the peasantry and growing dissent among Russia's intellectuals, middle classes, and workers spelled trouble for the years ahead.

■ DOCUMENT 19.3

A Serf Reacts to the Russian Emancipation Proclamation

In 1861, Tsar Alexander II issued a dramatic proclamation emancipating Russia's serfs. Many people anticipated great changes stemming from this proclamation. The following excerpt depicts the reaction of Aleksandr Nikitenko, a former serf.
■ **In what ways** *did various people react to the proclamation?* ■ **How** *does their reaction reveal aspects of Russian culture?*

5 March. A great day. The emancipation manifesto! I received a copy around noon. I cannot express my joy at reading this precious act which scarcely has its equal in the thousand-year history of the Russian people. I read it aloud to my wife, my children and a friend of ours in my study, under Alexander II's portrait, as we gazed at it with deep reverence and gratitude. I tried to explain to my ten-year-old son as simply as possible the essence of the manifesto and bid him to keep inscribed in his heart forever the date of March 5 and the name of Alexander II, the Liberator.

I couldn't stay at home. I had to wander about the streets and mingle, so to say, with my regenerated fellow citizens. Announcements from the governor-general were posted at all crossways, and knots of people were gathered around them. One would read while the others listened. I encountered happy, but calm faces every-where. Here and there people were reading the proclamation aloud, and, as I walked, I continually caught phrases like "decree on liberty," "freedom." One fellow who was reading the announcement and reached the place where it said that manor serfs were obligated to their masters for another two years, exclaimed indignantly, "The hell with this paper! Two years? I'll do nothing of the sort." The others remained silent. I ran into my friend, Galakhov. "Christ has risen!" I said to him. "He has indeed!" he answered, and we expressed our great joy to each other.

Then I went to see Rebinder. He ordered champagne and we drank a toast to Alexander II.

Source: Aleksandr Nikitenko, *The Diary of a Russian Censor* (1893).

SUMMARY

By the 1870s, the most successful political leaders had learned new lessons about the power of nationalistic sentiment. Nationalism was a mighty force more easily used than opposed. It could fuel successful movements for national unification, disintegrate multinational empires, enhance existing unity in already established nations, and strengthen central governments.

Shrewd political realists, rather than the idealists of earlier times, led successful nationalist struggles. These leaders relied on power politics, war, and diplomacy to achieve their aims. But such politicians, sometimes viewed as heroes who gamely shouldered the burden of unification, stood on ground that idealists and revolutionaries had broken in the years before 1850. Moreover, the hardest work was often carried out by nationalist groups, students, soldiers, intellectuals, journalists, and others who rose to the call of national unity. The costs for everyone were high. Many Italians, for example, lost their lives in the struggle for independence. Also tragic, those Italians who survived these turbulent years were left with a new nation that was far from rich and that still suffered from regional and political differences. Germany bought its unification with arms. From that point on, German nationalism remained linked with military prowess rather than liberal ideals. In the United States, Lincoln had preserved the Union—but only after a four-year nightmare that would mar American society for generations and cost Lincoln his life.

Other leaders, such as Napoleon III and Tsar Alexander II, recognized that reforms initiated from above could foster needed national unity and win them greater power. Moreover, Napoleon saw that real power flowed upward from a nation of citizens who deeply identified with their state and government. Increasingly, however, the cry "for the good of the nation" served as the only rationale for such leaders' policies and whims. As the era unfolded, even war could be presented to an unwary public as an act of national will and politics.

KEY TERMS

Realpolitik, p. 599   autocracy, p. 600   Dual Monarchy, p. 604   "Great Reforms", p. 610

REVIEW, ANALYZE, AND ANTICIPATE

REVIEW THE PREVIOUS CHAPTER

Chapter 18—"Coping with Change"—analyzed the struggles between competing ideologies and political forces during the period between Napoleon's fall and the revolutions of 1848.

1. *In what ways do you think the politics of this era reflect the efforts of governments to adjust to the changes initiated by the French Revolution and the industrial revolution?*

2. *How did the ideological struggles initiated during the first half of the century continue during the following decades?*

ANALYZE THIS CHAPTER

Chapter 19—"Nationalism and Statebuilding"—examines the efforts to build national unity and strength between 1850 and 1870.

1. *Analyze the methods used by leaders such as Cavour and Bismarck to achieve national unity. How do they compare with efforts during the revolutions of 1848?*

2. *How did leaders such as Napoleon III in France and Alexander II in Russia try to link nationalism and statebuilding?*

3. *In what ways was nationalism divisive in the Austrian and Ottoman Empires?*

ANTICIPATE THE NEXT CHAPTER

Chapter 20—"Mass Politics and Imperial Domination"—traces the spreading demands for democracy and the West's imperial expansion during the second half of the nineteenth century.

1. *What sorts of economic and social changes might be related to the rising nationalism and the increasing importance of politics during this period?*

2. *How might nationalism be related to both national and imperial expansion?*

BEYOND THE CLASSROOM

THE DRIVE FOR ITALIAN UNIFICATION

Clark, Martin. *The Italian Risorgimento.* New York: Pearson, 1998. A well-written, succinct summary.

Coppa, Frank J. *The Wars of Italian Independence.* New York: Longman, 1992. A thorough discussion of the subject.

Mack Smith, Denis. *Cavour.* London: Weidenfeld and Nicolson, 1985. An excellent biography of this important figure in Italian unification.

GERMANY "BY BLOOD AND IRON"

Blackbourn, David. *A History of Germany, 1780–1918.* London: Blackwell, 2002. An excellent political history and a fine analysis.

Carr, William. *The Wars of German Unification.* London: Longman, 1991. Analyzes the three wars that led to the unification of Germany.

Pflanze, Otto. *Bismarck and the Development of Germany. I: The Period of Unification, 1815–1871.* Princeton, NJ: Princeton University Press, 1990. An exhaustive biography and history of Germany during the period.

THE FIGHT FOR NATIONAL UNITY IN NORTH AMERICA

Bensel, Richard Franklin. *Yankee Leviathan: The Origins of Central State Authority in America, 1859–1877.* Cambridge: Cambridge University Press, 1990. A discussion of state formation and the extension of central state authority during the Civil War and Reconstruction.

McPherson, James. *Battle Cry of Freedom.* New York: Oxford University Press, 2003. A well-written one-volume history of the American Civil War.

GLOBAL CONNECTIONS

Jansen, Marius B., and Rozman, Gilbert, eds. *Japan in Transition: From Tokugawa to Meiji.* Princeton: Princeton University Press, 1986. A book of essays that examine the changes during the Meiji restoration.

DIVIDED AUTHORITY IN THE AUSTRIAN AND OTTOMAN EMPIRES

Shaw, Stanford J. *History of the Ottoman Empire and Modern Turkey. II: Reform, Revolution and Republic: The Rise of Modern Turkey, 1808–1875.* Cambridge: Cambridge University Press, 1983. An effective analysis of the causes for the Ottoman decline during the nineteenth century.

Sked, Alan. *The Decline and Fall of the Habsburg Empire, 1815–1918.* London: Longman, 2001. A particularly strong analysis of the Habsburg Empire during this period.

USING NATIONALISM IN FRANCE AND RUSSIA

Edgerton, Robert. *Death or Glory: The Legacy of the Crimean War.* New York: Perseus, 1999. Covers the war and its significance.

Kolchin, Peter. *Unfree Labor: American Slavery and Russian Serfdom.* Cambridge, MA: Harvard University Press, 1987. A comparative study of the two experiences.

Lincoln, W. Bruce. *The Great Reforms: Autocracy, Bureaucracy, and the Politics of Change in Imperial Russia.* DeKalb, IL: Northern Illinois University Press, 1990. Puts the social reforms during the reign of Alexander II in a broad political, social, and intellectual context.

Price, Roger. *People and Politics in France, 1848–1870.* Cambridge: Cambridge University Press, 2004. Clearly surveys the politics of the Second Empire in France.

www.mhhe.com/sherman3

- Unfamiliar words? See our Glossary at the back of the book for pronunciation and definitions.

- Need help studying? See our web page for map exercises, practice quizzes, and additional study resources.

- Need help writing a paper? Access hundreds of primary documents, maps, images, and a guide to writing history papers on our Primary Source Investigator site at **www.mhhe.com/psi.**

OPENING OF THE SUEZ CANAL, 1869

In 1869, after ten years of construction, the Suez Canal—linking the Mediterranean and Red Seas—opened. This drawing of the opening ceremony shows a crowd of traditionally dressed local inhabitants on the banks watching the line of new European boats, powered by steam as well as sails. European dignitaries, separated from this crowd, also attended the ceremonies. The canal, built by the French and later acquired by the British, shortened the sea route from Europe to India and the Far East by thousands of miles, and the new, large, smoke-belching steamboats carried cargo more rapidly and reliably than ever, facilitating the West's imperial expansion.

MASS POLITICS AND IMPERIAL DOMINATION

DEMOCRACY AND THE NEW IMPERIALISM, 1870–1914

STUDY	Democratic reforms ■ Politics of the extreme ■ Emigration ■ The new imperialism.
NOTICE	Connections between nationalism, democracy, and imperialism.

"We have conquered for ourselves a place in the sun," announced Germany's Kaiser William II (r. 1888–1919) in 1901. Addressing an audience from Hamburg's business community, he boasted that "it will now be my task to see to it that this place in the sun shall remain our undisputed possession, in order that the sun's rays may fall fruitfully upon our activity and trade in foreign parts, that our industry and agriculture may develop within the state." William was referring to Germany's territories, gained in the scramble for overseas conquests that had been going on over the previous two decades. His audience and many others in the industrialized Western world expected to gain wealth from this recent imperial expansion.

He also may have been reminding his listeners that the German nation had been unified in the 1860s through war and conquest (see Chapter 19). Indeed, underlying his words was an appeal to pride in the growing power of this new nation. Like other political leaders in the West, William had learned to use nationalism to gain support from listeners and readers.

Politicians such as William could no longer ignore public opinion, for democracy was on the rise. Between 1870 and 1914, demands for democracy, or political participation by common people, spread as more and more people struggled to gain access to politics. Now the new politics of nationalism combined with industrialism to multiply the power of the West and push it outward into Africa and Asia in a great imperial expansion. The West was rising to a new level of world dominance.

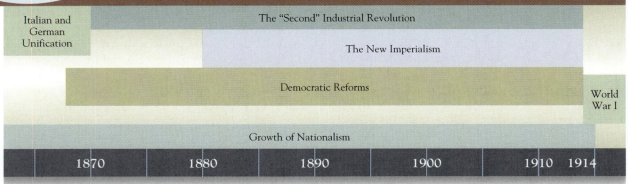

Italian and German Unification

The "Second" Industrial Revolution

The New Imperialism

Democratic Reforms

World War I

Growth of Nationalism

1870　　1880　　1890　　1900　　1910　1914

DEMANDS FOR DEMOCRACY

IN 1896, THE RUSSIAN STATESMAN Konstantin Pobedonostsev (1827–1907) published what would become a widely read attack on democracy. "What is this freedom by which so many minds are agitated, which inspires so many insensate actions, so many wild speeches . . . ?" His answer was democracy, "the right to participate in the government of the State." He complained that "the new Democracy now aspires to universal suffrage—a fatal error, and one of the more remarkable in the history of mankind."

However, between 1870 and 1914, it became increasingly clear to those who had long enjoyed political power in the West that, sooner or later, the beliefs of the masses counted in politics. Since the French Revolution in 1789, a widening pool of Europeans tasted political power, a trend that ruling elites had feared ever since. Some politicians, such as Pobedonostsev, tried to turn their backs on democracy. Others tried to tame it, and still others flourished with it.

During the 1870s and 1880s, three developments became entwined with demands for democracy. First, *Public education* many governments established national systems of free and compulsory public education at the primary-school level. With this policy, they hoped to create more patriotic citizens. They also wanted to provide citizens with the skills and discipline needed by modernizing economies and military establishments. Moreover, they wanted their voting electorate to be educated. To liberals especially, access to the schoolhouse and democracy went hand in hand.

Second, educated, voting citizens could read newspapers, and popular journalism responded to the call. Before 1850, newspapers were few, small, expensive, and written for a limited readership. By the end of the century, a new kind of newspaper had popped up everywhere—one that was cheap, sensational, and wildly popular. In the United States, publishers such as *Popular journalism* Joseph Pulitzer (1847–1911) and William Randolph Hearst (1863–1951) built influential newspapers featuring screaming headlines, flag-waving patriotism, an easy style, sensational news, and attention-getting columns. Other newspapers throughout Europe, especially in the capital cities, followed the same pattern. They catered to the newly educated public's hunger for news and, in turn, powerfully molded public opinion.

Third, politicians realized they had to appeal to the new voters. They devised innovative campaign strategies, such as crisscrossing the country by railroads and delivering stirring campaign speeches *Political campaigns* to cheering crowds in large halls and outdoor forums. They listened to newly formed interest groups—whether business organizations, reformers, or labor unions. These interest groups held rallies on their own, to gather support and gain influence through newspaper coverage of their meetings. Finally, politicians began creating all sorts of state institutions, from census bureaus to social security administrations, to satisfy the demands of their politically aroused societies and persuade new voters to support them. All these changes vastly reshaped parliamentary politics.

Such developments put pressure on politicians to adjust the way they conducted themselves, for democratic reform meant more than widening the right to vote and bringing new faces into government. To succeed in the new world of mass politics, politicians had to learn to monitor—and navigate—the shifting tides of public opinion. More and more, rising to and staying in political office meant pleasing interest groups, journalists, educated readers, and newly enfranchised voters.

LIBERAL DEMOCRACY IN WESTERN EUROPE

Would European societies ease toward a liberal democratic consensus? Many hoped so, particularly in western Europe, where Great Britain and France had experimented with democratic reforms, but in different ways.

Great Britain started the second half of the nineteenth century in a strong, stable position. It had avoided the revolutionary turmoil that swept over the European continent between 1848 and 1850, largely because the British adapted just enough to contain the pressures for radical change (see Chapter 18). Liberalism—stressing little governmental involvement in economic and social affairs, low taxes, and free trade—seemed to work well in Britain, and the island nation boasted the most modern economy in the world.

For most of the 1850s and 1860s, liberals controlled the British government. But they were more willing to call on national pride, sympathize with movements for national liberation abroad, and parade British naval might than to accommodate those who demanded entry into the political system. It was the Conservative Party, under Benjamin Disraeli (1804–1881), that finally decided to bend and take the credit for democratic reform before the Liberals themselves could grab it. The Conservatives passed a new measure—the Reform Bill of 1867—which doubled the electorate and gave the vote to the lower-middle class for the first time. In addition, they gathered support from the working class by passing laws that limited working hours, established sanitary codes, created housing standards, and aided labor unions. In 1884, the Liberal Party under William Gladstone (1809–1898) countered by pushing through another reform bill that gave two-thirds of adult males the vote. To sweeten the deal even further, the Liberals opened the army and civil service to talent and made primary education available to all.

Reform bills of 1867 and 1884

Having both jumped on the reform bandwagon, British Conservatives and Liberals now had to compete for power in new ways. For the first time, politicians such as Gladstone used the railways to campaign throughout the nation, speaking before crowds of thousands. A growing corps of journalists followed the campaigns, shaping public opinion by reporting speeches and scandals daily in cheap newspapers with mass circulation. New interest groups, mostly from the middle class, bent the ears of politicians who wanted their support in return.

Figure 20.1, a painting by Alfred Morgan, reveals some of these trends in British politics.

The artist depicts the political leader William Gladstone (wearing a tall hat, sitting stiffly, and staring straight ahead) riding in an omnibus. This form of transportation, which carried more than two dozen passengers at a time, was relatively inexpensive and available to all classes of people. The man (holding a newspaper), women, and children who share the bus with Gladstone are dressed well, but are not members of Britain's wealthy elite (who still ride in small carriages such as the one seen through the rear window). As this image indicates, Gladstone tried to appeal to the growing electorate by portraying himself as an upright, hardworking individual who allied himself with the people. Britain was moving toward democracy, but in ways that worried traditional politicians used to deciding things among their "own kind."

France's path toward democracy took more violent turns than Britain's. A birthplace of democracy, France nevertheless started the 1870s on a turbulent note. The Franco-Prussian War of 1870 spelled the end of Napoleon III's Second Empire and the emergence of the Third French Republic (see Chapter 19). The first elections, held in February 1871 after Napoleon III's fall and the surrender of Paris, resulted in a victory for the monarchists, who hoped to limit democracy and open the door for the restoration of a monarchy. Still the city of Paris refused to submit to the domination of conservative, rural France. It demanded home rule and set up its own city government, or commune.

France's Third Republic

The **Paris Commune** would gain a reputation as a democracy out of control or as an experiment in Marxist socialism. In reality, the Commune stood

■ FIGURE 20.1

Alfred Morgan, *One of the People.*

■ FIGURE 20.2

Altered photo portraying executions during the Paris Commune period.

handsome man on horseback, General Georges Boulanger, who became so popular that he might have overthrown the Republic had he been bolder and more skillful or had the republican leaders been less courageous. As it turned out, when he was summoned to answer charges of treason against the Republic, he fled to Belgium and eventually committed suicide on the grave of his late mistress.

Meanwhile, several forces reoriented politics toward the wider voting public. First, public schooling spread throughout France. Republican teachers replaced Catholic teachers, bringing in a common secular curriculum and promoting patriotism and republican virtues. Second, military service became compulsory and helped turn young, rural men into French citizens with new political awareness. Third, a popular national press took root in Paris and attracted readers throughout the nation. These papers reported all the political scandals, especially the sensational and far-reaching **Dreyfus affair** (see page 623), and soon readers in the provinces began avidly following national politics. In France, as in Britain, democratic institutions were spreading throughout the nation and redefining the nature of politics.

Spread of democratic institutions

for decentralizing power in France, self-governance, support of working-class organizations, and greater equality for women. Its roots lay in the city's resistance to the Germans between September 1870 and January 1871. During those horrific months, Parisians had braved starvation and isolation in the face of the German siege. Most of the rich fled the city. The lower classes not only resented this exodus, they also took over positions of power that the wealthy had abandoned. The February 1871 elections ended the German siege, but not the division between Paris and the rest of the nation. Parisians felt betrayed by France's new conservative government when it concluded the peace with Germany. When government troops tried to disarm them, they rebelled and fighting erupted. The government troops withdrew, and again Paris was put under siege, this time by French troops. Two months later, the government troops attacked, killing some 25,000 Parisians, arresting thousands more, and deporting more than 5,000 to distant penal colonies.

The Paris Commune

Both sides in the Paris conflict committed bitter reprisals. The "photograph" shown in Figure 20.2 purports to show Communards—including women and nonuniformed men—executing 62 hostages. In fact, the "photograph" is a photomontage—a composite photograph—used by government troops to justify retaliation against Communards.

The fall of the Paris Commune ended the immediate threat to the integrity of France, but not the political and social uncertainties that still lurked below the surface. A period of restless political struggle followed. At first, monarchists almost regained power, but they failed to agree on which of three possible royal houses (the Bourbon, the Orleanist, or the Bonaparte) they should rally around. By the end of the 1870s, liberals, elected by universal male suffrage, controlled the French Republic. Conservatives, however, refused to give up. In the late 1880s, they joined nationalists, supporters of the military, and opponents of parliament to rally around a

FOR AND AGAINST DEMOCRACY IN CENTRAL AND EASTERN EUROPE

In contrast to the western European governments, national leaders in central and eastern Europe were more autocratic. Monarchs and their ministers in these regions had the last word in political decision making. Like nations in western Europe, central and eastern Europe struggled with pressure to institute democratic reforms. In some cases, these nations took reluctant steps toward democracy; in others, they declined to change. In addition, the tensions between autocratic and democratic forces in central and eastern Europe became particularly entwined with aggressive nationalism. The cases of Germany, Austria, and Russia provide apt examples of the various ways in which this struggle manifested itself.

In Germany, the constitution stipulated universal suffrage, but real power rested with the king and his ministers. Bismarck, who dominated as Germany's chancellor between 1870 and 1890, supported universal male suffrage from the beginning only because "in a country with monarchical traditions and loyal sentiments" such as Germany, "universal suffrage would lead to . . . eliminating the influence of the liberal bourgeois classes." Bismarck believed that most workers and peasants would vote for his conservative policies.

Germany under Bismarck

Bismarck solidified the German states and people under Prussia. He also brought the law codes, currencies, and military forces of the lesser states into conformity with those of Prussia. He then turned to issues of ethnic divisions and cultural unity. Laws and schools pressured non-German language groups to give up their languages and traditions. In 1872, Bismarck struck out against Roman Catholics for being insufficiently nationalistic. Known as the **Kulturkampf** (the struggle for civilization), the roots of Bismarck's attack lay in Germany's Protestant-Catholic religious divisions and the newly vigorous papacy of Pius IX, who declared papal infallibility in 1870, opposed cooperation with Protestantism, and attacked the growth of state power. With support from liberals, Bismarck passed laws asserting the state's right to restrict religious orders, require civil marriage, and bring all education (including schools run by the Catholic Church) under state control. When the Roman Catholic clergy resisted, authorities arrested hundreds of priests and six bishops. Many of these measures backfired, however: They made the Roman Catholic Center Party stronger. In 1878, Bismarck repealed the most severe of the anti-Catholic laws, but only because he wanted support for a more important struggle—the fight against the democratically minded and socially radical Socialists.

Conflict with Catholic Church

Conflict with Socialists

In a twelve-year crusade against the Socialists, who attacked the autocratic nature of Germany's government and were gaining popularity in elections, Bismarck outlawed the Social Democratic Party's publications, organizations, and meetings, and set the German police force on them. When his repressive tactics did little to diminish Socialist votes, Bismarck tried to undercut the party's appeal to the working class by removing "the causes for socialism." Borrowing some of the Socialists' programs, between 1883 and 1889 he established a comprehensive system of social insurance that provided accident, sickness, and old-age benefits.

Ironically, in fighting against the Social Democrats, the conservative Bismarck made Germany a leader in enacting progressive social policies. Nevertheless, Bismarck's campaign against the Social Democratic Party would fail. The Socialists had built a solid following and continued to gain public support. In 1890, two years after the death of Kaiser William I, the new monarch, Kaiser William II dismissed the aging chancellor. William II, eager to rule himself, "dropped the pilot" of the German ship of state and ended an era in German history.

In Austria, liberalism spread during the 1870s along with the rise of the bourgeoisie in that country. Liberals supported the constitutional monarchy, parliamentary government, and restricted suffrage. They also believed that it was possible to hold a multinational empire together. In the 1880s, nationalistic demands from different language groups began to overwhelm liberals and play into the hands of conservatives. Parliamentary sessions in Austria frequently degenerated into shouting matches, in which representatives from different language groups hurled inkstands at one another. This nationalistic discontent proved even more intense in Hungary than in Austria. Moreover, the partnership between Austria and Hungary threatened to disintegrate altogether (see page 604). The introduction of universal male suffrage in 1907 only made the empire more difficult to govern. More often than not, the emperor and his advisors bypassed parliament and ruled by decree.

Nationalistic discontent in Austria

In Russia, Alexander II's "Great Reforms" did little to open the doors to democracy beyond the local level (see pages 608–609). Indeed, they may have sparked more dissatisfaction than celebration. For serfs, liberals, and intellectuals, the reforms did not go far enough. A group of sons and daughters of the aristocracy and middle classes decided to take action. In a well-intentioned but ill-fated movement, they traveled to rural areas in an effort to uplift the lives of country dwellers. They received a rude welcome in several ways: Rural people resented what they saw as condescending attention from inexperienced urban intellectuals, and the tsar's police promptly repressed them.

Radical action in Russia

Some of the young idealists fled; others remained and turned to terrorism. One group, The People's Will, defined terrorism as "the destruction of the most harmful persons in the Government, the protection of the party from spies, and the punishment of official lawlessness and violence." Vera Zasulich became an early heroine in this movement when she attempted to assassinate the St. Petersburg chief of police in 1878. Her action initiated a series of violent eruptions and assassinations, in which terrorists killed numerous bureaucrats and police officials, and the government brutally suppressed the rebels. The cycle of terrorism and repression turned Alexander II to a more conservative course, and he halted all further reforms. In 1881, members of The People's Will retaliated by murdering Alexander II with a bomb.

The new tsar, Alexander III (r. 1881–1894), blamed his father's death on softness and set out to erase every trace of liberalism and democracy in Russia. His secret police arrested thousands of suspects, and the tsar himself initiated a sweeping program of Russianization. Authorities forced minority groups to use the Russian language and persecuted followers of non-Orthodox religions, especially Jews. Russia, much more so than Austria, would not yet bend to the democratic winds blowing from the west.

Reaction under Alexander III

Insiders and Outsiders: Politics of the Extremes

During the late nineteenth century, those democratic winds in the West spread beyond what had been the mainstream of politics. New groups and causes emerged to challenge the established center of liberal and conservative politics. These new groups gained strength and complicated the trend toward democracy. To the political left of liberals stood the unions, socialists, and anarchists. To the political right of conservatives were anti-Semites and ultranationalists. Still outside, without the vote, were women, who increasingly demanded a voice in national politics.

These groups and causes appealed to large numbers of people, particularly those who had previously been left out of politics. They became so prominent that established political leaders could not ignore them. With the political spectrum widening, it seemed less and less likely that Europe's nations would find some consensus or social peace.

The Spread of Unions

Until the 1880s, labor unions were limited chiefly to skilled workers, organized by crafts, who proved moderate in their aims and methods. In the 1880s, unionization spread rapidly to unskilled workers. These new union members adopted more radical methods and turned toward socialist programs. Seeking more than mutual aid, they demanded a say in working conditions and wages. They went on strike and flexed their political muscle through the vote. One worker described an 1890 strike of textile workers in Bradford, England, that dragged on for six months.

Strikes

■ FIGURE 20.3
Paul Louis Delance, *Strike*, 1908.

"Twice and sometimes three times a week we had processions of the workpeople marching from near the millgates by several routes to the center of Bradford. The women strikers established a well-conducted soup kitchen, and the sympathy of the shopkeepers was very broad and the butchers gave their bones and greengrocers and grocers and bakers gave peas, lentils and loaves, and thus children were fed." As a man who employed thousands of dockers in Marseilles, France, explained, "The days of the employer's arbitrary power are past, unfortunately. . . . For long we could hope to subdue these trade unions that rose against our authority. . . . That too is finished, over."

Figure 20.3 captures some of the ideals of the new unions. This strike at Saint-Ouen, near Paris, France, is sympathetically portrayed by the artist, Paul Louis Delance. Workers, young and old, stream from smoke-belching factories carrying red flags, the symbol of their cause and of socialism. Their faces convey suffering and grim determination. The welfare of a woman and child—the core of the typical working-class family—represents the strikers' goal. The strikers are supported by humble people, heads bowed, upon whom a few rays of sunshine fall as if in blessing for the nobility of their cause.

As the end of the century approached, organized labor became a formidable force. Labor unions in Great Britain formed the National Trades Union Congress and became identified with the new Labour Party. In Germany, unions, especially among the unskilled workers, grew dramatically and coalesced into a national Marxist organization. In France, various unions banded together into the giant General Confederation of Labor, with a radical political program. In the United States, the abundance of cheap immigrant labor and the determined resistance by industrial capitalists hindered the emergence of unions. In 1886, however, Samuel Gompers founded the American Federation of Labor—the first successful national labor organization in America. By 1914, unions had become sufficiently large and organized to make them a major power, both in the workplace and at the polls.

Socialism Gains Strength

Like the labor unions, socialism also became a major force within the working class and in politics during the late nineteenth century. Most socialists looked to the ideas of Karl Marx for inspiration (see Chapter 18). Marx had argued that modern industrial society was splitting into two opposing classes: the capitalists, or owners of the means of production, and the workers. Capitalism, he explained, was bound to

The First International

be replaced by a socialist system through revolution by the working class. Marx helped union organizers to form the International Working Men's Association (the First International) in 1864. The organization fell apart in the 1870s, but in 1889, socialists formed the Second International. These organizations helped socialists unify and spread their cause. A sense of shared struggle and beliefs inspired them to form unions, create political parties, and fight powerful employers and strong politicians.

Yet, the strength of socialism varied in each country. In Britain, established politicians excluded the working classes or socialist thinkers from politics until the 1880s. Then a group of well-known intellectuals formed the **Fabian Society,** which advocated the adoption of socialist policies through politics rather than revolution. Beatrice Webb (1858–1943), one of the founders of the Fabians, explained that she became a socialist because of "the physical misery and moral debasement following in the tracks of the rack-renting landlord and capitalist profit maker in the swarming populations of the great centres of nineteenth century commerce and industry." Webb could see no way out of "the recurrent periods of inflation and depression— meaning for the vast majority of the nation, alternate spells of overwork and unemployment."

The Fabians

During the 1890s, both unions and socialists in Britain developed enough political muscle to form the Labour Party and elect members to Parliament. By 1906, Labour had pressured the Liberals, led by David Lloyd George (1863–1945), to adopt new policies providing accident, sickness, old-age, and unemployment insurance for workers. As Labour members of Parliament argued, these old men and women were "the veterans of industry, people of almost endless toil, who have fought for and won the industrial and commercial supremacy of Great Britain. Is their lot and end to be the everlasting slur of pauperism?" To pay for the new policies, the Liberals shifted the "heaviest burden to the broadest backs." A steeply graduated income tax and high taxes on inheritances landed on the rich. When Conservatives in the House of Lords resisted, the Liberal and Labour Parties passed a bill that stripped the House of Lords of most of its former power.

Britain's Labour Party

In France, socialism gained strength during the 1890s. During the following decade, socialist parties helped push France's republican government to enact a limited program of unemployment, old-age, accident, and sickness insurance for workers. By this time, the different wings of the French socialists had joined to form the United Socialist Party under the leadership of scholar-orator Jean Jaurès (see Biography). By 1914, the United Socialist Party

France and Jaurès

numbered 1.5 million voters and had 110 seats in the Chamber of Deputies.

Socialism enjoyed its greatest success in Germany. In 1890, Germany's main socialist party, the Social Democrats, won the vote of 20 percent of the electorate. Officially the party adhered to the idea that revolution was historically inevitable. A party leader, August Bebel, expressed the optimism of this view: "Every night I go to sleep with the thought that the last hour of bourgeois society strikes soon." In practice, however, the party usually followed the ideas of the "revisionist" socialist Eduard Bernstein (1850–1932). This German writer and politician urged socialists to cooperate with the capitalist classes to obtain immediate benefits for labor and advocated a gradual approach to socialism. By 1914, the Social Democrats polled some 4.5 million votes, making it the largest political party in Germany.

German Social Democrats

Even in conservative Austria, socialists gained strength in industrial areas for the same reasons they did elsewhere in the West. The plight of workers was their top priority. Anna Maier, who started a life of work in a tobacco factory when she was 13, captured this concern when she explained that "young girls were often abused or even beaten" on the job. One day Maier read a copy of the *Women Workers'* newspaper smuggled into the factory by one of the older women. Eventually, she managed to join the Social Democratic Party. After taking part in demonstrations, her factory manager took her "off a good job" and put her "in a poorer one," but as she later reported, "nothing stopped me." When the tobacco workers union formed in 1899, she joined them and became "a class-conscious fighter." Maier's story was repeated by many other workers throughout the West in the decades before 1914.

ANARCHISM: FREEDOM FROM ALL AUTHORITY

While sometimes associated with socialists, **anarchists** made more radical demands. Drawing on the ideas of leaders such as the Russian activist Mikhail Bakunin (1814–1876) and Russian theoretician Pyotr Kropotkin (1842–1921), they stressed the elimination of any form of authority that impinged on human freedom. "So long as there exist States, there will be no humanity," Bakunin argued. "The masses of the people will be de facto slaves even in the most democratic republics." Anarchists believed that human beings, once freed from the corrupting institutions that oppressed them, would naturally cooperate with one another. "Life will be open to all," an anarchist leader explained. "Everyone will take what he needs—this is the anarchist ideal."

Bakunin

Anarchism became particularly influential in Spain, Italy, and France, where it appealed to trade unionists,

BIOGRAPHY

Jean Jaurès (1859–1914)

CONSIDER

■ **Consider** *how Jaurès's life reflects both the promises of democracy and the political problems faced by people in this era.*

One observer described the French politician Jean Jaurès as such a spellbinding orator that "he could raise the masses and enchant the elite at the same time." Figure 20.4 shows Jaurès standing beneath the red flag of socialism, addressing a crowd in 1913. Jaurès's speeches in France's Chamber of Deputies sometimes lasted for hours. He also wrote so prolifically that it would take ninety volumes, four hundred pages each, to amass all his writing. Some called him an obvious genius. He called himself "a cultured peasant." Certainly an intellectual, he wore the typical middle-class long, black overcoat. However, the coat was usually dirty, his pants always too short, and his pockets forever stuffed with books and papers. Between the 1880s and 1914, he became one of France's most respected politicians.

Born in 1859 to a rural, middle-class family of little wealth, Jean excelled at school, winning a series of prizes and scholarships. He became a teacher in 1881 and then a professor of philosophy at the University of Toulouse in southern France in 1883. In 1885

■ FIGURE 20.4

Jean Jaurès.

Orator and Socialist Politician

he was elected to the Chamber of Deputies as an unaffiliated republican. Just 25, he was France's youngest deputy. That year he met Louise Bois, the daughter of a merchant, and a year later the couple married. Attracted to Paris by the political activity there, the couple settled in an apartment and eventually had two children.

Defeated in his 1889 bid for reelection to parliament, Jean became interested in socialism and made it the subject of his doctoral dissertation. He won fame for his support of striking miners at Carmaux in 1892. After this event, he was reelected to the Chamber of Deputies, this time as a socialist. He accepted the possibility of socialism by evolution rather than revolution: Class struggle might properly be replaced by democratic political struggle. To Jaurès and a growing number of other socialists, the forces of history suggested that socialism was inevitable. He rose in the Socialist Party, becoming a leader by 1900. In 1904, he helped found a newspaper, *L'Humanité*, which became France's chief socialist periodical. By 1908, he had solidified the party.

Jaurès became increasingly concerned with the problem of war. He argued that France wasted its resources on military preparations. "What will the future be like when the billions now thrown away in war preparations are spent on useful production to increase the well-being of the people?" he asked. He saw the West's recent imperial expansion into the non-Western world as a primary cause for wars. "The fever of imperialism has become a sickness. It is

the affliction of a badly organized society which cannot utilize its energies and productive forces at home." More and more, Jaurès championed pacifism and Franco-German reconciliation, but his stand won him and his followers ridicule and accusations of treason, particularly by right-wing nationalists.

During the evening of July 31, 1914, Jaurès began composing an antiwar appeal. At 9:00 P.M., he and a group of other socialist journalists met and decided to dine at a crowded cafe on the rue Montmartre. At 9:40 a young man, who was affiliated with a nationalist group, burst in and fired two shots, killing Jaurès. The French socialist leader was murdered on the very eve of the war he warned against.

artisans, agricultural laborers, and shopkeepers suffering from unemployment and declining wages. Its supporters favored direct action through unions and cooperatives rather than parliamentary politics. After the turn of the century, many anarchists hoped the

grand solution to their problems would come with a "general strike," as described by the popular French writer Georges Sorel (1847–1922). Such a strike, they believed, would force the capitalist system to grind to a sudden halt. A small wing of the anarchist movement went beyond hoping for a general strike and turned to violence. Among its victims were President Sadi Carot of France in 1894, King Umberto I of Italy in 1900, and President William McKinley of the United States in 1901.

ANTI-SEMITISM AND ULTRANATIONALISM

Usually at the opposite end of the political spectrum from socialism and anarchism, **anti-Semitism** often appealed to conservative nationalists. Followers of Judaism had long suffered from anti-Semitism—hostility toward or hatred of Jews. Since the Middle Ages, Jews had been accused of murdering Christ, segregated into special quarters known as ghettos, and persecuted. However, between 1789 and the 1870s, the spreading ideals of the Enlightenment and the French Revolution had enabled Jews to gain new rights and a degree of legal equality, though rarely full acceptance. At least in western and central Europe, this progress led many Jews to believe that finally they could join their nation-states as full citizens.

During the last decades of the nineteenth century, however, nationalism took on militant and authoritarian tones. All too easily, this spreading strain of na-tionalism strengthened racist and anti-Semitic thought. Comte de Gobineau (1816–1882), a Frenchman, and Houston Stewart Chamberlain (1855–1927), an Englishman who became a German citizen, wrote widely read tracts arguing that race determined much of history. The two men helped formulate the Aryan myth, which held that Germans belonged to a special race and therefore possessed superior qualities: "[T]he Germanic races belong to the most highly gifted group, the group usually termed Aryan. . . . Physically and mentally the Aryans are pre-eminent among all people; for that reason they are by right . . . the lords of the world." Chamberlain's ideas veered off into anti-Semitism, as did the thinking of other well-known racist writers. Their pseudoscientific thought—which labeled Jews as a separate, inferior race—became increasingly popular, as indicated by this excerpt from a speech delivered by an anti-Semitic member of the German parliament: "A Jew who was born in Germany does not thereby become a German; he is still a Jew. Therefore it is imperative that we realize that Jewish racial characteristics differ so greatly from ours that a common life of Jews and Germans under the same laws is quite impossible."

During the same period, anti-Semitic politics gained force, especially among artisans, small shopkeepers, rural workers, and others who felt threatened by liberalism and capitalism and saw Jews as being linked to both. These people scornfully called Jews outsiders and capitalists and blamed them for their own economic ills and fears. Ultranationalist politicians used anti-Semitism to rally crowds, shift the blame for failed policies away from themselves, and win votes.

Right-wing newspapers such as *La Libre Parole* popularized scandals as well as anti-Semitic stories that coalesced most dramatically in the Dreyfus affair. People throughout France followed every development of "the affair" day after day and year after year. In 1894, a group of bigoted army officers falsely accused and convicted a Jewish captain, Alfred Dreyfus, of treason and sent him to solitary imprisonment on Devil's Island in South America. Three years later, evidence of Dreyfus's innocence appeared. Nevertheless, high-ranking officers refused to reopen the case. Newspaper articles, sensational trials, accusations, and huge public demonstrations divided the nation between the political Left and Right. Republicans, socialists, and intellectuals, inspired by the famous French writer Émile Zola, who attacked the judgment of the military and judiciary in the case, rallied for Dreyfus. Nationalist, conservative, monarchist, and anti-Semitic forces supported the army. In 1899, a second court-martial again convicted Dreyfus, despite evidence of another officer's guilt in the affair. The president of the Republic pardoned Dreyfus, but it took seven more years to get Dreyfus fully acquitted.

The Dreyfus affair marked not only the battle over anti-Semitism, but the evolution of French politics. The victory for Dreyfus became a victory for republicanism and anti-clericalism. Electoral victories made republicans strong enough to separate church and state in 1905 and initiate a program of social legislation. Socialists, who had joined republicans in the Dreyfus case, gained greater legitimacy and popularity. The political power of monarchists and the Catholic Church had been dealt a debilitating blow.

For Jews, persecution was worse in central and eastern Europe. These regions had the highest Jewish population and the most aggressive strain of nationalism. Nationalistic anti-Semitic organizations, such as the Pan-German Association and the Christian Social Workers' Party, emerged in Germany. Anti-Semitic journals warned of the dangers to "the native-born Christian population" as Jews gained access to the press, to state offices, and to professions such as teaching and law. One anti-Semitic deputy in Germany's parliament explained in an 1895 speech that "every Jew who at this moment had not done anything bad may nevertheless under the proper conditions do precisely that, because his racial qualities drive him to do it."

In Austria, the Christian Socialist Party and the German National Party took a decidedly anti-Semitic stand. By the 1890s, a new breed of politics based on symbols, charisma, nationalism, racism, anticapitalism, and anti-Semitism had arisen. The election of Karl Lueger in 1897 as mayor of Vienna symbolized this political trend; Lueger campaigned

The Dreyfus affair

Central and eastern Europe

■ FIGURE 20.5

Samuel Hirszenberg, *The Black Banner*, 1905.

on an anti-Semitic platform and triumphed even in this bastion of Austrian liberalism.

Some of the most violent anti-Semitic acts occurred in Russia. Tsars Alexander III and Nicholas II (r. 1894–1917) sanctioned the persecution of Jews and required them to live in designated areas. Officials labeled Jews as outsiders and excluded them from mainstream society. Whenever anyone wanted to assign blame for their problems, they could point to the Jews. This hostility culminated in a series of pogroms, or organized mass attacks on Jews, led by anti-Semitic groups and government officials. Figure 20.5 shows a procession of Hasidic Jews in Russian-dominated Poland carrying

a coffin, which contains one of the victims of an anti-Semitic pogrom. The faces of people in the procession are of shock, horror, and desperation as well as mourning, and the sky echoes the ominous dangers still facing these people. The title of Hirszenberg's 1905 painting refers to "The Black Hundreds" who were the armed gangs of the "Union of the Russian People"—a right-wing, anti-Semitic political movement founded in 1905—and to "The Russian Banner," the newspaper of this organization, which also received "black money" from Russia's tsar. Between 1870 and 1914, these persecutions helped push more than 2 million eastern European Jews out of their homes and to the west, particularly to the United States (see Map 20.1).

Concerns about persecutions in eastern Europe as well as the weakening of Jewish identity through assimilation in western Europe gave rise to **Zionism,** a Jewish nationalist movement to create an inde-

Zionism and Herzl

pendent state for Jews in Palestine—the ancient homeland of the Jews. The Hungarian writer Theodor Herzl (1860–1904) became the leading figure in the Zionist movement. While in Paris covering the Dreyfus affair for an Austrian newspaper, he gained a greater sense of the strength of anti-Semitism and his own identity as a Jew. In 1896, he published an influential pamphlet, *The Jewish State: An Attempt at a Modern Solution of the Jewish Question,* urging formation of an international movement to make Palestine a Jewish homeland. He envisioned the homeland transformed into a socialist community of hard-working cooperatives. The following year he led the new World Zionist Organization to prominence. He gained a large following in eastern Europe, found financial support from several sources, and won cautious political support from British governmental officials. "It might be many years before the founding of the State is under way," Herzl warned. "In the meantime, Jews will be ridiculed, offended, abused, whipped, plundered, and

KEY DATES

POLITICAL AND SOCIAL DEVELOPMENTS

1864	First International Working Men's Association
1867	Britain's Second Reform Bill
1871	Paris Commune
1872–1878	Bismarck's *Kulturkampf*
1878	Romanian independence
1884	Britain's Third Reform Bill
1889	Second International
1897	World Zionist Organization founded
1897–1899	Dreyfus affair
1908	Hyde Park rally for women's suffrage
1914	World War I

slain in a thousand different localities." After Herzl's death in 1904, other leaders advanced his aims and secured more support—including the financial aid of donors such as the French banker Baron de Rothschild, and the cooperation of Arthur Balfour (1848–1930), Britain's prime minister. By 1914, some 85,000 Jews had immigrated to Palestine, primarily from eastern Europe.

STILL OUTSIDERS: WOMEN, FEMINISM, AND THE RIGHT TO VOTE

By 1914, most of the political groups that had been outside the mainstream of politics had gained a political voice. In the majority of Western countries, universal male suffrage had become the rule by 1914. However, women still remained on the political sidelines, hampered by an ideology that left them unequal economically, trapped in their own "separate sphere" by laws that declared them legally inferior, and excluded by political institutions that deprived them of the vote. Few men in any of the political parties, movements, or unions offered their support for women's suffrage.

During the last decades of the nineteenth century, many women finally turned to political activism. Numerous women—whether as individuals or as activist group members—were already calling themselves "feminist." Groups of feminists organized several movements to promote women's issues, demand legal equality of the

Political activism

sexes, and advocate social and political change. In 1878, representatives of these groups from twelve nations came together in Paris at the International Congress of the Rights of Women and initiated a period of increased activism and international cooperation. Although feminists were still a minority among women, their strength grew dramatically. In Britain and the United States, women with middle-class and aristocratic backgrounds fought especially hard for the right to vote. They argued that without the vote, women would continue to suffer from a range of inequalities. "The idea that the possession of political rights will destroy 'womanliness,' absurd as it may seem to us, is very deeply rooted in the minds of men," Brit-

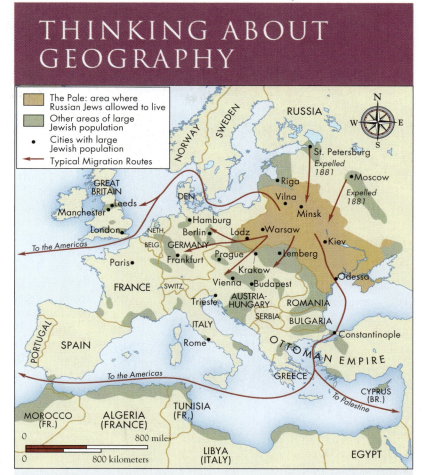

THINKING ABOUT GEOGRAPHY

Legend:
- The Pale: area where Russian Jews allowed to live
- Other areas of large Jewish population
- Cities with large Jewish population
- Typical Migration Routes

MAP 20.1 JEWISH MIGRATION, 1870–1914

This map shows areas and cities with large Jewish populations along with typical migration routes to the west and south.
■ **Notice** the heavy concentration of Jews in eastern Europe. **Consider** the significance of the particularly harsh anti-Semitic policies in these areas. **Why** might Jews have migrated primarily to the west and south?

ish writer Frances Power Cobbe (1822–1904) pointed out in 1884. Men, Cobbe explained, "really prize what women now are in the home and in society so highly that they cannot bear to risk losing it by any serious change in their condition." A few years later, Elizabeth Cady Stanton (1815–1902) expressed the views of many Americans in the women's suffrage movement: "If we are to consider [a woman] as a citizen, as a member of a great nation, she must have the same rights as all other members."

Another group of feminists tried to gain equality through social reform—focusing on the needs of the working class and often voicing socialist sympathies. Led by women such as Louise Michel (1830–1905) in France and Clara Zetkin (1857–1933) in Germany,

■ FIGURE 20.6

Emmeline Pankhurst.

and marching for the franchise. They continued despite scorn from men, ridicule by newspapers, rejection by politicians, cold shoulders from labor unions and socialists, and force by the police. Figure 20.6 shows a policeman arresting Emmeline Pankhurst. "We have tried every way," explained Pankhurst. "We have presented larger petitions than were ever presented for any other reform, we have succeeded in holding greater public meetings than men have ever had for any reform . . . we have faced hostile mobs at street corners . . . we have been ridiculed, we have had contempt poured upon us . . . we know that we need the protection of the vote even more than men have needed it."

In 1908, a rally for female suffrage drew some 250,000 women to Hyde Park in London. After 1910, feminism in Britain took a more public and violent turn as women resorted to window smashing, arson, assaults, bombing of railway stations, and chaining themselves to the gates of Parliament. Police arrested them, judges imprisoned them, and, when they went on hunger strikes, authorities force-fed them.

Still the British government as well as most other Western authorities refused to give in to the feminists' demands. Finland granted women the right to vote in 1906—the first victory for the women's suffrage movement—but other victories would take years. Women would not gain the vote until after 1918 in Britain, Germany, and the United States; until the 1940s in France; and until the 1970s in Switzerland.

EMIGRATION: OVERSEAS AND ACROSS CONTINENTS

By 1914, most Western societies had taken great, often reluctant, steps toward democracy. A swirl of forces—the growing pressures of nationalism, the spread of industry and commerce, and the competition for military might—fueled those steps and molded the politics that resulted. Some of those same forces also pushed a new wave of Europeans and their governments across the globe.

After the mid-nineteenth century, a great migration of people from Europe gained momentum. Europeans streamed overseas and across continents, hoping to start new and better lives. As they fanned across the globe, they brought money and great quantities of manufactured goods to nonindustrialized areas. Their governments did the same: Imperial powers raced to carve up Africa and establish control in Asia. With their new presence, wealth, and power, Europeans dominated the world as never before.

LEAVING EUROPE

Ever since the first sixteenth-century settlements, Europe had sent a sizable trickle of emigrants to the

they argued that only when workers as a whole gained freedom from economic and social oppression would women achieve justice. In 1885, Michel looked forward to a transforming revolution that would introduce a new era "when men and women will move through life together as good companions, and they will no more argue about which sex is superior than races will argue about which race is foremost in the world." Ten years later, Zetkin explained that proletarian women could attain "salvation only through the fight for the emancipation of labor."

The strongest women's suffrage movements arose in Great Britain. The movement was exemplified by organizations such as the National Union of Women's Suffrage Societies, led by Millicent Fawcett (1847–1929), and the more radical Women's Social and Political Union, led by Emmeline Pankhurst (1858–1928) and her two daughters. The leaders of these movements had reached a crucial conclusion: Being polite was not going to win them the right to vote. They worked as other political groups did, forming organizations, presenting petitions, pressuring politicians, forging alliances, holding demonstrations, publishing newspapers,

Suffrage movements

THINKING ABOUT ART

Eugène Laermans, *The Emigrants*, 1896

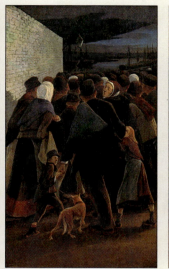

■ FIGURE 20.7

This triptych (three-paneled painting) by Eugène Laermans shows stages in the process of emigration that many Europeans experienced. In the right-hand panel (*The Exordium*), a parish priest addresses the crowd of departing villagers for the last time. For the priest, the news seems bad; this departure of his flock may mark the decline and possibly death of his village. In the background lies the village under dark clouds. The central panel (*The Exodus*) shows a seemingly endless line of humble men, women, and children carrying their meager belongings and dragging their pets. They march along the road and, for the last time, look back at their homeland and village in the distance. In the left-hand panel (*The Exile*), they crowd into the port. The darkening clouds to the west warn of a difficult voyage across the Atlantic and their unknown fate in new lands. ■ **Describe** the apparent mood of the emigrants in each panel. ■ According to what you see in this painting, **why** do you think these people might be emigrating? ■ **In what ways** might this painting be considered a realistic rather than an idealistic depiction of emigration across the Atlantic?

Americas. The trickle became a flowing stream in the mid-nineteenth century. Great numbers of British, Irish, and then German immigrants landed in the United States during the 1840s, 1850s, and 1860s. After 1870, the stream swelled into a rushing torrent, as peoples from southern and eastern Europe joined the flow. Between 1870 and 1914, some 30 million Europeans left their homelands and emigrated, mostly to the Americas and Australia.

What explains this immense movement? As suggested in Figure 20.7 by Belgian artist Eugène Laermans (1864–1940), many of the vast numbers of peasants and workers who emigrated overseas left Europe reluctantly. They felt pushed by the difficulties of their lives on the land and in the villages

Causes for the migration

more than pulled by the apparent opportunities in foreign lands. In several parts of Europe, such as Scandinavia, the British Isles, and southern Italy, the land could no longer support the expanding population. Moreover, the shift to commercial agriculture throughout Europe had left a flood of small farmers landless or unable to compete. Natural catastrophes also played a part. A deadly potato famine in Ireland in the late 1840s forced many Irish to flee their homeland to escape starvation. These hardships impelled people—even in relatively rich Western Europe countries such as Laermans' Belgium—to head for more promising shores. Many emigrated to the Americas, especially between 1880 and 1892.

Many opportunities, both real and imagined, also beckoned from across the oceans. Visions of free or

THINKING ABOUT DOCUMENTS

■ DOCUMENT 20.1

Kaiser William II Links Nationalism and Imperialism

For many people, the distance between the increasingly assertive nationalism of the late nineteenth century and the new imperialism of the period was short. The following speech at Hamburg in 1901, delivered by Kaiser William II of Germany, exemplifies this view. ■ **How** *does William II connect nationalism and imperialism?* ■ **By what means** *does he hope to spread German influence throughout the world?* ■ **In what ways** *might this speech appeal to both liberals and conservatives?*

In spite of the fact that we have no such fleet as we should have, we have conquered for ourselves a place in the sun. It will now be my task to see to it that this place in the sun shall remain our undisputed possession, in order that the sun's rays may fall fruitfully upon our activity and trade in foreign parts, that our industry and agriculture may develop within the state and our sailing sports upon the water, for our future lies upon the water. The more Germans go out upon the waters, whether it be in the races of regattas, whether it be in journeys across the ocean, or in the service of the battleflag, so much the better will it be for us. For when the German has once learned to direct his glance upon what is distant and great, the pettiness which surrounds him in daily life on all sides will disappear. Whoever wishes to have this larger and freer outlook can find no better place than one of the Hanseatic cities.[1] What we have learned out of the previous history of our development amounts really to what I already pointed out when I sent my brother to the East Asiatic station (Dec. 15, 1897). We have merely drawn the logical conclusions from the work which was left us by Emperor William the Great, my memorable grandfather, and the great man whose monument we have recently unveiled. These consequences lie in the fact that we are now making our efforts to do what, in the old time, the Hanseatic cities could not accomplish, because they lacked the vivifying and protecting power of the empire. May it be the function of my Hansa during many years of peace to protect and advance commerce and trade! . . .

As head of the empire I therefore rejoice over every citizen, whether from Hamburg, Bremen, or Lübeck, who goes forth with this large outlook and seeks new points where we can drive in the nail on which to hang our armour.

Source: C. Gauss, *The German Kaiser as Shown in His Public Utterances*, (New York: Charles Scribner's Sons, 1915), pp. 181–183.
[1]*The Hanseatic cities formed a league in the Late Middle Ages to facilitate trade.*

cheap land, already taken away from native peoples, attracted Europeans to the Americas, Australia, and New Zealand. People heard news of plentiful jobs in America's growing cities. Steamships and railroads made the trip faster and cheaper than ever, though not pleasant for the crowds who traveled in ships' bottom compartments with baggage and supplies.

Unfortunately for these hopeful travelers, reality often proved far less appealing than their dreams. New arrivals usually got only the most remote or poorest lands and the lowest-paying jobs. Lonely or adrift in their new world, they sent letters and money back home, maintaining ties to old communities for awhile or asking others to join them. Millions gave up the search for a better life or found reason to turn back; about one-third of those emigrating overseas from Europe eventually returned home.

THE NEW IMPERIALISM: THE RACE FOR AFRICA AND ASIA

In the 1880s, this mass migration of individuals was paralleled by an expansion of Western power into non-Western parts of the world. European nations raced to gain control over Africa and Asia especially. They subdued local opposition and reshaped the existing societies to fit their own purposes. They brought Western culture and institutions to Africa and Asia whether those peoples wanted them or not. By 1914, imperial powers had seized most of Africa and much of Asia, taking direct or indirect control over almost half a billion people.

Imperialism was not new. Since the fifteenth century, Europeans had been extending their influence over the globe. But the burst of expansion between about 1880 and 1914 was so rapid and extensive that historians call it the **new imperialism.**

MONEY AND GLORY

There were many forces driving this wave of imperialism. For one thing, as Document 20.1 indicates, people thought they could make money from it. "It is in order to foster the growth of the trade of this country, and to find an outlet for our manufacturers and our surplus energy, that our far-seeing statesmen and our commercial men advocate colonial expan-

Economic causes

sion," concluded a British colonial administrator. Industrial nations hungered for new markets, cheap raw materials, and juicy investment opportunities. Western manufacturers, merchants, financiers, shippers, investors, adventurers, and settlers thought they would find all these things in Africa and Asia, and European workers believed that the guaranteed markets would keep them employed. Political leaders, egged on by other pressures as well, usually agreed.

Yet the race for riches often proved more difficult than people expected. Many colonies cost European governments far more to acquire and maintain than riches received. The colonizing process got complicated politically as well. Imperial powers took some colonies not because they saw them as money-makers, but because they wanted to protect the borders of other, more lucrative colonies. In many such "buffer" colonies, loans were never paid off, mines never yielded enough minerals to cover their expenses, and markets proved not worth the cost of building railroads to reach them. But in the beginning, people hoped for great profits or at least security for money-making ventures in distant lands. Competition and the optimistic taking on of risks were at the heart of capitalism, and this led many Westerners and their nations into Africa and Asia.

Politics of imperialism

A different, probably more powerful competition—the drive for international prestige—also drove governments, cheered on by millions of their citizens, to snap up colonies. The renewed burst of imperialism came at precisely the time when nationalism was on the rise in Europe. As Document 20.2 suggests, nationalistic sentiment easily translated into a new struggle for imperial conquest—for remote islands, barren deserts, and impenetrable jungles as well as for more lucrative prizes. Governments used such conquests to display their muscle, especially when such a display was lacking at home. France's expansion, for example, helped French citizens feel compensated for losses suffered in the Franco-Prussian War. Italian conquests overseas promised to make up for Italy's failure to acquire first-rate power status on the Continent. Gaining colonies became a measure of status, proof of a nation's political and economic prowess. To be left behind in the imperial race marked a nation as second class. "[A]ll great nations in the fullness of their strength have desired to set their mark upon barbarian lands, and those who fail to participate in this great rivalry will play a pitiable role in the time to come," the nationalist German historian Heinrich von Treitschke announced. People in the West avidly followed the race for colonies. Newspapers reporting on incidents and conquests in Asia and Africa framed these developments as adventures and patri-

Nationalism and imperialism

otic causes. Thrilling stories about action overseas sold countless papers. In books and classrooms, people could see their national colors spreading across oceans and continents.

This competition for economic gain and international prestige gained a life of its own, a momentum that became hard to curb. When one nation moved into a new area, others followed, for fear of being left with nothing. To protect established colonies, imperial powers seized adjoining territories. To ensure supply lines to distant colonies, nations grabbed up islands, ports, and bases. To form alliances and collect bargaining chips for when disputes arose, imperial powers made colonial claims.

Finally, people found ways to justify imperialism. Westerners saw themselves as bringing "blessings" of their civilization to "backward" peoples. The British writer Rudyard Kipling (1865–1936) expressed the belief of many Westerners when he wrote of the "white man's burden" to civilize the "lesser breeds" of the earth. Missionaries took to heart the injunction to "Go ye into all the world and preach the gospel to every creature."

Justification

Figure 20.8, a cover illustration from a French Catholic magazine, *The Pilgrim*, reveals Westerners' idealized views of imperialism. Here a member of the White Sisters, a Catholic order, teaches already converted Ugandan girls how to use a sewing machine. The image plainly contrasts the devoted, beautiful European women and the humble, well-behaved children. The implied promise is that the West will bring the benefits of its technology, faith, and civilization to a new generation of thankful Africans.

Some people put imperialism in a less rosy context. These observers described colonial competition and conquest as part of an unavoidable, Darwinian struggle for survival of the fittest (see Document 20.3). In such a struggle, the white "race" would surely prevail, they believed. France's prime minister even claimed that "the superior races have rights over the inferior races," a view supported by many.

There were people who opposed imperialism. Intellectuals, reform clubs, and politicians such as Jean Jaurès called it an unjustifiably cruel and costly exploitation. However, such voices did not carry enough weight. Powerful economic interests and politicians had found imperial expansion irresistible, and most citizens were all too willing to support the adventure. Moreover, imperial conquest became so easy it seemed foolish not to take advantage of it.

Opposition to imperialism

THE TOOLS OF CONQUEST

Before 1850, it was either too difficult or not worth the effort for Westerners to penetrate into Africa's interior or extensively expand colonial holdings in

■ DOCUMENT 20.2

Economics and Imperialism in Africa

With new conquests made in the "scramble" for Africa, many people expected commerce to accelerate and new markets for manufactured goods to emerge. This attitude shows up in Lord Lugard's account of his experiences in colonial service. A British soldier and administrator, Lugard helped bring large parts of Africa into the British empire. ■ ***How** does Lugard connect nationalistic and economic motives for imperialism?* ■ ***How** does he respond to arguments against imperialism?* ■ ***What** are Lugard's perceptions of Africans?*

The Chambers of Commerce of the United Kingdom have unanimously urged the retention of East Africa on the grounds of commercial advantage. The Presidents of the London and Liverpool chambers attended a deputation to her Majesty's Minister for Foreign Affairs to urge "the absolute necessity, for the prosperity of this country, that new avenues for commerce such as that in East Equatorial Africa should be opened up, in view of the hostile tariffs with which British manufacturers are being everywhere confronted." Manchester followed with a similar declaration; Glasgow, Birmingham, Edinburgh, and other commercial centres gave it as their opinion that "there is practically no middle course for this country, between a reversal of the free-trade policy to which it is pledged, on the one hand, and a prudent but continuous territorial extension for the creation of new markets, on the other hand." . . .

This view has been strongly endorsed by some of our leading statesmen. Space forbids me to quote extracts from speeches by our greatest politicians, which I might else adduce as proof that they held the opinions of the Chambers of Commerce, which I have quoted, to be sound and weighty. . . .

The "Scramble for Africa" by the nations of Europe—an incident without parallel in the history of the world—was due to the growing commercial rivalry, which brought home to civilised nations the vital necessity of securing the only remaining fields for industrial enterprise and expansion. It is well, then, to realise that it is for our *advantage*—and not alone at the dictates of duty—that we have undertaken responsibilities in East Africa. It is in order to foster the growth of the trade of this country, and to find an outlet for our manufactures and our surplus energy, that our far-seeing statesmen and our commercial men advocate colonial expansion. . . .

There are some who say we have no *right* in Africa at all, that "it belongs to the natives." I hold that our right is the necessity that is upon us to provide for our ever-growing population—either by opening new fields for emigration, or by providing work and employment which the development of over-sea extension

entails—and to stimulate trade by finding new markets, since we know what misery trade depression brings at home.

While thus serving our own interests as a nation, we may, by selecting men of the right stamp for the control of new territories, bring at the same time many advantages to Africa. Nor do we deprive the natives of their birthright of freedom, to place them under a foreign yoke. It has ever been the key-note of British colonial method to rule through and by the natives, and it is this method, in contrast to the arbitrary and uncompromising rule of Germany, France, Portugal, and Spain, which has been the secret of our success as a colonising nation, and has made us welcomed by tribes and peoples in Africa, who ever rose in revolt against the other nations named. In Africa, moreover, there is among the people a natural inclination to submit to a higher authority. That intense detestation of control which animates our Teutonic races does not exist among the tribes of Africa, and if there is any authority that we replace, it is the authority of the Slavers and Arabs, or the intolerable tyranny of the "dominant tribe." . . .

* * *

So far, therefore, as my personal experience goes, I have formed the following estimate: (1) No kind of men I have ever met with—including British soldiers, Afghans, Burmese, and many tribes of India—are more amenable to discipline, more ready to fall into the prescribed groove willingly and quickly, more easy to handle, or require so little compulsion as the African. (2) To obtain satisfactory results a great deal of system, division of labour, supervision, etc., is required. (3) On the whole, the African is very quick at learning, and those who prove themselves good at the superior class of work take a pride in the results, and are very amenable to a word of praise, blame, or sarcasm.

Source: Captain F. D. Lugard, *The Rise of Our East African Empire*, vol. I (London: William Blackwood and Sons, 1893), pp. 379–382; 473.

Asia. After 1850, science and technology gave the industrialized nations the tools they needed to conquer and control nonindustrialized lands.

Steam-powered iron ships conveyed messages, materials, and people across oceans quickly and cheaply. Smaller steamboats took travelers up rivers. Railroads carried them across vast stretches of lands. The Suez Canal cut thousands of miles off journeys to Asia, and the Panama Canal promised much the same (see the drawing on p. 614). In 1800,

Transportation facilities

mail took as long as one year to get from London to India. In 1880, a telegram took just hours.

Innovations in weaponry also gave the West new clout. Europeans had long possessed more firepower than non-Western peoples. The new breech-loading rifles and machine guns multiplied that advantage. Local societies resisted, but with the destructive power of these new weapons, European soldiers numbering only a few hundred annihilated local forces in the thousands. Winston Churchill, Britain's future prime minister and an observer of the

Force

■ DOCUMENT 20.3

Progress and the Struggle of Race with Race

During the late nineteenth century, ideas about social Darwinism and eugenics—the study of hereditary "improvement" by selective breeding—spread in the West and were used to justify competition, war, and imperialism. Karl Pearson (1857–1936), trained as a mathematician, became an outspoken proponent of eugenics, claiming the best scientific thinking backed it. The following is an excerpt from his 1900 book, National Life from the Standpoint of Science. ■ ***In what ways** might Pearson's ideas justify imperialism?* ■ ***How** should competition and struggle take place according to Pearson?* ■ ***In what ways** might Pearson's ideas be considered racist today?*

"History shows me one way, and one way only, in which a high state of civilization has been produced, namely, the struggle of race with race, and the survival of the physically and mentally fitter race. . . . The struggle means suffering, intense suffering, while it is in progress; but that struggle and that suffering have been the stages by which the white man has reached his present stage of development, and they account for the fact that he no longer lives in caves and feeds on roots and nuts. This dependence of progress on the survival of the fitter race, terribly black as it may seem to some of you, gives the struggle for existence its redeeming features; it is the fiery crucible out of which comes the finer metal. You may hope for a time when the sword shall be returned into the plowshare, when American and German and English traders shall no longer compete in the markets of the world for their raw material and for their food supply, when the white man and the dark shall share the soil between them, and each till it as he lists. But, believe me, when that day comes mankind will no longer progress; there will be nothing to check the fertility of inferior stock; the relentless law of heredity will not be controlled and guided by natural selection. Man will stagnate; and unless he ceases to multiply, the catastrophe will come again; famine and pestilence, as we see them in the East, physical selection instead of the struggle of race against race, will do the work more relentlessly, and, to judge from India and China, far less efficiently than of old. . . ."

Source: Karl Pearson, *National Life from the Standpoint of Science*, London: A & C Black, 1901.

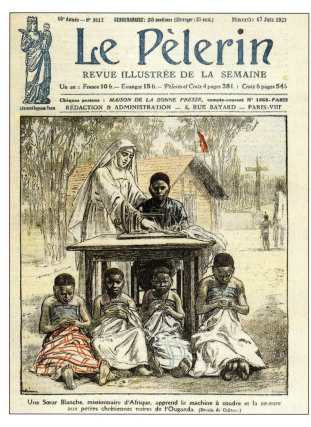

■ FIGURE 20.8

A European vision of imperialism.

1898 Battle of Omdurman in the Sudan, described the effects of the machine gun on natives: "It was not a battle but an execution. . . . The bodies were . . . spread evenly over acres and acres." In that particular battle, 11,000 Muslim tribesmen died, whereas only 28 British soldiers lost their lives. Many other battles, large and small, took place in the series of open and guerrilla wars over the years. Imperial powers usually prevailed, but conquest and control came with much bloodshed and brutality. As the British novelist Joseph Conrad wrote in his 1902 classic, *Heart of Darkness*, "The conquest of the earth, which mostly means the taking it away from those who have a different complexion or slightly flatter noses than ourselves, is not a pretty thing when you look into it much."

Disease, more than distance or resistance, had also kept Europeans out of most of Africa. But by 1830, the French had discovered the power of quinine to protect their soldiers from deadly *Medicine* malaria long enough to take Algeria in North Africa. After 1850, explorers, missionaries, traders, soldiers, and officials came into sub-Saharan Africa armed with the new medicine.

Various Europeans used these tools of conquest at different times. Sometimes missionaries and explorers entered new lands first; at other times, traders or even military officers made decisions on their own to move in. Once there, they called on home governments to provide support, enforce contracts, and protect private interests. Newspapers reported "atrocities" committed against the unwelcome intruders and stirred up European cries for revenge and protection of national honor. Western governments that had requested the cooperation of local political leaders and had been refused turned to force. Indirect control could quickly turn into direct control as problems arose. Control expanded even more as neighboring areas attracted the interest of the intruders.

Patterns of conquest

THE SCRAMBLE FOR AFRICA

Imperial control spread most dramatically in Africa. In the early nineteenth century, Africa was the seat of several vital civilizations. In the north were the long-established Islamic societies. In sub-Saharan Africa—particularly in the western and central Sudan, where the Sahara Desert gave way to grasslands and trade flourished—a rich array of societies and states had developed over the centuries. In most kingdoms of the Sudan and western Africa, Islam had become a major cultural influence. Trade and contact with Europeans affected Africa, but except for coastal and certain other limited areas, such as South Africa, most of Africa remained free from European control.

By the middle decades of the nineteenth century, however, the French had conquered and annexed Algeria in North Africa and had pushed their way up the Senegal River in the west. The British had taken the Cape Colony in South Africa from the Dutch during the Napoleonic Wars, and the Dutch settlers had moved northward into the interior (see Map 20.2). In the late 1870s, two developments initiated an international scramble to carve up Africa.

North Africa

The first occurred in Egypt. This North African state had long interested France and Britain as a market for European goods and investments and as a bridge to Asia. European bankers financed the construction of port facilities, railroads, and telegraph lines in Egypt, granting high-interest loans to Egypt's government. In 1869 the Suez Canal, built by a French company, opened and became the vital link from the Mediterranean Sea through Egypt to the Red Sea and the Indian Ocean (see the drawing on page 614). The British desired control over the canal so as to secure their lucrative position in India. In 1875, Great Britain took advantage of the Egyptian government's financial distress and purchased the Egyptian ruler's, or khedive's, controlling portion of the canal stock. Four years later, France and Britain seized Egypt's treasury to secure their investments. When nationalist groups in Egypt revolted, British troops occupied Egypt. Formally, the khedive remained in office, but after 1882, Britain held most of the real power. By then, 3,000 ships a year passed through the Suez Canal.

The British reshaped Egypt's economy so that it produced cotton, silk, and wheat for export in return for manufactured goods. They also disrupted local work life by hiring Egyptian laborers for their own projects—whether as railroad builders or servants. Worse, they insulted unfavored groups—such as Muslims and Arabs—by paying them less than favored groups.

The French reluctantly acquiesced to British control in Egypt in return for Britain's support of French ambitions in northwestern Africa. In the following years, Britain expanded south to secure Egypt and east to maintain its position in India and China. For similar reasons, France expanded from its stake in Algeria to Tunisia, Morocco, and most of northwestern Africa.

At the same time, King Leopold II of Belgium (r. 1865–1909), set out to get "a slice of this magnificent African cake." Hungry for ivory, rubber, hardwoods, palm oil, and glory, he initiated a new competition for acquisitions in sub-Saharan Africa by devouring the Congo. He had claimed that his purpose was "to open to civilization" central Africa, "to pierce the darkness which envelopes whole populations." In fact, his troops killed and mutilated thousands of local peoples in the process of conquest. An American missionary described the brutality with which Leopold's officials forced people into the forest to collect rubber: "The soldiers drive the people into the bush. If they will not go they are shot down, and their left hands cut off and taken as trophies."

Worried about missing out on the land grab, the other European powers voiced their own claims. The French centered their efforts in western Africa, the Germans in eastern Africa, and the British up and down the center "from Cairo to Cape-town." The Berlin Conference of 1885 formalized this scramble for Africa, setting ground rules for territorial acquisition on that continent. According to the conference, colonizers were supposed to have enough physical presence to control and develop an area before they could claim it. They also agreed to treat Africans according to humane standards, although they often used that declaration to disguise the exploitation and abuse they continued to commit.

Sub-Saharan Africa

By 1914, most of the huge continent had been carved up by the various European powers (see Map 20.3). The main exception was Ethiopia. There, Emperor Menelik II (r. 1889–1913) cleverly played one European power off against the other. In the process, he manipulated the Europeans into supplying his country with modern arms, which he then used to defeat the invading Italians in 1896.

For the Europeans, the costliest struggles occurred among themselves. The imperial powers averted most conflicts by diplomacy. In South Africa, however, even the most skilled diplomacy failed to keep the peace.

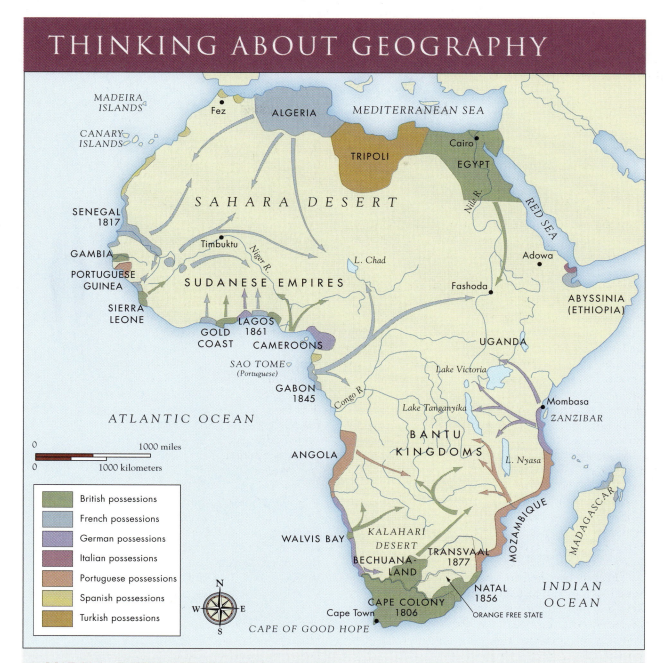

MAP 20.2 IMPERIALISM IN AFRICA, CA. 1885

Comparing Map 20.2, which shows European holdings in Africa in 1885, and Map 20.3, which shows European holdings in 1914, reveals the results of the Europeans' grab for African lands.
■ **Consider** which European nations became the main imperial powers in Africa. ■ **Notice** the dates of acquisition by the European powers. **What** do these dates reveal about the timing of the "scramble" for African lands? ■ **Locate** Britain's possessions. **How** do these reflect Britain's concern to protect its routes to India?

British settlers began to move into the South African Cape Colony early in the nineteenth century. The Dutch Boers (Afrikaners), who had settled there in the seventeenth century and resented Britain's abolition of slavery, trekked northward far into the interior, slaughtering the resisting Zulus in their way. Eventually, the British recognized the independence of the two Boer states, Transvaal and the Orange Free State.

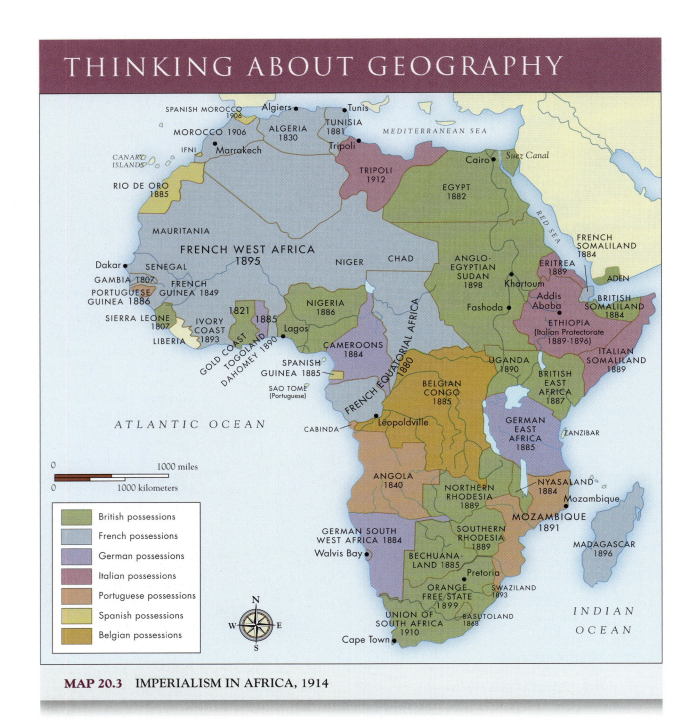

MAP 20.3 IMPERIALISM IN AFRICA, 1914

However, when rich gold mines were discovered in Transvaal in the 1880s, British immigrants flooded in. The British entrepreneur and empire builder Cecil Rhodes (1853–1902), backed by powerful interest groups concerned about growing German presence in southwestern Africa, decided to brush aside the two little Boer republics. But what the British thought would be an easy victory took three years (1899–1902) of military effort and involved severe casualties and enormous costs. Backed by 300,000 troops from India and the homeland, Brit-

Boer War

ain finally won the brutal contest and in the end treated the defeated Boers leniently. The British took them into partnership in the Union of South Africa, and the Boer hero, General Louis Botha (1862–1919), was elected the Union's first prime minister. Botha's government announced that it would "permit no equality between colored people and the white inhabitants," a policy that South Africa would hold on to for the next eighty years.

Europeans usually ruled directly over African societies so they could create the economic conditions they wanted. Colonial administrators trained cooperative tribes as their clerks, soldiers, and favored workers. These preferences often sparked bitter tribal jealousies and rivalries. Throughout Africa, Europeans made it clear by their words and actions that they considered themselves, their civilization, and their "race" superior to the Africans. Their dominance established, Europeans prided themselves on bringing Christianity and civilization to the "dark" continent. They had scant appreciation for the qualities of African societies and dismissed the Africans as inferior peoples useful only for manual labor. Often they treated them little better than slaves. They also established new political boundaries that ignored the long-standing social, cultural, and political realities of local peoples. Some officials even worked to "submerge" Africans from different societies "into a single colored working class," a policy that prevented Africans from maintaining kinship and community ties. Those Africans who resisted might be decimated in armed battle or dispossessed and forced onto reservations. Yet resentment and desperation led many Africans to rebel against their conquerors, despite the hopelessness of their situation. A warrior in South Africa explained the reasons for one of these rebellions: "Our King gone, we had submitted to the white people and they ill-treated us until we became desperate and tried to make an end of it all. We knew that we had very little chance because their weapons were so much superior to ours. But we meant to fight to the last, feeling that even if we could not beat them we might at least kill a few of them and so have some sort of revenge."

Dominance, conflict, and consequences

ESTABLISHING CONTROL IN ASIA

In Asia, Western powers usually got what they wanted by ruling through local elites. In these large, well-organized societies, where the potential for effective resistance remained great, Westerners' tampering with the established power structure was risky.

India

India was as linguistically and regionally diverse as Europe. Nevertheless, by the nineteenth century, the British had brought together a variety of states, territories, and tribal groups to create an Indian state under British control. The Indian subcontinent became Britain's richest imperial prize. Nearly twenty times larger than Great Britain and more than seven times as populous, India bought and sold more goods than any other British colony. Britain directed much of its imperial policy toward preserving this lucrative colony. Part of the reason Britain annexed new colonies in Africa and widened its sphere of influence in the Middle East was to protect India from other European states.

Until 1858, the British East India Company, a private-stock company, governed much of India. However, the great Sepoy Mutiny of 1857, the first large-scale uprising of Indians against British rule almost drove the British out of India. This prompted the British government to take direct control. Instead of meddling with the structure of Indian society, the British used India's elites to support their rule. They employed a half-million Indians to administer the huge country and built railroads, canals, ports, schools, and medical facilities. In one sense, India benefited in that population increased rapidly. On the other hand, living standards for most fell as population increases outstripped economic growth. The British paid low wages and labeled Indians as inferior—at best, in the words of the British historian and politician Thomas Macaulay, "a great people sunk in the lowest depth of slavery and superstition." Through use of tariffs, they forced India to collapse its own cotton industry and accept British imports of cotton cloth instead. They restructured India's economy to specialize in products the British wanted, such as jute, raw cotton, opium, tea, and wheat. As one Indian nationalist explained, "*Pax Britannica* [Britain's peace] has been established in this country in order that a foreign government may exploit the country."

Britain permanently altered this ancient civilization by creating a national unity, whether the Indians desired it or not. Moreover, British men and women in India imported their own cultural standards, lived separately from the "inferior" native societies, and expected the Indians they dealt with—from elites to servants—to

KEY DATES

IMPERIALISM AND THE NON-WESTERN WORLD

1839–1842	Opium Wars in China
1850–1864	Taiping Rebellion in China
1853	United States forces opening of Japan
1868	Meiji Restoration in Japan
1869	Suez Canal opens
1885	Berlin Conference
1896	Ethiopians defeat Italians
1898	Spanish-American War
1899–1900	Boxer Rebellion in China
1899–1902	Boer War
1904	Russo-Japanese War

adjust to British ways. For example, in her book, *The Complete Indian Housekeeper and Cook,* British author Flora Annie Steel boasted that "to show what absolute children Indian servants are," she has "for years adopted castor oil as an ultimatum," adding that this is "considered a great joke, and exposes the offender to much ridicule from his fellow-servants." Figure 20.9, a photo of Indian servants catering to a British gentleman, also indicates the gulf between the British ruling class and the Indians they governed. It also reveals the appeal of foreign service to the British, who at home may have enjoyed only modest social positions.

The British showed no inclination to grant India self-government. As a result, nationalism—already a potent force in Europe—rose in Asia. Indian dissatisfaction with British rule mounted steadily. In 1885, the nationalist Indian elite formed the Indian National Congress, which would launch a long struggle for Indian independence.

France followed the same pattern as Britain in its southeast Asia colonies. By the 1860s, open resistance to the intruding French became **Southeast Asia** hopeless. As one of Vietnam's leading statesmen explained in 1867, "The French have come, with their powerful weapons of war . . . no one can resist them. They go where they want, the strongest ramparts fall before them." During the 1880s and early 1890s, France took what would become Vietnam, Cambodia, and Laos and grouped them into the Union of Indochina under French control. As in India, medicine, sanitation, canals, roads, and other projects financed by the French led to population growth in Indochina. French rule also spawned economic dependence and resentment against the European assumption of superiority. A southeast Asian elite arose that, as in India, would struggle to expel Western rule.

China, with its highly structured society, strong central government, and large armed forces, had long kept Westerners at arm's length. Although the Chinese admitted some European traders and **China** Christian missionaries in the sixteenth and seventeenth centuries, they closed their doors rather tightly thereafter. At the beginning of the eighteenth century, China ranked among the world's most prosperous and powerful societies. The Chinese still considered their huge, populous country the center of civilization surrounded by lesser civilizations. As late as 1793, China's emperor could easily dismiss a proposed trade agreement with Britain: "Our Celestial Empire possesses all things in abundance. We have no need of barbarian products."

However, during the nineteenth century, population explosion, famine, rebellions, and poor leadership under the declining Qing (Ch'ing) dynasty weakened the ancient civilization. The country became a power vacuum that proved all too tempting to the Western powers. Armed with their guns and goods, Westerners streamed into China.

First, the British forced themselves on the Chinese. During the 1830s, Britain began trading Indian opium in China for tea, silver, silk, and other **Opium Wars** products. Soon opium became one of Britain's most important commodities (see Global Connections). Chinese officials tried to stop the economic drain, addiction, and criminal activities stemming from the opium trade by making the drug illegal. As the Chinese official in charge exclaimed to the British, "You do not wish opium to harm your own country, but you choose to bring that harm to other countries such as China. Why?" In response, Britain sent gunboats and troops armed with modern weapons. They easily defeated the Chinese in a series of clashes known as the Opium Wars. By the terms of the Treaty of Nanking (1842), which ended the conflict, the Chinese ceded Hong Kong to the British, opened several tariff-free ports to foreign trade, exempted foreigners from Chinese law, and paid Britain a large indemnity.

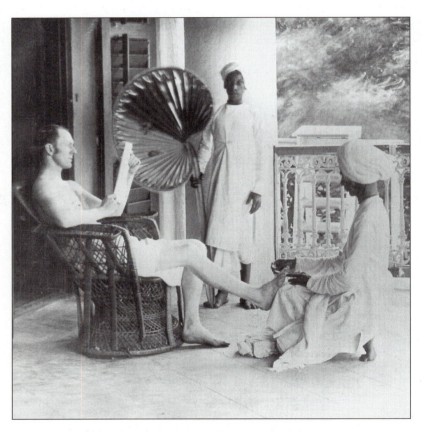

■ FIGURE 20.9
The British in India.

Opium and the West in China

CONSIDER

■ **Consider** how British merchants' selling of opium helped undermine the authority of China's government.

Opium, a narcotic derived from the opium poppy, was known and used—especially for medical purposes—in China for centuries. However, not until the nineteenth century did its use become so widespread that millions of Chinese became addicted to the drug. The West was not free from opium, either, for Europeans and Americans increasingly resorted to opium-based products such as morphine and laudanum to calm their nerves, ease aches and pains, and control their noisy children. During the nineteenth century, most of China's opium supply was imported by British merchants from colonial holdings in India.

Chinese officials made only half-hearted attempts to restrict the opium trade until 1838, when Emperor Daoguang finally banned importation of the drug. In 1839, an imperial official, Lin Zexu, wrote a letter to Britain's Queen Victoria complaining about the destructive impact of opium on China. "Unscrupulous" merchants, Lin wrote, are "so obsessed with material gain that they have no concern whatever for the harm they can cause to others." These merchants have flooded China with so much opium "that this poison has spread far and wide in all the provinces." Lin asked the queen to stop the trade and "destroy and plow under all of these opium plants." When Lin began confiscating and destroying imported opium, the British responded with force. As one of China's discouraged commissioners reported, "The ships of the barbarians are sturdy and their cannons fierce." By 1842, British firepower had overwhelmed the Chinese, and the Treaty of Nanjing legalized the opium trade and granted concessions to Britain and other Western powers.

The struggle against the British over opium was only the beginning of the wars and other upheavals China suffered during the nineteenth and twentieth centuries. Internal problems also increasingly plagued the vast country, weakening the government's ability to resist the West. In 1852, Zeng Guofan, a perceptive scholar and high official in Emperor Xianfeng's government, commented on the situation. Taxes, Zeng claimed, were overwhelming the people. Therefore, "people are complaining and angry, and often the resistance to tax payment bursts forth and mushrooms into full-fledged riot." More and more impoverished people were resorting to banditry to survive. Yet attempts to stop the lawlessness were useless because governmental soldiers "have always been in collusion with the bandits," Zeng maintained, and would soon release the bandits "in return for a handsome bribe." Moreover, people had lost faith in the justice system because so many "innocent men are condemned" and the people "[are unable] to have a wrong redressed." The next year, a series of disastrous uprisings struck China, the worst of which came with the Taiping Rebellion. Over the following ten years, the conflicts devastated large parts of the country. While the government eventually crushed the rebels, the country soon began losing lands and control to imperial powers.

Meanwhile, the destructive consequences of the opium trade mounted. Isabella Bird Bishop, a British traveler in China during the 1890s, reported on the situation. In addition to noting the continuing importation of opium into China by the British, Bishop observed that "The area devoted to the [opium-producing] poppy in Sze Chuan [province] is enormous." Moreover, its culture was "encroaching on the rice and arable lands" so much that "there was no longer a margin left on which to feed the population in years of a poor harvest." Even though the Chinese regarded the opium habit as a disease, Bishop continued, in that province "opium houses are as common as gin shops in our London slums." In the large cities of that province, she noted that eighty percent of men and forty percent of women were opium smokers. "It is obvious," she concluded, "that opium has come to stay."

To other observers throughout China and the West, it seemed equally clear that China was caught in the tightening grip of Western and Japanese imperialists as well as a powerful and addictive narcotic.

At mid-century, disaster struck. China suffered a devastating civil war—the Taiping Rebellion (1850–1864). Other subsequent rebellions extended the internal conflict another ten years. In the end, these wars took perhaps fifty million lives, and the famines that followed cost the lives of millions more. All this strife weakened the Qing dynasty and revealed the government's inability to control a nation threatened by external enemies and internal upheaval.

Taiping Rebellion

In the years that followed, China fought a series of wars against foreigners. It lost them all, and each defeat chipped away at its sovereignty and racked up yet more indemnities. The Western powers grabbed up spheres of influence and semi-independent treaty ports where all foreigners were exempt from Chinese jurisdiction. In addition, they built railroads to penetrate farther into China's heartland. As shown on Map 20.4, they also took lands on the huge country's periphery. By all these means, the French and British added to their possessions in south Asia, Russia gained territory in the north, and Japan snapped up Korea and Taiwan in the east.

The United States joined in the frenzy, grabbing the Philippine Islands after a war with Spain in 1898 and a long struggle against Filipino nationalist forces that cost the lives of perhaps 200,000 Filipinos. President William McKinley explained that the United States had the duty "to educate the Filipinos and uplift and Christianize them." To protect its commercial interests

The Philippines

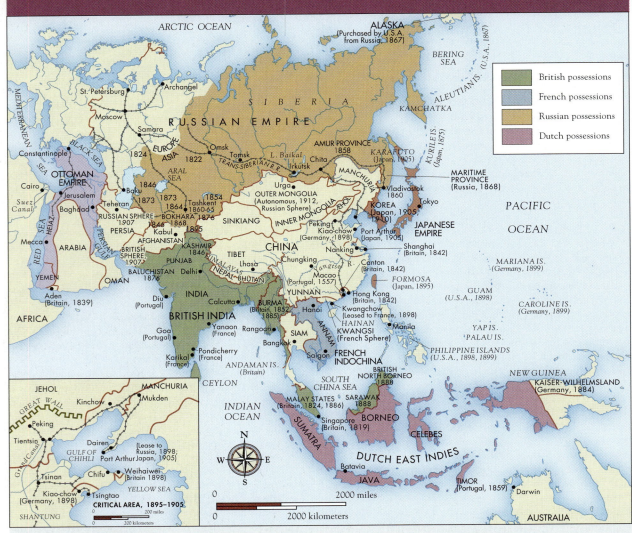

MAP 20.4 IMPERIALISM IN ASIA, 1840–1914

This map shows the expansion of imperialism in Asia by the Western powers and Japan. ■ **Which** powers gained the largest territorial interests in Asia by 1914? ■ **Notice** in particular the lands controlled by Russia, Britain, and Japan. **Where** might conflicts break out between these powers?

in Asia, the United States called for an "Open Door" policy that would avoid further territorial annexations by the imperial powers. Rivalry among the great powers themselves, as much as Chinese resistance, saved China from complete loss of its independence.

Meanwhile, Chinese nationalism rose in response to foreign aggression. In 1899–1900, the Boxer Rebellion, a serious uprising against Western influences, erupted. Furious at those who had betrayed Chinese religion and customs, the Boxers, a secret organization that believed in the spiritual power of the martial arts, killed thousands of Chinese Christians and a number of foreigners—all

with the encouragement of China's Dowager Empress. Figure 20.10, a painting by American artist John Clymer, depicts a battle between the Boxers—in the center, with swords and spears—and U.S. marines—in the lower right, with modern machine guns, rifles with bayonets, and revolvers. The Boxers, represented as wild and bloodthirsty, seem to burst out of the heavily populated Chinese society, while the steadfast U.S. marines fire from the outside into that society. Combined forces from the imperial powers brutally suppressed this nationalist movement and forced China to pay large indemnities.

Boxer Rebellion

Even propped up by imperial powers, the corrupt Chinese central government could not last. In 1911, reformers led by Sun Yat-sen (1866–1925), a Western-educated doctor, launched a revolution aimed at freeing China from foreign exploitation and modernizing its society. Rebellions swept most of China and pushed the corrupt, inept, disintegrating dynasty to its final collapse. Sun proclaimed a republic, but power soon dispersed among imperial generals who became warlords. China's struggles to cope with the encroaching world and its internal problems were far from over.

Japan, even more than China, had long refused direct contact with the West. At the beginning of the nineteenth century, the island nation remained in great part a feudal society ruled by the shogun—a strong military governor—and his military chieftains. The Japanese emperor had only limited powers. Though long influenced **Japan** by Chinese culture, Japan also had a sharply defined sense of identity: "[O]ur country is the source and fountainhead of all other countries, and in all matters it excels all the others," explained one Japanese writer.

In 1853, however, an American fleet under Admiral Perry (1794–1858) steamed into Tokyo Bay, uninvited and unwanted, and forced the Japanese to open their ports to Westerners (see Chapter 19). Impressed by the Americans' technological superiority, the Japanese reacted differently than the Chinese to the foreigners. In 1868, a group of young Japanese **The Meiji Restoration** overthrew the existing government and launched a social and political revolution from the top down. They ended the feudal structure of the country and began reorganizing Japanese society along modern Western lines (the **Meiji Restoration**). Taking what they considered the best features from the various Western nations, they patterned their business methods after those of the United States, their legal system after the French, and their navy after the British. They built an authoritarian government, an efficient military machine, and an educational system on the German model. They even required Western dress in court and imitated Western architecture in the rebuilding of Tokyo in 1872.

With stunning speed, Japan industrialized. Figure 20.11, a photograph of a Japanese silk-working factory, reveals how intensively—in form and substance—Japan adopted Western industrial methods. Men, dressed in formal Western attire, supervise women, who work on row after row of tightly spaced machines.

The industrialized nation soon began flexing its new muscle in Asia. Japan no longer viewed China as a source of culture to be respected, but a weakened land open to conquest and exploitation. In 1894, the Japanese invaded China, forcing it to pay a large indem-

■ FIGURE 20.10
John Clymer, *The Boxer Rebellion*, 1900.

■ FIGURE 20.11
Japanese silk factory, 1905.

nity and give up Korea and Taiwan. In 1904, after Russia angered Japan by increasing its presence in China's northern province of Manchuria, the Japanese attacked the tsar's **Russo-Japanese War** troops. To the world's surprise, Japan defeated the inept Russian forces both on land and at sea and became the dominant power in Manchuria. Industrialized, militaristic, and imperialistic, Japan took its place alongside other world powers by 1914.

THE LEGACY OF IMPERIALISM

With its technology, its industrial capitalism, and above all its aggressive nationalism, the West had subjected most of Africa and Asia to its domination between 1870 and 1914. In Australia and New Zealand, European powers had already established large settler colonies. As in North America, contact and clashes with the incoming settlers proved disastrous for the indigenous populations. In the Pacific, the pattern of imperial conquest that the West had established in Africa and Asia held true. Western adventurers, missionaries, traders, gunboats, troops, and businesses came, took over, and destroyed the world that native peoples had long known. Worse, the Westerners carried diseases that decimated Pacific populations.

Certainly, life in non-Western lands had not been idyllic before the intrusion of the West. As one Ndebele warrior in South Africa put it, "Even in our own time there were troubles, there was much fighting and many innocent people were killed." Many from the West in these lands may have been well meaning, and they may have brought elements of Western civilization that were of some benefit to people in the non-Western world. In 1900 Lord Curzon, the celebrated British viceroy of India, wrote about the consequences of British rule over India: "I do not see how any Englishmen, contrasting India as it now is with what it was . . . can fail to see that we came and have stayed . . . in obedience to . . . the decree of Providence, . . . for the lasting benefit of millions of the human race." In India, British rule probably prevented internal wars and promoted order. In Africa, Europeans did abolish slavery. Imperial powers built ports, railway lines, hospitals, schools, and sanitation facilities. Colonized peoples also learned about Western politics, economics, and education, eventually making use of them to assert their own liberation from imperial powers.

Yet rather than striving to understand and appreciate non-Western societies, most people in the West viewed them from a condescending, arrogant, or downright racist perspective. The colonized peoples had to endure being treated as menials and subordinates by men and women whose only necessary qualification was being Western. The insults to local peoples' self-respect and their relentless humiliation fueled resistance to Western control.

Western powers not only forcibly drew non-Western lands into a world economy, they also exploited the natural and human resources of the conquered lands and profoundly undermined the cultural, social, and religious traditions of the African and Asian peoples. In addition, they distorted non-Western economies to serve the demands of their own commerce. They imposed what one observer called "the European system of monotonous, uninterrupted labour," in which industries such as mining and railroad building subjected native laborers to inhumane and dangerous working conditions. Forced to migrate to find jobs in the alien economy, local workers left behind shattered families and communities. Political structures that had long functioned effectively in these lands broke down in just a few years.

By 1914, tens of thousands of colonial administrators, soldiers, and settlers relied directly on imperialism for their careers, status, and livelihood. They, along with Western tourists, enjoyed a sense of privilege and superiority over Africans and Asians. Many also enjoyed, though less often discussed, sexual contact with their colonized peoples. Indeed, most Westerners had come to view imperialism as normal and harmless. In their home countries, some people in the West visited the proliferating zoos with "exotic" animals, studied anthropology, viewed new works of art, and read literature that reflected interaction with non-Western lands. But few recognized how destructive it could be—not only to colonial peoples but also to themselves. In Asia, for example, Russia's expansion south brought it to the borders of British India and nearly ignited a war with that nation. Farther east, Russia pushed to the Sea of Japan and Manchuria; the action sparked hostilities with Japan. More than once, Britain, France, and Germany narrowly avoided war in Africa. Imperialism extended the already intense economic and political competition among the European states, heightening the potential for major conflict among these powers.

SUMMARY

In the years 1870–1914, more and more Westerners gained access to the political process. Nationalism opened these doors for them, as did the movement toward democracy. But the combination of nationalism and democracy had its dangers. In Britain, J. S. Mill warned that "the sentiment of nationality so far outweighs the love of liberty that the people are willing to abet their rulers in crushing the liberty and independence of any people not of their race or language." Many political leaders recognized nationalism and democracy as forces that they could use to their advantage. Others simply adjusted to them. Those who resisted did so at their own peril.

Europeans were also moving, not only to their own cities but out of Europe by the millions. Industrialization and the promise of wealth in new places combined with nationalism and mass politics to push the imperial West throughout the world as never before. As a result, Western power—economic, political, military, and imperial—expanded in an environment of intense international competition.

In the years just before 1914, the strain of this competition on Western societies grew obvious. Labor unrest, the movement for women's suffrage, politics of the extremes, civil violence, diplomatic crises, military threats, and a growing sense of uncertainty all pointed to trouble in the making. Yet this was a complex era. During this same period, the civilization that produced such uncertainty also created new engines of wealth, transformed its cities, and supported an explosion of creative thought and culture.

KEY TERMS

REVIEW, ANALYZE, AND ANTICIPATE

REVIEW THE PREVIOUS CHAPTER

Chapter 19—"Nationalism and Statebuilding"—analyzed the efforts to build national unity and strength between 1850 and 1870.

1. *In what ways did nationalism remain a powerful force in the decades after 1870?*

2. *Analyze how nationalism evolved during these later decades, comparing it with the nationalism of 1850–1870 as well as the ideology of nationalism of the early nineteenth century.*

ANALYZE THIS CHAPTER

Chapter 20—"Mass Politics and Imperial Domination"—examines the spreading demands for democracy and the West's imperial expansion between 1870 and 1914.

1. *In what ways were large numbers of people incorporated into politics during this period?*

2. *Why were some areas and groups still left out of the political arena in 1914?*

3. *Analyze the various causes for the rise of imperialism during this period.*

4. *For both Western and non-Western peoples, what consequences flowed from imperialism?*

ANTICIPATE THE NEXT CHAPTER

In Chapter 21—"Modern Life and the Culture of Progress"—the changes stemming from new industrial transformations and urban growth, as well as the culture of the West, will be traced.

1. *What sorts of social changes might be related to the statebuilding and rise of democracy during this period?*

2. *How might the continuing rise of science and technology support the West's imperial expansion?*

BEYOND THE CLASSROOM

DEMANDS FOR DEMOCRACY

Harrison, J.F.C. *Late Victorian Britain, 1875–1901.* London: Routledge, 1991. Examines British society and the experiences of the different social classes during the period.

Mayeur, Jean-Marie, and Madeleine Réberioux. *The Third Republic—From Its Origins to the Great War, 1871–1914.* Cambridge: Cambridge University Press, 1987. A solid survey of France during this period, stressing the politics of the republican government.

Wehler, Hans-Ulrich. *The German Empire, 1871–1918.* Leamington Spa, England: Berg Publishers, 1985. An important and controversial work that argues for continuity between the Second and Third Reichs.

INSIDERS AND OUTSIDERS: POLITICS OF THE EXTREMES

Hause, Steven C., and Anne R. Kenney. *Women's Suffrage and Social Politics in the French Third Republic.* Princeton, NJ: Princeton University Press,

1984. Examines all aspects of the women's suffrage movement in France from its origins to the years after the end of World War I.

Levine, Philippa. *Victorian Feminism.* Tallahassee: Florida State University Press, 1987. Examines women's involvement in various campaigns for their rights.

Lindemann, Albert S. *A History of European Socialism.* New Haven, CT: Yale University Press, 1983. An overview of the European socialist tradition from the Enlightenment to the 1980s.

Pulzer, P. *The Rise of Political Anti-Semitism in Germany and Austria.* Cambridge, MA: Harvard University Press, 1988. Studies the role of anti-Semitism in the world of central European politics.

Schorske, Carl E. *Fin-de-Siècle Vienna: Politics and Culture.* New York: Knopf, 1980. A classic study of the creative intellectual climate of Vienna that emphasizes the connections between culture and politics.

EMIGRATION: OVERSEAS AND ACROSS CONTINENTS

Hoerder, Dirk, and Leslie Page Moch, eds. *European Migrants—Global and Local Perspectives.* Boston: Northeastern University Press, 1996. A collection of articles by several scholars on the migrations of Europeans across the land and overseas.

Wolf, Eric. *Europe and the People Without History.* Berkeley, CA: University of California Press, 1983. An important cross-cultural perspective on the process and consequences of imperialism.

THE NEW IMPERIALISM: THE RACE FOR AFRICA AND ASIA

Doyle, Michael W. *Empires.* Ithaca, NY: Cornell University Press, 1986. A comparative examination of imperialism.

Headrick, Daniel R. *The Tentacles of Progress: Technology Transfer in the Age of Imperialism, 1850–1940.* New York: Oxford University Press, 1988. Argues that the poorer countries failed to develop under imperial rule despite the transfers of Western capital and technology.

Hochschild, Adam. *King Leopold's Ghost: A Study of Greed, Terror, and Heroism in Colonial Africa.* Boston: Houghton Mifflin, 1999. A chilling story of imperial brutality.

Wesseling, H.L. *Divide and Rule: The Partition of Africa, 1880–1914.* New York: Greenwood, 1996. A solid, well-written survey of this imperial conquest.

GLOBAL CONNECTIONS

Gelber, Harry. *Opium, Soldiers and Evangelicals.* London: Palgrave Macmillan, 2004. Revises standard views of the "Opium War."

www.mhhe.com/sherman3

- Unfamiliar words? See our Glossary at the back of the book for pronunciation and definitions.

- Need help studying? See our web page for map exercises, practice quizzes, and additional study resources.

- Need help writing a paper? Access hundreds of primary documents, maps, images, and a guide to writing history papers on our Primary Source Investigator site at **www.mhhe.com/psi**.

WILLIAM P. FRITH, *MANY HAPPY RETURNS OF THE DAY*

In this painting, a family gathers for a birthday. The rich clothing, carpeting, paintings on the wall, heavy
curtains, solid bricks showing through the window, and attentive servant on the left all mark this as an
urban middle-class home. In the center, haloed by a wreath, is the innocent "angel" birthday girl. Here is
the ideal of the happy home, the center of private life where men, women, and children celebrate together.
Yet the scene also reflects the contrasting gender spheres. The women and children gather comfortably. But
the father and grandfather—reading a newspaper—sit close to the window and to the outside, public world
of the modern city.

CHAPTER 21

MODERN LIFE AND THE CULTURE OF PROGRESS

WESTERN SOCIETY, 1850–1914

STUDY	The second industrial revolution ▪ The new urban landscape ▪ City life ▪ Private life ▪ Science and culture ▪ From optimism to uncertainty.
NOTICE	Connections between city life, private life, and culture.

In 1864, an observer described Milan in northern Italy as vibrant "without being feverish like Paris or London." Though Milan had become one of the great cultural centers in the newly unified Italian state, workers still lived along narrow, winding streets in the heart of this city. Everyone knew each other and spoke the local Milanese dialect. Citizens "huddled around the cathedral, like a family warming itself at the hearth."

This quaint image would not last long. Over the next thirty years, wide avenues and expensive "great white houses, all straight," replaced Milan's narrow streets and old dwellings. Each year thousands of immigrants—mostly peasants and artisans—streamed into the city looking for jobs and all kinds of other opportunities. In just one decade, the city's population grew by almost a third. By the 1890s, the center of Milan teemed with people from the city's outlying quarters and suburbs who traveled there to work, shop, or amuse themselves. They spoke the common Italian language and shoved "on and off the trams . . . day and night." More people purchased goods in the huge new department store near the cathedral than prayed in that Gothic church. Nearby, in the newly built Gallery, musicians, singers, businesspeople, shoppers, and diners congregated in the shops and cafes under a magnificent glass roof. Milan—like Paris, London, and other great cities in the West—had become a center of industry, growth, and culture—a thriving embodiment of modern life.

In the decades after 1850, industrialization pulled masses of Westerners to new jobs in cities like Milan. Urban growth began to overwhelm the West's centuries-old land-based society. In cities, the continuing spread of liberal ideas and the optimism of wealthy urban leaders created a culture of progress. Dominated by science, which seemed to promise so much, and by competitive values that served the up-and-coming middle class so well, this urban culture altered the ways people thought about the world and their place in it. Those who recognized these engines of change saw their civilization being pushed to modernity. In 1850, however, few understood what modernity meant or even how difficult the ride there could be.

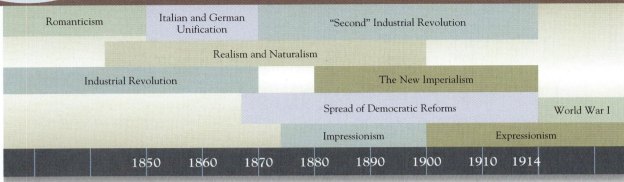

Romanticism		Italian and German Unification			"Second" Industrial Revolution					
			Realism and Naturalism							
Industrial Revolution					The New Imperialism					
					Spread of Democratic Reforms				World War I	
					Impressionism		Expressionism			
	1850	1860	1870	1880	1890	1900	1910	1914		

The Second Industrial Revolution

"Steam and electricity have conquered time and space to a greater extent during the last sixty years than all the preceding six hundred years," gushed a special issue of *The Illustrated London News* in 1897. Yet in 1850, most people knew little about the industrial revolution. Outside Britain and a few limited areas in the West, more people still lived in the countryside than in the cities, and more worked at home or in home workshops than in factories. Most had never set foot in a railway car. Even in the cities,

people probably made their living much as their parents had—as helpers in shops, domestics, artisans, merchants, and day laborers.

By 1914, this scenario had changed so drastically that even Britain had been left behind. Between 1850 and 1870, the coal mines, iron foundries, textile factories, steam engines, and railroads that had made Britain an industrial giant spread broadly into western and central Europe and North America. After 1870, new inventions, manufacturing processes, and methods for getting products to market and selling them rendered the earlier milestones of industrialization out of date. Science, technology, and industry marched hand in hand. Large-scale factories dwarfed the textile mills and iron foundries of the early industrial era, and huge department stores displayed endless goods to entice consumers. For the first time in history, people began to expect continuing economic growth. According to some historians, these developments created a "second industrial revolution."

Steel Leads the Way

Steel led the way in this new wave of industrialization. The Bessemer processes for removing impurities from molten iron speeded up and cheapened steel production, transforming it from an expensive luxury product into a strong, affordable improvement over iron. Figure 21.1, an 1880 photograph of the Krupp Steelworks, reveals the new technology and massive factories that produced steel and enabled countries such as Germany to become industrial leaders. On the left are the huge converters that turned iron into steel. Dwarfed in comparison, workers (in the foreground and around the converters)

■ FIGURE 21.1
The Krupp Steelworks, Germany, 1880.

toil to keep the process going. By 1914, the annual production of steel had risen more than fiftyfold since 1850. Figure 21.2 charts the growth of steel production between 1882 and 1912 and the countries that led in the creation of this crucial industrial material. Out of this steel, manufacturers made efficient tools and machines to fabricate metal, textile, leather, and wood products.

With advances in chemistry, textile manufacturers could now use inexpensive synthetic dyes to color their cloth, and paper manufacturers could process wood pulp more efficiently than ever. By 1914, new chemical-based fabrics and processes had *Chemicals* spawned a host of infant industries. Germany's chemical laboratories and their development of industrial uses for chemicals helped propel that nation ahead of Great Britain as an industrial leader.

Electricity and petroleum became practical sources of power, thanks to the invention of the electrical dynamo, the steam turbine, *Electricity and petroleum* and the internal combustion engine. By the end of the century, electric lamps glowed in city streets, large stores, and wealthy neighborhoods throughout Europe. Electricity powered factories and workshops and was the magic behind the refrigerators and vacuum cleaners starting to appear in middle-class homes.

NEW TRANSPORTATION AND COMMUNICATION NETWORKS

Getting around, moving things, and communicating became dramatically easier as well. Before 1850, few people had seen more of the world than they could view on foot or by cart or horseback. By 1914, millions traveled enormous distances each year. Even in China, Turkey, and *Railroad building* Brazil, trains chugged along, hauling people for astonishing stretches. This was the greatest era of railroad building in history, and with the railroads came hundreds of bridges and long tunnels. At the same time, huge steamships with steel hulls, turbine engines, and screw propellers replaced sailing ships. The opening of the Suez Canal (between the Mediterranean Sea and the Indian Ocean) in 1869 and the Panama Canal (between the Atlantic and Pacific Oceans) in 1914 cut thousands of miles off long sea voyages and brought the Western and non-Western worlds into closer contact.

However, the future lay with yet another revolutionary invention: the internal combustion engine. In 1887 the German inventor Gottlieb Daimler (1834–1900) attached his little combustion engine to *Internal combustion engine* a wagon—and the automobile was born. Two decades later in the United States, former bicycle mechanic Henry Ford (1863–1947) introduced the assembly line to the automobile industry. By 1914, cars, taxis, and trucks jammed city streets in Europe and America and created new demand for oil, rubber, and concrete.

Just as these new means of transportation linked millions of people physically, the telegraph and telephone connected them in a giant communication *Telegraph and telephone* network. In 1844, Samuel Morse sent a message by wire 40 miles from Baltimore to Washington. In 1866, ships laid telegraph cable across the Atlantic, enabling news to travel from London to New York as quickly as it had moved from one side of London to the other. Ten years later, Alexander Graham Bell (1847–1922), an American born in Scotland, invented the telephone.

THE BIRTH OF BIG BUSINESS

These telephone companies, railroads, shipping lines, steel mills, chemical plants, and new factories became too large for all but a very few individuals to finance. Capitalists now raised money by organizing corporations and selling shares of stock—partial ownership—to investors. Governments helped out by passing laws that limited stockholders' risk to only the money they invested. Luck helped, too, for the discovery of gold in California and Australia in the 1850s and 1860s, and in Alaska and South Africa later in the century, increased the supply of money. This was big business, and it was controlled by large banks and wealthy executives. These executives functioned much as heads of state, conferring with boards of directors and lesser

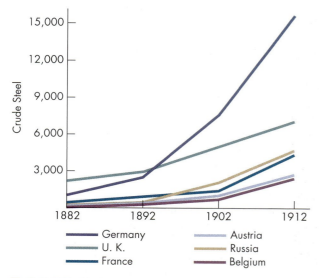

■ FIGURE 21.2

Steel production (thousands of metric tons).

executives. Under them were layers of managers who specialized in areas such as sales, finance, and production and who hired, fired, and supervised employees.

In this new world of business, the big and strong often destroyed the small and weak. Corporations combined into gigantic, monopolistic **Monopolies** trusts (called "cartels" in Germany) that commanded markets, prices, and wages. Rockefeller's Standard Oil trust in the United States and the I. G. Farben chemical cartel in Germany are examples of the spectacular business successes of the age. By 1914, big business controlled a large share of industrial production in the West. In Japan, too, which adapted quickly to Western industrialization, five giant corporations dominated three-quarters of that nation's industry.

THE LURE OF SHOPPING

With all the new technology, manufacturers habitually churned out more products than they could sell. So, **Department stores** merchants found new ways to create customer demand. Grandiose department stores, such as the Bon Marché in Paris and Bocconi's in Milan, rose up in major cities across the West. The stores displayed a dazzling array of enticing goods—ready-made clothes, furniture, rugs, umbrellas, stationery, toilet paper—a cornucopia of foreign and domestic temptations. Prices were fixed and aimed at the middle classes, but even members of the working class might afford some items. Posters announced "sales" to draw more people to their stores' massive glass and iron emporiums. Glossy catalogues mailed to potential customers in other cities and the countryside encouraged people to order the practical goods and the luxuries of modern urban life for delivery by the new national postal services.

As Figure 21.3 suggests, the stores become tourist attractions, places to spend leisure time, and leading promoters of consumption. This Parisian department store, with its dramatic central staircase, was designed like a theater for visitors as well as a building where a huge variety of goods could be purchased. Men, women, and children—themselves on display as much as the goods for sale—stroll through this monument to prosperity. By 1900, more than 15,000 people passed through the doors of the Bon Marché in Paris every day. Equally amazing, this shoppers' mecca was only one of twelve Parisian department stores that together employed almost 10,000 people. Department stores had come to represent the materialism of the cities.

WINNERS AND LOSERS IN THE RACE FOR WEALTH

In this intense economic struggle, some people flourished, others fell behind, and many worried about their future. Cycles of prosperity and recession made economic life precarious. New economic powers such as Germany and the United States rose to challenge and sometimes surpass mighty Britain, which failed to invest sufficiently in **Western and non-Western worlds** new processes and marketing techniques. Industrialization spread unevenly east to Russia—St. Petersburg alone would sprout more than nine hundred factories by 1914. Areas in southern and eastern Europe that held on to old ways of making a living fell further behind, although even in these poorer regions industrialization gained some footholds. Overseas, Australia and Canada began to industrialize, and Japan—with its new machines, factories, and railroads—became a major industrial power.

However, most of Latin America, Africa, and mainland Asia scarcely entered the industrial race before 1914. Although Latin America nations boasted some railway lines and substantial foreign trade, they lacked the machinery and manufacturing that marked industrial economies (see Global Connections, page 648). A similar pattern held in

■ FIGURE 21.3

A Paris department store.

mainland Asia and most of Africa, which produced cash crops and raw materials to trade to the industrialized West for manufactured goods but were unable to develop industrial economies.

Did this second industrial revolution make life better overall for Westerners? As we saw with our discussion of the first industrial revolution in Chapter 17, this question is difficult to answer. **New wealth** Statistically, the answer is yes. It certainly paid to be living in the industrializing nations of the West. In these thriving regions, most people benefited from the new wealth—even those living outside the cities. Food prices came down, and larger farms, chemical fertilizers, and threshing machines boosted harvests and lowered costs. Agricultural producers in North America, Argentina, and Australia sent inexpensive grains and meat in new, refrigerated ships. Prices for manufactured products also dropped as the new machines and processes made production more efficient. With declining prices came a rise in real wages for workers, which almost doubled in Britain between 1850 and 1914. Meat, dairy products, sugar, tea, and coffee were no longer luxuries. People snapped up previously out-of-reach manufactured goods. With care and luck, they even saved a bit of money for hard times.

Those hard times visited some more than others, and here the old pattern held true. The middle classes benefited more than the working classes, skilled workers more than unskilled, and owners of **Hard times** large farms more than agricultural laborers. Nor did the new wealth end misery for those at the bottom of the socioeconomic ladder. Many people remained mired in poverty. Among workers, few could expect to retire without sinking into dependence or impoverishment, let alone ease into the dream of a comfortable cottage with a small garden. The gaps between rich and poor were all too apparent. The upper 20 percent of the population generally received more of a nation's income than the remaining 80 percent. Every day the urban poor could see but not afford the fine apartments, carriages, and clothes of the wealthy.

THE NEW URBAN LANDSCAPE

City life became the new norm for masses of people in the West. Many rural villages declined or died, slowly in some areas, quickly in others. People from outside the local community moved in, bought the land, and hired migrant laborers to work it. Residents flocked to the cities, and those who had established themselves there stayed. An observer in 1899 reflected the experience of millions: "[T]he most re-markable social phenomenon of the present century is the concentration of population in cities." Europe's population ballooned from 270 million in 1850 to 450 million in 1914, and well over half of western Europeans lived in cities. In Britain, only 8 percent of the work force remained in the countryside. London, Europe's greatest urban center, grew from 2.5 million in 1850 to more than 4.5 million in 1914.

REBUILDING CITIES

As these numbers multiplied everywhere, even the physical foundations of cities changed. Urban centers grew out, up, and below ground. Milan, the thriving Italian center described at the beginning of this chapter, was not the only city to rebuild. Governments, entrepreneurs, and speculators tore apart centuries-old housing and winding streets in Paris, Vienna, Brussels, Stockholm, Barcelona, Cologne, and Mexico City. In place of these older features, they constructed broad, tree-lined avenues, parks, fashionable apartment houses, department stores, fancy cafes, government buildings, museums, hospitals, opera houses, schools, and libraries. New neighborhoods, open spaces, transportation systems, and underground water and sewer systems transformed the face and substance of city life.

Paris led the way in this wave of reconstruction. In the French capital, Emperor Napoleon III and his technocratic administrator, Baron Haussmann, initiated the most ambitious plans for demolishing some of the oldest and poorest neighborhoods. According to Napoleon, Haussmann, and their advisors, these reconstruction efforts offered several important benefits. Doctors and reformers argued that filth from overcrowding caused the diseases that often swept though Paris. Wide streets and open spaces, they explained, would let in much-needed fresh air. But those wide streets also gave governments a political advantage: They deterred people from again throwing up revolutionary barricades to fight the forces of order, as they had in 1848, and afforded troops ready access to working-class areas. Finally, reconstruction projects generated untold wealth for investors, speculators, influence brokers, schemers, architects, engineers, and workers from all over France.

As in Milan, the new construction drove the poor out of the center of Paris to the east end or into working-class suburbs. Wealthier Parisians felt little sympathy. After all, they reasoned, the capital city represented the nation in the eyes of citizens and visitors alike. As Haussman explained, "The splendor of this city reflects on the whole country." The power, wealth, beauty, and modernity of Paris must not be marred by images of poverty and misfortune.

Economic Transformation in Latin America

CONSIDER

■ **Consider** the effects of the "second industrial revolution" on Latin American nations. **Notice** what problems this economic transformation may have posed for Latin America.

In 1855, the Yankee speculator and entrepreneur Henry Meiggs arrived in Santiago, Chile, with ambitious plans to introduce railroads into that South American nation. By 1867, his company had built more than two hundred miles of railroad lines, many of them across Chile's difficult coastal mountain range. A year later, Meiggs moved north to Peru, which had only sixty miles of track under operation. At a banquet attended by the social elite of Lima, Peru's capital, he promised that his railroads would lead to "a great social revolution." He described the locomotive as "that irresistible battering ram of modern civilization" whose "whistle will awaken the native race from . . . lethargy. . . ." By the time of Meigg's death in 1877, this man whom Peruvians called the "Messiah of the Railway" had built over seven hundred miles of track, most of them up into the steep Andes and along two-mile-high plateaus. The entrepreneur had enlisted the help of capital and experts from Europe; machinery from the United States; and more than twenty thousand workers from Peru, Chile, Bolivia and China.

Chile's and Peru's experience with Meiggs and his railroads mirrors similar developments unfolding throughout Latin America between 1850 and 1914. People, money, and machinery flowed from Western Europe across the Atlantic to the Americas, and international trade mushroomed. Latin America's subsistence economies blossomed into market economies that exported crops and raw materials to Europe—such as bananas, coffee, sugar, tobacco, nitrates, copper, rubber, cocoa, wheat, and beef. In exchange, Europeans sent industrial goods. This transformation required new railroads, steamships utilities, communications, harbors, refrigeration facilities, and banks. However, Latin American countries lacked the capital to finance these investments. Spotting a hot opportunity, British, French, German, Belgian, and North American investors sent their money (sometimes in the hands of men such as Meiggs) to fill the voids.

Some larger Latin American countries flourished, thanks to all this trade and economic development. Argentina's economy, for example, expanded at about 5 percent per year between 1880 and 1914. And the population of major Latin American cities such as Montevideo, Uraguay; Buenos Aires, Argentina; Sao Paulo, Brazil; and Rio de Janerio, Brazil, more than tripled during the generation that preceded World War I. Not surprisingly, the large landowners and elites in these cities benefited the most from the new economic activity. So did foreigners. British companies owned most of Argentina's meat-processing plants, railways, and telegraph lines as well as many of its banks and merchant houses. This pattern showed up elsewhere in Latin America as well. In Mexico, for example, Belgian, Yankee, and English investors put up much of the money for that nation's railroads. The French controlled the large Mexican department stores; the Germans, the hardware business. North Americans dominated the cement industry, and the Spanish and French ran the textile industry.

Not everyone applauded these developments. "No one can deny the benefits that the railroads, the gas plants, the street cars, and the telegraph and telephone lines have brought to us," admitted the Argentine socialist Juan Bautista Justo in 1896. But "our country is tributary to England. Every year millions of gold pesos leave here and go to the stockholders of English enterprises that are established in Argentina." Others voiced the same sentiments elsewhere. Francisco Garcia Calderon, a Peruvian diplomat and writer, complained, "South America cannot dispense with the influence of the Anglo-Saxon North, with its exuberant wealth and its industries."

Despite such lamentations, there was no turning back. During the decade that followed World War I, Rudyard Kipling described Sao Paulo as "a metropolis" where "cars and trucks move everywhere, like electrons in the physics texts, across grids of streetcar lines." Outside the city coffee plantations stretched "as far as the eye could reach, the evenly-spaced twelve-foot trees and their reddening berries covered the rolling hills." The wave of economic transformation that began in Western Europe had swept through Latin America and was headed for the rest of the world.

SEWERS AND SUBWAYS

Below Europe's city streets, less glamorous but no less important projects hummed along. In 1850, most houses in Europe's major cities did not have running water. Sewage in cities such as Berlin still ran in open gutters, creating an atmosphere of filth and tremendous stench. During the following decades, these standards began to change. First in London and then elsewhere, engineers and workers built water and sewer systems. Doctors, reformers, and planners led the drive to bring in freshwater in aqueducts or pipes from sources upstream and to create hundreds of miles of underground sewers to carry waste downstream. These measures made urban life healthier and more comfortable than before.

More than water and waste moved below the city, however. In 1863, London's underground railway opened. Over the next fifty years, Paris and New York built subways of their own. Along with carriages, trams, and railroads, the efficient, predictable subways enabled people to shop and work in places farther from home than ever. People moved their residences out of crowded urban centers to city fringes and suburbs—whether upscale neighborhoods for the middle class or less expensive areas for workers.

City People

Who were these people filling the cities of the West? How did they make their way in life, so far away from the land and surrounded by industrial advances and new wealth? Part of the answer is revealed in Figure 21.4, a mid-century engraving of a typical Parisian apartment house. At this time, the city's various social classes still lived in close proximity but in different conditions. The drawing portrays the wealthy bourgeoisie living on the first (American second) floor in luxurious comfort; above them lives a bourgeois family of lesser means. The lower classes and aspiring artists—dancing and drinking instead of working, having too many children, and being unable to pay their bills—live on the bottom and upper floors in increasing poverty, thanks to their imprudence.

On Top of It All: The Urban Elite

At the top of the urban social order was a small, elite class of wealthy aristocrats and the richest of the bourgeoisie—the millionaire factory owners, merchants, and bankers. Amounting to less than 1 percent of the population, these people socialized together, turned to each other for help, and intermarried. Through strategic matchmaking, new wealth from the daughter or son of an American captain of industry or banker might enable an aristocratic family to maintain its position. More often, however, aristocrats kept their positions by making shrewd investments, serving governments, holding on to top spots in the military and diplomatic corps, and wisely managing their lands and businesses. They, along with members entering their ranks, had prestige but not the formal privileges that their eighteenth-century predecessors had enjoyed.

Those who had been born into aristocratic families clung to what was left of the old lifestyle. Those aspiring to the aristocratic life used their money to copy that lifestyle. These newly rich bought estate houses in the country and opulent townhouses along the best avenues and parks, attended fancy balls, took hunting trips to Africa, and supported large staffs of servants. They also kept up with the latest fashions and made grand gestures toward cultural and philanthropic activities. However, a few rules of the aristocratic game had changed. Obvious arrogance was frowned upon, as this elite made an effort to comply with middle-class morality. At the very least, they strove to appear responsible, domestic, and religious. Of course, their children got the best of everything. In every way, these elites were truly the upper crust, on top and intent on staying there.

Pride and Success: The "Solid" Middle Class

Well below this upper crust, the "solid" bourgeoisie held the better jobs, lived in the finer apartments, dined at fashionable restaurants, and commanded at least one good servant. These were the families of small factory owners, merchants, managers, doctors, druggists, local bankers, lawyers, professors, and architects who earned and spent more money than most.

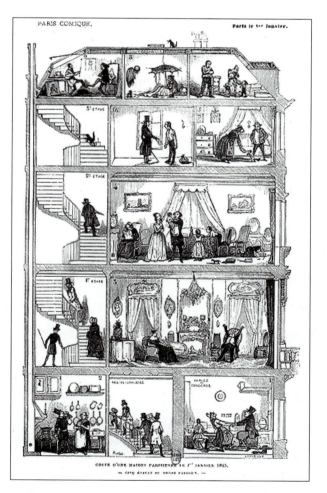

■ FIGURE 21.4

Bertall, The urban classes.

Worried about competitors from below, many middle-class men established "professional" associations designed to keep standards up and rivals down. Nor did they open their professions to women (see Document 21.1). Wives and daughters, they intoned, "best" not work for pay. Beliefs that women and men belonged in "separate spheres"—women at home, men in the public world of work—persisted. "Of all those acquirements, which more particularly belong to the feminine character," explained Isabella Mary Mayson Beeton in her best-selling advice book for women, "there are none which take a higher rank . . . than such as enter into a knowledge of household duties; for on these are perpetually dependent the happiness, comfort, and well-being of a family."

Women and work

Some women managed to swim against the current, however. They engaged in philanthropic activities—in support of the poor and uneducated, or against alcohol and prostitution. British philanthropist Angela Burdette-Coutts (1814–1906), for example, gave away a fortune to schools and housing for the poor. In France, many wealthy women followed the example of Empress Eugénie (consort of Napoleon III), who supported societies that provided assistance to new mothers. In the United States, educated middle-class women staffed hundreds of settlement houses in urban centers that helped immigrants adjust to the customs and language of their new country as well as middle-class values. Only a few women managed to carve out careers in business, teaching, writing, or painting. Exclusion from universities kept most ambitious upper-middle-class women from pursuing lucrative professions, though schools such as Queens College in Britain and the Female Medical

College of Pennsylvania promised some professional opportunities to women.

If not arrogant, this bourgeoisie was proud. Who else better represented their civilization? As they saw it, success flowed from character, ability, and effort; in a world open to talent, rewards came from achievement. These people praised discipline, control, and respectability, while attacking public drunkenness, emotional outbursts, and—especially in "Victorian" Britain—open displays of sexual affection. In addition, they respected Christian morality and marital fidelity. Cleanliness went hand in hand *Values* with purity and modernity, as did running water for regular baths and several changes of clothes. Certainly, they argued, all good people should live up to these standards, at least in appearance.

HARDWORKING AND HOPEFUL: THE LOWER MIDDLE CLASS

Those just below the solid bourgeoisie probably tried as hard as any group to succeed in modern society. These lower-middle-class people performed skilled services as tellers in banks, sorters in mailrooms, and salespeople in department stores. Reading, writing, and mathematical skills (and for more and more, the new typewriter) enabled thousands to become schoolteachers, postal workers, and clerks in places from government agencies and insurance firms to accounting offices and train stations. Some of these lower-paying "white-collar jobs" became open to educated women, particularly if they were unmarried.

Lower-middle-class people made their living in settings that sometimes resembled factories. Figure 21.5 shows clerks working in the offices of Cadbury's, the chocolate firm described in Chapter 17. In this huge room, all the chairs, desks, and tasks seem the same. All the clerks are men, and even their clothes look almost identical. Figure 21.6 shows a French telephone exchange, also set in a large room in which the chairs, fixtures, and activities are similar. Here the employees are all middle-class women, with the exception of male supervisors and a boy who delivers messages. As this image shows, even when jobs opened for middle-class women, they were often separate from men's work and of lower status.

With the heightening tempo of industrialization, these lower-middle-class occupations multiplied. People might move up the economic ladder, and better-off workers could hope to see their educated *Social mobility* children rising into this class. In turn, a few children from lower-middle ranks might move into the also-expanding solid middle class. Although moving up remained more

■ FIGURE 21.5
Modern office work for men.

■ DOCUMENT 21.1

John Stuart Mill Argues for Women's Rights

During the last decades of the nineteenth century, a number of observers commented on the position of women in Western societies and argued for women's rights. One of the most prominent and influential was John Stuart Mill, who published his essay, "The Subjection of Women," in 1869. In the following excerpt from that work, Mill places the question of women's subordination within the context of human progress and morality. ■ **Why,** *according to Mill, is the legal subordination of one sex to the other wrong?* ■ **In what ways** *is the liberation of women related to "the peculiar character of the modern world"?*

The principle which regulates the existing social relations between the two sexes—the legal subordination of one sex to the other—is wrong in itself, and now one of the chief hindrances to human improvement; and that it ought to be replaced by a principle of perfect equality, admitting no power or privilege on the one side, nor disability on the other.

" . . . The masters of all other slaves rely, for maintaining obedience, on fear; either fear of themselves, or religious fears. The masters of women wanted more than simple obedience, and they turned the whole force of education to effect their purpose. All women are brought up from the very earliest years in the belief that their ideal of character is the very opposite to that of men; not self-will, and government by self-control, but submission, and yielding to the control of others. All the moralities tell them that it is the duty of women, and all the current sentimentalities that it is their nature, to live for others; to make complete abnegation of themselves, and to have no life but in their affections. . . .

"For what is the peculiar character of the modern world—the difference which chiefly distinguishes modern institutions, modern social ideas, modern life itself, from those of times long past? It is, that human beings are no longer born to their place in life, and chained down by an inexorable bond to the place they are born to, but are free to employ their faculties, and such favourable chances as offer, to achieve the lot which may appear to them most desirable.

"If this general principle of social and economical sciences is . . . true, we ought to act as if we believed it, and not to ordain that to be born a girl instead of a boy, any more than to be born black instead of white, or a commoner instead of a nobleman, shall decide the person's position through all life. . . .

Source: John Stuart Mill, "The Subjection of Women," *Three Essays* (Oxford: Oxford University Press, 1975).

the exception than the rule, the possibilities were far greater than before 1850. By 1914, the middle classes overall had grown from between 3 and 10 percent of the population to more than 20 percent in much of the West.

THE "OTHER HALF": THE WORKING CLASSES

Unlike the elites and the middle classes, the working classes lived on crowded side streets, the poorer east side of cities such as London or Paris, or the edge of town where land and rents were cheaper. Though better off than before 1850, they still faced the threat of job loss, which could send them into poverty in an instant.

Even employed workers struggled to make ends meet. A new demand for certain skilled work helped some. Those who could read directions; build or repair machines; or who were printers, plumbers, or cabinetmakers earned respectable wages. They might also join unions and demand reforms. Other skilled workers lost out, for factory owners fit laborers to jobs that had become nothing more than mindless,

repetitive tasks. Automaker Henry Ford expressed the views of many industrial managers toward this kind of labor: "I could not possibly do the same thing day in and day out, but . . . to the majority of minds,

■ FIGURE 21.6

French telephone exchange.

repetition holds no terrors. . . . The average worker, I am sorry to say, . . . wants a job in which he does not have to think." Whether former artisans with obsolete skills or migrants from the countryside, these workers earned paltry wages and worked at an exhausting pace. They and their children tended to remain low-paid industrial laborers for the rest of their lives.

Despite legislation restricting women from certain jobs, many labored outside and inside the home. Jeanne Bouvier, a Frenchwoman born in 1865, worked as millions of other working-class women did. When she was 11 years old, she took her first job in a silk factory near Lyons. Three years later, she moved to Paris, where she worked as a domestic and then in the hatmaking industry. Later, she worked a twelve-hour day as a seamstress and did piecework on her own.

In addition to their jobs in factories and small shops, many women took in work at home finishing clothes, polishing items for sale, wrapping chocolates, or decorating toys. Some of the new machines of industry even added to the demand for this older piecework. For example, Singer's sewing machine, invented in the 1850s, enabled entrepreneurs to hire women for low wages to work at home or in small "sweatshops." Such women proved especially appealing to these employers because they were easy to fire and posed little threat of forming a union or going on strike.

Still more women worked in traditional urban jobs. Domestic servants could count on meals and housing and perhaps even some savings from their salaries. On the other hand, they suffered from the whims of their employers and the threat of sexual abuse. Women in laundries labored at drudgery for low wages, although some of them enjoyed the sense of comradeship that came with the job at times. The growth of cities may have increased the work available to these women, but the machinery of the industrial revolution did not yet ease job conditions for them.

Léon Frédérick (1856–1940), for a time Belgium's most famous painter, tried to encompass all stages of a worker's life in a large triptych (Figure 21.7). In the foreground of the central panel, children on the right play cards, while on the left they carry and nibble bread. Their parents and young couples stand just behind them, and in the background are the aged members of the working class whose ultimate fate is marked by the distant but approaching funeral coach. The left panel depicts the man's work world, where men of all ages, from adolescence to old age, engage in manual labor or observe it. In the foreground they are digging, and in the middle ground they struggle with heavy beams. Behind them are the factories where they work. The right panel shows the women's world, all mothering and nurturing with babies in their arms and at their breasts. Behind them are market stalls where they shop. Here is a vision of workers' lives in a nutshell: hard manual labor for men, child rearing and food preparation for women, and at the end, old age and death for all.

What to Do About "Them"

Members of the middle classes looked upon their working-class counterparts with a mixture of fear and sympathy: fear that these were "dangerous" people who might rise in revolt, commit crimes, or create disorder, and sympathy for the harshness of working-class life. Most middle-class people agreed with the popular writer Samuel Smiles that the working classes suffered from their own faults rather than injustices in the social system: "no laws . . . can make the idle industrious, the thriftless provident, or the drunken sober. Such reforms can only be effected by means of individual action, economy, and self-denial."

However, other members of the middle-class—especially younger, college-educated people who were also connected to religious causes—joined organizations to ease the plight of the urban poor. With high optimism and idealism, they established clinics, settlement houses, and maternal-wellness societies. Thousands of middle- and upper-class women visited the poor; ran schools; and inspected asylums, workhouses, and prisons. One Spanish charity worker wrote a guide for visitors to the poor: "In viewing their faults, vices, and crimes, we must ask ourselves this question: Would the poor be what they are, if we were what we ought to be?" Some of these workers spread birth-control information; others touted the benefits of religion. Women's groups in particular distributed prayer books to the poor or sold Bibles to raise money to aid the needy—a reflection of the still close link between the churches and charitable work. Still others tried to help the poor through political activism, joining socialist organizations such as the Fabian Society in London, which decried the capitalist system as unjust and inefficient.

Sports and Leisure in the Cities

Building Character Through Athletics

For turn-of-the-century Europeans who had the time and money, city life could be fun. New forms of recreation and sports not only offered entertaining diversions but also built character values important for industry and war. Soccer, rugby, and cricket, once

Léon Frédéric, *The Stages of a Worker's Life*, 1895

■ FIGURE 21.7

In 1895, Belgian artist Léon Frédéric completed these three panels depicting urban workers. ■ **In what ways** does the content of this work fit with its title, *The Stages of a Worker's Life?* ■ **Contrast** the roles played by men, women, and children in this painting. ■ **What** impression of working class life do you think the painter intended to convey to viewers? ■ **Consider** your own reaction to this painting.

games only for schoolchildren, became extremely popular, competitive team sports for adults. In 1901, over 100,000 attended a championship game of soccer in Britain. The emphasis on teamwork, competition, and discipline in the sports world reflected the qualities of industrial work and military service so prized during the era. Other new sports, such as bicycle and auto racing, stressed the speed and power of machines; by no coincidence, industrial firms sponsored some of these contests. Even the growth of scouting and, in Germany, the "wandering youth" clubs revealed the belief that good character required physical vigor and outdoor living. Accordingly, the modern Olympic games—stressing competition and nationalism—were established during this period, with the first games held in Athens in 1896.

Women's sports were less professional and less competitive than men's. Even scouting for girls was designed to instill homemaking values. But women did take to bicycles, despite warnings from the old guard that the loose clothing necessary for bicycling was unfeminine, that the activity would damage enthusiasts' ability to have children, and that women might inappropriately experience sexual pleasure from riding.

THE NEW TOURIST

Increasingly, people vacationed away from the cities. More and more, people left town. Those who had the means might imitate the eighteenth-century aristocratic habit of visiting the great cities, museums, and monuments of Europe. Others traveled to resorts on the Mediterranean coast, the Alps, or the shores of the Baltic Sea. By 1890, some 100,000 people visited the resort town of Vichy in central France to "take the waters" (cure their ills), relax, and socialize. Tourism became so popular that special books appeared, and professionally organized tours formed to guide people on their travels.

Workers usually lacked the time or money for such luxuries. Some managed short trips on trains that left cities every day for the coast, perhaps to Dieppe in France or Brighton in England, where piers and amusement parks beckoned. Most, however, stayed in the cities. There, some went to café concerts to see singers, comedians, jugglers, and acrobats. Others attended theaters featuring fast dancing or enjoyed boxing matches, vaudeville shows, and (after the turn of the century) movies.

PRIVATE LIFE: TOGETHER AND ALONE AT HOME

As the tempo of life in factories, stores, government offices, and streets increased, private life grew more precious. The individualism trumpeted by the liberal bourgeoisie accentuated the longing to withdraw from the public arena into the family, the home, and the self. The personal—one's body, sexuality, and internal life—became a subject of intense fascination. The home—the realm of the family protected by walls and locked doors—was the center of private life.

FAMILY: THE PROMISE OF HAPPINESS

People believed in the family. Like a religion, the family promised happiness in a difficult world, a meaning that would extend beyond death, and a sacred place free from intrusion by the outside world. As much as their means permitted, people celebrated the family through daily gatherings at meals and special occasions such as weddings, vacations, and birthdays (see the painting on p. 642). For individuals, these occasions marked points in their own life cycles. At more private moments, the family home served as a place where individuals shared emotions, or perhaps confessed silently or in a diary to themselves in the solitude of a bedroom.

More than ever, people recorded moments of private life in letters, diaries, and photographs. Families exchanged thousands of letters over a lifetime that told of children, deaths, visits, and health. Such correspondence held the family together when

Recording private life

travel and migration to different cities threatened to pull it apart. Diaries of the day reveal much self-concern and introspection. One French woman explained, "When I am alone, I have plenty to do in following the movement of my ideas and impressions, in exploring myself, in examining my dispositions and my various ways of being, in drawing the best out of myself, in registering the ideas that come to me by chance or that are suggested to me by my reading." People took photographs to capture family occasions—from baptisms to Sunday meals and partings—especially after the invention of the small Kodak camera in the 1880s. They carefully enshrined these photographs in frames and collected them in well-organized albums.

A HOME OF ONE'S OWN

The dream of family life and privacy required having a home of one's own—a private kingdom apart from city and society. But home had another purpose as well: It announced the material success of the bourgeoisie and the pleasures of private life.

As revealed in the 1877 painting of a Paris interior shown in Figure 21.8, the typical bourgeois apartment resembled an antique shop, overdecorated in no particular style and bulging with possessions. Heavy drapes hang over the walls and windows, multiple carpets cover the floors, fabrics ornament the mantelpieces and furniture, and tassels dangle everywhere. In such a home, family members could gaze at the many prints and paintings, enjoy music played by an elder daughter on the piano, read a novel in the library, and stay informed by subscribing to journals. Small, private gardens or potted plants and painted landscapes completed the picture by offering a way to appreciate nature.

Servants shared middle-class homes, but remained on the fringes of the family's private life. Relegated to their own small quarters in the attic or basement, servants had little freedom to move about the house at their leisure or take part in their employers' lives. Indeed, with the era's emphasis on both individualism and privacy, employers increasingly saw servants as potential intruders into private life. The bedroom and bathroom became off limits, and people complained about how hard it was to find "good," affordable servants. By the turn of the century, many middle-class families managed with just a single female domestic, or none at all.

Servants

■ FIGURE 21.8

Mihaly Munkacsy, *Paris Interior*, 1877.

■ DOCUMENT 21.2

Beeton's Guide for Women

Mrs. Beeton's Book of Household Management became the most popular "guidebook" for the proper middle-class woman in Victorian England. It covered topics from account keeping and the importance of cleanliness to strategies for hiring domestics. In the following selection, Isabella Beeton describes the overall role of the "mistress of a house," proper dress, and the correct treatment of servants. ■ **What** *qualities does Beeton stress?* ■ **What** *attitudes toward women does this selection reflect?*

1. As with the Commander of an Army, or the leader of any enterprise, so is it with the mistress of a house. Her spirit will be seen through the whole establishment; and just in proportion as she performs her duties intelligently and thoroughly, so will her domestics follow in her path. Of all those acquirements, which more particularly belong to the feminine character, there are none which take a higher rank, in our estimation, than such as enter into a knowledge of household duties; for on these are perpetually dependent the happiness, comfort, and well-being of a family.

* * *

13. The Dress of the Mistress should always be adapted to her circumstances, and be varied with different occasions. Thus, at breakfast she should be attired in a very neat and simple manner, wearing no ornaments. If this dress should decidedly pertain only to the breakfast-hour, and be specially suited for such domestic occupations as usually follow that meal, then it would be well to exchange it before the time for receiving visitors, if the mistress be in the habit of doing so.

* * *

19. The Treatment of Servants is of the highest possible moment, as well to the mistress as to the domestics themselves. On the head of the house the latter will naturally fix their attention, and if they perceive that the mistress's conduct is regulated by high and correct principles, they will not fail to respect her. If, also, a benevolent desire is shown to promote their comfort, at the same time that a steady performance of their duty is exacted, then their respect will not be unmingled with affection, and they will be still more solicitous to continue to deserve her favour.

Source: Isabella Beeton, *Mrs. Beeton's Book of Household Management* (Chancellor Press, 1982).

For the typical middle-class man, home was a retreat from public life, to be savored at the end of the workday or on weekends. For the middle-class woman, it was much more. Society glorified her domestic role more than ever. No longer would she be praised for doing "productive" work such as managing a husband's shop. Instead, she orchestrated every aspect of the family's home life, managing the meals, chores, visits, and guests. Her highest duty, however, was to bear and raise children. No longer was reproduction regarded as simply a natural function: It had become a complex, demanding activity. Most likely, a middle-class woman had fewer children than her mother, but she was expected to lavish greater attention on them. Her children would probably remain at home through adolescence, though many families sent their offspring to boarding schools. To help women meet all these expectations, books, magazines, pamphlets, and advice columns offered tips on how to attract a man and marry well; manage a household; sharpen "home economics" skills; and cultivate an appropriate social life that included teas, afternoon visits, and dinner parties.

At the same time, disturbing cross currents started to undermine this picture of the home and women's role in it. As Document 21.2 indicates, prominent people circulated new ideas about the restrictions imposed on women. Many women demanded more independent lives, even choosing to live outside the confines of the middle-class home. The British reformer Florence Nightingale (1820–1910) complained of "the petty grinding tyranny of a good English family," refused to marry, and helped found the modern profession of nursing (see the Biography in Chapter 19). A few occupations outside the home were gradually opened to middle-class women, and some women entered universities and professions. Growing numbers of "new women" lived in women's clubs or apartments, dressed more practically, and did more "daring" things such as traveling alone and entering the public space as activists.

> **Women's roles**

POOR HOUSING

Workers could not afford to draw such sharp lines between public and private life. Their homes, typically only one or two rooms in deteriorating buildings, rarely fulfilled all their needs. Often they relocated from one residence to another, carrying what they could. In some cases, they moved so as to search for something slightly better; in others, they sought to avoid a landlord demanding back rent.

The loss of a job might well doom a family to homelessness. With little hope of saving enough to pay for decent housing, workers tended to spend their extra money on clothes to "cut a good figure" and thereby present a well-groomed image in their public lives. For them, the city streets held far more promise than the buildings in which they lived. While the bourgeoisie retreated into homes or private clubs, workers used the public buildings, streets, and spaces of the city for their social and even private lives.

Working-class women enjoyed neither the space, furnishings, nor servants that graced the typical middle-class home. They usually worked at a factory or did poorly paid piece-work at home, where they could care for their children. If their children seemed more unruly and independent than those of the middle classes, moralists condemned these mothers for failing to create a "proper" home life. Such critics ignored the fact that working-class women lacked the money needed to cultivate the "ideal" family life. Worse, this disapproval helped employers justify paying these women less than men and treating them poorly.

Working-class women

INTIMACY AND MORALITY

Private life for working-class families was burdened by tensions involving basic survival. Middle-class families experienced tensions, too, but of a different sort. Founded on love, companionship, and intimacy, the middle-class family could become a pressure cooker of conflicting feelings and desires, of guilt and shame, of misunderstood communication and resentment. Family members often fought over money, but the confining expectations of intimacy could be worse. "Do not admit anyone else into our private life, into our thoughts," counseled a French man to his prospective wife in 1873. People understood such warnings. The home was a center of secrecy. More often than not, at the heart of that secrecy was sex.

For Britain's middle classes in particular, this era witnessed the height of **Victorian** sexual morality. Sex was supposed to be little discussed and limited to the marriage bed, enclosed in a separate "master" bedroom with locked doors. Sexual problems "shouldn't arise," but if they did, "enlightened" sufferers might turn to their doctor—the expert on sex, hygiene, and morality all rolled into one. Mixing moralisms with an image of scientific authority, most doctors confirmed the standard views of other commentators: healthy and prudent sexuality could take place only within the marriage. Affairs risked scandal (especially for the woman) and illegitimacy. Sex with prostitutes was unhygienic and somehow dangerous to the race. Doctors vaguely connected prostitu-

Victorian morality

tion, syphilis, tuberculosis, and alcoholism as physical and social "scourges," all resulting from "venereal excesses." Most often, they blamed women for being prostitutes, for forcing their husbands to visit prostitutes, or for having inappropriate sexual appetites.

Masturbation also caught the attention of doctors, priests, and parents. Physicians warned men that masturbation would drain their strength. They condemned masturbation by females even more strongly. To prevent youths from "abusing themselves," they prescribed orthopedic devices, special bandages, and belts.

As for homosexuality, people viewed it in an even worse light. Doctors labeled it a sickness or psychological disorder. Newspapers added to the public condemnation of homosexuality by reporting "scandalous" affairs among public figures and "uncovering" homosexual subcultures. The trial and imprisonment for gross indecency of the famed British author Oscar Wilde (1854–1900) in 1895 promoted a new awareness of homosexuality while revealing how far officials and the public would go to denounce it.

SEXUAL REALITIES

Despite these idealized, restrictive notions about proper sexual conduct, reality was quite different. Somehow people, especially the middle classes, discussed sex enough to limit births. While many used the old methods—abstinence and withdrawal—new information and methods also became available. Men began using condoms, and women douched or used diaphragms and sponges soaked in disinfectants. Many resorted to abortion as a method of birth control, particularly in cases of illegitimacy.

Birth control

These methods seem to have worked. The birthrate declined in these years. In France, for example, it dropped from 33 per 1,000 in 1800 to 19 per 1,000 in 1910. Many people chose to limit births for economic reasons. As people moved from farms to the cities, they no longer needed so many children to help with the work. In the cities, the increasing costs of raising children deterred couples from having large families. Yet successful birth control among the middle classes caused concern, for many worried that the "best" of society were not reproducing themselves as quickly as the "poor" and "uncompetitive." Commentators argued that "good" families needed more children. Nationalists complained that competing states or "alien peoples" would overwhelm their nation or "race" if "the fittest" did not increase their fertility.

Certainly actual sexual behavior failed to live up to the standards of Victorian moralists. The "best" people had "affairs," and illegitimacy remained high. Deadly sexually transmitted diseases rose and spread widely among all classes. In addition, prostitution thrived in many urban areas. Tens of thousands of prostitutes in the largest cities displayed themselves on streets and in city parks and in windows and doorways. Some worked in bars or elegant brothels for a more select clientele. Working-class women who lost jobs, domestic servants dismissed because of pregnancy, or young women on their own might turn to prostitution to survive. Men of all classes patronized prostitutes. Governments tried to control prostitution, requiring medical exams of prostitutes and limiting its practice to certain districts. Worse than these inconveniences were the risks of this life. Prostitutes were often subjected to violence, the most famous example of which was the serial killings committed by "Jack the Ripper" in London in the late 1880s.

By the end of the century, new attitudes, or perhaps the weight of reality, broke down some of the more restrictive notions of Victorian sexual propriety. More people accepted and expected mutual sexual enjoyment within marriage, and people became educated about the physical facts of sexual contact. *New attitudes* Books, pamphlets, and talks about sex enabled women and men to read about the subject and sometimes even discuss it openly. Doctors, psychologists, and intellectuals began to study sex and see that it played a major role in individuals' sense of identity.

PSYCHIC STRESS AND ALCOHOLISM

Growing concern with sex and private life in this period reflected a broader preoccupation with psychological well-being. Anxieties and emotional disorders seemed all too common. Women especially suffered from fits, paralysis, convulsions, numbness, headaches, oversensitivity to light, digestive disorders, and fatigue. Doctors listened, prescribed pills, and suggested expensive cures such as surgery and health-spa retreats. They sometimes blamed the complexities of city life or the noise and speed of modern life for these disturbing health problems. Other commentators suggested different causes. Within the confines of middle-class life, perhaps people worried too much about being judged by others. Or maybe the rapid changes of the era led to insecurity. Whatever the causes, the evidence of psychic stress was growing in diaries, in the rise of psychoanalysis, in the new descriptions of proliferating "mental illnesses," in the spread of psychiatric clinics, and in the mounting number of chronic patients in insane asylums.

Was widespread alcoholism a sign of psychic stress? Figure 21.9 an 1876 painting by Edgar Degas (1834–1917) of a woman drinking absinthe (a strong alcoholic beverage) in a Parisian cafe, seems to indicate a link between drinking and stress. Although a man sits nearby, the woman's face suggests that she is alone

■ FIGURE 21.9

Edgar Degas, *Absinthe*, 1876–1877.

and gloomy. In this evocative image, lines separating social drinking, addiction, and psychic stress blur. Drinkers now seemed more depressed than jovial, and drunkenness appeared to be everywhere—in the streets, at work, in bars, and, increasingly, behind closed doors. New temperance movements attacked the "scourge" of alcohol, and with legitimate reason. In France, the average person consumed more than 60 gallons of wine a year, not including the brandy, beer, and the more addictive absinthe shown in this painting. Even drugs such as opium, morphine, heroine, cocaine, and hashish gained footholds, especially among artists. Fear of drug-induced suicides led France to ban such drugs in 1908.

By no coincidence, the practice of **psychoanalysis** emerged during this period (see pages 666–667). Various other movements also focused on psychic stress. One of the best known and popular of these was Christian Science, founded in America by Mary Baker Eddy (1821–1910). Having suffered interminable ailments and nervous disorders as a youth, Eddy turned to a spiritual approach to healing in her adult years. As she explained in her best-selling book *Science and Health* (1875), "mind healing" could dispel sickness and pain. Whatever the causes and supposed cures, stress and emotional pain seemed too widespread to ignore, and many observers connected them to the pressures of modern life.

SCIENCE IN AN AGE OF OPTIMISM

Despite these concerns about the pressures of modern life, most observers embraced the new age enthusiastically. "I see no limit to the extent to which intelligence and will, guided by sound principles of investigation, and organized in common effort, may modify the conditions of existence, for a period longer than that now covered by history," announced British biologist T. H. Huxley (1825–1895) in 1893. "And much may be done to change the nature of man himself," he added.

The eighteenth-century optimism about science spread during the second half of the nineteenth century. Many people—especially members of the rising middle classes—felt certain that their generation would find solutions to the problems that had plagued human beings from the beginning. Scientists confirmed this optimism by making discoveries that answered fundamental questions and that could be translated into practical products, such as industrial goods and medicines. Intellectuals proffered new ways to explain the world and human beings' place in it. Writers and artists found answers to similar questions by looking hard at the lives of people in their changing world. These scientists, intellectuals, and artists thrived in big cities such as London, Paris, Berlin, Milan, and Vienna. In these cultural hubs, some taught in universities or conducted experiments in laboratories. Others might debate in learned societies, do research in libraries, or paint in studios. Still others chatted in cafés or simply wrote in back rooms. Their work generated provocative ideas and added to the sense that life could be understood more fully than ever before.

SCIENCE, EVOLUTION, AND RELIGION

The best news came from science. After 1850, word of scientific advances spread from elite circles to the broader public. Stunning discoveries emerged and directly affected people's lives. However, certain conclusions that appealed to some provoked outrage in others.

No one became a greater hero, or villain, than Charles Darwin (1809–1882). Born into a distinguished British family, Darwin studied medicine and theology. Yet these disciplines failed to challenge him. Instead, the world of plants and animals became his consuming passion. His answer to a single question—how have all living species come to be as they are today?—caused an intense controversy that still continues in some circles.

Darwin

In 1831, Darwin, despite frail health, began a voyage around the world as a ship's naturalist on the *Beagle*. He observed and collected fossils and specimens in different environments. He made his most important finds in South America and the Galapagos Islands off the coast of that continent. Gradually he developed his theory of evolution, which, for him, answered his question. In *On the Origin of Species by Natural Selection* (1859), he described the slow evolution of present plant and animal species from earlier, simpler forms through a process of natural selection. Survival, he explained, came from struggle. In the competition for survival, those that possessed the most useful characteristics in a given environment—for example, the horse with the longer legs—survived to produce the most offspring. Through this process, they transmitted their successful qualities to future generations.

These ideas were not completely new. By the mid-nineteenth century, many intellectuals had accepted the concept of a slow and gradual development of the earth's crust and its inhabitants. Liberalism included ideas about the competitive struggle among human beings for food and survival, something that Thomas Malthus had written about at the beginning of the century (see Chapter 17). In addition, Enlightenment thinkers had already popularized the notion of "progress." Many in the mid-nineteenth century already embraced the sense that the present had evolved in progressive stages from a lower past. But no one had ever before supplied an all-encompassing explanation, supported by convincing evidence, for the origin of plants and animals.

What about human beings? Most people believed that humans remained a species apart from all others. At first Darwin avoided the delicate question. In his 1871 work, *The Descent of Man*, he finally took the bold step, arguing that humans evolved from more primitive species by the same process as plants and animals. "Man still bears in his bodily frame the indelible stamp of his lowly origin," he proclaimed. No longer could people "believe that man is the work of a separate act of creation." Figure 21.10, one of many satirical cartoons on this topic, ridicules Darwin's idea that humans descended from other species by showing Darwin holding up a mirror to his close relative—a monkey—and depicting Darwin with the body of a monkey.

Though many people already believed in evolution, Darwin's claims became front-page news. Few ideas have provoked such widespread controversy. To some people, his ideas made sense. Much of the scientific world, for example, quickly accepted Darwin's theory of evolution. Dominant social groups everywhere also derived comfort from it. The rising bourgeoisie, for instance, seized upon evolution as a way to explain and justify its own success. Scientists, including Darwin, also found confirmation for their views that women were inferior to men and destined to play a dependent domestic role in the male-dominated family.

Controversy

As Document 21.3 suggests, philosophers and scholars also expanded Darwin's thesis and applied it to all human behavior, a doctrine known as **Social**

■ FIGURE 21.10

The controversy over Darwin's theories.

Darwinism. British philosopher Herbert Spencer (1820–1903) built a whole system of influential ideas around the concept of evolution; he and other Social Darwinists extended Darwin's theory far beyond its scientific foundations by making it the key to truth and progress. Spencer even saw the notion of survival of the fittest as justification for the harsh competitiveness of human society: "Under the natural order of things society is constantly excreting its unhealthy, imbecile, slow, vacillating, faithless members," he explained. Helping such people "encourages the multiplication of the reckless and incompetent . . . and discourages the multiplication of the competent and provident. . . ." Other Social Darwinists, such as British criminologist Francis Galton (1822–1911), suggested that the human race could be improved through selective breeding, or eugenics.

Social Darwinists

Darwin's ideas threatened many people wedded to traditional Christian beliefs. He tried to reassure his alarmed readers: "I see no good reason why the views given in this volume should shock the religious feelings of anyone." Though many Christians accepted some of Darwin's ideas, his views offended numerous others. Specifically, the notion of a long and mechanistic evolution of all present species, including human beings, from simpler forms seemed to contradict the account of divine creation given in the Bible: "If the Darwinian theory is true," complained one theologian, "Genesis is a lie, the whole framework of the book of life falls to pieces, and the revelation of God to man, as we Christians know it, is a delusion and a snare." Evolution, Darwin's critics cried, left God out of the world and diminished the uniqueness of human beings in it.

Darwinism and religion

Some of Darwin's opponents suppressed his books and the teaching of evolution in schools. The Catholic Church angrily rejected Darwin's theory along with many other ideas of the time. In 1864, Pope Pius IX (1846–1878) issued a *Syllabus of Errors* attacking the idea of evolution and secular education. He also railed against religious toleration, free speech, and much else: It is "an error to believe that the Roman Pontiff can and ought to reconcile himself to, and agree with, progress, liberalism, and modern civilization." In 1870, the First Vatican Council bolstered the pope's authority by declaring that, under certain circumstances, the pope's statements on issues of morality and faith should be considered divinely sanctioned truths.

Darwin's allies rushed to his defense. Thomas Huxley, a biologist, surgeon in the British navy, and president of a leading scientific society, popularized Darwin's work in dozens of vigorous and lucid books and pamphlets. Heaping withering scorn on opponents, Huxley called himself "Darwin's bull-dog." Alfred Russel Wallace (1823–1913), a Scottish naturalist, claimed that Darwin "is the Newton of natural history" who "established a firm foundation for all future study of nature."

Over time, many of Darwin's critics moderated their hostility to Darwin's findings. Toward the end of the century the Catholic Church, under Pope Leo XIII (1878–1903), even began taking the position that natural science was not the province of the church, that evolution could be taught as a hypothesis, and that parts of the Bible should be taken figuratively.

MYSTERIES OF THE MATERIAL AND HUMAN WORLD

Research multiplied in many fields besides natural science. Scientists focused especially on the nature of matter. Discovery after discovery in chemistry and physics led them to conclude that all matter was

THINKING ABOUT DOCUMENTS

■ DOCUMENT 21.3

Walter Bagehot on "Natural Selection" and Human History

Social Darwinism and related doctrines spread, especially among liberals, during the second half of the nineteenth century. The Englishman Walter Bagehot (1826–1877) won notice for presenting views shared by his liberal, middle-class contemporaries. The following is a selection from his 1873 work, Physics and Politics. ■ ***How*** *does Bagehot connect "natural selection" and human history?* ■ ***In what ways*** *might someone use Bagehot's argument to justify war or imperialism?*

. . . Three laws, or approximate laws, may, I think, be laid down. . . .

First. In every particular state of the world, those nations which are strongest tend to prevail over the others; and in certain marked peculiarities the strongest tend to be the best.

Secondly. Within every particular nation the type or types of character then and there most attractive tend to prevail; and the most attractive, though with exceptions, is what we call the best character.

Thirdly. Neither of these competitions is in most historic conditions intensified by extrinsic forces, but in some conditions, such as those now prevailing in the most influential part of the world, both are so intensified.

These are the sort of doctrines with which, under the name of "natural selection" in physical science, we have become familiar; and as every great scientific conception tends to advance its boundaries and to be of use in solving problems not thought of when it was started, so here, what was put forward for mere animal history may, with a change of form but an identical essence, be applied to human history. . . .

The strongest nation has always been conquering the weaker; sometimes even subduing it, but always prevailing over it. Every intellectual gain, so to speak, that a nation possessed was in the earliest times made use of—was invested and taken out—in war; all else perished. Each nation tried constantly to be the stronger, and so made or copied the best weapons, by conscious and unconscious imitation each nation formed a type of character suitable to war and conquest. Conquest improved mankind by the intermixture of strengths; the armed truce, which was then called peace, improved them by the competition of training and the consequent creation of new power. Since the long-headed men first drove the short-headed men out of the best land in Europe, all European history has been the history of the superposition of the more military races over the less military—of the efforts, sometimes successful, sometimes unsuccessful, of each race to get more military; and so the art of war has constantly improved. . . .

Source: Walter Bagehot, *Physics and Politics* (New York: 1873), pp. 44–46.

---

composed of atoms, that each atom was in turn made
Physics and chemistry
up of smaller particles that moved in circles like a miniature solar system, and that each chemical element of matter had a specific atomic weight. In 1870, the Russian chemist Dmitri Mendeleev (1834–1907) compiled a new chart showing the atomic weight of all the known elements and indicating by gaps the other elements that remained to be discovered. Chemists and physicists proved him right. Year after year, researchers discovered new elements that fit into the "Periodic Table." In the 1870s, James Clerk Maxwell (1831–1879) analyzed the relationship between light, magnetism, and electricity. His ideas led to a greater sense of physical unity in the universe and practical developments such as the development of the electronics industry.

The successes of Darwin and of chemists, physicists, and others in the natural sciences
Psychology
encouraged scholars to apply the same scientific techniques and principles to psychology, or the study of human behavior. One of the first to bring this discipline into the laboratory was

Wilhelm Wundt (1832–1920). In his laboratory at Leipzig, Wundt and his enthusiastic students tested human reactions and carried out carefully controlled and measured experiments on cats and dogs, assuming that the findings would also apply to human beings.

The Russian scientist Ivan Pavlov (1849–1936), pursuing Wundt's line of inquiry, discovered the conditioned reflex. Pavlov showed meat to a hungry dog until the dog's mouth watered. Then Pavlov rang a bell while showing the meat. Eventually, the dog's mouth would water when only the bell was rung. The implication was that many of our human responses are purely mechanical reflexes prompted by stimuli of which we are often unaware.

The field of sociology also acquired status as a social science. Auguste Comte (1798–1857) named the new discipline. He argued that humankind was entering a stage of history in which truths would be discovered by the scientific gathering of
Sociology
factual data. Humans and society, he said, are as susceptible to scientific investigation as minerals, plants, and the lower animals are. He believed

that his philosophy, which he called **positivism,** would reveal the laws of human relations and allow social scientists to engineer harmonious societies. Comte's followers, eager and numerous during the second half of the nineteenth century, placed great faith in statistics and amassed copious statistical data on numerous social problems. Like Comte, most of them believed that sure social knowledge would enable people to remake society for the better.

Historians such as the German Leopold von Ranke (1795–1886) strove to turn history into a social science. Ranke rejected history based on tradition or legend. He also attacked the notion that history could come in the form of a purposeful story about the progress of humanity, the working out of God's will, or other such themes. He argued that historical accounts should be based on an exhaustive accumulation and analysis of documentary evidence. Conclusions could be drawn only from facts, he insisted. In this way, Ranke believed, history would become coldly scientific and morally neutral. His attitude and methodology spread widely, particularly in Germany and the United States.

History

These scholars believed that individual and social behavior could best be studied by careful, objective observation, experimentation, and analysis. Like scientists, they considered themselves professionals with specialties rather than amateurs. They also formed societies and published their findings in their own journals. Part of what drove them was their faith that these findings would point the way to improving the quality of human life, and they conveyed that faith to a wider public. In this sense, these scholars and scientists shared and promoted the optimism of the period.

GERMS, CURES, AND HEALTH CARE

No field of science promised more new understanding and dramatic applications than medicine. At midcentury, medicine entered a golden age. The most important discovery came not from a doctor, but from a chemist. Louis Pasteur (1822–1895), the son of a French tanner, became interested in what happened to wine and beer during the fermentation process. In the 1860s, he discovered the airborne microorganisms responsible for fermentation and showed that bacteria caused milk to sour. He demonstrated that heating milk—"pasteurizing" it—destroyed the bacteria that caused diseases. His long years of work eventually enabled him to identify disease-producing organisms in humans and create vaccines to prevent diseases such as rabies. Here, finally, was the explanation for how people caught infectious diseases: germ theory.

Pasteur and germ theory

Many doctors and scientists, still wedded to old ideas and practices, dismissed Pasteur's findings. The German scientist, Robert Koch (1843–1910) confirmed the French chemist's conclusions, convincing doctors that bacteria indeed caused diseases. In the early 1880s, Koch discovered the bacteria responsible for two of the most deadly diseases of the time: tuberculosis and cholera. His students used the same research methods to find microbes that caused a list of other diseases from pneumonia and meningitis to syphilis.

Modern doctors of the late nineteenth century now understood that specific microorganisms ("germs") caused specific infectious diseases. In addition to this realization, new tools increased physicians' stature as scientists and improved their ability to diagnose ailments. The thermometer, for example, allowed them to measure body temperature, and the stethoscope let them hear what was going on inside the body. The microscope permitted examination of tissue samples, the X-ray (1896) revealed the body's internal structures, and the electrocardiograph (1901) recorded the workings of the heart.

The most advanced doctors realized that although they may know more about illnesses and the inner workings of the body, they still could do little to cure diseases. Aspirin (1899) reduced fever, inflammation, and minor pain; morphine controlled more serious pain; and barbiturates might induce sleep—but none of these constituted a medical cure. The first great exception was an antitoxin against diphtheria developed in Robert Koch's Berlin laboratory in 1891. For most diseases, however, cures lay in the future. The best that doctors could do was to stop prescribing poisonous pills and dangerous procedures such as bloodletting and purges.

Remedies

KEY DATES

WESTERN SOCIETY, 1850–1914

1853	Beginning of the rebuilding of Paris
1857	Flaubert, *Madame Bovary*
1859	Darwin, *On the Origin of Species*
1864	*Syllabus of Errors*
1860s	Pasteur's germ theory
1870	Periodic Table developed
1876	Telephone invented
1896	Modern Olympic games
1905	Einstein's theory of relativity
1913	Stravinsky, *Rite of Spring*

Within medicine, the field of surgery saw especially remarkable progress. During the 1860s and 1870s, the British surgeon Joseph Lister (1827–1912) developed procedures that included the use of antiseptics during operations. These procedures dramatically lowered the risk of infection from the operation itself. Over the following decades, surgeons applied Lister's methods with great success. No longer did they operate in dirty, blood-splattered back rooms, wearing black coats or street clothes. Increasingly, they washed their hands, worked in relatively sterile environments, and wore white surgical gowns, face masks, and rubber gloves to lessen the risks of infection.

Surgery

In Figure 21.11, an 1890 painting of an operating room in a Vienna hospital, a patient is being prepared for surgery. The doctors wear white coats rather than street clothes, and the patient is being anesthetized. However, old practices died slowly. Even though Joseph Lister had developed antiseptic procedures more than twenty years earlier, the surgeon and his assistants do not yet wear masks or gloves, and the surgical instruments have not been sterilized. Everyone in the scene is male; most medical schools still denied access to women. The picture also lacks religious symbols. All in all, it conveys a sense of solid confidence in modern science.

Medical advances also made a huge difference in the field of nursing. In hospitals, emergencies, and war, nurses often had the most direct contact with sufferers and the wounded. During the Crimean War (1853–1856), Florence Nightingale transformed nursing into a modern profession (see Chapter 19). Her reforms stressed cleanliness, fresh air, and discipline, and helped make nursing an attractive path to independence and service. A few years later, the philanthropist Dorothea Dix (1802–1887) led similar reform efforts in the United States during the Civil War, and in Switzerland a banker established the International Red Cross, creating new demand for professional nurses.

Nursing

By the turn of the century, much in medicine had gained the authority of science and was "professionalized." Better nursing gave the wounded a fighting chance at survival. Doctors who understood diseases and surgeons who performed operations safely now helped more than hurt their patients. Even so, many doctors insisted on practicing traditional medicine, and most remained too expensive for working-class families to afford except when they were in dire need. Many working-class women were forced to prescribe their own curative regime or find some inexpensive "cure."

CULTURE: ACCEPTING THE MODERN WORLD

Faith in science and technology reflected a growing sense that people could observe the facts of everyday life carefully, understand them, and use that understanding to control the world more successfully than ever before. Writers and artists also closely observed contemporary life in their books and paintings. During the second half of the nineteenth century, their focus included the methods of science and the realities of urban life. The romanticism of early-nineteenth-century culture—which had idealized love, religion, and the exotic—gave way to a gritty sense of realism (see Chapter 18). Realists felt free to look modern life full in the face and both praise its successes and criticize its failings.

REALISM AND NATURALISM: THE DETAILS OF SOCIAL LIFE

The age witnessed the rise of realistic and naturalistic literature, which explored the social dislocation brought about by the industrial revolution, commercial values, and city life. Eugène de Vogüé (1848–1910), a nineteenth-century

Literature

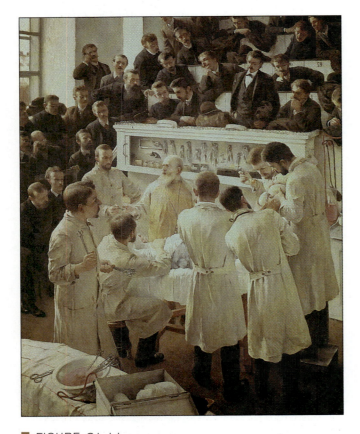

■ FIGURE 21.11

Albert Seligmann, *Operation by German Surgeon Theodor Billroth*, 1890.

French writer, explained that a realist "observes life as it is in its wholeness and complexity with the least possible prejudice on the part of the artist. It takes men under ordinary conditions, shows characters in the course of their everyday existence." Authors, often focusing on the unpleasant, sordid side of human nature and society, examined how environment and heredity together shaped people's lives. With scientific thoroughness, these writers examined people's public and private lives, their individual and social failings, and the hypocrisy of their religious and moral values.

The French novelist Gustave Flaubert (1821–1880), for example, deftly captured the full flavor of **realism.** His *Madame Bovary* (1857) related the illicit sex life of the wife of a small-town French physician in such full and unblushing detail that it scandalized a public not yet accustomed to such unrestrained revelations. *Madame Bovary* became a model for other novelists. Few writers, however, were as popular as Charles Dickens (1812–1870). As we saw in Chapter 17, Dickens's novels presented realistic descriptions of the middle and lower classes in Britain's urban, industrial society. For example, in *The Old Curiosity Shop,* he refused to shy away from the realities of nighttime in impoverished sections of cities, "when bands of unemployed labourers paraded in the roads . . . when carts came rumbling by, filled with rude coffins . . . or when orphans cried, and distracted women shrieked and followed in their wake, . . . when some called for bread, and some for drink to drown their cares. . . ."

Mary Ann Evans (1819–1880), writing under the pen name George Eliot, also wrote popular novels examining the realities of British social life. In *Middlemarch,* for instance, she linked psychological conflict to the determining social realities surrounding her characters. The Norwegian playwright Henrik Ibsen (1828–1906) presented another perspective on such realities. Ibsen ridiculed bourgeois society in his popular dramas. In *A Doll's House,* probably his best-known play, the heroine Nora rebels against her expected role in the "doll's house" that her stodgy, hypocritical, middle-class husband Helmer has created for her:

NORA: What do you consider my holiest duties?
HELMER: Need I tell you that? Your duties to your husband and children.
NORA: I have other duties equally sacred.
HELMER: Impossible! What do you mean!
NORA: My duties toward myself.
HELMER: Before all else you are a wife and a mother.
NORA: That I no longer believe. Before all else I believe I am a human being just as much as you are.

The French writer Émile Zola (1840–1902) explained that the naturalist novel, having evolved from the realistic novel, "substitutes for the study of the abstract man . . . the study of the natural man, governed by physical and chemical laws, and modified by the influences of his surroundings; it is in one word the literature of our scientific age. . . ." He wrote in almost clinical detail about the social problems spawned by industrialism. In one series of novels, he portrayed several generations of a working-class family battered by the forces of heredity and the environment. They struggle to survive, fighting poverty, strikes, alcoholism, and conflict among themselves.

Russia produced some especially talented writers who created stunning realistic literature. An example is Leo Tolstoy (1828–1910) and his masterpiece *War and Peace* (1865–1869). This sweeping novel about Russia during the Napoleonic Wars features scores of characters who battle impersonal social forces and the overwhelming details of everyday life. Even the strongest individuals in the story become ensnared in forces beyond their control. In other writings that reflected the social realities of his own times, Tolstoy attacked capitalism and materialism: "Money is a new form of slavery, and distinguishable from the old simply by the fact that it is impersonal. . . ."

Fyodor Dostoyevski (1821–1881), another legendary Russian author, focused more on psychological and moral realities in his novels. His characters—such as the anguished student Raskolnikov in *Crime and Punishment* (1866) who murders an old woman—struggle with moral conflicts in an age marked by spiritual bankruptcy. Like other realistic writers, Dostoyevski shone a spotlight on the harshness of modern life, particularly its power to overwhelm individuals.

Innovative painters also turned to realistic depictions of life on their canvases. The French artist Gustave Courbet (1819–1877), who believed | **Art** | that an artist should "never permit sentiment to overthrow logic," led the attack on romantic art by painting sober scenes of urban life and rural labor. In *The Stone Breakers* (Figure 21.12), he portrays rural laborers as a passerby might see them. Courbet claimed he "saw these people every day on my walk." Here an old worker—with patches on his pants and holes in his socks—breaks up stones, probably for use in building a road. His young assistant, who is "suffering from scurvy" according to Courbet, carries the stones away in a basket. The two men's tattered clothing and averted faces make them seem anonymous and therefore representative of many other workers. While there is dignity in their work, Courbet does not glorify either the stone breakers or nature. The scene, like the men's lives, is harsh. The image suggests that the young assistant is likely to end up the same as his old companion. Courbet and other realistic artists depicted everyday life on large canvases and thereby earned the wrath of those artists and critics who believed that only paintings of historical, mythological, religious, or exotic scenes should be considered "great art."

■ FIGURE 21.12
Gustave Courbet, *The Stone Breakers*, 1849.

■ FIGURE 21.13
Claude Monet, *The Pool at Argenteuil*, 1872.

IMPRESSIONISM: CELEBRATING MODERN LIFE

Like the realists and naturalists, impressionist paint-ers embraced modern life—but in a different way. Specifically, they applied a new understanding of color, light, and optics to their work. Their paint-ings—with their informal quality and emphasis on angles—suggested randomness of reality. Such art-ists ventured outside their studios to paint scenes. They especially sought to convey the impression of a view that the eye actually sees at first glance—the

"impression" created by light reflected off a surface at a single moment—rather than what the knowing brain interprets from visual cues, hence the name **impressionism** for this school of painting. The French artist Claude Monet (1840–1926) (see Biography) de-scribed the way he painted: "Try to for-get what objects you have before you—a tree, a house, a field, or whatever. Merely think, here is a little square of blue, here an oblong of pink, here a streak of yel-low, and paint it just as it looks to you . . . until it gives your own naive impres-sion of the scene before you."

Monet's *The Pool at Argenteuil* (Figure 21.13) is an example of many paintings of the suburban countryside—the places to which the urban bourgeoisie might travel on Sundays or vacations. In this scene near his home just outside of Paris, middle-class women carrying parasols stroll down a wide, tree-lined path bordering the Seine or wander over to a dock on the right where boats might be rented. Sailboats on the river suggest plea-sure, a bridge in the distance implies that the city is not far away. The bourgeoisie purchas-ers of Monet's paintings would recognize this sort of place, where civilization and country-side meet under a broad sky.

Impressionists also painted psychologically subtle portraits, bedroom and dance-hall inte-riors, urban parks, and city streets. *Boulevard des Capucines* (Figure 21.14), also by Monet, shows one of the straight, wide, tree-lined, fashionable boulevards constructed in Paris during the Second Empire under Napoleon III. Monet painted this winter scene while looking out the window of the studios where the first impressionist exhibition would be held in 1874 and where this painting would be shown. Only a few brush strokes suggest people, carriages, and building details—the impression that one might get glancing out an upper-floor window at an anonymous but vibrant urban scene below.

> Monet

FROM OPTIMISM TO UNCERTAINTY

The impressionists' delight in the beauty and charm of modern life fit well with the continuing belief in reason, individual rights, and progress that marked

BIOGRAPHY

Claude Monet (1840–1926)

CONSIDER

■ **Consider** how Monet's life, his paintings, and his popularity reflected European society during the second half of the nineteenth century.

As a boy growing up in Le Havre on France's north coast, Oscar Claude Monet was rebellious and daring. "My youth was essentially that of a vagabond," he wrote. "Never would I bend to a rule."

That pattern of assertive rebellion would stay with him. In 1857, the 16-year-old Claude announced to his father, a prosperous merchant, that he was going to Paris to become a painter. His father refused to help him financially, but Claude left home anyway. In Paris, he rejected academic art training, instead working with other young artists such as Pissarro and Renoir, with whom he would remain connected for many years.

In 1864, he met the 18-year-old Camille Doncieux, and the two moved in together. That year, Claude had his first paintings accepted at the official Salon, where prominent artists entered their paintings to be judged and—if accepted—offered for sale. Success at the Salon meant the possibility of earning a living as an artist. Despite this triumph, financial problems plagued the young Monet. He often had to hide in Paris or flee to the suburbs to escape from creditors. He perpetually wrote letters begging his family, friends, and other artists for money.

In the following years, Monet enjoyed some successes, but was disappointed whenever his paintings were turned down by the Salon. Depression often haunted him: "I am like a man going down the third time. . . . I see everything black. . . . Money is always lacking. Disappointments, insults, hopes, new disappointments." But in good times, he lived the bourgeois life and experienced private joys. In 1868, he wrote: "I am surrounded here by all that I love. I pass my time outdoors on the flint beach when the seas are heavy or when the boats go off to fish, or I even go into the country, which is so beautiful here. . . . I find in my tiny house a good fire and a good little family." Though he had a one-year-old son, Jean, with Camille, it took the prospect of money from an inheritance by Camille, guaranteed by a contract, before he finally married her in 1870.

In 1872, the Monets moved to Argenteuil, twenty minutes from Paris by train. Camille played the role of a middle-class housewife, rising early to serve breakfast to her husband and son, shopping, buying bread just before lunch, cleaning the house, preparing dinner, and reading the newspapers daily. Their son, Jean, dressed in long skirts as was the style of the time and riding his tricycle with a stuffed horse mounted on its front end, appeared on several of Monet's canvases, as did Camille. Every day, Monet painted by the shore of the river, sometimes accompanied by other visiting impressionists.

By 1874, Monet had turned his back on the official Salon. That year, he and other artists formed a group and mounted their own exposition. Monet was at the head of the group, which included Renoir and Pissarro. Critics attacked the paintings at the exposition, particularly one by Monet entitled *Impression: Sunrise*, for rejecting accepted standards of good art. Yet the group continued to paint and show together, earning a reputation for being rebellious artists and "bohemians" with inappropriate lifestyles.

Impressionist Painter

In 1878, the ailing Camille gave birth to a second son. A year later she died. Soon Monet became involved with another woman, Alice Hoschede, already married to a successful merchant and the mother of several children. The couple soon moved in together.

Monet was happy living with Alice, and his paintings began to sell well. He stopped showing his paintings with the other impressionist painters and moved to Giverny, northwest of Paris. There he created a large garden and pond, which he would paint for the rest of his life.

Monet gained a public reputation for being both brilliant and unyielding. When the government tried to award him the Legion of Honor, he refused. By 1890, he was recognized as France's premier painter, far more popular than any of his colleagues. His paintings commanded high prices. Now sporting a long, white beard, he became a revered figure. Despite his failing eyesight, he painted almost up until his death in 1926.

Monet made the bourgeoisie both the subject and the assumed audience of his paintings. Many of his landscapes featured the suburban fields, gardens, walks, and riverbanks that the bourgeoisie loved to visit (see Figure 21.13). Even his landscapes of southern France or the north coast were presented from the point of view of a tourist. Monet always emphasized the "modern" in his work. There was no horror in his depictions of the city, only a celebration of its boulevards, railway stations, and parks.

---

the decades after 1850. Economic growth, improving conditions in the cities, and new conquests by science buoyed a broad sense of moderate optimism about the world. However, from the 1880s on, signs of a disturbing new undercurrent rose to the surface of Western culture. Some of the West's best intellectuals, writers, and artists injected themes of pessimism and painful introspection into their work. They emphasized how strongly irrational forces guided human behavior. Though still a minority, these thinkers and critics undermined rather than overwhelmed the prevailing certainty and optimism of the period. They added to the growing social and political tensions of the turn-of-the-century decades described in Chapter 20.

■ FIGURE 21.14

Claude Monet, *Boulevard des Capucines*, 1873.

EVERYTHING IS RELATIVE

In part, this disillusionment stemmed from the growing feeling of uncertainty creeping into elite scientific circles—the sense that the more people learned, the less solid and reliable the material world became. The work of Albert Einstein (1879–1955) exposed this uncertainty in physics. A German who later fled to America, Einstein assailed time-honored concepts about the stability of matter and the nature of the physical universe. In 1905, while still earning a living as a patent clerk in Switzerland, he proposed what would become the seminal theory of relativity. According to this theory, time, space, and motion were relative to one another as well as to the observer—they were not the absolutes scientists had believed in for so long.

Einstein

Building on the work of the German physicist Max Planck (1858–1947), who had shown that heated bodies emit energy in irregular packets ("quanta") rather than a steady stream, Einstein also derived a groundbreaking formula, $E = mc^2$ (E = energy;

m = mass; c = speed of light). This formula blurred the distinction between mass and energy and described the immense energy contained within each atom. The atomic energy in a lump of coal, for example, was revealed to be some three billion times as great as the energy obtained by burning the coal. This unsettling notion later contributed to the development of the atomic bomb. By showing that matter could be transformed into energy, Einstein again challenged Newtonian physics. More conservative scientists, wedded to time-honored Newtonian physics, dismissed his theories. Eventually, however, Einstein's views gained support, further undermining scientists' assumptions about the physical nature of the universe.

SEX, CONFLICT, AND THE UNCONSCIOUS

Ideas about the human mind—the internal, mental universe—also took a disturbing turn in these years. Sigmund Freud (1856–1939), the Viennese neurologist, concluded that nervous disorders stemmed from psychological causes, not physiological sources as most doctors had believed. Basing his ideas on the words, experiences, and dreams of troubled patients, he founded psychoanalysis, which he described as "the scientific method by which the unconscious can be studied."

Freud and psychoanalysis

Freud argued that much of human behavior was irrational, unconscious, and instinctual. Conflict, he claimed, was a basic condition of life, particularly when it occurred between people's innate biological drives (such as sex or aggression) and their social selves. According to Freud, these conflicts developed on a mostly unconscious level and in stages during childhood. At war within all people are what Freud called the *id*, the *superego*, and the *ego*. The id is the source of our basic desires, the most important and disturbing of these being sexual. The superego imposes socially acceptable standards of behavior on the individual. The ego tries to find ways to satisfy both the demands of the id and the restraints of the superego. Typically, the mind responds to this conflict by repressing the id's desires from consciousness. However, the unconscious psychic struggle continues, creating a mental life of great tension.

Freud added fuel to his already controversial ideas by emphasizing the importance of sexual conflicts originating in childhood. He argued that children inevitably come into conflict with their parents, competing with the same-sex parent for the love of the opposite-sex parent. At an unconscious level, he claimed, this competition for the parent of the opposite sex strongly shapes the development of an individual's personality.

Freud believed that much psychic pain and many emotional disorders stemmed from the suppressed and frustrated drives of early life—frustrations that then festered outside of people's awareness. He concluded that the correct therapy for such disorders was to make the sufferer conscious of the facts and circumstances of his or her original frustration. Hence, he encouraged patients to talk about their dreams, for by interpreting dreams the unconscious could be revealed.

Freud's controversial explanation of human behavior had several disturbing implications: Neither adults nor children were innocent beings after all; too few people led happy lives; sex and aggression played powerful roles in children and adults alike; people cannot escape from internal conflict and frustration. Although he hoped that reason and understanding would ease humanity's psychological plight, Freud was far from an optimist. He eventually concluded that "the price of progress in civilization is paid in forfeiting happiness."

FEAR OF SOCIAL DISINTEGRATION

The French scholar Émile Durkheim (1858–1917), a founder of modern sociology, offered a different sort of warning about trends in modern society. Though a strong believer in science, Durkheim argued that industrial society—especially with its competitive individualism and lack of collective values—was weakening the ties that connected people with one another. As people became more concerned with their own freedom and advancement, he believed, the restraints and the spiritual beliefs that held traditional societies together would break down. This trend toward social disintegration, Durkheim warned, disoriented individuals, made them feel cut off from others, and left them without a sense of purpose. As a result, more and more people were experiencing despair, which in turn led to rising suicide rates. Like Freud, Durkheim believed that advancing civilization left psychic pain in its wake.

Durkheim

DISENCHANTMENT SETS IN

Perhaps the deepest sense of disenchantment with the optimistic, bourgeois, urban society of the nineteenth century emerged in philosophy. Friedrich Nietzsche (1844–1890), a brilliant German philosopher, is one example. Reason could not solve human problems, Nietzsche concluded. Instead, he believed in "will," which in his view enabled people to survive and the strongest among them to achieve power. Great leaders, he argued, rose through strength, intelligence, and above all, "the will to power." Nietzsche further claimed that if a superior society were to emerge, it would have to come about through the efforts of gifted individuals who would rise to positions of leadership because of their superior strength, will, and intelligence. Anything that contributes to power is good, he explained—be it strength of will, boldness, cunning, or intelligence. Likewise, whatever leads to weakness is bad—be it gentleness, modesty, generosity, or compassion.

Nietzsche

In Nietzsche's view, Christianity stood in the way of a better human society. "Christianity has taken the side of everything weak, base, ill-constituted; it has made an ideal out of opposition to the preservative instincts of strong life," he announced. "God is dead; we have killed him." For Nietzsche, the idea of the death of God was liberating: Now humans could cast off all conventions. Nietzsche also decried democracy for amounting to rule by the supposedly mediocre "masses . . . or the populace, or the herd, or whatever name you care to give them." He went on to attack many other accepted tenets of nineteenth-century civilization, such as liberalism,

■ FIGURE 21.15

James Ensor, *Intrigue*, 1890.

rationalism, and science. Although Nietzsche was not a nationalist or racist himself, others would later use his ideas to support militant nationalism and racism.

In France, the philosopher Henri Bergson (1859–1941) also questioned the limits of rational and scientific thinking. Gaining a large following by lecturing at the University of Paris, he argued that truth is best grasped through intuition and unconscious feelings rather than reason: "Science can teach us nothing of the truth; it can only serve as a rule of action." Society, Bergson said, needed the energy that only a spontaneous following of the "life

Bergson

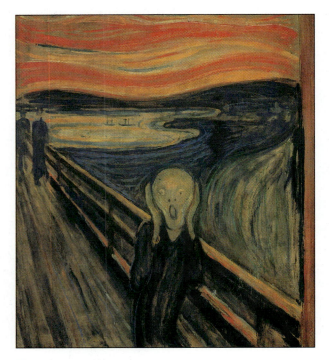

■ FIGURE 21.16

Edvard Munch, *The Scream*, 1893.

force" could provide. His views, like those of Nietzsche and others, reflected a growing criticism of the dominant ideas of middle-class society in the West.

ART TURNS INWARD

Many talented artists also turned away from the mainstream of nineteenth-century civilization. Their work grew more pessimistic and critical of middle-class life. The slogan "Art for art's sake" reflected the trend of various artistic movements such as **expressionism** and symbolism. They self-consciously attacked social and artistic taboos in ways that mystified much of the public. Their often introspective works proved understandable mainly to themselves and a small artistic elite. The Russian abstract expressionist painter Wassily Kandinsky (1866–1944) spoke for many of his fellow artists when he explained that his work was not intended to represent how things looked. "Look at the picture as a graphic representation of a mood and not as a representation of objects," he suggested.

Expressionism

Many artists focused on peripheral members of a society that seemed to be disintegrating, painting prostitutes, solitary drinkers, blind beggars, and circus performers. Moreover, threatening symbols of science, machinery, and speed began to crop up on canvases. Photography had already displaced traditional representation art. The French poet Guillaume Apollinaire explained that modern painters "avoid any representation of natural scenes . . . since everything is sacrificed by the artist to truth." Now avant-garde painters created distorted, subjective, and abstract images.

We can see evidence of these trends in expressionist paintings such as those by the Belgian artist James Ensor (1860–1949). In *Intrigue* (Figure 21.15), Ensor shows people as indistinct from the obnoxious masks they wear. In their everyday world of pretense, they gather together and exchange false smiles. Behind their masks lurk isolation and anxiety.

Like Ensor, the Norwegian artist Edvard Munch (1863–1944) expressed a deep current of horror in middle-class life, but in a deeper, more personal way. In *The Scream* (Figure 21.16), a wide-eyed figure standing on a bridge lets out a terrified shriek. The land, water, and sky—all distorted and painted in alarming colors—echo the cry of the figure. Munch described the feelings that inspired the scene: "I was tired and ill— I stood looking out across the fjord—the sun was setting—the clouds were colored red—like blood—I felt as though a scream went through nature. . . ." In this painting, themes of death, anxiety, loneliness, and fear coalesce. Munch once exclaimed, "How much of my art I owe to suffering!" Many other artists painted similarly anguished scenes, emphasizing social anxieties, urban loneliness, violence, horror, and a turning inward toward the unconscious. Their paintings penetrated through surface-level appearances into a deeper, disturbing psychic reality.

In music, expressionism also challenged artistic conventions and public tastes. The Russian composer Igor Stravinsky (1882–1971) led this movement in his music for the ballet *The Rite of Spring*. The premiere of the ballet on May 29, 1913, in Paris has been called the most notorious event of the twentieth century. Upon hearing the music—with its offbeat rhythm and unrestrained, dissonant sounds—the audience rose in outrage. Fights broke out, and many listeners stormed from the theater after complaining loudly. Yet among certain elites, Stravinsky became the leading composer of the day.

Like science and philosophy, art and music were slipping away from the grasp of ordinary people. The new understandings of modern life that seemed so promising a few decades earlier now appeared shadowed by doubt and even foreboding.

Music

SUMMARY

By 1914, industrialization, urban growth, and the culture of progress had pulled much of the West into new territory. Life in large parts of Europe and North America had undergone a huge transformation. Someone who had lived during the late eighteenth century would have found virtually everything about the turn-of-the-century West strange or even shocking. Most of us, however, would readily recognize early-twentieth-century Paris, Berlin, or New York as modern. Those cities—like our cities today—were part of a widespread urban society and culture dominated by the middle classes and marching to the quickening pace of economic transformation. The variety of public and private life within those cities has persisted to the present day.

People have called the years 1850–1914 the Age of Progress. The reasons are clear. Income for most people rose at least a little, and for some quite considerably, while the machines of industry pumped out endless new products that promised to ease the burdens of everyday life. Science promised even more and delivered findings that seemed to unlock the mysteries of both the physical and social world. Many of the cultural forms of the period gazed directly at the modern world and embraced it. In the 1920s, the French would look back to the two decades surrounding the turn of the century as "La Belle Époque"—the beautiful era.

Yet as we have seen, darker forces of change simmered below the optimistic surface during these same years. Just how much progress was achieved in politics is not so clear. Events in the summer of 1914 would expose that sense of dangerous uncertainty as all too well founded. Whether progress was made in the West's relations with the rest of the world is also in doubt. From outside the West, some questioned the very value of Western civilization. "In order to estimate the value of a civilization," explained a high Chinese official educated in European universities, "the question we must finally ask is not what great cities . . . it has built . . . what clever and useful implements . . . it has made . . . what institutions, what arts and sciences it has invested: the question . . . is what type of humanity, what kind of men and women it has been able to produce." These complex questions, too, would be immediately recognizable to us today. Modern times had arrived.

KEY TERMS

Victorian, p. 656

psychoanalysis, p. 657

Social Darwinism, p. 659

positivism, p. 661

realism, p. 663

impressionism, p. 664

expressionism, p. 668

REVIEW, ANALYZE, AND ANTICIPATE

REVIEW THE PREVIOUS CHAPTER
Chapter 20—"Mass Politics and Imperial Domination"—traced the spreading demands for democracy and the West's imperial expansion during the second half of the nineteenth century.

1. *How did politics adjust to the new industrial and urban realities of this period?*

2. *In what ways did imperialism support and reflect both the nationalism and industrialism of this period?*

ANALYZE THIS CHAPTER
Chapter 21—"Modern Life and the Culture of Progress"—traces the changes stemming from new industrial transformations and urban growth, as well as the culture of the West.

1. *Considering the material in this chapter and Chapter 17 (which focused on the industrial revolution), why do you think industrialization so quickly doomed traditional society in the West?*

2. *Analyze the impact of spreading industrialization on the various social classes during this period.*

3. *How did people adjust to the opportunities and pressures of life in the West's modernizing cities?*

4. *Do you think the title "The Culture of Progress" is an apt description of Western culture during this period? Why or why not?*

ANTICIPATE THE NEXT CHAPTER
In Chapter 22—"Descending into the Twentieth Century"—the story of World War I and the Russian Revolution will be told.

1. *What political and social tensions developing during the years before 1914 might have made Europe ripe for war?*

BEYOND THE CLASSROOM

THE SECOND INDUSTRIAL REVOLUTION
Hobsbawm, Eric J. *The Age of Capital, 1848–1875.* New York: New American Library, 1979. Includes detailed sections on industrialism as well as its social consequences.

Ville, Simon P. *Transport and the Development of the European Economy, 1750–1918.* Houndmills, UK: Macmillan, 1990. A comparative study of the major forms of transportation from 1750 to 1918 and their relationship to economic development.

Williams, Rosalind H. *Dream Worlds: Mass Consumption in Late Nineteenth-Century France.* Berkeley, CA: University of California Press, 1982. An exploration of the mental evolution of consumer society in late-nineteenth- and early twentieth-century France.

THE NEW URBAN LANDSCAPE
Olsen, Donald J. *The City as a Work of Art—London, Paris, Vienna.* New Haven, CT: Yale University Press, 1986. A well-illustrated examination of nineteenth-century urban growth and design.

Pinkney, David. *Napoleon III and the Rebuilding of Paris.* Princeton, NJ: Princeton University Press, 1972. A classic study of one of the most important urban renovations of the nineteenth century.

GLOBAL CONNECTIONS
Chasteen, John Charles. *Born in Blood and Fire: A Concise History of Latin America.* New York: Norton, 2001. A useful recent survey covering the period.

CITY PEOPLE
Joyce, P. *Visions of the People: Industrial England and the Question of Class, 1848–1914.* Cambridge: Cambridge University Press, 1991. An examination of working-class culture and language.

Pilbeam, Pamela. *The Middle Classes in Europe, 1789–1914.* Chicago: Lyceum Books, 1990. A thorough treatment of middle-class life in the major European nations.

PRIVATE LIFE: TOGETHER AND ALONE AT HOME
Gay, Peter. *The Bourgeois Experience: Victoria to Freud,* 2 volumes. New York: Oxford University Press, 1984–1986. Exhaustively researched volumes dealing with the varied experiences of middle-class life in America and Europe.

Perrot, Michelle, ed. *A History of Private Life, IV: From the Fires of Revolution to the Great War.* Cambridge, MA: Harvard University Press, 1990.

Richly detailed and well-illustrated essays on the nineteenth century and its division between public and private life.

Peterson, M. Jeanne. *Family, Love, and Work in the Lives of Victorian Gentlewomen.* Bloomington, IN: Indiana University Press, 1989. A portrayal that defies the stereotype that Victorian gentlewomen led productive lives, were well-educated and sexually knowledgeable.

SCIENCE IN AN AGE OF OPTIMISM
Bowler, Peter J. *Evolution—The History of an Idea,* rev. ed. Berkeley, CA: University of California Press, 2003. An outstanding survey of the subject that argues that the Darwinian revolution never really occurred.

Bynum, W.F. *Science and the Practice of Medicine in the Nineteenth Century.* Cambridge: Cambridge University Press, 1994. Examines the impact of the sciences on medicine.

Kern, Stephen. *The Culture of Time and Space, 1880–1918.* Cambridge, MA: Harvard University Press, 1983. A lively discussion of the impact of the new technology.

CULTURE: ACCEPTING THE MODERN WORLD
Dale, Peter A. *In Pursuit of a Scientific Culture: Science, Art, and Society in the Victorian Age.* Madison, WI: University of Wisconsin Press, 1989. Examines the connections between science, culture, and society during the second half of the nineteenth century.

Pool, Phoebe. *Impressionism.* New York: Thames and Hudson, 1985. A thorough analysis of impressionism, stressing its origins and legacy.

FROM OPTIMISM TO UNCERTAINTY
Burrow, J.W. *The Crisis of Reason: European Thought, 1848–1914.* New Haven: Yale University Press, 2000. An excellent survey of the subject.

Gay, Peter. *Freud—A Life for Our Time.* New York: Norton, 1988. A standard biography of Freud.

Hughes, H. Stuart. *Consciousness and Society: The Reorientation of European Social Thought, 1890–1930.* New York: Vintage Books, 1979. A classic examination of the intellectual revolt against scientific certainty.

www.mhhe.com/sherman3

- Unfamiliar words? See our Glossary at the back of the book for pronunciation and definitions.

- Need help studying? See our web page for map exercises, practice quizzes, and additional study resources.

- Need help writing a paper? Access hundreds of primary documents, maps, images, and a guide to writing history papers on our Primary Source Investigator site at **www.mhhe.com/psi.**

OTTO DIX, *WAR*, 1929–1932

The German expressionist painter Otto Dix (1891–1969) fought in the trenches of World War I and was wounded several times. In this triptych he depicts the destructiveness of war. In the panel on the left, soldiers march toward the bleak battlefront. Their fate is depicted in the following panels: the gore and destruction of the front lines, trenches that serve as coffins for the numberless dead, and the endless haunting nightmares of those who somehow survive. This painting all too accurately captured the reality of the period as experienced by millions of people.

DESCENDING INTO THE TWENTIETH CENTURY

WORLD WAR AND REVOLUTION, 1914–1920

STUDY	The path to total war ▪ The front lines ▪ The home front ▪ The losses of the war ▪ The peace settlement ▪ Revolutions in Russia.
NOTICE	Why this war is considered a historical watershed.

"Millions of men are going to be massacred in a War of the Worlds." As late as the first days of August 1914, only a few Westerners voiced such ominous warnings as these words by the French writer Marcel Proust. In 1917, the third year of the war that Proust had foretold, the young British poet and soldier Wilfred Owen became trapped in a hole on the still-raging battle lines with the shattered body of a fellow officer. As Owen put it, the officer "lay not only near by, but in various places around and about." Owen returned to England suffering from "shell shock," as nervous breakdowns were known. Yet, a year later, he chose to return to the front. In a letter to his mother, he explained why: "I came out in order to help these boys. . . ." He hoped "by watching their sufferings that I may speak of them as well as a pleader can."

Suffer the young soldiers did, and much of Western civilization agonized along with them. The "Great War" ended the era that had begun 125 years earlier with the French and industrial revolutions. It spawned a new round of revolution, destroyed several empires, and altered politics and society for the rest of the twentieth century. The consequences of this war even spread into the non-Western world, drawing in troops from Asia and Africa and changing how people around the globe viewed the West.

Why did entire nations send their people into this conflict? After all, the war was not inevitable, nor was it an accident. At the same time, some of the combatants reasoned that they had no choice in the matter. Indeed, the outbreak of the war seemed to pivot on something that happened one June day in 1914. By itself, that event would not have led nations to commit to such a costly endeavor. But people turned the event into a spark that ignited a deadly fire they could not put out.

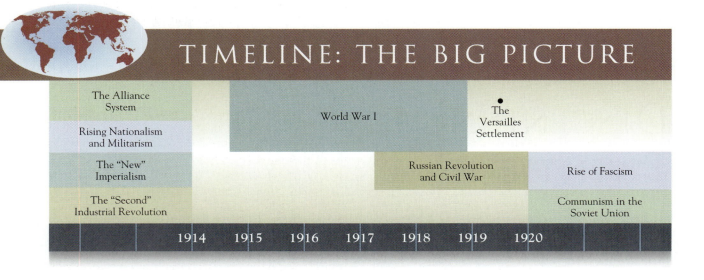

TIMELINE: THE BIG PICTURE

The Alliance System

Rising Nationalism and Militarism

The "New" Imperialism

The "Second" Industrial Revolution

World War I

The Versailles Settlement

Russian Revolution and Civil War

Rise of Fascism

Communism in the Soviet Union

1914 1915 1916 1917 1918 1919 1920

ON THE PATH TO TOTAL WAR

ON JUNE 28, 1914, 19-YEAR-OLD Gavrilo Princip, gun in hand, waited along a parade route in Sarajevo, the capital of the Austro-Hungarian province of Bosnia. Princip was a member of a Bosnian nationalist organization that had been trained by the Black Hand, a Serbian terrorist group. He was not alone. That day, Archduke Ferdinand, the heir to the Austro-Hungarian throne, was visiting Sarajevo. Princip, waiting with several conspirators, planned to kill the archduke to promote Slavic liberation from Austro-Hungarian control. As Ferdinand's open car passed by, Princip's co-conspirators lost their nerve and did not shoot. Then Ferdinand's driver took a wrong turn. Realizing his mistake, he stopped the car and, by chance, backed up to where Princip stood. Princip fired, killing Ferdinand and his wife.

In those years, several political leaders had been assassinated without great risk of war. Yet in just four weeks, this incident would lead Austria-Hungary, a second-rate power, to declare war on Serbia, a third-rate power in the southeast corner of Europe—the Balkans. Within one more week, most of Europe was engulfed by war. How could this incident in Sarajevo, far from the heart of Europe and not directly involving any of Europe's major powers, result in an all-out war that would end an era and transform Western society?

RIVALRIES AND ALLIANCES

Part of the answer lies in the national, economic, and imperial rivalry percolating in Europe at the time. Militant nationalism, intensifying since the mid-nineteenth century, encouraged countries to view one another as dangerous rivals in the struggle for power and prestige. Politicians used this nationalism to glaze over domestic problems and win public support. The growth of industrial capitalism created an environment of competitive economic struggle as nations tried to promote their industries and gain markets. The outburst of imperialism in the decades before 1914 pitted these rivals against one another in a race to acquire colonies and expand their arenas of influence around the world.

These rivalries fueled international affairs and pressured European states to form a system of alliances among themselves. The German statesman Otto von Bismarck initiated the alliances in the 1870s. Concerned about being encircled by enemies, he allied Germany with Austria-Hungary and Russia to avoid any possibility of a two-front war—to the east against Russia and to the west against France. With Bismarck's departure from office the new German kaiser—hoping to extend German influence over areas of concern to Russia—allowed the reinsurance treaty with Russia to lapse. This opened the door to major shifts in international relations. New alliances formed as European states tried to protect themselves and pursue their ambitions. Italy, looking for support against France in the competition for colonies, joined Germany and Austria-Hungary in 1882 to form the Triple Alliance. Russia, hoping to expand into southeastern Europe and gain access to the Mediterranean at the expense of the declining Ottoman Empire, came into conflict with Austro-Hungarian and German ambitions in the Balkans. By 1894, Russia had joined in a new alliance with France, which eagerly sought an ally in case of a clash with Germany. In 1904, Britain, threatened by the rise of Germany as a new naval, industrial, and imperial power, joined

The alliance system

its old rival France in an alliance called the Entente Cordiale. In 1905 and again in 1911, German challenges to French sovereignty over Morocco in North Africa created international crises that drew France and Britain closer together.

By 1914, Europe had divided itself into two powerful alliance systems: the Triple Entente, comprising France, Russia, and Great Britain; and the Triple Alliance, made up of Germany, Austria-Hungary, and Italy. On one hand, these alliances may have encouraged Europeans to believe that they could avert major wars. Between 1870 and 1914, a balance of power did generally prevail. Statesmen solved most conflicts diplomatically, and military scuffles remained brief and local. On the other hand, the alliance system gave smaller powers an opportunity to influence the decisions of larger powers; everyone feared that losing an ally—even a relatively weak supporter making decisions in its own interests—would upset the balance of power and make strong nations vulnerable.

Meanwhile, military might played a large part in politics in this world driven by competition and a struggle for international stature. Germany built a new navy; Britain kept ahead and in 1906 launched the Dreadnought, the first of a new class of battleships armed entirely with big guns; and *Military buildup* most powers reinforced their armies. Between 1870 and 1914, France and Germany more than doubled the size of their standing armies by requiring citizens to serve for set periods of time. Politicians justified huge expenditures for the military buildup with nationalistic slogans and claims that military spending promoted industry, jobs, and trade. Military staffs made plans emphasizing quick offensive thrusts and drew up timetables for mobilizing their forces in case of war. Most people assumed that any war that broke out would be short, like the Franco-Prussian War of 1870 (see pages 600–601), and that their own nation would win it. This armaments race and military planning only heightened the suspicion and fear brewing between nations. It also made national leaders feel ever more dependent on their allies for support in case of war.

CRISES IN THE BALKANS

These rivalries and hardening alliances became enmeshed in a series of crises that exploded in the Balkans (see Maps 22.1 and 22.2). Why the Balkans? This was Europe's most unstable area—a land of strong nationalistic aspirations felt by several peoples who had been long dominated by the declining Austro-Hungarian and Ottoman Empires. As the Ottoman Empire disintegrated during the late nineteenth and early twentieth centuries, various Balkan peoples, such as the Romanians, Bulgarians, and Serbs, had established independent nations. Peoples still under Ottoman or Austro-Hungarian rule agitated for their own independence or sought support from their linguistic kin—especially the Serbs—in these new Balkan states. The Ottoman Turks, newly united after a 1908 revolution led by the nationalistic Young Turks, struggled to maintain what power they still had in the area. The Austro-Hungarians feared dismemberment of their multinational empire by these nationalistic sentiments. They hoped to expand into the Balkans and thereby weaken any movements for independence among their own ethnic minorities. These hopes brought Austria-Hungary into conflict with Russia, which had long hungered for influence and expansion in the Balkans. Russia had fought two limited wars in pursuit of these aims during the second half of the nineteenth century. It also envisioned itself as the honorable, fraternal protector of Slavic peoples in the Balkans.

The first Balkan crisis erupted in 1908, when Austria-Hungary suddenly annexed two provinces, Bosnia and Herzegovina, which were home to Serbs, Croats, and others. Serbia had wanted to annex these territories, peopled by its own linguistic kin. Serbia appealed to Russia, and Russia threatened Austria-Hungary, whereupon Germany joined its ally and forced Russia to back down. The second Balkan crisis occurred in 1912–1913. The various Balkan states defeated Turkey in a war and then fought among themselves over the spoils. Victorious Serbia longed for more territory. Austria-Hungary thwarted the small country's expansion to the Adriatic Sea and threatened to annihilate Serbia. Again Serbia appealed to Russia, and again German pressure forced Russia to back down.

The assassination of Archduke Ferdinand on June 28, 1914, precipitated the third Balkan crisis. The government of Austria-Hungary, certain of Serbian involvement in the assassination, decided to crush Serbia and establish its own dominance in *Germany's blank check* the Balkans once and for all. But this plan would require the backing of Germany, for Russia might come to the support of its Serbian allies and defend its own interests in the Balkans. At a fateful conference in Berlin eight days after the Sarajevo shooting, the German government encouraged Austria-Hungary's scheme with a "blank check" of full support. Emboldened by Germany's backing and advice to act quickly, Austria-Hungary presented Serbia with an ultimatum that Serbia could not hope to meet. Upon hearing of Austria's demands on Serbia, Russia's foreign minister told Austria's ambassador, "You are setting fire to Europe." On July 28, even after Serbia had yielded on all but one of the ultimatum's terms (which would have allowed Austria to investigate Serbian involvement in the assassination plot), Austria-Hungary declared war.

MAP 22.1 THE BALKANS, 1878

MAP 22.2 THE BALKANS, 1914

Map 22.1 shows the Balkans in 1878, and fighting and territorial changes to 1913. Map 22.2 shows the same region in 1914 after new fighting resulted in further territorial changes. ■ **Notice** the shifting alliances and battlefronts indicated by the red arrows. **Consider** who gained the most and who lost the most. **Why** might this region be such a complex political and military cauldron?

Mobilization

To back Serbia against Austria-Hungary, Russia ordered its clumsy military establishment to mobilize. However, Russian military planning, which assumed a war against both Austria and Germany, did not allow for only partial mobilization against Austria. Russia's order of full mobilization on July 29 was almost the same as a declaration of war—especially to German military leaders.

Germany's main war plan assumed a two-front war against Russia and France, requiring the German army to knock France out of the fighting before Russia could bring the weight of its slow-moving forces against Germany. Therefore, Germany mobilized and sent ultimatums to Russia, demanding demobilization, and to

France, requiring a declaration of neutrality. When Russia failed to reply and France gave an unsatisfactory response, Germany declared war on Russia on August 1 and on France two days later. On August 4, when German troops violated Belgian neutrality on their way to attack France, Great Britain declared war on Germany.

Thus the great powers of Europe were sucked into a general war they did not want by the very alliances they had formed to protect themselves and feared to violate. The growing tensions in European societies—violent domestic politics, strikes, threats from the political Left and Right, and themes of uncertainty and disintegration expressed in the arts—all worsened matters.

One of the most ominous expressions of the growing tensions in the air came from German Expressionist Ludwig Meidner (1884–1966). In his 1913 canvas, *Apocalyptic Landscape* (Figure 22.1), the sky seems to explode as if under bombardment. Below, buildings shatter as the land quakes. People run in all directions over streets that echo the violence above. In the artist's words, this painting shows "big city life" where "life is lived at fever pitch," and reflects a time when "the great world storm was already baring its teeth and casting its harsh shadow over the whimpering land which was carrying my brush." These tensions made many Europeans, including many intellectuals and well-known observers, welcome war as a quick, all-encompassing relief. Facing these perils and tensions, Europe's stunningly inept political and military leaders made decisions based more on blind optimism and fear of humiliation than reason and concern for their nation's well-being. That "great world storm" described by Meidner soon arrived. At the time, few Europeans guessed how long the brutality would last.

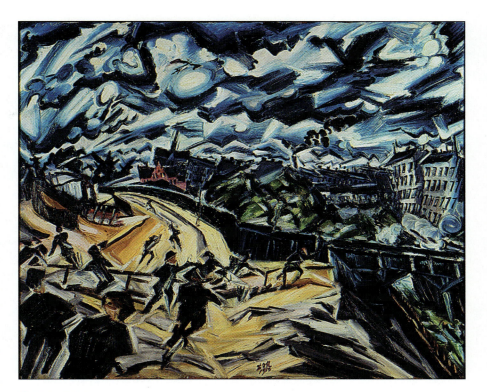

■ FIGURE 22.1

Ludwig Meidner, *Apocalyptic Landscape*, 1913.

THE FRONT LINES

OFF TO BATTLE

Almost everywhere in Europe, people greeted the declarations of war with outbursts of nationalistic joy.

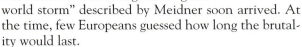 As the Austrian writer Stefan Zweig (1881–1942), a volunteer himself, recalled, "There were parades in the street, flags, ribbons, and music burst forth everywhere, young recruits were marching triumphantly, their faces lighting up at the cheering." Young men volunteered in droves, "honestly afraid that they might miss this most wonderful and exciting experience of their lives; that is why they hurried and thronged to the colors, and that is why they shouted and sang in the trains that carried them to the slaughter." Figure 22.2, a photograph of German volunteers marching down a Berlin street during the first weeks of the war, reveals the enthusiasm, optimism, and naivete of the young men. Well-dressed and raising their hats, they announce their bravery and celebrate their good fortune at being able to fight for their nation.

Celebrating war

KEY DATES

DEVELOPMENTS LEADING TO WORLD WAR I

1882	Triple Alliance
1894	Franco-Russian Alliance
1904	Entente Cordiale
1905	First Moroccan crisis
1908	Revolt in Ottoman Empire
	First Balkan crisis
1911	Second Moroccan crisis
1912	Second Balkan crisis
1914	Assassination of Archduke Ferdinand

Here, suddenly, was a way to end domestic divisions and renew one's sense of purpose in the world. Political opponents set their differences aside and came together to support the war effort. As Document 22.1 reveals, even socialists, long opposed to war and nationalistic calls, joined in the effort to promote national defense. In Germany, the socialists voted for war credits and

■ DOCUMENT 22.1

A Russian Socialist Supports the War Effort

At the beginning of World War I, there was tremendous popular enthusiasm and unity behind governments for the war effort. Even socialist parties—which had long argued that they would not support a nationalistic war entered into by a government dominated by capitalists—joined the effort. The following letter from V. Bourtzeff, a Russian Socialist, appeared in the London Times *about six weeks after the outbreak of the war in 1914.* ■ **Why** *does Bourtzeff support the war effort?* ■ **How** *does Bourtzeff justify his opposition to the government's policies and his support for the government in the war?*

To the editor of "The Times":

Sir—May I be allowed to say a few words in connection with the excellent letter by my compatriot, Professor Vinogradov, which appeared in your paper today (September 14)? Professor Vinogradov is absolutely right when he says that not only is it desirable that complete unity of feeling should exist in Russian political circles, but that this unity is already an accomplished fact.

The representatives of all political parties and of all nationalities in Russia are now at one with the Government, and this war with Germany and Austria, both guided by the Kaiser, has already become a national war for Russia.

Even we, the adherents of the parties of the Extreme Left, and hitherto ardent anti-militarists and pacifists, even we believe in the necessity of *this* war. *This* war is a war to protect justice and civilization. It will, we hope, be a decisive factor in our united *war against war*, and we hope that after it, it will at last be possible to consider seriously the question of disarmament and universal peace. There can be no doubt that victory, and decisive victory at that (personally I await this in the immediate future), will be on the side of the Allied nations—England, France, Belgium, Serbia, and Russia.

The German peril, the curse which has hung over the whole world for so many decades, will be crushed, and crushed so that it will never again become a danger to the peace of the world. The peoples of the world desire peace.

To Russia this war will bring regeneration. . . .

All the parties without any exceptions have supported the Government without even waiting for it to make any definite announcement about these crying needs. This is the measure of the belief of the people in the inevitableness of liberal reforms. The Government unfortunately still seems irresolute, and has up till now only done the minimum to justify the popular belief in it, but we are convinced that circumstances will develop in such a way that the Government will not be able to delay for long that which has become for Russia a *historical necessity*. And the sooner this happens the better.

Source: Frank A. Golder, *Documents of Russian History, 1914–1917,* trans. E. Aronsberg (Prentice-Hall, 1927), pp. 38–39.

---

agreed to suspend strikes until the end of the war. In France, socialists joined their old opponents to support a government of national defense, called the "Sacred Union." Russia's leading socialist party proclaimed,

■ FIGURE 22.2

German volunteers, August 1914.

"Our first duty is to preserve our nation's unity and integrity, and to defend her position as a world power." Most feminists also suspended their political demands and offered ardent support for the military cause. The troops, people assumed, would surely be home by Christmas. Indeed, the British government promised that life would go on as usual with no shortages and no new regulations. Each combatant expected to win.

Nations initially on the sidelines soon enlisted with one side or the other (see Map 22.3). Hoping to gain territory in a victorious fight, Turkey and Bulgaria joined Germany and Austria-Hungary to become the **Central Powers.** Italy, long a member of the Triple Alliance with Germany and Austria-Hungary, had declared its neutrality at the beginning of the war, claiming that Austria had violated the alliance by launching a war of aggression on Serbia. Italy shifted its loyalty to France and Britain after receiving better promises of victory spoils. This side, eventually joined by many other nations from

The Central Powers versus the Allies

THINKING ABOUT GEOGRAPHY

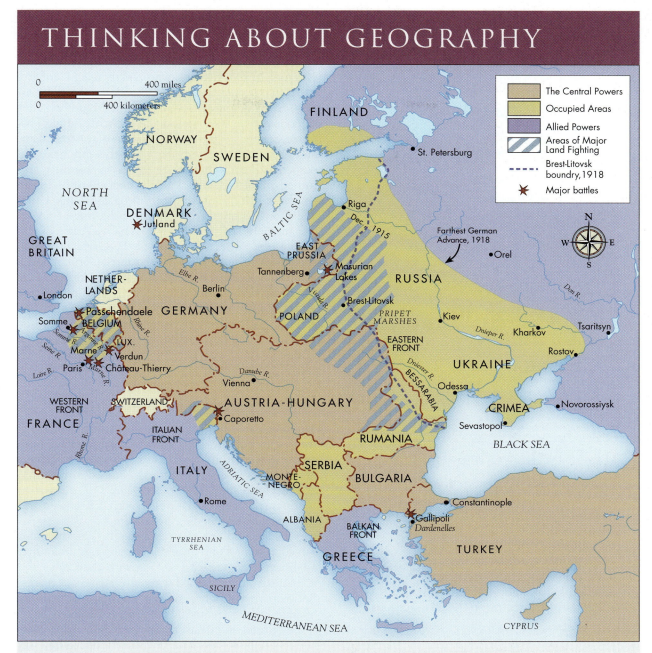

MAP 22.3   WORLD WAR I

This map shows the two alliances and the major fronts in World War I. ■ **Consider** what this map reveals about the surrounded position of the Central Powers and the importance of Turkey during the war. ■ **Locate** the major areas of fighting on the western and eastern fronts. **What** do these reveal about the different nature of the war on these two fronts? **Which** areas in Europe were most directly affected by the fighting?

the Americas and the non-Western world, became known as the **Allies.** The Allies had the advantage of sheer numbers, but the Central Powers were led by Germany's better equipped, well-trained army and could more easily move troops and coordinate military strategies.

The Schlieffen Plan

Anticipating a confrontation with both Russia and France, the German high command resorted to a military strategy known as the **Schlieffen Plan.** This plan called for a holding action against the slow-moving

THINKING ABOUT GEOGRAPHY

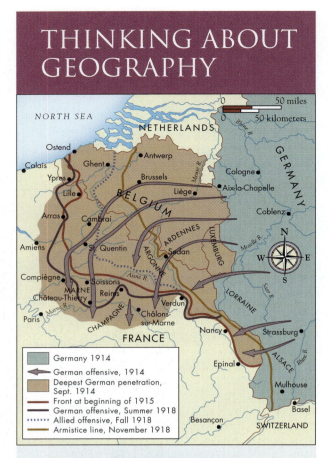

MAP 22.4 THE WESTERN FRONT

This map shows the western front at various stages of World War I. ■ **Notice** how far the Germans penetrated in their 1914 offensive and how close they came to capturing the French capital. ■ **Locate** the western front at the beginning of 1915—that line would change little over the next three years. ■ **What** countries were most directly affected by the fighting on the western front?

Russians while the main German forces thrust through neutral Belgium to knock out France. Then the Germans could concentrate on destroying Russia. Great Britain, her allies hobbled, would sue for peace, the Germans expected.

Day after day, the Schlieffen Plan worked. Four weeks after the outbreak of hostilities, German forces arrived just outside Paris ahead of schedule. Some surprises, however, lay in store for them. Stubborn Belgian resistance had held up the Germans long enough for the French to redeploy their forces to the north and for the British to send their small army across the Channel. Germans suffered unanticipated casualties and transportation problems. At a critical moment, the German command detached 100,000 of their best troops under generals Hindenburg (1847–1934) and Ludendorff (1865–1937) and sent them east to fight the Russians, who had invaded Germany with unexpected speed. Nearing Paris, the German First Army detoured from its planned route in order to concentrate its force on the French capital. This move opened a gap in the Germans' eastern flank and exposed its western flank. At this juncture, the desperate French armies seized the opportunity and turned on the Germans. Parisian taxicabs rushed army reserves to the front in the effort to save Paris. Units of Britain's army arrived to enter the fray at a crucial moment. In the bloody seven-day Battle of the Marne, the Allies at last halted the Germans, drove them back several miles, and shattered German hopes that the Schlieffen Plan would succeed. As Map 22.4 indicates, both sides extended their lines more than 400 miles from the Swiss border to the North Sea and dug in for the winter. Germany was now stuck with what it had tried so hard to avoid—a war on two fronts.

SLAUGHTER AND STALEMATE ON THE WESTERN FRONT

The defensive lines proved superior to offensive thrusts. To the surprise of almost everyone, the armies on the western front fought a war of attrition from their networks of trenches protected by barbed wire, mines, and machine guns. The trenches, up to thirty feet deep, became filled with mud, rats, human bodies, lice, waste, poison gas, and the stench of death. But they also served as homes and protection for troops under fire, as shown in Figure 22.3. Along with their rifles and grenades, soldiers carried wire cutters and gas masks. Between the trenches, mortar and massive artillery bombardments created a barren, pockmarked landscape of mud and death that few soldiers could cross and still hope to live. The British introduced tanks in 1916 but did not manage to use them effectively to cross trenches until the end of the war.

Trench warfare

Despite the defensive advantages of **trench warfare,** military commanders remained wedded to notions of an offensive breakthrough. Again and again, they sent troops scrambling out of their trenches, "over the top" and into "no-man's-land," where enemy machine-gun fire mowed them down by the thousands. Fritze Franke, a German soldier, described his experience of trench warfare in a November 1914 letter: "Every foot of ground contested, every hundred yards another trench; and everywhere bodies—rows of them! All the trees shot to pieces; the whole ground churned up a yard deep by the heaviest shells; dead animals; houses and churches . . . utterly destroyed . . . And every troop that advances in support must pass through a mile of this chaos, through this gigantic burial ground and the reek of corpses." Fololiyani Longwe, an African serving in the British army on the western front, described how soldiers stood "buried in a hole with only your head and hands outside, holding a gun" for days with "no food, no water," and "only death smelling all over the place." Wilfred Owen, the British poet whom we met at the beginning of the chapter, related how the brutal reality of the war wiped out old images of its glory. Owen warned that anyone who saw the suffering

> . . . [W]ould not tell with such high zest
> To children ardent for some desperate glory,
> The old Lie: Dulce et decorum est
> Pro patria mori. ("It is sweet and proper
> to die for one's country.")

Military leaders failed to realize that machine guns, modern artillery, mass mobilization, and trenches had utterly changed the nature of warfare. Acting on old assumptions and oblivious to these new military realities, generals ordered offensives again and again. Each time the charges moved lines only yards if at all, and each time the human costs were staggering. "We lie under the network of arching shells and live in a suspense of uncertainty," wrote German war veteran Erich Maria Remarque (1898–1970) in his novel *All Quiet on the Western Front*. "Over us Chance hovers." The wartime life expectancy of a front-line officer such as Wilfred Owen was only two months. After a year and a half of this mutual slaughter, nothing had changed.

In 1916, the Germans tried for a draining victory by attacking the French fortress at Verdun (see Map 22.3). Their plan was, in the words of the German commander, to "bleed to death" the French by forcing them to sustain massive casualties defending this historic strongpoint. During the ensuing nine-month battle, the Germans sometimes fired as many as a million shells in one day. The French managed to hold off the Germans, but 700,000 men on both sides lost their lives in the effort. "You found the dead embedded in the walls of the trenches, heads, legs, and half-bodies, just as they had been shovelled out of the way by the picks and shovels of the working party," recalled one French soldier.

Great battles of 1916

That same year the British attempted a breakthrough in the Battle of the Somme in northeastern France (see Map 22.3). They suffered 60,000 casualties, with more than 20,000 killed in just the first day. "As far as you could see there were all these bodies lying there—literally thousands of them . . . It didn't seem possible," wrote a British soldier. By fall, Britain had endured 400,000 casualties; France, 200,000; and

■ FIGURE 22.3

Trench warfare.

Germany, 500,000, in this one battle. It ended in a stalemate. "Here chivalry disappeared for always," wrote the German Ernst Jünger. In the Passchendaele offensive (see Map 22.3), the British again tried to break through the German "crust," losing some 400,000 soldiers in the effort. Like other great battles in the west, Passchendaele scarcely moved the front lines at all.

Neither the politicians nor the generals found the will to call a halt to the slaughter. Anything short of complete victory, they feared, would mean that all the deaths and casualties were in vain. The troops were not so stubborn. Sometimes they agreed to avoid battles. They even occasionally fraternized across the trenches, sang together, and allowed each other to eat meals in peace or collect the bodies of fellow soldiers in no-man's-land. They also were capable of making their outrage known to their superiors. After a new, disastrous offensive ordered by France's commander General Nivelle in April 1917, mutinies broke out in half the French divisions on the front. Thousands of soldiers were court-martialed and more than 500 sentenced to death, although most executions were never carried out. New commanders and troops tacitly agreed to stop these hopeless offensive onslaughts.

Figure 22.4 illustrates how all means, old and new, were used to fight this war. Here soldiers with plumed helmets sit astride horses while an airplane, used for **Weapons of war** bombing and intelligence, flies overhead. Armies would use poison gas, flame throwers, and tanks for the first time. Even dogs—75,000 of them—were employed to search for wounded men on the battlefronts.

On the seas, both sides in the war hoped for decisive victories. The British navy set up a blockade of Germany, and the Germans responded with the submarine. Germany and Britain never met in a conclusive naval showdown, however. In the Battle of Jutland, the only major naval battle of the war, the British fleet prevented the German fleet from breaking the blockade—but suffered serious losses as a result. Most of the massive struggle took place on the ground. After three years of fighting, neither side could break through on the western front. By then, the French alone had sustained more than 3.5 million casualties. Yet, the war dragged on.

VICTORY AND DEFEAT ON THE EASTERN AND SOUTHERN FRONTS

On the eastern front, as Map 22.3 indicates, the war proved far more mobile and offensive than in the west. In eastern Europe, the terrain did not favor trench warfare, and in any case the Russians lacked the resources to sustain such a defensive effort. Initially, Russia, with its huge but inadequately supplied army,

■ FIGURE 22.4
Old and new means of war.

pushed into German and Austro-Hungarian lands. By the end of August 1914, however, the reinforced German armies, bolstered by their superior technology and leadership, trapped the Russians at Tannenberg and administered a crushing defeat. The Russian commander, General Samsonov, committed suicide on the spot. Farther south, the Russians defeated an Austro-Hungarian army at Lemberg only to bring in a German army that delivered a series of hammer blows to the Russians. The Germans drove deep into Russia and inflicted immense casualties, making Generals Hindenburg and Ludendorff heroes. In the Balkans, German, Austrian, and Bulgarian forces eliminated Serbia from the war by the end of 1915. That same year, a disastrous Anglo-French effort to help the hard-pressed Russians by landing at Gallipoli and breaking through Turkish defenses at the nearby Dardanelles was beaten back by the Turks with heavy losses to the Allies (see Map 22.3).

In 1916, Russia made one more great effort against the Austro-Hungarian forces in the south. Under General Aleksei Brusilov, Russian armies almost forced the Austro-Hungarians to withdraw from the war. The Austro-Hungarians resorted to recruiting men over the **Russia's military collapse** age of 50 into the army, and in the end kept going only with German support. But the Russians could not sustain the effort. Lack of effective leadership, insufficient supplies, and desertions plagued Russia's armies. "Half of them have no rifles," Tsar Nicholas admitted, "the troops are losing masses and there is nobody to collect them on the battlefields." Germany's renewed push in 1917 resulted in massive Russian losses. These losses, along with internal strife that toppled the tsar, his government, and the succeeding provisional government (see pages 692–695) knocked Russia out of the war in December 1917. Nevertheless, for more than two years, the Russian effort had drawn German troops east, weakening the German forces in the west.

Meanwhile, in northeastern Italy, Austrian and German troops won some costly battles, but the Italian forces limited the Central Powers' advances (see Map 22.3). Farther south and east, Allied **Southern fronts** forces attacked the Ottoman Empire. In 1915, after an Anglo-French fleet failed to open the Dardanelle straits so Russia could receive supplies in her Black Sea ports, Britain sent a 400,000-man force of mostly Australian and New Zealand troops to Gallipoli. The invaders suffered terrible defeats at the hands of the Turkish defenders and were forced to evacuate. Even more crippling, malaria, cholera, dysentery, and other diseases spread among the troops fighting in the Middle

East. Eventually, the British, most notably the charismatic officer and writer T. E. Lawrence (1888–1935), stirred up Arab resentment into a desert revolt against the Ottoman Turks in Palestine and Mesopotamia. Together, British and Arab forces gradually gained the upper hand against the Ottoman Turks.

THE WAR SPREADS ACROSS THE GLOBE

The war itself soon spread outside of Europe and the Mediterranean basin, in great part thanks to the West's colonies and imperial interests throughout the world. In the South Atlantic, British and German naval forces clashed off the Falkland Isles. In Africa, minor battles erupted around Germany's colonies. In East Asia, Japan joined the war on the Allied side and promptly seized German holdings in the Pacific and China. When Russia seemed on the verge of falling apart, Japan also sent soldiers into the tsar's far eastern provinces. Britain and France drew troops from Canada, Africa, Asia, and Australia to fight on several fronts. More than 1 million Indian soldiers served under the British, particularly in the Middle East campaigns, and hundreds of thousands of African soldiers from French colonies served in Europe. The Western nations also called on workers from these lands, including a 200,000-man labor battalion from China, to work in France and elsewhere in the war effort.

However, non-Western peoples often resisted the European powers' efforts to gain their support. Nomadic tribes fled Russia's central Asian provinces rather than serve in the tsar's army. In French West Africa, local tribes revolted when the French tried to mobilize labor brigades. Moreover, non-Westerners did not automatically favor the Allied cause. Most of those who followed the conflict in Asia viewed World War I as a European civil war. In addition, they were likely to favor Germany over France and Britain, two nations who had a tradition of Asian conquest. Indeed, for the most part, the first world war remained a European affair. Raging on year after year, the conflict shattered the lives of soldiers and civilians alike.

WAR ON THE HOME FRONT

No Western society could come through such a protracted war unscathed. As the toll on lives and supplies climbed, whole societies had to mobilize to support the military effort. In this sense, World War I became the first **total war,** blurring the traditional distinctions between combatants and civilians and between battle lines and the home front. The first world war transformed

Total war

whole economies, societies, and governments, as well as the lives of soldiers.

MOBILIZING RESOURCES

After the first few months of hostilities, armies began to run out of ammunition, supplies, and troops. The French alone were firing more than 100,000 artillery shells a day—far more than their armaments factories could supply. Entire economies were reorganized to churn out huge quantities of bullets, guns, and machines in just days and weeks rather than the usual months and years. The war effort required untold quantities of other materials as well—everything from food and uniforms to trucks and coffins. Over all, the war demanded unprecedented industrial capability and organizational agility to produce and move supplies for the armed forces.

To varying degrees, the governments of the major powers took control of their economies. Government agencies, rather than the free marketplace, determined production, consumption, wages, and prices. In Germany, the War Raw Materials Board located, rationed, and distributed *Governments take control* raw materials. To meet the need for products that Germany could no longer import, such as rubber, the Board helped develop synthetic substitutes. In Britain, the Ministry of Munitions, led by David Lloyd George, supervised the armaments industry. The ministry's bureaucracy of 65,000 clerks controlled prices, supplies, and production of war materials.

This tightly controlled mobilization of resources also included people. Not only were men drafted into the armed services, but women and men on the home fronts were often required to work in accord with priorities determined by the government. Labor unions were brought into partnership with business and government. In addition, governments

KEY DATES

WORLD WAR I

1914	Battle of the Marne
1915	Italy joins Allies
1916	Battle of Verdun
1917	United States enters the war
1918	End of World War I
1919	Treaty of Versailles

suspended laws limiting the length of the workday and controlling workplace conditions. People were thus forced to work longer hours under dangerous circumstances.

Demand for troops on the front lines and labor on the home front altered traditional social and national boundaries. Although the war did not eliminate class conflict, social distinctions blurred as people from all walks of society joined the war effort and worked or fought side by side. Conventional national distinctions were sometimes violated: For awhile, the hard-pressed Germans forced thousands of Belgians to move and work in German factories. The war effort could even include children: Some German teachers organized their students to go through garbage and collect anything that might be useful. Perhaps most striking, officials challenged traditional gender roles by calling women into the labor force.

NEW GENDER ROLES

Gender roles changed radically under the pressures of all-out war. At first, many women were left on their own financially as their husbands marched off to battle. Later, when economies began straining with the war effort, women got new jobs previously reserved for men. Figure 22.5 shows women working in a large British armaments plant, producing the huge quantity of shells needed on the battle lines. Such women participated in all aspects of the munitions industries. They became army clerks and streetcar conductors and drove taxies and ran farms. Some served as firefighters at home and as nurses at the front. Others gained entry into white-collar jobs in banks, commercial businesses,

and urban offices. In Great Britain, the number of women working outside the home increased twenty-fold to some 5 million by 1918. In Russia, women made up over 40 percent of the labor force. Similar patterns held in other European countries.

These shifting labor patterns created new tensions over women's roles as men began fearing they would lose their jobs to women permanently. "Workmen have to be handled with the utmost tenderness and caution lest they should actually imagine . . . that women could do their work equally well," wrote a female British munitions factory worker in 1916. Women themselves often had conflicted feelings about their new role. Many gained a new sense of independence from earning a paycheck. Some displayed their newfound freedom by living alone, going out socially on their own, wearing shorter dresses, cutting ("bobbing") their hair, and smoking cigarettes. Others felt torn by the dual demands of service and family. "What exhausts women in wartime is not the strenuous and unfamiliar tasks that fall upon them, nor even the hourly dread of death for husbands or lovers or brothers or sons," recalled British writer Vera Brittain (1896–1970), who served as a nurse on the front lines. "It is the incessant conflict between personal and national claims which wears out their energy and breaks their spirit." By no coincidence, several nations would grant women the right to vote at the war's end.

MAINTAINING THE EFFORT

As the war persisted, governments became more involved in manufacturing consent and less tolerant of dissent. Propaganda specialists tried to inspire support for the war and hatred for the enemy. The more the propaganda succeeded in its aims, the harder it *Propaganda* became for governments to compromise or withdraw from the conflict. Officials deliberately manipulated information and censored private letters to shape public opinion about the war. In particular, they tried to create the impression that their own country was completely virtuous and that it was the other nations that were committing crimes against humanity. To combat war weariness, governments painted the enemy as evil incarnate and whipped up people's sense of outrage. There was no way, political leaders declared, that "good" people could ever make peace with such diabolical opponents.

Figure 22.6, a cover from a French magazine, is an example of such propaganda. The image depicts Germans as having committed atrocities during their march through Belgium and northern France. Here an innocent, horror-stricken, assaulted woman kneels

■ FIGURE 22.5
Women war workers.

on a blood-soaked crib and cradles the body of her murdered child. The empty wine bottles and helmet scattered on the ground around her leave no doubt that immoral German soldiers have committed these acts. The illustrator also blames the Germans for setting the homes and church of this village on fire while passing through. The glaring headline exhorts people to "Let Us Never Forget."

Governments also tried to promote dissent among their opponents and turn neutral countries into allies. Germany supported the Irish in their 1916 Easter Rebellion in Dublin for Irish independence, which British forces brutally crushed. Germany also aided the Bolsheviks against Russia's government. The British promoted rebellion among the Arabs against the Turks and used propaganda to help bring the Americans in on their side.

Victories or defeats on the front lines reflected the abilities of civilian societies to mobilize effectively for the war effort—materially, politically, and psychologically. Those nations less able to develop and sustain this vast home-front effort—such as the Austro-Hungarian and Russian empires—faltered first. They lacked the solid industrial base and organizational strength of Germany, France, and Great Britain. Over time, however, even the strongest nations weakened under the strains of total war. Food shortages spawned malnutrition, disease, and high infant mortality, especially in Germany, which acutely felt the impact of Britain's naval blockade. Governments tried to pay for the war by printing more money, thereby creating an inflation of prices.

By 1917, hunger and war weariness ignited strikes and domestic disorders throughout Europe. Beleaguered governments suspended civil liberties, ignored democratic procedures, and ruled by emergency police powers. In France, Georges Clemenceau (1841–1929) became a virtual dictator after November 1917. He sent troops against strikers and arrested those agitating for peace. "I wage war," he declared. "I wage nothing but war!" In Austria, political unity unraveled as different nationalities clamored for independence. In Germany, some socialist and Catholic legislators came out for peace, and generals Hindenburg and Ludendorff assumed control over the German war effort. By the end of 1917, Russia's whole war effort had collapsed. Clearly, World War I would be won or lost on the home front as well as on the battle lines.

Rising dissent

TO THE BITTER END

Early in 1917, the German high command grew desperate to bring the draining war to a victorious conclusion. The generals decided to launch an unrestricted submarine campaign against enemy and neutral shipping alike. Germany's leaders knew this policy could bring the United States into the war. Up to that point, the United States had remained

Let Us Never Forget

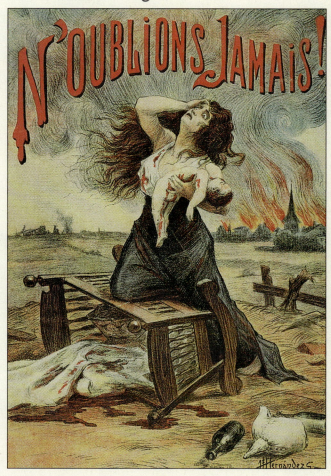

■ FIGURE 22.6

Numerous propaganda posters were produced on all sides of the war. This French poster depicts the fate of the Belgians when the Germans conquered the nation on the way to their main western adversary, France. ■ **What** kind of response do you think this scene was intended to stir in the viewer? ■ **Why** does the scene focus on a woman and her child rather than, for example, a battle scene? ■ **In what ways** are visual clues used to enable the viewer to read this picture as a dramatic series of events that have just occurred? ■ **Why** might propaganda posters such as this be effective?

BIOGRAPHY

Käthe Kollwitz (1867–1945)

CONSIDER

■ **Consider** how Kollwitz's life reflected the impact of World War I on European society.

By the eve of World War I, Käthe Kollwitz's prints, drawings, and posters had made her one of Germany's leading artists. "[M]y art has purpose," she said. "I want to be effective in this time when people are so helpless and in need of aid."

Käthe Schmidt was born in East Prussia in 1867. As a child, she often suffered from periods of depression, and these episodes continued well into her adulthood. Early on she learned to express her feelings in art. In 1891, Käthe married Dr. Karl Kollwitz, whom she would praise years later as her "life's comrade." Karl shared Käthe's socialist sympathies. That year, the couple moved to Berlin, where Karl took a job as a physician for a workers' health insurance fund and where Käthe gave birth to Hans in 1892 and Peter in 1896. Reflecting on the role of love in her life, she would later describe silently falling in love with women as well as men and the influence of bisexuality on the themes in her art.

Käthe earned her first public success as an artist between 1895 and 1898 with the publication of a series of prints, "The Weavers." These images recorded a doomed revolt of handloom weavers in the 1840s. Indeed, most of her works explored the plight of victims of social injustice, the cause of peace, and the sufferings of war and death. Not surprisingly, her art often offended the authorities, including the kaiser.

In early August 1914, just after World War I broke out, the Kollwitz family heard German soldiers singing as they marched in the streets (see pp. 677–678). Käthe wept in horror. During those same days, her youngest son, Peter, only 18 years old, volunteered for the army. On August 27, 1914, she wrote, "Where do all the women who have watched so carefully over the lives of their beloved ones get the heroism to send them to face the cannon? I am afraid that this soaring of the spirit will be followed by the blackest despair and dejection." A month later, she wrote, "It seems so stupid that the boys must go to war . . . how can they possibly take part in such madness?" Three weeks later, on October 22, 1914, Peter was killed in the war.

This loss of her son haunted Käthe for the rest of her life. In letters and diaries, she expressed endless grief for her fallen boy. She expanded her sorrow to embrace grieving mothers in all countries. Reflecting on the causes of the war, she described how Peter and others she knew had "subordinated their lives to the idea of patriotism. The English, Russian and French young men have done the same. The consequence has been this terrible killing and the impoverishment of Europe."

Artist and Witness to War

After her son's death, Käthe began a long struggle to create monumental sculptures in memory of Peter and other sons killed in the war. It would take her ten years to start work on the final forms for these sculptures and another eight years before the figures were completed in stone. Figures 22.7 and 22.8 are photographs of the two sculptures. At the opening ceremony, held in the Belgian cemetery where Peter was buried, Käthe stood before her stone figure of the mother: "I looked at her, my own face, and wept and stroked her cheeks."

When the war ended, she worried that "the peace will probably be very bad." For her the war, fought by Europe's youth, had destroyed "all that is most beautiful in Europe." In 1919, she became the first woman elected to the Prussian Academy of Arts. In 1928, she was further honored by being appointed head of a master class for graphic arts. In 1930, as the Nazis rose in strength, she wrote that "evil reaction is creeping into all areas." Käthe was forced to resign her prestigious position when Hitler came to power in 1933, and the Führer banned her work. In 1940 her grandson, Peter, the namesake of her son Peter killed in World War I, joined Germany's army as World War II erupted. He was killed on the Russian front in 1942. She continued her work almost until her death on April 22, 1945.

---

neutral but had become increasingly invested in the Allied cause through trade and loans. The sense that Germany and its partners were the aggressors, along with the 1915 sinking of the passenger liner *Lusitania* during a German submarine blockade of Britain, had also nudged American public opinion toward support of the Allies. Now Germany's high command gambled that they could defeat Britain and France before the Americans could send enough supplies and troops to Europe to make a difference. Indeed, Ludendorff and Hindenburg promised victory within only six months.

At about the same time, British intelligence turned over to the United States an alarming note that it claimed to have intercepted. In that document, called the Zimmermann note, Germany offered to grant U.S. territory to Mexico if Mexico agreed to attack the United States.

The U.S. enters the war

When German submarines began sinking American cargo ships, U.S. entry into the conflict was assured. On April 6, 1917, the United States declared war on Germany. President Woodrow Wilson promised to "make the world safe for democracy."

■ FIGURE 22.7

Käthe Kollwitz, *The Mourning Father*.

Like so many other people, Käthe Kollwitz had witnessed the great enthusiasm as soldiers first marched off to the Great War in August 1914. Also like countless millions of people, she had lost a loved one in that conflict. She, too, would live long

■ FIGURE 22.8

Käthe Kollwitz, *The Mourning Mother*.

enough to witness a terrible renewal of war. In her last letter, she wrote, "the war accompanies me to the end." She, along with far too many in the West, would never fully recover from the scars of World War I.

The Germans had good reason to think that they might prevail. By the beginning of 1918, the United States' contribution to the war was still relatively small. In addition, the Italians had suffered a disastrous blow at the Battle of Caporetto, almost putting them out of the war. Romania and Serbia had been defeated, and Russia had withdrawn from the war. Now Germany could at last focus its efforts on a one-front war. In the Atlantic, its U-boats (submarines) were sinking one-fourth of all ships taking supplies to Britain—350 ships went down in one month alone.

On the other hand, Germany's allies—the Austro-Hungarian and Ottoman Empires—were teetering, and Germany was suffering from lack of materials and food, thanks to Britain's naval blockade. The British had also discovered a way to foil the U-boats by using heavily escorted convoys armed with depth charges. Now the race was between Germany and the United States. Germany transferred troops from the Russian front in an effort to overwhelm Great Britain and France before waves of American troops could arrive, while the United States struggled to raise, train, and transport sufficient forces to France to stem the German tide.

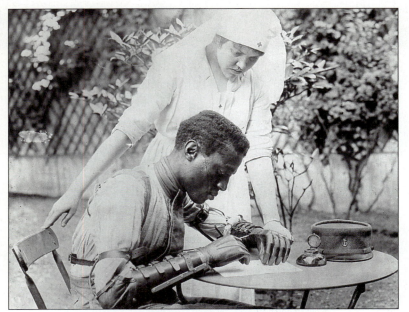

■ FIGURE 22.9
Casualty from the colonies.

In March 1918, Field Marshall Ludendorff launched, on the western front, the first of a series of massive German blows designed to end the war. The British and French were driven back with heavy losses. Desperate, they finally agreed to a unified command under France's General Ferdinand Foch (1851–1929). By mid-June, after the fourth of the great drives, the Allied lines were so badly battered that when the climactic fifth drive began along the Marne River in mid-July, Ludendorff wired the kaiser: "If the attack succeeds, the war will be over and we will have won it." When Foch heard the opening German barrage, he wired his government: "If the present German attack succeeds, the war is over and we have lost it." The Allies stopped the Germans by a narrow margin. Foch, now receiving a swelling stream of fresh American soldiers—more than 250,000 soldiers a month—immediately ordered a counterattack. British tanks helped break through German lines. The balance shifted. Suddenly, the Germans were in retreat. German strength and morale waned rapidly. That spring and summer, Germans suffered more than 2 million casualties.

Final battles

At the end of October, Germany's Bulgarian and Turkish allies surrendered. On November 3, Austria-Hungary, its ethnic minorities in revolt, also surrendered; a week later, the last Austro-Hungarian emperor abdicated. The next day, mutiny broke out in the German navy and spread to workers in German cities. Popular uprisings brought down the kaiser's government, and on November 9 he fled the country. On November 11, the new German Republic government accepted an armistice.

For many, however, even the last days of the war were too long. In Britain, Wilfred Owen's mother, like so many others, received news of her son's death (he was machine-gunned in a final attack) just as church bells began ringing for victory. Those last days would also leave a haunting legacy in Germany. German commanders manipulated reports from the front so that most of Germany's population remained unaware of the extent of their country's military collapse. The new civilian government of republicans and socialists in Germany would later be blamed by many Germans for the surrender. This development would in turn set the stage for future charges that Germany had not really lost the war but had been "stabbed in the back" by the very political forces that would rule Germany during the 1920s.

ASSESSING THE LOSSES

The war had shattered much of Europe. Some 10 million soldiers and another 10 million civilians perished from the war and its hardships. More than 50 percent of the Allied soldiers and 60 percent of the Central Powers soldiers mobilized became casualties. In France, half the men between the ages of 18 and 32 were killed. Russia lost almost 2 million soldiers, as did Germany. All across northern France and Belgium, war cemeteries spread, many with unmarked graves, others with elaborate monuments to the fallen such as those in Figures 22.7 and 22.8. Europe lost the cream of a generation of its future leaders. Colonial troops from Asia and Africa also suffered. Figure 22.9, showing a Senegalese soldier learning to use artificial limbs with the help of a Red Cross nurse, indicates the price many such veterans paid for their service. Almost 30,000 Senegalese soldiers died in the trenches fighting for France. Some 400,000 Africans serving the Allies as bearers of supplies and the wounded lost their lives.

For those left behind, the hardships persisted. Many survivors would have to spend the rest of their lives in veterans' hospitals. In many places, mutilated people, widows, and spinsters seemed the rule rather than the exception. Many survivors would remain obsessed by the experience of this war, like the British poet Siegfried Sassoon, who wrote, "The rank stench of those bodies haunts me still, And I remember things I'd best forget" (see Document 22.2). In addition to all the death and misery, the fighting brought incalculable financial and material losses. The war laid to waste a tenth of the richest region of France and devastated the most developed part of Russia. It also saddled European nations with heavy debts, especially to a new international creditor—the United States.

■ DOCUMENT 22.2

In the Trenches and Beyond

Some of the most poignant accounts of experiences on the front lines come from poets who have served in the military. Unlike many poets such as Rupert Brooke and Wilfred Owen, Siegfried Sassoon (1886–1967) survived World War I. But the experience would haunt him for the rest of his life. The following are excerpts from "The rank stench of those bodies haunts me still" and "Does it Matter?" ■ ***Which*** *images most vividly convey the war experience?* ■ ***How*** *does Sassoon describe the lives of maimed soldiers who return to society?*

"The rank stench of those bodies haunts me still"

The rank stench of those bodies haunts me still,
And I remember things I'd best forget.
For now we've marched to a green, trenchless land
Twelve miles from battering guns: along the grass
Brown lines of tents are hives for snoring men;

Wide, radiant water sways the floating sky
Below dark, shivering trees. And living-clean
Comes back with thoughts of home and hours of sleep.

To-night I smell the battle; miles away
Gun-thunder leaps and thuds along the ridge;
The spouting shells dig pits in fields of death,
And wounded men, are moaning in the woods.
If any friend be there whom I have loved, speed
God (send) him safe to England with a gash.

* * *

Does it Matter?

Does it matter?—losing your legs? . . .
For people will always be kind,
And you need not show that you mind

When the others come in after hunting
To gobble their muffins and eggs.

Does it matter?—losing your sight? . . .
There's such splendid work for the blind;
And people will always be kind,
As you sit on the terrace remembering
And turning your face to the light.

Do they matter?—those dreams from the pit? . . .
You can drink and forget and be glad,
And people won't say that you're mad;
For they'll know you've fought for your country
And no one will worry a bit.

Source: Siegfried Sassoon, "The rank stench of those bodies haunts me still" and "Does it Matter?" in *The Penguin Book of First World War Poetry,* 2nd ed., ed. Jon Silkin (London: Penguin Books, 1979), pp. 124–125, 131–132.

THE PEACE SETTLEMENT

No peace settlement could make up for the losses of World War I. Nevertheless, delegates who gathered at Versailles near Paris in January 1919 and the people they represented expected a resolution that could somehow justify those losses. Other burdens weighed on the delegates as well. The end of fighting did not stop wartime hatred and suffering. Starvation threatened central and eastern Europe. In addition, a growing fear of revolutionary communism haunted the delegates, who primarily represented the forces of order and wealth in their nations. Already in power in Russia, communists had a real chance of triumphing in Germany and in the newly independent states of eastern Europe.

GATHERING AT VERSAILLES

Although all thirty-two of the victorious Allies participated in the peace conference, the leaders of France, Great Britain, the United States, and Italy made the major decisions. Representatives of colonized peoples, ethnic and religious groups, women's organizations, and various national groups went to Versailles hoping for a hearing but received none. The vanquished Germany and Austria-Hungary were excluded from the talks, as was Russia, which had dropped out of the war a year earlier.

Premier Georges Clemenceau, the aged "Tiger of France," headed the French delegation. As host of the conference and leader of the nation that had done the most to defeat Germany, Clemenceau expected to dominate the decision making. The eloquent and fiery Prime Minister David Lloyd George led the British delegation. He also intended to dominate the conference. Premier Vittorio Orlando (1860–1952), head of the Italian delegation, wanted all the territory that the Allies had promised in the first place to draw Italy into the war. The idealistic President Woodrow Wilson (1856–1924), expecting approval of his "Fourteen Points" as the basis for peace, led the

American delegation. The United States had attained much prestige during the war and was the first non-European country in centuries to influence the fate of European nations.

A VICTORS' PEACE

A fundamental and bitter clash immediately developed between Clemenceau, who wanted a "hard peace" that would render Germany harmless, and Wilson, who wanted a "just" peace free of vindictiveness. Wilson and his advisors feared that a harsh settlement would leave Germany resentful, eager for revenge, or ripe for takeover by extreme political forces. He also believed that secret diplomacy and the alliance system had caused the war in the first place, and urged "open covenants of peace, openly arrived at." In his Fourteen Points, Wilson also called for the self-determination of peoples, armaments reduction, and a "general association of nations" to guarantee the safety of "great and small states alike." Lloyd George often sided with Wilson, but like Clemenceau wanted a victory worthy of the sacrifices made during the war.

Wilson's Fourteen Points

It took six months of hard work and wrangling to draw up the peace terms. Although the Treaty of Versailles reflected many of Wilson's ideals, it was more of a victors' peace reflecting France's desire for security and an eagerness to punish Germany. In what came to be known as the **war guilt clause,** the agreement forced Germany "and her allies" to accept full responsibility for the war. Germany lost all its overseas colonies and concessions; several victorious nations gained control over these territories in Africa and the Pacific. France regained Alsace and Lorraine, lost in the Franco-Prussian War of 1870. In addition, the victors would occupy German territory on the west bank of the Rhine for the next fifteen years. The Polish-speaking areas of eastern Germany were ceded to the resurrected Polish state, and a "Polish corridor" was cut through German territory to give Poland an outlet at Danzig to the Baltic Sea. Germany's armed forces were limited to 100,000 soldiers and saddled with severe armament limitations. Finally, Germany was held liable for reparations that in 1921 were set at $33 billion.

REDRAWING THE MAP OF EUROPE

As Map 22.5 reveals, the treaties dealt the harshest blow to Germany's allies because the territorial rearrangements were usually based on the principle of unifying national language groups. Austria-Hungary was cut down from a polyglot empire of 50 million—second in area only to Russia among the nations of Europe—to an Austria of 6.5 million German-speaking Austrians and a Hungary of 8 million Magyars. Many in Austria wanted their new country to merge with Germany, but the settlement specifically forbade this arrangement. The Czechs and Slovaks were joined into the new state of Czechoslovakia, which included sizable German and other minorities. Serbs, Croats, Slovenes, Bosnians, and others populated the new state of Yugoslavia. The Ottoman Empire lost its far-flung non-Turkish territories. Great Britain took administrative control over Mesopotamia and Palestine, and France took Lebanon and Syria. The Ottoman sultan's tottering regime soon fell to a revolt by Turkish nationalists led by the war hero of Gallipoli, Mustapha Kemel (1881–1938), who would create a secular Republic of Turkey in 1923. Perhaps unavoidably, all these new national boundaries created many internal ethnic divisions and pockets of discontent that would breed future conflicts.

Woodrow Wilson had placed his chief hopes for peace in an association of countries—the **League of Nations**—that he expected would guarantee borders and peaceably settle the tensions and conflicts that were certain to arise in the future. The League was incorporated into the treaty with Germany but had no military forces at its command. Its only weapons were economic sanctions and moral condemnations. Though perhaps well intentioned, the League was doomed almost from the beginning. The exclusion of Germany and the Soviet Union from the association weakened its potential effectiveness. In addition, the self-righteous President Wilson—reluctant to compromise with political opponents back in the United States and physically weakening—failed to persuade the isolationist American Senate to ratify the peace accords and join the League. What little faith Great Britain and France had in Wilson's ideas quickly disappeared.

The League of Nations

LEGACY OF THE PEACE TREATY

The peace settlement negotiated in Paris satisfied no one and left a legacy of deep resentments. France's Clemenceau considered the terms too lenient. Moreover, both Great Britain and the United States refused French pleas to join France in a defensive alliance. Not surprisingly, the French felt betrayed and abandoned. The Germans, for their part, considered the terms outrageous. Many Germans refused to believe that their armies had lost the war. The Germans also resented not being allowed to participate in the talks. Their representatives were presented with a humiliating settlement that they signed only after the Allies threatened to invade. Italy's leader, Orlando, walked out of the conference to protest broken Allied promises of more territorial gains. China refused to sign because the treaty gave the Japanese rights in the

THINKING ABOUT GEOGRAPHY

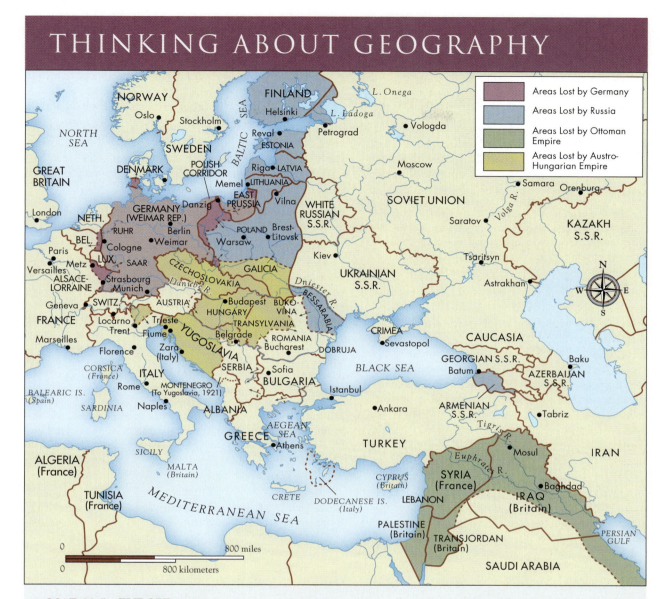

MAP 22.5   EUROPE, 1923

This map shows Europe after the settlement that ended World War I. ■ **Notice** the territorial losses suffered by the German, Russian, Ottoman, and Austro-Hungarian empires. **Do** these losses support the argument that the Versailles settlement was a harsh one? **What** areas might suffer from instability stemming from these new territorial arrangements? **Consider** the strategic problems facing the new eastern European states that hoped for support from France and Great Britain.

Chinese mainland, and Japan left offended because the conference refused to declare formally the equality of all races. Russia, which had suffered huge losses, had not even been invited to the conference, and the U.S. government failed to ratify the treaty.

John Maynard Keynes (1883–1946), an influential British economist who attended the talks, perhaps best summed up the flaws in the Paris agreement in his book *The Economic Consequences of the Peace* (1919)

(see Document 22.3). "[T]he treaty," Keynes warned, "includes no provisions for the economic rehabilitation of Europe—nothing to make the defeated Central Empires into good neighbors, nothing to stabilize the new States of Europe, nothing to reclaim Russia . . ."

World War I had unleashed passions and destruction of such magnitudes that possibly no settlement could have sufficed. Nowhere in the West did those passions rage stronger than in Russia, defeated

THINKING ABOUT DOCUMENTS

■ DOCUMENT 22.3

Keynes Warns of the Economic Consequences of the Peace

The various parties involved in the peace treaty talks after World War I came to agreements only after painful, protracted negotiations. Much of the debate centered on how to deal with Germany. In the following excerpt from his influential book The Economic Consequences of the Peace *(1919), economist John Maynard Keynes—an advisor to British prime minister Lloyd George at the Versailles Conference—assesses the different attitudes toward the peace terms.* ■ ***What** would be the consequences of high reparation payments from Germany, according to Keynes?* ■ ***What** role was the United States expected to play in the future?*

By fixing the Reparation payments well within Germany's capacity to pay, we make possible the renewal of hope and enterprise within her territory, we avoid the perpetual friction and opportunity of improper pressure arising out of Treaty clauses which are impossible of fulfilment, and we render unnecessary the intolerable powers of the Reparation Commission.

* * *

It would be objected, I suppose, by some critics that such an arrangement might go some way in effect towards realizing the former German dream of Mittel-Europa.

* * *

If we take the view that for at least a generation to come Germany cannot be trusted with even a modicum of prosperity, that while all our recent Allies are angels of light, all our recent enemies, Germans, Austrian, Hungarians, and the rest, are children of the devil, that year by year Germany must be kept impoverished and her children starved and crippled, and that she must be ringed round by enemies; then we shall reject all the proposals of this chapter, and particularly those which may assist Germany to regain a part of her former material prosperity and find a means of livelihood for the industrial population of her towns. But if this view of nations and of their relation to one another is adopted by the democracies of Western Europe, and is financed by the United States, heaven help us all.

* * *

I pass to a second financial proposal. The requirements of Europe are *immediate*. The prospect of being relieved of oppressive interest payments to England and America over the whole life of the next two generations (and of receiving from Germany some assistance year by year to the costs of restoration) would free the future from excessive anxiety. But it would not meet the ills of the immediate present—the excess of Europe's imports over her exports, the adverse exchange, and the disorder of the currency. It will be very difficult for European production to get started again without a temporary measure of external assistance. I am therefore a supporter of an international loan in some shape or form, such as has been advocated in many quarters in France, Germany, and England, and also in the United States. In whatever way the ultimate responsibility for repayment is distributed, the burden of finding the immediate resources must inevitably fall in major part upon the United States.

Source: John Maynard Keynes, *The Economic Consequences of the Peace* (Harcourt, Brace, and Howe, 1920).

by Germany in 1917 and still reeling from internal upheavals. There, revolution and civil war were forging a new union that would alter world affairs for the rest of the twentieth century.

REVOLUTIONS IN RUSSIA

In 1914, the Russian tsar Nicholas II and his advisors hoped that a short, painless war in the Balkans would overcome domestic divisions within Russia, strengthen the tsar's regime, and improve Russia's international stature. Instead, the "short, painless" fight turned into a massive conflagration that only compounded Russia's internal discord and revealed how far Russia had fallen behind other powers to the west. In addition, the greatest fears of the tsar, his government, and the aristocracy whose interests he represented came true: World War I devastated Russia militarily and brought the centuries-old Romanov dynasty crashing down.

THE FIRST WARNINGS: 1905

Long-simmering discontent made Russia ripe for violent upheaval. This discontent had its roots in the Russian government's historical resistance to change. Throughout the nineteenth century, Russia's government had usually tried to ignore rather than adapt to the liberalizing movements that swept most of Europe. The tsar ruled autocratically, relying on the nobility, the church, the army, and the bureaucracy without allowing a hint of political participation to the vast majority of Russian society. Industrialization, initiated in the 1880s and surging in the 1890s—

encouraged by the aggressive policies of Sergei Witte (1849–1915), the finance minister, and an infusion of foreign capital into Russia—stimulated the growth of the middle and working classes in cities such as Moscow and St. Petersburg. These people chafed against Russia's traditional society and archaic government. Frustrated Russian intellectuals turned to revolutionary doctrines and even terrorism in an effort to promote rapid change. Others hoped for more moderate liberal reforms. Still the tsarist government, particularly under Nicholas II (1894–1917), refused to bend.

A turning point came with the embarrassing defeat of the tsar's army and navy by Japan in the 1904–1905 Russo-Japanese War. The various liberal and radical groups took advantage of the government's weakness and clamored for reform. The mounting pressures for change finally exploded early in 1905. On Sunday, January 22, thousands of workers gathered in front of the tsar's palace in St. Petersburg to protest economic hardships. "We have become beggars; we have been oppressed; we are burdened by toil beyond our powers; we are scoffed at; we are not recognized as human beings; we are treated as slaves who must suffer their bitter fate and who must keep silence," complained the petitioners. Marchers sang "God save the tsar," but the tsar's troops fired on them, killing and wounding hundreds of women, men, and children. The violent event, known as "Bloody Sunday," was dramatically depicted by the Russian artist N. Vladimirov (Figure 22.10). On the right, a line of Tsar Nicholas II's troops shoot at the procession of workers. On the left, the unarmed workers, who sought to present peacefully a petition to the tsar at the Winter Palace in St. Petersburg, fall. Their blood darkens the snow as well as faith in the tsar as a protector of the people. In response, Father Georgi Gapon, a radical Orthodox priest, warned the tsar: "A sea of blood—unexampled—will be shed. Because of thee, because of thy whole family, Russia may perish."

Demands for reform increased, and in October, a general strike paralyzed the country for ten days. In the cities, workers organized themselves into councils, or **soviets.** Sailors mutinied on the battleship *Potemkin* as did soldiers in the army. At the same time, peasants in the countryside revolted and attacked wealthy landowners. Several officials were assassinated. With much of its army pinned down thousands of miles away in the Russo-Japanese War, the tsar's government wavered. Surrounded by dissension and revolt, Nicholas II yielded at last and issued a manifesto that promised civil liberties, a popularly elected Duma (parliament), and legalization of unions. These concessions

had little lasting meaning, however. The return of the Russian troops from the Far East and a fresh round of governmental repression restored order by 1907. The tsar and his advisors reduced the Duma to a nondemocratically elected body.

THE FALL OF THE TSAR

The few, half-hearted reforms were not enough, and discontent persisted in the years after 1905. In the months before the outbreak of World War I, strikes proliferated in Russia's cities. This turmoil probably encouraged the tsar to bring Russia into the war, for he immediately banned strikes and suspended the Duma, whose members still agitated for liberal reforms. As we saw earlier, Russia soon suffered staggering losses at the hands of the German armies. Its leadership, transportation facilities, supplies, and armaments simply could not withstand the demands of total war. Moreover, many non-Russian subjects living within the empire became more interested in establishing their own independent states than supporting the war effort.

In August 1915, a desperate Nicholas made a fatal mistake: He left the capital to take personal command of the army. The severity and depth of this error is revealed by the reaction of Russia's war minister. Reporting on the dire military situation to the council, the minister concluded, "Considering the present situation at the front and in the rear of the armies, one can expect an irreparable catastrophe momentarily." However, he added, "a far more horrible event threatens Russia." His stunned colleagues on the Council of Ministers waited for

■ FIGURE 22.10

Bloody Sunday, January 22, 1905.

the grim news. "This morning, His Majesty told me of his decision to personally assume the supreme command of the army." As a result of Nicholas's actions, the Russian people blamed the tsar for their country's military losses. Equally problematic, the inept, unpopular government in the capital now fell under the sway of Nicholas's wife, Alexandra. When the tsarina came under the influence of Grigori Efimovich Rasputin (ca. 1871–1916), a corrupt Siberian mystic who claimed to have the power to heal the tsar's hemophiliac son, things took a more bizarre turn. Even the tsar's aristocratic supporters, a group of whom finally murdered Rasputin late in 1916, demanded fundamental change.

In early March 1917, the dam broke. The strains of war drove hungry working women to initiate strikes and demonstrations. With industrialization, Petrograd (St. Petersburg), Moscow, and other Russian cities had grown rapidly. Women, who made up more than half of the labor force in Petrograd, | *The March revolution* | had to work long hours for low wages and then stand in long bread lines to buy food for their families. Rising prices and shrinking supplies, especially during the winters, translated into hunger and starvation. Figure 22.11 is a photograph of one of these demonstrations. Here women march down a Petrograd street demanding an increase of rations to soldiers' families.

Women rightly blamed the government for Russia's continuing involvement in the war and for the food shortages. On March 8, in recognition of International Women's Day, they made their voices heard. That day, 10,000 women marched into Petrograd, shouting, "Down with war and high prices! Down with starvation! Bread for workers!" The protesters also demanded an end to the rule of Nicholas II. Thousands of sympathizers, both women and men, joined the demonstrations in the wintry days of March 1917. Yet police and troops were reluctant to fire on the crowds, especially because so many of them were women. Many troops actually joined the demonstrators. The French ambassador to Russia reported watching "a disorderly mob carrying a red flag" marching toward an oncoming regiment of troops. But instead of restoring order, "the army was fraternizing with the revolt." Too many people had lost their respect for the rigid, poorly led autocracy. As Russia's Minister of Foreign Affairs put it, "The Emperor is blind!" Many of his colleagues agreed. On March 12, the Duma organized a provisional government, and three days later Nicholas II abdicated. Railroad workers took him and his family into custody.

THE PROVISIONAL GOVERNMENT

Most members of the provisional government hoped that Russia would move toward constitutional parliamentary democracy. Led by moderate liberals Pavel Milyukov (1859–1943) and Prince Georgi Lvov (1861–1925), these politicians represented the upper classes. The provisional government enacted into law civil liberties, religious freedom, equality before the law, union rights, and other liberal reforms. They also promised more fundamental social reforms and a constitution.

However, in addition to its inexperience, its rival factions, and the intensifying pressures for change, the provisional government labored under three key burdens. First, it had to share power with the soviets—the political | *The soviets* | organizations of workers, soldiers, and radical intellectuals— particularly the strong Petrograd soviet. The soviets favored socialist self-rule and stood against the upper classes represented by the provisional government. Second, the government chose to continue Russia's draining involvement in World War I. The links between these first two burdens came to light with the Petrograd soviet's issuance of Order Number 1 on March 14. This significant mandate declared that military officers would be democratically elected

■ FIGURE 22.11
Demonstrations in Petrograd, March 1917.

by soldiers and that military decisions would be democratically made. Order Number 1 further unraveled authority and discipline within Russia's armed forces. Third, neither the provisional government nor the soviets could control the peasantry, which made up some 80 percent of the population. Peasants refused to wait for the land-redistribution legislation that the government had promised. They seized land and hoarded food for themselves, worsening hunger in the cities as prices rose and supplies became more scarce. The peasantry's defiance also attracted soldiers, who deserted the front to make land claims of their own.

The provisional government failed to satisfy many. The peasants wanted still more land, and workers demanded more bread. Russia could no longer support the unpopular war effort, yet the government could not find a way to withdraw gracefully from it. Again and again the provisional government tried to rally the Russian troops to victory. In desperation, it even created the Women's Battalion of Death in an effort to shame male soldiers into greater effort. More than 80 percent of these women became casualties. The desertions continued.

In May, the liberal heads of the provisional government resigned and the moderate socialist Alexander Kerensky (1881–1970) became the leading figure in the government. Kerensky, however, faced new political divisions, for by this time many radical intellectuals had returned to Russia from the west, where they had fled from the tsar's repression, or rose from Russia's social ranks. They tried to push ideas and events in one direction or the other. Those who proved most influential came from a group of Marxist revolutionaries, the Social Democrats—in particular their minority faction, the Bolsheviks. This faction was led by Vladimir Ilich Ulyanov (1870–1924), known by his revolutionary name, Lenin.

Kerensky leads

THE RISE OF THE BOLSHEVIKS

Marxism had become influential among some Russian intellectuals, revolutionaries, and groups critical of Russia's tsarist autocracy toward the end of the nineteenth century. In 1898, Russian Marxists had formed the Social Democratic Party, whose principal leaders were Georgi Plekhanov (1857–1918) and his disciple Lenin. Repression by the tsar's government forced the Social Democrats into exile. At a London conference in 1903, the radical Bolshevik wing under Lenin split from the more moderate Mensheviks.

Until 1917, Lenin's **Bolsheviks** remained only a minor party within Russia. Its leaders were hunted down by the state police and shot, imprisoned, or exiled. For seventeen years, Lenin remained in exile in Switzerland, keeping his party alive from a distance and plotting the eventual overthrow of the tsar's gov-

ernment. During that time, he developed theoretical and tactical principles that the Bolsheviks would later use. Three of these principles set forth the most crucial guidelines and, for the most part, set Lenin's Bolsheviks apart from other Marxist organizations. First, the party should be an elite, highly trained, and constantly purged (cleaned of disloyal ideas and people) group of dedicated Marxist revolutionaries capable of instructing and leading the masses. This elite would not be seduced by short-term gains. Second, contrary to what Marx had argued, the socialist revolution need not include only the industrial working class. In Russia, it could be a dual revolution of workers and poor, land-hungry peasants—all part of an even broader socialist revolution that would sweep through other European countries. Third, the party should firmly oppose participation in the war, which Lenin considered a product of imperialist rivalries and a continuing civil war among capitalists.

Lenin's principles

In April 1917, the German government secretly transported Lenin from his place of exile in Switzerland to a Baltic port, from which he made his way to Russia, in an effort to worsen the chaos in Russia and remove Russia from the war. The Germans had good reason to consider Lenin a threat to stability in Russia. John Reed, a sympathetic American journalist and observer, described Lenin as "a strange popular leader—a leader purely by virtue of intellect; colorless, humorless, uncompromising and detached; without picturesque idiosyncrasies—but with the power of explaining profound ideas in simple terms, of analyzing a concrete situation." Back in Russia, Lenin refused to cooperate with the provisional government. Instead, he unleashed a barrage of compelling slogans such as "Peace to the Army," "Land to the Peasants," "Ownership of the Factories to the Workers," and "All Power to the Soviets." He argued that the time was ripe for a socialist revolution against capitalism. To achieve this revolution, he urged his followers to gain control over the soviets, particularly the powerful Petrograd soviet.

When Kerensky failed to extract Russia from the war, Bolshevik influence grew, especially among the Petrograd workers and soldiers. In July 1917, a massive popular demonstration against the provisional government erupted in that city. Most members of the Bolshevik Party supported the demonstration, though in the end the leadership did not. In these bloody "July Days," the provisional government put down the demonstrators with force. The Kerensky government arrested many Bolsheviks and impelled others, including Lenin, to flee to Finland.

Russia's July Days

Yet Kerensky soon suffered a fresh round of failures in the war as well as the threat of an impending coup d'état by General Lavr Kornilov (1870–1918). To avert disaster, in September the desperate Kerensky released the Bolsheviks and relied on the soviets to defend the capital against Kornilov. Kornilov's plans failed when most of his soldiers refused to follow his orders to attack Petrograd.

By October, many leading figures from larger socialist parties had become discredited through their association with the provisional government. This turn of events helped the Bolsheviks, under the leadership of Lenin and the brilliant Leon Trotsky (1879–1940), finally gain control over the Petrograd and Moscow soviets. Bolshevik women created a network to call for demonstrations, organize women in factories, and do paramilitary work. Lenin judged the time right for his next move.

On November 6, he and Trotsky launched a well-organized seizure of power. His Red Guards (workers' militia units) took over crucial control centers and arranged for the transfer of power to the soviets and Lenin. Within just hours, the deed was complete. Kerensky, unable to reorganize his forces, fled. Although some of the fighting was violent, the success of the Bolshevik revolution stemmed mostly from the revolutionaries' organizational talents, a lack of effective resistance by *The November revolution* the provisional government, and Trotsky's success in portraying the uprising as *defense* of the soviets rather than a Bolshevik *offensive*.

On November 7, the Bolshevik majority enthusiastically elected Lenin the head of the new government. The revolution won the endorsement of soviets throughout Russia. Figure 22.12, a painting by the Russian artist Vladimir Serov, shows Lenin, with Stalin standing behind him, proclaiming to the revolutionary forces the Bolsheviks' assumption of power in 1917. In this idealized re-creation of events, the artist has elevated Stalin to a prominent position just behind Lenin. The artist also portrays Lenin as a powerful orator towering above all others. The serious, impassioned crowd below, made up of women, sailors, soldiers, and workers, listens intently. The red flag of communism is held aloft in victory.

COMMUNISM AND CIVIL WAR

The Bolsheviks, who now called themselves Communists, immediately moved to fulfill their promises and consolidate their power. In place of the old tsarist hierarchy, they set up a pyramid of people's soviets, or councils. These councils were elected by universal suffrage but were actually dominated by relatively few Communist Party members. When national elections failed to return a Communist majority to the Constituent Assembly, Lenin had armed sailors disperse that elected body. Capitalism was abolished outright. A barter system of exchange replaced money, the value of the ruble having been destroyed by inflation and devaluation. Committees of workers responsible to party commissars took over management of industry and commerce. The government nationalized the land and turned over its management to local peasant

KEY DATES

THE RUSSIAN REVOLUTION

1904–1905	Russo-Japanese War
1905	General strike and revolution
1917	March revolution
	November revolution
1918	Treaty of Brest-Litovsk
1918–1920	Civil war

■ FIGURE 22.12

Vladimir Serov, *Lenin Proclaiming Soviet Power.*

committees, who then distributed it to individual peasants to be worked by their own labor. All crop surpluses were to be given to the state. Finally, the state expropriated church lands and enacted laws to establish the legal equality of the sexes—the first Western government to do so.

To buy time and free the new regime for the enormous task of refashioning Russian society, Lenin immediately opened peace negotiations with Germany. The Germans, realizing Russia's helplessness, demanded the harshest of terms. Lenin attempted to stall them, but in March 1918, when the Germans threatened to attack Petrograd and Moscow, he signed the Treaty of Brest-Litovsk. Russia lost Finland, Estonia, Latvia, Lithuania, the Ukraine, Bessarabia, the Polish provinces, and some of the Trans-Caucasian territory. Lenin had paid a high price for peace. These lands contained one-third of Russia's European population, three-fourths of its iron, and nine-tenths of its coal. In addition, Germany compelled Russia to pay a heavy indemnity. Lenin gambled that a socialist revolution in Germany would reverse some of these losses and provide the support that the fledgling socialist system desperately needed to survive in Russia.

Nevertheless, these hard peace terms were not the worst of Lenin's woes. A bitter civil war broke out in Russia following the peace with Germany (see Map 22.6). The Russian aristocracy, including most of the higher army officers, launched a series of uncoordinated attacks against the Bolshevik regime. These "White" forces were aided by various other groups disaffected by the revolution. They also had the support of French, British, Greek, Polish, Japanese, Czech, and U.S. troops that were in Russia for various reasons, but in great part to oppose the anticapitalist Bolshevik government. For decades afterward, the communists would remember how the outside world had turned against them during this vulnerable time.

Creating an emergency policy of "war communism," the Bolshevik government mobilized Russia's econ-

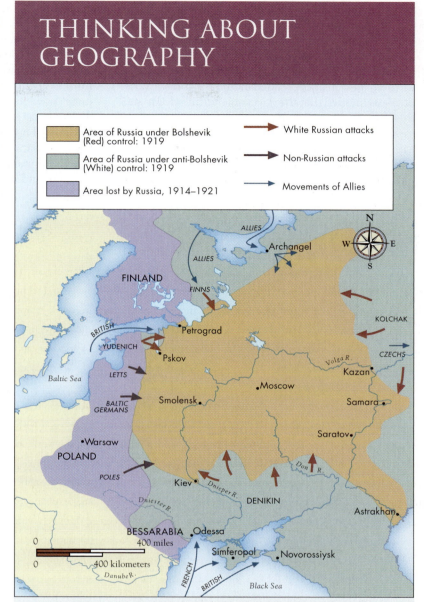

Area of Russia under Bolshevik (Red) control: 1919

Area of Russia under anti-Bolshevik (White) control: 1919

Area lost by Russia, 1914–1921

White Russian attacks

Non-Russian attacks

Movements of Allies

MAP 22.6   CIVIL WAR IN RUSSIA, 1919

This map shows Russia during the civil war. ■ **Notice** the different forces threatening the area controlled by the Bolsheviks. **Consider** why the Bolsheviks might emerge from the period with a sense of isolation from the West. ■ **What** strategy might have helped the forces opposing the Bolsheviks?

omy and society for the civil-war effort. Urban workers and troops swept through the countryside and confiscated grain from the peasantry to feed the cities and the army. The Bolsheviks sharply suppressed any internal opposition. A secret police force—the Cheka—unleashed the "Red Terror" to hunt down "class enemies" and ensure internal conformity to the Bolshevik regime. To avoid the possibility of White forces freeing the imprisoned Nicholas II and his family, the Bolshevik government ordered them executed. However, the "Red" armies faced numerous obstacles in their all-out effort to defeat the "Whites." When peasants realized that the government intended to seize their surpluses, for example, they resisted or refused to raise more crops than they needed for themselves. Moreover, the government had to contend with violent ethnic hatreds that further divided the country. Only with the greatest difficulty did the "Red" armies,

well organized by Trotsky, finally defeat the "Whites." In doing so, the Bolsheviks regained the Ukraine.

By 1920, World War I and the Russian civil war had ended. In addition to the deaths of two million Russian soldiers in the world war, some four to six million had lost their lives in the civil conflict. The once powerful nation lay defeated, impoverished, and exhausted. Starvation hung like a specter over millions. The fighting was over, but Russia and other Western nations now faced the challenge of rebuilding social stability in an environment of continuing political and economic turmoil.

SUMMARY

British historian Arnold Toynbee said that in the years before 1914, his generation expected that "life throughout the World would become more rational, more humane, and more democratic . . . that the progress of science and technology would make mankind richer . . . that all this would happen peacefully." World War I shattered that vision. The very technology and industrial prowess that had fueled the West's growth and sense of progress was turned to unimagined destruction. The war ended dreams of heroic battles and courageous military deeds: "Words such as glory, honor, courage, or hallow [became] obscene" in the face of how the war was fought and the carnage that resulted, wrote the American author and veteran Ernest Hemingway. Indeed, many survivors of World War I were haunted for the rest of their lives with a sense of belonging to a "lost generation."

Along with millions of human lives, the war destroyed or weakened European empires. The German, Austro-Hungarian, and Ottoman empires collapsed. Military losses and revolution ended the Russian empire, replacing it with the Soviet Union and Communist rulers who were transforming that society and would alter the political landscape throughout the world in the next decades. In the Far East, the Japanese gained lands and stature by expanding their empire at the expense of German colonies and China. In the Middle East, Africa, and Asia, the war and vague Allied declarations in support of national liberation stimulated struggles for national rights and independence. Even in the West, faith in imperialist ideals waned during and after the war. As one Indian diplomat explained, "there was no conviction left of the Europeans' superiority or sense of vision." From the outside looking in, Europe now seemed shrunken, vulnerable, and subject to unreasonable passions.

The calamities of those years were not limited to the war itself. In Turkey, the nationalistic government responded to Armenian demands for independence by deporting some 2 million Armenians from eastern Turkey. Probably one-third of these were massacred in what amounted to modern mass genocide; another third may have died during the forced march to Syria. In 1918, an influenza epidemic hit, killing some 27 million people worldwide. In central and eastern Europe, postwar starvation threatened millions despite relief efforts by the United States and the International Red Cross. The peace treaties "to make the world safe" and "to end all wars" left a legacy of disappointment and resentment. In the next two decades, these sentiments would draw Europe and the world once again into a maelstrom of violence.

KEY TERMS

Central Powers, p. 678

Allies, p. 679

Schlieffen Plan, p. 679

trench warfare, p. 680

total war, p. 683

war guilt clause, p. 690

League of Nations, p. 690

soviets, p. 693

Bolsheviks, p. 695

REVIEW, ANALYZE, AND ANTICIPATE

REVIEW THE PREVIOUS CHAPTERS
Chapter 20—"Mass Politics and Imperial Domination"—analyzed nationalism, the spreading demands for political inclusion, and imperialism during the second half of the nineteenth century.

Chapter 21—"Modern Life and the Culture of Progress"—examined new industrial transformations and urban life during this same period.

1. *In what ways did nationalism, industrialism, and imperialism create the forces underlying World War I?*

2. *After the experience of World War I, why might people look back on the decades preceding the war so longingly?*

ANALYZE THIS CHAPTER
Chapter 22—"Descending into the Twentieth Century"—tells the story of World War I and the Russian revolution.

1. *How might it be argued that several nations should bear responsibility for plunging the West into World War I? Which countries, if any, do you think were most responsible?*

2. *Why was this war so devastating, physically and psychologically?*

3. *Analyze the role of the home fronts. How did problems at the home fronts relate to problems on the battlefronts?*

4. *It is perhaps easier to understand why there was a revolution in Russia that toppled the tsar than why the Bolsheviks came to power several months later in a second revolution. How do you explain this?*

ANTICIPATE THE NEXT CHAPTER
In Chapter 23—"Darkening Decades"—the rise of fascism, the development of the Soviet Union, and the trials of nations struck by the Great Depression will be analyzed. World War II, which came at the end of these difficult decades, will also be examined.

1. *What potential problems did the peace settlement at the end of World War I create for the future? What might have been done differently?*

2. *What threats did the Russian revolution and communism seem to pose to other Western nations, and what might be the consequences of those perceived threats?*

BEYOND THE CLASSROOM

ON THE PATH TO TOTAL WAR
Ferguson, Niall. *The Pity of War: Explaining World War I.* New York: Basic Books, 1999. A thoughtful reassessment of the causes, course, and results of World War I.

Stevenson, David. *Cataclysm: The First World War as Political Tragedy* (New York: Basic Books, 2004). An excellent and comprehensive one-volume study of the war.

Strachan, Hew. *The First World War.* Oxford: Oxford University Press, 2003. A fine, very well written up-to-date survey.

THE FRONT LINES
Ellis, John. *Eye-Deep in Hell: Trench Warfare in World War I.* New York: Pantheon Books, 1989. An examination of the daily experiences of the trench soldier.

Keegan, John. *The First World War.* New York: Knopf, 1999. A highly respected military historian examines the realities of warfare, stressing experiences on the western front.

WAR ON THE HOME FRONT
Brayborn, Gail, and Penny Summerfield. *Out of the Cage: Women's Experiences in Two World Wars.* London: Pandora Press, 1987. Analyzes women's experiences in the two world wars and finds that the wars were economically and socially liberating for women.

Coetzee, Frans, and Marilyn Shevin-Coetzee, eds. *Authority, Identity and the Social History of the Great War.* Providence, RI: Berghahn Books, 1995. A comparative study of the experience and significance of the war in people's lives, especially for those on the home fronts.

Williams, John. *The Homefronts: Britain, France and Germany, 1914–1918.* London: Constable, 1972. Studies the effect of the ongoing struggle on the British, French, and German populations.

TO THE BITTER END
Becker, Jean-Jacques. *The Great War and the French People.* New York: St. Martin's Press, 1986. An examination of the impact of the war on the French.

Schmitt, Bernadotte E., and Harold C. Vedeler. *The World in a Crucible, 1914–1918.* New York: Harper & Row, 1984. Analyzes World War I as a total war and traces its economic, social, cultural, and diplomatic consequences.

ASSESSING THE LOSSES
Fussell, Paul. *The Great War and Modern Memory.* Oxford: Oxford University Press, 1975. A fascinating study of the British experience on the western front from 1914 to 1918 and the literary means by which it has been remembered.

Winter, J.M. *The Experience of World War I.* New York: Oxford University Press, 1988. A well-written examination of how the war was experienced by the peoples of the belligerent nations.

THE PEACE SETTLEMENT
MacMillan, Margaret. *Six Months That Changed the World.* New York: Random House, 2002. A new, very comprehensive account of the talks and the settlement.

Sharp, Alan. *The Versailles Settlement: Peacemaking in Paris, 1919.* New York: St. Martin's Press, 1991. A balanced overview that stresses the difficulties facing participants at the conference.

REVOLUTIONS IN RUSSIA
Fitzpatrick, Sheila. *The Russian Revolution, 1917–1932,* 2nd ed. Oxford: Oxford University Press, 1994. A brief and insightful treatment of this complex subject.

Lincoln, W. Bruce. *Red Victory: A History of the Russian Civil War.* New York: Simon and Schuster, 1989. Examines the Bolshevik triumph over internal conflicts.

Pipes, Richard. *The Russian Revolution.* New York: Vintage Books, 1991. Argues that the Bolshevik revolution was an authoritarian coup d'état.

www.mhhe.com/sherman3

- Unfamiliar words? See our Glossary at the back of the book for pronunciation and definitions.

- Need help studying? See our web page for map exercises, practice quizzes, and additional study resources.

- Need help writing a paper? Access hundreds of primary documents, maps, images, and a guide to writing history papers on our Primary Source Investigator site at **www.mhhe.com/psi.**

GEORGE GROSZ, *THE PILLARS OF SOCIETY*, 1926

In *The Pillars of Society*, German expressionist artist George Grosz (1893–1959) sarcastically and ominously depicted the leaders of Germany during the 1920s. The swastika on his tie, the sword in one hand and beer mug in the other, and the dreams of combat pouring out of his head identify the "old-guard" man in front as a Nazi. Behind him, in suits and ties, stand two other members of the dominant middle class. One, a dull journalist with a chamber pot on his head, holds a blood-stained palm leaf that suggests his hypocritical pacifism. The other, a parliamentarian with a head full of excrement, mindlessly clutches a German national flag. In the background, a corrupted military chaplain offers his blessings while murderous soldiers look on. The soldiers remind viewers of how violence and the catastrophic Great War provided a backdrop to German society in the 1920s.

CHAPTER 23

DARKENING DECADES

RECOVERY, DICTATORS, AND DEPRESSION, 1920–1939

STUDY	Postwar recovery ■ Dictatorships and fascism ■ Transforming the Soviet Union ■ The Great Depression ■ Nazism.
NOTICE	Connections between World War I, the rise of authoritarian governments, and the Great Depression.

"The Storm has died away," wrote French poet Paul Valéry in the years just after World War I, "and still we are restless, uneasy, as if the storm were about to break . . . we do not know what will be born, and we fear the future. . . ." Many in Europe shared Valéry's sense of "terrible uncertainty." The Great War was finally over, and people longed for the return of "normal" life. In 1919, almost any memory of the days before the war seemed rosy. Too much had changed, though; the pre-World War I era was gone forever.

In fact, the immediate postwar years would bring frustration and turmoil. In the victorious democracies, growing disillusionment and political bickering rather than dynamic action seemed the rule. Moreover, some of these nations faced dramatically rising resistance to foreign rule in their overseas holdings as colonial people, led by nationalistic intellectuals who combined Western ideas with their own cultural traditions, agitated for independence. Millions of people living in communist Russia still struggled just to survive, let alone transform that troubled nation. Elsewhere in the West, union, socialist, and communist movements alarmed those who feared change. As suggested by the painting on the facing page, many Europeans, especially in Italy, Germany, and east-central Europe, turned to right-wing leaders who attacked parliamentary government and raised the compelling banner of militant nationalism. Ahead, still unseen by most, lay the very dangers that people thought were over when the Great War ended.

World War I

Fascism in Italy

NEP in Soviet Union

Nazism in Germany

The Russian Revolution and Civil War

Collectivization and 5-year plans in USSR

World War II

The Locarno Era

The Great Depression

| 1915 | 1918 | 1921 | 1924 | 1927 | 1930 | 1933 | 1936 | 1939 | 1942 | 1945 |

TRYING TO RECOVER FROM THE GREAT WAR, 1919–1929

IN A HAUNTING PREVIEW OF troubles lurking over the era, Erich Maria Remarque, a German author and war veteran, described his life in Berlin during the early 1920s. "Prices have been soaring everywhere" and "poverty is greater than it was during the war." One afternoon he heard that demonstrations had been called for. In the streets, ominous rumors circulated that "troops have been concentrated at the barracks." Groups of strikers began marching through the streets. A disturbance broke out, people were yelling, and on corners speakers harangued small crowds. "Then suddenly everywhere is silence." A procession of maimed and wounded war veterans in the "faded uniforms of the front-line trenches" moved slowly toward him. Men with one arm carried white placards: "Where is the Fatherland's gratitude? The War Cripples are starving."

For Remarque and millions of others living in the post–World War I West, reality soon undermined the sense of liberation that the end of the war had brought. Families tried to care for their wounded sons, fathers, and brothers, and to endure the loss of those who had perished in battle. Many veterans came home angry. They had been promised moral "purification" during the war and compensation for their service after. Now they sensed that, in some ways, civilians did not fully appreciate their sacrifices. Too often, their old jobs had disappeared. For some, their wives or lovers had deserted them or developed a new, disturbing sense of independence. Many veterans, returning to homelands whose economies lay in ruins, struggled just to get enough food.

Indeed, economic uncertainty had settled like a pall over most of Europe. In the decades after the war, nations struggled to retool their economies from wartime needs back to ordinary requirements and to reestablish international trade. Enormous sums in veterans' pay, war-widow benefits, and unemployment insurance burdened government treasuries. In vain, the victors had hoped that high reparation payments from Germany would be enough to help them rebuild their economies or at least cover debts from the war. So, governments borrowed when they could and printed money that had no basis in actual wealth. The resulting inflation hurt the middle classes in particular. They watched in panic as rising prices drained away their life savings. Between 1914 and 1928, France's currency alone lost four-fifths of its value. Still more unlucky were the thousands of western European investors, especially in France, who had invested in Russian bonds and saw them turn worthless when the Bolsheviks came to power.

Economic uncertainty

Across Europe, recessions followed short periods of relative prosperity all too quickly. Unemployment persisted—in Britain, it remained above 10 percent in both good times and bad. Governments and employers pressured women to give up their wartime jobs or accept lower-paying positions so as to make way for men. Inflation and unemployment spun Germany's economy out of control. Among the Western powers, only the United States emerged from the war richer than ever. In Asia, Japan also emerged from the war stronger and richer—a new competitor looking to expand in East Asia and gain recognition as a great power. Europeans now looked to their governments for relief and leadership.

THE VICTORS JUST HOLD ON

Solutions to Europe's economic problems depended greatly on the politics of the postwar era. However, within the democracies, no one seemed to step forward with innovative ideas for change. Some people hoped that the addition of women to the voting roles in these countries (with the notable exception of France, Italy, and Sweden) would improve politics. In fact, however, women's suffrage seemed to change politics little if at all. Most women voted as men did, and relatively few women gained political office.

International relations showed the same lack of innovation as domestic politics. Although the dominant military power on the Continent, France still feared a resentful Germany and defensively held on to what it salvaged in the Versailles treaty following the war. The nation fiercely resisted any efforts by colonized people to move toward independence in its overseas holdings. Various conservative parties generally held power and domestic policies changed little from the prewar period. The conservatives concentrated on rebuilding France and trumpeting anti-German nationalism.

Defensive France

Great Britain might have worked with its ally France to find solutions to postwar problems, but each nation usually acted alone or in opposition to one another. Various political parties—Conservatives, Laborites, and Liberals—alternated in power in Britain. Sometimes they formed coalitions with each other, but none came forth with fresh solutions to the economic and diplomatic problems plaguing the British. Instead, Britain pulled away from extensive involvement in European affairs and tried to solve the Irish problem and to hold on to its restless colonies in Asia and Africa.

Britain and its empire

In the decades before World War I, British governments had attempted in vain to enact home rule for Ireland to quell growing demands for Irish independence. Leaders such as Constance Markievicz (1868–1926), a founder of republican and women's organizations, called on the Irish to "fix your mind on the ideal of Ireland free, with her women enjoying the full rights of citizenship in their own nation," warning that "our national freedom cannot, and must not, be left to evolution." In 1914, Parliament had finally passed the Irish Home Rule Bill, but postponed its implementation until after the war. In 1916, impatient Irish nationalists in Dublin rose up against the British, but were crushed (see p. 685). Executed leaders quickly became national martyrs, and the extremist organization Sinn Fein ("Ourselves Alone") gained leadership in the nationalist cause. Its military wing became the Irish Republican Army. When the Sinn Fein Party declared Irish independence in 1919, fighting broke out between the IRA and the British army. With the British cast in the role of oppressors, the bloodshed persisted for two years. In December 1921, a treaty created the Irish Free State, although the six predominantly Protestant counties of Ulster (Northern Ireland) remained tied to Great Britain. Even then, a civil war broke out between protreaty and antitreaty forces. This legacy of violence would haunt the British and Irish again and again.

The British also faced nationalist problems elsewhere in the world. In West Africa, nationalistic leaders pressured the British to establish representative institutions; the British agreed to new constitutions in Nigeria in 1923 and the Gold Coast in 1925. In North Africa, opposition to foreign rule forced the British to grant independence to Egypt in 1923. In the Middle East, Britain faced uprisings in Iraq and conflicts in Palestine, where Zionist immigrants bumped up against native Arabs. In Asia, nationalist parties developed into powerful political forces. Perhaps the strongest movement for national liberation emerged in India. Many Indians, hoping they would be rewarded with self-government, had fought for Britain in World War I, and the Indian economy had grown with India's support of Britain's war effort. Indian leaders, such as Mohandas Gandhi (1869–1948) and Jawaharlal Nehru (1889–1964), who had been westernized by education and experience while employed by British rulers, led the drive for independence. Gandhi used the tactic of civil disobedience—publicly and nonviolently breaking the law—to promote widespread sympathy for his cause. Even Britain's leaders, reacting to these pressures, began talking about granting self-rule to India.

The United States, for its part, could have taken a leadership role in international affairs. However, it refused to ratify the Versailles treaty, join the League of Nations, or involve itself extensively in tensions overseas. Europe's troubles came to center more and more on events in Germany, an unstable nation that would soon become enmeshed in a round of political and international turmoil.

The U.S. turns inward

CONTINUING CRISES IN GERMANY

Germany emerged from World War I defeated and angry. However, it had the potential to regain its strength quickly. More populous than France, Germany still had an intact industrial infrastructure. It also occupied an advantageous position in the postwar rearrangement of the European map. On its eastern borders lay weak nations newly created at the end of World War I. Farther east, Russia was isolated and preoccupied with shoring up its struggling new communist society.

Soon after the war, the Germans set up the **Weimar Republic** (named after the city where its

constitution was drawn up) as a model liberal democracy. Moderate Social Democrats led the republic, but they had inherited the taint of defeat from the outcome of the war. Moreover, many officials in the bureaucracy, judiciary, and army were the same people who had occupied these positions before 1918. They were not particularly dedicated to the new republic. Nationalists and right-wing parties looked on the new parliamentary system with contempt.

Challengers within Germany arose almost as soon as the Social Democrats came to power. From the Left, Rosa Luxemburg (1870–1919) and Karl Liebknecht (1871–1919) led an uprising of radical Marxists (Spartacists). The government responded with repression, using the Free Corps—right-wing paramilitary groups made up mostly of veterans—to murder the two leaders and put down the communist threat. Nevertheless, communists continued to stir discord for several more years. In 1920, the German government faced a new threat, this time from right-wing nationalists under Wolfgang Kapp (1858–1922). A general strike by workers in support of the government paralyzed the economy and ended Kapp's effort to take over Berlin.

Then economic and international crises added to Weimar's political woes. In January 1923, after the German government defaulted on the huge war reparations bill, French and Belgian troops responded by occupying the Ruhr Valley, Germany's richest industrial area. The Germans struck back with passive resistance—opposing the occupiers in every way but violence. Enraged, the French tried to create a secession movement from Germany in the Rhineland. Although the occupying forces failed to collect

any reparations, the occupation paralyzed Germany's economy, and wild inflation swept the country. At the crest of the inflation wave, four trillion German marks were worth only one dollar. People literally took wheelbarrows full of money to go shopping. Figure 23.1 reveals the extent of the inflation. Here children, apparently unaware of the economic turmoil throughout Germany, play with stacks of their nation's nearly worthless paper money. Within days, the inflation wiped out countless Germans' life savings. With a frightening hint of future events, Document 23.1 reveals some of the fears and political turmoil engendered by this uncertainty.

CONCILIATION AND A GLIMPSE OF PROSPERITY

Germany's international and economic picture looked bleak in 1923. But near the end of that year, a series of events unfolded that held out hope for international cooperation and a return to prosperity, not only for Germany but also for other nations in the West. In August, Gustav Stresemann (1878–1929) rose to leadership in the German government and offered to reconcile its differences with France.

Having lost more money and inter-

national standing than it had gained from its occupation of the Ruhr, France reversed its policy and agreed to cooperate with Stresemann. An international commission headed by Charles Dawes (1865–1951) of the United States drew up a plan for the occupying forces' withdrawal from Germany. The commission also arranged for international loans to Germany and set up a system by which Germany would pay lower reparations in installments. In 1925, Germany signed the Treaty of Locarno with France, Great Britain, Italy, and Belgium—an agreement that guaranteed Germany's existing frontiers with France and Belgium. Optimistic headlines in the *New York Times* declared, "France and Germany Ban War Forever." In 1926, the League of Nations admitted Germany and elected Stresemann its president. With international relations apparently normalized, France retreated, hoping that alliances with smaller eastern European states and the **Maginot Line**—a string of defensive fortresses on the French/German border it began building in the late 1920s—would contain the economically revived Germany.

Most of the remaining Western economies also perked up after 1924. In several countries, automobile manufacturing, aviation, synthetics, and electronics took off. Vac-

uum cleaners, washing machines, refrigerators, and electric irons—now often purchased

■ FIGURE 23.1

German inflation, November 1923.

■ DOCUMENT 23.1

Postwar Strains in Germany

Postwar dislocations and economic difficulties put enormous strains on European nations, particularly Germany. One of these hardships took the form of explosive inflation that struck Germany in 1923. This 1923 speech by Adolf Hitler—a minor but ambitious political figure at the time—reveals some of the anger and political uncertainty spawned by the inflation. ■ **What** *explanation and solution does Hitler offer for the painful problems facing Germans?* ■ **Are** *there any inconsistencies between this statement from 1923 and Hitler's later actions?*

"Germany is a people of children; a grown-up people would say: 'We don't care a fig for your paper-money. Give us something of value—gold! What have you after all to give us? Nothing? Thus have you defrauded us, you rogues and swindlers!' An awakened people with its last thirty marks—all that is left of the millions of its glory—would buy a rope and with it string up 10,000 of its defrauders!" Even the farmer will no longer sell his produce, "When you offer him your million scraps of paper with which he can cover the walls of his closet on his dung-heap, can you wonder that he says, 'Keep your millions and I will keep my corn and my butter.'" "The individual and the nation are delivered over to the international capital of the banks; despair seizes the whole people. We are on the eve of a second revolution. Some are setting their hopes on the star of the Soviet: that is the symbol of those who began the Revolution, to whom the Revolution has brought untold wealth, who have exploited it until to-day. It is the star of David, the sign of the Synagogue. The symbol of the race high over the world, a lordship which stretches from Vladivostok to the West—the lordship of Jewry. The golden star which for the Jew means the glittering gold."

"And when the people in its horror sees that one can starve though one may have milliards of marks, then it will perforce make up its mind and say: 'We will bow down no longer before an institution which is founded on the delusory majority principle, we want a dictatorship.' Already the Jew has a premonition of things to come: . . . he is saying to himself: If there must be a dictatorship, then it shall be a dictatorship of Cohen or Levi."

Source: Adolf Hitler, *The Speeches of Adolf Hitler*, vol. I, trans. and ed. by Norman Baynes (Oxford: Oxford University Press, 1942), pp. 72–73.

on installment plans—became the norm in middle-class homes. New production techniques spread, especially among big-business employers who began using the principles and methods of "scientific management" promoted by the American efficiency engineer Frederick W. Taylor (1856–1915). After conducting time and motion studies, Taylor and other industrial psychologists recommended a sharper division of labor and detailed control over every aspect of work in order to boost worker productivity. Taylor especially emphasized the division between thinking by managers and physical labor by workers: "We do not want any initiative [from workers]," he wrote. "All we want of them is to obey the orders we give them, do what we say and do it quick." These techniques may have made production more efficient, but for laborers, work became more mindless, dull, and repetitive than ever.

Outside of manufacturing, many people found jobs in the fast-growing service and housing sectors. Women in particular took positions as salesclerks, social workers, nurses, telephone operators, manicurists, hairdressers, and processors of convenience foods such as pudding mixes and dried cereals. Housing projects with indoor plumbing, electricity, and central heating sprang up throughout Europe—many of them boasted common-use day-care centers, laundries, and gardens. With all these developments, the West seemed to be back on the path of material progress that characterized the decades before World War I.

At the same time, several industries declined, unable to keep up with the new products, enhanced technology, and stiffer competition. Britain, especially, clung to its old expertise in metals and textiles and failed to invest in the rising new technologies. Its coal industry sank dramatically, sparking massive strikes that in 1926 turned into a general strike by miners and other industrial workers. The economies of nations outside of Europe—particularly in the United States, Canada, Australia, and Japan—benefited at Britain's and Europe's expense.

THE ROARING TWENTIES?

The popular culture of the 1920s reflected these complex political and economic changes of the postwar era. This uneasy, worrisome time has been called the "Jazz Age" and the "Roaring Twenties." Both terms convey the exuberance of the period's popular culture. They also hint at the superficial nature of the gaiety. This glittering culture had an edgy, frenetic quality that suggested a people haunted by a profound insecurity.

In Figure 23.2, a depiction of a cabaret scene, the German expressionist painter Otto Dix captures these contradictions of life during the 1920s. Berlin in particular became famous for cabarets such as this. In the painting, a couple dances to the music of a jazz band made up of black and white musicians, probably from America. European interest in American jazz and culture reflected the new international stature of the United States. To the right poses a "flapper," a fashionably thin woman whose dress and hair are cut short. She and the woman behind her smoking a cigarette stand alone, apparently independent. The scene suggests sexual abandon, yet the expressions on most people's faces are stiff, even apathetic. The picture conveys more of a sense of frenzy, decadence, and artificial celebration than relaxed happiness. The artist's deeper message is especially clear in the first panel (left) of this painting. In this smaller section, a crippled veteran leans on a crutch outside the cabaret and begs for assistance as the revelers pass him by with scarcely a glance in his direction. The canvas echoes a description of Berlin in that era by a leading German journalist, Hans Sahl: "It was a time of great misery, with legless war veterans riding the sidewalks on rolling planks, in a nation that seemed to consist of nothing but beggars, whores, invalids, and fat-necked speculators."

While millions of people read the proliferating practical books, popular fiction, and newspapers, no new forces of popular culture shaped and reflected national attitudes more than the radio and movies.

In France, the first radio broadcast station opened in 1920. It transmitted poor-quality sound to a limited audience, but by 1939, the number of radios in France had reached almost five million. The movie industry also flourished, particularly in Germany, Russia, France, and the United States. More than 100 million people saw a film each week.

The radio and movies

Filmmaking itself became an art form, a visual record of social attitudes, and an account of people's ambitions and dreams. Films were thoughtfully and cleverly edited to promote drama and show scenes from different perspectives. Increasingly, creating movies involved specialized roles, such as producer, director, and editor. Marketed actors became envied celebrities, and millions followed the lives and careers of these "movie stars." Many filmmakers projected their nations' self-images in stunning, creative ways—perhaps none more so than the legendary Russian Sergei Eisenstein (1898–1948). His epic films about the 1905 and 1917 revolutions in Russia represented the Soviet view of events in those "heroic" years.

Other films revealed deep-seated concerns about modern society. Figure 23.3, for example, shows an eerie, futuristic scene from the German director Fritz Lang's (1890–1976) film *Metropolis* (1925). This image emphasizes the overwhelming power of urban

■ FIGURE 23.2
Otto Dix, *Metropolis*, 1927.

architecture and technology and demonstrates cinema's potential to serve as an artistic medium. Here a solitary airplane flies through the stark canyons of buildings in a futuristic city. Humans are dwarfed out of sight in the impersonal world they have created. The image seems to complement visually lines from "The Waste Land" (1922), a work by one of the period's leading poets, T. S. Eliot (1888–1965):

> Unreal City,
> Under the brown god of a winter dawn,
> A crowd flowed over London Bridge, so many . . .
> And each man fixed his eyes before his feet.

On another level, this scene also hints at other harbingers of modernity: the advent of skyscrapers, already rising in New York City, and the daring flights being made in small planes. Just two years after this film was made, the solo flight across the Atlantic of the American pilot Charles Lindbergh (1902–1974) won acclaim on both sides of the ocean. Americans and Europeans alike saw embodied in Lindbergh and New York the promise of something young, exciting, and dynamic that just might push the West forward into a bright future.

Indeed, throughout the West, cities such as Berlin, Paris, and New York became even more dazzling cultural centers than before. Office buildings and skyscrapers shot up, some of them displaying striking new trends in architecture. Most influential was the German architect Walter Gropius (1883–1969), who in 1919 founded the **Bauhaus** school of art in Germany. This school created new standards for modern architecture and for the design of ordinary objects from chairs and lamps to dishes. In 1925, Gropius designed the building shown in Figure 23.4. Emphasizing clean, functional lines, this international style of architecture symbolized acceptance of the modern, industrial world. These buildings unabashedly displayed their efficient structure, prefabricated materials, and steel and glass features. Many architects would follow this new style over the next half-century in creating office buildings, workers' housing, and private homes.

The Bauhaus school

In addition to trends in entertainment and the arts, the "Roaring Twenties" implied new attitudes toward sex. Especially in leading cities, clothing fashions, often popularized in movies, exhibited these changing attitudes. Women's clothing, featuring thinner fabrics, shorter skirts, and tight-fitting styling, became more revealing. Along with the briefer fashions, women's hairstyles grew progressively

New attitudes toward sex

■ FIGURE 23.3

Fritz Lang's *Metropolis*.

shorter as well. Women discarded confining corsets that had long been in fashion and even donned trousers for sporting activities. Bathing suits, too, became increasingly skimpy. The "flapper," whom we saw in Figure 23.2, was now the new symbol of the ideal, free, sexually liberated woman.

The new focus on body image and sexual appeal intensified concerns about hygiene. People began regularly using toothbrushes, deodorants, and cosmetics. In addition, they bathed more often than before and shaved more closely. Tanned, thin women and muscular men became the new standards of health and sexual attractiveness.

As sex became more openly discussed and encouraged, people also searched for ways to revive declining birthrates and thereby replace the lives lost during the war. In France, for example, the government made distributing birth-control information illegal and abortion punishable by death. The French proclaimed a new holiday, "Mother's Day," an innovation that other Western countries soon copied. Many governments provided maternity benefits, and increasingly, births took place in hospitals under the control of specialized nurses and doctors. Separate rooms for testing, labor, delivery, and recovery made the process of giving birth almost factory-like. Doctors, nurses, and social workers told women the "best" way to care for their children, and child-rearing courses for girls became compulsory in some countries.

■ FIGURE 23.4

The Bauhaus Building, 1925.

THE ANXIOUS TWENTIES

Of all the forms of culture that gained currency during these years, high culture most powerfully reflected the stressful undercurrents of the postwar period. Many writers, intellectuals, and artists emphasized the uncertainty of the era and explored the widespread feelings of insecurity that people harbored.

Several philosophers, reacting to the horrors of the Great War, attacked nineteenth-century optimism and rationalism. These thinkers expanded on the ideas set forth earlier by Friedrich Nietzsche in Germany and Henri Bergson in France (see p. 661). The most widely read of the post-World War I philosophers was a German, Oswald Spengler (1880–1936). In his book *The Decline of the West* (1918), Spengler argued that all civilizations were like biological organisms, each with its own life cycle. Western civilization, he claimed, had passed its high point, and World War I signaled the beginning of its end. This sense of decay and crisis emerged in many other works, most notably in the Spanish writer José Ortega y Gasset's (1883–1955) *Revolt of the Masses* (1930). Gasset lamented the decline of liberal elites and the "accession of the masses to complete social power." The masses, he warned, were not equipped to lead, yet they now took control from qualified elites and demanded a dangerous conformity: "Anybody who is not like everybody, who does not think like everybody, runs the risk of being eliminated."

Sense of decay and crisis

Sigmund Freud's ideas (see Chapter 21) about the irrational, unconscious, and instinctual aspects of human thought and behavior—which had first emerged just before World War I—gained more acceptance during the 1920s. The unconscious and irrational played particularly prominent roles in the most acclaimed literature of the postwar era. The Irish writer James Joyce (1882–1941), German author Franz Kafka (1883–1924), and French writer Marcel Proust (1871–1922) created disquieting, introspective works of literature that elevated personal psychological experience over reason. In *Ulysses* (1922), Joyce in particular mastered the "stream of consciousness" technique, which displayed to the reader the rambling thoughts, free associations, and erotic fantasies going on in the mind of a character. At first critics and the public dismissed the novel as "morbid," "nonsense," and "foul." Eventually, however, this book about a single day in the lives of a group of Dubliners, which also served as a commentary on the human condition, was hailed as one of the century's greatest works of literature. In her novel *Mrs. Dalloway* (1925), British author Virginia Woolf used similar techniques to describe one day in the inner life of a woman, including fragmented conversations, partial remembrances, and fantasies (see Biography, p. 709).

Novels and memoirs of the Great War also proliferated during these years. As in *All Quiet on the Western Front* by the German author Erich Maria Remarque, these works emphasized themes of brutality and suffering, disillusionment with civilian life, and a sense that the war had spawned a generation of "lost souls." At the same time, Remarque's and others' books revealed a longing for the sense of purpose and comradeship that so often arises during a war effort but subsides in times of peace.

Similar themes marked artistic styles of the day. The **Dada** movement stressed the absence of purpose in life. Surrealist painters explored dreams and the world of the subconscious. Other painters, such as Käthe Kollwitz (see the Chapter 22 Biography) and Otto Dix (Figure 23.2), created moving images of suffering, destruction, and social despair.

In the 1920s, then, Western democratic societies struggled mightily both to come to terms with the consequences of the war and to move on to better days. In the early postwar years, the difficulties seemed overwhelming. Even with the revival of healthier economies and easing of international tensions after 1923, underlying doubt and insecurity persisted and made themselves plain in the period's cultural expression.

TURNING AWAY FROM DEMOCRACY: DICTATORSHIPS AND FASCISM, 1919–1929

The sense of unease and the difficult realities clearly burdened politics in the Western democracies, but things were far worse on the political front elsewhere

BIOGRAPHY

Virginia Woolf (1882–1941)

CONSIDER

■ **Consider** *why Virginia Woolf has won renown as a great writer and leading feminist.* **Notice** *connections between her ideas and historical developments in the decades after World War I.*

In 1938, the British writer Virginia Woolf looked back on her life and described herself as "fundamentally an outsider." By then, however, literary critics and the public alike had accepted this sensitive author's extraordinary works and honored her widely.

Born in 1882, Virginia Stephens was raised and educated within the Victorian literary world by her scholarly, well-connected parents. "Think how I was brought up!" she said, describing her isolated childhood. "No school; mooning about alone among my father's books; never any chance to pick up all that goes on in schools—throwing balls; ragging; slang; vulgarities; scenes; jealousies!" In adolescence, the gifted Virginia suffered from depressions and endured the first of the nervous breakdowns that would haunt her for the rest of her life.

In 1912, she married Leonard Woolf, also a writer and intellectual. They remained close over the years, the patient Leonard taking care of Virginia when she fell ill. The two also founded the Hogarth Press, which would publish works by some of the most important writers of the twentieth century, including T. S. Eliot, Sigmund Freud, and E. M. Forster. Their house in Bloomsbury became a gathering place for an influential group of writers, artists, and intellectuals who came to be known as the Bloomsbury group. Woolf acquired a reputation as a bit of a social snob, admitting that she enjoyed rubbing shoulders with the aristocracy because "the aristocrat is freer, more natural, more eccentric than we are." Within this group of intellectuals and social elites, some of her closest friends and lovers were women.

Woolf began her career as a writer in 1905 and published her first novel in 1915. Over the next twenty-five years, her many novels and essays gained critical and public recognition. Reflecting the growing interest in psychology and the life of the mind, she focused on England's intellectuals like herself, experimented with stream-of-consciousness narration in her novels, and emphasized the psychological and emotional underpinnings of her characters. After writing *Jacob's Room* (1922), she felt she had finally come into her own: "There's no doubt . . . that I have found out how to begin (at 40) to say something in my own voice." In some of her works, the action took place over just days. These included *Mrs. Dalloway* (1925), centering on a fashionable society woman, and *To the Lighthouse* (1927), her most autobiographical work of fiction. Other books, such as *Orlando* (1928) and *Between the Acts* (1941) covered large sweeps of English history. Woolf's characters embodied the traumas and challenges of the postwar years. For example, in *Mrs. Dalloway*, a shell-shocked war veteran, Septimus Smith, represents the millions of soldiers killed or maimed—in one way or another—in World War I.

Woolf's best-known nonfiction work, *A Room of One's Own* (1929), focuses on the role of women in literature, education, and twentieth-century society. "A woman must have money and a room of her own if she is to write fiction," she wrote. She went on to explore the hindrances faced by women writers and their need to depart from traditional literature "made by men out of their own needs for their own uses."

Writer and Self-Conscious Observer

During the 1920s and 1930s, Woolf closely followed world events. Having lived through the Great War of 1914–1918 and anticipating the upcoming conflagration that would become World War II, she argued that men—with their power and need to demonstrate their masculinity—caused wars. As a pacifist and antifascist, she became disgusted with the rise of rulers such as Hitler and Mussolini: "His eyes glare," she wrote. "His body, which is braced in an unnatural position, is tightly cased in a uniform. Upon the breast of that uniform are sewn several medals and other mystic symbols. His hand is upon a sword. He is called in German and Italian Führer and Duce; in our language Tyrant or Dictator."

Woolf's fears came true with the outbreak of World War II in 1939. She survived the terrifying bombing raids and threat of German invasion during the Battle of Britain. But she never broke free from her bouts of mental illness. On March 28, 1941, she filled her pockets with stones and drowned herself near her home. "I feel certain that I am going mad again," she had written in her suicide note. "And I shan't recover this time."

■ **FIGURE 23.5**
Virginia Woolf, 1925.

in Europe. Among the states of east-central and southern Europe, the strain of the postwar years became too much for the fragile democratic systems budding there.

AUTHORITARIANISM IN EAST-CENTRAL EUROPE

In 1919, Admiral Miklos Horthy (1868–1957), the reactionary former commander of the Austro-Hungarian navy, led forces, aided by anticommunist Allies and ambitious Romanians, that overthrew the newly formed regime led by the communist Béla Kun (1885–1937) in Hungary. Horthy's rule, like other right-wing authoritarian regimes that followed in Poland (1926) and Yugoslavia (1929), amounted to a dictatorship backed by the nation's military and conservative forces—the bureaucracy, high church, and wealthy elites. Why did these east-central European nations, most of which emerged from the dissolution of the Austro-Hungarian Empire during World War I with new democratic regimes, turn away from parliamentary democracy?

Part of the answer may be that the newly created nations in this area faced enormous economic problems. Although the old Austro-Hungarian Empire had suffered from ethnic and political divisions, it had functioned as an economic whole—its industrial areas trading with its agricultural regions. Now split up, the individual nations were mostly agricultural and too unproductive to create prosperity. Only Czechoslovakia, whose parliamentary system would survive the longest, boasted an advanced industrial economy.

Struggling with these problems, the new democratic regimes seemed divided and ineffective. Many conservative groups feared the kind of change represented by liberal democracy, socialism, and communism. Such changes promised to dilute conservatives' power, diminish their economic base, and undermine their beliefs in the traditional social order. This lack of experience with democracy and the strength of these conservative groups made these nations vulnerable to authoritarian men like Horthy, who promised order and advocated nationalism backed by armed force. One by one, the democratic governments fell to authoritarian takeovers. As in Horthy's regime, the new rulers sometimes used "White Terror" to silence opponents and often repressed Jews and other minority groups.

This rise of authoritarian governments during the 1920s spread beyond east-central Europe. The most dramatic and ominous move came in Italy. There, the charismatic Benito Mussolini (1883–1945) took power, bringing with him a new governance system and ideology: **fascism.**

THE RISE OF FASCISM IN ITALY

At its core, fascism in practice meant dictatorship by a charismatic leader. However it was more than that. It included a set of antidemocratic, anti-individualistic, and anticommunist ideas or attitudes. Fascist doctrine hailed "the people" while denouncing the principles of the French Revolution. Fascist leaders such as Alfredo Rocco (1875–1935) viewed the state as "a living organism" and rejected liberal democratic forms of government, complaining that the liberal state "is dissolving into a mass of small particles, parties, associations, groups and syndicates that are binding it in chains." The fascist call was to nationalism and military prowess. In Italy, people angry and dismayed by events following World War I heard this call and followed it.

Fascist doctrine

Italy had emerged from World War I a battered, disappointed victor. Its armies, on the verge of collapse, had nevertheless managed to hold on and ultimately contributed to the final Allied victory. However, the Treaty of Versailles denied Italy some of the territories on the Adriatic coast that the Allies had promised in return for Italy's contribution to the war effort. Many Italians felt that at Versailles, their nation lost its rightful status as a great power. All this left Italian nationalists bitter and convinced many more Italians that the war had not been worth the price Italy had paid.

Turmoil in Italy

Near-chaos within this troubled nation multiplied these disappointments. Italy's already weak economy staggered under a huge national debt. Its inflated

KEY DATES

FROM RECOVERY TO CRISIS

1919	Versailles Treaty
1921	Irish Free State
1922	Mussolini's march on Rome
1923	Munich putsch
	Egyptian independence
	Occupation of Ruhr
1929	Stock market crash
1933	Nazis gain power
1935	Nuremberg Laws
1938	*Kristallnacht*

currency, together with a shortage of consumer goods, made prices skyrocket. Hundreds of thousands of veterans could find no jobs. In the summer of 1919, disorder spread. Farmworkers threatened property owners by joining unions called "red leagues." Veterans and poor families began seizing idle lands. Banditry in the south grew out of control, and strikes plagued the cities. During the winter of 1920–1921, workers seized control of several hundred factories. Socialists and communists gained strength within industrial and rural unions.

Italy's newly elected government, plagued by political divisions, seemed powerless in the face of these pressures. Frightened landlords and factory owners, along with thousands of veterans and a middle class ravaged by inflation and insecurity, longed for vigorous leadership and a strong, dependable government. The vigorous leader who stepped forward was Benito Mussolini. The strong government was his fascist dictatorship.

Mussolini takes power

Mussolini was born into a family of socialist artisans; he received enough education to become a teacher and then a radical journalist. At the outbreak of World War I, he used the socialist paper he edited to advocate antimilitarism and to demand that Italy remain neutral during the war. A year later, he changed his mind, now convinced that "only blood makes the wheels of history turn." He broke from his socialist allies, started a new newspaper, and joined the army. After the war, he organized mostly unemployed veterans into the National Fascist Party—the term "fascist" alluding to Roman prowess, unity, and justice. His Fascist Party soon attracted enough support to bring down Italy's parliamentary government.

The appeal of Fascism

Why did Mussolini's political movement hold such appeal? The answer to this question is complex. Fascism attracted veterans hoping for a sense of renewal after the disappointments of the war and the immediate postwar years and appealed to young men who felt they had "missed out" on the war experience and therefore responded to the call of wounded national pride. "When I returned from the war—just like so many others—I hated politics and politicians, who . . . had betrayed the hopes of soldiers, reducing Italy to a shameful peace," explained Italo Balbo, a future associate of Mussolini. These men became the members and muscle of the new party. Factory owners, merchants, and landowners also embraced fascism when Mussolini vowed to save Italy from communism. These groups provided Mussolini with money when he organized squads of black-shirted "Fascisti" to terrorize rad-

ical workers and their liberal supporters. Finally, those who blamed the parliamentary government for Italy's postwar woes warmed to fascist promises to act decisively and create unity through nationalistic policies. Fascism seemed to offer a "third way"—a path above socialism and conventional parliamentary democracy—to security and success for Italy.

Figure 23.6 reveals some of the qualities that made Mussolini's Fascist movement attractive. Mussolini stands on a platform dressed in a white paramilitary uniform, his arm raised in the Fascist salute of exaggerated bravery. Below him stands his bodyguard of black-shirted party members in their paramilitary uniforms, holding knives up in the disciplined salute. All are posing for the crowd of onlookers to the left and photographers. The whole scene has been self-consciously set up to present an image of strong leadership and military prowess, and it suggests the appeal of ritual and participation in a mighty movement. Similar scenes would become common as fascist movements and authoritarian governments spread across Europe.

In 1922, building on this support, squads of black-shirted Fascists marched on Rome under Mussolini's vow that "either we are allowed to govern or we will seize power." The indecisive Italian king Victor Emmanuel III (r. 1900–1946) buckled under the pressure and appointed Mussolini prime minister. With great speed, the Fascist leader acquired extraordinary powers.

Between 1924 and 1926, Mussolini turned his office into a dictatorship. Under his rule, only the Fascist Party could engage in organized political activity. Il Duce (the leader) sent his secret police everywhere.

The Fascist system

■ FIGURE 23.6

Mussolini and his Black Shirts.

"Everything within the State," he demanded, and "Nothing outside the State." Mussolini next struck a deal with the powerful Catholic Church and signed the Lateran Treaty of 1929. In return for money and the right to teach religion in the public schools, the papacy finally recognized the existence of the Italian state. The agreement ended the sixty years of division between the church and the state since unification.

To guide Italy's economy toward self-sufficiency and industrialization while carefully protecting private property and profits, the Fascists worked closely with business leaders. They organized the different industries and trades into confederations, or "corporations." Each corporation included a syndicate of workers and one of employers, each in turn headed by a Fascist official. The Fascists also abolished all independent labor unions, strikes, and lockouts. Instead, compulsory arbitration under the party's direction now settled issues of wages and working conditions and disputes between labor and management. The complicated economic and political machinery that Mussolini put in motion for these purposes became known as the corporate state, or corporatism.

Although the state would gain a controlling hand in several major industries, Mussolini's corporate state mainly enlarged the bureaucracy and hamstrung workers' unions. A few well-publicized achievements, such as new railroads, highways, building projects, and educational reforms, hid more fundamental deficiencies. His ambitious agricultural policies generally failed to improve per capita output. People of property fared well, but workers, especially women, suffered declining income. Even though women flocked to hear him, Mussolini cut their wages by decree and banned them from several professions. Those who did not heed his call to take up their "maternal duties" were pushed toward low-paying jobs. Nevertheless, growing numbers of Italian women still managed to enter universities and find positions in the world of paid work.

By 1929, Mussolini stood unchallenged. Using films, radio addresses, biographies, newspapers, and schools, he amassed a huge following of supporters who repeated his reassuring phrase, "Mussolini is always right." Some artists and intellectuals supported at least his image of dynamic leadership. Mussolini also won a reputation among groups throughout Europe, South America, and the United States as someone who could "make the trains run on time," gain peace with the Catholic Church, and stand up to communist threats.

In reality, Mussolini—like many twentieth-century politicians—was more of an actor able to manipulate appearances than an effective ruler who could solve domestic or international problems. Many people immune to his charm saw him as merely a strutting, boasting carnival performer. Mussolini's vision of "historical destiny"—to create a Second Roman Empire and turn the Mediterranean into an Italian "lake"—perhaps most revealed a disturbing lack of touch with reality. Even with "Il Duce" in control, Italy was no major power.

To the east, the situation was entirely different. Russia had been a major power and might well rise again. Now transformed into a communist state and reformed into the Soviet Union by the Bolsheviks, its radical left-wing policies represented an even more frightening threat to capitalist democracies than the extreme right-wing politics of Italian Fascism.

TRANSFORMING THE SOVIET UNION: 1920–1939

In 1920, Russia's bloody civil war had finally ended. The suffering, however, dragged on. Industrial production sank to only 13 percent of pre-World War I levels. A famine struck, taking four to seven million lives. Countless thousands of veterans and city-dwellers roamed the countryside in search of food, shelter, and employment. "Green Armies" of peasants revolted against forced requisitions of their crops and restrictions against selling products at market prices. Workers struck against declining wages and lack of control over the factories. Sailors at the Kronstadt naval base mutinied, demanding political liberty. Many Communist Party and union members called for more democracy. How could Lenin's still vulnerable Communist government survive?

LENIN'S COMPROMISE: THE NEP

Lenin retreated. In 1921 he launched the **New Economic Policy** (NEP), a "temporary" compromise with capitalism. This policy allowed peasants to manage their own land and sell their own crops. In addition, small-scale industries could operate under private ownership, and money and credit were restored. Although the state still supervised the economy, the NEP provided enough capitalist incentive to pull the Russian economy out of chaos.

Lenin's retreat did not extend to politics, however. Russia remained a "dictatorship of the Proletariat," symbolized on Russia's flag by the red of socialism, the hammer of industrial workers, and the sickle of peasants. Lenin and the Communist Party elite maintained a tight grip on power and brutally suppressed any opposition. Local soviets submitted to the central government in Moscow, dominated by its 16-person Politburo and, above all, the secretariat of the Communist Party. The formal creation of the "Union of Soviet Socialist Republics" (USSR, or Soviet Union) in 1922 paid only lip service to desires for autonomy in "republics" such as the Ukraine, Armenia, and Georgia. Russia, home to four-fifths of the USSR's total population, dominated the Union.

Soviet society in the 1920s reflected its revolutionary origins as well as the temporary compromise with capitalism. The Communists had eliminated the old aristocracy, church, and traditional class distinctions. But party, military, and cultural elites enjoyed higher standards of living, better housing, and more educational opportunities than anyone else. Some peasants who took advantage of NEP opportunities also became relatively wealthy, as did their urban counterparts running small businesses.

Moreover, women enjoyed unprecedented legal equality. In addition to the right to vote, they received the right to equal pay, education, and professional opportunities. The government set up programs and agencies such as the Women's Bureau to promote equality, day care, housing, medical care, and information on birth control and divorce. Alexandra Kollontai (1872–1952), head of the Women's Bureau, urged collectivization of child-rearing and a new family form: "The narrow and exclusive affection of the mother for her own children must expand until it embraces all the children of the great proletarian family. In place of the indissoluble marriage based on the servitude of woman, we shall see rise in the free union [of two people] . . . equal in their rights and in their obligations. . . ."

These new policies all showed promise, but in fact the burdens on Soviet women probably increased. Programs to help them lacked the resources to make a real difference. Greater access to jobs rarely translated into higher-level positions. Women were still expected to retain their traditional burdens at home, their "second shift."

Although the NEP was a retreat from strict Communist policies, Lenin's regime still envisioned itself as leading the world into modernity. The government turned churches and great mansions into museums and meeting halls. Cultural activities promoted proletarian pride, the benefits of technology, and the glories of the future. Avant-garde artists created utopian visions by connecting images of mass production and social justice.

The NEP may have encouraged the outside world to end its isolation of Russia. Between 1922 and 1924, all Western nations recognized the Soviet Union except the United States, which remained aloof until 1933. Indeed, to many socialists throughout the West, the Soviet Union stood as a source of hope and inspiration.

The Struggle to Succeed Lenin

Lenin would not live to witness the results of the NEP. After a series of paralytic strokes, he died in 1924. Three of his chief associates—Leon Trotsky

(1879–1940), Nikolai Bukharin (1888–1938), and Joseph Stalin (1879–1953)—jockeyed to succeed him. Most observers assumed that the brilliant but arrogant Trotsky, who had led the Red Army during the civil war, would win. He argued that the Soviet Union must promote revolutions elsewhere in the West to survive and that the Soviet economy should be tightly controlled and massively industrialized from above. By contrast, the popular Bukharin, who had been appointed by Lenin to lead the NEP, argued for socialism by slow, careful steps. The shrewd political manipulator Stalin claimed a middle-of-the-road position between these two, but believed that Russia must survive alone—"socialism in one country." His opponents vastly underestimated him.

Stalin (a pseudonym meaning "man of steel") was born in Georgia the son of poverty-stricken ex-serfs. His mother managed to get him into an Orthodox seminary school, where he *Joseph Stalin* received a formal education. Expelled from the seminary because of his Marxist views, he joined revolutionary groups. Repeatedly arrested, he kept managing to escape. In 1917, he took advantage of the revolutionary turmoil and hastened to Petrograd from his exile in Siberia. A poor speaker and writer, he used daring and organizational talents to rise in the party. He played a prominent role in Russia's civil war and became executive secretary of the Communist Party. In this key position, he made himself master of the all-important party machinery and pursued his drive for power.

Toward the end of his life, Lenin warned that "Stalin is too rude" to lead. Nevertheless, after Lenin's death, Stalin cleverly played on the Soviet people's love of Lenin by posing as his heir and leading a movement to deify him. He also brought into the party new people, who thereby owed him a debt. Playing off his rivals against each other, he used his control over the Central Committee of the Communist Party to edge the overconfident Trotsky and his supporters on the Left out of powerful positions and, in 1927, expel them from the party. The next year, he turned against Bukharin and the Right. Party members who had doubts about Stalin accepted the need for party loyalty. By the end of 1928, Stalin had maneuvered himself into a position of dominance over the Communist Party and of dictatorship over the Soviet Union. Now he set out to transform the nation.

Stalin's Five-Year Plans

By 1928, Soviet industry had probably attained little more than 1913 levels of production. Stalin and his party leadership wanted much more. That year, he ended the NEP and launched the First **Five-Year Plan.** The fundamental goal of the plan could not have been more ambitious: "We do not want to be beaten. . . . Old Russia . . . was ceaselessly beaten for her backwardness. . . . We are fifty or a hundred years behind the advanced countries. We must make good this lag in ten years . . . or they crush us." The plan called for the rapid, massive industrialization of the nation. Goals included more than doubling industrial production, increasing the generation of electric power almost fivefold, and building 1,500 new factories within five years. To achieve the goals, the State Planning Commission, or Gosplan, would strictly regulate all aspects of production, including targeting crucial industries such as steel, regimenting the industrial labor force, and hiring foreign engineers to help build the new factories. The 1930s Soviet propaganda poster shown in Figure 23.7, "The Five-Year Plan in Four Years," portrays the idea that Stalin will lead Soviet industrial development against the threatening reactionary forces of capitalism and religion. As if preparing for another war, Stalin ordered the USSR's entire society to mobilize for industrialization.

To help accomplish the Five-Year Plan's goals (which included doubling agricultural production), the state took agriculture out of the control of individual peasants by consolidating their lands into huge collective farms that used modern machines. Elected managers and party officials ran the farms. Individuals could own tools, keep small gardens for fruits and vegetables, and raise pigs and chickens for private use or sale. By determining prices and distribution of crops, the state expected to use agricultural "surpluses" to pay for industrialization—to buy the equipment to build

Collectivization

factories, transportation facilities, and power plants. **Collectivization,** it was believed, would also push peasants to become industrial workers in the cities.

As Document 23.2 suggests, the process of collectivization proved ruinous. Hundreds of thousands of peasants, especially wealthier landowners derisively called *kulaks*, powerfully resisted the new policies. In protest, they even destroyed their own crops and livestock—some 50 percent of horses and cattle between 1929 and 1933. Officials terrorized such resisters into submission. "The expropriation of the kulaks is an integral part of the formation . . . of the collective farms," announced Stalin. The kulaks should be "eliminated as a class." Hundreds of thousands of peasants were killed and far more were exiled to Siberia, never to return. This violent battle of wills was accompanied by plummeting agricultural production and government pressure to increase agricultural exports at all costs to finance industrialization. The results were disastrous: Between 1930 and 1933, famine struck, taking the lives of four to six million people. An observer reported that in Ukrainian villages, peasants resorted to eating "dogs, horses, rotten potatoes, the bark of trees, grass—anything they could find . . . and no matter what they did, they went on dying, dying, dying." The effort to collectivize agriculture and the deadly hunger tore apart rural families, communities, and established ways of life. Nevertheless, Stalin finally got his way: More than half the land was collectivized within the first year, and over 90 percent after ten years.

To industrialize the Soviet Union, planners had to start almost from ground level and build up. They concentrated on producer goods such as engines and tractors rather than consumer goods such as shoes and clothes.

Mobilizing for industrialization

Gradually, steel mills, dams, power plants, foundries, mines, refineries, chemical factories, and railroads sprang up all over the Soviet Union. Technocrats and officials faced pressure to produce targeted results. The government fostered a sense of emergency to inspire people, especially the young, to work hard. Presenting the effort as a great adventure, officials pointed out that those who most contributed to the industrialization drive could achieve a status similar to that of the heroes of the 1917 revolution. The government moved "shock brigades" of enthusiastic, efficient workers from factory to factory to stimulate production, while the press celebrated new "Heroes of Labor" who exceeded production targets. Officials encouraged women to work on both the collective farms and in factories; by 1940, women made up almost half the labor force.

■ FIGURE 23.7

"The Five-Year Plan in Four Years."

■ DOCUMENT 23.2

Stalin Collectivizes Agriculture

As part of his campaign to collectivize agriculture, Stalin used massive coercion against the Russian kulaks (relatively rich independent peasants). Widespread destruction and death resulted. In the following excerpt, Lev Kopelev recounts his own participation in this collectivization drive. ■ **Why** *was this aspect of collectivization so devastating?* ■ **How** *does Kopelev justify his participation in the drive?* ■ **What** *insights into Soviet life during the early 1930s does this document provide?*

A team consisting of several young kolkhozniks [collective farmers] and members of the village soviet . . . would search the hut, barn, yard, and take away all the stores of seed, lead away the cow, the horse, the pigs.

In some cases they would be merciful and leave some potatoes, peas, corn for feeding the family. But the stricter ones would make a clean sweep. They would take not only the food and livestock, but also "all valuables and surpluses of clothing," including icons in their frames, samovars, painted carpets and even metal kitchen utensils which might be silver. And any money they found stashed away. Special instructions ordered the removal of gold, silver and currency. . . .

We were raised as the fanatical [believers] of a new creed, the only true *religion* of scientific socialism. The party became our church militant, bequeathing to all mankind eternal salvation, eternal peace and the bliss of an earthly paradise. It victoriously surmounted all other churches, schisms and heresies. The works of Marx, Engels and Lenin were accepted as holy writ, and Stalin was the infallible high priest.

. . . Stalin was the most perspicacious, the most wise (at that time they hadn't yet started calling him "great" and "brilliant"). He said: "The struggle for grain is the struggle for socialism." And we believed him unconditionally. And later we believed that unconditional collectivization was unavoidable if we were to overcome the capriciousness and uncertainty of the market and the backwardness of individual farming, to guarantee a steady supply of grain, milk and meat to the cities. And also if we were to reeducate millions of peasants, those petty landowners and hence potential bourgeoisie, potential kulaks, to transform them into laborers with a social conscience, to liberate them from "the idiocy of country life," from ignorance and prejudice, and to accustom them to culture, to all the boons of socialism. . . .

Source: Lev Kopelev, *The Education of a True Believer* (New York: Harper & Row, 1980), p. 123.

KEY DATES

THE SOVIET UNION

1918–1920	Civil war
1920–1921	Famine
1924	Death of Lenin
1928	Beginning of First Five-Year Plan
1930–1933	Famine
1934	Beginning of Great Purges

All elements of Soviet society were mobilized to support the effort to make the USSR an industrial power. Schools, adult education classes, newspapers, union meetings, and youth associations became saturated with official doctrines of Soviet communism, efficiency, and class pride. "We must make every school child aware of . . . how the great people of our epoch—Lenin, Stalin, and their companions in arms—organized the workers in the struggle for a new and happy life," explained a Soviet text on teaching methods. Officials, minor bureaucrats, and members of the secret police ranged everywhere and monitored progress. Within families—the "school for socialism"—mothers were urged to raise their children to fit into communist society. Earlier policies supporting women's choices were reversed. The state made abortion illegal and promoted traditional marriage and relationships. In this more repressive era, homosexuality became a crime.

The state also tightened controls over cultural productions, ending the experimentation of the 1920s. The Central Committee of the Communist Party told publishing houses that "books must be an instrument for the mobilization of the workers for the tasks of industrialization and collectivization." A government ministry took control over filmmaking to make sure movies promoted revolutionary enthusiasm and favorable views of the communist state. Socialist realism became the required orthodoxy in art. In this style, approved murals, art, and literature portrayed realistic images of people carrying out

■ FIGURE 23.8

Russian poster, *People's Dreams Have Come True!*

the dreams of a communist society. Figure 23.8 is an example of this effort to make art relevant and compelling to the working masses. In this idealized image, an older man (reminiscent of an aged Lenin) shows a boy the achievements of Stalin's programs. Above the two smiling figures is a well-known nineteenth-century painting of poverty-stricken peasants and workers hauling a ship up a river by ropes. By contrast, the new "social reality" can be seen outside the window, where steamships haul barges up a river and in the distance where modern facilities attest to the creation of modern industry. The eager boy, in a comradely embrace, wears the uniform of a Stalinist youth organization and represents the glowing future.

At the end of 1932, Stalin announced that all goals of the First Five-Year Plan had been accomplished several months ahead of time. He recited a list of accomplishments in iron, steel, tractors, automobiles, machine tools, chemicals, and aircraft production. "Our country has been converted from an agrarian into an industrial country," he proclaimed. These gains, however, came at a high price. For the hard-pressed workers, consumer goods beyond the necessities remained scarce. Clearly, some Soviet citizens—namely party members—benefited more than others. One refugee cynically compared life before and after the Bolshevik Revolution: "In Tsarist times there were the rich and the poor; under Soviet power there were the party members and the non-party members." Similar Second and Third Five-Year Plans would follow, this time with more emphasis on

consumer goods and armaments. The terrifying Great Purges would also follow.

BLOOD AND TERROR: THE GREAT PURGES

In 1934, Leonid Nikolayev assassinated Sergei Kirov (1888–1934), a high Soviet official. Stalin used the murder as an excuse to eliminate potential rivals. The incident introduced a long period of party purges, marked by terror, house arrests, bizarre show-trials, torture, imprisonments, and executions—all approved by Stalin.

Historians still debate Stalin's motives for the Great Purges. Stalin and party officials blamed difficulties during the five-year plans on many—engineers, technocrats, army officers, older party members, regional nationalists, foreign conspirators, saboteurs—and purged the accused. Lower-level officials probably contributed to the waves of purges by trying to rise at the expense of higher-level officials. Certainly Stalin worried about threats from within the party. He eradicated all potential opposition—real or imagined, and even on foreign soil. In 1940, Soviet agents assassinated Trotsky in Mexico.

By the time the **Great Purges** ended in 1939, authorities had killed some one million people. Another seven million died or languished in forced-labor camps; still more had been sent into exile. The terror spread throughout Soviet society, for everyone knew of someone accused and arrested. Almost all the original Bolshevik leaders and the Red Army's top officer corps were gone. New, younger figures beholden to Stalin now staffed the government, the Communist Party, and the military.

In the end, Stalin got most of what he wanted. By 1939, the Soviet Union had a fully planned economy, with the state determining production, prices, and distribution. Although officials announced successes whether they occurred or not, the USSR had in fact become the third-greatest industrial power in the world. More than 90 percent of peasants lived on collective, mechanized farms. Millions more had moved to the cities, where new housing, schools, libraries, and hospitals had sprung up. For the first time, most of the population could read. Within the Soviet Union, no one dared oppose Stalin, and now he had the armaments to face a new challenge already rising in the west. But the cost had been tremendous. Between 15 and 20 million people (some scholars argue that the figure might be much higher) had died from starvation, execution, or the harsh conditions in forced-labor camps and far more had suffered as a result of Stalin's policies.

THE GREAT DEPRESSION, 1929–1939

The forces to the west creating that challenge to the USSR had begun to coalesce and gather momentum, and the Soviets were not the only ones threatened by them. As we saw earlier, authoritarianism and fascism—fierce opponents of communism—had already started to rise in the 1920s. In 1929, a new crisis struck the Western democracies: the **Great Depression.** Reeling from years of hard times and pulling much of the world with them, Western societies began edging toward a new darkness that would more than rival the horrors of World War I.

CRASH!

In October 1929, the New York stock market crashed. In one month, stocks lost almost two-thirds of their value. The financial crisis quickly spread from the United States, the world's leading industrial nation and creditor, to Europe, where nations depended heavily on American loans and trade. The crash ended the relative prosperity since 1924 and provoked an unprecedented global depression. Within two years, thousands of banks and businesses throughout the West failed. Spending, production, employment, and income all dropped sharply. Plant closings, farm foreclosures, and joblessness haunted the Western nations. People's confidence in the economy died, and too often with it went their faith in themselves.

A complex series of events had led to the disaster. The postwar economic order was built on a fragile foundation of international credit, reparations payments, and foreign trade. Much of Europe remained dependent on the United States for credit. Germany in particular relied on American loans to support its reparation payments.

Causes of the economic collapse

In 1928, American investors began pulling their money out of Germany and demanding repayment of loans to invest in the unregulated, soaring U.S. stock market. Credit dried up in Germany and in east-central European nations tied to the German economy. The 1929 crash sent people running to banks to withdraw funds, further undermining credit. Soon the West's entire economic house of cards collapsed.

The collapse took much of the globe with it. Over the years, non-Western lands had become important suppliers of raw materials—such as rice, cotton, cocoa, rubber, oil, copper, and tin—for Western industry and urban populations. With their economies more and more dependent on international trade, these regions were now tied to the economic fate of the West. Ties to the West particularly marked industrialized Japan's economy. The lure of increasing trade with the United States during the 1920s had persuaded Japan to halt its imperial expansion in Asia. The Great Depression—which quickly slashed exports to the United States in half and left three million people unemployed—brought an end to Japan's prosperity and revived its imperial ambitions. Japan's leaders looked to make East Asian markets their own, by conquest if necessary.

Effects in non-Western lands

IN THE TEETH OF THE DEPRESSION

By 1932, Europe's economies had shrunk to one-half their 1929 size. Unemployment in the West rose to a shocking 22 percent, leaving 30 million people out of work. Along with their jobs, people lost their savings, their farms, and their homes. In Germany, Heinrich Hauser described how "an almost unbroken chain of homeless men extends the whole length of the great Hamburg-Berlin highway." One British woman echoed the feelings of many: "These last few years since I've been out of the mills . . . I've got no spirit for anything." Masses of people sank into poverty, and malnutrition and diseases spread. Families suffered from new tensions as men lost their traditional role as breadwinners. "When he was out of work," lamented a woman from Liverpool, "we were always having rows over the children."

Scenes of despair could be found everywhere. Figure 23.9, a painting by Isaac Soyer, shows people in a New York employment agency. Their faces reveal little hope as they wait—reading a newspaper, looking away in distraction, or staring ahead in resignation. The dreary room offers no consolation, and the scene through the window suggests there is little to look forward to on the city streets.

In eastern and central Europe, hard-pressed farmers and unemployed workers looked for scapegoats. They blamed Jews, whom they saw as controlling the banks, bureaucracy, jobs, and policies responsible for the depression. People also pointed their fingers at socialists, communists, big business, and even modernity. Ethnic groups and major powers turned on one another, and throughout the West, popular protests by desperate, angry people spread.

■ FIGURE 23.9

Isaac Soyer, *Employment Agency*, 1937.

SEARCHING FOR SOLUTIONS

At first, governments met the depression the old way: by balancing the budget and increasing tariffs on imported goods. However, these policies just made matters worse by dampening spending and hindering trade. A moratorium on reparations and war debts in August 1931 came too late to do much good. Imperial powers such as Britain and France turned to their colonial holdings for secure trade and profits, only to meet rising demands for independence in India, Iraq, Vietnam, Algeria, and elsewhere. The British economist John Maynard Keynes (1883–1946) argued for new policies—more government expenditures financed by budget deficits to stimulate consumer spending and raise employment—but few listened to his still little-known ideas.

After 1932, new regimes in the United States, Britain, and Germany adopted policies to increase government spending and provide some relief. Similar policies had already enabled Scandinavian democracies to weather the depression with relative ease. However, even with these measures, most Western democracies recovered slowly and not fully until the late 1930s, thanks to spending for rearmament. Figure 23.10 indicates that France and the United States in particular had difficulty raising industrial production to figures approaching pre-1929 levels. By then, these democracies faced new threats that made even the anxious 1920s look like "roaring" good times. The most ominous menace came from Germany.

NAZISM IN GERMANY

In 1928, Germany's fascist party, the Nazis (National Socialists), won less than 3 percent of the vote in national elections. Five years later, the party and its leader, Adolf Hitler, gained power and ended German democracy —all through legal means. How did this happen?

THE YOUNG ADOLF HITLER

The story of Nazism's rise begins with the life of Adolf Hitler (1889–1945). Hitler was born to a middle-aged Austrian customs official and his much younger wife. When his father died in 1905, Hitler quit school and traveled to Vienna, where he hoped to become an artist or architect. Denied admission to the art academy, he lived on his orphan's pension, selling postcards and hanging wallpaper. He compulsively followed daily routines and would do so for the rest of his life. He also picked up nationalistic, anti-Semitic, and racist ideas circulating in Vienna that he embraced with deadly seriousness.

When World War I broke out, Hitler "thanked heaven out of an overflowing heart." For this ardent German nationalist, here was a righteous crusade to end a life of drifting. He served as a courier in the German army and was decorated three times. War's end found him in a hospital recovering from a poison gas attack. He revered World War I as "the greatest of all experiences." As for Germany's defeat at the end of the conflict, he blamed Jews and Marxists, who he felt sure had "stabbed Germany in the back."

THE BIRTH OF NAZISM IN GERMANY'S POSTWAR YEARS

Hitler spotted opportunities in Germany's turbulent postwar years. Several right-wing groups had formed that offered extreme solutions to Germany's problems and that threatened the newly formed parliamentary government of the Weimar Republic. In 1919, while working in Munich as an informer for the army, Hitler joined one of those groups—the German Workers' Party. A year later, he rose to leadership in the party and renamed it the National Socialist German Workers' Party, or the **Nazi Party** (despite the party's name, it was neither socialist in the traditional sense nor well-supported by urban workers). Hitler also organized a paramilitary wing—the SA "stormtroopers"— to back the party. Copying Mussolini's techniques, the SA troopers wore brown shirts and carried pagan symbols (the swastika). They marched through the streets, sang patriotic songs, and beat up communists, socialists, and anyone else they considered their opponents.

Nothing yet marked this small group as destined for success. Nevertheless, in 1923 Hitler and the popular war hero Field Marshal Ludendorff made an ambitious grab for power. From a beer hall in Munich, the Nazis marched on the local government. Republican troops easily put down this "Beer Hall Putsch," and Hitler, after a highly publicized trial, spent nearly a year in jail. While in prison, he wrote *Mein Kampf (My Struggle)*, a work that set forth the core of his Nazi doctrine.

Nazism, like other brands of fascism, assaulted the liberal, democratic tradition in the West. According to Nazi doctrine, the political order should be dominated by a single party headed by a dictatorial leader (Hitler) who appealed to the masses. In *Nazi doctrine* addition, Germany should rearm, redress the "injustices" of the Versailles treaty, and conquer the Slavic people to the east to gain "living space" (**Lebensraum**). At the center of Hitler's beliefs lurked biological racism and anti-Semitism. He glorified the mythical German "Aryan race" as superior and destined to conquer all other peoples in the struggle for racial supremacy. He also condemned the Jews as corrupt, landless parasites who created Marxist communism, caused Germany's humiliating defeat in World War I, and propagated liberalism.

THE GROWTH OF THE NAZI PARTY

Hitler exited jail in 1924 determined to acquire power from within, "legally." Between 1925 and 1929, the Nazi Party grew in numbers somewhat, but still remained a small splinter group. Then in October 1929, Germany's foreign minister, Gustav Stresemann, whose effective leadership for five years held center parties of the Weimar Republic together, died. That same month, the New York stock market crashed. Soon the Great Depression had Germany in its grip. It spelled the end of American loans and ignited unemployment and panic. Internal divisions immobilized parliamentary government, and the political extremes on both the Left and Right rapidly gained strength.

In 1930, the aged president Paul Hindenburg, Germany's military commander during World War I and no friend to democracy, authorized rule by decree over Germany's unstable parliament. In elections held that year, the Nazis won a startling 18.3 percent of the vote—up from 2.6 percent in 1928. Hindenburg turned to conservative politicians to lead the republic, but they failed to govern effectively. The moder-

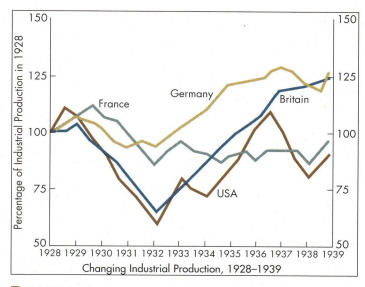

■ FIGURE 23.10

Industrial production, 1928–1939.

ates, socialists, and communists, for their part, could not unify into a strong political force. In 1932, the Nazi Party became the largest political organization in Germany, winning an astonishing 37.3 percent of the vote. In elections for the office of president, Hitler gained 13.5 million votes against Hindenburg's 19 million.

THE APPEAL OF NAZISM

Hitler and the doctrine of Nazism captured the imaginations of many Germans, especially young people and displaced veterans eager to achieve some measure of social stature in the new elite. Indeed, Hitler presented Nazism as "the organized will of the youth." He also appealed to the millions of Germans—the lower-middle class in particular—who had been traumatized by the Great Depression.

Much of Hitler's appeal stemmed from the alluring promises he made—promises that offered comfort and reassurance to a people in desperate need. He claimed that he would get rid of the despised war reparations, economic hardship, incompetent leadership, threats from the Left, and parliamentary government. In addition, he vowed to restore national unity and order in Germany and revive both the German people's shattered pride and their military might. Document 23.3 suggests how Hitler and the Nazi Party used nationalism and anti-Semitism to gain support.

To wealthy industrial leaders and landowners who feared the growing strength of unions, socialists, and communists, Hitler and his party held less of a personal attraction. Instead, Nazism represented the lesser of

■ DOCUMENT 23.3

Goebbels' Nazi Propaganda Pamphlet

Propaganda was strongly emphasized by the Nazis as a method of acquiring and maintaining power. Joseph Goebbels (1897–1945), an early leader in the Nazi party, was made chief of propaganda in 1929, minister for propaganda and national enlightenment in 1933, and a member of Hitler's cabinet council in 1938. The following is an excerpt from a 1930 pamphlet, written by Goebbels, describing why the Nazis are nationalists and against Jews. ■ **How** *does this document reflect the character of life in Germany during the 1920s?* ■ **To whom** *was this document designed to appeal and* **in what ways** *might it be a convincing piece of propaganda?*

WHY ARE WE NATIONALISTS?

We are NATIONALISTS because we see in the NATION the only possibility for the protection and the furtherance of our existence.

The NATION is the organic bond of a people for the protection and defense of their lives. He is nationally minded who understands this IN WORD AND IN DEED.

Today, in GERMANY, NATIONALISM has degenerated into BOURGEOIS PATRIOTISM, and its power exhausts itself in tilting at windmills. It says GERMANY and means MONARCHY. It proclaims FREEDOM and means BLACK-WHITE-RED.

WE ARE NATIONALISTS BECAUSE WE, AS GERMANS, LOVE GERMANY. And because we love Germany, we demand the protection of its national spirit and we battle against its destroyers.

* * *

WHY DO WE OPPOSE THE JEWS?

We are the ENEMIES OF THE JEWS, because we are fighters for the freedom of the German people. THE JEW IS THE CAUSE AND THE BENEFICIARY OF OUR MISERY. He has used the social difficulties of the broad masses of our people to deepen the unholy split between Right and Left among our people. He has made two halves of Germany. He is the real cause for our loss of the Great War.

The Jew has no interest in the solution of Germany's fateful problems. He CANNOT have any. FOR HE LIVES ON THE FACT THAT THERE HAS BEEN NO SOLUTION. If we would make the German people a unified community and give them freedom before the world, then the Jew can have no place among us. He has the best trumps in his hands when a people lives in inner and outer slavery. THE JEW IS RESPONSIBLE FOR OUR MISERY AND HE LIVES ON IT. . . .

WE ARE ENEMIES OF THE JEWS BECAUSE WE BELONG TO THE GERMAN PEOPLE. THE JEW IS OUR GREATEST MISFORTUNE.

It is not true that we eat a Jew every morning at breakfast.

It is true, however, the he SLOWLY BUT SURELY ROBS US OF EVERYTHING WE OWN.

THAT WILL STOP, AS SURELY AS WE ARE GERMANS.

Source: From Louis L. Snyder, *The Weimar Republic*. Reprinted by permission of D. Van Nostrand Co. (New York, 1966), pp. 201–203. Copyright © 1966 by Litton Educational Publishing, Inc.

---

two distasteful options in the minds of these groups. Many such people who voted for the Nazis did so as a way to vote *against* the Weimar Republic, the terms of the Versailles treaty, and the communist path, rather than *for* the Nazi ideology. Indeed, most of these Germans probably would have preferred to elect more traditional conservatives, but none of the existing candidates passed muster.

Whatever the appeal, those drawn to Hitler and the Nazis either ignored the party's strident nationalism, racism, and anti-Semitic fervor or embraced those sentiments. After all, such calls had been heard throughout central and eastern Europe for decades. However, many Germans failed to detect the especially virulent quality of the Nazis' version of these feelings. Even experienced politicians never saw the danger in the situation. In fact, some conservative leaders, such as Franz von Papen, supported Hitler under the assumption that they could control him. As they would discover, they were greatly mistaken.

HITLER TAKES POWER

In January 1933, President Hindenburg offered Hitler the chancellorship, and the Nazi leader accepted. Jubilant stormtroopers marched through Berlin's streets, holding their blazing torches high. In his new position, Hitler immediately called for another round of parliamentary elections. Now in official control of the state police and the agencies of information, the Nazis used propaganda and terror to confuse and frighten voters. As Hitler explained it, "Terror at the place of employment, in the factory, in the meeting hall, and on the occasion of mass demonstrations will always be successful."

Five days before the elections, Hitler discredited the communists by accusing them of burning the Reichstag building. He used the fire to justify the suspension of civil liberties and the arrest of many communists. On election day, the Nazis gained 44 percent of the vote; with their nationalist allies, they now had enough for a majority. The Reichstag quickly passed an enabling act granting Hitler the power to make laws on his own for four years. He soon outlawed all other political parties, and when Hindenburg died in 1934, Hitler became the sole leader of the German government. That same year, Hitler ordered Heinrich Himmler (1900–1945) and a handpicked private armed force, the elite **SS,** to "blood purge" his own paramilitary organization, the SA. Hitler saw the leader of the SA, Ernst Röhm (1887–1934) as a rival with plans to establish control over the army. That "Night of the Long Knives" eliminated potential opponents to Hitler within the party and the powerful SA as a rival to the reviving German army. Now the army swore allegiance to Hitler. The Nazi leader's dictatorship was complete.

LIFE IN NAZI GERMANY

His power consolidated, Hitler proceeded to turn Germany into a police state. The government abolished freedom of speech, press, and assembly. An elaborate and all-powerful secret police, the Gestapo, uncovered and destroyed opposition. Nazi officials took over top positions in the government and pressured churches to conform to the new order. Professional organizations of doctors, teachers, lawyers, and engineers were transformed into Nazi associations. Officials even pushed people into joining Nazi leisure-time organizations.

The Nazis set out to bring family and private life under their control. As one step, the German Women's Bureau established guidelines for "proper" womanhood. Women, the bureau proclaimed, belonged at home where they could fulfill their primary duties as homemakers, as subordinates to their husbands, and as producers of children. According to Guida Diehl, the leader of a pro-Nazi women's organization, "A woman's honor rests on the province specifically entrusted to her . . . love, marriage, family, motherhood . . . The German man wants to

Family and private life

know . . . that it is worthwhile to live and die for such German womanhood." Officials launched campaigns to honor and reward pregnant women, prevent birth control, and "improve racial stock." The government provided subsidies for large, "racially German" families. Women who gave birth to more than four children received the bronze Honor Cross of the German Mother; more than six warranted a silver medal, and more than eight, the coveted gold. In 1937, the Nazi Art Council of the Reich demanded that painters cease depicting families with only two children. A new program in 1938 went so far as to encourage SS soldiers to breed children with "racially fit" women outside of marriage.

Nazi youth organizations such as the Hitler Youth and the League of German Girls expanded rapidly, absorbing the majority of teenage boys and girls by the late 1930s. Boys were molded into Nazi supporters with military values and sometimes encouraged to spy on their teachers and parents. "I don't want an intellectual education" for boys, Hitler said. "They must learn in the face of the most difficult trials to conquer the fear of death for my sake." Girls were trained to become housewives and mothers, which the Nazis saw as the perfect complement to the loyal, fearless German soldier.

Nazi youth organizations

Hitler inspired and manipulated people with his stirring, inflammatory speeches, rallies, parades, and symbols. His organizers choreographed mass meetings such as the one at Buckeberg in 1934, shown in Figure 23.11, to whip up excitement and a sense of belonging

■ FIGURE 23.11
Adolf Hitler at Buckeberg.

THINKING ABOUT ART

Felix Nussbaum, *Self-Portrait with Jewish Identity Card, 1943*

■ FIGURE 23.12

This painting depicts the German artist Felix Nussbaum within prison walls holding up his Jewish identity card.
■ **What** might be the significance of the yellow Star of David and the identity card in understanding the evolving Nazi policy toward Jews in Germany? ■ **Why** might the artist have portrayed himself so directly looking out at the viewers? ■ **What** feelings might viewers experience upon seeing this painting?

among the populace. In this photograph, Hitler leads

Promoting Nazism and Hitler

a procession of Nazi elites between two lines of honor guards and swastika banners. At such rallies, Hitler made a carefully staged, dramatic entrance and delivered a long, emotionally charged speech. "It is the belief in our people that has made us small men great, that has made us poor men rich, that has made brave and courageous men out of us wavering, spiritless, timid fold," he proclaimed at the Nuremberg rally in 1936. Listeners described feeling "eternally bound to this man." The ministry of propaganda, under Joseph Goebbels (1897–1945), reinforced the psychological power of the rallies by controlling information and spreading Nazi ideology through the press, radio, films, textbooks, pamphlets, and posters. For ex-

ample, the ministry commissioned Leni Riefenstahl (1902–2003) to create the documentary film *Triumph of the Will* (1935), which portrayed the Nazis and their leaders as awe inspiring and gloriously on the march. Goebbels also painted an image of Hitler as the people's heroic leader, the one who could even be trusted to limit any excesses by overzealous extremists within the Nazi Party itself.

In addition to promoting enthusiasm for their leader and ideology, the Nazis attacked "decadent" modern art and the popular culture of the Jazz Age. Only those whose works conformed to Nazi tastes— usually sentimental, pro-Nazi subject matter—could exhibit, publish, or perform. Officials promoted the burning of liberal books, sometimes even those of Germany's greatest literary figures of the eighteenth and nineteenth centuries, such as Goethe and Schiller. The Nazi minister of culture told university professors, "From now on it will *not* be your job to determine whether something is true but whether it is in the spirit of the [Nazi] revolution." Although some intellectuals and artists supported these policies, many opposed them and left Germany.

Both to solidify their power and to carry out their racist ideas, the Nazis targeted many groups for repression. For example, they sent communists, socialists, resisting Catholics, Jehovah's Witnesses, and the Roma ("Gypsies") to concentration camps. Mixed-race children, criminals, prostitutes, alcoholics— all considered genetically inferior or "community aliens"—became candidates for sterilization. Homosexuality warranted at least incarceration or castration. A frightening glimpse of the future for all these groups came in 1939 when the Nazis created euthanasia programs designed to eliminate the mentally ill, handicapped, aged, and incurably ill.

Nazi repression and persecution

No group, however, was more systematically repressed than the Jews. According to Joseph Goebbels, Jews had "corrupted our race, fouled our morals, undermined our customs, and broken our power." He blamed them as "the cause and the beneficiary of our misery." In 1933, the government excluded Jews from higher education and public employment. By 1935, most Jewish professionals in Germany had lost their jobs. That year the **Nuremberg Laws** took citizenship away from Jews, forced them to wear a yellow Star of David on their clothes, and forbade marriage or sexual relations between Jews and non-Jews. In 1938, an episode of unrestrained violence revealed the mounting intensity of the Nazis' anti-Semitism. Incited by Goebbels, who blamed Jews for the assassination of a German diplomat in Paris, Nazi stormtroopers vandalized Jewish residences, synagogues, and places of business, smashing windows and plundering shops during the night of November 9–10. The troops then attacked Jews themselves, killing dozens and imprisoning tens of thousands in concentration camps.

After this attack—known as **Kristallnacht,** or Crystal Night, for its images of shattered glass—the Nazi government increasingly restricted Jews' movements, eliminated their jobs, and confiscated their assets. By 1939, over half of Germany's Jews had emigrated, even though they had to leave their possessions behind, pay hefty emigration fees, and face rejection in other countries. Soon, though, it became too late to escape Germany.

Figure 23.12 depicts the repression closing in on the Jews. The man in this painting—a self-portrait of the German artist Felix Nussbaum (1904–1944)—grimly regards the viewer. In one hand, he holds up his identity card, which in red letters states that he is Jewish. The yellow Star of David on his coat also identifies him as Jewish to the public. The walls of a prison yard tower above him. Beyond the walls, barbed wire, a truncated tree, and a blackening sky all hint at the dark future facing this man and others like him. Nussbaum completed this painting in 1943 while in hiding from the Nazis; less than a year later the Nazis arrested, imprisoned, and then killed him, along with his parents and brother.

What did ordinary Germans think of this repression and persecution? Historians still debate this question. Although many people seemed to share Hitler's attitudes, at least to a degree, most people outside the persecuted groups may not have understood Hitler's extreme, ultimate purpose. Certainly some knew and many should have known. A few Germans objected. However open resistance was dangerous. For those who disagreed with Hitler, it was much easier and safer to retreat into private life and apathy. Moreover they, and many other Germans, found reason to overlook Hitler's repressive measures and support him in his efforts to revive their prostrate nation.

REBUILDING AND REARMING THE NEW GERMANY

Governmental expenditures fueled economic recovery, but Hitler's main goal was rearmament. Superhighways, hospitals, sports stadiums, and apartment houses sprang up all over Germany; so did rearmament plants that created jobs for millions. To make Germany self-sufficient in case of another war, the Nazis supported the development of synthetics for the manufacture of such items as rubber and petroleum that Germany would otherwise have to import. The planned conquest to the east, Hitler hoped, would provide needed raw materials and eventually pay for Germany's government expenditures.

For the most part, the Nazis left business organizations and the capitalist economy alone. However, big business, forced to bow to the will of governmental policy, did lose some freedom. The real assault was on independent labor unions, which the government abolished and replaced with the Nazi Labor Front.

All these efforts worked. Germany regained the economic and military strength to make it a great power. By 1935, Hitler had taken Germany out of the League of Nations and the Geneva Disarmament Conference. Unwilling to back the letter of the Versailles treaty with force, the Allies offered only muted opposition to Hitler's renunciation of the Versailles disarmament provisions. The next year, he initiated a secret Four-Year Plan to prepare Germany for war. By 1939, the Nazis had increased armaments expenditures thirtyfold. Hitler felt ready to flex his newly developed muscles. His aggressive ambitions, combined with disturbing events outside Germany, were pushing the world toward war.

SUMMARY

During the 1920s, the West struggled to recover from the terrible World War I years. But any optimism generated by the end of the war was quickly tempered by problems such as inflation and unemployment in much of Europe. In southern, central, and eastern Europe, political turmoil created even more uncertainty. In the Soviet Union, crippled by the war and a devastating civil war, the Bolshevik regime faced an overwhelming task of rebuilding and creating a new kind of society. Even among the victors in western Europe and North America, the search for some return to "normalcy" brought frustrations and, at best, temporary moments of vibrancy, stability, and renewal. Most of the strong moments ended with the stock market crash of 1929, which ushered in the Great Depression.

By the early 1930s, the West had divided into three camps: the capitalist democracies, the fascist and authoritarian nations of central and eastern Europe, and the communist Soviet Union. As hardships from the Depression deepened and persisted, the capitalist democracies weakened, the authoritarian nations became ominously belligerent, and the communist Soviet Union under Joseph Stalin pursued—at terrible cost—its ambitious policies of agricultural collectivization and industrial five-year plans. But no country seemed to grow stronger, and for many in a more frightening way, than Germany under Adolf Hitler and the Nazis. The decade would not end before a return to the horrors that so many had hoped were behind them when that terrible storm lifted in 1918.

KEY TERMS

REVIEW, ANALYZE, AND ANTICIPATE

REVIEW THE PREVIOUS CHAPTER

Chapter 22—"Descending into the Twentieth Century"—told the story of World War I and the Russian revolution.

1. *In what ways were the forces unleashed by World War I responsible for the rise of authoritarian governments in Europe?*

2. *How might one argue that during the 1920s and the 1930s, the West never recovered from World War I?*

ANALYZE THIS CHAPTER

Chapter 23—"Darkening Decades"—traces the rise of fascism, the development of the Soviet Union, and the trials of nations struck by the Great Depression. This story culminates with World War II.

1. *Do you think the 1920s was a period of real recovery and cultural flowering or more of a haunted, anxious decade? Why?*

2. *Analyze the main qualities of German Nazism. How do you explain its rise and the acquisition of power by Hitler?*

3. *Why do you think Stalin initiated the Five-Year Plans? What were the purposes of those plans?*

4. *In what ways was the Great Depression much more than an economic downturn?*

ANTICIPATE THE NEXT CHAPTER

In Chapter 24, Into the Fire Again: World War II, 1939–1945, the devastating war that spread across the globe will be examined.

1. *What hints of the coming conflict can be found in Chapter 23?*

2. *Do you think the rise of fascism in Italy and the Nazis in Germany made World War II inevitable? Why?*

BEYOND THE CLASSROOM

TRYING TO RECOVER FROM THE GREAT WAR, 1919–1929

Kitchen, Martin. *Europe Between the Wars: A Political History.* London: Longman, 1988. An economic and political history of the interwar period.

Mommsen, Hans. *The Rise and Fall of Weimar Democracy.* Chapel Hill, NC: University of North Carolina Press, 1996. Argues that Weimar collapsed because of a skewed political culture inherited from imperial Germany.

TURNING AWAY FROM DEMOCRACY: DICTATORSHIPS AND FASCISM, 1919–1929

Lyttelton, Adrian. *The Seizure of Power: Fascism in Italy, 1919–1929,* 2nd ed. New York: Scribners, 1988. A narrative history of how Mussolini came to power and consolidated it, with in-depth chapters on ideology.

Paxton, Robert O. *The Anatomy of Fascism.* New York: Knopf, 2004. A fine, comparative analysis of fascism and fascist movements.

Payne, Stanley G. *A History of Fascism, 1914–1945.* Madison, WI: University of Wisconsin Press, 1995. Excellent in its European and global perspective on fascist movements.

TRANSFORMING THE SOVIET UNION: 1920–1939

Applebaum, Anne. *Gulag: A History.* New York: Doubleday, 2003. A recent study that vividly analyzes the Soviet Union's forced-labor camps.

Lewin, Moshe. *The Making of the Soviet System: Essays in the Social History of Interwar Russia.* London: Methuen, 1985. A thoughtful analysis by a noted scholar.

Thurston, Robert W. *Life and Terror in Stalin's Russia, 1934–1941.* New Haven, CT: Yale University Press, 1996. An attempt to revise accepted interpretations of Stalin and the Great Terror as the product of an evil mastermind.

Tucker, Robert C. *Stalin in Power: The Revolution from Above, 1928–1941.* New York: Norton, 1990. The second volume of an exhaustive and acclaimed analysis of Stalin, stressing the policies of collectivization and industrialization.

THE GREAT DEPRESSION, 1929–1939

Eichengreen, Barry. *Golden Fetters: The Gold Standard and the Great Depression, 1919–1939.* New York: Oxford University Press, 1992. Argues that the gold standard was the obstacle to financial stability and economic prosperity in the interwar period.

Kindleberger, Charles. *The World in Depression, 1929–1939.* 2nd ed. Berkeley, CA: University of California Press, 1986. A wide-ranging account that argues that problems in the system of international exchange played the most important role in causing the Great Depression.

NAZISM IN GERMANY

Evans, Richard J. *The Third Reich in Power, 1933–1939.* New York: Penguin, 2005. An excellent recent examination of life in Nazi Germany during the 1930s.

Fischer, Klaus P. *Nazi Germany: A New History*. New York: Continuum, 1995. A highly regarded examination of Nazi Germany.

Kershaw, Ian. *The Nazi Dictatorship*, 3rd ed. London: Edward Arnold, 1993. A thoughtful examination of the historiography of Nazism.

Koonz, Claudia. *Mothers in the Fatherland: Women, the Family, and Nazi Politics*. New York: St. Martin's Press, 1987. Studies Nazi ideology regarding women as well as women's responses to it.

www.mhhe.com/sherman3

- Unfamiliar words? See our Glossary at the back of the book for pronunciation and definitions.

- Need help studying? See our web page for map exercises, practice quizzes, and additional study resources.

- Need help writing a paper? Access hundreds of primary documents, maps, images, and a guide to writing history papers on our Primary Source Investigator site at **www.mhhe.com/psi.**

HORST STREMPEL, *NIGHT OVER GERMANY*, 1945

This 1945 painting by German artist Horst Strempel (1904–1975) depicts the fate of Germany in World War II. More broadly, it conveys the human suffering brought on by that horrendous conflict. In the left panel, a man huddles in terror and stares out from a confined space. Behind him mysterious figures loom in the darkness. In the right panel, a family peers out of a similar space, despair etched in their faces. The figures in the central panel mutely express that same despair, while the background hints at the misery and destruction of war. Below these individuals huddle more people, seemingly trapped but perhaps hoping for rescue. Strempel's painting, like World War II itself, has roots in World War I and echoes the stunning depiction of that conflict by Otto Dix, shown on page 672.

CHAPTER 24

INTO THE FIRE AGAIN: WORLD WAR II, 1939–1945

STUDY	Causes of the war ■ Axis victories ■ Struggle and horror behind the front lines ■ Turning the tide of war ■ Peace and the aftermath of war.
NOTICE	Connections between World War I and World War II, and the consequences of both conflicts.

In September 1938, British prime minister Neville Chamberlain flew home from a conference with leaders of France, Germany, and Italy. At the airport north of London, he announced to cheering crowds that an agreement at that meeting, known as the Munich conference, had achieved "peace for our time." British newspapers proclaimed him a hero.

Less than a year later, Chamberlain delivered another speech on the same topic. But this time, he made a painful admission to Britain's House of Commons. "This is a sad day for all of us, and to none is it sadder than to me," he confessed. "Everything that I have worked for, everything that I have hoped for . . . has crashed into ruins." The events that had devastated Chamberlain had just taken place in Eastern Europe. On September 1, 1939, Germany had invaded Poland. Now Chamberlain was announcing Britain's declaration of war against Germany. He made his point clear: "I trust I may live to see the day when Hitlerism has been destroyed and a liberated Europe has been reestablished."

Chamberlain, who died in 1940, would not see that day. War raged in Europe and across the globe for more than five years. Some viewed this conflict as a chance to reverse the results of the Great War of 1914–1918. Others deemed it a dreaded return of that "war to end all wars." But for most, this new contest would prove unique in its horrors and far worse than World War I. Inhumanity—from indiscriminate bombing to programmed genocide—gained the upper hand in the West, Asia, and the Pacific between the late 1930s and 1945. In the end, the conflict would take the lives of tens of millions of people and leave lasting scars on many nations and individuals. The painting shown on the facing page not only echoes Otto Dix's image of World War I (see page 672), it also evokes the suffering of those who survived the violence and hardship inflicted by World War II.

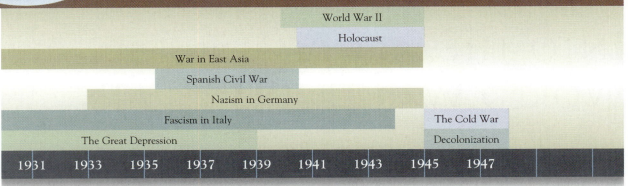

World War II

Holocaust

War in East Asia

Spanish Civil War

Nazism in Germany

Fascism in Italy

The Cold War

The Great Depression

Decolonization

1931　1933　1935　1937　1939　1941　1943　1945　1947

THE ROAD TO WAR, 1931–1939

"For us Germans the dictated Treaty of Versailles is not a law," announced Hitler to the German Reichstag on September 1, 1939. Throughout his speech—in which he sought to explain why German forces has just invaded Poland—Hitler jumped back and forth between the Great War of 1914–1918 and the present conflict, referring to himself as "the first soldier of the German Reich." He made clear his intent to reverse the results of World War I: "I have once again put on that uniform which was always so sacred and dear to me. I shall not lay it aside until after the victory—or I shall not live to see the end. . . ." What happened in the West and the world that led to that moment?

As we saw in Chapter 23, in the tense years of the 1920s and 1930s a new wave of authoritarian governments had washed across eastern and southern Europe; by 1938, only Czechoslovakia remained a parliamentary democracy. Many of these regimes included elements of fascism, but most were simple dictatorships by royal or military figures. Fascist movements, such as the Cross of Fire organization in France and the "Rex" Party in Belgium, also sprouted up in western Europe.

The democratic nations turned inward as they grappled with the depression and political divisions within their own borders. After 1934, communists in those nations sought to form alliances with socialists and moderates against the growing strength of fascism. The **Popular Front** in France is an example of such a partnership. The Front governed from 1936 to 1938. It was unable to pull the nation out of the depression, however, and ultimately fell from power. Its defeat left France more politically divided and discouraged than ever.

INTERNATIONAL AFFAIRS BREAK DOWN

For France and the other democracies, international affairs soon slipped out of control. Rearmament spread, aggression became the order of the day, and neither the democratic powers nor the League of Nations responded forcefully to stop it.

In 1931, Japan initiated the new pattern. Many in Japan had long viewed China as their immediate rival—an enemy with the potential to stand in the way of their ambitions for economic and political dominance in east Asia. On the orders of young officers, the Japanese army invaded Manchuria in northern China and began a drive for conquest. *Japan on the march* Crowds in Japan cheered the news of the Manchurian campaign, and a heightened sense of nationalistic militarism gradually pervaded Japanese political life. The League of Nations condemned Japan but took no action. By 1937, China had managed to shake off the most onerous Western controls over the country but still bore the scars of decades of a sporadic, bloody civil war. China's dominant Nationalist Party under Jiang Jieshi (Chiang Kai-shek) (1887–1975) had expended much of its strength opposing the growing Chinese Communist Party, led by Mao Zedong (1893–1976). In the early 1930s, Jiang had almost vanquished the Communists, but Mao and the core of his movement held on.

In 1937, Japanese troops invaded China proper. Less than six months later, the Japanese Imperial Army captured Nanking, capital city of China's Nationalist government. Over the following six weeks, Japanese army officers gave their troops free rein of the city. An American reporter in Nanking described the Japanese victory as "accompanied by the mass killing of the defenders, who were piled up among the sandbags, forming a mound six feet high." Victory did not end the slaughter: "Thousands of prisoners were executed by the Japanese . . . the killing of civilians was widespread . . . Nanking's streets were littered with dead." In what probably amounted to a deliberate policy, the Japanese carried out mass killings and executions of up to 300,000 Chinese soldiers and civilians, and raped thousands of women.

Appalled, the rival Chinese Communists and Nationalists finally forged an alliance against the Japanese, and the Soviet Union provided military assistance to China against its powerful rival in the east. Nevertheless, city after city in China fell to Japanese bombs and invading armies. With its expanding industrial economy hungry for new markets, Japan was determined to create "a new order in East Asia" under its domination. To secure its position, it moved to form an alliance with two other aggressive, authoritarian states: Italy and Germany.

In 1935, Mussolini ordered his troops to invade Ethiopia in East Africa, hoping to win popularity at home despite the unemployment and failing social policies there. Ethiopia appealed to the League of Nations for protection. The League condemned Il Duce's actions, but the democratic powers did not follow up with enough action to stop him. Indeed, these responses to his aggression only pushed Mussolini toward Hitler, and in 1936 the two leaders agreed to a friendship alliance—the Rome-Berlin **Axis.** In 1939, that alliance solidified into the military "Pact of Steel." To show unity with Hitler, Mussolini promptly adopted anti-Semitic racial laws for Italy. To further his own military ambitions, he invaded Albania.

Italy invades Ethiopia

CIVIL WAR IN SPAIN

In 1936, civil war broke out in Spain. Five years earlier, Spain had become a democratic republic for the first time. But when the Popular Front, made up of radicals, socialists, and communists, won election in 1936, a group of generals led by the conservative Francisco Franco (1892–1975) launched an armed rebellion against the new government. Franco's nationalist rebels enjoyed the support of the fascist Falange Party, the army, the church, and most of the wealthy elites; nevertheless, they could not easily overturn the popular Loyalists—the supporters of the Popular Front government.

The Spanish civil war soon became an international battlefield. Hitler and Mussolini, spotting an opportunity to advance the cause of fascism, gain an ally, and test their new weapons, sent arms and troops to aid Franco. At one point in 1937, Germans manning new airplanes on behalf of Franco's nationalists attacked the small Spanish town of Guernica, raining death on the civilian population there. The slaughter

became the subject matter of one of the most haunting paintings of the twentieth century, *Guernica* (1937), by the Spanish artist Pablo Picasso (1881–1973). This 25-foot-long mural in black and white (Figure 24.1) captures the worst features of this war—terror, brutality, disjointedness, lack of direction, and despair. On the left, a woman shrieks while holding a dead child. In the center, a warrior and horse lie shattered into fragments as the wounded sorrowfully look on. On the right, a woman plummets from a burning building. The image expresses both a wailing lament and a warning: modern war not only kills indiscriminately, but targets civilians in order to terrorize all into submission.

The Loyalists appealed to the other Western democracies for aid, but no help came. These nations hoped to maintain good relations with Italy and Germany and thus committed to a policy of neutrality, even though the fascist powers only pretended to agree. Unofficial Loyalist support came from some 40,000 idealistic volunteers, such as the Garibaldi Brigade and the Lincoln Brigade, who traveled to Spain from abroad and fought as individuals in the Loyalist cause. Otherwise, only the Soviet Union (until 1938) and Mexico provided assistance. The Loyalists also suffered from internal divisions between competing communists, anarchists, and liberals. In 1939, after three years of slaughter and atrocities on both sides, Franco's rebels finally beat down the last of the Loyalist resistance (see Map 24.1). The authoritarian Franco ruled Spain until his death in 1975.

TRYING TO COPE WITH GERMANY

In March 1936, Hitler gambled by ordering his armed forces into the Rhineland, that part of Germany on the west bank of the Rhine River that the Treaty of Versailles had deemed a demilitarized zone (see Map 24.2). France fretted and fumed but, lacking Britain's support, did nothing. Hitler's bold gamble paid off. With a new confidence, he turned to the three countries that bordered Germany to the east: Austria, Czechoslovakia, and Poland.

In 1938, the Nazis incorporated Austria without opposition, annexing the 6.5 million Austrians to the German Reich (empire) (see Map 24.2). Hitler then claimed a portion of Czechoslovakia—the Sudetenland—that included 3.5 million German-speaking people. The Czechs, however, surprised him by rushing to their defenses. For months, Hitler churned out a barrage of propaganda that painted the German-speaking Czechs as a persecuted minority. He threatened and roused his people to readiness for war, finally vowing to march if the Sudetenland was not surrendered to him.

A difficult question now arose for the rest of Europe as it watched Hitler's actions: What should be

Pablo Picasso, *Guernica*, 1937

■ FIGURE 24.1

Pablo Picasso's painting reveals the horrors of the Spanish civil war by focusing on a 1937 bombing raid on the town of Guernica. ■ **What** realities of the attack does Picasso depict in this painting? ■ **What** impressions of war was Picasso seeking to convey to viewers? ■ **How** does this painting differ from a traditional battle scene? ■ **In what ways** might details of this painting serve as a warning?

done? For complex reasons, no one had the nerve to oppose Hitler with force. For one thing, World War I had made many Europeans reluctant to risk general war again. In addition, disagreement swirled over the justice of Hitler's demands. Some people agreed with Germany that the Versailles treaty was too harsh, and sympathized with those who wanted to appease Germany's injured feelings. Many other people saw Hitler as sometimes reasonable and as a force that at least might be used to stop the spread of communism. British prime minister Neville Chamberlain (1869–1940), aware of Britain's lack of armed forces and public support to halt Hitler, tried for a compromise with the German ruler.

On September 29, 1938, the leaders of Germany, Italy, France, and Britain met in Munich to resolve the Sudetenland question. In the end, the two democratic powers chose **appeasement**—giving in to Hitler's

Appeasement at Munich

demands in hopes of satisfying him. Hitler grabbed the piece of Czechoslovakia that he wanted. British and French leaders, underestimating Hitler's territorial ambitions and determination

to go to war, felt pleased with the agreement. Their nations still suffered from the Great Depression and could not endure another conflict, they told themselves. Moreover, many Europeans—particularly the British and French—considered a renewal of horrors akin to those of the Great War of 1914–1918 unacceptable. However, the Czechoslovak and Soviet governments expressed outrage; they hadn't been invited to attend the conference. The agreement would force the Czechs to capitulate. For Stalin, the deal confirmed the continuing unwillingness of the Western democracies to unite with the Soviet Union against the growing fascist threat.

Back in Britain, Chamberlain announced that the **Munich conference** agreement had "saved Czechoslovakia from destruction and Europe from Armageddon." Across Europe, crowds cheered, celebrating what they saw as the preservation of peace. But a few months later, Hitler showed his true colors: With no warning, he sent forces to overrun the remainder of the Czechoslovakian Republic (see Map 24.2).

When Hitler next threatened Poland, Great Britain got tough and promised to come to Poland's aid. They

THINKING ABOUT GEOGRAPHY

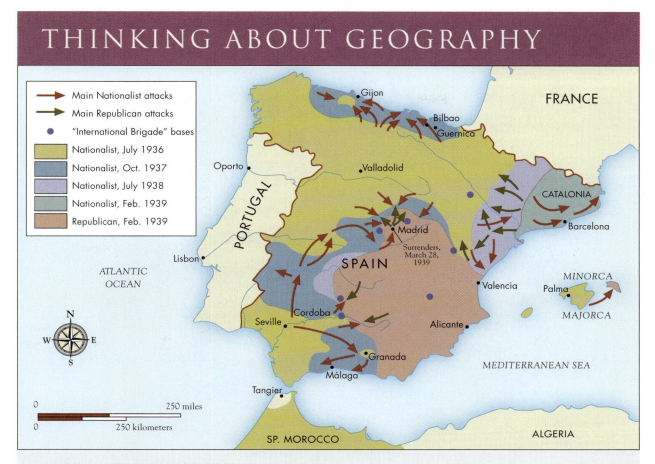

MAP 24.1   THE SPANISH CIVIL WAR, 1936–1939

This map shows the evolution of the Spanish civil war between 1936 and 1939. ■ **Notice** that Franco's Nationalist forces first moved north from Spanish Morocco and southern Spain, then east to Republican strongholds. **Consider** the importance of France's unwillingness to help the Republican forces.

turned to the Soviets for help, but it was too late. Isolated or excluded for too long from international affairs and disillusioned by France's and Britain's weak response to German aggression, Stalin stunned the world by signing a nonaggression pact with Hitler on August 23, 1939. In return for the Soviet Union's neutrality while Germany carved up Poland, Hitler gave Stalin a free hand to reannex territories in eastern Europe—including eastern Poland—that Russia had lost during World War I (see Map 24.2). By making thïs cynical pact with his greatest ideological enemy, Nazi Germany, Stalin may have gambled that the Soviet Union could stay on the sidelines, growing in strength, while the fascist and democratic capitalists destroyed one another.

Nazi-Soviet nonaggression pact

At dawn on September 1, the Germans launched an all-out attack on Poland by land, sea, and air.

Hitler remained convinced that France and Britain would not go to war over Poland. He was wrong. Two days later, Great Britain and France declared war on Germany. In a poem titled "SEPTEMBER 1, 1939," poet W. H. Auden (1907–1973) moaned that

> *The unmentionable odor of death*
> *Offends the September night*

World War II had begun.

AXIS VICTORIES, 1939–1942

Perhaps the war initiated in 1914 never quite ended, and the 1920s were just a pause in three decades of fighting and crises after 1914. Maybe if the depression had not struck, Hitler and the Nazis would not have come to power, the democracies would have

MAP 24.2   GERMAN EXPANSION, 1936–1939

This map shows German expansion between 1936 and September 1939, as well as territory annexed by the Soviet Union thanks to the Nazi-Soviet nonaggression pact of August 1939. ■ **Consider** how vulnerable these developments left Poland. ■ **How** might the steps in Germany's expansion be distinguished? ■ **What** nations might feel most threatened by further German aggression?

continued to grow, and war could have been averted. Tragically, the war that did break out in September 1939 would blaze six long years and encompass the globe as never before.

TRIUMPH OF THE GERMAN BLITZKRIEG

The German **blitzkrieg**—a "lightning war" of highly coordinated air strikes and rapid deployment of tanks and motorized columns—overwhelmed Polish forces.

The French and British mobilized their armies along the German border, and the British fleet blockaded Germany by sea—all to no avail.

For the next six months, in what became known as the "phony war," almost no military action took place. France and Great Britain seemed paralyzed. Meanwhile, the Soviet Union took advantage of its agreement with Hitler and reannexed territories in Poland and eastern Europe—including Estonia, Latvia, and Lithuania—that Russia had lost in

World War I. When Finland refused to yield strategic territories, the Soviets attacked. The Finns put up a determined resistance, and it took several months for the Soviet army finally to defeat these stubborn soldiers.

In April 1940, the Germans suddenly overran both Denmark and Norway. German planes fended off

The Battle of France

Britain's fleet, inflicting heavy losses. The next month, German armies assaulted Luxembourg, the Netherlands, Belgium, and France. Tiny Luxembourg offered no resistance, while the Dutch fought heroically but fell after six days. To support the beleaguered Belgians, the British army and a large part of the French army moved into Belgium. The French trusted that their Maginot Line of fortresses would hold along the German border. However, the line proved useless against the highly mobile German tanks. The Germans skirted the fortresses to the north through the Ardennes Forest. German General Erwin Rommel recalled the breakthrough: "The tanks now rolled in a long column through the line of fortifications. . . . Our artillery was dropping heavy harassing fire on villages and the road far ahead. . . . Engines roared, tank tracks clanked and clattered . . . civilians and French troops, their faces distorted with terror, lay huddled in the ditches." And then, he noted, "the flat countryside lay spread out around us under the cold light of the moon. We were through the Maginot Line."

The German blitzkrieg drove quickly to the English Channel, cutting off Allied armies in Belgium and then trapping them at Dunkirk, a seaport in Northern France. A flotilla of military and civilian ships, including fishing boats and pleasure craft, rescued 330,000 British and French troops off the beach at Dunkirk.

The Battle of France ended after only five weeks. Although almost equal in numbers to the Germans, the French seemed demoralized from the beginning of the war. According to one French journalist, they felt abandoned by the British, "who were ready to fight to the last French soldier." On June 16, 1940, the aged, right-wing Marshal Philippe Pétain became premier of France and quickly surrendered to Hitler. Figure 24.2 shows triumphant German troops on the march through Paris that year. In the background stands France's Arch of Triumph, a reminder of past victories now vastly overshadowed by Germany's occupying forces. With the surren-

■ FIGURE 24.2

German troops parading down Champs-Elysees after the fall of Paris, 1940.

der, Germany took the northern half of France and the entire Atlantic coast. The new authoritarian French regime would govern the remaining unoccupied portion of France from the city of Vichy. French general Charles de Gaulle escaped to Great Britain and declared himself leader of the Free French government in exile.

France's collapse left Great Britain to face Germany alone. The audacious and eloquent Winston Churchill (1874–1965), who had replaced Neville Chamberlain as prime minister, warned his people of the serious struggle to come: "This is no war of chieftains or of princes, of dynasties or national ambition; it is a war of peoples and of causes."

The Battle of Britain

The Germans, determined to gain control of the English Channel and prepare for an invasion of Britain unleashed massive air attacks against Britain in July 1940. As the Battle of Britain erupted, Churchill rallied his country, offering his "blood, toil, tears, and sweat" and vowing that "we shall never surrender."

For almost two months that fall, the Germans bombed London every night. A British civilian described some of the ordeal: "Bombs fell by day as well as by night. We became accustomed to the sudden drone of an airplane in the middle of the morning, the screech of a bomb, the dull crash of its explosion and the smell of cordite that filled the air a moment later." Figure 24.3 reveals some of the effort involved

■ FIGURE 24.3

The Battle of Britain.

fleet in southern Italy. The Greeks also contributed to the rout, driving the Italians back into Albania.

In response, Germany's forces streamed into the Balkans and North Africa. Hitler had several goals in mind for this move. He coveted the Balkans for their rich supplies of raw materials, especially the Romanian oil fields. He also hoped to save the Italian forces in North Africa and take the Suez Canal, Britain's lifeline to its empire. Hungary and Romania yielded to Hitler's threats and joined the Axis alliance in November 1940; Bulgaria did the same in March 1941. Yugoslavia and Greece refused, and they were overrun by German forces within a few weeks. Germany's Afrika Korps drove the British back into Egypt. Pro-German movements broke out in Iraq, Iran, and French Syria. At this point, however, Hitler hurled his main forces against the Soviet Union, giving the British a breathing spell to recoup their strength in North Africa and the eastern Mediterranean.

in the Battle of Britain. A group of three women and one man pull in a barrage balloon. Weighted cables dangling beneath the balloon hinder low-level flights by German bombers. In the background are buildings destroyed by bombings, but numerous smokestacks in the distance indicate that Britain's ability to fight survives. In cellars and subway stations, the British people holed up while their planes and antiaircraft guns, now aided by radar, fought off the Germans. Boosted by the high morale of the people, the increased output of aircraft factories, and Churchill's leadership, the island nation miraculously held. By November, the British had prevailed.

WAR IN NORTH AFRICA AND THE BALKANS

Even though Italy was not yet ready to take on another major war, Mussolini did not want to miss out on the spoils of an easy victory. He, too, invaded France as it fell to the Germans. Then in September 1940, his armies in Africa moved east from Libya into Egypt. A few weeks later, they attacked Greece from Albania.

However, Mussolini's forces met disaster at every turn. Mobile British forces routed Italian armies in North Africa, and British planes crippled the Italian

OPERATION BARBAROSSA: GERMANY INVADES THE SOVIET UNION

The eventual conquest of the Soviet Union had always been uppermost in Hitler's thoughts, despite his deceptive pact with the USSR. Even before that 1939 deal, Hitler revealed his true intentions to a group of associates: "Everything I do is directed against Russia. If the West is too stupid and blind to understand that, I shall be forced to reach an agreement with the Russians and strike at the West. Once [the West] is defeated, [I shall] turn my concentrated forces against the Soviet Union." Conquest of the Soviet Union would bring Germany "living space" as well as vast industrial and agricultural resources. It would also eliminate any threat from Nazism's great ideological enemy. And it would afford Germany access to millions of Jews—Hitler's "blood enemy—living in the Soviet Union. Still, the Nazi leader had hoped to subdue the British before turning to the Soviets. Failing that, he decided to invade the Soviet Union anyway.

In June 1941, the Germans launched Operation Barbarossa, sending more than three million soldiers, 3,700 tanks, and 2,500 planes against the USSR. Hitler expected to crush Soviet resistance in six weeks, well before the notorious Russian winter set in. "You only have to kick in the door, and the whole rotten structure will come crashing down," he claimed. But he also warned his generals, "The war against Russia will be . . . one of ideologies and racial differences and will have to be conducted with unprecedented, unmerciful and unrelenting harshness."

Stalin had long suspected that Hitler would someday turn against him, yet he believed that a German invasion was impossible before spring 1942, when Britain would be too crippled to constitute much of a diversion to German forces. Moreover, recent evidence suggests that Stalin himself may have planned to turn the tables on Hitler and launch his own full-scale preemptive attack on German forces in Eastern Europe. In the days before the June invasion by Germany, Stalin refused to believe numerous reports from many sources that Hitler's forces were about to attack. He even ignored warnings from some of his top generals.

On the morning of June 22, the Germans launched their assault. Caught off guard, Stalin delayed his response. For a few days, he disappeared from the public eye. Finally, he urged the Soviet people to rally to "the Great Patriotic War." Not everyone rose to the challenge. Indeed, the Ukrainians and some other Soviet groups initially greeted the Germans as liberators. The German forces quickly shattered Soviet armies. On July 3, the chief of Germany's General Staff wrote in his journal, "The Russian Campaign has been won in the space of two weeks." In just the first twenty days of the campaign, 600,000 Soviet soldiers lost their lives.

Even in the face of such destruction, most Soviet peoples put up a determined resistance. The weather worked against the enemy. The September mud season slowed German troops and tanks, and the unusually harsh winter that followed caught the invaders unprepared. Nevertheless, the German war machine crunched forward. By December 1, it had come within sight of Moscow and had nearly surrounded Leningrad (see Map 24.3). A confident Hitler announced the imminent, permanent destruction of the USSR.

Once again, the weather intervened. The winter tightened its grip, subjecting the lightly-clothed and weakly-supplied Nazis to frigid temperatures. Moreover, Japan's decision not to go to war against the USSR saved the Soviets from a disastrous two-front struggle. Stalin could now move troops from the Far East to the west. The combination of punishing weather and Russian counterattacks forced the Germans to halt and in some places even retreat—but only temporarily. By then, German forces had slaughtered more than three million Soviet soldiers and captured another three million. But the Soviet forces were not yet broken.

JAPAN ATTACKS

Farther east, events were brewing that would add yet another dimension to the war. Specifically, Western imperial presence in Asia and the Pacific had frustrated Japan's dreams of expansion. The resource-poor island nation depended on foreign raw materials and markets to fuel its industrial economy. During the 1930s, the Great Depression had weakened Japan's democratic regime and made the army a more potent political as well as military force. As military men gained control of the government, Japan's foreign policy shifted to expansionism (see Global Connections). By 1939, Japan had conquered the populous coastal areas of China and pushed Chinese forces well into the interior. When the war in Europe weakened European colonial powers—which controlled much of southeast Asia, with its wealth of essential resources such as oil, tin, and rubber—Japan joined the Rome-Berlin Axis. It quickly occupied French Indochina and threatened the Dutch East Indies. The United States responded with a total economic embargo on all exports to Japan, threatening Japan's oil supplies in particular.

Hoping that the war in Europe would induce the United States to cede dominance to the Japanese in southeast Asia, Japan struck. On December 7, 1941, Japanese air forces surprised the American fleet anchored in Pearl Harbor, Hawaii, crippling the U.S. naval and air forces. President Franklin D. Roosevelt (1882–1945) called it "a day *The U.S. enters the war* that will live in infamy." The United States immediately declared war on Japan and within days Germany and Italy declared war on the United States. Several Latin American nations joined the United States in the Grand Alliance against the Axis.

The long-isolationist United States had an army with limited capabilities. In addition, it had sent huge quantities of arms, equipment, and food across the Atlantic in its role as "the arsenal of democracy." Roosevelt agreed with Churchill to make the war in Europe the United States' first priority, and Americans started mobilizing their country's vast resources for the fight.

Meanwhile, the Japanese conquered a vast area in southeast Asia and the Pacific (Map 24.4), creating "The Greater East Asia Co-Prosperity Sphere." Japan claimed to be liberating Asia from the imperial West, but it dominated the new territories through nationalist leaders ready to collaborate with Japan's occupation forces and treated the conquered peoples as inferior subjects. Scoring victory after victory, the Japanese and Germans seemed to be winning the war.

The Rise of Japanese Ultranationalism

CONSIDER

■ **Consider** *why the arguments of Japanese ultranationalists might have appealed to various political and military groups.*
Notice *how Western imperialist practices were used to justify Japanese expansion.*

During the 1920s, Japanese liberals who supported the international system established at the end of World War I held most of the power in the island nation's government. However, ultranationalists and militarists rejected the "Western" system and argued for an expanding Japanese empire in east Asia. These opponents of the system gained increasing power, especially after the Great Depression struck in 1929 and weakened Japan's economy.

During the 1930s, as some Western nations expressed alarm over Japanese expansionist moves, Hashimoto Kingoro, a leading ultra-nationalist, challenged them to reexamine their thinking. Western nations, Hashimoto proclaimed, were in no position to complain about Japan's desire to take territories it needed: "[W]e may wish to ask the white race just which country it was that sent warships and troops to India, South Africa, and Australia and slaughtered inno-cent natives, bound their hands and feet with iron chains, lashed their backs with iron whips, proclaimed these territories as their own, and still continues to hold them to this very day?" Okawa Shumei, another leading ultranationalist, built on Hashimoto's reasoning. A "struggle between the great powers of the East and the West," Okawa claimed, "which will decide their existence, is at present, as in the past, absolutely inevitable" if a better world for Asia is to come about. In Okawa's view, Japan's proper role in this new world was clear: "Heaven has decided on Japan as its choice for the champion of the East. Has not this been the purpose of our three thousand long years of preparation?"

Over the course of the 1930s, liberals lost ground to the ultranationalists and militarists, who increasingly took over Japan's government. In 1931, Japanese troops created an "incident" in Manchuria that ignited a war with China and led to the establishment by the Japanese of a puppet state, Manchukuo, in Manchuria. In 1937, Japan again attacked China, launching a full-scale but undeclared war against the beleaguered nation. Soon Japan had seized large areas of east and north China. In 1940, Japan allied itself with the two main ultranationalist powers in the West: Nazi Germany and Fascist Italy.

The following year, just a few months before the Japanese attack on Pearl Harbor, Japan's Ministry of Education distributed "The Way of Subjects"—required reading for all Japanese high school and university students. The pamphlet revealed the think-ing behind Japanese ultranationalism. The document pointed to the harmful "influx of European and American culture into this country," by which the authors meant individualism, liberalism, and materialism. Thanks to these outside influences, "the traditional character of the country was much impaired and the virtuous habits and customs bequeathed by our ancestors were affected unfavorably." Japan's mission, the document continued, was "the emancipation of East Asian nations." Throughout Asia, "hopes to be free of the shackles and bondage of Europe and America were ablaze."

In 1942, at the height of its power, the Japanese government created a plan for the establishment of the Greater East Asia Co-Prosperity Sphere that echoed ultranationalist thought. The plan asserted that "the Japanese empire is the center and pioneer of Oriental moral and cultural reconstruction." Moreover, Japan's mission was "to cause East Asia to return to its original form of independence and co-prosperity by shaking off the yoke of Europe and America." By this time, Japan controlled much of east and south Asia as well as the Pacific Basin. But this year also saw the beginning of the end of Japan's power, for U.S. military might had begun turning the tide against Japan. Ultranationalist dreams and policies finally collapsed in the summer of 1945. That year, American planes dropped atomic bombs on Hiroshima and Nagasaki, defeating Japan and ending World War II.

BEHIND THE LINES: THE STRUGGLE AND THE HORROR

By 1942, Hitler ruled most of continental Europe from the English Channel to the outskirts of Moscow (see Map 24.3). In administrating his lands, he pursued two primary goals. First, he hunted for ways to keep Germany supplied with war materials and maintain the standard of living for Germans without having to call on them to make unpopular sacrifices. Second, he sought to fulfill his racist agenda. To these ends, he implemented his "New Order," a program of economic exploitation and racial imperialism in the lands that he now controlled. He used conquered peo-ples according to their ranking in his racial hierarchy. Those most directly related to the Nazi conception of the "Aryan race," such as Scandinavians, Anglo-Saxons, and Dutch, were treated well and might be absorbed into the Nazi Empire as partners with the Germans. He considered the "Latin races," such as the French, inferior but tolerable as supportive cogs in the New Order. Slavs ranked toward the bottom of Hitler's hierarchy; they were to be isolated, shoved aside, treated like slaves, or killed.

Hitler's "New Order"

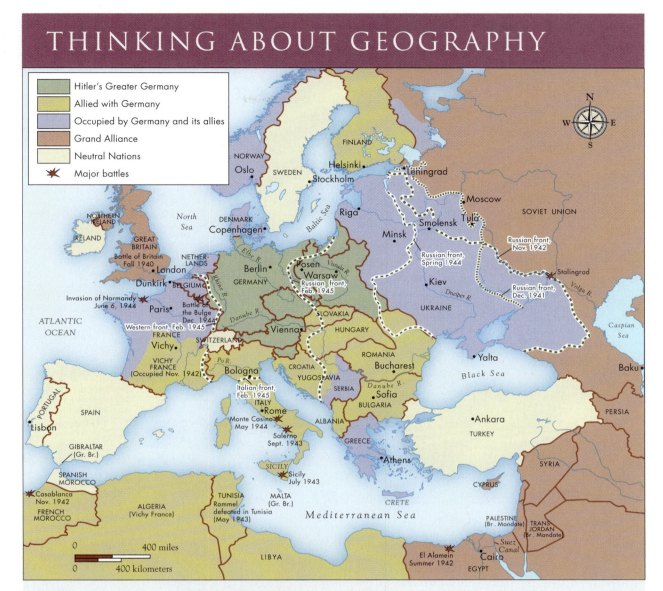

MAP 24.3   WORLD WAR II IN EUROPE

This map shows Hitler's empire at its height in 1942, the front lines in the following years as the Allies closed in on Germany in 1945, and major battles of the war. ■ **What** does this indicate about the military problems facing Hitler after 1942? ■ **Compare** the eastern, southern, and western fronts. How might the fighting have differed in these three areas? ■ **Locate** the western, Italian, and Russian fronts in February 1945, just a few months before the end of the war. **What** might these troop locations suggest about spheres of influence during the postwar decades?

THE HOLOCAUST

Lowest on Hitler's racial scale were the Jews, and they fared the worst in Hitler's scheme. Nazis herded Jews into ghettos in German, Polish, and Russian cities. For a while, the Nazis envisioned forced emigration of Jews, perhaps to the island of Madagascar off the east coast of Africa, to solve the "Jewish problem."

In 1941, such ideas ended and Hitler initiated a policy of genocide, which came to be known as the **Holocaust.** Mobile SS squads under Reinhard Heydrich (1904–1942) and Heinrich Himmler began the wholesale killing of Jews, along with Slavic prisoners of war, in Poland and Russia. Firing squads shot victims en masse. Dissatisfied with the pace of the killings, the Germans began using mobile vans that murdered

THINKING ABOUT GEOGRAPHY

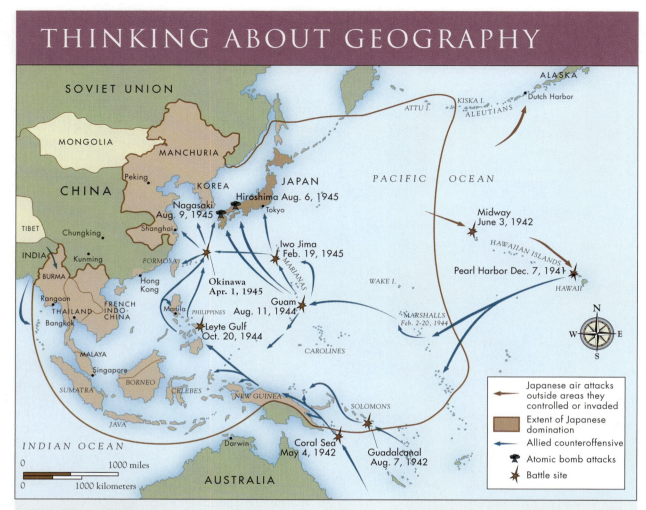

MAP 24.4   WORLD WAR II IN THE PACIFIC

This map shows Japan's empire at its height in 1942 and the course of the Allied counteroffensive that led to Japan's defeat in 1945. ■ **What** problems did the Japanese face trying to control their far-flung territories? ■ **Consider** what strategy the Allies used in their counteroffensive against the Japanese. **Why** did this strategy differ from that used in Europe?

people by gas. Finally, when that method still did not seem efficient enough, the Nazis used large gas chambers that killed thousands at a time. Heydrich, the Plenipotentiary for the Preparation of the Final Solution of the European Jewish Question, promised that this campaign—"a historic moment in the struggle against Jewry"—would be carried out "effectively but silently."

The Nazis built six huge death camps in what had been Poland. From gathering points all over Europe, unknowing victims were crowded into cattle cars where they soon became dehydrated, disoriented, and terrorized; many died in transit. Upon their arrival, officials divided families, segregated people by sex,

and made the first "selection." "Inside the camp, one's first view was fixed on a mountain of children's shoes," recalled a woman survivor. "To tell the truth I did not understand what that meant." Those who could not work as the Nazis wanted—therefore more women, children, and elderly—were sent to the "showers"—the Nazis' euphemism for the gas chambers. Officials especially targeted pregnant women to prevent the birth of more Jews. They sent the rest, now physically and mentally terrorized, to the work camps.

Death camps

The scale and depravity of this programmed inhumanity, torture, and death were unprecedented; thus the victims simply could not grasp it until it was too

■ DOCUMENT 24.1

The Nazi Death Camps

In 1942, the Nazis began a new phase in their campaign to murder Jews and others. Their "final solution" took the form of death camps where Nazis could kill on a larger scale. Testimonies from witnesses paint vivid pictures of the horrors that occurred daily in these camps. The first account below is from Abraham Bomba, who in 1942 was transported with his family from a Polish ghetto to the Treblinka death camp, where his job was to cut women's hair before they were gassed. He escaped in 1943 and later described his experiences at the camp. The second account comes from a French doctor, André Lettich, whose job was to remove corpses from the crematoria at Birkenau. ■ **Why** *did the Nazis use prisoners for these tasks?* ■ **How** *do you explain the reasons behind the procedures used in these camps?* ■ **What** *might be the significance of these actions, which occurred on such a large scale?*

1. Filling the Treblinka Gas Chambers

The gas chamber . . . was all concrete. There was no window. [It] had two doors . . . [and] the people went in to the gas chamber from the one side . . . [and] they pushed in as many as they could. It was not allowed to have the people standing up with their hands down because there was not enough room, but when the people raised their hand[s] . . . there was more room. . . . And on top of that they throw in kids, 2, 3, 4 years old. . . . The whole thing took . . . between five and seven minutes. The door opened up . . . from the other side. People working in Treblinka number two took out the corpses. Some of them dead and some of them still alive. They dragged them to the ditches . . . big ditches, and they covered them. That was the beginning of Treblinka.

2. The "Shower Room"

"Until the end of January 1943, there were no crematoria in Birkenau. In the middle of a small birch forest, about two kilometres from the camp, was a peaceful looking house, where a Polish family had once lived before it had been either murdered or expelled. This cottage had been equipped as a gas chamber for a long time.

"More than five hundred metres further on were two barracks: the men stood on one side, the women on the other. They were addressed in a very polite and friendly way: 'You have been on a journey. You are dirty. You will take a bath. Get undressed quickly.' Towels and soap were handed out, and then suddenly the brutes woke up and showed their true faces: this horde of people, these men and women were driven outside with hard blows and forced both summer and winter to go the few hundred metres to the

'Shower Room.' Above the entry door was the word 'Shower'. One could even see shower heads on the ceiling which were cemented in but never had water flowing through them.

"These poor innocents were crammed together, pressed against each other. Then panic broke out, for at last they realised the fate in store for them. But blows with rifle butts and revolver shots soon restored order and finally they all entered the death chamber. The doors were shut and, ten minutes later, the temperature was high enough to facilitate the condensation of the hydrogen cyanide, for the condemned were gassed with hydrogen cyanide. This was the so-called 'Zyklon B', gravel pellets saturated with twenty per cent of hydrogen cyanide which was used by the German barbarians.

"Then, SS *Unterscharführer* Moll threw the gas in through a little vent. One could hear fearful screams, but a few moments later there was complete silence. Twenty to twenty-five minutes later, the doors and windows were opened to ventilate the rooms and the corpses were thrown at once into pits to be burnt. But, beforehand the dentists had searched every mouth to pull out the gold teeth. The women were also searched to see if they had not hidden jewelry in the intimate parts of their bodies, and their hair was cut off and methodically placed in sacks for industrial purposes."

Sources: (1) United States Holocaust Memorial Museum, "The Holocaust," in *Holocaust Encyclopedia*, www.ushmm.org/wk/index. (2) J. Noakes and G. Pridham, eds., *Nazism, 1919–1945: A Documentary Reader*, vol. 3, in *Foreign Policy, War, and Racial Extermination* (Exeter: University of Exeter Press, 1995), pp. 78–79.

late. Some Jews rebelled—in the Warsaw ghetto and the Treblinka camp, for example. They and others who fought back may have made important moral statements, but they stood no real chance against the Nazis. The masses of Jews trapped in ghettos or camps, their strength sapped by hunger and illness, had little choice. For many, the only way to maintain a shred of dignity against the degradation and death was silence. The Nazis had trapped these victims in a merciless, thoroughly organized system from which few escaped.

Struggling to survive in the camps, many people tried to help one another, though the desperate conditions at

times also brought out the worst in people. In this surreal world, the Germans applied assembly-line methods to the destruction of millions of human beings. A French doctor described the killing process at the Auschwitz-Birkenau camp: Once prisoners were herded and forced into the gas chambers, "the massive oak double doors are shut. For two endless minutes one can hear banging on the walls and screams which are no longer human. . . . Five minutes later the doors are opened. The corpses, squashed together and distorted, fall out like a waterfall" (see Document 24.1). In a particularly brutal twist, the Nazis forced Jewish prisoners to carry out much of the dirty work of killing. Nazi guards subjected their captives to torture and abuse, and German doctors conducted gruesome experiments on camp prisoners.

In the end, almost all prisoners slaved in the camps on starvation rations until they died or were sent to the gas chambers when no longer useful to their captors. In Auschwitz alone, the largest of these camps, the Nazis murdered more than 12,000 people a day and more than one million Jews by the end of the war. Although Jews were the Nazis' main target, many people from non-Jewish groups—communists, gypsies, Jehovah's Witnesses, Soviet prisoners of war, Slavs, homosexuals—suffered the same fate. Later, Rudolf Hoss, commander of the Auschwitz camp, would describe the order for mass killings as "something extraordinary, something monstrous. However the reasoning behind the order of this mass annihilation seemed correct to me . . . I wasted no thoughts about it." Ultimately these genocidal efforts took priority over even the war effort and continued right up until the last days of the war.

Figure 24.4 is a photograph taken after World War II ended. Here American officials force German civilians living near the Landsberg camp to stand witness to the Nazis' shocking atrocities. Who knew about the brutal realities of the camps during the war? The Nazis had gone to great lengths to cover up the process of killing, swearing everyone involved to secrecy and presenting more benign concentration camps outside Poland for international inspection. As reports of what really was happening filtered out, many people expressed disbelief. Atrocities on such a mass scale seemed impossible.

But it had taken thousands of officials, bureaucrats, soldiers, police, and SS guards to carry out the murders. At least these thousands knew. Indeed, many concentration- and death-camp officials followed orders with enthusiasm, competing for approval from their superiors. Several large German companies, including the industrial giant I. G. Farben, benefited from contracts with the camps. Authorities on the outside who might have tried to help did nothing. At some point British and American commanders probably knew. While the full extent of the Holocaust may not have been clear, from almost the beginning Allied leaders had received information about the Nazi killing program from numerous sources. After 1942, Western newspapers published reports about mass murders and the death camps. Allied governments could have responded to pleas from Jewish leaders to bomb gas chambers or railway lines leading to the death camps. But they claimed that other military targets were more important.

COLLABORATION AND RESISTANCE

Collaborating governments often copied or cooperated with the Nazis. In some countries, such as Croatia, officials willingly rounded up Jews and carried out the killing themselves. The anti-Semitic government of Vichy France under Pétain transported thousands of Jews to Nazi death camps. In almost all conquered lands, the Nazis managed to find individuals who would collaborate with them.

However, many others resisted. The Danes saved most of the Jews living in their lands. In Italy, officials often ignored Nazi directives, despite Mussolini's alliance with Hitler. Numerous stories, such as the experience of the young Anne Frank hiding in the Netherlands, record individual heroism and tragedy. Resistance organizations rose in almost every occupied territory, particularly in France, Yugoslavia, and the Soviet Union. At great risk, men and women alike established underground networks, provided intelligence to the Allied forces, conducted guerrilla actions, aided escaping prisoners, sabotaged German military installations, and engaged Nazi forces that might have been used on the war fronts. Communists, such as those in Yugoslavia under the command of Josip Broz (Tito—see Biography), often formed the core of the most determined resistance movements.

■ FIGURE 24.4

Landsberg concentration camp, 1945.

BIOGRAPHY

Josip Broz (Tito) (1892–1980)

CONSIDER

■ **Consider** how Tito's life reveals the ties between war, ideology, and politics during this period.

Josip Broz was a hunted resistance leader for years. Born in Croatia in 1892 to a peasant family, the young Josip became an apprentice to a locksmith and then worked as a mechanic. In World War I, he served as a platoon leader in the Austro-Hungarian army, was severely wounded, and was taken prisoner by the Russians. Already a socialist, he joined Russia's Red Army during the revolution and civil war. He also married a Russian woman, with whom he would have a son. In 1920, he returned to Croatia, became a trade-unionist, joined the Communist Party of Yugoslavia, and soon rose to a position of leadership. Eight years later, he was arrested and imprisoned for six years for his communist activity—the police had discovered bombs in his apartment. He again traveled to the Soviet Union, where he rose through the ranks as a loyal Stalinist during the purges. In 1937, he became the head of Yugoslavia's Communist Party. During his underground party work, Josip assumed the pseudonym Tito.

When Hitler invaded Yugoslavia and the Soviet Union, Tito announced, "We do not recognize the various Fascist puppet governments." He called on the Communist Party of Yugoslavia to organize the "partisans," a guerrilla resistance movement against Axis forces. Figure 24.5 shows Tito, standing on the far right, with his staff of fellow fighters. At the same time, he entered into a virtual civil war with a competing, more conservative resistance movement. Although Tito won this struggle between resistance movements, it may have cost more lives than the battle against the Nazis. While fighting occupying forces, he organized a provisional communist government that would stand ready to take over at the end of the war. With the help of Soviet troops, Tito's forces drove the retreating Germans from Yugoslavia.

In 1945, Yugoslavia became a federal republic, with Tito as its leader and virtual dictator. He turned the new republic into a one-party, communist state on the model of the Soviet Union. Eventually balking at Stalin's plans to purge Yugoslav leadership and undermine his authority, Tito led Yugoslavia on a separate course after 1948. Unlike Stalin, he emphasized more relaxed, decentralized control over his nation and its economy, yet he tolerated no opposition to his rule. In the 1950s and 1960s, he became a spokesperson for nations such as Egypt, Indonesia, and India who refused to align themselves with either the United States or the Soviet Union in the Cold War. He served as president of Yugoslavia until his death in 1980.

Yugoslavia would not long survive his passing. Conflict between ethnic groups had long plagued this region of Europe. Such tensions had helped ignite World War I, had contributed to the rise of authoritarian leaders of both the Right and Left during the 1930s and 1940s, and had taken thousands of lives during the resistance struggles of World War II. Now that conflict led to the undoing of the federation. Yugoslavia broke up in 1991 in a series of bloody civil wars that would drag on for years.

Communist Leader and Yugoslav Dictator

■ FIGURE 24.5

Tito and the Yugoslav resistance.

Tito's organization became one of the most effective resistance forces in Europe.

But the price of fighting back was high. The Germans infiltrated resistance groups and brutally crushed any hints of threats. Collective retribution for attacks against German leaders deterred many. In one case, the Nazis massacred 7,000 people in one town in retaliation for the killing of 10 Germans by Yugoslav partisans. In some places, such as Ukraine, Greece, and Yugoslavia, resistance groups with different political agendas fought among themselves, eroding their ability to oppose the Nazis.

MOBILIZING THE HOME FRONTS

Even more than in World War I, whole societies mobilized for the war effort in the 1940s. Governments controlled production and rationed goods. As labor shortages arose, women again assumed jobs normally reserved for men (see Document 24.2). Political

■ DOCUMENT 24.2

Women Go to Work in the Factories

In World War II, the major combatants recognized that victory hinged on the ability to increase industrial production. With so many men serving in the armed forces, nations called on women to work in jobs traditionally reserved for men. In this account, Elizabeth Hawes describes her experiences in an American airplane engine plant in 1943. ■ **What** *impressed Hawes most about the experience?* ■ **What** *might have been the consequences of such experiences for women and other groups?* ■ **How** *did men react to Hawes?*

Now that I've worked a few months in a plant—on the graveyard shift too—the only wonder to me is that all the women in the USA aren't storming the factory gates. I'm convinced that any healthy woman can work in a factory—and like it. My biggest regret is that I had to leave because I'd agreed to do some writing. My biggest ambition is to get back.

It was a great pleasure to me that nobody gave a darn who anyone was. . . . Of course there are little discords. The foremen and subforemen are honestly scared to death of us women. When first you arrive they look at you out of the corner of their eyes. . . . Every woman machinist has to endure sheer torture from her fellow male employees at one point in her career. . . .

The men see that now you think you're a mechanic. Some honestly don't believe the Lord ever intended women to be mechanics. Others are infuriated by your presumption that you can do their work. . . . [The women] are working for money—money to feed their kids, money to keep their homes together—so their sons and husbands can fight. . . .

I want to go back to Wright's new plant because I think the women who work in war plants, and the men who first help them and then work with them are the luckiest people in the world. There's an equality developing there unlike any I've ever seen. Joe was an Italian—Nel, a Negro—Suzy, Irish—there were Germans, Poles, Hungarians, Gentiles, Jews. Slowly you could see there was no difference between any two of us. Gradually everybody was beginning to work as one unit. When you see something like that happening you feel you're not just doing a job to help win the war. You also have the profound pleasure of seeing the future peace being worked out before your eyes.

Source: Elizabeth Hawes, "My Life on the Midnight Shift," *Woman's Home Companion* (August 1943), pp. 24, 27.

---

leaders acquired unusual powers and discouraged dissent. Even outside the Nazi Empire, some groups of citizens fell victim to the suspicion that the war engendered. In the United States, for example, government agents removed Japanese Americans living on the West Coast from their homes and businesses and placed them in camps. Propaganda on all sides painted distorted, racist pictures of the enemy and whipped up civilian support of the troops.

Britain, taking the brunt of German aggression early on, mobilized thoroughly. The government drafted men between the ages of 18 and 50 and women between 20 and 30 into military or civilian war service. Women accounted for most of the increase in Britain's labor force. The government also enlisted scientists to help break the German code and work on an atomic bomb.

The Soviet Union tried everything to brace itself against the Germans. Hundreds of thousands of Russian women served in the Soviet armed forces; millions took jobs, replacing men sent to the front. In October 1941, the Soviets managed an astounding feat: They dismantled more than 500 factories in Moscow and elsewhere and reassembled them in the east, away from the encroaching German troops. By 1943, Soviet factories were turning out 2,000 tanks a month.

The United States, less threatened geographically by the war, mobilized unevenly; still, it boosted its wartime production by 400 percent in two years and sent large quantities of supplies to its British and Soviet allies. Germany was also slower to mobilize its citizens. In the early years, Hitler instead relied on quick victories and spoils from conquered lands to fulfill his nation's needs. Millions of conscripted foreigners and prisoners of war served as Germany's laborers. Only after 1942 did Hitler turn to full mobilization, multiplying Germany's production over the following two years despite concentrated Allied bombing.

TURNING THE TIDE OF WAR, 1942–1945

The now global war was fought in three major theaters: the Soviet Union, the Mediterranean and western Europe, and the Pacific. The turning points in all theaters came between June and August 1942. The largest, bloodiest battles occurred in the Soviet Union and were fought by some nine million soldiers. The

Germans had already conquered most of that nation's lands west of the Volga River, leaving nearly half of the Soviet people under German rule.

THE EASTERN FRONT AND THE BATTLE OF STALINGRAD

The Germans, refreshed and reequipped, resumed their offensive against the Soviet Union in June 1942, this time in the southern sector of the USSR. In July, one German soldier expressed confidence that "the Russian troops are completely broken," and "the Führer knows where the Russians' weak point is." The soldier recorded in his diary that he fully expected German forces to "take Stalingrad and then the war will inevitably soon be over." In early August, as German forces pushed forward, he and others anticipated the rewards of victory: "What great spaces the Soviets occupy, what rich fields there are to be had here after the war's over." By mid-August, they had reached the outskirts of Stalingrad on the Volga River. However, this soldier noted that the "doomed" Russian divisions "are continuing to resist bitterly."

The Battle of Stalingrad became the greatest of the war and raged for seven months. "Not a step backward," ordered Stalin. He spared no resource, including the many women who served on the front lines as combat soldiers, tankers, and snipers. Indeed, some airforce regiments were made up entirely of women. The most revered pilot, Lily Litvak, shot down twelve German planes.

Figure 24.6 provides a sense of the battle as well as the Soviets' use of propaganda. In this staged photograph, one Russian soldier has fallen for the cause. Two others, despite the danger, heroically fight on with their rifle, machine gun, and hand grenades. The photograph avoids the reality of how brutal and ignoble much of this battle was. It also suggests that these front-line soldiers willingly sacrificed themselves for the cause and that all Soviets should make their own sacrifices for the war effort. While the scene omits the gore of the struggle, it reveals the close quarters, amid the rubble of a ruined city, in which the soldiers had to fight.

As the Russian winter again approached, Hitler ordered his army not to retreat. That decision took a huge toll on the German army. By the end of October, the German soldier's diary entries revealed a change in his optimistic attitude: "Who would have thought three months ago that instead of the joys of victory we would have to endure such sacrifice and torture, the end of which is nowhere in sight." The Germans mounted their final assault on November 11 and penetrated to the Volga. But a stalemate ensued, and dragged on until November 19, when the Russians launched their long-planned encircling offensive. Though the Russian winter loomed, Hitler ordered his forces to stand firm. That decision took a huge toll on the German army. In December, the same German soldier complained, "Everybody is racked with hunger. Frozen potatoes are the best meal." Just before his death, he wrote, "The soldiers look like corpses or lunatics, looking for something to put in their mouths. They no longer take cover from Russian shells; they haven't the strength to walk, run away and hide."

In January 1943, the Russians finally surrounded the remainder of the 300,000-man German army, now reduced by casualties to 80,000. German Sixth Army commander General Friedrich Paulus sent a note to the German high command: "Further defense senseless. Collapse inevitable. Army requests immediate permission to surrender in order to save lives of remaining troops." Hitler replied: "Surrender is forbidden. Sixth Army will hold their positions to the last man." A few days later, the German Sixth Army surrendered.

■ FIGURE 24.6

Russian soldiers, the Battle of Stalingrad.

The Soviets lost one million soldiers in the bitter struggle over Stalingrad. And Germany never recovered from the massive loss of men and material, and morale suffered during the epic seven-month battle. Over the next two and a half years, Soviet forces slowly beat back the invaders (see Map 24.3).

THE SOUTHERN FRONTS

In North Africa, the German general Rommel's (1891–1944) tough Afrika Korps fought to within 65 miles of the Egyptian coastal city of Alexandria. But in August 1942, at the Battle of El Alamein, the British forces, bolstered by supplies from the United States, held. Over the following months, British and newly arriving American forces managed to push the Germans back, and in May 1943, the cornered Afrika Korps surrendered.

The Mediterranean

■ FIGURE 24.7

Leonard Henry Rosoman, *A House Collapsing on Two Firemen, Shoe Lane London EC4.*

The war-weary Stalin now urged Britain and America to open up a major western front in France to take the pressure off his forces. Instead in an effort to protect British interests in the Mediterranean without risking a battle against major German forces, the Allies attacked Italy. First, they moved from the island of Sicily up into the southern Italian mainland. In July 1943, the Italian government arrested Mussolini, and two months later Italy surrendered. However, strong German forces still held most of the country. German commandos rescued Mussolini and set him up as the head of a puppet government in the north. The Allies' progress slowed through the Italian mountains, and the rest of the Italian campaign became a long and costly effort.

Meanwhile, Allied planes rained bombs on German targets. These dangerous missions took a heavy toll on both sides. In 1943, for example, only one-third of British crews flying planes across the channel would survive their first tour of duty. In late July of that same year, systematic bombing raids by British and American air forces set off a devastating firestorm in the German city of Hamburg. A survivor described what happened: The sky became "absolutely hellish" in minutes. "No noise made by humans—no outcry—could be heard. It was like the end of the world." The firestorm killed 40,000 people. Figure 24.7, a painting by British artist Leonard Henry Rosoman, suggests what civilians faced in cities subjected to heavy bombing. On the left, buildings that have stood for decades collapse in flames. Below, two firemen, armed with only a hose, fight a conflagration that is about to engulf them. While Rosoman set this in London, which endured indiscriminate rocket attacks until the last months of the war, similar and even worse scenes took place in Hamburg and many other cities.

THE WESTERN FRONT

On June 6, 1944 (**D-day**), American, British, and Canadian forces under General Dwight Eisenhower (1890–1969) finally swept across the British channel to make a run at German forces holding France. Hitler, overextended in Russia and the Mediterranean, had to defend a 3,000-mile coastline in the west. Forced to gamble on where the Allies would invade, he bet on Calais, where the English Channel was narrowest. Instead, the invasion—supported by an armada of more than 6,000 vessels and 12,000 aircraft—came on the Normandy beaches. Hitler's "Atlantic Wall" of defenders took a huge toll on the invaders. In many cases, lead companies suffered 90 percent casualties; boats and tanks were often destroyed before their troops could even fire a shot. One American soldier reported that within the first ten minutes, "every officer and sergeant of the leading company had been killed or wounded . . . It had become a struggle for survival and rescue."

Despite these losses, the Allies established a north-western European front. Two months later, they opened a new front in southern France. Aided by French forces and resistance fighters, the Allies pushed the Germans out of most of France before year's end. Meanwhile, Allied bombs pulverized German cities and crippled Germany's transportation network.

Under the steady onslaught, Germany began running out of oil and soldiers. Early in 1945, American and British forces at last succeeded in crossing the Rhine into Germany. By that time, the Russians had swept through most of eastern and southeastern Europe. Along the 1,500 miles between Stalingrad and Berlin lay the wreckage of Hitler's once mighty war machine. Figure 24.8, a painting by Canadian artist Charles Fraser Comfort, reveals the fate of so many combatants toward the end of World War II. Comfort, who accompanied Canadian troops in Europe, saw firsthand the horrors of war. In this haunting image, a German soldier lies dead among barbed wire on a desolate battlefield. His ravaged remains imply that the battle is long over and that his struggle was in vain. The image echoes scenes from World War I, suggesting ways in which the two wars were tragically related.

Germany defeated

Still, Hitler would not give up. Even in the case of Berlin, he refused to evacuate civilians from the cities, despite the deaths and hardships that would result, so that his troops would feel compelled to fight even more desperately—a tactic Stalin had already used. On April 20, 1945, Berlin civilians heard the approaching Soviet troops. "Our fate is rolling in from the east," reported one woman in her diary. "What was yesterday a distant rumble has now become a constant roar. We breathe the din; our ears are deafened to all but the heaviest guns."

Germany finally surrendered on May 8, and the war in Europe ended. In what one survivor described as "the carcass of Berlin," Hitler, his wife, Eva Braun, and several other top Nazis committed suicide. In Italy, Italian partisans had already shot Mussolini and his mistress.

THE WAR IN THE PACIFIC

In the Pacific, the turning point of the war came in the late spring of 1942 (see Map 24.4). American and Australian troops stopped the Japanese army in New Guinea, and the Americans turned back Japanese naval forces in the Battle of the Coral Sea, northeast of Australia. Soon, American ships, aided by intelligence from intercepted cipher transmissions, positioned themselves off Midway Island to ambush the incoming Japanese. At first, the Japanese fared well, destroying two-thirds of the American planes. Then, aided by luck, dive-bombers from American aircraft carriers spotted four Japanese carriers with their planes being refueled and rearmed. The encounter proved a disaster for the Japanese. In just five minutes, the course of the Pacific war was reversed. Three Japanese carriers went down, followed later by the fourth. The Japanese lost the advantage permanently. The U.S. arms industry was already on its way to outproducing the Japanese and creating an overwhelmingly strong fleet. The Battle of Midway condemned the Japanese to fight defensively for the rest of the war.

Battle of Midway

In August 1942, the Americans attacked Guadalcanal in the Solomon Islands northeast of Australia. Capitalizing on their growing naval superiority and having broken the Japanese code, the Americans conducted an island-hopping campaign toward Japan. One American Marine described the "brutal, primitive hatred" that developed between the Japanese and American soldiers in this costly campaign,

■ FIGURE 24.8

Charles Fraser Comfort, *Dead German on the Hitler Line*, ca. 1944.

■ DOCUMENT 24.3

We Shall Plunge into Enemy Ships

During the last year of the war in the Pacific, the Japanese responded to widespread losses by resorting to suicide attacks on U.S. ships. The Kamikaze Special Attack Corps carried out these attacks. Heiichi Okabe was a member of that corps, and on February 22, 1945, he wrote the following letter. ■ ***How*** *do you explain Okabe's thoughts expressed here?* ■ ***Compare*** *his "duty" to that of other soldiers.* ■ ***Do you agree*** *with his statement that he is "just a human being" and neither hero nor fool?*

I am actually a member at last of the Kamikaze Special Attack Corps. My life will be rounded out in the next thirty days. My chance will come! Death and I are waiting. The training and practice have been rigorous, but it is worthwhile if we can die beautifully and for a cause.

I shall die watching the pathetic struggle of our nation. My life will gallop in the next few weeks as my youth and life draw to a close. . . .

The sortie has been scheduled for the next ten days. I am a human being and hope to be neither saint nor scoundrel, hero nor fool—just a human being. As one who has spent his life in wistful longing and searching, I die resignedly in the hope that my life will serve as a "human document."

The world in which I lived was too full of discord. As a community of rational human beings it should be better composed. Lacking a single great conductor, everyone lets loose with his own sound, creating dissonance where there should be melody and harmony.

We shall serve the nation gladly in its present painful struggle. We shall plunge into enemy ships cherishing the conviction that Japan has been and will be a place where only lovely homes, brave women, and beautiful friendships are allowed to exist.

What is the duty today? It is to fight.
What is the duty tomorrow? It is to win.
What is the daily duty? It is to die.

We die in battle without complaint. I wonder if others, like scientists, who pursue the war effort on their own fronts, would die as we do without complaint. Only then will the unity of Japan be such that she can have any prospect of winning the war.

Source: Rihihei Inoguchi and Tadashi Nakajima, *The Divine Wind* (Annapolis, MD: United States Naval Institute, 1958), pp. 207–208.

---

which "resulted in savage, ferocious fighting with no holds barred." As the battles raged on Pacific islands, "the fierce struggle for survival . . . eroded the veneer of civilization and made savages of us all."

In October 1944, the Japanese fleet made a final, desperate effort near the Philippines, but American forces annihilated it in the Battle of Leyte Gulf. However, as the United States and its allies closed in on the Japanese home islands, the most brutal land battles of the war lay ahead: Iwo Jima and Okinawa. During these battles, Japanese soldiers often fought to the death or took their own lives rather than surrender. During the battle of Okinawa, Japanese pilots volunteered to fly almost 2,000 **kamikaze** missions in which they dive-bombed their planes into Allied ships (see Document 24.3). The Allies lost dozens of ships and thousands of soldiers to these desperate tactics.

Isolated, exposed, and subjected to ceaseless air and sea attacks, Japan was doomed. In February, 1945, the United States began massive bombing raids on Japan's home islands, igniting huge firestorms that destroyed vast sections of Japan's cities and killed hundreds of

The atomic bomb

thousands of people. After Germany surrendered in May 1945, American and British troops rushed to the Far East. In mid-July, American and British scientists finished developing and testing the atom bomb, a new, powerful weapon the two countries had been working on for several years. To avoid the heavy casualties that a direct assault on the Japanese home islands would cause, the United States decided to use the bomb to shock Japan into surrender—a decision that has sparked controversy ever since.

While some Japanese political leaders recognized the hopelessness of continuing the war and pressed the government to pursue a peace settlement, Japan's military leaders promised a bloody fight to the finish. The fighting on Okinawa had convinced many American soldiers that the enemy would not give up. As one survivor of that battle put it, "Japan would have to be invaded with the same gruesome prospects." Moreover, President Truman and his advisors had more in mind than saving American lives. They also wanted Japan's unconditional surrender and hoped to impress the Soviet Union, an ally but also a potential opponent, with a display of unprecedented power. The bomb would serve those purposes. At the same time, many of the scientists who developed the weapon opposed using it. So did General Dwight Eisenhower: "First, the Japanese were ready to surrender and it wasn't necessary to hit them with that awful thing. Second, I hated to see our country be the first to use such a weapon."

On August 6, 1945, a U.S. plane dropped an atomic bomb that destroyed the Japanese city of Hiroshima and some 80,000 of its inhabitants; tens of thousands more died later from the effects of radiation. One survivor, Yamaoka Michiko, described the horror: "There were people, barely breathing, trying to push their intestines back in. People with their legs wrenched off. Without heads. Or with faces burned and swollen out of shape. The scene I saw was a living hell." Three days later, a second atomic bomb demolished the industrial city of Nagasaki, killing an additional 50,000. On August 8, the Soviet Union declared war on Japan and sent

troops into Manchuria. The Japanese finally surrendered on August 15, 1945.

Peace and the Legacy of War

In 1945, Europe lay prostrate as some 50 million refugees drifted across the land and countless people faced starvation and homelessness. Memories of lost loved ones and homes, the horrors of the concentration camps, the hardships of occupation, and *Europe in shambles* the echoes of mass bombings would haunt people for the rest of their lives.

Outrage, fear, and violence continued to stalk Europe. Many resistance fighters and Soviet troops executed surrendering Nazi soldiers on the spot. Angry officials and ordinary people hunted down and punished collaborators after only summary trials. To shame women they suspected of sleeping with German soldiers, irate citizens shaved off women's hair and marched them through the streets. The Soviets, Poles, and Czechoslovakians pushed 13 million ethnic Germans out of homes in Eastern Europe toward the west. One eyewitness described how "families with children, packages, hand wheelbarrows, horse-drawn wagons, and bicycles were making their way, and were being assaulted" as they fled along the roads to Germany. Stalin's officials sent thousands of returning Soviet prisoners to forced-labor camps or to the executioner for being "contaminated" by dangerous, anti-Soviet ideas. Jews who had managed to survive often found their homes destroyed, and they still suffered from flagrant anti-Semitism.

With agricultural and nonmilitary industrial production at a fraction of their prewar levels, Western Europe looked to the United States for loans, relief, defense, and leadership. Eastern Europe, in even worse shambles, was falling under the dominance of the Soviet Union. Political leaders and diplomats involved in the peace settlement hoped this time to avoid the "mistakes" made at the close of World War I. The main challenge facing them was to find a way to deal with defeated nations without spawning new conflicts.

The Settlement

The leaders of Great Britain, the United States, and the Soviet Union shaped postwar Europe in two wartime conferences at Teheran in December 1943 and Yalta in February 1945, and one postwar conference

KEY DATES

CONFLICT AND WAR

1931	Japan invades Manchuria
1935	Italy invades Ethiopia
1936	German troops reoccupy Rhineland
1936–1938	Popular Front in France
1936–1939	Spanish civil war
1937	Japanese-Chinese war begins
1938	Munich conference
1939	Russo-German pact
	Invasion of Poland
1940	Dunkirk
	France falls
	Battle of Britain
1941	Germans invade Soviet Union
	Pearl Harbor bombed
1942	Battle of Stalingrad begins
	Battle of Midway
1944	Normandy invasion
1945	Yalta conference
	United Nations founded
	Atomic bomb dropped on Hiroshima

at Potsdam in July 1945. They agreed to accept only unconditional surrender by Germany and Japan and to require complete restructuring of the aggressors' governments. Germany, which had proved so powerful in two world wars, would be disarmed and divided. The Soviet Union, having suffered so much from Germany's massive invasion, demanded and received pledges of territories on its western border as well as reparations from Germany. To further weaken Germany and recognize the impact of the war, Poland's border with Germany was pushed westward. Finally, a **United Nations** organization was founded in 1945 by fifty-one nations to promote international peace and cooperation. Figure 24.9, a 1947 poster marking the second anniversary of the organization's birth, reveals the high hopes of its founders. Caring hands plant a tree of peace and union, each leaf representing the flag of a member nation. People hoped that as the "sapling" grew, new "leaves" and maturity would strengthen the young organization.

On other matters, however, discord among the wartime allies created a more ominous view of the future. The most crucial disagreements came over the fate of the Eastern European countries. Stalin argued that because the Soviet Union had endured invasions through these countries in both world wars, he

needed them to serve as a "buffer zone" of states loyal to the USSR. The United States and Great Britain demanded complete independence and democracy for these countries. Concessions on both sides at the Yalta Conference in February 1945 left Eastern Europe vaguely "democratic" but "friendly" to the Soviet Union. This arrangement quickly proved unworkable. Two nations—Poland and Bulgaria—were already under communist control, and pro-Soviet "coalition governments" quickly formed in other Eastern European states.

Discord over Eastern Europe

At the final conference at Potsdam in July 1945 (the war ended without a formal peace treaty), Stalin had the upper hand. President Roosevelt had died. Although the American president, Harry Truman, firmly demanded free elections in all of Eastern Europe, he had been in office only three months. Churchill might have been able to exert more pressure on Stalin, but the newly elected Clement Attlee replaced him during the conference. Stalin, insisting that the Soviet Union must obtain complete security against Germany and any potential Eastern European allies, refused to budge on the issue: "A freely elected government in any of these East European countries would be anti-Soviet," he admitted, "and that we cannot allow."

U.S. leaders had trouble swallowing the reality behind Stalin's words. In fact, Eastern Europe was already behind Soviet lines and occupied by Soviet troops by war's end, just as Western Europe remained behind Anglo-American lines and within the United States' and Britain's sphere of influence. "Everyone imposes his own system as far as his armies can reach," observed Stalin privately. "It cannot be otherwise."

THE LEGACY OF WAR

Human beings have waged war on each other since the beginnings of civilization. But World War II, especially when viewed in connection with its twentieth-century predecessor, World War I, shook the West and the world as nothing before.

One crucial difference stemmed from technology. Bloody battles, massacres, torture, and cruelty were not new to the twentieth century. But for the first time, combatants had developed weapons to translate these acts into tens of millions of deaths on and off the battlefields. The use of chemicals, machines, and organizations to inflict a wide range of horrors on so many people so quickly was also unprecedented.

Certainly World War I set a well-remembered precedent for the decision makers of the Second World War. The 1914–1918 conflict had become a relentless mutual slaughter with single battles costing hundreds of thousands of lives and total deaths surpassing 20 million. Those years of war also carried in their wake genocidal

■ FIGURE 24.9
Henri Eveleigh, United Nations poster, 1947.

actions by the Turks against the Armenians and Allied blockades for months after the end of the war that inflicted widespread starvation on defeated nations.

The two decades after World War I brought to power regimes in Russia, Germany, and Japan that hinted at what a second world conflict might wreak on humanity. In Russia, transformed into the Soviet Union, Stalin inflicted a terror-famine on Ukraine, which cost millions of lives, and established the system of slave-labor camps (the Gulag) that also killed and imprisoned millions more. In Germany, the rise of the Nazis to power under Adolf Hitler in 1933 soon led to concentration camps, anti-Semitic terror, and policies of euthanasia. In Japan, the initiation of war against China in 1937 resulted in what is generally called "The Rape of Nanking."

The outbreak of war in Europe in 1939 led to even worse acts and consequences. Violence raged across oceans and continents. The death toll alone was staggering. More than 60 million people—some scholars argue that the actual figure might be much higher—were killed during World War II.

Even more ominous, far more civilians than soldiers died, owing in part to the tactics and weapons of modern war. The drive to inflict massive damage led to indiscriminate carpet and fire bombings. These raids not only made little distinction between military and civilian targets; they literally flattened German and Japanese cities such as Dresden and Tokyo. The search for revolutionary superweapons also bore frightening fruit. The atomic bomb—the weapon that finally ended the war in the Pacific—made it all too clear that human beings now had the ability to inflict unimaginable destruction with a single blow.

Meanwhile, the 11 to 12 million deaths resulting from the Nazis' genocidal program revealed a new capacity for bureaucratized and industrialized killing. Only a relatively few individuals survived the death camps to "tell the story, to bear witness." They and the rest of humanity have had to find ways to live with the realization, in the words of the Auschwitz survivor Primo Levi, "that such a crime should exist," and that it had been "introduced irrevocably into the world of things that exist."

More broadly, terror—of combatants and civilians alike—became a standard tactic during World War II. Officially sanctioned mass rape—in particular by advancing Russian forces in retaliation against the Germans and by Japanese soldiers against the Chinese—made the experience of war all the more vicious. Rape took tragic forms. For example, some 300,000 women, most of them from Korea, were forced to "serve" the Japanese military as "comfort women."

After World War II, it was clear that humans had acquired the capacity to annihilate peoples and civilizations. This realization called into question some of the very developments that had most characterized the West over the previous two centuries: science (used to destroy lives), industrialization (which made the war machines possible), nationalism (which mutated into militarism), ideological beliefs (which justified everything from sacrifice to terror and genocide), and humanism (which seemed irrelevant in the face of blatant inhumanity). In the European heart of the West, many people prayed that a conflict on the scale of World War II would never strike again. But even as they hoped, tensions between two countries that had once lay at the peripheries of the West—the Soviet Union and the United States—suggested that peace might prove short-lived.

SUMMARY

World War II devastated much of Europe and left scars across the globe from North Africa and the Middle East to East Asia, the Pacific, and even the Caribbean. The first battles erupted in Asia when the Japanese, eager to expand their empire, invaded China. Then Nazi Germany and Fascist Italy struck in Europe. The Axis powers piled up victories until the Allies, with their superior industrial might and manpower, finally turned the tide.

The war took a staggering toll. Twenty-seven million Soviets, perhaps many more, perished in the struggle. German armies had left the Soviet Union's cities in smoking ruins and ravaged its countryside. Despite aid from the United States and Great Britain, the Soviets produced 90 percent of their supplies themselves. They had turned the tide against the Germans in Europe well before the Americans and British opened a western front in France. Understandably, the Soviets maintained that they had sacrificed more than any other nation to defeat Germany.

Other countries also sustained terrible losses. Some 15 million Chinese died. Germany gave up six million lives; Japan almost two million. Poland suffered horribly: In addition to losing hundreds of thousands of ordinary citizens, its elites were systematically rounded up and executed by both the Soviets and the Germans.

At war's end, tens of millions of Europeans were uprooted and homeless. Western and non-Western societies, weary and bloodied, now faced an overwhelming task: to recover from the devastation of the war and regain some sense of order. The road ahead looked hard. In Asia, rumblings of national revolutions had already begun. There, the Japanese invaders had inadvertently emboldened nationalists by demonstrating that an Asian people could defeat Western overlords. Such developments all unfolded under the shadow of a sobering new realization: Through modern warfare and new technology, human beings now had the power to obliterate the entire world.

KEY TERMS

Popular Front, p. 728

Axis, p. 729

appeasement, p. 730

Munich conference, p. 730

blitzkrieg, p. 732

Holocaust, p. 737

D-day, p. 744

kamikaze, p. 746

United Nations, p. 748

REVIEW, ANALYZE, AND ANTICIPATE

REVIEW THE PREVIOUS CHAPTER
Chapter 23—"Darkening Decades"—traced the rise of fascism, the development of the Soviet Union, and the trials of nations struck by the Great Depression.

1. *How might one argue that World War II stemmed directly from World War I and the Great Depression?*

2. *What qualities of fascism and authoritarian governments fed the forces for war in the 1930s?*

ANALYZE THIS CHAPTER
Chapter 24—"Into the Fire Again"—studies the causes, course, and consequences of World War II.

1. *Analyze some of the thinking behind Japanese aggression during the 1930s and 1940s.*

2. *How was the Holocaust connected to Hitler's Nazi ideology and the course of World War II?*

3. *How did the Allies turn the tide and defeat the Axis powers in World War II?*

4. *What problems faced negotiators trying to design a settlement at the end of World War II?*

ANTICIPATE THE NEXT CHAPTER
Chapter 25—"Superpower Struggles and Global Transformations" —will examine the Cold War competition between the United States and the Soviet Union and the recovery of the West from World War II. The chapter will also analyze changes stemming from the end of colonialism.

1. *For the decades to come, what do you think were the most important consequences of World War II?*

2. *In what ways did World War II set up the United States and the Soviet Union as potential superpowers? Were they likely to continue as allies? Why or why not?*

BEYOND THE CLASSROOM

THE ROAD TO WAR, 1931–1939
Crozier, Andrew. *The Causes of the Second World War.* London: Blackwell, 1997. A book with good detail within a world context.

Neville, Peter. *Hitler and Appeasement: The British Attempt to Prevent the Second World War.* New York: Continuum, 2005. Defends British efforts to avoid war and places "appeasement" in a broad context.

Watt, Donald Cameron. *How War Came: The Immediate Origins of the Second World War.* London: Heinemann, 1989. A helpful coverage of events directly leading to the war.

AXIS VICTORIES, 1939–1942
Keegan, John. *The Second World War.* New York: Viking, 1990. A book that is particularly good on battles and strategy.

Weinberg, Gerhard L. *A World at Arms: A Global History of World War II.* New York: Cambridge University Press, 1994. Excellent in its global perspective and its examination of the Nazi plan for world order.

GLOBAL CONNECTIONS
Irokawa, Daikichi. *The Age of Hirohito: In Search of Modern Japan.* New York: The Free Press, 1995. A broad study that covers the topic and more.

BEHIND THE LINES:
THE STRUGGLE AND THE HORROR
Yahil, Leni. *The Holocaust: The Fate of European Jewry.* New York: Oxford University Press, 1990. A comprehensive look at the persecution of the Jews before and during World War II.

Jackson, Julian. *France: The Dark Years, 1940–1944.* New York: Oxford University Press, 2003. A fine study of collaboration and resistance in France.

TURNING THE TIDE OF WAR, 1942–1945
Beevor, Anthony. *The Fall of Berlin 1945.* New York: Penguin, 2003. An effective narrative covering the final siege against Berlin.

Frank, R. B. *Downfall: The End of the Imperial Japanese Empire.* New York: Penguin, 2001. A balanced account of the end of the war in the Pacific.

Overy, Richard. *Russia's War: A History of the Soviet War Effort, 1941–1945*. New York: Penguin, 1998. A well-written account of the war on the Eastern Front.

Peace and the Legacy of War

Glover, Jonathan. *Humanity: A Moral History of the Twentieth Century*. New Haven: Yale University Press, 2000. A superb analysis of the grave challenges from the twentieth century that combines psychological, philosophical, and historical perspectives.

Winter, Jay, and Emmanuel Sivan. *War and Remembrance in the Twentieth Century*. Cambridge: Cambridge University Press, 1999. A series of interdisciplinary essays focusing on memory and loss in twentieth-century wars.

www.mhhe.com/sherman3

• Unfamiliar words? See our Glossary at the back of the book for pronunciation and definitions.

• Need help studying? See our web page for map exercises, practice quizzes, and additional study resources.

• Need help writing a paper? Access hundreds of primary documents, maps, images, and a guide to writing history papers on our Primary Source Investigator site at **www.mhhe.com/psi.**

THE GLOBAL CONTEXT

FORMING THE PRESENT

CONSIDER
■ **Consider** the four major developments on which this essay focuses. **What** other developments might be added to this discussion?

The end of World War II marked the dawn of a new era that we can best understand by widening our focus from the West to the entire world. Between 1945 and the first decade of the twenty-first century, four key developments dominated interactions among civilizations around the globe. First, peoples throughout the world increasingly believed that being modern meant becoming Westernized. Second, more and more non-Western peoples agitated to free themselves from Western imperial control. Third, contradictory political beliefs emerged that pitted democratic capitalism against Marxist communism. And, fourth, a vast movement of ideas, technologies, labor, capital, and goods across borders further blurred lines between the West and the non-Western world.

The decades after 1945 witnessed an affirmation of the civilization located in the West and uncertainty about its borders and defining characteristics. In many areas of the world, Western civilization became a model for change and modernization. Indeed some people used the term "modernization"—for example, the spread of cutting-edge science, technology, and industry—interchangeably with "Westernization". The West's enduring power further affirmed its standing in the world. Despite the devastation in the European heartland wrought during World War II, the West had emerged as the globe's politically, economically, and militarily dominant player. But with Europe prostrate, the West's centers of power shifted to what once had been its peripheries—across the Atlantic to the United States and east to the Soviet Union.

At the same time, what defined the West's borders and unique characteristics became less and less clear. Great numbers of people moved in and out of the West, carrying different ways of life with them. Meanwhile, elements of Western culture—liberalism and Marxism, sneakers and hamburgers, movies and the Internet—spread into and saturated other cultures. This mingling of culture, ideas, and institutions made it difficult to discern where the West ended and other civilizations began. Nevertheless, most historians think of the West at this time as consisting of Europe and those areas (such as the Americas, Australia, and New Zealand) where Europeans arrived, adapted, dominated, and almost crushed preexisting cultures and peoples.

Outside of the West, two main struggles dominated the decades after 1945. Both involved the West in one way or another. The first struggle was for national liberation, as peoples in Africa, Asia, and elsewhere threw off their Western colonial rulers. This process sometimes required extended armed combat; other times, it took the form of a peaceful transfer of power. Most such victories left problematic legacies that would plague the freed countries for decades. For example, many newly liberated nations in Africa and Asia would experience great difficulty achieving political stability and developing the economic means to support their populations.

The second struggle that extended beyond the West came with a battle for political power and ideological control that pitted nations headed by the United States (with its system of democratic capitalism) against those allied with the Soviet Union (which had adopted state-directed communism). This complex conflict, known as the Cold War, spread to such places as far-flung as South-East Asia, Korea, Cuba, and Angola.

Connections between the West and the rest of the world became so extensive after 1945 that many call that period the age of globalism. But in reality, waves of globalism had struck earlier. The first began in the late fifteenth century, as Western powers moved out of Europe to establish imperial or commercial links across the seas. The second wave came in the nineteenth century. In those years, industrialism and imperial ambitions pushed Western nations to increase their influence and control over much of the world. People, goods, and ideas flowed between the West and other civilizations. World War I and the economic problems of the 1920s and 1930s dampened this second age of globalism. The new age that began after World War II renewed the flood of ideas, trade, and peoples across borders, with technology bringing hourly if not instant communications around the globe. By the end of the century, for example, goods could be designed in one country, financed internationally, produced in yet another nation, sold in faraway markets, and serviced via phones and the Internet from still different points of the globe.

The West remained at the core of this new globalism. However, other areas of the world began coming to the fore. Some in parts of Asia took over industrial produc-

EARTH FROM SPACE
This world map view of the Earth is a composite of many different NASA satellite images.
Go to www.mhhe.com/psi/Sherman to study an interactive version of maps of the world and of contemporary Europe.

tion and technology first developed in the West and success-fully adapted it. Others in parts of the Middle East controlled crucial, wealth-making assets such as oil. Still others in parts of the Islamic world reacted in a backlash against the West. In addition to these developments, all civilizations—Western and non-Western alike—would soon face challenges they could not have imagined previously. Perhaps none were more threatening to the entire human species than the spread of nuclear arms and such dramatic environmental changes as global warming.

DISCUSSION QUESTIONS

■ **What** areas of the world are generally considered of the West today?

■ In the satellite image above, **identify** areas that border the Pacific Ocean and that might be considered part of the modernized world. **Refer also** to the maps of Europe and the world at the back of this book for more detail.

■ Starting from Europe, **scan** the rest of the world, first to the south, then the east, and finally to the west. **In what ways** has the West touched and affected various parts of the globe over the three ages of globalism? **How** might our present age of globalism resemble previous ages of globalism? **How** might it differ?

DON EDDY, *NEW SHOES FOR H*, 1974

In this 1974 painting, Don Eddy uses the artistic style known as photo-realism to depict a shoe-store display in New York City. Reflected in the store window are cars, buses, a department store sign (S. Klein), office and apartment buildings, and a pedestrian in blue jeans—all in all, a typically vibrant street scene in a leading Western city of the era.

CHAPTER | 25

SUPERPOWER STRUGGLES AND GLOBAL TRANSFORMATIONS

THE COLD WAR, 1945–1980s

STUDY	The Cold War ■ Recovery in Eastern and Western Europe ■ Decolonization ■ Relativity in thought and culture ■ Protests, problems, and politics ■ Postindustrial society ■ Scientific breakthroughs.
NOTICE	How the Cold War colored this period.

In 1974, a retired Frenchwoman, Françoise Giroud, contrasted her early life as a stenographer in the 1930s with the lives of young women of the 1970s. "[T]here is simply no comparison. . . . A month of paid vacation, . . . organized travel, . . . paperback books, . . . blue jeans and the T-shirts, instant mashed potatoes, the transistor, . . . the boyfriend who has a [used car], . . . and the Pill! It's not a better world; it's another world altogether." This new world that Giroud described boasted unheard-of material well-being, international peace throughout most of the West, innovative day-to-day conveniences, and striking new medical knowledge. The painting on page 754 is an apt illustration of this new age. The image reveals a wealthy, commercial society awash in consumer goods. In effect, the painting offers a view of reality from different perspectives, paralleling the efforts that many Westerners made to understand their rapidly changing world.

Yet these decades also had their dark side. Nations around the world labored to recover from the devastation of World War II. As they did so, a new menace emerged—growing tensions between the United States and the Soviet Union that for decades would overshadow international relations and everyday life. At the same time, colonial peoples took advantage of Europe's weakness and changing attitudes toward imperialism and demanded their independence in ways the West could not ignore. New nations and international organizations soon emerged throughout the world, and global interactions grew so complex that the traditional lines between Western and non-Western societies blurred more than ever.

TIMELINE: THE BIG PICTURE

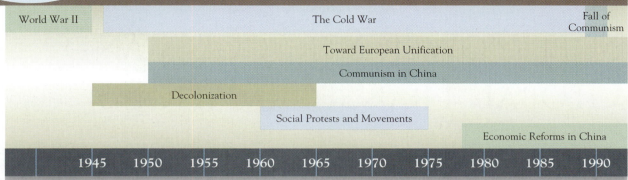

World War II	The Cold War								Fall of Communism
Toward European Unification									
Communism in China									
Decolonization									
Social Protests and Movements									
Economic Reforms in China									

| 1945 | 1950 | 1955 | 1960 | 1965 | 1970 | 1975 | 1980 | 1985 | 1990 |

ORIGINS OF THE COLD WAR

"AT THE PRESENT MOMENT IN world history nearly every nation must choose between alternative ways of life," announced U.S. President Harry Truman on March 12, 1947. Ominously, he added, "The choice is too often not a free one," referring to what he termed the "coercion and intimidation" used to force "total-itarian regimes" on the peoples of several countries. Eight months later, his secretary of state, George Marshall, pointed to the heart of the problem: "The present line of division in Europe is roughly the line upon which the Anglo-American armies coming from the west met those of the Soviet Union coming from the east. . . . Developments in the European countries to the east of that line bear the unmistakable imprint of an alien hand." According to Truman and Marshall, the "alien hand" over eastern Europe belonged to the Soviet Union, only two years earlier an ally of the United States in World War II.

The conflict over the fate of Eastern Europe drove a sharp wedge between the World War II allies. Long-standing antagonisms and new differences soon combined to break down further any cooperation between the Western democracies and the Soviet Union. Ever since the communists had come to power in 1917, they and the capitalist democracies had viewed each other as opponents (see Chapter 23). As ideologies, communism and capitalism had always been in direct opposition. As practiced in the Soviet Union under Lenin and Stalin, the political system of communism took a dictatorial form, in sharp contrast to the democracies of Great Britain and the United States. Hitler's invasion of the Soviet Union in World War II and the United States' entry into the war only temporarily united Great Britain, the United States, and the Soviet Union. The three powers joined as allies more in opposition to Nazi Germany than in agreement over principles or goals. Not surprisingly, when negotiations over war aims and settlement terms took place, the history of hostility, distrust, and fear between the capitalist and communist powers caused problems. After the war, when the threat of Nazi Germany no longer held the Allies together, tensions worsened.

In 1945, the U.S. cut off all aid to the USSR. The rhetoric of discord between the powers increased. The next year, Winston Churchill, speaking at a small college in Missouri, warned the world of an **Iron Curtain** descending from the Baltic to the Adriatic Seas, dividing Europe between communist East and capitalist West.

Churchill's warning proved apt. Within the next few years, Soviet-backed communist parties in Eastern Europe pushed their opponents aside and rose to power; only communist Yugoslavia and Albania would manage to follow independent courses. In Western Europe, despite the presence of popular communist parties, American-backed anticommunist politicians controlled the governments. In Greece, the two sides clashed as the British and the Americans supported the repressive anticommunist monarchy in an armed conflict against the Greek communists. The **Cold War** had begun.

THE HEART OF THE COLD WAR

At the heart of the Cold War lay a troubled Germany. As Map 25.1 indicates, the peace settlement had divided the aggressor nation into four occupation zones: American, Soviet, British, and French. The city of Berlin, in the Russian zone, was also divided into the same four sectors. Sharp disagreements soon surfaced among the occupiers. The Soviets alarmed

THINKING ABOUT GEOGRAPHY

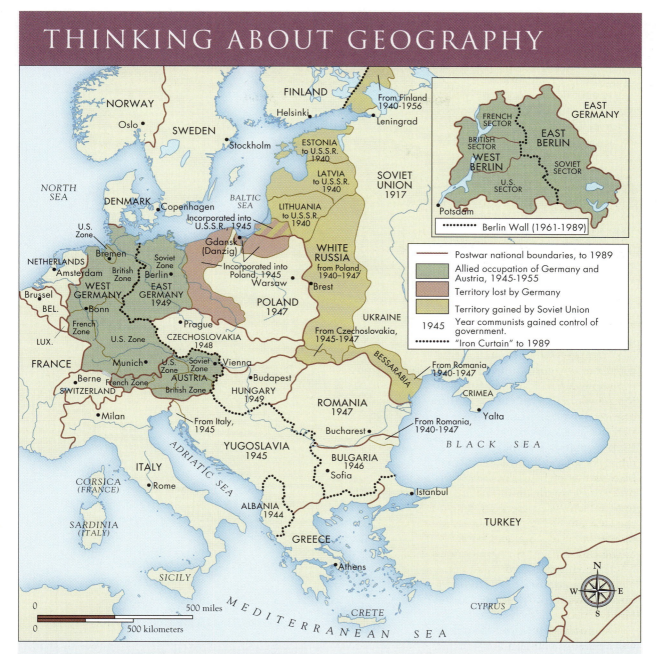

MAP 25.1 EUROPE AFTER WORLD WAR II

This map shows Europe after World War II and the dates communists gained control of governments in Eastern Europe. ■ **Notice** the territories acquired by the Soviet Union as well as those lost by Germany. ■ **Notice** that Austria, Germany, and Berlin were divided into American, British, French, and Soviet zones. ■ **Locate** Berlin. **Why** might this city be of such strategic, political, and symbolic importance? **What** predicament faced the western zones of Berlin when the Soviets cut off land traffic from the west? ■ **Evaluate** the size and potential importance of a unified Western Germany and Eastern Germany.

their allies by grabbing valuable resources from Germany, including entire factories, and transporting them to the Soviet Union as reparations for war losses rather than waiting for cash payments. The

Soviets also hoped to keep their old enemy Germany economically weak and fully divided. The United States and Britain, on the other hand, set out to restore and integrate economically the western sectors of Germany, seeing those regions as essential allies in the growing split with the USSR.

Matters came to a head in 1948 when the U.S. and Britain tried to spur economic recovery by introducing a new currency in the western zones of Germany despite Soviet opposition. Stalin countered by

The Berlin blockade and the division of Germany

blockading the three western zones of Berlin. From June 1948 to May 1949, the Soviets stopped all land traffic across their zone from the West to Berlin. In response, the Western powers mounted a daring and continuous airlift that carried supplies to the city. If "Berlin falls," warned the American military commander General Lucius Clay, "western Germany will be next . . . if we withdraw, our position in Europe is threatened. . . . Communism will run rampant." The **Berlin airlift** eventually prompted the Soviet Union to back down.

In September 1949, the Western allies followed through on their plan to merge the three western zones of Germany and to create an independent West German state—the German Federal Republic. One month later, the Soviet Union established the German Democratic Republic in its eastern zone, completing the division of Germany into the capitalist West and communist East.

Meanwhile, the Cold War chill was already spreading across the rest of Europe. In 1947, the U.S. president Harry Truman (1884–1972) initiated the Truman Doctrine, a policy that offered military and economic aid to countries threatened by a communist takeover. "The peoples of a number of countries of the world have recently had totalitarian regimes forced upon them against their will," he warned. "[I]t must be the policy of the United States to support

The Cold War spreads

free peoples who are resisting attempted subjugation by armed minorities or by outside pressures." His immediate concern was the civil

THINKING ABOUT GEOGRAPHY

Map legend:
- NATO Alliance, 1955
- ★ Original EEC Members, 1957
- Communist Bloc (Members of Warsaw Pact and COMECON)

MAP 25.2   EUROPE DURING THE COLD WAR

This map shows how the Cold War had divided Europe by the 1950s. ■ **What** connections between military and economic cooperation are revealed by this map? **Consider** why the Soviet Union was so anxious to maintain control over its Eastern European allies. **Why** was Turkey such an important member of NATO? ■ **Notice** what nations are not part of the alliance organizations. **Consider** the possible reasons for this.

war in Greece, where local communists aided by neighboring Yugoslavia were making gains against the royalist government. His larger goal was to create a military ring of "**containment**" around the Soviet Union and its satellite states.

■ DOCUMENT 25.1

The Cold War and Nuclear Weapons

The intensity of the Cold War and the existence of nuclear weapons on both sides spread fear throughout the West during the 1950s and early 1960s. Observers debated whether nuclear weapons would deter attacks from the opposing side, whether the contestants could agree to disarm, and whether unilateral destruction of nuclear weapons made the most sense. In the following selection from a 1956 debate, Philip Toynbee of Great Britain argues for the last position. ■ **What** *does Toynbee's argument reveal about the level of fear during the Cold War?* ■ **How** *does Toynbee justify a policy of unilateral nuclear disarmament?* ■ **How** *might his opponents have responded to this argument?*

It is obvious, surely, that this is an issue which has nothing whatever to do with party politics and nothing whatever to do with our estimations of American and Russian society. In the terrible context of nuclear war even the vital differences between Communism and Western freedom become almost unimportant. We would infinitely prefer our Western system of freedom and privacy to prevail in the world; and if we are spared we shall have an opportunity of trying to ensure that it does so. But even if it didn't prevail *mankind* would still be given the opportunity of prevailing. Mr. Kennan has said that anything would be better than a policy which led inevitably to nuclear war. But surely anything is better than a policy which allows for the *possibility* of nuclear war.

The issue has nothing do to with politics. It has little to do with causes and highmindedness. Those who have had at least a partial vision of our destruction are like people who have leant out of the window of an express train and seen that a bridge is down a little further along the line. They are urging the driver and their fellow-passengers that the train should be stopped. But the others

reply, many of them from behind their newspapers, that the train can't possibly be stopped because they have important engagements in the city. As for the bridge, it may not be down after all, and even if it is the train will probably manage to jump across it somehow. Besides, it does no good to the reputation of our railways if express trains are to be halted in this way. And finally, we ought surely to be aware that there is another express train coming in the opposite direction which will certainly fall down into the river just as soon as we do.

At the very least, then, let those who wish to continue with the arms-race be prepared with competent methods of killing off their mutilated families before killing their mutilated selves. Only when we see that they have made these preparations shall we be able to believe that they have faced the implications of their policy.

Source: Philip Toynbee, *The Fearful Choice* (London: Victor Gollancz, 1956), pp. 21–22.

That same year, Truman's secretary of state, George Marshall (1880–1959), launched the **Marshall Plan,** a package of massive economic aid to European nations designed both to strengthen them and tie them to American influence. The Soviet Union forbade Eastern European governments to accept the aid and soon established the Council for Mutual Economic Assistance (COMECON), a Soviet version of the Marshall Plan for Eastern Europe.

In 1949, the United States organized the **North Atlantic Treaty Organization (NATO),** a military alliance among the United States, Canada, and most of the nations of Western Europe against the Soviet Union. Within a few years, Greece and Turkey had joined the alliance. After West Germany signed on in 1955, the Soviet Union countered NATO by creating its own military alliance in Eastern Europe, the Warsaw Pact. Now thousands of troops in each alliance—backed by the presence and might of the two superpowers—faced each other along a line dividing Eastern and Western Europe. It had taken only a few years for each side in the Cold War to forge

economic, political, and military ties among its allies and form two hostile camps (see Map 25.2).

The Cold War would color international relations and everyday life for more than four decades. Andrei Zhdanov (1896–1948), a powerful Soviet official, described the official Soviet view of the Cold War in 1947: U.S. goals were "domination in all countries marked out for American expansion" and "the creation in peacetime of numerous [military] bases . . . for aggressive purposes against the USSR." John Foster Dulles (1888–1959), President Dwight Eisenhower's secretary of state, presented the U.S. view in 1953: "Soviet communism . . . is the gravest threat that has ever faced . . . Western civilization, or indeed, any civilization . . . dominated by a spiritual faith." Compromise between such extreme, hostile views seemed impossible.

As Document 25.1 suggests, terror lurked just below the surface of the Cold War. By 1949, both superpowers had the atomic bomb; by 1953, the hydrogen bomb. Each country supported growing military

Cold War weapons

■ FIGURE 25.1

André Fougeron, *Peace Must Be Saved*, 1948.

budgets and stockpiled huge caches of weapons, including intercontinental ballistic missiles (ICBMs) that could carry nuclear warheads. The danger rippled outward as other nations—Britain, France, India, China, Israel, and Pakistan—also developed nuclear weapons. As U.S. President John F. Kennedy (1917–1963) admitted in 1962, "The decision to use any kind of a nuclear weapon . . . presents such a risk of it getting out of control so quickly. . . ." In fact, the Cold War was fought in all ways except open military conflict between the United States and the Soviet Union. Networks of spies fanned out over the globe. Political struggles anywhere, even purely internal matters, became arenas for defining a victory or defeat in the Cold War. The competition expanded to include nonpolitical activities as well, such as space exploration and the Olympic Games.

Cold War posturing and imagery also saturated the media. In Figure 25.1, a 1948 poster created for the French Communist Party, atomic bombs hover over the prostrate victim, spreading death (the crosses in the background) and destruction (the burning buildings). The poster warns France against any form of alliance with Germany, which the communists

claimed would amount to preparation for war against the Soviet Union. From the United States, the Voice of America radio station spread anticommunist messages throughout Europe, while the station's Soviet counterpart presented its own views. Most European governments controlled the news on their radio and television programs.

All this led to a pervasive sense of suspicion and fear. Novels, movies, and television shows featuring spies and international intrigue proliferated. In the United States, for example, Senator Joseph McCarthy (1908–1957) led a massive name-calling campaign between 1950 and 1954 "to uncover" communists and communist sympathizers; these "fellow travelers," McCarthy claimed, had infiltrated every aspect of American life, from the armed services to Hollywood movie studios. Atomic bomb drills in American schools and bomb shelters in city basements and suburban backyards completed the picture of a Western democratic nation menaced by communism and the Soviet Union.

THE GLOBAL IMPACT OF THE COLD WAR

The Cold War quickly spread around the globe as each side searched for allies and victories wherever they could find them (see Map 25.3). No area escaped from the worldwide competition, but events in Asia and Latin America especially reveal the far-reaching impact of the Cold War. In both areas, the United States forged anticommunist alliances while the Soviet Union supported communist governments and revolutionary movements. More than once, the contest fueled crises and armed conflict in these areas.

Japan had emerged from World War II defeated on sea and land, the shocked victim of history's first two atomic bombs used for military purposes. Because the United States by far had played the major role in the defeat of Japan, it refused to share the occupation and govern-ing of the Japanese islands with its former allies. The U.S. quickly promoted political democratization and used financial aid to help Japan rebuild and conform to U.S. policies. In this way, Japan, like West Germany, would become a link in the Cold War containment "chain" that the U.S. was forging around the Soviet Union. The strategy paid off handsomely. During the 1950s and 1960s, Japan became a firm ally and used its modern industries and skilled labor to make an astounding economic recovery that surpassed that of even West Germany.

China, just across the Sea of Japan, moved in a different direction. The civil war between Mao Zedong's zealous Communist forces and Jiang Jieshi's conservative Nationalist forces was suspended during World

The Cold War in Asia

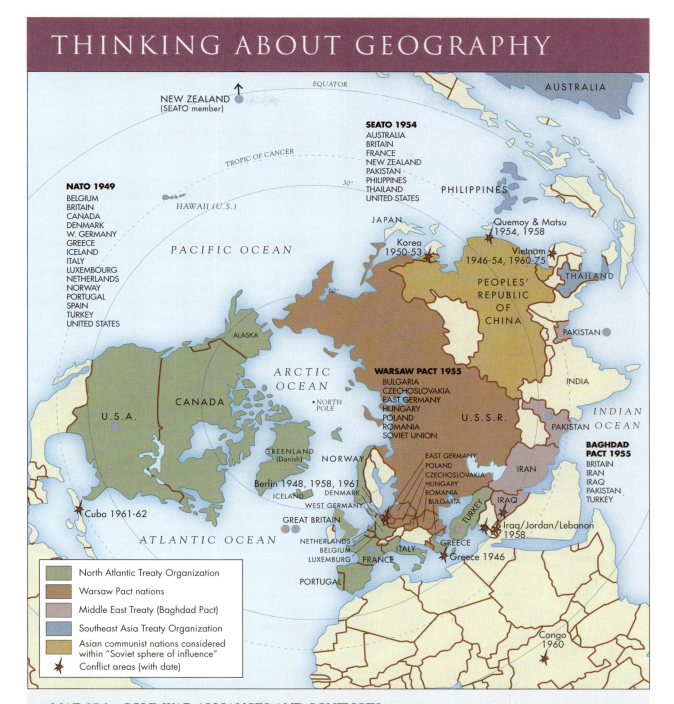

NEW ZEALAND (SEATO member)

EQUATOR

AUSTRALIA

SEATO 1954
AUSTRALIA
BRITAIN
FRANCE
NEW ZEALAND
PAKISTAN
PHILIPPINES
THAILAND
UNITED STATES

PHILIPPINES

NATO 1949
BELGIUM
BRITAIN
CANADA
DENMARK
W. GERMANY
GREECE
ICELAND
ITALY
LUXEMBOURG
NETHERLANDS
NORWAY
PORTUGAL
SPAIN
TURKEY
UNITED STATES

TROPIC OF CANCER

HAWAII (U.S.)

30°

JAPAN

Quemoy & Matsu 1954, 1958

Korea 1950-53

Vietnam 1946-54, 1960-75

THAILAND

PACIFIC OCEAN

PEOPLES' REPUBLIC OF CHINA

PAKISTAN

ALASKA

60°

ARCTIC OCEAN

NORTH POLE

WARSAW PACT 1955
BULGARIA
CZECHOSLOVAKIA
EAST GERMANY
HUNGARY
POLAND
ROMANIA
SOVIET UNION

INDIA

CANADA

U.S.S.R.

INDIAN OCEAN

PAKISTAN

U.S.A.

GREENLAND (Danish)

NORWAY

EAST GERMANY
POLAND
CZECHOSLOVAKIA
HUNGARY
ROMANIA
BULGARIA

IRAN

BAGHDAD PACT 1955
BRITAIN
IRAN
IRAQ
PAKISTAN
TURKEY

Berlin 1948, 1958, 1961

ICELAND

DENMARK

WEST GERMANY

Cuba 1961-62

GREAT BRITAIN

TURKEY

IRAQ

Iraq/Jordan/Lebanon 1958

ATLANTIC OCEAN

NETHERLANDS
BELGIUM
LUXEMBURG

FRANCE

ITALY

GREECE

Greece 1946

PORTUGAL

Congo 1960

- North Atlantic Treaty Organization
- Warsaw Pact nations
- Middle East Treaty (Baghdad Pact)
- Southeast Asia Treaty Organization
- Asian communist nations considered within "Soviet sphere of influence"
- ★ Conflict areas (with date)

MAP 25.3   COLD WAR ALLIANCES AND CONFLICTS

This map shows the Cold War alliances that spread across the globe during the 1940s and 1950s and areas where conflicts related to the Cold War broke out. ■ **Notice** which countries are part of anticommunist organizations, and that several of these nations are members of more than one organization. **Consider** the geopolitical advantages and disadvantages held by each side.

War II. Mao's forces waged a more incessant guerrilla warfare against the Japanese than the Nationalists did and thereby gained a growing following among the Chinese people. After the surrender of Japan in

1945, the bitter, internal struggle for the control of China began anew. The United States supported the Nationalists, while ever-increasing numbers of Chinese supported the Communists. In 1949, the

THINKING ABOUT GEOGRAPHY

MAP 25.4 VIETNAM AND SOUTHEAST ASIA

This map shows Vietnam and its neighbors during the 1950s, 1960s, and 1970s, when war wracked the area. ■ **Consider** why Cambodia and Laos became involved in the conflicts. ■ **Notice** China to the north. **Why** might the U.S. bombings of Hanoi and Haiphong have been strategically risky?

People's Republic of China and joined in an alliance with the Soviet Union. With Soviet aid, he began the daunting task of industrializing and communizing China.

Less than a year later, the Cold War merged with simmering internal forces in nearby Korea to produce a major conflict that embroiled both the new Chinese communist regime and the United States. At the end of World War II, in accordance with the Yalta agreements, Soviet troops occupied Korea north of the thirty-eighth parallel while American forces controlled the south. The Soviets and Americans withdrew by 1949, leaving North and South Korea as armed client states rather than a united Korean nation. The new governments of the North and South, each ruled by dictators, talked loudly of conquering each other.

The Korean War

In 1950, the Soviet-backed North Korean communists—with the approval of both Stalin and Mao—suddenly invaded U.S.-backed South Korea. The determined, well-armed North Korean communists easily defeated the South Koreans. Supported by the UN, the U.S. quickly intervened. The American and UN forces soon overcame the North Koreans, but as their troops approached the Korean-Chinese border and threatened to bomb North Korean sanctuaries in China, the Chinese entered the fray. They pushed the U.S. and UN forces back to the thirty-eighth parallel, where a stalemate developed. By the time of the armistice in 1953, the war had cost some 1.5 million casualties on each side and had left much of Korea in ruins.

These experiences with Korea and China prompted the U.S. to involve itself in nearby Vietnam, Laos, and Cambodia. The U.S. feared that the fall of one nation in that region to communism would, like a row of dominoes, lead to the fall of other adjacent nations. "Vietnam represents the cornerstone of the Free World in Southeast Asia, the keystone to the arch, the finger in the dike," warned then Senator John F. Kennedy in 1956. "Burma, Thailand, India, Japan, the Philippines, and obviously Laos and Cambodia are among those whose security would be threatened if the red tide of Communism overflowed into Vietnam. . . ."

Accordingly, the U.S. helped the French fight against Vietnamese nationalists. Vietnam had been a French colony before World War II and, under the leadership of Ho Chi Minh (1890–1969) and his Vietnamese Communist Party, had fought for its independence from France in the years after World War II. After suffering a series of defeats, France finally agreed to withdraw in 1954. The 1954 Geneva Accords provisionally gave Ho Chi Minh's communists control of the nation north of the seventeenth latitude and provided for elections throughout the whole country in 1956. The U.S. refused to sign the accords, and

The Vietnam War

victorious Communists swept over the entire Chinese mainland. Jiang's Nationalists fled to the nearby island of Taiwan, where they came under the protection of the U.S. navy. Mao promptly proclaimed the

Ngo Dihn Diem (1901–1963), who took power in the south where the remnants of the old French-supported Associated State of Vietnam had fled, refused to hold the elections. The nation was divided between the North, ruled by the victorious Ho Chi Minh, and the South, under an authoritarian, anticommunist government that tried to maintain the aristocratic society of a vanishing era (see Map 25.4).

The unpopular regime in the South relied for its survival on the economic and political support of the United States and its allies. Military aid and armed forces soon followed, as the United States sought to increase its influence not only in South Vietnam but also in Laos and Cambodia, which had gained freedom from the French. During the mid-1960s, the U.S. sent more than 500,000 troops to Vietnam. American planes dropped more explosives there than had been used by all combatants during World War II, pummeling the tiny nation. Still, the opposing North Vietnamese—helped by material aid from the Soviet Union and China—proved skilled and tenacious fighters, and the war dragged on.

Throughout the West, the United States drew harsh criticism from antiwar demonstrators for its relentless—and apparently futile—assaults on Vietnam. Figure 25.2, a 1968 collage titled *Miss America*, is one example of the reproach aimed at the United States. In this disturbing image, the well-known German artist Wolf Vostell uses photo-journalism to convey his message. In the center, a National Front for the Liberation of Southern Vietnam (contemptuously called the "Viet Cong" by its enemies) suspect in South Vietnam is being executed. At the bottom, U.S. troops loom over crumpled corpses. Above is a mutilated image of a woman. The title of the work implies a mangling of American innocence, beauty, and honor by the daily, brutal realities of Vietnam published in newspapers and beamed into televisions around the world.

The cost, futility, and unpopularity of the Vietnam War put increasing pressure on U.S. leaders to end American involvement in the conflict. In 1973, after long negotiations, the U.S. and Vietnamese forces finally signed peace agreements, and the United States withdrew its forces. The civil war in Vietnam, however, persisted for another two years before the communists swept to victory—not only in Vietnam but also in neighboring Laos and Cambodia.

The Cold War tide shifted in Asia several times.

China's "Great Leap Forward" China, which had backed the Vietnam communists, had continued in its own direction. During the 1950s, China was engaged in trying to meet overly ambitious goals in industry and agriculture. To that end, it communized its society even more completely than had ever been attempted in the Soviet Union. In a plan called the "Great Leap Forward," China's huge and burgeoning population was

THINKING ABOUT ART

Wolf Vostell, *Miss America*, 1968

■ FIGURE 25.2

In this 1968 collage, German artist Wolf Vostell conveys impressions of the war in Vietnam. ■ **Why** do you think Vostell titled this work *Miss America*? ■ **What** might the artist have intended the viewer to understand by juxtaposing photos of events in Vietnam over an image of this woman? ■ **Do you think** this collage should be viewed primarily as a thoughtful, realistic depiction of the war, or as a piece of propaganda, and **why**?

set to building irrigation dams and ditches, steel mills, factories, railroads, schools, and hospitals at a frenetic pace. In 1959, an alternating cycle of droughts and flooding struck, producing one of the deadliest famines in history; some 20 million Chinese may have died of starvation and malnutrition over the next three years. Overzealous local party officials provoked resentment and resistance among the already harried populace, and for years the Communist Party hierarchy was wracked by a power struggle between moderates and radicals. In 1966, Mao tried to reignite the revolutionary spirit by launching the Great Proletarian Cultural Revolution. He empowered youthful zealots to cleanse China of those who did not enthusiastically support him. Over several years, millions of people suffered humiliation or death.

Mao's Cultural Revolution

At the same time, relations between China and the Soviet Union began to cool. As early as 1956, China started criticizing the USSR, which that year under Nikita Khrushchev (1894–1971) began backing away from Stalin's harshest policies. Mao denounced Moscow for softening toward the capitalistic, imperialist West and for abandoning strict Marxist-Leninist principles. In 1960, the Soviet Union began to withhold promised economic and technological aid to China. When China exploded its first nuclear device in 1964, the two communist nations moved further apart, and by 1968, they were embroiled in border disputes.

The Chinese-Soviet split

With the Soviet Union a common enemy, China and the U.S. tentatively looked to one another for support. During the 1970s, China normalized relations with the U.S., replaced Taiwan in the UN, and, after the death of Mao in 1976, initiated policies emphasizing economic decentralization and free-market activities. Figure 25.3 symbolizes the new, assertive strength of communist China. In this striking photograph, a 90-foot statue of Chairman Mao Zedong towers over marchers celebrating the twenty-first anniversary of the communists' victory in China.

■ FIGURE 25.3

Victory parade in China, 1970.

The Cold War soon took another turn in central Asia, where the Soviet Union became entangled in its own version of the Vietnam War. In 1979, Soviet troops intervened to support a communist coup in Afghanistan, a nation on the USSR's southern border that the Soviets considered within their own sphere of influence. They promptly became locked into a ten-year war against tenacious guerrilla forces backed by the U.S. Central Intelligence Agency. In 1989 the Soviets finally withdrew, leaving Afghanistan in shambles and wracked by internal violence.

Soviets in Afghanistan

Even the Latin American countries, far from the conflicts in Asia and long considered "friends" by the United States, got pulled into the Cold War. At the end of World War II, the governments of independent Latin American states were republics in name. In reality, however, most of them were right-wing dictatorships, representing the interests of the well-to-do bourgeoisie, the landowning classes, and the professional military. The Roman Catholic Church, which had been a powerful conservative force in this region during the nineteenth century, had grown more liberal during the twentieth century. Sometimes it even exerted its influence in social and economic reform movements. In the years following World War II, the poor in Latin America became increasingly restless. Many of them turned to communism, encouraged by the Soviet Union. The United States, on the other hand, supported the conservative governments.

The Cold War in Latin America

Over the next four decades, the U.S. intervened in or invaded several Latin American nations to shore up conservative forces in its global struggle against communism. The Soviets, for their part, supported sympathetic revolutionary movements and regimes. Of all the Latin American countries, Cuba became the most volatile staging ground for the intensifying feud between the superpowers. In 1959, Marxist rebel leader Fidel Castro ousted the American-supported dictatorship in Cuba and launched a sweeping program of social and economic reforms. The new program included the seizure of property owned by citizens and corporations of the United States. The U.S. government promptly terminated aid to the island nation, and Castro turned to the Soviets for help. These developments threatened the Americans in two crucial ways. First, a revolutionary, left-wing regime backed heavily by the Soviet Union had suddenly gained a beachhead in Latin America—a mere 90 miles away from the U.S. mainland. Second, the Americans worried that Castro's success would embolden other opposition and revolutionary movements—also typically led by Marxists—throughout Latin America. Such uprisings would lead to more Cold War victories for the communists. Three years after the Cuban revolution, the U.S. government

Crisis in Cuba

sponsored the Bay of Pigs invasion, an ill-fated attempt by Cuban refugees to topple the Castro regime.

Tensions soon reached a new high in the Caribbean. On October 12, 1962, a U.S. spy plane discovered Soviet missiles being installed in Cuba. Privately, President Kennedy admitted: "What difference does it make? They've got enough to blow us up now anyway. . . . This is a political struggle as much as military." Although the U.S. had missiles on Russia's border in Turkey, the Americans decided that Soviet missiles in Cuba were intolerable. With the USSR's ships steaming toward the Caribbean, the U.S. navy under orders to intercept them to prevent the arrival of more missiles in Cuba, and American forces mobilizing, people around the world braced themselves for a possible nuclear war. On October 27, the U.S. Joint Chiefs of Staff urged an all-out attack on Cuba if the Soviets did not immediately remove the missile bases. Two days later, USSR leader Nikita Khrushchev backed down, and an agreement ended the crisis.

DÉTENTE

The two superpowers would not again come so close to war with each other. Indeed, at times Cold War tensions relaxed as each side backed away from the sort of conflict that promised to devastate each nation and much of the world. Nuclear test-ban treaties in the 1960s and strategic arms limitation talks in the 1970s eased fears of confrontation. The Helsinki agreement in 1975 confirming Europe's political frontiers, and recognizing certain human rights seemed to solidify a period of **détente**—growing cooperation between Cold War adversaries. But détente went only so far. The 1980s witnessed a return to combative rhetoric and policies with the Soviet invasion of Afghanistan and the tougher anticommunist policies of the Reagan administration in the United States. By the middle of that decade, few saw any end to the Cold War.

EAST AND WEST: TWO PATHS TO RECOVERY IN EUROPE

Under the long shadow of the Cold War, Europeans again tried to return to normal life after World War II. Beyond the astounding number of deaths and widespread destruction, whole cities—such as Berlin, in the heart of Europe—had been devastated. "Nothing is left in Berlin," wrote a reporter for the *New York Herald Tribune* in 1945. "There are no homes, no shops, no transportation, no government buildings. . . . Berlin can now be regarded only as a geographical location heaped with mountainous mounds of debris." Realists declared that economic recovery alone might take twenty-five years. Others wondered whether European society would ever recover.

European nations followed two main paths toward recovery that reflected Cold War differences and the politics underlying those differences. In the Soviet Union and Eastern Europe, communist governments promised clear planning and an unquestionable sense of direction under firm party direction. In Western Europe, the capitalist democracies relied on an alliance of the free market and governmental controls to transform their societies from the wartime devastation. Each path would have its successes and problems.

TIGHT CONTROL IN THE SOVIET UNION AND EASTERN EUROPE

Nowhere was the damage and upheaval from World War II worse than in the Soviet Union and Eastern Europe. Soviet citizens longed for an end to wartime deprivations and Stalin's strict controls. Eastern Europeans living along the USSR's border wondered uneasily what to expect as their governments and economies came under the rule of communist parties controlled by Moscow.

Stalin refused to relax his grip over the Soviet Union. He asserted dictatorial control, crushing the merest hint of political dissent and purging those whom he perceived as potential threats. Prisons and forced-labor camps overflowed with his victims. Nor did his economic policies—tight planning and extreme sacrifice for heavy industrialization—change. To help rebuild what the war had destroyed in the Soviet Union, Stalin drained off economic resources from the Eastern European states.

Those countries under Soviet dominance—the "satellite" states—were required to cooperate with the Soviet Union. Single-party "people's democracies" in Poland, East Germany, Czechoslovakia, Hungary, Romania, Yugoslavia, and Albania initiated Soviet-style economic planning, nationalization, collectivization of agriculture, and industrialization. Officials allowed little contact with Western Europe.

Nevertheless, Eastern Europe refused to become a mere appendage to the Soviet Union. These nations harbored strong desires for national autonomy and they often resented Soviet restrictions. Within these states, discontent also rose over the persistent shortage of consumer goods, low wages, and poor working conditions. The Soviets and their followers often had difficulty maintaining control as resistance flared into open rebellions.

Yugoslavia snapped first. The Soviet Union had a weak foothold there because the Yugoslav Resistance had liberated the nation from Nazi control almost on its own. In 1948, Yugoslavia's strong and popular dictator, Tito (see Biography in Chapter 24), stood up to Stalin's threats and headed his nation on an independent course. Tito's decentralized form of communism stressed more local control and worker participation in management than the Soviet model.

In 1953, Joseph Stalin, the man who had led the Soviet Union for a quarter-century, died. In the Soviet Union, millions mourned Stalin as the leader who had saved them from Nazism. However, some Eastern Europeans saw his death as an opportunity to step up their demands for greater independence. Workers in East Berlin initiated protests against governmental efforts to increase workloads without raising wages. Crowds soon gathered in the streets, demanding political reform and a loosening of ties to the USSR. Police and Soviet tanks promptly crushed these uprisings.

The death of Stalin and new opportunities

In Moscow, potential successors to Stalin jockeyed for power. They quickly agreed to eliminate the dreaded head of the secret police, Lavrenti Beria (1899–1953), and restricted that organization's terrorist activities. After two years of collective leadership, Nikita Khrushchev, the son of a miner, moved up from the party bureaucracy to emerge as Stalin's successor. In a 1956 unpublished speech to startled communist leaders, Khrushchev denounced the "cult of personality" fostered by Stalin. He also accused Stalin of using "the most cruel repression, violating all norms of revolutionary legality . . . mass arrests and deportations of many thousands of people, executions without trial." Khrushchev slightly loosened government control of Soviet cultural life; authors such as Boris Pasternak (1890–1960) even managed to publish works that implied some criticism of the Soviet regime. New policies also stressed the production of consumer goods, increased housing, and better health care. Workers throughout the USSR gained more freedom to move from one job to another.

Eastern Europeans hoped that this de-Stalinization would spell a relaxation of Soviet control over their nations. In Poland, worker strikes against wage cuts expanded into demands for political change in 1956, and the Soviets threatened to intervene. Nevertheless, Poland's Communist Party elected the moderate Wladyslaw Gomulka (1905–1982) instead of the Soviet candidate. Gomulka refused to cave in to Soviet demands but promised military loyalty. A compromise left Poland within the Soviet sphere of control while enjoying some new levels of economic and cultural independence—including increased toleration of the Roman Catholic Church.

Protests and uprisings in Eastern Europe

Next, Hungarians issued a challenging demand for independence. When Hungary's communist leaders called on troops to put down protesters in the streets, the troops refused to fire and instead switched sides. A new government under the reforming communist Imre Nagy (1896–1958) initiated major economic and political reforms that included the introduction of a multiparty system. Nagy even proposed to withdraw

■ FIGURE 25.4
The Berlin Wall.

Hungary from the Warsaw Pact—Moscow's military alliance with its Eastern European satellites. The Hungarians had crossed the line. The Soviets sent in tanks and troops, slaughtering thousands and forcing hundreds of thousands to flee to the West. Nagy was hanged, and the lesson was made crystal clear: Cooperate with Moscow or pay the highest penalty.

In 1961, relations between East and West hit a new low. Under orders from Khrushchev, the East German government erected a 100-mile, heavily armed wall in Berlin to keep its citizens from fleeing to the West. Berlin had served as an escape route for 2.6 million people, especially professionals and the well educated who sought a higher standard of living in Western Europe. Figure 25.4 shows the **Berlin Wall,** topped by barbed wire, as it curves around the historic Brandenburg Gate. To the left is East Berlin. Between the wall and a wire fence is the lane where guards were ordered to shoot anyone trying to flee to the West. The wall graphically marked the division of Germany and symbolized the hostility between Western and Eastern Europe.

The Berlin Wall

In 1964, competitors within the Communist Party's Central Committee suddenly ousted Khrushchev, who had been weakened by foreign policy embarrassments such as the Cuban missile crisis, and installed the more conservative Leonid Brezhnev (1906–1982). The new Soviet leader took a firm line in dealing with Soviet satellites in Eastern Europe. Most of these states posed no problem for him. East Germany, for example, closely followed the Soviet line while developing its industrial capacity, and it became the richest nation in Eastern Europe. Hungary remained tranquil, orienting its economy toward consumer goods, loosening state control, and introducing limited capitalistic practices at the local level.

Other satellite states caused conflict—none more than Czechoslovakia. In 1968, reformers gained control of the Czechoslovak Communist Party and replaced the country's Stalinist leader with Alexander Dubcek, who believed that communism could be made compatible with internal party democracy and personal freedom. In this **Prague Spring** uprising, the Dubcek government initiated economic decentralization, greater national independence, democratic reforms, and elimination of censorship—"socialism with a human face." The reforms gained enthusiastic support within Czechoslovakia, especially among optimistic students and intellectuals thirsting for free speech.

The Prague Spring

Like Hungary in 1956, Dubcek's reforms went too far for the USSR's comfort. Especially fearful that the Prague Spring could inspire similar movements throughout Eastern Europe, the Soviets sent in Warsaw Pact troops to reverse Dubcek's policies and halt Czechoslovakia's steps toward independence. Figure 25.5 shows Soviet tanks rumbling through Prague in August 1968. Czechoslovakian citizens stand on the sidewalks watching as the tanks overwhelm any potential resistance in the streets. Fire burns in the background, adding to this image of the Soviets using brute force to compel Czechoslovakia back into line. The Czechs reacted with passive resistance; they could do little more. The Soviets removed Dubcek and his liberal supporters from power, and Brezhnev established his "Doctrine": Soviet intervention is justified in order to ensure the survival of socialism in another state. The conservative Brezhnev would make sure that Eastern Europe, like the Soviet Union itself, would not stray too far from the tightly controlled communist path followed since the early post–World War II years.

■ FIGURE 25.5
Soviet tanks in Prague.

PARLIAMENTARY POLITICS AND PROSPERITY IN THE WESTERN DEMOCRACIES

Western European nations proceeded on a strikingly different course to recovery, dictated both by Cold War considerations and the internal histories of those societies. In 1945, most Western European nations quickly returned to prewar democratic forms of government, and political parties leaning toward the center of the political spectrum soon gained control. In some countries, one political party dominated for long stretches of time—the Christian Democrats reigned in West Germany for two decades, for example, and in Italy for four decades following World War II. In other countries, major parties alternated in power, as the Labor and Conservative parties did in Britain. Some governments lasted only months, as happened in France, though the same group of well-known politicians usually rotated into the high offices of new governments and worked with a stable bureaucracy that carried out policy.

Initially, communist parties also gained strength after the war, especially in France and Italy. In France, elections in 1945 resulted in a sweeping victory for parties of the Left, including the communists, as well as the retirement of the conservative general Charles de Gaulle, who had set up a government in Paris in 1944. In Italy, the communists also emerged from World War II strong. For decades, the Italian Communists would command 25 to 35 percent of the vote and win local elections. But after 1947, when the Cold War heated up, these communist parties in France, Italy, and elsewhere were systematically excluded from participation in national governments.

In the struggle to repair their broken economies, European nations benefited greatly from U.S. aid. Having emerged from the war the world's preeminent economic power, the U.S. pumped almost $13 billion of Marshall Plan aid into Western Europe between 1947 and 1952. More than a sense of humanity motivated the Americans. The economic aid also served U.S. Cold War interests by supporting anticommunist forces. The aid came with strings attached: international cooperation and freer trade by *U.S. aid and economic recovery* the recipients. By demanding these conditions, the U.S.—now producing more than half the world's industrial goods—gained unprecedented access to large European markets.

Europeans helped themselves as well. Drawing on lessons from the Great Depression, World War II, and the British economist John Maynard Keynes, governments adopted policies to dampen recessions by deficit spending ("priming the pump") and to counter inflation by tightening expenditures and interest rates. Several European states, from France to Norway, went even further by engaging in economic planning. This typically included nationalizing certain industries. In France, for example, major banking and insurance companies, coal mines, and gas and electrical utilities came under government control. In such countries, technocrats—bureaucrats with technological or scientific expertise—made economic decisions that were once the province of business owners or parliaments. Other nations avoided such extensive planning. West Germany, for example, broke up prewar corporate cartels instead and pressured labor and management to cooperate for industrial peace.

At the same time, most European nations created social programs to protect citizens from severe hardship and to promote social peace. These **welfare state** programs had roots in the late nineteenth century, when governments had begun taking responsibility for the inequities of capitalism. Concerned about declining population growth, Europeans also wanted to encourage women to have more children. In the years after World War II, many governments followed Sweden's early lead and initiated programs providing health-care benefits and family allowances as well as prenatal care, maternity benefits, child care, and nursery schooling.

The welfare state

Nowhere was the welfare state more dramatically introduced than in Britain. Having shared the toil and suffering of World War II under the effective governmental direction of the economy, British citizens believed that everyone should get a piece of the prosperity that they expected would follow the war. In 1945, they elected a Labor government under Clement Attlee (1883–1967). The new government soon nationalized about 20 percent of Britain's economy and initiated what some called "cradle-to-grave" social-welfare policies. All British citizens could now look to governmental support during times of need—whether those times involved raising children, suffering job loss or accidents, paying for adequate housing, or ensuring adequate resources for retirement. Above all, Britain's National Health Service guaranteed free medical care to all.

Scandinavian countries continued to lead, going the furthest in ensuring a decent standard of living for everyone in both good times and bad. By contrast, the Americans swam against the tide. Prosperous, with its high-spending military in close alliance with big business, the United States strenuously resisted programs smacking of socialism. Not until the 1960s did it pursue moderate social reform, such as new educational programs, low-income housing projects, and limited governmental support of medical services.

Of course, all social programs came at a price. Taxes rose, particularly for the middle and upper classes, and government bureaucracies ballooned. Moreover, critics questioned the quality of the services provided, particularly medical care. Yet once established, most social programs served enough people and gained sufficient political backing to become permanent fixtures.

The nations of Western Europe recognized that cooperation offered the best hope for competing economically in a world of superpowers. Encouraged by the Marshall Plan, these countries moved toward economic integration. In 1950, France and West Germany created the French-German Coal and Steel Authority to remove tariff barriers and manage coal and steel resources regionally. Jean Monnet (1888–1979), the architect of this organization, held high hopes: "If only the French could lose their fear of German industrial domination, then the greatest obstacle to a united Europe would be removed. . . . It could, in fact, become the germ of European unity." In 1952, the organization expanded into the European Coal and Steel Community with the addition of Italy, Belgium, Luxembourg, and the Netherlands. Five years later, these same six nations signed the Treaty of Rome establishing the **European Economic Community** (the EEC, also referred to as the Common Market). The treaty proposed to eliminate tariff barriers, cut restrictions on the flow of labor and capital, and integrate the economies of the member nations.

Beginning European economic integration

The Common Market ended tariff and immigration barriers ahead of schedule, and its member nations enjoyed increased trade, productivity, and industrial production. In 1967, the organization combined with other cooperative bodies to form the European Community (EC) to work toward even greater economic and political integration. As Document 25.2 indicates, optimistic supporters hoped that the European Community would make Western Europe an independent regional power that might economically and even politically challenge its superpower ally, the United States, as well as the opposing Soviet bloc in Eastern Europe.

ASSESSING THE PATHS TAKEN

Throughout Europe, early fears about how long reconstruction would take proved unfounded (see Figure 25.6). The Soviet and East European economies expanded after the war, though not as rapidly as Eastern Europeans expected or hoped. The Soviets applied advanced science, technology, and engineering to establish a strong industrial base, support a huge military, and build large urban projects. Some Eastern European nations, such as East Germany and Czechoslovakia, also developed extensive industrial bases and even outperformed the Soviets.

The Eastern-bloc nations

■ DOCUMENT 25.2

A Warning About the United States

By the mid-1960s, many Europeans sensed that the United States, although friendly, had grown overbearing in some ways. U.S. economic institutions, capital, and culture were invading Europe, even though Europe had recovered from the devastation of World War II. This sense was particularly strong in France, as evidenced by the following selection from Jean-Jacques Servan-Schreiber's The American Challenge. *This widely popular book was first published in 1967.* ■ **What** *does this document suggest about Europeans' perceptions of the United States?* ■ **How** *does Servan-Schreiber plan to confront the American challenge?*

Europeans can regain control over their destiny in this confrontation with the American challenge only by taking stock of themselves and, as we will now try to describe, by hard work and patience. What we must do is not so hard to explain, for the path of our counterattack can be clearly marked out.

1. Creation of large industrial units which are able both in size and management to compete with the American giants.

2. Carrying out "major operations" of advanced technology that will ensure an independent future for Europe.

3. At least a minimum of federal power to protect and promote European business.

4. Transforming the relationship between business, the university, and the government.

5. Broader and more intensive education for young people; specialized and continuing education for adults.

6. Finally, as the key to everything else, the liberation of imprisoned energies by a revolution in our methods of organization—a revolution to revitalize the elites and even relations between men. . . .

To build a powerful and independent Europe means strengthening the economic and political bonds of the Common Market. No single nation is strong enough to support efficient production in all areas of advanced technology, for the national framework is too narrow and cannot provide adequate markets for such products. Also, the growing diversification of these products demands a specialization that makes any attempt at national self-sufficiency virtually impossible. . . .

Our back is to the wall. We cannot have both economic self-sufficiency and economic growth. Either we build a common European industrial policy, or American industry will continue taking over the Common Market.

Source: J.J. Servan-Schreiber, *The American Challenge,* trans. Ronald Steel (New York: Atheneum House, 1969), pp. 153–154, 156.

Although communism stood for the end to class differences, some citizens within each nation were, in the words of British author George Orwell, "more equal" than others. Certainly the Communist Party elite and professionals enjoyed better services and a higher standard of living than everyone else. But all citizens gained access to education, free medical care, and job security under communism. Subsidies made their usually overcrowded housing inexpensive, and unemployment and abject poverty virtually disappeared.

Women participated fully in economic life in these nations, often outnumbering men in the labor force. Moreover, a majority of doctors and teachers were women. Far more women engaged in manual labor such as logging and heavy construction work than their counterparts did in the West. They also received family allowances, maternity benefits, and child-care support. Outside the higher levels of government, Soviet women gained widespread political representation in parliamentary bodies, especially in local government. Nevertheless, women's pay lagged behind men's and women usually remained responsible for traditional domestic duties.

But even with all these improvements, Eastern-bloc nations could not keep up with their citizens' growing desires for a higher standard of living and more independence. Eastern Europeans had relatively few choices in consumer goods, food, and housing. In satellite nations, longing for autonomy from the Soviet Union persisted. Within each nation, Soviet-backed regimes—for the most part dictatorships—labored under questions about their political legitimacy. For many people, a sense of isolation from the West and a stifling of free expression within their own societies dampened cultural life in those nations.

In the capitalist democracies of Western Europe, government spending and welfare-state programs, as well as U.S. aid, fueled a strong revival (see Figure 25.6). Europeans used this money, their growing store of new technology, and their skilled workforce to **Western Europe** rebuild factories and transportation networks into models of efficiency. Falling tariff barriers and a population enlarged by increased birthrates created new demand for consumer goods. Food and clothing prices declined, jobs abounded, and wages rose. By 1955, the standard of living for even those in the bottom half of society rose. In just a decade, Western Europe had recovered fully from the economic devastation of the war.

During the 1960s, some Western European nations achieved unimagined levels of prosperity. West

Country	1938	1953	1963	1980
Britain	181	258	330	441
France	74	98	194	362
Germany	214	224	416	747
West Germany		180	330	590
East Germany		44	86	157
Italy	46	71	150	319
Poland	19	31	66	169
Sweden	21	28	48	83
Soviet Union	152	328	760	1630

■ FIGURE 25.6

European industrial production, 1938–1980.
Figures are a percentage of British industrial output in 1900.

Germany, Switzerland, and Sweden became the wealthiest nations in Europe. People in northern Italy spoke of their own "economic miracle." On the other hand, areas farther south still wedded to more traditional agricultural economies lagged behind, and once-mighty Britain—reeling from the loss of overseas trade and investments, and hampered by the antiquated state of most of its mines and factories—suffered a relative decline.

Overall, however, Western Europe took on the look and substance of wealth. Industries such as electronics, automobiles, plastics, petroleum, prefabricated housing, and airlines flourished. Newly restored city centers attracted hordes of shoppers, suburban commuters, tourists, and pedestrians. The number of cars on Europe's streets jumped tenfold from fewer than five million in 1945 to over 50 million by 1970. Stores overflowed with a cornucopia of foods and clothing. Electronic gadgets—from electric can openers to hand-held audiotape players—cropped up everywhere. The proliferation of restaurants, theaters, travel, and hotels reflected the affluence and the widespread standard of a forty-hour workweek and four weeks of paid vacation each year.

The good economic news outweighed almost everything else in Western Europe, and nothing helped its politicians more, for economic growth became the key measure of political success. Moreover, as observers and visitors looked at the paths to recovery taken in Eastern and Western Europe, the West's stunning prosperity clearly contrasted with the slower growth in the East. However, Western Europe also had problems that reflected its decline from the heights of power and certainty. Not only had these nations forfeited leadership to the United States, they lost their colonial empires as well.

THE TWILIGHT OF COLONIALISM

Even before World War II, national liberation movements around the globe had gathered momentum. When Germany defeated imperial nations such as France and the Netherlands, and Japan conquered Western holdings in Asia and the Pacific, Europe's control over its colonial territories weakened. The United Status further undermined the imperial powers by pushing them to dismantle their empires at war's end. At the same time, the Soviet Union continued to spread its decades-old denunciation of Western imperialism throughout the world. In the United Nations, sentiment grew toward the view that colonial "subjugation, domination and exploitation constitutes a denial of fundamental human rights." In the colonies, people seethed with anger against the Europeans. "Leave this Europe where they are never done talking of Man, yet murder men everywhere they find them," wrote the French West Indian philosopher Frantz Fanon (1925–1961) in his widely read book *The Wretched of the Earth.* "For centuries they have stifled almost the whole of humanity. . . . Look at them today swaying between atomic and spiritual disintegration." The last emperor of Vietnam, Bao Dai, warned his French overlords about "this desire for independence which is in everyone's heart and which no human force can any longer restrain."

Despite the intensity of these sentiments, many European settlers felt they had lived in the colonies too long to cede control to the local populations. Several political leaders in Europe agreed with Winston Churchill's sentiments: "I did not become the king's first minister in order to preside over the liquidation of the British Empire." The French announced that "the attainment of 'self-government' in the colonies, even in the distant future, must be excluded." The struggle to end colonialism was on.

REVOLTS IN SOUTHERN ASIA

At the end of World War II, national liberation revolts threatened the huge British, Dutch, and French empires in southern Asia. Of the Western imperial powers, only the United States escaped direct embroilment in this revolt by granting independence to the Philippines in 1946.

In India, the world's second most populous country, Mohandas K. Gandhi (1869–1948) led the independence movement. Educated in Great Britain, this astute middle-class Hindu used passive resistance and civil disobedience rather than direct violence *India* to pressure British officials to grant Indian independence. In 1947, Britain's Labor government finally freed India, partitioned into the separate states of India and Pakistan because of growing political divisions between Hindus and Muslims. Great Britain also relinquished Ceylon (Sri Lanka), Burma (Myanmar), and Malaya.

Independence, however, did not end problems in this troubled region. Religious and national strife soon broke out between Hindu India and Muslim Pakistan. Gandhi tried to quell the hostilities, but a fanatical Hindu nationalist assassinated him in 1948. Open war between the two states erupted in 1949 over possession of the disputed state of Kashmir. The United Nations managed to stop the shooting but failed to resolve the dispute, which would simmer for decades. This conflict, as well as border clashes with China, persuaded India to accept military aid from both the United States and the Soviet Union. India and Pakistan also faced the huge tasks of unifying their populations—divided by languages, caste, and class—and helping their millions of poverty-stricken and illiterate citizens.

In the rich and populous Dutch East Indies, nationalist leaders had established underground organizations during the wartime Japanese occupation. These leaders now stepped in and declared independence when the invaders left. The Dutch resisted fiercely for four years before yielding control. In 1949, they finally recognized the Republic of Indonesia as an independent nation.

Indonesia

A similar but more painful pattern emerged in France's Asian empire after the Japanese left Indochina in 1945. As we have seen (p. 762), the popular Indochinese nationalists, led by Soviet-educated communist Ho Chi Minh (1890–1969), proclaimed the independent Democratic Republic of Vietnam. Heavy fighting between the French imperialists and communist nationalists ensued. In 1954, France finally admitted defeat, pulling out of Vietnam and freeing the neighboring countries of Laos and Cambodia.

Vietnam

CONFLICT IN THE MIDDLE EAST

In the Middle East, Britain had been the dominant imperial power since World War I. However, under pressure from nationalists who had agitated for full independence since the first decades of the twentieth century, the British relaxed their control in the years before World War II. At the end of the war, British influence remained strong in several states, but only Cyprus, Palestine, and the Suez Canal were still official British possessions. Moreover, Britain was making a pronounced bid for Arab friendship, and to that end helped to form the League of Arab States in 1945. Yet, the admission of tens of thousands of Jews into Palestine under the Balfour Declaration of 1917—a British promise to create a "national home" for Jews in Palestine—made Palestine a new trouble spot.

Palestine was the ancient home of the Jews—a people with a long history of being displaced by others. In the seventh century, the Islamic Arabs conquered Palestine and lived there until the twentieth century. In the late nineteenth century, a new movement—Zionism—emerged to restore Palestine as the national home for the Jews (see pp. 623–625). During the anti-Semitic persecutions of the Hitler era, Jewish refugees poured into Palestine and bought land, enraging the dispossessed Arabs. The British were caught between their obligations to the Arab nationalists in Palestine and the Jewish settlers eager to reclaim Palestine as their homeland.

Palestine

In 1948, the beleaguered British finally turned Palestine over to the United Nations. The Jews immediately proclaimed the State of Israel and accepted the boundary lines that the United Nations drew up dividing Palestine between the Jews and the Arabs. However, the League of Arab States protested this arrangement, and fighting broke out between the two sides. Although outnumbered, the well-organized Jewish forces held on. After a year, the United Nations brokered a truce. During the conflict, Israel had gained some territory and had expelled more than a half-million Palestinian Arabs. Most of these refugees, not welcomed by neighboring Arab states, settled in rough camps just outside Israel's new borders. The vigorous new nation, with financial help from abroad and a social-democratic government at home, began building modern cities and a strong economy. The Arab nations, however, refused to recognize Israel, and Palestine nationalists, without a country of their own, continued to conduct border raids on the fledgling nation. Conflicts stemming from the birth of the Israeli state would drag on for decades (see Map 25.5).

Israel founded

These conflicts only compounded the broader anti-Western sentiment percolating in the region, especially in nearby Egypt, where Britain still controlled the Suez Canal. In 1952, a military coup in Egypt brought the dynamic nationalist leader Gamel Abdul Nasser (1918–1970) to power. Although Nasser kept much political power for himself, he promised parliamentary institutions, drew up a constitution guaranteeing individual rights, and distributed land to the poorer peasantry. In 1956, when the United States refused to support his plans to develop the Egyptian economy, he seized the Suez Canal. As he saw it, control of the canal would not only enrich Egypt but would also symbolize Egypt's independence and Arab nationalism.

Egypt

Nasser's bold action provoked a military attack by Israel, Britain, and France. Cold War rivalries quickly came into play when the Soviet Union threatened to

THINKING ABOUT GEOGRAPHY

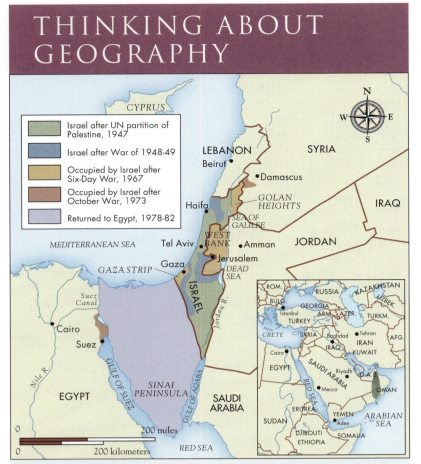

MAP 25.5 THE ARAB-ISRAELI CONFLICT, 1947–1982

This map shows some of the results of the various Arab-Israeli conflicts between 1947 and 1982. ■ **Consider** which states in the area might be most involved in these conflicts. **Who** gained the most and suffered the greatest losses of territory? **Why** might Jerusalem, the West Bank, and the Golan Heights be of such importance to the parties involved?

LIBERATING AFRICA

As in Asia and the Middle East, movements for national liberation stirred in Africa, where France and Britain held the most territory. France faced its greatest challenge in North Africa, where the largely Islamic population seethed with

The French in North Africa

nationalistic unrest. In the face of this growing force, France granted independence to Morocco and Tunisia in 1956 but drew the line at Algeria. The imperial power had held Algeria for over a century and considered it part of France rather than just a colony. In addition, more than a million French settlers lived there. They feared loss of property and reprisals from the eight million Islamic Algerians in the case of France's withdrawal. Complicating matters, the French military was determined to hold Algeria so as to repair the damage that France's reputation had sustained in Vietnam. At the same time, Arab nationalists living in Algeria believed that, with enough resolve, they just might oust the colonialist regime.

A long, bloody stalemate resulted. As one French soldier noted, "There's this staggering fact: The entire Arab population is joining the resistance against us." When the French government eventually showed a willingness to compromise, disgruntled colonial army officers threatened to overthrow the government in Paris. In 1958, as France's government teetered on the verge of collapse, retired general Charles de Gaulle was recalled to power. The World War II hero alone had the stature and legitimacy to negotiate with the forces of Arab nationalism. He granted Algeria independence in 1962, and freed almost all the other remaining French colonies.

Britain experienced similar challenges to its authority in its African colonies. The Labor government tried to prepare for the gradual freeing of British territories by sharing power with Africans in the civil service and bolstering funds for educational and economic

Britain dismantles its empire

development. The experience with Nasser in Egypt and a rebellion in Kenya from 1951 to 1956 finally persuaded the British to hasten their departure from

intervene on the side of Egypt. At this point, the United States pressured the three invading powers to retreat. Though defeated militarily, Nasser ended up a national hero and the leader of the Arab world for standing up to Israel and the Western powers. Moreover, Britain lost the canal and soon its last holdings in the Middle East, and the Soviets gained influence in the region.

When war broke out again in 1967 and 1973—between Egypt (with its Arab allies) and Israel—the Soviet Union and the United States rushed billions more dollars of arms and advisors to their respective allies. The area had become another crucible of superpower competition that would continue to generate anti-Western resentment.

Africa. By 1965, Britain had formally dismantled its African empire.

Yet even with most imperialists gone, trouble still brewed on the African continent. Sizable white minorities living in Rhodesia and South Africa clung desperately to their power over black majorities. In Rhodesia, despite persist- *Rhodesia and South Africa* ent guerrilla attacks by angry members of the black majority, the exclusively white regime held on until 1980. In long-independent South Africa, the prosperous white minority held fast to its power over the nonwhite majority (see Global Connections). The white minority harshly suppressed the increasingly restless black majority and enforced **apartheid** (racial segregation). This policy earned the all-white South African government decades of heated protests from nonwhites and condemnation throughout the world. Only in the 1990s would the white government under F.W. de Klerk at last allow the popular African National Congress, headed by the venerated Nelson Mandela, to assume leadership. By then, all European powers had pulled out of Africa. As Map 25.6 shows, their departure ended Europe's domination of Africa and Asia.

Decolonization did not end Western influence in the non-Western world or bring peace and prosperity to the previously subject *The legacy of colonialism* peoples. Newly independent nations were often left with illogical borders drawn arbitrarily by nineteenth-century European imperialists, depleted economies, and internal political divisions that drew in Cold War agents from both sides to exploit the chaos. Especially in Africa, ethnic conflict sometimes flared up into bloody civil wars, such as in Nigeria where the Ibos in the eastern region attempted to secede and set up the independent Republic of Biafra. Because the newly freed countries—especially in Africa—were generally left without internally generated political institutions, instability, bloodshed, and rule by military strongmen often resulted. In southern and southeastern Asia, religious and political differences broke out into wars in the years after liberation. Growing but impoverished populations lived under the threat of hunger and in bad weather, starvation. Droughts, for example, in the huge sub-Saharan region of northern Africa during the 1970s, 1980s, and 1990s, brought famine and death to tens of thousands. Most former colonies remained "Third World" nations—relatively poor, supplying raw materials to industrialized nations and dependent on the wealthier countries' goods and aid. Interaction between Western and non-Western peoples had transformed life on both sides, and resentments nurtured by years of colonial suppression still lingered in many non-Western nations.

A SENSE OF RELATIVITY IN THOUGHT AND CULTURE

Decolonization forced Western Europeans to reevaluate themselves and their civilization. So did the rise of the United States and the Soviet Union as superpowers and the ensuing Cold War that quickly cast its shadow over the West and the world. In these decades of such accelerating change, thoughtful people struggled to understand and define their lives and the culture in which they lived. The idea of universal truths that had prevailed in earlier times gave way to a growing sense that truth was relative—to the individual, to time, and to place. Increasingly, intellectuals, scholars, and writers argued that values were defined by the cultures in which they arose, *Sartre and Camus* judgments stemmed from individual perceptions, and conclusions hinged on the evidence selected. In these subtle senses, the postwar decades stressed shifting meanings rather than certainties.

EXISTENTIALISM: RESPONSIBILITY AND DESPAIR

During the 1940s and 1950s, the philosophy of existentialism captured much attention in the West. Originating in an era marked by war, depression, mass death, and the decline of traditional standards of morality and religious beliefs, **existentialism** offered a stark interpretation of reality. France's Jean-Paul

KEY DATES

GLOBAL RELATIONS

1947	India gains independence
1948	Israel founded
1949	Indonesia gains independence
	Communist victory in China
1950–1953	Korean War
1954	France withdraws from Vietnam
1956	Egypt seizes the Suez Canal
1962	Algeria gains independence
1966	Mao's Cultural Revolution
1973	Oil crisis
1975	End of Vietnam War
1979	Invasion of Afghanistan

Apartheid in South Africa

CONSIDER

■ **Consider** *the nature of apartheid and its purposes.* **Notice** *the forces that brought an end to apartheid.*

In 1960, the United Nations formally recognized that "the people of the world ardently desire the end of colonialism in all its manifestations." Within a few years, most of Africa would be free from white control. However, events unfolded in a strikingly different way in South Africa. Marked by its unique history, that society still labored under "apartheid."

Since its virtual independence from Britain and unification in 1910, the Union of South Africa came increasingly under the political influence of Afrikaners. These whites traced their roots back to the seventeenth century, when their Dutch ancestors had established colonies in South Africa. They were committed to ensuring their own domination over black Africans. Meanwhile, as the political winds shifted, cheap labor, cheap energy, gold, diamonds, and governmental aid fueled the country's industrialization and urbanization.

These trends culminated in 1948 with the electoral victory of the radical Afrikaner National Party. Building on established policies, the party put into practice the officially sanctioned system of apartheid (which means "separation" in Afrikaans). Through apartheid, the National Party sought to rigidly segregate people by color in order to keep nonwhites (which included blacks, Indians, and people of mixed heritage) completely subordinated to whites. Apartheid dictated where people of different groups could live, work, and go to school. It determined whom people might marry and what lavatories they could use. After 1958, Afrikaner leader Hendrik Verwoerd created "grand apartheid," which sent black South Africans to live in a patchwork of small ethnic states. He claimed that the Bible justified this policy. "We have a very fine position in South Africa; we've got land, we've got a country and we are obliged by the love commandment to provide exactly the same to black people." However, grand apartheid kept more than 85 percent of the land in the hands of the white minority and treated blacks in white areas as "foreign" migrant workers.

The African National Congress (ANC), founded in 1912 by black Africans "for the purpose of creating national unity and defending our rights and privileges," actively opposed apartheid. The South African government severely repressed the ANC and other black activist groups. In 1962, government forces captured one of the ANC leaders, Nelson Mandela (1918–). At his first trial in 1963, Mandela proclaimed, "I have cherished the ideal of a democratic and free society in which all persons live together in harmony and with equal opportunities. . . . It is an ideal for which I am prepared to die." During his second trial, in 1964, Mandela cited the English Magna Carta and the American Bill of Rights in support of his cause. He also castigated the apartheid system: "The lack of human dignity experienced by Africans is the direct result of the policy of white supremacy." That year, Mandela was sentenced to life imprisonment. He soon became an internationally recognized symbol of the struggle to end apartheid; his image could be found in homes from Africa to Europe and the Americas.

For a while, repression by the white regime quelled most black protests. However, in 1976, an 18-month uprising initiated by black schoolchildren in Soweto further spread South Africa's worldwide reputation for heartless repression. In 1978, the United Nations imposed a mandatory arms embargo against South Africa in an effort to weaken the white regime. Over the years, nation after nation cut economic ties with the country.

In 1989, National Party leader F.W. de Klerk (1936–) became president of South Africa and began dismantling apartheid. Ultimately, however many forces destroyed apartheid. Demographic trends shifted the balance of power: Though population growth tripled under apartheid, the percentage of white people declined from 21 to 14. Moreover, black African opposition movements sapped the white government's energy. International isolation also weakened the regime, and, as de Klerk explained, "the decline and collapse of Communism in Eastern Europe and Russia put a new complexion on things." In 1990, de Klerk released Mandela from jail and legalized the ANC. De Klerk, Mandela, and others created a new constitution, ending white minority rule, and in 1994, South Africa held open elections. Sally Motlana, long an ANC activist, spoke for many about her new freedom: "I never dreamt that one day I would be sitting here with other human beings and regarded as a human being. For all those years I've been made to feel that I was not part of the human race." Voters resoundingly chose Mandela, making him the first black president of South Africa. Still vital and determined despite twenty-seven years of imprisonment, the new president proclaimed his nation "free at last."

Sartre (1905–1980) (see Figure 25.10) became the most influential proponent of this body of thought. In novels, plays, and philosophical works, Sartre argued that there is no meaning to existence, no universal right or wrong. As he saw it, individuals are born and simply exist. They must make their own decisions, define their own purpose and values, and take responsibility for their actions. "Man cannot escape from the sense of complete and profound responsibility . . . one ought always to ask oneself what would happen if everyone did as one is doing." In the end, according to Sartre, one simply dies without there being any philosophical meaning to death. The French writer Albert Camus (1913–1960) also popularized existentialism in novels and plays such as *The Stranger* (1942) and *The Plague* (1947). He stressed the plight

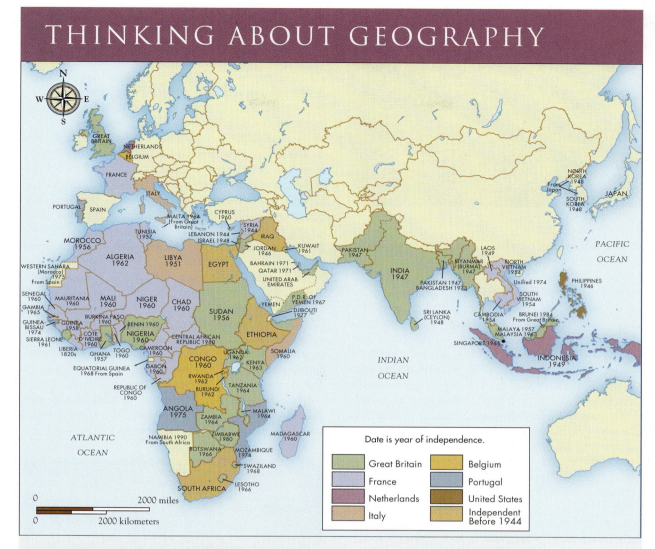

MAP 25.6 DECOLONIZATION

This map shows the colonial empires held by Western powers before World War II and the dates when the former colonies gained their independence. ■ **Consider** how decolonization diminished the political reach of Europe. ■ **Which** former colonies became particularly volatile zones of conflict? **How** might that be related to decolonization?

of the responsible individual seeking understanding and identity in an amoral, purposeless world.

The sense of despair that existentialist assumptions often engendered came forth graphically in the Theater of the Absurd, which dispensed with linear plots, definable action, and conventional sets and costumes. Samuel Beckett's (1906–1989) plays are good examples of this genre. In "Waiting for Godot" (1952), two tramps wait for someone who never arrives. There is no purpose in what they do, for people in this culture no longer shared a sense of meaning. In Beckett's "Endgame" (1958), one char-

Theater of the Absurd

acter adrift in a world out of control describes his situation: "All life long the same questions, the same answers." In this absurd life, all responsibility rested with individuals, who had to make their own choices and decide how best to use their time on Earth.

A CULTURE OF CONTRASTS AND CRITICISM

The uncertainty and relativity implied by existentialism emerged not only in theater but in other cultural forms. Writers, artists, and critics often disagreed with each other and with popular taste. In cinema,

■ FIGURE 25.7

Jackson Pollock, *Convergence*, 1952.

crowds. Figure 25.7 is one of Pollock's best-known works. Pollock explained why he avoided realistic representations of recognizable objects: "The modern artist is living in a mechanical age and we have a mechanical means of representing objects in nature such as the camera and photograph. The modern artist . . . is working and expressing an inner world . . . expressing his feelings rather than illustrating."

Pop art, with its images of everyday objects such as hamburgers in advertisements, also gained attention but bewildered audiences. Figure 25.8, by the American artist Andy Warhol (1928–1987), looks like nothing more than rows of soup cans. From another perspective, however, viewers might interpret it as an image of striking, colorful unity that reproaches our commercial, prepackaged society with its standardized tastes.

Such paintings sometimes drew popular ridicule. One American news magazine, *Time*, called Jackson Pollock "Jack the Dripper." On one level, this popular rejection of bold new artistic forms was nothing new. Indeed, artistic styles that were once unpopular and considered avant-garde or elite—such as nineteenth-century post-impressionism and the twentieth-century paintings of Pablo Picasso—now attracted admiring crowds.

A related, but more puzzling, pattern emerged in literature and music. For example, the "new novel," which consciously avoided clear plots and well-defined

a stream of what critics dismissed as undistinguished movies nevertheless poured forth year after year. Yet cinema was perhaps the most original art form produced during the twentieth century. In the late 1940s and 1950s, several thoughtful movies, such as *The Bicycle Thief* by Italian filmmaker Vittorio de Sica, stressed the realistic struggles of ordinary people. During the 1960s and 1970s, the works of filmmakers such as Ingmar Bergman in Sweden, Federico Fellini and Liliana Cavani in Italy, Jean-Luc Godard in France, and Stanley Kramer in the United States exemplified the potential of cinema as a sophisticated, creative, artistic medium. These films contrasted sharply with the flashy artificiality of innumerable Hollywood movies—although many Hollywood motion pictures did feature stunning re-creations of the past, finely honed acting, and a creative mix of lighting, sound, and special effects.

Many educators and commentators hoped that television would become a worthy cultural and educational medium as well. By the 1960s, people spent on average fifteen to thirty hours per week watching television. To be sure, numerous situation comedies, adventure shows, dramas, and game shows celebrated the joys, anguish, and pains of everyday life—as well as violence, romance, and fantasy. Yet most television critics were disappointed. Like radio and newspapers, television crossed lines between serious news, politics, and entertainment alike. TV had an especially powerful impact on politics. Politicians sought or purchased TV exposure, shortened and simplified their messages, and cultivated an image created with the help of media and advertising professionals.

In the more traditional cultural fields, a similar pattern of conflict over new works emerged. Some of the most critically acclaimed works seemed inaccessible to ordinary people. In art, abstract expressionistic paintings, such as those created by the American artist Jackson Pollock (1912–1956), who dripped paint onto canvases, drew attention but not

■ FIGURE 25.8

Andy Warhol, *100 Campbell Soup Cans*, 1962.

characters, gained critical acclaim but attracted little popular attention. Yet other, hard-to-categorize novels that critics praised just as heartily—for example, works by German author Günter Grass, French author Marguerite Duras, and British author Doris Lessing—won wide popularity. In music, the dissonant, atonal music of Arnold Schoenberg (1874–1951) garnered few fans compared with the hugely popular rock and roll, whereas jazz—a creation of African-American culture that emphasized sophisticated improvisation and rhythm—enjoyed a large following.

Literature and music

Perhaps cultural products and tastes, like the civilization they reflected, were changing too fast for most people. To be sure, many Westerners worried about the speed of and the forces behind cultural changes. In Europe especially, people talked about maintaining their own cultural tastes and identities in the face of "Americanization." They complained about the Hollywood movies, blue jeans, Coca-Cola, hamburgers, and fast food that poured from the United States into Europe. They also bemoaned the drain of intellectuals and artists moving to the United States. However, they could do little about the rapid spread of ideas, tastes, talent, and culture across political boundaries. Western Europeans found themselves losing the control they once had, and even the relative stability and prosperity gained in the 1950s and 1960s came under attack.

Americanization

Protests, Problems, and New Politics: The 1960s to the 1980s

As the two postwar decades came to a close, the course of history in the West shifted. Events in the 1970s and 1980s unfolded in a context similar to that of the earlier decades: Cold War competition led by the United States and the USSR. Each side represented different political and economic systems that divided Europe and much of the world. Each side also marched to the beat of economic growth—more rapid in the capitalist West than the communist East. However, within this same context, economic and political trouble was afoot. During the late 1960s and early 1970s, the road to social peace grew bumpy.

A Flurry of Social Protests and Movements

During these years, the gap between the ideals and realities of democracy, equality, and prosperity became more obvious and irritating than before. In some cases, unprecedented access to education fueled a growing awareness of this gap, while in others prosperity itself gave people the confidence to demand change. Often the well-publicized efforts of one group to force change inspired similar efforts by others. Protest movements frequently began in the United States and attracted close attention throughout the West. These dissatisfied groups voiced their demands with an assertiveness that shook several Western societies and even threatened governments.

The first of the great social movements began in the United States during the 1950s. There, African Americans initiated the civil rights movement, which inspired several other protest and liberation efforts in the West. The civil rights movement stemmed from America's long failure to integrate its large black population. African-American veterans returning from World War II felt particularly frustrated with the discrimination they again faced at home.

The civil rights movement

In 1954, the Supreme Court took a major step in the fight against discrimination by outlawing racial segregation in public schools. "Separate educational facilities are inherently unequal," the court concluded. A year later, a quiet act by a courageous individual set a series of additional changes in motion. A black civil rights activist, Rosa Parks, took a seat in the white-only section of a bus in Montgomery, Alabama. A year-long boycott of segregated public transportation by African Americans in Montgomery followed, the first of many mass actions throughout the U.S. in the 1950s and 1960s.

White resistance to the black struggle for equality flared up in the American South, and more than once the federal government had to send troops and marshals there to overcome white resistance. White opposition also mounted in the large industrial cities of the North. Many whites fled to the suburbs to avoid integration. In 1964 and 1965, Congress passed a series of civil rights acts that guaranteed voting rights for all and broadly outlawed racial discrimination. Still, the turmoil continued. Racially charged riots broke out in major cities. The violence reached a climax in 1968 following the murder of Martin Luther King, Jr. (1929–1968), the prominent African-American leader.

In the face of growing opposition and divisions within its own ranks, the civil rights movement lost steam in the 1970s, but not before inspiring other groups such as Spanish-speaking Americans, Native Americans, young people, and women. The protests by youths became especially threatening. Like the civil rights movement, these protests began in the United States. Soon, however, they spread throughout the West.

College students, whose numbers in the West more than tripled during the 1950s and 1960s, created movements of their own. The sheer mass of this first postwar generation of students and the emergence

Student movements

■ DOCUMENT 25.3

An Oxford Student Explains Revolutionary Attitudes

The period between the mid-1960s and early 1970s was marked by intense political, social, and revolutionary activism. Perhaps most striking, university students throughout the West organized radical attacks on the status quo. The following selection by Tariq Ali, a student at Oxford and a leading revolutionary socialist, demonstrates the more extreme attitudes among these activists. ■ *In what ways are Ali's views revolutionary?* ■ *What developments of the 1960s does his analysis reflect?*

What is absolutely clear is that the revolutionary movement is in a period of upswing throughout the world. The war in Vietnam, the events of May 1968 in France and the invasion of Czechoslovakia symbolize this upswing. Vietnam is at the moment the battle-front against imperialism. France showed the extreme vulnerability of monopoly capitalism and the strength of the working class. Czechoslovakia has initiated the struggle for political revolutions in Eastern Europe and the Soviet Union itself. . . .

Those of us who form the hard core of today's new revolutionaries are still Marxists, but we abhor Stalinism; we believe in Leninism but prefer the emphasis to be upon 'democracy' rather than 'centralism';

we are Guevarist but can appreciate and analyse the mistakes made by Che. We are puzzled by the tendency among many Left factions in the developed countries to devote as much time and energy to attacking each other as to attacking capitalism. The new revolutionaries fight against sectarian tendencies. And what is most important of all, we are not to be bought off by the State. WE mean business.

Source: Tariq Ali, *The New Revolutionaries* (New York: William Morrow, 1969), pp. 314–315.

---

of a separate youth culture helped give these young people an acute sense of their own power. The civil rights movement and growing opposition to the Vietnam War provided causes and experiences for many. In 1964, students at the University of California at Berkeley attacked the restrictive values, social inequities, and competitive impersonality of the university and the traditional society it represented. Many found support in the writings of well-known social theorists such as Herbert Marcuse (1898–1979), who criticized modern Western society as too restrictive and overly commercialized. Students also decried racism, poverty, and the growing American participation in the Vietnam War. Sometimes the protests turned into riots when authorities used force. Similar demonstrations soon boiled up across the United States.

In 1968, the unrest spread to the campuses and streets of capitals from Tokyo and Mexico City to London, Amsterdam, Milan, and Berlin. Even in Eastern Europe—especially in Czechoslovakia— youthful protesters added to dissident movements demanding social change and political democratization. "We are intensely aware, in a way perhaps not possible for the older generation, that humanity stands on the edge of a new era," declared students at the University of British Columbia in Canada. Document 25.3 reveals the views of some of the radical student groups. The most dramatic confrontations took place in Paris—the "Days of May" uprisings. Fed up with the rigid, overcrowded university system and fearing that many would miss out on France's new prosperity after graduation, Parisian

students rampaged through the streets of the French capital. Charles de Gaulle, president of France since 1958, met the demonstrators with police repression. The students then gained the support of sympathetic workers, who in turn demanded higher wages and an end to police brutality. This alliance between students and workers paralyzed France and even threatened to overturn the government. But the danger was short-lived. Agreements to raise wages appeased workers and siphoned them off from the movement, and the government once more regained control. However, the protests provoked major reforms in higher education and probably played a role in de Gaulle's resignation a year later.

Like the civil rights movement, student activism waned in the 1970s. As universities adopted reforms that met many of the protesters' demands and the war in Vietnam came to an end, the sparks of protest faded. Among women, however, an international feminist movement was still gaining momentum.

Although feminism had a lengthy history in the West, the traditionally defined domestic role of women still had not changed much, even as late as the *The women's liberation movement* 1950s. In 1956, a London journalist wrote, "Today, the spirit of the old pioneers [of feminism] is so dead it seems a miracle it ever existed." In most Western nations, the dominant message from pulpits, welfare offices, doctors, and governmental officials was the same: Women should stay at home and serve as the anchor of the family, defining their social identity through their husband and focusing on raising children. But that age-old message increasingly came under attack as women gained access to higher education, experience in various protest and liberation movements, and greater awareness of the social restrictions on their lives.

One key to this increasing awareness came from new books. In 1949, the French writer Simone de Beauvoir (1908–1986) (see Biography) published *The Second Sex*, the century's most pivotal analysis of the condition of women. In this powerful book, de Beauvoir uncovered the myths that had relegated women to second-class status relative to men. "There is an absolute human type, the masculine . . . He is the Subject, . . . she is the Other." De Beauvoir argued that women remained in cultural and economic dependence to men and therefore did not live as free human beings. The passive role assigned to women, she explained, forced them to live according to standards set up by men. De Beauvoir recommended a difficult, but rewarding role for women: a life of work, self-definition, and independence.

The Second Sex became the fundamental text for feminist movements in the 1960s. Other writers, such as the American Betty Friedan, popularized de Beauvoir's ideas and added to them. In her widely read book *The Feminine Mystique* (1963), Friedan urged women to escape the confines of home, go back to school, get new careers, and become more independent.

These ideas struck a chord, especially among many middle-class women. Increasing life expectancy and fewer children meant that more of these women than ever were living longer and devoting less of their lives to raising a family. They now had the time and resources to seek fulfillment outside the home—if they could find a way to break down traditional barriers. As more women enrolled in universities and pursued careers, discrimination against them on the job because of their gender only heightened their sense of injustice and outrage.

Starting in the late 1960s, women in several Western nations founded organizations, conducted marches, held rallies, started journals, opened feminist bookstores, and pressured officials to recognize their needs. Figure 25.9 shows one of many demonstrations. Women—many in slacks and jeans rather than traditional dresses—along with a few supportive men march through the streets of Paris. Carrying banners, signs, and balloons, they announce their purposes—equal pay with men for equal work—and unity. In 1969, an English women's group described the essence of the women's liberation movement: "We are economically oppressed: In jobs we do full work for half pay, in the home we do unpaid work full time. We are commercially exploited by advertisements, television and the press; legally we often have only the status of children. We are brought up to feel inadequate,

■ FIGURE 25.9

The women's movement in France.

educated to narrower horizons than men. This is our specific oppression as women. It is as women that we are, therefore, organizing."

Such efforts inspired a barrage of specific demands, including full citizenship in the political arena, equitable wages, and access to new careers. Despite opposition from conservative and religious groups, women pushed controversial issues such as day care, maternal leave, legalized abortion, and liberalized divorce into the spotlight of public discourse. They also protested stereotypical portrayals of femininity and widespread assumptions—among women and men alike—that raised the barriers facing them. Finally, they persuaded universities to introduce women's studies programs and prompted scholars in numerous academic disciplines to include feminist perspectives in their books.

By the early 1980s, the sharp edge of women's movements had dulled, but many long-term victories were already theirs. Women had gained greater control over fertility and sexuality from governments, churches, and male-dominated medical establishments. Moreover, lesbians demanded and received some recognition of their rights. As French author Monique Wittig noted in 1979, without feminism, lesbian culture and society "would still be as secret as they have always been." More women than ever flocked to universities, began careers in law, medicine, education, government, and business, and won political office. "Every girl now thinks in terms of a job. This is progress," said one Swedish vocational counselor. "They don't intend to be housewives for some future husband."

STAGNANT GROWTH AND RISING INFLATION

While the protest movements inspired optimism among their proponents and anger among conservative opponents, disturbing economic developments

BIOGRAPHY

Simone de Beauvoir (1908–1986)

CONSIDER

■ **Consider** what de Beauvoir's life reveals about the position and role of intellectuals during the twentieth century.

Simone de Beauvoir was born in 1908 to a devoutly Catholic mother and an intellectual father who practiced law. Later, after rebelling against her family's middle-class values, Simone wrote that her mother "held dear all those bourgeois, Catholic, pious, well-thinking ideas which I was learning to detest," while her father gave her "a taste for the intellectual life." World War I ruined the family financially. Realizing that she needed to support herself, de Beauvoir went to college. Reforms in 1924 gave women new access to higher education, and de Beauvoir, a brilliant student, seized the opportunity.

In 1929, while completing her degree in philosophy at the Sorbonne, Simone met and fell in love with Jean-Paul Sartre—a dazzling speaker and leader of a circle of rebellious intellectuals. "What is unique between Simone de Beauvoir and me," Sartre would later say, "is the equality of our relationship." The two vowed that "neither of us would conceal anything from the other." De Beauvoir had already concluded that "bourgeois marriage is an unnatural institution . . . that doubles one's domestic responsibilities, and, indeed all one's social chores." Neither did she want children: "I was too self-sufficient."

Through the 1930s, the couple's teaching careers in various parts of France kept them apart. De Beauvoir admitted that she and Sartre avoided getting involved in politics until 1939 when "history took hold of me and never let go thereafter." When the Germans invaded France the following year, de Beauvoir fled Paris along with thousands of others. Shortly thereafter, the Germans captured and imprisoned Sartre. Freed in 1942, he joined de Beauvoir, who had returned to Paris.

In 1944, de Beauvoir became a full-time writer. By then she had already published the successful novel, *She Came to Stay* (1943), in which she discussed connections between personal life and existentialism—the philosophy she, Sartre, and their intellectual circle often discussed. Sartre had also published numerous well-received works. In 1946, the couple founded and edited the influential review, *Les Temps Moderne*. Between 1946 and 1949, de Beauvoir researched and wrote her thousand-page study

Intellectual and Feminist

of women, *The Second Sex* (1949). By this time, de Beauvoir and Sartre had become France's—and perhaps the West's—leading intellectual couple (see Figure 25.10).

During the 1960s, de Beauvoir rejected formal participation in feminist groups, believing instead that socialism would lead women and men alike to full liberation. In the 1970s, disillusioned with socialism and impressed with the strength of the feminist movement, she changed her mind. She served as president of the French League of Women's Rights and editor of feminist journals and remained active in the feminist cause for the rest of her life.

In 1980, Sartre died. Their 50-year relationship was not idyllic. Both had lovers, and their relationship was not equal. Much of the time, the companionship of Sartre and de Beauvoir had more of a verbal than physical intimacy. "That was why it lasted so long," said de Beauvoir just weeks before her own death in 1986.

■ FIGURE 25.10

Jean-Paul Sartre and Simone de Beauvoir.

---

spawned worry and doubt. A new phenomenon that became known as "stagflation"—stagnant economic growth paired with rising inflation—spread in the West. The main culprit was oil and its central role in providing cheap energy for the Western economy. During the 1950s and 1960s, Western interests had kept oil prices low by expanding production and discouraging oil-producing countries in the Middle East, Africa, and South America from presenting a united front to raise prices. The low prices encouraged many users of coal to switch to oil and helped control inflation.

In 1973, a war broke out in the Middle East between Israel and its Arab opponents. Middle Eastern oil-producing states, now organized into the Arab-dominated **Organization of Petroleum Exporting**

Countries (OPEC), began to punish the West for supporting Israel in this conflict. As they limited production and increased prices, the cost of oil rose sixfold between 1973 and 1975. Prices again surged in 1979, spurring global inflation that particularly distressed the poorer nations of Asia and Africa and sent Western nations into a downward spiral of debt. Western economies, also facing disruptions in the international monetary system and growing competition from Japan, fell into recession.

The oil crisis

In Europe and the U.S., expectations of perpetual economic growth and limitless natural resources gave way to doubt. Indeed, the very forces that had brought prosperity for some threw others out of work. For example, the increased automation of industrial plants, the substitution of oil for coal, and the growing use of computers often eliminated more jobs than they created. The "green revolution" in agriculture boosted productivity but also forced people off the land and into the urban labor market. Equally alarming, large transnational corporations cut jobs as they moved their plants to regions offering cheap labor.

All these forces worsened unemployment, which by the early 1980s hit a whopping 10 percent and higher in many Western nations. In Britain—once an economic giant—unemployment stayed at more than 12 percent year after year through the 1980s.

Growing unemployment

Unions weakened, unable to protect workers in this perilous economic climate. The gap between rich and poor widened, and for many people—especially lower-wage earners—the economic good times seemed over. Least able to protect themselves were immigrant workers.

As is common during periods of economic uncertainty, wealthier nations turned against "outsiders." During the prosperity of the 1950s and 1960s, Western Europeans had opened their doors to desperate immigrants from southern Europe, Turkey, North Africa, and former colonies lured north by the promise of work. Immigrants filled the jobs that British, French, German, and Swiss workers passed over—the hardest, lowest-paid work in factories and fields, undesirable night shifts, street cleaning, and garbage collecting. Immigrant women were particularly vulnerable to exploitation in these jobs and in positions as domestics. Immigrant workers also labored under obligations to send money back home. Many, having heard myths about "lands of plenty," assumed that some day they would return home rich.

Turning against immigrants

In fact, officials often denied them social services and discouraged them from settling permanently. West Germany refused to grant citizenship to even those "immigrants" born in Germany. In the 1970s and 1980s, many governments, fearing worsening unemployment in their own countries, slammed the door shut against immigrants. The millions of foreign-born residents or "outsiders" who managed to arrive in the West increasingly suffered racial and anti-immigrant attacks.

THE NEW POLITICAL LANDSCAPE

Reacting to social movements and uneasy about their economic fate during the 1970s and 1980s, voters throughout the West turned to political parties that they had once ignored or even disdained. Socialists, who accommodated these voters by toning down their radical message, gained the most from this new development. In 1969, the Social Democrats in West Germany won control for the first time in almost fifty years. During the 1970s, under Willy Brandt (1913–1992) and Helmut Schmidt, they eased Cold War tensions by pursuing a policy of increased diplomatic and economic relations with Eastern Europe and the Soviet Union. By the late 1970s and early 1980s, Spain, Portugal, and Greece had also elected new Socialist governments that endured and led these nations into the European Common Market. In 1981, socialists under the leadership of François Mitterrand (1916–1996) came into power in France. They nationalized industries, shortened working hours, and enacted progressive social programs. However, persisting inflation and high unemployment soon led them to reverse some of these policies.

Turning to the Left

Communist parties in Western Europe also tried to adapt to voters' demands so as to garner popularity. In Italy, Spain, and France, the communists turned to "Eurocommunism," supporting more moderate policies and vowing to cooperate with other leftist parties. They even gave up the Soviet model and its call to worldwide revolution and promised to work within Western democratic institutions and economic systems that blended free enterprise and state planning. For a while during the late 1970s and early 1980s, communists gained strength in Italy and played roles in governments in Spain and France.

Britain turned the other way. In 1979, voters handed a sweeping victory to the Conservatives and their right-wing leader, Margaret Thatcher, Britain's first female prime minister. Thatcher initiated policies to diminish state control over the economy, crush union power, and cut spending for Britain's welfare state. Some state-owned and subsidized industries were "privatized"—sold to private enterprise. Thatcher also cut taxes on the wealthy, hoping to encourage investment and a "trickling down" of wealth to the rest of British society. Bitter strikes and urban riots by workers and the unemployed decrying her hard policies did not dissuade her.

Turning to the Right

Across the Atlantic, Thatcher found an ideological ally in Ronald Reagan, elected president of the United States in 1980. Reagan pursued similarly conservative policies, reversing some of the liberal social policies of the 1960s, moving against unions, privatizing governmental services, cutting taxes, increasing military spending, and reviving Cold War posturing against the Soviet Union. Thatcher's and Reagan's partially successful efforts in the 1980s to limit governmental spending on social programs marked the beginning of a gentle but broad turn toward conservative politics in the West.

Despite the changes, some groups still felt left out of politics. They demanded attention, even at the price of violence. In the 1970s and *Terrorism* 1980s, political terrorism spread across the West, conducted by groups such as the Red Brigades in Italy, the Red Army Faction in West Germany, and the Palestine Liberation Organization (PLO). Many of these groups had radical political goals. Others, such as the militant Basque separatists in Spain and the Kurdish rebels in Turkey, demanded national liberation. All desperately wanted recognition and had concluded that only assassinations, abductions, and bombings would achieve their aims. Terrorists killed several prominent Western businessmen and politicians. The most stunning of these incidents occurred in Italy, where in 1978 the Red Brigades murdered Aldo Moro (1916–1978), Italy's leading politician.

No area in Europe suffered more from terrorism than Northern Ireland. There the Roman Catholic minority struggled fiercely to gain equality with the Protestant majority. Many Roman Catholics demanded total separation from Britain and union with Ireland. The Provisional Wing of the Irish Republican Army (IRA) conducted a long campaign of terror to this end. As the Protestants fought fiercely to maintain their supremacy, violence begot even more violence. Hundreds on both sides died, and hopes for a harmonious solution sank.

Governments responded to terrorists, sometimes with violence and occasionally by making deals. Security measures increased, as did the presence of armed police, and occasionally governments were able to penetrate the urban anonymity of modern society to capture terrorists. For the most part, however, terrorism remained an exceptional means of protest that never gained enough support to threaten governments.

POSTINDUSTRIAL SOCIETY

The political fluctuations of the 1970s and 1980s reflected more than just economic ups and downs or politicians' efforts to garner popular support. Underlying many changes during this period was a fun-

damental development: The industrial societies of the West had begun transforming themselves into **postindustrial societies.** This term refers to a culmination of economic and social changes occurring in the West over several decades. Traditional manufacturing industries declined in importance as more competitive plants employing cheap labor opened outside of Europe and North America. In place of manufacturing, demand for financial, health, educational, informational, and consumer services mushroomed—all services at which the West excelled. Well-educated and handsomely paid professionals, managers, and financiers rose to prominent positions in corporations and government, joining or replacing property owners and entrepreneurs as key economic figures. The bulk of the middle class—most of them well educated and with white-collar jobs—also grew in number and wealth. Industrial workers saw their jobs disappearing while demand for service employees expanded. Yet many of these service employees, who seemed "white collar" or "middle class" in their appearance or lifestyle, made the same income or even less than blue-collar workers. Traditional class lines were blurring.

Changing Fortunes in the Postindustrial Society

Some people gained more than others in this mobile society. The gap between rich and poor may have narrowed between the 1940s and 1960s, but that gap remained formidable and even increased in the 1970s and 1980s. Only the growing numbers of married women entering the paid workforce maintained or improved most families' standard of living after the early 1970s. Nor did overall prosperity solve problems of economic discrimination. Women generally received only two-thirds to three-fourths of men's salaries for the same work. Minority and immigrant groups still occupied the most poorly paid jobs. In many Western cities, a core of impoverished slum dwellers remained. Often without regular jobs and marked by their race or ethnic origin, they suffered the worst problems of urban life.

For most people in postindustrial societies, however, material life improved. Housing mushroomed, in France alone increasing to a half-million new units per year during the 1970s. New apartments had distinct rooms—bedroom, kitchen, living room, bathroom—and were not just for the middle class. Most homes boasted running water, indoor toilets, a bath or shower, and heating as well as an array of appliances. In the 1980s, one Italian woman reflected in amazement how her children "have grown up in a world in which washing machine, refrigerator, vacuum cleaner, and television set are taken for granted."

Daily patterns of life also changed as more and more people lived and worked in different parts of the cities and their expanding suburbs. People commuted on crowded trains or by car through traffic jams. "I'm running, running . . . from home to bus, from bus to metro, bus again. Metro again. To work and back," complained a Soviet woman in 1969. The neighborhood cafes or pubs where people used to gather after work steadily lost customers, as did local, small stores where shoppers knew the merchants and each other. In their place, restaurants, supermarkets, and shopping malls sprang up, adding to the sense of urban anonymity.

The Baby Boom and the Booming Cities

Underlying the development of this postindustrial society were shifting populations that fueled economic growth and transformed patterns of life. Skyrocketing birthrates that had started during the war years led to the so-called **baby boom** soon after. An increase in life expectancy and the influx of immigrants added to the population growth. Europe's population, for example, increased from 264 million during the war to 320 million in the early 1970s. But the baby boom and the rapid jump in population did not last long.

By the 1960s, birthrates began to decline as people returned to the long-term pattern of choosing to have fewer children. In the 1970s, these rates fell to less than half the pre–World War II figures in some areas.

Fewer of those populations lived on farms anymore. By 1955, less than a quarter of the population worked in agriculture. Over the next thirty years, that figure would fall to below 10 percent almost everywhere. Thanks to mechanization, fertilizers, pesticides, new seeds, and larger farms, dwindling numbers of farmers produced more than enough for everyone else, as well as surpluses for export. Rural economies could no longer offer employment to more than a small minority of the population. Once the heart of Western civilization, rural areas became places that city people traveled through and nostalgically imagined. Small country towns dominated by church steeples tried to stay viable by attracting tourists, people wanting second homes, or small industries looking to relocate. With the spread of highways, telephones, televisions, and computers, rural life retained only a hint of the isolation that formerly distinguished it from city life.

As they had for decades, people left rural areas and small towns in droves and headed for the cities. These migrations spread well beyond national borders. Wealthy northern European cities absorbed waves of newcomers from southern Italy, Greece, Turkey, and Africa, just as cities in North America took in Latin Americans and Asians. These immigration trends added to the traditional urban problems of congestion, overburdened transportation systems, pollution, and crime. Large parts of great cities deteriorated while the surrounding suburbs, with their own industrial plants, corporate offices, apartment complexes, and housing projects, expanded. Despite these problems, cities and suburbs generally boasted more comfortable housing and working conditions than ever before.

The Shifting Foundations of Family and Private Life

Along with this movement of people and transformation of cities, the very foundations of family and private life within postindustrial society began to shift. After the baby boom years of the 1940s and 1950s, families became smaller as people, aided by more widely available birth-control devices, chose to limit births. Families also became less stable, as married people used changing attitudes and laws concerning divorce to break apart more often. Many people decided to put off or avoid marriage altogether. Increasing numbers of single parents and same-sex partners now headed households.

The old family structure, in which the man wielded authority, weakened and began to be replaced by a sense of the family as a democratic partnership of

■ FIGURE 25.11
Family watching television.

equals. Married women streamed out of their roles as housekeepers, child rearers, and supporters of their "breadwinning" husbands. They now took paying jobs outside the home not only for the income, but for the equality and independence that paid employment offered. Especially within the middle classes, work outside the home became a sign of emancipation for women. With these changes, some homes became zones of domestic cooperation; others witnessed new battles between couples over household chores and child rearing. Overall, however, the burdens of housework and child care still rested primarily with women.

The process of raising children also changed. Children spent more years than ever in school to acquire the skills needed to excel in the competitive postindustrial society, a shift that made them financially dependent on their parents into their late teens and even early twenties. With nursery schools becoming standard, children now started school at age three rather than age six. More than ever, the socialization, training, and career choices of youths were taking place outside the home.

Within the home, an individual's private life became no longer secondary to family life. Figure 25.11 presents the image of the small family together watching television. The television as much as the kitchen became a center of nightly family gatherings. But this image may also depict a decline of family interaction. Larger apartments and houses let family members spend more time than ever in separate rooms, coming together only for meals or TV watching. Much of home life became private, with individuals spending most time apart and alone rather than joining other family members.

Growing concern for private satisfactions

This growing concern for private satisfactions, which fit so well with the competitive economic individualism of postindustrial society, also played a role in the frequent separation of families. More often than ever, the ties holding marriages together began breaking apart. With love as the primary motive for marriage, the declining intensity of love that often occurs with time seemed enough to warrant divorce. As the sexual satisfaction of both partners became a core purpose of marriage, trouble in this domain also became a volatile source of discord and divorce.

Legal changes and statistics reflected these new realities. The grounds for divorce eased in most places to the point where mutual consent was enough. By the 1980s, between 25 and 50 percent of those who married would eventually get divorced. The old image of the breadwinning father, the homemaking wife, and the dependent children bonded together in a life-long relationship remained true for only a minority of the population.

THE "SEXUAL REVOLUTION" AND THE YOUTH CULTURE

Within or outside marriage, people gained new degrees of sexual freedom. Innovative methods of contraception, particularly the birth-control pill and the intrauterine device (and abortion, especially in Eastern Europe), achieved widespread acceptance in the 1960s and further separated sexual pleasure from reproduction. Manuals, sex education in schools, and the portrayal of sex in movies, books, magazines, and marketing materials became far more explicit than ever, reflecting the changing attitudes toward sex. Many conservative and religious groups strongly opposed these developments and the increase in premarital sex, though they were losing this battle by the 1970s. They also lost ground to gays, lesbians, and others who demanded respect and freedom.

Young men and women coming of age in the late 1950s and the 1960s, an era sometimes called "the sexual revolution," led these widespread changes in sexual values. Their clothing—flowered shirts and beads for men, blue jeans and mini skirts for women—and long hairstyles symbolized their new sexual freedom as well as the wider challenge of their youth culture to "the older generation."

Young people's taste in music and movies also announced a break between generations. In the United States, Elvis Presley led the explosion in rock and roll's popularity in the late 1950s. With his suggestive dancing, slicked back hair, and devoted following of young, screaming fans, Presley embodied eroticism and sexual abandon. The Beatles and other popular rock groups had a similar impact. Social dancing evolved from a carefully choreographed, chaste ritual to a no-holds-barred celebration of the body and sexuality. In popular movies, brooding, sullen young actors such as James Dean and Marlon Brando portrayed rebellious youths and became icons of the expanding youth culture.

BREAKTHROUGHS IN SCIENCE

The postindustrial society and the changing patterns of urban life that characterized it owed much to the many scientific breakthroughs of the period following World War II. More than ever, science became linked to economics and the needs of large institutions—from governments and industrial corporations to universities. These links were particularly strong in "big science." Before World War II, most scientific research was carried out by individuals or small groups of scientists in a university setting. The application of their discoveries by engineers and technicians came later. After the war, funds for scientific research poured in from government and big business, forming what some called the military-industrial-university complex. With the influx of money and interest, the number of scientists jumped fivefold between 1945 and 1985, and the fields they entered divided into more and more subspecialties. Organized teams of scientists, technicians, and managers worked in large research laboratories, using expensive equipment and aiming for specific goals. The results were stunning.

The rise of big science

FROM THE UNIVERSE ABOVE TO THE UNIVERSE WITHIN

Cold War competition especially fueled the massive effort to put satellites and humans into space. By the 1960s, satellites spun around the earth, providing a steady stream of military surveillance, weather observations, communications, and scientific information. The "space race" between the United States and the Soviet Union climaxed with a televised walk on the moon's surface in 1969. While taking his first step, the American astronaut Neil Armstrong spoke his now-famous words: "That's one small step for man, one giant leap for mankind." Figure 25.12 shows an American astronaut standing on the surface of the moon. One of the first things he did was to plant the United States flag and pose with it for a photograph. The image announced how daring and powerful the combination of government, science, and nationalism could be. Subsequent unmanned voyages carried spacecraft to planets throughout the solar system and beyond.

Government money funded other scientific and technological efforts as well. Teams of physicists used powerful particle accelerators to explore the subatomic world. From innovations in radar systems during World War II came microwave technology, which became central to the television and long-distance telephone industries. Work on the atomic bomb led to nuclear power plants.

Similar efforts by teams of scientists and individuals led to fundamental discoveries in fields such as genetics. In 1953, the structure of DNA, the material in chromosomes that contains hereditary information, was discovered. This implied that the characteristics of all living things, including humans, could be controlled, and it opened the controversial possibility of tampering with this molecule to create new forms of life. Research into gene splitting and genetic engineering would turn this possibility into reality. During the 1980s and 1990s, scientists introduced cloning—reproducing an organism from cells of that organism in a laboratory.

THE INFORMATION REVOLUTION

Much of the new scientific work depended on computers, which became the core of the "**information revolution.**" The computer first emerged in the 1940s as a tool for storing and manipulating information. Encouraged by business and government during the 1950s and 1960s, its scientific and economic impact widened. With miniaturization during the 1970s and 1980s, computers the size of a notebook could outpower their room-size predecessors. These new "personal computers" cropped up on desktops and in briefcases everywhere. Now most people involved in science, scholarship, and business relied on computers, and the new devices became the core of a booming, worldwide industry.

TRANSFORMING MEDICINE

In the decades after World War II, medicine also entered new territory—itself becoming a big business with strong links to science and economics. Long gone were the days of visits by horse-and-buggy doctors. Now most physicians saw patients in offices, clinics, and especially hospitals, which employed medical personnel working in coordinated teams with

■ FIGURE 25.12

Americans on the moon, 1969.

complex machines. The era of the family doctor also faded. Now patients consulted more prestigious specialists. Finally, doctors gained a new degree of power to battle medical problems. Whereas in earlier centuries physicians may have done more harm than good with their treatments, now medicine became a major lifesaver in the Western and non-Western world.

The keys to these changes were antibiotic drugs and vaccines. In the 1930s, researchers discovered that sulfa drugs could cure infectious diseases. Penicillin and other antibiotics soon followed. By the 1940s, once fatal illnesses such as meningitis and pneumonia could be cured by antibiotic drugs. Tuberculosis, a disease so deadly that it was called the "white plague," was almost eliminated by a vaccine and antibiotics. In 1977, smallpox was literally eradicated throughout the globe. The spotlight on medicine shifted from traditional infectious diseases to cancer, heart disease, arthritis, and AIDS.

New surgical techniques also offered more hope than in previous centuries. Antibiotics let surgeons perform lung and other operations that had been too risky before because of the danger of infection. By the 1960s, open heart surgery and heart bypass operations became almost routine. Then organ replacement—first kidneys and then even hearts—became possible. Dr. Jan H. Louw described the first successful human heart transplant in 1967 and the use of electric shock to start the transplanted heart: "It was like turning the ignition switch of a car." Surgery became more a process of continuous repair and replacement than cutting and removing.

Expensive new machines for diagnosis and treatment complemented all the new medical techniques. Ultrasound machines, CT scanners (which combined X rays with computer analysis), and MRI devices that used radio waves gave doctors a window into the body without having to open it up. Dialysis machines and pacemakers offered new hope to kidney and heart patients.

For those suffering from mental illnesses, effective medications emerged in the 1950s. Doctors prescribed a growing list of these psychotropic drugs for people with schizophrenic and manic-depressive conditions. Though the success of these drugs was far from complete, they contributed to the closing of many mental hospitals and asylums.

By the 1980s, medicine had become dominated by large hospitals, groups of doctors, insurance companies, and governmental agencies. Health "consumers" expected more and more from medicine—including "cures" for most ailments and what many saw as a right to live to retirement and a robust old age. Nations devoted more resources than ever to medicine—often more than 10 percent of the national income. Britain's minister of health once complained, "There is virtually no limit to the amount of health care an individual is capable of absorbing."

In several senses, then, the evolution of medicine since World War II reflected broader qualities of the era. Science, and especially "big science," enabled doctors to expand and even revolutionize the field. Medicine also relied on the overall prosperity and governmental support of those decades, which enabled people to demand, and the healthcare industry to provide, so many services. The very growth of this service industry as well as the high status and income enjoyed by its leading practitioners echoed the development of the postindustrial society, with its stress on services and technical expertise. Finally, like much else, Western medicine spilled across borders and into the non-Western world—though also in ways that highlighted the disparities of wealth between the Western and non-Western worlds and the conflicts that often arose when those different cultures met.

SUMMARY

The decades between 1945 and 1989 witnessed a quickening pace of change as more people than ever were drawn into the swirl of politics, economic development, and urban life. The Cold War, whose contours came into sharp focus after 1945, cast a pall over the entire era. Each side represented different paths to recovery after World War II and competitive ideologies that had their roots in the nineteenth century. Yet despite people's worst fears, the Cold War never ignited into an actual conflagration between the two superpowers. As we will see, it evaporated with surprising rapidity in the late 1980s.

During these decades, Western society became more technocratic, affluent, welfare-oriented, and culturally open—characteristics that also had first come to light at the end of the nineteenth century. Western Europe, in particular, managed this transformation despite ceding leadership to the United States and losing its colonial empires. Although Western Europe's status in the world declined, it remained a strikingly prosperous, dynamic region.

As the final decade of the twentieth century approached, the West as a whole remained powerful and was often envied abroad. At the same time, it had become clear that the Western powers could no longer act without taking into account the concerns, power, and problems of the non-Western world. Soon, stunning developments in Eastern Europe would mark 1989 as the dawn of a new historical era.

KEY TERMS

REVIEW, ANALYZE, AND ANTICIPATE

REVIEW THE PREVIOUS CHAPTER

Chapter 24—"Into the Fire Again"—analyzed the devastating war that encompassed the world.

1. *In what ways did World War II set the stage for the Cold War and the different paths followed by Western and Eastern Europe?*

2. *In what ways did World War II hasten decolonization in the following decades?*

ANALYZE THIS CHAPTER

Chapter 25—"Superpower Struggles and Global Transformations"—traces the Cold War competition between the United States and the Soviet Union. Within this context, the recovery of the West and the end of colonialism are examined.

1. *How did Cold War tensions influence international affairs in the Western and non-Western worlds?*

2. *In what ways did Western life during these decades represent a triumph of Western industrialization and political democracy? What sorts of problems persisted despite this triumph?*

3. *Compare and evaluate the two paths followed by Western and Eastern Europe during this period.*

4. *Evaluate the process of decolonization. What problems faced the newly independent nations of the non-Western world?*

ANTICIPATE THE NEXT CHAPTER

In Chapter 26—"Into the Twenty-First Century"—the collapse of communism and the intense interaction between the Western and non-Western worlds is examined.

1. *What forces developing in these decades might lead to the collapse of communism in Europe?*

2. *Which of the major developments during the decades between 1945 and the 1980s seem most relevant to today's world? Which seem like part of the already distant past? Why?*

BEYOND THE CLASSROOM

ORIGINS OF THE COLD WAR

Gaddis, John Lewis. *The Cold War: A New History.* New York: Penguin, 2005. A recent, authoritative history of the Cold War.

Hitchcock, William. *Struggle for Europe: The Turbulent History of a Divided Continent, 1945 to the Present.* New York: Knopf, 2004. A well-written survey of the period.

Patterson, Thomas G. *On Every Front: The Making and Unmaking of the Cold War.* New York: W.W. Norton, 1992. Analyzes both the domestic and foreign policy aspects of the Cold War.

EAST AND WEST: TWO PATHS TO RECOVERY IN EUROPE

Hosking, Geoffrey. *The First Socialist Society: A History of the Soviet Union from Within.* Cambridge, MA: Harvard University Press, 1990. A comprehensive history of the USSR from its origins to its demise.

Judt, Tony. *Postwar: A History of Europe Since 1945.* New York: Penguin, 2005. Excellent, extensive treatment of the period, emphasizing how post–World War II Europe dealt with its own past and modernization.

Rothschild, Joseph. *Return to Diversity: A Political History of East Central Europe Since World War II,* 2nd ed. New York: Oxford University Press, 1993. A history of states in this region that stresses the growing conflicts between nationalist ambitions and communist rule.

THE TWILIGHT OF COLONIALISM

Ansprenger, Franz. *The Dissolution of the Colonial Empires.* London: Routledge, 1989. Stresses the legacy of inequality and cells of poverty created by imperialism, but also asserts that imperialism helped to create a global economy.

Springhall, John. *Decolonization since 1945: The Collapse of European Empires.* London: Palgrave Macmillan, 2001. A good overview with colony by colony coverage.

A SENSE OF RELATIVITY IN THOUGHT AND CULTURE

Maltby, R., ed. *Passing Parade: A History of Popular Culture in the Twentieth Century.* New York: New Oxford Press, 1989. Excellent in its breadth of coverage.

Stromberg, Roland N. *After Everything: Western Intellectual History Since 1945.* New York: St. Martin's Press, 1986. An excellent survey of ideas and ideology in the postwar period.

GLOBAL CONNECTIONS

Maier, Karl. *Into the House of the Ancestors: Inside the New Africa.* New York: John Wiley and Sons, 1998. A balanced and well-supported account.

PROTESTS, PROBLEMS, AND NEW POLITICS: THE 1960s TO THE 1980s

Caute, David. *The Year of the Barricades: A Journey Through 1968.* New York: Harper & Row, 1988. Examines the revolutionary upheavals in a period called "year one" of the revolution.

de Beauvoir, Simone. *The Second Sex*. New York: Knopf, 1963. A classic and important examination of women's confinement to the periphery throughout history.

Lovenduski, Joni. *Women and European Politics: Contemporary Feminism and Public Policy*. Amherst, MA: University of Massachusetts Press, 1986. Compares the movement for women's liberation in the 1960s with previous women's movements.

Pulzer, Peter. *German Politics, 1945–1995*. Oxford: Oxford University Press, 1995. Examines both West and East Germany during the period and covers the process of reunification.

POSTINDUSTRIAL SOCIETY

Hoffman, Stanley, and Paschalis Kitromilides. *Culture and Society in Contemporary Europe*. London: Allen & Unwin, 1981. A wide-ranging, interpretative survey connecting cultural and social developments.

Ruggie, Mary. *The State and Working Women: A Comparative Study of Britain and Sweden*. Princeton, NJ: Princeton University Press, 1984. Compares the legislative and political events affecting women in Britain and Sweden.

BREAKTHROUGHS IN SCIENCE

Porter, Roy. *The Cambridge Illustrated History of Medicine*. Cambridge: Cambridge University Press, 1996. A well-written and well-illustrated survey by several noted scholars.

Ziman, John. *The Force of Knowledge: The Scientific Dimension of Society*. Cambridge: Cambridge University Press, 1976. A useful examination of connections between science and society during the postwar years.

www.mhhe.com/sherman3

• Unfamiliar words? See our Glossary at the back of the book for pronunciation and definitions.

• Need help studying? See our web page for map exercises, practice quizzes, and additional study resources.

• Need help writing a paper? Access hundreds of primary documents, maps, images, and a guide to writing history papers on our Primary Source Investigator site at **www.mhhe.com/psi.**

THE BERLIN WALL, NOVEMBER 1989

In November 1989, as revolutions swept Eastern Europe and ended the Cold War, Germans from East and West climbed over the Berlin Wall near the Brandenburg Gate. Demonstrators wrote "In the Name of the People" on the wall, crediting popular will for finally tearing down the decades-old barrier. By writing in English, they announced the importance of this historical event to the watching world.

CHAPTER 26

INTO THE TWENTY-FIRST CENTURY

THE PRESENT IN PERSPECTIVE

STUDY	The collapse of communism ▪ Realignments in the West ▪ The world and the West from a global perspective.
NOTICE	The consequences flowing from the fall of communism.

"The 20th century is now over." The historian John Lukacs made this announcement in a 1991 issue of the *New York Times*. By "20th century," Lukacs meant the 75-year era that began in 1914 and ended in 1989. The year 1914 marked the outbreak of World War I, which for most historians represented the beginning of the twentieth century. That conflict and World War II dominated the period. "The Russian Revolution, the atom bomb, the end of the colonial empires, the establishment of the Communist states, the emergence of the two superpowers, the division of Europe and of Germany—all of these were the consequences of the two world wars, in the shadow of which we were living, until now," wrote Lukacs. The year 1989 saw the nations of Eastern Europe break from their Soviet ties and from communism. In just two more years, the Soviet Union itself would fall apart.

Other developments, also with roots in the past, added to the sense that the world had just lived through the closing of one historical era and the opening of another. The movement toward economic integration in Western Europe, the growing strength of the newly unified Germany, and the changing position of the United States altered international relations. Beyond the West, the Pacific Rim—particularly East Asia—gained enormous economic clout. In the Islamic world, stretching from North Africa through the Middle East to Indonesia, mounting pressures posed a variety of threats to stability in those regions and beyond. From a global perspective, three regional power centers had emerged—Europe, North America, and East Asia. Almost everywhere, people, problems, cultures, and histories spilled across national borders, challenging those living in the Western and non-Western worlds to broaden their understanding of the world and their place in it.

TIMELINE: THE BIG PICTURE

● The Fall of Communism

The Cold War   ● German Reunification

● Disintegration of Soviet Union

Civil Wars in Former Yugoslavia

Growing Importance of Computers and "The Information Revolution"

Toward European Unification

| 1989 | 1990 | 1991 | 1995 | 1996 | 1997 | 1998 | 1999 | 2000 | 2004 | 2006 |

THE COLLAPSE OF COMMUNISM

OF ALL THESE DEVELOPMENTS, THE collapse of communism in the Soviet Union and Eastern Europe arguably had the most dramatic and far-reaching global impact. In a startling public announcement early in November 1989, East Germany's communist leader succumbed to months of growing pressure and ordered the Berlin Wall, the most powerful symbol of the Cold War, torn down. A reporter described the scene (see the photo on page 790): "Nearby, before the Brandenburg Gate . . . people climbed up onto the rim of the wall during the night of November 9 . . . taking pickaxes to it." Then the cranes and bulldozers came. "People stared unbelieving, as East German cranes lifted away the slabs of concrete. . . ." As the wall crumbled, another observer described the Berlin border crossings: "The streets were packed with people streaming past the East German border guards. . . . Cars from East Berlin slowed to a crawl alongside the crowds of West Berliners waiting just over the white stripe painted on the asphalt, cheering every car . . . handing cans of beer to the drivers." In those first heady days, millions of East Germans crossed the border, some to stay, others to return again and again "loaded down with full plastic shopping bags." The mayor of West Berlin declared, "This [is] the greatest historical event since the French Revolution."

Everywhere in Eastern Europe, communist governments were collapsing. The Soviet bloc, which had seemed so impenetrable, quickly dissolved. Soon the Soviet Union itself would break apart.

UNDERMINING COMMUNISM IN THE SOVIET UNION

What explains this massive historical reversal? The story begins in the Soviet Union where communist power was most firmly entrenched. During the two or three decades following World War II, the Soviet Union, like other communist nations, enjoyed economic growth and relative prosperity (see Chapter 25). The USSR boasted impressive factories and elaborate technical projects such as dams, railway systems, military hardware, and manned rockets. Rapid industrialization, which pulled peasants and women into the urban workforce by the millions, boosted productivity.

However, during the 1970s and 1980s, central planning and collectivization—the hallmarks of the Soviet economic system—failed to match new consumer demands. Keeping up with the rapidly changing, technologically sophisticated economy of the 1970s and 1980s required flexibility, a willingness to experiment with new production methods, and local decision making—all of which the Soviet economic system lacked. Instead, economic decisions came from high officials more sensitive to political pressures than economic realities. Central planners, pursuing out-of-date strategies or unaware of changes in grassroots needs, often ordered factories to produce goods that did not meet consumers' demands. Local plant managers, struggling to get needed materials and labor, suffered long delays while distant officials made decisions. Workers, their jobs guaranteed, had little incentive to work hard or even show up consistently. Similar problems plagued agriculture, where collectivization discouraged effective decision making and hard work. As the rate of economic growth declined, embarrassed Soviet planners had to import grain again and again from the capitalist West. Government leaders worried that the Soviet economy would never catch up with formidable capitalist competitors such as the United States, Germany, and Japan.

Problems with central planning

Worse, everyday dissatisfactions spread. Soviet workers had money but not the selection or quality of goods that they wanted and that they knew were available to people in the West. Instead, they regularly stood in lines for as long as two hours a day just to buy basic supplies.

Spreading dissatisfaction Even urban professionals, managers, and technicians, although relatively wealthy and well educated, experienced similar frustrations. Far too obviously, only a small corps of Communist Party officials and privileged elites enjoyed access to the most desirable goods and services in this supposedly egalitarian society, fueling resentment. For everyone else, the only alternative was the thriving, but expensive and illegal, black market. Faith in the communist system, even among members of the Communist Party, began to evaporate. "I'm not a good Party member because I don't believe in Communism . . . nor do a lot of Party members," admitted one 40-year-old Communist in 1990. "Joining the Party was for me entirely a calculated way of furthering my career."

Three pivotal developments during the late 1970s and 1980s exacerbated the problems undermining the Soviet brand of communism. First,

Growth of dissent the spread of modern communications broke down the old Stalinist policy of enforced isolation from the rest of the world and fueled the growing dissident movement. By watching television, people saw for themselves the material wealth enjoyed by Western nations. They also perceived the swirling cultural and intellectual currents that officials tried to stifle within the Soviet Union. Yet photocopiers and computers spread information easily, making censorship difficult. Privately published manuscripts criticizing Soviet life circulated among the educated elite. The dissident movement grew, led by the Nobel Prize-winning physicist Andrey Sakharov (1921–1989) and others. Dissidents demanded more democracy, greater civil liberties, and some independence for nationalities within the Soviet Union. Although such demands earned Sakharov and others exile, the dissident movement persisted. Moreover, among many people not yet ready to join the dissident movement, the increasingly obvious contradictions between the official party line and the harsh realities of Soviet life engendered cynicism and apathy.

Second, military and wartime expenditures increasingly burdened the Soviet economy. In the 1980s, the United States under President Ronald Reagan vigorously pursued the Cold War arms

Military burdens race, forcing the Soviets—with their fundamentally weaker economy—to struggle to keep up. At the same time, the 1979 Soviet invasion of Afghanistan turned into a costly military quagmire. The widely condemned conflict wore on for years, straining the USSR's economy and diminishing the Soviet leadership's popularity.

Third, the quality of the Soviet leadership declined in the 1970s and 1980s. Leonid Brezhnev weakened noticeably and repeatedly fell ill in the seven years before his death in 1982. Most of his colleagues were long established in their offices. Brezhnev's immediate successors, **Declining leadership** Yuri Andropov (1982–1984) and Konstantin Chernenko (1984–1985), each died shortly after assuming office. These older men were reluctant to alter the USSR's course or to make way for a younger generation of reformers. But in 1985, a new leader—Mikhail Gorbachev—was appointed head of the Soviet Union. Just 54 years old, he had very different ideas about how the Soviet Union should operate.

GORBACHEV LAUNCHES REFORMS

Born into a peasant family, Mikhail Gorbachev studied law as a youth at the University of Moscow. He moved rapidly up through the Communist Party ranks, eventually taking responsibility for agricultural policy. Charming and astute, he became a capable manipulator of people and events. Britain's prime minister Margaret Thatcher recognized him as a man "with whom we can do business." Gorbachev also had bold plans to lead the Soviet Union in new directions. Soon after assuming power in 1985, he replaced a third of the old party leadership with new supporters. By then, he shared the views of reformers who recognized the fundamental economic problems plaguing the Soviet Union. In his willingness to grapple with problems, Gorbachev echoed Khrushchev's attack on Stalinism some thirty years earlier. Nevertheless, he had no intention of loosening the party's hold on power.

Gorbachev embarked on a three-pronged policy: *perestroika* ("restructuring"), *glasnost* ("openness" to discussion), and disarmament. All three were intended to bring the Soviet economy up to the standard of Western capitalist societies. No one—not even Gorbachev— **Perestroika** imagined the consequences that would flow from these daring reforms.

Perestroika involved a thorough restructuring of the Soviet economy. The program's goals included decentralizing planning, allowing market forces rather than officials to set prices, and putting control of land and agricultural practices into the hands of families and cooperatives rather than large state farms. In short, *perestroika* would create a mixed economy featuring a blend of socialist planning and a capitalist, free market. Gorbachev knew that the transformation would take time and cause short-term pain, including further shortages of consumer goods, inflation, and unemployment. To gather the political backing and the financial resources he needed to carry out the program, he initiated *glasnost* and an arms-reduction plan.

Glasnost curtailed censorship, encouraged freer discussion of everything from culture to politics, and

Glasnost

opened the doors to the partial democratization of the Communist Party and the Soviet political system. Officials freed dissidents such as Andrey Sakharov. Some governmental proceedings were made visible to the public and even televised. In the spring of 1989, the government held the first open elections since 1917, which resulted in the defeat of numerous communist dignitaries. Gorbachev hoped that *glasnost* would elevate his prestige internationally, win him foreign political and financial support, and inspire intellectuals and workers at home to accept his bold restructuring of the Soviet economy.

His arms-reduction plan served the same ends. In meetings with U.S. presidents almost every year

Arms reduction

between 1985 and 1991, Gorbachev pushed for more and more reductions in both countries' military stockpiles. These meetings bore fruit: Both the USSR and the U.S. agreed to limit nuclear weapons and conventional forces not only on their own soil but also in Europe. At the same time, Gorbachev tried to extract Soviet forces from the war in Afghanistan. The effort took four years, but in 1989 the last Soviet troops finally came home. These feats burnished Gorbachev's reputation at home and abroad and promised to ease the USSR's heavy burden of military expenditures.

Figure 26.1 shows Gorbachev, at the height of his popularity, standing next to his wife. On this visit to Prague, he reaches out to greet people in the crowd. Czechoslovakian officials, including the nation's president, Gustav Husak (just behind Gorbachev), smile and seem to back him up. Gorbachev made many visits such as this to make his policies known and to drum up support.

However, implementing *perestroika* proved more difficult than Gorbachev and his supporters expected. Entrenched officials resisted the changes, as did many Soviet individuals whose jobs and incomes were threatened by economic restructuring. Gorbachev's promises also raised the Soviet people's expectations to impossible heights. Some reformers even criticized him for moving too slowly.

To complicate matters, ethnic groups and republics within the Soviet Union began agitating for national autonomy and the freedom to express their own

Demands for autonomy

cultural beliefs. Peoples from central Asia and Armenia to the Baltic republics had long harbored resentments against the Soviet state. Most of these republics had been forced to join the Soviet

■ FIGURE 26.1

Gorbachev in Czechoslovakia, 1987.

Union during the devastating civil wars of 1917–1921. When Gorbachev weakened the monopoly power of the Communist Party, he undermined the principal institution holding the multinational Soviet Union together. Emboldened by Gorbachev's promised leniency in Eastern Europe, the republics took action. The greatest threat came from elites in Latvia, Lithuania, and Estonia on the Baltic coast who led demands for political autonomy. As tensions mounted, events in Eastern Europe took a dramatic turn, overshadowing developments in the Soviet Union.

REVOLUTIONS IN EASTERN EUROPE

Ever since coming under the USSR's control, many people living in the communist nations of Eastern Europe had yearned to reclaim their national autonomy. Moreover, economic and cultural problems similar to those undermining communism in the Soviet Union plagued these societies and their governments. Though dissent did not always result in public protests, strikes, or demonstrations, it still simmered. In 1978, the Czechoslovakian playwright Václav Havel (see Biography) mocked the words of the *Communist Manifesto:* "A spectre is haunting eastern Europe: the spectre of what in the West is called 'dissent.'" Underground publications demanding honesty and civil rights circulated through intellectual and artistic circles in Poland, Hungary, and Czechoslovakia.

Two developments in the late 1980s strained the communist regimes trying to maintain control over these satellite states. First, economic difficulties mounted as Eastern European governments labored to keep prices artificially low. To make matters worse, foreign loans from the West to Eastern European nations such as Poland became more expensive

Economic problems

and began drying up. When those governments finally tried to increase prices without raising wages, public opposition mushroomed. Second, Gorbachev revoked the long-standing Brezhnev Doctrine. In 1989, he made his intentions clear: "Any interference in domestic affairs and any attempts to restrict the sovereignty of states, both friends and allies or any others, are inadmissible." Gorbachev had decided to

Revoking the Brezhnev Doctrine let events in Eastern Europe unfold without Soviet intervention. For reformers and dissenters, this policy was a green light to action.

Poland led the way in the rush for liberation. This nation already had a history of protest movements that made it a weak link in the Soviet chain. In 1980, shipyard workers in Gdansk struck against rising consumer-goods prices. The strikers orga-

Poland leads nized a noncommunist union, Solidarity, under the leadership of Lech Walesa. Support for Solidarity spread throughout the nation, forcing the government to recognize the new organization and accede to some of its demands. When the union pushed for more, resistance from Moscow and conservative elements in the Polish government stiffened. In late 1981, General Wojciech Jaruzelski, the new leader of the Polish Communist Party, declared martial law, arrested Walesa, and outlawed Solidarity.

However, the union survived these reversals. Early in 1989, with the Polish economy in crisis, negotiations began between Jaruzelski and Solidarity, still led by Walesa. The Polish Catholic Church, which had maintained a position in the nation and indeed enhanced its own prestige with the visit of Pope John Paul II in 1979, helped mediate discussions. The talks resulted in the legalization of Solidarity and, in June, new elections. Solidarity's stunning victory at the polls prompted Jaruzelski to ask the union to form a new government. A few months later, the communist leader stepped down, and the Communist Party gave up power in Poland without a fight.

Hungary soon followed suit. This satellite state already had a mixed economy, with almost one-third of its wealth coming from a private sector of small enterprises, crafts, and family agriculture. Reformers within the Hungarian Communist Party

Hungary gained some power in 1988 and removed the old leader, János Kádár, from office. In the summer and fall of 1989, Hungary held elections, established a multiparty political system, and initiated economic reforms to open the country to private enterprise. Figure 26.2, a poster published by the Hungarian Democratic Forum, captures the sense of ushering out a bygone era. The poster announces the fall of communism in Hungary with the words "Comrades, It's Over," and with the depiction of the back of a departing man's head. The military hat symbolizes

■ FIGURE 26.2

Istvan Orosz, *Comrades, It's Over*, 1989.

the confining authority of the old regime, and the wide neck perhaps represents the resentment against communist officials who had enjoyed special privileges.

Next came Czechoslovakia. In the fall of 1989, student demonstrators took to the streets demanding academic freedom and human rights. When police responded with clubs and tear gas, the demonstrators turned against them and other authorities. Workers and employers alike joined the students in the streets of Prague and in the great St. Wenceslas Square in the city center. In November, the call went out for a general strike. Within a few days, the hard-line Communist government resigned. Václav Havel, the playwright

The "velvet revolution" in Czechoslovakia

and dissident leader who had been imprisoned for his views, and Alexander Dubcek, who had tried to liberalize Czechoslovakia in 1968, quickly rose to power. As in Poland and Hungary, the fall of the communist regime in Czechoslovakia was bloodless—a "velvet revolution."

In East Germany, the wealthiest and most powerful of the Eastern European states, even people who

BIOGRAPHY

Václav Havel (1936–)

CONSIDER

■ **Consider** how Havel's life reveals the forces behind the fall of communism in Eastern Europe.

In May 1989, Czechoslovakian authorities released the playwright and dissident leader Václav Havel from jail. Just seven months later, the nation elected him as its new president. The well-known American author Arthur Miller called Havel "the world's first surrealist president" in reference to his unusual literary and intellectual background. *Time* magazine described him as "the conscience of Prague." Havel referred to himself as a mere writer who lacked "any of the necessary qualities" of a politician. "I've always understood my mission to be to speak the truth about the world I live in, to bear witness to its terrors and its miseries— in other words, to warn rather than hand out prescriptions for change."

Václav was born in 1936 into a well-known, middle-class family of engineers. With the advent of the communist regime in 1948, the family lost much of their property and position. Havel thanked "the apparent disadvantage of coming from a bourgeois background and growing up in a Communist state" for enabling him to see "the world . . . as it really is."

At age 13, Havel began writing poetry and philosophy. Over the next several years, he developed an interest in the theater and started writing plays. In 1956, he met his future wife, Olga Splichalova, who would become the first person to read each of his manuscripts.

In the early 1960s, Havel wrote plays and articles while attending night classes at the Academy of Performing Arts. The boyish, blue-eyed writer often stayed up all night working or talking with friends in beer pubs. Soon he earned acclaim as one of Czechoslovakia's most successful playwrights. His best-known works included *The Garden Party*, *The Increased Difficulty of Concentration*, *The Memorandum*, and *Largo Desolato*.

Havel also acquired a reputation as a dissident in 1965 by publicly criticizing the Writers' Union for acting "as a broker between politics and literature" rather than "defending the right of literature to be literature." During the "Prague Spring" of 1968 (see Chapter 25),

Playwright, Dissident, and Politician

Havel published a bold article suggesting the end of single-party rule in Czechoslovakia. Warsaw Pact troops crushed that moment of liberation, and the new, repressive regime banned Havel's works.

In the 1970s, Havel helped establish an underground press that published many disapproved and hard-to-find works. He wrote several influential essays on totalitarianism and dissent, including "The Power of the Powerless." Further, he argued that the communist regime in Czechoslovakia was based on fundamental lies, though he had faith that truth could penetrate these lies. In 1977 he became a founding spokesman for Charter 77, signed by hundreds of Czechs, Slovaks, and intellectuals from other countries. The charter called for people to do all they could for human rights

East Germany did well under communism, wanted to head west by the thousands. An American woman residing in East Germany described the growing dissatisfaction. "Too many . . . things were wrong. . . . Too much was missing from the shops. . . . There were no spare parts to fix home appliances or cars. Assembly lines were halted for want of supplies from auxiliary plants. It was the same on building sites, and the workers stood idle and furious. What good was this kind of socialism? Why did everything work so smoothly in the Germany next door?" When Hungary opened its borders with Austria in September 1989, tens of thousands of East Germans used that escape route to stream into the West. "They had been watching it longingly on West German television all their young lives. They knew from the commercials exactly how they would furnish their homes and make them shine."

In October 1989, antigovernment demonstrations spread throughout East Germany. People brandished signs proclaiming "We are the people." Long-suppressed criticism of the state's feared "security" forces surfaced. The hard-line communist leader was ousted from office. In November 1989, his communist successor bowed to the inevitable and ordered the Berlin Wall torn down. Joyful demonstrators celebrated for days. Soon, communists lost power, and within a year East and West Germany had reunified.

The rest of Eastern Europe also quickly followed. In Bulgaria, an internal coup deposed the Stalinist ruler. In Romania, the relatively independent but dictatorial communist leader, Nicolae Ceausescu, ordered troops to fire on demonstrators, setting off a bloody revolution. His overthrow cost many lives and ended with the execution of Ceausescu and his wife. The following year, Albania's independent but highly Stalinist regime also collapsed.

The freeing of Eastern Europe took less than a year. One after another, these nations cut the ties binding them to the USSR, enacted democratic reforms, in Eastern Europe. Officials labeled the publication as "reactionary," something "delivered to Western agents as instructed by anti-Communist and Zionist headquarters." Police quickly rounded up and interrogated signers.

Havel spent most of the period from 1977 to 1983 in prison for his human rights activities. Nevertheless, his wife Olga continued the underground publishing. Václav would later publish a book of his letters to her. Not long after his release, he reflected on his prison experience: "[A]ll that heroic time in prison was in fact one long chain of worries, fears, and terrors . . . and despite all this, I know that, if it were necessary, I would go back to prison again. . . ."

His words were prophetic. In February 1989, Havel once more languished in a prison cell for his criticisms of the communist regime. Yet his fortunes were about to change. Not far from the walls of his prison, student demonstrators marched angrily through the city streets. A petition campaign somehow persuaded authorities to release Havel in May. He soon took up his role again as a leader of the dissidents, circulating petitions demanding democratic reforms.

In November 1989, he helped found the Civic Forum, which led the opposition movement in Czechoslovakia. Before the end of the year, the Czech parliament elected Havel president, completing his stunning transition from prison cell to the halls of government. Figure 26.3 shows Havel in December 1989. As the newly elected president of Czechoslovakia, he reads the names of the nation's new, noncommunist government members to the crowd. In his 1990 New Year's address, he announced, "People, your government has returned to you!"

■ FIGURE 26.3

Václav Havel addressing the crowd, 1989.

Through the 1990s, the people again and again reelected Havel president. Some critics saw him as too much of an intellectual. Still, he gained a worldwide reputation as a moral spokesperson for Europe who stressed "the tolerant coexistence of different cultural identities" and the "ties that link everything in this world together."

and introduced capitalism into their economies (see Map 26.1). The repercussions of these events echoed throughout the Soviet Union, quickly pushing developments beyond the control of Gorbachev and his supporters.

THE SOVIET UNION DISINTEGRATES

The Soviet leader had managed only halting steps in his effort to restructure the Soviet economy—*perestroika*. High officials announced plans to move the economy away from central planning and then delayed the plans in the face of determined opposition by hard-liners. These officials also worried about the difficulties—including unemployment, inflation, and dislocation—that the transition would cause. Gorbachev watered down his reforms to the satisfaction of no one. The waffling and controversy only worsened the frustrations of hard-liners and

Problems with reform

reformers alike. Reformers who wanted Gorbachev to move faster grew disgusted with the moderate pace of change, while the old communist guard became increasingly alienated. As the economy began to spin out of control, the Soviet leader's popularity dwindled.

Gorbachev tried pushing through promising political reforms as part of his *glasnost* policy, but, as with *perestroika*, each step taken to enact reforms opened the door further for new expressions of dissatisfaction. In 1990, he persuaded the Communist Party's Central Committee to eliminate the party's constitutional monopoly on political power. He created a new, strong presidency—an office separate from the Communist Party hierarchy. Equally daring, he called for new elections.

All these changes democratized Soviet politics and undermined the power of the Communist Party—in the process exposing the corruption of the old Soviet regime. Party members resigned in droves. These

THINKING ABOUT GEOGRAPHY

MAP 26.1   EASTERN EUROPE, 1989

This map shows the upheavals that toppled the communist regimes in Eastern Europe. ■ **Notice** the extent of public protests and demonstrations. ■ **Consider** which Western European states might gain more influence in Eastern Europe as Soviet control over the area disappeared. **Why** might several of these states be interested in joining Western European organizations such as NATO and the European Community?

At the same time, movements for independence gained momentum within several ethnic groups and nationalities throughout the USSR. The Soviet Union contained more than a hundred ethnic groups, as well as some 50 million Muslims in central Asia.

Independence movements

Many of these groups considered themselves separate nations and the Soviet Union as a collection of nations rather than a single whole. The republics of Estonia, Lithuania, and Latvia led in pressing Moscow for independence. In 1991, the Ukraine joined the Russian Republic in declaring itself independent. Ethnic conflict and nationalistic demands spread in the Soviet republics of Armenia, Azerbaijan, Moldova, Georgia, and elsewhere. Though Gorbachev resisted these demands and tried to quell the ethnic conflicts, the situation had gone beyond anyone's control. In the spring of 1991, he proposed a compromise: the "Treaty of Union," in which all the Soviet republics would be independent but held together as a confederation.

In August 1991, with the Treaty of Union about to take effect, communist hard-liners from inside the government and the KGB tried to oust Gorbachev. Within three days, the hard-liners' ineptitude and the opposition marshaled by Russian president Yeltsin doomed the coup to failure. Indeed, Gorbachev's authority was slipping away to Yeltsin even at this moment. In late 1991, after the two leaders stripped

Hard-liners' coup

the Communist Party of much of its power, Gorbachev resigned.

In the end, no one, including the once-dominant Russians, wanted to save the old Soviet Union. Gorbachev had unleashed the forces of revolution, and he—along with the USSR itself—became revolution's victim. In 1999, Gorbachev would look back and explain, "Communism—as the inventors of the theory imagined it—never existed anywhere. . . . What did exist was Stalinist socialism. That system had exhausted itself and was doomed to disappear." Map 26.2 shows what became of the for-

policies also facilitated the rise of Gorbachev's chief rival, Boris Yeltsin, the newly elected president of the Russian Republic. A charismatic, liberal reformer, Yeltsin publicly resigned from the Communist Party in July 1990. In another bold move, he declared the Russian Republic an independent state.

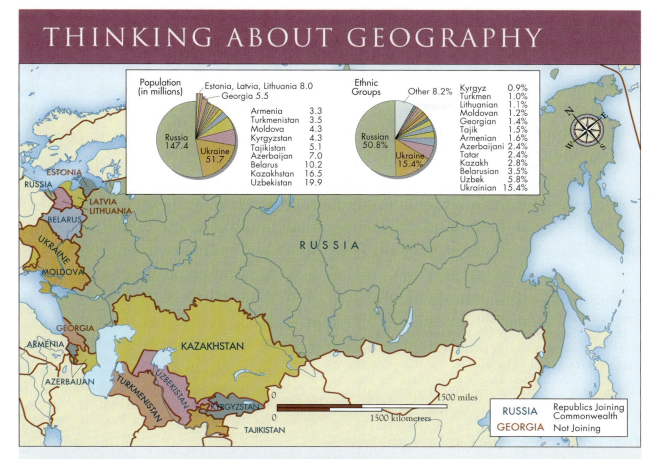

Population (in millions)

Estonia, Latvia, Lithuania 8.0
Georgia 5.5

Russia 147.4
Ukraine 51.7

Armenia   3.3
Turkmenistan   3.5
Moldova   4.3
Kyrgyzstan   4.3
Tajikistan   5.1
Azerbaijan   7.0
Belarus   10.2
Kazakhstan   16.5
Uzbekistan   19.9

Ethnic Groups   Other 8.2%

Russian 50.8%
Ukraine 15.4%

Kyrgyz   0.9%
Turkmen   1.0%
Lithuanian   1.1%
Moldovan   1.2%
Georgian   1.4%
Tajik   1.5%
Armenian   1.6%
Azerbaijani   2.4%
Tatar   2.4%
Kazakh   2.8%
Belarusian   3.5%
Uzbek   5.8%
Ukrainian   15.4%

RUSSIA — Republics Joining Commonwealth
GEORGIA — Not Joining

MAP 26.2 THE DISSOLUTION OF THE SOVIET UNION, 1991

This map shows the division of territory resulting from the disintegration of the former Soviet Union. ■ **Notice** which states became the largest and potentially the most powerful in the former USSR. **Which** areas might be most influenced by European states to the west and Islamic states to the south? ■ **Notice** the ethnic divisions in the former Soviet Union. **What** problems might ethnicity pose after the breakup of the USSR?

mer Soviet Union. Most of the republics within the old structure joined the new Commonwealth of Independent States, a loose confederation. A few republics, such as the Baltic states, broke away altogether.

LIFE AFTER THE COLLAPSE OF COMMUNISM

After the celebrations in the former communist bloc ended, people awoke to new, dismaying realities. In his 1990 inaugural address, Václav Havel had issued a warning that applied just as much to other nations in Eastern Europe as it did to Czechoslovakia: "Our country is not flourishing. . . . Entire branches of industry are producing goods which are of no interest to anyone, while we are lacking the things we need. A state which calls itself a workers' state humiliates

and exploits workers. Our obsolete economy is wasting the little energy we have available. . . . We have polluted our soil, our rivers and forests. . . ." Leaders in Eastern Europe and the former USSR faced a crucial problem: how to institute capitalism and liberal democracy in nations with little experience of either.

The economic transition proceeded quickly in Poland and Hungary, but more moderately in Bulgaria, Romania, and Albania. Almost everywhere, however, it brought pain. *Eastern Europe* When governments closed the doors of inefficient state industries or sold them, many workers lost their jobs. The removal of price controls also provoked instant inflation that especially hurt those living on fixed incomes. Some people took advantage of new opportunities that came with the transition; for example, former communist officials in particular benefited from lucrative insider deals. Several cities—such as Prague in the Czech Republic, with its domes, spires, cobblestone alleys, pubs, cafes, and secondhand bookstores—also fared well with the heightened tourism to such areas. But too many people had let themselves expect more than the eradication of communism could deliver. In the face of widespread bitterness, governments struggled to gain stability and institute unpopular but apparently necessary economic policies such as closing state industries and allowing prices to rise.

In the former Soviet Union, people were unaccustomed to democratic politics, managers were unfamiliar with the market economy, and many officials resisted reform. The economy stumbled badly. Year after year, Russia's economic output decreased, as did its population. Removing price controls and pri-

The former Soviet Union vatizing industry had eliminated lines in front of stores and created economic opportunities for some. However, prices skyrocketed beyond the reach of average consumers, the Russian currency lost its value, and some 30 percent of the population struggled to subsist on approximately $1 per day.

The collapse of communism proved particularly stressful for Russian men. From Communist Party officials and generals to physicists and professors, men who had once enjoyed status, security, and relative wealth lost these benefits in the turmoil of the postcommunist era. Life expectancy for Russian men plummeted to fifty-eight years, a decline that was "the steepest and most severe ever documented anywhere in the world" according to one researcher. Alcoholism more than tripled in the years after the collapse. For women, the story was different. Although many women suffered from unemployment when state industries folded, perhaps their losses were not

so great and were eased by new opportunities. In any case, they seemed to manage the transition better than men, maintaining a life expectancy of seventy-three years. Indeed, a growing elite of women entered managerial positions and earned increasing salaries.

Boris Yeltsin retained a precarious hold on power as president of Russia and, despite illnesses, was re-elected in 1996. But the Russian people resisted his inconsistent efforts at reform. In the parliament, *Yeltsin's problems* with its tangled array of different political parties, fragmentation ruled. Moreover, "reformed" communists retained positions of power, as they did in Eastern European states such as Serbia, Bulgaria, and Lithuania. With control disintegrating, lawlessness—from street crime to organized crime—rapidly spread. By 1998, the fumbling Yeltsin had lost his popularity and much of his power as the Russian economy verged on collapse. When he resigned on the last day of 1999, turning power over to Vladimir Putin, many Russians yearned for the power, order, and stability that communism had brought. While rich oligarchic figures and organized crime still sapped Russia's wealth, Putin, supported by an increasingly loyal bureaucracy and some genuine popularity, provided some functional stability and considerable respect within and outside Russia. He effectively supported Russia's evolving market economy and legal system. Although he moved against the independent media and undermined political opposition, he provided a welcome relief from Yeltsin, whose uneven and unpopular reign witnessed the collapse of basic industries and social services along with the growth of crime and widespread corruption. By 2006, political stability and increasing wealth from oil propelled Russia's economy forward.

NATIONALISM UNLEASHED

Despite its drawbacks, communism had provided many people with a sense of unity and security. As Document 26.1 suggests, its fall opened a void that nationalistic sentiments rose to fill. As had often been the case in nineteenth- and twentieth-century history, nationalism provoked heated conflict along with a feeling of belonging. Ethnic and cultural struggles raged in several republics of the former Soviet Union. In Azerbaijan, the Azerbaijanis and Armenians clashed. The most violent outburst came in secessionist Chechnya, where Russians fought an unpopular war with Chechnyans demanding their independence. The indecisive two-year conflict cost some 80,000 deaths and 250,000 wounded, although the Chechnyans gained many of their goals. In 1999, another draining war broke out between Chechnyans and Russians.

■ DOCUMENT 26.1

The Perils of the New Nationalism

In recent years, many commentators have noted a growth of nationalism and movements for political separatism. Of course, nationalistic trends have been common in the West since the nineteenth century. But there seems to be something different about this new impulse. In the following selection, Eric Hobsbawm analyzes this new nationalism, emphasizing four reasons for its strength.
■ **How** *have recent events encouraged political separatism?* ■ **What** *consequences might these movements have?*

There are today four rather different reasons such sentiments, and their political expression in separatism, are widely supported. The first is that the collapse of the Communist system, which imposed political stability over a large part of Europe, has reopened the wounds of World War I, or, more precisely, of the misconceived and unrealistic peace settlements after it. The explosive nationalist issues in Central and Eastern Europe today are not ancient ethnic conflicts but those created during the formation of the successor states to the collapsing multiethnic Habsburg, Ottoman and Czarist Russian empires. . . . What has made those problems acute is not the strength of national feeling, which was no greater than in countries like Britain and Spain, but the disintegration of central power, for this forced even Soviet or Yugoslav republics that did not dream of separation, like Kazakhstan and Macedonia, to assert independence as a means of self-preservation. . . .

The second reason is more general, though probably more important in the West than in the East. The massive population movements of the past forty years—within and between countries and continents—have made xenophobia into a major political phenomenon, as the earlier mass migrations of 1880–1920 did to a smaller extent. Xenophobia encourages ethnic nationalism, since the essence of both is hostility to other groups (the "not-we"). . . .

The third reason is that the politics of group identity are easier to understand than any others, especially for peoples who, after several decades of dictatorship, lack both political education and experience. In Central Europe, argues Miroslav Hroch, a leading Czech historian, language is once again replacing complicated concepts like constitutions and civil rights. Nationalism is among the simple, intuitively comprehensible beliefs that substitute for less understandable political programs. It is not the only one.

The fourth reason is perhaps the most fundamental. To quote the Czech historian: "Where an old regime disintegrates, where old social relations have become unstable, amid the rise of general insecurity, belonging to a common language and culture may become the only certainty in society, the only value beyond ambiguity and doubt." In the former Communist countries this insecurity and disorientation may derive from the collapse of the predictable planned economy and the social security that went with it.

Source: Eric Hobsbawm, "The Perils of the New Nationalism," *The Nation* 255:537+, September 4, 1992.

In Eastern Europe also, nationalistic, ethnic, and religious rivalries opened old wounds and created new divisions. Maps 26.3 and 26.4 reveal some of these problems. In 1993, the Slovak minority in Czechoslovakia, pushed by ambitious Slovak politicians, voted for independence. Czechoslovakia reluctantly agreed to divide itself into the Czech Republic and Slovakia. In Romania, ethnic friction between the Romanian majority and the Hungarian minority flared up.

The bloodiest conflicts broke out in Yugoslavia, where chaotic civil wars marked the disintegration of that country. Figure 26.4, a chart listing the many ethnic groups living in Yugoslavia, reveals the complexity of ethnic divisions in the country. In some regions, one ethnic group made up the vast majority of the population, but in other areas several ethnic groups lived as large minorities. The six republics that constituted Yugoslavia had been

Civil wars in Yugoslavia

held together under communist rule since World War II (see Map 26.4). With the death of Tito in 1980 and the fall of communism in the rest of Eastern Europe in 1989, Yugoslavia began to crack. In 1991, Slovenians, angered by the refusal of the dominant Serbian communists to liberalize economic and political policies, detached themselves from Yugoslavia. Peoples in Croatia, Bosnia-Herzegovina, and Macedonia followed suit. War soon erupted between the religiously Orthodox Serbs, attempting to expand the territory they controlled, and their long-time Catholic Croatian rivals to the northwest. Trapped between the two antagonists were the mostly Muslim Bosnians and other peoples who lived as minorities in these areas.

The war for a "Greater Serbia" raged with appalling brutality. The worst fighting took place in Bosnia-Herzegovina. On this bloody battlefield, the Serbs initiated a policy of **ethnic cleansing,** driving Muslim Bosnians from their homes; placing them in concentration camps; and raping, murdering, and starving

MAPS 26.3 AND 26.4 DISINTEGRATION OF CZECHOSLOVAKIA AND YUGOSLAVIA, 1991–2007

These maps show how Czechoslovakia divided into the Czech Republic and Slovakia, and the disintegration of Yugoslavia. ■ **Compare** the maps. **How** do you explain the different paths to the breakup of these two nations? ■ **Consider** why problems in this area of Europe led to war at the beginning as well as the end of the twentieth century.

Legend for lower map:
- Former border of Yugoslavia
- Border of Bosnia-Herzegovina
- Dayton Agreement inter-entity boundary (November 1995)
- Bosnian Serb territory, after Dayton
- Croat-Muslim Federation portion of Bosnia, after Dayton

Ethnic group	Percentage
Serbians	36
Croatians	20
Bosnians (Muslim)	9
Slovenes	8
Albanians	8
Macedonians	6
Montenegrins	3
Hungarians	2
Others	8

■ FIGURE 26.4

Ethnic groups in Yugoslavia, 1991.

Nations truck and blue-helmeted soldiers—one carrying a medical kit. Almost surrounded by barbed wire, the troops try to provide aid to civilians—all women and children—standing along the road.

The Bosnians, supported by aid from the Islamic world, fought back desperately for more than four years. Only a Western embargo and NATO intervention brought an uneasy end to the violence and peace accords in 1996. The conflict had killed 250,000 people, displaced 3 million, and left 800,000 antipersonnel mines embedded in the land. Moreover, peace still depended on the continued presence of international troops. In 1997, a NATO commander in Bosnia warned that "if we withdraw our forces, there will be slaughter in the streets," and predicted that complete recovery would take decades.

them. In 1992, a Serb guard at one concentration camp proudly explained, "We won't waste our bullets on them. . . . They have no roof. There is sun and rain, cold nights, and beatings two times a day. We give them no food and no water. They will starve like animals." A survivor reported seeing "corpses piled one on top of another. . . . The bodies eventually were gathered with a forklift . . . this happened almost every day." Figure 26.5 reveals the suffering from the war and the international effort to do something about it. In the foreground, a woman throws her arms and head back in anguish. Behind her is a white United

Just two years later, the brutality unleashed in Bosnia rose again in nearby Kosovo—another region within Yugoslavia. Serbians, led by President Slobodan Milosevic, met rising demands for independence from the Albanian majority in Kosovo with overwhelming military force. Renewing the practice of "ethnic cleansing," Serbian troops slaughtered thousands of Kosovar Albanians and forced hundreds of thousands to flee to neighboring states.

After diplomacy failed, NATO unleashed its military resources for the first time in its fifty-year history. Member air forces, led by the United States, opened a three-month bombing campaign on Serbian forces and on Serbia itself. Milosevic finally agreed to terms and withdrew his forces. Protected by NATO troops, the Kosovar Albanians streamed back to their badly damaged land, bringing with them few hopes for ethnic cooperation in the region. In 2000, Vojislav Kostunica defeated Milosovec in Yugoslavia's presidential election, and soon Milosovec found himself standing trial for war crimes before an international tribunal in The Hague, Netherlands.

REPERCUSSIONS AND REALIGNMENTS IN THE WEST

Repercussions from the collapse of communism spread around the world. As communism lost its credibility, nations still committed to the Soviet model, such as Cuba and North Korea, were left isolated. Capitalism gained renewed respect and even inspired awe in both the Western and non-Western worlds. For many, the collapse of communism in Eastern Europe and the USSR signified the final triumph of capitalism. With the end of the Cold War, the contours of domestic and international politics began to shift.

THE UNITED STATES UNCHALLENGED AND GERMANY RISING

With the former Soviet forces in decline and the Warsaw Pact dissolved, the United States and Germany rose in stature. The United States emerged as the world's only military superpower. It flexed its military muscle in 1991 by leading a United Nations-authorized coalition that repelled Iraq's invasion of tiny, neighboring Kuwait. In the short war, the U.S.-dominated coalition easily defeated Saddam Hussein's forces. In 2001 and 2003, it again demonstrated its military might in Afghanistan and Iraq (see pages 802–804). The U.S. also contributed to international peacekeeping efforts by sending forces to troubled areas such as Somalia, Haiti, Bosnia, and Kosovo. Despite years of large budget deficits and apparent decline, the U.S. economy rebounded in the mid-

■ FIGURE 26.5

Civil war in Bosnia-Herzegovina, 1995.

1990s to a position of leadership that inspired envy the world over.

Germany's influence and potential also rose. In 1990, German unification confirmed Germany as a European and world economic leader—in exports, in balance of trade, and in gross domestic product. Emerging victorious from the first national elections, the former West German chancellor Helmut Kohl and his conservative Christian Democrats vowed to bring eastern Germany's economy up to the high standard enjoyed in the West. The costs of the transition mushroomed far beyond expectations; as state industries collapsed in the East, unemployment and the cost of welfare benefits shot up. Nevertheless, the reunified state still ranked as the top economic power in Europe. Clearly, Germany stood poised to exert new influence in Eastern Europe and the European Community.

POLITICS SHIFT TO THE RIGHT

In the United States, Germany, and elsewhere in the West, politics shifted to the Right. The reasons behind this change were complex, but economic forces played a major role. Despite the continued overall prosperity enjoyed in the West, many nations suffered from high unemployment and declining growth rates during the 1980s and 1990s. In part, the free flow of trade and capital had created a new international labor market that operated outside the control of national governments and labor unions, resulting in the loss of many business opportunities and manufacturing jobs in the West. As global economic competition stiffened and nations struggled to stay in the game, many people blamed costly social programs—often supported by the political Left—for their nation's economic problems. The changes wrought by the postindustrial society, especially the shift from manufacturing to services, also weakened labor unions—the Left's traditional source of support. The previous sense that government was obligated to provide for rich and poor alike—a belief that had fueled the post–World War II welfare state—faded along with memories of those older times. Government regulation of economic affairs and the cost of social programs came under question everywhere.

Conservatives began scoring record successes at the polls. Citing the apparent triumph of capitalism, they attacked expensive programs and sometimes fanned the flames of anti-immigrant senti-ments, playing on the popular perception that foreign-born newcomers took jobs. France's right-wing National Front, led by Jean-Marie LePen, attained particular prominence by blam-ing immigrants from North Africa and elsewhere for France's economic problems. The traditional commu-nist parties in Western Europe declined, and socialist parties, whether in power or not, moderated their policies to shore up their popularity. In Austria, Italy, Germany, and Spain, conservative and right-wing politicians gained popularity. Even when traditional parties of the Left regained power, as they did in many countries during the late 1990s, their platforms were more muted and conservative than in the past. No nation ventured as far down the conservative path as Great Britain and the United States. In Great Britain, the Conservatives led by Margaret Thatcher and her successor dominated throughout most of the 1980s and 1990s, cutting taxes, attacking social programs, and selling state-owned industries to private inves-tors. When the Labor Party finally came to power in Great Britain in 1997, it pursued only mild changes. In the United States, Republicans rolled back liberal programs and Democrats scrambled to adopt more conservative platforms. The sharply conservative administration of George W. Bush came to power in 2001. Mostly in the name of economic development and the war against terrorism, it aggressively pursued many policies initiated by the Reagan administration in the 1980s, including loosening of environmental protections, reducing social programs, lowering taxes in ways that favored the wealthy and corporations, increasing military spending, and cutting into the protection of civil liberties.

By the mid-1990s, this conservatism had merged with a broader questioning of traditional politics in the West. As anxieties over economic problems in-tensified and as scandals rocked governments, people voted for unknowns or stopped voting altogether. Es-pecially in France, Italy, and Austria, candidates who voiced disenchantment with the standard politics of the Left and Right attracted popular support. In 2000, for example, a populist right-wing party in Aus-tria gained enough support to join with conservatives and form a government—much to the dismay of tra-ditional parties throughout Europe. All these shifts in domestic politics gained much attention. However,

Questioning traditional politics

events beyond state borders would soon overshadow these internal concerns throughout Europe.

TOWARD EUROPEAN INTEGRATION

The end of the Cold War may have left the United States the world's sole superpower, but it also strength-ened the movement toward unity that had been unfold-ing in Europe since the 1950s. According to Michael Naumann, in 2002 the editor of a leading German magazine, the "huge influence of the world's single superpower, the United States, will push Europeans together." Moreover, many Europeans agreed with Michel Albert, a leading French official and industri-alist, who in 1991 argued, "If the aim is to harness cap-italism without impairing its efficiency, it is no longer to the nation-state that we must look, but to Europe."

In 1992, the 12 members of the European Com-munity (EC) eliminated all major internal barriers to trade, the flow of capital, and the movement of people. That same year, the EC joined with the seven-member European Free Trade Association to form the European Economic Area, creating the world's largest trading bloc and paving the way for several new countries to seek full membership (see Map 26.5). Between 1999 and 2004, a number of East-ern European nations, such as Poland, the Czech Republic, Hungary, Lithuania, and Slovakia joined NATO and were accepted for membership in the European Union. Also in 1992, France and Germany formed a joint army corps, the European Corps, open to other participants in the European Union. With the Maastricht Treaty of 1992 (which changed the name of the EC to the European Union), most mem-bers of the **European Union (EU)** agreed to estab-lish a common currency (the **Euro**) controlled by a central European bank by 1999. The plan required great economic discipline, above all controlling the large yearly budget deficits most nations ran. By 2002, people in most countries of the European Union carried Euros in their pockets, wallets, and purses.

Figure 26.6 shows the new monetary unit of the Eu-ropean Union. In the center of the print are Euro bills of various denominations, designed simply and neu-trally, with a blend of buildings and bridges instead of any faces or heroes, so as not to favor any coun-try. Swirling around them are the currencies—represented by colorful bills with historical and national symbols—the Euro replaced. To some crit-ics, this image represented a danger of European integration—the merging of unique, colorful nations with their own flavors into a bland, homogenized union controlled by faceless bureaucrats.

The potential of the European Union seemed tre-mendous. In 2006, the member nations had more than 450 million inhabitants and a combined gross national product greater than that of the United States. Perhaps in response to the growing power of the European Union, the United States joined with Mexico and Canada in 1994 to create a new free-trade zone—the **North American Free Trade Agreement (NAFTA).** Not everyone embraced the idea of such alliances. Many Europeans opposed further integration, clinging to national preferences and warning against the dangers of giving up sovereignty to an international body of bureaucrats. To be sure, the European nations had great difficulty joining forces to put down the crisis in Bosnia, but their joint action as part of a NATO force to quell the violence in Kosovo in 1999 led to a vow by the leaders of fifteen European countries to make the European Union a military power for the first time. The Union adopted plans to build its own military of up to 60,000 troops. Moreover, by that same year, the European Union had opened its arms to possible membership for Turkey as well as virtually all of central and eastern Europe. Despite many reservations, most Europeans seemed willing to cooperate. The statement by a German woman early in 2002 reflected the sense of many: "I feel German, but also European." However, in 2005 French and Dutch voters rejected a newly drafted constitution designed to strengthen the European Union. This signaled broad ambivalence about taking further steps toward European integration and, in particular, concerns about welcoming the populous, Muslim, and relatively poor Turkey into the Union—and the potential influx of immigrants and migrant workers that might follow.

THINKING ABOUT GEOGRAPHY

Member of the European Union

Applied for Membership

MAP 26.5   THE EUROPEAN UNION, 2007

This map shows the European Union in 2007 and nations that applied for membership. ■ **Notice** how inclusive membership is. **Which** nations form the most important core of a potentially united Europe? **How** economically and politically powerful might a united Europe be? ■ **Consider** the significance of several Eastern European nations' joining this association.

THE WORLD AND THE WEST FROM A GLOBAL PERSPECTIVE

As they took further steps toward unity, Europeans had more in mind than competing with the United States. They also knew that they had to meet the changes sweeping through much of the Western and

non-Western worlds. Since the end of colonialism, European nations could no longer rely on colonies as controllable markets. By the 1990s, all nations faced a global economy marked by the presence of multinational enterprises beyond the command of individual states. Waves of huge corporate buyouts

■ FIGURE 26.6
The Euro, 1999.

and mergers increased this concentration of economic power. By 2000, small handfuls of these corporations controlled more than half the global market in oil, automobiles, electronics, multimedia, and personal computers. Westerners also confronted new competitors, from Latin America to East Asia, who wielded growing economic and political clout. In addition, various international agencies and organizations such as the International Monetary Fund, the World Bank, and the World Trade Organization wielded great economic clout over financial aid and international commerce that affected governments, corporations, and ordinary people throughout the world. Finally, the pace of global economic integration and change had quickened, complicating international business for everyone. Certain technological advances, above all the development of the computer, the Internet, and genetic engineering, had the potential of creating the equivalent of a third industrial revolution. By 2000, the mushrooming use of computers and the Internet in business and commerce had already transformed many economies. Increasingly, goods could be designed in one country, financed internationally, produced overseas, sold worldwide, and serviced through phones and the Internet from numerous locations. All these changes tended to blend local and national markets into global markets and called into question the very issue of national identity. Even in the poorest nations, signs of this **globalization** proliferated. As just one example, workers in new manufacturing plants owned by multinational corporations wore the same brand-name athletic shoes and drank the same beverages as their Western counterparts. Moreover as Document 26.2 suggests, thanks to films, television, radio, computers, cellular phones, fax machines, satellites, and travel, ideas and images flowed across international borders as easily as money, goods, and services, further blurring the distinctions between cultures.

Globalization

EAST ASIA AND THE RISE OF THE PACIFIC RIM

The greatest challenge to the West's economic dominance came from East Asia. Since the 1960s, Japan had grown into a major economic power. Year after year, this island nation enjoyed the world's largest favorable balance of trade. By the 1980s, it boasted the world's second-largest gross domestic product. A giant in automobile production and electronics, Japan replaced the United States as the world's topmost creditor nation. Although reversals brought Japan's economic momentum to a virtual standstill during the 1990s, and even a decline during the 2001 and 2002 world economic slowdown, the nation still led the world in per capita gross domestic product.

By the 1990s, other regions on the periphery of the Pacific Ocean attracted wealthy investors with their political stability, cheap and disciplined labor force, and openness to capitalism. Multinational corporations opened offices and made investments throughout this so-called Pacific Rim. Hong Kong, Taiwan, South Korea, Malaysia, Indonesia, and Singapore all boomed, drawing manufacturing jobs away from Europe and the United States in industries such as electronics, textiles, plastics, metals, computers, automobiles, and leather goods. Visitors found thriving cities such as Kuala Lumpur in Malaysia—with the world's two tallest buildings marking its skyline and its high-rise apartment houses serviced by climate-controlled malls—"unrecognizable to anyone who knew it 30 years ago." On the outskirts of such glittering urban centers, satellite communities and industrial parks rose where jungles used to thrive. Similar developments transformed other great cities of East Asia, from Singapore and Bangkok to Jakarta and Hong Kong.

Yet no country experienced a more stunning economic transformation than China. In 1978, the successors to Mao, led by Deng Xiaoping (1904–1997), had initiated the "Four Modernizations" program to foster rapid economic development and greater productivity. The program departed dramatically from Mao's economic policies by decentralizing decision making and introducing a market-oriented economy into the countryside and, later, into some urban areas. By the mid-1980s, these policies had opened China to tourism and foreign investment, stimulated new economic growth, and created greater economic freedom within China. Agreements with Japan and the United States rapidly expanded trade as well. For the first time, Chinese farmers produced a surplus of food for export. In certain areas of the country, particularly the "New Economic Zones" in the southeast, capitalistic investments and manufacturing practices spurred

The economic transformation of China

■ DOCUMENT 26.2

The Information Revolution Inspires Visions of New Potential

Perhaps the most important new technological development affecting people is the computer. In addition to their use in science, scholarship, and business, computers have fueled the "information revolution." In recent years, computers—along with other means of communication—have demonstrated their potential to create an "information highway." Crossing political borders, this highway might facilitate a convergence of cultures throughout the world. In the following selection, Howard H. Frederick extols the potential of this technology. ■ ***How** might computers and other machines change old notions of community?* ■ ***What** is the nature of "global civil society?"*

What we call "community" used to be limited to face-to-face dialogue among people in the same physical space, a dialogue that reflected mutual concerns and a common culture. For thousands of years, people had little need for long-distance communication because they lived very close to one another. The medieval peasant's entire life was spent within a radius of no more than twenty-five miles from the place of birth. Even at the beginning of our century, the average person still lived in the countryside and knew of the world only through travelers' tales.

Today, of course, communications technologies have woven parts of the world together into an electronic web. No longer is community or dialogue restricted to a geographical place. With the advent of the fax machine, telephones, international publications, and computers, personal and professional relationships can be maintained irrespective of time and place. Communication relationships are no longer restricted to place, but are distributed through space. Today we are all members of many global "non-place" communities.

In the last decade there has emerged a new kind of global community, one that has increasingly become a force in international relations. We speak of the emergence of a global civil society, that part of our collective lives that is neither market nor government but is so often inundated by them. Still a global civil society is best represented in the global "NGO Movement," nongovernmental organizations and citizens advocacy groups uniting to fight planetary problems whose scale confounds local or even national solutions. Previously isolated from one another, nongovernmental organizations (NGOs) are flexing their muscles at the United Nations and other world forums as their power and capacity to communicate increase. . . .

Source: Howard Frederick. Paper presented at the Annual Conference of the Peace Studies Association, Institute for Global Communications, February 28, 1992.

---

high rates of growth. By 2002, China had become the world's most important manufacturing nation.

Nevertheless, China made these economic reforms without corresponding political reforms. Whether that practice could continue was called into question in 1989, when students and intellectuals demanding political reform organized massive demonstrations in Beijing. After a brief standoff, the government, supported by China's rural population and most of the army, violently crushed the demonstrations and jailed the leaders. In the years that followed, as China's leadership aged and pressures for political reform persisted, analysts watched carefully for change within the great Asian country. By the first decade of the twenty-first century, China stood as a rapidly growing economic power with tremendous political potential on the international stage.

THE CHALLENGE OF ISLAM

Other areas of the world presented different challenges to the West. In particular, several Islamic nations in North Africa and the Middle East developed a new assertiveness and a willingness to make their dissatisfaction with Western ways known. They had long resented the former Western imperial powers' condescension toward them. The West's support of Israel only irritated an already raw nerve.

The emergence of combative leaders in states such as Libya, Syria, Iran, and Iraq—some of whom advocated Islamic or Pan-Arab unity against Israel and Western influence—stepped up tensions further. Moreover, in nations from Algeria and Turkey to Afghanistan and Pakistan, Islamic fundamentalists had gained strength. Western secular notions such as individualism, capitalism, materialism, commercialism, gender equality, and sexual freedom were flooding across airwaves and borders into the Islamic world. These notions seemed to insult and threaten fundamentalists' traditional and religious beliefs. Condemning westernization and the secularization of life in their countries, they demanded a return to traditional symbols of their conservative views, such as the veil that they required women to wear in public. Iran's fundamentalist leader Ayatollah Ruholla Khomeini (1900–1989), who had come to power as the leader of a revolution in 1979, epitomized rejection of the West. "With the Qur'an in one hand and a gun in the other, defend your dignity and honor" against the "oppressive powers" of the West, he told his nation in 1980. He especially castigated the United States, labeling it the "great Satan" because it had supported Israel and had intervened several times in the region. Finally, many Middle Eastern Islamic states possessed the crude-oil reserves on which the West and Asia depended, and they used the precious resource to command international respect and attention. The potential of Middle Eastern states to pull Western nations into armed conflict was made all too clear in 1990 when Iraq invaded oil-rich Kuwait, prompting a UN-backed military response, and again in 2003 with the U.S.-led invasion of Iraq.

INTERNATIONAL TERRORISM AND WAR

On the morning of September 11, 2001, coordinated teams of terrorists hijacked four U.S. American airliners. They slammed two of the planes into Manhattan's famed World Trade Center (Twin Towers) office buildings and a third into the Pentagon, headquarters of the U.S. Department of Defense in Washington D.C. Passengers apparently brought down the fourth plane before it could reach its target. Nearly 3,000 people lost their lives in the attacks, most of them perishing when the Twin Towers collapsed later that morning. Blame soon fell on the shoulders of a well-financed international terrorist group, **al-Qaeda,** which professed a radical version of Islamic fundamentalism, under the leadership of Osama bin Laden.

The forces behind this tragedy and the responses to it were complex, and historians can make only tentative analyses at this point. However, analysts point to the intensifying anger toward the West among radical Islamic fundamentalists as one major underlying force for the attack. Islamic fundamentalists had long lamented what they saw as the West's "corruption" of regimes within the Islamic world. Authoritarian governments that fundamentalists viewed as too secular and too connected to the West ruled most Islamic states. Fundamentalism found growing support among people who were outraged by this supposed perversion of Islamic law and who were enraged at the reality of masses of people living far below the wealthy elites in these countries.

Most Muslim leaders and clerics rejected violence and terrorism. But against the overwhelming military, political, and economic forces that Western nations and nonfundamentalist Islamic states could marshal, terrorism seemed a legitimate and even religiously justified way to assert some fundamentalists' point of view. For a group such as al-Qaeda, terrorism might catalyze widespread fundamentalist revolts that would bring down "corrupt" governments in the Islamic world.

A second force came in the form of the festering Israeli-Palestinian conflict. This struggle deepened Islamic fundamentalists' rage toward the West—in particular the United States. In various ways, Israel and the Arab world had been at odds since the mid-twentieth century (see Chapter 25). Moreover, Israel had long been perceived as a Western "outpost" in the Middle East. *Israeli-Palestinian conflict* The close relationship between Israel and the United States encouraged that perception, and many held the United States partly responsible for the sufferings of Palestinians. For example, al-Qaeda's Osama bin Laden railed against "the crusader-Jewish alliance, led by the United States and Israel."

Fueled by these forces and religious enthusiasm, terrorist organizations grew in the 1980s and 1990s and adopted bolder tactics aimed at both military and civilian targets. Some of these groups gained strength and reach through financial support by wealthy patrons. The growing availability of modern communications and military technology also enhanced their power.

During the first years of the new century, tensions grew. After efforts to forge a U.S.-sponsored settlement of the Israeli-Palestinian dispute collapsed in 2000, a new, more deadly round of violence erupted between Israelis and Palestinians (see Map 26.6). Day after day, pictures, reports, and stories of the conflict focusing on Palestinian deaths at the hands of the Israelis spread across the Islamic world. In Israel, suicidal terrorists bombed shopping centers, restaurants, and buses. Within Palestinian areas, the death tolls from missiles, planes, and guns fired by the well-armed and trained Israeli forces rose dramatically. By 2004, much of the violence had subsided, and in 2005 Israel unilaterally withdrew from the Gaza Strip. However, in 2006 an election gave the militant Islamic organization Hamas—considered a terrorist group by many in the West—governing power in Palestine, raising tensions again. That same year, a war broke out in Lebanon between Israel and Hezbollah, a radical Islamic organization apparently backed by Iran and Syria.

The devastating attacks of September 11, 2001, against the United States were intended to strike at symbols of U.S. "imperial" power. The United States answered the attacks by declaring war against terrorism. President George W. Bush vowed to pursue terrorists wherever they lurked in the world and punish those who harbored them. Drawing on the sympathy and support of many nations, the U.S. military launched a massive aerial assault on al-Qaeda strongholds in Afghanistan, as well as on the Taliban, the radical fundamentalist regime that ruled the mountainous nation (see Map 26.7).

Afghanistan had a history of strife. During the 1980s, the Afghani people had endured a long, bloody war against Soviet invaders (see page 764). The im-

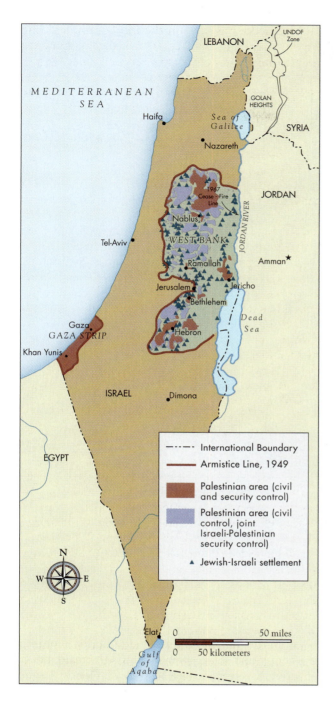

MAP 26.6   ISRAEL AND THE OCCUPIED TERRITORIES, 2007

This map shows Israel, the occupied territories of the West Bank, and the Gaza Strip. It also shows areas of varying Palestinian and Israeli control as well as Jewish-Israeli settlements. ■ **Notice** the location of settlements and the divided areas of Palestinian and Israeli control. **Consider** the difficulties facing Palestinians and Israelis trying to establish a permanent peace. **Consider** how any settlement might affect surrounding states with large numbers of Palestinian refugees.

other terrorists and regimes might acquire and wield "weapons of mass destruction." He warned that other states might also feel the force of U.S. military power in the future.

In March 2003, the United States took another step in the name of its "war on terror." The U.S. military, backed by British forces and the token support of other nations, attacked Iraq. During the months leading up to the war, the Bush administration, building on fears stemming from the September 11, 2001, terrorist attacks, cited the development and existence of terrifying weapons of mass destruction (chemical, biological, and nuclear) in Iraq that threatened the United States and the whole international community. Administration officials also claimed that Iraqi leader Saddam Hussein's dictatorial regime had links with international terrorist organizations such as al-Qaeda. The United States, officials said, had a duty to rid the world of Iraq's violent, brutal regime. Under these justifications for invading Iraq lay a vision within Bush administration of aggressively and, if necessary, single-handedly reforming oil-rich Iraq. Other authoritarian regimes in the strategic Middle East, administration officials hoped, would then transform themselves into democracies or at least reform. These new regimes would become friends of the United States and its allies as well as stable sources of oil (see Map 26.7).

Within weeks, U.S. and British air and ground forces overwhelmed Iraqi defenders and toppled Saddam Hussein and the Baathist Party, which had ruled Iraq with an iron fist for more than twenty years. Although President Bush declared victory in June 2003, achieving peace, stability, or international acclaim in the months that followed proved daunting. The United States, backed by Great Britain, refused to

poverished, war-torn country again suffered from the turmoil following the Soviet withdrawal in the late 1980s. In the mid-1990s, the Taliban seized power in most of Afghanistan, and there al-Qaeda found a home.

War in Afghanistan

In 2001 and 2002, the U.S. military, using anti-Taliban Afghan forces for much of the campaign on the ground, crushed most of the al-Qaeda and Taliban forces harbored within Afghanistan. However, President George W. Bush declared the war on terrorism far from over, pointing to the possibility that

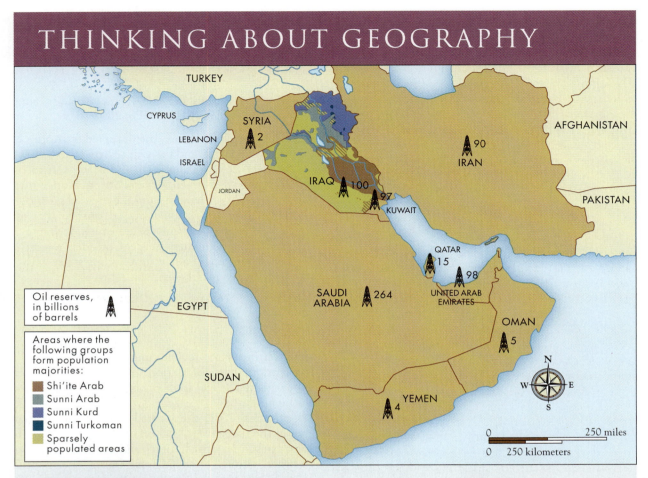

Oil reserves, in billions of barrels ⛏

Areas where the following groups form population majorities:

■ Shi'ite Arab
■ Sunni Arab
■ Sunni Kurd
■ Sunni Turkoman
■ Sparsely populated areas

MAP 26.7   THE MIDDLE EAST AND IRAQ, 2003

This map shows the Middle East, estimated oil reserves in several nations, and ethnoreligious groups in Iraq at the beginning of the U.S.-led invasion in 2003. ■ **Why** might the Middle East be of such strategic importance? **In what ways** might the war in Iraq change this region? **What** problems face those in Iraq who are trying to establish a stable, unified nation?

cede authority over the stabilization and rebuilding of Iraq to the United Nations. Many potential allies who had opposed the war in the first place—including France, Germany, Russia, India, Turkey, and most Arab states—refused to lend a hand under those conditions. The cost and responsibility for the process fell squarely on the shoulders of the United States and Great Britain, though other allies provided some support. Within Iraq, guerrilla and suicide attacks steadily raised the death toll into the thousands each month. Looting and sabotage further undermined efforts to establish security and promote recovery. By 2007, Iraq seemed on the verge of civil war.

Moreover, U.S. ambitions to usher in a new "democratic" government met with mounting discord among factions within Iraq. Historic rivalries between majority Arabs and minority Kurds in the north, and

between the majority Shiites and minority Sunnis in the center and south stymied efforts to create a new, effective government (see Map 26.7). Finally despite the eventual capture of Saddam Hussein in December 2003 and extensive searches, U.S. investigators could find no weapons of mass destruction or links to the sort of international terrorist organizations that carried out the 9/11 plot.

Only time will enable us to make firm judgments about the U.S. actions in Iraq and the policies underlying them. However, these actions and policies may prove to have greater historical significance than the toppling of Saddam Hussein's regime. First, the Bush administration set what many critics worldwide considered dangerous precedent by initiating a **preemptive war,**

Preemptive war unilateralism, and the occupation

based on the *assertion* that Iraq had imminent plans to attack the United States, or, even worse, a "preventive war," based on the *possibility* that Iraq might attack some time in the distant future. In these relatively nonthreatening circumstances, such a war violated long-established rules of international relations and dashed ambitions of those hoping to strengthen international barriers to the outbreak of wars.

Second, the Bush administration not only failed to win important UN and international support for the war. It also appeared to punish those who disagreed with its foreign policies—including long-time major allies such as France and Germany. Indeed, the United States seemed to discard the principles of internationalism that had informed global diplomacy since the end of World War II. In place of those principles, it appeared to favor a kind of **unilateralism** in which the world's only superpower pursued its own interests regardless of its allies' views and interests. The administration's abandonment of the Kyoto Protocol, which sought to limit global-warming emissions; its plans to develop an antiballistic missile shield and a new class of nuclear weapons; its desertion of international efforts to strengthen rules against biological weapons, land mines, and small arms; and its attacks on the International Criminal Court all added to the impression that the United States had decided to go it alone.

Third, the way the United States government justified its invasion of Iraq and what many in the world saw as the destructive mishandling of the occupation that followed diminished the sympathy and support for the United States after the September 11 attacks. Moreover, the bloodshed and political turmoil that reigned in Iraq year after year during the presence of U.S. led coalition forces served to increase the regional influence of Iran, still ruled by a fundamentalist regime that now embarked on a policy to develop its own atomic resources. These developments, along with veiled threats by the United States government to launch strikes against Iran, cast a darkening shadow over the Middle East.

Terrorism and the war in Afghanistan also had implications for the long-simmering problems between neighboring Pakistan, a predominantly Muslim nation, and India, a primarily Hindu country, over Kashmir. These two nations' struggle for control over Kashmir (See Map 26.8) had sparked armed conflict several times over previous decades. The growing threat of terrorism made the area even more volatile. In 2002, the two sides again seemed on the verge of war. This time, however, both Pakistan and India had demonstrated to each other and the world their ability to use nuclear weapons.

Crisis over Kashmir

To many people around the world, it seemed clear that terrorism—and the conflicts, poverty, and political tensions that fueled it as well as reactions to it—had greater global significance than ever before. Bombings in Bali in 2002, Madrid in 2004, and London in 2005 added to their fears about terrorism. The images of peace and security that many people had envisioned after the fall of communism gave way to a new sense of vulnerability in a world that seemed to be slipping out of control.

ACROSS BORDERS: CULTURAL CONFLICT AND CONVERGENCE

All these developments—in the Middle East, North Africa, and East Asia—revealed the West's inextricable ties with the non-Western world. They also posed new challenges to the dominance that the West had enjoyed for so long. Perhaps most important, they illustrated a problem that spread well beyond any one region: the chafing of local cultures against global and even national influences. On one level, globalization meant the invasion

Resistance to globalization

KEY DATES

THE WEST AND THE WORLD

1991	Persian Gulf War
1992	Maastrich Treaty
1994	NAFTA created
	Mandela president of South Africa
1999	Euro introduced
2000	Palestinian uprisings
2001	Terrorist attacks in United States
	War in Afghanistan
2002	Kashmir crisis
	Terrorist bombing in Bali
2003	Invasion of Iraq
2004	Terrorist bombings in Madrid
	European Union adds ten new members
2005	Terrorist bombings in London
	Pope John Paul II dies
	France and the Netherlands reject new European constitution
2006	Israel invades Lebanon
2007	Power-sharing agreement in Northern Ireland

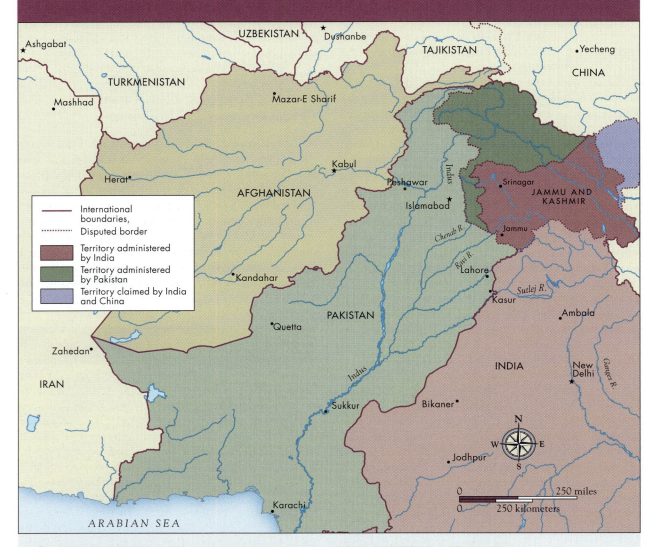

MAP 26.8   AFGHANISTAN, KASHMIR, AND SOUTH-CENTRAL ASIA, 2002

This map shows Afghanistan, Kashmir, and the surrounding areas in 2002. ■ **What** might be difficult about controlling conflicts in these areas? **Consider** what might be of strategic significance about this region. **Consider** why the conflict over Kashmir might be of such importance.

of Western culture into centuries-old but vulnerable non-Western cultural legacies. Figure 26.7 reveals this tenuous mixture and clash of cultures in Mexico. A descendant of the Olmecs, who once dominated parts of Mexico some three thousand years ago, prepares to dance as a jaguar to bring rain. The boy's clay-covered body is being stamped with ashes by an adult using a Coca Cola bottle—one of the most recognized symbols of Western commerce. This image was soon transmitted by a Western photographer to a magazine with circulation in the millions, perhaps encouraging Western tourists and companies to invade this traditional culture even further. On another level, nationalism and religious fundamentalism revealed a deep resistance to globalization. The struggles of minorities to retain their own sense of identity in the face of demands for national and religious conformity within their own nations reflected a parallel resistance to outside meddling. In one terrifying variation of this pattern, in the central African state of Rwanda, ethnic

Hutu extremists slaughtered more than 500,000 ethnic Tutsi during the mid-1990s; fighting and civil war plagued the area for years. Another variation of this violence occurred in the western Sudan region of Darfur, where political disputes between Arabs and non-Arab rebels arose. Between 2004 and 2006, government-backed Arab militias carried out a systematic campaign that killed 300,000 non-Arab farmers and displaced two million people. In the West and elsewhere, these multilayered resentments and struggles formed a complex backdrop for other emerging developments.

Immigration While ethnic conflict and nationalism intensified in several parts of the globe, cultural differences among Western nations and between Western and non-Western peoples also softened with an increase in international contacts. People migrated in droves to the West and other wealthier areas of the world, such as the oil-rich Middle East, and crossed countless borders in the search for work. The new immigration opened doors for many people, but it also had its dark side. The opening of frontiers within Europe during the 1990s and the desperation of millions throughout the world made the movement of people difficult to control.

■ FIGURE 26.7
The clash of cultures.

Illegal immigration skyrocketed to more than 10 million people a year globally. For example, immigrants from Iran, Turkey, Iraq, Pakistan, Bangladesh, Albania, and elsewhere risked dangerous boat passages and expulsion to reach places such as Italy's long, exposed southern coast. "We lived like animals. . . . If we had not brought some biscuits and water, we would have starved," said a Kurdish immigrant in 1997. Some of the thousands who crossed North American borders each year—legally and illegally—told similar stories.

Germany in particular drew people from Turkey, Yugoslavia, Italy, Eastern Europe, and Russia and attracted asylum-seekers from many other parts of the world. In 1997, almost 9 percent of Germany's population were immigrants, many of whom remained unassimilated and yet alienated from their lands of origin. One Turkish woman who worked in her father's pizzeria in Berlin described the situation: "People like me are foreigners in Turkey. . . . There you are not a real Turk, and here you are not a complete German. We are somewhere in between." Her father agreed: "Even if I had a German passport, I would still feel like a foreigner and be regarded as a foreigner."

By 2005, some 20 million Muslims lived in Western Europe, many of whom were frustrated by bleak job prospects, outraged by discrimination, and yearning for a sense of respect. A French youth of Algerian descent living in one of the rough housing projects just outside of Paris explained: "You wake up every morning looking for work. But why? There isn't any." Like millions of other Arab and African immigrants and their French-born children and grandchildren, he had not been well integrated into French society. In 2005 and 2006, groups of young immigrants displayed their frustration in riots. Figure 26.8 shows French youths burning vehicles in protest and battling police in one of France's many immigrant communities, Aulnay sous Bois, just northeast of Paris. The photograph suggests the combination of defiance and anger that rose to the surface in these French neighborhoods.

During these same decades, a common popular culture, especially among the youth in American, European, and non-Western cities, spread with increasing speed across all borders. The worldwide popularity of Hollywood movies, Disney products, soccer, Nintendo computer games, hamburgers, pizza, shopping malls, noodle soup, Nike shoes, Benetton clothes, TV series, and rock and roll all reflected this standardization **Popular culture** of cultural tastes. The spread of English as the world's second language and the beaming of television shows across borders by satellite facilitated the convergence of cultures. No medium offered more potential for this crossing of cultural lines in the future than the Internet. Instantaneous electronic communication and

Youths set vehicles ablaze near Paris, France, in 2005.

access to burgeoning informational, commercial, and scientific resources on the World Wide Web seemed to have dissolved time and space as well as national borders, spawning what some observers called the "global village."

The easing of more traditional forms of travel also added to the meeting of cultures, particularly for middle-class tourists who journeyed throughout the world, visited museums, and absorbed at least visual images of different nations' cultural past and present. Figure 26.9, an illustration for the *Sophisticated Traveler* supplement to the *New York Times,* captures this sense of historical and cultural convergence. In this composite of six masterpieces of Western art, the artist makes a playful statement about the blending of Western cultures. Most of this image's components, which span three thousand years of Western history, are probably familiar to the millions of museum-going, "sophisticated" middle-class travelers for whom this magazine is intended.

Other cultural changes also set off the 1990s as unique. In the arts, what was once seen as modern in 1914 or even as late as midcentury—the glass skyscrapers and the abstract paintings of Mondrian and Pollock, for example—now seemed old and taken for granted. Artistic and intellectual movements adopted the "postmodern" label. In the *Postmodernism*
arts, followers of **postmodernism** became less concerned with austere principles. Architects, for example, rejected the pure forms and plain glass walls of the modern style in favor of buildings with elaborate shapes and ornamentation. Intellectuals and critics sympathetic to postmodernism attacked all ideologies—from liberalism to Marxism—and even the intellectual foundations of most academic disciplines as outmoded, oppressive distortions of the truth. Skeptical that objective truth was possible, they claimed that science itself was infected by the dominant values and beliefs of the culture that produced it.

BEYOND BORDERS: UNCERTAINTY AND OPPORTUNITY IN A SHRINKING WORLD

The spreading webs of communications and the goods and services radiating out from the West promised satisfactions galore for anyone who wanted to—and could afford to—participate. However, recessions during the 1980s and after 2000 reminded Westerners and non-Westerners

■ FIGURE 26.9
Marco Ventura, *Mona Lisa Contemplating the Bust of Nefertiti as God Creates Order out of Chaos on a Starry Night on the Island of La Grande Jatte as the Infanta Margarita Looks On,* 1993.

THINKING ABOUT GEOGRAPHY

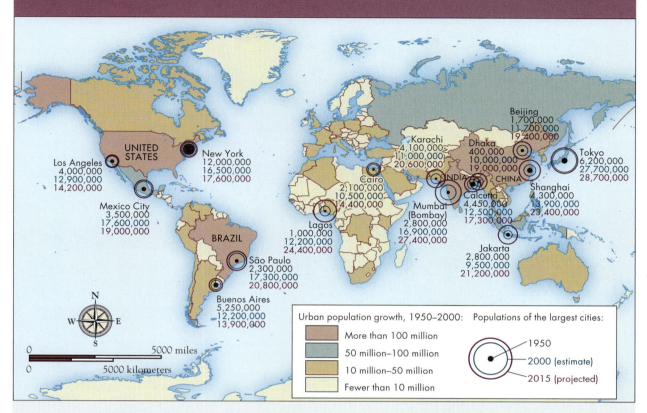

United States
Los Angeles
4,000,000
12,900,000
14,200,000

New York
12,000,000
16,500,000
17,600,000

Mexico City
3,500,000
17,600,000
19,000,000

Brazil
São Paulo
2,300,000
17,300,000
20,800,000

Buenos Aires
5,250,000
12,200,000
13,900,000

Cairo
2,100,000
10,500,000
14,400,000

Lagos
1,000,000
12,200,000
24,400,000

Karachi
4,100,000
11,000,000
20,600,000

India

Mumbai
(Bombay)
2,800,000
16,900,000
27,400,000

Calcutta
4,450,000
12,500,000
17,300,000

Dhaka
400,000
10,000,000
19,000,000

Beijing
1,700,000
11,700,000
19,400,000

China

Shanghai
4,300,000
13,900,000
23,400,000

Tokyo
6,200,000
27,700,000
28,700,000

Jakarta
2,800,000
9,500,000
21,200,000

Urban population growth, 1950–2000:
- More than 100 million
- 50 million–100 million
- 10 million–50 million
- Fewer than 10 million

Populations of the largest cities:
- 1950
- 2000 (estimate)
- 2015 (projected)

0   5000 miles
0   5000 kilometers

MAP 26.9   THE GROWTH OF CITIES

This map shows those areas with the largest urban populations and the growth of population in the world's largest cities. ■ **Notice** where the greatest growth of large cities has been and is expected to occur. ■ **Consider** what problems this growth of urban population poses for the West and the world.

alike that economic growth could not be taken for granted. Despite the West's overall prosperity, inflation and declining personal incomes for the bottom half of society spawned social discontent in these decades. In most of Europe, unemployment continued to hover above 10 percent and reached as high as 20 percent during the 1990s. Unions everywhere lost membership and clout, leaving more workers than ever without protection in a shifting, competitive marketplace.

In addition, with international economic ties proliferating, problems in one area of the world quickly made themselves felt in other regions. For example, the financial crisis and economic turmoil that struck Asia in 1998 spread rapidly, creating huge losses for investors and trading partners throughout the world. More recently, economic development in the West and elsewhere heightened demand for energy derived from oil and natural gas. Most Western nations consume far more oil than they produce, and nations with rising economies such as China and India want the oil-fueled wealth enjoyed in the West. In a competitive international arena, they vie for supplies from major producers such as Saudi Arabia, Iran, Iraq, Russia, Venezuela, and Nigeria. Webs of politics, arms, money, and influence surround this growing international need for oil. The relatively affluent West, with its multinational corporations, could no longer ignore nations scourged by crushing debts, pressing economic needs, and unmet demands. The evolving global economic landscape added to the uncertainty. Despite the rise of East Asia and India, the gap between the affluent, industrialized nations of the northern latitudes and the poorer, developing nations of the south widened. Incomes in most nations in sub-Saharan Africa and

Growing international economic ties

THINKING ABOUT GEOGRAPHY

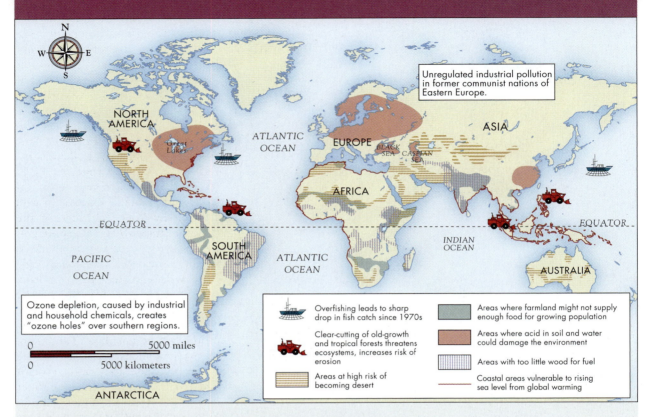

Unregulated industrial pollution in former communist nations of Eastern Europe.

Ozone depletion, caused by industrial and household chemicals, creates "ozone holes" over southern regions.

Overfishing	Overfishing leads to sharp drop in fish catch since 1970s
Clear-cutting	Clear-cutting of old-growth and tropical forests threatens ecosystems, increases risk of erosion
Desert	Areas at high risk of becoming desert
Farmland	Areas where farmland might not supply enough food for growing population
Acid	Areas where acid in soil and water could damage the environment
Wood	Areas with too little wood for fuel
Coastal	Coastal areas vulnerable to rising sea level from global warming

MAP 26.10   GLOBAL ENVIRONMENTAL PROBLEMS

This map indicates widespread environmental problems, most stemming from industrialization, exploitation of natural resources, urbanization, and population increases. ■ **Which** areas of the world are affected more than others by environmental problems? **How** interconnected are these difficulties? ■ **What** environmental problems are not adequately revealed by this map? ■ **Consider** what might be done to diminish these problems.

Latin America actually declined from 1960s levels. In 2005, more than 2 billion people in the world subsisted on the equivalent of less than $1 per day.

As world population in 2006 passed 6.5 billion—more than double that at the end of World War II—the poorer southern half of the globe carried the heaviest burden of population growth. Figure 26.10 shows population changes for major areas of the world since 1900 and estimates population figures for the mid-twenty-first century. Europe, with declining birthrates, will experience a drop in population, while Asia and Africa will gain the most. Many Western nations—particularly the United States—have relied on immigration to bolster population figures.

The distinction between Europe and the rest of the world in population trends is also reflected in the process of urbanization (see Map 26.9). Although the

Major Area	1900	1950	1998	2050
	Population (in millions)			
Asia	947	1402	3585	5268
Africa	133	221	749	1766
Europe	408	547	729	628
Latin America	74	167	504	809
North America	82	172	305	392
Oceania	6	13	30	46
World (total)	1650	2522	5902	8909

■ FIGURE 26.10

Population changes across the twentieth and twenty-first centuries.

■ FIGURE 26.11

Muir Glacier, Alaska, in 1941 (*top*) and 2004 (*bottom*).

runoff from industrial sites and cities. Even the monuments of ancient Greece and Rome were rapidly deteriorating and crumbling from the onslaught of fumes and vibrations of city life. In Eastern Europe and the Soviet Union, environmental problems had been virtually ignored for decades. The collapse of communism in those areas revealed staggering environmental degradation. In many Western countries the growing importance of Green parties pushed environmental concerns into the political spotlight.

As Map 26.10 shows, environmental problems extended well beyond the West. Thirteen of the fifteen cities with the worst air pollution in the world were in Asia. Of the estimated 2.7 million people worldwide who died each year from illnesses caused by air pollution, the majority were Asians. Each year, Asia lost 1 percent of its forests. As humanity consumed more and more resources and disrupted the globe's natural balance, thousands of plant and animal species became extinct each year (see Document 26.3). Humanity's need for more and more energy also led many nations to rely increasingly on nuclear power. The 1986 accident at the Chernobyl plant in the Soviet Union shed new light on the potential dangers of nuclear power—the accident released two hundred times the radiation of the two bombs dropped in World War II.

Many observers believe that **global warming** has become our most threatening environmental problem. Most scientists agree that in recent decades the Earth's atmosphere has heated up at an alarming rate in great part thanks to the *Global warming* heat-trapping so-called "greenhouse gases," such as carbon dioxide, that have been created through the combustion of coal and petroleum products. Factories, power plants, urban growth, and gas-guzzling motor vehicles in the West and in rapidly developing nations such as China and India add to those greenhouse gases every day. According to most scientists, the warming process is probably irreversible, and unless slowed by policies that crucial nations seem unwilling to adopt, could produce dramatic climate changes, resulting in the melting of ice sheets and glaciers, coastal flooding, widening

wealthy areas of the West once experienced the most rapid urban growth, other parts of the world gained the lead during the last half of the twentieth century. Moreover, in 1950, six out of the ten largest cities were in Europe and the U.S.; by 2000 most of the world's largest cities were in the non-Western world, a trend likely to grow in the future.

Economic growth, population increases, and urbanization created alarming environmental problems in the late twentieth century (see Map 26.10). The earth's air, water, and seas became more and more polluted, while acid rain, caused by smoke and fumes, damaged more than one-third of Germany's remaining forests. Great rivers such as the *Environmental costs* Rhine and the Danube became like sewers, and waters such as the Mediterranean and Black seas were fouled by

Charles Michael Helmken, *Loveaidspeople*, 1989

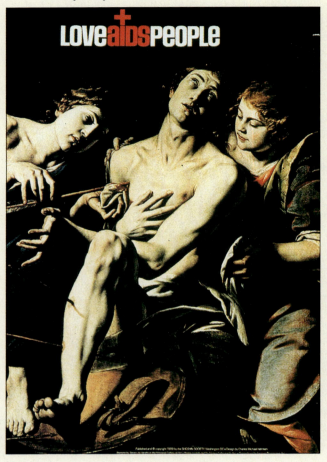

■ FIGURE 26.12

This 1989 poster was designed to increase public awareness of AIDS and attitudes toward people affected by AIDS. ■ **How** do you explain the meaning of the title, *Loveaidspeople*, and how the title has been depicted by the artist? ■ **Why** might the artist have referred back to the Christian martyr Saint Sebastian in this poster? ■ **How** might the viewer understand some of the details and coloring of this poster?

taken in August 1941. On the bottom is a photograph taken from the same vantage point in August 2004. The glacier had retreated more than seven miles, allowing ocean water to fill the valley. What remained of the glacier, now in the distance, had thinned by more than 875 yards. Some experts feel that such dramatic environmental developments will diminish or destroy our ability to sustain Earth's population. Global warming is "the single biggest challenge facing the planet, the equal in every way to the nuclear threat that transfixed us during the past half-century and a threat we haven't even begun to deal with," warned one distinguished scientist.

People have turned to science and government to solve these environmental problems, but thus far the results have been mixed at best. On one hand, scientists and governmental officials finally recognized the severity of these problems and have begun to address them by committing more funds to research and coming to agreements on new regulations to minimize the damage. On the other hand, anxieties about the environment have often conflicted with a stronger desire of many people for continued economic growth. Businesses and governments, reflecting this desire, have often proved reluctant to commit to expensive environmental-protection programs.

Like the environment, health issues have also received an ambivalent response. In the last few decades of the twentieth century, many officials and commentators recognized that an aging population, particularly in the West, presented a growing health problem that would strain medical facilities and budgets, **AIDS** but they were unsure what to do. With certain health problems—the worldwide AIDS (Acquired Immune Deficiency Syndrome) epidemic is just one example—recognition of the dangers often came too late. Even then, many efforts to address such crises proved half-hearted. Again, AIDS is an apt example. Between 1978 and 2006, 26,000,000 people died from this disease. AIDS became the most deadly epidemic in recent global history, yet many people initially denied its existence or criticized those who had contracted it. The AIDS poster in Figure 26.12, *Loveaidspeople*, uses Renaissance painter Tanzio da Varallo's painting of the Christian martyr Saint Sebastian, to protest these attitudes. In this poignant image, a modern-day AIDS victim has been wounded by the "arrows" of officials and social attitudes that condemn both the third-century martyr and the twentieth-century AIDS victim as "morally dirty" and "sinful." The poster makes an urgent plea for assistance for AIDS sufferers. After several years, some help began to arrive, but not nearly enough. In 2006, the United Nations estimated that 40 million people in the world were living with AIDS or HIV, the virus that causes AIDS. In some sub-Saharan countries of Africa, one in four adults were infected.

droughts, worsening hurricanes, and rapid extinction of plant and animal species by the end of this century. Figure 26.11 shows one example of the many glaciers that have been melting throughout the world. On the top is a photograph of the Muir Glacier in Alaska

■ DOCUMENT 26.3

Ecological Problems Threaten Nature

Over the past decades, modern civilization has been exacting a higher and higher price from nature. Scholars point out that the planet's air and water are becoming polluted, species are being diminished or destroyed, and vital natural resources are being depleted. In the following selection, Thomas Berry, a Christian theologian, assessed the seriousness of these problems. ■ ***What*** *does Berry mean by the earth deficit?* ■ ***What*** *has caused these problems?*

The reality of our present economy is such that we must have certain forebodings not simply as regards the well-being of the human community but even of the planet itself in its most basic life systems. . . .

In the natural world there exists an amazing richness of life expression in the ever-renewing cycle of the seasons. There is a minimum of entropy. The inflow of energy and the outflow are such that the process is sustainable over an indefinite period of time—so long as the human process is integral with these processes of nature, so long is the human economy sustainable into the future. The difficulty comes when the industrial mode of our economy disrupts the natural processes, when human technologies are destructive of earth technologies. In such a situation the productivity of the natural world and its life systems is diminished. When nature goes into deficit, then we go into deficit. . . .

. . . the earth deficit is the real deficit, the ultimate deficit, the deficit so absolute in some of its major consequences as to be beyond adjustment from any source in heaven or earth. Since the earth system is the ultimate guarantor of all deficits, a failure here is a failure of last resort. Neither economic viability nor improvement in life conditions for the poor can be realized in such circumstances. They can only worsen, especially when we consider rising population levels throughout the developing world.

This deficit in its extreme expression is not only a resource deficit but the death of a living process, not simply the death of *a* living process but of *the* living process—a living process which exists, so far as we know, only on the planet earth. This is what makes our problems definitively different from those of any other generation of whatever ethnic, cultural, political or religious tradition or of any other historical period. For the first time we are determining the destinies of the earth in a comprehensive and irreversible manner. The immediate danger is not *possible* nuclear war but *actual* industrial plundering.

Source: Thomas Berry, "Wonderworld as Wasteland: The Earth in Deficit," *Cross Currents*, Winter 1985–1986, pp. 408–410.

In the face of frightening diseases, environmental degradation, economic uncertainty, and devastating weaponry, many people looked to the new century with cynicism or dread. Some found it all too easy to imagine even the violent destruction of all life on Earth, as Figure 26.13 suggests. This painting, by American artist Jennifer Bartlett, shows a firestorm sweeping away everything in its path. Sculptural objects are dashed to the floor between the viewer and the canvas. In a world that still had unimaginably destructive weapons of war at its fingertips, this scene may well have offered a visual warning of the potential for holocaust that hung over the West and the rest of the world as the twenty-first century began.

Perhaps in response to these anxieties, the last two decades of the twentieth century saw a renewal of religious commitment among many people. In the United States and Europe, evangelical Christianity—with its emphasis on personal salvation and spiritual experience—became the fastest growing

■ FIGURE 26.13

Jennifer Bartlett, *Spiral: An Ordinary Evening in New Haven*, 1989.

religious movement. In Russia, an outpouring of religious sentiment within the Orthodox Church followed the collapse of communism. Islamic fundamentalism, calling for a return to traditional ways and a rejection of alien ideologies, intensified in lands from West Africa to East Asia. All of these movements reflected a hunger for a sense of meaning and a clarity of values by which to live in an uncertain time.

Movements of religious revival

Yet, despite these anxieties, there were also reasons to look to the coming century with hope and optimism. After all, the West had surmounted major obstacles. It had enjoyed more than fifty years of relative peace and had managed to avert the dreaded clash of superpowers during the Cold War. In Eastern Europe, most nations had gained their long-sought independence with a minimum of violence. In some areas, seemingly hopeless problems showed signs of being solved. For example, in Northern Ireland, Protestants and Catholics created a power-sharing government, ending a decades-long bitter conflict.

Accomplishments and optimism

For many people around the world, the standard of living had risen to unprecedented levels. Although social equality still remained only an ideal, the Western promise of continually improving well-being for everyone seemed to hold firm. The increasing human life span and rising numbers of elderly—in part thanks to the global increase in food production and better access to health care—attested to that well-being. Moreover, many women gained access to opportunities once available only to men: By the late 1990s, roughly equal numbers of women and men in the West received higher education and pursued paying careers. Women's presence in professional life and in politics continued to grow. True, traditionalists worried about the destruction of the family as an institution, citing the growing prevalence of two-career parents, a rise in cohabitation and single motherhood, and accelerating divorce rates. Nevertheless, family structures persisted, although many of them took new forms such as "an emotionally bound partnership."

Continuing scientific discoveries suggested that the West and the rest of the world could look forward to dramatic developments in the future. Perhaps most stunning was the prospect of changes stemming from the decoding of the human genome—determining the chemical sequence of the DNA in every cell of the human body. In 2001, this costly, long-term project carried out by hundreds of scientists in six countries was completed. With this "blueprint" of human life, scientists hoped to revolutionize medicine and gain new insights into human nature.

Overall, the West has gained a much needed appreciation of its place in the world, and human beings around the globe have new tools to understand themselves within a widening universe. Technology, trade, and instant com-munications provide growing opportunities for cooperation across national boundaries. As the twenty-first century opens, life offers more options to more people than ever.

SUMMARY

In 1989, history in the West abruptly shifted course. The communist regimes in Eastern Europe fell, severing these nations' ties to the Soviet Union and sparking unprecedented political and economic reforms. Two years later, the Soviet Union itself disintegrated. The Cold War ended and along with it, a sharply defined historical era stretching back to 1914. The end of the Cold War renewed the commitment to democracy and capitalism in the West, accelerated the existing movement toward unification in Europe, and left the United States standing as the sole military superpower in the world.

But the collapse of communism did not end all the anxieties present during the Cold War era. The transition in Eastern Europe and the Soviet Union proved rocky, and Westerners realized that despite their lofty global position, they could no longer keep the rest of the world at arm's length. Indeed, the West's global status began to change, as statistics reveal. In 1950, some 30 percent of the world's population lived in Europe and North America. In 1997, that figure dropped below 20 percent and continued to decline. As peoples around the world interacted more and more, cultures mingled, producing both conflict and convergence; our time may mark the beginning of a new global society. The relentless human desire for limitless economic growth and material security also left its mark on the environment in ways that spread concern across national boundaries. Western civilization, so long centered on the western tip of the Eurasian continent, now seemed to be just one of many lights shining on this shrinking globe. As one era closed and another opened, great challenges faced all of humanity. Whether and how the West—and the world—would embrace these challenges remained to be seen.

KEY TERMS

REVIEW, ANALYZE, AND ANTICIPATE

REVIEW THE PREVIOUS CHAPTER

Chapter 25—"Superpower Struggles and Global Transformations"—analyzed the Cold War competition between the United States and the Soviet Union. Within the Cold War context, the recovery of the West and end of colonialism were analyzed.

1. *How might you argue that developments since 1989 are not the beginning of a new historical era and that instead, they are a continuation of trends that first emerged in the post–World War II decades?*

2. *Do you think that the collapse of communism and the end of the Cold War should have been predictable by the early 1980s? Why?*

ANALYZE THIS CHAPTER

Chapter 26—"Into the Twenty-First Century"—traces the collapse of communism and the intense interaction between the Western and non-Western worlds.

1. *Analyze the consequences of the collapse of communism outside Eastern Europe and the Soviet Union.*

2. *In what ways has much of Europe become integrated, and what steps remain to achieve full integration?*

3. *What forces are pulling the world together? How do these forces compare with those dividing the world?*

ANTICIPATE THE FUTURE

It is always difficult to predict the future, but history can sometimes provide grounds for reasonable guesses.

1. *In the near future, what might be the consequences of continuing steps toward the unification of Europe?*

2. *Judging from developments since 1989, which problems do you think will prove the most serious in the years to come? Why? Do you think there is good reason for optimism? Why or why not?*

BEYOND THE CLASSROOM

THE COLLAPSE OF COMMUNISM

Brown, Archie. *The Gorbachev Factor.* New York: Oxford University Press, 1996. An examination of Gorbachev's role in the collapse of communism.

Garton Ash, Timothy. *In Europe's Name: Germany and the Divided Continent.* London: Jonathan Cape, 1993. Stresses the history of tensions between East and West Germany as background to their reunification.

Remnick, David. *Lenin's Tomb: The Last Days of the Soviet Empire.* New York: Random House, 1994. Journalistic coverage of the final period before the collapse of the Soviet empire, stressing the role played by Yeltsin.

Service, Robert. *Russia: Experiment with a People.* Cambridge, MA: Harvard University Press, 2003. Solid, scholarly coverage of Russia since 1991.

Silber, Laura, and Little, Allan. *Yugoslavia: Death of a Nation.* New York: TV Books/Penguin USA, 1996. An account of the nation's ethnic troubles.

Stokes, Gale. *The Walls Came Tumbling Down: The Collapse of Communism in Eastern Europe.* Oxford: Oxford University Press, 1993. Analyzes the decline and fall of communism in Eastern Europe since 1968.

REPERCUSSIONS AND REALIGNMENTS IN THE WEST

Caplan, Richard, and John Feffer, eds. *Europe's New Nationalism: States and Minorities in Conflict.* New York: Oxford University Press, 1996. A collection of essays by scholars on the growth of nationalism in Europe after the collapse of communism.

Cheles, Juciano, et al., eds. *The Far Right in Western and Eastern Europe,* 2nd ed. London: Longman, 1995. A comparative study of fringe movements in these areas.

Dinan, Desmond. *Europe Recast: A History of the European Union.* New York: Lynne Rienner Publishers, 2003. A well-written overview.

THE WORLD AND THE WEST FROM A GLOBAL PERSPECTIVE

Campos, Jose Edgardo, and Hilton L. Root. *The Key to the Asian Miracle: Making Shared Growth Credible.* Washington, D.C.: Brookings Institution, 1996. An interesting analysis of economic development in Asia and its connections to the West.

Cohen, Daniel. *Globalization and Its Enemies.* Boston: MIT Press, 2006. A brilliant discussion of the promises and problems of globalization in a broad historical context.

Friedman, Thomas L. *The Lexus and the Olive Tree.* New York: Farrar, Straus, Giroux, 1999. An engaging, boldly interpretive analysis of globalism.

Mandelbaum, Michael. *The Case for Goliath: How America Acts as the World's Government in the 21st Century.* New York: Perseus, 2005. A sharp, challenging interpretation of America's changing role in world affairs.

McNeill, J.R. *Something New Under the Sun: An Environmental History of the Twentieth-Century World.* New York: W.W. Norton, 2000. An important union of historical and environmental perspectives.

Purdum, Todd S. *A Time of Our Choosing: America's War in Iraq.* New York: Times Books/Henry Holt, 2003. A useful guide to the war in Iraq.

www.mhhe.com/sherman3

- Unfamiliar words? See our Glossary at the back of the book for pronunciation and definitions.

- Need help studying? See our web page for map exercises, practice quizzes, and additional study resources.

- Need help writing a paper? Access hundreds of primary documents, maps, images, and a guide to writing history papers on our Primary Source Investigator site at **www.mhhe.com/psi.**

GLOSSARY

Note to users: Terms that are foreign or difficult to pronounce are transcribed in parentheses directly after the term itself. The transcriptions are based on the rules of English spelling; that is to say, they are similar to the transcriptions employed in the *Webster* dictionaries. Each word's most heavily stressed syllable is marked by an acute accent.

A

Absolute monarch (máh-nark) A seventeenth- or eighteenth-century European monarch claiming complete political authority.

Absolutism (áb-suh-loo-tism) (Royal) A government in which all power is vested in the ruler.

Abstract expressionism (ex-présh-un-ism) A twentieth-century painting style infusing nonrepresentational art with strong personal feelings.

Acropolis (uh-króp-uh-liss) The hill at the center of Athens on which the magnificent temples—including the Parthenon—that made the architecture of ancient Athens famous are built.

Act of Union Formal unification of England and Scotland in 1707.

Afrikaners Afrikaans-speaking South Africans of Dutch and other European ancestry.

Age of Reason The eighteenth-century Enlightenment; sometimes includes seventeenth-century science and philosophy.

Agora In ancient Greece, the marketplace or place of public assembly.

Agricultural revolution Neolithic discovery of agriculture; agricultural transformations that began in eighteenth-century western Europe.

Ahura Mazda In Zoroastrianism, the beneficial god of light.

Ahriman In Zoroastrianism, the evil god of darkness.

Akkadian (uh-káy-dee-un) A Semitic language of a region of ancient Mesopotamia.

Albigensians (al-buh-jén-see-unz) A medieval French heretical sect that believed in two gods—an evil and a good principle—that was destroyed in a crusade in the thirteenth century; also called Cathars.

Alchemy (ál-kuh-mee) The medieval study and practice of chemistry, primarily concerned with changing metals into gold and finding a universal remedy for diseases. It was much practiced from the thirteenth to the seventeenth century.

Allies (ál-eyes) The two alliances against Germany and its partners in World War I and World War II.

Al-Qaeda A global terrorist network headed by Osama bin Laden.

Anarchists (ánn-ar-kissts) Those advocating or promoting anarchy, or an absence of government. In the late nineteenth and early twentieth century, anarchism arose as an ideology and movement against all governmental authority and private property.

Ancien Régime (áwn-syáwn ráy-zhéem) The traditional political and social order in Europe before the French Revolution.

Antigonids (ann-tíg-un-idz) Hellenistic dynasty that ruled in Macedonia from about 300 B.C.E. to about 150 B.C.E.

Anti-Semitism (ann-tye-sém-i-tism) Prejudice against Jews.

Apartheid "Separation" in the Afrikaans language. A policy to rigidly segregate people by color in South Africa, 1948–1989.

Appeasement Attempting to satisfy potential aggressors in order to avoid war.

Aramaic (air-uh-máy-ik) A northwest Semitic language that spread throughout the region. It was the language that Jesus spoke.

Archon (áhr-kahn) A chief magistrate in ancient Athens.

Areopagus (air-ee-áh-pa-gus) A prestigious governing council of ancient Athens.

Arete (ah-ray-táy) Greek term for the valued virtues of manliness, courage, and excellence.

Arianism (áir-ee-un-ism) A fourth-century Christian heresy that taught that Jesus was not of the same substance as God the father, and thus had been created.

Assignats (ah-seen-yáh) Paper money issued in the National Assembly during the French Revolution.

Astrolabe (áss-tro-leyb) Medieval instrument used to determine the altitudes of celestial bodies.

Augury (áh-gur-ee) The art or practice of foretelling events though signs or omens.

Autocrat (áuto-crat) An authoritarian ruler.

Autocracy (au-tóc-ra-cee) Government under the rule of an authoritarian ruler.

Axis World War II alliance whose main members were Germany, Italy, and Japan.

B

Baby boom The increase in births following World War II.

Babylonian Captivity Period during the fourteenth century in which seven popes chose to reside in Avignon instead of Rome. Critics called this period the "Babylonian Captivity" of the papacy.

Bailiffs Medieval French salaried officials hired by the king to collect taxes and represent his interests.

Balance of power Distribution of power among states, or the policy of creating alliances to control powerful states.

Balkans States in the Balkan Peninsula, including Albania, Bulgaria, Greece, Romania, and Yugoslavia.

Baroque (ba-róak) An artistic style of the sixteenth and seventeenth centuries stressing rich ornamentation and dynamic movement; in music, a style marked by strict forms and elaborate ornamentation.

Bastard feudalism (feúd-a-lism) Late medieval corruption of the feudal system replacing feudal loyalty with cash payments.

Bastille (bas-téel) The royal prison symbolizing the old regime that was destroyed in the French Revolution.

Bauhaus (bóugh-house) An influential school of art emphasizing clean, functional lines founded in Germany by the architect Walter Gropius just after World War I.

Bedouin (béd-oh-in) An Arab of any of the nomadic tribes of the deserts of North Africa, Arabia, and Syria.

Berlin airlift The airborne military operation organized to supply Berlin's Western-occupied sectors during the Soviet Union's 1948 Berlin blockage.

Berlin Wall The wall erected in 1961 to divide East and West Berlin.

Bessemer (béss-uh-mer) **process** A method for removing impurities from molten iron.

Black Death Name given the epidemic that swept Europe beginning in 1348. Most historians agree that the main disease was bubonic plague, but the Black Death may have incorporated many other diseases.

Blackshirts Mussolini's black-uniformed Fascist paramilitary forces in the 1920s and 1930s.

Blitzkrieg (blíts-kreeg) "Lighting war," a rapid air and land military assault used by the Germans in World War II.

Boers (boars) Dutch settlers in south Africa.

Bolshevik (bówl-shuh-vick) "Majority faction," the Leninist wing of the Russian Marxist Party; after 1917, the Communist Party.

Bourgeoisie (boor-zhwa-zée) The middle class.

Boxers A nineteenth-century Chinese secret society that believed in the spiritual power of the martial arts and fought against Chinese Christians and foreigners in China.

Boyar A Russian noble.

Brezhnev (bréhzh-nyeff) **Doctrine** Policy that justified Soviet intervention in order to ensure the survival of socialism in another state, initiated by USSR leader Brezhnev in 1968.

Brownshirts Hitler's brown-uniformed paramilitary force in the 1920s and 1930s.

Burschenschaften (bóor-shen-shàhf-ten) Liberal nationalist German student unions during the early nineteenth century.

C

Cabinet system Government by a prime minister and heads of governmental bureaus developed by Britain during the eighteenth century.

Caesaropapism (see-zer-oh-pápe-ism) The practice of having the same person rule both the state and the church.

Cahiers (kye-yéah) Lists of public grievances sent to the French Estates General in 1789.

Caliph (káy-liff) A title meaning "successor to the Prophet" given to Muslim rulers who combined political authority with religious power.

Capitalists Those promoting an economic system characterized by freedom of the market with private and corporate ownership of the means of production and distribution that are operated for profit.

Capitularies (ka-pít-chew-làir-eez) Royal laws issued by Charlemagne and the Carolingians.

Caravel (care-uh-véll) A small, light sailing ship of the kind used by the Spanish and Portuguese in the fifteenth and sixteenth centuries.

Carbonari (car-bun-áh-ree) A secret society of revolutionaries in nineteenth-century Italy.

Cartel (car-téll) An alliance of corporations designed to control the market place.

Cartesian (car-tée-zhen) **dualism** A philosophy developed by René Descartes in the seventeenth century that defines two kinds of reality: the mind, or subjective thinking, and the body, or objective physical matter.

Catacombs Underground burial places. The term originally referred to the early Christian burial locations in Rome and elsewhere.

Cathars (cáth-arz) A medieval French dualist heretical sect; also called Albigensians.

Central Powers World War I alliance, primarily of Germany, Austria, and the Ottoman Empire.

Centuriate (sen-chúr-ee-ate) **Assembly** An aristocratic ruling body in ancient Rome that made the laws.

Chancellor A high-ranking official—in Germany, the prime minister.

Chartists English reformers of the 1830s and 1840s who demanded political and social rights for the lower classes.

Checks and balances A balanced division of governmental power among different institutions.

Chivalry (shív-el-ree) Code of performance and ethics for medieval knights. It can also refer to the demonstration of knightly virtues.

Christian humanists During the fifteenth and sixteenth centuries, experts in Greek, Latin, and Hebrew who studied the Bible and other Christian writings in order to understand the correct meaning of early Christian texts.

Civil Constitution of the Clergy New rules nationalizing and governing the clergy enacted during the French Revolution.

Civic humanists Those practicing a branch of humanism that promoted the value of responsible citizenship in which people work to improve their city-states.

Classical style A seventeenth- and eighteenth-century cultural style emphasizing restraint and balance, and following models from ancient Greece and Rome.

Cold War The global struggle between alliances headed by the United States and the Soviet Union during the second half of the twentieth century.

Collectivization The Soviet policy of taking agricultural lands and decisions away from individual owners and placing them in the hands of elected managers and party officials.

Comecon (cómm-ee-con) The economic organization of communist eastern European states during the Cold War.

Committee of Public Safety Ruling committee of twelve leaders during the French Revolutionary period of the Terror.

Common law Laws that arise from customary use rather than from legislation.

Common market The European Economic Community, a union of western European nations initiated in 1957 to promote common economic policies.

Commonwealth of Independent States A loose confederation of several former republics of the disintegrated Soviet Union founded in 1991.

Commune (cómm-yune) A medieval or early modern town; a semi-independent city government or socialistic community in the nineteenth and twentieth centuries.

Communist Manifesto A short, popular treatise written by Karl Marx and Friedrich Engels in 1848 that contained the fundamentals of their "scientific socialism."

Complutensian Polyglot (comm-plue-tén-see-an pólly-glàht) **Bible** An edition of the Bible written in 1520 that had three columns that compared the Hebrew, Greek, and Latin versions.

Compurgation (comm-pur-gáy-shun) A Germanic legal oath taken by twelve men testifying to the character of the accused.

Concert of Europe The alliance of powers after 1815 created to maintain the status quo and coordinate international relations.

Conciliar (conn-síll-ee-ar) **movement** The belief that the Catholic Church should be led by councils of cardinals rather than popes.

Concordat (conn-córe-dat) A formal agreement, especially between the pope and a government, for the regulation of church affairs.

condotierri (conn-duh-tyáy-ree) From the fourteenth to the sixteenth century, the captain of a band of mercenary soldiers, influential in Renaissance Italy.

Congress of Vienna The peace conference held between 1814 and 1815 in Vienna after the defeat of Napoleon.

Conquistadors (conn-kéy-stah-doors) Spanish adventurers in the sixteenth century who went to South and Central America to conquer indigenous peoples and claim their lands.

Conservatism An ideology stressing order and traditional values.

Constitutionalism The idea that political authority rests in written law, not in the person of an absolute monarch.

Constitutional monarchy Government in which the monarch's powers are limited by a set of fundamental laws.

Consuls (cónn-sul) The appointed chief executive officers of the Roman Republic.

Containment The Cold War strategy of the United States to limit the expansion and influence of the Soviet Union.

Continental System Napoleon's policy of preventing trade between continental Europe and Great Britain.

Contra posto (cón-tra páh-sto) A stance of the human body in which one leg bears weight, while the other is relaxed. Also known as counterpoise, it was popular in Renaissance sculpture.

Copernican (co-pér-nick-an) **revolution** The change from an earth-centered to a sun-centered universe initiated by Copernicus in the sixteenth century.

Corn Laws British laws that imposed tariffs on grain imports.

Corporate state Mussolini's economic and political machinery to manage the Italian economy and settle issues between labor and management.

Corsair A swift pirate ship.

Cossacks The "free warriors" of southern Russia, noted as cavalrymen.

Cottage industry Handicraft manufacturing usually organized by merchants and performed by rural people in their cottages.

Coup d'état (coo-day-táh) A sudden taking of power that violates constitutional forms by a group of persons in authority.

Creoles (crée-ohlz) People of European descent born in the West Indies or Spanish America, often of mixed ancestry.

Crusades From the late eleventh century through the thirteenth century, Europeans sent a number of military operations to take the Holy Land (Jerusalem and its surrounding territory) from the Muslims. These military ventures in the name of Christendom are collectively called the Crusades.

Cult of sensibility The eighteenth-century emphasis on emotion and nature forwarded by several European artists and authors.

Cuneiform (cue-née-uh-form) A writing system using wedge-shaped characters developed in ancient Mesopotamia.

Curia Regis (kóo-ree-uh régg-ees) A medieval king's advisory body made up of his major vassals.

Cynicism (sín-uh-sism) A Hellenistic philosophy that locates the search for virtue in an utter indifference to worldly needs.

Cyrillic (suh-ríll-ik) **alphabet** An old Slavic alphabet presently used in modified form for Russian and other languages.

D

Dada (dáh-dah) An early twentieth-century artistic movement that attacked traditional cultural styles and stressed the absence of purpose in life.

Dauphin (dough-fán) Heir to the French throne. The title was used from 1349 to 1830.

D-Day The day of the Allied invasion of Normandy in World War II—June 6, 1944.

Decembrists (dee-sém-brists) Russian army officers who briefly rebelled against Tsar Nicholas I in December 1925.

Decolonization The loss of colonies by imperial powers during the years following World War II.

Declaration of the Rights of Man and Citizen France's revolutionary 1789 declaration of rights stressing liberty, equality, and fraternity.

Deductive reasoning Deriving conclusions that logically flow from a premise, reasoning from basic or known truths.

Deism (dée-iz-um) Belief in a God who created the universe and its natural laws but does not intervene further; gained popularity during the Enlightenment.

Demotic A form of ancient Egyptian writing used for ordinary life. A simplified form of hieratic script.

Détente (day-táhnt) The period of relative cooperation between Cold War adversaries during the 1960s and 1970s.

Devotio moderno (day-vóh-tee-oh moh-dáir-noh) A medieval religious movement that emphasized internal spirituality over ritual practices.

Diaspora The dispersion of the Jews after the Babylonian conquest in the sixth century B.C.E. The term comes from the Greek word meaning "to scatter."

Diet The general legislative assembly of certain countries, such as Poland.

Directory The relatively conservative government during the last years of the French Revolution before Napoleon gained power.

Division of labor The division of work in the modern process of industrial production into separate tasks.

Doge (dóhj) The chief magistrate of the Republic of Venice during the Middle Ages and Renaissance.

Domesday (dóomz-day) **Book** A record of all the property and holdings in England, commissioned by William the Conqueror in 1066 so he could determine the extent of his lands and wealth.

Drachma (dróck-mah) Hellenistic coin containing either 4.3 grams (Alexander's) or 3.5 grams (Egypt's) of silver.

Dreyfus (dry'-fuss) **affair** The political upheaval in France accompanying the unjust 1894 conviction of Jewish army officer Alfred Dreyfus as a German spy that marked the importance of anti-Semitism in France.

Dual monarchy The Austro-Hungarian Empire; the Habsburg monarchy after the 1867 reform that granted Hungary equality with Austria.

Il Duce (ill dóoch-ay) "The Leader," Mussolini's title as head of the Italian Fascist Party.

Duma Russia's legislative assembly in the years prior to 1917.

E

Ecclesia (ek-cláy-zee-uh) The popular assembly in ancient Athens made up of all male citizens over 18.

Edict of Nantes (náwnt) Edict issued by French king Henry IV in 1598 granting rights to Protestants, later revoked by Louis XIV.

Émigrés (em-ee-gráy) People, mostly aristocrats, who fled France during the French Revolution.

Emir (em-éar) A Muslim ruler, prince, or military commander.

Empirical method The use of observation and experiments based on sensory evidence to come to ideas or conclusions about nature.

Ems (Em's) **Dispatch** Telegram from Prussia's head of state to the French government, edited by Bismarck to look like an insult, that helped cause the Franco-Prussian War.

Enclosure Combining separate parcels of farmland and enclosing them with fences and walls to create large farms or pastures that produced for commerce.

encomienda (en-koh-mee-én-da) A form of economic and social organization established in sixteenth-century Spanish settlements in South and Central America. The encomienda system consisted of a royal grant that allowed Spanish settlers to compel indigenous peoples to work for them. In return, Spanish overseers were to look after their workers' welfare and encourage their conversion to Christianity. In reality, it was a brutal system of enforced labor.

Enlightened absolutism (áb-suh-loo-tism) Rule by a strong, "enlightened" ruler applying Enlightenment ideas to government.

Enlightenment An eighteenth-century cultural movement based on the ideas of the Scientific Revolution and that supported the notion that human reason should determine understanding of the world and the rules of social life.

Entente Cordiale (on-táhnt core-dee-áhl) The series of understandings, or agreements, between France and Britain that led to their alliance in World War I.

Entrepreneur (on-truh-pren-óor) A person who organizes and operates business ventures, especially in commerce and industry.

Epic (épp-ik) A long narrative poem celebrating episodes of a people's heroic tradition.

Epicureanism (epp-uh-cúre-ee-an-ism) A Hellenistic philosophy that held that the goal of life should be to live a life of pleasure regulated by moderation.

Equestrians (ee-quést-ree-ans) A social class in ancient Rome who had enough money to begin to challenge the power of the patricians.

Essenes (Ess-éenz) Members of a Jewish sect of ascetics from the second century B.C.E. to the second century C.E.

Estates Representative assemblies, typically made up of either the clergy, the nobility, the commoners, or all three meeting separately.

Estates General The legislature of France from the Middle Ages to 1789. Each of the three Estates—clergy, nobility, and bourgeoisie—sent representatives.

Ethnic cleansing The policy of brutally driving an ethnic group from their homes and from a certain territory, particularly prominent during the civil wars in the Balkans during the 1990s.

Eugenics (you-génn-iks) The study of hereditary improvement.

Euro (yóu-roe) The common currency of many European states, established in 1999.

Eurocommunism The policy of western European Communist parties of supporting moderate policies and cooperating with other Leftist parties during the 1970s and 1980s.

European Economic Community The E.E.C., or Common Market, founded in 1957 to eliminate tariff barriers and begin to integrate the economies of western European nations.

European Union (EU) The community of European nations that continued to take steps toward the full economic union of much of Europe during the late twentieth century.

Evolution Darwin's theory of biological development through adaptation.

Existentialism (ekk-siss-ténn-sha-lism) A twentieth-century philosophy asserting that individuals are responsible for their own values and meanings in an indifferent universe.

Expressionism A late nineteenth- and early twentieth-century artistic style that emphasized the objective expression of inner experience through the use of conventional characters and symbols.

F

Fabian (fáy-bee-an) **Society** A late nineteenth-century group of British intellectuals that advocated the adoption of socialist policies through politics rather than revolution.

Factory system Many workers producing goods in a repetitive series of steps and specialized tasks using powerful machines.

Falange (fa-láhn-hey) A Spanish fascist party that supported Francisco Franco during the Spanish civil war.

Fascism (fáh-shism) A philosophy or system of government that advocates a dictatorship of the extreme right together with an ideology of belligerent nationalism.

Fealty (fée-al-tee) In the feudal system, a promise made by vassals and lords to do no harm to each other.

Federates In the late Roman Empire, treaties established with many Gothic tribes allowed these tribes to settle within the Empire. The tribes then became "federates," or allies of Rome.

Fibula (pl. fibulae) An ornamented clasp or brooch, favored by the ancient Germanic tribes to hold their great cloaks closed.

Fief (feef) In the feudal system, the portion—usually land—given by lords to vassals to provide for their maintenance in return for their service.

Five Year Plan The rapid, massive industrialization of the nation under the direction of the state initiated in the Soviet Union in the late 1920s.

Forum The central public place in ancient Rome which served as a meeting place, market place, law court, and political arena.

Fourteen Points U.S. president Wilson's plan to settle World War I and guarantee the peace.

Frankfurt Assembly Convention of liberals and nationalists from several German states that met in 1848 to try to form a unified government for Germany.

Free companies Mercenary soldiers in the Middle Ages and Renaissance who would fight for whoever paid them. They were called "free" to distinguish them from warriors who were bound by feudal ties to a lord.

Free Corps (core) Post–World War I German right-wing paramilitary groups made up mostly of veterans.

Free trade International trade of goods without tariffs, or customs duties.

Fronde (frawnd) Mid-seventeenth century upheavals in France that threatened the royal government.

Fundamentalists Those who believe in an extremely conservative interpretation of a religion.

G

Galley A large medieval ship propelled by sails and oars.

General will Rousseau's notion that rules governing society should be based on the best conscience of the people.

Gentry People of "good birth" and superior social position.

Geocentric Earth-centered.

Gerousia (gay-róo-see-uh) Ruling body in ancient Sparta made up of male citizens over age 60.

Gestapo (guh-stóp-po) Nazi secret police in Hitler's Germany.

Girondins (zhee-roan-dán) Moderate political faction among leaders of the French Revolution.

Glasnost (gláz-nost) Soviet leader Gorbachev's policy of political and cultural openness in the 1980s.

Globalization Twentieth-century tendency for cultural and historical development to become increasingly worldwide in scope.

Global warming The heating of the earth's atmosphere in recent decades, caused in part by the buildup of carbon dioxide and other "greenhouse gases" produced by burning fossil fuels.

Glorious Revolution In 1688, English Parliament offered the crown of England to the Protestant William of Orange and his wife Mary, replacing James II. This change in rule was accomplished peacefully, and clarified the precedent that England was a constitutional monarchy with power resting in Parliament.

Gosplan The Soviet State Planning Commission, charged with achieving ambitious economic goals.

Gothic (góth-ik) A style of architecture, usually associated with churches, that originated in France and flourished from the twelfth to the sixteenth century. Gothic architecture is identified by pointed arches, ribbed vaults, stained-glass windows, and flying buttresses.

Grand tour An educational travel taken by the wealthy to certain cities and sites, particularly during the seventeenth and eighteenth centuries.

Great Chain of Being A traditional Western-Christian vision of the hierarchical order of the universe.

Great Depression The global economic depression of the 1930s.

Great fear Panic caused by rumors that bands of brigands were on the loose in the French countryside during the summer of 1789.

Great Purges The long period of Communist Party purges in the Soviet Union during the 1930s, marked by terror, house arrests, show-trials, torture, imprisonments, and executions.

Great Reforms Reforms instituted by Russia's tsar Alexander II in 1861 that included freeing Russia's serfs.

Great Schism (skíz-um) Period in the late Middle Ages from 1378–1417 when there were two (and at times three) rival popes.

Greek Fire A Byzantine naval weapon made of combustible oil that was launched with a catapult or pumped through tubes to set fire to enemy ships.

Guild An association of persons of the same trade united for the furtherance of some purpose.

Guillotine (ghée-oh-teen) A device for executing the condemned used during the French Revolution.

H

Hacienda (ha-see-én-da) Large landed estates in Spanish America that replaced encomiendas as the dominant economic and social structure.

Haj (hodge) The Muslim annual pilgrimage to Mecca, Medina, and other holy sites.

Hasidim (hah-see-déem) Sect of Jewish mystics founded in Poland in the eighteenth century in opposition to the formalistic Judaism and ritual laxity of the period.

Heliocentric (hee-lee-oh-sén-trick) Pertaining to the theory that the sun is the center of the universe.

Hellenes (Héll-eenz) The name ancient Greeks assigned to themselves, based on their belief that they were descended from a mythical King Hellen.

Hellenistic Of or related to the period between the fourth century B.C.E. and the first century B.C.E.

Helot (héll-ots) A serf in ancient Sparta.

Heresy A religious belief that is considered wrong by orthodox church leaders.

Hermetic doctrine Notion popular in the sixteenth and seventeenth centuries that all matter contains the divine spirit.

Hieratic (high-rát-ick) A form of ancient Egyptian writing consisting of abridged forms of hieroglyphics, used by the priests in keeping records.

Hieroglyph (hígh-roe-gliff) A picture or symbol used in the ancient Egyptian writing system—means "sacred writing."

Hijra (hídge-rah) (also *Hegira*) Muhammad's flight from Mecca to Medina in 622 B.C.E.

Holocaust (hóll-o-cost) The extermination of some 6 million Jews by the Nazis during World War II.

Holy Alliance Alliance of Russia, Austria, and Prussia to safeguard the principles of Christianity and maintain the international status quo after the Napoleonic Wars.

Homeopathy (home-ee-áh-pa-thee) Medical treatment emphasizing the use of herbal drugs and natural remedies.

Hoplites (hóp-light) Ancient Greek infantrymen equipped with large round shields and long thrusting spears.

Hubris Excessive pride, which for the ancient Greeks brought punishment from the gods.

Huguenots (húgh-guh-nots) French Protestants of the sixteenth, seventeenth, and eighteenth centuries.

Humanists Students of an intellectual movement based on a deep study of classical culture and an emphasis on the humanities (literature, history, and philosophy) as a means for self-improvement.

Hundred Years' War A series of wars between England and France from 1337 to 1453. France won and England lost its lands in France, thus centralizing and solidifying French power.

I

Icon (éye-con) A sacred image of Jesus, Mary, or the saints that early Christians believed contained religious power.

Iconoclasm (eye-cónn-o-claz-um) A term literally meaning "icon breaking" that refers to an eighth-century religious controversy in Byzantium that argued that people should not venerate icons.

Ideogram (eye-dée-o-gram) A hieroglyph symbol expressing an abstract idea associated with the object it portrays.

Ideograph A written symbol that represents an idea instead of expressing the sound of a word.

Ideology (eye-dee-áh-lo-gee) A set of beliefs about the world and how it should be, often formalized into a political, social, or cultural theory.

Imam Muslim spiritual leader, believed by Shi'ites to be a spiritual descendant of Muhammad who should also be a temporal leader.

Imperialism The policy of extending a nation's authority by territorial acquisition or by the establishment of economic and political control over other nations or peoples.

Impressionism A nineteenth-century school of painting originating in France that emphasized capturing on canvas light as the eye sees it.

Indo-European Belonging to or constituting a family of languages that includes the Germanic, Celtic, Italic, Baltic, Slavic, Greek, Armenian, Iranian, and Indic groups.

Inductive reasoning Drawing general conclusions from particular concrete observations.

Indulgence A certificate issued by the papacy that gave people atonement for their sins and reduced their time in purgatory. Usually indulgences were issued for performing a pious act, but during the Reformation, critics accused the popes of selling indulgences to raise money.

Industrial revolution The rapid emergence of modern industrial production during the late eighteenth and nineteenth centuries.

Information revolution A rapid increase in the ability to store and manipulate information accompanying the development of computers during the second half of the twentieth century.

Inquisition A religious court established in the thirteenth century designed to root out heresy by questioning and torture.

Intendant (ann-tawn-dáunt) A French official sent by the royal government to assert the will of the monarch.

Internationalism The principle of cooperation among nations for their common good.

Ionia (eye-ówn-ee-uh) Ancient district in what is now Turkey that comprised the central portion of the west coast of Asia Minor, together with the adjacent islands.

Iron Curtain The dividing line between Eastern and Western Europe during the Cold War.

Islamic fundamentalism A movement within Islam calling for a return to traditional ways and a rejection of alien ideologies that gained strength during the second half of the twentieth century.

J

Jacobins (jáck-o-bins) A radical political organization or club during the French Revolution.

Jacquerie (zhak-rée) The name given to the peasant revolt in France during the fourteenth century.

Jansenism A religious movement among French Catholics stressing the emotional experience of religious belief.

Jesuits (jéh-zu-it) Members of the Catholic religious order the Society of Jesus, founded by Ignatius Loyola in 1534.

Jihad (jée-hod) Islamic holy war in which believers feel they have the authority to fight to defend the faith.

Joint-stock company A business firm that is owned by stockholders who may sell or transfer their shares individually.

Journeyman A worker in a craft who has served his or her apprenticeship.

Joust A medieval contest in which two mounted knights combat with lances.

Junkers (yóong-kers) Prussian aristocracy.

Justification by faith The belief that faith alone—not good works—is needed for salvation. This belief lies at the heart of Protestantism.

K

Kamikaze (kah-mih-káh-zee) Usually refers to suicidal attacks on Allied ships by Japanese pilots during World War II.

Kore (kóh-ray) (pl. *korai*) Greek word for maiden that refers to an ancient Greek statue of a standing female, usually clothed.

Kouros (kóo-ross) (pl. *kouroi*) Greek word for a young man that refers to an ancient Greek statue of a standing nude young man.

Kristallnacht (kriss-táhl-nahkt) The "night of the broken glass"—a Nazi attack on German Jewish homes and businesses in 1938.

Kulak (kóo-lock) A relatively wealthy Russian peasant labeled by Stalin during the period of collectivization as a "class enemy."

Kulturkampf (kool-tóur-kahmpf) Bismarck's fight against the Catholic Church in Germany during the 1870s.

L

Laissez-faire (léss-say-fair) "Hands-off." An economic doctrine opposing governmental regulation of most economic affairs.

Laudanum (láud-a-numb) Opium dissolved in alcohol, used as a medicine in the eighteenth and nineteenth centuries.

League of Nations A post–World War I association of countries to deal with international tensions and conflicts.

Lebensraum (láy-benz-rowm) "Living space." Hitler's policy of expanding his empire to the east to gain more land for Germans.

Legume (lég-yoom) A pod, such as that of a pea or bean, used as food.

Levée en masse (le-váy awn máhss) General call-up of all men, women, and children to serve the nation during the French Revolution.

Levellers Revolutionaries who tried to "level" the social hierarchy during the English civil war.

Liberalism A nineteenth- and twentieth-century ideology supporting individualism, political freedom, constitutional government, and (in the nineteenth century) laissez-faire economic policies.

Liege (léezh) **lord** In the feudal system, a lord who has many vassals, but owes allegiance to no one.

Linear perspective An artistic technique used to represent three-dimensional space convincingly on a flat surface.

Lollards Followers of the English church reformer John Wycliffe who were found heretical.

Long March An arduous Chinese communist retreat from south China to north China in 1934 and 1935.

Luddism The smashing of machines that took jobs away from workers in the first half of the nineteenth century.

M

Ma'at (máh-aht) An Egyptian spiritual precept that conveyed the idea of truth and justice, or, as the Egyptians put it, right order and harmony.

Maccabean (mack-uh-bée-en) **Revolt** Successful Jewish revolt led by Judas Maccabeus in the mid-second century B.C.E. against Hellenistic Seleucid rulers.

Magi (máyj-eye) Ancient Persian astrologers or "wise men."

Maginot (máh-zhin-oh) **Line** A string of defensive fortresses on the French/German border that France began building in the late 1920s.

Magna Carta The Great Charter that English barons forced King John of England to sign in 1215 that guaranteed certain rights to the English people. Seen as one of the bases for constitutional law.

Marshall Plan A package of massive economic aid to European nations offered in 1947 to strengthen them and tie them to American influence.

Marxism A variety of socialism propounded by Karl Marx stressing economic determinism and class struggle—"scientific socialism."

Megalith An archaeological term for a stone of great size used in ancient monuments.

Meiji (máy-jee) **Restoration** The reorganizing of Japanese society along modern Western lines; initiated in 1868.

Mendicant orders Members of a religious order, such as the Dominicans or Franciscans, who wandered from city to city begging for alms rather than residing in a monastery.

Mercantilism (mírr-kan-till-ism) Early modern governmental economic policies seeking to control and develop the national economy and bring wealth into the national treasury.

Mercator projection (mer-káy-ter) A method of making maps in which the earth's surface is shown as a rectangle with Europe at the center, causing distortion toward the poles.

Mesolithic Of or pertaining to the period of human culture from about 15,000 years ago to about 7000 B.C.E. characterized by complex stone tools and greater social organization. "Middle Stone Age."

Methodism A Protestant sect founded in the eighteenth century that emphasized piety and emotional worship.

Metics (métt-iks) Foreign residents of Athens.

Miasma (my-ázz-ma) Fumes from waste and marshes blamed for carrying diseases during the eighteenth and the first half of the nineteenth centuries.

Middle Passage The long sea voyage between the African coast and the Americas endured by newly captured slaves.

Minoan (mínn-oh-an) A civilization that lived on the island of Crete from 2800 to 1450 B.C.E.

Mir (mere) Russian village commune.

Missi dominici (mée-see do-min-ée-kee) Royal officials under Charlemagne who traveled around the country to enforce the king's laws.

Mithraism (míth-ra-ism) A Hellenistic mystery religion that appealed to soldiers and involved the worship of the god Mithra.

Mughals (móe-gulls) Islamic rulers of much of India in the sixteenth, seventeenth, and eighteenth centuries.

Munich conference The 1938 conference where Britain and France attempted to appease Hitler by allowing him to dismantle Czechoslovakia.

Mycenean (my-sen-ée-an) A civilization on the Greek peninsula that reached its high point between 1400 and 1200 B.C.E.

Mystery religions Ancient religions that encouraged believers to cultivate a deep connection with their deity. Initiates swore not to reveal the insights they had gained during rites and ceremonies; the shroud of secrecy resulted in the name "mystery" religions.

N

Napoleonic (na-po-lee-ón-ik) **Code** The legal code introduced in France by Napoleon Bonaparte.

Nationalism A nineteenth- and twentieth-century ideology stressing the importance of national identity and the nation-state.

Natural law Understandable, rational laws of nature that apply to the physical and human world.

Nazi Party Hitler's German National Socialist Party.

Neolithic (nee-oh-líth-ik) Of or denoting a period of human culture beginning around 7000 B.C.E. in the Middle East and later elsewhere, characterized by the invention of farming and the making of technically advanced stone implements. "New Stone Age."

Neoplatonism (nee-oh-pláy-ton-ism) Views based on the ideas of Plato that one should search beyond appearances for true knowledge; stressed abstract reasoning.

New Economic Policy Lenin's compromise economic and social policy for the USSR during the 1920s—the NEP.

New imperialism The second wave of Western imperialism, particularly between 1880 and 1914.

Night of August 4 Surrender of most privileges by the French aristocracy at a meeting held on August 1, 1789.

Nominalism (nóm-in-al-ism) A popular late medieval philosophy based on the doctrine that the universal, or general, has no objective existence or validity, being merely a name expressing the qualities of various objects resembling one another in certain respects. Also called New Nominalism.

North American Free Trade Agreement (NAFTA) The 1994 agreement between the United States, Mexico, and Canada to create a free trade zone.

North Atlantic Treaty Organization (NATO) A military alliance against the Soviet Union initiated in 1949.

Nuremberg Laws Hitler's anti-Jewish laws of 1935.

O

Ockham's razor A principle that states that between alternative explanations for the same phenomenon, the simplest is always to be preferred.

October Revolution The 1917 Bolshevik revolt and seizure of power in Russia.

Old regime (re-zhéem) European society before the French Revolution.

Oligarchy (áh-luh-gar-kee) Rule by a small group or by a particular social class—often wealthy middle classes, as in ancient Greek or medieval European cities.

Operation Barbarossa (bar-bar-óh-ssa) The German invasion of the USSR during World War II.

Optimates (ahp-tuh-máht-ays) The nobility of the Roman empire. Also refers to the political party that supported the nobility. Contrast with the *populares*.

Ordeal An ancient form of trial in which the accused was exposed to physical dangers which were presumed to be harmless if the accused was innocent. Ordeals might include grasping hot pokers, trial by battle, immersion in water, and other similar challenges.

Organization of Petroleum Exporting Countries (OPEC) An Arab-dominated organization of Middle Eastern oil-producing states that became effective during and after the 1970s.

Ostracism (áhs-tra-sism) A political technique of ancient Greece by which people believed to be threats to the city-state were chosen for exile by popular vote.

P

Paleolithic (pay-lee-oh-líth-ik) Of or pertaining to the period of human culture beginning with the earliest chipped stone tools, about 750,000 years ago, until the beginning of the Mesolithic, about 15,000 years ago. "Old Stone Age."

Pantheon (pán-thee-on) A great temple in Rome built in 27 B.C.E. and dedicated to all the gods. In 609 C.E., it was rededicated as a Christian church called Santa Maria Rotunda.

Paris Commune The revolutionary government of the city of Paris, first in the 1790s, and then in 1871.

Parlement (parl-máwn) A French court of law during the Old Regime.

Parliament Britain's legislature, including the House of Commons and House of Lords.

Parthenon (párth-uh-non) A famous Doric temple of Athena on the Acropolis in ancient Athens.

Patricians The ancient Roman aristocracy who populated the Senate and were particularly powerful during the Republic.

Pax Romana ("pocks" or "packs" row-máhn-ah) Literally, "Roman Peace." Two hundred years of relative, internal peace within the Roman Empire beginning with the rule of Caesar Augustus.

Peace of Paris The 1919 peace settlement after World War I.

Peers Members of the House of Lords in England.

Perestroika (pair-ess-trói-ka) Gorbachev's policy of "restructuring" the Soviet economy during the 1980s.

Petrine (pée-tryn) **doctrine** The belief that the popes, bishops of Rome, should lead the church because they are the successors of Peter, who many claim was the first bishop of Rome.

Phalanstery (fa-láns-ter-ee) The model commune envisioned by the French utopian socialist Fourier.

Phalanx (fáy-langks) An ancient Greek formation of foot soldiers carrying overlapping shields and long spears.

Pharaoh The title of the rulers of ancient Egypt. Also refers to the household and administration of the rulers.

Pharisees (fáir-uh-sees) Members of an ancient Jewish sect that rigidly observed purity laws, including dietary rules. They also believed in the resurrection of the just and the existence of angels.

Philosophes (fee-low-zóff) Leading French intellectuals of the Enlightenment.

Phonogram A character or symbol used to represent a speech sound used in ancient writing.

Physiocrats (fízz-ee-oh-crats) Eighteenth-century French economic thinkers who stressed the importance of agriculture and favored free trade.

Pictogram A picture representing an idea used in ancient writing.

Pietism (píe-uh-tism) An eighteenth-century Protestant movement stressing an emotional commitment to religion.

Plebeians (pleb-ée-an) The members of the urban lower classes in ancient Rome.

Plebiscite (pléb-uh-sight) A direct vote that allows the people to either accept or reject a proposed measure.

Pogrom ('puh-grúhm'; also 'póe-grom') An organized persecution or massacre of Jews, especially in eastern Europe.

Polis (póe-liss) (pl. *Póleis* [póe-lease]) An ancient Greek city-state.

Poor Laws Eighteenth- and nineteenth-century British laws enacted to deal with the poor.

Populares (pop-you-lahr-ays) In Roman history the political party of the common people. Also refers to the people themselves. Contrast with the *optimates*.

Popular Front The political partnership of parties of the left, particularly in France and Spain, during the 1930s.

positivism A mid-nineteenth century theory of sociology holding that scientific investigation could discover useful fundamental truths about humans and their societies.

Postindustrial societies Late twentieth-century societies that moved from manufacturing to services led by professionals, managers, and financiers.

Postmodernism A later twentieth-century approach to the arts stressing relativism and multiple interpretations.

Pragmatic Sanction The international agreement secured by the Habsburg emperor in the 1730s to ensure that his daughter would succeed him without question.

Prague Spring The brief period of democratic reforms and cultural freedom in Czechoslovakia during 1968.

Predestination Doctrine claiming that since God is all-knowing and all-powerful, he must know in advance who is saved or damned. Therefore, the salvation of any individual is predetermined. This doctrine is emphasized by Calvinists.

Preemptive War War initiated by one side on the justification that another side was on the verge of attack.

Prefect Powerful agents of the central government stationed in France's departments.

Preventive War War initiated by one side on the justification that another side might attack sometime in the future.

Principate (prínce-a-pate) The governmental system of the Roman Empire founded by Octavian (also known as Caesar Augustus).

Privateer An armed private vessel commissioned by a government to attack enemy ships.

Protestant Of or pertaining to any branch of the Christian church excluding Roman Catholicism and Eastern Orthodox.

Psychoanalysis Pioneered by Sigmund Freud, a method of investigating human psychological development and treating emotional disorders.

Ptolemaic (ptah-luh-máy-ik) **system** The traditional medieval earth-centered universe and system of planetary movements.

Ptolemies (ptáh-luh-meez) Hellenistic dynasty that ruled in Egypt from about 300 B.C.E. to about 30 B.C.E.

Purgatory In Roman Catholic theology, a state or place in which those who have died in the grace of God expiate their sins by suffering before they can enter heaven.

Purge Expelling or executing political party members suspected of inefficiency or opposition to party policy.

Puritans In the sixteenth and seventeenth centuries, those who wanted to reform the Church of England by removing all elaborate ceremonies and forms. Many Puritans faced persecution and were forced to flee to the American colonies.

Q

Quadrant An instrument for taking altitude of heavenly bodies.

Quadrivium (quad-rív-ee-um) The medieval school curriculum that studied arithmetic, music, geometry, and astronomy after completion of the trivium.

Quadruple (quad-róo-pull) **Alliance** Alliance of Austria, Prussia, Russia, and France in the years after the Napoleonic Wars to maintain the status quo.

Qur'an (also Koran) The Muslim holy book recorded in the early seventh century by the prophet Muhammad.

Quietism (quíet-ism) A movement among seventeenth-century Spanish Catholics that emphasized the emotional experience of religious belief.

R

Racism Belief that racial differences are important and that some races are superior to others.

Raison d'état (ráy-zawn day-táh) "Reason of state." An eighteenth- and nineteenth-century principle justifying arbitrary or aggressive international behavior.

Rationalism The belief that, through reason, humans can understand the world and solve problems.

Realism A medieval Platonist philosophy that believed that the individual objects we perceive are not real, but merely reflections of universal ideas existing in the mind of God. In the nineteenth century this referred to a cultural style rejecting romanticism and attempting to examine society as it is.

Realpolitik (ray-áhl-po-lee-teek) The pragmatic politics of power; often a self-interested foreign policy associated with Bismarck.

Redshirts Garibaldi's troops used in the unification of Italy.

Reform Bill of 1832 English electoral reform extending the vote to the middle classes of the new industrial cities.

Reichstag (ríkes-tahg) German legislative assembly.

Reign of Terror The violent period of the French Revolution between 1792 and 1794.

Relativity Einstein's theory that all aspects of the physical universe must be defined in relative terms.

Relics In the Roman Catholic and Greek Orthodox churches, valued remnants of saints or other religious figures. Relics usually are parts of bodies, but may also include objects that had touched sacred bodies or that were associated with Jesus or Mary, such as remnants of the True Cross.

Renaissance Literally, "rebirth." The term was coined in Italy in the early fourteenth century to refer to the rebirth of the appreciation of classical (Greek and Roman) literature and values. It also refers to the culture that was born in Italy during that century that ultimately spread throughout Europe.

Resistance movements Underground opposition to occupation forces, especially to German troops in conquered European countries during World War II.

Restoration The conservative regimes in power after the defeat of Napoleon in 1815 that hoped to hold back the forces of change or even turn back the clock to prerevolutionary days.

Risorgimento (ree-sor-jee-mén-toe) A nineteenth-century Italian unification movement.

Rococo (roe-coe-cóe) A style of art developed from the baroque that originated in France during the eighteenth century that emphasized elaborate designs to produce a delicate effect.

Romanesque (Roman-ésk) A style of architecture usually associated with churches built in the eleventh and twelfth centuries and that was inspired by Roman architectural features. Romanesque buildings were massive, with round arches, barrel vaulted ceilings, and dark interiors.

Romanticism A cultural ideology during the first half of the nineteenth century stressing feeling over reason.

Rosetta Stone A tablet of black basalt found in 1799 at Rosetta, Egypt, that contains parallel inscriptions in Greek, ancient Egyptian demotic script, and hieroglyphic characters. The stone provided the key to deciphering ancient Egyptian writing.

Rostra The speaker's platform in the Forum of ancient Rome.

Roundheads Members or supporters of the Parliamentary or Puritan party in England during the English civil war (1642).

Royal absolutism The seventeenth- and eighteenth-century system of elevated royal authority.

S

Sacraments In Christianity, rites that were to bring the individual grace or closeness to God. In Roman Catholicism and Greek Orthodoxy there are seven sacraments: baptism, confirmation, the Eucharist, penance, extreme unction, holy orders, and matrimony. Protestants in general acknowledge only two sacraments: baptism and the Lord's Supper.

Sadducees (sád-juh-sees) Members of an ancient Jewish sect that emphasized worship at the Temple in Jerusalem. They rejected new ideas such as resurrection, insisting on only those ideas that could be found in the Torah.

Saga A medieval Scandinavian story of battles, customs, and legends, narrated in prose and generally telling the traditional history of an important Norse family.

Salon (suh-láhn) Seventeenth- and eighteenth-century social and cultural gatherings of members of the upper and middle classes.

Sans-culottes (sawn-key-lóht) Working-class people of Paris during the French Revolution.

Sarcophagus (sar-kóff-a-gus) A stone coffin.

Satellite states Eastern European states under the control of the Soviet Union during the Cold War.

Satrap (sát-trap) An ancient Persian governor in charge of provinces called "satrapies."

Schlieffen (shléaf-en) **Plan** German military strategy in World War I that called for a holding action against Russia while German forces moved through Belgium to knock out France.

Scholasticism The dominant medieval philosophical and theological movement that applied logic from Aristotle to help understand God's plan. It also refers to the desire to join faith with reason.

Scientific Revolution The new sixteenth- and seventeenth-century methods of investigation and discoveries about nature based on observation and reason rather than tradition and authority.

Scutage (skyóot-ij) Medieval payment in lieu of military service.

Seleucids (se-lóo-sids) Hellenistic dynasty that ruled in Asia from about 300 B.C.E. to about 64 B.C.E.

Semitic (sem-ít-ik) Of or pertaining to any of a group of Caucasoid peoples, chiefly Jews and Arabs, of the eastern Mediterranean area.

Septuagint (sep-tu-eh-jint) A Greek translation of the Hebrew scriptures (the Old Testament), so named because it was said to be the work of 72 Palestinian Jews in the third century B.C.E., who completed the work in seventy days.

Serfs Medieval peasants who were personally free, but bound to the land. They owed labor obligations as well as fees.

Shi'ite (shée-ite) **Muslims** Those who accepted only the descendants of 'Ali, Muhammad's son-in-law, as the true rulers. It was not the majority party in Islam but did prevail in some of the Muslim countries.

Shire An English county.

Sinn Fein (shín féign) "Ourselves Alone." An extremist twentieth-century Irish nationalist organization.

Skepticism (skép-ti-cism) The systematic doubting of accepted authorities—especially religious authorities.

Second Reich (rike) German regime founded in 1871 and lasting until the end of World War I.

Sepoy (sée-poy) **Mutiny** The 1857 uprising of Indians against British rule.

Social Darwinism The effort to apply Darwin's biological ideas to social ideas stressing competition and "survival of the fittest."

Socialists Those promoting or practicing the nineteenth- and twentieth-century ideology of socialism, stressing cooperation, community, and public ownership of the means of production.

Socratic method The method of arriving at truth by questioning and disputation.

Solidarity A Polish noncommunist union that became the core of resistance to the communist regime during the 1980s.

Sophists (sóff-ists) Fifth-century B.C.E. Greek philosophers who were condemned for using tricky logic to prove that all things are relative and success alone is important.

Sovereignty (sóv-rin-tee) The source of authority exercised by a state; complete independence and self-government.

Soviet A workers' council during the 1905 and 1917 Russian revolutions and part of the structure of government in the Soviet Union.

SS The Schutzstaffel, Hitler's elite party troops of the 1930s and 1940s.

Stadholder (stáhd-holder) A governor of provinces in the Dutch United Provinces.

Statutory law Laws established by a king or legislative body. Contrast with common law.

Stoicism (stów-i-cism) A Hellenistic philosophy that advocated detachment from the material world and an indifference to pain.

Strategoi (stra-táy-goy) Generals in ancient Athens who eventually took a great deal of political power.

Struggle of the Orders The political strife between patrician and plebeian Romans beginning in the fifth century B.C.E. The plebeians gradually won political rights as a result of the struggle.

Sturm und drang (shtúrm unt dráhng) "Storm and stress." A literary movement in late eighteenth-century Germany.

Sumptuary (súmp-chew-air-ee) **laws** Laws restricting or regulating extravagance (for example, in food or dress), often used to maintain separation of social classes.

Sunna (sóon-a) A collection of sayings and traditions of the prophet Muhammad that delineates the customs adhered to by Muslims.

Supply and demand Adam Smith's liberal economic doctrine that demand for goods and services will stimulate production (supply) in a free-market system.

Surrealism (sur-rée-a-lism) A twentieth-century literary and artistic style stressing images from the unconscious mind.

Symphony A long sonata for orchestra.

Syncretism (sín-cre-tism) The attempt or tendency to combine or reconcile differing beliefs, as in philosophy or religion.

Syndicalism (sín-di-cal-ism) A late nineteenth-century anarchist ideology envisioning labor unions as the center of a free and just society.

T

Taliban The strict, fundamentalist Islamic regime that ruled most of Afghanistan from 1996 to 2001.

Tennis Court Oath Oath taken by members of the French Estates General not to dissolve until they had created a constitution for France.

Tetradrachma (tet-ra-drák-ma) Hellenistic coin worth four drachmas.

Tetrarchy (tét-rar-key) The governmental system of the Roman Empire founded by Diocletian that divided the empire into four administrative units.

Theocracy (thee-áh-kruh-see) Government by priests claiming to rule by divine authority.

Theme A division for the purpose of provincial administration in the Byzantine Empire.

Thermidorian (ther-mi-dór-ee-an) **Reaction** The overthrow of Robespierre and the radicals in July 1794, during the French Revolution.

Third Estate Commoners, or all people except the nobility and clergy, in early modern European society.

Third French Republic The republican government established in 1871 and lasting until Germany's defeat of France in 1940.

Torah (tór-uh) The first five books of the Jewish sacred scriptures, comprising Genesis, Exodus, Leviticus, Numbers, and Deuteronomy.

Tories A conservative British political party during the eighteenth and nineteenth centuries.

Totalitarianism A twentieth-century form of authoritarian government using force, technology, and bureaucracy to effect rule by a single party and controlling most aspects of the lives of the population.

Total war A form of warfare in which all the forces and segments of society are mobilized for a long, all-out struggle.

Transubstantiation (trán-sub-stan-chee-áy-shun) In the Roman Catholic and Greek Orthodox churches, the belief that the bread and wine of the Eucharist were transformed into the actual body and blood of Christ.

Trench warfare An almost stagnant form of defensive warfare fought from trenches.

Triangular trade Trade pattern between European nations and their colonies by which European manufactured goods were traded for raw materials (such as agricultural products) from the Americas or slaves from Africa.

Tribune An official of ancient Rome chosen by the common people to protect their rights.

Triple Alliance Alliance of Germany, Austria-Hungary, and Italy in the years before World War I.

Triumvirate (try-úm-vir-ate) A group of three men sharing civil authority, as in ancient Rome.

Trivium (trív-ee-um) The basic medieval curriculum that studied grammar, rhetoric, and logic; after completion, students could proceed to the quadrivium.

Troubadour (tróo-buh-door) Poets from the late twelfth and early thirteenth centuries who wrote love poems, meant to be sung to music, that reflected the new sensibility of courtly love, which claimed that lovers were ennobled.

Truman Doctrine U.S. policy initiated in 1947 that offered military and economic aid to countries threatened by a communist takeover with the intention of creating a military ring of containment around the Soviet Union and its satellite states.

Tsar The emperor of Russia.

Twelve Tables According to ancient Roman tradition, popular pressure in the fifth century B.C.E. led to the writing down of traditional laws to put an end to patrician monopoly of the laws. The resulting compilation—the Twelve Tables—was seen as the starting point for the tradition of Roman law.

U

Ultra-royalism The nineteenth-century belief in rule by a monarch and that everything about the French Revolution and Enlightenment was contrary to religion, order, and civilization.

Unconscious According to Freud, that part of the mind of which we are not aware; home of basic drives.

Unilateralism Actions or policies taken by one nation in its own interests regardless of the views and interests of its allies.

United Nations (UN) An international organization founded in 1945 to promote peace and cooperation.

Universal A metaphysical entity that does not change, but that describes particular things on earth—for example, "justice" or "beauty." Explained by the ancient Greeks and examined by subsequent philosophers. (Also called "forms" or "ideas.")

Utilitarianism (you-till-a-táre-ee-an-ism) A nineteenth century liberal philosophy that evaluated institutions on the basis of social usefulness to achieve "the greatest happiness of the greatest number."

Utopian (you-tópe-ee-an) **socialism** A form of early nineteenth-century socialism urging cooperation and communes rather than competition and individualism.

V

Vassal In the feudal system, a noble who binds himself to his lord in return for maintenance.

Versailles (ver-sígh) **treaty** Peace treaty between the Allies and Germany following World War I.

Victorian Referring to the period of Queen Victoria's reign in Britain, 1837–1901.

Vulgate (vúll-gate) A version of the Latin Bible, primarily translated from Hebrew and Greek by Jerome.

W

War guilt clause Article 231 of the Treaty of Versailles that places all blame on Germany for causing World War I.

Warsaw Pact A military alliance in Eastern Europe controlled by the Soviet Union and initiated in 1955.

Waterloo Site in Belgium of a decisive defeat of Napoleon in 1815.

Weimar (wy'e-mar) **Republic** The liberal German government established at the end of World War I and destroyed by Hitler in the 1930s.

Welfare state Governmental programs to protect citizens from severe economic hardships and to provide basic social needs.

Wergeld (véhr-gelt) In Germanic law, the relative price of individuals that established the fee for compensation in case of injury.

Whigs A British political party during the eighteenth and nineteenth centuries.

Witan The ancient Anglo-Saxon men who participated in the Witenagemot.

Witenagemot (wí-ten-uh-guh-mote) Ancient Anglo-Saxon assembly of nobles.

Z

Zealots (zéll-ets) An ancient Jewish sect arising in Palestine in about 6 C.E. that militantly opposed Roman rule and desired to establish an independent Jewish state. The sect was wiped out when the Romans destroyed Jerusalem in 70 C.E.

Zemstva (zémst-fah) Municipal councils established in Russia in the second half of the nineteenth century.

Ziggurat (zíg-gur-raht) A pyramid-shaped Mesopotamian temple.

Zionism A late nineteenth and twentieth-century Jewish nationalist movement to create an independent state for Jews in Palestine.

Zollverein (tsóll-ver-rhine) Nineteenth-century German customs union headed by Prussia.

Zoroastrianism (zorro-áss-tree-an-ism) An ancient Persian religion that had a belief in two gods: a god of light named Ahura Mazda, and an evil god named Ahriman.

CREDITS

PHOTOS

Collection/Science, Industry & Business Library. New York Public Library; p. 551: Trade Union Congress, London, UK/Bridgeman Art Library; p. 554: Print Collection. Miriam and Ira D. Wallach. Division of Art Prints and Photographs, New York Public Library, Astor, Lenox and Tilden Foundations; p. 556: Naudet, Caroline. Voyage Et Conduite D'Un Moribund Pour L'autre Monde. 1988-102-116. Philadelphia Museum of Art: The William H. Helfand Collection; p. 558: Merrymakers, 1870. Carolus-Duran. Founders Society Purchase, Robert H. Tannahill Foundation Fund. Photograph © 1989 The Detroit Institute of Arts; p. 561: Cadbury Ltd.

Chapter 18
p. 564: Museen der Stadt Wien, Vienna, Austria; p. 567: AKG London; p. 573: The British Library; p. 576: Bayerische Staatsgemaldesammlungen, Neue Pinakothek, Munich; p. 577 top: Yale Center for British Art, Paul Mellon Collection, USA/Photo: Bridgeman Art Library; p. 577 bottom: Staatliche Museen zu Berlin - Preussischer Kulturbesitz, Nationalgalerie/F.V. 42. Foto: Jurgen Liepe/Bildarchiv Preussischer Kulturbesitz; p. 581: The Granger Collection; p. 583: Giraudon/Art Resource, NY; p. 584: Giraudon/Art Resource, NY; p. 587: Giraudon/Art Resource, NY; p. 589: Giraudon/Art Resource, NY; p. 592: Hamburger Kunsthalle, Hamburg, Germany/Bridgeman Art Library.

Chapter 19
p. 594: Photo: Joerg P. Anders. Nationalgalerie, Staatliche Museen zu Berlin, Berlin, Germany/Bildarchiv Preussischer Kulturbesitz/Art Resource, NY; p. 598: Culver Pictures; p. 603: Bismarck Museum/Bildarchiv Preussischer Kulturbesitz; p. 604 top: Museum of the City of New York; p. 604 bottom: Charles Giroux, American, 1850s-1880s, Cotton Plantation, 1850s, Oil on canvas, 55.56 x 92.07 cm (21 7/8 x 36 1/4 in.), Museum of Fine Arts, Boston, Gift of Martha C. Karolik for the M. and M. Karolik Collection of American Paintings, 1815-1865, 1947, 47.1144; p. 607: Staedtische Kunsthalle, Mannheim, Germany/Erich Lessing / Art Resource, NY; p. 609 top: The Granger Collection; p. 609 bottom: Novosti/Sovfoto; p. 611: The Wellcome Library.

Chapter 20
p. 614: Mary Evans Picture Library; p. 617: Christie's Images, London, UK/Bridgeman Art Library; p. 617: Hulton/Getty Images; p. 620: Erich Lessing/Art Resource, NY; p. 622: Roger Viollet/Getty Images; p. 624: The Jewish Museum of New York/Art Resource, NY; p. 626: Culver Pictures; p. 627: Koninklijk Museum voor Schone Kunsten, Anver/Lukas; p. 631: Mary Evans Picture Library; p. 636: Hulton/Archive/Getty Images; p. 639 top: Marine Corps Historical Society; p. 639 bottom: Keystone-Mast Collection (14757), UCR/California Museum of Photography, University of California at Riverside.

Chapter 21
p. 642: Harrogate Museums and Art Gallery, North Yorkshire, UK/Bridgeman Art Library; p. 644: Ullstein Bilderdienst; p. 646: Tallandier; p. 649: Bibliotheque Nationale de France; p. 650: Cadbury Ltd.; p. 651: Musee de la Poste; p. 653: Musee d'Orsay/Reunion des Musees Nationaux/Art Resource; p. 654: Magyar Nemzeti Galeria (Hungarian National Gallery), Budapest. Photo by Mester Tibor; p. 657: Erich Lessing/Art Resource, NY; p. 659: The Granger Collection; p. 662: Erich Lessing/Art Resource, NY; p. 664 top: Sachsische Landesbibliothek-Staats-und Universitats Bibliothek Dresden; p. 664 bottom: Erich Lessing/Art Resource, NY; p. 666: Scala/Art Resource, NY; p. 668 top: © Copyright ARS, NY. Copyright Giraudon/Art Resource, NY; p. 668 bottom: © Copyright ARS, NY. The Scream. 1893. Copyright Erich Lessing/Art Resource, NY.

Chapter 22
p. 672: © Copyright ARS, NY. The War. Copyright Erich Lessing/Art Resource, NY; p. 677: © Ludwig Meidner-Archiv, Jüdisches Museum der Stadt Frankfurt am Main/Gift of Clifford Odets/Los Angeles County Museum of Art; p. 678: Ullstein Bilderdienst; p. 681: Roger Viollet/Getty Images; p. 682: Imperial War Museum, London; p. 684: Imperial War Museum, London; p. 685: Mary Evans Picture Library; p. 687: Sachsische Landesbibliothek-Staats-und Universitats Bibliothek Dresden; p. 688: Bettmann/Corbis; p. 693: Sovfoto/Eastfoto; p. 694: Sofoto/VA; p. 696: TASS/Sovfoto/Eastfoto.

Chapter 23
p. 700: Photo: Joerg P. Anders. Nationalgalerie, Staatliche Museen zu Berlin, Berlin, Germany/Art Resource, NY. (c) VAGA, NY; p. 704: AKG London; p. 706: Erich Lessing/Art Resource, NY; p. 707: Transit Films GmbH, Munich and the Friedrich-Wilhelm-Murnau-Foundation, Wiesbaden, Germany; p. 708: AKG London; p. 709: Mansell/Time Life Pictures/Getty Images; p. 711: AP Images; p. 714: The Fotomas Index; p. 716: RUSU 2225, Poster Collection, Hoover Institution Archives; p. 718: Isaac Soyer, Employment Agency, 1937. Oil on canvas. 34 1/4 x 45 in. (87 x 114.3 cm.) Whitney Museum of American Art, New York; purchase. 37.44; p. 721: Heinrich Hoffman/TimePix/Getty Images; p. 722: Felix Nussbaum. Selbstbildnis mit Judenpass, August 1943. Als Besitzvermerk is anzugeben/Owner: Felix-Nussbaum-Haus Osnabrueck mit der Sammlung der Niedersaachsischen Sparkassenstiftung.

Chapter 24
p. 726: Photo: Joerg P. Anders. © ARS, NY/Nationalgalerie, Staatliche Museen zu Berlin, Berlin, Germany/Bildarchiv Preussischer Kulturbesitz/Art Resource, NY; p. 730: © ARS, NY. Copyright John Bigelow Taylor/Art Resource, NY; p. 733: Bettmann/Corbis; p. 734: Imperial War Museum, London. IWM ART LD 2750; p. 740: AP Images; p. 741: Imperial War Museum, London; p. 743: Archive Photos/Hulton Archive/Getty Images #71986845; p. 744: The Art Archive / Imperial War Museum; p. 745: Canadian War Museum, Ottawa, Canada/The Bridgeman Art Library; p. 748: Musee d'Histoire Contemporaine, BCIC, Universite de Paris, France.

Chapter 25
p. 754: Don Eddy, American, b.1944. New Shoes for H. Acrylic on canvas, 973-4, 111.7 x 121.9 cm. © The Cleveland Museum of Art, 2002. Purchased with a grant from the National Endowment for the Arts and matched by gifts from members of The Cleveland Society for Contemporary Art, 1974.53; p. 760: Musee d'Histoire Contemporaine, BCIC, Universite de Paris, France; p. 763: Museum Ludwig, Koln; p. 764: Goksin Sipahiouglu/Sipa Press; p. 766: Bettmann/Corbis; p. 767: Joseph Koudelka/Magnum Photos; p. 776 top: © 2003 The Pollock-Krasner Foundation/Artists Rights Society (ARS), New York. Copyright Art Resource, NY; p. 776 bottom: © 2003 Andy Warhol Foundation for the Visual Arts/ARS, NY/TM Licensed by Cambell's Soup Co. All rights reserved. Copyright Art Resource, NY; p. 779: G. Pierre/Corbis SYGMA; p. 780: Gianni Giansanti/Sygma/Corbis; p. 784: Archive Photos/Getty Images; p. 785: NASA.

Chapter 26
p. 790: Regis Bossu/Corbis SYGMA; p. 794: P. Aventurier/Gamma; p. 795: Musee d'Histoire Contemporaine, BCIC, Universite de Paris, France; p. 797: AP Images; p. 803: J. Jones/Corbis SYGMA; p. 806: Anthony Edwards/The Image Bank/Getty Images; p. 813: Kenneth Garrett/National Geographic Image Collection; p. 814 top: Eric Travers/Pascal Le Floch/epa/Corbis; p. 814 bottom: Marco Ventura/The Artworks USA, Inc.;

p. 817 left: William O. Field; p. 817 right: Bruce F. Molnia/USGS; p. 818: Courtesy of the National Library of Medicine; p. 819: Jennifer Bartlett. Spiral: An Ordinary Evening in New Haven, 1989. Painting: oil on canvas, tables: painted wood and steel, cones: break formed hot rolled welded steel painting: 108″ x 192″, tables: 30″ x 32″ x 35″, 39″ x 41″ x 35″ cones: 20″ x 30″ x 21″, © J. Bartlett. Private Collection, Greenwich, CT. Courtesy of the Paula Cooper Gallery, NY

TEXTS

Chapter 10

Luca Landucci, A Florentine Diary From 1450 to 1516, Trans. Alice de Rosen Jervice, The Orion Publishing Group Ltd. All attempts to find the rightsholder were unsuccessful.

Chapter 11

Used by permission of Elisabeth M. Wengler.

From Readings in Christianity, 1st edition by Van Voorst. 1997. Reprinted with permission of Wadsworth, a division of Thomson Learning: www.thomsonrights.com. Fax 800 730-2215.

Chapter 13

J.B. Bossuet, Politics Drawn from the Very Words of Holy Scripture, 1709 in Brian Tierney and Joan Scott, Western Societies: A Documentary History, Vol II, McGraw-Hill, 1984, pp. 11-13. Used by permission of The McGraw-Hill Companies, Inc.

J.M. Thompson, Lectures on Foreign History, 1494-1789, Blackwell, 1956, pp. 172-174.

Chapter 14

Giorgio de Santillana, The Crime of Galileo, University of Chicago Press, 1955. Used by permission of University of Chicago Press.

Jean Antoine Nicholas Caritat Marquis de Condorcet, Sketch for a Historical Picture on the Progress of the Human Mind, tr. June Barraclough, Weidenfeld and Nicolson (Orion Books), 1955, pp. 236-237, 244.

Chapter 17

Sidney, Pollard and Colin Holmes, Documents of European Economic History, Source: vol. 1, St. Martin's Press, 1968. Reproduced with permission of Palgrave Macmillan

Chapter 22

Frank A. Golder, Documents of Russian History 1914-1917, Peter Smith Publisher, Inc., Goucester, MA 1964. Reprinted by permission of Peter Smith Publisher, Inc.

"Does It Matter", from Collected Poems of Siegfried Sassoon by Siegfried Sassoon, copyright 1918, 1920 by E.P. Dutton. Copyright 1936, 1946, 1947, 1948 by Siegfried Sassoon. Used by permission of Viking Penguin, a division of Penguin Group (USA) Inc.; Copyright Siegfried Sassoon by kind permission of the Estate of George Sassoon.

Chapter 23

Used by permission of Chatham House.

Page 123 from The Education of a True Believer by Lev Kopelev and translated by Gary Kern. English translation copyright © 1980 by Harper & Row, Publishers, Inc. Reprinted by permission of HarperCollins Publishers.

Louis L. Snyder, The Weimar Republic, D. Van Nostrand Co., 1966.

Chapter 24

Nazism 1919-1945: A Documentary Reader, Volume 3: Foreign Policy, War and Racial Extermination. Edited by J. Noakes and G. Pridham. ISBN: 0 85989 602 1. Reprinted by permission.

Elizabeth Hawes, "My Life on the Midnight Shift," Woman's Home Companion, August 1943.

Reprinted by permission from Rihihei Inoguchi and Tadashi Nakajima, The Divine Wind (Annoplis, Md: Naval Institute Press, © 1958).

Chapter 25

Philip Toynbee, The Fearful Choice, Victor Gollancz, Ltd., 1956.

The American Challenge by Jean Jacques Servan-Schreiber. English Translation copyright © 1968 by Atheneum House. Originally published in French as Le Defi Americain Copyright © 1967 by Editions Denoel. Reprinted by permission of Georges Borchardt, Inc., for Editions Denoel.

INDEX

Note: Page numbers for figures and maps are indicated in *italic* type.

abortion, 656, 707, 784
absinthe, 657
abstract expressionism, 776
Académie des Sciences in France, 451
acid rain, 817
Adam, 305
Addison, Joseph, 453
Adolphus, Gustavus, 364
Adriatic Sea, 418
Afghanistan, 803, 807
   2002, *812*
    al-Qaeda strongholds in, 808
    Soviet invasion of, 764, 773, 793
    Soviet withdrawal from, 794, 800
    war against Soviet invaders, 808–9, 811
Africa
    birth control, 390
    imperialism in, 630, 632–35, *633, 634*
    lack of industrial economies, 646–47
    legacy of colonialism, 773
    liberation, 772
    struggle for national liberation, 752
    trade with Muslims, 500
African Americans, civil rights movement, 777
African National Congress, 773
African National Congress (ANC), 773, 774
Africans
    conversion to Christianity, 391
    as pirates, 396
African slave trade, 320, 388–90, 396, 425, 483, 500, 585
Afrika Korps, 744
Afrikaner National Party, 774
Afrikaners, 774
Age of Reason, 441, 442
Agoult, Marie d', 575
agricultural revolution, 486–87, 540
agriculture
    new approaches to, 486
AIDS (Acquired Immune Deficiency Syndrome), 786, 818
airplanes, 707
air pollution, 817
Akbar, 422
Alaska, 645
Albania, 756
    liberation, 796
    "people's democracies," 765
Alberti, Leon Battista, 306, 320, 322, 325
    On Building, 323
Albret, Michel, 804
Alcalá de Henares, 354
alchemy, 327, 443, 452
alcoholic beverages, 388

alcoholism, 656, 657
Alexander I, Tsar, 530, 565, 566, 568, 569, 581
Alexander II, Tsar, 610–11, 619
Alexander III, Tsar, 619, 624
Alexander VI, Pope, 316, 354
Alexandra, 694
Alfonso the Magnanimous, 316
algebra, 327
Algeria, 631, 772, 773, 807
Algiers, 396
Algonquin language, 390
Ali, Mehemet, 582
Alighieri, Dante: *Divine Comedy*, 321
alliance system, 674–75
alpaca, 383
al-Qaeda, 808, 809
Alsace, 602, 690
alternative medicine, 556
American colonists, 381
    commercial regulations and taxes, 496
    expansion and battles with Amerindians, 479
    push westward, 482
    revolt of, 527
American constitution
    Bill of Rights, 497
American Federation of Labor, 620
Americanization, 777
"Americanization," 777, 813–14
American Revolution, 478, 496–97, 506, 571
Americas
    conquest of the Great Empire, 385–86
    indigenous empires in, ca. 1500, *384*
Amerindians, 381–83
    death from disease and overwork under Spanish imperialists, 386, 388
    enforced labor for Spanish, 386–87
    human sacrifice, 383
    planting wheat in America, 397
Amherst, Lord, 538
Amsterdam, 394, 434, 435, 448
Anabaptists, 349
anarchism, 621, 623
Anatolia, 500
Anatomical Theatre, 448
anatomy, 447–48
Andes Mountains, 382
Andropov, Yuri, 793
anesthetics, 556
Angelo del Tovaglia, 310
Angevin dynasty, 304, 315
Anglican Church, 352, 353
Angola, 752
Anguissola, Sofonisba, 322
Anne, Queen, 433, 452, 478
Anne, Saint, 345
antibiotic drugs, 786

anti-Catholicism, 424, 425
anti-immigrant sentiments, 804
anti-Semitism, 719, 720, 722, 747, 749, 771
    and ultranationalism, 623–25
antiseptic procedures, 662
antitoxins, 661
Antwerp, 357
apartheid, South Africa, 773, 774
Apollinaire, Guillaume, 668
appeasement policy, 730
aqueducts, 648
Arabic numerals, 327
Arab-Israeli conflict, 1947-1982, *772*
Aragon, 315, 354
Aragon dynasty, 304
architecture
    domed, 324
    eighteenth-century European, 491–92
    Gothic, 574
    human scale, 323
    Renaissance, 322–24
Arch of Triumph, 733
Ardennes Forest, 733
Argenteuil, 665
Argentina, 527, 648
Aristotle, 326, 442, 443
Arkwright, Richard, 541
Armenia, 713, 798, 800
Armstrong, Neil, 785
Arnaud du Tilh, 342
Arndt, Ernst Moritz, 572
Arobé, Don Francisco de, portrait of, *373*
art
    "Art for art's sake," 668
    expressionism, 668
    modern, 776
    nineteenth century, 663–64, 668
artisans, 406
    workshops, 320
Arundel, earl of, 423
Aryan myth, 623
"Aryan race," 719
Asia
    air pollution, 817
    financial crisis, 815
    lack of industrial economies, 646–47
    nationalist parties, 703
    struggle for national liberation, 752
    Western imperialism in, 635–39, *638*
    wood-block printing, 311
aspirin, 661
assembly line, 645
Assembly of Notables, 513
assignats, 511
Associated Shipwright's Society, 551
Astell, Mary: A *Serious Proposal to the Ladies*, 461
astrolabe, 377
astrology, 309, 327, 442, 443, 452

astronomy, 444, 445
asylum-seekers, 813
Atahualpa, 386, 387
atheism, 458
athletics, 652–53
atomic bomb, 746, 747, 749, 759
atomic energy, 666
atoms, 660
Attlee, Clement, 748, 768
Auden, W. H., 731
Augsburg, Peace of, 364
Augustine, 358
Augustus Caesar, 313
Aulnay sous Bois, 813
Aurangzeb, 422
Auschwitz, 740, 749
Auschwitz-Birkenau, 739
Austen, Jane, 557
Austerlitz, Battle of, 524
Australia, 500, 627, 628, 639, 645, 646
Austria, 338, 580, 623
    alliance with France, 473, 474
    annexation of Lombardy and Venetia,
      581
    annexation of Polish territory, 471
    Bohemian lands, 548
    Compromise of 1867, 604
    declaration of war on Napoleon, 530
    defeat by Prussia in 1866, 604
    expansion of control, 417–19
    invasion by Germany, 729
    nationalistic discontent in, 619
    populist right-wing party, 804
    revolution of 1848, 588, 590
    socialists in, 621
    spread of liberalism during 1870s, 619
Austria-Hungary, 468, 604, 607, 674
    declaration of war on Serbia, 675
    language groups of, 606
    in World War I, 678, 688, 690
Austrian Empire, 471, 500
    1721-1772, 475–83
Austrian Netherlands (Belgium), 506, 567
Austrian Succession, War of, 478
Austro-Prussian War, 600, 607
autocracy, 600
automobile, 645
auto racing, 653
Avignon, 316, 330
Azerbaijan, 798, 800
Aztec Empire, 381, 383
    Cortes and, 385–86, 387
    destruction of, 386
    human sacrifice, 385
    location of, 384

Babur, 422
baby boom, 783
"babyfarmers," 559
Bach, John Sebastian, 493
Bacon, Francis: *New Instrument,* 449, *450*
bacteria, 661
Baden-Baden, Germany, 555
Bagehot, Walter: *Physics and Politics, 660*
Bailly, Jean-Sylvain, 507, 517
Bakhta'war Khan, 422
Bakunin, Mikhail, 621
balance of power, 468

balance of trade, 394
Balbo, Italo, 711
Balboa, Vasco Núñez de, 379
Balfour, Arthur, 625
Balfour Declaration of 1917, 771
Bali, terrorist bombing in, 811
Balkans, 194, 296, 297, 471
    1878, 676
    1914, 676
    crises in, 675–77
    nationalism, 604
Ball, John, 348, 427
Baltic Sea, 421, 422
Balzac, Honoré de, 553
Bangkok, 806
bank checks, 394
banking, growth of, 394–95
Bank of Amsterdam, 394
Bank of England, 394
Bank of France, 523
Bank of Sweden, 394
Bao Dai, 770
baptism, 346
Barbados, 388
barbiturates, 661
Barcelona, 647
Barlow, Arthur, 384
baroque art, 357, 358, 414
baroque music, 493
baroque style, 492
Bartlett, Jennifer: *Spiral: An Ordinary
    Evening in New Haven, 819*
Basque separatists, 782
Bastille, 508
    fall of, 513
    storming of, 502
Bath, England, 555
Bauhaus Building, *708*
Bauhaus school, 707
Bayle, Pierre
    Historical and Critical Dictionary,
      454–55
    News from the Republic of Letters, 454
bayonets, 474
Beagle, 658
Beatles, 784
Beatrice, 321
Beauharnais, Josephine de, 521
Bebel, August, 621
Beccaria, Cesare, 470
    On Crimes and Punishments, 459–60
Beckett, Samuel
    "Endgame," 775
    "Waiting for Godor," 775
Beethoven, Ludwig van, 576
    Pastoral Symphony, 575
Beeton, Isabella Mary Mayson, 650, 655
beggary, 367, 490
Beijing, 807
Belgian Congo, 632
Belgian provinces, Netherlands, 583
Belgium, 361, 362, 434, 506
    independence, 583
    industrialization, 546–47
    revolutions in, 586
    "Rex" Party, 728
Belgrade, 338
Bell, Alexander Graham, 645

Bellini, Gentile: *Procession of Eucharist,
    310, 314*
Bentham, Jeremy, 571, 572
Benwell, J. A.: Florence Nightingale in the
    military hospital, 1856, *611*
Benzoni, Girolamo, 382
Bergman, Ingmar, 776
Bergson, Henri, 668, 708
Beria, Lavrenti, 766
Berlin, 706, 756, 765
Berlin airlift, 758
Berlin blockade, 758, 782
Berlin Conference of 1885, 632, 635
Berlin Wall, *766,* 782
    fall of, 792, 796
    November 1989, *790*
Bernstein, Eduard, 621
Berruguete, Pedro, Federico da Montefeltro
    and his son Guidobaldo, *302*
Berry, Thomas: "Wonderworld as Waste-
    land: The Earth in Deficit," 819
Bertall: The urban classes, *649*
Bessarabia, 697
Bessemer process, 644
Bible
    first printed, 311
    Genesis, 305
    King James, 425
bicycle, 653
The Bicycle, 776
big business, birth of, 645–46
big science, rise of, 785
bin Laden, Osama, 808
biological racism, 719
Birkenau, 739
Birmingham, England, 552
birth control, 656, 707, 783
birth-control pill, 784
Bishop, Isabella Bird, 637
Bismarck, Otto wvon, 599–603, 604,
    618–19, 674
    conflict with Catholic Church, 619
    conflict with socialists, 619
    Kulturkampf, 624
    master of politics in, 601
Black Death, 305, 392
Black Hand, 674
"The Black Hundreds," 624
black-lung disease, 554
Black Sea, 421, 422, 468, 471
Blanc, Louis, 587, 588, 590
blast furnace, 541
bloodletting, 555
Bloomsbury group, 709
"Bobbies," 553–54
Boccaccio, Giovanni, 315
Bocconi's, Milan, 646
Boer War, 634, 635
Bohemia, 362, 588
Bois, Louise, 622
Boleyn, Anne, 351, 352, 353
Bolívar, Simón, *527*
Bolivia, 387
Bolsheviks, 695–96, 697–98
Bomba, Abraham, 739
Bonald, Louis de, 569
Bonaparte, Joseph, 527, 529
Bonaparte, Louis-Napoleon, 590, 606, 607

revolt of the nobility, 505
taxation system, 504
"tennis court oath," 507
unpopular kings, 506
France, interwar period and World War II
Cross of Fire, 728
declaration of war on Germany, 731
Popular Front, 728, 747
post-WW I, 703
surrender to Hitler, 733, 747
Francesco of Mantua, 308
Franche-Comté (Burgundy), 415
Francisco, Don, 373
Francis I of France, 316, 329, 331, 332, 338, 341, 342–43, 349, 354, 360
Franco, Francisco, 729
Franco-Prussian Alliance, 677
Franco-Prussian War, 601, 607, 617, 629, 675
Franics Joseph, 604
Frank, Anne, 740
Franke, Fritze, 680
Frankfurt Assembly, 589, 590
Franklin, Benjamin, 455
fraternal societies, 551
Frédéric, Léon: *The Stages of a Worker's Life*, 653
Frederick II (Frederick the Great), 457, 471, 472–74, 478, 484
Frederick II Hohenstaufen, Emperor, 262
Frederick I of Prussia, 411, 417
Frederick the Wise of Saxony, 347
Frederick William I, 471
Frederick William IV, 588, 590
free trade, 459, 585
French and Indian War, 482
French Calvinists (Huguenots), 350, 360, 410, 411, 415
French Communist Party, 760
French garden, 492
French-German Coal and Steel Authority, 768
French League of Women's Rights, 780
French Revolution, 502, 503, 504–10, 569, 570, 571
attack on Catholic Church, 518
beheadings, 515
Committee of Public Safety, 517, 518
declaration of rights of man and citizen, 509
end of old order, 509–10
"Great Fear," 509
internal and external threats, 515
key dates, 513
Law of the Maximum, 517
levée en masse, 518
National Convention, 514, 516–17
and nationalism, 572
Parisian women march to Versailles, *510*
peasant revolts, 509
radical Republicans, 514–16, *519*
reactions to outside France, 512
Republic of Virtue, 518
resistance to the Republic, 519–20
revolutionary symbols, 518–19

rules for family life and education, 518
sister republics, 519
spread outside of France, 519
storming of Bastille, 508–9
the Terror, 513, 516–18, 520
Thermidorian reaction, 520
underlying causes, 505–7
war and the breakdown of order, 513–14
the "White" Terror, 520–21, 710
women's march to Versailles, 510
French Syria, 734
French telephone exchange, *651*
French warship, eighteenth-century, *476*
Freud, Sigmund, 666–67, 708, 709
Friedan, Betty: *The Feminine Mystique*, 779
Friedland, Battle of, 525
Frith, William Powell
Many Happy Returns of the Day, *642*
The Railway Station, *544*
Fronde revolts, 411, 412
Fuggers, 394

Galapagos Islands, 658
Galilei, Galileo, 442, 445–46, 451, 452
Dialogue on the Two Chief Systems of the World, 446
and Kepler, 446
Trial of before the Inquisition, *447*
galleys, 377
Gallipoli, 682, 690
Gallque, Andres Sánchez: *The Mulatto Gentlemen of Esmeraldas*, *373*
Galton, Francis, 659
Gama, Vasco da, 374, 377, 396
Gandhi, Mohandas, 703, 770, 771
Gapon, Georgi, 693
Garibaldi, Giuseppe, 595, 597, 598, 599
Garibaldi Brigade, 729
Gaskell, Elizabeth, 553
Gasset, José Ortega y: *Revolt of the Masses*, 708
Gaudeloupe, 483
Gaza Strip, 808, 809
Gdansk shipyards, 795
gender roles, and WW I, 684
"general strike," France, 622
General Workers' Brotherhood, Germany, 551
genetic engineering, 785, 806
Geneva, 349
Geneva Accords, 762
"gentry," 423
Geoffrin, Madame Marie-Thérèse, 462
George I, 433, 493
George II, 478
George III, 496, 538
Georgia, 713, 798
German Confederation, 567, 580, 600
German Democratic Republic, 758
German Empire, 601–3
German Federal Republic, 758
German Hanoverian line, 478
German hospital, 1746, *489*
Germanic Confederation, 598–603
Germanic kingdoms
peasant revolts, 347, 348, 364

rage against papal exploitation, 344
German inflation, November 1923, *704*
German Jews, expulsion of, 318
German nationalism, 347, 572
German National Party, 623
German Reformed Church, 346–48
German Republic, 688
German states
industrialization, 546–47
quest for unification, 598–603
reaction and repression in, 580
revolution of 1848, 588–89
unification, 607
German volunteers, August 1914, 678
German Women's Bureau, 721
German Workers' Party, 718
Germany, 678
under Bismarck, 618–19
"blank check" of full support for Austria-Hungary, 675
blockade of, 682
Christian Democrats, 803
cottage industry, 488
expansion, 1936-1939, *732*
immigration in 1990s, 813
liberals and nationalists rally for reform, 591
progressive social policies, 619
Social Democrats, 621
unification of, *602*
unions, 620
universal male suffrage, 618
War Raw Materials Board, 683
World War I, 676
Germany, post-World War I
conciliation, 704
Free Corps, 704
inflation, 704
reparations, 690
Weimar Republic, 704
Germany, post-World War II
after collapse of communism, 803
and the cold War, 756–58
crises, 703–4, 705
division of, 758
four occupation zones, 756
unification, 803
Germany, World War II
Afrika Korps, 734
"Atlantic Wall," 744
defeat of, 745
invasion of Poland, 727
invasion of Russia, 743–44
invasion of Soviet Union, 734–35, 747
Nazism, 718–23
reoccupation of Rhineland, 747
troops parading down Champs-Elysees after the fall of paris, *733*
germ theory, 661
Giotto di Bondone, 304, 315, 322, 325, 328
Lamentation over Christ, *325*
Girondins, 514, 516, 517, 520
Giroud, François, 755
Giroux, Charles: *Cotton Plantation*, 604
Giverny, 665
Gladstone, William, 617

growth from 1850 to 1914, 647
Irish quarter, 553
Paddington Station, 544
plague of 1665, 431, 433
police force, 553
Renaissance, 332–33
terrorist bombings in, 811
underground railway, 648–49
London Daily News, 561
Longwe, Fololiyani, 681
Lorenzo the Magnificent de'Medici, 313,
316, 317, 380
Lorraine, 602, 690
Lorraine, Claude, 414
*The Marriage of Isaac and Rebekah
(The Mill)*, 415
Louis, king of Holland, 525
Louisiana, 526
Louis IX, 317
Louis-Philippe, 583, 586, 587, 591
Louis XIII, 410, 411
Louis XI ("Louis the Spider"), 303, 316,
329, 331
Louis XIV, 361, 404, 409, 410, 411–17,
413, 431
assessing, 417
death, 416, 468
diminishing of stature in late reign,
476
on horseback at Versailles, *414*
on monarchical rights and duties, 412
religious persecutions, 454
revocation of the Edict of Nantes,
415
wars of aggression, 415
Louis XV, 468, 476, 477, 504, 506
Louis XVI, 477, 504, 506, 507–8, 510,
512, 513
execution of, 513, *515*
Louis XVIII, 530, 580, 582
Loutherbourg, Philip James de: *The Coal-
brookdale Ironworks at Night*, 541
Louvois, Marquis of, 415
Louw, Jan H., 786
Low Countries, 329, 434
Lucas Cranach the Younger: *Martin Luther
and the Wittenberg Reformers*, 347
Ludd, Ned, 551
Luddism, 551
Luddite riots, 581
Ludendorff, Erich, 680, 682, 685, 686, 688,
719
Lueger, Karl, 623–24
Lugard, Lord, 630
Lukacs, John, 791
Lusitania, 686
Luther, Martin, 344, 345–46, 347, 349,
350, 354, 358, 365–66, 367,
368, 445
"Against the Robbing and Murdering
Hordes of Peasants," 348
Ninety-Five Theses, 346
Lutheranism, 343, 346, 348, 353
Lutzen, 364
Luxembourg, 361, 506
Luxemburg, Rosa, 704
luxury goods, global demand for, 392
Lvov, Prince Georgi, 694

Lyons, 516
Lyrical Ballads, 575

Maastricht Treaty of 1992, 804, 811
Macartney, George, 538
Macaulay, Thomas Babington, 574,
584, 635
Macedonia, 801
Machiavelli, Niccoló, 333
The Prince, 317, 328
machine gun, 630, 631
Mackenzie, William Lyon, 603
Madonna of Impruneta, 309
Madrid, 359, 811
Magellan, Ferdinand, 379, 380, 396
Magenta, battle of, 597
magic, 443
Maginot Line, 704, 733
Magna Carta, 429
Magyars (Hungarians), 588, 590, 604, 690
Maier, Anna, 621
Maine, 381
Maine, Battle of the, 683
Maistre, Joseph de: *Essay on the Generative
Principle of Political Constitutions*,
569, 570
maize, 381, 382, 397, 398
malaria, 631
Malaya, 771
Malaysia, 806
Malinche, 385, 386
Malleus Maleficarum, 368–69
Malta, 396
Malthus, Thomas, 571, 658
Essay on the Principle of Population,
548
Manchester, 535, 552, 553
Manchukuo, 736
Manchuria, 639
Mandela, Nelson, 773, 774, 811
Manet, Edouard: *The Execution of Emperor
Maximilian*, 607
Manhattan Island, 381
manic-depressive condition, 786
Mantegna, Andrea: *The Cardinal Francesco
Gonzaga Returning from Rome*, 321
Mantua, Duchy of, 307, 309, 321
manufacturing, eighteenth century,
487–88
manure, 487
Mao Zedong, 728, 760–62, 764, 773, 806
Marat, Jean-Paul, 513, 520
Marcuse, Herbert, 778
Marguerite of Navarre, 351
Marguerite of Navarre, Queen, 350
Maria Theresa, 471–73, 478, 489
Maria Theresa of Austria, 474
Marie Antoinette, 506, 513, *515*
Marie de l'Incarnation, 390
Marie de Médicis, 410
Marie-Louise of Austria, 525
maritime battles, eighteenth century,
474–75
Markievicz, Constance, 703
Marne River, 688
marriage
arranged, 366

middle-class, 557
and Protestant Reformation, 365–66
"Marseillaise," 518
Marshall, George, 756, 759
Marshall Plan, 759, 767, 768, 782
Marsilio Ficino, 308–9
Martin, John: *The Bard*, 577
Martini, Francesco di Giorgio, 323
Martinique, 483
Marx, Karl, 620–21
The Communist Manifesto, 578–79
Das Kapital, 579
Marxists, 704
Mary, 329, 362
Mary ("Bloody Mary"), 352
Mary of Scotland, Queen, 424
masturbation, 656
maternal-wellness societies, 652
maternity benefits, 707
mathematics, 327
Maximilian, Emperor, 607
Maximilian of Bavaria, 362
Maxwell, James Clerk, 660
Maya, 381, 383
Mazarin, Cardinal Jules, 411, 412
Mazzini, Giuseppe, 573–74, 584, 589
McCarthy, Joseph, 760
McKinley, William, 623, 637
measles, 398
the Medici, 313, 314, 316, 325, 327,
379, 394
Medici, Catherine 'de, 360
Medici, Cosimo de', 308, 309, 313, 316,
317, 451
Medici, Lorenzo de', 313, 316, 317, 380
medicine, 447, 631
alternative, 556
golden age, 661–62
in industrial age, 554–57
nineteenth century, 555–56
remedies, 661
transformation after WW II, 785–86
Mediterranean Sea, 632
Meidner, Ludwig: *Apocalyptic Landscape*,
677
Meiggs, Henry, 648
Meiji, 605
Meiji Restoration, 635, 639
Meissonier, Jean-Louis-Ernest: *Memory of
Civil War (The Barricade)*, 589
Melchior, 349
Melchiorites, 349
Melozzo da Forlí: *Sixtus IV Receives Platina,
Keeper of the Vatican Library*, 317
men
modern office work for, 650
sphere of in nineteenth century, 558
Mendeleev, Dmitri, 660
mendicant orders, 269–70
Menelik II, Emperor, 632
Mennonites, 349
mental illnesses, 657
Menzel, Adolph: *The March Casualties
Lying in State*, 590, 592
mercantilistic economic policies, 393, 394,
414, 417, 419, 459
Mercator, Gerhard, 401
mercator maps, 400

Mercator projection of the world in 1608, *401*
mercenaries, 312, 318, 329, 340, 341, 342
Merian, Maria Sibylla, 389, 390, 395, 399, 450
    Metamorphosis of the Insects of Surinam, 399, 400
Meshica, 383
Mesopotamia, 683, 690
mestizos, 397, 398
Methodism, 495–96
Metternich, Prince Clemens von, 565, 566, 567, 568, 569, 570, 580, 581, 588
Metz, 601
Mexico, 381, 388, 648, 686
    clash of cultures, 812, *813*
    conversion of indigenous peoples, 390
Mexico City, 383, 647
Meytens, Martin: *Maria Theresa and Her Family, 473*
"miasma," 555
Michel, Louise, 625, 626
Michelangelo, 305–6, 317, 322, 323, 326, 328
    Creation of Adam, 306
    David, 324, 325
microorganisms ("germs"), 661
microscope, 448
microwave technology, 785
Middle Ages (400-1400)
    bankers, 394
middle class, 395, 643
    changing roles for women and men in nineteenth century, 557–59
    growth of, 349
    in industrial age, 649–51
    values, 559, 650
    view of working-class counterparts, 652
Middle East
    2003, *810*
    oil resources, 753
Middle East War, 780
Middle Passage, 480
Midway, Battle of, 745, 747
Midway Island, 745
Milan, 309, 312, 314–15, 319, 547, 643, 647
military draft, 340
military strategies, 303
Mill, James, 548
Mill, John Stuart, 571, 572–73
    caricature drawing of, *573*
    On Liberty, 572–75
    The Subjection of Women, 573, 651
    A System of Logic, 572
Miller, Arthur, 796
Milosevic, Slobodan, 803
Milyukov, Pavel, 694
Mirabeau, Count, 507
missionaries, 629, 631
    in Asia, 391
    in China, 391
    in Japan, 391
    in New World, 390–91
"Mississippi Bubble," 476
Mississippi Company, 476

Missolonghi, 582
Mitterrand, François, 781
modernity, 643, 707
Moldovia, 798
Molière, Jean-Baptiste, 414
Moluccas, 377
monarchies
    absolutism, 409
    twilight of, 483–86
monasteries
    dissolution of in England by Henry VIII, 352
Mondrian, 814
Monet, Claude
    Boulevard des Capucines, 664, 666
    Impression: Sunrise, 665
    The Pool at Argenteuil, 664
Mongol Empire, 419
Monnet, Jean, 768
monoculture, 389
monopolies, 646
Monroe, James, 569
Monroe Doctrine, 569
Montesquieu, Baron de, 470, 570
    attack on discrimination against Jews, 458
    Persian Letters, 455
    political thought, 458
    The Spirit of the Laws, 458, 459
Montevideo, 648
Montezuma II, 385
Montreal, 381
moon
    Americans on, 1969, *785*
    landings, 782, 785
morality, 656
More, Thomas, 328, 344, 352
    Utopia, 332
Morgan, Alfred: *One of the People, 617*
Moro, Aldo, 782
Morocco, 632
    crises, 677
    independence, 772
morphine, 657, 661
Morse, Samuel, 645
Moscow, 297, 548, 693, 735
"Mother's Day," 707
Motlana, Sally, 774
moveable type, 311
Mozart, Wolfgang Amadeus, 493, 494
The Mozarts, 495
MRI devices, 786
Mrs. Beeton's Book of Household Management, 655
Mughals, 422, 482, 500
Muir Glacier, Alaska, in 1941 and 2004, *817, 818*
multinational corporations, 781, 805, 806, 815
multinational enterprises, 805
Mun, Thomas
    "Discourse on England's Treasure by Foreign Trade," 393
Munch, Edvard: *The Scream,* 668
Mundus Novus, 379
Munich conference, 730, 747
Munich putsch, 710
Munkacsy, Mihaly: *Paris Interior,* 654

Munster, 349
music
    baroque, 493
    classical, 493
    eighteenth century Europe, 492–93
    expressionism, 669
    gospel, 391
    modern, 777
    romantic, 575
muskets, 339, 340, 474
Muslim Bosnians, 801
Muslim societies, 199–200, 771
    immigrants in Western Europe, 813
Mussolini, Benito, 709, 710, *711–12,* 729, 734, 744, 745
mutual aid societies, 551
mystics, 358

Nagasaki, 736, 747
Nagy, Imre, 766
Nahuatl, 385
Nain, Louis le: *The Cart, 406, 407*
Naples, Kingdom of, 312, 315–16, 329, 411, 451, 581, 586, 597
Napoleonic Civil Code, 523, 524, 525, 528, 558
Napoleonic War, 524–26
Napoleon III, 597, 600, 601, 606–7, 617, 647
Nasser, Gamel Abdul, 771–72
National Assembly of France, 507, 508, 509, 510, 511, 512
National Front for the Liberation of Southern Vietnam ("Viet Cong"), 763
nationalism, 571–74, 579, 580, 596, 615
    after collapse of communism, 800–803
    Asian, 636
    Balkans, 604
    Chinese, 638
    cultural, 572–73
    economic, 394
    ethnic, 801
    in France and Russia, 605–12
    French, 572
    German, 347, 572
    ideologies of, 571–74
    "new," 801
    Ottoman Empire, 604–5
    and romanticism, 576
    and statebuilding, key dates, 607
    twentieth century, 674
    vs. liberalism, 591–92
national liberation, 573
National Trades Union Congress, 551, 620
National Union of Women's Suffrage Societies, 626
nation-states, building, 596
Native Americans, 777
NATO, 782, 803, 804, 805
Natural History of Brazil, 400
naturalism, 662
naturalist novel, 663
natural selection, 660
Nauder, Caroline: *Journey of a Dying Man to the Other World,* 555–56
Naumann, Michael, 804

Poussin, Nicolas, 414
poverty, 647
power loom, 541
Pragmatic Sanction, 471
Prague, Soviet tanks in, *767*
Prague Spring, 767, 796
predestination, 349–50
preemptive war, 810–11
prefect, 523
Presbyterian churches, 424
Presbyterian Scottish practice, 425
Presley, Elvis, 784
"Prester John," 375, 376
"Prince of the Humanists," 343
Princip, Gavrilo, 674
principalities, 312
printing industry, 309
printing press, 311, 375, 443, 493
printing shop, late fifteenth century, *311*
privateers, 396
propaganda, 684
prostitution, 656, 657
    nineteenth century, 559–60
Protestant Bohemia, 362
Protestant Dutch Republic, 362
Protestant electors, 362
Protestantism, 346, 353, 359
    ideals of education, 366
    and idol worship, 350
    "priesthood of all believers," 346
    reformers, 358
    reliance on individual conscience,
        350
    religious ideas, 346–47
    revitalization of, 424
    sacraments, 346
    in Swiss cantons, 349
    views of sovereignty, 429
Protestant Reformation, 347, 348, 354,
        360, 443
    and anxiety and spiritual insecurity,
        367–68
    life after, 365–69
    and link between education and
        work, 366–67
    and new definitions of courtship and
        marriage, 365–66
    politics of the age of, 364
Protestant "work ethic," 367
Proust, Marcel, 673, 708
Prussia, 468, 580, 599
    1721-1772, 475–83
    annexation of Polish territory, 471
    and Congress of Vienna, 567
    Hohenzollern kings, 580
    Junkers, 580
    revolution of 1848, 588, 590
    wars for unification, 600
Prussian Academy of Arts, 686
pseudoscience, 327
psychic stress, 657
psychoanalysis, 657, 667
psychology, 660
psychotropic drugs, 786
Ptolemy
    Geography, 375, 378

image of the world, *376*
    map of, 377, 400
Ptolemy of Alexandria, 442
public education, 616
public health, nineteenth century, 556–57
Pugachev, Yemelyan, 471
Pulitzer, Joseph, 616
pulmonary tuberculosis (consumption),
    556
Punch, 573
purgatory, 345, 358
Puritans, 424, 425, 426
Putin, Vladimir, 800
putting-out system, 487, 545
pyramids, 383
Pythagoras, 326

Qianlong (Ch'ien Lung), Emperor, 538
Qianolong, 500
Qing (Ch'ing) dynasty, 500, 538, 636, 637
quadrant, 376
Quadruple Alliance (Concert of Europe),
    569, 586
Quakers, 423
Quebec, 381, 482
queens
    Renaissance, 332
Queens College, Britain, 650
Quesnay, François, 459
Quietism, 496
quinine, 631
Qur'an, 422

Rabelais, François, 329–31
    Gargantua, 331
Racine, Jean, 414
radio, 706
Radischev, Alexander: *A Journey from St.
    Petersburg to Moscow*, 470–71
railroads, 543–45, 547, 548, 628, 630,
    645, 648
Raleigh, Walter, 396
Ramsay, Allan: *Jean-Jacques Rousseau, 461*
Ranke, Leopole von, 661
Raphael, 328
    School of Athens, 326–27
Rasputin, Grígori Efimovich, 694
rationalism, 708
Raynal, Abbé Guillaume, 460
Razin, Stenka, 419
Reagan, Ronald, 765, 782, 793, 804
realism, 305, 314, 325, 662, 663
Realpolitik, 599
reason, cult of, 518
Red Army, 698, 713, 716
Red Army Faction, West Germany, 782
Red Brigades, Italy, 782
Red Guards, 696
Red Sea, 632
"Red Shirts," 597, 598
"Red Terror," 697
Reed, John, 695
reformers, radical, 349
Reichstag, 600, 721
relics, 346
religion
    and Darwinism, 659

and the new science, 451–52
    and skepticism, 454–55
religious fundamentalism, 807, 808,
    812, 820
religious mysticism, 358, 575
religious patronage, 309
religious reform
    sixteenth century, 343
    in Switzerland, 348
religious revivals, 495–96
    late eighteenth and early nineteenth
        centuries, 574–75
    twenty-first century, 820
Remarque, Erich Maria, 702
    All Quiet on the Western Front,
        681, 708
Rembrandt van Rijn: *Syndics of the Cloth
    Guild*, 436
Renaissance, 303, 304–5, 443
    activism, 306, 312
    age of accelerated change, 304
    architecture, 322–24
    artists and writers, 322, 328
    art of diplomacy, 316
    banking and commerce, 319
    children's lives, 321–22
    classical rebirth, 305, 306
    culture and science, 322–29
    domes, 323
    economic boom times, 318–19
    family, 320–21
    growing intolerance, 318
    individualism, 305, 311–17, 318–22,
        325–26
    Italian origins, 305
    marriage alliances, 320
    medieval antecedents, 304
    multifaceted movement, 305–6
    of "New Monarchies" of the North:
        1453-1640, 329–33
    painting, 325–27
    realism, 306
    revival of slavery, 319–20
    rising crime, 318
    science, 327
    sculpture, 324–27
    secular spirit, 306
    study and self-improvement, 307
    town planning, 324
Renaissance London, 332–33
Renaissance queens, 332
Renaissance rulers, 316
Renoir, Auguste, 665
repartimiento, 387
Republic of Biafra, 773
Republic of Florence, 325
Republic of Turkey, 690
republics, 108, 312
resistance organizations, 740–41
rhetoric, 307
Rhodes, Cecil, 314, 634
Rhodesia, 773
Ricardo, David, 548, 571
Ricci, Matteo, 391
Richardson, Samuel: *Pamela, or Virtue
    Rewarded*, 491